Fodor's 96 California

"When it comes to information on regional history, what to see and do, and shopping, these guides are exhaustive."

—*USAir Magazine*

"Usable, sophisticated restaurant coverage, with an emphasis on good value."

—Andy Birsh, *Gourmet Magazine* columnist

"Valuable because of their comprehensiveness."

—*Minneapolis Star-Tribune*

"Fodor's always delivers high quality...thoughtfully presented...thorough."

—*Houston Post*

"An excellent choice for those who want everything under one cover."

—*Washington Post*

Fodor's Travel Publications, Inc.
New York • Toronto • London • Sydney • Auckland

Fodor's California

Editor: Daniel Mangin

Contributors: Dianne Aaronson, Steven K. Amsterdam, Robert Andrews, Colleen Dunn Bates, Christopher Billy, Robert Blake, William P. Brown, John Burks, Deke Castleman, Lori Chamberlain, Toni Chapman, Bruce David Colen, Albert M. Columbo, Jon and Noonie Corn, Karen Croft, Pamela Faust, Janet Foley, Alan Frutkin, Sheila Gadsden, Claudia Gioseffi, Dennis Harvey, Pamela Hegarty, Patrick Hoctel, Mary Jane Horton, Edie Jarolim, Jacqueline Killeen, Jane E. Lasky, Amy McConnell, Ellen Melinkoff, Maribeth Mellin, Marty Olmstead, Tracy Patruno, Jim Peters, Marcy Pritchard, Mary Ellen Schultz, M. T. Schwartzman (Gold Guide editor), Kathryn Shevelow, Aaron Shurin, Sharon Silva, Dan Spitzer, Dinah Spritzer, Alison B. Stern, Aaron Sugarman, Robert Taylor, Casey Tefertiller, Bobbi Zane

Creative Director: Fabrizio La Rocca

Cartographer: David Lindroth

Cover Photograph: Catherine Karnow/Woodfin Camp

Text Design: Between the Covers

Copyright

ISBN 0-679-02993-1

Special Sales

Fodor's Travel Publications are available at special discounts for bulk purchases for sales promotions or premiums. Special editions, including personalized covers, excerpts of existing guides, and corporate imprints, can be created in large quantities for special needs. For more information contact your local bookseller or write to Special Markets, Fodor's Travel Publications, 201 East 50th Street, New York, NY 10022. Inquiries from Canada should be directed to your local Canadian bookseller or sent to Random House of Canada, Ltd., Marketing Department, 1265 Aerowood Drive, Mississauga, Ontario L4W 1B9. Inquiries from the United Kingdom should be sent to Fodor's Travel Publications, 20 Vauxhall Bridge Road, London SW1V 2SA, England.

MANUFACTURED IN THE UNITED STATES OF AMERICA

10 9 8 7 6 5 4 3 2 1

CONTENTS

Maps

ON THE ROAD WITH FODOR'S

A GOOD TRAVEL GUIDE is like a wonderful traveling companion. It's charming, it's brimming with sound recommendations and solid ideas, it pulls no punches in describing lodging and dining establishments, and it's consistently full of fascinating facts that make you view what you've traveled to see in a rich new light. In creating *California '96,* we at Fodor's have gone to great lengths to provide you with the very best of all possible traveling companions—and to make your trip the best of all possible vacations.

About Our Writers

Colleen Dunn Bates, who revised the Central Coast chapter, has southern California roots that go back to the mid-19th century—her great-great-great-grandfather was the first white settler in Ventura County. Like many California natives, Colleen is a lifelong surfer, "Though as the mother of two young daughters I don't get in the water as much these days," she says. On shore, Bates is the author of the upcoming *Unofficial Guide to Dining in Los Angeles* and writes for several publications, among them *Shape, Westways, Travel and Leisure,* and *Cooking Light.*

Deke Castleman, who updated the Lake Tahoe and Mojave Desert chapters, grew up in New York and Boston but fled the East Coast for the wide-open spaces of the American West. He discovered the region's many wonders while engaged in a variety of occupations—door-to-door vacuum-cleaner salesman in central California, tour guide at Alaska's Denali National Park, and locksmith on Lake Tahoe's north shore. Deke recently moved to Las Vegas, where he is senior editor of Huntington Press, a gambling publishing company. He spends his spare time exploring the Mojave Desert.

Claudia Gioseffi, who updated the Wine Country and Monterey Bay chapters, brings an art, food, and wine background to *California '96.* The author of an ongoing series of artist profiles for Caldwell Snyder Galleries of New York and San Francisco, Claudia had the first solo exhibit of her own paintings in 1995. Her travel writings have appeared in *Country Bed & Breakfast Inns.* A food writer and the former editor of the *Epicurean Rendezvous* guides, the San Francisco resident managed to cover every important restaurant in California, Florida, and New York—without gaining an ounce.

Jane E. Lasky, who updated the Los Angeles and Orange County chapters, is a syndicated newspaper columnist, television producer, and author of several travel books. She also publishes articles in many national magazines such as *Vogue, Connoisseur, Los Angeles, Travel and Leisure,* and *Esquire.*

Marty Olmstead, who revised the North Coast and Far North chapters, is the former travel editor of *San Francisco Focus* magazine, for which she crisscrossed the state many times. Accounts of her voyages around the globe have appeared in *Travel and Leisure,* the *Los Angeles Times, Geo, Glamour,* and the *San Francisco Chronicle.* Since 1989, she has lived in Sonoma County, which she "appreciates for its role in California's history and its proximity to grapes—the North Coast's most famous (legal) crop."

Bobbi Zane, who revised the Palm Springs chapter and wrote the Gold Country chapter, has been visiting the state's southern desert region since her grandfather, a Hollywood producer, took her on weekend getaways to La Quinta Resort. She became intrigued with the "haunting history to be discovered at every turn" in the Gold Country while working for a Sacramento television station in the 1960s. She returns to the area yearly. Bobbi's byline has appeared in the *Los Angeles Times, Los Angeles Daily News,* and *Orange County Register.* For Fodor's she has contributed to *California's Best Bed & Breakfasts* and *Fodor's Los Angeles '95.* With her husband, Gregg, she publishes *Yellow Brick Road,* a monthly newsletter about bed-and-breakfast inns.

Daniel Mangin, the editor of *California '96* and a contributor to the San Francisco chapter, is a longtime transplant from the East Coast. He first traversed California as the stage manager and lighting director of two '70s punk rock bands, one of which, he reminisces with nary a trace of regret, "hit just short of the big time. One year we stayed at low-budget motels, the next year it was four-star hotels with private butlers and antique furniture (we were well-behaved rockers). The experience taught me what travelers of all budgets need and expect." Since he left behind life in the fast lane, Daniel, who writes about the arts for several San Francisco Bay Area and national publications, has co-authored *Sunday in San Francisco* and edited *California's Best Bed & Breakfasts,* both for Fodor's.

We'd also like to thank Alan Frutkin, who braved a winter storm (and a hair-raising first experience with tire chains) to update the Sierra National Parks chapter, and associate editor Fionn Davenport, whose diligence was exceeded only by his sardonic ways.

What's New

Big things are happening at Fodor's—and in California.

A New Design

If this is not the first Fodor's guide you've purchased, you'll immediately notice our new look. More readable and easier to use than ever? We think so—and we hope you do, too.

New Takes on California

The changes go beyond design, though. This year's edition of *California '96* features a completely revamped Gold Country chapter that focuses on three sections of famed Highway 49 easily accessible from the state's capital, Sacramento. Although visitors often overlook the region, it's a great destination for families, with reasonably priced dining and lodging options, plenty of history, and a fine mix of indoor and outdoor activities.

We've also expanded coverage of the San Jose–Silicon Valley area, added more shopping and dining options in Santa Barbara, and discovered a swinging weekend nightlife scene in formerly staid Palm Springs. There are extended chapters on San Francisco, Los Angeles, and San Diego, with plenty of information for a week's stay, but this book has been written primarily for those travelers who plan to visit several regions of the state.

Let Us Do Your Booking

Our writers have scoured California to come up with an extensive and well-balanced list of the best B&Bs, inns, resorts, and hotels, both small and large, new and old. But you don't have to beat the bushes to come up with a reservation. Now we've teamed up with an established hotel-booking service to make it easy for you to secure a room at the property of your choice. It's fast, it's free, and confirmation is guaranteed. If your first choice is booked, the operators can line up your second right away. Just call 800/FODORS–1 or 800/363–6771 (0800/89–1030 when in Great Britain; 0014/800–12–8271 when in Australia; 1800/55–9101 when in Ireland).

Travel Updates

In addition, just before your trip, you may want to order a Fodor's Worldview Travel Update. From local publications all over California, the lively, cosmopolitan editors at Worldview gather information on concerts, plays, opera, dance performances, gallery and museum shows, sports competitions, and other special events that coincide with your visit. See the order blank at the back of this book, call 800/799–9609, or fax 800/799–9619.

And in California

SAN FRANCISCO➢ The $62 million **San Francisco Museum of Modern Art** (SFMOMA) across 3rd Street from the **Center for the Arts at Yerba Buena Gardens,** which opened in January 1995, was an instant hit. The new building, designed by internationally celebrated Mario Botta, gives the city's collection of 20th-century art a world-class setting for the first time—within a few months, the attendance figures for the new museum had already surpassed recent yearly totals at the museum's cramped Civic Center quarters.

The new Yerba Buena Gardens complex, with its inviting grass esplanade, its growing number of art galleries and museums, and its performance spaces, which host events ranging from computer-assisted jazz improvisations to re-created settings from the *Star Wars* movies, has transformed a tired South of Market neighborhood of residential hotels and marginal industries into a new civic center for the arts.

The newest additions to the neighborhood are the **Cartoon Art Museum,** with exhibits ranging from 19th-century political satire to the latest in underground comic books, and the California Historical Society's library and gallery (slated to open in January 1996), with rotating exhibitions of paintings and artifacts covering the gold rush and other events in the state's history.

Union Square's transformation from a shopping district serving San Francisco's old guard to a livelier neighborhood for international visitors was dramatized by the closing of the I. Magnin department store early in 1995. Across the square, the newest arrival is a three-level **"Nike Town"** (expected to open in April 1996), a virtual retail theater of athletic wear and video entertainment.

Facing another corner of the square, a **Borders Books and Music** store and a **Disney Store** have taken over a former airline ticketing office at Powell and Stockton streets. The landmark **Gump's,** which has specialized in Asian art goods since the 1860s, moved a block east on Post Street into retail space that resembles a lantern-filled Oriental courtyard; the store's venerable, gilded, 18th-century Buddha statue, newly refurbished, made the move, too.

Performing-arts organizations are changing locations this year, primarily because civic buildings are being seismically upgraded. The **War Memorial Opera House** closes in January 1996 for an expected 18 months. The **San Francisco Opera** will perform its 1996 season nearby in the Bill Graham Civic Auditorium and Orpheum Theatre. The **San Francisco Ballet,** which normally performs a winter season at the Opera House, will be performing at three temporary locations until 1997. Meanwhile, the **American Conservatory Theater** hopes to return to its rebuilt Geary Theater—which was damaged by the Loma Prieta earthquake—in 1996. On the northwestern edge of the city, the California **Palace of the Legion of Honor** was scheduled to open in the fall of 1995.

The long-delayed **Underwater World** at **Pier 39,** slated to open in the spring of 1996, will offer visitors views, from a transparent tunnel, of some 2,000 marine species in a 700,000-gallon aquarium. Another new attraction at Pier 39 is *San Francisco: The Movie,* a 35-minute, 70-millimeter travelogue projected onto an oversize screen.

LOS ANGELES➢ Los Angeles has always been a newsworthy city, but this has been especially true during the past five years. From the ravages of riots and fires to the devastation of the Northridge earthquake, the eyes of the world have focused on this city for reasons other than its signature silver-screen status.

Topping itself, in 1995, a more-outrageous-than-usual event took place: the **double murder trial of L.A. resident O.J. Simpson.** For months television sets throughout the world were tuned to what became the country's new addiction. Of course, when tourists arrived here, O.J.'s and the late Nicole Brown's homes were among the first sights to see. However, rubbernecking soon ended when neighbors of this famous pair demanded that the police re-route the barrage of invaders who were intruding on the privacy of the residential area.

Determined to prove that there are better ways to spend time in sunshine city, **community efforts have been made to lure visitors downtown.** Hollywood Boulevard, for example, has undergone megachanges in order to diminish its bad rap as a seedy place. In fact, some of the glamour of Hollywood's heyday is slowly being restored. As well, the streets are on a continual cleanup program; more than a hundred trees have been planted; and new lampposts shaped like massive movie kliegs have gone up around the strip. Also, high in the Hills, the four-story-tall HOLLYWOOD sign had its youth restored with a face-lift in 1995.

Meanwhile, across town, atop the Santa Monica Mountains, finishing touches on the $400 million **Getty Center Museum** are taking place in preparation for its 1997 opening, when one of the world's most renowned art collections will be unveiled.

Among the city's other improvements are several attractions at local theme parks. **Six Flags Magic Mountain,** in Valencia, opened Hurricane Harbor, a water extravaganza. Across the San Fernando Valley at **Universal Studios,** the multimillion-dollar Waterworld: A Live Sea War Spectacular promises to be one of the most ambitious (and wettest) stunt shows ever. The attraction, scheduled to open by 1996, includes a sea plane crash that stops just 2 feet short of the audience.

If you care to spend a day on an island, **Catalina is closer than ever,** thanks to Catalina Express. Their new, state-of-the-art high-speed cruising boats can get you to Avalon Harbor in less than one hour.

Meanwhile, **Disneyland** has also been busy, with the opening of the treacherous Indiana Jones Adventure. It delivers action and thrills to the participant, who chooses which route to take, so guests will never experience the same ride twice. Another Disney project is the building of the avant-garde Frank Gehry–designed **Disney Concert Hall,** which will be the home of the Los Angeles Philharmonic in 1997.

SAN DIEGO➢ The event that's sure to change the quality of life in San Diego in 1996 (at least for a month) is the **Republican National Convention.** The GOP will gather August 10–17, and some 25,000 people are expected to descend on the city and, it's hoped, spend at least part of their time crowding the city's attractions and nightspots. The official noisemaking and platform-building will take place in the San Diego Convention Center.

The downtown San Diego skyline continues to change in subtle and startling ways. Although hotel and office-tower construction seems to have peaked in this newly developed area, growth and refinement of already existing sites are continuing apace. At press time, downtown's **Horton Plaza** was undergoing a $16 million renovation, most of the work concentrated on converting the former Robinsons-May building into a 120,000-square-foot dining/entertainment/fashion complex. A new **Planet Hollywood** restaurant littered with movie and television memorabilia recently opened as part of the expansion. Other additions to Horton Plaza will include a 14-screen movie-theater complex.

In 1995 the 150-acre **Arco Training Center** for Olympic athletes had its grand opening. Overlooking Lower Otay Lake, 10 miles east of San Diego Bay, the facility is a warm-weather counterpart to the U.S. Olympic centers in Lake Placid, New York, and Colorado Springs, Colorado. Guests can survey the complex and watch athletes training for events; guided tours begin at the visitor center.

There's always something new at the **San Diego Zoo.** At the zoo's newest habitat, **Hippo Canyon**—a 2-acre African rain forest opened at the base of Tiger River in 1995—you can watch the huge but surprisingly graceful beasts frolicking underwater. These newcomers, however, are likely to be overshadowed for a while by two glamorous visitors who arrived in the spring: **Shi Shi and Bay Yun,** a pair of giant pandas on 12-year loan from the People's Republic of China.

One of San Diego's most delightful museums was scheduled to move to new quarters in late 1995. The **Mingei International Museum of World Folk Art,** one of only five facilities in the world devoted to this subject, is planning to move from the University Towne Center into Balboa Park's House of Charm. Get up-to-date information on the new facility by calling the museum's current number (☎ 619/453–5300).

SACRAMENTO➢ Preservation remains a priority in the state's capital. Looking to its past for inspiration, Sacramento has facilitated the rehabilitation of street after tree-shaded street of **Victorian and Edwardian mansions** and smaller homes surrounding the **Capitol** building.

Three decades in the making, the refurbished **Old Sacramento** now successfully recaptures the feeling of riverfront life during the gold rush. Shops lining gaslit cobblestone streets fulfill the same functions they did a century and a half ago, purveying merchandise needed by visitors passing through. The centerpiece of the area remains the 100,000-square-foot **California State Railroad Museum,** the largest and most comprehensive collection of its kind in the nation.

As the gateway to the Gold Country, Sacramento is gearing up for the three-year-long **California Gold Discovery to Statehood Sesquicentennial** celebration, set to run throughout the Golden State from 1998 to 2000.

How to Use This Book

Organization

Up front is the **Gold Guide,** comprising two sections on gold-color paper chock-full of information about traveling in general and specifically at your destination. Both are in alphabetical order by topic. **Important Contacts A to Z** gives you addresses and telephone numbers of organizations and companies that offer detailed information and publications, plus information about arriving and departing from your destination. **Smart Travel Tips A to Z** gives you specific tips on how to get the most out of your travels as well as information on how to accomplish what you need to in your destination.

Chapters in *California '96* are arranged in a north-to-south order, except for those covering the North Coast and Far North regions, which are organized from south to north. The Wine Country chapter is divided into two tours of the Napa Valley and one covering Sonoma County vineyards. Each chapter covers exploring, shopping, sports, dining, lodging, and arts and nightlife and ends with a section called Essentials, which tells you how to get there and get around and gives you important local addresses and telephone numbers.

At the end of the book, you'll find Portraits, essays about San Francisco, Los Angeles, and San Diego, followed by suggestions for pre-trip reading, both fiction and non-fiction, and movies you can rent to get you in the mood for your travels.

Stars

Stars in the margin are used to denote highly recommended sights, attractions, hotels, and restaurants.

Restaurant and Hotel Criteria and Price Categories

Restaurants and lodging places are chosen with a view to giving you the cream of the crop in each location at each price range. Because prices in California vary widely from region to region or between a city and outlying areas, we have included separate charts in each chapter tailored to the range of dining and lodging possibilities in that area.

Hotel Facilities

Note that in general you incur charges when you use many hotel facilities; we want to let you know what facilities a hotel has to offer, but don't always specify whether or not there's a charge. When planning a resort vacation that entails a stay of several days, it's wise to ask what's included in your rates.

Dress Code in Restaurants

Under the **What to Wear** heading at the beginning of the individual chapters' dining sections you'll find out what's most common in that area. In general, we note dress code only when men are required to wear a jacket or a jacket and tie.

Credit Cards

The following abbreviations are used: **AE,** American Express; **D,** Discover; **DC,** Diners Club; **MC,** MasterCard; and **V,** Visa.

Please Write to Us

Everyone who has contributed to *California '96* has worked hard to make the text accurate. All prices and opening times are based on information supplied to us at press time, and Fodor's cannot accept responsibility for any errors that may have occurred. The passage of time will bring changes, so it's always a good idea to call ahead and confirm information when it matters—particularly if you're making a detour to visit specific sights or attractions. When making reservations at a hotel or inn, be sure to mention if you have a disability or are traveling with children, if you prefer a private bath or a certain type of bed, or if you have specific dietary needs or any other concerns.

Were the restaurants we recommended as described? Did our hotel picks exceed your expectations? Did you find a museum we recommended a waste of time? Positive and negative, we would love your feedback. If you have complaints, we'll look into them and revise our entries when the facts warrant it. If there's a special place you've happened upon that we haven't included, we'll pass the information along to the writers so they can check it out. So please send us a letter or postcard (we're at 201 East 50th Street, New York, NY 10022). We'll look forward to hearing from you. And in the meantime, have a wonderful trip!

Karen Cure

Karen Cure
Editorial Director

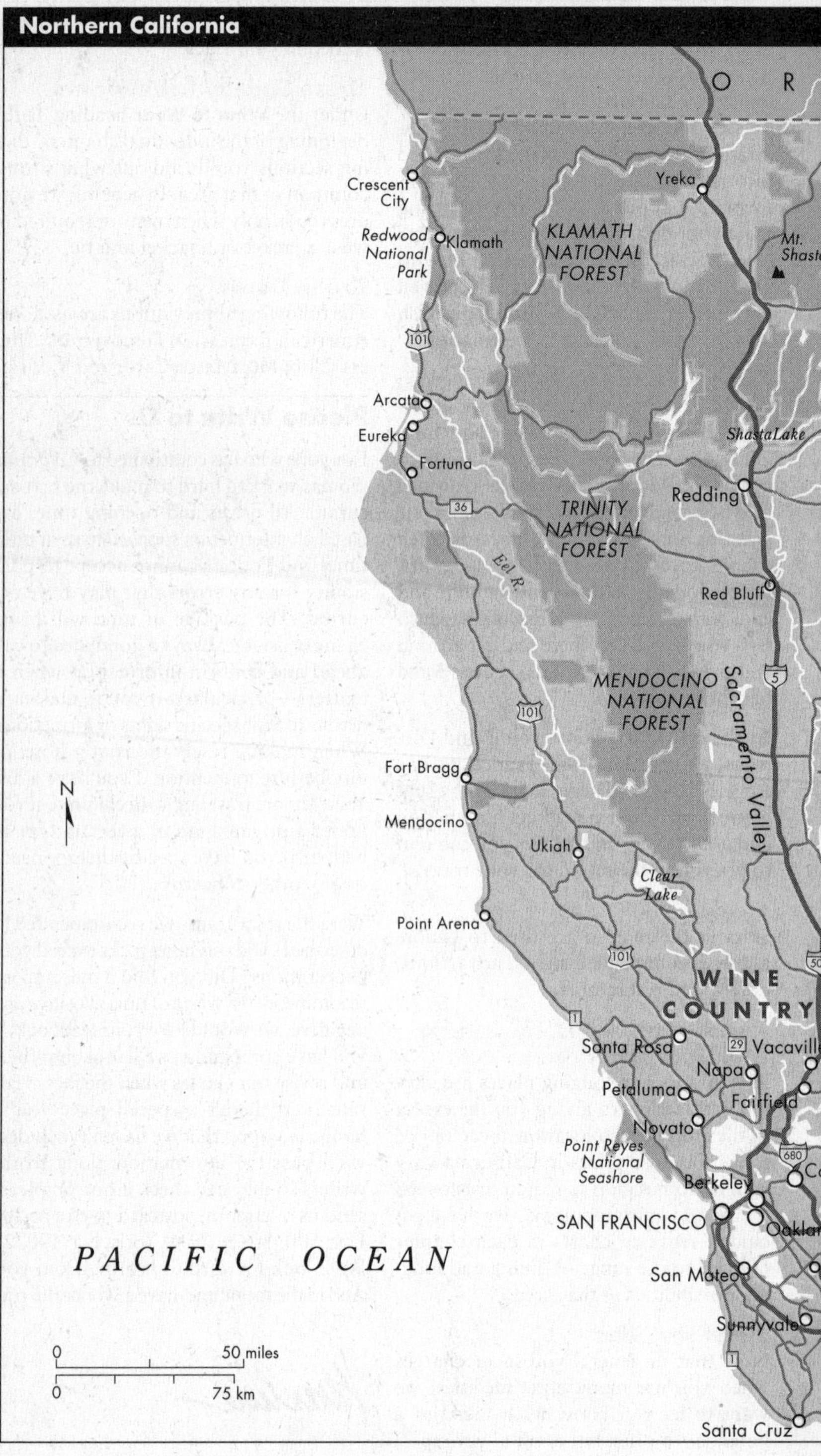
Northern California
O R
Crescent City
Yreka
Redwood National Park
Klamath
KLAMATH NATIONAL FOREST
Mt. Shasta
101
Arcata
Eureka
Fortuna
Shasta Lake
Redding
36
TRINITY NATIONAL FOREST
Eel R.
Red Bluff
5
MENDOCINO NATIONAL FOREST
Sacramento Valley
101
Fort Bragg
N
Mendocino
Ukiah
Clear Lake
Point Arena
101
505
WINE COUNTRY
1
Santa Rosa
29
Vacaville
Napa
Petaluma
Fairfield
Novato
Point Reyes National Seashore
680
Berkeley
SAN FRANCISCO
PACIFIC OCEAN
San Mateo
Sunnyvale
0
50 miles
0
75 km
1
Santa Cruz

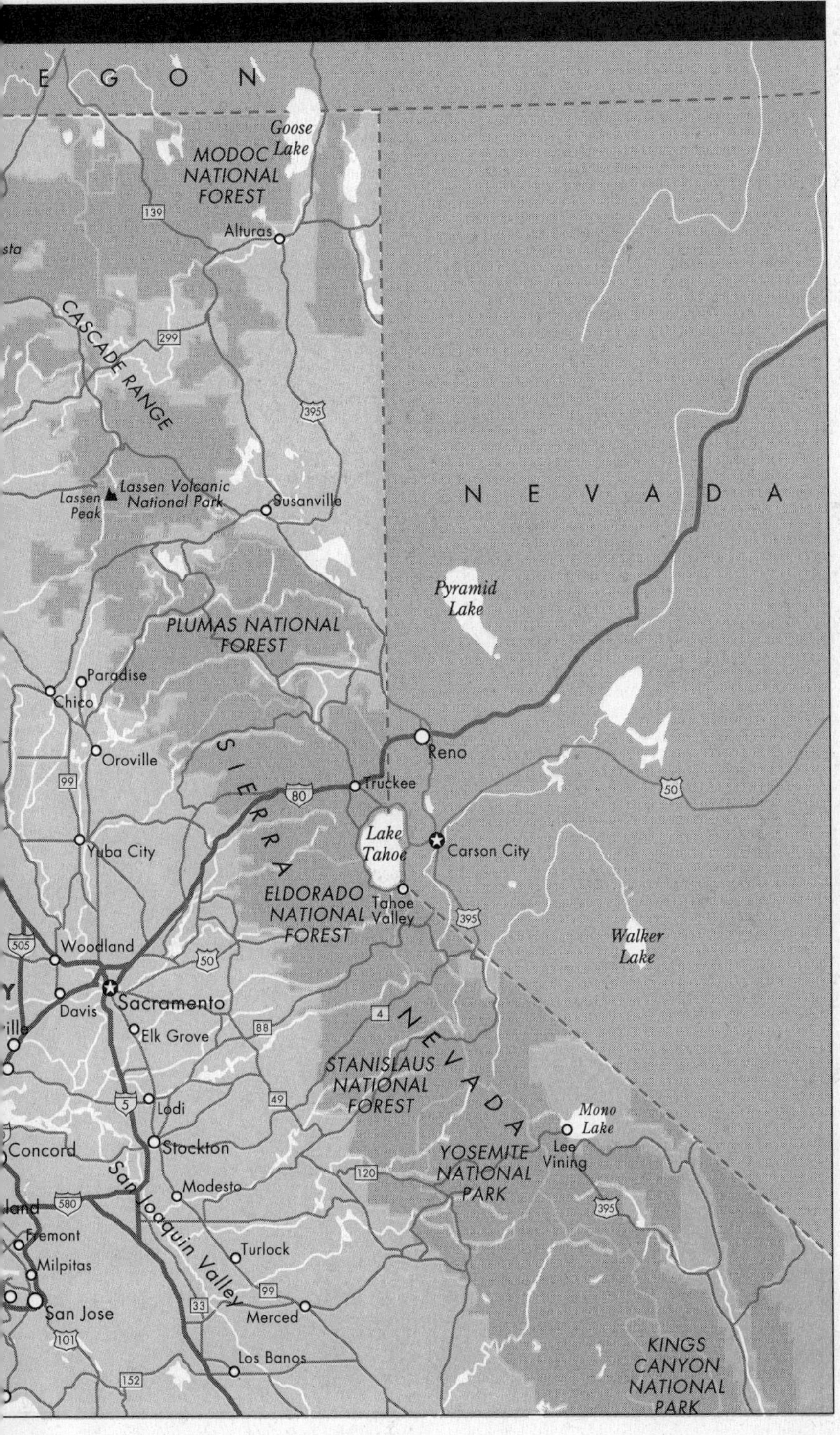

EGON
Goose Lake
MODOC NATIONAL FOREST
139
Alturas
CASCADE RANGE
299
395
Lassen Peak
Lassen Volcanic National Park
Susanville
NEVADA
Pyramid Lake
PLUMAS NATIONAL FOREST
Paradise
Chico
Oroville
SIERRA
Reno
99
80
Truckee
50
Lake Tahoe
Carson City
Yuba City
ELDORADO NATIONAL FOREST
Tahoe Valley
395
Walker Lake
505
Woodland
50
Sacramento
Davis
4
NEVADA
Elk Grove
88
STANISLAUS NATIONAL FOREST
5
Lodi
49
Mono Lake
Concord
Stockton
YOSEMITE NATIONAL PARK
Lee Vining
San Joaquin Valley
120
Modesto
580
395
Fremont
Turlock
Milpitas
99
33
San Jose
Merced
101
Los Banos
152
KINGS CANYON NATIONAL PARK

Southern California

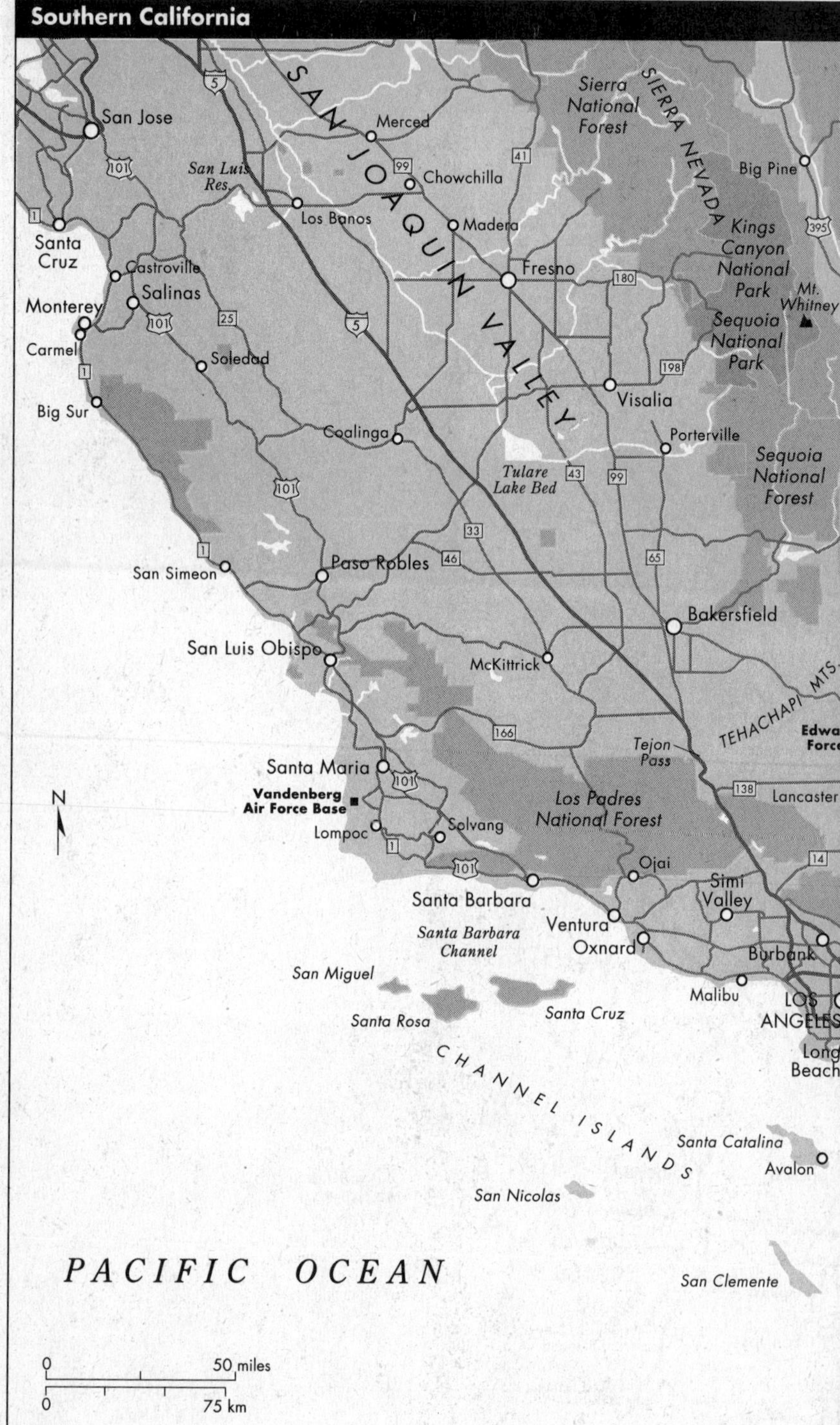

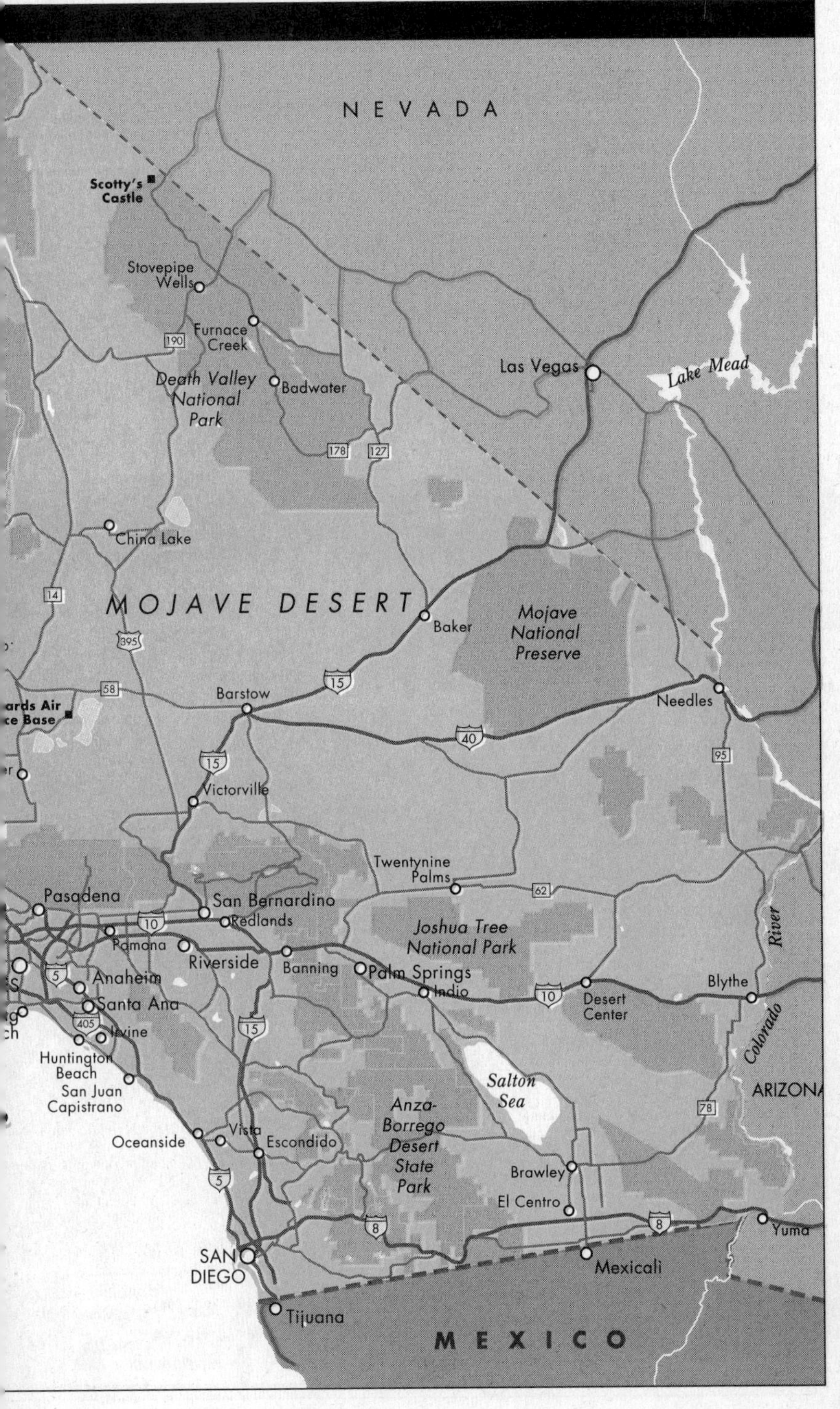
NEVADA
Scotty's Castle
Stovepipe Wells
Furnace Creek
190
Death Valley National Park
Badwater
178
127
Las Vegas
Lake Mead
China Lake
14
MOJAVE DESERT
Baker
Mojave National Preserve
395
58
Barstow
15
Needles
40
95
Victorville
Twentynine Palms
62
Pasadena
San Bernardino
Redlands
10
Joshua Tree National Park
Pomona
Riverside
Banning
Palm Springs
Indio
Blythe
Desert Center
River
Colorado
5
Anaheim
Santa Ana
405
Irvine
Huntington Beach
San Juan Capistrano
Salton Sea
Anza-Borrego Desert State Park
ARIZONA
78
Oceanside
Vista
Escondido
Brawley
El Centro
8
Yuma
SAN DIEGO
Mexicali
Tijuana
MEXICO

The United States

ONTARIO
CANADA
QUÉBEC
NEW BRUNSWICK
Fredericton
Québec
MAINE
Montréal
Augusta
Ottawa
Montpelier
VT.
Concord
N.H.
Boston
MASS.
R.I.
Providence
Lake Superior
MINNESOTA
Duluth
MICHIGAN
WISCONSIN
Lake Huron
Toronto
Lake Ontario
Albany
Hartford
CONN.
St. Paul
Green Bay
Lake Michigan
Minneapolis
Buffalo
NEW YORK
Lake Erie
Milwaukee
Lansing
Madison
Detroit
Cleveland
New York
N.J.
PENNSYLVANIA
Trenton
IOWA
Chicago
Pittsburgh
Harrisburg
Philadelphia
OHIO
Dover
Des Moines
Omaha
INDIANA
Baltimore
MD.
DEL.
Columbus
Annapolis
ILLINOIS
Indianapolis
WEST VIRGINIA
Washington, D.C.
Springfield
Charleston
Richmond
Mississippi R.
Cincinnati
Topeka
Frankfort
Norfolk
Louisville
VIRGINIA
Kansas City
Jefferson City
St. Louis
Ohio R.
KENTUCKY
MISSOURI
Raleigh
Nashville
NORTH CAROLINA
TENNESSEE
Tulsa
Columbia
ARKANSAS
Memphis
SOUTH CAROLINA
Little Rock
Tennessee R.
Savannah R.
Atlanta
ATLANTIC OCEAN
Birmingham
GEORGIA
MISSISSIPPI
Savannah
Montgomery
ALABAMA
Jackson
Jacksonville
Baton Rouge
Mobile
Tallahassee
FLORIDA
Orlando
New Orleans
Houston
LOUISIANA
Bahama Islands
Miami
Nassau
Gulf of Mexico
N
0
200 miles
0
300 km

World Time Zones

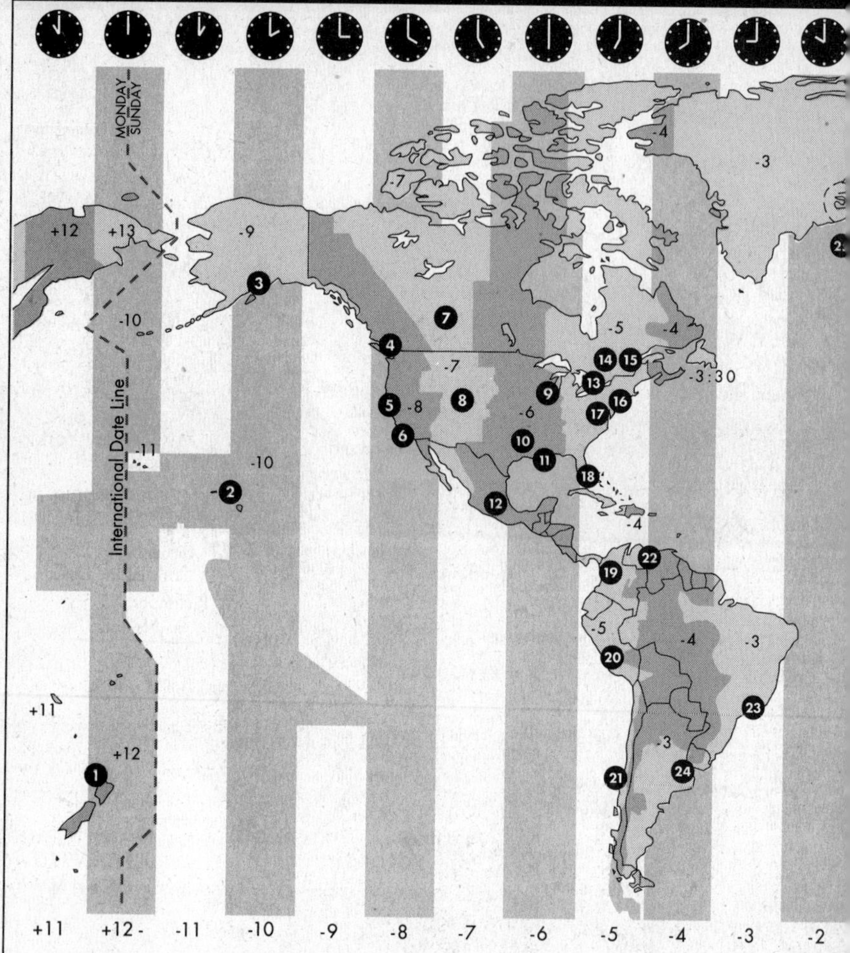

Numbers below vertical bands relate each zone to Greenwich Mean Time (0 hrs.).
Local times frequently differ from these general indications,
as indicated by light-face numbers on map.

Algiers, **29**
Anchorage, **3**
Athens, **41**
Auckland, **1**
Baghdad, **46**
Bangkok, **50**
Beijing, **54**
Berlin, **34**
Bogotá, **19**
Budapest, **37**
Buenos Aires, **24**
Caracas, **22**
Chicago, **9**
Copenhagen, **33**
Dallas, **10**
Delhi, **48**
Denver, **8**
Djakarta, **53**
Dublin, **26**
Edmonton, **7**
Hong Kong, **56**
Honolulu, **2**
Istanbul, **40**
Jerusalem, **42**
Johannesburg, **44**
Lima, **20**
Lisbon, **28**
London (Greenwich), **27**
Los Angeles, **6**
Madrid, **38**
Manila, **57**

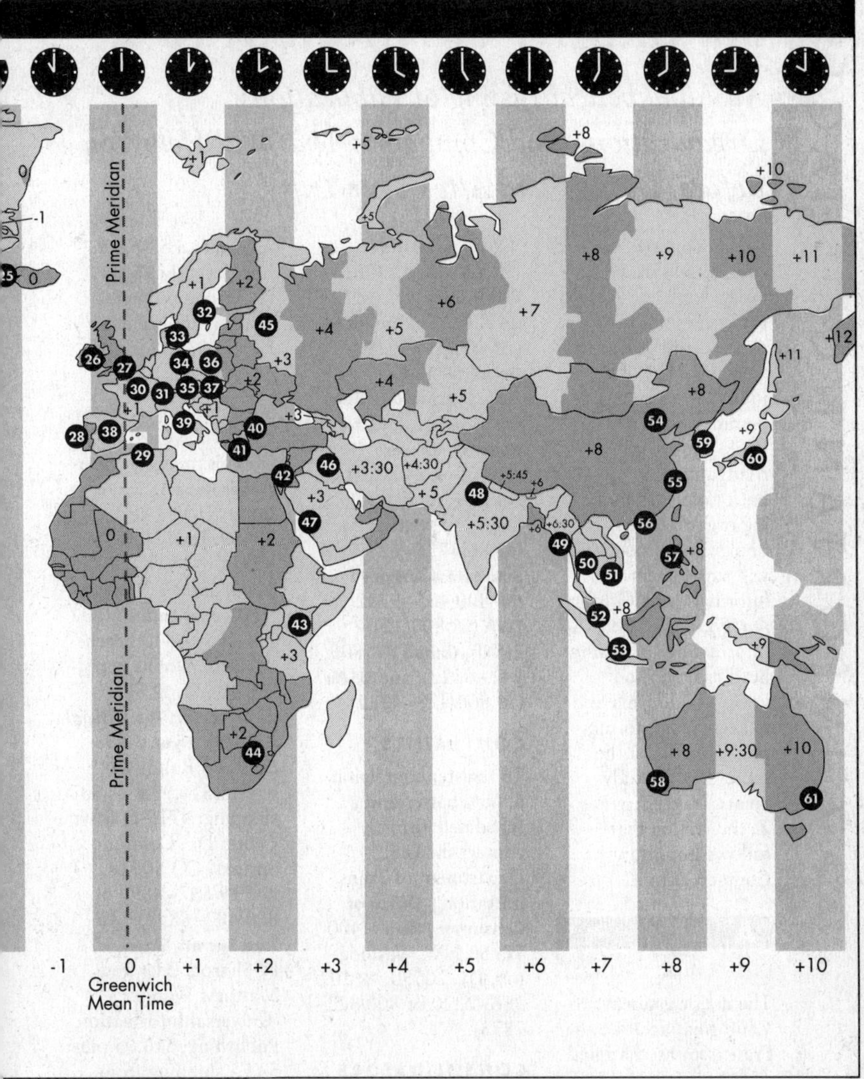

Mecca, **47**
Mexico City, **12**
Miami, **18**
Montréal, **15**
Moscow, **45**
Nairobi, **43**
New Orleans, **11**
New York City, **16**

Ottawa, **14**
Paris, **30**
Perth, **58**
Reykjavík, **25**
Rio de Janeiro, **23**
Rome, **39**
Saigon (Ho Chi Minh City), **51**

San Francisco, **5**
Santiago, **21**
Seoul, **59**
Shanghai, **55**
Singapore, **52**
Stockholm, **32**
Sydney, **61**
Tokyo, **60**

Toronto, **13**
Vancouver, **4**
Vienna, **35**
Warsaw, **36**
Washington, D.C., **17**
Yangon, **49**
Zürich, **31**

IMPORTANT CONTACTS A TO Z

An Alphabetical Listing of Publications, Organizations, and Companies That Will Help You Before, During, and After Your Trip

No single travel resource can give you every detail about every topic that might interest or concern you at the various stages of your journey—when you're planning your trip, while you're on the road, and after you get back home. The following organizations, books, and brochures will supplement the information in *California '96*. For related information, including both basic tips on visiting California and background information on many of the topics below, study Smart Travel Tips A to Z, the section that follows Important Contacts A to Z.

A

AIR TRAVEL

The major gateways to California include San Francisco International Airport (SFO) and Los Angeles International Airport (LAX). Flying time is roughly six hours from New York and four hours from Chicago. Flying between San Francisco and Los Angeles takes one hour.

CARRIERS

Carriers serving California include **Air Canada** (☎ 800/776–3000), **Alaska Airlines** (☎ 800/426–0333), **America West** (☎ 800/235–9292), **American** (☎ 800/433–7300), **British Airways** (☎ 800/247–9297), **Continental** (☎ 800/525–0280), **Delta** (☎ 800/221–1212), **Japan Air Lines** (☎ 800/525–3663), **Midwest Express** (☎ 800/452–2022), **Northwest** (☎ 800/225–2525), **Reno Air** (☎ 800/736–6247), **Southwest Airlines** (☎ 800/435–9792), **TWA** (☎ 800/221–2000), **United** (☎ 800/241–6522), and **USAir** (☎ 800/428–4322).

COMPLAINTS

To register complaints about charter and scheduled airlines, contact the U.S. Department of Transportation's **Office of Consumer Affairs** (400 7th St. NW, Washington, DC 20590, ☎ 202/366–2220 or 800/322–7873).

CONSOLIDATORS

Established consolidators selling to the public include **TFI Tours International** (34 W. 32nd St., New York, NY 10001, ☎ 212/736–1140 or 800/745–8000).

PUBLICATIONS

For general information about charter carriers, ask for the Office of Consumer Affairs' brochure **"Plane Talk: Public Charter Flights."** The Department of Transportation also publishes a 58-page booklet, **"Fly Rights"** ($1.75; Consumer Information Center, Dept. 133B, Pueblo, CO 81009).

For other tips and hints, consult the Consumers Union's monthly **"Consumer Reports Travel Letter"** ($39 a year; Box 53629, Boulder, CO 80322, ☎ 800/234–1970) and the newsletter **"Travel Smart"** ($37 for 1st year; 40 Beechdale Rd., Dobbs Ferry, NY 10522, ☎ 800/327–3633); ***The Official Frequent Flyer Guidebook,*** by Randy Petersen ($14.99 plus $3 shipping; 4715-C Town Center Dr., Colorado Springs, CO 80916, ☎ 719/597–8899 or 800/487–8893); ***Airfare Secrets Exposed,*** by Sharon Tyler and Matthew Wonder (Universal Information Publishing; $16.95 plus $3.75 shipping from Sandcastle Publishing, Box 3070-A, South Pasadena, CA 91031, ☎ 213/255–3616 or 800/655–0053); and ***202 Tips Even the Best Business Travelers May Not Know,*** by Christopher McGinnis ($10 plus $3 shipping; Irwin Professional Publishing, 1333 Burr Ridge Pkwy., Burr Ridge, IL 60521, ☎ 708/789–4000 or 800/634–3966).

B

BETTER BUSINESS BUREAU

For local contacts, consult the **Council of Better Business Bureaus** (4200 Wilson Blvd., Arlington, VA 22203, ☎ 703/276–0100).

BUS TRAVEL

Greyhound (☎ 800/231–2222) provides service to and throughout California.

C

CAR RENTAL

Major car-rental companies represented in California include **Alamo** (☎ 800/327–9633, 0800/272–2000 in the U.K.), **Avis** (☎ 800/331–1212, 800/879–2847 in Canada), **Budget** (☎ 800/527–0700, 0800/181–181 in the U.K.), **Hertz** (☎ 800/654–3131, 800/263–0600 in Canada, 0181/679–1799 in the U.K.), and **National** (☎ 800/227–7368, 0181/950–5050 in the U.K., where it is known as Europcar). In Los Angeles and San Diego, rates for an economy car with unlimited mileage begin at $25 a day and $170 a week. In San Francisco, rates begin at $30 and $175.

CHILDREN AND TRAVEL

FLYING

Look into **"Flying With Baby"** ($5.95 plus $1 shipping; Third Street Press, Box 261250, Littleton, CO 80126, ☎ 303/595–5959), cowritten by a flight attendant. **"Kids and Teens in Flight,"** free from the U.S. Department of Transportation's Office of Consumer Affairs, offers tips for children flying alone. Every two years the February issue of ***Family Travel Times*** (*see* Know-How, *below*) details children's services on three dozen airlines.

KNOW-HOW

Family Travel Times, published 10 times a year by Travel With Your Children (annual subscription $55; TWYCH, 45 W. 18th St., New York, NY 10011, ☎ 212/206–0688), covers destinations, types of vacations, and modes of travel.

The ***Family Travel Guides*** catalogue ($1 postage; ☎ 510/527–5849) lists about 200 books and articles on family travel. Also check out ***Take Your Baby and Go! A Guide for Traveling with Babies, Toddlers and Young Children,*** by Sheri Andrews, Judy Bordeaux, and Vivian Vasquez ($5.95 plus $1.50 shipping; Bear Creek Publications, 2507 Minor Ave., Seattle, WA 98102, ☎ 206/322–7604 or 800/326–6566).

LOCAL INFORMATION

Consult the lively by-parents, for-parents ***Where Should We Take the Kids? California*** ($17; Fodor's Travel Publications, ☎ 800/533–6478 and in bookstores). Helpful city guides include ***The Parents' Guide to L.A.,*** ($19.95 plus $4–$5 shipping; Mani Flattery Publications, c/o SCB Distributors, 15612 South New Century Dr., Gardena, CA 90248, ☎ 310/532-9400), which includes discount coupons for area attractions; ***Sacramento With Kids,*** by Dierdre Honnold (spring 1996 edition, $11.95 plus $2 shipping and 7¾% sales tax for CA residents; Wordwrights International, Box 1941, Carmichael, CA 95609, ☎ 916/483–4961); and ***San Jose With Kids*** ($11.95 plus $2 shipping and 7¾% sales tax for CA residents; also from Wordwrights).

San Francisco/Peninsula Parent (Box 1280, Millbrae 94030, ☎ 415/342–9203), ***Parents Press*** (1454 6th St., Berkeley 94710, ☎ 510/524–1602), ***Parents Monthly*** (8611 Folsom Blvd., Suite A, Sacramento 95826, ☎ 916/383–7012), ***L.A. Parent*** (Box 3204, Burbank 91504, ☎ 818/846–0400), and ***San Diego Family Press*** (Box 23960, San Diego 92193, ☎ 619/685–6970) are monthly newspapers that list activities for children. These free papers can be found in racks at many libraries and some supermarkets; they are available by mail for a small fee.

TOUR OPERATORS

Contact **Grandtravel** (6900 Wisconsin Ave., Suite 706, Chevy Chase, MD 20815, ☎ 301/986–0790 or 800/247–7651), which has tours for people traveling with grandchildren ages seven to 17.

Rascals in Paradise (650 5th St., Suite 505, San Francisco, CA 94107, ☎ 415/978–9800 or 800/872–7225) arranges family trips to several California resorts and ranches with children's programs. Child care—if desired—is included.

Travelling With Children (2313 Valley St., Berkeley, CA 94702, ☎ 510/848–0929 or, in CA, 800/499–0929, FAX 510/848–0935) offers consultation services and makes reservations for California guest ranches, house rentals, rafting trips, Disneyland packages, and other family vacations.

CUSTOMS

CANADIANS

Contact **Revenue Canada** (2265 St. Laurent Blvd. S, Ottawa, Ontario K1G 4K3, ☎ 613/993–0534) for a copy of the free brochure **"I Declare/Je Déclare"** and for details on duties that exceed the standard duty-free limit.

U.K. CITIZENS

HM Customs and Excise (Dorset House, Stamford St., London SE1 9NG, ☎ 0171/202–4227) can answer questions about U.K. customs regulations and publishes **"A Guide for Travellers,"** detailing standard procedures and import rules.

D

FOR TRAVELERS WITH DISABILITIES

COMPLAINTS

To register complaints under the provisions of the Americans With Disabilities Act, contact the U.S. Department of Justice's **Public Access Section** (Box 66738, Washington, DC 20035, ☎ 202/514–0301, FAX 202/307–1198, TTY 202/514–0383).

DISCOUNT PASSES

The **National Park Service** (Box 37127, Washington, DC 20013-7127) provides a Golden Access Passport free to those who are medically blind or have a permanent disability; the passport covers the entry fee for the holder and anyone accompanying the holder in the same private vehicle and a 50% discount on camping and some other user fees. Apply for the passport in person at a national recreation facility that charges an entrance fee; proof of disability is required.

ORGANIZATIONS

FOR TRAVELERS WITH HEARING IMPAIRMENTS➢ Contact the **American Academy of Otolaryngology** (1 Prince St., Alexandria, VA 22314, ☎ 703/836–4444, FAX 703/683–5100, TTY 703/519–1585).

FOR TRAVELERS WITH MOBILITY IMPAIRMENTS➢ Contact the **Information Center for Individuals with Disabilities** (Fort Point Pl., 27–43 Wormwood St., Boston, MA 02210, ☎ 617/727–5540, 800/462–5015 in MA, TTY 617/345–9743); **Mobility International USA** (Box 10767, Eugene, OR 97440, ☎ and TTY 503/343–1284, FAX 503/343–6812), the U.S. branch of an international organization based in Belgium (*see below*) that has affiliates in 30 countries; **MossRehab Hospital Travel Information Service** (1200 W. Tabor Rd., Philadelphia, PA 19141, ☎ 215/456–9603, TTY 215/456–9602); the **Society for the Advancement of Travel for the Handicapped** (SATH, 347 5th Ave., Suite 610, New York, NY 10016, ☎ 212/447–7284, FAX 212/725–8253); the **Travel Industry and Disabled Exchange** (TIDE, 5435 Donna Ave., Tarzana, CA 91356, ☎ 818/344–3640, FAX 818/344–0078); and **Travelin' Talk** (Box 3534, Clarksville, TN 37043, ☎ 615/552–6670, FAX 615/552–1182).

FOR TRAVELERS WITH VISION IMPAIRMENTS➢ Contact the **American Council of the Blind** (1155 15th St. NW, Suite 720, Washington, DC 20005, ☎ 202/467–5081, FAX 202/467–5085) or the **American Foundation for the Blind** (15 W. 16th St., New York, NY 10011, ☎ 212/620–2000, TTY 212/620–2158).

IN THE U.K.

Contact the **Royal Association for Disability and Rehabilitation** (RADAR, 12 City Forum, 250 City Rd., London EC1V 8AF, ☎ 0171/250–3222) or **Mobility International** (Rue de Manchester 25, B1070 Brussels, Belgium, ☎ 00–322–410–6297), an international clearinghouse of travel information for people with disabilities.

PUBLICATIONS

Several free publications are available from the U.S. Information Center (Box 100, Pueblo, CO 81009, ☎ 719/948–3334): **"New Horizons for the Air Traveler with a Disability"** (address to Dept. 355A), describing legally mandated changes; the pocket-size **"Fly Smart"** (Dept. 575B), good on flight safety; and the Airport Operators Council's worldwide **"Access Travel: Airports"** (Dept. 575A).

Fodor's ***Great American Vacations for Travelers with Disabilities*** ($18; available in bookstores or call 800/533–6478) details accessible attractions, restaurants, and hotels in Los Angeles, San Diego, San Francisco, and Yosemite National Park. The 500-page ***Travelin' Talk Directory*** ($35; ☎ 615/552–6670) lists people and organizations who help travelers with disabilities. For specialist travel agents worldwide, consult the ***Directory of Travel Agencies for the Disabled*** ($19.95 plus $2 shipping; Twin Peaks Press, Box 129, Vancouver, WA 98666, ☎ 206/694–2462 or 800/637–2256). The Sierra Club publishes ***Easy Access to National Parks*** ($16 plus $3 shipping; 730 Polk St., San Francisco, CA 94109, ☎ 415/776–2211 or 800/935–1056).

"Around the Town with Ease" gives accessibility ratings to the 109 most visited Los Angeles sites. Send $2 to the Junior League of Los Angeles (Gate 12, Farmer's Market, 6301 W. 3rd St., Los Angeles 90036, ☎ 213/937–5566). Accessible San Diego (2466 Bartel St., San Diego 92123, ☎ 619/279–0704, TTY 800/735–2922) publishes the 34-page **"Access Guide for Travelers with Disabilities"** (cost: $5).

San Francisco Convention and Visitors Bureau (Box 429097, San Francisco 94142-9097, ☎ 415/974–6900, TTY 415/392–0328) has free pamphlets and booklets with information about public transportation and the accessibility of various attractions. These include the slightly dated but still helpful **"Guide to San Francisco for the Person Who Is Disabled."** The California State Coastal Conservancy (Publications Dept., 1330 Broadway, Suite 1100, Oakland 94612, ☎ 510/286–1015) publishes the free booklet **"Wheelchair Riders Guide to San Francisco Bay and Nearby Shorelines."**

TRAVEL AGENCIES AND TOUR OPERATORS

The Americans with Disabilities Act requires that travel firms serve the needs of all travelers. However, some agencies and operators specialize in making group and individual arrangements for travelers with disabilities, among them **Access Adventures** (206 Chestnut Ridge Rd., Rochester, NY 14624, ☎ 716/889–9096), run by a former physical-rehab counselor; **Tailored Tours** (Box 797687, Dallas, TX 75379, ☎ 214/612–1168 or 800/628–8542); and **Travel Trends** (2 Allan Plaza, 4922 51st Ave., Leduc, Alberta T9E 6X2, ☎ 403/986–9000 or 800/661–2109 in Canada), which has group tours and is especially good for cruises. In addition, many general-interest operators and agencies (*see* Tour Operators, *below*) can also arrange vacations for travelers with disabilities.

FOR TRAVELERS WITH HEARING IMPAIRMENTS➢ One agency is **International Express** (7319-B Baltimore Ave., College Park, MD 20740, ☎ and TTY 301/699–8836, FAX 301/699–8836), which arranges group and independent trips.

FOR TRAVELERS WITH MOBILITY IMPAIRMENTS➢ A number of operators specialize in working with travelers with mobility impairments: **Hinsdale Travel Service** (201 E. Ogden Ave., Suite 100, Hinsdale, IL 60521, ☎ 708/325–1335 or 800/303–5521), a travel agency that will give you access to the services of wheelchair traveler Janice Perkins; and **Wheelchair Journeys** (16979 Redmond Way, Redmond, WA 98052, ☎ 206/885–2210), which can handle arrangements worldwide.

FOR TRAVELERS WITH DEVELOPMENTAL DISABILITIES➢ Contact the nonprofit **New Directions** (5276 Hollister Ave., Suite 207, Santa Barbara, CA 93111, ☎ 805/967–2841).

DISCOUNTS

Options include **Entertainment Travel Editions** (fee $28–$53, depending on destination; Box 1068, Trumbull, CT 06611, ☎ 800/445–4137), **Great American Traveler** ($49.95 annually; Box 27965, Salt Lake City, UT 84127, ☎ 800/548–2812), **Moment's Notice Discount Travel Club** ($25 annually, single or family; 163 Amsterdam Ave., Suite 137, New York, NY 10023, ☎ 212/486–0500), **Privilege Card** ($74.95 annually; 3391 Peachtree Rd. NE, Suite 110, Atlanta, GA 30326, ☎ 404/262–0222 or 800/236–9732), **Travelers Advantage** ($49 annually, single or family; CUC Travel Service, 49 Music Sq. W, Nashville, TN 37203, ☎ 800/548–1116 or 800/648–4037), and **Worldwide Discount Travel Club** ($50 annually for family, $40 single; 1674 Meridian Ave., Miami Beach, FL 33139, ☎ 305/534–2082).

G

GAY AND LESBIAN TRAVEL

ORGANIZATION

The **International Gay Travel Association** (Box 4974, Key West, FL 33041, ☎ 800/448–8550), a consortium of 800 businesses, can supply names of travel agents and tour operators.

PUBLICATIONS

The premier international travel magazine for gays and lesbians is ***Our World*** ($35 for 10 issues; 1104 N. Nova Rd., Suite 251, Daytona Beach, FL 32117, ☎ 904/441–5367). The 16-page monthly **"Out & About"** ($49 for 10 issues; ☎ 212/645–6922 or 800/929–2268) covers gay-friendly resorts, hotels, cruise lines, and airlines.

Many California cities large and small have lesbian and gay publications available in sidewalk racks and at bars and other social spaces; most have extensive events and information listings. The papers include ***San Francisco Bay Times*** (288 7th St., San Francisco 94103, ☎ 415/626–8121), ***Mom Guess What Newspaper*** (1725 L St., Sacramento 95814, ☎ 916/441–6397), ***Edge*** (6434 Santa Monica Blvd., Los Angeles 90038, ☎ 213/962–6994), ***Bottom Line*** (1243 N. Gene Autry Trail, Palm Springs 92262, ☎ 619/323–0552), and ***Gay & Lesbian Times*** (3636 5th Ave., Suite 101, San Diego 92103, ☎ 619/299–6397).

SWITCHBOARDS/HOT LINES

For general information, contact the **Gay and Lesbian Community Services Center** (1625 N. Schrader Blvd., Los Angeles 90028, ☎ 213/993–7400), the **Lambda Community Center** (1931 L St., Sacramento 95814, ☎ 916/442–0185), **Lesbian and Gay Men's Community Center** (3916 Normal St., San Diego 92103, ☎ 619/692–4297), or, in the San Francisco Bay Area, the **Pacific Center Lesbian, Gay and Bisexual Switchboard** (☎ 510/841–6224).

TOUR OPERATORS

Cruises and resort vacations are handled by **R.S.V.P. Travel Productions** (2800 University Ave. SE, Minneapolis, MN 55414, ☎ 800/328–7787) for gays, **Olivia** (4400 Market St., Oakland, CA 94608, ☎ 800/631–6277) for lesbian travelers. For mixed gay and lesbian travel, contact **Toto Tours** (1326 W. Albion, Suite 3W, Chicago, IL 60626, ☎ 312/274–8686 or 800/565–1241), which has group tours worldwide.

TRAVEL AGENCIES

The largest agencies serving gay travelers are **Advance Travel** (10700 Northwest Freeway, Suite 160, Houston, TX 77092, ☎ 713/682–2002 or 800/695–0880), **Islanders/Kennedy Travel** (183 W. 10th St., New York, NY 10014, ☎ 212/242–3222 or 800/988–1181), **Now Voyager** (4406 18th St., San Francisco, CA 94114, ☎ 415/626–1169 or 800/255–6951), and **Yellowbrick Road** (1500 W. Balmoral Ave., Chicago, IL 60640, ☎ 312/561–1800 or 800/642–2488). **Skylink Women's Travel** (746 Ashland Ave., Santa Monica, CA 90405, ☎ 310/452–0506 or 800/225–5759) works with lesbians.

I

INSURANCE

Travel insurance covering baggage, health, and trip cancellation or interruptions is available from **Access America** (Box 90315, Richmond, VA 23286, ☎ 804/285–3300 or 800/284–8300), **Carefree Travel Insurance** (Box 9366, 100 Garden City Plaza, Garden City, NY 11530, ☎ 516/294–0220 or 800/323–3149), **Near Travel Services** (Box 1339, Calumet City, IL 60409, ☎ 708/868–6700 or 800/654–6700), **Tele-Trip** (Mutual of Omaha Plaza, Box 31716, Omaha, NE 68131, ☎ 800/228–9792), **Travel Insured International** (Box 280568, East Hartford, CT 06128-0568, ☎ 203/528–7663 or 800/243–3174), **Travel Guard International** (1145 Clark St., Stevens Point, WI 54481, ☎ 715/345–0505 or 800/826–1300), and **Wallach & Company** (107 W. Federal St., Box 480, Middleburg, VA 22117, ☎ 703/687–3166 or 800/237–6615).

IN THE U.K.

The **Association of British Insurers** (51 Gresham St., London EC2V 7HQ, ☎ 0171/600–3333; 30 Gordon St., Glasgow G1 3PU, ☎ 0141/226–3905; Scottish Provident Bldg., Donegall Sq. W, Belfast BT1 6JE, ☎ 01232/249176; and other locations) gives advice by phone and publishes the free **"Holiday Insurance,"** which sets out typical policy provisions and costs.

L

LODGING

APARTMENT AND VILLA RENTAL

Among the companies to contact are **Hometours International** (Box 11503, Knoxville, TN 37939, ☎ 615/588–8722 or 800/367–4668), **Rent-a-Home International** (7200 34th Ave. NW, Seattle, WA 98117, ☎ 206/789–9377 or 800/488–7368), **Vacation Home Rentals Worldwide** (235 Kensington Ave., Norwood, NJ 07648, ☎ 201/767–9393 or 800/633–3284), and **Villas and Apartments Abroad** (420 Madison Ave., Suite 1105, New York, NY 10017, ☎ 212/759–1025 or 800/433–3020). Members of the travel club **Hideaways International** ($99 annually; 767 Islington St., Portsmouth, NH 03802, ☎ 603/430–4403 or 800/843–4433) receive two annual guides plus quarterly newsletters and arrange rentals among themselves.

CAMPING

MISTIX (Box 85705, San Diego, CA 92186-5705) handles camping reservations, which in many cases are required, in California's national (☎ 800/365–2267) and state (☎ 800/444–7275) parks. The *California RV and Camping Guide,* available free from the **California Travel Parks Association** (Box 5648, Auburn, CA 95604, ☎ 916/823–1076, FAX 916/823–6331), has information about nearly 400 private parks and campgrounds throughout the state and bordering areas of Oregon and Nevada.

HOME EXCHANGE

Principal clearinghouses include **HomeLink International/Vacation Exchange Club** ($60 annually; Box 650, Key West, FL 33041, ☎ 305/294–1448 or 800/638–3841), which gives members four annual directories, with a listing in one, plus updates; **Intervac International** ($65 annually; Box 590504, San Francisco, CA 94159, ☎ 415/435–3497), which has three annual directories; and **Loan-a-Home** ($35–$45 annually; 2 Park La., Apt. 6E, Mount Vernon, NY 10552-3443, ☎ 914/664–7640), which specializes in long-term exchanges.

M

MONEY MATTERS

ATMS

For specific **Cirrus** locations in the United States and Canada, call 800/424–7787. For U.S. **Plus** locations, call 800/843–7587 and enter the area code and first three digits of the number you're calling from (or of the calling area where you want an ATM).

WIRING FUNDS

Funds can be wired via **American Express MoneyGram℠** (☎ 800/926–9400 from the U.S. and Canada for locations and information) or **Western Union** (☎ 800/325–6000 for agent locations or to send using MasterCard or Visa, 800/321–2923 in Canada).

P

PARKS

For information on specific national parks, monuments, and recreation areas, contact the **National Park Service** (Fort Mason, Bldg. 201, San Francisco, CA 94123, ☎ 415/556–0560). For information on state parks, beaches, and recreation areas, contact the **California State Park System** (Dept. of Parks and Recreation, Box 942896, Sacramento 94296, ☎ 916/653–6995). For campsite reservation numbers, *see* Lodging, *above*.

PASSPORTS AND VISAS

U.K. CITIZENS

For fees, documentation requirements, and to get an emergency passport, call the **London passport office** (☎ 0171/271–3000). For visa information, call the **U.S. Embassy Visa Information Line** (☎ 0891/200–290; calls cost 49p per minute or 39p per minute cheap rate) or write to the **U.S. Embassy Visa Branch** (5 Upper Grosvenor St., London W1A 2JB). If you live in Northern Ireland, write to the **U.S. Consulate General** (Queen's House, Queen St., Belfast BTI 6EO).

PHOTO HELP

The **Kodak Information Center** (☎ 800/242–2424) answers consumer questions about film and photography.

R

RAIL TRAVEL

Amtrak (☎ 800/872–7245) trains (the *Zephyr,* from Chicago via Denver, and the *Coast Starlight,* traveling between Los Angeles and Seattle) stop in Oakland (Jack London Sq., 245 2nd St.) and Emeryville (5885 Landregan St.); shuttle buses connect the Emeryville station and the Ferry Building on the Embarcadero at the foot of Market Street in San Francisco.

S

SENIOR CITIZENS

EDUCATIONAL TRAVEL

The nonprofit **Elderhostel** (75 Federal St., 3rd Floor, Boston, MA 02110, ☎ 617/426–7788), for people 60 and older, has offered inexpensive study programs since 1975. The nearly 2,000 courses cover everything from marine science to Greek myths and cowboy poetry. Fees for programs in the United States and Canada, which usually last one week, run about $300, not including transportation.

ORGANIZATIONS

Contact the **American Association of Retired Persons** (AARP, 601 E St. NW, Washington, DC 20049, ☎ 202/434–2277; $8 per person or couple annually). Its Purchase Privilege Program gets members discounts on lodging, car rentals, and sightseeing, and the AARP Motoring Plan furnishes domestic trip-routing information and emergency road-service aid for an annual fee of $39.95 per person or couple ($59.95 for a premium version).

For other discounts on lodgings, car rentals, and other travel products, along with magazines and newsletters, contact the **National Council of Senior Citizens** (membership $12 annually; 1331 F St. NW, Washington, DC 20004, ☎ 202/347–8800) and **Mature Outlook** (subscription $9.95 annually; 6001 N. Clark St., Chicago, IL 60660, ☎ 312/465–6466 or 800/336–6330).

PUBLICATIONS

The 50+ Traveler's Guidebook: Where to Go, Where to Stay, What to Do, by Anita Williams and Merrimac Dillon ($12.95; St. Martin's Press, 175 5th Ave., New York, NY 10010, ☎ 212/674–5151 or 800/288–2131), offers many useful tips. ***The Mature Traveler*** ($29.95; Box 50400, Reno, NV 89513, ☎ 702/786–7419), a monthly newsletter, covers travel deals.

SPORTS

FISHING

California has abundant fishing options: deep-sea fishing expeditions, surf fishing from the shore, and freshwater fishing in streams, rivers, lakes, and reservoirs. You'll need a California fishing license. State residents pay $23.25 ($2 for senior citizens and those on limited income), but nonresidents must fork over $64.25 for a one-year license. Both residents and nonresidents can purchase a one-day license for $8.25. For information, contact the **Department of Fish and Game** (3211 S St., Sacramento 95816, ☎ 916/227–2244). The department can also advise you on hunting licenses and regulations.

STUDENTS

GROUPS

Major tour operators include **Contiki Holidays** (300 Plaza Alicante, Suite 900, Garden Grove, CA 92640, ☎ 714/740–0808 or 800/466–0610).

HOSTELING

Contact **Hostelling International–American Youth Hostels** (733 15th St. NW, Suite 840, Washington, DC 20005, ☎ 202/783–6161) in the United States, **Hostelling International–Canada** (205 Catherine St., Suite 400, Ottawa, Ontario K2P 1C3, ☎ 613/237–7884) in Canada, and the **Youth Hostel Association of England and Wales** (Trevelyan House, 8 St. Stephen's Hill, St. Albans, Hertfordshire AL1 2DY, ☎ 01727/855215 and 01727/845047) in the United Kingdom. Membership ($25 in the U.S., C$26.75 in Canada, and £9 in the U.K.) gets you access to 5,000 hostels worldwide that charge $7–$20 nightly per person.

I.D. CARDS

To get discounts on transportation and admissions, get the **International Student Identity Card** (ISIC) if you're a bona fide student or the **International Youth Card** (IYC) if you're under 26. In the United States, the ISIC and IYC cards cost $16 each and include basic travel accident and illness coverage, plus a toll-free travel hot line. Apply through the Council on International Educational Exchange (*see* Organizations, *below*). Cards are available for $15 each in Canada from Travel Cuts (187 College St., Toronto, Ontario M5T 1P7, ☎ 416/979–2406 or 800/667–2887) and in the United Kingdom for £5 each at student unions and student travel companies.

ORGANIZATIONS

A major contact is the **Council on International Educational Exchange** (CIEE, 205 E. 42nd St., 16th Floor, New York, NY 10017, ☎ 212/661–1450) with locations in Boston (729 Boylston St., Boston, MA 02116, ☎ 617/266–1926), Miami (9100 S. Dadeland Blvd., Miami, FL 33156, ☎ 305/670–9261), Los Angeles (1093 Broxton Ave., Los Angeles, CA 90024, ☎ 310/208–3551), 43 college towns nationwide, and the United Kingdom (28A Poland St., London W1V 3DB, ☎ 0171/437–7767). Twice a year, it publishes *Student Travels* magazine. The CIEE's Council Travel Service offers domestic air passes for bargain travel within the United States and is the exclusive U.S. agent for several student-discount cards.

Campus Connections (325 Chestnut St., Suite 1101, Philadelphia, PA 19106, ☎ 215/625–8585 or 800/428–3235) specializes in discounted accommodations and airfares for students. The **Educational Travel Centre** (438 N. Frances St., Madison, WI 53703, ☎ 608/256–5551) offers rail passes and low-cost airline tickets, mostly for flights departing from Chicago.

In Canada, also contact **Travel Cuts** (*see above*).

PUBLICATIONS

See the ***Berkeley Guide to California*** ($17.50; Fodor's Travel Publications, ☎ 800/533–6478 or from bookstores).

T

TOUR OPERATORS

Among the companies selling tours and packages to California, the following have a proven reputation, are nationally known, and offer plenty of options.

GROUP TOURS

For deluxe escorted tours to California, contact **Maupintour** (Box 807, Lawrence, KS 66044, ☎ 913/843–1211 or 800/255–4266) and **Tauck Tours** (11 Wilton Rd., Westport, CT 06880, ☎ 203/226–6911 or 800/468–2825). Another operator falling between deluxe and first class is **Globus** (5301 South Federal Circle, Littleton, CO 80123, ☎ 303/797–2800 or 800/221–0090). In the first-class and tourist range, try

RI 02860, ☎ 401/728–3805 or 800/832–4656), **Domenico Tours** (750 Broadway, Bayonne, NJ 07002, ☎ 201/823–8687 or 800/554–8687) and **Mayflower Tours** (1225 Warren Ave., Downers Grove, IL 60515, ☎ 708/960–3430 or 800/323–7604). For budget- and tourist-class programs, contact **Cosmos** (*see* Globus, *above*).

PACKAGES

Independent vacation packages are available from major tour operators and airlines. Contact **American Airlines Fly AAway Vacations** (☎ 800/321–2121), **SuperCities** (139 Main St., Cambridge, MA 02142, ☎ 617/621–0099 or 800/333–1234), **Continental Airlines' Grand Destinations** (☎ 800/634–5555), **Delta Dream Vacations** (☎ 800/872–7786), **Certified Vacations** (Box 1525, Ft. Lauderdale, FL 33302, ☎ 305/522–1414 or 800/233–7260), **United Vacations** (☎ 800/328–6877), **Kingdom Tours** (300 Market St., Kingston, PA 18704, ☎ 717/283–4241 or 800/872–8857), and **USAir Vacations** (☎ 800/455–0123).

Funjet Vacations, based in Milwaukee, Wisconsin, and **Gogo Tours,** based in Ramsey, New Jersey, sell packages to California only through travel agents. For rail packages, try Amtrak (☎ 800/872–7245).

FROM THE U.K.➢ Tour operators offering packages to San Francisco include **British Airways Holidays** (Astral Towers, Betts Way, London Rd., Crawley, West Sussex RH10 2XA, ☎ 01293/518–022), **Jetsave** (Sussex House, London Rd., East Grinstead, West Sussex RH19 1LD, ☎ 01342/312033), **Key to America** (1–3 Station Rd., Ashford, Middlesex TW15 2UW, ☎ 01784/248–777), **Kuoni Travel Ltd.** (Kuoni House, Dorking, Surrey RH5 4AZ, ☎ 01306/742–222), and **Premier Holidays** (Premier Travel Center, Westbrook, Milton Rd., Cambridge CB4 1YG, ☎ 01223/516–688).

Travel agencies that offer cheap fares to California include **Trailfinders** (42–50 Earl's Court Rd., London W8 6FT, ☎ 0171/937–5400), **Travel Cuts** (295a Regent St., London W1R 7YA, ☎ 0171/637–3161; *see* Students, *above*), and **Flightfile** (49 Tottenham Court Rd., London W1P 9RE, ☎ 0171/700–2722).

THEME TRIPS

ADVENTURE➢ **All Adventure Travel** (5589 Arapahoe, #208, Boulder, CO 80303, ☎ 800/537–4025), with more than 80 operator members, can book camping, canoeing, sailing, and hiking trips in California. **Trek America** (Box 8189, Rockaway, NJ 07866, ☎ 201/983–1144 or 800/221–0596) arranges inland and Pacific coast hiking and camping tours.

BALLOONING➢ **Napa Valley Balloons** (Box 2860, Yountville, CA 94599, ☎ 707/944–0228 or 800/253–2224) and **Sonoma Thunder Wine Country Balloon Safaris** (6984 McKinley St., Sebastopol, CA 95472, ☎ 707/538–7359 or 800/759–5638) float over Wine Country valleys toward a champagne brunch. **Del Mar Balloons** (Box 2103, Del Mar, CA 92014, ☎ 619/259–3115 or 800/400–3115) flies mornings over the Temecula Valley, at sunset over coastal Del Mar. **Fantasy Balloon Flights** (83710 Avenue 54, Thermal, CA 92274, ☎ 619/398–6322 or 800/462–2683) covers San Diego, Palm Springs, and Temecula.

BICYCLING➢ Affordable weeklong California cycling vacations are sold by **Cycle America** (Box 485, Cannon Falls, MN 55009, ☎ 800/245–3263). Mountain and road biking in northern California is available from **Timberline Bicycle Tours** (7975 E. Harvard, #J, Denver, CO 80231, ☎ 303/759–3804). For bike tours that stop at inns or campsites overnight, contact **Backroads** (1516 5th St., Suite A550, Berkeley, CA 94710, ☎ 510/527–1555 or 800/462–2848). For deluxe cycling trips, contact **Butterfield & Robinson** (70 Bond St., Toronto, Ontario M5B 1X3, ☎ 416/864–1354 or 800/387–1147).

FISHING➢ **Rod & Reel Adventures** (3507 Tully Rd., Modesto, CA 95356, ☎ 209/524–7775 or 800/356–6982) can arrange ocean or river packages.

FOOD & WINE➢ *See* Chapter 4, The Wine Country.

GOLF➢ **Best Golf Tours** (332 Forest Ave., Laguna Beach, CA 92651, ☎ 714/752–8881 or 800/227–0212) sells design-your-own packages of Palm Springs courses. **Golf America, Inc.** (8070 La Jolla Shores Dr., Suite 449, La Jolla, CA 92037, ☎ 619/454–2026 or 800/435–5775) has the same for Palm Springs and San Diego courses.

HORSEBACK RIDING➢ **FITS Equestrian** (685 Lateen Rd., Solvang, CA 93463, ☎ 805/688–9494 or 800/666–3487) has several California programs.

LEARNING VACATIONS➢ **The Smithsonian National Associate Program** (1100 Jefferson Dr. SW, Room 3045, Washington, DC 20560, ☎ 202/357–4700), the **National Wildlife Federation** (1400 S. 16th St., NW, Washington, DC 20036, ☎ 703/790–4363 or 800/245–5484), and **Earthwatch** (680 Mount Auburn St., Box 403SI, Watertown, MA 02272, ☎ 617/926–8200 or 800/776–0188) operate natural-history programs led by specialists in a variety of scientific fields. **Oceanic Society Expeditions** (Fort Mason Center, Bldg. E, San Francisco, CA 94123, ☎ 415/441–1106 or 800/326–7491) runs natural-history, whale-watching, and dolphin-research expeditions.

MOTORCYCLING➢ **Western States Motorcycle Tours** (1823 W. Seldon La., Phoenix, AZ 85021, ☎ and fax 602/943–9030) includes California in its tours of the wild, wild West.

MUSIC➢ **Dailey-Thorp Travel** (330 W. 58th St., New York, NY 10019, ☎ 212/307–1555; book through travel agents) has San Francisco opera packages that include dining at fine restaurants and sightseeing.

RAFTING➢ **Outdoor Adventure River Specialists** (Box 67, Angels Camp, CA 95222, ☎ 800/346–6277) has trips on the Tuolomne, Merced, Stanislaus, American, and (California) Salmon rivers. **Whitewater Voyages** (Box 20400, El Sobrante, CA 94820, ☎ 800/488-7238, FAX 510/758-7238) has voyages on 11 California rivers. A variety of California river trips are also available from **Access to Adventure** (92520 Highway 96, Somes Bar, CA 95568, ☎ 916/469–3322 or 800/441–9463) and **Action Whitewater Adventures** (Box 1634, Provo, UT 84603, ☎ 800/453–1482, FAX 801/375–2251).

SAILING➢ Whale watching and yachting in northern California are the specialties of **Bay & Delta Charters** (3020 Bridgeway, Suite 271, Sausalito, CA 94965, ☎ 415/332–7187 or 800/762–6287).

WHALE WATCHING➢ **Pacific Sea-Fari Tours** (2803 Emerson St., San Diego, CA 92106, ☎ 619/226–8224) sails out of San Diego to the Sea of Cortez and San Ignacio Lagoon in search of gray whales.

ORGANIZATIONS

The **National Tour Association** (546 E. Main St., Lexington, KY 40508, ☎ 606/226–4444 or 800/682–8886) and the **United States Tour Operators Association** (USTOA, 211 E. 51st St., Suite 12B, New York, NY 10022, ☎ 212/750–7371) can provide lists of member operators and information on booking tours.

PUBLICATIONS

Consult the brochure **"Worldwide Tour & Vacation Package Finder"** from the National Tour Association (*see above*) and the Better Business Bureau's **"Tips on Travel Packages"** (publication No. 24-195, $2; 4200 Wilson Blvd., Arlington, VA 22203).

TRAVEL AGENCIES

For names of reputable agencies in your area, contact the **American Society of Travel Agents** (1101 King St., Suite 200, Alexandria, VA 22314, ☎ 703/739–2782).

V VISITOR INFORMATION

Contact the **California Division of Tourism** (Box 1499, Sacramento, CA 95812, ☎ 800/462–2543 or 916/322–2881, FAX 916/322–3402), from which you can order (free; ☎ 800/862–2543) a travel package including the magazine-size *Golden*

California Visitors Guide, a state map, and booklets with details about accommodations, skiing, special events, and state parks. In addition, there are visitors bureaus and chambers of commerce throughout the state; see individual chapters for listings.

In the United Kingdom, also contact the **United States Travel and Tourism Administration** (Box 1EN, London W1A 1EN, ☎ 0171/495–4466). For a free USA pack, write the USTTA at Box 170, Ashford, Kent TN24 0ZX. Enclose stamps worth £1.50.

W

WEATHER

For current conditions and forecasts, plus the local time and helpful travel tips, call the **Weather Channel Connection** (☎ 900/932–8437; 95¢ per minute) from a touch-tone phone.

SMART TRAVEL TIPS A TO Z

Basic Information on Traveling in California and Savvy Tips to Make Your Trip a Breeze

The more you travel, the more you know about how to make trips run like clockwork. To help make your travels hassle-free, Fodor's editors have rounded up dozens of tips from our contributors and travel experts all over the world, as well as basic information on visiting California. For names of organizations to contact and publications that can give you more information, *see* Important Contacts A to Z, *above.*

A

AIR TRAVEL

If time is an issue, **always look for nonstop flights,** which require no change of plane and make no stops. If possible, **avoid connecting flights,** which stop at least once and can involve a change of plane, although the flight number remains the same; if the first leg is late, the second waits.

CUTTING COSTS

The Sunday travel section of most newspapers is a good source of deals.

MAJOR AIRLINES➢ The least-expensive airfares from the major airlines are priced for round-trip travel and are subject to restrictions. You must usually **book in advance and buy the ticket within 24 hours** to get cheaper fares, and you may have to **stay over a Saturday night.** The lowest fare is subject to availability, and only a small percentage of the plane's total seats are sold at that price. It's good to **call a number of airlines, and when you are quoted a good price, book it on the spot**—the same fare on the same flight may not be available the next day. Airlines generally allow you to change your return date for a $25 to $50 fee, but most low-fare tickets are nonrefundable. However, if you don't use it, you can apply the cost toward the purchase price of a new ticket, again for a small charge.

CONSOLIDATORS➢ Consolidators, who buy tickets at reduced rates from scheduled airlines, sell them at prices below the lowest available from the airlines directly—usually without advance restrictions. Sometimes you can even get your money back if you need to return the ticket. Carefully read the fine print detailing penalties for changes and cancellations. If you doubt the reliability of a consolidator, **confirm your reservation with the airline.**

ALOFT

AIRLINE FOOD➢ If you hate airline food, **ask for special meals when booking.** These can be vegetarian, low cholesterol, or kosher, for example; commonly prepared to order in smaller quantities than standard catered fare, they can be tastier.

JET LAG➢ To avoid this syndrome, which occurs when travel disrupts your body's natural cycles, try to maintain a normal routine. At night, **get some sleep.** By day, move about the cabin to **stretch your legs, eat light meals, and drink water—not alcohol.**

SMOKING➢ Smoking is banned on all flights within the United States of less than six hours' duration and on all Canadian flights; the ban also applies to domestic segments of international flights aboard U.S. and foreign carriers. Delta has banned smoking system-wide.

C

CAMERAS, CAMCORDERS, AND COMPUTERS

LAPTOPS

Before you depart, **check your portable computer's battery,** because you may be asked at security to turn on the computer to prove that it is what it appears to be. At the airport, you may prefer to **request a manual inspection,** although security X-rays do not harm hard-disk or floppy-disk storage.

PHOTOGRAPHY

If your camera is new or if you haven't used it for a while, **shoot and develop a few rolls of film** before you leave. Always **store film in a cool, dry place**—never in the car's glove compartment or on the shelf under the rear window.

Every pass through an X-ray machine increases film's chance of clouding. To protect it, carry it in a clear plastic bag and **ask for hand inspection at security.** Such requests are virtually always honored at U.S. airports. Don't depend on a lead-lined bag to protect film in checked luggage—the airline may increase the radiation to see what's inside.

VIDEO

Before your trip, **test your camcorder, invest in a skylight filter to protect the lens, and charge the batteries.** (Airport security personnel may ask you to turn on the camcorder to prove that it's what it appears to be.)

Videotape is not damaged by X-rays, but it may be harmed by the magnetic field of a walk-through metal detector, so **ask that videotapes be hand-checked.**

CHILDREN AND TRAVEL

In many ways California is made to order for traveling with children: Kids love Disneyland, the San Diego Zoo, the Monterey Aquarium, the San Francisco cable cars, the city-owned gold mine in Placerville, and the caverns at Lake Shasta.

BABY-SITTING

For recommended local sitters, **check with your hotel desk.**

DRIVING

If you are renting a car, **arrange for a car seat when you reserve.** Sometimes they're free.

FLYING

On domestic flights, children under two not occupying a seat travel free, and older children currently travel on the lowest applicable adult fare.

BAGGAGE➢ In general, the adult baggage allowance applies for children paying half or more of the adult fare.

SAFETY SEATS➢ According to the Federal Aviation Administration, it's a good idea to **use safety seats aloft.** Airline policy varies. U.S. carriers allow FAA-approved models, but airlines usually require that you buy a ticket, even if your child would otherwise ride free, because the seats must be strapped into regular passenger seats.

FACILITIES➢ When making your reservation, **ask for children's meals and a freestanding bassinet** if you need them; the latter are available only to those with seats at the bulkhead, where there's enough legroom. If you don't need a bassinet, **think twice before requesting bulkhead seats**—the only storage for in-flight necessities is in the inconveniently distant overhead bins.

LODGING

Most hotels allow children under a certain age to stay in their parents' room at no extra charge, while others charge them as extra adults; be sure to **ask about the cut-off age.**

CUSTOMS AND DUTIES

IN CALIFORNIA

British visitors aged 21 or over may import the following into the United States: 200 cigarettes or 50 cigars or 2 kilograms of tobacco; 1 U.S. liter of alcohol; gifts to the value of $100. Restricted items include meat products, seeds, plants, and fruits. Never carry illegal drugs.

BACK HOME

IN CANADA➢ Once per calendar year, when you've been out of Canada for at least seven days, you may bring in C$300 worth of goods duty-free. If you've been away fewer than seven days but more than 48 hours, the duty-free exemption drops to C$100 but can be claimed any number of times (as can a C$20 duty-free exemption for absences of 24 hours or more). You cannot combine the yearly and 48-hour exemptions, use the C$300 exemption only partially (to save the balance for a later trip), or pool exemptions with family members. Goods claimed under the C$300 exemption may follow you by mail; those claimed under the lesser exemptions must accompany you.

Alcohol and tobacco products may be included in the yearly and 48-hour exemptions but not in the 24-hour exemption. If you meet the age requirements of the province through which you reenter Canada, you may bring in, duty-free, 1.14 liters (40 imperial ounces) of wine or liquor *or* 24 12-ounce cans or bottles of beer or ale. If you are 16 or older, you may bring in, duty-free, 200 cigarettes, 50 cigars or cigarillos, and 400 tobacco sticks or 400 grams of manufactured tobacco. Alcohol and tobacco must accompany you on your return.

An unlimited number of gifts valued up to C$60 each may be mailed to Canada duty-free. These do not count as part of your exemption. Label the package "Unsolicited Gift—Value under $60." Alcohol and tobacco are excluded.

IN THE U.K.➢ From countries outside the EU, including the United States, you may import duty-free 200 cigarettes, 100 cigarillos, 50 cigars or 250 grams of tobacco; 1 liter of spirits or 2 liters of fortified or sparkling wine; 2 liters of still table wine; 60 milliliters of perfume; 250 milliliters of toilet water; plus £136 worth of other goods, including gifts and souvenirs.

D

FOR TRAVELERS WITH DISABILITIES

California is a national leader in making attractions and facilities accessible to people with disabilities. Since 1982 the state building code has required that all areas for public use be made accessible. State laws more than a decade old provide special privileges, such as license plates allowing special parking spaces, unlimited parking in time-limited spaces, and free parking in metered spaces. Insignia from states other than California are honored.

When discussing accessibility with an operator or reservationist, **ask hard questions.** Are there any stairs, inside *or* out? Are there grab bars next to the toilet *and* in the shower/tub? How wide is the doorway to the room? To the bathroom? For the most extensive facilities, meeting the latest legal specifications, **opt for newer facilities,** which more often have been designed with access in mind. Older properties or ships must usually be retrofitted and may offer more limited facilities as a result. Be sure to **discuss your needs before booking.**

DISCOUNT CLUBS

Travel clubs offer members unsold space on airplanes, cruise ships, and package tours at as much as 50% below regular prices. Membership may include a regular bulletin or access to a toll-free hot line giving details of available trips departing from three or four days to several months in the future. Most also offer 50% discounts off hotel rack rates. Before booking with a club, **make sure the hotel or other supplier isn't offering a better deal.**

DIVERS' ALERT

Scuba divers take note: **Do not fly within 24 hours of scuba diving.**

G

GAY AND LESBIAN TRAVEL

San Francisco, Los Angeles, West Hollywood, San Diego, and Palm Springs are among the California cities with visible lesbian and gay communities. *See* Gay and Lesbian Travel *in* Important Contacts A to Z, *above,* for a list of local publications and switchboards.

I

INSURANCE

Travel insurance can protect your investment, replace your luggage and its contents, or provide for medical coverage should you fall ill during your trip. Most tour operators, travel agents, and insurance agents sell specialized health-and-accident, flight, trip-cancellation, and luggage insurance as well as comprehensive policies with some or all of these features. Before you make any purchase, **review your existing health and home-owner policies** to find out whether they cover expenses incurred while traveling.

BAGGAGE

Airline liability for your baggage is limited to $1,250 per person on domestic flights. On international flights, the airlines' liability is $9.07 per pound or $20 per kilogram for checked baggage (roughly $640 per 70-pound bag) and $400 per passenger for unchecked baggage. However, this excludes valuable items such as jewelry and cameras that are listed in your ticket's fine print. You can buy additional insurance from the airline at check-in, but first **see if your homeowner's policy covers lost luggage.**

FLIGHT

You should **think twice before buying flight insurance.** Often purchased as a last-minute impulse at the airport, it pays a lump sum when a plane crashes, either to a beneficiary if the insured dies or sometimes to a surviving passenger who loses eyesight or a limb. Supplementing the airlines' coverage described in the limits-of-liability paragraphs on your ticket, it's expensive and basically unnecessary. Charging an airline ticket to a major credit card often automatically entitles you to coverage and may also embrace travel by bus, train, and ship.

HEALTH

FOR U.K. TRAVELERS➢ According to the Association of British Insurers, a trade association representing 450 insurance companies, it's wise to **buy extra medical coverage when you visit the United States.** You can buy an annual travel-insurance policy valid for most vacations during the year in which it's purchased. If you go this route, make sure it covers you if you have a preexisting medical condition or are pregnant.

TRIP

Without insurance, you will lose all or most of your money if you must cancel your trip due to illness or any other reason. Especially if your airline ticket, cruise, or package tour is nonrefundable and cannot be changed, it's essential that you **buy trip-cancellation-and-interruption insurance.** When considering how much coverage you need, look for a policy that will cover the cost of your trip plus the nondiscounted price of a one-way airline ticket should you need to return home early. Read the fine print carefully, especially sections defining "family member" and "preexisting medical conditions." Also **consider default or bankruptcy insurance,** which protects you against a supplier's failure to deliver. However, such policies often do not cover default by a travel agency, tour operator, airline, or cruise line if you bought your tour and the coverage directly from the firm in question.

L

LODGING

Hotels in cities may or may not provide parking facilities, and there is usually a charge if they do. Motels, which are more common along the highways and outside cities, have parking space but may not have some of the amenities that hotels typically have—on-site restaurants, lounges, and room service.

Bed-and-breakfasts and inns have become extremely popular in California. These are not usually economy lodgings—their prices are often at the top of the scale. Most typically, they are large, older homes, renovated and charmingly decorated with antiques, with a half-dozen guest rooms. The price usually includes breakfast, which may be a Continental breakfast—juice, coffee, and some simple pastries—or a four-course feast. Baths may be private or shared. Sometimes the inn is a renovated hotel from the last century with a dozen rooms; occasionally it is a Victorian farmhouse with only three guest rooms. Few B&Bs allow smoking; virtually none take pets.

APARTMENT AND VILLA RENTALS

If you want a home base that's roomy enough for a family and comes with cooking facilities, **consider a furnished rental.** It's generally cost-wise, too, although not always—some rentals are luxury properties (economical only when your party is large). Home-exchange directories do list rentals—often second homes owned by prospective house swappers—and some services search for a house or apartment for you (even a castle if that's your fancy) and handle the paperwork. Some send an illustrated catalogue and others send photographs of specific properties, sometimes at a charge; up-front registration fees may apply.

HOME EXCHANGE

If you would like to find a house, an apartment, or other vacation property to exchange for your own while on vacation, **become a member of a home-exchange organization,** which will send you its annual directories listing available exchanges and will include your own listing in at least one of them. Arrangements for the actual exchange are made by the two parties to it, not by the organization.

M

MONEY AND EXPENSES

ATMS

Chances are that you can **use your bank card at ATMs** to withdraw money from an account and get cash advances on a credit-card account if your card has been programmed with a personal identification number, or PIN. Before leaving home, **check on frequency limits** for withdrawals and cash advances.

On cash advances you are charged interest from the day you receive the money from ATMs as well as from tellers. Transaction fees for ATM withdrawals outside your home turf may be higher than for withdrawals at home.

TRAVELER'S CHECKS

Whether or not to buy traveler's checks depends on where you are headed; **take cash to rural areas and small towns, traveler's checks to cities.** The most widely recognized are American Express, Citicorp, Thomas Cook, and Visa, which are sold by major commercial banks for 1% to 3% of the checks' face value—it pays to **shop around.** Both American Express and Thomas Cook issue checks that can be countersigned and used by you or your traveling companion. Record the numbers of the checks, cross them off as you spend them, and keep this information separate from your checks.

WIRING MONEY

You don't have to be a cardholder to send or receive funds through MoneyGram℠ from American Express. Just go to a MoneyGram agent, located in retail and convenience stores and in American Express Travel Offices. Pay up to $1,000 with cash or a credit card, anything over that in cash. The money can be picked up within 10 minutes in cash or check at the nearest MoneyGram agent. There's no limit, and the recipient need only present photo identification. The cost, which includes a free long-distance phone call, runs from 3% to 10%, depending on the amount sent, the destination, and the method of payment.

Money sent from the United States or Canada will be available for pickup at agent locations in 100 countries within 15 minutes. Once the money is in the system, it can be picked up at any one of 25,000 locations. Fees range from 4% to 10%, depending on the amount you send.

P

PACKAGES AND TOURS

A package or tour to California can make your vacation less expensive and more convenient. Firms that sell tours and packages purchase airline seats, hotel rooms, and rental cars in bulk and pass some of the savings on to you. In addition, the best operators have local representatives to help you out at your destination.

A GOOD DEAL?

The more your package or tour includes, the better you can predict the ultimate cost of your vacation. Make sure you know exactly what is included, and **beware of hidden costs.** Are taxes, tips, and service charges included? Transfers and baggage handling? Entertainment and excursions? These can add up.

Most packages and tours are rated deluxe, first-class superior, first class, tourist, and budget. The key difference is usually accommodations. If the package or tour you are considering is priced lower than in your wildest dreams, **be skeptical.** Also, **make sure your travel agent knows the hotels** and other services. Ask about location, room size, beds, and whether it has a pool, room service, or programs for children, if you care about these. Has your agent been there or sent others you can contact?

BUYER BEWARE

Each year consumers are stranded or lose their money when operators go out of business—even very large ones with excellent reputations. If you can't afford a loss, take the time to **check out the operator**—find out how long the company has been in business, and ask several agents about its reputation. Next, **don't book unless the firm has a consumer-protection program.** Members of the United States Tour Operators Association and the National Tour Association are required to set aside funds exclusively to cover your payments and travel arrangements in case of default. Nonmember operators may instead carry insurance; look for the details in the operator's brochure—and the name of an underwriter with a solid reputation. Note: When it comes to tour operators, **don't trust escrow accounts.** Although there are laws governing those of charter-flight operators, no governmental body prevents tour operators from raiding the till.

Next, **contact your local Better Business Bureau and the attorney general's office** in both your own state and the operator's; have any complaints been filed? Last, **pay with a major credit card.** Then you can cancel payment, provided that you can document your complaint. Always **consider trip-cancellation insurance** (*see* Insurance, *above*).

BIG VS. SMALL➢ An operator that handles several hundred thousand travelers annually can use its purchasing power to give you a good price. Its high volume may also indicate financial stability. But some small companies provide more personalized service; because they tend to specialize, they may also be experts on an area.

USING AN AGENT

Travel agents are an excellent resource. In fact, large operators accept bookings only through travel agents. But it's good to **collect brochures from several agencies,** because some agents' suggestions may be skewed by promotional relationships with tour and package firms that reward them for volume sales. If you have a special interest, **find an agent with expertise in that area;** the American Society of Travel Agents can give you leads in the United States. (Don't rely solely on your agent, though; agents may be unaware of small niche operators, and some special-interest travel companies only sell direct.)

SINGLE TRAVELERS

Prices are usually quoted per person, based on two sharing a room. If traveling solo, you may be required to pay the full double-occupancy rate. Some operators eliminate this surcharge if you agree to be matched up with a roommate of the same sex, even if one is not found by departure time.

PACKING FOR CALIFORNIA

The most important single rule to bear in mind in packing for a California vacation is to **prepare for changes in temperature.** An hour's drive can take you up or down many degrees, and the variation from daytime to nighttime in a single location is often marked. Take along sweaters, jackets, and clothes for layering as your best insurance for coping with variations in temperature. Include shorts or cool cottons unless you are packing for a midwinter ski trip. Always tuck in a bathing suit; most lodgings have a pool, spa, and sauna.

While casual dressing is a hallmark of the California lifestyle, in the evening men will need a jacket and tie for many good restaurants, and women will be more comfortable in something dressier than regulation sightseeing garb.

Considerations of formality aside, bear in mind that **San Francisco and other coastal towns can be chilly** at any time of the year, especially in summer, when the fog is apt to descend and stay.

Bring an extra pair of eyeglasses or contact lenses in your carry-on luggage, and if you have a health problem, **pack enough medication** to last the trip. In case your bags go astray, **don't put prescription drugs or valuables in luggage to be checked.**

LUGGAGE

Free airline baggage allowances depend on the airline, the route, and the class of your ticket; ask in advance. In general, on domestic flights you are entitled to check two bags—neither exceeding 62 inches, or 158 centimeters (length + width + height), or weighing more than 70 pounds (32 kilograms). A third piece may be brought aboard; its total dimensions are generally limited to less than 45 inches (114 centimeters), so it will fit easily under the seat in front of you or in the overhead compartment. In the United States, the FAA gives airlines broad latitude to limit carry-on allowances and tailor them to different aircraft and operational conditions. Charges for excess, oversize, or overweight pieces vary.

SAFEGUARDING YOUR LUGGAGE➢ Before leaving home, **itemize your bags' contents** and their worth, and label them with your name, address, and phone number. (If you use your home address, cover it so that potential thieves can't see it.) Inside your bag, **pack a copy of your itinerary.** At check-in, **make sure that your bag is correctly tagged** with the airport's three-letter destination code. If your bags arrive damaged or not at all, file a written report with the airline before leaving the airport.

PASSPORTS AND VISAS

CANADIANS

No passport is necessary to enter the United States.

U.K. CITIZENS

British citizens need a valid passport. If you are staying fewer than 90 days and traveling on a vacation, with a return or onward ticket, you will probably not need a visa. However, you will need to fill out the Visa Waiver Form, 1-94W, supplied by the airline.

While traveling, **keep one photocopy of your passport's data page** separate from your wallet and leave another copy with someone at home. If you lose your passport, promptly call the nearest embassy or consulate, and the local police; having the data page can speed replacement.

R

RENTING A CAR

CUTTING COSTS

To get the best deal, **book through a travel agent and shop around.** When pricing cars, **ask where the rental lot is located.** Some off-airport locations offer lower rates—even though their lots are only minutes away from the terminal via complimentary shuttle. You may also want to **price local car-rental companies,** whose rates may be lower still, although service and maintenance standards may not be up to those of a national firm. Also **ask your travel agent about a company's customer-service record.** How has it responded to late plane arrivals and vehicle mishaps? Are there often lines at the rental counter, and, if you're traveling during a holiday period, does a confirmed reservation guarantee you a car?

INSURANCE

When you drive a rented car, you are generally responsible for any damage or personal injury that you cause as well as damage to the vehicle. Before you rent, **see what coverage you already have** by means of your personal auto-insurance policy and credit cards. California has outlawed the sale of collision damage waiver policies.

SURCHARGES

Before picking up the car in one city and leaving it in another, **ask about drop-off charges or one-way service fees,** which can be substantial. Note, too, that some rental agencies charge extra if you return the car before the time specified on your contract. To avoid a hefty refueling fee, **fill the tank just before you turn in the car.**

FOR U.K. CITIZENS

In the United States you must be 21 to rent a car; rates may be higher for those under 25. Extra costs cover child seats, compulsory for children under five (about $3 per day), and additional drivers (about $1.50 per day). To pick up your reserved car you will need the reservation voucher, a passport, a U.K. driver's license, and a travel policy covering each driver.

S

SENIOR-CITIZEN DISCOUNTS

To qualify for age-related discounts, **mention your senior-citizen status up front** when booking hotel reservations, not when checking out, and before you're seated in restaurants, not when paying your bill. Note that discounts may be limited to certain menus, days, or hours. When renting a car, **ask about promotional car-rental discounts**—they can net lower costs than your senior-citizen discount.

STUDENTS ON THE ROAD

To save money, **look into deals available through student-oriented travel agencies.** To qualify, you'll need to have a bona fide student I.D. card. Members of international student groups also are eligible. *See* Students *in* Important Contacts A to Z, *above.*

T

TELEPHONES

LONG-DISTANCE

The long-distance services of AT&T, MCI, and Sprint make calling home relatively convenient and let you avoid hotel surcharges; typically, you dial an 800 number.

TIPPING

At restaurants, a 15% tip is standard for waiters; up to 20% may be expected at more expensive establishments. The same goes for taxi drivers, bartenders, and hairdressers. Coat-check operators usually expect $1; bellhops and porters should get 50¢ to $1 per bag; hotel maids in upscale hotels should get about $1 per day of your stay. On package tours, conductors and drivers usually get $10 per day from the group as a whole; check whether this has already been figured into your cost. For local sightseeing tours, you may individually tip the driver-guide $1 if he or she has been helpful or informative. Ushers in theaters do not expect tips.

W

WHEN TO GO

Any time of the year is the right time to go to California. There won't be skiable snow in the mountains between Easter and Thanksgiving; there will usually be rain in December, January, and February in the lowlands, if that bothers you; it will be much too hot to enjoy Palm Springs or Death Valley in the summer. But San Francisco, Los Angeles, and San Diego are delightful year-round; the Wine Country's seasonal variables are enticing; and the coastal areas are almost always cool.

The climate varies amazingly in California, not only over distances of several hundred miles but occasionally within an hour's drive. A foggy, cool August day in San Francisco makes you grateful for a sweater, tweed jacket, or light wool coat. Head north 50 miles to the Napa Valley to check out the Wine Country, and you'll probably wear shirt sleeves and thin cottons.

Daytime and nighttime temperatures may also swing widely apart. Take Sacramento, a city that is at sea level but in California's Central Valley. In the summer, afternoons can be very warm indeed, in the 90s and occasionally over 100°. But the nights cool down, often dropping 40°.

It's hard to generalize much about the weather in this varied state. Rain comes in the winter, with snow at higher elevations. Summers are dry everywhere. As a rule, compared to the coastal areas, which are cool year-round, inland regions are warmer in summer and cooler in winter. As you climb into the mountains, there are more distinct variations with the seasons: Winter brings snow, autumn is crisp, spring is variable, and summer is clear and warm.

CLIMATE

The following are average daily maximum and minimum temperatures for the major California cities.

Climate in California

LOS ANGELES

Jan.	64F	18C	May	69F	21C	Sept.	75F	24C
	44	7		53	12		60	16
Feb.	64F	18C	June	71F	22C	Oct.	73F	23C
	46	8		57	14		55	13
Mar.	66F	19C	July	75C	24C	Nov.	71F	22C
	48	9		60	16		48	9
Apr.	66F	19C	Aug.	75C	24C	Dec.	66F	19C
	51	11		62	17		46	8

SAN DIEGO

Jan.	62F	17C	May	66F	19C	Sept.	73F	23C
	46	8		55	13		62	17
Feb.	62F	17C	June	69F	21C	Oct.	71F	22C
	48	9		59	15		57	14
Mar.	64F	18C	July	73F	23C	Nov.	69F	21C
	50	10		62	17		51	11
Apr.	66F	19C	Aug.	73F	23C	Dec.	64F	18C
	53	12		64	18		48	9

SAN FRANCISCO

Jan.	55F	13C	May	66F	19C	Sept.	73F	23C
	41	5		48	9		51	11
Feb.	59F	15C	June	69F	21C	Oct.	69F	21C
	42	6		51	11		50	10
Mar.	60F	16C	July	69F	21C	Nov.	64F	18C
	44	7		51	11		44	7
Apr.	62F	17C	Aug.	69F	21C	Dec.	57F	14C
	46	8		53	12		42	6

1 Destination: California

RESTLESS NIRVANA

COASTAL CALIFORNIA began its migration from somewhere far to the south millions of years ago. It's still moving north along the San Andreas fault, but you have plenty of time for a visit before Santa Monica hits the Arctic Circle. If you've heard predictions that some of the state may fall into the Pacific, take the long view and consider that much of California has been in and out of the ocean throughout its history. The forces that raised its mountains and formed the Central Valley are still at work.

Upheaval has always been a fact of life in California—below ground and above. Floods, earthquakes, racial strife, immigration woes, high unemployment, and Orange County's scandal-ridden bankruptcy are but a few of the high-profile traumas—not to mention that famous celebrity murder case—that have tarnished California's image in recent years. Things got so bad in the early 1990s that U Haul declared a shortage of trucks because so many residents were abandoning the Golden State. This was just fine with the many natives whose "Welcome to California: Now Go Home" bumper stickers had greeted several decades of arrivals—few states have grown as rapidly as California, which had a population of approximately 7 million as World War II came to a close and now is home to more than 32 million.

From the outside looking in, it may have seemed that, along with its AAA bond rating, California might lose its appeal as a travel destination. But even in difficult times—the worst of which appear to be over—the Golden State just has too much to offer to be written off: dramatic coastline; rugged desert and mountain regions; Hollywood glitz and Palm Springs glamour; a potpourri of Pacific Rim, European, and Latin American influences; a temperate climate; and a fabled history as a conduit for fame and fortune, hope and renewal.

California has always been a place where initiative—as opposed to class, family, or other connections—is honored above all else. The state has lured assertive types who metaphorically or otherwise have come seeking "gold"—in the Sacramento foothills, in Hollywood, and, more recently, in the Silicon Valley. To be sure, not everyone achieves the mythical California dream, but neither is it totally an illusion. The sense of infinite possibility, as much a by-product of the state's varied and striking landforms as media hype, is what most tourists notice on their first trip. It's why so many return—sometimes forever.

More so than most of its residents are willing to admit, California is a land of contradiction, where "reality" is a matter of opinion—which is why the cinema, an enterprise based wholly on the manipulation of reality, is the perfect signature industry for the state. Take for instance two books in many local libraries about the historic chain of 21 California missions established by Spanish Catholic priests, most notably Father Junípero Serra. One book is titled *California's Missions: Their Romance and Beauty.* Its author details Serra's strategy "to convert and civilize the Indians" who resided in late-18th-century California. The other tome, *The Missions of California: A Legacy of Genocide,* disputes the contentions of "mission apologists" and illustrates how on levels physical and spiritual the mission system "was the first disaster for the Indian population of California."

The truth? It's likely somewhere in between (though recent scholarship has tended to show Serra and other missionaries in a less favorable light). The treatment of other groups over the years has been equally problematic, and the scapegoating of "foreigners"—often by first-generation Californians with no sense of the irony of their declarations—is a cyclical blot on the state's conscience. California's move to the forefront of the controversy over affirmative action has given many across the nation the impression that its residents wish only to roll back the clock. But the circumstances here are more complex than they appear on the surface because the state has a more diverse population than many others in the Union. California may very well play an integral role in the formulation of more equitable and up-to-date anti-discrimination policies. In any case, as with the debate over immigration and the previous "taxpayer revolts" of the 1970s and 1980s, the state's residents have forced discussion of an issue that citizens elsewhere have brooded over but not confronted.

California is a restless nirvana. The sun shines and all is beautiful, then the earth shakes and all is shattered. It's time to rebuild. And the state bounces back—San Francisco from the 1906 and 1989 quakes, Los Angeles from ones in 1971 and 1994. Billions are made during the Cold War defense boom, then communism collapses, bases close, and unemployment skyrockets. It's time to diversify. And the state does, making new overtures to Asia and Latin America.

And to tourists, who find that although California isn't perfect—what place is?—it's a source of endless diversion, natural and man-made. "Wow!" is a word one hears often here—at Half Dome in Yosemite, during the "Backdraft: 10,000 Degrees of Excitement" experience at Universal Studios, in the pleasingly symmetrical courtyard of the J. Paul Getty Museum, or among the redwoods of Humboldt County. If Texans like things "big" and New Yorkers like a little style, what delights Californians most is drama—indoors or out.

There is no way to take in this "show" in one trip, so don't try. Seventy-five percent of California's visitors return at least once, an impressive quotient of satisfied customers. As you travel through California's various regions you will get a sense of the great diversity of cultures, the ongoing pull between preservation and development, and the state's unique place in the landscapes of geography and the imagination.

WHAT'S WHERE

Keep in mind the very long distances. If you drive between San Francisco and Los Angeles on Highway 1, remember that it is not only more than 400 miles but also a difficult road to drive. Scenic routes, such as Highway 1 along the coast, Highway 49 in the Gold Country, and Highways 50 and 120 across the Sierra Nevada, require attention to driving and enough time for frequent stops.

The Central Coast

Between Big Sur and Santa Barbara is a spectacular stretch of Highway 1, requiring concentration and nerve to drive. Don't expect much in the way of dining, lodging, shopping, or even history until you get to Hearst Castle. Santa Barbara flaunts its Spanish-Mexican heritage. There's a well-restored mission, and almost all of downtown (including some pleasant shopping areas) is done in Spanish-style architecture. The centerpiece is the Santa Barbara Courthouse, built in the 1920s and displaying some beautiful tile work and murals.

The Far North

The two main attractions in the Far North are Mt. Shasta, a large volcano that dominates the scenery of the northern part of the state, and Lassen Volcanic National Park. The park is at the southern end of the Cascade Range and is particularly interesting because of the record of past volcanic activity and evidence of current geothermal activity (such as the Sulphur Works). Like the North Coast, this region best suits those interested in nature; dining, lodging, and nightlife options are limited. Keep in mind also that much of the Far North can be very hot in summer.

Lake Tahoe

Lake Tahoe is famous for its deep blue water and as the largest alpine lake on the continent. It stands up well to its reputation, despite crowded areas around the Nevada casinos. Lake Tahoe is just under a four-hour drive from San Francisco along I–80; the traffic to the lake on Friday afternoon and to San Francisco on Sunday is horrendous. If you plan to visit in winter, remember to carry chains in your car; they are sometimes required even on the interstate. Summertime is generally cooler here than in the foothills, though sometimes it does get hot. Luckily, there are lots of beaches where you can swim.

Los Angeles

In certain lights Los Angeles displays its Spanish heritage, but much more evident is its cultural vibrancy as a 20th-century center on the Pacific Rim. Hollywood, the beaches, and Disneyland are all within an hour's drive. Also here are Beverly Hills, noted for its shops and mansions, important examples of 20th-century domestic architecture, and freeways. Dining options are improving, if still not up to the range of San Francisco's choices. Despite the city's reputation for a laid-back lifestyle, a visit here can be fairly overwhelming because of the size and variety of the region. Careful planning will help.

The Mojave Desert and Death Valley

When most people assemble their "must-see" list of California attractions, the desert isn't often among the top contenders. What with its heat and vast, sparsely populated tracts of land, the desert is no Disneyland. But that's precisely why it deserves a closer look. The natural riches here are overwhelming: rolling waves of sand dunes, black cinder cones thrusting up hundreds of feet into the air from a blistered desert floor, riotous sheets of wildflowers, bizarrely shaped Joshua trees basking in an orange glow at sunset, and an abundant silence that is both dramatic and startling.

Monterey Bay

The Monterey Peninsula, a two- or three-hour drive south of San Francisco, offers some of the state's most luxurious resorts and golf courses, interesting historic sites, and beautiful coastal scenery. Monterey was the capital during Spanish and Mexican rule and the state constitution was written here. Point Lobos is among the state's most treasured parks. Depending on which way you look, scenic 17-Mile Drive is rustic (cypress trees, craggy coastal views) or just plain elegant (the Crocker Marble Palace, the Pebble Beach Golf Links). There are many good restaurants in Monterey and Carmel and plenty of places to shop. The weather is usually mild, though visitors should prepare themselves for fog and cool temperatures.

The North Coast

California's North Coast is a dramatically beautiful region whose main industries are tourism, fishing, and logging. There are no large cities, no large amusement parks, few luxury resorts. There isn't even much swimming, because of a cold current that runs down the coast for most of the state (turning out to sea before it reaches southern California beaches). What you will find are a scenic drive along Highway 1 and U.S. 101, many small inns, uncrowded state beaches and parks, some good art galleries, and restaurants serving imaginative dishes featuring locally produced ingredients. This is a region for leisurely exploring. The Russians settled this region briefly in the 19th century, and you will find reminders of their presence.

Palm Springs Desert Resorts

Palm Springs and the new cities nearby are filling up with resorts with elaborate gardens, waterfalls, serpentine sidewalks, and golf courses. This is a different type of "desert experience" than you'll get in the outlying areas, but with all their creature comforts, great winter weather, and many outdoor activities, the desert resorts are a good base for exploration. Joshua Tree National Park is an easy day trip from Palm Springs. The northern part is High Desert and the southern part Low Desert, so you can see the difference between these very different types of terrain.

Sacramento and the Gold Country

The Gold Country, also known as the Mother Lode, is the gold-mining region of the Sierra Nevada foothills. This is a less expensive, if also less sophisticated, region but not without its pleasures, natural and man-made. Spring brings wildflowers, and in fall the hills are colored by bright-red berries and changing leaves. The hills are golden in the summer—and hot. Dining has improved remarkably in recent years, and many fine bed-and-breakfast inns have sprung up. The Gold Country has a mix of indoor and outdoor activities, one of the many reasons it's a great place to take the kids. We've included Sacramento, the state capital, in the Gold Country chapter because it is adjacent and because its history is one with that of the Gold Rush.

San Diego

Spanish missionary Father Junípero Serra founded his first mission in Alta California (as opposed to Baja California, which is still part of Mexico) in San Diego in 1769. Some of the city's past is preserved in its

Old Town section, but more than a century ago San Diego's focus moved closer to the water. A great place to take the kids, San Diego's daytime attractions include historical sites from Mexican and Victorian times, one of the best zoos in the country, and fine beaches. Dining and nightlife have improved in recent years, so the good times continue when the sun goes down.

San Francisco

San Francisco is a sophisticated city offering world-class hotels and the greatest concentration of excellent restaurants in the state. The town has an undeserved reputation as the kook capital of the United States, yet it's the country's number-one tourist destination. Why? To use the vernacular, the vibe here is cool, from North Beach coffeehouses to Chinatown tea emporiums, Golden Gate Park, and Haight Street's head shops (yes, they're still around). People in San Francisco know how to have a good time; the high spirits can't help but rub off on visitors.

The Wine Country

The Wine Country is one of California's most popular tourist regions. Many Sonoma and Napa Valley wineries are beautiful sites for meals, picnics, or tastings, and there are top-notch bed-and-breakfasts and restaurants in the area. There are many ways to explore the region: hiking and bicycling for the active set and balloon, train, and glider rides for those seeking a less strenuous overview. People here know how to pamper themselves: In Calistoga and other towns are resorts and health spas with mud baths, massages, sulfur whirlpool baths, and other rejuvenating treatments.

Yosemite

The highlight for many travelers to California is a visit to one of the Sierra Nevada's national parks. Yosemite is the state's most famous park and every bit as sublime as one expects. Its Yosemite-type or U-shape valleys were formed by the action of glaciers on the Sierra Nevada during recent ice ages. Other examples are found in Kings Canyon and Sequoia national parks (which are adjacent to each other and usually visited together). At all three parks there are fine groves of Big Trees (*Sequoiadendron gigantea*), some of the largest living things in the world. The parks are open year-round, but large portions of the higher backcountry are closed in winter. Yosemite Valley is only 4,000 feet high, so winter weather is mild, and the waterfalls are beautiful when hung with ice.

PLEASURES & PASTIMES

Beaches

With almost 1,000 miles of coastline, California is well supplied with beaches. They are endlessly fascinating: You can walk on them, lie and sun on them, watch seabirds and hunt for shells, dig clams, or spot seals and sea otters at play. From December through March you can witness the migrations of the gray whales.

What you can't always do at these beaches is swim. From San Francisco and northward, the water is simply too cold for all but extremely hardy souls. Even along the southern half of the coast, some beaches are too dangerous for swimming because of the undertow. Look for signs and postings and take them seriously. Park rangers patrol beaches and enforce regulations, such as those prohibiting alcohol, dune buggies, fires, and pets (dogs must be on leash at all times).

Access to beaches in California is generally excellent. The state park system includes many fine beaches, and oceanside communities have their own public beaches. In addition, through the work of the California Coastal Commission, many stretches of private property that would otherwise seal off the beach from outsiders have public-access paths and trails. Again, the best advice is to look for signs and obey them.

Dining

Over the past decade, California's name has come to signify a certain type of modern, healthful, sophisticated cuisine, using the freshest of local ingredients, creatively combined and served in often stunning presentations. In coastal areas, most restaurants' menus feature at least some seafood, fresh off the boat. California is also a major agricultural state, so local produce is usually excellent.

San Francisco and Los Angeles have scores of top-notch restaurants—an expensive meal at one of these gourmet shrines is often the high point of a trip to California. The Wine Country, just north of San Francisco, and Santa Barbara are also known for superb restaurants.

Don't neglect the culinary bounty of California's mixed ethnic population—notably Mexican and Chinese, but also Japanese, Scandinavian, Italian, French, Belgian, English, Thai, and German restaurants.

You can pick up some singularly Californian taste treats at shops or roadside stands: date shakes along Highway 111 near Thermal (in the Palm Springs desert resorts area), French-fried artichoke hearts on the Monterey Peninsula, salmon jerky along the North Coast, garlic ice cream during Gilroy's Garlic Festival, cinnamon churros and other Mexican treats on Olvera Street in Los Angeles, and San Francisco's famous sourdough bread.

Fishing

California has abundant fishing options: deep-sea fishing expeditions, surf fishing from the shore, and freshwater fishing in streams, rivers, lakes, and reservoirs. You'll need a California fishing license (*see* Important Contacts A to Z *in* the Gold Guide).

Golf

Golf is a year-round sport in California. Though its most famous courses are in the Pebble Beach and Palm Springs desert resorts areas, there are championship courses all over the state. (*See* Participant Sports in each chapter for listings of courses.)

Hot-Air Ballooning

Hot-air ballooning is gaining in popularity, although it is not cheap: A ride costs in excess of $100. More and more of the large, colorful balloons drift across the valleys of the Wine Country, where the air drafts are particularly friendly to this sport, as well as in San Diego, the Palm Springs area, and the Gold Country. (*See* Essentials in each chapter for a list of companies providing this service.)

Parks

Much of California's wilderness and even portions of urban areas such as San Francisco are managed by the National Park Service or the California Department of Parks and Recreation (*see* Important Contacts *in* the Gold Guide for addresses). Camping possibilities are abundant, though reservations are essential in the most popular areas.

NATIONAL PARKS➢ There are eight national parks in California: Death Valley, Joshua Tree, Lassen, Redwood, Sequoia, Kings Canyon, Yosemite, and the Channel Islands. National monuments include Cabrillo, in San Diego; Devil's Postpile, 7,600 feet up in the eastern Sierra Nevada; Lava Beds, in northeastern California; Muir Woods, north of San Francisco; and Pinnacles, in western central California.

California has three national recreation areas: Golden Gate, with 87,000 acres both north and south of the Golden Gate Bridge in San Francisco; Santa Monica Mountains, with 150,000 acres from Griffith Park in Los Angeles to Point Mugu in Ventura County; and Whiskeytown-Shasta-Trinity, with 240,000 acres, including four major lakes. Point Reyes National Seashore is on a peninsula near San Francisco.

STATE PARKS➢ California's state-park system includes more than 200 sites; many are recreational and scenic, others historic or scientific. Among the popular sites are Angel Island in San Francisco Bay, reached by ferry from San Francisco or Tiburon; Anza-Borrego Desert, 600,000 acres of the Colorado Desert northeast of San Diego; Big Basin Redwoods, California's first state redwood park, with 300-foot trees, near Santa Cruz; Empire Mine, one of the richest mines in the Mother Lode, in Grass Valley; Hearst Castle at San Simeon; Leo Carrillo Beach, north of Malibu; and Pismo Beach, with surfing, clamming, and nature trails. Most state parks are open year round.

Shopping

In California's big cities, opportunities abound to shop for internationally known brands of clothing, jewelry, leather goods, and perfumes, often in shops or boutiques set up by French, Italian, British, or American designers. San Francisco and Los Angeles are centers of clothing manufacture; if you're a bargain hunter, you'll want to explore the factory outlets in both cities.

If you are shopping for something unique to California, look at the output of its many resident artists and craftspeople. You can find their creations from one end of the state to the other in fine city galleries, in small neighborhood shops, in out-of-the-way mountain studios, at roadside stands, and at county fairs. Paintings, drawings, sculpture, wood carvings, pottery, jewelry, handwoven fabrics, handmade baskets—the creativity and the output of California's artisans seem endless.

Skiing

Snow skiing in the Lake Tahoe area and elsewhere is generally limited to the period between Thanksgiving and late April, though in years of heavy snowfall like 1995 skiers can still hit the trails as late as July.

Water Sports

Swimming and surfing, scuba diving, and skin diving in the Pacific Ocean are favorite year-round California pleasures in the southern part of the state, although these become seasonal sports on the coast from San Francisco northward. Sailboats are available for rent in many places along the coast and inland.

River rafting—white-water and otherwise—canoeing, and kayaking are popular, especially in the northern part of the state, where there are many rivers.

Wine Tasting

You can visit wineries in many parts of the state, not only in the Wine Country north of San Francisco. Vintners associations in the Gold Country, Santa Barbara, Santa Cruz, and other wine-growing areas provide brochures (see individual chapters for details) with lists of wineries that open for tastings. Wineries and good wine stores will package your purchases for safe travel or shipping.

FODOR'S CHOICE

No two people will agree on what makes a perfect vacation, but it can be helpful to know what others think. Below is a list of Fodor's Choices. We hope you'll have a chance to experience some of them yourself while visiting California. We have tried to offer something for everyone and from every price category. For more detailed information about each entry, refer to the appropriate chapters within this guidebook.

Lodging

★ **Hotel Bel-Air, Los Angeles.** This secluded celebrity mecca's extensive exotic gardens and creek complete with swans give it the ambience of a top-rated resort. $$$$

★ **Ritz-Carton Hotel, Laguna Niguel.** The classiest hotel along the coast, the Ritz draws guests from around the world with its sweeping oceanside views, gleaming marble, and stunning antiques. $$$$

★ **Post Ranch Inn, Big Sur.** This luxurious retreat has the ultimate in environmentally correct architecture. Each unit has its own hot tub, stereo system, private deck, and massage table. $$$$

★ **Hotel Majestic, San Francisco.** One of San Francisco's original grand hotels, this five-story yellow-and-white Edwardian looks like a wedding cake. Most rooms contain a fireplace and are decorated with a period feel. $$$

★ **Torrey Pines Inn, La Jolla.** This inn commands a view of miles and miles of coastline. It's adjacent to a public golf course, a state beach, and a nature reserve. $$

★ **San Simeon Pines Motel, Cambria.** Set amid 9 acres of pines and cypresses, this motel-style resort near Hearst Castle has its own golf course and is directly across from Leffingwell Landing, a state picnic area on the rocky beach. $–$$

Scenic Drives

★ **17-Mile Drive, Carmel.** The wonders are both man-made and natural as this road winds its way through Carmel and Pebble Beach.

★ **Highway 1 from Big Sur to San Simeon.** The twisting section of coastal highway affords some breathtaking ocean vistas before arriving at Hearst Castle.

★ **Highway 49, the Gold Country.** California's pioneer past comes to life in the many towns along this 325-mile highway at the base of the Sierra foothills.

★ **Kings Canyon Highway.** During the summer, the stretch of Highway 180 in Kings Canyon National Park from Grant Grove to Cedar Grove is spectacular.

★ **Mulholland Drive, Los Angeles.** One of the most famous thoroughfares in Los Angeles winds through the Hollywood Hills, across the spine of the Santa Monica Mountains, stopping just short of the Pacific Ocean.

Historic Buildings

★ **Coit Tower, San Francisco.** This landmark, dedicated as a monument to the city's volunteer firefighters, was a gift to San Francisco by one of its most eccentric residents, Lillie Hitchcock Coit. The tower's WPA-era murals are as striking as the view.

★ **Lachryma Montis (General Vallejo's Home), Sonoma.** The last Mexican governor of California built this large Victorian Gothic house with a white marble fireplace in every room.

★ **Griffith Park Observatory and Planetarium, Los Angeles.** One of the largest telescopes in the world is open to the public for free viewing every clear night. In the planetarium—immortalized in *Rebel Without a Cause*—dazzling daily shows duplicate the starry sky.

★ **Hearst Castle, San Simeon.** One of California's most popular tourist attractions—in its heyday a playground for the rich and famous—sits in solitary splendor on the 127 acres that were the heart of newspaper magnate William Randolph Hearst's 250,000-acre ranch.

★ **Hotel del Coronado, San Diego.** Coronado Island's most prominent landmark was the world's first electrically lighted hotel.

★ **Mann's Chinese Theater, Hollywood.** The architecture of the former "Grauman's Chinese" is a fantasy of pagodas and temples. Its courtyard is open for browsing of celebrity cement hand- and footprints.

★ **Mission Santa Barbara.** The gem of the chain of 21 Spanish missions established in California is still active as a Catholic church.

★ **California State Capitol, Sacramento.** The lacy plasterwork of the rotunda of this 1869 structure has all the complexity and color of a Fabergé egg. Outside, the 40-acre Capitol Park is one of the oldest gardens in the state.

Lovely Sights

★ **Buena Vista Carneros Winery, Sonoma.** This is the site where modern California wine making began.

★ **El Capitan and Half Dome, Yosemite National Park.** Yosemite's two most famous peaks are also its most photographed.

★ **View from Emerald Bay Lookout, Lake Tahoe.** This aquatic cul-de-sac is famed for its jewel-like shape and colors.

★ **Golden Gate Bridge Vista Point and Marin Headlands, Marin County.** On a clear day, San Francisco glistens from this vantage point at the bridge's north end. From here you can hike (or drive) around the headlands overlooking the Golden Gate.

★ **Huntington Library, Art Gallery, and Gardens, Pasadena.** The botanical splendors here include the 12-acre Desert Garden and 1,500 varieties of camellias. Indoors, there's a Gutenberg Bible in the library, and the original *Blue Boy* by Gainsborough hangs in the gallery.

★ **La Jolla Cove at sunset.** It's beautiful any time of day, but as the sun goes down over the cove and its towering palms, the view is a postcard come to life.

Restaurants with Fabulous Atmosphere

★ **Café Beaujolais, Mendocino.** All the rustic charm of peaceful, backwoods Mendocino is here, with great country cooking to boot. The ever-evolving dinner menu is cross-cultural. Sunday brunch is superb. $$$–$$$$

★ **Stars, San Francisco.** Jeremiah Tower's eatery is a must on every traveling gourmet's itinerary. The dining room has a clublike ambience, and the food ranges from grills to ragouts to sautés. $$$

★ **George's at the Cove, La Jolla.** A wall-length window in the elegant main dining room, renowned for its fresh seafood specials, overlooks the cove. There's also an informal café and outdoor terrace, also with sweeping views of the coast. $$–$$$

★ **Granita, Malibu.** Wolfgang Puck's coastal outpost has striking interior details and a menu that favors seafood, along with the chef's signature California-inspired dishes. $$–$$$

★ **Greens at Fort Mason, San Francisco.** The expansive bay views alone would be worth a visit to this beautiful restaurant owned and operated by the Zen Buddhist Center of Marin County. The bonus: a wide, eclectic, and creative spectrum of meatless cooking. The homemade breads promise nirvana. $$–$$$

★ **Samoa Cookhouse, Samoa (near Eureka).** Get a feel for dining during the heyday of the North Coast logging industry at this lumberman's hangout that dates back to the late 19th century. The Samoa's cooks serve substantial meals family-style at long wooden tables. $

FESTIVALS AND SEASONAL EVENTS

WINTER

JANUARY➢ Palo Alto's annual **East-West Shrine All-Star Football Classic** (1651 19th Ave., San Francisco 94122, ☎ 415/661–0291) is America's oldest all-star sports event. In Pasadena, the 107th annual **Tournament of Roses Parade and Football Game** (391 S. Orange Grove Blvd., Pasadena 91184, ☎ 818/449–7673) takes place on New Year's Day 1996, with lavish flower-decked floats, marching bands, and equestrian teams, followed by the Rose Bowl game. From December or January through March, hundreds of gray whales migrate along the California coast, and visitors turn out in force for **whale watching** (call California Division of Tourism, ☎ 800/462–2543; San Francisco Visitors Bureau, ☎ 415/391–2000; or San Diego Visitors Bureau, ☎ 619/276–8200).

FEBRUARY➢ The legendary **AT&T Pebble Beach National Pro-Am** golf tournament (Box 869, Monterey 93942, ☎ 408/649–1533) begins in late January and ends in early February. In San Francisco, home of the largest concentration of Chinese-Americans in the country, the climax to the annual **Chinese New Year Celebration** is the Golden Dragon Parade (Chinese Chamber of Commerce, 730 Sacramento St., San Francisco 94108, ☎ 415/982–3000). This year is the Year of the Rat. Los Angeles also has a Chinese New Year Parade (Chinese Chamber of Commerce, 977 N. Broadway, Suite E, Los Angeles 90012, ☎ 213/617–0396). Indio's **National Date Festival and Fair** (46-350 Arabia St., Indio 92201, ☎ 619/863–8247) is an exotic county fair with an Arabian Nights theme; it features camel and ostrich races, an Arabian Nights fantasy production, and date exhibits and tastings.

SPRING

MARCH➢ **Snowfest** in North Lake Tahoe (Box 7590, Tahoe City 96145, ☎ 916/583–7625) is the largest winter carnival in the West, with skiing, food, fireworks, parades, and live music. The finest female golfers in the world compete for the richest purse on the LPGA circuit at the **Nabisco Dinah Shore Golf Tournament** in Rancho Mirage (2 Racquet Club Dr., Rancho Mirage 92270, ☎ 619/324–4546). The **Mendocino/Fort Bragg Whale Festival** (Fort Bragg–Mendocino Coast Chamber of Commerce, Box 1141, Fort Bragg 95437, ☎ 707/961–6300) features whale-watching excursions, marine art exhibits, wine and beer tastings, crafts displays, and a chowder contest.

APRIL➢ A large cast presents the **Ramona Pageant,** a poignant love story based on the novel by Helen Hunt Jackson, on weekends in late April and early May on a mountainside outdoor stage (Ramona Pageant Association, 27400 Ramona Bowl Rd., Hemet 92544, ☎ 909/658–3111). More than 1,200 costumed revelers re-create a springtime 16th-century country fair, the popular **Renaissance Pleasure Faire** (☎ 800/523–2473), from late April to mid-June in the foothills of the San Bernardino Mountains. A similar Elizabethan harvest fair is held in northern California (at press time its location was undetermined) from late August to mid-October.

MAY➢ The **Music At the Wineries** festival in the Gold Country boosts spirits with a world-class jazz session on the 20th in Plymouth (Box 217, Sutter Creek 95685, ☎ 209/267–0211). Inspired by Mark Twain's story "The Notorious Jumping Frog of Calaveras County," the **Jumping Frog Jubilee** in Angels Camp (39th District Agricultural Association, Box 489, Angels Camp 95222, ☎ 209/736–2561) is for frogs and trainers who take their competition seriously. Sacramento hosts the **Dixieland Jazz Jubilee** (Sacramento Traditional Jazz Society, 2787 Del Monte St., West Sacramento 95691, ☎ 916/372–5277) on Memorial Day weekend; it's the world's largest Dixieland festival, with 125 bands from around the world. In Monterey, the squirmy squid is the main attraction for the Memorial Day weekend **Great Monterey Squid Festival** (2600 Garden Rd., Suite 208, Monterey 93940, ☎ 408/649–6547). You'll see squid cleaning and cooking demonstrations, taste treats, plus the usual festival fare: entertainment, arts and crafts, educational exhibits.

SUMMER

JUNE➢ Starting in late May and running into early June is a national ceramics competition and exhibition called **Feats of Clay** in the Gold Country (175 Almond St., Auburn, CA 95603, ☎ 916/645–9713). During the first weekend in June, Pasadena City Hall Plaza hosts the **Chalk It Up Festival.** Artists use the pavement as their canvas to create masterpieces that wash away when festivities have come to a close. There are also musical performances and exotic dining kiosks, the proceeds of which benefit the homeless (The Light-Bringer Project, 539 E. Villa St., Cottage 27, Pasadena 91101, ☎ 818/449–3689). A wine event for serious sippers, the **Napa Valley Wine Auction** in St. Helena features open houses, wine tasting, and the auction. Pre-registration by April 1 is required (Napa Valley Wine Auction, Box 141, St. Helena 94574, ☎ 707/963–5246). Each year on Father's Day is the **Tour of Nevada City Bicycle Classic** (Nevada City Chamber of Commerce, 132 Main St., Nevada City 95959, ☎ 916/265–2692 or 800/655–6569).

JULY➢ During the **Carmel Bach Festival,** the works of Johann Sebastian Bach and 18th-century contemporaries are performed for three weeks; events include concerts, recitals, and seminars (Box 575, Carmel 93921, ☎ 408/624–1521). During the last weekend in July, Gilroy, the self-styled Garlic Capital of the World, celebrates its smelly but delicious product with the **Gilroy Garlic Festival** (Box 2311, Gilroy 95021, ☎ 408/842–1625), featuring such unusual concoctions as garlic ice cream.

AUGUST➢ The **California State Fair** (Box 15649, Sacramento 95852, ☎ 916/263–3000) showcases the state's agricultural side, with high-tech exhibits, rodeo, horse racing, carnival, and big-name entertainment. It runs 18 days from August to Labor Day in Sacramento. The **Old Spanish Days' Fiesta** (Box 21557, Santa Barbara 93121, ☎ 805/962–8101) is the nation's largest all-equestrian parade. The citywide celebration features costumes, several parades, a carnival, fiesta breakfast, rodeo, dancers, and a Spanish marketplace.

AUTUMN

SEPTEMBER➢ In Guerneville, jazz fans and musicians jam at Johnson's Beach for the **Russian River Jazz Festival** (☎ 707/869–3940). The **San Francisco Blues Festival** (☎ 415/826–6837) is held at Fort Mason in late September. The **Los Angeles County Fair** in Pomona (Box 2250, Pomona 91769, ☎ 909/623–3111) is the largest county fair in the world. It features entertainment, exhibits, livestock, horse racing, food, and more.

OCTOBER➢ San Francisco's **Grand National Rodeo, Horse, and Stock Show** (Cow Palace, 2600 Geneva Ave., Daly City 94014, ☎ 415/469–6057) is a 10-day, world-class competition, with 3,000 top livestock and horses. In Carmel, speakers and poets gather for seminars, a banquet, and book signing at the **Tor House Poetry Festival** (Box 2713, Carmel 93921, ☎ 408/624–1813), which honors the poet Robinson Jeffers. The climax of this weekend event is a walk on the beach, where participants picnic and read the poet's work aloud.

NOVEMBER➢ The **Death Valley '49er Encampment,** at Furnace Creek, commemorates the historic crossing of Death Valley in 1849, with fiddlers' contest and an art show (Death Valley National Park, Box 579, Death Valley 92328, ☎ 619/786–2331). Pasadena's **Doo Dah Parade,** a fun-filled spoof of the annual Rose Parade, features the Lounge Lizards, who dress as reptiles and lip-sync to Frank Sinatra favorites, and West Hollywood cheerleaders in drag (Light-Bringer Project, 539 East Villa St., Cottage

27, Pasadena 91101, ☎ 818/449–3689).

DECEMBER➢ For the **Newport Harbor Christmas Boat Parade** in Newport Beach (1470 Jamboree Rd., Newport Beach 92660, ☎ 714/729–4400), more than 200 festooned boats parade through the harbor nightly December 17–23. In Columbia in early December, the **Miner's Christmas Celebration** includes a Victorian Christmas feast at the City Hotel, lamplight tours, theater, children's piñata, costumed carolers, and Las Posados Nativity Procession (Columbia Chamber of Commerce, Box 1824, Columbia 95310, ☎ 209/532–4301). The internationally acclaimed El Teatro Campesino (Box 1240, San Juan Bautista 95045, ☎ 408/623–2444) annually stages its nativity play **La Virgen Del Tepeyac** in the Mission San Juan Bautista.

2 The North Coast

The North Coast's main industries are tourism, fishing, and logging. There are no large cities, no large amusement parks, few luxury resorts. There isn't even much swimming, because of a cold current that runs down the coast for most of the state (turning out to sea before it reaches southern California beaches). What you will find are a scenic drive along Highway 1 and U.S. 101, many small inns, uncrowded state beaches and parks, some good art galleries, and restaurants serving imaginative dishes featuring locally produced ingredients. This is a region for leisurely exploring.

Updated by
Marty
Olmstead

WITHIN THE NEARLY 400 MILES of California coastline between the San Francisco Bay and the Oregon border are some of the most beautiful and rugged landscapes in America. Here in the aptly named Redwood Empire are primeval forests of the world's tallest trees. The nearby shoreline holds a wealth of secluded coves and beaches from which you may well see gray whales migrating, seals sunning, and hawks soaring. The area is also rich in human history, having been the successive domain of Native American Miwoks and Pomos, Russian traders, Hispanic settlers, and more contemporary fishing folk and lumberjacks, all of whom have left legacies that can be seen today. For those in search of untamed natural beauty, great fishing, abundant wildlife, and elegant country inns, the North Coast is a bit of heaven.

This region is sparsely populated, with only 10 towns of more than 700 inhabitants. Traditionally, residents have made their living from fishing and timber. But today the local economy suffers from the loss of jobs these industries are facing. Tourism, however, is doing well. Some of California's most original restaurants are sprouting up on the North Coast, and locals are lovingly restoring the area's many Victorian mansions to lodge the increasing number of visitors.

EXPLORING

Exploring the northern California coast is easiest in a car. Highway 1 is a beautiful, if sometimes slow and nerve-racking, drive. You'll want to stop frequently to appreciate the views, and there are many portions of the highway along which you won't drive faster than 20–40 mph. You can still have a fine trip even if you don't have much time, but be realistic and don't plan to drive too far in one day (*see* Getting Around *in* North Coast Essentials, *below*).

We've arranged the exploring section for a trip from San Francisco heading north. The first section follows Highway 1 north past Fort Bragg to its intersection with U.S. 101. The second section follows U.S. 101 through the Redwood Empire.

The North Coast via Highway 1

Numbers in the margin correspond to points of interest on the North Coast maps.

To reach Highway 1 heading north from San Francisco, cross the
Golden Gate Bridge and proceed north on U.S. 101 to the Stinson
Beach/Highway 1 exit. Follow Highway 1 north, and as it winds up-
1 hill, you will see a turnoff for **Muir Woods.** Muir Woods National Monument and the adjoining Mt. Tamalpais State Park are described (as
2 day trips) in Chapter 5. Past this turnoff, the town of **Stinson Beach**
has the most expansive sands (4,500 feet) in Marin County. On any
hot summer weekend, every road to Stinson Beach is jam-packed, so
factor this into your plans. Along Bolinas Lagoon, you will find the
3 **Audubon Canyon Ranch,** a 1,000-acre wildlife sanctuary. In the spring,
the public is invited to take to the trails to see great blue heron and
great egret tree nestings. There is a small museum with displays on the
geology and natural history of the region, a natural history bookstore,
and a picnic area. ☎ *415/868–9244. Donation requested.* ⏲ *Mid-Mar.–mid-July, weekends and holidays 10–4.*

At the northern edge of Bolinas Lagoon, a couple of miles beyond the Audubon Canyon Ranch, take the unmarked road running west from Highway 1, which leads to the sleepy town of **Bolinas.** Some residents of Bolinas are so wary of tourism that whenever the state tries to post signs, they tear them down. Birders should head down Mesa Road to
4 the **Point Reyes Bird Observatory,** a sanctuary and research center within the National Seashore harboring nearly 225 species of bird life. ☎ *415/868–0655.* ☛ *Free. Banding May–Nov., daily; Dec.–Apr., weekends and Wed., weather permitting. Visitor center open daily 8–6.*

On the way back to Bolinas, go right on Overlook Drive and right again
5 on Elm Avenue until you come to **Duxbury Reef,** known for its fine tide pools.

Returning to Highway 1, you will pass pastoral horse farms. About ⅓
6 mile past Olema, look for a sign marking the turnoff for the **Bear Val-**
★ **ley Visitors Center** at the **Point Reyes National Seashore.** Here you'll find exhibits of park wildlife as well as helpful rangers who can advise you about beaches, visits to the lighthouse for whale watching (the season for gray-whale migration is mid-December–mid-April), hiking trails, and camping. (Camping, for backpackers only, is free; reservations should be made through the visitor center.) No matter what your interests, the beauty of this wilderness is worth your time. A reconstructed Miwok Indian Village is a short walk from the visitor center. It provides insight into the daily lives of the first human inhabitants of this region. The lighthouse is a 30- to 40-minute drive from the visitor center, across rolling hills that resemble Scottish heath. On busy weekends during the season, parking near the lighthouse may be difficult. The view alone lures most people to make the effort of walking down—and then back up—the hundreds of steps from the cliff tops to the lighthouse below; but if you choose to skip the descent, you can still see the whales from the cliff. ☎ *415/663–1092.* ☛ *Free. Visitor center open weekdays 9–5, weekends 8–5.*

If you decide to stay overnight in this area, there are good country inns and decent restaurants (not to mention great hiking) in and around the towns of **Inverness,** where the architecture and cuisine reflect the influence of the once-sizable Czech population, and in **Point Reyes Station.**

The Russian River empties into the Pacific at the fishing town of **Jenner.** If you are lucky, you may spot seals sunning themselves off the banks of the estuary. Travelers who wish to move on to the Wine Country (*see* Chapter 4) from here can take Highway 116 east from Jenner.

Highway 1 between Jenner and Gualala is the most dramatic stretch of North Coast shoreline. The road is one long series of steep switchbacks after another, so take your time, relax, and make frequent stops to enjoy the unparalleled beauty of this wild coast.

About 12 miles north of Jenner is a must-see for history buffs. Built in
7 1812, Russia's major fur-trading outpost in California, **Fort Ross,** has been painstakingly reconstructed by the state park service. The Russians brought Aleut sea-otter hunters down from their Alaskan bailiwicks to hunt pelts for the czar. In 1841, with the area depleted of seal and otter, the Russians sold their post to John Sutter, later of Gold Rush fame. After a local Anglo rebellion against the Mexicans, the land fell under U.S. domain, becoming part of the state of California in 1850. At Fort Ross, you will find a restored Russian Orthodox chapel, a redwood stockade, officers' barracks, a blockhouse, and an excellent museum. *Fort Ross State Historical Park,* ☎ *707/847–3286.* ☛ *$5 per*

The North Coast

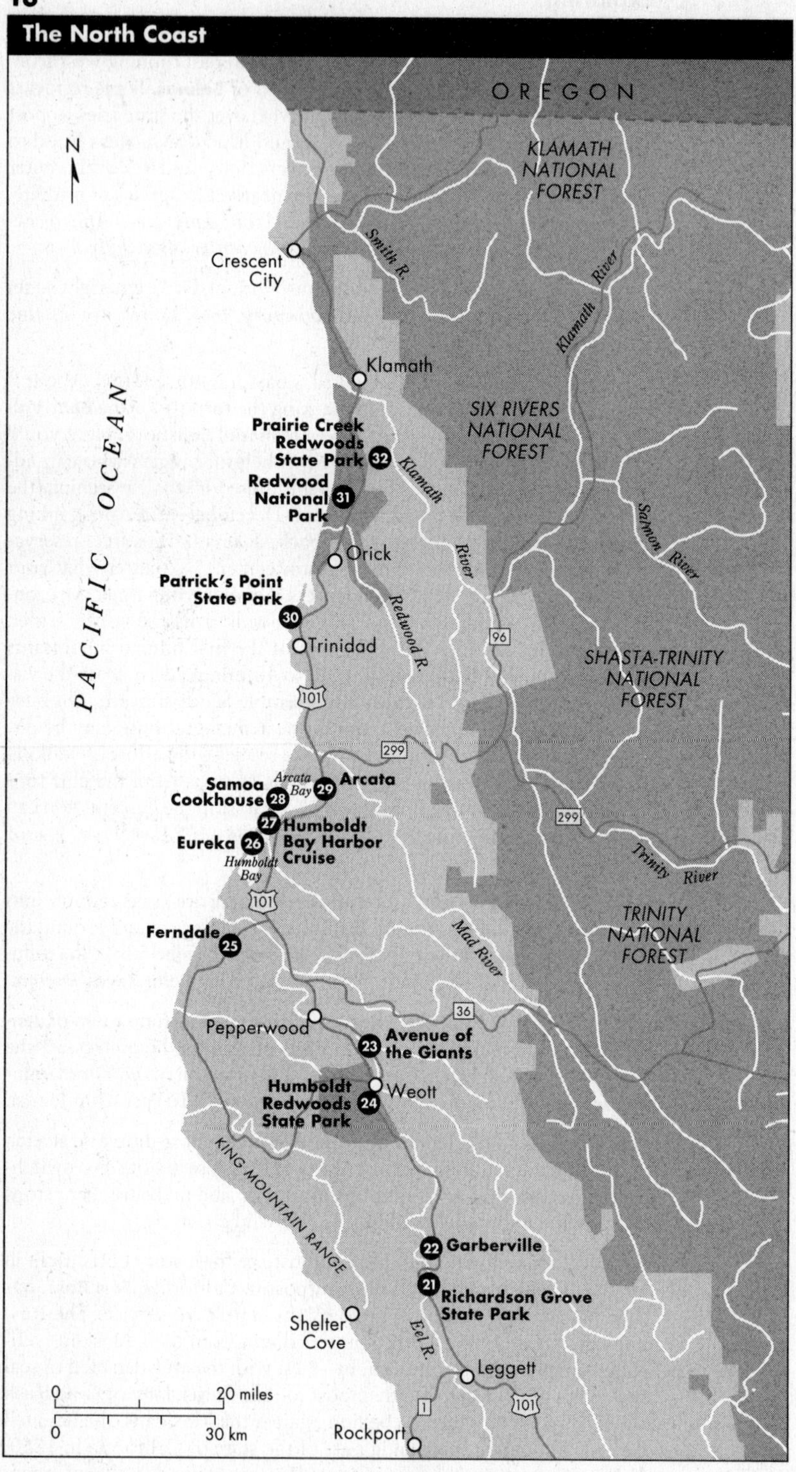
OREGON
KLAMATH NATIONAL FOREST
N
Crescent City
Smith R.
Klamath River
Klamath
SIX RIVERS NATIONAL FOREST
PACIFIC OCEAN
Prairie Creek Redwoods State Park 32
Klamath
Redwood National Park 31
Salmon River
Orick
River
Patrick's Point State Park 30
Redwood R.
96
Trinidad
SHASTA-TRINITY NATIONAL FOREST
101
299
Samoa Cookhouse 28
Arcata Bay
29 Arcata
27 Humboldt Bay Harbor Cruise
Eureka 26
Humboldt Bay
299
Trinity River
101
TRINITY NATIONAL FOREST
Ferndale 25
Mad River
36
Pepperwood
23 Avenue of the Giants
Humboldt Redwoods State Park 24
Weott
KING MOUNTAIN RANGE
22 Garberville
21 Richardson Grove State Park
Shelter Cove
Eel R.
Leggett
1
101
Rockport
0
20 miles
0
30 km

North Coast South

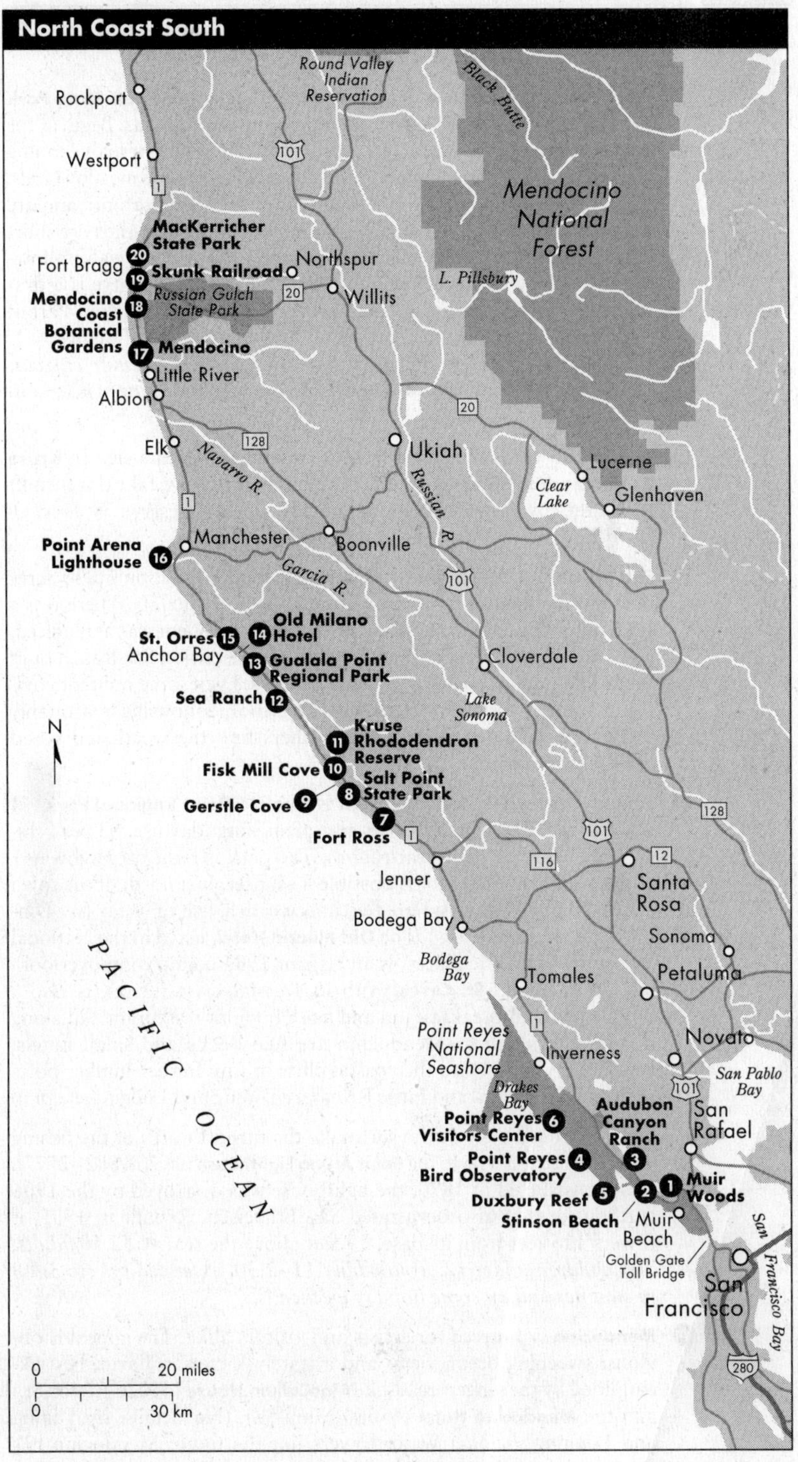
Round Valley Indian Reservation
Black Butte
Rockport
Westport
Mendocino National Forest
MacKerricher State Park
20
Fort Bragg
19 Skunk Railroad
Northspur
Willits
L. Pillsbury
Mendocino Coast Botanical Gardens 18
Russian Gulch State Park
17 Mendocino
Little River
Albion
Elk
Navarro R.
Ukiah
Russian R.
Lucerne
Clear Lake
Glenhaven
Point Arena Lighthouse 16
Manchester
Boonville
Garcia R.
Old Milano Hotel 14
St. Orres 15
Anchor Bay
13 Gualala Point Regional Park
Cloverdale
Sea Ranch 12
Lake Sonoma
11 Kruse Rhododendron Reserve
Fisk Mill Cove 10
8 Salt Point State Park
Gerstle Cove 9
7
Fort Ross
Jenner
Santa Rosa
Bodega Bay
Sonoma
Bodega Bay
Tomales
Petaluma
PACIFIC OCEAN
Point Reyes National Seashore
Inverness
Novato
San Pablo Bay
Drakes Bay
Point Reyes Visitors Center 6
Audubon Canyon Ranch 3
San Rafael
Point Reyes Bird Observatory 4
Duxbury Reef 5
1 Muir Woods
Stinson Beach 2
Muir Beach
Golden Gate Toll Bridge
San Francisco
San Francisco Bay
N
0 20 miles
0 30 km

vehicle (day use), $4 senior citizens. ⏲ *Daily 10–4:30; closed Dec. 25 and Jan. 1. No dogs allowed past parking lot.*

8 About 19 miles north of Jenner, the 6,000-acre **Salt Point State Park** offers a glimpse of nature virtually untouched by humans. Begin at the
9 park's **Gerstle Cove,** where you'll probably catch sight of seals sunning themselves on the beach's rocks, and deer roaming in the meadowlands. The unusual formations in the sandstone are called "tafoni" and are the product of hundreds of years of erosion. Next, take the *very* short
10 drive to Salt Point's **Fisk Mill Cove,** where a five-minute walk following the trail uphill brings you to a bench from which there is a dramatic overview of Sentinel Rock and the pounding surf below. Part of the wonder of this spot is that it's all less than a mile off Highway 1. ☎ *707/847–3221.* ☛ *$5 per vehicle (day use), $4 senior citizens. Camping: $14 peak season, $12 off-season, $2 senior-citizen discount.* ⏲ *Daily sunrise–sunset.*

11 About 200 yards beyond Fisk Mill Cove, look for the sign to **Kruse Rhododendron Reserve.** If you're around here in May, take this turnoff to see the towering pink flowers in this 317-acre reserve. ☛ *Free.* ⏲ *Daily.*

12 **Sea Ranch** is a development of pricey second homes, on 5,000 acres overlooking the Pacific about 10 miles south of Gualala. There was a great outcry by conservationists when this development was announced, and much controversy ensued. To appease the critics, Sea Ranch built accessible public trails down to the beaches. Even some militant environmentalists deem architect Charles Moore's housing reasonably congruent with the surroundings; others find the weathered wood buildings beautiful.

13 An excellent whale-watching spot is **Gualala Point Regional Park** (☎ 707/785–2377), where there is also picnicking (day use: $3 per vehicle) and camping ($14 year-round). The park is right off Highway 1 and is well marked; entry is possible 8–sunset. Just north of the town of Gualala on Highway 1 are two inns worth a visit or a stay (*see* Din-
14 ing and Lodging, *below*). The **Old Milano Hotel,** listed in the National Registry of Historic Places, is an elegant 1905 country inn overlook-
15 ing Castle Rock. **St. Orres,** with its Russian-style turrets, is also a unique bed-and-breakfast inn and has a popular restaurant. All along this stretch north to Mendocino are fine B&Bs and small hotels, perched in and around the coastal cliffs of tiny former lumber ports such as Elk, Albion, and Little River (*see* Dining and Lodging, *below*).

For a dramatic view of the surf, take the turnoff north of the fishing
16 village of Point Arena to the **Point Arena Lighthouse** (☎ 707/882–2777). First constructed in 1870, the lighthouse was destroyed by the 1906 earthquake that also devastated San Francisco. Rebuilt in 1907, it towers 115 feet from its base, 50 feet above the sea. ☛ *$2.50 adults, 50¢ children under 12. Tours daily 11–2:30, extended hrs (to 3:30) in summer and on some holiday weekends.*

★ 17 **Mendocino** is a mecca for artists and visitors alike. The appeal is obvious: sweeping ocean views and a stately Victorian flavor, best exemplified by the gingerbread-like **MacCallum House** (45020 Albion St.) and the **Mendocino Hotel** (45080 Main St.). (For details, *see* Dining and Lodging, *below.*) Water towers dot the town; Mendocino has never had an underground public water system. The town is most easily and best seen on foot, and there are numerous art galleries to stop in while walking around. The **Mendocino Art Center** (45200 Little

Lake St., ☏ 707/937–5818) has exhibits, art classes, concerts, and a theater. The **Kelley House Museum** (45007 Albion St., ☏ 707/937–5791; ☛ $1; open June–Sept., daily 1–4, Oct.–May, Fri.–Mon. 1–4) is a refurbished 1861 structure displaying historical photographs of Mendocino's logging days, antique cameras, Victorian-era clothing, furniture, and artifacts. Also on Albion Street is the green and red **Chinese Joss Temple,** dating to 1882. Another restored structure, the **Ford House,** built in 1854, is on Main Street and serves as the visitor center for Mendocino Headlands State Park (☏ 707/937–5397; open year-round, daily 11–4, with possible temporary midweek closings in winter; history walks Sat. at 1 PM). The park itself consists of the cliffs that border the town; access is free.

18 Off Highway 1, between Mendocino and Fort Bragg, are the **Mendocino Coast Botanical Gardens.** The gardens were established as a private preserve in 1962. In 1982 the Mendocino Coast Park District acquired 17 acres, and the Coastal Conservancy added another 30 acres in 1991. Along 2 miles of coastal trails, with ocean views and observation points for whale watching, is a splendid array of flowers, with the rhododendron season at its peak from April to June, and perennials in bloom from May to September. Fuchsias, heather, and azaleas are resplendent here. This is a fine place to stop for a picnic. ☏ *707/964–4352.* ☛ *$5 adults, $4 senior citizens, $3 children 13–17 and students.* ⏲ *Mar.–Oct., daily 9–5; Nov.–Feb., daily 9–4.*

Fort Bragg is the commercial center of Mendocino County. While Mendocino boomed with bed-and-breakfasts, art galleries, and tourists, this loggers' town retained its old-fashioned, workaday character. It is
19 also headquarters of the famous and popular **Skunk Railroad,** on which you can take scenic half- or full-day tours through redwood forests inaccessible by automobile. A remnant of the region's logging days, the Skunk Railroad line dates from 1885 and travels a route from Fort Bragg on the coast to the town of Willits, 40 miles inland. A fume-spewing, self-propelled train car that shuttled passengers along the railroad got nicknamed the Skunk Train, and the entire line has been called that ever since. Excursions are now given on historic trains and replicas of the Skunk Train motorcar that are more aromatic than the original. In summer you have a choice of going partway to Northspur, a three-hour round-trip, or making the full seven-hour journey to Willits and back. (You can also travel one-way from Fort Bragg to Willits, or vice versa.) *California Western Railroad Inc., Fort Bragg,* ☏ *707/964–6371. Fort Bragg–Willits: departs daily 9:20 AM.* ☛ *$26 adults, $12 children 5–11. Fort Bragg–Northspur: departs 2nd Sat. in June–1st Mon. in Sept., daily 9:20 AM and 1:40 PM; Sept. 5–early June, 10 AM and 2 PM.* ☛ *$21 adults; $10 children 5–11.*

★ 20 **MacKerricher State Park** is 3 miles north of Fort Bragg on the outskirts of Cleone. It includes 10 miles of sandy beach and several square miles of dunes. Fishing (at two freshwater lakes, one stocked with trout), canoeing, hiking, jogging, bicycling, camping (143 sites available), and harbor seal watching at Laguna Point are among the popular activities—many of which are wheelchair accessible. Whales can often be spotted December through mid-April from the nearby headland. Rangers lead nature hikes throughout the year. *3 mi north of Fort Bragg on Hwy. 1,* ☏ *707/937–5804.*

North on Highway 1 from Fort Bragg, past the coastal mill town of **Westport,** the road cuts inland around the **King Range,** a stretch of mountain so rugged that it was impossible to build the intended major highway through it. Highway 1 joins the larger U.S. 101 at the town of Leggett and continues north into the redwood country of Humboldt and Del Norte counties.

The Redwood Empire

21 **Richardson Grove State Park,** north of Leggett, along U.S. 101, marks
your first encounter with the truly giant redwoods, but there are even
22 more magnificent stands farther north. A few miles below **Garberville,**
perched along Eel River, is an elegant Tudor resort, the **Benbow Inn**
(*see* Dining and Lodging, *below*). Even if you are not staying here, stop
in for a drink or meal and a look at the architecture and gardens.

23 For an unforgettable treat, take the turnoff for the **Avenue of the Gi-**
ants just north of Garberville. Along this stretch of two-lane blacktop
you will find yourself enveloped by some of the tallest trees on the planet,
24 the coastal redwoods. This road cuts through part of the **Humboldt Red-**
woods State Park, 51,222 acres of redwoods and waterways, and follows the south fork of the Eel River. The visitor center near **Weott** (☎
707/946–2263) is open in the spring and summer and can provide information on the region's recreational opportunities, and flora and
★ fauna. **Founders Grove** contains some of the tallest trees in the park.
The grove's highest tree, at 362 feet, fell in 1991.

25 Detour 5 miles west of U.S. 101 from Fortuna to **Ferndale.** This stately town, which has just about recovered from a 1992 earthquake that centered here, maintains some of the most sumptuous Victorian homes in California, many of them built by 19th-century timber barons and Scandinavian dairy farmers. The queen of them all is the **Gingerbread Mansion** (400 Berding St.), once a hospital and now refurbished as a bed-and-breakfast (*see* Dining and Lodging, *below*). A beautiful, sloped **graveyard** sits on Ocean Avenue west of Main Street. Numerous shops carry a local map for self-guided tours of this lovingly preserved town.

The **Ferndale Museum** has a storehouse of antiques from the turn of the century. *515 Shaw Ave.,* ☎ *707/786–4466.* ☛ *$1 adults, 50¢ children 6–16.* ⏲ *Oct.–June 1, Wed.–Sat. 11–4, Sun. 1–4; also Tues. 11–4 in summer.*

26 With 28,500 inhabitants, **Eureka** ranks as the North Coast's largest city. It has gone through cycles of boom and bust, first with mining and later with timber and fishing. There are nearly 100 elegant Victorian buildings here, many of them well preserved or refurbished. The most splendid (and most photographed in the state) is the **Carson Mansion** (at M and 2nd Sts.), built in 1885 by the Newsom brothers for timber baron William Carson. The house is now occupied by a private men's club. Across the street is another Newsom extravaganza popularly known as the **Pink Lady.** For proof that contemporary architects still have the skills to design lovely Victoriana, have a look at the **Carter House** B&B inn (3rd and L Sts.; *see* Dining and Lodging, *below*) and keep in mind that it was built in the 1980s, not the 1880s. The **Chamber of Commerce** can provide maps of the town and information on how to join organized tours. *2112 Broadway,* ☎ *707/442–3738 or 800/356–6381.* ⏲ *Weekdays 9–5.*

★ **Old Town Eureka** is one of the most outstanding Victorian-era commercial districts in California, with buildings dating from the 1860s to 1915. The **Clarke Museum** has an extraordinary collection of northwestern California Native American basketry and contains artifacts from Eureka's Victorian, logging, and maritime heritages. *240 E. St.,* ☎ *707/*

443–1947. ☛ *Donations accepted.* ⏲ *Feb.–Dec., Tues.–Sat. and July 4 noon–4.*

At the south end of Eureka stands **Fort Humboldt,** which guarded settlers against the Indians and is now a state historic park. Ulysses S. Grant was posted here in 1854. On the fort's grounds are re-creations of the logging industry's early days, including a logging museum, some ancient steam engines, and a logger's cabin. *3431 Fort Ave.,* ☎ *707/445–6567.* ⏲ *Daily 9–4; call ahead to arrange a tour.*

27 To explore the waters around Eureka, take a **Humboldt Bay Harbor Cruise.** You can observe some of the region's bird life while sailing past fishing boats, oyster beds, and decaying timber mills. *Pier at C St.,* ☎ *707/445–1910 or 707/444–9440.* ☛ *$8.50 adults, $7.50 senior citizens and children 12–17, $5.50 children 6–11. Departs May–Sept., daily 1, 2:30, and 4. Cocktail-cruise fare: $5.50. Departs daily 5:30.*

28 Across the bridge in Samoa is the **Samoa Cookhouse** (☎ 707/442–1659), an example from about the 1860s of the cookhouses that once stood in every lumber and mill town. There is a museum displaying antique culinary artifacts, and breakfast, lunch, and dinner are served family style at long wood tables. (*See* Dining and Lodging, *below.*)

29 Just north of Eureka is the pleasant college town of **Arcata,** home of Humboldt State University. One of the few California burgs that retain a town square, Arcata also has some restored Victorian buildings. The town square holds a farmer's market on Tuesday evenings and Saturday mornings May through November. For a self-guided tour, pick up a map from the **Chamber of Commerce.** *1062 G St.,* ☎ *707/822–3619.* ⏲ *Weekdays 10–4.*

After taking the turnoff for the town of **Trinidad,** follow the road a mile to one of the most splendid harbors on the West Coast. First visited by a Portuguese expedition in 1595, the waters here are now sailed by fishing boats trolling for salmon. Picturesque Trinidad Bay's harbor cove and rock formations look both raw and tranquil. ⏲ *Daily sunrise–sunset.*

30 Twenty-five miles north of Eureka is **Patrick's Point State Park.** Set on a forested plateau almost 200 feet above the surf, the park affords good whale and sea-lion watching. There are also tide pools and a small museum with natural history exhibits. ☎ *707/677–3570.* ☛ *$5 per vehicle (day use), $4 senior citizens. Camping: $14 per car, $12 senior citizens ($2 less in winter).*

31 Those continuing north will pass through the 113,200 acres of **Redwood National Park.** After 115 years of intensive logging, this vast region of tall trees came under government protection in 1968, marking the California environmentalists' greatest victory over the timber industry. The park encompasses three state parks (Prairie Creek Redwoods, Del Norte Coast Redwoods, and Jedediah Smith Redwoods) and is more than 40 miles long. *Redwood National Park Headquarters, 1111 2nd St., Crescent City, CA 95531,* ☎ *707/464–6101.*

For detailed information about Redwood National Park, stop at the **Redwood Information Center** between the park entrance and the town of Orick (☎ 707/488–3461). There you can also get a free permit to drive up the steep, 17-mile road (the last 6 miles are gravel) to reach the **Tall Trees Grove,** where a 3-mile round-trip hiking trail leads to the world's first-, third- and fifth-tallest redwoods. Whale watchers will find the deck of the visitor center an excellent observation point, and birders will enjoy the nearby **Freshwater Lagoon,** a popular layover for migrating waterfowl.

Within **Lady Bird Johnson Grove,** just off Bald Hill Road, is a short circular trail to resplendent redwoods. This section of the park was dedicated by, and named for, the former first lady. For additional spectacular scenery, take Davison Road along a stunning seascape to **Fern Canyon.** This gravel road winds through 4 miles of second-growth redwoods, then hugs a bluff 100 feet above the pounding Pacific surf for another 4 miles.

32 To reach the entrance to Redwood's **Prairie Creek Redwoods State Park,** take the Elk Prairie Parkway exit off the U.S. 101 bypass. Extra space has been paved alongside the parklands, providing fine vantage points from which to observe an imposing herd of **Roosevelt elk** grazing in the adjoining meadow. **Revelation Trail** in Prairie Creek is fully accessible to visitors with disabilities.

The route through the redwoods and sea views will ultimately lead past the Klamath River, home of the famous king salmon, to Del Norte County's largest town, **Crescent City.**

Travelers continuing north to the Smith River near the Oregon border will find fine trout and salmon fishing as well as a profusion of flowers. Ninety percent of America's lily bulbs are grown in this area.

SHOPPING

In the charming town of **Inverness,** Shaker Shops West (5 Inverness Way, ☎ 415/669–7256) has an exceptional array of reproduction Shaker furniture and gift items. There is a turn-of-the-century sensibility to the fine works exhibited here; it's open Tuesday–Saturday 11–5, Sunday noon–5. In **Point Reyes Station,** Gallery Route One (11101 Hwy. 1, ☎ 415/663–1347) is a nonprofit cooperative of 24 area artists in all media, open Friday through Monday from 11 to 5, Thursday through Monday in summer.

Mendocino has earned a reputation as the artistic center of the North Coast. So many fine artists exhibit their wares here, and the streets of this compact town are so easily walkable, that you're sure to find a gallery with something that strikes your fancy. You might start at the Mendocino Art Center (45200 Little Lake St., ☎ 707/937–5818), where artists teach courses and display their creations.

The Victorian village of **Ferndale,** in the Redwood Empire, is a magnet for fine painters, potters, and carpenters. Just walk down Main Street and stop in to browse at any of the stores along its three principal blocks. Golden Gait Mercantile (421 Main St., ☎ 707/786–4891) seems to be lost in a time warp, what with Burma Shave products and old-fashioned long johns as well as penny candy. For gifts, you can't do better than Withywindle (358 Main St., ☎ 707/786–9610), which sells local stoneware, porcelain, jewelry, and wearable art. The shopkeepers also specialize in gift baskets crammed with various gourmet products from the shelves.

Eureka has several fine art shops and galleries in the district running from C to I streets between 2nd and 3rd streets. One of note is the Old Town Art Gallery (233 F St., ☎ 707/445–2315). Another recommended gallery is the Humboldt Cultural Center (422 1st St., ☎ 707/442–2611 or 707/442–0278). Specialty shops in Old Town include Restoration Hardware (417 2nd St., ☎ 707/443–3152), the original store that has since branched out. This is the place to find attractive and functional home and garden accessories and clever polishing and cleaning products. The Irish Shop (2nd and E Sts., ☎ 707/443–8343) fills a large corner store with myriad imports from the Emerald Isle, mostly fine woolens.

For its size, **Arcata** has an impressive array of shops, particularly on the streets flanking its modest plaza. Fabrics, clothing, home furnishings, and books are the best bets here. The most exceptional shop is Plaza Design (808 G St., ☎ 707/822–7732), which specializes in gifts, papers and innovative furnishings.

SPORTS

Bicycling

For the hardy rider who wishes to take in the full beauty of the North Coast by mountain bike, there are a number of rental services in San Francisco and the major North Coast towns. Some rental shops on the coast are **Trailhead Rentals** (88 Bear Valley Rd., corner of Hwy. 1, Olema, ☎ 415/663–1958) and **Catch-a-Canoe and Bicycles Too** (Stanford Inn by the Sea, Mendocino, ☎ 707/937–0273).

Camping

Campground reservations for all state parks are usually necessary in summer. For reservations, call MISTIX, ☎ 800/444–7275.

Canoeing

Among the many canoe liveries of the North Coast is **Catch-a-Canoe and Bicycles Too** (Stanford Inn by the Sea, Mendocino, ☎ 707/937–0273).

Fishing

For ocean fishing, there are plenty of outfits from which you can charter a boat with equipment provided. Among them are **Bodega Bay Sportfishing** (☎ 707/875–3344), **Noyo Fishing Center** (Fort Bragg, ☎ 707/964–7609), **Lost Coast Landing** (Shelter Cove, ☎ 707/986–7624; closed winter), and **Blue Pacific Charters** (Eureka, ☎ 707/442–6682). You can fish for salmon and steelhead in the rivers. There's particularly good abalone diving around Jenner, Fort Ross, Point Arena, Westport, Shelter Cove, and Trinidad.

Golf

Among others, there are courses open to the public at **Bodega Harbour Golf Links** (18 holes, Bodega Bay, ☎ 707/875–3538), **Little River Inn** (9 holes, Little River, ☎ 707/937–5667), **Benbow Inn** (9 holes, Garberville, ☎ 707/923–2124), and **Eureka Golf Course** (18 holes, ☎ 707/443–4808).

Horseback Riding

Numerous stables and resorts offer guided rides on the North Coast, including **Five Brooks Stables** (Point Reyes, ☎ 415/663–1570), **Chanslor Guest Ranch** (Bodega Bay, ☎ 707/875–2721), **Ricochet Ridge Ranch** (Cleone, ☎ 707/964–7669), and **Lazy L Ranch** (Arcata, ☎ 707/822–6736).

River Tours

Eel River Delta Tours (Eureka, ☎ 707/786–4187) emphasizes wildlife and history in the estuary.

Whale Watching

From any number of excellent observation points along the coast, you can watch whales during their annual migration season from December through April. Another option is a **whale-watching cruise.** Some cruises run June–November to the Farallon Islands to watch the blue- and humpback-whale migration. Possibilities include the **Oceanic Society Expeditions** (San Francisco, ☎ 415/474–3385). **New Sea Angler and Jaws** (Bodega Bay, ☎ 707/875–3495) runs cruises on weekends December–April.

BEACHES

Although the waters of the Pacific along the North Coast are fine for seals, most humans find the temperatures downright arctic. But when it comes to spectacular cliffs and seascapes, the North Coast beaches are second to none. So pack a picnic and take in the pastoral beauty of the wild coast. Explore tide pools, watch for seals, or dive for abalone. Don't worry about crowds: On many of these beaches you will have the sands largely to yourself.

The following beaches are particularly recommended and are listed in a south-to-north order:

Muir Beach. Located just off Highway 1, 3 miles from Muir Woods. Small but scenic.

Duxbury Reef. Tide pools. From Bolinas, take Mesa Road off Olema–Bolinas Road; make a left on Overlook Drive and a right on Elm Avenue to the beach parking lot.

Point Reyes National Seashore. Limantour Beach is one of the most beautiful of Point Reyes sands.

Tomales Bay State Park. Take Sir Francis Drake Boulevard off Highway 1 toward Point Reyes National Seashore, then follow Pierce Point Road to the park.

Fort Ross State Park. About 9 miles north of Jenner.

Sea Ranch Public Access Trails and Beaches. Off Highway 1 south of Gualala.

Manchester State Beach. About 9 miles north of Point Arena.

MacKerricher State Park. About 3 miles north of Fort Bragg (*see* North Coast via Highway 1 *in* Exploring, *above*).

Agate Beach. A 3-mile beach with tide pools. Set within Patrick's Point State Park off U.S. 101 about 25 miles north of Eureka.

DINING AND LODGING

Dining

For years, the better dining establishments of the North Coast specialized in fresh salmon and trout. With the growth of the tourist industry, a surprising variety of fare ranging from Japanese to Continental cuisine is now being served at good restaurants charging reasonable prices. During the winter months, December to mid-March, tourism slackens on the North Coast; consequently, restaurant days and/or hours are often reduced. It is best to call ahead to check the schedule.

WHAT TO WEAR

Unless otherwise noted, dress is informal.

CATEGORY	COST*
$$$$	over $35
$$$	$25–$35
$$	$15–$25
$	under $15

per person for a three-course meal, excluding drinks, service, and 7¼% tax

Lodging

The North Coast has some of the most attractive lodging in the country, with a price range to accommodate virtually every pocketbook. You will find elaborate Victorian homes, grand old hotels, and modest motels. Many bed-and-breakfasts along the coast are sold out on weekends months in advance, so reserve early. Budget travelers will find youth hostels in Point Reyes National Seashore, Klamath, and Leggett (summer only).

CATEGORY	COST*
$$$$	over $100
$$$	$75–$100
$$	$50–$75
$	under $50

**All prices are for a standard double room, excluding 10% tax.*

Albion

DINING

$$$ **Ledford House.** This restaurant specializes in new American cuisine, which the manager translates as "doing whatever we want." The menu is divided into hearty bistro dishes—mainly stews and pastas—and equally large-portioned examples of California cuisine: ahi tuna, grilled meats, and the like. Ledford House is on a bluff with views—and the auditory accompaniment—of the crashing waves. ✕ *3000 N. Hwy. 1,* ☏ *707/937–0282. Reservations advised. AE, MC, V. Closed Mon. in summer, Mon. and Tues. in winter. No lunch.*

DINING AND LODGING

$$$$ ★ **Albion River Inn.** Overlooking the sea, this attractive inn is composed of modern, two-room cabins overlooking the dramatic bridge and seascape where the Albion River empties into the Pacific. Rooms are bright and have fireplaces. All but two have decks facing the ocean. Six have a Jacuzzi for two, and eight have double tubs. The decor ranges from antique furnishings to wide-back willow chairs. A full breakfast is included. In the glassed-in dining room, which serves grilled dishes and fresh seafood, the views are as spectacular as the food. *3790 N. Hwy. 1, Box 100, 95410,* ☏ *707/937–1919, 800/479–7944 (from northern CA only),* FAX *707/937–2604. 20 rooms. Restaurant (no lunch). AE, MC, V.*

Arcata

DINING

$$ **Abruzzi.** Salads and hefty pasta dishes take up most of the menu at this upscale Italian restaurant just off the town square. Abruzzi serves *panini* (Italian sandwiches) at lunch, and pastas (such as linguine pescara, with a spicy seafood-and-tomato sauce) for lunch and dinner. The dining room and large bar are comfortably decorated in dark colors and wood, lit by candles. ✕ *791 8th St., at the corner of H St. (entrance on H St.),* ☏ *707/826–2345. Reservations advised. AE, D, DC, MC, V. No lunch weekends.*

$ **Crosswinds.** This restaurant serves good Continental cuisine in a casual, sunny Victorian setting, to the tune of live, classical music. ✕ *10th* *and I Sts.,* ☎ *707/826–2133. Reservations advised on weekends. MC, V. Closed Mon. No dinner.*

LODGING

$$ **Hotel Arcata.** The rooms of this conveniently located historic landmark overlooking the town square have character, with their flowered bedspreads and claw-foot bathtubs. The hotel is owned by the Yurok tribe, a Native American nation based north of Arcata. Rates include use of a nearby health club as well as (on weekdays) Continental breakfast. *708 9th St., 95521,* ☎ *707/826–0217 or 800/344–1221,* FAX *707/826–1737. 32 rooms. Restaurant. AE, D, DC, MC, V.*

Bodega Bay

DINING AND LODGING

$$$–$$$$ **Inn at the Tides.** This complex of modern condominium-style buildings offers spacious rooms with high, peaked ceilings and uncluttered decor. All the rooms here have a view of the harbor, and some have fireplaces. Continental breakfast is included. The inn's two restaurants serve excellent seafood dishes. *800 Hwy. 1, Box 640, 94923,* ☎ *707/875–2751 or 800/541–7788,* FAX *707/875–2669. 86 rooms. 2 restaurants, room service, refrigerators, pool, hot tub, sauna, coin laundry. AE, MC, V.*

Cazadero

DINING AND LODGING

$$$$ ★ **Timberhill Ranch.** The winding country road that leads from Highway 1 to Timberhill Ranch gives visitors just enough time to ease into the restful pace of this secluded resort. Simple and serene, Timberhill has 15 cabins decorated with quilts and fresh flowers. Each has a fireplace and private patio where guests can enjoy the breakfast brought to them on a golf cart—perhaps sharing croissants with the resident ducks and geese that waddle up from the ranch's huge pond. The Timberhill's inspired six-course dinners, once served in the spacious wood-and-stone lodge, now take place by candlelight in a separate new dining room. The walk back to your cabin under starlight is so quiet you can hear leaves fall to the ground. *35755 Hauser Bridge Rd. (Timber Cove Post Office), 95421,* ☎ *707/847–3258,* FAX *707/847–3342. 15 cottages. Refrigerators, minibars, pool, outdoor hot tub, tennis courts, hiking. Modified American Plan, picnic lunches additional. AE, MC, V.*

Crescent City

DINING

$–$$ **Harbor View Grotto.** This glassed-in dining hall overlooking the Pacific prides itself on its fresh fish entrées. ✕ *155 Citizen's Dock Rd.,* ☎ *707/464–3815. MC, V. No lunch.*

LODGING

$–$$ **Curly Redwood Lodge.** This lodge was built from a single, huge redwood tree, which produced 57,000 board feet of lumber. The decor in the guest rooms also makes the most of that tree, with paneling, platform beds, and dressers built into the walls. The rooms are a decent size, and there is a fireplace in the lobby. *701 Redwood Hwy. S, 95531,* ☎ *707/464–2137,* FAX *707/464–1655. 36 rooms. AE, DC, MC, V.*

Elk

DINING AND LODGING

$$$$ **Harbor House.** Constructed in 1916 by a timber company to entertain its guests, this redwood ranch-style house has a dining room with a view of the Pacific. Five of the six rooms in the main house have fireplaces, and some are furnished with antiques original to the house. There

are also four smallish cottages with fireplaces and decks. The path to the inn's private beach takes you through the lovely garden. Breakfast and dinner are included in the cost of the room. The restaurant ($$$$), which serves California cuisine, is highly recommended; reservations are required and there's limited seating for those not spending the night. ☎ *5600 S. Hwy. 1, 95432,* ☎ *707/877-3203. 10 rooms. No credit cards.*

LODGING

$$$–$$$$ **Elk Cove Inn.** Private, romantic cottages are perched on a bluff above the pounding surf. One room's shower has a full-length window that shares this magnificent view of the Pacific. Skylights, wood-burning stoves in some rooms, and hand-embroidered cloths are just some of the amenities. The 1883 Victorian home features four rooms with spacious dormer windows and window seats, a parlor, and ocean-view deck. A Victorian-style gazebo is perched on the edge of the bluff. A full gourmet breakfast is included. *6300 S. Hwy. 1, Box 367, 95432,* ☎ *707/877-3321. 4 cabin rooms, 4 rooms in Victorian building. No credit cards.*

Eureka

DINING

$$–$$$ ★ **Restaurant 301.** Mark and Christi Carter, owners of Eureka's fanciest hotels, also run one of the town's best restaurants. Most of the vegetables and herbs used in the food are grown at the hotel's greenhouse and nearby ranch, to provide the kitchen with the freshest possible ingredients. Try the superbly presented fish or duck, and don't skip the appetizers—especially the warm goat cheese and pâté. ✕ *301 L St.,* ☎ *707/444-8062. Reservations advised during summer. AE, D, DC, MC, V. Closed Tues. and Wed. No lunch.*

$$ **Cafe Waterfront.** A small corner café with checkered tablecloths and a long bar with TV, Cafe Waterfront is snugly located across from the marina. Sandwiches and affordable seafood dishes are the mainstays of the menu. ✕ *102 F St.,* ☎ *707/443-9190. Reservations advised Thurs.–Sat. MC, V.*

$$ **Lazio's.** Another restaurant with a prow-of-the-ship theme, Lazio's is notable for its hefty classic seafood and steak dinners, complete with soup, salad, and potatoes. Nouvelle cuisine it's not. ✕ *327 2nd St., at E St.,* ☎ *707/443-9717. Reservations advised Fri. and Sat. MC, V.*

$$ **Ramone's.** A bakery and café by day, Ramone's is a casual bistro at night, serving some of Eureka's best California cuisine. The menu changes about twice a week and emphasizes fish, meats, pasta, and seasonal vegetables. ✕ *209 E St.,* ☎ *707/445-1642. Reservations advised. MC, V. Closed Mon. and Tues. (bakery closed holidays only).*

$ ★ **Samoa Cookhouse.** The recommendation here is more for atmosphere, of which there is plenty: This local lumberman's hangout dates back to the early years of the century. The Samoa's cooks serve three substantial meals family-style at long wooden tables. Meat dishes dominate the menu. Save room (if possible) for dessert. ✕ *Short drive from Eureka, across Samoa Bridge, off U.S. 101 on Samoa Rd. (via the R St. Bridge),* ☎ *707/442-1659. AE, D, MC, V.*

LODGING

$$$–$$$$ **An Elegant Victorian Mansion.** This restored Eastlake mansion in a residential neighborhood east of the Old Town, a National Historic Landmark, lives up to its name. Each room is splendidly decked out in period furnishings and wall coverings, down to the carved wood beds, fringed lamp shades, and pull-chain commodes. The innkeepers may even greet you in vintage clothing and surprise you with old-fashioned ice-

cream sodas in the afternoon. An original watercolor in the Van Gogh Room is said to be by the master himself, and the owners further lure you into their time warp with silent movies on tape, old records played on the windup Victrola, croquet on the rose-encircled lawn, and guided tours of local Victoriana in their antique automobile. The Victorian flower garden boasts more than 100 rosebushes. Gourmet breakfast is included. *14th and C Sts., 95501, 707/444–3144 or 800/386–1888. 4 rooms share 4 baths. Sauna, massage, croquet, bicycles, laundry service. MC, V.*

$$$–$$$$ ★ **Carter House, Hotel Carter, and Cottage.** Between two small inns and one hotel, the Carter family is single-handedly raising property values in downtown Eureka. The Carter House, built in 1982 following the floor plan of a San Francisco mansion, has an antiques-laden sitting area and gorgeous rooms with heirloom furniture. The Cottage two doors down, an original Victorian, contains three rooms and a big sitting area decorated in contemporary style, with lots of rustic wood and southwestern motifs. The hotel, catercorner to the Carter House, has an airy, elegant lobby and suites. Handsome brocaded spreads cover the beds; some rooms have fireplaces and whirlpool tubs. A large breakfast, served in the hotel's sunny dining room, is included with a night's stay in any of the three buildings. *Hotel: 301 L St., 95501, and fax 707/444–8062; 23 rooms. Carter House: 1033 3rd St., 707/445–1390; 5 rooms. Cottage: 3rd St., 707/445–1390; 3 rooms. All 3: AE, D, DC, MC, V.*

Ferndale

LODGING

$$$$ **Gingerbread Mansion.** The exterior of this classic Victorian bed-and-breakfast has the most playful paint job on the North Coast. The mansion's carved friezes set off its gables, and turrets dazzle the eye. Inside, comfortable parlors and spacious bedrooms are laid out in flowery Victorian splendor. Some have views of the mansion's elegant English garden, and one has side-by-side bathtubs. After the 1992 earthquake, innkeeper Ken Tolbert replaced the old Franklin stoves with coal-burning fireplaces designed to look Victorian; he also added wallpaper and carpeting of materials more suitable to the building's period. Ask about off-season rates. *400 Berding St., off Brown St., Box 40, 95536, 707/786–4000. 9 rooms. Breakfast included. Bicycles. AE, MC, V.*

$$$ **Victorian Inn.** This hostelry occupies the second floor of a beautifully renovated Victorian building on Ferndale's perfectly preserved Main Street. The rooms, which are very affordable, are decorated in muted colors and have antique armoires, feather comforters, original moldings, and some claw-foot tubs. Downstairs are the inn's casual bar and restaurant. *400 Ocean Ave., at Main St., 707/725–9686 or 800/576–5949, FAX 707/786–4648. 12 rooms. MC, V.*

Fort Bragg

DINING

$$ **The Restaurant.** The name may be generic, but this place isn't. California cuisine is served in a dining room that doubles as an art gallery and features a jazz brunch on Sunday. *418 N. Main St., 707/964–9800. Reservations advised. MC, V. Closed Wed. No lunch Sat., Mon., Tues.*

LODGING

$$$–$$$$ **Grey Whale Inn.** Once a hospital, this comfortable, friendly abode doesn't look or feel anything like one today. Each room is individually decorated with floral spreads or handcrafted quilts. The two penthouse rooms are exceptionally spacious. Three rooms have fireplaces, four

have an ocean view, and the deluxe room has a private, two-person whirlpool tub and sundeck. Rooms off Main Street are quieter. Generous buffet breakfast is included. *615 N. Main St., 95437, ☎ 707/964–0640 or 800/382–7244, FAX 707/964–4408. 14 rooms. Billiards, living room with fireplace. AE, D, MC, V.*

Garberville

DINING

$ **Woodrose Cafe.** This unpretentious eatery, a local favorite, serves basic breakfast items and healthy lunches. Dishes include chicken, pasta, and vegetarian specials. ✕ *911 Redwood Dr., ☎ 707/923–3191. Closed weekends. No dinner. No credit cards.*

DINING AND LODGING

$$$$ ★ **Benbow Inn.** Set alongside the Eel River one highway exit south of Garberville, this three-story Tudor-style manor resort is the equal of any in the region. A magnificent fireplace warms the bar-lobby of this national historic landmark, and all rooms are furnished with antiques. The most luxurious rooms are on the terrace, with fine views of the Eel River; some have fireplaces, and 18 have TV with VCR. Guests have canoeing, tennis, golf, and pool privileges at adjacent property. The wood-paneled dining room offers American cuisine with the focus on fresh salmon and trout dishes. *445 Lake Benbow Dr., 95442, ☎ 707/923–2124 or 800/355–3301. 55 rooms. Restaurant ($$–$$$), lobby lounge, refrigerators, lake. AE, D, MC, V. Closed early Jan.–mid-Mar.*

Gualala

DINING AND LODGING

$$$–$$$$ **Sea Ranch Lodge.** South of Gualala, the lodge is set high on a bluff, affording ocean views. Some rooms have fireplaces, and some have hot tubs. Handcrafted wood furnishings and quilts create an earthy, contemporary look. The restaurant, which overlooks the Pacific, serves good seafood and homemade desserts. Guests receive a complimentary wine and fruit basket upon arrival. It is close to beaches, trails, and golf. *60 Sea Walk Dr., Box 44, Sea Ranch 95497, ☎ 707/785–2371 or 800/732–7262, FAX 707/785–2243. 20 rooms. Restaurant ($$$). AE, MC, V.*

$$–$$$$ **St. Orres.** Located 2 miles north of Gualala, St. Orres is one of the North Coast's most eye-catching inns. Reflecting the area's Russian influence, St. Orres's main house is crowned by two onion-domed towers. The exterior is further accented by balconies, stained-glass windows, and wood-inlaid towers. Two of the rooms overlook the sea, while the other six are set over the garden or forest; all the rooms in the main house share baths. There are also 11 rustic cottages behind the main house in tranquil woods; eight have woodstoves or fireplaces. Those traveling with children are placed in the cottages. Breakfast is included with the room rate; for dinner, the inn's restaurant is so popular that even patrons with reservations are sometimes kept waiting. It serves dinner only, a fixed-price meal ($$$$) with a choice of five entrées (meat or fish) plus soup and salad. *Hwy. 1, Box 523, 95445, ☎ 707/884–3303, FAX 707/884–3903. 8 rooms, 11 cottages. Restaurant (closed Wed. in winter), hot tub, sauna, beach. MC, V.*

LODGING

$$$$ **Whale Watch Inn.** This elegant inn lives up to its name—most rooms here claim views (through cypress trees) down the coast, where whales often come close to shore on their northern migration in early spring. Year-round, the scent of pine and salt-sea air fills the rooms, all of which have fireplaces and small decks; some have whirlpool baths or kitchens.

A 132-step stairway leads down to a small, virtually private beach. Set amid 2½ acres, the Whale Watch maintains well-kept gardens that bloom even in winter. A full breakfast is brought to guests in their rooms. *35100 Hwy. 1, 95445, ☎ 707/884–3667 or 800/942–5342, FAX 707/884–4815. 12 rooms, 6 suites. AE, MC, V.*

$$$–$$$$ ★ **Old Milano Hotel.** Overlooking Castle Rock and a spectacular coast just north of Gualala and set amid English gardens, the Old Milano is one of California's premier bed-and-breakfasts. Established in 1905, this elegantly rustic mansion is listed in the National Registry of Historic Places. Rooms are tastefully furnished and appointed with exceptional antiques (this hotel may not be appropriate for children); five of the upstairs rooms look out over the ocean, and another looks over the gardens. All upstairs rooms share bathrooms. The downstairs master suite has a private sitting room and a picture window framing the sea. Those in search of something different might consider the caboose with a wood-burning stove. A cottage also comes complete with woodstove. The private outdoor hot tub has an unforgettable view of the surf. Breakfast is included, and dinners are offered Wednesday through Sunday (also Tuesday in summer). *38300 Hwy. 1, 95445, ☎ 707/884–3256. 9 rooms. Hot tub. MC, V. No smoking.*

$$–$$$ **Sea Ranch Escape.** The Sea Ranch houses, sparsely scattered on a grass meadow fronting a stretch of ocean, are a striking sight from Highway 1. The structures inspired a generation of natural wood architecture. Groups or families can rent fully furnished houses for two nights (minimum) or more. Linen, housekeeping, and catering services are available for a fee, or you can stock up on provisions from one of the markets in Gualala and make use of the full kitchens. All houses have TVs and VCRs; some have hot tubs and some take pets. Rates are most expensive next to the surf; prices recede with distance from the beach, although all the houses have views of the surrounding meadows and forest. *60 Sea Walk Dr., Box 238, Sea Ranch 95497, ☎ 707/785–2426 or 800/732–7262, FAX 707/785–2124. 55 houses. MC, V.*

Inverness

DINING

$ **Grey Whale.** If you're driving through the area, this casual place is a good stop for pizza, salad, pastries, and espresso. ✕ *Sir Francis Drake Blvd., in center of town, ☎ 415/669–1244. MC, V.*

DINING AND LODGING

$$–$$$$ ★ **Manka's.** A series of three intimate, wood-paneled dining rooms, glowing with candlelight and piano music, provides the setting for creative American-regional cuisine. Specialties include caribou, pheasant, and other unusual game grilled in the fireplace, line-caught fish, and homemade desserts. Two of the four smallish guest rooms above the restaurant have private decks that look onto Tomales Bay. Rooms in the Redwood Annex and two cabins are also available. *30 Calendar Way, ☎ 415/669–1034. Restaurant (reservations advised; closed Tues. and Wed. year-round and Sun.–Thurs. in Jan; no lunch; MC, V; $$$$).*

LODGING

$$$$ **Blackthorne Inn.** An adult-size fantasy tree house, this imaginative structure is highlighted by a 3,500-square-foot deck with stairways to higher decks. The solarium was made with timbers from San Francisco wharves; the outer walls are salvaged doors from a railway station. A glass-sheathed, octagonal tower called the Eagle's Nest crowns the inn. Buffet breakfast is included. *266 Vallejo Ave., Box 712, Inverness Park 94937, ☎ 415/663–8621. 5 rooms, 2 share bath. Hot tub. MC, V.*

$$$$ **Ten Inverness Way.** In a lovely 1904 shingle-style house, set on a quiet side street, you will find this homey, low-key B&B. The comfortable living room has a classic stone fireplace and player piano, and a weekend-cabin feel. The cozy rooms are highlighted by such homespun touches as patchwork quilts, lived-in-looking antiques, and sky-lighted dormer ceilings. The inn's proximity to Point Reyes hiking trails and Mt. Vision is a big draw for many guests. Full breakfast is included. *10 Inverness Way, Box 63, 94937, ☎ 415/669–1648. 5 rooms. Hot tub. MC, V.*

Jenner

DINING

$$–$$$ ★ **River's End.** At the right time of year, diners can view sea lions lazing on the beach below from this rustic restaurant. The excellent fare is eclectic/German—seafood, venison, and duck dishes. The brunches here are exceptional. ✕ *Hwy. 1, north end of Jenner, ☎ 707/865–2484. MC, V. Closed Jan.–Feb. 13.*

LODGING

$$$–$$$$ **Fort Ross Lodge.** The lodge, about 1½ miles north of the old Russian fort, is somewhat dated and wind-bitten, but all but four of its rooms have fireplaces and spectacular views of the Sonoma shoreline; some have private hot tub on back patio. Seven hill suites have sauna, hot tub, and fireplace. *20705 Hwy. 1, 95450, ☎ 707/847–3333. 22 rooms. Refrigerators. AE, MC, V.*

$–$$ **Stillwater Cove Ranch.** Sixteen miles north of Jenner, overlooking Stillwater Cove, this former boys' school has been transformed into a pleasant, if spartan, place to lodge. Peacocks stroll the grounds. *22555 Hwy. 1, 95450, ☎ 707/847–3227. 7 rooms. No credit cards.*

Klamath

LODGING

$ **Hostelling International—Redwood National Park.** The California coast's northernmost hostel, this turn-of-the-century inn is a stone's throw from the ocean. It's actually located within Redwood National Park, so hiking begins just beyond its doors. The living room is heated by a woodstove. Lodging is dormitory style. *14480 U.S. 101 at Wilson Creek Rd., 95548, ☎ and fax 707/482–8265. No credit cards.*

Little River

DINING

$$–$$$ **Little River Restaurant.** This tiny restaurant across from the Little River Inn is attached to the post office and gas station. Despite its modest appearance, this eatery serves some of the best dinners in the Mendocino area, featuring steaks and fresh seafood. ✕ *Hwy. 1, ☎ 707/937–4945. Reservations advised. No credit cards. Closed Tues.–Thurs. and Dec. No lunch.*

LODGING

$$$$ ★ **Glendeven.** This tranquil inn sits at the north end of Little River. The New England–style main house has five rooms, all with private bath, three with fireplace. The converted barn features a two-bedroom suite with kitchen and an art gallery. The 1986 Stevenscroft building has a high-peaked, gabled roof and weathered barnlike siding. The four rooms within all have fireplaces. The owners, both designers, have decorated the guest rooms with antiques, contemporary art, and ceramics. Breakfast is included. *8221 N. Hwy. 1, 95456, ☎ 707/937–0083, FAX 707/937–6108. 9 rooms, 1 suite. AE, MC, V.*

$$$$ **Heritage House.** This famous resort, where the movie *Same Time, Next Year* was filmed, has attractive cottages with stunning ocean views. There is a lovely dining room, also with a Pacific panorama, serving break-

fast and dinner, which are included with the room rate for guests; others should make reservations in advance. The meal is prix fixe. Each room's decor is unique, but all are appointed with plush furnishings, and many have private decks, fireplaces, and whirlpool tubs. ☎ *Hwy. 1, 95456,* ☎ *707/937–5885,* FAX *707/937–0318. 72 rooms. Reserve well in advance. Restaurant ($$$$). MC, V. Closed Jan.–mid-Feb.*

Mendocino

DINING

$$$–$$$$ ★ **Cafe Beaujolais.** All the rustic charm of peaceful, backwoods Mendocino is here, with great country cooking to boot. The ever-evolving dinner menu is cross-cultural and includes such delicacies as Yucatecan Thai crab cakes and a barbecued rock-shrimp-filled corn crepe with avocado and blood orange pico de gallo. Owner Margaret Fox runs the marvelous mail-order Cafe Beaujolais bakery—be sure to take home a package or two of her irresistible *panforte,* made with almonds, hazelnuts, or macadamia nuts. Sunday brunch (not offered year-round) here is superb. ✕ *961 Ukiah St.,* ☎ *707/937–5614. Reservations advised. No credit cards. Hrs vary, so call ahead. Closed most of Dec. No lunch late fall–mid-May.*

$$–$$$ **955 Ukiah St.** The interior of this smart restaurant beside Cafe Beaujolais is woodsy, and the California cuisine creative. Specialties include pastas topped with original sauces and fresh fish, such as Pacific red snapper, wrapped in phyllo dough and topped with pesto and lemon sauce. ✕ *955 Ukiah St.,* ☎ *707/937–1955. MC, V. Closed Mon. and Tues. July–Nov., Mon.–Wed. Dec.–June. No lunch.*

DINING AND LODGING

$$$–$$$$ **MacCallum House.** The most meticulously restored Victorian exterior in Mendocino, this splendid 1882 inn, complete with gingerbread trim, transports you back to another era. Its comfortable period furnishings and antiques provide a turn-of-the-century ambience. In addition to the main house, individual cottages and barn suites are set around a garden with a gazebo. The menu at the firelit, redwood-paneled restaurant changes quarterly. The focus is on fresh local seafood. ☎ *45020 Albion St., Box 206, 95460,* ☎ *707/937–0289. 21 rooms. Restaurant (closed Jan.–mid-Feb. and Wed.–Thurs. most of the year; no lunch; $$$), bar. MC, V.*

$$–$$$ **Mendocino Hotel.** From the outside, this fine hotel looks like something out of the Wild West with a period facade and balcony that overhangs the raised sidewalk. Inside, an elegant atmosphere is achieved by stained-glass lamps, Remington paintings, polished wood, and Persian carpets. All but 14 of the rooms have private baths, and the 19th-century decor is appealing. There are also deluxe garden rooms with fireplaces and TVs. The wood-paneled dining room, fronted by a glassed-in solarium, serves fine fish dishes and the best wild-berry cobblers in California. ☎ *45080 Main St., Box 587, 95460,* ☎ *707/937–0511 or 800/548–0513,* FAX *707/937–0513. 51 rooms. Restaurant ($$–$$$), bar, room service. AE, MC, V.*

LODGING

$$$$ ★ **Headlands Inn.** A magnificently restored Cape Cod–style building erected in 1868, the inn combines 19th-century charm and contemporary comforts. All rooms have private baths, feather beds, and fireplaces; some overlook a garden and the pounding surf, and others offer fine village views. There is also a private cottage on the premises. Gourmet breakfast is served in your room, and afternoon tea is served in the charming sitting room upstairs. ☎ *Howard and Albion Sts., Box 132, 95460,* ☎ *707/937–4431. 5 rooms. No credit cards.*

$$$$ ★ Stanford Inn by the Sea. The comfortable wood-paneled rooms at this rustic, two-story lodge have decks with ocean views, traditional furnishings with four-poster or sleigh beds, fireplaces or woodstoves, and an appealing selection of paintings by local artists. The tourist attractions of Mendocino are just a short walk away. Complimentary buffet breakfast is served in the sitting room downstairs. ☎ *Just south of Mendocino, east on Comptche–Ukiah Rd. (off Hwy. 1), Box 487, 95460, ☎ 707/937–5615 or 800/331–8884, FAX 707/937–0305. 24 rooms. Refrigerators, indoor pool, hot tub, sauna, bicycles. AE, D, DC, MC, V.*

$$$–$$$$ Brewery Gulch Inn. This 1860s farmhouse bed-and-breakfast, a short drive from town, has retained its old-fashioned rural character, complete with chickens, which supply the eggs for breakfast. Antiques, wood floors, and hand-sewn quilts enhance cozy rooms, two with fireplace. *9350 N. Hwy. 1, 94560, ☎ 707/937–4752. 5 rooms, 2 share bath. MC, V.*

$$$–$$$$ Joshua Grindle Inn. Mendocino's oldest B&B stands on a 2-acre hilltop near the Highway 1 turnoff into town. The original farmhouse has five guest rooms, a parlor, and a dining room. Two outbuildings, the Watertower (an upper room has windows on all four sides) and the Cottage, have five additional rooms. Furnishings throughout the inn are simple but comfortable American antiques: Salem rockers, wing chairs, steamer-trunk tables, painted pine beds. Full breakfast is included. *44800 Little Lake Rd., 95460, ☎ 707/937–4143. 10 rooms. MC, V.*

$$–$$$ Mendocino Village Inn. This refurbished 1882 Queen Anne Victorian inn has a potpourri of styles, with one room providing a southwestern motif, another reminiscent of a whaling captain's quarters, and a third with California mission–style furnishings. There also is a two-story water-tower suite. Eight of the rooms have fireplaces or woodstoves, some have ocean views, and others look out on the garden. Breakfast is included. *44860 Main St., Box 626, 95460, ☎ 707/937–0246; in CA, 800/882–7029. 13 rooms, 2 share bath. No credit cards.*

Muir Beach

DINING AND LODGING

$$$$ ★ Pelican Inn. This atmospheric Tudor-style B&B is a five-minute walk from Muir Beach. Each room has Oriental scatter rugs, English prints, heavy velvet draperies, hanging tapestries, and half-tester beds. Even the bathrooms are special, with Victorian-style hardware and hand-painted tiles in the shower. Locals and tourists compete at darts in the ground-floor pub, which has a wide selection of brews, sherries, and ports. A rustic wood hall and a glassed-in solarium, both warmed by fireplaces, serve as dining quarters—the Pelican's fare is sturdy English, from fish-and-chips to prime rib and Yorkshire pudding. Rates include full English breakfast. *10 Pacific Way at Hwy. 1, 94965, ☎ 415/383–6000. 7 rooms. Restaurant (closed Mon.; $$–$$$). MC, V.*

Point Reyes National Seashore

LODGING

$ Point Reyes Hostel. Located within the national seashore and a mere 2 miles from Limantour Beach, this is the best deal for budget travelers. Lodging is dorm style in an old clapboard ranch house. The family room is limited to families with children five and under and must be reserved well in advance. *Box 247, Pt. Reyes Station, 94956, ☎ 415/663–8811. Send $9 per adult per night with reservation request; state your gender. Shared kitchen. No credit cards.*

Point Reyes Station

DINING

$–$$ **Station House Cafe.** This very fine local hangout serves breakfast, lunch, and dinner inside or on a brick patio. Fresh shellfish, grilled meats, and scrumptious chocolate cake highlight the dinner menu; pancakes, waffles, and muffins are among the breakfast specialties. ✕ *11180 Hwy. 1,* ☎ *415/663–1515. MC, V.*

Shelter Cove

LODGING

$–$$$ **Shelter Cove Beachcomber Inn.** There are five rooms in this converted private home. Two have full kitchens, two have minikitchens (toaster, microwave, refrigerator), and one has a refrigerator and coffeemaker. Four have ocean views. The inn is near the marina—where you can arrange fishing expeditions—and it's an easy walk to the beach. Register at the Shelter Cove General Store. 🏨 *Write c/o 7272 Shelter Cove Rd., Shelter Cove 95589,* ☎ *707/986–7733. Take the Redway exit from Hwy. 101 to Shelter Cove. 5 rooms. MC, V.*

Stinson Beach

DINING

$–$$$ ★ **Stinson Beach Grill.** A great selection of beer and wine, art on the walls, and outdoor seating are among the draws here, but the food is memorable, too. Seafood and several types of oysters are served at lunch and dinner; the evening menu includes pasta, lamb, chicken, or other hearty dishes. ✕ *3465 Rte. 1,* ☎ *415/868–2002. AE, MC, V.*

$–$$ **Sand Dollar.** This pleasant pub serves great hamburgers and other sandwiches for lunch and decent seafood for dinner. An added attraction is the outdoor dining deck. ✕ *Hwy. 1,* ☎ *415/868–0434. MC, V.*

Tomales Bay

LODGING

$$$ **Tomales Country Inn.** Secluded by trees—pine, fir, and acacia—this Queen Anne house (built entirely of redwood) is decorated with original art, some of it local. One of the nicer rooms has an Eastlake walnut bed and a view of a small park. The very private third-floor room looks out over the inn's gardens, a local church, and surrounding hills and pastures. Room rates include Continental breakfast. 🏨 *25 Valley St., Box 376, 94791,* ☎ *and fax 707/878–2041. 5 rooms, 3 share bath. No credit cards. Closed Dec. 20–28.*

Trinidad

DINING

$$–$$$ ★ **Larrupin' Cafe.** Larrupin' has earned a widespread reputation for its Cajun ribs and fresh fish dishes, served in a bright yellow, two-story house on a quiet country road 2 miles north of Trinidad. ✕ *1658 Patrick's Point Dr.,* ☎ *707/677–0230. Reservations required. No credit cards. Closed Mon.–Wed. No lunch.*

$–$$ **Merryman's Dinner House.** Fresh fish and a romantic oceanfront setting make this a perfect spot for hungry lovers. ✕ *100 Moonstone Beach,* ☎ *707/677–3111. No credit cards. No lunch; no dinner weekdays Oct.–Mar.*

$–$$ **Seascape.** With its glassed-in main room, and a deck for alfresco dining, this is an ideal place to take in the splendor of Trinidad Bay. The breakfasts are great, the lunches substantial, and the dinners feature good seafood. ✕ *At pier,* ☎ *707/677–3762. MC, V.*

LODGING

$$$$ **Trinidad Bed and Breakfast.** Overlooking Trinidad Bay, this Cape Cod–style shingle house, built in 1949, has an unforgettable ocean view.

The innkeepers offer a wealth of information about the nearby wilderness, beach, and fishing habitats. The living room is warmed by a crackling fireplace. Breakfast is included. ☎ *560 Edwards St., Box 849, 95570,* ☎ *707/677-0840. 2 rooms and 2 suites (1 with fireplace). Reserve well in advance. D, MC, V.*

Valley Ford

LODGING

$$–$$$ **Inn at Valley Ford.** The rooms at this small B&B, a Victorian farmhouse built in the late 1860s, are named after literary figures, characters, or periods—books commemorating each chamber's theme grace its bookshelves. Bird-watching is a favorite pastime here: Blue herons, egrets, hawks, and owls make Valley Ford their home. Room rates include a full gourmet breakfast, including the inn's specialty, old-fashioned cream scones. ☎ *14395 Hwy. 1, Box 439, 94972,* ☎ *707/876-3182. 4 rooms share 2 baths, 1 cottage suite has a private bath. DC, MC, V.*

THE ARTS AND NIGHTLIFE

Eureka, Ferndale, and Mendocino have long-standing repertory theater companies that generally perform contemporary and classic American plays. As for nightlife, if you're hankering for a swinging, raucous time, the North Coast may not be the place for you. Below are some watering holes favored by locals and visitors that should meet the needs of those not quite ready for a good night's sleep after exploring the forest and sea.

Bolinas

Smiley's Schooner Saloon. The *only* nightlife in Bolinas, Smiley's has a CD sound system and live music on Friday and Saturday. *41 Wharf Rd.,* ☎ *415/868-1311.*

Eureka

Lost Coast Brewery & Café. This bustling microbrewery is the best place in town to relax with a pint of strong ale or porter. The brewery also serves soups, salads, and light meals for lunch and dinner, all reasonably priced. *617 4th St.,* ☎ *707/445-4480.*

North Coast Repertory Theatre. This group performs five plays per season (Sept.–June), plus a "Summer Showcase" production in July and August. *300 5th St.,* ☎ *707/442-6278.*

Ferndale

Ferndale Repertory Theatre. The North Coast's oldest company presents mysteries, comedies, musicals, and dramas on weekends year-round. *477 Main St.,* ☎ *707/725-2378.*

Garberville

Benbow Inn. In this elegant Tudor mansion, you can hear a pianist nightly while you are warmed by a romantic fireplace. *445 Lake Benbow Dr.,* ☎ *707/923-2124.*

Mendocino

Caspar Inn. Live music, from rock to jazz to ska, is featured nightly at this popular spot between Mendocino and Fort Bragg. *Caspar St. at Hwy. 1,* ☎ *707/964-5565.*

Mendocino Theatre Company. This community theater has been around for two decades. Its repertoire ranges from classics like *Uncle Vanya* to more recent works like *Other People's Money.* It's located in the

Mendocino Arts Center *45200 Lower Little Lake St., 95460,* ☎ *707/937–4477. Tickets $9–$13.*

Patterson's Pub. This Irish-style watering hole is a friendly gathering place day or night, though it does become boisterous as the evening wears on. *10485 Lansing St.,* ☎ *707/935–4782.*

Muir Beach

Pelican Inn. Set just outside Muir Beach, this is an English-style pub and restaurant, with imported brews on tap, a dartboard, a stone fireplace, a genial host, and friendly regulars. *10 Pacific Way at Hwy. 1,* ☎ *415/383–6000. Closed Mon.*

Point Reyes Station

Western Saloon. If you are in town on the weekend, you can dance your jeans off at this favorite local pub. There's live music on Friday and Saturday nights. Other nights it's a friendly place to meet West Marinites. *11201 Hwy. 1,* ☎ *415/663–1661.*

NORTH COAST ESSENTIALS

Arriving and Departing

By Car

If Mendocino is your northernmost destination, the most scenic drive from San Francisco is via Highway 1, but with its twists and turns, it's slow going, and you should allow at least a full day to get there. Those who wish to explore Point Reyes National Seashore en route might consider an overnight stay at Inverness or another town along the way. You can return directly to San Francisco in about 3½ hours from Mendocino by taking Highway 1 south to Highway 128, which cuts inland and passes through picturesque farm and forest lands. At Cloverdale, Highway 128 intersects with U.S. 101, which continues south to San Francisco.

If Eureka or a point near the Oregon border is your destination, the quickest way from San Francisco is via U.S. 101. This takes a good six to seven hours if you drive straight through. Those with the time and inclination should opt for the more scenic but much slower Highway 1, which ultimately intersects with U.S. 101 at Leggett. It would be backbreaking to cover the latter route in less than two days.

By Plane

United Express (☎ 800/241–6522) has regular nonstop flights from San Francisco to Eureka/Arcata. This is the fastest and most direct way to reach the redwood country. **Hertz** (☎ 800/654–3131) rents cars at the Eureka-Arcata airport (no ☎) in McKinleyville.

Getting Around

By Car

Although there are excellent services along Highway 1 and U.S. 101, gas stations and mechanics are few and far between on the smaller roads.

Important Addresses and Numbers

Emergencies

For **emergency services** on the North Coast, dial **911.**

Visitor Information

Eureka/Humboldt County Convention and Visitors Bureau (1034 2nd St., Eureka, CA 95501, ☎ 800/346–3482, 800/338–7352 in CA).

Fort Bragg–Mendocino Coast Chamber of Commerce (Box 1141, Fort Bragg, CA 95437, ☎ 800/726–2780).

Redwood Empire Association (in the Cannery, 2801 Leavenworth St., 2nd Floor, San Francisco, CA 94133, ☎ 415/543–8334, FAX 415/543–8337).

West Marin Chamber of Commerce (Box 1045, Point Reyes Station, CA 94956, ☎ 415/663–9232).

The Redwood Empire Association (*address above*) is an excellent source of information on the North Coast. Its San Francisco office is filled with brochures, and the staff is knowledgeable. For $3, the association will send you its visitor's guide to the region, or you can pick it up for free at its office (open weekdays 9–5) and at other stores and tourism offices throughout the North Coast.

3 The Far North

The two main attractions in the Far North are Mt. Shasta, a large volcano that dominates the scenery of the northern part of the state, and Lassen Volcanic National Park. The park is at the southern end of the Cascade Range and is particularly interesting because of the record of past volcanic activity and evidence of current geothermal activity (such as the Sulphur Works). Like the North Coast, this region best suits those interested in nature; dining, lodging, and nightlife options are limited. Keep in mind also that much of the Far North can be very hot in summer.

SOARING MOUNTAIN PEAKS, wild rivers brimming with fish, and almost infinite recreational possibilities make the Far North a sports lover's paradise. You won't find many hot nightspots or cultural enclaves, but you will find some of the best hiking, fishing, and hunting the state has to offer. Some Bay Area families return to this region year after year. Many enjoy the outdoors from their own piece of paradise—a private houseboat. A good number of retirees have chosen to live out their golden years here.

Updated by Marty Olmstead

The towering, snow-covered Mt. Shasta dominates the land. Visible for 100 miles, it qualifies the otherwise flat and fast trip through the valley along I–5 as a scenic drive. The 14,000-foot dormant volcano is surrounded by national and state parks. The natural and artificially created wonders include the sulfur vents and bubbling mud pots of Lassen Volcanic National Park and the immense Shasta Dam.

Almost all the towns in the Far North are small and friendly, made up of third- and fourth-generation descendants of '49ers who never cared to leave. Proud of their Gold Rush history, each town, no matter how small, has a museum filled with an impressive collection of artifacts donated by locals. California's Far North is the kind of place where people say hello to you as you walk down Main Street.

EXPLORING

The Far North encompasses three vast counties (Tehama, Shasta, and Trinity), land that stretches from the valleys east of the Coast Range to the Nevada border, and from the almond and olive orchards north of Sacramento to the Oregon border. The entire state of Ohio would fit into this section of California.

Redding, the urban center of the Far North, offers the greatest selection of restaurants and the largest concentration of hotels and motels. You'll experience the true flavor of this outdoor country in the smaller towns, though. Many visitors make the outdoors their home for at least part of their stay. Camping, houseboating, and animal-pack trips into the wilderness are very popular.

This exploring section is arranged south-to-north, following the mostly flat and fast I–5 with the addition of two daylong side trips. The valley around Redding is hot in the summer and mild in the winter, but cooler temperatures prevail at the higher elevations to the east and north. Be aware that many restaurants and museums in this region have limited hours and sometimes close for stretches of the off-season.

Red Bluff and Lassen Volcanic National Park

Numbers in the margin correspond to points of interest on the Far North map.

1 The turnoff for **Red Bluff** from I–5 will take you past a neon-lit motel row, but persevere and explore the roads to the left of the main drag, where you'll discover gracefully restored Victorian structures, a fine museum, and an Old West–style downtown.

The **Kelly-Griggs House Museum** is a restored 1880s Victorian dwelling with an impressive collection of antique furniture, housewares, and clothing arranged as though a refined Victorian family were still in residence: An engraved silver tea server waits at the end table; a "Self Instructor

The Far North

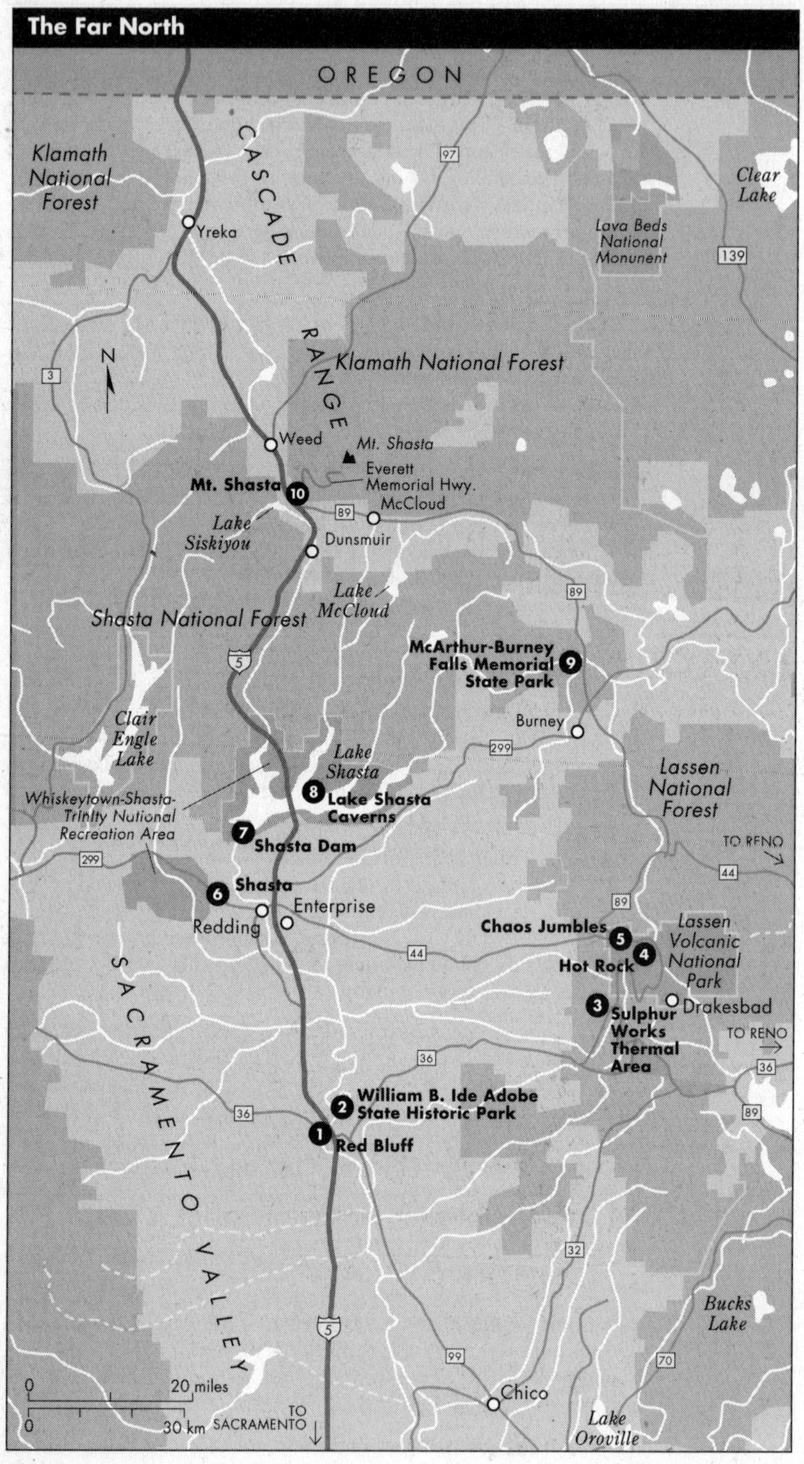
OREGON
CASCADE RANGE
Klamath National Forest
Yreka
97
Clear Lake
Lava Beds National Monument
139
Klamath National Forest
3
Weed
Mt. Shasta
Everett Memorial Hwy.
Mt. Shasta 10
McCloud
89
Lake Siskiyou
Dunsmuir
Lake McCloud
Shasta National Forest
89
McArthur-Burney Falls Memorial State Park 9
5
Burney
299
Clair Engle Lake
Lake Shasta
8 Lake Shasta Caverns
Lassen National Forest
Whiskeytown-Shasta-Trinity National Recreation Area
7 Shasta Dam
TO RENO
299
44
6 Shasta
89
Enterprise
Redding
Chaos Jumbles 5
Lassen Volcanic National Park
Hot Rock 4
44
SACRAMENTO VALLEY
3 Sulphur Works Thermal Area
Drakesbad
TO RENO
36
36
2 William B. Ide Adobe State Historic Park
36
89
1 Red Bluff
32
Bucks Lake
5
99
70
0 20 miles
0 30 km
TO SACRAMENTO
Chico
Lake Oroville

in Penmanship" teaching the art of graceful, flowing handwriting sits on the desk; and costumed mannequins seem frozen in conversation in the upstairs parlor. The museum's collection also includes finely carved china cabinets and Native American basketry. *Persephone,* the painting over the fireplace, is by Sarah Brown, daughter of abolitionist John Brown, whose family settled in Red Bluff after his execution. The Brown home is part of the self-guided tour of Red Bluff Victoriana; maps are available here. *311 Washington St.,* ☏ *916/527–1129. Donation suggested.* ⏲ *Thurs.–Sun. 1–4.*

Two miles north of town on the banks of the Sacramento River is the
2 **William B. Ide Adobe State Historic Park,** a memorial to the first and only president of the short-lived California Republic of 1846. The Bear Flag Party proclaimed California a sovereign nation, no longer under the dominion of Mexico, and the republic existed for 25 days with Ide as chief executive before it was occupied by the United States. The flag concocted for the republic has survived, with only minor refinements, as California's state flag. What is thought to be Ide's adobe home was built in the 1850s and now displays period furnishings and artifacts of the era. Also on the park grounds are a friendly donkey named Lucy and a living-history museum with a blacksmith's workshop. *21659 Adobe Rd.,* ☏ *916/529–8599.* ☛ *$3 donation requested per vehicle.* ⏲ *8 AM–sunset year-round (park and picnic facilities). Home open 11–4 in summer; in winter, look for ranger on park grounds to unlock the house.*

Take Highway 36 east from Red Bluff to Highway 89, which mean-
★ ders north for 34 miles through **Lassen Volcanic National Park,** offering a look at three sides of the world's largest plug volcano. Except for the Nordic ski area, the park is largely inaccessible from late October to early June because of snow. Highway 89 through the park is closed to cars in winter but open to intrepid cross-country skiers, conditions permitting.

In 1914 the 10,457-foot Mt. Lassen began a series of 300 eruptions that went on for seven years. Molten rock overflowed the crater, and the mountain emitted clouds of smoke and hailstorms of rocks and volcanic cinders. Proof of the volcano's volatility becomes evident shortly
3 after you enter the park at the **Sulphur Works Thermal Area.** Boardwalks take you over bubbling mud and hot springs and through the nauseating sulfur stink of steam vents. Five miles farther along Highway 89 you'll find the start of the **Bumpass Hell Trail,** a 3-mile round-trip hike to the park's most interesting thermal-spring area, where you'll see hot and boiling springs, steam vents, and mud pots. The trail climbs and descends several hundred feet.

Back on the road, continue through forests and past lakes, looking out
4 for deer and wildflowers, to **Hot Rock.** This 400-ton boulder tumbled down from the summit during the volcano's active period and was still hot to the touch when locals found it. Although cool now, it's still an
5 impressive sight. Five miles on is **Chaos Jumbles,** created 300 years ago when an avalanche from the Chaos Crags lava domes spread hundreds of thousands of rocks 2 to 3 feet in diameter over 2 square miles.

An important word of warning: Stay on trails and boardwalks near the thermal areas. What may appear to be firm ground may be only a thin crust over scalding mud, and serious burns could result if you step through it. Be especially careful with children!

Lassen is a unique, lovely, and relatively uncrowded national park, but services are rather sparse. In the southwest corner of the park, at the winter-sports area, there is a café and a gift shop that's open during the summer and the ski season. At the Manzanita Lake campground another store, open only in summer, offers gas and fast food. *Lassen Volcanic National Park, Box 100, Mineral 96063-0100, ☏ 916/595–4444. ☛ $5 per car in summer, free in winter.*

The Shasta Area

6 A few miles west of Redding on Highway 299 are the ruins of the gold-mining town of **Shasta,** now a **state historic park** with a few restored buildings. A museum located in the old courthouse has an eclectic array of California paintings as well as memorabilia, including period newspapers advertising "Gold Dust Bought and Sold," a *Prairie Traveler* guidebook with advice on encounters with Indians, and the 1860 census of this once-prosperous town. Continue down to the basement to see the iron-bar jail cells, and step outside for a look at the scaffold where murderers were hanged. *☏ 916/243–8194. ☛ $2 adults, $1 children 6–12. ⏲ Mar.–Oct., Thurs.–Mon. 10–5; Nov.–Feb., Fri.–Sun. 10–5.*

★ 7 Take the Center Valley/Shasta Dam exit west off I–5 about 12 miles north of Redding and follow the signs to **Shasta Dam.** You'll be able to see the mammoth construction from several points; this is the second-largest and the fourth-tallest concrete dam in the United States.

Whether you drive across the dam or park at the landscaped visitors area and walk across, you'll see three Shastas: the dam, the lake spreading before you, and the mountain presiding over it all. At twilight the sight is magical, with Mt. Shasta gleaming above the not-quite-dark water and deer frolicking on the hillside beside the dam. The dam is lighted after dark, but there is no access from 10 PM to 6 AM. In addition to providing fact sheets, the **Visitor Information Center** (☏ 916/275–4463) has photographic and historic displays weekends 9 to 5, weekdays 8 to 5. Daily guided tours of the dam are given on weekends on the hour from 9 to 3 and on weekdays at 10, noon, 2, and 3:30.

★ **Lake Shasta** has 370 miles of shoreline and 21 varieties of fish. You can rent fishing boats, ski boats, sailboats, canoes, paddleboats, Jet Skis, and Windsurfer boards at one of the many marinas and resorts along the shore. But Lake Shasta is known as the houseboat capital of the world, and around here the houseboat is king.

Houseboats come in all sizes except small. The ones that sleep 12 to 14 people are 55 feet by 14 feet; the smallest sleep six. As a rule these moving homes come with cooking utensils, dishes, and most of the equipment you'll need to set up housekeeping on the water. (You supply food and linens.) Renters are given a short course in how to maneuver the boats before they set out on cruises; it's not difficult.

The houseboats are slow moving, and life aboard is leisurely. You can fish, swim, sunbathe on the flat roof, or just sit on the deck and watch the world go by. The shoreline of Lake Shasta is beautifully ragged, with countless inlets; exploring it is fun, and it's not hard to find privacy.

Expect to spend a minimum of $200 a day for a craft that sleeps six. There is usually a three-night minimum in peak season. Contact the Shasta Cascade Wonderland Association (*see* Important Addresses and Numbers *in* Far North Essentials, *below*) for specifics.

8 Stalagmites, stalactites, odd flowstone deposits, and crystals entice visitors of all ages to the **Lake Shasta Caverns.** The two-hour tour includes a catamaran ride across the McCloud arm of Lake Shasta and a bus ride up Grey Rock Mountain to the cavern entrance. The cav-

erns are a constant 58°F year round, making them an appealingly cool retreat on a hot summer day. All cavern rooms are well lit, and the crowning jewel is the spectacular cathedral room. The guides are friendly, enthusiastic, and informative. *Take the Shasta Caverns Rd. exit from I–5. ☎ 916/238–2341 or 800/795–2283. ☛ $12 adults, $6 children 4–12. ⏲ Daily 9–4; May–Sept. tours conducted on the hr, Oct.–Apr. tours at 10, noon, and 2.*

Take the Highway 299 East exit off I–5 just north of Redding, past
★ 9 the town of Burney, and turn north on Highway 89 to get to **McArthur-Burney Falls Memorial State Park.** It's a two-hour round-trip drive from I–5, so you may want to plan to spend the day here. Just inside the southern boundary of the park, Burney Creek wells up from the ground and divides into two cascades that fall over a 129-foot cliff and into a pool below. The thundering water creates a mist at the base of the falls, often highlighted by a rainbow. Countless ribbonlike falls stream from hidden moss-covered crevices, creating an ethereal backdrop to the main cascades. Each day, 100 million gallons of water rush over these falls; Theodore Roosevelt proclaimed them "the eighth wonder of the world." A self-guided nature trail descends to the foot of the falls. There is a lake and beach for swimming. A campground, picnic sites, trails, and other facilities are available. The camp store is open Memorial Day–Labor Day. *24898 Hwy. 89, Burney 96013, ☎ 916/335–2777. ☛ $5 per vehicle (day use). Camping: May–Sept., $14 per night; Oct.–Apr., $12 per night. Campground reservations (necessary in summer) are made through MISTIX, ☎ 800/444–7275.*

If you drive up the valley on I–5, past the 130-million-year-old granite outcroppings of Castle Crags towering over the road, through the
10 quaint old railroad town of Dunsmuir, you'll reach the town of **Mt. Shasta,** nestled at the base of the huge mountain. If you are interested in hiking on Mt. Shasta, stop at the **Forest Service Ranger Station** (204 W. Alma St., ☎ 916/926–4511) as you come through town for the latest information on trail conditions, or call the **Fifth Season Mountaineering Shop** in Mt. Shasta City (☎ 916/926–3606), which also offers a recorded 24-hour climber-skier report (☎ 916/926–5555).

The central Mt. Shasta exit east leads out of town along the **Everett Memorial Highway.** This scenic drive climbs to almost 8,000 feet, and the views of the mountain and the valley below are extraordinary.

If you are wondering where all those eye-catching pictures of Mt. Shasta reflected in a lake are shot, take the central Mt. Shasta exit west and follow the signs to **Lake Siskiyou.** This is the only man-made lake in California created solely for recreational purposes. On the way, stop at the oldest **trout hatchery** in California. The pools there literally swarm with more than 100,000 trout.

Off the Beaten Track

McCloud began as a lumber-company town in the late 1800s and was one of the longest-lived company towns in the country. In 1965 the U.S. Plywood Corp. acquired the town, its lumber mill, and the surrounding forest land and allowed residents to purchase their homes. The immense mill has been cut back to a computerized operation, but the spirit of the townsfolk has kept McCloud from becoming a ghost town. Picturesque hotels, churches, a lumber baron's mansion, and simple family dwellings have been renovated, and the 60,000-pound Corliss steam engine that powered the original mill's machinery stands as a monument behind the town's small museum. On Main Street, you'll find an enormous old-style dance hall and a classic small-town soda fountain. To reach this time-capsule town, take the Highway 89 exit east from I–5 just south of the town of Mt. Shasta.

SPORTS

Fishing

For licenses, current fishing conditions, guides, or special fishing packages, contact the **Fly Shop** (4140 Churn Creek Rd., Redding 96002, ☎ 916/222–3555), the **Fishin' Hole** (3844 Shasta Dam Blvd., Central Valley 96019, ☎ 916/275–4123), or **Shasta Cascade Wonderland Association** (*see* Important Addresses and Numbers *in* Far North Essentials, *below*).

Golf

Churn Creek Golf Course (7335 Churn Creek Rd., Redding, ☎ 916/222–6353) is a nine-hole, par-36 course. Carts are available. **Gold Hills Country Club** (1950 Gold Hills Dr., Redding, Oasis Rd. exit from I–5, ☎ 916/246–7867) is an 18-hole, par-72 course. Carts, club rentals, driving range, pro shop, and restaurant are available. **Lake Redding Golf Course** (1795 Benton Dr., Redding, in Lake Redding Park, ☎ 916/243–5531) is a nine-hole, par-31 course. Pull carts, electric carts, and rentals are available.

Mountain Climbing

Shasta Mountain Guides (1938 Hill Rd., Mt. Shasta 96067, ☎ 916/926–3117) leads hiking and ski-touring groups to the snow-covered, 14,161-foot summit of Mount Shasta.

Raft/Canoe Rentals

Park Marina Watersports (2515 Park Marina Dr., Redding, ☎ 916/246–8388).

Skiing

Mt. Shasta Ski Park. On the southeast flank of Mt. Shasta are three lifts on 300 skiable acres. The terrain is 20% beginner, 60% intermediate, 20% advanced. Top elevation is 6,600 feet; its base, 5,500 feet; its vertical drop, 1,100 feet. The longest run is 1.2 miles. Night skiing goes till 10 PM Wednesday–Saturday. There is a ski school with a beginner's special: lifts, rentals, lessons. The "Powder Pups" program is for ages four–seven. Lodge facilities include food and beverages, ski shop, and rentals. *Hwy. 89 exit east from I–5, just south of Mt. Shasta,* ☎ *916/926–8610. Snow phone 916/926–8686.*

Snowshoe Tours

National Park Service rangers conduct snowshoe tours at Mt. Lassen Ski Park. A variety of natural history topics are covered. ☎ *916/595–4444. No reservations.* ☛ *$1 donation for upkeep of snowshoes.* ⏲ *Jan.–Apr., Sat. at 1:30 PM.*

DINING AND LODGING

Dining

Cafés and simple, informal restaurants are ample in the Far North. Most of the fast-food restaurants are clustered in Redding, though they are also found along I–5 in some of the larger communities. The restaurants listed here are of special interest because of their food and/or unique atmosphere. Reservations aren't necessary except where noted.

WHAT TO WEAR

Dress is always informal in the Far North.

CATEGORY	COST*
$$$$	over $35
$$$	$25–$35
$$	$15–$25
$	under $15

**per person for a three-course meal, excluding drinks, service, and 7¼% tax*

Lodging

Motel chains, such as Best Western and Motel 6, have branches in many of the communities in the Far North, though Redding has the greatest selection by far. Upscale hotels with business facilities are found only in Redding.

CATEGORY	COST*
$$$$	over $100
$$$	$75–$100
$$	$50–$75
$	under $50

**All prices are for a standard double room, excluding 8% tax.*

Dunsmuir

LODGING

$$ ★ Railroad Park Resort. At this railroad buff's delight, antique cabooses have been converted into cozy, wood-paneled motel rooms in honor of Dunsmuir's railroad legacy. Nine railcars have been transformed into a modestly *Orient Express*–style dining room and a lounge. The landscaped grounds feature a huge logging steam engine, a restored water tower, and a fishing pond. *100 Railroad Park Rd., 96025, ☎ 916/235–4440 or 800/974–7245, FAX 916/235–4470. 24 cabooses, 4 cabins. Pool, hot tub. AE, D, MC, V.*

Lake Shasta

DINING

$$ **Tail O' the Whale.** Reminiscent of a ship's prow, this restaurant overlooking the lake is distinguished by its nautical decor. Seafood, prime rib, poultry, and Cajun pepper shrimp are the specialties. ✕ *10300 Bridge Bay Rd., Bridge Bay exit from I–5, ☎ 916/275–3021. Reservations advised for summer Sun. brunch. MC, V.*

Lassen Volcanic National Park

LODGING

$$$$ **Drakesbad Guest Ranch.** The only lodging inside the park is the 100-year-old guest ranch at Drakesbad, near its southern border on Lake Almanor, and isolated from most of the park. Rooms in the lodge, bungalows, and cabins don't have electricity; they're lighted by kerosene lamps. But the accommodations are clean and comfortable and include furnace heat and either half or full bath. Reservations should be made well in advance (the waiting list can be up to two years long); all meals are included. *Booking office: 2150 N. Main St., Suite 5, Red Bluff 96080, ☎ 916/529–1512, FAX 916/529–4511. 19 rooms. Dining room, pool, badminton, horseback riding, horseshoes, Ping-Pong, volleyball, fishing. MC, V. Closed early Oct.–early June.*

Mt. Shasta

DINING

$–$$ **Lily's.** In a light-filled, white clapboard house complete with picket fence, Lily's serves pastas (the house specialty is spinach fettuccine with artichoke hearts or scallops), salads (Thai noodle, Caesar), and Mexican, Italian, Asian, and American entrées. ✕ *1013 S. Mt. Shasta Blvd., ☎ 916/926–3372. MC, V.*

$–$$ **Michael's Restaurant.** Wood paneling, candlelight, and wildlife prints by local artists create an unpretentious setting for such Italian specialties as stuffed calamari, filet-mignon scaloppine, linguine pesto, and other Continental dishes. ✕ *313 N. Mt. Shasta Blvd., ☎ 916/926–5288. AE, D, MC, V. Closed Sun., Mon.*

$ ★ **Marilyn's.** This charming, homespun eatery in the shadow of Mt. Shasta is one of the best old-style diners north of the Bay Area. Local historical memorabilia lines the walls. Neighborly waitresses serve large portions of delicious food in carved wooden booths. Much of the town comes in for breakfast; complete dinners including soup and salad cost less than $10. ✕ *1136 S. Mt. Shasta Blvd., ☎ 916/926–2720. MC, V.*

LODGING

$$ **Tree House Best Western.** The clean, standard rooms at this motel, a half mile from the center of the town of Mt. Shasta, are decorated with natural wood furnishings and a range of colors. *111 Morgan Way at I–5 and Lake St., Box 236, 96067, ☎ 916/926–3101 or 800/528–1234, FAX 916/926–3542. 95 rooms, Restaurant, lounge, indoor pool. AE, D, DC, MC, V.*

$$ ★ **Wagon Creek Inn.** This lodgepole pine log home in a quiet residential neighborhood 2 miles outside town is one of the area's newest and most affordable inns, with crisp, country decor; a living room with fireplace, television, and VCR; and laid-back hospitality. Generous Continental breakfast is included. *1239 Woodland Park Dr., 96067, ☎ 916/926–0838 or 800/995–9260. 3 rooms, 2 share bath. MC, V.*

Red Bluff

DINING

$$–$$$ **Hatch Cover.** Offering views of the adjacent Sacramento River, this attractive establishment is decorated in dark-wood paneling to resemble a ship's interior. The menu features seafood, but you can also get steaks and combination plates. Check out the exotic after-dinner drinks. ✕ *202 Hemsted Dr., ☎ 916/223–5606. From the Cypress Ave. exit off I–5, turn left, then right on Bechelli La., and left on Hemsted Dr. AE, D, MC, V. No lunch weekends.*

$ **Snack Box.** This renovated Victorian building is cheerfully decorated in country-French blue and dusty rose. The paintings on the wall, like the omelets, soups, and sandwiches, are created by the owner. ✕ *257 Main St., 1 block from Kelly-Griggs Museum, ☎ 916/529–0227. No credit cards. No dinner.*

Redding

DINING

$–$$ **Jack's Grill.** Although it looks like a dive from the outside, this steak house and bar is immensely popular with residents throughout the territory, who come in for the famous 16-ounce steaks. The place is usually jam-packed and noisy. ✕ *1743 California St., ☎ 916/241–9705. AE, MC, V. Closed Sun. No lunch.*

LODGING

$$$–$$$$ **Red Lion Motor Inn.** Nicely landscaped grounds and a large, attractive patio area with outdoor food service are the highlights here. The rooms are spacious and comfortable. Misty's, the lobby's fancy restaurant, is popular among locals for its steak Diane. *1830 Hilltop Dr., Hwy. 44/299 exit east from I–5, 96002, ☎ 916/221–8700 or 800/547–8010, FAX 916/221–0324. 194 rooms with bath. Restaurant ($$$), coffee shop, lounge, room service, pool, wading pool, hot tub, putting green. Pets allowed; mention when booking room. AE, D, DC, MC, V.*

$$–$$$ **Oxford Suites.** This hotel with more than 100 suites (and 24 studios) offers excellent value. All rooms have two televisions, a VCR, and refrigerator. Most have microwave ovens, and three have whirlpool tubs. Complimentary beer and wine and a full buffet breakfast are included. Advance reservations are recommended. *1967 Hilltop Dr., 96002, ☎ 916/221–0100 or 800/762–0133, FAX 916/221–8265. 139 rooms. Lounge, snack bar, pool, hot tub. AE, D, DC, MC, V.*

$$ **La Quinta.** This motel's spacious lobby has a cozy sitting area. Rooms are all tastefully decorated with dark-wood furniture; the spotless, white-tile bathrooms have full-length mirrors. *2180 Hilltop Dr., ☎ 916/221–8200 or 800/531–5900. 145 rooms. Pool, hot tub. AE, D, DC, MC, V.*

Camping

There are an infinite number of camping possibilities in the Far North's national and state parks, forests, and recreation areas. You'll find every level of rusticity, too, from the well-outfitted campgrounds in McArthur-Burney State Park, which have hot water, showers, and flush toilets, to isolated campsites on Lake Shasta that can be reached only by boat.

There are seven campgrounds within Lassen Volcanic National Park. Reservations are not accepted; it's first come, first served. For campground and other information, contact **Lassen Volcanic National Park** or the **Shasta Cascade Wonderland Association** (*see* Important Addresses and Numbers *in* Far North Essentials, *below*).

NIGHTLIFE

Although the larger hotels in Redding usually have weekend dance bands geared to the younger set, there's not much nightlife in this outdoors country where the fish bite early. Country-western fans will enjoy **The Derringer** (2655 Bechelli La., behind the bowling alley, Redding, ☎ 916/221–2727), which features live music Wednesday through Saturday and recorded music other nights. There's a $2 cover charge on weekends, $1 weeknights. If C&W isn't your cup of tea, check out the bar at **Jack's Grill** (*see* Dining and Lodging, *above*), which is almost always jumping.

FAR NORTH ESSENTIALS

Arriving and Departing

By Bus

Greyhound Lines (☎ 800/231–2222) buses travel I–5, serving Red Bluff, Redding, Dunsmuir, and Mt. Shasta City. In Redding, a city bus system, "The Ride" (☎ 916/241–2877), serves the local area daily except Sunday.

By Car

I–5, an excellent four-lane divided highway, runs up the center of California through Red Bluff and Redding and continues north to Oregon. Lassen Park can be reached by Highway 36 from Red Bluff or, except in winter, Highway 44 from Redding; Highway 299 leads from Redding to McArthur-Burney Falls. These are very good two-lane roads that are kept open year-round. If you are traveling through this area in winter, however, always carry snow chains in your car.

By Plane

Redding Municipal Airport (☎ 916/224–4321) is served by **United Express** (☎ 800/241–6522) and **Reno Air** (☎ 800/736–6247), which flies daily from San Francisco with a connection in San Jose. Major car-rental agencies are located at the airport.

By Train

There are **Amtrak** (☎ 800/872–7245) stations in Redding (1620 Yuba St.) and Dunsmuir (5750 Sacramento Ave.).

Important Addresses and Numbers

Emergencies

Dial 911 for police, fire, and medical help.

Visitor Information

Lassen Volcanic National Park (Box 100, Mineral 96063-0100, ☎ 916/595–4444).

Mt. Shasta Convention and Visitors Bureau (300 Pine St., Mt. Shasta 96067, ☎ 916/926–4865 or 800/926–4865).

Northern Buttes District Office, State of California Department of Parks and Recreation (400 Glen Dr., Oroville 95966, ☎ 916/538–2200).

Red Bluff–Tehama County Chamber of Commerce (100 Main St., Box 850, Red Bluff 96080, ☎ 916/527–6220 or 800/655–6225).

Redding Convention and Visitors Bureau (777 Auditorium Dr., Redding 96001, ☎ 916/225–4100 or 800/874–7562).

Shasta Cascade Wonderland Association (14250 Holiday Rd., Redding 96003, ☎ 916/275–5555 or 800/326–6944).

Siskiyou County Visitors Bureau (808 W. Lennox St., Yreka 96097, ☎ 916/842–7857 or 800/446–7475).

4 The Wine Country

The Wine Country is one of California's most popular tourist regions. Many Sonoma and Napa Valley wineries are beautiful sites for meals, picnics, or tastings, and there are top-notch bed-and-breakfasts and restaurants in the area. There are many ways to explore the region: hiking and bicycling for the active set and balloon, train, and glider rides for those seeking a less strenuous overview. People here know how to pamper themselves: In Calistoga and other towns are resorts and health spas with mud baths, massages, sulfur whirlpool baths, and other rejuvenating treatments.

Updated by Claudia Gioseffi

IN 1862, after an extensive tour of the wine-producing areas of Europe, Count Agoston Haraszthy de Mokcsa reported a promising prognosis to his adopted California: "Of all the countries through which I passed, not one possessed the same advantages that are to be found in California. . . . California can produce as noble and generous a wine as any in Europe; more in quantity to the acre, and without repeated failures through frosts, summer rains, hailstorms, or other causes."

The "dormant resources" that the father of California's viticulture saw in the balmy days and cool nights of the temperate Napa and Sonoma valleys are in full fruition today. While the wines produced here are praised and savored by connoisseurs throughout the world, the area continues to be a fermenting vat of experimentation, a proving ground for the latest techniques of grape growing and wine making.

Ever more competitive, the vintners constantly hone their skills, aided by the scientific know-how of graduates of the nearby University of California at Davis, as well as by the practical knowledge of the grape growers. They experiment with planting the vine stock closer together and with canopy management of the grape cluster, as well as with cold fermentation in stainless-steel vats, and new methods of fining, or filtering, the wine.

For many, wine making is a second career—since any would-be wine maker can rent the cumbersome, costly machinery needed to stem and press the grapes. Many say making wine is a good way to turn a large fortune into a small one, but that hasn't deterred the doctors, former college professors, publishing tycoons, and airline pilots who come to try their hand at it.

Twenty years ago, Napa Valley had no more than 20 wineries; today there are almost 10 times that number. In Sonoma County, where the web of vineyards is looser, there are more than 100 wineries, and development is now claiming the cool Carneros region at the head of the San Francisco Bay, deemed ideal for growing the chardonnay grape. Grape growers now produce their own wines instead of selling their grapes to larger wineries. As a result, smaller producers can make excellent, reasonably priced wines, while the larger wineries consolidate land and expand their varietals.

In the past, the emphasis was on creating wines to be cellared, but today so-called drinkable wines, which can be enjoyed relatively rapidly, are more commonly produced. These are served in the first-class restaurants that have proliferated in the valley as a result of the thriving tourist industry.

In addition to state-of-the-art viticulture and dining, the Wine Country is steeped in California history. The town of Sonoma is filled with remnants of Mexican California and the solid, ivy-covered, brick wineries built by Haraszthy and his disciples. Calistoga is a virtual museum of Steamboat Gothic architecture, replete with the fretwork and clapboard beloved of gold-rush prospectors and late 19th-century spa goers. St. Helena is home to a later architectural fantasy, the beautiful Art Nouveau mansion of the Beringer brothers. The latter-day postmodern extravaganza of Clos Pegase is in Calistoga.

Tourism's growth has produced tensions, and some residents look askance at projects like the Wine Train between Napa and St. Helena. Still, the area's natural beauty, recalling the hills of Tuscany and

Provence, will always draw tourists—from the spring, when the vineyards bloom yellow with mustard flowers, to the fall, when fruit is ripening. Haraszthy was right: This is a chosen place.

EXPLORING

Like the wines they produce, each of the regions within the Wine Country has its own flavor. Napa Valley is larger, more commercial, and a bit more sophisticated than Sonoma County; with more than 200 wineries, it is the undisputed capital of American wine production. Still, the valley has its fair share of small, quirky towns. Calistoga feels like an Old West frontier town, with wooden-plank storefronts and people in cowboy hats; St. Helena is posh, with tony shops and elegant restaurants; Yountville is small, concentrated, and redolent of American history.

While Napa Valley is upscale and elegant, Sonoma County is overalls-and-corduroy, with an air of rustic innocence; and yet its Alexander, Dry Creek, and Russian River valleys are no less productive of award-winning vintages. Here, family-run wineries treat visitors like personal friends, and tastings are usually free. The Sonoma countryside also offers excellent opportunities for hiking, biking, camping, and fishing.

Since there are more than 400 wineries in this region, it pays to be selective when planning your visit. Better to mix up the wineries with other sights and diversions—a picnic, a trip to the village museum, a ride in a hot-air balloon—than to try to visit them all in one day.

Numbers in the margin correspond to wineries on the Wine Country map.

Unless otherwise noted, visits to the wineries listed are free.

Napa Valley

The town of **Napa** is the gateway into the valley that's famed for its unrivaled climate and neat rows of vineyards. The towns in the valley are small, and their Victorian Gothic architecture makes the area feel like a distant world.

Yountville

A few miles north of Napa is the small town of **Yountville.** Turn west off Highway 29 at the Veterans Home exit and then up California Drive
1 to **Domaine Chandon,** owned by the French champagne producer Moet-Hennessy and Louis Vuitton. Tours of the sleek modern facilities on this beautifully maintained property include sample flutes of the méthode champenoise sparkling wine. Champagne is $3–$4 per glass, hors d'oeuvres are complimentary, and an elegant restaurant beckons gourmets. *California Dr., Yountville,* ☎ *707/944–2280. Restaurant closed Mon. and Tues. Nov.–Apr. and closed entirely Jan. 1–25. No dinner Mon. and Tues. May–Oct. Tours daily 11–5, except Mon. and Tues. Nov.–Apr. Closed major holidays.*

Vintage 1870, a 26-acre complex of boutiques, restaurants, and gourmet stores, is on the east side of Highway 29. The vine-covered brick buildings were built in 1870 and originally housed a winery, livery stable, and distillery. The original mansion of the property is now **Compadres Bar and Grill,** and the adjacent **Red Rock Cafe** is housed in the train depot Samuel Brannan built in 1868 for his privately owned Napa Valley Railroad. The remodeled railroad cars now accommodate guests at the Napa Valley Lodge (*see* Lodging, *below*).

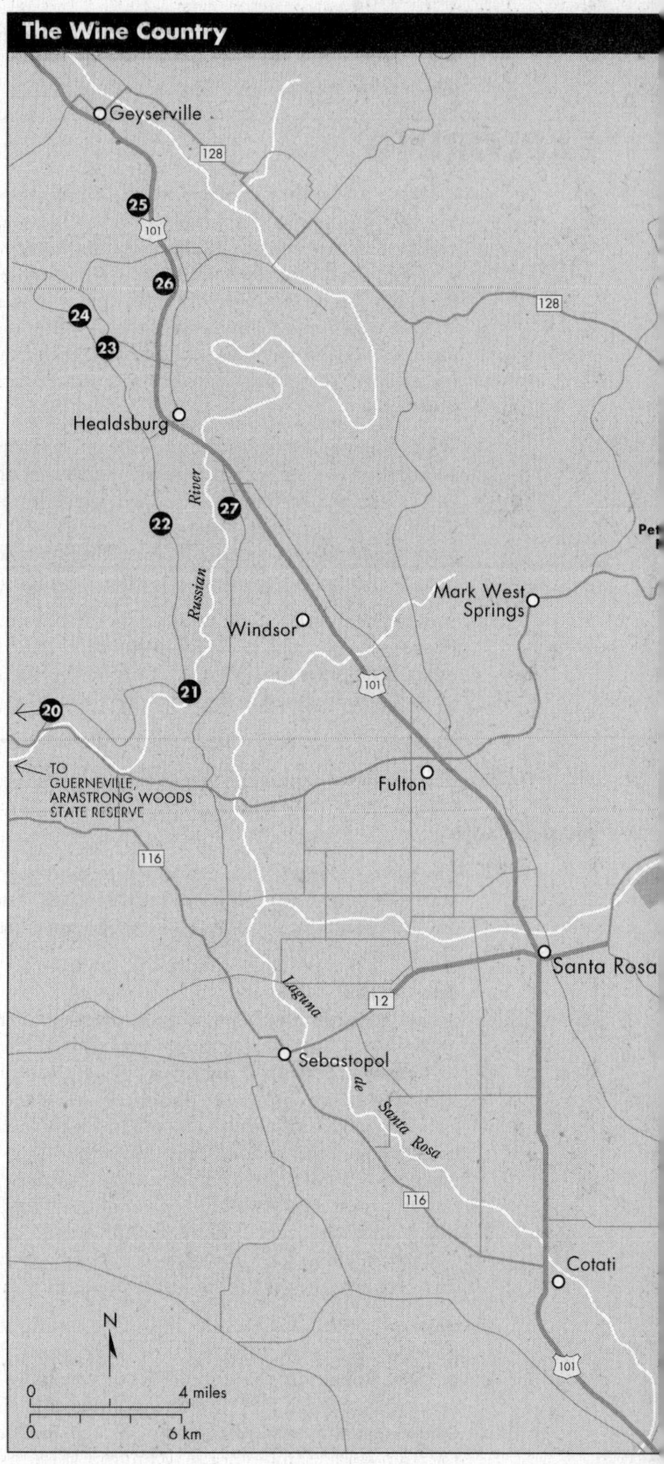
The Wine Country
Geyserville
128
25
101
26
24
23
128
Healdsburg
River
27
22
Russian
Mark West Springs
Windsor
101
21
20
TO GUERNEVILLE, ARMSTRONG WOODS STATE RESERVE
Fulton
116
Santa Rosa
Laguna
12
Sebastopol
de
Santa Rosa
116
Cotati
N
101
0
4 miles
0
6 km

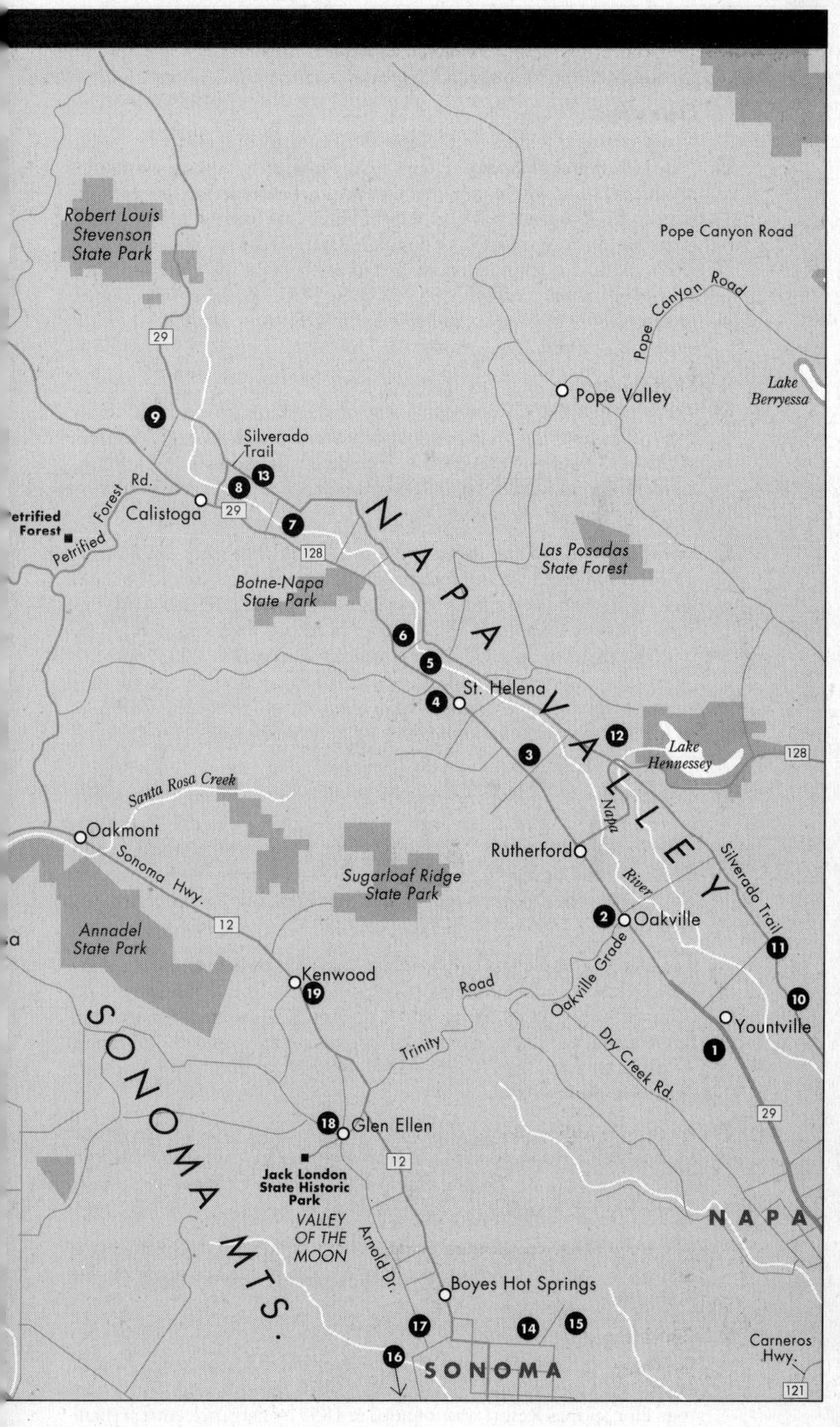

Robert Louis Stevenson State Park
Pope Canyon Road
Pope Canyon Road
Pope Valley
Lake Berryessa
29
Silverado Trail
Rd.
Forest
Petrified
Petrified Forest
Calistoga
29
128
NAPA VALLEY
Las Posadas State Forest
Botne-Napa State Park
St. Helena
Lake Hennessey
128
Santa Rosa Creek
Oakmont
Sonoma Hwy.
Sugarloaf Ridge State Park
Rutherford
Napa
River
Silverado Trail
Oakville
Annadel State Park
12
Oakville Grade
Kenwood
Road
Trinity
Yountville
Dry Creek Rd.
29
SONOMA MTS.
Glen Ellen
12
Jack London State Historic Park
VALLEY OF THE MOON
Arnold Dr.
NAPA
Boyes Hot Springs
Carneros Hwy.
SONOMA
121

Washington Square, at the north end of Yountville, is a complex of shops and restaurants; **Pioneer Cemetery,** birthplace of the town's founder, George Yount, is across the street.

Oakville

Many premier wineries lie along the route from Yountville to St.
2 Helena. At **Robert Mondavi,** tasters are encouraged to take the 60-minute production tour with complimentary tasting before trying the reserved wines ($1–$5 per glass). In-depth, three- to four-hour tours and gourmet lunch tours are also popular. Afterward, visit the art gallery, and look for the summer concerts that are held on the grounds. *7801 St. Helena Hwy., Oakville, ☎ 707/259–9463. Reservations advised in summer. ⏲ May–Oct., daily 9–5:30; Nov.–Apr., daily 9:30–4:30; closed major holidays.*

St. Helena

3 The wine made at **V. Sattui** is sold only on the premises; the tactic draws crowds, as does the huge gourmet delicatessen with its exotic cheeses and pâtés. Award-winning wines include dry Johannisberg Rieslings, zinfandels, and Madeiras. *1111 White La., St. Helena, ☎ 707/963–7774. ⏲ Daily 9–5; closed Dec. 25.*

4 **Beringer Vineyards** has been operating continually since 1876. Tastings are held in the Rhine House mansion, where hand-carved oak and walnut furniture and stained-glass windows feature Belgian Art Nouveau at its most opulent. The Beringer brothers, Frederick and Jacob, built the mansion in 1883 for the princely sum of $30,000. Tours are given every 30 minutes and include a visit to the deep limestone tunnels in which the wines mature. *2000 Main St., St. Helena, ☎ 707/963–4812. ⏲ Daily 9:30–4; summer hrs are sometimes extended to 5; closed major holidays.*

5 The **Charles Krug Winery** opened in 1861 when Count Haraszthy loaned Krug a small cider press. The oldest winery in the Napa Valley, it is run by the Peter Mondavi family. The gift shop stocks everything from gourmet food baskets with local produce and "grape" pasta to books about the region and its wines. *2800 N. Main St., St. Helena, ☎ 707/963–5057. ⏲ Daily 10:30–5; closed major holidays.*

The town of St. Helena boasts many Victorian buildings. Don't overlook the **Silverado Museum,** two blocks east from Main Street on Adams. Its Robert Louis Stevenson memorabilia consist of more than 8,000 artifacts, including first editions, manuscripts, and photographs. *1490 Library La., ☎ 707/963–3757. ☛ Free. ⏲ Tues.–Sun. noon–4; closed major holidays.*

6 **Freemark Abbey Winery** was founded in the 1880s by Josephine Tychson, the first woman to establish a winery in California. *3022 St. Helena Hwy. N, St. Helena, ☎ 707/963–9694. ⏲ Mar.–Dec., daily 10–4:30; Jan. and Feb., Thurs.–Sun. 10–4:30. 1 tour daily at 2 PM.*

The **Hurd Beeswax Candle Factory** is next door, with two restaurants and a gift shop that specializes in handcrafted candles made on the premises.

Calistoga

Calistoga, at the head of the Napa Valley, is noted for its mineral water, hot mineral springs, mud baths, steam baths, and massages. The Calistoga Hot Springs Resort was founded in 1859 by maverick entrepreneur Sam Brannan, whose ambition was to found "the Saratoga of California." He tripped up the pronunciation of the phrase at a formal banquet—it came out "Calistoga"—and the name stuck. One of his cottages, preserved as the **Sharpsteen Museum,** has a magnificent diorama of the resort in its heyday. *1311 Washington St., ☎ 707/942–5911. Donations accepted. ⏲ May–Oct., daily 10–4; Nov.–Apr., daily noon–4.*

7 **Sterling Vineyards** sits on a hilltop to the east near Calistoga. The pristine white Mediterranean-style buildings are reached by an enclosed gondola from the valley floor; the view from the tasting room is superb and the gift shop is one of the best in the valley. *1111 Dunaweal La., Calistoga, ☎ 707/942–3300. Tram fee: $6 adults, children under 16 free. ⏲ Daily 10:30–4:30; closed major holidays.*

8 At **Clos Pegase,** neoclassicism sets the tone. The winery, designed by architect Michael Graves, the exemplar of postmodernism, and commissioned by Jan Schrem, a publisher and art collector, pays homage to art, wine, and mythology. *1060 Dunaweal La., Calistoga, ☎ 707/942–4981. ⏲ Daily 10:30–5; closed major holidays.*

9 **Chateau Montelena** is a vine-covered 1882 building set amid Chinese-inspired gardens, complete with a lake, red pavilions, and arched bridges. It's a romantic spot for a picnic, but be sure to reserve in advance. *1429 Tubbs La., Calistoga, ☎ 707/942–5105 or 800/222–7288. ⏲ Daily 10–4. Tours at 11 and 2 by appointment only.*

Calistoga Gliders gives participants a bird's-eye view of the entire valley. On clear days, visibility extends to the San Francisco skyline, the snowcapped Sierra peaks, and the Pacific Ocean. *1546 Lincoln Ave., ☎ 707/942–5000. Fees: $110–$150 for 2 passengers, depending on length of ride. ⏲ Daily 9 AM–sunset (weather permitting); closed Thanksgiving and Dec. 25.*

Although paying to wallow in mud may sound like an odd thing to do, it's a chic and popular pastime in the Napa Valley. At **Indian Springs** $85 entitles enthusiasts to a mud bath, a mineral-water shower, and a mineral-water whirlpool, followed by time in the steam room, blanket wrap, and a half-hour massage. The spa has 16 cottages with studio or one-bedroom units and a larger structure with six rooms. *1712 Lincoln Ave., Calistoga, ☎ 707/942–4913. Reservations recommended for spa treatments. ⏲ Daily 9–7.*

Silverado Trail

The **Silverado Trail,** which runs parallel to Highway 29 north from Napa, takes you away from the crowds to some distinguished wineries.

10 At **Clos du Val,** French owner Bernard Portet produces a celebrated cabernet sauvignon. *5330 Silverado Trail, ☎ 707/259–2200. ⏲ Daily 10–5.*

11 In 1993 the World Wine Championships gave **Stag's Leap Wine Cellars** a platinum award for their 1990 Reserve Chardonnay, designating it the highest-ranked premium chardonnay in the world. Their proprietary red table wine, Cask 23, consistently earns accolades from *Connoisseur* and *The Wine Spectator* as well. *5766 Silverado Trail, ☎ 707/944–2020. Tasting fee: $3. Tours by appointment. ⏲ Daily 10–4; closed major holidays.*

12 The wine at **Rutherford Hill Winery** is aged in French oak barrels stacked in more than 30,000 square feet of caves—the largest such caves in the nation. Tours of the caves can be followed by a picnic in the orchards: Choose among oak, olive, or madrone. *200 Rutherford Hill Rd. (off the Silverado Trail), Rutherford, ☎ 707/963–7194. ⏲ Weekdays 10–4:30, weekends 10–5. Tour times vary seasonally; call for detailed information.*

13 A Swiss-owned winery, **Cuvaison** specializes in chardonnay, merlot, and cabernet sauvignon for the export market. Two small picnic areas on the grounds look out over Napa Valley. *4550 Silverado Trail,* ☎ *707/942–6266.* ⏲ *Daily 10–5. Tours by appointment.*

Sonoma

Rustic Sonoma is anchored by its past. As the site of the last and the northernmost of the 21 missions established by the Franciscan order of Fra Junípero Serra, its central plaza includes the largest group of old adobes north of Monterey. The **Mission San Francisco Solano,** whose chapel and school were used to bring Christianity to the Indians, is now a museum with a fine collection of 19th-century watercolors. *114 Spain St. E,* ☎ *707/938–1519.* ☛ *$2 adults, $1 children 6–12; includes the Sonoma Barracks on the central plaza and General Vallejo's home, Lachryma Montis (*see below*).* ⏲ *Daily 10–5; closed major holidays.*

TIME OUT The four-block **Sonoma Plaza** is an inviting array of shops and food stores that overlook the shady park and attract gourmets from miles around. You can pick up the makings for a first-rate picnic here. The **Sonoma French Bakery** (466 1st St. E, ☎ 707/996-2691) is famous for its sourdough bread and cream puffs. The **Sonoma Cheese Factory** (2 Spain St., ☎ 707/996-1000), run by the same family for four generations, makes Sonoma jack cheese and a tangy Sonoma Teleme. Great swirling baths of milk and curds are visible through the windows, along with flat-pressed wheels of cheese.

A few blocks west (and quite a hike away) is the tree-lined approach to **Lachryma Montis,** which General Mariano Vallejo, the last Mexican governor of California, built for his large family in 1851. The Victorian Gothic house is secluded in the midst of beautiful gardens; opulent Victorian furnishings, including a white marble fireplace in every room, are particularly noteworthy. The state purchased the home in 1933. *Spain St. W,* ☎ *707/938–1519.* ☛ *$2 adults, $1 children 6–12.* ⏲ *Daily 10–5; closed major holidays.*

14 The **Sebastiani Vineyards,** originally planted by Franciscans of the Sonoma Mission in 1825, were bought by Samuele Sebastiani in 1904. The Sebastianis are renowned producers of red wines, and Sylvia Sebastiani has recorded her good Italian home cooking in a family recipe book, *Mangiamo,* to complement them. Tours include a look at an unusual collection of impressive carved oak casks. *389 4th St. E,* ☎ *707/938–5532.* ⏲ *Daily 10–5; last tour at 4:30; closed major holidays.*

15 The landmark **Buena Vista Carneros Winery** (follow signs from the plaza), set among towering trees and fountains, is a must-see in Sonoma. It was here, in 1857, that Count Agoston Haraszthy de Mokcsa laid the basis for modern California wine making, bucking the conventional wisdom that vines should be planted on well-watered ground by instead planting on well-drained hillsides. Chinese laborers dug tunnels 100 feet into the hillside, and the limestone they extracted was used to build the main house. Although their wines are produced elsewhere in the Carneros region today, the winery offers tours, a gourmet shop, an art gallery, and great picnic spots. *18000 Old Winery Rd.,* ☎ *707/938–1266.* ⏲ *Daily 10:30–4:30.*

Carneros

In the Carneros region of the Sonoma Valley, south of Sonoma, the wines
16 at **Gloria Ferrer Champagne Caves** hark back to a 700-year-old stock of Ferrer grapes. The wines here are aged in a "cava," or cellar, where

several feet of earth maintain a constant temperature—an increasingly popular alternative to temperature-controlled warehouses. *23555 Carneros Hwy. 121,* ☎ *707/996–7256. Tasting fees by the glass and the type of champagne.* ⏲ *Daily 10:30–5:30. Tours every hr from 11 to 4.*

17 One of the newer wineries in Sonoma Valley is **Viansa,** opened by a son of the famous Sebastiani family who decided to strike out on his own. Reminiscent of a Tuscan villa, the winery's ocher-colored building is surrounded by olive trees and overlooks the valley. Inside is an Italian food and gift market. *25200 Arnold Dr., Sonoma,* ☎ *707/935–4700.* ⏲ *Daily 10–5.*

Glen Ellen and Kenwood

Continue north on Highway 12 through lush Sonoma Valley, where writer Jack London lived for many years; much around here has been named for him. The drive along Highway 12 takes you through orchards and rows of vineyards, with oak-covered mountain ranges flanking the valley. Some 2 million cases of wine are bottled in this area annually, and the towns of Glen Ellen and Kenwood are rich in history and lore. **Glen Ellen,** with its century-old Jack London Bar, is nestled at the base of the hill leading to Jack London State Park and the Benziger Family Winery. Nearby is Grist Mill Inn, a historic landmark with shops, and Jack London Village, with a charming bookstore filled with London's books and memorabilia. **Kenwood** is home to several important wineries, a historic train depot, and several eateries and shops specializing in locally produced gourmet products.

In the hills above Glen Ellen—known as the Valley of the Moon—lies **Jack London State Historic Park.** The House of Happy Walls is a museum of London's effects, including his collection of South Sea artifacts. The ruins of Wolf House, which London designed and which mysteriously burned down just before he was to move in, are nearby, and London is buried on the property. *2400 London Ranch Rd.,* ☎ *707/938–5216. Parking: $5 per car, with discounts for senior citizens.* ⏲ *Park: Daily 9:30–sunset, museum: daily 10–5. Museum closed major holidays.*

18 The **Benziger Family Winery** specializes in premium estate and Sonoma County wines. Its Imagery Series is a low-volume release of unusual red and white wines distributed in bottles with art labels by well-known artists from all over the world. *1883 London Ranch Rd., Glen Ellen,* ☎ *707/935–3000. Complimentary tasting of Sonoma County wines; tasting fees vary.* ⏲ *Daily 10–4:30.*

19 The beautifully rustic grounds at **Kenwood Vineyards** complement the attractive tasting room and the artistic bottle labels. While Kenwood produces all premium varietals, it is best known for its signature Jack London Vineyard reds—pinot noir, zinfandel, cabernet and merlot, and a unique Artist Series Cabernet. *9592 Sonoma Hwy., Kenwood,* ☎ *707/833–5891. Free tasting, no tours.* ⏲ *Daily 10–4:30.*

Santa Rosa, Healdsburg, and Guerneville

Santa Rosa is the Wine Country's largest city and a good bet for moderately priced hotel rooms, especially for those who have not reserved in advance. Healdsburg, with its pastoral treasures, remains undeveloped and relatively untrafficked. Guerneville is a sleepy little hamlet along the Russian River.

The **Luther Burbank Home and Gardens** commemorate the great botanist who lived and worked on these grounds for 50 years, single-handedly developing the modern techniques of hybridization. Arriving as a young man from New England, he wrote: "I firmly believe . . . that this is the chosen spot of all the earth, as far as nature is concerned." The Santa Rosa plum, the Shasta daisy, and the lily of the Nile agapanthus are among the 800 or so plants he developed or improved. In the music room of his house, a Webster's Dictionary of 1946 lies open to a page on which the verb "burbank" is defined as "to modify and improve plant life." Head north on Santa Rosa Avenue off Highway 12. *Santa Rosa and Sonoma Aves.,* ☎ *707/524–5445. Gardens free and open Nov.–Mar., daily 8–5; Apr.–Oct., daily 8–7. Guided tours of the house and greenhouse: $2, children under 12 free; tours Apr.–Oct., Wed.–Sun. 10–3:30. Garden tours Fri. and Sat. at 10:15* AM.

The wineries of Sonoma County, located along winding roads, are not immediately obvious to the casual visitor; a tour of the vineyards that lie along the Russian River is a leisurely and bucolic experience. For a free map of the area, contact **Russian River Wine Road** (Box 46, Healdsburg 95448, ☎ 707/433–6782).

20 For a historical overview, start at the imposing **Korbel Champagne Cellars,** which displays photographic documents of the North West Railway in a former train stop on its property. *13250 River Rd., Guerneville,* ☎ *707/887–2294.* ⏲ *Oct.–Apr., daily 9–4:30; May–Sept., daily 9–5. Tours on the hr 10–3.*

Armstrong Woods State Reserve, just outside of Guerneville, contains 752 acres of virgin redwoods and is the best place in the Wine Country to see California's most famous trees. More redwood country lies west of Guerneville, along the Russian River Road (Highway 116), which leads to the Pacific Ocean and the rugged Sonoma coast. A string of small towns along this are loaded with bed-and-breakfasts, seafood restaurants, and interesting sights. **Duncan Mills** is an old logging and railroad town with a complex of shops and a small museum in an old train depot. At the coast is **Jenner,** where the Russian River meets the Pacific. A colony of harbor seals makes its home here March through June.

East of Guerneville, turn left off River Road onto Westside Road, which winds past a number of award-winning wineries.

21 **Davis Bynum Winery,** in business since 1965, specializes in Russian River valley wines and is noted for its merlots and pinot noirs. *8075 Westside Rd., Healdsburg,* ☎ *707/433–5852.* ⏲ *Daily 10–5.*

22 The **Hop Kiln Winery** is in an imposing hops-drying barn, which was built during the early 1900s and has been used as a backdrop for films. *6050 Westside Rd., Healdsburg,* ☎ *707/433–6491.* ⏲ *Daily 10–5.*

23 **Dry Creek Vineyard** is one of California's leading producers of white wines and well known for its fumé blanc. The winery's reds, especially zinfandels and cabernets, have also begun to earn notice. Flowering magnolia and redwood trees provide an ideal setting for a picnic. *3770 Lambert Bridge Rd., Healdsburg,* ☎ *707/433–1000.* ⏲ *Daily 10:30–4:30.*

24 The **Robert Stemmler Winery,** which draws on German traditions of wine making, specializes in pinot noir. Picnic facilities, available by appointment only, are small and private, shaded by towering redwood trees. *3805 Lambert Bridge Rd., Healdsburg (Dry Creek Rd. exit from Hwy. 101, northwest 3 mi to Lambert Bridge Rd.),* ☎ *707/433–6334.* ⏲ *Weekdays by appointment only; weekends 10:30–4:30.*

25 **Lytton Springs Winery** produces the archetype of Sonoma zinfandel, a dark, fruity wine with high alcohol content. Though the origin of this varietal is still disputed—some claim it was transplanted from stock in New England—the vines themselves are distinctive—gnarled and stocky, many of them over a century old. *650 Lytton Springs Rd., Healdsburg, ☎ 707/433–7721. ⏲ Daily 11–4.*

26 Five miles north of Healdsburg, **Clos du Bois** produces the fine estate chardonnays of the Alexander and Dry Creek valleys that have been mistaken for great French wines. *19410 Geyserville Ave., Box 940, Geyserville, ☎ 707/857–3100 or 800/222–3189. ⏲ Daily 10–4:30. No tours.*

27 South of Healdsburg, off U.S. 101, is **Piper Sonoma,** a state-of-the-art winery specializing in méthode champenoise sparkling wines. *11447 Old Redwood Hwy., Healdsburg, ☎ 707/433–8843. ⏲ Daily 10–5.*

TIME OUT Once you've seen, heard about, and tasted enough wine for one day, head over to **Kozlowski's Farms** (5566 Gravenstein, Hwy. 116N, ☎ 707/887–1587), in Forestville, where jams are made from every berry imaginable. Originally in Forestville but now located in Santa Rosa, **Brother Juniper's** (463 Sebastopol Ave., Santa Rosa, ☎ 707/542–9012) makes a heavenly "Struan" bread of polenta, malted barley, brown rice, buttermilk, wheat bran, and oats.

What to See and Do with Children

In the **Bale Grist Mill State Historic Park,** a partially restored 1846 flour mill is powered by a 36-foot overshot waterwheel. Short paths lead from the access road to the mill and the old pond site. *3 mi north of St. Helena on Hwy. 29, ☎ 707/942–4575. ☛ $2 adults, $1 children 6–17. ⏲ Daily 10–5. Waterwheel demonstrations most weekends. Call ahead for schedule and other special tour arrangements.*

Old Faithful Geyser of California blasts a 60-foot tower of steam and vapor about every 40 minutes; the pattern is disrupted if there's an earthquake in the offing. One of just three regularly erupting geysers in the world, it is fed by an underground river that heats to 350°F. The spout lasts three minutes. Picnic facilities are available. *1299 Tubbs La., 1 mi north of Calistoga, ☎ 707/942–6463. ☛ $5 adults, $4 senior citizens, $2 children 6–11. ⏲ Daily 9–6 during daylight saving time, 9–5 in winter. Call first if you're traveling from a distance to make sure the geyser will be active when you arrive.*

The **Petrified Forest** contains the remains of the volcanic eruptions of Mount St. Helena 3.4 million years ago. The force of the explosion uprooted the gigantic redwoods, covered them with volcanic ash, and infiltrated the trees with silicas and minerals, causing petrification. Explore the museum, then picnic on the grounds. *4100 Petrified Forest Rd., 5 mi west of Calistoga, ☎ 707/942–6667. ☛ $3 adults, $2 senior citizens, $1 children 4–11. ⏲ Summer, daily 10–6; winter, daily 10–4:30.*

The **Redwood Empire Ice Arena** in Santa Rosa is a skating rink with a twist. It was built by local resident Charles Schulz, creator of *Peanuts.* The Snoopy Gallery and gift shop, with Snoopy books, clothing, and life-size comic strip characters, is delightful. *1667 W. Steele La., ☎ 707/546–7147. ☛ 7.50 ages 12 and over, $6.50 ages under 12. ⏲ Daily, public skating.*

A steam train at **Train Town** runs for 20 minutes through a forested park with trestles, bridges, and small animals. *20264 Broadway (Hwy.*

12), 1 mi south of Sonoma Plaza, ☎ *707/938–3912.* ☛ *$3.50 adults, $2.50 children under 16 and senior citizens.* ⏲ *Mid-June–Labor Day, daily 10:30–5; Sept.–mid-June, Fri.–Sun. 10:30–5 (weather permitting); closed Dec. 25.*

Howarth Memorial Park, in Santa Rosa, has a lake where canoes, rowboats, paddleboats, and small sailboats can be rented for $6 an hour. The children's area has a playground, pony rides, a petting zoo, a merry-go-round, and a miniature train. Fishing, tennis, and hiking trails are also available. *Summerfield Rd. off Montgomery Rd.,* ☎ *707/543–3282. Amusements: 75¢–$1. Park open daily in good weather; children's area open summer, Wed.–Sun.; spring and fall, weekends.*

Off the Beaten Track

Breathtaking views of both the Sonoma and Napa valleys are evident from all of the hairpin turns of the **Oakville Grade,** which twists along the range dividing the two valleys. The surface of the road is good, and those who are comfortable with mountain driving will enjoy this half-hour excursion. Driving the road at night, however, can be difficult. Trucks are advised not to attempt it at any time.

Robert Louis Stevenson State Park, on Highway 29, 3 miles northeast of Calistoga, encompasses the summit of Mount St. Helena. It was here, in an abandoned bunkhouse of the Silverado Mine, that Stevenson and his bride, Fanny Osbourne, spent their honeymoon in the summer of 1880. The stay inspired Stevenson's "The Silverado Squatters," and Spyglass Hill in *Treasure Island* is thought to be a portrait of Mount St. Helena. The park's 3,000 acres are undeveloped except for a fire trail leading to the site of the cabin, which is marked with a marble tablet, and then on to the summit. Picnicking is permitted, but fires are not.

SHOPPING

Don't expect bargains at the wineries, where prices are generally as high as at retail outlets. Residents report that the area's supermarkets stock a wide selection of local wines at lower prices. For connoisseurs seeking extraordinary values, the **All Seasons Cafe Wine Shop** (☎ 707/942–6828) in Calistoga is a true find. Gift shops in the larger wineries offer the ultimate in gourmet items. Most wineries will ship purchases.

SPORTS AND THE OUTDOORS

Ballooning

This whimsical pastime has fast become part of the scenery in the Wine Country, and many hotels arrange excursions. Most flights take place soon after sunrise, when the calmest, coolest time of day offers maximum lift and soft landings. Prices depend on the duration of the flight, number of passengers, and services (some companies provide extras such as pickup at your lodging or champagne brunch after the flight). Expect to spend about $165 per person. Companies that provide flights include **Balloons Above the Valley** (Box 3838, Napa 94558, ☎ 707/253–2222 or 800/464–6824 in CA), **Napa Valley Balloons** (Box 2860, Yountville 94599, ☎ 707/944–0228 or 800/253–2224 in CA), **American Balloon Adventures** (Box 795, Calistoga 94515, ☎ 707/942–6546 or 800/333–4359), **Once in a Lifetime** (Box 795, Calistoga 94515, ☎ 707/942–6541 or 800/659–9915), and **Napa's Great Balloon Escape** (Box 795, Calistoga 94515, ☎ 707/253–0860 or 800/564–

9399), featuring a catered brunch finale at the Silverado Country Club, overlooking the golf course.

Bicycling

One of the best ways to experience the countryside is on two wheels, and the Eldorado Bike Trail is considered one of the best. Reasonably priced rentals are available in most towns.

Golf

Although the weather is mild year-round, rain may occasionally prevent your teeing off in the winter months. Call to check on greens fees at **Fountaingrove Country Club** (1525 Fountaingrove Pkwy., Santa Rosa, ☎ 707/579–4653), **Oakmont Golf Club** (west course: 7025 Oakmont Dr., Santa Rosa, ☎ 707/539–0415; east course: 565 Oak Vista Ct., Santa Rosa, ☎ 707/538–2454), **Silverado Country Club** (1600 Atlas Peak Rd., Napa, ☎ 707/257–0200), or the **Chardonnay Club** (2555 Jameson Canyon Rd., Napa, ☎ 707/257–8950), a favorite among Bay Area golfers.

DINING

Revised by Karen Croft

Restaurants in the Wine Country have traditionally reflected the culinary heritage of early settlers from Italy, France, and Mexico. Star chefs from urban areas are the most recent influx of immigrants, bringing creative California cuisine, seafood, and an eclectic range of American-regional and international fare. Food now rivals wine as the prime attraction in the region, with restaurants offering fresh produce, meats, and prime ingredients from local farms. Where reservations are indicated to be essential, you may need to reserve a week or more ahead; during the summer and early fall harvest seasons you may need to book several months ahead.

Those on a budget will find an appealing range of reasonably priced eateries. Gourmet delis offer superb picnic fare, and brunch is a cost-effective strategy at high-end restaurants.

What to Wear

With few exceptions (which are noted), dress is informal.

CATEGORY	COST*
$$$$	over $40
$$$	$25–$40
$$	$16–$25
$	under $16

**per person for a three-course meal, excluding drinks, service, and 7½% sales tax*

Calistoga

$$$–$$$$ ★ **All Seasons Cafe.** Bistro cuisine has a California spin in this sun-filled setting with marble tables and a black-and-white checkerboard floor. A seasonal menu featuring organic greens, wild mushrooms, local game birds, house-smoked beef and salmon, and homemade breads, desserts, and ice cream from their on-site ice-cream plant is coupled with a superb listing of local wines at bargain prices. For lunch there's a tempting selection of pizza, pasta, and sandwiches. ✕ *1400 Lincoln Ave.,* ☎ *707/942–9111. Reservations advised on weekends. Brunch Fri.–Sun. MC, V. Closed Wed.*

$$$ ★ **Catahoula Restaurant and Saloon.** Inside the Mount View Hotel and Spa, this homey new restaurant, named after Louisiana's state dog, is the brainchild of chef Jan Birnbaum, whose credentials include stints at the Quilted Giraffe in New York and at the Campton Place in San

Francisco. Using a large wood-burning oven as a stove, Birnbaum churns out California-Cajun dishes such as spicy gumbo Ya Ya with andouille sausage, oven braised lamb shank with red beans, whole roasted fish, and oven-roasted chili squid salad with honey-caramelized endive. Save room for tantalizing desserts such as chocolate-sour cherry bread pudding or a wood-fired chocolate s'more that will bring you back to the campfire. Sit at the counter and watch the chef cook—it's the best entertainment in town. ✕ *1457 Lincoln Ave.* ☏ *707/942–2275. Reservations required. MC, V. Closed Tues.*

$–$$ Silverado Restaurant & Tavern. In a setting straight out of a spaghetti western, savvy locals and seasoned wine connoisseurs linger over an award-winning wine list with more than 700 selections priced just above retail. The eclectic menu includes egg rolls, chicken-salad sandwiches, Caesar salad, and great burgers. ✕ *1374 Lincoln Ave.,* ☏ *707/942–6725. Reservations advised. MC, V. Closed Thurs.*

$ Boskos Ristorante. Set in a restored sandstone building that dates back to the 1800s, this family-style eatery dishes up homemade pasta, pizza, and garden-fresh salads. *Glorioso* (pasta shells with garlic, mushrooms, and red chilies) is a favorite entrée. Leave room for the homemade chocolate cheesecake. ✕ *1364 Lincoln Ave.,* ☏ *707/942–9088. No reservations. No credit cards.*

Geyserville

$–$$ Château Souverain Café. A spectacular view of Alexander Valley vineyards, an outdoor terrace for tranquil summer lunches, and reasonable prices make chef Martin Courtman's French country menu triply irresistible. Try braised lamb shanks, garlic and black pepper penne pasta, or grilled buckwheat polenta with Gorgonzola cheese. ✕ *400 Souverain Rd. (Independence La. exit west from Hwy. 101),* ☏ *707/433–3141. Reservations advised. AE, MC, V. Closed Mon.–Thurs. and Jan.*

Healdsburg

$$$$ Restaurant at Madrona Manor. This country inn with 21 rooms serves breakfast to guests only, but others can sample great food from the brick oven, smokehouse, orchard, and kitchen garden, including local Sonoma produce, Campbell lamb, and choice seafood. Chef Todd Muir turns out dishes fit for a wine baron: smoked lamb salad, Dungeness crab mousse, acorn squash soup, oven-roasted pork tenderloin, and Grand Marnier crème caramel. The 1881 Victorian mansion, surrounded by 8 acres of wooded and landscaped grounds, provides a storybook setting for a candlelight dinner or brunch on the outdoor deck. The seasonal menu is à la carte. ✕ *1001 Westside Rd. (take central Healdsburg exit from Hwy. 101, turn left on Mill St.),* ☏ *707/433–4231. Reservations advised. Sun. brunch Apr.–Oct. AE, D, DC, MC, V. No lunch.*

$–$$ Bistro Ralph. Ralph Tingle, once executive chef of the defunct Fetzer Vineyards Sun Dial Grill in Mendocino, has created a culinary hit with his California home-style cuisine. The small, frequently changing menu includes Szechuan pepper calamari, braised lamb shanks with mint essence (using locally ranched Bruce Campbell lamb), and sea bass braised with ginger and carrot juice. Wine is used liberally in the cooking, and the wine list features picks from small local wineries. ✕ *109 Plaza St.,* ☏ *707/433–1380. Reservations advised. MC, V. No lunch weekends.*

$–$$ Samba Java. This lively café manages to fit a lot of tables, colorful decor, and culinary action into a very small space. The menu, which represents an eclectic range of California cuisine, is based largely on Sonoma ingredients and changes daily. Breads and preserves are made in-house, as are the succulent roasted pork loin with a sweet-potato *galette* (razor-thin slices layered with olive oil and herbs) and wilted bitter greens, and the mocha swirl cheesecake. ✕ *109A Plaza St.,* ☏

707/433–5282. Reservations accepted for dinner; lunch reservations for 6 or more only. Breakfast served weekends. AE, MC, V. No lunch Mon., no dinner Sun.–Wed.

Napa

$$$ **Silverado Country Club.** There are two restaurants and a bar and grill at this large, famous resort. The elegant Vintner's Court, with Pacific Rim cuisine, serves dinner only; there is a seafood buffet on Friday night and a champagne brunch on Sunday. Royal Oak serves steak and seafood for dinner nightly. The bar and grill is open for breakfast and lunch year-round; in the summer, lunch offerings include an outdoor barbecue with chicken and hamburgers. ✕ *1600 Atlas Peak Rd. (follow signs to Lake Berryessa),* ☎ *707/257–0200. Reservations required for 2 restaurants only. AE, D, DC, MC, V. Vintner's Court closed Mon. and Tues. No dinner Sun.*

$$–$$$ **La Boucane.** Chef-owner Jacques Mokrani has created a gorgeous little gem of a restaurant in a restored 1885 Victorian decorated with period antiques. Classic French cuisine (rack of lamb, champagne-crisp duck) is delivered with style in a candlelit dining room enhanced by silver, linen, and a red rose on each table. ✕ *1778 2nd St. (at Jefferson St. in downtown Napa),* ☎ *707/253–1177. Reservations advised. MC, V. Closed Sun. and Jan. No lunch.*

$–$$ **Bistro Don Giovanni.** Rumor has it that Alice Waters' first venture in the Wine Country, Table 29, failed because there weren't enough Napa Valley selections on the wine list. Giovanni and Donna Scala, the culinary couple behind the success of Ristorante Piatti, have avoided this problem, with a wine list that's as locally representative as their menu is eclectic. The ambience is casual Mediterranean, with terra-cotta tile floors, high ceilings, and a full bar stocked with Napa Valley wines, as well as a spacious outdoor patio with an expansive view of the valley. Ingredients such as pesto, goat cheese, and shrimp top individual pies from the wood-burning pizza oven. The carpaccio is a standout. Winning items include pastas and grilled entrées such as pork chops with garlic-infused mashed potatoes. Don't miss the delectable fruit-crisp dessert, which changes daily. ✕ *4110 St. Helena Hwy. 29,* ☎ *707/224–3300. Reservations advised. AE, DC, MC, V.*

$ **Jonesy's Famous Steak House.** This spacious and informal local favorite with a children's menu has been providing entertainment for aviation buffs, steak lovers, and kids of all ages since 1946. One entire wall has an expanse of windows with a prime view of the Napa County Airport landing strip. Inside, prime steaks, weighted down with Sacramento River rocks to keep juices in, are seared over a dry grill. Roasted chicken, homemade soups, and fresh fish round out the fare. ✕ *2044 Airport Rd. (halfway between Napa and Vallejo, off Hwy. 29),* ☎ *707/255–2003. Reservations advised. AE, D, DC, MC, V. Closed Mon. and 1 wk at Christmas.*

Oakville

$$ ★ **Stars Oakville Cafe.** Jeremiah Tower, father of California Cuisine, and Peter Hall have transformed an old building next to the Oakville Grocery store into a country café with glazed tile floors, white walls, lots of flowers, and picture windows that look into the kitchen. Wood-burning ovens turn out rustic fare for a daily-changing menu that features roasted leg of lamb, roast salmon, and roast pumpkin-filled pasta with white truffle oil. The wine list is stellar, and desserts (brownie-steamed pudding, pumpkin cheesecake) are sublime. Space heaters on the tented outdoor patio add comfort to alfresco dining, and the adjacent garden with olive and lemon trees, lavender, and an antique aviary is the perfect setting for an after-dinner stroll. ✕ *7848 St. Helena Hwy. 29*

(corner of Hwy. 29 and Oakville Crossroad), ☎ *707/944–8905. Reservations required weekends, advised weekdays. AE, D, DC, MC, V. No lunch Tues. and Wed.*

Rutherford

$$–$$$$ ★ **Auberge du Soleil.** The dining room of this 50-room inn is a setting of Mediterranean elegance: earth tones, wood beams, and outdoor deck with panoramic views of the valley. The frequently changing menu, which features local produce, includes roasted lobster sausage and rosemary-roasted rack of lamb. A moderately priced bar menu offers slow-roasted garlic with homemade pretzels and pan-seared salmon sandwiches, and the extensive wine list represents French, Italian, and Napa Valley wines. ✕ *180 Rutherford Hill Rd. (off Silverado Trail just north of Rte. 128),* ☎ *707/963–1211. Reservations advised. AE, D, MC, V.*

St. Helena

$$$$ **Restaurant at Meadowood.** This sprawling resort looks like a scene from an F. Scott Fitzgerald novel, complete with croquet lawns, and provides the perfect setting for weekend brunch. Refined French cuisine with a California twist is offered on a prix fixe in either a dining room with a cathedral ceiling, a fireplace, and lush greenery, or outdoors on a terrace overlooking the golf course. A lighter menu of pizzas and spa food can be had at breakfast and lunch (and early dinners Friday and Saturday) at a second, less formal and less expensive Meadowood restaurant, the Grill. ✕ *900 Meadowood La.,* ☎ *707/963–3646. Reservations required. AE, D, DC, MC, V.*

$$$$ **Terra.** The delightful twosome who own this lovely, unpretentious restaurant housed in a century-old stone foundry learned their culinary skills at the side of chef Wolfgang Puck. Hiro Sone was head chef at L.A.'s Spago, and Lissa Doumanie was the pastry chef. Together, they offer an enticing array of southern French and northern Italian favorites, highlighting Hiro's Japanese-French-Italian finesse. Favorites are pear and goat cheese salad with warm pancetta and sherry vinaigrette, and fillet of salmon with Thai red-curry sauce and basmati rice. Save room for Lissa's desserts. ✕ *1345 Railroad Ave.,* ☎ *707/963–8931. Reservations advised. MC, V. Closed Tues. No lunch.*

$$$$ **Trilogy.** Chef-owner Diane Pariseau pairs one of the best and most extensive contemporary wine lists in the valley with superb renditions of California-French cuisine on a prix fixe menu that changes daily. Pariseau deftly juxtaposes flavors and textures; her all-star entrées, such as grilled chicken breast on a nest of sautéed apples and green peppercorns, or grilled tuna steak with olive oil and sweet red pepper puree, are artfully presented. The secluded dining room feels like a gracious country home, with a mere 10 tables. ✕ *1234 Main St.,* ☎ *707/963–5507. Reservations required. MC, V. Closed Mon. and 3 wks in Dec. No lunch weekends.*

$$$ ★ **Showley's.** In a building that dates from 1860, this homey, family-run restaurant has two dining rooms, the smaller of which has a bar. The seasonal menu reflects the owner-chef's interest in international flavors as well as local products (there's a fig tree out back that inspired an annual fig menu in late summer). Fresh fish and meats are noteworthy, especially the garlic chicken, tenderloin of pork, and roast monkfish with garlic-mashed potatoes. Starters are equally well prepared, especially the *chile en nogada,* which is stuffed with pork, pine nuts, and chutney and served with a walnut–crème fraîche sauce. Desserts to try are the famous chocolate phyllo pastry "hoo hoo" layered with Valrhona chocolate pastry cream and fresh raspberries, or the home-

made ice creams that change flavors each season. ✕ *1327 Railroad Ave., ☏ 707/963–1200. Reservations advised. AE, D, MC, V.*

$$ ★ **Brava Terrace.** Owner and chef Fred Halpert was one of the instigators of the culinary renaissance in the Wine Country. American-born, French-trained Halpert has created a menu that features produce plucked from the restaurant's own garden to enliven his trademark pasta, risotto, and cassoulet dishes. The chocolate-chip crème brûlée provides a grand finale. Brava has a comfortably casual ambience with a full bar, a large stone fireplace, a romantic outdoor terrace, and a heated deck with views of the valley floor and Howell Mountain. ✕ *3010 St. Helena Hwy. (Hwy. 29, ½ mi north of St. Helena), ☏ 707/963–9300. Reservations advised. AE, D, DC, MC, V. Closed Wed. Nov.–Apr. and Jan. 16–25.*

$$ ★ **Tra Vigne.** This Napa Valley fieldstone building has been transformed into a striking, extremely popular trattoria with a huge wood bar, impossibly high ceilings, and plush banquettes. Homemade mozzarella, olive oil, and vinegar, and house-cured pancetta and prosciutto contribute to a one-of-a-kind tour of Tuscan cuisine. Although getting a table without a reservation is sometimes difficult, drop-ins can sit at the bar. The outdoor courtyard in summer is a sun-splashed Mediterranean vision of striped umbrellas and awnings, crowded café tables, and rustic pots overflowing with flowers. The Cantinetta delicatessen in the corner of the courtyard offers wine by the glass and gourmet picnic fare. ✕ *1050 Charter Oak Ave. (off Hwy. 29), ☏ 707/963–4444. Reservations suggested in dining room. D, DC, MC, V.*

Santa Rosa

$$$ **Cafe Lolo.** Voted the best new restaurant in Sonoma County by the *Press Democrat* and winner of the best Sonoma County wine list award at the 1994 Sonoma County Harvest Fair, this small, clean, downtown café also caught the eye of *The Wine Spectator* and the *San Francisco Chronicle* that same year. Tables are elegantly dressed in white linen, but the mood is casual. Chef-owner Michael Quigley's lunch and dinner menus include fresh seafood, daily changing risotto and pasta dishes, free-range chicken, rabbit, and lots of goat cheese and local produce. ✕ *620 5th St., ☏ 707/576–7822. Reservations advised. AE, MC, V. Closed Sun. No lunch Sat.*

$$–$$$ **John Ash & Co.** The thoroughly regional cuisine here emphasizes beauty, innovation, and the seasonal availability of food products grown in Sonoma County and in the restaurant's organic garden. In spring, local lamb is roasted with hazelnuts and honey; in fall, farm pork is roasted with fresh figs and Gravenstein apples. Desserts are delicious and the wine list extensive. With patio seating outside and a cozy fireplace indoors, the slightly formal restaurant looks like a Spanish villa amid the vineyards and is a favorite spot for Sunday brunch. ✕ *4330 Barnes Rd. (River Rd. exit west from Hwy. 101), ☏ 707/527–7687. Reservations advised. AE, MC, V. No lunch Mon.*

$–$$ **Lisa Hemenway's.** A shopping center on the outskirts of town seems an unlikely location for a restaurant find, but Hemenway, who trained under John Ash (*see* John Ash & Co., *above*), has created a light and airy eatery with soft wine-country colors and a garden view from the patio. The fare, which is updated every four months, represents American and international cuisine, from grilled sea bass with Singapore curry to red chili crepes and tapas. The adjacent café, Tote Cuisine, has a vast selection of tempting takeouts for picnickers. ✕ *714 Village Ct. Mall (east on Hwy. 12, at Farmer's La. and Sonoma Ave.), ☏ 707/526–5111. Reservations advised. Sun. brunch. AE, MC, V.*

$ Mixx. Great service and an eclectic "mix" of dishes define this small restaurant with large windows, booth and table seating, high ceilings, and French blown-glass chandeliers. Nightly homemade pasta and seafood dishes are offered, along with regional specialties such as grilled Cajun prawns and New Mexican stuffed chilies—all based on locally grown ingredients and served with Napa Valley wine. ✕ *135 4th St. (at Davis behind the mall on Railroad Sq.),* ☎ *707/573–1344. Reservations advised. No lunch weekends. AE, MC, V.*

Sonoma

$$$ Grille at Sonoma Mission Inn & Spa. There are two restaurants at this famed resort (*see* The Cafe, *below*). The Grille offers formal dining in a light, airy setting with original art on the walls, French windows overlooking the pool and gardens, and a patio for alfresco dining. Wine Country cuisine changes seasonally to feature favorites like Sonoma leg of lamb and basil-roasted chicken with garlic-mashed potatoes. On weekends, a prix fixe menu pairs each course with the appropriate wine from the restaurant's extensive selection. A special spa menu caters to health-conscious gourmets. ✕ *18140 Hwy. 12 (2 mi north of Sonoma at Boyes Blvd.),* ☎ *707/938–9000. Reservations strongly advised. Sun. brunch. AE, DC, MC, V.*

$$ Eastside Oyster Bar & Grill. Chef-owner Charles Saunders, renowned for his stint at the Grille at Sonoma Mission Inn (*see above*), has received rave reviews for his creative culinary flair and health-conscious approach. Specialties include a surprisingly delicate Hangtown fry (plump oysters on a bed of greens and beets with a Sonoma mustard vinaigrette), creative renditions of roast chicken or Sonoma lamb, and stellar salads and vegetarian dishes. Inside, the restaurant has a fireplace and an intimate bistro atmosphere; outside there's a wisteria-draped terrace where diners enjoy a picture-window view into the pastry kitchen. ✕ *133 E. Napa St. (just off downtown plaza square),* ☎ *707/939–1266. Reservations advised. Sun. brunch. AE, DC, MC, V.*

$$ Kenwood Restaurant & Bar. This is where Napa and Sonoma chefs eat on their nights off. Both in tastes and looks it evokes the mood of a sunny hotel dining room in the south of France. Patrons indulge in country French cuisine such as braised rabbit and warm sweetbread salad in the airy dining room, or head through the French doors to the patio, which affords a memorable view of the vineyards. ✕ *9900 Hwy. 12, Kenwood,* ☎ *707/833–6326. Reservations advised. MC, V. Closed Mon.*

$$ Ristorante Piatti. On the ground floor of the remodeled El Dorado Hotel, a 19th-century landmark building, this is the Sonoma cousin of the Yountville Piatti (*see below*). Pizza from the wood-burning oven and northern Italian specials (spit-roasted chicken, ravioli with lemon cream) are served in a rustic Italian setting with an open kitchen and bright wall murals, or on the award-winning outdoor terrace. ✕ *405 1st St. W (facing the plaza),* ☎ *707/996–2351. Reservations advised. AE, MC, V.*

$ The Cafe. This is Sonoma Mission Inn's (*see above*) second restaurant, with an informal bistro atmosphere, overstuffed booths, ceiling fans, and an open kitchen renowned for its country breakfasts, pizza from the wood-burning oven, and tasty California renditions of northern Italian cuisine. ✕ *18140 Sonoma Hwy. (2 mi north of Sonoma on Hwy. 12 at Boyes Blvd.),* ☎ *707/938–9000. Reservations advised for dinner; accepted for 6 or more for breakfast and lunch. Sun. brunch. AE, DC, MC, V.*

$ La Casa. Whitewashed stucco, red tile, and serapes adorn this restaurant just around the corner from Sonoma's plaza. There's bar seating, a patio out back, and an extensive menu of traditional Mexican food:

chimichangas and snapper Veracruz for entrées, sangria to drink, and flan for dessert. ✕ *121 E. Spain St.,* ☎ *707/996–3406. Reservations advised. AE, DC, MC, V.*

Yountville

$$$$ ★ Domaine Chandon. Part of the world-renowned winery, this large, formal dining room caters to wine and food aficionados with a daily-changing menu of expertly prepared, artfully presented, French-inspired California cuisine. Sonoma duck breast is served with polenta and green-olive sage juice; venison is wrapped in pancetta and drizzled with huckleberry sauce. Desserts are a must: Try the hot gooey chocolate cake with double vanilla ice cream, or the daily-made sorbets. ✕ *California Dr. (Yountville exit off Hwy. 29, toward Veterans' Home),* ☎ *707/944–2892. Reservations essential. Jacket required. AE, D, DC, MC, V. No lunch Mon. and Tues. Nov.–Apr.*

$$$$ ★ French Laundry. Inside an old converted brick building surrounded by lush gardens, fresh flowers, and gentle lighting make patrons feel like well-tended houseguests being treated to an exquisite meal. The prix fixe menu, which costs $46 for five courses, $38 for four (lunch is $33 for four courses and $28 for three), includes canapés such as "bacon and eggs"—quail eggs paired with bacon and served atop tiny silver spoons; entrées such as pan-roasted Virginia striped bass with sweet peppers and black olives, or thyme-scented eggplant with potato gnocchi; and for dessert, "coffee and doughnuts" (cinnamon sugared doughnuts with cappuccino ice cream) or warm chocolate truffle cake with caramel cream. ✕ *6640 Washington St.,* ☎ *707/944-2380. Reservations recommended. AE, MC, V. Closed Mon.*

$$ Mustard's Grill. Grilled fish, steak, local fresh produce, and an impressive selection of wines are offered in a noisy bistro with a black-and-white marble floor and upbeat artwork. Expect to encounter a crowd, since this is a wine makers' hangout. ✕ *7399 St. Helena Hwy., Napa Valley (Hwy. 29, 1 mi north of Yountville),* ☎ *707/944–2424,* FAX *707/944–0828. Reservations advised well in advance. D, DC, MC, V.*

$$ Ristorante Piatti. A small, stylish trattoria with a pizza oven and open kitchen, this cheery place is full of good smells and happy people. Its authentic regional Italian cooking—from antipasti to grilled chicken to tiramisù—is the perfect cure for a jaded appetite. The homemade pastas are the best bet. ✕ *6480 Washington St.,* ☎ *707/944–2070. Reservations advised. AE, MC, V.*

$ The Diner. One of the best-known and most-appreciated stop-offs in the Napa Valley, this breakfast-centric eatery has local sausages and house potatoes that are not to be missed. Healthful versions of Mexican and American classics are served for dinner. ✕ *6476 Washington St.,* ☎ *707/944–2626. Reservations accepted for 6 or more; expect a wait for seating. No credit cards. Closed Mon.*

LODGING

Not surprisingly, staying in the Wine Country is expensive. Most inns, hotels, and motels are exquisitely appointed, and many are fully booked long in advance of the summer season. Since Santa Rosa is the largest population center in the area, it has the largest selection of rooms, many at moderate rates. Try there if you've failed to reserve in advance or have a limited budget. For those seeking something more homey (and also a bit more expensive), check out the dozens of bed-and-breakfast inns that have been established in the Victorian homes and old hotels of the Wine Country (the tourist bureaus of Sonoma and Napa counties both provide information and brochures). Breakfast, which is included in the price of B&Bs, often features local produce and specialties. Families should note, however, that small children are often discouraged as guests at B&Bs. For all accommodations in the area, rates are lower on weeknights and about 20% less in the winter.

CATEGORY	COST*
$$$$	over $100
$$$	$80–$100
$$	$50–$80
$	under $50

**All prices are for a standard double room, excluding 12% tax.*

Calistoga

$$$–$$$$ ★ Brannan Cottage Inn. This exquisite Victorian cottage with lacy white fretwork, large windows, and a shady porch is the only one of Sam Brannan's 1860 resort cottages still standing on its original site. Rooms, which have private entrances, are adorned with elegant stenciled friezes of stylized wildflowers. Full breakfast is included. *109 Wapoo Ave., 94515, ☎ 707/942–4200. 6 rooms. Breakfast room. MC, V (for room payment; reservations held by mailed check only).*

$$–$$$ Calistoga Spa and Inn. One of the oldest hot-springs spa resorts in Calistoga is a longtime favorite of northern Californians and tourists alike. Its rooms are functional but well maintained. The main lure is the spa itself, where there are separate fees. "The works" includes mud bath, steam room, mineral bath, blanket wrap, and massage. *1006 Washington St., 94515, ☎ 707/942–6269. 57 rooms. 4 mineral pools (83°–106°), poolside)steam bath, exercise room. MC, V.*

$$ Comfort Inn Napa Valley North. All the rooms in this motel have one king- or two queen-size beds, and many have vineyard views. Continental breakfast is included. There are rooms for nonsmokers and travelers with disabilities as well as discounts for senior citizens. Guests have access (for a fee) to a full-scale spa across the street. *1865 Lincoln Ave., 94515, ☎ 707/942–9400 or 800/228–5150, FAX 707/942–5262. 54 rooms with bath. Pool, hot tub, sauna, steam room. AE, D, DC, MC, V.*

$$ Mountain Home Ranch. This rustic ranch, established in 1913, is set on 300 wooded acres, with hiking trails, a creek, and a fishing lake. The seven cabins spread over the grounds are ideal for families; each has a full kitchen and bath, and the majority have wood-burning fireplaces. There is just one TV, in the dining room, and no phones. In summer, the modified American plan (full breakfast and dinner) is used; otherwise, Continental breakfast is included. Special children's rates are available. *3400 Mountain Home Ranch Rd., 94515 (north of town on Hwy. 128, left on Petrified Forest Rd., right on Mountain Home Ranch Rd., to end; 3 mi from Hwy. 128), ☎ 707/942–6616, FAX 707/942–9091. 6 rooms in main lodge, 11 cabins. 2 pools, tennis court. MC, V. Closed Dec. and Jan.*

Glen Ellen

$$$–$$$$ Beltane Ranch. On a slope of the Mayacamas range on the eastern side of the Sonoma Valley lies this 100-year-old house built by a retired San Francisco madam. Part of a working cattle and grape-growing ranch—the nearby Kenwood Winery has a chardonnay made from the ranch's grapes—the Beltane is surrounded by miles of trails through oak-studded hills. Innkeeper Rosemary Woods and her family, who have lived on the premises for 50 years, have stocked the comfortable living room with dozens of books on the area. The rooms, all with private baths and antique furniture, open onto the building's wraparound porch. *11775 Sonoma Hwy. (Hwy. 12), 95442, ☎ 707/996–6501.*

4 rooms. Tennis court, hiking, horseshoes. No credit cards, but personal checks accepted.

$$$–$$$$ **Glenelly Inn.** Just outside the hamlet of Glen Ellen, this sunny little establishment, built as an inn in 1916, offers all the comforts of home—including a hot tub in the garden. Mother and daughter innkeepers Ingrid and Kristi Hallamore serve breakfast in front of the common room's cobblestone fireplace and local delicacies in the afternoons. On sunny mornings, guests may eat outside, under the shady oak trees. ☐ *5131 Warm Springs Rd., 95442,* ☎ *707/996–6720. 8 rooms. Breakfast room, outdoor hot tub. MC, V.*

Healdsburg

$$$$ **Madrona Manor.** A splendid, three-story, 1881 Victorian mansion, carriage house, and outbuildings sit on 8 wooded and landscaped acres. Mansion rooms are recommended: All nine have fireplaces, and five contain the antique furniture of the original owner. The approach to the mansion leads under a stone archway and up a flowered hill; the house overlooks the valley and vineyards. Full breakfast is included, and a fine restaurant on the premises serves dinner (*see* Dining, *above*). Pets are allowed. ☐ *1001 Westside Rd., Box 818, 95448,* ☎ *707/433–4231 or 800/258–4003,* FAX *707/433–0703. 21 rooms. Restaurant, pool. AE, D, DC, MC, V.*

$$ **Best Western Dry Creek Inn.** Continental breakfast and a bottle of wine are complimentary at this three-story Spanish Mission–style motel, and there's also a coffee shop next door. Small pets are allowed. Midweek discounts are available, and direct bus service from San Francisco's airport can be arranged. ☐ *198 Dry Creek Rd., 95448,* ☎ *707/433–0300 or 800/528–1234; in CA, 800/222–5784;* FAX *707/433–1129. 102 rooms with bath. Pool, hot tub, coin laundry. AE, D, DC, MC, V.*

Napa

$$$$ **Napa Valley Marriott.** Since Marriott took over this former Sheraton motel, the lounge has been redecorated in Marriott's trademark sports-bar-and-grill style. A convenient restaurant remains on the premises, and live music is still featured in the lounge. Rooms are available for travelers with disabilities, and all guests are entitled to a pay-per-movie service. ☐ *3425 Solano Ave., 94558 (1 block west off Hwy. 29; take Redwood-Trancas exit),* ☎ *707/253–7433 or 800/228–9290,* FAX *707/258–1320. 191 rooms. Pool, hot tub, 2 tennis courts. AE, D, DC, MC, V.*

$$$$ **Silverado Country Club.** This luxurious 1,200-acre resort in the hills east of the town of Napa offers cottages, kitchen apartments, and one- to three-bedroom efficiencies, many with fireplaces. There are also two dining rooms, a lounge, a sundries store, eight pools, 22 tennis courts, and two championship golf courses designed by Robert Trent Jones. Fees are charged for golf, tennis, and bike rentals. ☐ *1600 Atlas Peak Rd., 94558 (6 mi east of Napa via Hwy. 121),* ☎ *707/257–0200 or 800/532–0500,* FAX *707/257–2867. 277 condo units. 3 restaurants. AE, D, DC, MC, V.*

$$$–$$$$ **Best Western Inn.** This immaculate modern redwood motel with spacious rooms has a restaurant on the premises, and same-day laundry and valet service. Suites are available, as are rooms for nonsmokers and travelers with disabilities. Small pets are allowed. ☐ *100 Soscol Ave., 94558 (from the direction of the Golden Gate Bridge, take Imola Ave./Hwy. 121 exit east from Hwy. 29 to junction of Hwy. 121 and Soscol),* ☎ *707/257–1930 or 800/528–1234,* FAX *707/255–0709. 68 rooms. Pool, spa, free parking. AE, D, DC, MC, V.*

$$$ **Chateau Hotel.** This French country inn–style modern motel offers Continental breakfast, in-room refrigerators, facilities for travelers with disabilities, and discounts for senior citizens. ☐ *4195 Solano Ave., 94558 (west of Hwy. 29; exit at Trower Ave.),* ☎ *707/253–9300 or 800/253–6272 in CA. 115 rooms. Refrigerators, pool, hot tub. AE, D, DC, MC, V.*

Rutherford

$$$$ ★ **Auberge du Soleil.** As you sit on a wisteria-draped deck sipping a late-afternoon glass of wine, with acres of terraced olive groves and rolling vineyards at your feet, you'll swear you're in Tuscany. ☐ *180 Rutherford Hill Rd., 94573,* ☎ *707/963–1211 or 800/348–5406,* FAX *707/963–8764. 50 rooms. Pool, hot tub, massage, steam room, 3 tennis courts, exercise room. AE, D, MC, V.*

$$$$ **Rancho Caymus Inn.** California-Spanish in style, this inn has well-maintained gardens and large suites with kitchens and whirlpool baths. Well-chosen details include decorative handicrafts, beehive fireplaces, tile murals, stoneware basins, and llama-hair blankets. ☐ *1140 Rutherford Rd., Box 78, 94573 (junction of Hwys. 29 and 128),* ☎ *707/963–1777 or 800/845–1777,* FAX *707/963–5387. 26 rooms. 2-night minimum Apr.–Nov. AE, DC, MC, V.*

St. Helena

$$$$ **Harvest Inn.** This Tudor-style inn with 47 fireplaces overlooks a 14-acre vineyard and hills beyond. Although the property is set close to a main highway, the lush landscaping and award-winning brick and stonework create an illusion of remoteness. Most rooms have wet bars, refrigerators, antique furnishings, and fireplaces. Pets are allowed in certain rooms for a $20 fee. Complimentary breakfast is served in the breakfast room and on the patio overlooking the vineyards. ☐ *1 Main St., 94574,* ☎ *707/963–9463 or 800/950–8466,* FAX *707/963–4402. 55 rooms. 2 pools, 2 hot tubs. AE, D, MC, V.*

$$$$ **Meadowood Resort.** Set on 256 wooded acres, with a golf course, croquet lawns, and hiking trails, this is a vacation getaway. The hotel is a rambling country lodge reminiscent of a turn-of-the-century New England seaside cottage, and separate bungalow suites are clustered on the hillside. Half the suites and some rooms have fireplaces. ☐ *900 Meadowood La., 94574,* ☎ *707/963–3646 or 800/458–8080,* FAX *707/963–3532. 82 rooms. 2 restaurants, bar, room service, 2 pools, hot tub, massage, sauna, steam room, 9-hole golf course, 7 tennis courts, croquet, health club. AE, D, DC, MC, V.*

$$$$ ★ **Wine Country Inn.** Surrounded by a pastoral landscape of vineyards and hills dotted with old barns and stone bridges, this New England–style inn feels peaceful. Rural antiques fill all of the rooms, most of which overlook the vineyards with either a balcony, patio, or deck. Most rooms have fireplaces, and some have private hot tubs. A hearty country breakfast is served buffet-style in the sun-splashed common room, and wine tastings are scheduled in the afternoons. With no TV, this is a place for readers and dreamers. ☐ *1152 Lodi La., 94574,* ☎ *707/963–7077 or 800/473–3463,* FAX *707/963–9018. 24 rooms. Pool, hot tub. MC, V.*

$$$–$$$$ **El Bonita Motel.** Hand-painted grapevines surround the windows at this roadside motel, and flower boxes overflow with new colors every season. While most rooms have private whirlpools, the outdoor pool is available only in summer. There are 16 rooms in the main motel and six smartly furnished garden rooms with kitchenettes. ☐ *195 Main St., 94574,* ☎ *707/963–3216 or 800/541–3284,* FAX *707/963–8838. 42 rooms. Kitchenettes, pool, hot tub, sauna. AE, D, DC, MC, V.*

$$$–$$$$ **Hotel St. Helena.** The oldest standing wooden structure in St. Helena, this restored 1881 hostelry aims at Old World comfort. It is completely furnished with antiques and decorated in rich, appealing tones of burgundy. Complimentary Continental breakfast is included. Smoking is discouraged—the only evidence of the New World. *1309 Main St., 94574, ☎ 707/963–4388, FAX 707/963–5402. 18 rooms, 4 with shared bath. AE, DC, MC, V.*

$$–$$$$ **Cinnamon Bear Bed and Breakfast.** Built in 1904 in the classic Arts and Crafts style, this house is decorated with the 1920s in mind. The beds are covered with antique quilts and the rooms are filled with toys of the period. Claw-foot tubs and a cozy fireplace in the parlor complete the mood. Full breakfast is included. Rooms for nonsmokers are available. *1407 Kearney St., 94574 (from Main St., Hwy. 29, turn west on Adams St., then 2 blocks to Kearney), ☎ 707/963–4653. 3 rooms. MC, V.*

Santa Rosa

$$$$ **Vintners Inn.** Set on 50 acres of vineyards, this French provincial inn has large rooms, many with wood-burning fireplaces, and a trellised sundeck. Breakfast is complimentary, and the noteworthy John Ash & Co. (*see* Dining, *above*) tempts guests to other meals. Guests can get discounted passes to an affiliated health club nearby, and VCRs can be rented for a small fee. *4350 Barnes Rd., 95403 (River Rd. exit west from U.S. 101), ☎ 707/575–7350 or 800/421–2584, FAX 707/575–1426. 44 rooms. Restaurant, hot tub. AE, DC, MC, V.*

$$$ ★ **Fountaingrove Inn.** A redwood sculpture and a wall of cascading water are the focal points of this elegant, comfortable inn in the heart of the Sonoma valley. Rooms have work spaces with modem jacks. Buffet breakfast is included, and an elegant restaurant offers a piano and a stellar menu. Guests have access to a nearby 18-hole golf course, a tennis court, and a health club nearby, for a fee. Golf packages are available, as are discounts for senior citizens. *101 Fountaingrove Pkwy. (near U.S. 101), 95403, ☎ 707/578–6101 or 800/222–6101, FAX 707/544–3126. 85 rooms. Restaurant, room service, pool, hot tub, meeting rooms. AE, DC, MC, V.*

$$–$$$ ★ **Los Robles Lodge.** This pleasant, relaxed motel has comfortable rooms overlooking a pool set into a grassy landscape. Pets are allowed, except in executive rooms, which have whirlpools. Rooms for nonsmokers are available. *1985 Cleveland Ave., 95401 (Steele La. exit west from Hwy. 101), ☎ 707/545–6330 or 800/255–6330, FAX 707/575–5826. 104 rooms. Restaurant, coffee shop, pool, outdoor hot tub, nightclub, coin laundry. AE, D, DC, MC. V.*

$$ **Best Western Hillside Inn.** Ten of the rooms at this small, cozy, landscaped motel have balconies or patios. Kitchenettes and suites are available. *2901 4th St., 95409 (at Farmers La., 2 mi east off U.S. 101 on Hwy. 12), ☎ 707/546–9353 or 800/528–1234. 35 rooms. Restaurant, pool, sauna, shuffleboard. AE, DC, MC, V.*

Sonoma

$$$$ **Sonoma Mission Inn & Spa.** This classy 1920s resort blends Mediterranean and old-California architecture for a look that's early Hollywood: Gloria Swanson would fit right in. Despite its unlikely location off the main street of tiny, down-home Boyes Hot Springs, the hotel's extensive spa facilities and treatments attract guests from all over. Ask for a room in one of the newer buildings: They are much larger and more attractive than the smallish standard rooms in the main building. Don't miss the pool, which is heated by warm mineral water pumped from underground wells, or the well-equipped fitness pavilion. *18140 Hwy. 12 (just north of Sonoma), Box 1447, 95476, ☎ 707/938–9000 or*

800/358–9022; in CA, 800/862–4945; FAX 707/996–5358. 170 rooms. 2 restaurants, 2 bars, coffee shop, 2 pools, 2 hot tubs, sauna, steam room, 2 tennis courts, health club. AE, DC, MC, V.

$$$$ **Thistle Dew Inn.** A half block from Sonoma Plaza, this turn-of-the-century Victorian home is filled with collector-quality arts-and-crafts furnishings. Owners Larry and Norma Barnett live on the premises, and Larry cooks up creative, sumptuous breakfasts and serves hors d'oeuvres in the evenings. Four of the six rooms have private entrances and decks, and all have queen-size beds with antique quilts, private baths, and air-conditioning. Welcome bonuses include a hot tub and free use of the inn's bicycles. Smoking is not permitted indoors. *171 W. Spain St., 95476, ☎ 707/938–2909 or 800/382–7895 in CA. 6 rooms. AE, MC, V.*

$$$–$$$$ **Best Western Sonoma Valley Inn.** Just one block from the historical town plaza, this comfortable hotel features balconies, handcrafted furniture, wood-burning fireplaces, and whirlpool baths. Continental breakfast and complimentary quarter bottles of wine are included. Kitchenettes and rooms for nonsmokers are available. *550 2nd St. W, 95476, ☎ 707/938–9200 or 800/334–5784, FAX 707/938–0935. 72 rooms. Pool, hot tub, coin laundry. AE, D, DC, MC, V.*

$$$–$$$$ ★ **El Dorado Hotel.** In 1990 Claude Rouas, the owner of Napa's acclaimed Auberge du Soleil, opened this small hotel with its popular restaurant, Ristorante Piatti (*see* Dining, *above*). Rooms reflect Sonoma's mission era, with Mexican-tile floors and white walls. The best rooms are numbers 3 and 4, which have big balconies overlooking Sonoma Plaza. Only four of the rooms—the ones in the courtyard by the pool—have bathtubs; the rest have showers only. *405 1st St. W (on Sonoma Plaza), ☎ 707/996–3030 or 800/289–3031, FAX 707/996–3148. 27 rooms. Restaurant, pool. AE, MC, V.*

$$–$$$ **Vineyard Inn.** Built as a roadside motor court in 1941, this inn with red-tile roofs brings a touch of Mexican village charm to an otherwise lackluster location at the junction of two main highways. Set in the heart of Sonoma's Carneros region, across from two vineyards, it is the closest lodging to Sears Point Raceway. Rooms have queen-size beds. Continental breakfast is provided. *23000 Arnold Dr. (at the junction of Hwys. 116 and 121), 95476, ☎ 707/938–2350 or 800/359–4667. 9 rooms, 3 suites with wet bar, 1 resident suite with kitchenette. Breakfast room. AE, MC, V.*

Yountville

$$$$ **Napa Valley Lodge.** Spacious rooms overlook the vineyards and the valley in this hacienda-style lodge, which has a tile roof, covered walkways, balconies, patios, and colorful gardens. Freshly brewed coffee is provided to guests, along with a Continental breakfast and the morning paper. Some rooms have fireplaces; others have wet bars. *2230 Madison St. at Hwy. 29, 94599, ☎ 707/944–2468 or 800/368–2468, FAX 707/944–9362. 55 rooms. Refrigerators, pool, hot tub, sauna, exercise room. AE, D, DC, MC, V.*

$$$$ **Vintage Inn.** All the rooms at this luxurious inn have fireplaces, whirlpool baths, refrigerators, private verandas or patios, hand-painted fabrics, window seats, and shuttered windows. A welcome bottle of wine, Continental breakfast with champagne, and afternoon tea are all complimentary. In season, bike rentals and hot-air ballooning are available. *6541 Washington St., 94599, ☎ 707/944–1112 or 800/351–1133, FAX 707/944–1617. 80 rooms with bath. Pool, spa, tennis court. AE, D, DC, MC, V.*

THE ARTS AND NIGHTLIFE

Galleries throughout the Wine Country display the work of local artists: painters, sculptors, potters, and jewelry makers. The **Luther Burbank Performing Arts Center** in Santa Rosa (50 Mark West Springs Rd., 95403, ☏ 707/546–3600; box office open Mon.–Sat. noon–6 and approximately 1 hr before most events) offers a full events calendar featuring concerts, plays, and other performances by locally and internationally known artists. Send away for the calendar in advance if you're planning a trip. For the symphony, ballet, and other live theater performances throughout the year, call the **Spreckels Performing Arts Center** in Rohnert Park (☏ 707/584–1700 or 707/586–0936; box office open Tues.–Sat. noon–5). The most highly recommended theater groups among the valley's 30 ensembles include **Cinnebar** in Petaluma (☏ 707/763–8920), **Main Street Theatre** in Sebastopol (☏ 707/823–0177), **SRT** (Summer Repertory Theatre) in Santa Rosa (☏ 707/527–4307), and the **Actors Theatre,** also in Santa Rosa (☏ 707/523–4185). In addition to the sounds at local music clubs and the larger hotels, wineries often schedule concerts and music festivals during the summer. Popular music aficionados might also try the **Mystic Theatre** in Petaluma, where Chris Isaak sometimes plays (☏ 707/765–6665), and movie lovers can take in a foreign or first-run film at the **Raven Theatre** in Healdsburg (☏ 707/433–5448). The **Sebastiani Theatre,** on historic Sonoma square (☏ 707/996–2020), features first-run movies and hosts special events during the year.

Many believe that the best way to savor evenings in the Wine Country is to linger over an elegant dinner, preferably on a patio under the stars, at one of the restaurants for which the area is justly famous.

WINE COUNTRY ESSENTIALS

Arriving and Departing

By Bus

Greyhound-Trailways (☏ 800/231–2222) runs buses—two per day—from the Transbay Terminal at 1st and Mission streets to Sonoma and Santa Rosa.

By Car

Three major paths cut through the Wine Country: U.S. 101 north from Santa Rosa, Highways 12 and 121 through Sonoma County, and Highway 29 north from Napa.

From San Francisco, cross the Golden Gate Bridge, go north on U.S. 101, east on Highway 37, and north on Highway 121. To reach many of the Sonoma wineries listed above, head north at 121's junction with Highway 12. Other Sonoma wineries are along Highway 121 as it proceeds east toward Highway 29. Head north at Highway 29 to reach the Napa Valley's wineries. Another route runs over the San Francisco–Oakland Bay Bridge and along I–80 to Vallejo, where Highway 29 leads north to Napa.

From the east, take I–80 and then turn northwest on Highway 12 for a 10-minute drive through a hilly pass to Highway 29. From the north, take U.S. 101 south to Geyserville, and follow Highway 128 southeast into the Napa Valley.

By Plane

The closest large airports are in San Francisco and Oakland.

Getting Around

By Bus

Sonoma County Area Transit (☎ 707/585–7516) and **Napa Valley Transit** (☎ 707/255–7631) provide local transportation between towns in the Wine Country.

By Car

Although traffic on the two-lane country roads can be heavy, the best way to get around the Wine Country is by private car. Rentals are available at the airports and in San Francisco, Oakland, Santa Rosa, and Napa. The **Rider's Guide** (484 Lake Park Ave., Suite 255, Oakland 94610, ☎ 510/653–2553) produces tapes about the history, landmarks, and wineries of the Sonoma and Napa valleys that you can play in your car (maps also provided). The tapes are available at some local bookstores, including Rand McNally Map & Travel at 595 Market, or can be ordered directly from Rider's Guide for $12.95 (Napa tape) and $11.95 (Sonoma tape), plus $2 postage.

Guided Tours

Full-day guided tours of the Wine Country usually include lunch and cost about $50. The guides, some of whom are winery owners themselves, know the area well and may show you some lesser-known cellars. Reservations are usually required.

Gray Line (350 8th St., San Francisco 94103, ☎ 415/558–9400) has bright-red double-decker buses that tour the Wine Country.

Great Pacific Tour Co. (518 Octavia St., San Francisco 94102, ☎ 415/626–4499) offers full-day tours of Napa and Sonoma, including a summer picnic lunch and a winter restaurant lunch, in passenger vans that seat 14.

HMS Tours (707 4th St., Santa Rosa 95404, ☎ 707/526–2922 or 800/367–5348) offers customized tours of the Wine Country, for four or more people, by appointment only.

Napa Valley Wine Train (1275 McKinstry St., Napa 94559, ☎ 707/253–2111 or 800/427–4124) allows you to enjoy lunch, dinner, or a weekend brunch on one of several restored 1915 Pullman railroad cars that now run between Napa and St. Helena on tracks that were formerly owned by the Southern Pacific Railroad. Round-trip fare costs $24 during dinner and $30 during brunch and lunch; meals of three to five courses cost between $26 and $47.50. During the winter, service is limited to Thursday–Sunday. There is a special car for families with children on weekend brunch trips and weekday lunch trips.

Wine Country Wagons (Box 1069, Kenwood 95452, ☎ 707/833–2724, FAX 707/833–1041) offers four-hour horse-drawn wagon tours that include three wineries and end at a private ranch, where a lavish buffet lunch is served. Tours depart daily at 10 AM, May through October; advance reservations are required.

Important Addresses and Numbers

Emergencies

Dial **911** for **fire, police, ambulance,** and **paramedics.**

Visitor Information

Calistoga Chamber of Commerce (1458 Lincoln Ave., Calistoga 94515, ☎ 707/942–6333).

Healdsburg Chamber of Commerce (217 Healdsburg Ave., Healdsburg 95448, ☏ 707/433–6935 or 800/648–9922 in CA).

Napa Valley Conference and Visitors Bureau (1310 Napa Town Center, Napa 94559, ☏ 707/226–7459).

St. Helena Chamber of Commerce (1080 Main St., Box 124, St. Helena 94574, ☏ 707/963–4456 or 800/767–8528, FAX 707/963–5396).

Sonoma County Convention and Visitors Bureau (5000 Roberts Lake Rd., Rohnert Park 94928, ☏ 707/586–8100 or 800/326–7666, FAX 707/586–8111).

Sonoma Valley Visitors Bureau (453 1st St. E, Sonoma 95476, ☏ 707/996–1090).

5 San Francisco

San Francisco is a sophisticated city offering world-class hotels and the greatest concentration of excellent restaurants in California. The town has a reputation as the "kook" capital of the United States, yet it's the country's number-one tourist destination. Why? To use the vernacular, the vibe here is cool, from North Beach coffeehouses to Chinatown tea emporiums, Golden Gate Park, and Haight Street's head shops (yes, they're still around). People in San Francisco know how to have a good time; the high spirits can't help but rub off on visitors.

IN ITS FIRST LIFE, SAN FRANCISCO was little more than a small, well-situated settlement. Founded by Spaniards in 1776, it was prized for its natural harbor, so commodious that "all the navies of the world might fit inside it," as one visitor wrote. The discovery of gold in the Sierra foothills in 1848 transformed the sleepy little settlement into a city of 30,000. As millions of dollars' worth of gold was panned and blasted out of the hills, a "western Wall Street" sprang up. Just as gold production began to taper off, prospectors turned up a rich vein of silver in Virginia City, Nevada, and surrounding areas. San Francisco, the nearest financial center, prospered again. Nowadays, the city prides itself on its role as a Pacific Rim capital, and overseas investment has become a vital part of its financial life. In terms of both geography and culture, San Francisco is about as close as you can get to Asia in the continental United States.

Loose, tolerant, and even licentious are words that are used to describe San Francisco; bohemian communities thrive here. As early as the 1860s, the "Barbary Coast"—a collection of taverns, whorehouses, and gambling joints along Pacific Avenue close to the waterfront—was famous, or infamous. North Beach, the city's Little Italy, became the home of the Beat Movement in the 1950s. Lawrence Ferlinghetti's City Lights, a bookstore and publishing house, still stands on Columbus Avenue. The Haight-Ashbury district became synonymous with hippiedom, giving rise to such legendary bands as the Jefferson Airplane, Big Brother and the Holding Company (fronted by Janis Joplin), and the Grateful Dead. Thirty years later, the Haight's history and its name still draw neo-hippies, as well as skinheads and post-punkers with black lips and blue hair.

Technically speaking, San Francisco is only California's fourth-largest city, behind Los Angeles, San Diego, and nearby San Jose. But that statistic is misleading: The Bay Area, which stretches from the bedroom communities north of Oakland and Berkeley south through Silicon Valley (the cluster of Peninsula cities that have become the center of America's computer industry) and San Jose, is really one continuous megacity, with San Francisco as its heart—its hub.

The Gay and Lesbian Freedom Day Parade, each June, vies with the Chinese New Year Parade, in February, as the city's most elaborate. They both get competition from Japantown's Cherry Blossom Festival, in April; the Columbus Day and St. Patrick's Day parades; the late-May Carnaval in the Hispanic Mission District; and the May Day march, a labor celebration in a labor town. The mix of ethnic, economic, social, and sexual groups can be bewildering, but the city's residents—whatever their origin—face it with aplomb and even gratitude (though, to be sure, this wasn't always the case). Everybody in San Francisco has an opinion about where to get the best burrito or the hottest Szechuan eggplant or the strongest cappuccino, and even the most staid citizens have learned how to appreciate good camp. Nearly everyone smiles on the fortunate day they arrived on, or were born on, this windy, foggy patch of peninsula.

EXPLORING

By Toni Chapman

Updated by Dennis Harvey

You could live in San Francisco a month and ask no greater entertainment than walking through it," waxed Inez Hayes Irwin, the author of *The Californiacs,* an effusive 1921 homage to the state of California and the City by the Bay. Her claim remains as true as ever today: As in the '20s, touring on foot is the best way to experience this diverse metropolis.

San Francisco is a relatively small city, with just over 750,000 residents nested on a 46.6-square-mile tip of land between San Francisco Bay and the Pacific Ocean. San Franciscans cherish the city's colorful past, and many older buildings have been spared from demolition and nostalgically converted into modern offices and shops. Longtime locals rue the sites that got away—spectacular railroad and mining-boom-era residences lost in the '06 quake, the elegant Fox Theater, Playland at the Beach. But despite acts of God, the indifference of developers, and the mixed record of the city's Planning Commission, much of architectural and historical interest remains. Bernard Maybeck, Julia Morgan, Willis Polk, and Arthur Brown, Jr., are among the noted architects whose designs still grace the city's downtown and neighborhoods.

San Francisco's charms are great and small. First-time visitors won't want to miss Golden Gate Park, the Palace of Fine Arts, the Golden Gate Bridge, or a cable-car ride on Nob Hill. A walk down the Filbert Steps or through Macondray Lane, though, or a peaceful hour gazing east from Ina Coolbrith Park can be equally inspiring.

It's no accident that the San Francisco Bay Area has been a center for the environmental movement. An awareness of geographical setting permeates life in San Francisco, where views of the surrounding mountains, ocean, and bay are ubiquitous. Much of the city's neighborhood vitality comes from the distinct borders provided by its hills and valleys, and many areas are so named: Nob Hill, Twin Peaks, Eureka Valley, the East Bay. San Francisco neighborhoods are self-aware, and they retain strong cultural, political, and ethnic identities. Locals know this pluralism is the real life of the city. Experiencing San Francisco means visiting the neighborhoods: the colorful Mission District, gay Castro, countercultural Haight Street, serene Pacific Heights, bustling Chinatown, and still-exotic North Beach.

The famed 40-plus hills can be a problem for drivers who are new to the terrain. Cable cars, buses, and trolleys can take you to or near many of the area's attractions. Many of the following exploring tours include information on public transportation.

Union Square

Numbers in the margin correspond to points of interest on the Downtown San Francisco map.

★ Since 1850 **Union Square** has been the heart of San Francisco's downtown. Its name derives from a series of violent pro-Union demonstrations staged in this hilly area just prior to the Civil War. Union Square is where you will find the city's finest department stores and its most elegant boutiques. There are 40 hotels within a three-block walk of the square, and the downtown theater district is nearby.

The square itself is a 2.6-acre oasis planted with palms, boxwood, and seasonal flowers, and peopled with a kaleidoscope of characters: office workers sunning and brown-bagging, street musicians, several very vocal preachers, and a fair share of panhandlers. Throughout the year, the square hosts numerous public events: fashion shows, free noontime concerts, ethnic celebrations, and noisy demonstrations. Auto and bus traffic is often gridlocked on the four streets bordering the square. Post, Stockton, and Geary are one-way, while Powell runs in both directions until it crosses Geary, where it then becomes one-way to Market Street. Union Square covers a convenient but costly four-story underground garage. Close to 3,000 cars use it on busy holiday shopping and strolling days.

1 Any visitor's first stop should be the **San Francisco Visitors Information Center** (☏ 415/391–2000) on the lower level of Hallidie Plaza at Powell and Market streets. It is open daily (except holidays), and the multilingual staff will answer specific questions as well as provide maps, brochures, and information on daily events. Visitors can pick up coupons for substantial savings on tourist attractions, as well as pamphlets (and, depending on the season, discount vouchers) for most of the downtown hotels. The office provides 24-hour recorded information (☏ 415/391–2001).

2 The **cable-car terminus** at Powell and Market streets is the starting point for two of the three operating lines. The Powell-Mason line climbs up Nob Hill, then winds through North Beach to Fisherman's Wharf. The Powell-Hyde car also crosses Nob Hill, but then continues up Russian Hill and down Hyde Street to Victorian Park across from the Buena Vista Cafe and near Ghirardelli Square.

There are 39 cars in the three lines, and the network covers just 12 miles. Most of the cars date from the last century, although the cars and lines had a complete overhaul during the early 1980s. There are seats for about 30 passengers, with usually that number standing or straphanging. If possible, plan your cable-car ride for mid-morning or mid-afternoon during the week to avoid crowds. In summertime there are often long lines to board any of the three systems. Buy your ticket ($2, good in one direction) at nearby hotels or at the police/information booth near the turnaround. (*See* Getting Around *in* San Francisco Essentials, *below*.)

A two-block stroll, heading north of the cable-car terminus along
3 bustling Powell Street, leads to **Union Square.** At center stage, the Victory Monument by Robert Ingersoll Aitken commemorates Commodore George Dewey's victory over the Spanish fleet at Manila in 1898. The 97-foot Corinthian column, topped by a bronze figure symbolizing naval conquest, was dedicated by Theodore Roosevelt in 1903 and withstood the 1906 earthquake.

After the earthquake and fire in 1906, the square was dubbed "Little St. Francis" because of the temporary shelter erected for residents of the St. Francis Hotel. Actor John Barrymore was among the guests pressed into volunteering to stack bricks in the square. His uncle, thespian John Drew, remarked, "It took an act of God to get John out of bed and the United States government to get him to work."

4 The **Westin St. Francis Hotel,** on the southwest corner of Post and Powell, was built in 1904 and was gutted by the 1906 disaster. The hotel has known its share of notoriety as well. Silent comedian Fatty Arbuckle's career plummeted faster than one of the St. Francis's glass-walled elevators after a wild 1921 party in one of the hotel's suites went awry. In 1975 Sara Jane Moore, standing among a crowd outside the hotel, attempted to shoot then-president Gerald Ford. As might be imagined, no plaques commemorate these events in the establishment's lobby. The ever-helpful staff will, however, gladly direct you to the traditional teatime ritual—or, if you prefer, to champagne and caviar—in the dramatic art deco Compass Rose lounge. Elaborate Chinese screens, secluded seating alcoves, and soothing background music make it an ideal time-out after frantic shopping or sightseeing.

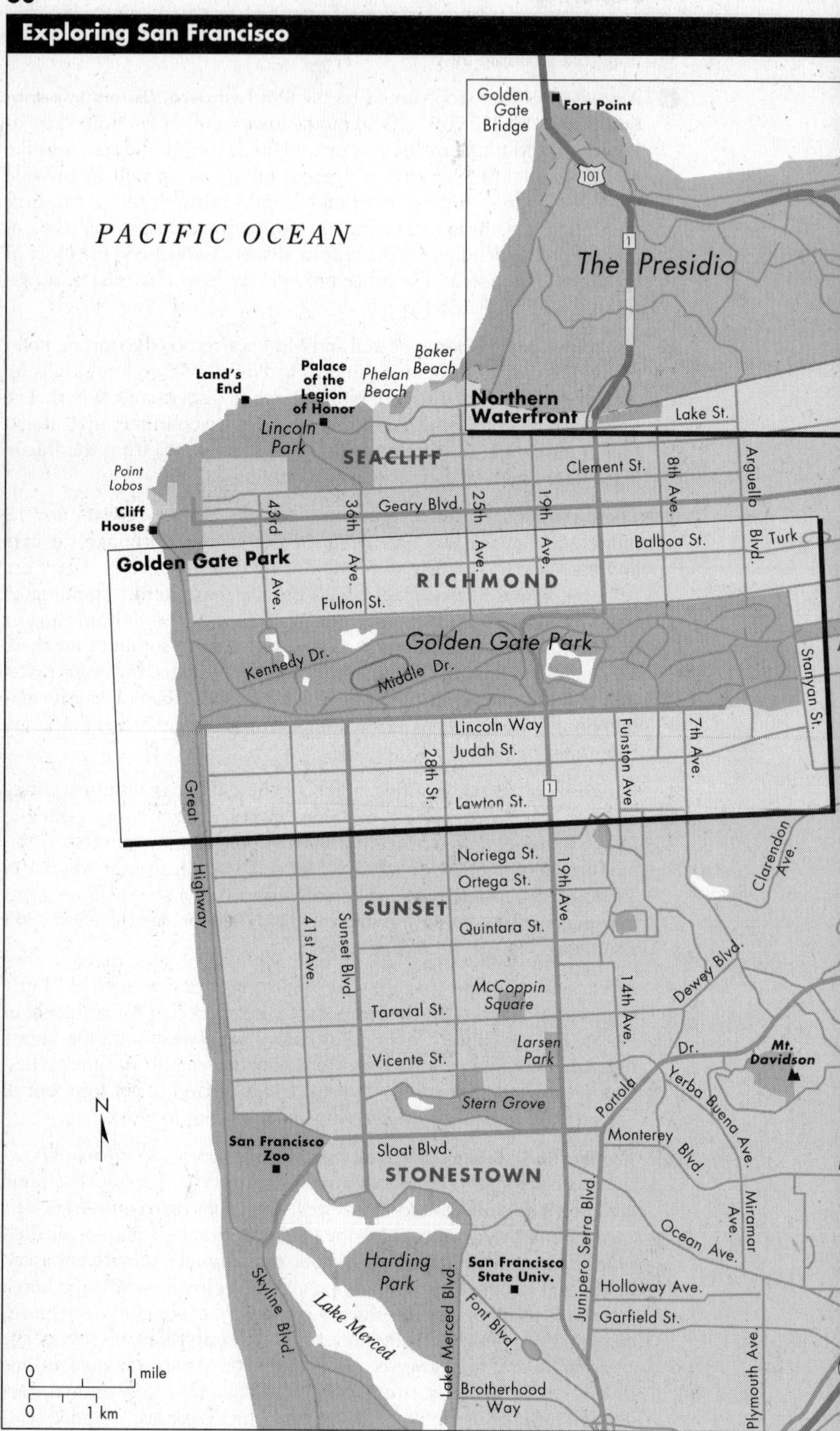
Golden Gate Bridge
Fort Point
101
PACIFIC OCEAN
The Presidio
Baker Beach
Phelan Beach
Land's End
Palace of the Legion of Honor
Northern Waterfront
Lake St.
Lincoln Park
SEACLIFF
Clement St.
8th Ave.
Arguello Blvd.
Point Lobos
Cliff House
Geary Blvd.
43rd Ave.
36th Ave.
25th Ave.
19th Ave.
Balboa St.
Turk
Golden Gate Park
RICHMOND
Fulton St.
Golden Gate Park
Kennedy Dr.
Middle Dr.
Stanyan St.
Lincoln Way
Judah St.
28th St.
Funston Ave
7th Ave.
Lawton St.
Great Highway
Noriega St.
Ortega St.
19th Ave.
Clarendon Ave.
SUNSET
41st Ave.
Sunset Blvd.
Quintara St.
McCoppin Square
Dewey Blvd.
14th Ave.
Taraval St.
Larsen Park
Vicente St.
Dr.
Mt. Davidson
Stern Grove
Portola
Yerba Buena Ave.
N
San Francisco Zoo
Sloat Blvd.
Monterey Blvd.
STONESTOWN
Junipero Serra Blvd.
Miramar Ave.
Ocean Ave.
Harding Park
Lake Merced Blvd.
San Francisco State Univ.
Holloway Ave.
Skyline Blvd.
Lake Merced
Font Blvd.
Garfield St.
Plymouth Ave.
0 1 mile
0 1 km
Brotherhood Way

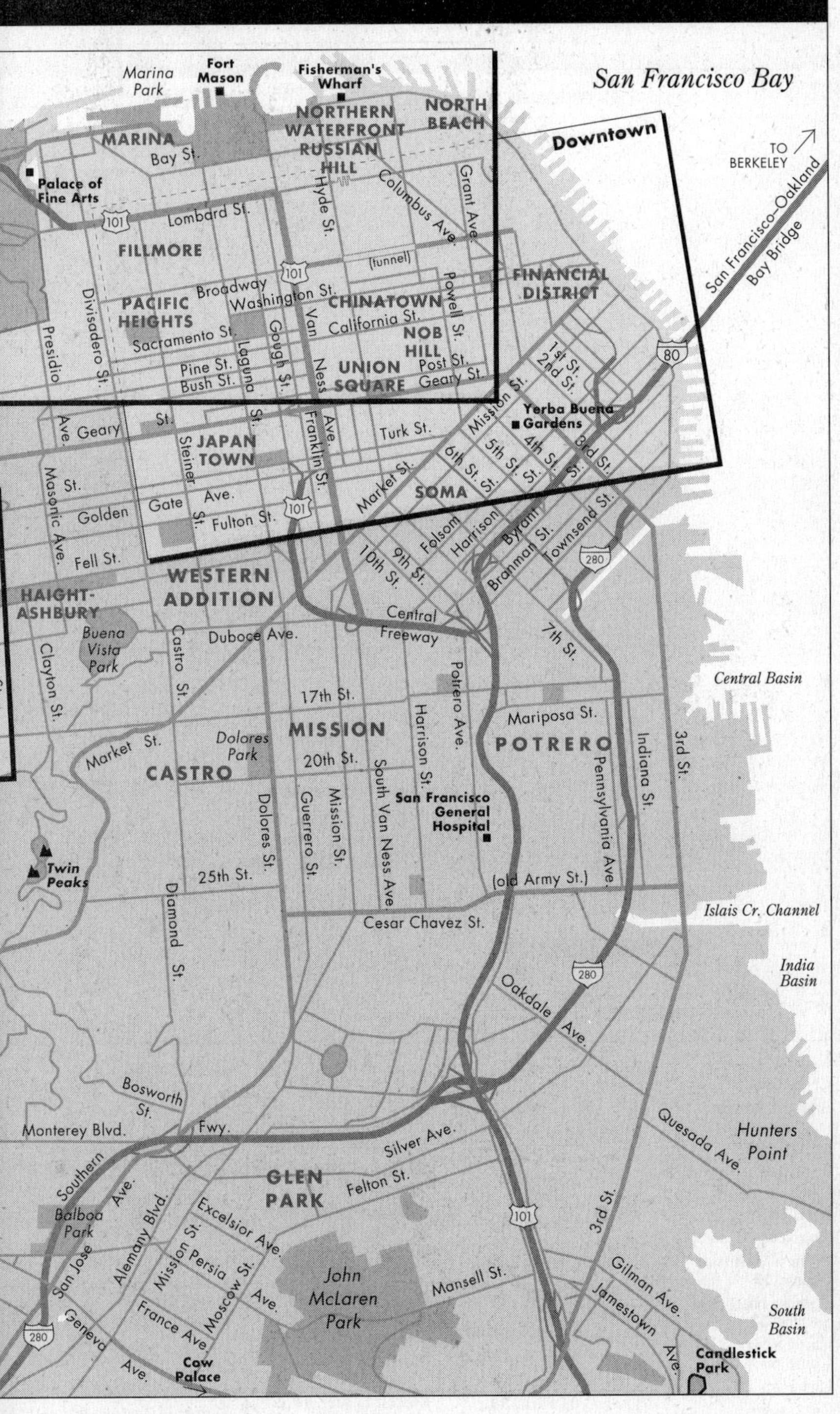
San Francisco Bay
Downtown
TO BERKELEY
San Francisco–Oakland Bay Bridge
Marina Park
Fort Mason
Fisherman's Wharf
NORTHERN WATERFRONT
NORTH BEACH
RUSSIAN HILL
MARINA
Bay St.
Palace of Fine Arts
Lombard St.
Columbus Ave.
Grant Ave.
Hyde St.
FILLMORE
(funnel)
FINANCIAL DISTRICT
Broadway
Washington St.
CHINATOWN
Powell St.
PACIFIC HEIGHTS
California St.
NOB HILL
Presidio
Divisadero St.
Sacramento St.
Laguna
Gough St.
Van Ness Ave.
UNION SQUARE
Post St.
Geary St.
Pine St.
Bush St.
1st St.
2nd St.
Mission St.
Yerba Buena Gardens
Geary St.
JAPAN TOWN
Steiner St.
Franklin St.
Turk St.
6th St.
5th St.
4th St.
3rd St.
Masonic Ave.
Golden Gate Ave.
Fulton St.
Market St.
SOMA
Folsom
Harrison
Bryant
Townsend St.
Fell St.
10th St.
9th St.
Brannan St.
WESTERN ADDITION
HAIGHT-ASHBURY
Buena Vista Park
Castro St.
Duboce Ave.
Central Freeway
7th St.
Clayton St.
17th St.
Potrero Ave.
Central Basin
Mariposa St.
MISSION
Harrison St.
Dolores Park
POTRERO
Indiana St.
3rd St.
Market St.
20th St.
Pennsylvania Ave.
CASTRO
South Van Ness Ave.
San Francisco General Hospital
Dolores St.
Guerrero St.
Mission St.
Twin Peaks
25th St.
(old Army St.)
Islais Cr. Channel
Diamond St.
Cesar Chavez St.
India Basin
Oakdale Ave.
Bosworth St.
Quesada Ave.
Hunters Point
Monterey Blvd.
Fwy.
Silver Ave.
Southern
GLEN PARK
Felton St.
Balboa Park
Ave.
Alemany Blvd.
Excelsior Ave.
3rd St.
San Jose
Mission St.
Persia Ave.
Moscow St.
John McLaren Park
Mansell St.
Gilman Ave.
Jamestown Ave.
South Basin
Geneva Ave.
France Ave.
Cow Palace
Candlestick Park
101
80
280

Downtown San Francisco

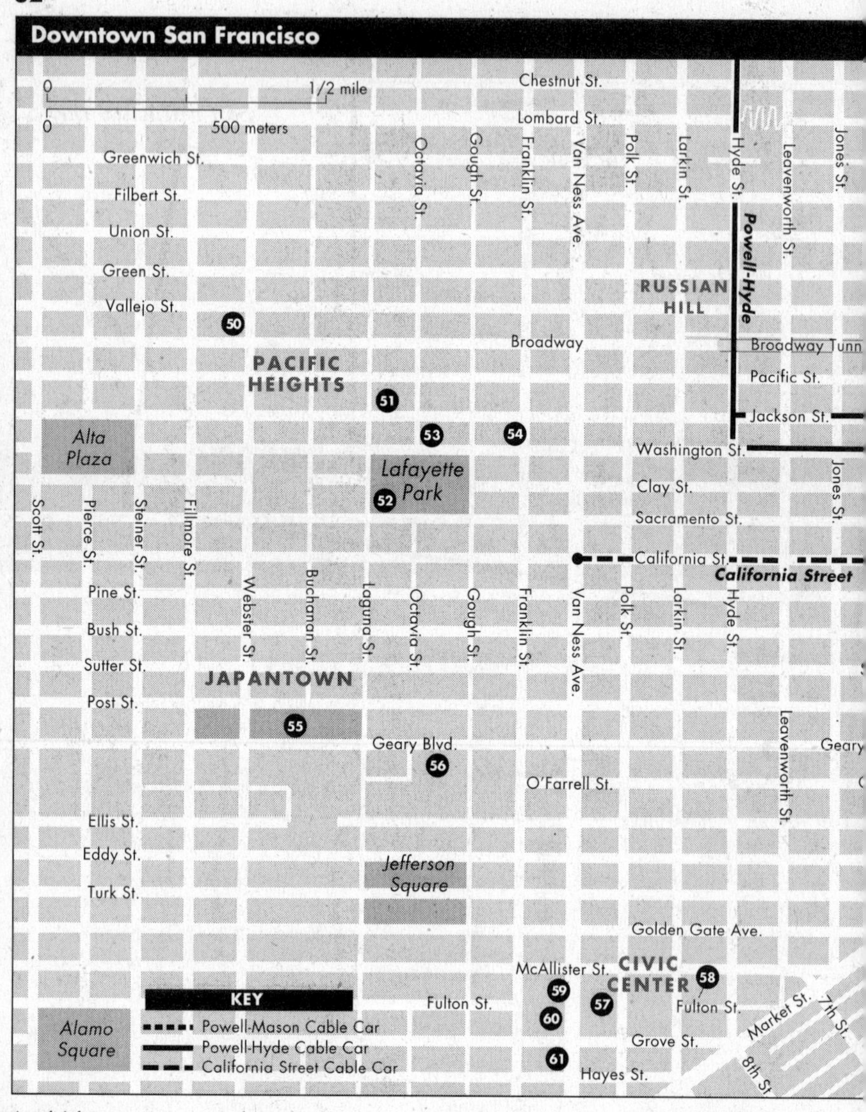

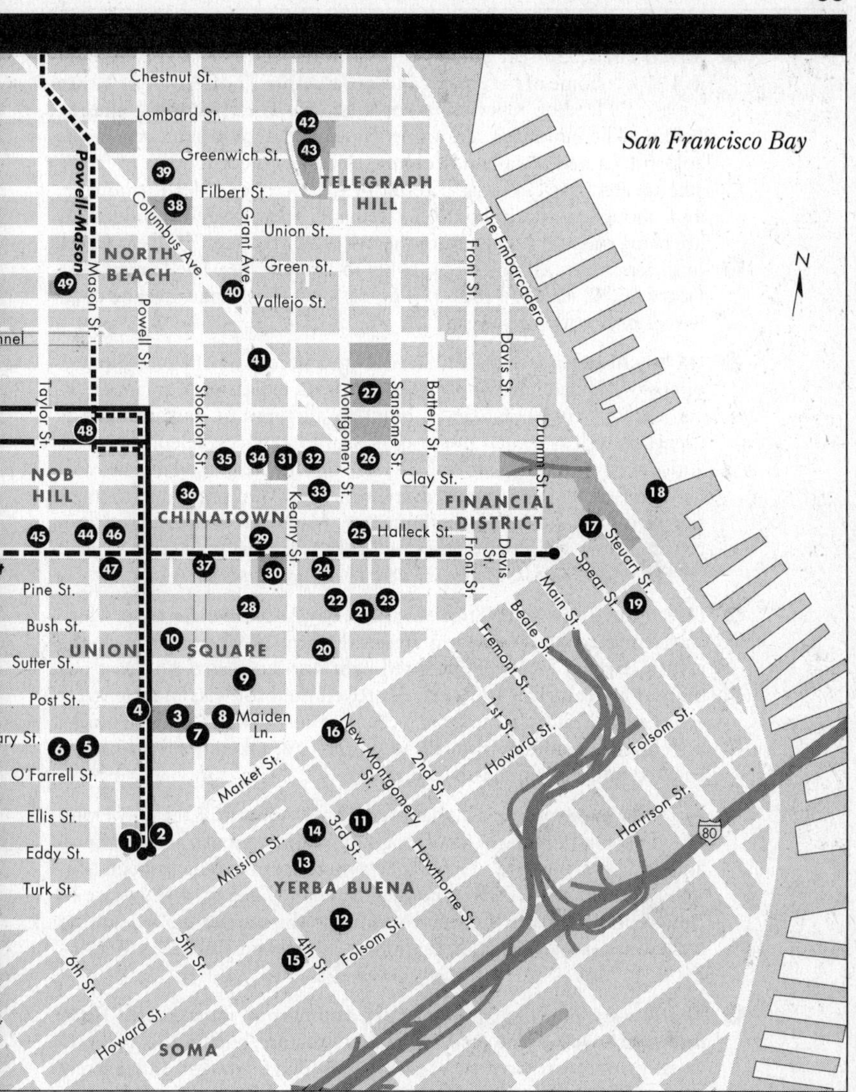

San Francisco Bay
Chestnut St.
Lombard St.
Greenwich St.
Filbert St.
Union St.
Green St.
Vallejo St.
TELEGRAPH HILL
NORTH BEACH
Powell-Mason
Columbus Ave.
Grant Ave.
Mason St.
Powell St.
Taylor St.
Stockton St.
Montgomery St.
Sansome St.
Battery St.
Front St.
Davis St.
Drumm St.
The Embarcadero
NOB HILL
CHINATOWN
FINANCIAL DISTRICT
Clay St.
Halleck St.
Kearny St.
Steuart St.
Spear St.
Main St.
Beale St.
Fremont St.
1st St.
Pine St.
Bush St.
Sutter St.
Post St.
O'Farrell St.
Ellis St.
Eddy St.
Turk St.
UNION SQUARE
Maiden Ln.
Market St.
New Montgomery St.
2nd St.
3rd St.
Howard St.
Folsom St.
Harrison St.
Mission St.
YERBA BUENA
Hawthorne St.
4th St.
5th St.
6th St.
SOMA
80

Both the Geary and Curran theaters are a few blocks west on Geary
5 Street. The 1,038-seat **Geary** (415 Geary St., ☎ 415/749–2228), built
in 1910, is home of the American Conservatory Theater, one of North
America's leading repertory companies (*see* The Arts and Nightlife,
below). The building's serious neoclassical design is lightened by the
colorful, carved terra-cotta columns depicting a cornucopia of fruits.
The theater was closed as a result of the October 1989 earthquake,
and, though the main box office remains open, current productions
are being run at the Stage Door theater (420 Mason St.) and elsewhere
6 until repairs are complete, probably in January '96. The **Curran** (445
Geary St., ☎ 415/474–3800) is noted for showcasing traveling companies of Broadway shows.

7 **TIX Bay Area** has a booth on the Stockton Street side of Union Square, opposite Maiden Lane. It provides half-price day-of-performance tickets (cash or traveler's checks only) to all types of performing-arts events, as well as regular full-price box-office services. Telephone reservations are not accepted for half-price tickets. Also available are $10 Golden Gate Park Cultural Passes, which provide admission to all of the park's museums at a discount rate. MUNI Passports (short-term tourist passes for all city buses and cable cars) are sold here as well. ☎ *415/433–7827.* ⏲ *Tues.–Thurs. 11–6, Fri. and Sat. 11–7.*

8 Directly across Stockton Street from TIX Bay Area is **Maiden Lane,** which runs from Stockton to Kearny streets. Known as Morton Street in the raffish Barbary Coast era, this red-light district reported at least one murder a week. The 1906 fire destroyed the brothels, and the street emerged as Maiden Lane, now a chic and costly mall. The two blocks are closed to vehicles from 11 AM until 5 PM; takeout snacks can be enjoyed under umbrella-shaded tables.

Note **140 Maiden Lane**: This handsome brick structure is the only Frank Lloyd Wright building in San Francisco. With its circular interior ramp and skylights, it is said to have been a model for the Guggenheim Museum in New York. It now houses the Circle Gallery, a showcase of contemporary artists. Be sure to examine the unique limited-edition art jewelry designed by internationally acclaimed Erté. ☎ *415/989–2100.* ⏲ *Mon.–Sat. 10–6, Sun. noon–5.*

9 At 301 Sutter Street, on the corner of Grant Avenue, is the colorful **Ham-
mersmith Building.** The small beaux arts structure, built in 1907, is noteworthy for its extensive use of glass and its playful design. Sutter Street
is lined with prestigious art galleries, antiques dealers, smart hotels,
and noted designer boutiques. Art deco aficionados will want to head
one block up Sutter Street for a peek at the striking medical-dental of-
10 fice building at **450 Sutter Street.** Handsome Mayan-inspired designs
cover both the exterior and interior surfaces of the 1930 terra-cotta
skyscraper.

South of Market (SoMa) and the Embarcadero

The vast tract of downtown land **South of Market** Street along the waterfront and west to the Mission District is also known by the acronym SoMa (inspired by New York City's south-of-Houston SoHo). For years the industrial South of Market area west of 4th Street was a stomping ground for alternative artists. Although many artists moved away when urban renewal started in earnest, they still hang out in SoMa and show their work in several galleries on the cutting edge of San Francisco's art scene, among them **Capp Street Project** (525 2nd St., ☎ 415/495–7101).

★ 11 The **San Francisco Museum of Modern Art** (SFMOMA) took center stage in the SoMa arts scene in January 1995, winning immediate international acclaim for its adventuresome programming, which includes traveling exhibits and film/video series. The strong permanent collection—including works by Matisse, Picasso, O'Keeffe, Frida Kahlo, Jackson Pollock, and Warhol—is now seen to much greater advantage than the old Civic Center building allowed. The striking Modernist structure, designed by Swiss architect Mario Botta, features a stepped-back burnt-sienna brick facade and a central tower constructed of alternating bands of black and white stone. Inside, natural light from the tower floods the central atrium and some of the museum's galleries. A grand staircase leads from the atrium up to four floors of galleries. Accessible from the street, SFMOMA's café provides a comfortable, reasonably priced refuge for drinks and light meals. *151 3rd St.,* ☎ *415/357–4000.* ☛ *$7 adults, $3.50 senior citizens and students over 12; free 1st Tues. of month.* ⏲ *Daily 11–6, Thurs. until 9 (*☛ *1/2-price 5–9); closed major holidays.*

12 **Moscone Convention Center,** on Howard Street between 3rd and 4th streets, the site of the 1984 Democratic convention, is distinguished by a contemporary glass-and-girder lobby at street level (all exhibit space is underground) and a monolithic, column-free interior. In 1992 the center finished a $150 million expansion project that doubled its size and incorporated a new building with underground exhibit space, across Howard Street.

★ 13 Above the new exhibit space is the **Yerba Buena Gardens** complex (in the block surrounded by 3rd, Mission, Howard, and 4th streets). A large expanse of green is surrounded by a circular walkway lined with benches and sculptures. A waterfall memorial to Martin Luther King, Jr., is the focal point of the gardens; above it are two restaurants and an overhead walkway that traverses Howard Street to Moscone Cen-
14 ter's main entrance. On the eastern side of the block is the **Center for the Arts** (701 Mission St., ☎ 415/978–2787), which showcases dance, music, performance, theater, visual arts, film, video, and installations—from the community-based to the international.

15 Just across 4th Street from the Moscone Center is the **Ansel Adams Center,** which showcases historical and contemporary photography, as well as an extensive permanent collection of Adams's work. *250 4th St.,* ☎ *415/495–7000.* ☛ *$4 adults, $3 students, $2 ages 12–17 and senior citizens.* ⏲ *Tues.–Sun. 11–5, 1st Thurs. of month 11–8.*

Heading east on Market Street toward the waterfront, the venerable
16 **Sheraton Palace Hotel** (at the corner of New Montgomery St., ☎ 415/392–8600) has a storied past, some of which is recounted in small cases off the main lobby; President Warren Harding died here while still in office in 1923. Worth a look is the glass-domed Garden Court restaurant on the ground floor. Maxfield Parrish's wall-size painting, *The Pied Piper,* graces the wall in the hotel's Pied Piper Bar.

Market Street, which bisects the city at an angle, has consistently challenged San Francisco's architects. One of the most intriguing responses sits diagonally across Market Street from the Palace. The tower of the **Hobart Building** (582 Market St.) combines a flat facade and oval sides. Farther east on Market Street between Sutter and Post is another classic solution, Charles Havens's triangular **Flatiron Building** (540–548 Market St.). At **388 Market** is a sleek, modern variation on the theme designed by Skidmore, Owings, and Merrill.

Facing the Embarcadero is the **Hyatt Regency Hotel** (Embarcadero 5),
17 part of the huge **Embarcadero Center** complex. The Hyatt, designed by John Portman, is noted for its huge lobby and 20-story hanging garden. On the waterfront side of the hotel is **Justin Herman Plaza,** where arts-and-crafts shows and performances by street musicians take place on weekends year-round.

After the 1989 Loma Prieta earthquake, the Embarcadero freeway was torn down, making the foot of Market Street clearly visible for the first
18 time in 30 years. The trademark of the port is the quaint **Ferry Building** that stands at the Embarcadero. The clock tower is 230 feet high and was modeled by Arthur Page Brown after the campanile of Seville's cathedral. The four great clock faces on the tower, powered by the swinging of a 14-foot pendulum, stopped at 5:17 on the morning of April 18, 1906, and stayed that way for 12 months. The 1896 building survived the quake and is now the headquarters of the Port Commission and the World Trade Center.

A waterfront promenade that extends from this point to the San Francisco–Oakland Bay Bridge is great for jogging, in-line skating, watching sailboats on the bay, or enjoying a picnic. Check out the beautiful pedestrian pier adjacent to Pier 1, with its old-fashioned lamps, wrought-iron benches, and awe-inspiring views of the bay. Ferries from behind the Ferry Building sail to Sausalito, Larkspur, and Tiburon.

Continuing down the promenade, notice the curiously styled Audiffred Building at the corner of Mission Street and the Embarcadero. (Boulevard restaurant occupies the first floor.) It was built by a homesick gentleman as a reminder of his native France. A few doors down, an old brick YMCA building is now the Harbor Court Hotel. Cross the Embarcadero at Howard Street, and turn right on Steuart Street.

Across Steuart Street from the main entrance to the hotel is the new—
19 and old—**Rincon Center.** Two modern office-apartment towers overlook a small shopping and restaurant mall behind an old post office built in the Streamline Moderne Style. A stunning five-story rain column draws immediate attention inside the mall. In the "Historic Lobby" (which formerly housed the post office's walk-up windows) is a mural by Anton Refregier. One of the largest WPA-era art projects, its 27 panels depict California life, from the days when Indians were the state's sole inhabitants through World War I.

The Financial District and Jackson Square

The heart of San Francisco's Financial District is Montgomery Street. It was here in 1848 that Sam Brannan proclaimed the historic gold discovery on the American River. At that time, all the streets below Montgomery between California and Broadway were wharves. At least 100 ships were abandoned by frantic crews and passengers all caught up in the '49 gold fever. Many of the wrecks served as warehouses or were used as foundations for new constructions.

The Financial District is roughly bordered by Kearny Street on the west, Washington Street on the north, and Market Street on the southeast. On workdays it is a congested canyon of soaring skyscrapers, gridlock traffic, and bustling pedestrians. Evenings and weekends are peaceful times to admire the distinctive architecture. Unfortunately, the museums in corporate headquarters are closed at those times.

20 Head down Sutter Street toward the Financial District to see the **Hallidie Building** (130 Sutter St., between Kearny and Montgomery Sts.),

named for cable-car inventor Andrew Hallidie. The building, best viewed from across the street, is believed to be the world's first all-glass curtain-wall structure. Willis Polk's revolutionary design hangs a foot beyond the reinforced concrete of the frame.

21 The **Mills Building and Tower** (220 Montgomery St.) was the outstanding prefire building in the Financial District, erected in 1891. The original Burnham and Root design was white marble and brick, but it was actually built as a 10-story all-steel construction with its own electric plant in the basement. Damage from the 1906 fire was slight; its walls were somewhat scorched but were easily refurbished. Two compatible additions east on Bush Street were added in 1914 and 1918 by Willis Polk, and in 1931 a 22-story tower completed the design.

22 The **Russ Building** (235 Montgomery St.) was called "the skyscraper" when it was built in 1927. The Gothic design was modeled after the Chicago Tribune Tower and until the 1960s was San Francisco's tallest—at just 31 stories.

Ralph Stackpole's monumental 1930 granite sculptural groups, *Earth's*
Fruitfulness and *Man's Inventive Genius,* flank another imposing
23 structure, the 301 Pine Street **Pacific Stock Exchange** (which dates
from 1915), on the south side of Pine Street at Sansome Street. The
Stock Exchange Tower around the corner at 155 Sansome Street, a 1930
modern classic by architects Miller and Pfleuger, features an art deco
gold ceiling and black marble-walled entry.

24 The granite-and-marble **Bank of America** building dominates the territory bounded by California, Pine, Montgomery, and Kearny streets. The 52-story polished red granite complex is crowned by a chic cocktail lounge and restaurant. Inside, impressive original art is displayed, while outdoor plazas showcase avant-garde sculptures. In the mall, a massive abstract black granite sculpture designed by the Japanese artist Masayuki has been dubbed the "Banker's Heart" by local wags.

Soaring 52 stories above the Financial District, the Bank of America's **Carnelian Room** (☎ 415/433–7500) offers elegant and pricey dining with a nighttime view of the city lights. This is an excellent spot for a drink at sunset. By day, the room is the exclusive Banker's Club, open to members or by invitation.

25 A quick but interesting stop is the **Wells Fargo Bank History Museum,** which displays samples of nuggets and gold dust from major mines, a mural-size map of the Mother Lode, original art by western artists Charlie Russell and Maynard Dixon, mementos of the poet bandit Black Bart, and letters of credit and old bank drafts. The showpiece is the red, century-old Concord stagecoach that in the mid-1850s carried 18 passengers from St. Joseph, Missouri, to San Francisco in three weeks. *420 Montgomery St.,* ☎ *415/396–2619.* ☛ *Free.* ⏲ *Banking days 9–5.*

26 The city's most-photographed high-rise is the 853-foot **Transamerica Pyramid** at 600 Montgomery Street, between Clay and Washington streets at the end of Columbus Avenue. Designed by William Pereira and Associates in 1972, the controversial $34 million symbol has become more acceptable to local purists over time. There is a public viewing area on the 27th floor, but call building management (☎ 415/983–4100) first—recent elevator-system renovations have closed the floor for an undetermined period. A redwood grove along the east side of the building is a nice place to unwind.

In the Gay '90s San Francisco earned the title "the Wickedest City in
the World." The saloons, dance halls, cheap hotels, and brothels of its
Barbary Coast attracted sailors and gold rushers. Most of this red-light
district was destroyed in the 1906 fire; what remains is now part of
27 **Jackson Square.** A stroll through this district recalls some of the romance and rowdiness of early San Francisco.

Directly across Washington Street from the Transamerica redwood grove is Hotaling Place, a tiny alley east of and parallel to Montgomery Street. The alley is named for the head of the **A. P. Hotaling and Company whiskey distillery,** which was located at 451 Jackson. A plaque on the side of the building repeats a famous query about its surviving the quake: "If, as they say, God spanked the town/for being over-frisky,/Why did He burn the churches down/and spare Hotaling's Whisky?" The **Ghirardelli Chocolate Factory** was once housed at 415 Jackson.

Chinatown

San Francisco is home to one of the largest Chinese communities out-
★ side Asia. While Chinese culture is visible throughout the city, **Chinatown,** bordered roughly by Bush, Kearny, Powell and Broadway,
remains the community's spiritual and political center. Recent immigrants from Southeast Asia have added new character and life to the
neighborhood.

Visitors usually enter Chinatown through the green-tiled dragon-
28 crowned **Chinatown Gate** at Bush Street and Grant Avenue. To best
savor this district, explore it on foot (it's not far from Union Square),
even though you may find the bustling, noisy, colorful stretches of Grant
and Stockton streets north of Bush difficult to navigate. Parking is extremely hard to find, and traffic is impossible. As in Hong Kong, most
families shop daily for fresh meats, vegetables, and bakery products.
The street shines with good-luck crimson and gold; giant beribboned
floral wreaths mark the opening of new bakeries, bazaars, and banks.
Note the dragon-entwined lampposts, the pagoda roofs, and street signs
with Chinese calligraphy.

Dragon House Oriental Fine Arts and Antiques (455 Grant Ave.), several doors up from the Chinatown gate, is an excellent place to start your Chinatown visit. Its collection of ivory carvings, ceramics, and jewelry dates back 2,000 years and beyond. The shop's display window is a history lesson in itself.

29 The handsome brick **Old St. Mary's Church** at Grant and California
streets served as the city's Catholic cathedral until 1891. Diagonally
30 across California Street from the church is **St. Mary's Park,** a tranquil
setting for local sculptor Beniamino (Benny) Bufano's heroic stainless-
steel and rose-color granite *Sun Yat-sen.* The 12-foot statue of the founder
of the Republic of China was installed in 1937 on the site of the Chinese leader's favorite reading spot during his years of exile in San
Francisco.

Head down Grant Avenue, turn right on Clay Street, continue one block
31 to Kearny Street, and turn left to reach **Portsmouth Square.** This is
where Captain John B. Montgomery raised the American flag in 1846.
Note the bronze galleon atop a 9-foot granite shaft. Designed by Bruce
Porter, the sculpture was erected in 1919 in memory of Robert Louis Stevenson, who often visited the site during his 1879–80 residence. In the morning, the park is crowded with people performing solemn t'ai chi exercises.
By noontime, dozens of men huddle around mah-jongg tables.

32 From here you can walk to the **Chinese Cultural Center,** which frequently displays the work of Chinese-American artists as well as traveling exhibits of Chinese culture. The center also offers $15 Saturday-afternoon (2 PM) walking tours of historic points in Chinatown. *In the Holiday Inn, 750 Kearny St., ☎ 415/986–1822. ☛ Free. ⏲ Tues.–Sat. 10–4.*

In an alley parallel to and a half block south of the side of the Holi-
33 day Inn, the **Chinese Historical Society** traces the history of Chinese immigrants and their contributions to the state's rail, mining, and fishing industries. *650 Commercial St., parallel to Clay St. off Kearny, ☎ 415/391–1188. ☛ Free. ⏲ Tues.–Sat. noon–4.*

The original Chinatown burned down after the 1906 earthquake; the first building to set the style for the new Chinatown is near Portsmouth
34 Square, at 743 Washington Street. The three-tier pagoda, called the **Old Chinese Telephone Exchange** (now the Bank of Canton), was built in 1909. The exchange's operators were renowned for their "tenacious memories," about which the San Francisco Chamber of Commerce boasted in 1914: "These girls respond all day with hardly a mistake to calls that are given (in English or one of five Chinese dialects) by the name of the subscriber instead of by his number—a mental feat that would be practically impossible to most high-schooled American misses."

TIME OUT Dim sum, a variety of pastries filled with meat, fish, and vegetables, is the Chinese version of a smorgasbord. In most dim sum restaurants, stacked food-service carts patrol the premises; customers select from the varied offerings, and the final bill is tabulated by the number of different saucers on the table. A favorite on Pacific Avenue, two blocks north of Washington Street, is **New Asia.** *772 Pacific Ave., ☎ 415/391–6666. ⏲ For dim sum 8:30 AM–3 PM.*

Waverly Place is noted for ornate painted balconies and Chinese tem-
35 ples. **Tien Hou Temple** was dedicated to the Queen of the Heavens and the Goddess of the Seven Seas by Day Ju, one of the first three Chinese to arrive in San Francisco in 1852. As you enter the temple (it's on the third floor), elderly ladies can often be seen preparing "money" to be burned as offerings to various Buddhist gods. A (real) dollar placed in the donation box on their table will bring a smile. Notice the wood carving suspended from the ceiling, depicting a number of gods at play. *125 Waverly Pl. ⏲ Daily 10–4.*

Throughout Chinatown you will notice herb shops that sell an array of Chinese medicines. The **Great China Herb Co.** (857 Washington St.), around the corner from the Tien Hou Temple, is one of the largest. All day, sellers fill prescriptions from local doctors, measuring exact amounts of tree roots, bark, flowers, and other ingredients with their hand scales, and adding up the bill on an abacus (an ancient calculator). The shops also sell "over-the-counter" treatments for the common cold, heartburn, hangovers, and even impotence.

The other main thoroughfare in Chinatown, where locals shop for everyday needs, is Stockton Street, which parallels Grant Avenue. This is the real heart of Chinatown. Housewives jostle one another as they pick apart the sidewalk displays of Chinese vegetables. Double-parked trucks unloading crates of chickens or ducks add to the all-day traffic jams.
36 Noteworthy architecture includes the elaborate **Chinese Six Companies** (843 Stockton St.), with its curved roof tiles and elaborate cornices. Around the corner at 965 Clay Street is the handsome, redbrick **Chinatown YWCA,** designed by architect Julia Morgan, who was also responsible for the famous Hearst Castle at San Simeon, California.

It's an easy 15-minute walk back downtown to Union Square via the
37 **Stockton Street Tunnel,** which runs from Sacramento Street to Sutter
Street.

North Beach and Telegraph Hill

Among the first immigrants to Yerba Buena during the early 1840s were young men from the northern provinces of Italy. Many settled in what is now known as North Beach (and which really was a beach back then). The Genoese started the still-active fishing industry in the newly renamed boomtown of San Francisco, as well as a much-needed produce business. Later the Sicilians emerged as leaders of the fishing fleets and eventually as proprietors of the seafood restaurants lining Fisherman's Wharf. Meanwhile, their Genoese cousins established banking and manufacturing empires.

38 **Washington Square** may well be the daytime social heart of what was
once considered "Little Italy"—though in the early morning, the dominating sight is a hundred or more older Asian neighbors engaged in
t'ai chi. Nevertheless, by mid-morning groups of conservatively dressed
elderly Italian men arrive to sun and sigh at the state of their immediate world. Nearby, laughing playmates of a half-dozen cultures race
through the grass with Frisbees or colorful kites. Camera-toting tourists
39 focus their lenses on the adjacent Romanesque splendor of **Sts. Peter
and Paul,** often called the Italian Cathedral: Completed in 1924, its
twin-turreted terra-cotta towers are local landmarks.

Surrounding streets are packed with savory Italian delicatessens, bakeries, Chinese markets, coffeehouses, and ethnic restaurants. Wonderful aromas fill the air; coffee beans roasted at **Graffeo** at 735 Columbus Avenue are shipped to customers all over the United States. Stop by the **Panelli Brothers deli** (1419 Stockton St.) for a memorable, reasonably priced meat-and-cheese sandwich to go. **Florence Ravioli Factory** (1412 Stockton St.) features garlic sausages, prosciutto, and mortadella, as well as 75 tasty cheeses and sandwiches to go. **Victoria** (1362 Stockton St.) has heavenly cream puffs and eclairs. Around the corner on Columbus Avenue is **Molinari's,** noted for the best salami in town and a mouthwatering array of salads: Be prepared for a wait.

40 South of Washington Square and just off Columbus Avenue is the **St. Francis of Assisi Church** (610 Vallejo St.). This 1860 Victorian Gothic building stands on the site of the frame parish church that served the gold-rush Catholic community.

Over the years, North Beach has attracted creative individualists. The
Beat Movement of the 1950s was born, grew up, flourished, then fal-
tered here. Though most Beat gathering places are gone and few of the
original leaders remain, poet Lawrence Ferlinghetti still holds court at
41 his **City Lights Bookstore** (261 Columbus Ave.).

TIME OUT Cafés are a way of life in North Beach. **Caffe Puccini** (411 Columbus Ave.) could be Italy: Few of the staff speak English. Their caffé latte (coffee, chocolate, cinnamon, and steamed milk) and strains of Italian operas recall *Roman Holiday*.

42 **Telegraph Hill** rises from the east end of Lombard Street to about 300 feet and is capped with the landmark Coit Tower, dedicated as a monument to the city's volunteer firefighters. Early during the Gold Rush, an eight-year-old who would become one of the city's most memorable eccentrics, Lillie Hitchcock Coit, arrived on the scene. Legend relates that at age 17, "Miss Lil" deserted a wedding party and chased down

the street after her favorite engine, Knickerbocker No. 5, clad in her bridesmaid finery. She was soon made an honorary member of the Knickerbocker Company and after that always signed herself "Lillie Coit 5" in honor of her favorite fire engine. Lillie died in 1929 at the age of 86, leaving the city about $100,000 of her million-dollar-plus estate to "expend in an appropriate manner . . . to the beauty of San Francisco." The money was used to build Coit Tower.

The Greenwich stairs lead up to Coit Tower from Filbert Street, and there are steps down to Filbert Street on the opposite side of Telegraph Hill. Views are superb en route, but most visitors should either taxi up to the tower or take the Muni Bus 39-Coit at Washington Square. To catch the bus from Union Square, walk to Stockton and Sutter streets, board the Muni No. 30, and ask for a transfer to use at Washington Square (Columbus Ave. and Union St.) to board the No. 39-Coit. Public parking is limited at the tower, and on holidays and weekends long lines of cars and buses wind up the narrow road.

★ 43 **Coit Tower** stands as a monument not only to Lillie Coit and the city's firefighters but also to the influence of the political and radical Mexican muralist Diego Rivera. Fresco was Rivera's medium, and it was his style that unified the work of most of the 25 artists who painted the murals of labor-union workers in the tower. The murals were commissioned by the U.S. government as a Public Works of Art Project, and the artists were paid $38 a week. Ride the elevator to the top of the hill to enjoy the panoramic view of both the Bay Bridge and Golden Gate Bridge; directly offshore is the famous Alcatraz, and just behind it is Angel Island.

Walk down the Greenwich Steps to Montgomery Street, and turn right. At the corner where the Filbert Steps intersect, you'll find an Art Deco masterpiece at 1360 Montgomery Street. Descend the Filbert Steps amid roses, fuchsias, irises, and trumpet flowers—courtesy of Grace Marchant, who labored for nearly 30 years to create one of San Francisco's hidden treasures.

Nob Hill

Nob Hill is within walking distance of Union Square. Once called the Hill of Golden Promise, it became Nob Hill during the 1870s when "the Big Four"—Charles Crocker, Leland Stanford, Mark Hopkins, and Collis Huntington—built their hilltop estates. It is still home to many of the city's elite as well as four of San Francisco's finest hotels.

In 1882 Robert Louis Stevenson called Nob Hill "the hill of palaces." But the 1906 earthquake and fire destroyed all the palatial mansions. The shell of one survived: The Flood brownstone (1000 California St.) was built by the Comstock silver baron in 1886 at a reputed cost of $1.5 million. In 1909 the property was purchased by the prestigious
44 **Pacific Union Club.** The 45-room exclusive club remains a bastion of the wealthy and powerful. Adjacent is a charming small park noted for its frequent art shows.

45 Neighboring **Grace Cathedral** (1051 Taylor St.) is the seat of the Episcopal church in San Francisco. The soaring Gothic structure, built on the site of Charles Crocker's mansion, took 53 years to build. The gilded bronze doors at the east entrance were taken from casts of Ghiberti's Gates of Paradise on the baptistery in Florence. Architect Lewis Hobart's grand design was finally achieved in 1995 after workers completed a sweeping set of stairs leading up to the doors. The cathedral's superb rose window is illuminated at night.

46 The **Fairmont Hotel** (California and Mason Sts.) has a legendary history. Its dazzling opening was delayed a year by the 1906 quake, but since then the marble palace has hosted presidents, royalty, and local nabobs. Prices are up a bit, though: On the eve of World War I, you could get a room for as low as $2.50 per night—meals included. Nowadays, prices run as high as $6,000—this being for a night in the eight-room penthouse suite that was showcased regularly in the TV series *Hotel*. The apartment building on the corner of Sacramento Street across from the Fairmont is also a media star. In 1958 it was a major location in Alfred Hitchcock's *Vertigo* and was more recently (1993) featured in the BBC production of Armistead Maupin's homage to San Francisco, *Tales of the City*.

On the Fairmont's other flank at California and Mason streets is the **Mark**
47 **Hopkins Inter-Continental Hotel,** which is remembered fondly by thousands of World War II veterans who jammed the Top of the Mark lounge (*see* Skyline Bars *in* Nightlife, *below*) before leaving for overseas duty.

48 The **Cable Car Museum,** at the corner of Washington and Mason streets, is a brief but engaging stopover on the way to Russian Hill. On exhibit are photographs, old cars, and other memorabilia from the system's 121-year history, and an overlook allows visitors to observe the cables that haul the city's cars in action. *1201 Mason St., at Washington St., ☎ 415/474-1887. ☛ Free. ⏲ Nov.–Mar., daily 10–5; Apr.–Oct., daily 10–6; closed some holidays.*

If you're in the mood for another hill, walk four blocks north on Mason Street to Vallejo Street and you'll be on Russian Hill. Slowly
49 start climbing the Vallejo Steps up to attractive **Ina Coolbrith Park.** An Oakland librarian and poet, Ina introduced both Jack London and Isadora Duncan to the world of books. For years she entertained literary greats in her Macondray Lane home near the park. In 1915 she was named poet laureate of California.

Pacific Heights

★ **Pacific Heights** forms an east–west ridge along the city's northern flank from Van Ness Avenue to the Presidio and from California Street to the bay. Some of the city's most expensive and dramatic real estate, including mansions and town houses priced at $1 million and up, are located here. Grand old Victorians, expensively face-lifted, grace tree-lined streets—although here and there glossy, glass-walled high-rise condos obstruct the view.

A good place to begin a tour of the neighborhood is at the corner of Webster Street and Pacific Avenue. You can get here from Union Square by taking Muni Bus 3 from Sutter and Stockton to Jackson and Fillmore streets. Head one block east on Jackson to Webster Street.

North on Webster Street, at 2550, is the massive Georgian brick mansion built in 1896 for William B. Bourn, who had inherited a Mother Lode gold mine. The architect, Willis Polk, was responsible for many of the most traditional and impressive commercial and private homes built from the prequake days until the early 1920s. (Be sure to see his 1917 Hallidie Building, 130 Sutter Street; *see* Financial District and Jackson Square, *above*. Polk also designed Bourn's Woodside estate, Filoli, *see* Filoli and Stanford *in* Excursions, below.)

Broadway uptown, unlike its North Beach stretch, is home to some important addresses, including a consulate and, on the northwest corner,
50 two classic showplaces. **2222 Broadway** is the three-story Italian Re-

naissance palace built by Comstock mine heir James Flood, later donated to a religious order. Ten years later, the Convent of the Sacred Heart purchased the Baroque brick Grant house (2220 Broadway) and both serve as school quarters today. A second top-drawer school, the Hamlin (2120 Broadway), occupies another Flood property.

Return east on Broadway past the Hamlin School and turn right (south) on Buchanan Street, then left on Jackson Street to Laguna Street.
51 The massive red sandstone **Whittier Mansion,** at 2090 Jackson Street, was one of the most elegant 19th-century houses in the state, built so solidly that only a chimney toppled over during the 1906 earthquake.

52 One block south on Laguna, at Washington Street, is **Lafayette Park,** a four-block-square oasis for sunbathers and dog-and-Frisbee teams. During the 1860s, a tenacious squatter, Sam Holladay, built himself a big wooden house in the center of the park. Holladay even instructed city gardeners as if the land were his own and defied all orders to leave. The house was finally torn down in 1936.

As you walk east on Washington street along the edge of Lafayette Park,
53 the most imposing residence is the formal French **Spreckels Mansion** (2080 Washington St.). Sugar heir Adolph Spreckels's wife, Alma, was so pleased with her house that she commissioned architect George Applegarth to design the city's European museum, the California Palace of the Legion of Honor in Lincoln Park. Alma, one of the city's great iconoclasts, is the model for the bronze figure atop the Victory Monument in Union Square.

Continue east on Washington Street two more blocks to Franklin
54 Street and turn left. At 2007 Franklin is the handsome **Haas-Lilienthal House.** Built in 1886, at an original cost of $18,500, this grand Queen Anne survived the 1906 earthquake and fire and is the only fully furnished Victorian open to the public. The carefully kept rooms offer an intriguing glimpse of turn-of-the-century taste and lifestyle. A small display of photographs on the bottom floor proves that this elaborate house was modest compared with some of the giants that fell to the fire. It is operated by the Foundation for San Francisco's Architectural Heritage, whose volunteers conduct tours of the house two days a week, as well as an informative two-hour tour of the eastern portion of Pacific Heights on Sunday afternoon. ☏ *415/441–3004.* ☛ *$5 adults, $3 senior citizens and children under 12.* ⏲ *Wed. noon–4 (last tour at 3:15), Sun. 11–5 (last tour at 4:15). Pacific Heights tours ($5 adults, $3 senior citizens and children) leave the house Sun. at 12:30 PM.*

The **Coleman House** at 1701 Franklin Street is an impressive twin-turreted Queen Anne mansion built for a gold-rush mining and lumber baron. At 1818 and 1834 California are two stunning **Italianate Victorians.** A block farther at 1990 California is the Victorian-era **Atherton House,** perhaps the oddest combination of architectural elements—among them Queen Anne and Stick-Eastlake—in all of Pacific Heights.

Japantown

Japanese-Americans began gravitating to the neighborhood known as the Western Addition prior to the 1906 earthquake; the early immigrants who arrived about 1860 named San Francisco Soko. After the 1906 fire had destroyed wooden homes in other parts of the stricken city, many survivors settled in the Western Addition. By the 1930s the pioneers had opened shops, markets, meeting halls, and restaurants and established Shinto and Buddhist temples. Japantown was virtually disbanded during World War II when many of its residents, including second- and third-generation Americans, were "relocated" in camps. Today **Japantown,** or "Nihonmachi," is centered on the slopes of Pacific Heights, north of Geary Boulevard, between Fillmore and Laguna streets. The Nihonmachi Cherry Blossom Festival is celebrated two weekends every April with a calendar of ethnic events.

To reach Japantown from Union Square, take Muni Bus 38-Geary or Bus 2, 3, or 4 on Sutter Street, westbound to Laguna. Japantown and the Western Addition are at their best during the day. Though the hotel, restaurant, and Kabuki movie complex are relatively safe in the evenings, the proximity of the often-hostile street gangs in the Western Addition poses a threat late at night, when cabs are scarce.

The buildings around the traffic-free **Japan Center Mall** between Sutter and Post streets are of the shoji screen school of architecture, and
Ruth Asawa's origami fountain sits in the middle. The mall faces the
55 three-block-long, 5-acre **Japan Center.** The three-block cluster includes
an 800-car public garage and shops and showrooms selling Japanese
products: electronic products, cameras, tapes and records, porcelains,
pearls, and paintings.

The center is dominated by its Peace Plaza and Pagoda located between the Tasamak Plaza and Kintetsu buildings. The five-tier, 100-foot Peace Pagoda overlooks the plaza, where seasonal festivals are held. The pagoda, which draws on the tradition of miniature round pagodas dedicated to eternal peace by Empress Koken in Nara more than 1,200 years ago, was designed by the Japanese architect Yoshiro Taniguchi "to convey the friendship and goodwill of the Japanese to the people of the United States." A cultural bridge modeled after Florence's Ponte Vecchio spans Webster Street, connecting the Kintetsu and Kinokuniya buildings.

TIME OUT At **Isobune** (☎ 415/563–1030), on the second floor of the Kintetsu Building, "sushi boats" float by the customers, who take what they want and pay per boat at the end of the meal. The inexpensive but superb **Mifune** (☎ 415/922–0337), diagonally across from Isobune, serves both hot and cold noodle dishes, either boiled and served in broth or prepared toss-fried, with bits of greens and meat added for flavor.

Walk back east on Geary Boulevard's north side to Gough Street—an
enclave of expensive high-rise residential towers known as Cathedral
56 Hill. Dramatic **St. Mary's Cathedral,** on the south side of Geary, was
dedicated in 1971 at a cost of $7 million. The impressive Italian traver-
tine Catholic cathedral seats 2,500 people around the central altar. Above
the altar is a spectacular cascade made of 7,000 aluminum ribs. Four
magnificent stained-glass windows in the dome represent the four elements: the blue north window, water; the light-colored south window,
the sun; the red west window, fire; and the green east window, earth.

Civic Center

San Francisco's Civic Center stands as one of the country's great city, state, and federal building complexes with handsome adjoining cultural institutions—a realization of the theories of turn-of-the-century proponents of the "City Beautiful."

57 Facing Polk Street, between Grove and McAllister streets, **City Hall** is
a French Renaissance Revival masterpiece of granite and marble, modeled after the Capitol in Washington. Its dome, which is even higher
than the Washington version, dominates the area. In front of the build-

ing (closed for seismic upgrading until at least 1998) are formal gardens with fountains, walkways, and seasonal flower beds. Brooks Hall was constructed under this plaza in 1958 to add space for the frequent trade shows and other events held in the Bill Graham Civic Auditorium, on Grove Street. The seismic upgrades of both buildings were scheduled for completion by early 1996.

Across the plaza from City Hall on Larkin Street is the main branch
58 of the **San Francisco Public Library.** (A new library is being built directly across Fulton Street; at press time, the old library was scheduled for closing from December 31, 1995, until the new one opened on April 16, 1996.) History buffs should visit the San Francisco History Room and Archives, where historic photographs, maps, and other memorabilia are displayed. ☎ *415/557–4400 (415/557–4567 for archive).* ⏲ *Mon. 10–6, Tues.–Thurs. 9–8, Fri. 11–5, Sat. 9–5, Sun. noon–5.*

On the west side of City Hall, across Van Ness Avenue, are the Veterans Building, the Opera House, and Davies Symphony Hall. The north-
59 ernmost of the three is the **Veterans Building** (401 Van Ness Ave.), the third and fourth floors of which formerly housed the San Francisco Museum of Modern Art. The mayor's office and other city departments have moved into this space while City Hall is being repaired. Herbst Theatre, on the first floor, remains a popular venue for lectures and readings, classical ensembles, and dance performances. In 1995 the 50th anniversary of the signing of the United Nations Charter was commemorated with celebrations in the theater.

An ornate horseshoe carriage entrance on its south side separates the
60 Veterans Building from the **War Memorial Opera House** (301 Van Ness Ave.), which opened in 1932. Modeled after European counterparts, the opera house has a vaulted and coffered ceiling, a marble foyer, and two balconies. The Opera House will be closed for seismic retrofitting and renovation from January '96 through July '97; San Francisco Opera and the San Francisco Ballet will perform their regular seasons at several alternative venues. (*See* The Arts and Nightlife, *below.*)

61 South of Grove Street, still on Van Ness, is the 2,750-seat **Louise M. Davies Symphony Hall,** home of the San Francisco Symphony. The glass-encased wraparound lobby, visible from the street, is just a precursor of the sleek, futuristic wonders inside: 59 adjustable Plexiglas acoustical disks hang from the ceiling like hanging windshields. Tours are available of Davies Hall and the adjacent Performing Arts Center, which encompasses the Opera House and Herbst Theatre. *201 Van Ness Ave.,* ☎ *415/552–8338. Cost: $3 adults, $2 senior citizens and students. Tours of Davies Hall Wed. and Sat. by appointment. Tours of Davies Hall and the Performing Arts Center every ½ hr Mon. 10–2.*

The Northern Waterfront

Numbers in the margin correspond to points of interest on the Northern Waterfront map.

For the sight, sound, and smell of the sea, hop the Powell-Hyde cable car from Union Square to the end of the line. From the cable-car turnaround, Aquatic Park and the National Maritime Museum are immediately to the west; Fort Mason, with its several interesting museums, is just a bit farther west. Those who wish to explore the more commercial attractions can head to nearby Ghirardelli Square or Fisherman's Wharf. Be sure to wear good walking shoes and a jacket or sweater for mid-afternoon breezes or foggy mists.

San Francisco is famous for the arts and crafts that flourish on the streets. Each day more than 200 of the city's innovative jewelers, painters, potters, photographers, and leather workers offer their wares for sale. You'll find them at Fisherman's Wharf, Union Square, Embarcadero Plaza, and the Cliff House. Be wary: Some of the items are from foreign factories and may be overpriced; bargaining is often a wise idea.

❶ The **National Maritime Museum** exhibits ship models, photographs, maps, and other artifacts chronicling the development of San Francisco and the West Coast through maritime history. *Aquatic Park, at the foot of Polk St.,* ☎ *415/556–3002 (if no answer call 415/929–0202).* ☛ *Free.* ⏲ *Daily 10–5, until 6 in summer.*

★ ❷ The museum includes the **Hyde Street Pier** (two blocks east), where historic vessels are moored. The highlight of the pier, one of the wharf's best bargains, is the *Balclutha,* an 1886 full-rigged, three-mast sailing vessel that sailed around Cape Horn 17 times. The *Eureka,* a side-wheel ferry, and the *C.A. Thayer,* a three-masted schooner, can also be boarded. ☎ *415/929–0202.* ☛ *$3 adults, $1 children 12–18; senior citizens free. (Note: Travelers with a National Park Service Golden Eagle Pass enter the pier free.)* ⏲ *Fall–spring, daily 10–5; summer, daily 10–6.*

❸ Spend some time strolling through **Ghirardelli Square,** which is across Beach Street from the National Maritime Museum. This charming complex of 19th-century brick factory buildings, once the home of the aromatic Ghirardelli Chocolate Company, has been transformed into a network of specialty shops, cafés, restaurants, and galleries. Two unusual shops in the Cocoa Building are **Xanadu Gallery** and **Folk Art International**: Both display museum-quality tribal art from Asia, Africa, Oceania, and the Americas. Also of interest, on the Lower Plaza level of the Cocoa Building, is the **Creative Spirit Gallery** (☎ 415/441–1537), a space sponsored and run by the National Institute of Art and Disabilities to showcase works by artists with disabilities. Nearby, in Ghirardelli's Rose court, is the **California Crafts Museum** (☎ 415/771–1919), which honors the state's craft artists.

❹ Just east of the Hyde Street Pier, **The Cannery** is a three-story structure built in 1894 to house what became the Del Monte Fruit and Vegetable Cannery. Shops, art galleries, and unusual restaurants ring the courtyard today, and the **Museum of the City of San Francisco** can be found on the third floor. The first independent museum on the history of the city, it displays historical items, maps, and photographs, including the 8-ton head of the Goddess of Progress statue that toppled from City Hall just before the 1906 earthquake. *2801 Leavenworth St.,* ☎ *415/928–0289.* ☛ *Free ($2 donation suggested).* ⏲ *Wed.–Sun. 10–4.*

❺ The mellow **Buena Vista Cafe** (2765 Hyde St., ☎ 415/474–5044) claims to be the first U.S. establishment to serve Irish coffee; the late San Francisco columnist Stan Delaplane is credited with importing the Gaelic concoction. The café opens at 9 AM weekdays, 8 AM weekends, and serves a great breakfast. It is always crowded, but try for a table overlooking nostalgic Victorian Park with its cable-car turntable.

For an even more sweeping view of the bay, walk five (steep) blocks up Hyde street to Lombard Street. This puts you at the top of one of
❻ San Francisco's signature sites, the **"Crookedest Street in the World."** Stretching the length of just one block, the street drops down the east face of Russian Hill in eight switchbacks to Leavenworth Street.

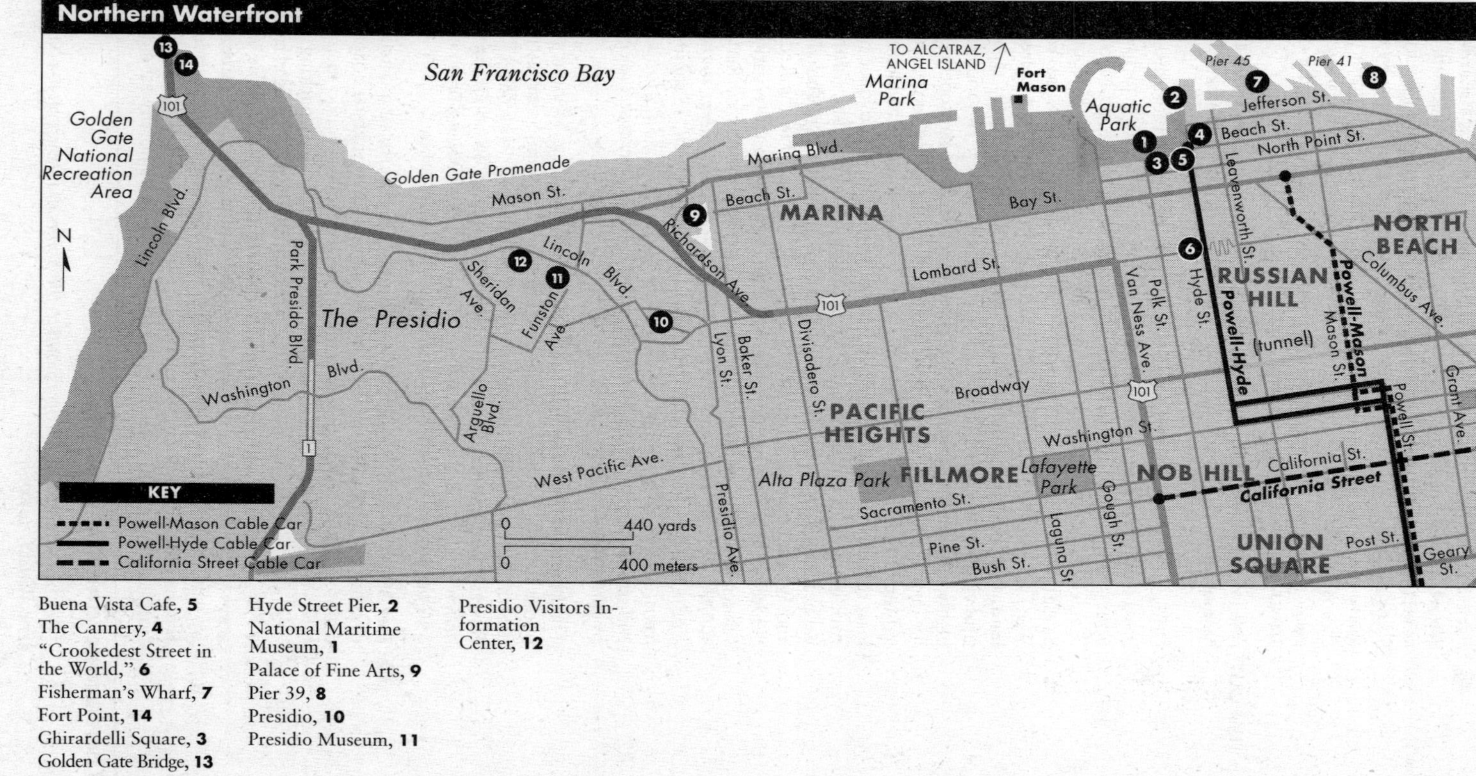

Buena Vista Cafe, **5**
The Cannery, **4**
"Crookedest Street in the World," **6**
Fisherman's Wharf, **7**
Fort Point, **14**
Ghirardelli Square, **3**
Golden Gate Bridge, **13**
Hyde Street Pier, **2**
National Maritime Museum, **1**
Palace of Fine Arts, **9**
Pier 39, **8**
Presidio, **10**
Presidio Museum, **11**
Presidio Visitors Information Center, **12**

7 Back on the waterfront, at Taylor and Jefferson streets, is **Fisherman's Wharf,** home of numerous seafood restaurants, as well as sidewalk crab pots and counters that offer take-away shrimp and crab cocktails. Ships creak at their moorings; seagulls cry out for a handout. By midafternoon, the fishing fleet is back to port. T-shirts and sweats, gold chains galore, redwood furniture, acres of artwork—some original—beckon visitors. Wax museums, fast-food favorites, and amusing street artists provide diversions for all ages.

TIME OUT Fine live music—R&B, blues, rock—floods the wharf from **Lou's Pier 47 Restaurant** (300 Jefferson St., ☎ 415/771-0377). The food's okay, too.

Cruises are an exhilarating way to see the bay. Among the cruises offered by the **Red and White Fleet,** berthed at Pier 43½, are frequent one-hour swings under the Golden Gate Bridge and along the Northern Waterfront. More interesting—and just as scenic—are the tours to Sausalito, Angel Island, Tiburon, Muir Woods, and the Napa Valley ★ Wine Country. Perhaps best of all is the popular tour of **Alcatraz Island.** The boat ride to the island is brief (15 minutes) but affords beautiful views of the city, Marin County, and the East Bay. The audio tour, highly recommended, features observations of guards and prisoners about life in one of America's most notorious penal colonies. A separate, ranger-led tour surveys the island's ecology. Plan your schedule to include at least three hours for the visit and boat rides combined. Advance reservations, even in the off-season, are strongly recommended. (Note: as we headed to press, the Blue and Gold Fleet (*see below*) acquired Red and White. Subject to regulatory approval, during 1996 the Red and White boats will be repainted blue and gold, though no reservation or service changes are expected.) *Recorded information on all Red and White tours, ☎ 415/546–2628 or 800/229–2784. Alcatraz tours (including audio guide) are $10 adults and children 12–18, $8 senior citizens, $4.50 children 5–11; without audio, subtract $3.25 for adults and senior citizens, $1.25 for children 5–11. Add $2 per ticket to charge by phone at 415/546–2700.*

The **Blue and Gold Fleet,** berthed at Pier 39, conducts 1¼-hour tours under both the Bay and Golden Gate bridges. Friday and Saturday night dinner-dance cruises run April–mid-December. ☎ *415/781–7877. Reservations not necessary. Bay Cruise: $16 adults; $8 senior citizens, active military, and children 5–18. Summertime dinner-dance cruise: $40 per person (group rates available). Daily departures.*

8 **Pier 39** is the most popular of San Francisco's waterfront attractions, drawing millions of visitors each year to browse through its dozens of shops. **Only in San Francisco** is the place for San Francisco memorabilia. Ongoing free entertainment, accessible validated parking, and nearby public transportation ensure crowds most days. Opening in spring 1996 is a new attraction: **Underwater World** at Pier 39. Moving walkways will transport visitors through a space surrounded on three sides by water. The focus will be on indigenous San Francisco Bay marine life, from fish and plankton to sharks. Above water, don't miss the sea lions that bask and play on the docks on the pier's northwest side.

The Marina and the Presidio

Numbers in the margin correspond to the points of interest on the Northern Waterfront map.

9 San Francisco's rosy, rococo **Palace of Fine Arts** is at the very end of the Marina, near the intersection of Baker and Beach streets. The

palace is the sole survivor of the 32 tinted plaster structures built for the 1915 Panama-Pacific International Exposition. Bernard Maybeck designed the Roman Classic beauty, and in the ensuing 50 years the building fell into disrepair. It was reconstructed in concrete at a cost of $7 million and reopened in 1967, thanks to legions of sentimental citizens and a huge private donation that saved the palace from demolition. The massive columns, great rotunda, and swan-filled lagoon have been used in countless fashion layouts and recent films.

The interior houses a fascinating hands-on museum, the **Exploratorium,** which has been called the best science museum in the world. The curious of all ages flock here to play with and learn from some of the 600 exhibits. Be sure to include the dark, touchy-feely Tactile Dome in your visit, and inquire about the program of films and lectures. ☎ *415/561–0360 for general information, 415/561–0362 for required reservations for Tactile Dome.* ☛ *$9 adults, $7 students over 18 and senior citizens with ID, $5 children 6–17, $2.50 children 3–5; free 1st Wed. of month.* ⊙ *Tues.–Sun. 10–5, Wed. 10–9:30, legal Mon. holidays 10–5.*

If you have a car, now is the time to use it for a drive through the
10 **Presidio.** (If not, Muni Bus 38 from Union Square will take you to Park Presidio Boulevard; from there use a free transfer to Bus 28 into the Presidio.) Now part of the Golden Gate National Recreation Area, the Presidio was a military post for more than 200 years. Don Juan Bautista de Anza and a band of Spanish settlers first claimed the area in 1776. It became a Mexican garrison in 1822 when Mexico gained its independence from Spain, until U.S. troops forcibly occupied it in 1846. The U.S. Sixth Army was stationed here until October 1994.

The more than 1,400 acres of rolling hills, majestic woods, and attractive redbrick army barracks present an air of serenity in the middle of the city. There are two beaches, a golf course, and picnic sites. The former **Officers' Club,** a long, low adobe built around 1776, was the Spanish commandante's headquarters and may be the oldest standing building in the city.

11 The **Presidio Museum,** housed in a former hospital built in 1863, focuses on the role played by the military in San Francisco's development. Behind the museum are two cabins that housed refugees from the 1906 earthquake and fire. Photos on the wall of one depict rows and rows of temporary shelters at the Presidio and in Golden Gate Park following the disaster. *On the corner of Lincoln Blvd. and Funston Ave.,* ☎ *415/556–0856.* ☛ *Free.* ⊙ *Wed.–Sun. 10–4.*

12 Four blocks west on Lincoln lies the new **Presidio Visitors Information Center,** offering maps, brochures, and schedules for guided walking and bicycle tours. *On the corner of Lincoln Blvd. and Montgomery,* ☎ *415/556–0865.* ☛ *Free.* ⊙ *Daily 10–5.*

★ 13 Muni Bus 28 will take you to the **Golden Gate Bridge** toll plaza. Nearly 2 miles long, connecting San Francisco with Marin County, the bridge's art deco design is simple but powerful, made to withstand winds of more than 100 miles per hour. Though frequently gusty and misty (walkers should wear warm clothing), the bridge offers unparalleled views of the Bay Area. The east walkway offers a glimpse of the San Francisco skyline as well as the islands of the bay. The view west confronts you with the wild hills of the Marin headlands, the curving coast south to Land's End, and the majestic Pacific Ocean. A vista point on the Marin side affords a spectacular view of the city.

14 Though **Fort Point,** designed to mount 125 cannons with a range of up to 2 miles, was constructed during the years 1853–61 to protect San Francisco from sea attack during the Civil War, it was never used for that purpose. Standing under the shadow of the Golden Gate Bridge, the national historic site is now a museum filled with military memorabilia. Guided group tours and cannon drills are offered daily by national park rangers. The top floor affords a superb view of the bay. ☎ *415/556–1693.* ☛ *Free.* ⏲ *Wed.–Sun. 10–5.*

From here, hardy walkers may elect to stroll about 3½ miles along the scenic Golden Gate Promenade to Aquatic Park and the Hyde Street cable-car terminus.

Golden Gate Park

Numbers in the margin correspond to points of interest on the Golden Gate Park map.

It was a Scotsman, John McLaren, who became manager of Golden Gate Park in 1887 and transformed the brush and sand into the green civilized wilderness we enjoy today. Here you can attend a polo game or a Sunday band concert and rent a bike, boat, or roller skates. On Sunday, some park roads are closed to cars and come alive with joggers, bicyclists, skaters, museum goers, and picnickers. There are tennis courts, baseball diamonds, soccer fields, a buffalo paddock, and miles of trails for horseback riding in this 1,000-acre park.

Because it is so large, the best way for most visitors to see it is by car. Muni buses provide service, though on weekends there may be a long wait. On Market Street, board westbound Bus 5-Fulton or Bus 21-Hayes and continue to Arguello and Fulton streets. Walk south about 500 feet to John F. Kennedy Drive.

From May through October, free guided walking tours of the park are offered every weekend by the Friends of Recreation and Parks (☎ 415/221–1311).

The oldest building in the park and perhaps San Francisco's most
1 elaborate Victorian is the **Conservatory,** a copy of London's famous Kew Gardens. Originally brought around the Horn for the estate of James Lick in San Jose, the ornate greenhouse was purchased from the Lick estate with public subscription funds and erected in the park. In addition to a tropical garden, there are seasonal displays of flowers and plants and a permanent exhibit of rare orchids. ☎ *415/752–8080.* ☛ *$1.50 adults, 75¢ senior citizens and children 6–12; free 1st and last ½ hr.* ⏲ *Daily 9–5.*

The eastern section of the park has three museums. Purchase of a $10 Golden Gate Park Cultural Pass gains you one-day admission to all three, plus the Japanese Tea Garden and the Conservatory—a substantial savings (for adults) if you are planning to visit all these attractions. Purchase your pass at any of the museums or at TIX Bay Area in Union
2 Square. The **M. H. de Young Memorial Museum** specializes in American art, with paintings, sculpture, textiles, and decorative arts from Colonial times through the 20th century. More than 200 paintings highlight the work of American masters, including Copley, Eakins, Bingham, and Sargent. Don't miss the room of landscapes, dominated by Frederic Church's moody, almost psychedelic *Rainy Season in the Tropics,* or the wonderful gallery of American still lifes, including the trompe l'oeil paintings of William Harnett. The de Young also has a dramatic collection of tribal art from Africa, Oceania, and the Americas, including

pottery, basketry, sculpture, and ritual clothing and accessories. An ongoing textile installation, *Unraveling Yarns: The Art of Everyday Life,* contains more than 60 samples of fiber art from around the world. In addition to its permanent collections, the museum hosts selected traveling shows—often blockbuster events that involve long lines and additional entrance fees. The museum shop offers a wide selection of art objects, and the **Cafe de Young,** which has outdoor seating in the Oakes Garden, serves a complete menu of light refreshments until 4 PM. ☎ *415/863–3330 for 24-hr information.* ☛ *$6 adults, $4 senior citizens, $3 ages 12–17; free 1st Wed. of month. Note: One entrance charge admits you to the de Young, Asian Art, and Legion of Honor museums on the same day.* ⏲ *Wed.–Sun. 10–5, 1st Wed. of month only, 10–8:45.*

3 The **Asian Art Museum,** located in galleries adjoining the de Young, contains a world-famous collection of more than 12,000 sculptures, paintings, and ceramics from 40 countries, illustrating major periods of Asian art. One standout permanent exhibit is the Leventritt collection of blue and white porcelains. On the second floor are treasures from Iran, Turkey, Syria, India, Tibet, Nepal, Pakistan, Korea, Japan, Afghanistan, and Southeast Asia. ☎ *415/668–8921.* ☛ *Collected when entering the de Young.* ⏲ *Wed.–Sun. 10–5., 1st Wed. of month 10–8:45.*

TIME OUT ★ 4 The **Japanese Tea Garden,** next to the Asian Art Museum, is an ideal place to rest after touring the museums. This charming 4-acre village was created for the 1894 Mid-Winter Exposition. Small ponds, streams, and flowering shrubs create a serene landscape. The cherry blossoms in spring are exquisite. The Tea House, where tea and cookies are served, is popular and busy. ☎ *415/752-1171.* ☛ *$2.50 adults and children 13–17, $1.50 senior citizens and children 6–12.* ⏲ *Summer, daily 9–6; winter, daily 9–5.*

5 The **California Academy of Sciences,** directly opposite the de Young Museum, is one of the top five natural-history museums in the country, with both an aquarium and a planetarium. The Steinhart Aquarium, with its dramatic 100,000-gallon Fish Roundabout, is home to 14,000 creatures, including a living coral reef with colorful fish, giant clams, tropical sharks, and a rainbow of hard and soft corals. The Space and Earth Hall has an "earthquake floor" that enables visitors to experience a simulated California earthquake. The Wattis Hall presents rotating natural-history, art, and cultural exhibits. In the Wild California Hall, a 14,000-gallon aquarium tank shows underwater life at the Farallones (islands off the coast of northern California), life-size elephant-seal models, and video information on the wildlife of the state. The innovative Life Through Time Hall tells the story of evolution from the beginnings of life on earth through the age of dinosaurs to the age of mammals. A popular attraction at the Academy is the permanent display of cartoons by Far Side creator Gary Larson. There is an additional charge for Morrison Planetarium shows (depending on the show, up to $2.50 adults, $1.25 senior citizens and students, ☎ 415/750–7141 for daily schedule). Laserium (☎ 415/750–7138 for schedule and fees) presents evening laser-light shows at Morrison Planetarium, accompanied by rock, classical, and other types of music; educational shows outline laser technology. A cafeteria is open daily until one hour before the museum closes, and the Academy Store offers a wide selection of books, posters, toys, and cultural artifacts. ☎ *415/750–7145.* ☛ *$7 adults, $4 senior citizens and students 12–17, $1.50 chil-*

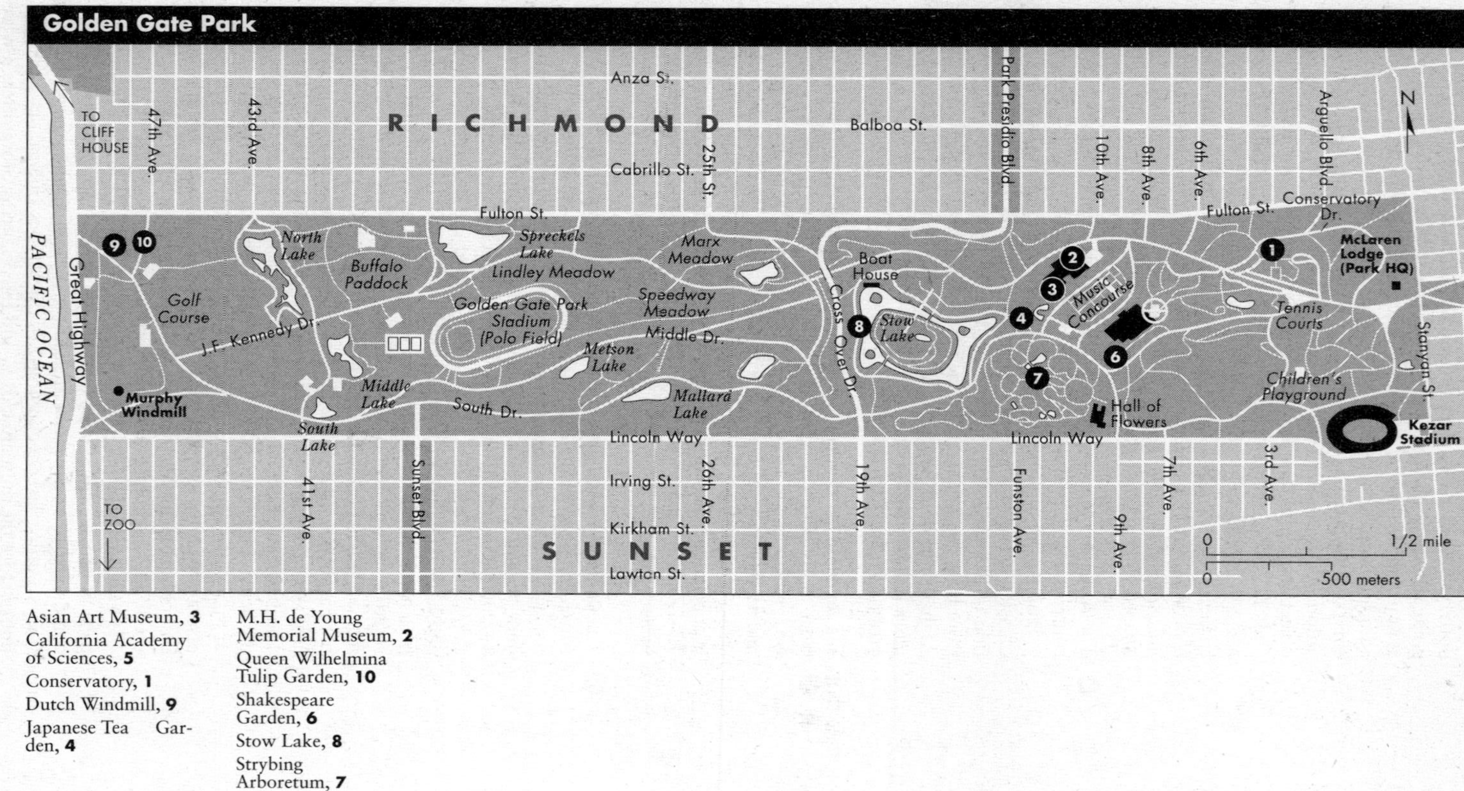

Asian Art Museum, **3**

California Academy of Sciences, **5**

Conservatory, **1**

Dutch Windmill, **9**

Japanese Tea Garden, **4**

M.H. de Young Memorial Museum, **2**

Queen Wilhelmina Tulip Garden, **10**

Shakespeare Garden, **6**

Stow Lake, **8**

Strybing Arboretum, **7**

dren 6–11; $2 discount with Muni transfers; free 1st Wed. of month. ⏲ *July 4–Labor Day, daily 10–7; Labor Day–July 4, daily 10–5.*

6 A short stroll from the Academy of Sciences will take you to the free **Shakespeare Garden.** Two hundred flowers mentioned by the Bard, as well as bronze-engraved panels with floral quotations, are set throughout the garden.

7 **Strybing Arboretum** specializes in plants from areas with climates similar to that of the Bay Area, such as the west coast of Australia, South Africa, and the Mediterranean. Six thousand plants and tree varieties bloom in gardens throughout the grounds. *9th Ave. at Lincoln Way,* ☏ *415/661–1316.* ☛ *Free.* ⏲ *Weekdays 8–4:30, weekends and holidays 10–5. Tours leave the bookstore weekdays at 1:30, weekends at 10:30 and 1:30.*

The western half of Golden Gate Park offers miles of wooded greenery and open spaces for all types of spectator and participant sports.
8 Rent a paddleboat or stroll around **Stow Lake.** The Chinese Pavilion, a gift from the city of Taipei, was shipped in 6,000 pieces and assembled on the shore of Strawberry Hill Island in Stow Lake in 1981. At the very western end of the park, where Kennedy Drive meets the Great
9 Highway, is the beautifully restored 1902 **Dutch Windmill** and the pho-
10 togenic **Queen Wilhelmina Tulip Garden.**

Lincoln Park and the Western Shoreline

No other American city provides such close-up viewing of the power and fury of the surf attacking the shore. From Land's End in Lincoln Park you can look across the Golden Gate (the name was originally given to the opening of San Francisco Bay long before the bridge was built) to the Marin Headlands. From the Cliff House south to the San Francisco Zoo, the Great Highway and Ocean Beach run along the western edge of the city.

The wind is often strong along the shoreline, summer fog can blanket the ocean beaches, and the water is cold and usually too rough for swimming. Carry a sweater or jacket and bring binoculars.

At the northwest corner of the San Francisco Peninsula is **Lincoln Park.** At one time all the city's cemeteries were here, segregated by nationality. The cemeteries have given way to an 18-hole golf course with large and well-formed Monterey cypresses lining the fairways. There are scenic walks throughout the 275-acre park, with particularly good views from **Land's End** (the parking lot is at the end of El Camino del Mar). The trails out to Land's End, however, are for skilled hikers only: Landslides are frequent, and danger lurks along the steep cliffs.

Also in Lincoln Park is the **California Palace of the Legion of Honor.** The building itself—modeled after the 18th-century Parisian original—is architecturally interesting and spectacularly situated on cliffs overlooking the ocean and the Golden Gate Bridge. The museum, which recently reopened after extensive renovations, contains 27 galleries of mostly European paintings, drawings, sculpture, tapestries, and porcelain. Collection highlights also include ancient Egyptian, Greek, and Roman art. ☏ *415/863–3330 for 24-hr information.* ☛ *$6 adults, $4 senior citizens, $3 ages 12–17; free 2nd Wed. of month. Note: One entrance fee admits you to the de Young, Asian Art, and Legion of Honor museums on the same day.* ⏲ *Tues.–Sun. 10–5 and the first Sat. of month 10–8:45.*

★ The **Cliff House** (1066 Point Lobos Ave.), where the road turns south along the western shore, has existed in several incarnations. The original, built in 1863, and several later structures were destroyed by fire. The present building has restaurants, a pub, and a gift shop. The lower dining room overlooks Seal Rocks (the barking marine mammals sunning themselves are actually sea lions).

An adjacent attraction is the **Musée Mécanique,** a collection of antique mechanical contrivances, including peep shows and nickelodeons. The museum carries on the tradition of arcade amusement at the Cliff House. ☎ *415/386–1170.* ☛ *Free.* ⏲ *Weekdays 11–7, weekends 10–8.*

Two flights below the Cliff House are a fine observation deck and the Golden Gate National Recreation Area **Visitors Center,** which contains interesting and historic photographs of the Cliff House and the glass-roofed **Sutro Baths.** This complex, which comprised six enormous baths, 500 dressing rooms, and several restaurants, covered 3 acres just north of the Cliff House. The baths were closed in 1952 and burned in 1966. You can explore the ruins on your own or take ranger-led walks on weekends. The Visitors Center offers information on these and other trails. ☎ *415/556–8642.* ⏲ *Daily 10–4:30.*

Because traffic is often heavy in summer and on weekends, you might want to take the Muni system from the Union Square area out to the Cliff House. On weekdays, take the Muni Bus 38-Geary Limited to 48th Avenue and Point Lobos and walk down the hill. On weekends and during the evenings, the Muni Bus 38 is marked "48th Avenue." Don't take Bus 38 bus marked "Ocean Beach," though, or you'll have to walk an extra 10 minutes to get to the Cliff House.

TIME OUT The Cliff House (☎ 415/386–3330) has several restaurants and a busy bar. The **Upstairs Room** features a light menu with a number of omelet suggestions. The lower dining room, the **Seafood & Beverage Co. Restaurant,** has a fabulous view of Seal Rocks. Reservations are recommended, but you may still have to wait for a table, especially at midday on Sunday.

Below the Cliff House are the **Great Highway** and **Ocean Beach.** Stretching 3 miles along the western (Pacific) side of the city, this is a beautiful beach for walking, running, or lying in the sun—but not for swimming. Although dozens of surfers head to Ocean Beach each day, you'll notice they are dressed head-to-toe in wet suits, as the water here is extremely cold. Across the highway from the beach is a new path that winds through landscaped sand dunes from Lincoln Avenue to Sloat Boulevard (near the zoo)—an ideal route for walking and bicycling.

At the Great Highway and Sloat Boulevard is the **San Francisco Zoo,** which was first established in 1889 in Golden Gate Park. At its present home there are 1,000 species of birds and animals, more than 130 of which have been designated endangered species. Among the protected are the snow leopard, Sumatran tiger, jaguar, and the Asian elephant. A favorite attraction is the greater one-horned rhino, next to the African elephants. Another popular zoo resident is Prince Charles, a rare white tiger and the first of its kind to be exhibited in the West.

Gorilla World is one of the largest and most natural gorilla habitats of any zoo in the world. The circular outer area is carpeted with natural African Kikuyu grass, while trees and shrubs create communal play areas. The Primate Discovery Center houses 14 endangered species in atriumlike enclosures.

There are 46 "storyboxes" throughout the zoo that, when turned on with blue and red keys ($2), recite animal facts and basic zoological concepts in four languages—English, Spanish, Cantonese, and Tagalog.

The children's zoo has a minipopulation of about 300 mammals, birds, and reptiles, plus an insect zoo, a baby-animal nursery, and a beautifully restored 1921 Dentzel Carousel. A ride astride one of the 52 hand-carved menagerie animals costs $1.

Zoo information, ☎ *415/753–7083.* ☛ *$6.50 adults, $3 children 12–15 and senior citizens, $1 children 6–12; free 1st Wed. of month.* ⏲ *Daily 10–5.* ☛ *Children's zoo: $1.* ⏲ *Daily 11–4.*

Mission Dolores

Mission Dolores, on palm-lined Dolores Street, is the sixth of the 21 missions founded by Father Junípero Serra. The adobe building, begun in 1782, was originally known as Mission San Francisco de Assisi. Completed in 1791, its ceiling depicts original Costanoan Indian basket designs, executed in vegetable dyes. There is a small museum, and the mission cemetery maintains the graves of mid-19th-century European immigrants. *Dolores and 16th Sts.,* ☎ *415/621–8203.* ☛ *$1.* ⏲ *Daily 9–4.*

SHOPPING

By Sheila Gadsden

Updated by Alan Frutkin

Shopping in San Francisco means much more than driving to the local mall. Scattered among the city's diverse neighborhoods are clusters of stores of every stripe: major department stores, fine fashion boutiques, discount outlets, art galleries, and specialty stores for crafts, vintage items, and more. The *San Francisco Chronicle* and *Examiner* advertise sales; for smaller innovative shops, check the San Francisco *Bay Guardian.* Store hours are slightly different everywhere, but standard shopping times are between 10 AM and 5 or 6 PM Monday through Wednesday, Friday, and Saturday; between 10 AM and 8 or 9 PM Thursday; and from noon until 5 PM Sunday. Stores on and around Fisherman's Wharf often have longer hours in summer.

The Castro/Noe Valley

Often called the gay capital of the world, the Castro is a major destination for nongay travelers as well. The Castro is filled with clothing boutiques, home accessory stores, and small, quirky specialty stores, including **A Different Light** (489 Castro St., ☎ 415/431–0891), one of the country's premier gay and lesbian bookstores.

Just south of the Castro on 24th Street in Noe Valley is an enclave of gourmet food stores, used record shops, and clothing boutiques. Much of Armistead Maupin's *Tales of the City* was filmed in this villagelike neighborhood, whose small shops and relaxed street life evoke a '70s mood.

Chinatown

Racks of Chinese silks, toy trinkets, colorful pottery, baskets, and carved figurines are displayed in racks on the sidewalks, alongside herb stores that specialize in ginseng and roots. Dominating all are the sights and smells of food: crates of bok choy, tanks of live crabs, and hanging whole chickens.

Embarcadero Center

Five modern towers of shops, restaurants, and offices plus the Hyatt Regency Hotel make up the Embarcadero Center, downtown at the end of Market Street. What the center lacks in charm, it makes up for in sheer quantity. Its 175 establishments include such nationally known stores as **The Limited** and **Ann Taylor,** as well as West Coast–based businesses such as the **Nature Company.**

Fisherman's Wharf

San Francisco's Fisherman's Wharf is host to a number of shopping and sightseeing attractions: **Pier 39,** the **Anchorage, Ghirardelli Square,** and **The Cannery.** Each offers shops, restaurants, and a festive atmosphere as well as such outdoor entertainment as musicians, mimes, and magicians.

The Haight

Haight Street is always an attraction for visitors, if only to see the sign at Haight and Ashbury streets—the geographic center of flower power during the 1960s. These days, in addition to renascent tie-dyed shirts, you'll find high-quality vintage clothing, funky jewelry, used-book and record stores, and reproductions of Art Deco accessories (*see* Vintage Fashion, Furniture, and Accessories, *below*).

Jackson Square

Once the raffish Barbary Coast, tiny, now-gentrified Jackson Square is presently home to a dozen or so of San Francisco's finest retail antiques dealers, mostly located in two-story town houses.

Japantown

The three-block **Japan Center** complex includes an 800-car public garage and shops and showrooms selling Japanese products: cameras, tapes and records, new and old porcelains, pearls, antique kimonos, tansu chests, and paintings. Among the favorites: **Soko Hardware** (1698 Post St., ☎ 415/931–5100), run by the Ashizawa merchant family since 1925, specializes in beautifully crafted Japanese tools for gardening and carpentry; **Kinokuniya,** on the second floor of the Kinokuniya Building, the center's western-most structure (1581 Webster St., ☎ 415/567–7625), may have the finest selection of English-language books on Japanese subjects in the United States.

The Marina District

Chestnut Street, one block north of Lombard Street, caters to the shopping whims of Marina District residents. **Red Rose Gallerie** (2251 Chestnut St., ☎ 415/776–6871) specializes in "tools for personal growth," including body scents, exotic clothing, and audiotapes for rejuvenating the mind. Shops stretch from Fillmore Street to Broderick Street.

The Mission

Known as one of the city's sunniest neighborhoods, the Mission is also one of its most ethnically diverse, with a large Latino population and a sprinkling of everything else. In addition to those with a hunger for inexpensive Mexican food, the area draws bargain shoppers with its many used clothing, furniture, and alternative bookstores.

North Beach

Shopping here is clustered tightly around Washington Square and Columbus Avenue. Most of the businesses are small clothing stores, antiques and vintage shops, or such eccentric specialty shops as **Quantity Postcard** (1441 Grant Ave., ☎ 415/986–8866), which carries 15,000 different postcards.

Pacific Heights

Pacific Heights residents seeking practical services head straight for Fillmore and Sacramento streets, where private residences alternate with good bookstores, fine clothing and gift shops, thrift stores, and art galleries. **Sue Fisher King Company** (3067 Sacramento St., ☎ 415/922–7276) has an eclectic collection of home accessories, and **Yountville** (2416 Fillmore St., ☎ 415/922–5050) specializes in sporty children's clothing from local and European designers. The Fillmore Street shopping area runs between Post Street and Pacific Avenue. Most shops on the western end of Sacramento Street are between Lyon and Maple streets.

South of Market

Dozens of discount outlets, most of them open seven days a week, have sprung up along the streets and alleyways bordered by 2nd, Townsend, Howard, and 10th streets. A good place to start is the **Six Sixty Center** (660 3rd St.), two floors of shops offering everything from designer fashions to Icelandic sweaters.

At the other end of the spectrum, the newly opened SFMOMA shop (151 3rd St.) carries an exclusive line of watches and jewelry, as well as its artists' monographs, contemporary gift items, and extensive book collection. The gift shop at the Center for the Arts at Yerba Buena Gardens (701 Mission St.) carries an outstanding line of handmade jewelry and crafts, including an unusual selection of glass tableware.

Union Square

Serious shoppers head straight to Union Square, San Francisco's main shopping artery and the site of most department stores. Neiman Marcus, on the southeast corner of Union Square, is noted for its high-quality merchandise. **Macy's,** with entrances on Geary, Stockton, and O'Farrell streets, has huge selections of clothing, plus extensive furniture and household accessories departments. The men's department occupies its own building across Stockton Street.

Opposite is the **F.A.O. Schwarz** children's store, with its extravagant assortment of life-size stuffed animals, animated displays, and steep prices. A half block down Stockton Street from F.A.O. Schwarz is the new **Virgin Megastore,** which has four floors of music, entertainment, and software in a building also housing a **Planet Hollywood** restaurant. Also livening up the already lively Union Square area: a huge new **Disney Store,** selling memorabilia and other merchandise from the famous movie studio. The Disney space, across Post Street from the Westin St. Francis Hotel, includes a 45,000-square-foot **Borders Books and Music** store. Across Powell Street from Disney, **Saks Fifth Avenue** caters to the upscale shopper. Nearby are the pricey international boutiques of Hermès of Paris, Gucci, Celine of Paris, Alfred Dunhill, Louis Vuitton, and Cartier. Scheduled to open in April 1996 is the three-level **"Nike Town,"** which will combine athletic-wear sales and video and other entertainments.

Across from the cable-car turntable at Powell and Market streets is the **San Francisco Shopping Centre,** with the fashionable **Nordstrom** department store, the two-floor **Warner Bros.** shop, and more than 35 other businesses. Underneath a glass dome at Post and Kearny streets is **Crocker Galleria,** a complex of 50 shops (including **Ralph Lauren** and **Gianni Versace**) and restaurants.

Union Street

Out-of-towners sometimes confuse Union Street with downtown's Union Square. In fact, Union Street is just a short stretch of tony boutiques—a tiny, neighborhood version of Union Square. Nestled at the foot of a hill between Pacific Heights and the Marina District, the street is lined with contemporary fashion and custom jewelry shops, along with a few antiques shops and art galleries. At **Enchanted Crystal** (1895 Union St., ☎ 415/885–1335), an in-house glass blower adds his wares to a large collection of jewelry, ornaments, and American crafts.

SPORTS, FITNESS, BEACHES

Participant Sports and the Outdoors

By Casey Tefertiller

Updated by Dianne Aaronson

Joggers, bicyclists, and aficionados of virtually all sports can find their favorite pastimes within driving distance, and often within walking distance, of downtown hotels. Golden Gate Park has numerous paths for runners and cyclists. For information on participant sports, check the monthly issues of *City Sports* magazine, available free at sporting-goods stores, tennis centers, and other recreational sites. The most important running event of the year is the *Examiner* Bay-to-Breakers race on the third Sunday in May. For information on this race, call 415/512–5000, ext. 2222.

Bicycling

Two bike routes are maintained by the San Francisco Recreation and Park Department (☎ 415/666–7201). One route goes through Golden Gate Park to Lake Merced; the other goes from the south end of the city to the Golden Gate Bridge and beyond. Many shops along Stanyan Street rent bikes.

Boating and Sailing

Stow Lake (☎ 415/752–0347) in Golden Gate Park has rowboat, pedal boat, and electric boat rentals. The lake is open daily for boating, but call for seasonal hours. San Francisco Bay offers year-round sailing, but tricky currents make the bay hazardous for inexperienced navigators. Boat rentals and charters are available throughout the Bay Area and are listed under "boat rentals" in the Yellow Pages. A selected charter is **A Day on the Bay** (☎ 415/922–0227). **Cass' Marina** (☎ 415/332–6789) in Sausalito has a variety of sailboats that can be rented or hired with a licensed skipper. Local sailing information can be obtained at the **Eagle Cafe** on Pier 39.

Fishing

Numerous fishing boats leave from San Francisco, Sausalito, Berkeley, Emeryville, and Point San Pablo. Lines can be cast from San Francisco Municipal Pier, Fisherman's Wharf, or Aquatic Park. Trout fishing is possible at Lake Merced (rent rods at boathouse at 1 Harding Blvd., ☎ 415/753–1101). One-day licenses, good for ocean fishing only, are available for $5.50 on the charters; sporting-goods stores sell complete state licenses—seasonal passes that permit both ocean and freshwater fishing—for $24.95. Two sportfishing charters are **Lovely**

Martha's Sportsfishing (☎ 415/871–4445) and **Wacky Jacky** (☎ 415/586–9800). Most charters depart daily from Fisherman's Wharf during the salmon-fishing season, March through October.

Fitness

The drop-in fee at the **24-hour Nautilus** center (1335 Sutter, ☎ 415/776–2200) is $15. The club has aerobics classes, fitness equipment, sauna, Jacuzzi, and steam room. The **Embarcadero YMCA** (169 Steuart St., ☎ 415/957–9622) offers racquetball, an indoor track, a swimming pool, and aerobics classes. The $12 drop-in fee includes use of the sauna and whirlpool. At the **Women's Training Center** (2164 Market St., ☎ 415/864–6835), the $10 day fee includes use of the sauna.

Golf

Call 415/750–4653 for computerized reservations at any of the following public courses: **Harding and Fleming parks** (Lake Merced Blvd. and Skyline Blvd.), an 18-hole, par-72 course and a nine-hole executive course, respectively; **Lincoln Park** (34th and Clement Sts.), 18 holes, par 68; **Golden Gate Park** (47th Ave. at Fulton St.), a "pitch and putt" nine-holer; or **Sharp Park,** in Pacifica (Hwy. 1, at the foot of Sharp Park Rd.), 18 holes, par 72. **Glen Eagles Golf Course** (2100 Sunnydale Ave.), a full-size 18-holer in McLaren Park, can be reached at 415/587–2425. At press time, the 18-hole **Presidio Golf Course** (☎ 415/561–4653), just opened to the public, had become an instant hit.

Tennis

The San Francisco Recreation and Park Department maintains 130 free tennis courts throughout the city. The largest set of free courts is at **Dolores Park** (18th and Dolores Sts.), with six courts available on a first-come, first-served basis. There are 21 public courts in **Golden Gate Park**; reservations and fee information can be obtained by calling 415/753–7101.

Spectator Sports

Baseball

The **San Francisco Giants** play at Candlestick Park (☎ 415/467–8000). The **Oakland A's** play at the Oakland Coliseum (☎ 510/638–0500). City shuttle buses marked Ballpark Special run from numerous bus stops (☎ 415/673–6864 for directions). Candlestick Park is often windy and cold, so take along extra layers of clothing. The Oakland Coliseum can be reached by taking BART trains to the Coliseum stop.

Basketball

The **Golden State Warriors** play NBA basketball at the Oakland Coliseum Arena from October through April. Tickets are available through BASS (☎ 510/762–2277). BART trains to the Coliseum stop are the easiest method of travel.

Football

The **San Francisco 49ers** play at Candlestick Park, but the games are almost always sold out far in advance, so call first (☎ 415/468–2249).

The **Oakland Raiders** returned to the Oakland Coliseum in 1995 after a 13-year sojourn in Los Angeles. Tickets (☎ 510/639–7700) are as hard to come by as they were in the team's glory years.

Hockey

San Jose Sharks play their home games at the San Jose Arena (☎ 408/287–4275 for directions). Many of the games sell out (☎ 510/762–2277 for tickets).

Beaches

Baker Beach

Baker Beach is not recommended for swimming: Watch for larger-than-usual waves. In recent years, the north end of the beach has become popular with nude sunbathers. (Though this is not legal, such laws are seldom enforced.) The beach is in the southwest corner of the Presidio, beginning at the end of Gibson Road, which turns off Bowley Street. Weather is typical for the bay shoreline: summer fog, usually breezy, and occasionally warm. Picnic tables, grills, day-camp areas, and trails are available. The mile-long shoreline is ideal for jogging, fishing, and building sand castles.

China Beach

From April through October, China Beach, south of Baker Beach, offers a lifeguard, gentler water, changing rooms, and showers. It is also listed on maps as Phelan Beach.

Ocean Beach

South of the Cliff House, Ocean Beach stretches along the western (ocean) side of San Francisco. It has a wide beach with scenic views and is perfect for walking, running, or lying in the sun—but not for swimming.

DINING

By Jacqueline Killeen and Sharon Silva

San Francisco probably has more restaurants per capita than any other city in the United States, including New York. Practically every ethnic cuisine is represented. That makes selecting restaurants a difficult task indeed. We have chosen several restaurants in each popular style of dining in various price ranges, in most cases because of the superiority of the food, but in some instances because of the view or ambience.

Parking accommodations are mentioned only when a restaurant has made special arrangements; otherwise you're on your own. There is usually a charge for valet parking. Validated parking is not necessarily free and unlimited; often there is a nominal charge and a restriction on the length of time.

In January 1995, smoking was banned in most Bay Area workplaces, including restaurants. Bars, however, were excluded from the ordinance.

Restaurants do change their policies about hours, credit cards, and the like. It is always best to make inquiries in advance.

The price ranges listed below are for an average three-course meal. A significant trend among more expensive restaurants is the bar menu, which provides light snacks—hot dogs, chili, pizza, and appetizers—in the bar for a cost that is often less than $15 for two.

CATEGORY	COST*
$$$$	over $50
$$$	$30–$50
$$	$20–$30
$	under $20

**per person for a three-course meal, excluding drinks, service, and 8½% sales tax*

American

Civic Center

$$$ ★ **Stars.** This is the culinary temple of Jeremiah Tower, the superchef who claims to have invented California cuisine. Stars is a must on every traveling gourmet's itinerary, but it's also where many of the local movers and shakers hang out, a popular place for post-theater dining, and open till the wee hours. The dining room has a clublike ambience, and the food ranges from grills to ragouts to sautés—some daringly creative and some classical. Dinners here are pricey, but those on a budget can order a hot dog at the bar. ✕ *150 Redwood Alley,* ☏ *415/861–7827. Reservations accepted up to 2 wks in advance, some tables reserved for walk-ins. AE, DC, MC, V. No lunch weekends. Valet parking at night.*

$–$$ **Stars Cafe.** Highlights at this lower-priced satellite of Stars restaurant are pizzas from the wood-burning oven and desserts by Stars' noted pastry chef Emily Luchetti. ✕ *500 Van Ness Ave.,* ☏ *415/861–4344. Reservations accepted for 5 or more for lunch, 2 or more for dinner. AE, DC, MC, V.*

Embarcadero North

$$ **Fog City Diner.** This is where the diner and grazing crazes began in San Francisco, and the popularity of this spot knows no end. The long, narrow dining room emulates a luxurious railroad car with dark wood paneling, huge windows, and comfortable booths. The cooking is innovative, drawing its inspiration from regional cooking throughout the United States. The sharable "small plates" are a fun way to go. ✕ *1300 Battery St.,* ☏ *415/982–2000. Reservations advised. D, DC, MC, V.*

$$ **MacArthur Park.** Year after year San Franciscans acclaim this as their favorite spot for ribs, but the oak-wood smoker and mesquite grill also turn out a wide variety of all-American fare, from steaks and hamburgers to seafood. Takeout is also available at this handsomely renovated pre-earthquake warehouse. ✕ *607 Front St.,* ☏ *415/398–5700. Reservations advised. AE, DC, MC, V. No lunch weekends and most major holidays. Valet parking at night.*

Embarcadero South

$$–$$$ **Boulevard.** Renowned chef Nancy Oakes's menu is seasonally in flux, but you can be certain to find her signature juxtaposition of aristocratic fare—foie gras is a favorite—with homey comfort foods like pot roast and wood-roasted meats and fowl. For those who can't find or afford a table during regular hours, Boulevard offers a less formal weekday afternoon bar service that features pizza, oysters, burgers, or perhaps a baked potato stuffed with goat cheese. ✕ *1 Mission St.,* ☏ *415/543–6084. Reservations accepted up to 6 wks in advance. AE, DC, MC, V. Closed major holidays. No lunch weekends. Valet parking.*

Financial District

$$$ **Cypress Club.** Fans of John Cunin have flocked here since 1990, when Masa's longtime maître d' opened his own place, which he calls a "San Francisco brasserie." This categorizes the contemporary American cooking somewhat, but the decor defies description. It could be interpreted as anything from a parody of an ancient temple to a futuristic space war. ✕ *500 Jackson St.,* ☏ *415/296–8555. Reservations advised. AE, DC, MC, V. No lunch. Valet parking at night.*

Nob Hill

$$–$$$ ★ **Ritz-Carlton Restaurant and Dining Room.** There are two distinctly different places to eat in this neoclassical Nob Hill showplace. The Restaurant, a cheerful, informal spot with a large garden patio for outdoor dining, serves breakfast, lunch, dinner, and a Sunday jazz brunch,

Aequarello, **8**
Alain Rondelli, **56**
Appam, **42**
Aqua, **27**
Bistro M, **61**
Boulevard, **30**
Cafe Adriano, **5**
Café Marimba, **4**
California Culinary Academy, **45**
Campton Place, **34**
Capp's Corner, **12**
Cypress Club, **17**
Des Alpes, **13**
Faz, **37**
Fleur de Lys, **44**
Fog City Diner, **18**
Fringale, **40**
Gaylord's, **2, 29**
Greens, **1**
Harbor Village, **28**
Harris', **7**
Hawthorne Lane, **39**
Hayes Street Grill, **54**
The Heights, **63**
Helmand, **16**
Hong Kong Flower Lounge, **57**
Hyde Street Bistro, **9**
Il Fornaio, **19**
Izzy's Steak & Chop House, **6**
Kabuto Sushi, **58**
Kuleto's, **35**
Kyo ya, **38**
La Folie, **11**
Le Central, **36**
Le Soleil, **59**
LuLu, **41**
MacArthur Park, **21**
Manora, **49, 50**
Masa's, **33**
Maykadeh, **15**
McCormick & Kuleto's, **3**
Mifune, **55**
Millennium, **48**
Moose's, **14**
Pacific, **32**
Postrio, **43**
R & G Lounge, **24**
Ritz-Carlton Restaurant and Dining Room, **20**
Square One, **22**
Stars, **46**
Stars Cafe, **47**
Straits Cafe, **62**
Tadich Grill, **26**
Thepin, **53**
Ton Kiang, **60, 61**

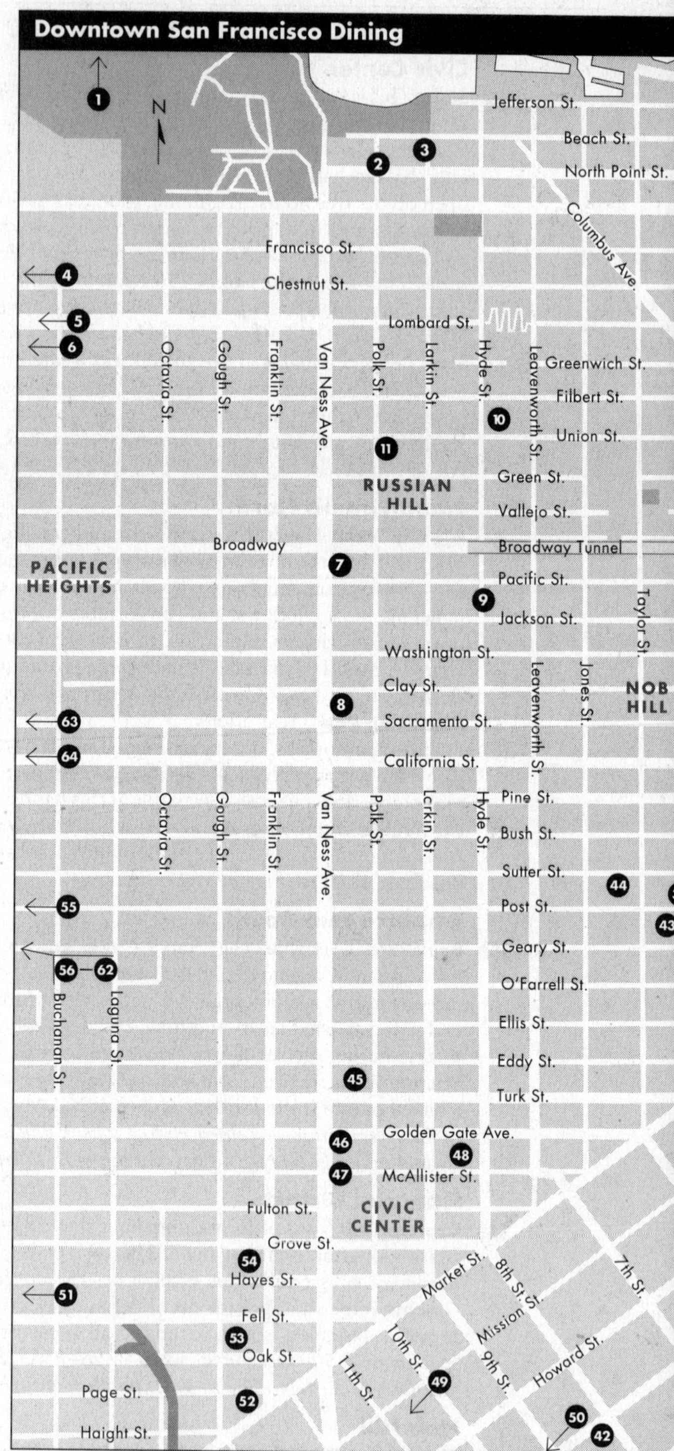

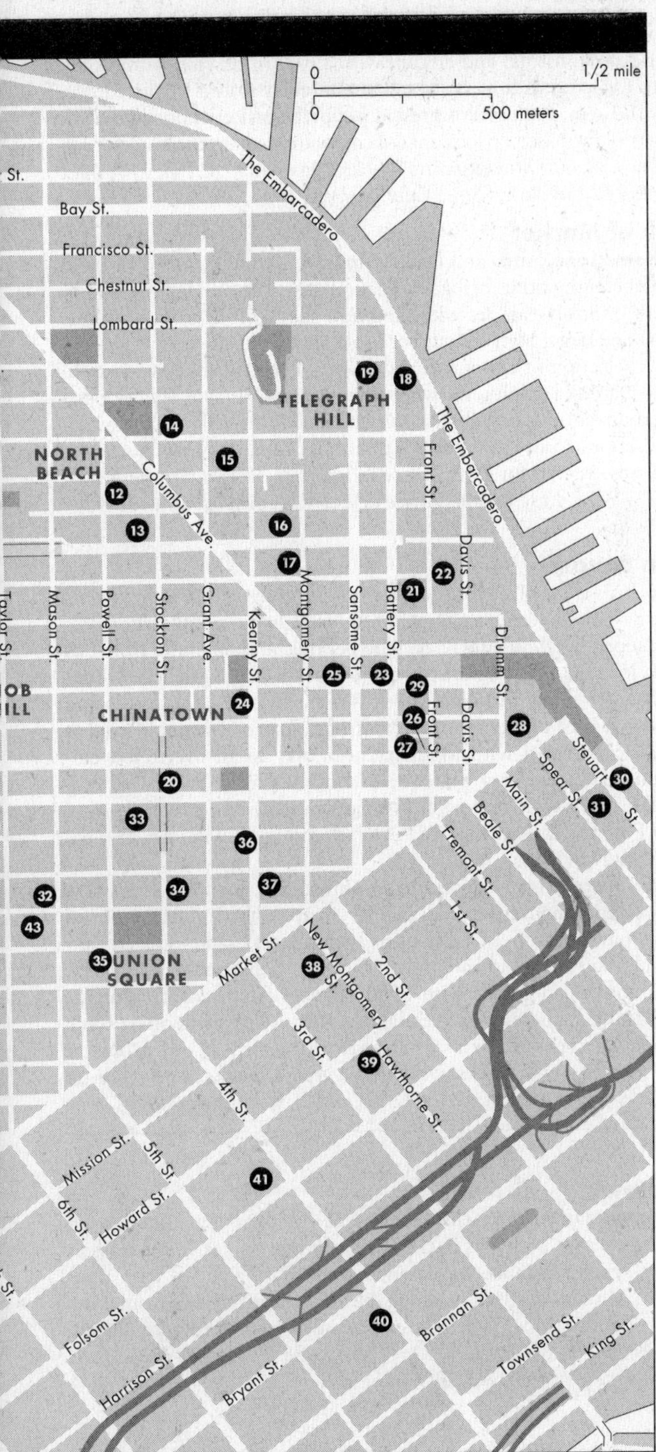

Vertigo, **25**
Vivande Porta Via, **64**
Wu Kong, **31**
Yaya Cuisine, **51**
Yank Sing, **23**
Zarzuela, **10**
Zuni Café & Grill, **52**

with piano music at lunchtime and a jazz trio at weekend dinners. The Dining Room, formal and elegant with a harpist playing, serves only two- to five-course dinners, which are uniquely priced by the course, not by the item. Both rooms present a superb version of northern California cooking based on local ingredients with Mediterranean and Asian overtones. ✕ *600 Stockton St.,* ☎ *415/296–7465. AE, D, DC, MC, V. Dining Room closed Sun. Valet parking.*

South of Market

$$$ **Hawthorne Lane.** Anne and David Gingrass, two of Postrio's original trio of chefs (the other being Wolfgang Puck), have joined the booming bevy of SoMa eateries with their new spot a block from Moscone Center. The large, high-ceiling bar looks into a private courtyard and offers a selection of country-rustic classics like artichokes with aioli, cracked crab, and onion soup, while patrons in the intimate, light-flooded dining room have views of both courtyard and kitchen. The menu, which they describe as San Franciscan, is not unlike the East-West cuisine the Gingrasses created for Postrio (*see below*). ✕ *22 Hawthorne St.,* ☎ *415/777–9779. Reservations advised. MC, V. No lunch weekends. Valet parking.*

Union Square

$$$–$$$$ ★ **Postrio.** This is the place for those who want to see and be seen; there's always a chance to catch a glimpse of some celebrity, including Postrio's owner, superchef Wolfgang Puck, who periodically commutes from Los Angeles to make an appearance in the restaurant's open kitchen. A stunning three-level bar and dining area is highlighted by palm trees and museum-quality contemporary paintings. Attire is formal; food is Puckish Californian with Mediterranean and Asian overtones, emphasizing pastas, grilled seafood, and house-baked breads. A substantial breakfast and bar menu (with great pizza) are served here, too. ✕ *545 Post St.,* ☎ *415/776–7825. Reservations advised. AE, D, DC, MC, V. Valet parking.*

$$$ ★ **Campton Place.** This elegant, ultrasophisticated small hotel put new American cooking on the local culinary map. Chef Todd Humphries carries on the innovative traditions of opening chef Bradley Ogden with great aplomb and has added his own touches, such as embellishing traditional American dishes with ethnic flavors from recent immigrations. Breakfast and brunch are major events. A bar menu offers some samplings of appetizers, plus a caviar extravaganza. ✕ *340 Stockton St.,* ☎ *415/955–5555. Reservations suggested, 2 wks in advance on weekends. Jacket required. AE, D, DC, MC, V. Valet parking.*

Chinese

Chinatown

$–$$ **R&G Lounge.** Downstairs (entrance on Kearny Street) is a no-tablecloth dining room that is always packed at lunch and dinner. In the classier upstairs space (entrance on Commercial Street) a menu with photographs helps diners decide among the many exotic dishes, from dried scallops with seasonal vegetables to steamed bean curd with shrimp meat. ✕ *631 B Kearny St.,* ☎ *415/982–7877 or 415/982–3811. Reservations accepted. AE, DC, MC, V.*

Embarcadero North

$$ ★ **Harbor Village.** Classic Cantonese cooking, dim-sum lunches, and fresh seafood from the restaurant's own tanks are the hallmarks of this 400-seat branch of a Hong Kong establishment. The setting is opulent, with Chinese antiques and teak furnishings. ✕ *4 Embarcadero Center,* ☏ *415/781–8833. Reservations not accepted for lunch on weekends. AE, DC, MC, V. Validated parking in Embarcadero Center Garage.*

Embarcadero South

$$ **Wu Kong.** Tucked away in the splashy art deco Rincon Center, Wu Kong features the cuisine of Shanghai and Canton. Specialties include dim sum, braised yellow fish, and the incredible vegetarian goose—one of Shanghai's famous mock dishes, created from paper-thin layers of dried bean-curd sheets and mushrooms. ✕ *101 Spear St.,* ☏ *415/957–9300. Reservations advised. AE, DC, MC, V. Validated parking at Rincon Center garage.*

Financial District

$$ **Yank Sing.** The city's oldest teahouse has grown by leaps and branches with the popularity of dim sum, and each branch presently offers some 70 varieties of the little morsels each day. The Battery Street location seats 300, and the older, smaller Stevenson Street site has been rebuilt in high-tech style. ✕ *427 Battery St.,* ☏ *415/362–1640; 49 Stevenson St.,* ☏ *415/541–4949. Reservations advised. AE, DC, MC, V. No dinner. Stevenson site closed weekends.*

Richmond District

$$ **Hong Kong Flower Lounge.** This outpost of a famous Asian restaurant chain is known in particular for its seafood—crabs, shrimp, catfish, lobsters, scallops—which is plucked straight from tanks and prepared in a variety of ways, from classic to contemporary. A good array of dim sum is offered at midday. ✕ *5322 Geary Blvd.,* ☏ *415/668–8998. Reservations advised. AE, D, DC, MC, V.*

$ **Ton Kiang.** This restaurant serves regional Hakka specialties like salt-baked chicken, braised stuffed bean curd, wine-flavored dishes, delicate fish and beef balls, and casseroles of meat and seafood cooked in clay pots. Do not overlook the seafood offerings, such as salt-and-pepper squid or shrimp, braised catfish, or stir-fried crab. Of the two branches on Geary Boulevard, the newest, at 5821, is more stylish and serves excellent dim sum. ✕ *3148 Geary Blvd.,* ☏ *415/752–4440; 5821 Geary Blvd.,* ☏ *415/387–8273. Reservations advised. MC, V.*

French

Civic Center

$$–$$$ **California Culinary Academy.** A historic theater houses one of the most highly regarded professional cooking schools in the United States. Well-dressed patrons (men wear jackets) watch the student chefs at work on the double-tier stage while dining on classic French cooking offered as a prix fixe meal or a bountiful buffet in the theaterlike Carême Room. An à la carte informal grill is located on the lower level. ✕ *625 Polk St.,* ☏ *415/771–3500. Reservations advised (2–4 wks in advance for Fri.-night buffet). AE, DC, MC, V. Closed weekends.*

Financial District

$$ **Le Central.** This is the quintessential bistro: noisy and crowded, with nothing subtle about the cooking. But the garlicky pâtés, leeks vinaigrette, cassoulet, and grilled blood sausage with crisp french fries keep the crowds coming. ✕ *453 Bush St.,* ☏ *415/391–2233. Reservations advised. AE, DC, MC, V. Closed Sun.*

Lower Pacific Heights

$$$ **The Heights.** This sophisticated French eatery is the domain of chef-owner Charles Solomon, who arrived from New York highly recommended. At comfortably spaced tables in three small but light-filled dining rooms, customers can work their way through a six-course tasting menu or choose from an à la carte menu that changes regularly. A fricassee of wild mushrooms with sweetbreads and a vegetable pot-au-feu are particularly tasty appetizers; lavender-scented roast duck atop braised pears and steelhead trout with lobster sauce may follow. Don't overlook the dessert list; the homemade ice creams and delicate puff-pastry creations are sublime. ✕ *3235 Sacramento St.,* ☏ *415/474-8890. Reservations advised. AE, D, DC, MC, V. Closed Mon. No lunch. Valet parking.*

Midtown

$$$ ★ **La Folie.** This pretty storefront café showcases the nouvelle cuisine of Roland Passot, a former sous-chef at Illinois's famous Le Français. Much of the food is edible art—whimsical presentations in the form of savory terrines, *galettes* (flat, round cakes), and napoleons—or elegant accompaniments such as bone-marrow flan. ✕ *2316 Polk St.,* ☏ *415/776–5577. Reservations advised. AE, D, DC, MC, V. Closed Sun. No lunch.*

North Beach

$ **Des Alpes.** Basque dinners are offered here, with soup, salad, *two* entrées—sweetbreads on puff pastry and rare roast beef are a typical pair—ice cream, and coffee included in the budget price. It's a haven for trenchermen and a pleasant spot, with wood-paneled walls and bright, embroidered cloths on the tables. Service is family style. ✕ *732 Broadway,* ☏ *415/788–9900. Reservations advised on weekends. D, DC, MC, V. Closed Mon., Dec. 25. No lunch.*

Richmond District

$$–$$$ ★ **Alain Rondelli.** Chef Rondelli, formerly of Ernie's, has adapted his background in classic yet contemporary French cooking to the agricultural abundance and Asian-Hispanic influences of California, with a zap of jalapeño chili here, a bit of star anise there. Two-part entrées are a Rondelli signature: a breast of chicken followed up with a confit of the leg in a custard tart, for example. ✕ *126 Clement St.,* ☏ *415/387–0408. Reservations advised. MC, V. Closed Mon., Tues.*

South of Market

$$$ **Bistro M.** Chef Michel Richard serves French cuisine—executed with a California accent—for breakfast, lunch, and dinner. In the evening, the Alsatian onion tart and sardine rillettes with brioche toasts are superb first courses, followed by the imaginative oxtail in ziti terrine. Be sure to leave room for Richard's signature crunchy napoleon. ✕ *Hotel Milano, 55 5th St.,* ☏ *415/543–5554. Reservations advised. AE, D, DC, MC, V. No lunch Sun. Valet parking.*

$$ ★ **Fringale.** The bright-yellow paint on this dazzling bistro stands out like a beacon on an otherwise bleak industrial street, attracting a Pacific Heights–Montgomery Street clientele. They come for the French Basque–inspired creations of Biarritz-born chef Gerald Hirigoyen, whose ultimate crème brûlée is a hallmark. ✕ *570 4th St.,* ☏ *415/543–0573. Reservations required. AE, MC, V. Closed Sun., Dec. 25. No lunch Sat.*

Union Square

$$$$ ★ **Fleur de Lys.** The menu changes constantly at this award-winning restaurant, but such dishes as lobster soup with lemongrass, Maryland

crab cakes, and pork tenderloin with black beans bear witness to Keller's international scope. The intimate dining room, like a sheikh's tent, is encased with hundreds of yards of paisley. ✕ *777 Sutter St.,* ☎ *415/673–7779. Weekend reservations advised 2 wks in advance. Jacket required. AE, DC, MC, V. Closed Sun., most major holidays. No lunch. Valet parking.*

$$$$ ★ Masa's. Chef Julian Serrano carries on the tradition of the late Masa Kobayashi. In fact, some Masa regulars say her cooking is even better. Presentation is as important as the food itself in this pretty, flower-filled dining spot in the Vintage Court Hotel. ✕ *648 Bush St.,* ☎ *415/989–7154. Reservations accepted up to 2 months in advance. Jacket and tie. AE, D, DC, MC, V. Closed Sun., Mon., and 1st 2 wks of Jan. No lunch. Valet parking.*

$$$ Pacific. Takayoshi Kawai, former sous-chef at Masa's, crafts sophisticated yet unstuffy dishes that combine French techniques and California ingredients. For those on a budget, a three-course, prix fixe menu offers a tasty solution, as does breakfast. ✕ *Pan Pacific Hotel, 500 Post St.,* ☎ *415/929–2087. Reservations advised. AE, D, DC, MC, V. Complimentary valet parking.*

Greek and Middle Eastern

Financial District

$$ Faz. Creamy *baba ghannooj* (eggplant spread), beef-and-rice-filled dolmas, and a Persian-inspired platter of feta cheese, pungent olives, and garden-fresh herbs are all great courses here. The signature house-smoked fish platter includes salmon, trout, and sometimes sturgeon. ✕ *161 Sutter St.,* ☎ *415/362–0404. Reservations advised. AE, DC, MC, V. Valet parking at night. Closed Sun. No lunch Sat.*

North Beach

$–$$ Maykadeh. Lamb dishes with rice are the specialties in this authentic Persian restaurant, whose setting is so elegant that the modest check comes as a great surprise. ✕ *470 Green St.,* ☎ *415/362–8286. Reservations advised. MC, V. Valet parking at night.*

$ Helmand. Authentic Afghani cooking, elegant surroundings with white napery and rich Afghan carpets, and amazingly low prices make Helmand worth checking out. Don't miss the *aushak* (leek-filled ravioli served with yogurt and ground beef). The lamb dishes are also exceptional. ✕ *430 Broadway,* ☎ *415/362–0641. Reservations advised. AE, MC, V. No lunch weekends. Free validated parking at night at Helmand Parking, 468 Broadway.*

Indian

Northern Waterfront and Embarcadero

$$ Gaylord's. A vast selection of mildly spiced northern Indian food is offered here, along with meats and breads from the tandoori ovens and a wide range of vegetarian dishes. The dining rooms are elegantly appointed with Indian paintings and gleaming silver service. The Ghirardelli Square location offers bay views. ✕ *Ghirardelli Sq.,* ☎ *415/771–8822; Embarcadero 1,* ☎ *415/397–7775. Reservations advised. AE, D, DC, MC, V. No lunch Sun. at Embarcadero. Validated parking at Ghirardelli Sq. garage and Embarcadero Center garage.*

South of Market

$$ **Appam.** A traditional north Indian cooking style, *dum pukt,* literally "breath of steam," is the specialty of this attractive restaurant, which also offers a lovely garden for sunny lunchtime dining. Curries such as a fragrant salmon *mouli,* a coconut milk–based curry, flavored with onions, tomatoes, and tamarind, or a duck leg paired with apricots, are sealed inside clay pots. The pots are then placed inside a double-walled oven, and the foods cook in their own steam. Service can be ragged. ✕ *1261 Folsom St.,* ☎ *415/626–2798. Reservations accepted. AE, MC, V. Closed Sun.*

Italian

Cow Hollow/Marina

$$ ★ **Café Adriano.** House-made *strongozzi* (thick spaghetti) with a spicy Umbrian tomato sauce or *stracci* (pasta squares) with scallops are among the specialties here. Irresistible antipasti might include venison carpaccio with a garlicky mayonnaise. Roast leg of lamb with eggplant puree and simply cooked sea bass are main-course staples. ✕ *3347 Fillmore St.,* ☎ *415/474–4180. Reservations advised. MC, V. Closed Mon. No lunch.*

Embarcadero North

$$ **Il Fornaio.** An offshoot of the Il Fornaio bakeries, this handsome tile-floored, wood-paneled complex combines a café, bakery, and upscale trattoria with outdoor seating. The Tuscan cooking features pizzas from a wood-burning oven, superb house-made pastas and gnocchi, and grilled poultry and seafood. Anticipate a wait, but take solace in the moderate prices. ✕ *Levi's Plaza, 1265 Battery St.,* ☎ *415/986–0100. Reservations advised. AE, DC, MC, V. Valet parking.*

Lower Pacific Heights

$$$ **Vivande Porta Via.** The regularly changing menu at Vivande includes such satisfying southern Italian plates as the classic Sicilian pasta *alla Norma* (with eggplant) or spaghetti with fresh tuna and olives, and such northern specialties as risotto with radicchio, pancetta, and pine nuts. ✕ *2125 Fillmore St.,* ☎ *415/346–4430. Reservations advised. MC, V.*

Midtown

$$–$$$ **Acquarello.** This exquisite restaurant is one of the most romantic spots in town. The service and food are exemplary, and the menu covers the full range of Italian cuisine, from northern Italy to the tip of the boot. Desserts are exceptional. ✕ *1722 Sacramento St.,* ☎ *415/567–5432. Reservations advised. AE, D, DC, MC, V. Closed Sun., Mon., major holidays. No lunch.*

North Beach

$ **Capp's Corner.** At one of the last of the family-style trattorias, diners sit elbow to elbow at long oilcloth-covered tables to feast on bountiful, well-prepared five-course dinners. For calorie counters or the budget-minded, a simpler dinner includes a tureen of minestrone, salad, and pasta. ✕ *1600 Powell St.,* ☎ *415/989–2589. Reservations advised. AE, D, DC, MC, V. No lunch weekends. Parking validation available.*

Russian Hill

$$ **Hyde Street Bistro.** The ambience says quintessential neighborhood bistro, but the food is part *gasthaus,* part trattoria, and closely in line with the Austro-Italian tradition of Italy's northeastern Frioli region. Strudels and spaetzles are served alongside pastas and polentas, potato dumplings are paired with a Gorgonzola sauce, and the pastries belie the chef-owner's Austrian roots. ✕ *1521 Hyde St.,* ☎ *415/441–7778. Reser-*

vations advised. AE, MC, V. Closed 3 days at Christmas. No lunch. Valet parking.

Union Square

$$ **Kuleto's.** The contemporary cooking of northern Italy, the atmosphere of old San Francisco, and a terrific bar menu showcasing contemporary and traditional antipasti have made this spot off Union Square a hit. Publike booths and a long, open kitchen fill one side of the restaurant; a gardenlike setting with light splashed from skylights lies beyond. Grilled seafood dishes are among the specialties. Breakfast is also served. ✕ *221 Powell St.,* ☎ *415/397–7720. Reservations advised. AE, D, DC, MC, V.*

Japanese

Financial District

$$–$$$ ★ **Kyo-ya.** Rarely replicated outside Japan, the refined experience of dining in a fine Japanese restaurant has been introduced with extraordinary authenticity at this showplace within the Sheraton Palace Hotel. The range is spectacular—encompassing tempuras, one-pot dishes, deep-fried and grilled meats, and a choice of some three-dozen sushi selections. The lunch menu is more limited than dinner but does offer a *shokado,* a sampler of four classic dishes encased in a handsome lacquered lunch box. ✕ *Sheraton Palace Hotel, 2 New Montgomery St., at Market St.,* ☎ *415/546–5000. Reservations advised. AE, D, DC, MC, V. Closed weekends.*

Japantown

$ **Mifune.** Thin, brown soba (buckwheat) and thick, white udon (wheat) are the specialties at this North American outpost of an Osaka-based noodle empire. Seating is at rustic wooden tables, where diners can be heard slurping down big bowls of such traditional Japanese combinations as fish cake–crowned udon and *tenzaru* (cold noodles and hot tempura served on lacquered trays with gingery dipping sauce). ✕ *Japan Center Mall, Kintetsu Bldg., 1737 Post St.,* ☎ *415/922–0337. No reservations. AE, D, DC, MC, V.*

Richmond District

$$ **Kabuto Sushi.** Behind his black-lacquered counter, master chef Sachio Kojima flashes his knives with the grace of a samurai warrior. In addition to exceptional sushi and sashimi, traditional Japanese dinners are served in the adjoining dining room with both Western seating and, in a shoji-screened area, tatami seating. ✕ *5116 Geary Blvd.,* ☎ *415/752–5652. Reservations advised for dinner. MC, V. Closed Mon. No lunch.*

Mediterranean

Civic Center

$$–$$$ ★ **Zuni Café & Grill.** Zuni's Italian-Mediterranean menu and its unpretentious atmosphere pack in the crowds from early morning to late evening. A spacious, window-filled balcony dining area overlooks the large bar, where shellfish, one of the best oyster selections in town, and drinks are dispensed. A second dining room houses the giant pizza oven and grill. Even the hamburgers have an Italian accent—they're topped with Gorgonzola and served on herbed focaccia buns. ✕ *1658 Market St.,* ☎ *415/552–2522. Reservations advised. AE, MC, V. Closed Mon., major holidays.*

Embarcadero North

$$–$$$ ★ **Square One.** Chef Joyce Goldstein introduces an ambitious new menu daily, with dishes based on the classic cooking of the Mediterranean countries, sometimes straying to Asia and Latin America. The dining room, with its views of the open kitchen and the Golden Gateway commons, is an understated setting for some of the finest food in town—and an award-winning wine list. A bar menu is available. ✕ *190 Pacific Ave., ☎ 415/788–1110. Reservations advised. AE, DC, MC, V. No lunch weekends. Valet parking at night.*

Financial District

$$ **Vertigo.** The Transamerica Pyramid houses one of the city's most stunning restaurants, a three-tier space with see-through ceilings, a park-like entrance, and an inviting French and Italian menu with Asian accents. A seasonal menu combines the freshest possible ingredients—especially seafood—in creative combinations. A first course of grilled shrimp with a salad of fennel and tangerine might be followed by salmon in crunchy coriander crust, or lamb loin with goat cheese–potato gratin. A bar menu offers afternoon snacks such as Dungeness crab cakes and corn-wheat pizzas. ✕ *600 Montgomery St., ☎ 415/433–7250. Reservations advised. AE, D, DC, MC, V. Valet parking. Closed Sun. No lunch Sat.*

North Beach

$$ ★ **Moose's.** Along with a host of local luminaries, Tom Brokaw, Walter Cronkite, Tom Wolfe, and Senator Dianne Feinstein head for Moose's when they're in town. And the food impresses as much as the clientele: A Mediterranean-inspired menu highlights innovative appetizers, pastas, seafood, and grills. The surroundings are classic and comfortable, with views of Washington Square and Russian Hill from a front café area and, in the rear, facing the open kitchen, counter seats for singles. There's live music at night and a fine Sunday brunch. ✕ *1652 Stockton St., ☎ 415/989–7800. Reservations advised 6–8 wks in advance. AE, DC, MC, V. No lunch Mon. Valet parking.*

South of Market

$–$$ ★ **LuLu.** Chef Reed Hearon has brought a touch of the French-Italian Riviera to a spacious and stunningly renovated San Francisco warehouse. Diners feast on a signature dish of sizzling mussels roasted in an iron skillet, plus pizzas and pastas with "would you believe it" embellishments, and wood-roasted poultry, meats, and shellfish. Sharing dishes family-style is the custom here. For those who like a quieter ambience, Hearon has opened a little bistro, LuLu Bis, just next door, where four-course prix fixe dinners are served at communal tables. ✕ *816 Folsom St., ☎ 415/495–5775. Reservations advised 1–2 wks in advance. AE, DC, MC, V. No Sun. lunch at LuLu. No lunch at LuLu Bis.*

Mexican/Latin American/Spanish

Cow Hollow/Marina

$$ **Café Marimba.** The regional specialties at Reed Hearon's colorful bistro include silken *mole negro* (sauce of chiles and chocolate) from Oaxaca, served in tamales and other dishes; shrimp prepared with roasted onions and tomatoes in the style of Zihuatenejo; and chicken with a marinade from Yucatán, stuffed into one of the world's greatest tacos. ✕ *2317 Chestnut St.,* ☏ *415/776–1506. Reservations advised. MC, V. Closed Thanksgiving, Dec. 25. No lunch Mon. Valet parking.*

Russian Hill

$$ **Zarzuela.** This small, crowded storefront serves nearly 40 different hot and cold tapas, plus some dozen main courses. There is a tapa to suit every palate, from poached octopus atop new potatoes and hot, garlic-flecked shrimp to slabs of Manchego cheese with paper-thin slices of serrano ham. The paella of saffron-scented rice weighed down with prawns, mussels, and clams is guaranteed to make the most unsentimental Madrileño homesick. ✕ *2000 Hyde St.,* ☏ *415/346-0800. Reservations accepted for 6 or more. MC, V. Closed Sun.*

Seafood

Civic Center

$$ **Hayes Street Grill.** Eight to 15 different kinds of seafood are chalked on the blackboard each night at this extremely popular restaurant. The fish is served simply grilled, with a choice of sauces ranging from tartar to a spicy Szechuan peanut concoction. Appetizers are unusual, and desserts are lavish. ✕ *320 Hayes St.,* ☏ *415/863–5545. Reservations advised several wks in advance. AE, D, DC, MC, V. Closed some holidays. No lunch weekends.*

Financial District

$$$ ★ **Aqua.** This quietly elegant and ultrafashionable spot is possibly the city's most important seafood restaurant ever. Chef-owner George Morrone has a supremely original talent for creating contemporary versions of French, Italian, and American classics: Expect mussel, crab, or lobster soufflés; lobster gnocchi with lobster sauce; shrimp and corn madeleines strewn in a salad; and ultrarare *ahi* tuna paired with foie gras. Desserts are miniature museum pieces. ✕ *252 California St.,* ☏ *415/956–9662. Reservations essential. AE, DC, MC, V. Closed Sun. No lunch Sat. Valet parking at night.*

$$ **Tadich Grill.** Owners and locations have changed many times since this old-timer opened during the Gold Rush era, but the 19th-century atmosphere remains, as does the kitchen's special way with seafood. Simple sautés are the best choices, or the cioppino during crab season. There is seating at both the counter and in private booths, but expect long lines for a table at lunchtime. ✕ *240 California St.,* ☏ *415/391–2373. No reservations. MC, V. Closed Sun.*

Northern Waterfront

$$ **McCormick & Kuleto's.** This seafood emporium in Ghirardelli Square is a visitor's dream come true: a fabulous view of the bay from every seat in the house; an old San Francisco atmosphere; and some 30 varieties of fish and shellfish prepared in at least 70 globe-circling ways, from tacos, pot stickers, and fish cakes to grills, pastas, and stew. The food has its ups and downs, but even on foggy days you can count on the view. ✕ *Ghirardelli Sq.,* ☏ *415/929–1730. Reservations advised. AE, D, DC, MC, V. Validated parking in Ghirardelli Sq. garage.*

Southeast Asian

Civic Center

$–$$ **Thepin.** The stylish dining room at Thepin sparkles with linen napery, fresh flowers, Thai artwork, and a wine list that surpasses the Asian norm. Notable are the duck dishes and the curries, each prepared with its own mixture of freshly blended spices. ✕ *298 Gough St.,* ☎ *415/863–9335. Reservations advised. AE, MC, V. Closed major holidays. No lunch weekends.*

$–$$ ★ **Le Soleil.** The food of Vietnam is the specialty of this pastel, light-filled restaurant. Try the excellent raw-beef salad; crisp, flavorful spring rolls; a simple stir-fry of chicken and aromatic fresh basil leaves; or large prawns simmered in a clay pot. ✕ *133 Clement St.,* ☎ *415/668–4848. Reservations accepted. MC, V.*

$–$$ **Straits Cafe.** This popular restaurant serves the unique fare of Singapore, a cuisine that combines the culinary traditions of China, India, and the Malay archipelago. That exotic mix translates into complex curries, rice cooked in coconut milk, sticks of fragrant *satay* (skewers of chicken or beef), and seafood noodle soups. ✕ *3300 Geary Blvd.,* ☎ *415/668–1783. Reservations advised. AE, MC, V.*

South of Market

$ **Manora.** When this homey Thai café way out on Mission Street first opened, crowds from all over town lined up for a table to try the extensive selection of carefully prepared dishes. Now the same great food is offered at a more conveniently located Manora, not far from the Performing Arts Center. Good choices are the fish cakes and curries. ✕ *3226 Mission St.,* ☎ *415/550–0856; 1600 Folsom St.,* ☎ *415/861–6224. MC, V. Closed Mon. and lunch at Mission St.; no lunch weekends at Folsom St.*

Steak Houses

Marina

$$ **Izzy's Steak & Chop House.** Izzy Gomez was a legendary San Francisco saloon keeper, and his namesake eatery carries on the tradition with terrific steaks, chops, and seafood, plus all the trimmings—such as cheesy scalloped potatoes and creamed spinach. ✕ *3345 Steiner St.,* ☎ *415/563–0487. Reservations accepted. AE, DC, MC, V. No lunch. Validated parking at Lombard Garage.*

Midtown

$$$ ★ **Harris'.** Ann Harris knows her beef. She grew up on a Texas cattle ranch and was married to the late Jack Harris of Harris Ranch fame. In her own large, New York–style restaurant she serves some of the best dry-aged steaks in town, but don't overlook the grilled seafood or poultry. There is also an extensive bar menu. ✕ *2100 Van Ness Ave.,* ☎ *415/673–1888. Reservations advised. AE, DC, MC, V. No lunch. Valet parking.*

Vegetarian

Civic Center

$$ **Millennium.** Millennium offers a vegetarian menu of low-fat, dairy-free dishes made with organic ingredients that keeps herbivores and carnivores alike satisfied. Pastas, polenta, and grilled vegetables are among the most successful dishes. For true believers, there is *seitan* (a whole-wheat meat substitute) steak in marsala sauce, a chocolate mousse cake made from tofu, and organic wines and beers. A Continental breakfast is served Monday through Friday and brunch is offered on Sunday. ✕ *Abigail Hotel, 246 McAllister St.,* ☎ *415/487–9800. Reservations accepted. MC, V.*

Marina

$$ ★ **Greens.** This beautiful restaurant with expansive bay views is owned and operated by the Zen Buddhist Center of Marin County. The dining room offers a wide, eclectic, and creative spectrum of meatless cooking, and the bread promises nirvana. Dinners are à la carte on weeknights, but only a five-course prix fixe dinner is served on Saturday. ✕ *Bldg. A, Fort Mason,* ☎ *415/771–6222. Reservations advised. MC, V. No lunch Mon., no dinner Sun. Public parking at Fort Mason Center.*

LODGING

By Patrick Hoctel

Few cities in the United States can rival San Francisco's variety in lodging. There are plush hotels ranked among the finest in the world, renovated older buildings that have the charm of Europe, bed-and-breakfasts in the city's Victorian "Painted Ladies," and the popular chain hotels found in most cities in the United States.

One of the brightest spots in the lodging picture is the transformation of handsome early 20th-century downtown high-rises into small, distinctive hotels that offer personal service and European ambience. Another is the recent addition of ultradeluxe modern hotels such as the Miyako and the Mandarin Oriental, which specialize in attentive Asian-style hospitality.

The **San Francisco Convention and Visitors Bureau** (☎ 415/391–2000) publishes a free lodging guide with a map and a listing of all hotels. Call to order and also to find out what's happening that week in San Francisco.

Because San Francisco is one of the top destinations in the United States for tourists as well as business travelers and convention goers, reservations are always advised, especially during the May–October peak season.

San Francisco's geography makes it conveniently compact. No matter what their location, the hotels listed below are on or close to public transportation lines. Some properties on Lombard Street and in the Civic Center area have free parking, but a car is more a hindrance than an asset in San Francisco.

Although not as high as the rates in New York, San Francisco hotel prices may come as a surprise to travelers from less urban areas. Average rates for double rooms downtown and at the wharf are in the $120 range. Adding to the expense is the city's 12% transient occupancy tax, which can significantly boost the cost of a lengthy stay. The good news is that because of the hotel building boom of the late 1980s, there is now an oversupply of rooms, which has led to much discounting of prices. Check for special rates and packages when making reservations.

For those in search of true budget accommodations (under $50), try the Adelaide Inn (*see* Union Square/Downtown, *below*) or the **YMCA Central Branch.** *220 Golden Gate Ave., 94102, ☎ 415/885–0460. 106 rooms, 6 with bath. Café, pool, sauna, steam room, health club. MC, V.*

An alternative to hotels and motels is staying in private homes and apartments, available through **American Family Inn/Bed & Breakfast San Francisco** (Box 420009, San Francisco 94142, ☎ 415/931–3083), **Bed & Breakfast International–San Francisco** (Box 282910, San Francisco 94128-2910, ☎ 415/696–1690 or 800/872–4500, FAX 415/696–1699).

CATEGORY	COST*
$$$$	over $175
$$$	$120–$175
$$	$80–$120
$	under $80

**All prices are for a standard double room, excluding 12% tax.*

Union Square/Downtown

The largest variety and greatest concentration of hotels is in the city's downtown hub, Union Square, where hotel guests can find the best shopping, the theater district, and convenient transportation to every spot in San Francisco.

$$$$ ★ Campton Place Hotel. Behind a simple brownstone facade with white awning, quiet reigns. Highly attentive, personal service—from unpacking assistance to nightly turndown—begins the moment uniformed doormen greet guests outside the marble-floored lobby. The rooms, small but well appointed, are decorated with Asian touches in subtle tones of gold and brown, with double-pane windows, Chinese armoires, and good-size writing desks. From the ninth floor up, there are only four rooms to a floor. They overlook an atrium, which lends a cozy, residential feel. The hotel is a 10-minute walk from the Moscone Center and the new Yerba Buena Center complex. The Campton Place Restaurant, listed prominently in *Condé Nast Traveler*'s "50 American Restaurants Worth the Journey," is famed for its breakfasts. *340 Stockton St., 94108, ☎ 415/781–5555 or 800/235–4300, FAX 415/955–5536. 117 rooms. Restaurant, bar. AE, DC, MC, V.*

$$$$ ★ Four Seasons Clift. The Clift towers over San Francisco's theater district, its crisp, forest-green awnings and formal door service subtle hints of the elegance within. In the busy lobby, where dark paneling and four enormous chandeliers lend a note of grandeur, everything runs smoothly. The Clift is noted for its swift personalized service; a phone call will get you anything from complimentary limousine service to a chocolate cake. Rooms, some rich with dark woods and burgundies, others refreshingly pastel, all have large writing desks, plants, and flowers. Be sure to sample a cocktail in the famous Art Deco Redwood Room lounge, complete with chandeliers and a sweeping redwood bar. *495 Geary St., 94102, ☎ 415/775–4700 or 800/332–3442, FAX 415/441–4621. 329 rooms. Restaurant, lounge, exercise room, meeting rooms. AE, DC, MC, V.*

$$$$ Westin St. Francis. Host to the likes of Emperor Hirohito, Queen Elizabeth II, and many presidents, the St. Francis, with its imposing facade, black marble lobby, and gold-topped columns, looks more like a great public building than a hotel. The effect is softened by the columns and exquisite woodwork of the Compass Rose bar and restaurant; since its inception, this has been a retreat from the bustle of Union Square, especially for those in a romantic frame of mind. An extensive refurbishment of the entire hotel is likely to continue for several more years but will result in a sandstone resurfacing of the exterior, and improved guest rooms. Many of the rooms in the original building are small by modern standards, but all retain their original Victorian-style moldings and bathroom tiles. The rooms in the modern tower are larger, with brighter, lacquered furniture. ☎ *335 Powell St., 94102,* ☎ *415/397–7000 or 800/228–3000,* FAX *415/774–0124. 1,200 rooms. 5 restaurants, 5 lounges, room service, exercise room, business services. AE, DC, MC, V.*

$$$ ★ **Galleria Park.** A few blocks east of Union Square, this hotel is close to the Chinatown gate and the Crocker Galleria, one of San Francisco's most elegant shopping areas. The staff is remarkably pleasant and helpful. The French country-style rooms all have floral bedspreads and white furniture that includes a writing desk. Four floors are nonsmoking. Guests are invited to enjoy the lobby's inviting fireplace or the adjacent Bentley's Seafood Grill. ☎ *191 Sutter St., 94104,* ☎ *415/781–3060 or 800/792–9639,* FAX *415/433–4409. 162 rooms, 15 suites. 2 restaurants, jogging. AE, D, DC, MC, V.*

$$$ **Holiday Inn–Union Square.** Given the rather undistinguished, '60s-style facade of this convention-oriented hotel right on the cable-car line, the charming, 19th-century English decor of the rooms comes as a surprise. Back rooms on upper floors have commanding views of the bay; from the front rooms, you can see west all the way to the avenues. Every room has a large writing desk and most have two phones. ☎ *480 Sutter St., 94108,* ☎ *415/398–8900 or 800/243–1135,* FAX *415/989–8823. 400 rooms. Restaurant, lounge, health club. AE, D, DC, MC, V.*

$$$ **Inn at Union Square.** With its dark-timber double doors and its tiny but captivating lobby with trompe l'oeil bookshelves painted on the walls, this inn feels like someone's home. Comfortable, Georgian-style rooms promote indolence with sumptuous goose-down pillows; brass lion's-head door knockers are a unique touch. Complimentary Continental breakfast, afternoon tea, and evening wine and hors d'oeuvres are served in front of a fireplace in a sitting area on each floor. ☎ *440 Post St., 94102,* ☎ *415/397–3510 or 800/288–4346,* FAX *415/989–0529. 30 rooms. No smoking. AE, DC, MC, V.*

$$$ **Petite Auberge.** "The Teddy Bears' Picnic" might be an alternate name for this whimsical re-creation of a French country inn a couple of blocks uphill from Union Square. The lobby, festooned with teddies of all shapes, sizes, and costumes, sets the tone; the country kitchen and side garden create a pastoral atmosphere despite the downtown location. Rooms are small, but each has a teddy bear, bright flowered wallpaper, an old-fashioned writing desk, and a much-needed armoire—there's little or no closet space. The atmosphere borders on precious but doesn't stray past the mark. Next door, at 845 Bush Street, is a sister hotel, the 26-room **White Swan Inn,** similar in style but with an English-country flavor and larger rooms. ☎ *863 Bush St., 94108,* ☎ *415/928–6000,* FAX *415/775–5717. 26 rooms. Breakfast rooms. AE, DC, MC, V.*

$$$ **Prescott Hotel.** A gourmet's delight might be the best way to describe this plush hotel, thanks to its partnership with Wolfgang Puck's Postrio (*see* Dining, *above*), which consistently hovers near the top of San Francisco's best-restaurant lists. Cuisine-conscious guests can order room service from Postrio and avoid trying to make a reservation. Thankfully, guests also have access to the health club next door at the Press Club. The Prescott's rooms, which vary only in size and shape, are traditional in style, with dark, rich color schemes. Each bed is backed by a partially mirrored wall and has a boldly patterned spread; the bathrooms have marble-top sinks and gold fixtures. The Prescott's personalized service

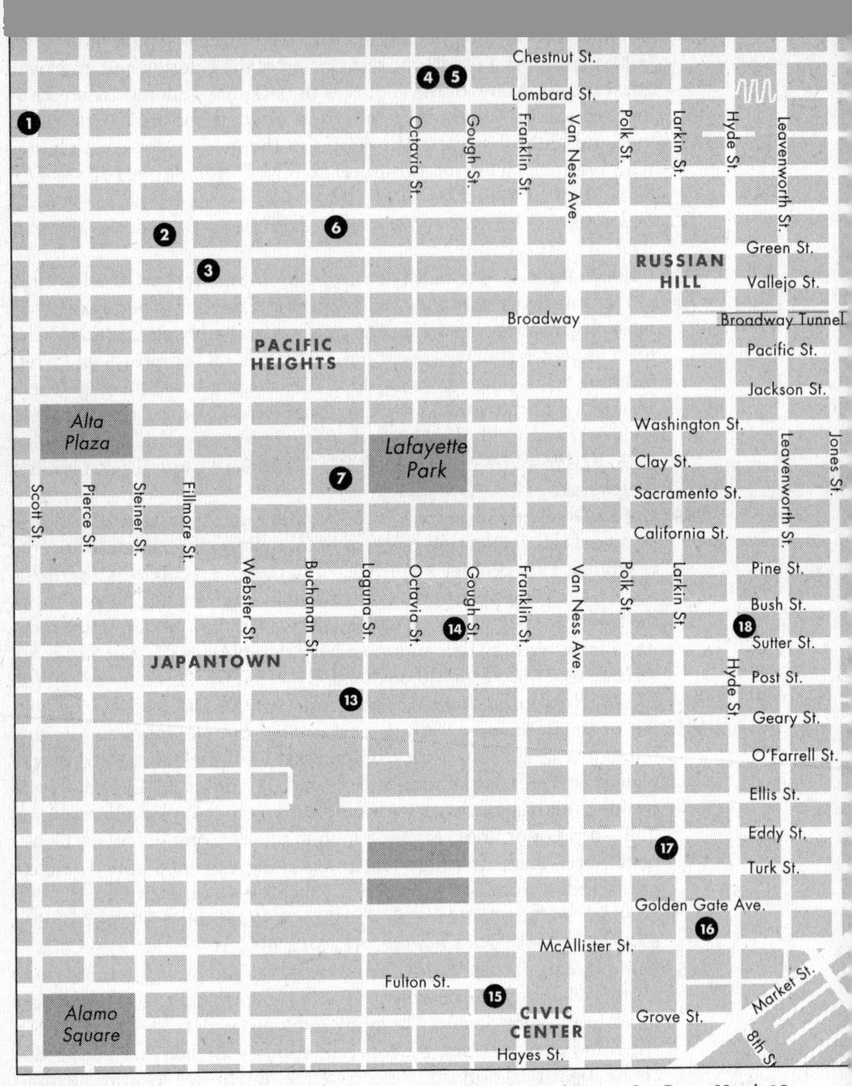

Abigail Hotel, **16**
Adelaide Inn, **20**
Bed and Breakfast Inn, **6**
Campton Place Hotel, **39**
The Cartwright, **28**
Chancellor Hotel, **36**
Clarion Hotel, **45**
Crown Sterling Suites–Burlingame, **49**
Days Inn, **46**
Edward II Inn, **1**
Fairmont Hotel and Tower, **25**
Four Seasons Clift, **32**
Galleria Park, **40**
Grant Plaza, **30**
Harbor Court Hotel, **44**
Holiday Inn–Union Square, **38**
Hotel Diva, **31**
Hotel Majestic, **14**
Hotel Sofitel–San Francisco Bay, **50**
Huntington Hotel, **23**
Hyatt at Fisherman's Wharf, **9**
Hyatt Regency, **43**
Inn at the Opera, **15**
Inn at Union Square, **35**
King George, **33**
La Quinta Motor Inn, **48**
Mandarin Oriental, **42**
The Mansions Hotel, **7**
Marina Inn, **4**
Mark Hopkins Inter–Continental, **24**
Marriott at Fisherman's Wharf, **8**
Miyako Hotel, **13**
Nob Hill Lambourne, **29**
Petite Auberge, **22**
Phoenix Inn, **17**
Prescott Hotel, **19**
Radisson Hotel, **47**
Ritz–Carlton San Francisco, **26**
San Francisco Airport Hilton, **51**
San Remo Hotel, **12**
Sheraton Palace, **41**
Sherman House, **3**
Sir Francis Drake, **37**
Town House Motel, **5**
Travelodge Hotel at Fisherman's Wharf, **11**
Tuscan Inn, **10**
Union Street Inn, **2**
Vintage Court, **27**
Westin St. Francis, **34**
White Swan Inn, **21**
York Hotel, **18**

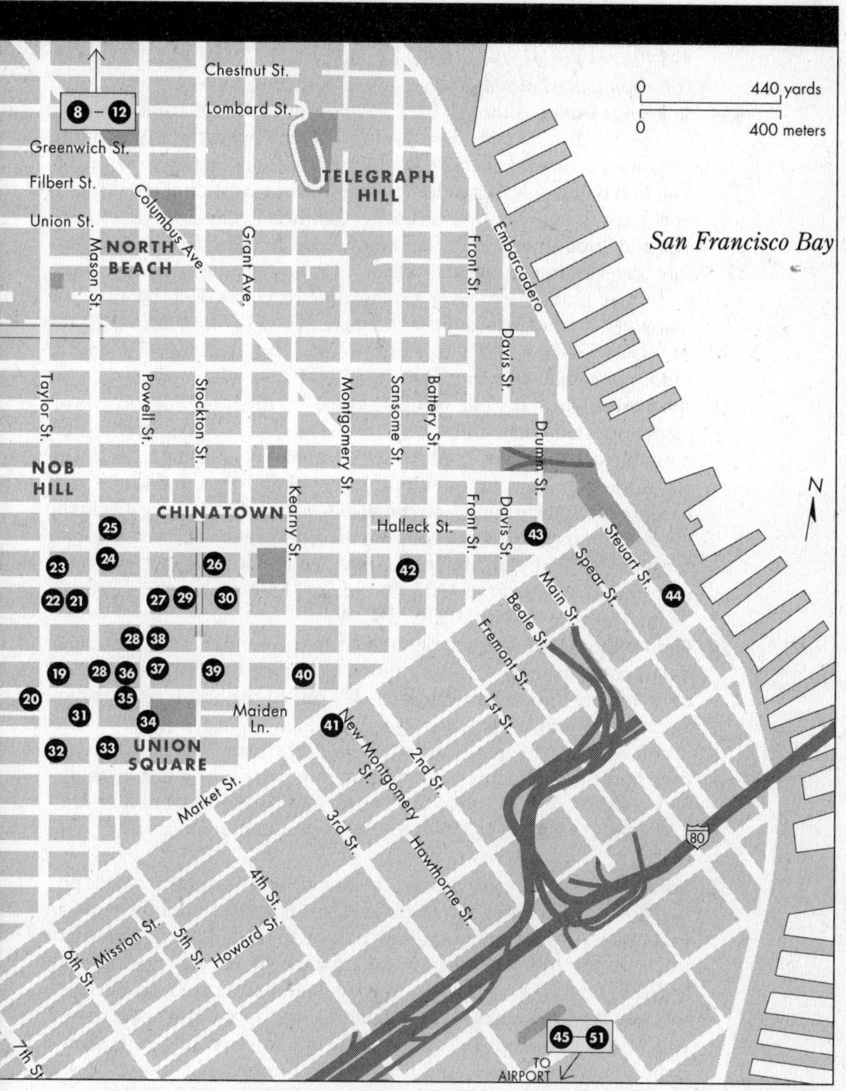

8 – 12
Chestnut St.
Lombard St.
Greenwich St.
Filbert St.
Union St.
TELEGRAPH HILL
NORTH BEACH
Columbus Ave.
Mason St.
Grant Ave.
Front St.
Embarcadero
San Francisco Bay
0 440 yards
0 400 meters
Davis St.
Taylor St.
Powell St.
Stockton St.
Montgomery St.
Sansome St.
Battery St.
Drumm St.
NOB HILL
CHINATOWN
Kearny St.
Halleck St.
Front St.
Davis St.
Steuart St.
Spear St.
Main St.
Beale St.
Fremont St.
1st St.
Maiden Ln.
New Montgomery St.
2nd St.
UNION SQUARE
Market St.
3rd St.
Hawthorne St.
4th St.
Howard St.
5th St.
Mission St.
6th St.
7th St.
80
45 – 51
TO AIRPORT
N

includes complimentary limousine service to the Financial District. ☎ *545 Post St., ☎ 415/563–0303 or 800/283–7322, FAX 415/563–6831. 166 rooms. Restaurant, lounge. AE, D, DC, MC, V.*

$$$ Sir Francis Drake. Although Beefeater-costumed doormen and dramatic red theater curtains still adorn the front of the Drake, the inside has undergone a profound change. The lobby is still opulent, with wrought-iron lion balustrades, chandeliers, and Italian marble, but guest rooms now have the flavor of a B&B, with California colonial-style furnishings and floral-print fabrics. The decor seems designed to appeal to pleasure travelers, but business travelers will appreciate the modem hookups and voice mail. Party-giver extraordinaire Harry Denton runs the renowned Starlite Roof supper club here. *450 Powell St., 94102, ☎ 415/392–7755 or 800/268–7245, FAX 415/391–8719. 417 rooms. 2 restaurants, meeting room. AE, D, DC, MC, V.*

$$ The Cartwright. "It's like being at home" is the motto of this conveniently located hotel, a block northwest of Union Square and just off the cable-car line. This is only true, however, if your home is filled with authentic European antiques, fluffy terry-cloth robes, and floral-print bedspreads and curtains, with English tea from 4 to 6 every day in the library. Guests may choose rooms with old-fashioned carved-wood or brass beds. Complimentary Continental breakfast is served in the lobby. *524 Sutter St., 94102, ☎ and fax 415/421–2865 or 800/227–3844. 114 rooms. AE, D, DC, MC, V.*

$$ Chancellor Hotel. This family-owned and -oriented hotel, although not as grand as some of its neighbors, more than lives up to its promise of comfort without extravagance—it's one of the best buys on Union Square. The moderate-size rooms have high ceilings and Edwardian decor, with peach, green, and rose color schemes; the ceiling fans and deep bathtubs are a treat. Connecting rooms are available for couples with children. *433 Powell St., 94102, ☎ 415/362–2004 or 800/428–4748, FAX 415/362–1403. 140 rooms. Restaurant, lounge. AE, D, DC, MC, V.*

$$ Hotel Diva. A beige awning and beaten-and-burnished silver facade give this hotel a slick, high-tech look that sets it apart from others in San Francisco. Although the Diva's proximity to the landmark Curran attracts theater folk and others of an artistic bent, it's also popular with tourists and business travelers. The black-and-silver color scheme with touches of gray extends to the nightclub-esque lobby and to the rooms, which vary in size and are comfortable but not fussy. Black-lacquered armoires, writing desks, and headboards complete the mood. *440 Geary St., 94102, ☎ 415/885–0200 or 800/553–1900, FAX 415/346–6613. 125 rooms. Restaurant, lounge, exercise room, business services, meeting room. AE, D, DC, MC, V.*

$$ King George. Behind the George's white-and-green Victorian facade, the rooms are compact but nicely furnished in classic English style, with walnut furniture and a pastel-and-earth-tone color scheme. British and Japanese tourists and suburban couples seeking a weekend getaway frequent this adult-oriented hotel. *334 Mason St., 94102, ☎ 415/781–5050 or 800/288–6005, FAX 415/391–6976. 144 rooms. AE, D, DC, MC, V.*

$$ Vintage Court. This bit of the Napa Valley just off Union Square has lavish rooms decorated in a Wine Country theme, and each afternoon complimentary wine is served in front of a crackling fire in the lobby. Complimentary French Continental breakfast is served each morning, and for fine food, guests need go no farther than the lobby to get to Masa's (*see* Dining, *above*), one of the city's most celebrated French restaurants. Guests have access to an affiliated health club one block away. *650*

Bush St., 94108, ☎ 415/392–4666 or 800/654–1100, FAX 415/433–4065. 106 rooms. Restaurant, lounge. AE, D, DC, MC, V.

$$ York Hotel. This family-owned hotel several blocks west of Union Square is perhaps the most gay-friendly of San Francisco's downtown hotels; it's also popular with European tourists and businesspeople, who appreciate such touches as the complimentary limousine service. The gray-stone facade and ornate, high-ceiling lobby give the hotel a touch of elegance. The moderate-size rooms are a tasteful mix of Mediterranean styles, with a terra-cotta, burgundy, and forest-green color scheme. The Plush Room cabaret, where well-known entertainers perform, is the York's drawing card. *940 Sutter St., 94109, ☎ 415/885–6800 or 800/808–9675, FAX 415/885–2115. 96 rooms. Lounge, exercise room, nightclub. AE, D, DC, MC, V.*

$ Adelaide Inn. The bedspreads at this quiet retreat may not match the drapes or carpets, and the floors may creak, but the rooms are sunny, clean, and cheap: $42–$48 for a double. Tucked away in an alley, this funky European-style pension hosts many guests from Germany, France, and Italy. *5 Isadora Duncan Ct. (off Taylor between Geary and Post Sts.), 94102, ☎ 415/441–2474 or 415/441–2261, FAX 415/441–0161. 18 rooms with shared bath. Breakfast room, refrigerators. AE, MC, V.*

$ ★ Grant Plaza. Serious Asian-cuisine aficionados take note—this bargain hotel in the shadow of the Chinatown gate has small but clean, attractively furnished rooms from $39. The Grant stands midway between the shopping options of Union Square and the Italian cafés and restaurants of North Beach. *465 Grant Ave., 94108, ☎ 415/434–3883 or 800/472–6899, FAX 415/434–3886. 72 rooms. AE, MC, V.*

Financial District

$$$$ Hyatt Regency. The gray concrete, bunkerlike exterior of the Hyatt Regency at the foot of Market Street is an unlikely introduction to the spectacular 17-story atrium lobby inside. Embarcadero Center (with its 125 shops) is right next door. Rooms, some with bay-view balconies, are decorated in two styles. Both have cherry-wood furniture, but one strikes a decidedly more masculine tone with a black-and-brown color scheme; the other has soft rose-and-plum combinations. *5 Embarcadero Center, 94111, ☎ 415/788–1234 or 800/233–1234, FAX 415/398–2567. 803 rooms. 2 restaurants, lounge. AE, D, DC, MC, V.*

$$$$ Mandarin Oriental. The Mandarin comprises the top 11 floors (38–48) of San Francisco's third-tallest building, the First Interstate Center, so no matter what room you're in, you'll get some of the most panoramic vistas of the city and beyond. The front and back towers of this structure are connected by a sky bridge. Rooms in the front tower fill up quickly because of their dramatic, sweeping view from the ocean all the way to the Golden Gate Bridge and beyond to Angel Island; the Mandarin Rooms in each tower are favorites because their bathtubs are flanked by windows. The California-style rooms have an Asian color scheme: light, creamy yellow with black accents and wood tones. *222 Sansome St., 94104, ☎ 415/885–0999 or 800/622–0404, FAX 415/433–0289. 154 rooms, 4 suites. Restaurant, lounge. AE, D, DC, MC, V.*

$$$$ Sheraton Palace. One of the city's grand old hotels—with a guest list that has included Enrico Caruso, Woodrow Wilson, and Al Jolson—the Palace has a pool with a skylight, a health club, and a business center. The Garden Court restaurant, with its leaded-glass, domed ceiling, is famous for its lavish buffet breakfasts. With their 14-foot ceilings, the rooms are splendid on a smaller scale. Modern amenities are carefully integrated into the classic decor, from the TV inside the mahogany armoire to the telephone in the marble bathroom. ⊞ *2 New Montgomery St., 94105,* ☎ *415/392–8600 or 800/325–3535,* FAX *415/543–0671. 550 rooms. 3 restaurants, 2 lounges, room service, health club. AE, D, DC, MC, V.*

$$$ ★ **Harbor Court Hotel.** Within shouting distance of the Bay Bridge and the hot South of Market area with its plentiful nightclubs and restaurants, this boutique-style hotel, formerly a YMCA, is noted for the exemplary service of its warm, friendly staff. The small rooms, some with bay views, have a sage-green color scheme and partial canopy beds resting on wood casements. The adult-oriented Harbor Court attracts corporate types (especially on weekdays) as well as the average traveler. Guests have free access to YMCA facilities (including a 150-foot heated indoor pool) on one side of the hotel, and Harry Denton's Bar and Grill on the other side. There's a complimentary limousine service to the Financial District. ⊞ *165 Steuart St.,* ☎ *415/882–1300 or 800/346–0555,* FAX *415/882–1313. 131 rooms. Business services. AE, D, DC, MC, V.*

Nob Hill

Synonymous with San Francisco's high society, Nob Hill contains some of the city's best-known luxury hotels. All offer spectacular city and bay views and noted gourmet restaurants. Cable-car lines that cross Nob Hill make transportation a cinch.

$$$$ **Fairmont Hotel and Tower.** Perched atop Nob Hill and queen of all she surveys, the Fairmont has the most awe-inspiring lobby in the city, with a soaring, vaulted ceiling; towering, hand-painted, faux-marble columns; gilt mirrors; red-velvet upholstered chairs; and a grand, wraparound staircase. The tower rooms, which have spectacular city and bay views, reflect a more modern style than their smaller Victorian counterparts in the older building. The Tonga Room, site of San Francisco's busiest happy hour, is a must-see. ⊞ *950 Mason St., 94108,* ☎ *415/772–5000 or 800/527–4727,* FAX *415/772–5013. 596 rooms. 5 restaurants, room service, 5 lounges, spa, health club. AE, D, DC, MC, V.*

$$$$ **Huntington Hotel.** Across from Grace Cathedral and the small but captivating Huntington Park, the redbrick, ivy-covered Huntington provides a quiet alternative to the larger, more famous hotels down the street. Regulars here return year after year for the attentive personal service that is the hallmark of this hotel. Rooms and suites, all individually appointed, reflect the Huntington's traditional style, albeit with a '90s bent. The opulent materials, such as soft leathers, raw silks and velvets, are mixed and matched in a color scheme of cocoa, gold, and burgundy. Guests have access to the health club at the Fairmont, across the street. ⊞ *1075 California St., 94108,* ☎ *415/474–5400 or 800/227–4683; in CA, 800/652–1539;* FAX *415/474–6227. 140 rooms. Restaurant, lounge. AE, D, DC, MC, V.*

$$$$ **Mark Hopkins Inter-Continental.** The circular drive to this Nob Hill landmark across from the Fairmont leads to a lobby with floor-to-ceiling mirrors and marble floors. The rooms, with dramatic neoclassical furnishings of gray, silver, and khaki and bold leaf-print bedspreads, lead into bathrooms lined with Italian marble. Even-number rooms on high floors have views of the Golden Gate Bridge. No visit would be complete without a gander at the panoramic views from the Top of the Mark, *the* rooftop lounge in San Francisco since 1939. ⊞ *999 California St., 94108,* ☎ *415/392–3434 or 800/327–0200,* FAX *415/421–3302. 392 rooms. Restaurant, 2 lounges, exercise room. AE, D, DC, MC, V.*

$$$$ ★ Ritz-Carlton, San Francisco. Rated one of the top three hotels in the world by *Condé Nast Traveler,* the Ritz-Carlton is a stunning tribute to beauty, grandeur, and warm, attentive service. Beyond the neoclassical facade, crystal chandeliers and museum-quality 18th-century oil paintings adorn an opulent lobby. Rooms are elegant and spacious, and every bath is appointed with double sinks, hair dryers, and vanity tables. A maid service cleans twice a day, and guests staying on the butler level enjoy the added luxury of their own butler. The hotel's Dining Room is a worthy destination in its own right. *600 Stockton St., at California St., 94108, ☎ 415/296–7465 or 800/241–3333, FAX 415/291–0288. 336 rooms. 2 restaurants, 3 lounges, indoor pool, health club, shops. AE, D, DC, MC, V.*

$$$ Nob Hill Lambourne. This urban retreat designed with the traveling executive in mind takes pride in taking care of business while offering stress-reducing pleasures. Personal computers, fax machines, personalized voice mail, laser printers, and a fully equipped boardroom help guests maintain their edge, and the on-site spa, with massages, body scrubs, herbal wraps, manicures, and pedicures, helps them take it off. Rooms have queen-size beds with divine double-padded, hand-sewn mattresses and contemporary furnishings in Mediterranean colors. A deluxe Continental breakfast is complimentary. *725 Pine St., at Stockton, 94108, ☎ 415/433–2287 or 800/274–8466, FAX 415/433–0975. 20 rooms. Kitchenettes. AE, D, DC, MC, V.*

Fisherman's Wharf/North Beach

Fisherman's Wharf, San Francisco's top tourist attraction, is also the most popular area for lodging. All accommodations are within a couple of blocks of restaurants, shops, and cable-car lines. Because of city ordinances, none of the hotels exceeds four stories; thus, this is not the area for fantastic views of the city or bay. Reservations are always necessary, sometimes weeks in advance during peak summer months, when hotel rates rise by as much as 30%. Some street-side rooms can be noisy.

$$$$ Hyatt at Fisherman's Wharf. Location is the key to this hotel's popularity with business travelers and families: It's within walking distance of Ghirardelli Square, the Cannery, Pier 39, Aquatic Park, and docks for ferries and bay cruises. It's also across the street from the cable-car turnaround and bus stop. The moderate-size guest rooms, a medley of greens and burgundies with dark woods and brass fixtures, have double-pane windows to keep out the often considerable street noise. Each floor has a laundry room. The Marble Works Restaurant, which still has the original facade of the 1906 Musto Marble Works, is next door and has a children's menu. *555 N. Point St., 94133, ☎ 415/563–1234 or 800/233–1234, FAX 415/563–2218. 313 rooms. Restaurant, sports bar, pool, outdoor hot tub, health club. AE, D, DC, MC, V.*

$$$ Marriott at Fisherman's Wharf. Behind an unremarkable sand-color facade, the Marriott strikes a grand note in its lavish, low-ceiling lobby, with marble floors and English club-style furniture. With the Transamerica Pyramid downtown to its left and the Cannery nearby on its right, the hotel is well situated for business and pleasure. Rooms, all with turquoise, blue, and white color schemes, have dark natural wood, Asian art touches, and either a king-size bed or two double beds. *1250 Columbus Ave., 94133, ☎ 415/775–7555 or 800/228–9290, FAX 415/474–2099. 255 rooms. Restaurant, lounge, health club. AE, D, DC, MC, V.*

$$$ **Tuscan Inn.** The major attraction here is the friendly, attentive staff, which provides services such as a complimentary limousine to the Financial District. The condolike exterior of the inn, made of reddish brick with white concrete, gives little indication of the charm of the relatively small, Italian-influenced guest rooms, with their white-pine furniture and floral bedspreads and curtains. Two floors are smoke-free. Room service is provided by Cafe Pescatore, the Italian seafood restaurant off the lobby. Morning coffee, tea, and biscotti are complimentary, and wine is served in the early evening. 🏨 *425 N. Point St., 94133,* ☎ *415/561–1100 or 800/648–4626,* FAX *415/561–1199. 220 rooms. Restaurant, meeting rooms. AE, D, DC, MC, V.*

$$ **Travelodge Hotel at Fisherman's Wharf.** Taking up an entire city block, the Travelodge is the only bayfront hotel at Fisherman's Wharf and is known for its reasonable rates. The higher-priced rooms on the third and fourth floors have balconies that provide unobstructed views of Alcatraz and overlook a landscaped courtyard and pool. The rooms at this family-oriented hotel with an 80% international clientele have either a king-size bed or two double beds and are simply and brightly furnished with blond, lacquered-wood furniture, lime-green leather chairs, and southwestern curtains and bedspreads. 🏨 *250 Beach St., 94133,* ☎ *415/392–6700 or 800/578–7878,* FAX *415/986–7853. 250 rooms. 3 restaurants, pool, free parking. AE, D, DC, MC, V.*

$ ★ **San Remo Hotel.** A guest recently described a sojourn at the San Remo as being "like staying at Grandma's house." This three-story, blue-and-white Italianate Victorian just a couple of blocks from Fisherman's Wharf has reasonably priced rooms and a down-home, slightly tatty elegance. The somewhat cramped rooms are crowded with furniture: vanities, rag rugs, pedestal sinks, ceiling fans, antique armoires, and brass, iron, or wooden beds. The rooms share six black-and-white tiled shower rooms, one bathtub chamber, and six scrupulously clean toilets with brass pull chains and oak tanks. Special rates are available for longer stays. 🏨 *2237 Mason St., 94133,* ☎ *415/776–8688 or 800/352–7366,* FAX *415/776–2811. 62 rooms, 61 with shared baths. AE, DC, MC, V.*

Lombard Street/Cow Hollow

Lombard Street, a major traffic corridor leading to the Golden Gate Bridge, stretches through San Francisco's poshest neighborhoods: Pacific Heights, Cow Hollow, and the Marina District.

$$$$ ★ **Sherman House.** This magnificent landmark mansion on a low hill in residential Pacific Heights is San Francisco's most luxurious small hotel. Rooms are individually decorated with Biedermeier, English Jacobean, or French Second Empire antiques. Tapestry-like canopies over four-poster beds, wood-burning fireplaces with marble mantels, and black-granite bathrooms with whirlpool baths complete the picture. The six romantic suites attract honeymooners from around the world, and the elegant in-house dining room serves superb French-inspired cuisine. 🏨 *2160 Green St., 94123,* ☎ *415/563–3600 or 800/424–5777,* FAX *415/563–1882. 14 rooms. Dining room. AE, DC, MC, V.*

$$$ **Bed and Breakfast Inn.** Hidden in an alleyway off Union Street between Buchanan and Laguna, this ivy-covered, dark-green-and-white Victorian with black trim claims the title of San Francisco's first B&B. Pierre Deux and Laura Ashley are the inspirations of the English-country-style rooms, which are full of antiques, plants, and floral paintings. The Mayfair, a private flat above the main house, comes complete with a living room, kitchenette, latticed balcony, and spiral stair-

case leading to a sleeping loft. The Garden Suite, a larger, more deluxe flat, is a recent addition. ⊞ *4 Charlton Ct., 94123,* ☏ *415/921–9784. 5 rooms with bath, 4 rooms with shared bath, 2 flats. Breakfast room. No credit cards.*

$$ Edward II Inn. Banners of the English king and the state of California fly from the rooftop of this picturesque B&B. A variety of English-country-style accommodations is available, including 14 small pension rooms with private bath, 10 with shared bath; six suites with one or two bedrooms, whirlpool baths, living rooms, kitchens, and wet bars; a carriage-house annex with apartment suites; and a three-bedroom, one-bath cottage suite perfect for traveling families. Two junior suites in the main building are especially popular, as is the pub. ⊞ *3155 Scott St., at Lombard St., 94123,* ☏ *415/922–3000 or 800/473–2846,* FAX *415/931–5784. 31 rooms, 19 with bath. AE, MC, V.*

$$ ★ Union Street Inn. This ivy-draped, Edwardian 1902 home affords a cozy intimacy that has made it popular with honeymooners and other romantics. Of the six rooms, one standout is the Wildrose, which has a king-size brass bed, persimmon-and-mauve decor, and a garden view that can be seen from the whirlpool tub. The very private Carriage House, which also has its own whirlpool tub, is separated from the main house by an old-fashioned English garden. An elaborate complimentary Continental breakfast is served to guests in the parlor, in the garden, or in their rooms. Special rates are available for longer stays. Off-season prices are considerably lower. ⊞ *2229 Union St., 94123,* ☏ *415/346–0424,* FAX *415/922–8046. 6 rooms with private bath. Breakfast room. AE, MC, V.*

$ Marina Inn. This inn five blocks from the marina offers B&B-style accommodations at motel prices. English-country-style rooms are sparsely appointed with a queen-size two-poster bed, private bath, small pinewood writing desks, nightstands, and armoires; the wallpaper and bedspreads are aggressively floral. Some of the rooms facing Octavia and Lombard streets have bay windows. A complimentary Continental breakfast is served in the central sitting room, and a barbershop and beauty salon are on the premises. ⊞ *3110 Octavia St., at Lombard St., 94123,* ☏ *415/928–1000 or 800/274–1420,* FAX *415/928–5909. 40 rooms. Lounge. AE, MC, V.*

$ Town House Motel. What this family-oriented motel lacks in luxury and ambience it makes up for in value: The rooms are simply furnished and well kept. Like its grander neighbor, the Marina Inn, this motel is convenient to many sights of interest, although its blaring blue facade may put off some visitors. The modest, medium-size rooms have a pastel, southwestern color scheme, lacquered-wood furnishings, and either a king-size bed or two doubles. Continental breakfast is complimentary. ⊞ *1650 Lombard St., 94123,* ☏ *415/885–5163 or 800/255–1516,* FAX *415/771–9889. 24 rooms. Free parking. AE, D, DC, MC, V.*

Civic Center/Van Ness

The governmental heart of San Francisco, flanked by a boulevard of cultural institutions, is enjoying a renaissance that has engendered fine restaurants, fashionable nightspots, and well-situated small hotels.

$$$ ★ Hotel Majestic. One of San Francisco's original grand hotels, this five-story yellow-and-white Edwardian with gingerbread and scrollwork looks like a wedding cake. Most rooms contain a fireplace and either a large, hand-painted, four-poster, canopied bed or two-poster bonnet twin beds, and most have a mix of French Empire and English antiques and custom furniture. The hotel's Cafe Majestic, which evokes turn-of-the-century San Francisco, has been called "San Francisco's most romantic restaurant." ☐ *1500 Sutter St., 94109,* ☎ *415/441–1100 or 800/869–8966,* FAX *415/673–7331. 57 rooms. Restaurant, lounge. AE, DC, MC, V.*

$$$ ★ **Inn at the Opera.** This seven-story hotel a block or so from City Hall hosts the likes of Pavarotti and Baryshnikov, as well as lesser lights of the music, dance, and opera worlds. Behind the yellow faux-marble front and red carpet are rooms of various sizes, decorated with creamy pastels and dark wood furnishings. Even the smallest singles have queen-size beds. The bureau drawers are lined with sheet music, and every room is outfitted with terry-cloth robes, microwave ovens, mini-bars, fresh flowers, and a basket of apples. Those in the know say the back rooms are the quietest. ☐ *333 Fulton St., 94102,* ☎ *415/863–8400 or 800/325–2708; in CA, 800/423–9610;* FAX *415/861–0821. 48 rooms. Restaurant, lounge. AE, DC, MC, V.*

$$$ ★ **Miyako Hotel.** Next to the Japantown complex and near Fillmore Street, this pagoda-style hotel is frequented by Asian travelers and others with a taste for the East. Some guest rooms are in the tower building; others are in the garden wing, which has traditional seasonal gardens. Japanese-style rooms have futon beds with tatami mats; Western rooms have traditional beds with mattresses. Both types of rooms feature Japanese touches such as shojis; most have their own soaking rooms with a bucket and stool and a Japanese tub (1 foot deeper than Western tubs). A chocolate set on a haiku by the bedside awaits each guest. ☐ *1625 Post St., at Laguna St., 94115,* ☎ *415/922–3200 or 800/533–4567,* FAX *415/921–0417. 218 rooms. Restaurant, lounge. AE, D, DC, MC, V.*

$$ **The Mansions Hotel.** This twin-turreted Queen Anne was built in 1887 and today houses one of the most unusual hotels in the city. Rooms, which contain an odd collection of furnishings, vary in theme from the tiny Tom Thumb Room to the opulent Josephine Suite, the favorite of such celebrities as Barbra Streisand. Owner Bob Pritikin's pig paintings and other "porkabilia" are scattered throughout the hotel. Other nice touches are the sculpture and flower gardens, and the nightly concerts. Full breakfast is included. ☐ *2220 Sacramento St., 94115,* ☎ *415/929–9444,* FAX *415/567–9391. 21 rooms. Dining room, cabaret. AE, D, DC, MC, V.*

$$ **Phoenix Inn.** Dubbed the "hippest hotel" in San Francisco by *People* magazine, this turquoise-and-coral hideaway on the fringes of the Tenderloin district is a little bit south-of-the-equator and a little bit *Gilligan's Island*—probably not the place for a traveling executive, even though it bills itself as an urban retreat in a resortlike environment. Its bungalow-style rooms, decorated with casual, handmade, bamboo furniture and original art by San Francisco artists, have white beamed ceilings, white wooden walls, and vivid tropical-print bedspreads. All rooms face a pool (with a mural by Francis Forlenza on its bottom) adjacent to a courtyard and sculpture garden. An in-house cable channel plays films made in San Francisco and films about bands on the road. Miss Pearl's Jam House restaurant and bar is a good place to hear reggae and indulge in Jamaican delights. ☐ *601 Eddy St., 94109,* ☎ *415/776–1380, 415/861–1560, or 800/248–9466,* FAX *415/885–3109. 44 rooms. Restaurant, bar, lounge, pool, free parking. AE, D, DC, MC, V.*

$ **Abigail Hotel.** This hotel, a former B&B, retains its distinctive atmosphere with an eclectic mix of faux-stone walls, a faux-marble front desk, and an old-fashioned telephone booth in the lobby. Hissing steam radiators, sleigh beds, and antiques complete the mood. Room 211—the hotel's only suite—is the most elegant and spacious. The new

Millennium Restaurant, right off the lobby, has proven to be a hit with its gourmet organic cuisine. 🏨 *246 McAllister St., 94102,* ☎ *415/861–9728 or 800/243–6510,* FAX *415/861–5848. 60 rooms. Restaurant. AE, D, DC, MC, V.*

The Airport

Because they cater primarily to midweek business travelers, the airport hotels often cut weekend prices drastically; be sure to inquire. A full complement of services and airport shuttle buses is provided by all of the following chain hotels.

In the $$$ range: **Crown Sterling Suites–Burlingame** (150 Anza Blvd., Burlingame 94010, ☎ 415/342–4600 or 800/433–4600, FAX 415/343–8137), **Hotel Sofitel–San Francisco Bay** (223 Twin Dolphin Dr., Redwood City 94065, ☎ 415/598–9000 or 800/763–4835, FAX 415/598–0459), **San Francisco Airport Hilton** (San Francisco International Airport, Box 8355, 94128, ☎ 415/589–0770 or 800/445–8667, FAX 415/589–4696).

In the $$ range: **Clarion Hotel** (401 E. Millbrae Ave., Millbrae 94030, ☎ 415/692–6363 or 800/223–7111, FAX 415/697–8735), **Radisson Hotel** (1177 Airport Blvd., Burlingame 94010, ☎ 415/342–9200 or 800/333–3333, FAX 415/342–1655).

In the $ range: **Days Inn** (777 Airport Blvd., Burlingame 94010, ☎ 415/342–7772 or 800/325–2525, FAX 415/342–2635), **La Quinta Motor Inn** (20 Airport Blvd., South San Francisco 94080, ☎ 415/583–2223 or 800/531–5900, FAX 415/589–6770).

THE ARTS AND NIGHTLIFE

The Arts

By Robert Taylor

The best guide to arts and entertainment events in San Francisco is the "Datebook" section, printed on pink paper, in the Sunday *Examiner and Chronicle*. The *Bay Guardian* and *S.F. Weekly*, free and available in racks around the city, list more neighborhood, avant-garde, and budget-priced events. For up-to-date information about cultural and musical events, call the Convention and Visitors Bureau's *Cultural Events Calendar* (☎ 415/391–2001).

Half-price tickets to many local and touring stage shows go on sale (cash only) at 11 AM, Tuesday–Saturday, at the TIX Bay Area booth on the Stockton Street side of Union Square, between Geary and Post streets. TIX is also a full-service ticket agency for theater and music events around the Bay Area (open until 6 PM Tues.–Thurs., 7 PM Fri.–Sat.). For recorded information about TIX tickets, call 415/433–7827.

The city's charge-by-phone ticket service is **BASS** (☎ 510/762–2277 or 415/776–1999), with one of its centers in the TIX booth mentioned above and another at **Tower Records** (Bay St. at Columbus Ave.), near Fisherman's Wharf. Other agencies downtown are the **City Box Office** at 153 Kearny Street, Suite 402 (☎ 415/392–4400), and **Downtown Center Box Office** in the parking garage at 325 Mason Street (☎ 415/775–2021). The opera, symphony, the ballet's *Nutcracker*, and touring hit musicals are often sold out in advance; tickets are usually available within a day of performance for other shows.

While the city's major commercial theaters are concentrated downtown, the opera, symphony, and ballet perform at the Civic Center.

Theater

San Francisco's "theater row" is a single block of Geary Street west of Union Square, but a number of commercial theaters are located within walking distance, along with resident companies that enrich the city's theatrical scene. The three major commercial theaters are operated by the Shorenstein-Nederlander organization, which books touring plays and musicals, some of them before they open on Broadway. The most venerable is the **Curran** (445 Geary St., ☎ 415/474–3800). The **Golden Gate** is a stylishly refurbished movie theater (Golden Gate Ave. at Taylor St., ☎ 415/474–3800), now primarily a musical house. The 2,500-seat **Orpheum** (1192 Market St., near the Civic Center, ☎ 415/474–3800) is used for the biggest touring shows.

The smaller commercial theaters, offering touring shows plus some local performances, are the **Marines Memorial Theatre** (Sutter and Mason Sts., ☎ 415/441–7444) and **Theatre on the Square** (450 Post St., ☎ 415/433–9500). For commercial and popular success, nothing beats *Beach Blanket Babylon,* the zany revue that has been running since 1974 at **Club Fugazi** (678 Green St., in North Beach, ☎ 415/421–4222). Conceived by the late Steve Silver, it is a lively, colorful musical mix of cabaret, show-biz parodies, and tributes to local landmarks. (*See* Cabarets *in* Nightlife, *below.*)

The city's major nonprofit theater company is the **American Conservatory Theater (ACT),** which was founded in the mid-1960s and quickly became one of the nation's leading regional theaters. It presents a season of approximately eight plays in rotating repertory from October through late spring. ACT's ticket office is at 405 Geary Street (☎ 415/749–2228), next door to its **Geary Theater,** which is scheduled to reopen in 1996 after a $24 million reconstruction to repair damage from the 1989 earthquake. ACT may also continue performing at its interim theaters, the nearby **Stage Door Theater** (420 Mason St.) and the **Marines Memorial Theatre** (Sutter and Mason Sts.).

The leading producer of new plays is the **Magic Theatre** (Bldg. D, Fort Mason Center, Laguna St. at Marina Blvd., ☎ 415/441–8822).

The city boasts a wide variety of specialized and ethnic theaters that work with dedicated local actors and some professionals. Among the most interesting are **The Lamplighters,** the delightful Gilbert and Sullivan troupe that often gets better reviews than touring productions of musicals, performing at **Presentation Theater** (2350 Turk St., ☎ 415/752–7755); the **Lorraine Hansberry Theatre** (620 Sutter St., ☎ 415/474–8800), which specializes in plays by black writers; the **Asian American Theatre** (405 Arguello Blvd., ☎ 415/751–2600); and two stages that showcase gay and lesbian performers: **Theatre Rhinoceros** (2926 16th St., ☎ 415/861–5079) and **Josie's Cabaret & Juice Joint** (3583 16th St., ☎ 415/861–7933). The **San Francisco Shakespeare Festival** offers free performances on summer weekends in Golden Gate Park (☎ 415/666–2222).

Avant-garde theater, dance, opera, and "performance art" turn up in a variety of locations, not all of them theaters. The major presenting organization is the **Theater Artaud** (499 Alabama St., in the Mission District, ☎ 415/621–7797), which is situated in a huge, converted machine shop. Some contemporary theater events, in addition to dance and music, are scheduled at the theater in the **Center for the Arts at Yerba Buena Gardens** (3rd and Howard Sts., ☎ 415/978–2787). A more adventurous venue is **George Coates Performance Works** (110

McAllister St., ☎ 415/863–4130), which combines theater, film, video, and electronic music in a former church in the Civic Center.

Berkeley Repertory Theatre (☎ 510/845–4700), across the bay, is the American Conservatory Theater's major rival for leadership among the region's resident professional companies. It performs an adventurous mix of classics and new plays in a modern, intimate theater at 2025 Addison Street near BART's downtown Berkeley station. It's a fully professional theater, with a fall–spring season. Tickets are available at the TIX booth in San Francisco's Union Square. The Bay Area's most professional outdoor summer theater, **California Shakespeare Festival,** performs in an amphitheater east of Oakland, on Gateway Boulevard just off state Highway 24 (☎ 510/548–3422).

Music

Davies Symphony Hall at Van Ness Avenue and Grove Street is the home of the San Francisco Symphony. The symphony and other musical groups also perform in the smaller, 928-seat Herbst Theatre in the War Memorial Building at Van Ness Avenue and McAllister Street. Other musical ensembles can be found all over the city: in churches and museums, in restaurants and parks, and in outreach series in Berkeley and on the peninsula.

San Francisco Symphony (Davies Symphony Hall, Van Ness Ave. at Grove St., ☎ 415/431–5400; tickets: $8–$65, at the box office or through BASS, ☎ 415/776–1999 or 510/762–2277). The symphony performs September through May. California-born Michael Tilson Thomas, who is known for his innovative programming of 20th-century and American works, became music director in September 1994. Guest conductors often include Edo de Waart and Riccardo Muti. Soloists include artists of the caliber of Andre Watts, Peter Serkin, and Pinchas Zukerman. Special events include a summer festival built around a particular composer, nation or musical period, and summer Pops Concerts in the nearby Civic Auditorium.

Old First Concerts (Old First Church, Van Ness Ave. at Sacramento St., ☎ 415/474–1608; tickets also at TIX booth, Union Square). This is a well-respected Friday evening and Sunday afternoon series of chamber music, vocal soloists, new music, and jazz, takes place in a church and feels like a community gathering.

Stern Grove (Sloat Blvd. at 19th Ave., ☎ 415/252–6252). This is the nation's oldest continual free summer music festival, offering 10 Sunday afternoons of symphony, opera, jazz, pop music, and dance. The amphitheater is in a eucalyptus grove below street level; remember that summer in this area near the ocean can be cool.

Opera

San Francisco Opera (Van Ness Ave. at Grove St., ☎ 415/864–3330). Founded in 1923, and the resident company at the War Memorial Opera House in the Civic Center since it was built in 1932, the Opera gives approximately 70 performances of 10 operas, beginning on the first Friday after Labor Day. The Opera frequently embarks on co-productions with European opera companies.

In addition to the fall season, the Opera schedules occasional summer festivals. Ticket prices range from about $35 to $100. Standing-room tickets (less than $10) are always sold at 10 AM for same-day performances, and patrons often sell extra tickets on the Opera House steps just before curtain time. Note that the Opera House will be closed in

1996 for repairs; performances will take place at the Bill Graham Civic Auditorium, a block east at Grove and Polk Streets, and also at the Orpheum. The full-time box office is located at 199 Grove Street, at the corner of Van Ness Avenue.

Dance

San Francisco Ballet (☎ 415/703–9400) has regained much of its luster under artistic director Helgi Tomasson, and both classical and contemporary works have won admiring reviews. The company's primary season runs February–May; its repertoire includes such full-length ballets as *Swan Lake* and a new production of *Sleeping Beauty,* and the annual December presentation of the *Nutcracker* is one of the most spectacular in the nation. The ballet will perform in several Bay Area locations until December 1997, when its usual home base, the War Memorial Opera House, reopens after reconstruction. Tickets and information are available at the ballet's administration and rehearsal building, 455 Franklin Street, behind the Opera House.

Nightlife

By Daniel Mangin

Updated by Dennis Harvey

San Francisco provides a potpourri of evening entertainment, from ultrasophisticated cabarets to bawdy bistros that reflect the city's gold-rush past. With the exception of the hotel lounges and discos noted below, casual dress is the norm. Bars generally close between midnight and 2 AM. Bands and performances usually begin between 8 and 10 PM. The cover charge at smaller clubs ranges from $3 to $7, and credit cards are rarely accepted. At the larger venues the cover may go up to $30, and tickets can often be purchased through BASS (☎ 415/776–1999 or 510/762–2277).

For information on who is performing where, check the following sources: The Sunday San Francisco *Examiner and Chronicle*'s pink "Datebook" insert lists major events and cultural happenings. The free alternative weeklies, the *Bay Guardian* and *SF Weekly,* are terrific sources for current music clubs and comedy. Another handy reference for San Francisco nightlife is *Key* magazine, offered free in most major hotel lobbies. For a phone update on sports and musical events, call the Convention and Visitor Bureau's *Events Hotline* (☎ 415/391–2001).

Although San Francisco is a compact city with the prevailing influences of some neighborhoods spilling into others, the following generalizations should help you find the kind of entertainment you're looking for. **Nob Hill** is noted for its plush piano bars and panoramic skyline lounges. **North Beach,** infamous for its topless and bottomless bistros, also maintains a sense of its beatnik past, and this legacy lives on in atmospheric bars and coffeehouses. **Fisherman's Wharf,** while touristy, is great for people-watching and attracts plenty of street performers. **Union Street** is home away from home for singles in search of company. South of Market (**SoMa,** for short) has become a hub of nightlife, with a bevy of highly popular nightclubs, bars, and lounges in renovated warehouses and auto shops. Gay men will find their scene at **Castro** and **Polk streets.**

Rock, Pop, Folk, and Blues

The **Blue Lamp** (561 Geary St., ☎ 415/885–1464), a downtown "hole in the wall," has an aura of faded opulence. Fare ranges from '20s blues to original rock and roll.

Bottom of the Hill (1233 17th St., at Texas St., ☎ 415/626–4455), "two minutes south of SoMa" in the Potrero Hill District, showcases some of the city's best local alternative rock and blues.

DNA Lounge (375 11th St., near Harrison St., ☎ 415/626–1409), a longtime, two-floor SoMa haunt, was recently revamped to include new murals and a larger VIP lounge. Alternative independent rock, funk, and rap are the music of choice here. Live bands play most nights at 10 PM; other nights the club is open for dancing to recorded music—until 4 AM on weekends.

The Fillmore (1805 Geary Blvd., at Fillmore St., ☎ 415/346–6000), one of San Francisco's most famous rock music halls, reopened in 1994 after several years of retrofitting. Today it serves up a varied menu of national and local acts: rock, reggae, grunge, jazz, comedy, folk, acid house, and more.

Freight and Salvage Coffee House (1111 Addison St., Berkeley, ☎ 510/548–1761), one of the finest folk houses in the country, is worth a trip across the bay. Some of the most talented practitioners of folk, blues, Cajun, and bluegrass perform here, among them Taj Mahal, Iris DeMent, Laurie Lewis, and Greg Brown.

Great American Music Hall (859 O'Farrell St., between Polk and Larkin Sts., ☎ 415/885–0750) is one of the great eclectic nightclubs, not only in San Francisco but in the entire country. Here you will find truly top-drawer entertainment, running the gamut from the best in blues, folk, and jazz to alternative rock with a sprinkling of outstanding comedians. The colorful marble-pillared emporium (built in 1907 as a bordello) will also accommodate dancing to popular bands. Past headliners include B. B. King, Van Morrison, the Spin Doctors, and George Clinton.

Last Day Saloon (406 Clement St., between 5th and 6th Aves., ☎ 415/387–6343) offers an attractive setting of wooden tables and potted plants, along with major entertainers and a varied schedule of blues, Cajun, rock, and jazz. Illustrious performers of the past have included Taj Mahal, Big Head Todd & the Monster, Motherhips, Maria Muldaur, and Pride and Joy.

Slim's (333 11th St., ☎ 415/621–3330), one of SoMa's most popular nightclubs, specializes in what it labels "American roots music"—blues, jazz, classic rock, and the like. The club has expanded its repertoire in recent years, with national touring acts playing alternative rock and roll and a series of "spoken word" concerts. Co-owner Boz Scaggs helps bring in the crowds and famous headliners. The box office doubles as a general BASS ticket outlet.

Jazz

Cafe du Nord (2170 Market St., at Sanchez St., ☎ 415/861–5016), once a Basque restaurant, now hosts some of the liveliest jam sessions in town. The atmosphere in this basement poolroom-bar is decidedly casual, but the music, provided mostly by local talent, is strictly top-notch.

Eleven (374 11th St., ☎ 415/431–3337), an Italian restaurant–cum–casual jazz showcase, joined the ranks of SoMa hot spots at the end of 1993. The various funky, salsafied, and trad sounds here are called "Live Loft Jazz," because the stage is 12 feet off the ground.

Heart and Soul (1695 Polk St., ☎ 415/673–6788), a sleek, plush "1940s big-city retro room," captures the ambience of another era with just a hint of lounge-revival irony. The kitchen serves excellent appetizers and meals, while local and national combos and vocalists play jazz from 1940s through the '60s.

Jazz at Pearl's (256 Columbus Ave., near Broadway, ☎ 415/291–8255) is one of the few reminders of North Beach's days as a hot spot for cool tunes. Sophisticated and romantic, the club's picture windows overlook City Lights Bookstore across the street. The talent level is remarkably high, especially considering that there is rarely a cover.

Kimball's East (5800 Shellmound St., Emeryville, ☎ 510/658–2555), in a shopping complex in Emeryville just off Highway 80 near Oakland, hosts jazz greats such as Wynton Marsalis and Hugh Masekela and popular vocalists such as Lou Rawls and Patti Austin. With an elegant interior and fine food, it's one of the Bay Area's most luxurious supper clubs.

Up and Down Club (1151 Folsom St., ☎ 415/626–2388), a hip restaurant and club whose owners include supermodel Christy Turlington, books up-and-coming jazz artists downstairs Wednesday through Monday. There's a bar and dancing to a DJ upstairs Wednesday through Saturday.

Cabarets

Club Fugazi (678 Green St., ☎ 415/421–4222) is most famous for *Beach Blanket Babylon,* a wacky musical revue that has become the longest-running show of its genre. A send-up of San Francisco moods and mores, *Beach Blanket* has now run for two decades. While the choreography is colorful and the songs witty, the real stars of the show are the exotic costumes—worth the price of admission in themselves. Order tickets as far in advance as possible; the revue has been sold out up to a month in advance. Those under 21 are admitted only to the Sunday matinee.

Coconut Grove (1415 Van Ness Ave., ☎ 415/776–1616) has a chic, '40s supper-club ambience. Tom Jones, Connie Stevens, Diahann Carroll, and other pop icons are among the past headliners.

Eichelberger's (2742 17th St., ☎ 415/863–4177) bills itself as a "classic supper club with a San Francisco twist." The "twist" is presumably its full schedule of cabaret acts after dining hours upstairs. The line-up ranges from drag chanteuses to veteran jazz stylists.

Finocchio's (506 Broadway, ☎ 415/982–9388), an amiable, world-famous club, has been generating confusion with its female impersonators since 1936. The scene at Finocchio's is decidedly retro, which for the most part only adds to its charm.

Josie's Cabaret and Juice Joint (3583 16th St., at Market St., ☎ 415/861–7933), a small, stylish café and cabaret in the predominantly gay Castro District, books performers who reflect the countercultural feel of the neighborhood. National talents stopping through have included Lypsinka, lesbian comic Lea Delaria, and transsexual performance artist Kate Bornstein.

Comedy Clubs

Cobb's Comedy Club (2801 Leavenworth St., at the corner of Beach St., ☎ 415/928–4320), in the Cannery, books super stand-up comics such as Margaret Smith, Dana Gould, Jake Johannsen, and Dom Irrera.

Punch Line (44-A Battery St., between Clay and Washington Sts., ☎ 415/397–7573), a launching pad for the likes of Jay Leno and Whoopi Goldberg, features some of the area's top talents—several of whom are certain to make a national impact. Note that weekend shows often sell out; it is best to buy tickets in advance at BASS outlets (☎ 510/762–2277) or from the club's new charge line (☎ 415/397–4337). Admission is for those 18 and over only.

Dancing Emporiums

Cesar's Latin Palace (3140 Mission St., ☎ 415/648–6611), in the Mission District, lures all kinds of dancers with its salsa-style Latin music. Latin dance lessons from 9 to 10 PM are included in the price of admission Friday and Saturday nights. Sunday is Brazilian Night. Note: No alcohol is served here.

Metronome Ballroom (1830 17th St., ☎ 415/252–9000) is at its most lively on weekend nights, when ballroom dancers come for lessons and revelry. The ambience is lively but mellow at this smoke- and alcohol-free spot.

Oz (335 Powell St., between Geary and Post Sts., ☎ 415/774–0116), on the top floor of the St. Francis Hotel—accessible via glass elevator—has marble floors and a splendid panorama of the city. Dancers can recharge on cushy sofas and bamboo chairs. The fine sound system belts out progressive house music.

Sound Factory (525 Harrison St., ☎ 415/543–1300) became an instant hit when it opened in SoMa in 1993. Musical styles change with the night and sometimes the hour. Depending on who's up in the DJ booth, you're likely to hear anything from garage and deep house to '70s disco. Two "virtual reality pods" offer refuge; live bands also perform at special events. Some nights the venue becomes an alcohol-free, after-hours club.

Piano Bars

Act IV Lounge (333 Fulton St., near Franklin St., ☎ 415/553–8100), in the Inn at the Opera Hotel, is a popular spot for a romantic rendezvous. The focal point of this tastefully appointed lounge is a crackling fireplace.

Redwood Room (Taylor and Geary Sts., ☎ 415/775–4700), in the Four Seasons Clift Hotel, is a classy Art Deco lounge with a low-key but sensuous ambience. Klimt reproductions grace the walls, and mellow sounds fill the air.

Ritz-Carlton Hotel (600 Stockton St., ☎ 415/296–7465) has a tastefully appointed lobby lounge where a harpist plays during high tea, daily from 2:30 to 5 PM. The lounge shifts to piano (with occasional vocal accompaniment) for cocktails until 11:30 weeknights and 1:30 AM weekends.

Washington Square Bar and Grill (1707 Powell St., on Washington Sq., ☎ 415/982–8123), affectionately known as the "Washbag" among San Francisco politicians and newspaper folk, hosts pianists performing jazz and popular standards.

Skyline Bars

Carnelian Room (555 California St., ☎ 415/433–7500), on the 52nd floor of the Bank of America Building, offers what is perhaps the loftiest view of San Francisco's magnificent skyline. Enjoy dinner or cocktails at 781 feet above the ground; reservations are a must for dinner.

Crown Room (California and Mason Sts., ☎ 415/772–5131), the aptly named lounge on the 29th floor of the Fairmont Hotel, is one of the most luxurious of the city's skyline bars. Just riding the glass-enclosed Skylift elevator is a drama in itself.

Top of the Mark (California and Mason Sts., ☎ 415/392–3434), in the Mark Hopkins Hotel, was immortalized by a famous magazine photograph as a hot spot for World War II service people on leave or about to ship out. Now folks can dance to the sounds of that era on weekends. There's live music Wednesday through Saturday night and dancing to standards from the '20s, '30s, and '40s Friday and Saturday. The view is superb seven nights a week.

San Francisco's Favorite Bars

Locals patronize all of the places listed above, but there are several joints they hold near and dear:

Buena Vista (2765 Hyde St., ☎ 415/474–5044), the Wharf area's most popular bar, introduced Irish coffee to the New World—or so they say. Because it has a fine view of the waterfront, it's usually packed with tourists.

Cypress Club (500 Jackson St., off Columbus Ave., ☎ 415/296–8555) is an eccentric restaurant-bar where sensual, '20s-style opulence clashes with Fellini/Dali frivolity. The decor alone makes it worth a visit, but it's also a fine spot for a before-dinner or after-theater chat. Raymond Chandler's *The Big Sleep* inspired the club's name.

Edinburgh Castle (950 Geary St., near Polk St., ☎ 415/885–4074), cherished by Scots all over town, pours out happy and sometimes baleful Scottish folk tunes the likes of which can be heard nowhere for miles; Fridays feature bagpipe performances. There are plenty of Scottish brews from which to choose. You can work off your fish-and-chips with a turn at the dart board.

House of Shields (39 New Montgomery St., ☎ 415/392–7732), a saloon-style bar, attracts an older, Financial District crowd after work. It closes at 8 PM weekdays, 6 PM Saturday.

Vesuvio Cafe (255 Columbus Ave., between Broadway and Pacific Ave., ☎ 415/362–3370), near the legendary City Lights Bookstore, is little altered since its heyday as a haven for the Beat poets.

Gay and Lesbian Nightlife

LESBIAN BARS

The Box (715 Harrison St., ☎ 415/647–8258), a long-running one-nighter, moved to new digs in 1994, but "Mixtress" Page Hodel still keeps the dressed-to-sweat crowd in constant motion with house, hip-hop, and funk sounds. Expect to find a mixed, increasingly male crowd.

Club Q (177 Townsend St., ☎ 415/647–8258), a dance party from Page Hodel's One Groove Productions, is geared to "women and their friends."

G-Spot (9th and Harrison Sts., ☎ 415/863–6623), inside the Stud, is a hot spot (aka Girlspot) on Saturday night, when a mostly lesbian crowd dances to pop (Whitney Houston, etc.), with a bit of techno-beat. Note: The Stud also has a women's night on Thursdays.

Red Dora's Bearded Lady Café and Cabaret (485 14th St., at Guerrero St., ☎ 415/626–2805), a neighborhood venue, serves a predominantly lesbian and gay clientele. It's also a gallery with mostly women's work, and a music outlet for local independent labels. The kitchen serves inexpensive vegetarian fare.

GAY MALE BARS

Alta Plaza Bar & Grill (2301 Fillmore St., ☎ 415/922–1444) is an upper Fillmore restaurant-bar that caters to nattily dressed guppies (gay yuppies) and their admirers.

Elephant Walk (Castro St., at 18th St., no ☎), one of the Castro's cozier bars, is among the few where the music level allows for easy conversation.

Midnight Sun (4067 18th St., ☎ 415/861–4186), one of the Castro's longest-standing and most popular bars, has giant video screens riotously programmed. Don't expect to hear yourself think.

N Touch (1548 Polk St., ☎ 415/441–8413), a tiny dance bar, has long been popular with Asian-Pacific Islander gay men. Video screens alternately play mildly erotic videos and MTV.

EXCURSIONS

Sausalito

By Robert Taylor

The San Francisco Convention and Visitors Bureau describes Sausalito's location as "the Mediterranean side of the Golden Gate." With its relatively sheltered site on the bay in Marin County, just 8 miles from San Francisco, it appeals to Bay Area residents and visitors for the same reason: It is so near and yet so far. As a hillside town with superb views, an expansive yacht harbor, the aura of an artist's colony, and ferry service, Sausalito might be a resort within commuting distance of the city. It is certainly the primary excursion for visitors to San Francisco, especially those with limited time to explore the Bay Area. Mild weather encourages strolling and outdoor dining, although morning fog and afternoon winds can roll over the hills from the ocean, funneling through the central part of town once known as Hurricane Gulch.

There are substantial homes, including Victorian mansions, in Sausalito's heights, but the town's raffish reputation predates them. Discovered in 1775 by Spanish explorers and named Saucelito (Little Willow) for the trees growing around its springs, Sausalito was a port for whaling ships during the 19th century. In 1875 the railroad from the north connected with ferryboats to San Francisco and the town became an attraction for the fun-loving. Even the chamber of commerce recalls the time when Sausalito sported 25 saloons, gambling dens, and bordellos. Bootleggers flourished during Prohibition in the 1920s, and shipyard workers swelled the town's population during the 1940s, when tour guides divided the residents into "wharf rats" and "hill snobs."

Ensuing decades brought a bohemian element with the development of an artists' colony and a houseboat community. Sausalito has also become a major yachting center, and restaurants attract visitors for fresh seafood as well as spectacular views. Sausalito remains a friendly and casual small town, although summer traffic jams can fray nerves. If possible, visit on a weekday—and take the ferry.

Exploring

Numbers in the margin correspond to points of interest on the Sausalito map.

Bridgeway is Sausalito's main thoroughfare and prime destination, with the bay, yacht harbor, and waterfront restaurants on one side and more restaurants, shops, hillside homes, and hotels on the other. It is only a few steps from the ferry terminal to the tiny landmark park in
1 the center of town: the **Plaza Vina del Mar,** named for Sausalito's sister city in Chile. The park features a fountain and two 14-foot-tall statues of elephants created for the 1915 Panama-Pacific International Exposition in San Francisco.

2 Across the street to the south is the Spanish-style **Sausalito Hotel,** which has been refurbished and filled with Victorian antiques. Between the hotel
3 and the **Sausalito Yacht Club** is another unusual historic landmark, a drinking fountain inscribed with the words, "Have a Drink on Sally." It's in remembrance of Sally Stanford, the former San Francisco madam who later ran Sausalito's Valhalla restaurant and became the town's mayor—although, as suggested by a sidewalk-level bowl that reads "Have a Drink on Leland," the fountain may actually be in remembrance of her dog.

Alta Mira, **5**
Bay Model, **7**
Plaza Vina del Mar, **1**
Sausalito Hotel, **2**
Sausalito Yacht Club, **3**
Valhalla, **4**
Village Fair, **6**

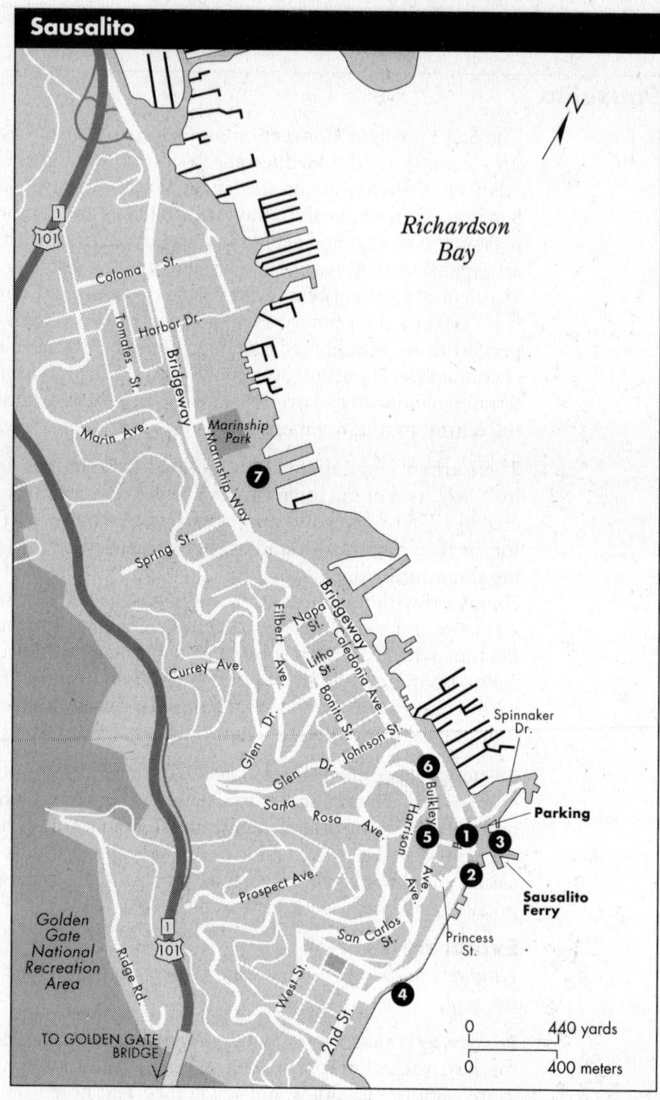

South on Bridgeway, toward San Francisco, an esplanade along the water affords picture-perfect views. Farther south are a number of restaurants on piers, including—near the end of Bridgeway at Richardson Street—what was the **Valhalla** and is the oldest restaurant in Sausalito. Built in 1893 as "Walhalla," it was one of the settings for the film *The Lady from Shanghai* in the 1940s, Sally Stanford's place in the 1950s, and most recently a Chart House restaurant.

North on Bridgeway from the ferry terminal are yacht harbors and, parallel to Bridgeway a block to the west, the quieter Caledonia Street, with its own share of cafés and shops. There is a pleasant, grassy park with a children's playground at Caledonia and Litho streets, with a food shop nearby for picnic provisions.

Along the west side of Bridgeway are flights of steps that climb the hill to Sausalito's wooded, sometimes rustic and sometimes lavish residential

neighborhoods. The stairway called Excelsior, just across the street from
5 Vina del Mar Park, leads to the **Alta Mira,** a popular Spanish-style hotel and restaurant with a spectacular view (*see* Dining, *below*).

Where there isn't a hillside house or a restaurant or a yacht in Sausalito, there is a shop. Mostly along Bridgeway and Princess Street, they offer a wide assortment of casual and sophisticated clothing, posters and paintings, imported and handcrafted gifts, and the expected vari-
6 ety of T-shirts, ice cream, cookies, and pastries. The **Village Fair** (777 Bridgeway) is a four-story former warehouse that has been converted into a warren of clothing, crafts, and gift boutiques. Crafts workers often demonstrate their talents in the shops, and a winding brick path—Little Lombard Street—connects various levels. The shopping complex is a haven during wet weather.

Sausalito's reputation as an art colony is enhanced by the **Art Festival** held during the three-day Labor Day weekend in September. It attracts more than 35,000 visitors to the waterfront area, and ferry service is extended to the site during the festival. Details are available from the Sausalito Chamber of Commerce (333 Caledonia St., 94965, ☎ 415/332–0505).

7 North on Bridgeway, within a few minutes' drive, is the **Bay Model,** a 400-square-foot replica of the entire San Francisco Bay and the San Joaquin–Sacramento River delta, which is used by the U.S. Army Corps of Engineers to reproduce the rise and fall of tides, the flow of currents, and the other physical forces at work on the bay. Housed in a former World War II shipyard building, the Bay Model is next to a display of shipbuilding history. At the same site is the Wapama, a World War I–era steam freighter being restored by volunteers. *2100 Bridgeway, ☎ 415/332–3871. ☛ Free. ⏲ Tues.–Fri. 9–4, weekends 10–6; closed Sun. in winter.*

Along the shore of Richardson Bay, between the Bay Model and U.S. 101, are some of the 400 houseboats that make up Sausalito's "floating homes community." In the shallow tidelands, most of them float only about half the time, but their constant presence ensures a trademark view of the rustic, the eccentric, the flamboyant, and the elegant.

Just south of Sausalito, facing a cove beneath the Golden Gate Bridge, the **Bay Area Discovery Museum** fills five former military buildings with entertaining and enlightening hands-on exhibits. Youngsters and their families can crew on a boat, explore in and under a house, and make multitrack recordings. From San Francisco take the Alexander Avenue exit from U.S. 101 and follow signs to East Fort Baker. *☎ 415/487–4398. ☛ $5. ⏲ Wed.–Sun. 10–5, and Tues. 10–5 in summer; closed major holidays.*

Dining

Restaurants by the bay or perched on Sausalito's hillside feature prime views and fare that covers the waterfront. Most menus contain at least one heart-healthy pick on every menu. Casual dress is acceptable.

CATEGORY	COST*
$$$$	over $30
$$$	$20–$30
$$	$10–$20
$	under $10

**per person for a three-course meal, excluding drinks, service, and 7¼% sales tax*

$$$ Gate Five. The 80% seafood menu at this cozy, East Coast–style harborside restaurant includes Maine lobster, New England clam chowder, and fresh mussels. Ask to sit near one of the two fireplaces. ✕ *305 Harbor Dr.,* ☏ *415/331–5355. AE, DC, MC, V.*

$$$ Mikayla. Part of a hotel complex that includes a classic Victorian, a cluster of cottages, and terraced gardens stepping down the hillside, this upscale restaurant serves up fine American cuisine with French overtones and all-star views of the bay. The light, airy dining terrace with retractable roof and sliding glass walls is a great spot to splurge on a Sunday brunch buffet. ✕ *801 Bridgeway,* ☏ *415/331–5888. Reservations advised. AE, D, DC, MC, V. No lunch Mon.–Sat.*

$$–$$$ Alta Mira. This Sausalito landmark, in a Spanish-style hotel a block above Bridgeway, has spectacular views of the bay from the heated front terrace and the windowed dining room. It's a favored destination Bay Area–wide for Sunday brunch (try the famed eggs Benedict and Ramos Fizz), an alfresco lunch, or cocktails at sunset. The California-Continental cuisine includes succulent rack of lamb, duckling, seafood salad, and a stellar Caesar salad. ✕ *125 Bulkley Ave.,* ☏ *415/332–1350. Reservations advised. AE, DC, MC, V.*

$$ Spinnaker. Spectacular bay views, homemade pastas, and seafood specialties like fresh grilled salmon are the prime attractions in this contemporary building on a point beyond the harbor, near the yacht club. You may see a pelican perched on one of the pilings just outside. ✕ *100 Spinnaker Dr.,* ☏ *415/332–1500. Reservations advised. Sun. brunch. AE, DC, MC, V.*

$–$$ Margaritaville. Exotic drinks and every Mexican favorite you'd ever crave from fajitas and enchiladas to *camarones rancheros* (fresh Pacific prawns sautéed in a flavorful red sauce) are on the bill of fare in a tropically hip setting with views of the marina and the bay. ✕ *1200 Bridgeway,* ☏ *415/331–3226. Reservations accepted for 6 or more. AE, DC, MC, V.*

$ Lighthouse Coffee Shop. This budget-priced coffee shop serves breakfast and lunch (omelets, sandwiches, and burgers) every day from 6:30 (7 on weekends). Most find the down-to-earth atmosphere and simple fare (including Danish meatballs, herring, and salmon open-faced sandwiches) a welcome break from tourist traps and seafood extravaganzas. ✕ *1311 Bridgeway,* ☏ *415/331–3034. No reservations. No credit cards. No alcohol.*

Sausalito Essentials

ARRIVING AND DEPARTING

By Bus: Golden Gate Transit (☏ 415/332–6600) travels to Sausalito from 1st and Mission streets and other points in the city.

By Car: Cross the Golden Gate Bridge and head north on U.S. 101 to the Sausalito exit, then go south on Bridgeway to municipal parking near the center of town. The trip takes 20 to 45 minutes one-way. (Bring change for the parking lots' meters.)

By Ferry: Golden Gate Ferry (☏ 415/332–6600) crosses the bay from the Ferry Building at Market Street and the Embarcadero; **Red and White Fleet** (☏ 415/546–2896) leaves from Pier 41 at Fisherman's Wharf. The trip takes 15–30 minutes.

GUIDED TOURS

Most tour companies include Sausalito on excursions north to Muir Woods and the Napa Valley Wine Country. Among them are **Gray Line** (☏ 415/558–9400) and **Great Pacific Tour Co.** (☏ 415/626–4499).

Muir Woods

One hundred and fifty million years ago, ancestors of redwood and sequoia trees grew throughout the United States. Today the *Sequoia sempervirens* can be found only in a narrow, cool coastal belt from Monterey to Oregon. (*Sequoiadendron gigantea* grows in the Sierra Nevada.) **Muir Woods National Monument,** 17 miles northwest of San Francisco, is a 550-acre park that contains one of the most majestic redwood groves in the world. Some redwoods in the park are nearly 250 feet tall and 1,000 years old. This grove was saved from destruction in 1908 and named for naturalist John Muir, whose campaigns helped to establish the national park system. His response: "This is the best tree-lover's monument that could be found in all of the forests of the world. Saving these woods from the axe and saw is in many ways the most notable service to God and man I have heard of since my forest wandering began."

Exploring

Muir Woods is a pedestrian's park; no cars are allowed in the redwood grove itself. Beginning from the park headquarters, 6 miles of easy trails cross streams and pass through ferns and azaleas as well as magnificent stands of redwoods, including Bohemian Grove and the circular formation called Cathedral Grove. The main trail along Redwood Creek is 1 mile long, paved, and wheelchair accessible. All the trails connect with an extensive network of hiking tails in Mt. Tamalpais State Park. No picnicking or camping is allowed, but snacks are available at the visitor center, along with a wide selection of books and exhibits. The weather is usually cool and often wet, so dress warmly and wear shoes appropriate for damp trails. Pets are not allowed. ☏ *415/388–2595.* ⏲ *Daily 8 AM–sunset.*

Muir Woods Essentials

ARRIVING AND DEPARTING

By Car: Take U.S. 101 north to the Mill Valley–Muir Woods exit. The trip takes 45 minutes one-way when the roads are clear, but allow extra time for traffic on summer weekends. The park staff recommends visiting before 10 AM and after 4 PM to avoid congestion. Note that the narrow, winding entrance road cannot accommodate some larger recreation vehicles.

GUIDED TOURS

Most tour companies include Muir Woods on excursions to the Wine Country, among them **Gray Line** (☏ 415/558–9400) and **Great Pacific** (☏ 415/626–4499).

Berkeley

By Robert Taylor

Berkeley and the University of California are not synonymous, although the founding campus of the state university system dominates the city's heritage and contemporary life. But the city of 100,000 facing San Francisco across the bay has other interesting features for visitors. Berkeley is culturally diverse and politically adventurous, a breeding ground for social trends, a continuing bastion of the counterculture, and an important center for Bay Area writers, artists, and musicians. Indeed, the city's liberal reputation and determined spirit have led detractors to describe it in recent years as the People's Republic of Berkeley.

Named for George Berkeley, the Irish philosopher and clergyman who crossed the Atlantic to convert the Indians and wrote "Westward, the course of empire takes its way," the city grew with the university. The latter was created by the state legislature in 1868 and established five years later on a rising plain of oak trees split by Strawberry Canyon. The central campus occupies 178 acres of the scenic 1,282-acre property, with most buildings located from Bancroft Way north to Hearst Street and from Oxford Street east into the Berkeley Hills. The university has more than 30,000 students and a full-time faculty of 1,600. It is considered one of the nation's leading intellectual centers and a major site for scientific research.

Exploring

Numbers in the margin correspond to points of interest on the Berkeley map.

1 The visitor center (☎ 510/642–5215) in **University Hall** at University Avenue and Oxford Street is open weekdays 8:30–4:30. There are maps and brochures for self-guided walks; 1½-hour student-guided tours leave Monday, Wednesday, and Friday at 10 AM and 1 PM.

2 At **Sproul Plaza,** just inside the campus at Telegraph Avenue and Bancroft Way, the lively panorama of political and social activists, musicians, class-bound students, and food vendors along Bancroft Way gives credence to U.C. Berkeley's reputation as a "university within a park."

TIME OUT Some people insist that without its cafés Berkeley would simply collapse. No fewer than 55 peacefully coexist within 1 square mile of the U.C. campus. Cafés of all persuasions serve every kind of coffee concoction, along with light meals. They are where people read, discuss, and debate, or eavesdrop on others doing the same. A few among the many: **Caffe Mediterraneum** (2475 Telegraph Ave., ☎ 510/549–1128) is a relic of '60s-era Berkeley but far enough from campus to pull in a mostly nonstudent crowd. Allen Ginsberg wrote while imbibing here. **Caffe Strada** (2300 College Ave., ☎ 510/843–5282) has a sprawling patio where frat boys, sorority sisters, and foreigners meet and greet; try the iced white-chocolate mocha. The **Musical Offering** (2430 Bancroft Way, ☎ 510/849–0211) serves light meals and coffee; in back there's a music store specializing in classical CDs and cassettes.

The university's suggested tour circles the upper portion of the central campus, past buildings that were sited to take advantage of vistas to the Golden Gate across the bay. The first campus plan was proposed by Frederick Law Olmsted, who designed New York's Central Park; over the years the university's architects have also included Bernard Maybeck and Julia Morgan (who designed Hearst Castle at San
3 Simeon). Beyond Sproul Plaza is the bronze **Sather Gate,** built in 1909, and the former south entrance to the campus; the university expanded a block beyond its traditional boundary in the 1960s. Up a walkway
4 to the right is vine-covered **South Hall,** one of two remaining buildings that greeted the first students in 1873.

5 Just ahead is **Sather Tower,** popularly known as the Campanile, the campus landmark that can be seen for miles. The 307-foot tower was modeled on St. Mark's tower in Venice and was completed in 1914. The carillon, which was cast in England, is played three times a day. In the lobby of the tower is a photographic display of campus history. An elevator takes visitors 175 feet up to the observation deck. ☛ *50¢.* ⏲ *Daily 10–3:15.*

Bancroft Library, **6**
Botanical Garden, **13**
Cody's Books, **15**
Earth Sciences Building, **7**
Faculty Glade, **11**
Hearst Greek Theatre, **12**
Lawrence Hall of Science, **14**
Leopold Records, **17**
Moe's, **16**
Paleontology Museum, **8**
The Phoebe Apperson Hearst Museum of Anthropology, **9**
Sather Gate, **3**
Sather Tower, **5**
South Hall, **4**
Sproul Plaza, **2**
The University Art Museum, **10**
University Hall (Visitors Center), **1**

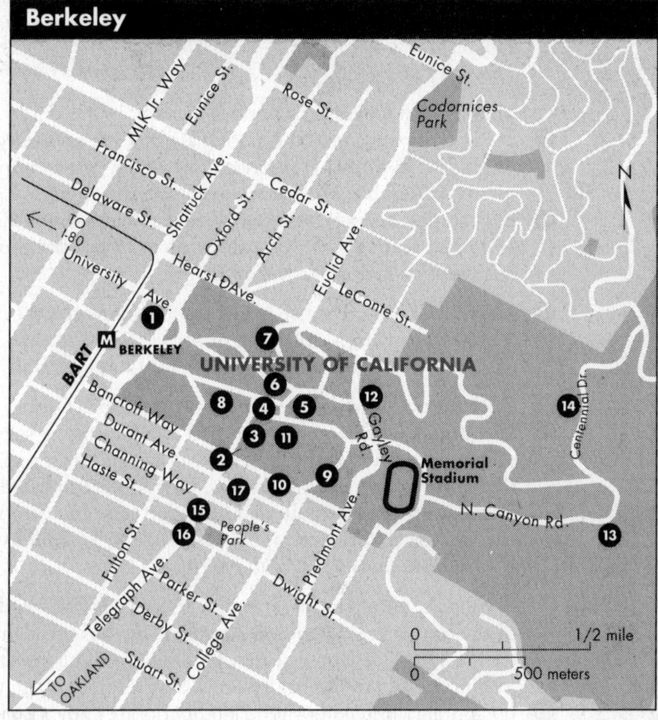

6 Opposite the Campanile is **Bancroft Library,** with a rare-book collection and a changing series of exhibits that may include a Shakespeare first folio or a gold-rush diary. On permanent display is a gold nugget purported to be the one that started the rush to California when it was discovered on January 24, 1848.

7 Across University Drive to the north is the **Earth Sciences Building,** with a seismograph for measuring earthquakes. Another scientific wonder
8 is the **Paleontology Museum,** whose public displays line the lobby and hall of the Valley Life Sciences Building south of University Drive. The casted skeleton of a 40-foot Tyrannosaurus rex hangs in the building's three-story atrium. ☎ *510/642–1821.* ☛ *Free.* ⏲ *When the university is in session, weekdays 8–5, Sat. 1–4.*

The university's two major museums are on the south side of campus
9 near Bancroft Way. The **Phoebe Apperson Hearst Museum of Anthropology** (formerly the Lowie), in Kroeber Hall, has a collection of more than 4,000 artifacts. Items on display may cover the archaeology of ancient America or the crafts of Pacific Islanders. The museum also houses the collection of artifacts made by Ishi, the lone survivor of a California Indian tribe who was brought to the Bay Area in 1911. ☎ *510/642–3681. Nominal admission charge.* ⏲ *Wed. and Fri.–Sun. 10–4:30, Thurs. 10–9.*

10 The **University Art Museum** is a fan-shaped building with a spiral of ramps and balcony galleries. It houses a collection of Asian and Western art, including a major group of Hans Hofmann's abstract paintings, and also displays touring exhibits. On the ground floor is the Pacific Film Archive, which offers daily programs of historic and contemporary films. *2626 Bancroft Way,* ☎ *510/642–0808;* ☎ *510/642–1124*

for film-program information. ☛ *Museum: $6, $4 senior citizens, free Thurs. 11* AM*–noon and 5–9.* ⏲ *Museum: Wed. and Fri.–Sun. 11–5, Thurs. 11–9.*

Many of the university's notable attractions are outdoors. Just south
11 of the Campanile near the rustic Faculty Club is **Faculty Glade** on the south fork of Strawberry Creek, one of the best examples of the university's attempt to preserve a parklike atmosphere. East of the cen-
12 tral campus, across Gayley Road, is the **Hearst Greek Theatre,** built in 1903 and seating 7,000. Sarah Bernhardt once performed here; now it is used for major musical events.

13 Above the Greek Theatre in Strawberry Canyon is the 30-acre **Botanical Garden,** with a collection of some 25,000 species. It's a relaxing gathering spot with benches and picnic tables. ⏲ *Daily 9–4:45.*

Perched on a hill above the campus on Centennial Drive is the fortresslike
14 **Lawrence Hall of Science,** which is a laboratory, a science education center, and—most important to visitors—a dazzling display of scientific knowledge and experiments. Displays are updated regularly. On weekends there are additional films, lectures, and demonstrations, especially for children. ☎ *510/642–5132.* ☛ *$6 adults, $4 senior citizens and students.* ⏲ *Weekdays 10–5.*

Beyond the university, Berkeley is a rewarding city to explore. Just south of the campus on **Telegraph Avenue** is the busy student-oriented district, full of cafés, bookstores, poster shops, and street vendors with traditional and trendy crafts items. Shops come and go with the times,
15 but among the neighborhood landmarks are **Cody's Books** (2454 Tele-
16 graph Ave.), with its adjacent café; **Moe's** (2476 Telegraph Ave.), with
17 a huge selection of used books; and **Leopold Records** (2518 Durant Ave.), one of the Bay Area's best music stores—along with nearby **Amoeba Music** (2455 Telegraph Ave.) and **Rasputin's Records** (2350 Telegraph Ave.). This district was the center of student protests during the 1960s, and on the street it sometimes looks as if that era still lives (it can be unruly at night). People's Park, one of the centers of protest, is just east of Telegraph between Haste Street and Dwight Way.

Dining

Food is a priority in Berkeley, where specialty markets, cheese stores, charcuteries, coffee vendors, produce outlets, innovative restaurants, and ethnic eateries abound. The most popular gourmet ghetto is along Shattuck Avenue, a few blocks north of University Avenue. University Avenue itself has become a corridor of good Indian, Thai, and Cambodian restaurants. You'll find lots of students, interesting coffeehouses, and cheap eats on Telegraph, Durant, and Berkeley avenues near the campus. Casual dress is considered politically correct wherever you dine.

CATEGORY	COST*
$$$$	over $30
$$$	$20–$30
$$	$10–$20
$	under $10

**per person for a three-course meal, excluding drinks, service, and 8¼% sales tax*

$$–$$$$ **Chez Panisse Café & Restaurant.** President Clinton has joined the ranks of luminaries who have dined at this legendary eatery, but like anyone else without a reservation, he sat in the upstairs café. Alice Waters is still the mastermind behind the culinary wizardry, with Jean-Pierre

Moullé lending hands-on talent as head chef. In the downstairs restaurant, where redwood paneling, a fireplace, and lavish floral arrangements create the ambience of a private home, dinners are prix fixe and pricey, but the cost is lower on weekdays and almost halved on Monday. The daily-changing menu includes local rock cod with ginger sauce, sirloin roast with red wine sauce, pasta specialties, and roast truffled breast of guinea hen. Upstairs in the café the atmosphere is informal, the crowd livelier, the prices lower, and the menu more simple, with dishes such as calzone with goat cheese, mozzarella, prosciutto, and garlic. ✕ *1517 Shattuck Ave., north of University Ave. Restaurant (downstairs): ☎ 510/548–5525; reservations required; no lunch. Café (upstairs): ☎ 510/548–5049; same-day reservations; Fri. and Sat. dinner, walk-ins only. 15% service charge added to each bill. AE, D, DC, MC, V. Closed Sun.*

$$$ **Rivoli.** Husband-and-wife team Wendy Rucker and Roscoe Skipper use native California ingredients in French- and Italian-inspired dishes for a menu that changes weekly. Highlights are linguine with scallops; braised veal stew; ricotta tart with prosciutto, figs, salsa verde, and mizuna; and rigatoni with eggplant, olives, and feta cheese. Desserts include a pear granita with ginger snaps, bittersweet chocolate tiramisù with expresso crème anglaise, and home-style hot-fudge sundae. ✕ *1539 Solano Ave., ☎ 510/526–2542. Reservations advised. AE, MC, V. No lunch.*

$$ **Spenger's Fish Grotto.** This rambling, boisterous seafood restaurant is known for hearty portions of fairly ordinary food. It's a wildly popular place, though, so expect a wait in its combination oyster–sports bar, or opt for the take-out section next door and eat your fish alfresco on the Berkeley pier at the foot of University Avenue. ✕ *1919 4th St., near University Ave. and I–80, ☎ 510/845–7771. Reservations for 5 or more. AE, D, DC, MC, V.*

$$ **Venezia Caffe & Ristorante.** This family-friendly eatery was one of the first to serve fresh pasta in the Bay Area, and it continues to offer a wide range of tasty selections (don't miss the house-made chicken sausage). The large dining room looks like a Venetian piazza, with a fountain in the middle, murals on the walls, and laundry hanging overhead. Children get their own menu, free antipasti, and crayons. ✕ *1799 University Ave., ☎ 510/849–4681. Reservations advised. AE, DC, MC, V. No lunch weekends.*

Berkeley Essentials

ARRIVING AND DEPARTING

By Car: Take I–80 east across the Bay Bridge, then the University Avenue exit through downtown Berkeley to the campus, or take the Ashby Avenue exit and turn left on Telegraph Avenue to the traditional campus entrance; there is a parking garage on Channing Way. The trip takes a half hour one-way (except in rush hour).

By Public Transportation: BART (☎ 415/992–2278) trains run under the bay to the downtown Berkeley exit; transfer to the Humphrey Go-Bart shuttle bus to campus. The trip takes from 45 minutes to one hour one-way.

Oakland

Originally the site of ranches, farms, a grove of redwood trees, and, of course, clusters of oaks, Oakland has long been a warmer and more spacious alternative to San Francisco. By the end of the 19th century, Mediterranean-style homes and gardens had been developed as summer estates. With swifter transportation, Oakland became a bedroom community for San Francisco; then it progressed to California's fastest-growing industrial city. In recent decades, Oakland has struggled to upgrade its image as a tourist destination. However, the major attractions remain the same as they ever were: the parks and civic buildings around Lake Merritt, which was created from a tidal basin in 1898; the port area, now named Jack London Square, where the author spent much of his time at the turn of the century; and the scenic roads and parks along the crest of the Oakland-Berkeley hills. Also in the hills is the castlelike Claremont Resort Hotel, a landmark since 1915, as well as more sprawling parks with lakes and miles of hiking trails.

Exploring

Numbers in the margin correspond to points of interest on the Oakland map.

1 If there is one reason to visit Oakland, it is to explore the **Oakland Museum of California,** an inviting series of landscaped buildings that display the state's art, history, and natural science. It is the best possible introduction to a tour of California, and its dramatic and detailed exhibits can help fill the gaps on a brief visit. The natural-science department displays a typical stretch of California from the Pacific Ocean to the Nevada border, including plants and wildlife. A breathtaking film, *Fast Flight,* condenses the trip into five minutes. The museum's sprawling history section includes everything from Spanish-era artifacts and a gleaming fire engine that battled the flames in San Francisco in 1906 to 1960s souvenirs of the "summer of love." The California Dream exhibit recalls a century of inspirations. The museum's art department includes mystical landscapes painted by the state's pioneers, as well as contemporary visions. There is a pleasant museum café for lunch and outdoor areas for relaxing. *1000 Oak St., at 10th St., ☎ 510/834–2413. ☛ $4 adults, $2 children 7–18. ⏲ Wed.–Sat. 10–5, Sun. noon–7.*

2 Near the museum, **Lake Merritt** is a 155-acre oasis surrounded by parks and paths, with several outdoor attractions on the north side.
3 The **Natural Science Center and Waterfowl Refuge** attracts birds by the hundreds during winter months. *At the foot of Perkins St., ☎ 510/238–3739. ⏲ Daily 10–5.*

4 **Children's Fairyland** is a low-key amusement park with a puppet theater, small merry-go-round, and settings based on nursery rhymes. *Grand Ave. at Park View Terr., ☎ 510/452–2259. ☛ $3 adults, $2.50 children 1–12. ⏲ Summer, Tues.–Fri. 10–4:30, weekends 10–5:30; days and hrs vary rest of year; open Mon. on school holidays.*

5 The **Lakeside Park Garden Center** has a Japanese garden and many native flowers and plants. *666 Bellevue Ave., ☎ 510/238–3208. ☛ Free. ⏲ Daily 10–3 or later in summer; closed Thanksgiving, Dec. 25, Jan. 1.*

Jack London, although born in San Francisco, spent his early years in Oakland before shipping out for adventures that inspired *The Call of the Wild, The Sea Wolf, Martin Eden,* and *The Cruise of the Snark.*
6 He is commemorated with a bronze bust on what is now called **Jack London's Waterfront,** at the foot of Broadway. A livelier landmark is
7 **Heinhold's First and Last Chance Saloon,** one of his hangouts. Next door is the reassembled Klondike cabin in which he spent a winter. Restaurants cluster around the plaza, and the nearby Jack London Village has specialty shops and restaurants. The best local collection of the author's letters, manuscripts, and photographs is in the Jack London Room at the Oakland Main Library (125 14th St., ☎ 510/238–

Children's Fairyland, **4**
Heinhold's First and Last Chance Saloon, **7**
Jack London's Waterfront, **6**
Lake Merritt, **2**
Lakeside Park Garden Center, **5**
Natural Science Center and Waterfowl Refuge, **3**
Oakland Museum of California, **1**

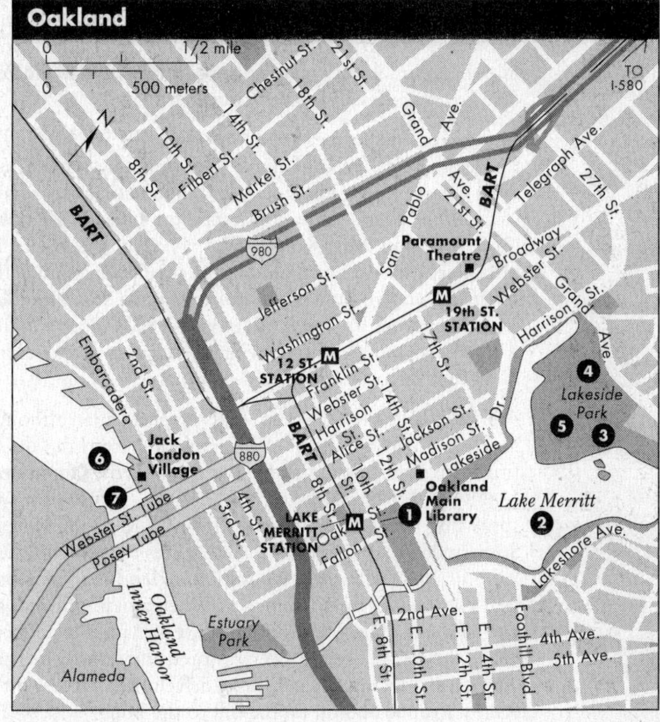

3134). Oakland's downtown has been undergoing redevelopment for many years and is finally becoming a destination for visitors and residents alike. A number of community events have settled down at the plaza at Jack London Square, ranging from boat and auto shows to a farmers' market every Sunday. Other areas for shopping, browsing, or just relaxing at a café can be found on Lake Shore Avenue northeast of Lake Merritt, Piedmont Avenue near the Broadway exit from I–580, and College Avenue west of Broadway in North Oakland, which neighbors BART's Rockridge station. From the station, the local Bus 51 will take visitors to the University of California campus, about 1½ miles away in Berkeley.

The East Bay Regional Park District (☏ 510/562–7275) offers 46 parks in an area covering 60,000 acres to residents and visitors. In the Oakland hills is **Redwood Regional Park,** accessible from Joaquin Miller Road off Highway 13, to which Ashby Avenue will lead you. In the Berkeley hills is the 2,000-acre **Tilden Park,** which includes a lake and children's playground and is accessible from Grizzly Peak Boulevard off Claremont Avenue. There are scenic views of the Bay Area from roads that link the hilltop parks: Redwood Road, Skyline Boulevard, and Grizzly Peak Boulevard. Parks are open daily during daylight hours.

OFF THE BEATEN TRACK

Given the city's reputation for Victorian and Craftsman housing, visitors to Oakland are generally surprised by the profusion of Art Deco architecture in the neighborhood around the 19th Street BART station downtown. Some of these buildings have fallen into disrepair, but the **Paramount Theater** (2025 Broadway, ☏ 510/465–6400) is a masterpiece of the Art Deco style and remains open and operating as a venue for concerts and performances of all kinds. For $1 you can take a two-hour tour of the building, given the first and third Saturday of each month. For information about performances, check the free weekly *East Bay Express,* or call the box office.

In the years just after the Second World War, Oakland gave birth to the gritty, hurts-so-bad-I-think-I'm-gonna-die soulful music known as West Coast blues, and the style still flourishes in clubs and bars all over town. One consistently good spot for blues is **Eli's Mile High Club** (3629 Martin Luther King Jr. Way, ☎ 510/655–6661). Reputedly *the* birthplace of West Coast blues, it's a small, basic club with a pool table, soul food, and music Wednesday–Sunday. At **Your Place Too** (5319 Martin Luther King Jr. Way, ☎ 510/652–5837) there are 50¢ beers and a warped pool table (complete with resident pool shark), along with nightly blues and the occasional hard-core band.

A drive through the Oakland Hills is spectacular, although a wide area north from Broadway is still recovering from the devastating 1991 firestorm. One landmark that was saved is the **Claremont Resort Hotel** (Ashby and Domingo Aves., ☎ 510/843–3000). From a distance, the sprawling white building with towers and gables looks like a castle. Surrounded by 22 acres of lush grounds tucked into the south Berkeley hills, the Claremont is on the Oakland–Berkeley border, and for years both cities have claimed it. When a new entrance was built on a different side of the building, the address changed from Berkeley to Oakland. The 1915 hotel has been restored and refurbished and turned into a resort spa facility. To get there, drive north on Claremont Avenue to Ashby Avenue and on up the hill to the hotel.

Dining

Oakland's ethnic diversity is reflected in its restaurants and cafés. There is a thriving Chinatown a few blocks northwest of the Oakland Museum, a number of seafood restaurants at Jack London Square, and fare to fit any palate, penchant, or pocketbook on Piedmont and College Avenues. Dress is casual.

CATEGORY	COST*
$$$$	over $30
$$$	$20–$30
$$	$10–$20
$	under $10

**per person for a three-course meal, excluding drinks, service, and 8¼% sales tax*

$$–$$$ Bay Wolf. A favorite for 20 years, this converted home has a redwood deck out front, elegantly understated dining rooms inside, and a kitchen garden out back. The menu changes frequently to feature fresh seasonal ingredients and Mediterranean cuisine with a twist: Try pork loin salad with stuffed squash; grilled eggplant, peppers, and couscous; or pan-roasted salmon with artichokes, asparagus, spring carrots, and sorrel sauce. ✕ *3853 Piedmont Ave., ☎ 510/655–6004. Reservations advised. MC, V. No lunch weekends.*

$–$$$ Oliveto Café & Restaurant. This is one of the East Bay's most interesting Italian restaurants, fashioned after a rustic stucco casa in Tuscany and situated on the corner of a bustling gourmet marketplace. In the formal dining room upstairs, gourmets indulge in chef Paul Bertolli's tagliatelle with smoked ham, ravioli with pumpkin, or chicken cooked under a brick. The café at street level is the place to see and be seen sipping wine or espresso, or snacking on pizzas and pastries. ✕ *5655*

College Ave., ☏ 510/547–5356. Reservations advised for restaurant. AE, DC, MC, V. No lunch weekends in restaurant.

$$ ZZA's Trattoria. Pizzas, salads, house-smoked chicken, and homemade pasta, ravioli, and lasagna are served in this fun, family-oriented restaurant on the shore of Lake Merritt. There's a wild neon sign over the open kitchen, along with butcher-paper table covers and crayons, and customers' artwork on the walls. ✕ *552 Grand Ave., ☏ 510/839–9124. Same-day reservations for 6 or more. MC, V. No lunch Mon., Tues., weekends.*

$–$$ Lantern Restaurant. Fine Hong Kong cuisine can be had downstairs at the oldest restaurant in Oakland's Chinatown, but the dim sum (steamed dumplings, spring rolls, and assorted exotic delicacies) served in the enormous upstairs dining room is the big deal here. Point to what you want as the carts roll by and pay by the plate. ✕ *814 Webster St., ☏ 510/451–0627. D, DC, MC, V.*

$–$$ Rockridge Cafe. This casual café is known for burgers, breakfasts, and mighty fine pie. ✕ *5492 College Ave., ☏ 510/653–1567. Reservations for 6 or more. MC, V. Sun. brunch.*

Oakland Essentials

ARRIVING AND DEPARTING

By Car: Take I–80 across the Bay Bridge, then I–580 to the Grand Avenue exit for Lake Merritt. To reach downtown and the waterfront, take the I–980 exit from I–580. The trip takes 45 minutes.

By Public Transportation: Take the BART to Oakland City Center station or to Lake Merritt station for the lake and Oakland Museum. The trip takes 45 minutes one-way.

Filoli and Stanford

One of the few great country houses in California that remain intact in its original setting is **Filoli** in Woodside. Built for wealthy San Franciscan William B. Bourn in 1916–19, it was designed by Willis Polk in a Georgian style, with redbrick walls and a tile roof. The name is not Italian but Bourn's acronym for "fight, love, live." As interesting to visitors as the house (which you might remember from the television series *Dynasty*) are the 16 acres of formal gardens. The gardens were planned and developed over a period of more than 50 years and preserved for the public when the last private owner, Mrs. William P. Roth, deeded Filoli to the National Trust for Historic Preservation.

The gardens rise south from the mansion to take advantage of the natural surroundings of the 700-acre estate and its vistas. Among the designs are a sunken garden, walled garden, woodland garden, yew alley, and a rose garden developed by Mrs. Roth with more than 50 shrubs of all types and colors. A focal point of the garden is a charming teahouse designed in the Italian Renaissance style. Spring is the most popular time to visit, but daffodils, narcissi, and rhododendrons are in bloom as early as February, and the gardens remain attractive in October and November. *Cañada Rd., near Edgewood Rd., Woodside, ☏ 415/364–2880. ☛ $8 adults, $4 children. ⏲ For tours mid-Feb.–mid-Nov., Tues.–Sat. Reservations necessary; spring tours may fill several wks in advance. Call for openings. Filoli is often open for unguided visits and nature hikes on the estate; call for information.*

Stanford University, 30 miles south of San Francisco, also has its roots among the peninsula's estates. Originally the property was former California governor Leland Stanford's farm for breeding horses. For all its stature as one of the nation's leading universities, Stanford is still known as "the Farm." Founded and endowed by Leland and Jane Stanford in 1885 as a memorial to their son, Leland, Jr., who died of typhoid fever, the university was opened in 1891. Frederick Law Olmsted conceived the plan for the grounds and Romanesque sandstone buildings, joined by arcades and topped by red-tile roofs.

The center of the 8,200-acre campus is the inner quadrangle, a group of 12 original classroom buildings later joined by Memorial Church, whose facade and interior walls are covered with mosaics of biblical scenes. Free walking tours leave daily at 11 AM and 3:15 PM from the **Visitor Information Booth** (☎ 415/723–2560 or 415/723–2053) at the front of the quadrangle. The main campus entrance, Palm Drive, is an extension of University Avenue from Palo Alto.

Dining

El Camino Real (Highway 82) is the peninsula's major commercial thoroughfare, lined with cafés, restaurants, and fast-food franchises. Palo Alto also has its fair share of pleasant cafés, some with outdoor dining, mostly along University Avenue and its cross streets, just east of El Camino Real.

CATEGORY	COST*
$$$	$20–$30
$$	$10–$20
$	under $10

**per person for a three-course meal, excluding drinks, service, and 8¼% sales tax*

$$–$$$ **Flea Street Cafe.** Specialties here change seasonally and may include herb-roasted Cornish game hen with sage jalapeño gravy and red-onion cornbread stuffing, fettuccine with duck sausage and pippin apples, and—for Sunday brunch—house-baked buttermilk biscuits, homemade jams, and seductive pancake, egg, and omelet creations. Young diners have access to a fully stocked toy chest. ✕ *Alameda de las Pulgas, Menlo Park (take Sand Hill Rd. west from the Stanford shopping center or east from I–280, turn right on Alameda),* ☎ *415/854–1226. Reservations advised. MC, V. Closed Mon. No lunch Sat.*

$$–$$$ **Il Fornaio Cucina Italiana.** This popular eatery has a casually rustic look, with food as the visual focus. Buy gourmet fare to go or stay here to sample superb antipasti, pizza, pasta, and calzone baked to perfection in a wood-burning oven. There is also a charming café area just inside the front door for coffee and snacks. ✕ *520 Cowper St., Palo Alto,* ☎ *415/853–3888. Reservations strongly advised. Weekend brunch. AE, DC, MC, V.*

$$–$$$ **Village Pub.** In this pleasant restaurant near Filoli, patrons elbow up to a carved oak bar to sample the ale, or relax in the stylishly simple modern dining room to savor creative California-rustic renditions of duck, fresh seafood, steak, and pasta. ✕ *2967 Woodside Rd. (¾ mi from I–280W), Woodside,* ☎ *415/851–1294. Reservations advised. AE, DC, MC, V. No lunch weekends.*

$ **Vicolo Pizzeria.** An upscale little hangout, Vicolo has whimsical, faux-Italian decor, more than 30 varieties of gourmet toppings on tasty cornmeal crust, and sidewalk seating in good weather. ✕ *473 University Ave. (near Cowper St.), Palo Alto,* ☎ *415/324–4877. No reservations. No credit cards.*

San Francisco Peninsula Essentials

ARRIVING AND DEPARTING

By Car: The most pleasant direct route down the peninsula is I–280, the Junípero Serra Freeway, which passes along Crystal Springs reservoir. Take the Edgewood Road exit for Filoli, and Alpine Road for Stanford.

By Public Transportation: Take the **CalTrain** (☎ 800/660–4287) from 4th and Townsend streets to Palo Alto, then the shuttle bus to Stanford campus. Filoli is best reached by car.

Silicon Valley

By Claudia Gioseffi

In the spring of 1938, Dave and Lucile Packard, joined by William Hewlett, made room in back of their house for what would eventually become Hewlett-Packard, a pioneer company in the high-tech and electronics revolutions. Another milestone was marked 39 years later when Steve Jobs and Steve Wozniak emerged from a small garage in Cupertino with something called Apple. Ultimately these computer companies and others grew big enough to replace sleepy Santa Clara County's fruit growers and cattle ranchers with an industry that changed the world.

El Camino Real, Highway 101, and the more picturesque I–280 link the Silicon Valley's key towns: Sunnyvale, Cupertino, Santa Clara, and San Jose. Many of the sights here are suitable for a day trip from San Francisco, but the region's attractions warrant a closer look. Moderate year-round temperatures make Silicon Valley ideal for viticulture—and for enjoying the great outdoors.

The center of the valley is San Jose, California's third-largest city. Despite its reputation as a charmless, suburban Los Angeles of the north, San Jose is buffered by city parks and gardens, and in addition to the industrial parks, computer companies, and corporate headquarters, it is home to museums, symphonies, theaters, and wineries.

Exploring

SANTA CLARA

Santa Clara's offerings include two major attractions at opposite ends of the sightseeing spectrum: the mission, founded in 1777, and Paramount's Great America, northern California's answer to Disneyland.

In **Paramount's Great America** 100-acre theme park there are six roller coasters, a triple-arm Ferris wheel, and several exciting water rides. The latest rides are the "Rip Roaring Rapids," which takes you on a white-water river in oversize inner tubes; the "Vortex" stand-up roller coaster; a movie-themed *Top Gun* roller coaster, whose cars travel along the outside of a 360-degree loop track; a *Days of Thunder* racing-simulator theater, which combines film, a giant-screen image, special effects, and moving seats to simulate a stock-car race; and a Nickelodeon-style interactive amusement arena based on the cable network's popular kids show *Double Dare*. The park is served by Santa Clara County Transit and BART (the Fremont station). *Great America Pkwy., between U.S. 101 and Hwy. 237 (6 mi north of San Jose),* ☎ *408/988–1776.* ☛ *$25.95 adults, $18.95 senior citizens, $12.95 children 3–6. Parking $5.* ⏲ *Weekends Mar.–May and Sept.–Oct., daily in summer. Opens at 10 AM; closing times vary with season. AE, MC, V.*

Visitors to the **Intel Museum,** just a couple miles south of Great America, can learn how computer chips are made and follow the development of Intel Corporation's microprocessor, memory, and systems product lines. *Robert Noyce Bldg., 2200 Mission College Blvd. (exit off Montague Expressway ½ mi north of Hwy. 101),* ☎ *408/765–0503.* ☛ *Free.* ⏲ *Weekdays 8–5.*

Downtown Santa Clara's attractions are on or near the green campus of Santa Clara University. Founded in 1851 by Jesuits, this was California's first college. In the center of the campus is the **Mission Santa Clara de Assis,** the eighth of 21 California missions founded under the direction of Father Junípero Serra. In the mid-1770s, Franciscan friars raised grapes here for sacramental wines; the olive and fig trees they planted at this time remain. Also on the campus is a notable art museum, the **de Saisset,** with a permanent collection that includes California mission artifacts. The museum also has a full calendar of temporary exhibits. *Campus: 500 El Camino Real. Mission:* ☎ *408/554–4023.* ☛ *Free.* ⏲ *Weekdays 8–6. De Saisset Museum:* ☎ *408/554–4528.* ☛ *Free.* ⏲ *Tues.–Sun. 11–4.*

From the Santa Clara University campus, follow El Camino Real north and then west to Lincoln Street. Civic Center Park is on the right, and a few blocks north of that is the Civic Center, which holds Santa Clara's City Hall.

Across from the Civic Center, skylights cast natural light for viewing the exhibitions in the **Triton Museum of Art.** A permanent collection of 19th- and 20th-century sculpture by artists from the Bay Area is displayed in a 7-acre garden, which you can see through a curved-glass wall at the rear of the building. Indoors there are rotating exhibits of contemporary works in a variety of media and a permanent collection of 19th- and 20-century American artists, many from California. *1505 Warburton Ave.,* ☎ *408/247–3754.* ☛ *Free for most exhibitions.* ⏲ *Tues. 10–9, Wed.–Fri. 10–5, weekends noon–5.*

The **Santa Clara Historic Museum,** next door, exhibits artifacts and photos that trace the history of the region. *1509 Warburton Ave.,* ☎ *408/248–2787.* ☛ *Free.* ⏲ *Daily 1–4.*

SAN JOSE

A good way to explore San Jose is to hop on the light rail that connects San Jose State University on one end with the Center for Performing Arts on the other; its route will give you a good overview of the city, and the convention center stop will drop you in the center of downtown, where you can explore on foot.

The **Children's Discovery Museum,** near the convention center, exhibits interactive installations on space, technology, the humanities, and the arts. Children can dress up in period costumes, create jewelry from recycled materials, or play on a real fire truck. *180 Woz Way, at Auzerais St.,* ☎ *408/298–5437.* ☛ *$6 adults, $5 senior citizens, $4 children 2–18.* ⏲ *Tues.–Sat. 10–5, Sun. noon–5.*

The **Tech Museum of Innovation,** across from the convention center, presents high-tech information through hands-on lab exhibits that are fun and accessible, allowing visitors to discover and demystify disciplines such as microelectronics, biotechnology, robotics, and space exploration. *145 W. San Carlos St.,* ☎ *408/279–7150.* ☛ *$6 adults, $4 students and senior citizens.* ⏲ *Tues.–Sun. 10–5.*

In collaboration with New York's Whitney Museum, the **San Jose Museum of Art** is exploring the development of 20th-century American art with exhibits of pieces from the permanent collections of both. The series will run through the year 2000 and will include works by such American artists as Andrew Wyeth, Edward Hopper, and Georgia O'Keeffe. *110 S. Market St.,* ☎ *408/294–2787.* ☛ *$5 adults; $3 senior citizens, students, and children 6–17.* ⏲ *Tues.–Wed. 10–5, Thurs. 10–8, Fri.–Sun. 10–5.*

Silicon Valley

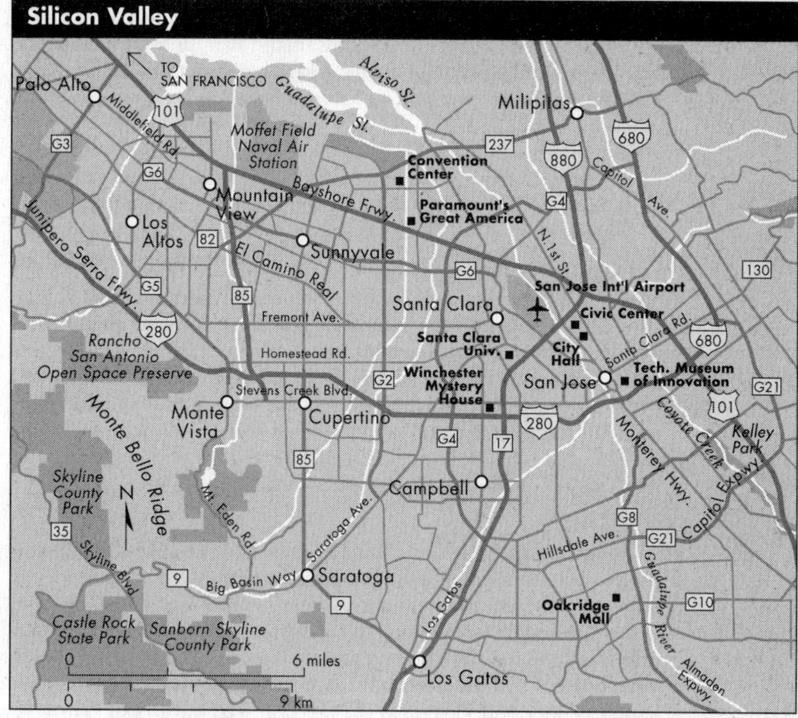

On the north end of town lies the **Winchester Mystery House.** Convinced that spirits would harm her if construction ever stopped, firearms-heiress Sarah Winchester constantly added to her house. For 38 years beginning in 1884, she kept hundreds of carpenters working around the clock, creating a bizarre, 160-room Victorian labyrinth with stairs going nowhere and doors that open into walls. *525 S. Winchester Blvd. (between Stevens Creek Blvd. and I–280), ☎ 408/247–2101. ☛ $12.50 adults, $9.50 senior citizens, $6.50 children 6–12. ⏲ Daily 9:30–4; later in summer.*

The **Egyptian Museum and Planetarium** offers some mysteries of its own in the West Coast's largest collection of Egyptian and Babylonian antiquities, including mummies and an underground replica of a pharaoh's tomb. The planetarium offers programs like the popular "Celestial Nile," which describes the significant role astrology played in ancient Egyptian myths and religions. *1600 Park Ave., at Naglee Ave. off Hwy. 82 (The Alameda) southeast of I–80, ☎ 408/947–3636. ☛ (museum only): $6 adults, $4 senior citizens and students, $3.50 children 7–15. Planetarium entry fees and show times vary. ⏲ Daily 9–5; planetarium open weekdays only.*

On 176 acres of rolling lawns on the east side of San Jose, off I–280, is **Kelley Park,** a haven for families and picnickers. On the grounds is the creative **Happy Hollow Park & Zoo,** with theme rides, puppet shows, a riverboat replica, and events specially planned for children from two to 10 years old. Also in the park is the **Japanese Friendship Garden,** with fish ponds and a teahouse inspired by Japan's Korakuen Garden. Occupying 25 acres of the park is the **San Jose Historical Museum,** which re-creates San Jose in the 1880s with a collection of original and replicate Victorian homes and shops, a firehouse, and a trolley line. The dusty Main Street recalls small-town America without the brightly painted gloss of amusement-park reproductions. *Kelley Park: 1300 Senter Rd. ☛ free, parking $3 on holidays and in summer. Happy Hollow Park: ☎ 408/295–8383, ☛ $3.50, $3 senior citizens, free for visitors under 2 and over 75. ⏲ Apr.–Oct., Mon.–Sat. 10–5, Sun. 11–6; Nov.–Mar., Mon.–Sat. 10–5, Sun. 10–5. Historical Museum: ☎ 408/287–2290, ☛ $4 adults, $3 senior citizens, $2 children 4–17. ⏲ Weekdays 10–4:30, weekends noon–4:30.*

SARATOGA

Saratoga, 10 miles west of San Jose, is a quaint former artists' colony chock-full of antiques shops, upscale jewelry stores, and art galleries. The Zen-style **Hakone Gardens** are nestled on a steep hillside just south of downtown. Designed in 1918 by a man who had been an imperial gardener in Japan, the gardens have been carefully maintained, with *koi* (carp) ponds and sculptured shrubs. *21000 Big Basin Way, ☎ 408/741–4994. ☛ Free. Parking: $3 Mon., Wed.–Fri.; $5 weekends; free Tues. ⏲ Weekdays 10–5, weekends 11–5.*

WINERIES

Although most people don't think of wine in connection with Silicon Valley, the area's vintages are gaining attention. Many of the wineries represent generations of vintners, whose families began making wine in Europe long before coming to California. Prominent wineries that offer tours and tastings (some on weekends only, so call ahead) are **Ridge Vineyards** (17100 Montebello Rd., Cupertino, ☎ 408/867–3233), **Byington Winery and Vineyards** (21850 Bear Creek Rd., Los Gatos, ☎ 408/354–1111), **Mirassou Champagne Cellars** (300 College Ave., Los Gatos, ☎ 408/395–3790), **J. Lohr Winery** (1000 Lenzen Ave., ☎ 408/288–5057; tasting daily 10–5), and **Mirassou Vineyards** (3000 Aborn Rd., ☎ 408/274–4000).

Dining

Though Silicon Valley's billboard-strewn highways lined with motels and fast-food franchises can look like a surreal suburban landscape, the Bay Area's reputation as a world-class culinary center remains intact at its southernmost tip.

CATEGORY	COST*
$$$$	over $30
$$$	$20–$30
$$	$10–$20
$	under $10

**per person for a three-course meal, excluding drinks, service, and 8¼% sales tax*

SAN JOSE

$$$$ ★ **Emile's.** Swiss chef and owner Emile Mooser is well versed in the classic marriage of food and wine and will make your wine selection from the restaurant's extensive list for you. House specialties include house-cured gravlax and rack of lamb. Romantic lighting and walls hand-painted with gold leaves create an intimate and elegant backdrop. ✕ *545 S. 2nd St., ☎ 408/289–1960. Reservations advised. AE, MC, V. Closed Sun. and Mon. Lunch Fri. only.*

$$$ **Paolo's Restaurant.** Not far from the cultural centers, this casual eatery caters to those with curious palettes. The bar menu offers small plates that give you several different tastes in a hurry—great for a snack before or after the theater. The Italian entrées and the parklike dining room—filled with plants and overlooking a patio, lush greenery, and

the Guadalupe River—deserve more leisurely appreciation. ✕ *333 W. San Carlos St., ☏ 408/294–2558. Reservations advised. AE, D, DC, MC, V. No lunch weekends.*

$$ Henry's World Famous Hi-Life. This vintage rib-and-steak joint is where the Sharks eat after each game. Located in a 120-year-old building two blocks from San Jose Arena, it has been owned and operated by the same family since 1960. The interior is funky and rustic, the atmosphere friendly and fun. Try the sweet barbecue sauce. ✕ *301 W. St. John St., ☏ 408/295–5414. Reservations for 8 or more. MC, V. No lunch Sat.–Mon.*

$$ Scott's Seafood Grill & Bar. Young, upwardly mobile types fill the clean-lined, oak-and-brass dining room here. Seafood and shellfish are the specialties; the fresh calamari (dusted with flour and lightly fried in garlic, lemon butter, and wine) and the oyster bar are noted attractions. Meat eaters will appreciate the juicy steaks. ✕ *185 Park Ave., 6th Floor, ☏ 408/971–1700. Reservations accepted. AE, D, DC, MC, V. No lunch weekends.*

$ Original Joe's. Hearty Italian specialties, along with steaks, chops, and hamburgers, are served in large portions until 1:30 AM in a warm cognac-and-green dining room. ✕ *301 S. 1st St., ☏ 408/292–7030. No reservations. AE, D, MC, V.*

SANTA CLARA

$$$ Birk's. High-tech sensibilities will appreciate the modern open kitchen and streamlined, multilevel dining area. The menu is traditional, strong on grilled and smoked meat, fish, and fowl. Try the smoked prime rib, served with garlic mashed potatoes and creamed spinach, or the rotisserie-grilled chicken or ribs. ✕ *3955 Freedom Circle at Hwy. 101 and Great America Pkwy., ☏ 408/980–6400. Reservations advised. AE, D, DC, MC, V. No lunch weekends.*

$ Pizzeria Uno. Some say that eating at one is eating at them all. Still, Pizzeria Uno is consistent, reliable, and tasty. You can get the same gourmet deep-dish pizzas here as in the Chicago flagship, classic pies that predate Wolfgang Puck's versions by 45 years. ✕ *2570 El Camino Real, ☏ 408/241–5152. Reservations for 10 or more. AE, D, DC, MC, V.*

SARATOGA

$$$$ Le Mouton Noir. Anything but the black sheep that its name suggests, this romantic French-country restaurant is filled with aspiring and established foodies and wine connoisseurs, and the kitchen turns out classic, contemporary French cuisine. Fine examples of the seasonal menu are the seafood dishes and the roast rack of lamb with a light, caramelized fennel and raspberry sauce. ✕ *14560 Big Basin Way, near Hwy. 9, ☏ 408/867–7017. Reservations advised. AE, DC, MC, V. No lunch Sun. and Mon.*

Lodging

All the big hotel chains are represented in the valley: Best Western, Howard Johnson, Marriott, Days Inn, Hilton, Holiday Inn, Quality Inn, and Sheraton. Many dot the King's Highway–El Camino Real. If character is more important than luxury, seek out a smaller inn.

CATEGORY	COST*
$$$$	over $175
$$$	$110—$175
$$	$75—$110
$	under $75

**All prices are for a standard double room, excluding 9½% room tax (10% in San Jose).*

$$$$ **Fairmont Hotel.** If you're accustomed to the best, this is the place to stay. The rooms have every imaginable comfort, from down pillows and custom-designed comforters to oversize bath towels changed twice a day. *170 S. Market St., at Fairmont Pl., San Jose 95113, ☎ 408/998–1900 or 800/527–4727, FAX 408/287–1648. 500 rooms, 41 suites. 4 restaurants, lounge, no-smoking floors, room service, fitness center, business services, valet parking. AE, D, DC, MC, V.*

$$$ **Hotel De Anza.** This lushly appointed French Mediterranean–style hotel, opened in 1931, has an Art Deco facade, hand-painted ceilings, and an enclosed terrace with towering palms and dramatic fountains. You'll also find many business amenities, including computers, cellular phones, and secretarial services. *233 W. Santa Clara St., San Jose 95113, ☎ 408/286–1000 or 800/843–3700, FAX 408/286–0500. 100 rooms. Restaurant, jazz club, exercise room, breakfast buffet, complimentary late-night snacks, valet parking. AE, DC, MC, V.*

$$$ ★ **Inn at Saratoga.** This five-story, European-style inn is actually only 10 minutes from the cultural action of Saratoga, yet with its aura of calm, it feels far from bustling Silicon Valley. All rooms have secluded sitting alcoves overlooking a peaceful creek, and the hotel's sun-dappled patio provides a quiet retreat. Modern business conveniences are available but discreetly hidden. *20645 4th St., Saratoga 95070, ☎ 408/867–5020 or 800/338–5020; in CA, 800/543–5020; FAX 408/741–0981. 46 rooms. Business services, meeting room. AE, DC, MC, V.*

$$ **Biltmore Hotel & Suites.** This hotel's central Silicon Valley location makes it a popular choice for business travelers. Attractions include a sports bar and 16 meeting rooms. *2151 Laurelwood Rd., Santa Clara 95054, ☎ 408/988–8411 or 800/255–9925, FAX 408/988–0225. 128 rooms, 134 suites. Restaurant, lounge, pool, hot tub, fitness center, airport shuttle, parking. AE, D, DC, MC, V.*

$$ **Sundowner Inn.** This hotel offers voice mail, computer data ports, and remote-control televisions with ESPN, HBO, CNN, Nintendo, and VCRs, which you can use to play complimentary tapes. Mountain bikes and a library full of best-sellers are also available. The complimentary breakfast buffet is served poolside. *504 Ross Dr., Sunnyvale 94089, ☎ 408/734–9900 or 800/223–9901, FAX 408/747–0580. 105 rooms, 12 suites. Restaurant, no-smoking rooms, pool, sauna, exercise room, laundry, meeting room. AE, D, DC, MC, V.*

$ **Motel 6.** This motel has all the basics and is conveniently located. *3208 El Camino Real, Santa Clara, 95051, ☎ 408/241–0200 or 800/437–7486. 99 rooms. Pool, parking. AE, D, DC, MC, V.*

The Arts and Nightlife

The San Jose arts calendar is packed with everything from film festivals to jazz festivals, and there are many nightclubs and dance floors within the larger hotels. Throughout the rest of the valley there is plenty to do after the sun goes down. The daily and Sunday editions of the *San Jose Mercury News* carry extensive cultural listings.

ARTS

If you're traveling in summer, try not to miss the **Mountain Winery Concert Series** (14831 Pierce Rd., Box 1852, Saratoga 95070, ☎ 408/741–5181), where music is performed under the moon and stars on a stage surrounded by grapevines. The series hosts internationally known country, jazz, blues, and opera acts. Be sure to buy tickets well in advance, as shows always sell out.

The **Flint Center at DeAnza College** (21250 Stevens Creek Blvd., Cupertino, ☎ 408/864–8816) showcases nationally known dance, music, and theater acts. There is also a top-notch lecture series with celebrity speakers from the worlds of entertainment, education, and politics. Designed by the Frank Lloyd Wright Foundation, the **Center for Performing Arts** (255 Almaden Blvd., San Jose) is the venue for performances of the **San Jose Civic Light Opera** (1717 Technology Dr., ☎ 408/453–7108), the **San Jose Symphony** (99 Almaden Blvd., Suite 400, ☎ 408/288–2828), and the **San Jose Cleveland Ballet** (Almaden Blvd. and Woz Way, ☎ 408/288–2800). The **San Jose Repertory Theatre** (1 N. 1st St., Suite 1, ☎ 408/291–2255), the only professional resident theater in Silicon Valley, performs at the **Montgomery Theater** (corner of San Carlos and Market). For schedules and tickets, call the companies directly or phone BASS (☎ 408/998–2277). The season generally runs from September through June.

NIGHTLIFE

ComedySportz (3428 El Camino Real, Santa Clara, ☎ 408/725–1356) is a comedy club and sports bar combined. The **Plumed Horse** (14555 Big Basin Way, Saratoga, ☎ 408/867–4711; Mon.–Sat.) is known for good jazz and blues. Try the **New West Melodrama and Comedy Vaudeville Show** (157 W. San Fernando St., San Jose, ☎ 408/295–7469) for a fresh take on the Old West.

Silicon Valley Essentials

ARRIVING AND DEPARTING

By Car: U.S. 101, I–280 (the Junípero Serra Freeway), and I–880 (Highway 17) connect the valley with the San Francisco Bay Area. The drive south from San Francisco to San Jose on I–280 takes 60 minutes depending on traffic, which gets heavy during rush hour. The drive north from Monterey on U.S. 101 takes about 90 minutes. Highway 1, which runs along the California coast, takes longer but is far more scenic.

By Plane: San Jose International Airport (☎ 408/277–4759), just 3 miles from downtown San Jose, is served by the light-rail system in addition to airport shuttle services such as **Express Airport Shuttle** (☎ 408/378–6270) and **South & East Bay Airport Shuttle** (☎ 408/559–9477).

By Train: Although Silicon Valley is as much a car culture as Los Angeles, commuter services are available. **CalTrain** (☎ 800/660–4287) runs from 4th and Townsend streets in San Francisco to San Jose's light-rail system.

GETTING AROUND

In San Jose, **light-rail vehicles** serve most major attractions, shopping malls, historic sites, and downtown. Trolley fare is 50¢ for all ages. For more information call the **Transit Information Center** (4 N. 2nd St., San Jose, ☎ 408/321–2300).

VISITOR INFORMATION

For information about recreational events, contact the **Santa Clara Chamber of Commerce and Convention & Visitors Bureau** (2200 Laurelwood Rd., Santa Clara, 95054, ☎ 408/970–9825) or the **Visitor Information Center** (1515 El Camino Real, Box 387, Santa Clara, 95050, ☎ 408/296–7111). The **San Jose Visitor and Business Center** (☎ 408/283–8833) publishes a bimonthly calendar of ethnic festivals and outdoor events, and the **San Jose Convention and Visitors Bureau** (333 W. San Carlos St., Suite 1000, San Jose 95110, ☎ 408/295–9600) produces an annual events calendar. For schedules of around-the-clock activities, call the **San Jose Tourist Bureau's FYI Hotline** (☎ 408/295–2265).

Marine World Africa USA

Animals of the land, sea, and air perform in shows, roam in natural habitats, and stroll among park visitors with their trainers at this popular 160-acre wildlife theme park. Among the "stars" are killer whales, dolphins, camels, elephants, sea lions, chimpanzees, and a troupe of human water-skiers (April–October). "Shark Experience" takes visitors on a walk through an acrylic tunnel that traverses a 300,000-gallon coral reef habitat with 15 species of sharks and rays and 100 species of tropical fish.

Owned by the Marine World Foundation, a nonprofit organization devoted to educating the public about the world's wildlife, the park is a family attraction, with entertaining but informative shows and close-up looks at exotic animals. For additional sightseeing, visitors can reach the park on a high-speed ferry from San Francisco, a trip that offers unusual vistas through San Francisco Bay and San Pablo Bay. *Marine World Pkwy., Vallejo,* ☎ *707/643–6722.* ☛ *$24.95 adults, $20.95 senior citizens 60 and over, $16.95 children 4–12.* ⏲ *Summer, daily 9:30–6:45; rest of year and some school holidays, Wed.–Sun. 9:30–5.*

Marine World Africa USA Essentials

ARRIVING AND DEPARTING

By Bus: Greyhound Lines (☎ 800/231–2222) runs buses from downtown San Francisco to Vallejo. You can take the **BART** train (415/992–2278) to El Cerrito Del Norte Station and transfer to **Vallejo Transit** line (☎ 707/648–4666) to get to the park.

By Car: Take I–80 east to Marine World Parkway in Vallejo. The trip takes one hour one-way. Parking is $4 at the park.

By Ferry: Blue and Gold Fleet's (☎ 415/705–5444) high-speed ferry departs mornings each day that the park is open, from Pier 39 at Fisherman's Wharf. It arrives in Vallejo an hour later. Round-trip service allows five hours to visit the park. Excursion tickets cost $22.50–$39 and include park admission.

SAN FRANCISCO ESSENTIALS

Arriving and Departing

By Bus

Greyhound (☎ 800/231–2222) serves San Francisco from the Transbay Terminal at 1st and Mission streets.

By Car

Route I–80 finishes its westward journey from New York's George Washington Bridge at the Bay Bridge, which links Oakland and San Francisco. U.S. 101, running north–south through the entire state, enters the city across the Golden Gate Bridge and continues south down the peninsula, along the west side of the bay.

By Plane

The major gateway to San Francisco is the **San Francisco International Airport** (☎ 415/761–0800), just south of the city, off U.S. 101. **Oakland Airport** (☎ 510/577–4000) is across the bay but not much farther away from downtown San Francisco (via I–880 and I–80), although traffic on the Bay Bridge may at times make travel time longer.

Carriers serving San Francisco include **Alaska Air** (☎ 800/426–0333), **American** (☎ 800/433–7300), **Continental** (☎ 800/525–0280), **Delta**

(☎ 800/221–1212), **Southwest** (☎ 800/435–9792), **TWA** (☎ 800/221–2000), **United** (☎ 800/241–6522), and **USAir** (☎ 800/428–4322).

Southwest, United, and other major carriers serve the Oakland Airport.

BETWEEN THE AIRPORT AND DOWNTOWN

SFO Airporter (☎ 415/495–8404) provides bus service between downtown and the airport, making the round of downtown hotels. Buses run every 20 minutes from 5 AM to 11 PM, from the lower level outside the baggage-claim area. The fare is $8 one-way, $14 round-trip.

For $11 ($8 per additional passenger), **SuperShuttle** will take you from the airport to anywhere within the city limits of San Francisco. The quickest way to catch a shuttle is to follow ground transportation signs to the exterior traffic islands on the upper (departure) level of each of SFO's terminals. The dark blue vans (with yellow letters) stop here. Or call 415/871–7800 for directions. To go to the airport, make reservations (☎ 415/558–8500) 24 hours in advance.

Taxis to or from downtown take 20–30 minutes and average $30.

By Train

Amtrak (☎ 800/872–7245) trains (the *Zephyr,* from Chicago via Denver, and the *Coast Starlight,* traveling between Los Angeles and Seattle) stop at the Emeryville (5885 Landregan St.) and Oakland (245 2nd St., in Jack London Sq.) stations. Shuttle buses connect the Emeryville station and San Francisco's Ferry Building (30 Embarcadero, at the foot of Market St.).

Getting Around

By Bus and Light Rail

The **San Francisco Municipal Railway System,** or **Muni** (☎ 415/673–6864), includes buses and trolleys, surface streetcars, and the new below-surface streetcars, as well as cable cars. There is 24-hour service, and the fare is $1 for adults, 35¢ for senior citizens and children 5–17. The exact fare is always required; dollar bills or change are accepted. Eighty-cent tokens can be purchased (in rolls of 10, 20, or 40) to reduce the cost of transferring; otherwise you must pay $1 each time you board a bus or light-rail vehicle.

A $6 pass good for unlimited travel all day on all routes can be purchased from ticket machines at cable-car terminals and at the Visitor Information Center in Hallidie Plaza (Powell and Market Sts.).

The **Bay Area Rapid Transit,** or **BART,** system (☎ 415/992–2278 in San Francisco) sends air-conditioned aluminum trains at speeds of up to 80 miles an hour under the bay to Oakland, Berkeley, Concord, Richmond, and Fremont, with extensions expected to open this year southeast to Castro Valley and Dublin. Trains also travel south from San Francisco as far as Daly City. Wall maps in the stations list destinations and fares (90¢–$3.45). Trains run Monday–Saturday 6 AM–midnight, Sunday 9 AM–midnight.

A $3 excursion ticket buys a three-county tour. You can visit any of the 34 stations for up to four hours as long as you exit and enter at the same station.

By Cable Cars

Cable cars are popular, crowded, and an experience to ride: Move toward one quickly as it pauses, wedge yourself into any available space, and hold on! The sensation of moving up and down some of San Francisco's steepest hills in a small, open-air, clanging conveyance is not to be missed.

The fare (for one direction) is $2 for adults and children. Exact change is preferred, but operators will make change. There are self-service ticket machines (which do make change) at a few major stops and at all the terminals. The one exception is the busy cable-car terminal at Powell and Market streets; purchase tickets at the kiosk there. Be wary of street people attempting to "help" you buy a ticket.

The Powell-Mason line (No. 59) and the Powell-Hyde line (No. 60) begin at Powell and Market streets near Union Square and terminate at Fisherman's Wharf. The California Street line (No. 61) runs east and west from Market Street near the Embarcadero to Van Ness Avenue.

By Car

Driving in San Francisco can be a challenge because of the hills, the one-way streets, and the traffic. Take it easy, remember to curb your wheels when parking on hills, and use public transportation whenever possible. This is a great city for walking and a terrible city for parking. On certain streets, parking is forbidden during rush hours. Look for the warning signs; illegally parked cars are towed. Downtown parking lots are often full and always expensive. Finding a spot in North Beach at night, for instance, may be impossible.

The best approach to renting a car in San Francisco is not to, at least for a day or two. First see how well suited the cable cars are to this city of hills, how well the Muni buses and streetcars get you around every neighborhood, how efficiently BART delivers you practically anywhere on the bay. Chances are that you won't want a car, unless you're preparing to take excursions into Marin County, the Wine Country, or Silicon Valley.

Guided Tours

Orientation

Golden Gate Tours (☎ 415/788–5775) uses both vans and buses for its 3½-hour city tour, offered mornings and afternoons. You can combine the tour with a bay cruise. Customers are picked up at hotels and motels. Senior-citizen and group rates are available. Cost: $25 adults, $12 children under 12, $20.50 senior citizens. Tours daily. Make reservations the day before. Cruise combo: $30 adults, $15 children under 12, $28 senior citizens.

Gray Line (☎ 415/558–9400) offers a variety of tours of the city, the Bay Area, and northern California. The city tour, on buses or double-decker buses, lasts 3½ hours and departs from the Transbay Terminal at 1st and Mission streets five to six times daily. Gray Line also picks up at centrally located hotels. Cost: $26 adults, $13 children. Tours daily. Make reservations the day before.

Gray Line-Cable Car Tours sends motorized cable cars on a one-hour loop from Union Square to Fisherman's Wharf and two-hour tours including the Presidio, Japantown, and the Golden Gate Bridge. Cost: $15 and $22 adults, $7.50 and $11 children. No reservations necessary.

The Great Pacific Tour (☎ 415/626–4499) uses 13-passenger vans for its daily 3½-hour city tour. Bilingual guides may be requested. They pick up at major San Francisco hotels. Tours are available to Monterey, the Wine Country, and Muir Woods. Cost: $27 adults, $25 senior citizens, $20 children 5–11. Tours daily. Make reservations the day before, or, possibly, the same day.

Tower Tours (☎ 415/434–8687) uses 20-passenger vans for city tours, 25-passenger buses for trips outside San Francisco to Muir Woods and Sausalito, the Wine Country, Monterey and Carmel, and Yosemite. The city tour runs 3½ hours. The Wine Country tour includes the historic Sonoma town square. Cost: $25 adults, $12 children. Tours daily. Make reservations the day before.

Special-Interest

Near Escapes (Box 193005-K, San Francisco 94119, ☎ 415/386–8687) plans unusual activities in the city and around the Bay Area. Recent tours and activities included tours of a Hindu temple in the East Bay, the Lawrence Berkeley Laboratory, the aircraft maintenance facility at the San Francisco Airport, and the quicksilver mines south of San Jose. Send $1 and a self-addressed, stamped envelope for a schedule for the month you plan to visit San Francisco.

WALKING

Castro District. Trevor Hailey (☎ 415/550–8110) leads a 3½-hour tour focusing on the history and development of the city's gay and lesbian community, including restored Victorian homes, shops and cafés, and the NAMES Project, home of the AIDS memorial quilt. Tours depart at 10 AM Tuesday–Saturday from Castro and Market streets. Cost: $30, including brunch.

Chinatown with the "Wok Wiz." Cookbook author Shirley Fong-Torres leads a 3½-hour tour of Chinese markets, other businesses, and a fortune-cookie factory (☎ 415/355–9657). Cost: $35, including lunch; $25 without lunch. Shorter tours start at $15.

Chinese Cultural Heritage Foundation (☎ 415/986–1822) offers two walking tours of Chinatown. The Heritage Walk leaves Saturday at 2 PM and lasts about two hours. The Culinary Walk, a three-hour stroll through the markets and food shops, plus a dim sum lunch, is held every Wednesday at 10:30 AM. Heritage Walk: $12 adults, $2 children under 12. Culinary Walk: $25 adults, $10 children under 12.

City Guides (☎ 415/557–4266), a free service sponsored by Friends of the Library, offers the greatest variety of walks, seven days a week. They include Chinatown, North Beach, Coit Tower, Pacific Heights mansions, Japantown, the Haight–Ashbury, historic Market Street, the Palace Hotel, and downtown roof gardens and atriums. Schedules are available at the San Francisco Visitors Center at Powell and Market streets and at library branches.

Important Addresses and Numbers

Doctors

Two hospitals with 24-hour emergency rooms are **San Francisco General Hospital** (1001 Potrero Ave., ☎ 415/206–8000) and the **Medical Center at the University of California, San Francisco** (500 Parnassus Ave., at 3rd Ave., near Golden Gate Park, ☎ 415/476–1000).

Physician Access Medical Center (26 California St., ☎ 415/397-2881) is a drop-in clinic in the Financial District, open weekdays 7:30 AM–5:30 PM. **Access Health Care** (☎ 415/565–6600) provides drop-in medical care at Davies Medical Center, Castro Street at Duboce Avenue, daily 8 AM–8 PM.

Emergencies

For **police** or **ambulance,** telephone 911.

24-Hour Pharmacies

Several **Walgreen Drug Stores** have 24-hour pharmacies, including stores at 500 Geary Street near Union Square (☎ 415/673–8413) and 3201 Divisadero Street at Lombard Street (☎ 415/931–6417). Also try the Walgreen pharmacy at 135 Powell Street near Market Street (☎ 415/391–7222), which is open Monday–Saturday 8 AM–midnight, Sunday 9 AM–9 PM.

Visitor Information

Contact the **San Francisco Convention and Visitors Bureau** (201 3rd St., Suite 900, 94103, ☎ 415/974–6900). The attractive 80-page *San Francisco Book* ($2; from the SFCVB at Box 6977, 94101) includes up-to-date information on theater offerings, art exhibits, sporting events, and other special events.

The **Redwood Empire Association Visitor Information Center** (The Cannery, 2801 Leavenworth St., 2nd Floor, 94133, ☎ 415/543–8334) covers San Francisco and surrounding areas, including the Wine Country, the redwood groves, and northwestern California. For $3 they will send *The Redwood Empire Visitor's Guide*; or pick it up at their office for free.

6 Sacramento and the Gold Country

The Gold Country, also known as the Mother Lode, is the gold-mining region of the Sierra Nevada foothills. This is a less expensive, if also less sophisticated, region but not without its pleasures, natural and man-made. Spring brings wildflowers and in fall the hills are colored by bright-red berries and changing leaves. The hills are golden in the summer—and hot. Dining has improved remarkably in recent years and many fine bed-and-breakfast inns have sprung up. The Gold Country has a mix of indoor and outdoor activities, one of the many reasons it's a great place to take the kids.

By Bobbi Zane

JAMES MARSHALL TURNED UP a gold nugget in the tailrace of a sawmill he was constructing for John Sutter along the American River and ushered in a whole new era for California. Before January 24, 1848, what became the Golden State had been a beautiful but sparsely populated land over which Mexico and the United States were still wrestling. With Marshall's discovery and its subsequent confirmation by President James Polk in his State of the Union speech on December 5, 1848, prospectors came to seek their fortunes in the Mother Lode.

As gold fever seized the nation, California's total population of 15,000 swelled to 265,000 within three years—44,000 newcomers arrived by ship in San Francisco in the first 10 months alone, the majority of them men under 40, either unattached or with families back east. Most spent about two years in California before returning home—usually with empty pockets or having barely broken even. Many historians have noted that the consequences of the Gold Rush were more than monetary: The '49ers who remained in the state contributed to a freer culture that eschewed many of the constricting conventions and values of the eastern states.

Originally, the term "Mother Lode" denoted a gold-bearing quartz vein 120 miles long between Mariposa to the south and Auburn to the north. It ranged in width from 2 miles to only a few yards. By 1865 it had yielded more than $750 million in gold. As prospectors headed farther afield, the entire Gold Rush region came to be known as the Mother Lode. Ironically, neither Sutter nor Marshall got rich from the discovery.

The boom brought on by the Gold Rush lasted scarcely 20 years, but it changed California forever. It produced 546 mining towns, of which fewer than 250 remain. The hills were alive, not only with prospecting and mining but also with business, the arts, literature, plenty of gambling, and a fair share of crime. Opera houses went up alongside brothels, and the California State Capitol in Sacramento was built with the gold dug out of the hills. Some of the nation's most treasured writers—Mark Twain and Bret Harte among them—began their careers writing about the mining camps. Gold Rush lore immortalized notorious bandits: Legend has it that Joaquin Murieta's crime spree—he robbed miners by day, then partied by night at local saloons, a few of which are still extant—followed an assault on him and his family by Yankee prospectors. When the law finally caught up with the debonair Black Bart, who targeted Wells Fargo stagecoaches and left behind poems (signed "Black Bart—PO-8") at his crime scenes, he turned out to be a well-known San Franciscan.

The northern California cities of Sacramento, San Francisco, and Stockton grew quickly to meet the needs of the surrounding gold fields. Saloon keepers and canny merchants recognized that the real gold was to be made from the '49ers' pockets. Potatoes and onions sold for as much as $1 apiece, making entrepreneurs like storekeeper Samuel Brannan millionaires. Much important history was made in Sacramento, the key center of commerce during this period. Pony Express riders ended their nearly 2,000-mile journeys in the city in the 1860s. The Transcontinental Railroad, conceived here by the Big Four (Leland Stanford, Mark Hopkins, Collis P. Huntington, and Charles Crocker) was linked in 1869.

By the 1960s, the scars left on the Gold Country landscape by mining had largely healed. To promote tourism, townspeople began restoring vintage structures, historians developed museums, and the state established parks and recreation areas that preserved this extraordinary episode in American history. The Gold Country, flourishing once again, generously rewards leisurely exploration.

EXPLORING

Highway 49 winds the 325-mile north–south length of the historic mining area, linking the towns of Sierraville and Mariposa. The highway, often a twisty, hilly, two-lane road, begs for a convertible with the top down. It's most scenic in spring when the hillsides are ablaze with wildflowers or when the autumn light lends them a golden hue. Summers are beautiful, too, but also hot: Temperatures in the 90s and even the 100s are common all summer long.

Visitors flock to Nevada City, Auburn, Coloma, Placerville, Sutter Creek, and Columbia on weekends, not only to relive the past but also to shop for antiques, explore museums and art galleries, experience traditional celebrations, and stay over at bed-and-breakfast inns. The best of these inns, which occupy former mansions, miners' cabins, and other historic buildings, yield clues about life as it was lived 150 years ago. As 20th-century hostelries, they provide a level of elegance, comfort, and cuisine the average miner might never have thought possible.

Old Sacramento and its museums provide an overview of Gold Rush life, but the real heart of the Gold Country lies along Highway 49. If you're pressed for time, the tour of Auburn, Coloma, and Placerville can easily be done as a day trip from Sacramento.

Sacramento

Numbers in the margin correspond to points of interest on the Sacramento map.

Downtown Sacramento is ideal for walking. Its flat, wide streets are laid out in a grid, so it's easy to locate sights. Along the Sacramento River (take the J St. exit off I–5), **Old Sacramento** is a 28-acre area with more than 100 restored buildings, shops, and restaurants. Wood sidewalks and horse-drawn carriages on cobblestone streets lend the district a late 19th-century feel, and river cruises and train rides bring Gold Rush history to life. *Call the Event Hotline,* ☎ *916/558–3912, for train and cruise schedules.*

1 The **Visitor Information Center** (1104 Front St., ☎ 916/442–7644) is housed in a former steamship depot. ⏲ *Daily 9–5.*

2 The **Eagle Theater** (925 Front St.) was the first building constructed as a theater in California. It opened in 1849. A reconstruction was completed in 1976, and the theater remains in regular use today. The
3 building housing the **Discovery Museum** (officially called the Sacramento Museum of History, Science, and Technology) was once City Hall, containing the mayor's offices, council chambers, a jail, and policemen's quarters, among other things. The museum presents a streamlined introduction to the history of Sacramento and its surroundings, complete with gold pans with which you can sift, an Indian thatched hut, memorabilia from the world wars, and a colorful stack of turn-of-the-century cans of local produce. There are also ever-changing child-oriented hands-on science exhibits. *101 I St.,* ☎ *916/264–7057.* ☛ *$3.50 adults, $2 children 6–17.* ⏲ *Wed.–Sun. noon–5.*

The Gold Country

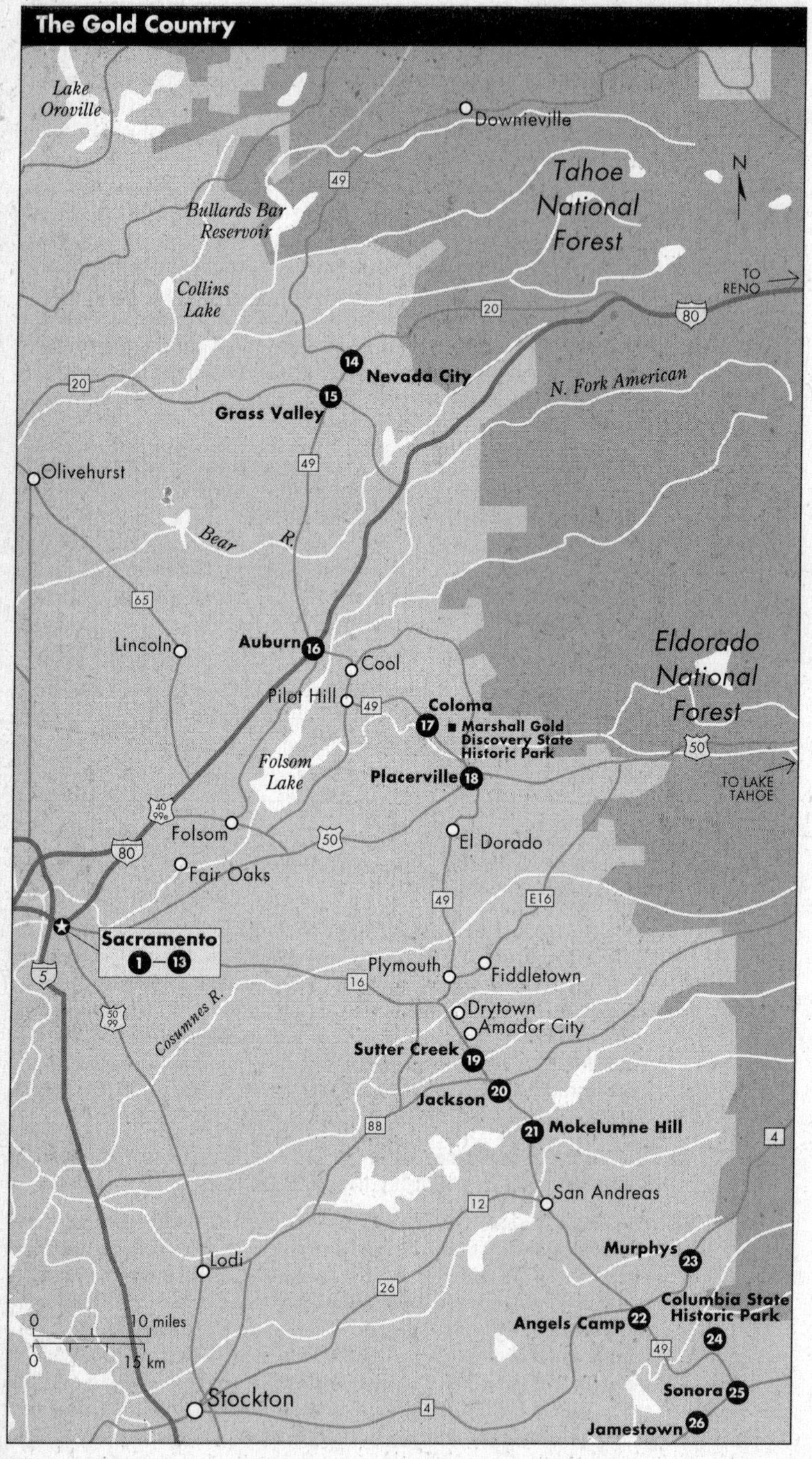

Lake Oroville
Downieville
Tahoe National Forest
N
Bullards Bar Reservoir
49
Collins Lake
TO RENO
20
80
14 Nevada City
15 Grass Valley
20
N. Fork American
Olivehurst
49
Bear R.
65
Lincoln
Auburn 16
Cool
Pilot Hill
49
Coloma
17 ■ Marshall Gold Discovery State Historic Park
Eldorado National Forest
50
Folsom Lake
Placerville 18
TO LAKE TAHOE
40 99e
Folsom
50
El Dorado
80
Fair Oaks
49
E16
Sacramento
1 – 13
Plymouth
Fiddletown
16
5
Drytown
Amador City
50 99
Cosumnes R.
Sutter Creek 19
Jackson 20
88
21 Mokelumne Hill
4
San Andreas
12
Murphys 23
Lodi
26
Columbia State Historic Park
0 10 miles
0 15 km
Angels Camp 22
24
49
Sonora 25
Stockton
4
Jamestown 26

Sacramento

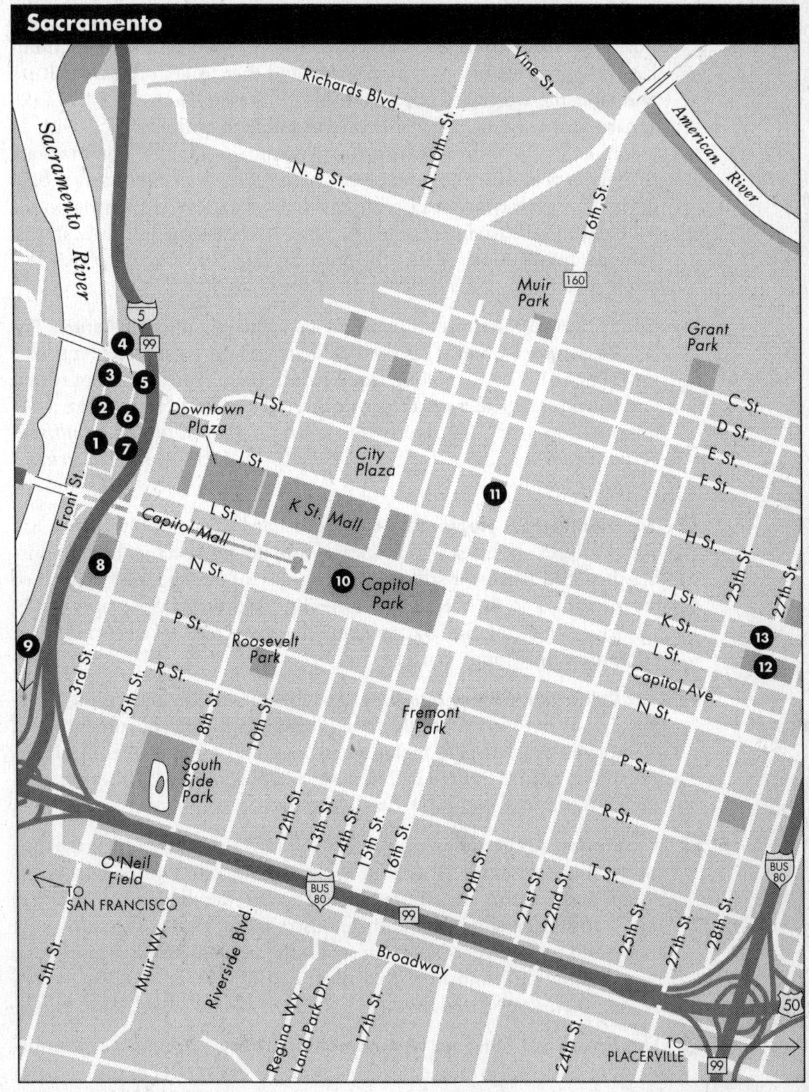

B.F. Hastings Building, **6**
California Military Museum, **7**
California State Railroad Museum, **4**
Crocker Art Museum, **8**
Eagle Theater, **2**
Governor's Mansion, **11**
Huntington, Hopkins & Co. Store, **5**
Sacramento Museum of History, Science and Technology, **3**
State Capitol building, **10**
State Indian Museum, **13**
Sutter's Fort, **12**
Towe Ford Museum of Automotive History, **9**
Visitor Information Center, **1**

★ 4 What is now the **California State Railroad Museum** was once the terminus of the Transcontinental and Sacramento Valley railroads. Exhibits here trace the history of the railroads and their role in the Gold Rush and later the westward expansion of the United States. The 100,000-square-foot museum is the largest of its kind in North America, with 21 locomotives and railroad cars on display, and 46 exhibits. You can walk through a post-office car and peer into the cubbyholes and canvas bags of mail, or go through a sleeping car that simulates the swaying on the roadbed and the flashing lights of a passing town at night. Allow at least a couple hours to experience the museum fully. *125 I St., ☎ 916/448–4466. ☛ $5 adults, $2 children 6–12. ⏲ Daily 10–5.*

Your ticket to the railroad museum also gets you into the **Central Pacific Passenger Station,** a restored 1876 depot across the street (entrance on Front St.). There's rolling stock to admire, a typical waiting room, and a little café. Rides on a steam-powered excursion train make a 40-minute loop along the riverfront. *Train fare: $4 adults, $2 children. Trains run May–Labor Day, weekends 10–5; Oct.–Apr., 1st weekend of month, noon–3.*

5 The **Huntington, Hopkins & Co. Store** hardware exhibit (111 I St.; open daily 11–5) gives a good idea of supplies prospectors bought during the Gold Rush—it still stocks a variety of merchandise typical of
6 the period. The **B. F. Hastings Building** (2nd and J Sts.; open daily 10–5) includes the first Sacramento chambers of the California State Supreme Court, built in 1854.

7 The **California Military Museum** specializes in militia and military history, from before statehood to modern times. The documents and memorabilia on display include uniforms and military memorabilia. *1119 2nd St., ☎ 916/442–2883. ☛ $2.25 adults, $1.50 senior citizens, $1 children 8–17. ⏲ Tues.–Sun. 10–5.*

★ 8 The **Crocker Art Museum,** a few blocks from Old Sacramento, is the oldest art museum in the American West, with a collection of European, Asian, and Californian art, including *Sunday Morning in the Mines,* a large canvas depicting the mining industry of the 1850s. The museum's lobby and magnificent ballroom retain the original 1870s woodwork, plaster moldings, and imported tiles. *216 O St., ☎ 916/264–5423. ☛ $4.50 adults, $2 children 7–17. ⏲ Thurs. 10–9, Wed.–Sun. 10–5.*

9 The **Towe Ford Museum of Automotive History** contains a collection of more than 170 vintage cars, including every model manufactured by the Ford company for 50 years, starting from 1903. *2200 Front St., ☎ 916/442–6802. ☛ $5 adults, $4.50 senior citizens, $2.50 children 14–18, $1 children 5–13. ⏲ Daily 10–6.*

10 The **California State Capitol** was built in 1869 and underwent extensive restoration in the late 1970s and early 1980s. The lacy plasterwork of the rotunda, 120 feet high, has the complexity and color of a Fabergé Easter egg. Underneath the gilded dome are magnificent marble floors, glittering chandeliers, monumental staircases, original artwork, replicas of 19th-century state offices, and legislative chambers decorated in the style of the 1890s. There are free guided tours of the building and the 40-acre Capitol Park, dating to 1870 and one of the oldest gardens in the state. The park contains a rose garden, an impressive display of camellias (Sacramento's city flower), and the California Vietnam Veterans Memorial. *Capitol Mall and 10th St., ☎ 916/324–0333. ☛ Free. Hourly tours daily 9–4.*

11 The **Governor's Mansion,** built in 1877 and used by the state's chief executives from the early 1900s until 1967, is a 15-room Victorian house with furnishings that reflect the tastes of its various residents over those years. *16th and H Sts., ☏ 916/323–3047. ☛ $2 adults, $1 children 6–12. Hourly tours daily 10–4.*

★ 12 **Sutter's Fort,** Sacramento's earliest settlement, was founded by Swiss immigrant John Augustus Sutter in 1839. Self-guided tours with audio wands explain the exhibits, which include a blacksmith's shop, bakery, prison, living quarters, and livestock areas. Costumed docents sometimes reenact fort life, demonstrating crafts, food preparations, and maintenance of early firearms. *27th and L Sts., ☏ 916/445–4422. ☛ $2 adults, $1 children 6–12. ⏲ Daily 10–5.*

13 Directly behind Sutter's Fort, the **State Indian Museum** displays arts and crafts made by California's earliest inhabitants. *2601 K St., ☏ 916/324–0971. ☛ $2 adults, $1 children 6–17. ⏲ Daily 10–5.*

Highway 49

Numbers in the margin correspond to points of interest on the Gold Country map.

Three sections of Highway 49 are described here, starting in the north with the Nevada City/Grass Valley area. The middle tour of Highway 49, less than an hour's drive from Sacramento, includes the Gold Discovery site at Coloma and includes a side trip to the region's wineries and vineyards. The southern tour explores some of the Gold Country's best-preserved towns. The three tours could be completed in one day, though we don't recommend it. If time is a factor, choose the excursion that intrigues you the most.

Tour 1: Nevada City and Grass Valley

14 Charming **Nevada City,** about 30 miles north of I–80 on Highway 49, was once known as the Queen City of the Northern Mines. Its narrow, winding downtown streets are lined with iron-shuttered brick buildings containing antiques shops, galleries, a winery, bookstores, boutiques, bed-and-breakfast inns, and many restaurants. Horse-drawn carriage tours add to the romance, as do gas-powered streetlights. A walking tour map, available at the Chamber of Commerce (132 Main St., ☏ 916/265–2692) and elsewhere in town, points out the most interesting old buildings. Among these are **Firehouse Museum No. 1** (214 Main St., ☏ 916/265–5468; ⏲ Daily 11–4), which houses a collection of Gold Rush artifacts.

At one point in the 1850s, Nevada City had a population of nearly 10,000, enough to support a lively cultural community. The **Nevada Theatre** on Broad Street is California's oldest theater in continuous use. Behind the theater is the **Miners Foundry** (325 Spring St.), built in 1856, a cavernous building that now serves as a cultural center presenting plays, concerts, and a wide range of events that include a Victorian Christmas fair, a teddy-bear convention, antiques shows, and themed period parties.

TIME OUT During the Gold Rush and the period that followed, the hills around Nevada City were dotted with vineyards and wineries. Now there's only one left. Wines produced from local grapes can be tasted at **Nevada City Winery,** located in the **Miners Foundry Garage.** *321 Spring St., ☏ 916/265-9463. ⏲ For tasting daily noon–5.*

15 Four miles south along Highway 49, **Grass Valley** contrasts sharply with Nevada City, its historic downtown now surrounded by urban sprawl. More than half of California's total gold production was extracted from the mines of Nevada County. Grass Valley's Empire Mine and the North Star Power House and Pelton Wheel Exhibit (*see below*) are among the Gold Country's most fascinating exhibits.

The **Nevada County Chamber of Commerce** is housed in a reproduction of the home on this site owned by notorious dancer Lola Montez when she moved to Grass Valley in the early 1850s. Lola was no great talent—her popularity among miners derived from her revealing "Spider Dance"—but her loves, which reportedly included composer Franz Liszt, were legend. She had arrived in California not too long after, according to one account, being "permanently retired from her job as Bavarian king Louis's mistress," literary muse, and political adviser. Seems she pushed too hard for democracy, which contributed to his overthrow and her banishment as a witch! Or so the story went. The memory of licentious Lola lingers on in Grass Valley, as does her bathtub. *248 Mill St., ☏ 916/273–4667.*

Built in 1851, the landmark **Holbrooke Hotel** (212 W. Main St., ☏ 916/273–1353) in its day hosted not only Lola Montez but Mark Twain, Ulysses S. Grant, and a stream of U.S. presidents. Its saloon is one of the oldest still operating west of the Mississippi.

★ The **Empire Mine,** worked from 1850 right up to 1956, was one of California's richest quartz mines. An estimated 5.8 million ounces of gold were extracted from its 367 miles of underground passages. The mine is now a State Historic Park. Tours allow you to peer into the mine's deep recesses and to view the owner's "cottage," with its exquisite woodwork. The visitor center has mining exhibits and a picnic area. *10791 E. Empire St. (Empire St. exit south from Hwy. 49), ☏ 916/273–8522. ☛ $2 adults, $1 children 6–12. ⏲ Summer, daily 9–6; winter, daily 10–5. Tours and lectures daily in summer on the hr 11–4; weekends only in winter at 1 and 2.*

The **North Star Power House and Pelton Wheel Exhibit** boasts a 32-foot-high Pelton wheel, the largest ever built. It was used to power mining operations and was a forerunner of the modern water turbines that generate hydroelectricity. Period mining equipment and a stamp mill are also on display, as well as the largest operational Cornish pumps in the country, part of the legacy of the tin miners who migrated here from Cornwall in England. There are hands-on displays for children and a picnic area. *Allison Ranch Rd. and Mill St. (Empire St. exit north from Hwy. 49), ☏ 916/273–4255. Donation requested. ⏲ May–Oct., daily 10–5.*

TIME OUT A tradition for more than 20 years, **Mrs. Dubblebee's Pasties** (251 S. Auburn St., Grass Valley, ☏ 916/272-7700) is famous for its Cornish pasties, with flaky, buttery crusts. Besides the traditional beef-filled pasties there are wonderful English scones and sweet pastries.

Tour 2: Auburn, Coloma, and Placerville

Our second Highway 49 tour can be done in one day by making a loop from and back to Sacramento via I–80, Highway 49, and U.S. 50.

16 **Auburn,** at the intersection of Highway 49 and I–80 (going south on Highway 49; after it crosses under I–80 turn right on Lincoln Way), is the Gold Country town most accessible to travelers on the interstate. An important transportation center during the Gold Rush, Auburn has

a small old town with narrow, climbing streets, cobblestones, wooden sidewalks, and many original buildings.

The town's standout structure is the **Placer County Courthouse,** on Maple Street off Lincoln Way. The classic gold domed building houses the **Placer County Museum,** which documents the area's history—Native American, railroad, agricultural, and mining—from the early 1700s to 1900. *101 Maple St., ☎ 916/889–6500. ☛ Free (at press time; may go up to $1 adults, 50¢ children). ⏲ Tues.–Sun. 10–4.*

From the Placer County Museum, head east on Maple Street, which becomes Auburn-Folsom Road after it crosses Lincoln Way. Several blocks down is the **Bernhard Museum Complex,** whose centerpiece is the former Traveler's Rest Hotel, built in 1851 and occupied by the Bernhard family from 1868 to 1957. The Bernhard Residence and adjacent winery buildings reflect family life in the late-Victorian era; a carriage house displays several period conveyances. *291 Auburn-Folsom Rd., ☎ 916/889–4156. ☛ $1 adults, 50¢ senior citizens over 65 and children 6–16. ⏲ Tues.–Fri. 11–3, weekends noon–4.*

The Bernhard complex entrance fee is also good for the **Gold Country Museum** (head back north on Auburn-Folsom Road and make a right on High Street), housed in a small WPA-era building. The museum, worth a look, surveys life in the mines and includes a walk-through mine tunnel, a gold-panning stream, and a replica saloon. *1273 High St., ☎ 916/889–4134. ☛ $1 adults, 50¢ children 6–16 and senior citizens over 65. ⏲ Tues.–Fri. 10–3:30, weekends 11–4.*

17 Twenty-five miles farther on Highway 49 is **Coloma,** where the California Gold Rush started. "My eye was caught with the glimpse of something shining in the bottom of the ditch," James Marshall recalled later. Unfortunately, Marshall himself never found any more "color," as it came to be called.

★ Most of Coloma lies within **Marshall Gold Discovery State Historic Park.** Although it's often crowded with tourists in summer, Coloma hardly resembles the mob scene it was in 1848 when 2,000 prospectors had staked out claims along the streambed. Its population swelled rapidly to 10,000, supporting 13 hotels, three banks, and many stores and businesses. But when reserves of the precious metal dwindled, prospectors left as quickly as they had come. The park now contains a working replica of John Sutter's mill, about 100 yards from where James Marshall first saw gold; a self-guided trail leads to a monument marking his discovery. The museum here is not as interesting as the outdoor exhibits. *☎ 916/622–3470. ☛ $5 per car day-use fee, $4 senior citizens. ⏲ Daily 8 AM–sunset (park). Museum open summer, daily 10–5; Labor Day–Memorial Day, daily 10–4:30.*

A scenic but slow and twisty portion of Highway 49 leads south 10
18 miles into **Placerville,** where in 1849 4,000 miners had staked out every gully and hillside. Then a rip-roaring camp consisting of log cabins, tents, and clapboard houses, the town was known as Hangtown, a graphic allusion to the summary nature of frontier justice. It took on the name Placerville in 1854 and became an important supply center for the miners where several American industrialists—Mark Hopkins, Philip Armour, and John Studebaker—got their start.

Today, Placerville has the distinction of being one of the only cities in
★ the world to own a gold mine. The **Gold Bug Mine,** with a fully lighted shaft, is open for touring. A shaded stream runs through the park, and there are picnic facilities. *9/10 mi off U.S. 50, north on Bedford Ave. to*

Gold Bug Park, ☎ *916/642–5232.* ☛ *$1 adults, 50¢ children 5–16, for self-guided tour of mine.* ⏲ *May–Sept., daily 10–4; late Mar.–Apr. and late Sept.–Oct., weekends 10–4.*

If you have the time, take a leisurely drive around **Apple Hill,** an area filled with orchards and vineyards, where roadside stands sell fresh produce. Head east on U.S. 50 from Placerville, and get off at the Camino exit (about 5 miles east of Highway 49). During the fall harvest season the Apple Hill Growers Association (4103 Carson Rd., Camino, ☎ 916/644–7692) open their orchards for apple-picking, picnicking, and wine and cider tasting. Many sell baked items and picnic food.

WINERY EXCURSION

The most concentrated Gold Country wine touring area lies in the rolling hills of the Shenandoah Valley, just east of Plymouth, about 16 miles south of Placerville. Take Shenandoah Road east of Highway 49 and follow the signs. This section of Amador County contains 17 wineries, mostly family-run operations on scenic back roads. Robust zinfandel is the primary grape grown here, but wineries also produce chardonnay and cabernet sauvignon. Most are open weekend afternoons; several have shady picnic areas, gift shops, and galleries or museums.

Sobon Estate (14430 Shenandoah Rd., ☎ 209/245–6554; open daily 10–5) also operates the **Shenandoah Valley Museum,** illustrating pioneer life and wine making in the valley. **Charles Spinetta Winery** (12557 Steiner Rd., ☎ 209/245–3384; open Tues.–Sun. 10–5) has a wildlife gallery. Fourteen more wineries are located farther east in El Dorado County; they're tucked into the hillsides around Placerville along back roads, north and south of U.S. 50. Maps are available from the **Amador County** and **El Dorado County** chambers of commerce (*see* Visitor Information *in* Sacramento and Gold Country Essentials, *below*) or the two wineries above.

Tour 3: Sutter Creek to Jamestown

The southern portion of the Gold Country tour begins just below Plymouth, where State Highway 16 from Sacramento meets Highway 49.

★ 19 **Sutter Creek** is a charming conglomeration of balconied buildings, Victorian homes, and neo–New England structures. The stores along Highway 49 (called Main Street in the town proper) are worth visiting to hunt for works by the many local artists and craftspeople. The **Sutter Creek Visitor's Center** in **Knight Foundry** (81 Eureka St., 95685, ☎ 800/400–0305; open daily 9–4) has maps showing historic buildings in town and offers self-guided tours of the foundry, machine shop, and blacksmith shop.

As you drive south from Sutter Creek, Highway 49 climbs sharply, twists and turns, and then rewards you with a wonderful view, first of the
20 headframes of the Kennedy Mine and then of **Jackson,** the Amador county seat. Jackson once had the world's deepest and richest mines. While it wasn't the Gold Country's rowdiest town, the party lasted longer in Jackson than anywhere else: "Girls dormitories" and nickel slots flourished until the mid-1950s. Now the heart of Jackson's historic section is the National Hotel (2 Water St.), which operates an old-time saloon in the lobby; the hotel is especially active on weekends, when people come from miles around to participate in the Saturday-night singalongs. Jackson also has a number of aboveground pioneer cemeteries where the early Italian and Serbian miners were buried. The terraced cemetery on the grounds of the handsome **St. Sava Serbian Orthodox Church** (724 N. Main St.) is the most impressive.

The **Amador County Museum,** built in the late 1850s as a private home, still has many of the original furnishings and contains a working model of the Kennedy Mine. *225 Church St., 95642,* ☎ *209/223–6386.* ☛ *Museum: free; building with mine: $1 adults, 50¢ children.* ⏲ *Wed.–Sun. 10–4.*

21 Seven miles south along Highway 49 is **Mokelumne Hill.** Once one of the largest of the Gold Rush towns, "Moke Hill" now feels frozen in time; unlike its many gussied-up counterparts along Highway 49, it hasn't been gentrified and sanitized. Mokelumne Hill is almost but not quite a ghost town—its single downtown block is largely unreconstructed, the few sidewalks planked.

22 Twenty miles south is **Angels Camp,** famed chiefly for its jumping-frog contest held each May, based on Mark Twain's "The Jumping Frog of Calaveras County." At the north end of town is a museum with minerals and early artifacts and a large collection of carriages; you can pick up a guide to other points of interest here. ☎ *209/736–2963.* ☛ *$1 adults, 25¢ children.* ⏲ *Mar.–Labor Day, daily 10–3; Labor Day–Mar., Wed.–Sun. 10–3.*

23 East on Highway 4, and less than 10 miles up the road, is **Murphys,** a well-preserved town of white picket fences, Victorian houses, and interesting shops. In **Murphys Historic Hotel and Lodge** (*see* Lodging, *below*), the guest register records the visits of Horatio Alger and Ulysses S. Grant, who joined the 19th-century swarms visiting the giant sequoias in **Calaveras Big Trees State Park** about 15 miles farther east on Highway 4. ☎ *209/795–2334. Day use: $5 per car.* ⏲ *Daily dawn to dusk; campsites available.*

The **Kautz Ironstone Winery and Caverns** in Murphys are worth a visit even if you don't like wine; tours take visitors into aging underground tunnels cooled by a waterfall from a natural spring. *Six Mile Rd., 95247,* ☎ *209/728–1251.* ⏲ *Daily 11 to 5.*

Another spectacle of nature, 4 miles out of Murphys, on the Vallecito–Columbia highway, is **Moaning Cavern,** a vast underground chamber with ancient crystalline rock formations. ☎ *209/736–2708.* ☛ *$6.25 adults, $3 children 6–12.* ⏲ *Summer, daily 9–6; winter, daily 10–5.*

Back on Highway 49 as you drive south, a breathtaking ride across the Stanislaus River bridge yields views of the Melones Reservoir. It's a vivid example of the rugged terrain in a part of California where the rivers have dug deep canyons. Horse-drawn wagons must have found it rough going.

★ 24 A well-marked turnoff leads to **Columbia State Historic Park,** a pleasingly executed mix of preservation and restoration. The "Gem of the Southern Mines" comes as close to a Gold Rush town in its heyday as you can get. You can ride a stagecoach and pan for gold, street musicians give lively performances in summer, and there is a blacksmith working at his anvil. Restored or reconstructed buildings include a Wells Fargo Express office, Masonic temple, stores, saloons, two elegant hotels, a firehouse, churches, a school, and a newspaper office. All are staffed to simulate a working 1850s town. The Fallon Theater presents plays year-round. ☎ *209/532–0150.* ☛ *Free.* ⏲ *Daily 8:30–5; closed Thanksgiving and Dec. 25. Museum open 10–5.*

25 Highway 49 is the main street in **Sonora,** one of the earliest—and hard as it might be to believe today—wildest towns in the region. Religion found its way here, too: The board-and-batten **St. James Episcopal Church,** built in 1859, is the second-oldest wood-frame church in California.

The road turns west for a few miles out of Sonora and heads to
26 **Jamestown,** which many will recognize from the movies or television—it's often used as a location for westerns. The town's **Railtown 1897 State Historic Park** includes 26 acres of trains, a station, a roundhouse, and facilities for maintaining trains. There are slide presentations, guided tours, and train excursions on the weekends. ☎ *209/984–3953.* ☛ *Self-guided tours are free; train excursions; $9 adults, $4.50 children.* ⏲ *Daily 10–4.*

SHOPPING

Sacramento has two major shopping malls. **Downtown Plaza,** comprising the K Street Mall along with many specialty shops and restaurants, has brought locals to the center city for shopping and entertainment; there's a Thursday-night market, and in winter an outdoor ice-skating rink is set up. **Arden Fair Mall,** located in the North Area (a major district bisected by I–80, north and east of downtown Sacramento) is Sacramento's largest shopping center, anchored by Nordstrom and Weinstock's department stores. **Pavilions Mall** (Fair Oaks Blvd. and Howe Ave.) and **Town and Country Village** (Marconi Ave. and Fulton Ave.) have numerous boutiques. Among the T-shirt and yogurt emporiums in Old Sacramento are some interesting art galleries and bookstores. The **Artists' Collaborative Gallery** (1007 2nd St., ☎ 916/444–3764) has ever-changing exhibits by top local artists and craftspeople. **Bookmine** (1015 2nd St., ☎ 916/441-4609) sells used and rare books.

DINING AND LODGING

Dining

Given the small population of the Gold Country, the number of good restaurants is disproportionately large, especially in Nevada City. American, Italian, and Mexican fare is common, but Gold Country chefs also prepare ambitious Continental, French, and California cuisine, with an emphasis on innovation and the freshest ingredients. Outside Sacramento, national fast-food chains are few and far between. It's not difficult, though, to find the makings for a good picnic in most Gold Country towns.

WHAT TO WEAR

Dress is casual unless otherwise noted.

CATEGORY	COST*
$$$$	over $35
$$$	$25–$35
$$	$15–$25
$	under $15

**per person for a three-course meal, excluding drinks, service, and 7¼% tax*

Lodging

Among the treasures of the Gold Country today are its inns, many of them beautifully restored buildings dating back to the 1850s and 1860s and furnished with period pieces. If you came here for the history, there's no better way to get a taste of it. In Sacramento, most of the lodgings listed are in the downtown area, close to Old Sacramento, the Capitol, and Sutter's Fort.

CATEGORY	COST*
$$$$	over $100
$$$	$75–$100
$$	$50–$75
$	under $50

**All prices are for a standard double room, excluding 7¼% tax (12% in Sacramento).*

Amador City

DINING

$$ Ballads. Contemporary American cuisine is served here—a seasonally changing selection of seafood, poultry, and meat, as well as vegetarian dishes. Appetizers include smoked duck with red-onion marmalade, polenta with wild-mushroom ragout, and spinach salad with scallops and peppers. The imaginative presentation and an interesting wine list are additional draws. ✕ *14220 Hwy. 49,* ☏ *209/267–5403. Reservations advised. AE, MC, V. Closed Wed. No lunch.*

DINING AND LODGING

$$–$$$ **Imperial Hotel.** This hotel, dating from 1879, has whimsically decorated rooms that mock Victorian excesses in a 20th-century way. Antique furnishings include iron and brass beds, gingerbread flourishes, and in one room art deco appointments. The two front rooms, which can be noisy, have balconies. The modern bathrooms have hair dryers and towel warmers. The hotel's fine restaurant serves meals in a bright Victorian-style dining room and on the patio outdoors. The menu changes quarterly; the fare ranges from vegetarian to country-hearty to trendy cuisine. Breakfast is included in the lodging rates; there is a two-night minimum weekends. 🏨 *Box 195, Hwy. 49, 95601,* ☏ *209/267–9172 or 800/242–5594,* FAX *209/267–9249. 6 rooms. Restaurant ($$$), bar. AE, D, DC, MC, V.*

Angels Camp

LODGING

$$$ **Cooper House.** Surprises abound inside this board-and-batten cottage tucked into a hillside above town. Its wainscoting, ceiling beams, floors, moldings, and unusual angled doors are striking examples of Craftsman-style woodworking. Authentic antiques include a Limbert desk and chair; original art hangs on the walls. Two rooms open to the gardens. Room rates include breakfast and afternoon wine-and-appetizer sampling. 🏨 *1184 Church St., Box 1388, 95222,* ☏ *209/736–2145. 3 rooms. AE, D, MC, V.*

Auburn

DINING

$$–$$$ ★ **Latitudes.** This fine restaurant serves delicious, light multicultural cuisine in an elegant, off-white 1870 Victorian. There are no red-meat dishes, but the varied menu (which changes monthly) includes seafood, chicken, and turkey prepared with Mexican spices, curries, cheese, or teriyaki sauce. The beer and wine list is as extensive and eclectic as the menu. The Sunday brunch here is deservedly popular. An ever-changing display of local art graces the dining-room walls. ✕ *130 Maple St.,* ☏ *916/885–9535. AE, MC, V. No lunch Sat.; no dinner Mon. and Tues.*

$$ **Awful Annie's.** In good weather, sit outside and take in the view of old-town Auburn at this popular spot for breakfast (a specialty: omelets with chili) or a lunch of soup, sandwich, and/or salad. ✕ *160 Sacramento Way,* ☏ *916/888–9857. AE, MC, V. No dinner.*

LODGING

$$$–$$$$ **Powers Mansion Inn.** This elegant Victorian hints at the opulence the Gold Rush gentry enjoyed. Two light-filled parlors have gleaming oak floors, Asian antiques, and ornate Victorian chairs and settees. Photos on the walls relate the story of the gold fortune that built the mansion. A second-floor maze of narrow corridors leads to the guest rooms, which have brass and pencil-post beds with satin spreads. Breakfasts such as eggs Benedict and french toast are included in the room rate. *164 Cleveland Ave., 95603, ☎ 916/885–1166, FAX 916/885–1386. 11 rooms. AE, MC, V.*

$$ **Auburn Inn.** This beige and brown multistory inn is exceptionally well maintained. The decor is contemporary, in teal and pastel colors. There are king- and queen-size beds, suites, and no-smoking rooms. *1875 Auburn Ravine Rd., Foresthill exit north from I–80, 95603, ☎ 916/885–1800 or 800/272–1444, FAX 916/888–6424. 81 rooms. Pool, spa, coin laundry. AE, D, DC, MC, V.*

Coloma

DINING AND LODGING

$$$–$$$$ ★ **Vineyard House.** The site of an early, prize-winning winery, this 1878 country inn became an important hotel and the social center of the area, home of Robert Chalmers, a state senator in the 1880s. Said to be haunted by Chalmers, or perhaps his destitute widow Louisa, the inn is a popular weekend destination. The cellar bar, once used as a jail, is especially busy. The restaurant is popular locally for its traditional American food—chicken, beef, seafood, and pasta. Rooms, located upstairs, are furnished with antiques. Room rates include breakfast. *Box 517, 530 Cold Springs Rd., off Hwy. 49, 95613, ☎ 916/622–2217, FAX 209/622–5379. 7 rooms, 6 with shared bath. Restaurant (usually closed Mon.–Wed.; no lunch), bar. No pets. Smoking restricted. AE, MC, V.*

LODGING

$$$–$$$$ **Coloma Country Inn.** A restored Victorian bed-and-breakfast built in 1852, this inn is set on 5 acres of state parkland. Guests can fish and canoe at the inn's pond. Rooms have antique double beds and private sitting areas; the decor features quilts, stenciled friezes, and fresh flowers. There are two suites. Hot-air ballooning and white-water rafting can be arranged. Room rates include full country breakfast. Note: Advance notice is needed for children. *Box 502, 345 High St., 95613, ☎ 916/622–6919. 7 rooms, 2 with shared bath. No pets. No smoking. No credit cards.*

Columbia

DINING AND LODGING

$$–$$$ **City Hotel.** The rooms in this restored 1856 hostelry are elaborately furnished with period antiques. Two rooms have balconies overlooking Main Street, and the four parlor rooms open onto a second-floor sitting room. Rooms have private half baths with showers nearby; robes and slippers are provided. Continental breakfast (included in room rate) is served in the upstairs parlor; lunch, dinner, and weekend brunch are available in the restaurant, which is generally considered one of the best in the Gold Country. It serves French-accented California cuisine. The wine cellar, one of the finest in the state, contains a huge collection of California wines. The What Cheer Saloon is right out of a western movie. *Main St., Columbia State Park, Box 1870, 95310, ☎ 209/532–1479, FAX 209/532–7027. 10 rooms with ½ bath. Restaurant (closed Mon.; $$$), bar, saloon. No pets. AE, MC, V.*

LODGING

$$–$$$ **Fallon Hotel.** The state of California restored this 1857 hotel to Victorian grandeur. The lobby and rooms are furnished with 1890s antiques. Each accommodation has a private half bath; there are men's and women's showers. Continental breakfast is served; if you occupy one of the five balcony rooms, you can sit outside with your coffee and watch the town wake up. One room is equipped for visitors with disabilities. *Washington St., Columbia State Park, next to Fallon House Theater, Box 1870, 95310, ☎ 209/532–1470. 14 rooms with ½ bath. No smoking. AE, MC, V.*

Grass Valley

LODGING

$$$ ★ **Murphy's Inn.** An immaculate white house in a leafy setting (there is a giant sequoia in the backyard and some eye-catching topiaries), this outstanding bed-and-breakfast, built in 1866, was once the mansion of a gold-mine owner. Some guest rooms have the original wallpaper, four have fireplaces, and many have gas chandeliers. The spacious veranda is festooned with ivy. There are award-winning full breakfasts; Belgian waffles and eggs Benedict are specialties. *318 Neal St. (Colfax 174 exit from Hwy. 49/20 south, left on S. Auburn St.), 95945, ☎ 916/273–6873, FAX 209/273–6873. 8 rooms. No pets (kennel facilities nearby). No smoking. AE, MC, V.*

Jackson

DINING

$–$$ **Upstairs Restaurant.** Chef Layne McCollum, who learned his trade at the California Culinary Institute, takes a creative approach to contemporary American dining in this intimate (12 tables) restaurant. Fresh flowers, white table linens, and soft music accompany gourmet fowl, fresh seafood, and meat, with daily specials. The baked-brie-and-roast-garlic appetizer and homemade soups are specialties. Local wines are featured, and the chef blends and roasts exotic coffees daily. ✕ *164 Main St., 95642, ☎ 209/223–3342. Reservations advised. AE, D, DC, MC, V. Closed Mon.*

$ **Rosebud's Cafe.** The decor is art deco, black and white with touches of red, and the music is from the '30s and '40s in this casual, homey café. The classic American food includes hot roast beef, turkey, and meat loaf with mashed potatoes smothered in gravy, as well as charbroiled burgers and hot sandwiches. Omelets are a specialty. Freshly baked pies and espresso or gourmet coffees round out the menu; local wines are served. ✕ *26 Main St., 95641, ☎ 209/223–1035. MC, V. No dinner.*

LODGING

$$–$$$ **Court Street Inn.** Listed on the National Register of Historic Places, this conveniently situated B&B Victorian has tin ceilings, a redwood staircase, Oriental rugs, and antique furnishings. The cozy first-floor Muldoon Room has a fireplace and king-size bed; Blair Room features a large whirlpool, a Wedgwood stove, and a queen-size brass bed. The Indian House is a two-bedroom guest cottage with a large bathroom. Full breakfast is included, as well as evening refreshments by the grand piano. *215 Court St., 95642, ☎ 209/223–0416 or 800/200–0416. 7 rooms. TV by request, radio with tape player, robes, outdoor hot tub. No smoking indoors. AE, MC, V.*

$$ **Best Western Amador Inn.** This sprawling two-story modern motel is conveniently located right on the highway. Rooms are nicely decorated; many have fireplaces. *200 S. Hwy. 49, Box 758, 95642, ☎ 209/223–*

0211, 800/543–5221, FAX 209/223–4836. 118 rooms. Restaurant, pool, laundry service. AE, D, DC, MC, V.

Jamestown

DINING AND LODGING

$$ **National Hotel.** One of California's 10 oldest continuously operated hotels, the National has been in business since 1859. Decor is simple—brass beds, patchwork quilts, and lace curtains. Although not all rooms have private baths, those that don't have antique washbasins. Breakfast is included in the room rate. The saloon, with its original 19th-century redwood bar, is a great place to linger. The popular restaurant serves mountain-size portions: great hamburgers and fries, salads, Italian entrées. *77 Main St., Box 502, 95327, ☎ 209/984–3446; in CA, 800/894–3446; FAX 209/984–5620. 11 rooms, 6 share bath. Restaurant (reservations required), TV by request. Not all rooms have phones. AE, D, DC, MC, V.*

LODGING

$$–$$$ **Royal Hotel.** Although it dates from the 1920s, this charming small hotel has light, airy Victorian decor. There are 16 rooms in the main building and three cottages—one of which is especially romantic. Guests can enjoy a large private garden area, and complimentary Continental breakfast is served on weekends. There are no TVs and no in-room phones. *18239 Main St., Box 219, 95327, ☎ 209/984–5271. 16 rooms, 9 with shared bath. Coin laundry. AE, MC, V.*

$$ **Railtown Motel.** This is a modern, typical motel, good for families. It's clean, but don't expect luxury. Ground-floor rooms have a double-size spa bath. *Willow St. at Main St., Box 1129, 95327, ☎ 209/984–3332. 20 rooms. Pool, spa. AE, MC, V.*

Murphys

DINING AND LODGING

$$–$$$ **Murphys Historic Hotel and Lodge.** This picturesque stone hotel, built in 1855, figured in Bret Harte's story "A Night at Wingdam." The register contains signatures of Ulysses S. Grant, Mark Twain, and bandit Black Bart. Accommodations are in the historic hotel and a modern motel-style addition. The older rooms are furnished with antiques, many large, heavy, and hand-carved. The hotel has a friendly old-time saloon, full-service dining room, and conference facilities. Continental breakfast is included in the room rate. *457 Main St., Box 329, 95247, ☎ 209/728–3444, 800/532–7684, FAX 209/728–1950. 29 rooms (9 historic rooms share baths). AE, D, DC, MC, V.*

LODGING

$$$$ **Dunbar House 1880.** The oversize rooms in this elaborate Italianate-style home are decorated in an eclectic selection of antiques, with brass beds, down comforters, wood-burning stoves, and claw-foot tubs. One bathroom has its own daybed. Broad wraparound verandas encourage lounging, as do colorful gardens and shady elm trees. The Cedar's sunporch has a two-person whirlpool tub and a view of a white-flowering almond tree; in Sequoia, you can gaze at the garden while soaking in a bubble bath. Breakfast (included) is an elegant affair. *271 Jones St., Box 1375, 95247, ☎ 209/728–2897; 800/225–3764, ext. 321; FAX 209/728–1451. 4 rooms. Refrigerators, TVs with VCR. AE, MC, V.*

Nevada City

DINING

$$–$$$$ **Country Rose Cafe.** The exterior of this old brick and stone building, whose original iron shutters date from Gold Rush days, harmonizes well with the antiques inside. The café's lengthy French country menu includes seafood, beef, lamb, chicken, and ratatouille. In the summer, there is outdoor service on a verdant patio. ✕ *300 Commercial St.,* ☎ *916/265–6248. Reservations advised. AE, MC, V. No lunch Sun.*

$$ **Friar Tuck's.** This local gathering spot, which opened in 1974, is one of the area's oldest restaurants. The cozy bar feels like an English pub, with its elaborately carved wood antique back bar, originally in a Liverpool pub. A guitar player sings nightly; sometimes patrons join in. The dining area is like a catacomb, with cubicles defined by old beams, brick walls, and arches. The menu's hearty offerings include fondue, Iowa beef, Hawaiian fish specials, and Tuck's bouillabaisse. ✕ *111 N. Pine St.,* ☎ *916/265–9093. Reservations accepted. AE, MC, V. No lunch.*

$$ ★ **Potager at Seleya's.** The food is consistently fresh and good at this sophisticated restaurant in an elegant Victorian setting. The menu lists a variety of fish, fowl, meat, and pasta dishes, creatively prepared. Appetizers include wild mushrooms gratin and potager (soup). Beef Wellington, salmon roulade, and loin of lamb are featured entrées. Caesar salads are mixed at your table; breads and desserts are baked on the premises. The adjacent Potager to Go (☎ 916/265–0558) prepares gourmet deli luncheon items daily. ✕ *320 Broad St.,* ☎ *916/265–5697. Reservations advised. AE, MC, V. No lunch. Closed Mon. and major holidays.*

$ **Cirino's.** This popular restaurant serves American-Italian food—seafood, pasta, and veal dishes—in an informal bar-and-grill atmosphere. The handsome Brunswick back bar is of Gold Rush vintage. ✕ *309 Broad St.,* ☎ *916/265–2246. Reservations advised. AE, MC, V.*

$ **Posh Nosh.** Fresh bread baked daily, deli fare, and California cuisine are the highlights here. Anything on the lunch menu is available for takeout: sandwiches, salads, and bagel baskets. There's a good wine list, as well as 20 varieties of imported beer and a dozen domestic brands. The dinner menu includes fresh seafood and vegetarian selections. You can dine on the garden patio in nice weather. ✕ *318 Broad St.,* ☎ *916/265–6064. Reservations advised for dinner. AE, MC, V.*

LODGING

$$$–$$$$ ★ **Flume's End.** This unique inn was built at the end of a historic flume that once brought water into the mines. The hillside setting, on 3 wooded acres with an adjacent waterfall, is soothing. Rooms are on several levels, most with creek views. Two have Jacuzzis. The decor is eclectic Victorian, homey and casual, with romantic nooks. The large common rooms have a piano and fireplace for guests to gather around. Room rates include a full breakfast. No pets are allowed, and smoking indoors is not permitted. 🏨 *317 S. Pine St., 95959,* ☎ *916/265–9665. 6 rooms. TV in parlor, guest refrigerator. MC, V.*

$$$–$$$$ **Red Castle Inn.** A state landmark, this 1860 Gothic Revival mansion stands on a hillside overlooking Nevada City. Its brick exterior is trimmed with white icicle woodwork, and its porches and gardens add to the charm. The rooms, some of which overlook the town, have antique furnishings and are elaborately decorated. A full buffet breakfast is served. No pets are allowed. 🏨 *109 Prospect St., 95959,* ☎ *916/265–5135. 8 rooms, 2 with shared bath. MC, V.*

$$–$$$ **Northern Queen Inn.** This bright, pleasant, two-story motel has a lovely creek-side setting. Accommodations include new and remodeled motel units; eight two-story chalets and eight rustic cottages with efficiency kitchens are located in a secluded, wooded area. ☎ *400 Railroad Ave., Sacramento St. exit off Hwy. 49, 95959,* ☎ *916/265–5824,* FAX *916/265–3720. 85 rooms. Restaurant, refrigerators, pool, spa. No pets. AE, DC, MC, V.*

Placerville

DINING

$$$ ★ **Zachary Jacques.** The location is not easy to find, but call ahead for directions—it's worth the effort. The country-French menu changes seasonally and features fresh fish and vegetables. Appetizers may include escargot or mushrooms prepared in several ways, as well as prawns and goat cheese. Traditionally prepared, classic entrées include roast rack of lamb, *daube Provençale* (beef stew), scallops and prawns in lime butter, and chateaubriand garni. ✕ *1821 Pleasant Valley Rd.,* ☎ *916/626–8045. Reservations advised. AE, MC, V. Closed Mon. No lunch.*

$$ ★ **Smith Flat House.** The recommendation here is for atmosphere. Once the last milepost on the Lake Tahoe Wagon Road, this place has been an inn, restaurant, dance hall, Pony Express office, and store—the restrained decor still suggests the 19th century. Located in the cellar saloon is a mine shaft, now filled with water, leading to the heart of the Mother Lode. Occasional ghostly happenings have been reported. The dinner menu is limited, but there is an extensive lunch menu, featuring a build-your-own-sandwich option. On Saturday there's a barbecue lunch. ✕ *2021 Smith Flat Rd.,* ☎ *916/621–0667 or 916/621–0471. Reservations advised. AE, DC, MC, V. No lunch Mon.*

$ **Lyons.** This reliable chain restaurant serves prime rib, steaks, chicken, and fried shrimp; for lunch, there are sandwiches, burgers, and salads. Breakfasts are hearty. It's clean, centrally located, and open 24 hours a day. ✕ *1160 Broadway,* ☎ *916/622–2305. No reservations. AE, D, MC, V.*

$ **Powell Bros. Steamer Co.** This seafood restaurant sports a nautical-theme decor, old brick walls, and dark wood. The menu is primarily shellfish, served in stews, pastas, chowders, cocktails, and sandwiches, and cooked in big steamers—nothing is fried. ✕ *425 Main St.,* ☎ *916/626–1091. No reservations. MC, V. Closed Sun.*

LODGING

$$$ **Chichester-McKee House.** This 1892 Queen Anne was the first house in Placerville with built-in plumbing; an entrance to a gold mine lies underneath the dining-room table. Rooms are furnished with a mix of antiques and reproductions; a window seat and an Amish oak bed with a handmade fishnet canopy make Yellow Rose the most appealing room despite the faint traffic sounds. Be aware that there is a steep walk from the parking lot to the inn. After a hearty breakfast (included), guests can walk a few blocks to downtown Placerville or drive to nearby Apple Hill for a wine tasting. ☎ *800 Spring St., 95667,* ☎ *916/626–1882 or 800/831–4008. 3 rooms with ½ bath share full bath. Air-conditioning. No pets. No smoking indoors. AE, D, MC, V.*

$$ **Best Western Placerville Inn.** This motel's serviceable rooms are done in the chain's trademark pastels; the pool comes in handy during the hot summer months. There is a coffee shop–restaurant on the premises. ☎ *6850 Greenleaf Dr. near U.S. 50's Missouri Flats exit, 95667,* ☎ *916/622–9100 or 800/528–1234,* FAX *916/622–9376. 105 rooms. Pool, hot tub. AE, D, DC, MC, V.*

$$ **Days Inn.** Rooms in this downtown motel are clean and comfortable. Continental breakfast is included; there is a coffee shop next door. ☎ *1332 Broadway, U.S. 50 east from Hwy. 49, then Schnell School exit*

south, 95667, ☎ *916/622–3124 or 800/325–2525,* FAX *916/622–2080. 45 rooms. AE, D, DC, MC, V.*

Sacramento

DINING

$$$ ★ **Biba.** Owner Biba Caggiano is an authority on Italian cuisine, author of several cookbooks, and star of a national TV show on cooking. The Capitol crowd flocks here for her delicate pasta dishes, baked spinach lasagna, and homemade tortellini. Caggiano also offers a great osso buco, rabbit tenderloin, and grilled pork loin, as well as regional specialties. ✕ *2801 Capitol Ave.,* ☎ *916/455–2422. Reservations advised. AE, MC, V. No smoking. Closed Sun. No lunch weekends.*

$$$ **Rio City Café.** This bright restaurant on an old Sacramento wharf has dual attractions: eclectic lunch and dinner menus and huge, floor-to-ceiling windows with river views. When the weather's good you can enjoy your meals at water's edge. Rio City serves both light and hearty fare: grilled vegetables on pasta, sautéed ahi with pomegranate sauce, and baked stuffed chicken breast. Sunday brunch is a full buffet with omelet bar, prime rib, salads, and desserts. ✕ *1110 Front St.,* ☎ *916/442-8226. Reservations advised. AE, D, DC, MC, V.*

$$–$$$ **California Fats.** This is the better of two Old Sacramento restaurants operated by the younger generation of the Fat family (*see* Frank Fat's, *below*). The extensive Pacific Rim–influenced menu is full of different flavors: seared ahi and glazed duck from a wood-fired oven, pizza, pastas with overtones of ginger and coriander, and venison in cashew crust, in addition to steaks and seafood. The restaurant's decor portrays the history of Chinese immigrants with vibrant colors, railroad ties, a 30-foot-high waterfall, Ping-Pong-ball wall screens, and bowling-ball tables. ✕ *1015 Front St.,* ☎ *916/441–7966. Reservations accepted. AE, MC, V.*

$$–$$$ **Frank Fat's.** Known as the "third house" of the California legislature where lawmakers, lobbyists, and media have been making deals for more than 50 years, Frank Fat's is known as much for its watering-hole qualities as its so-so Chinese food. The menu emphasizes Cantonese cuisine, but there are items from other regions of China. Signature dishes include brandy-fried chicken, stir-fried clams in black bean sauce, plus a couple of items from the American menu: New York steak and banana cream pie. ✕ *806 L St.,* ☎ *916/442–7092. Reservations advised. AE, MC, V. No lunch weekends.*

$$ **Aïoli Bodega Española.** One of several new eateries located near the Capitol, this corner storefront is popular with the young crowd who graze on a large selection of hot and cold tapas while sipping sherry, port, or sangria. Entrées include a selection of paellas, grilled meat, and seafood. ✕ *1800 L St.,* ☎ *916/447-9440. Reservations advised. AE, DC, MC, V. No lunch weekends.*

$$ **Harlow's.** This popular spot serves California-Italian cuisine, with extraordinary seafood specials, tortellini, and wonderful cheesecake. Dining can be noisy and crowded, but the service is excellent, and people-watching is fun, especially at the bar. ✕ *2714 J St.,* ☎ *916/441–4693. Reservations advised. AE, D, DC, MC, V.*

$$ **Paragary's Bar and Oven.** Pizza is the specialty at this casual, noisy restaurant that's popular with the downtown state-worker crowd for lunch or dinner. You won't go hungry here—pasta, dessert, and even appetizer portions are enormous. The restaurant's namesake Randy Paragary also owns the nearby (and also popular) Capitol Grill. ✕ *1401 28th St.,* ☎ *916/457–5737. Reservations advised. AE, D, DC, MC, V. No lunch weekends.*

$–$$ **Centro.** While the cuisine may not be as authentic as claimed, Centro stretches the concept of Mexican food beyond tacos and burritos. Unusual items include adobo marinated pork, black bean and chipotle chili tamales, and salmon Veracruzana. This is a bright, noisy industrial-style storefront with a pair of motorcycles in the window. ✕ *2730 J St., ☎ 916/442–2552. Reservations advised for lunch. AE, DC, MC, V. No lunch weekends.*

LODGING

$$$–$$$$ **Abigail's Bed and Breakfast Inn.** This 1912 Colonial Revival mansion sits on a tree-shaded street near the Capitol. Two parlors flank a grand staircase leading to comfortably furnished upstairs bedrooms with pencil-post or canopied beds. One room has a Jacuzzi. Innkeeper Susanne Ventura is a most attentive host. Full breakfast and afternoon refreshments are included. *2120 G St., 95816, ☎ 916/441–5007 or 800/858–1568, FAX 916/441–0621. 5 rooms. Air-conditioning, TVs available, outdoor hot tub. AE, D, DC, MC, V.*

$$$–$$$$ **Amber House Bed & Breakfast Inn.** Two artistic-themed residences comprise this bed-and-breakfast located in a historic district near the Capitol. The original house, called the Poet's Refuge, is a Craftsman-style home with five bedrooms decorated in literary themes. There are stained-glass windows, wood floors, and a fireplace in the living room. Next door, a 1913 Mediterranean-style home has a French Impressionist motif: Bright rooms are swathed in colors reminiscent of the paintings of Degas, Van Gogh, and Renoir. Several rooms have double Jacuzzis or VCRs. Complimentary breakfast and beverages are included. *1315 22nd St., 95816, ☎ 916/444–8085 or 800/755–6526, FAX 916/447–1548. 9 rooms. Air-conditioning, TVs, bicycles. AE, D, DC, MC, V.*

$$$–$$$$ **Delta King.** This grand old riverboat, now permanently moored at Old Sacramento's waterfront, once transported passengers between Sacramento and San Francisco. It was refurbished in the 1980s to its former elegance, with original grand staircase, mahogany paneling, and brass fittings. The best of the 44 staterooms are on the river side toward the back of the boat. The restaurant is locally popular, though the cuisine and service are uneven. Rates include Continental breakfast. *1000 Front St., 95814, ☎ 916/444–5464 or 800/825–5464, FAX 916/444–5314. 44 rooms. Restaurant, bar, parking (fee), meeting rooms. AE, D, DC, MC, V.*

$$$–$$$$ ★ **Hyatt Regency at Capitol Park.** Located across the street from the Capitol and adjacent to the Convention Center, this is the premier hotel in Sacramento with its dramatic marble-and-glass lobby and luxuriously appointed rooms. The best rooms have Capitol Park views. The service here is outstanding. *1209 L St., 95814, ☎ 916/443–1234 or 800/233–1234, FAX 916/321–6631. 500 rooms. 2 restaurants, lounge, air-conditioning, pool, hot tub, exercise room, nightclub, conference center. AE, D, DC, MC, V.*

$$$–$$$$ **Radisson.** This sprawling hotel has been recently refurbished and considerably upgraded. Mediterranean-style two-story buildings clustered around a large artificial lake on the 18-acre landscaped site contain fairly large rooms, with art deco appointments and furnishings. Many have patios or balconies. The hotel has a busy conference center plus an annex across the freeway. It's a good headquarters for attending events at Cal Expo or visiting the North Area. *500 Leisure La., 95815, ☎ 916/922–2020 or 800/333–3333, FAX 916/649–9463. 314 rooms. 2 restaurants, air-conditioning, pool, exercise room, boating, bicycles, conference center. AE, D, DC, MC, V.*

$$–$$$ **Best Western Ponderosa.** Many consider this family-owned motel the best value downtown. Rooms are nicely appointed; many open to a

courtyard surrounding the pool. Continental breakfast is included. ☎ *1100 H St., 95814,* ☎ *916/441–1314 or 800/528–1234,* FAX *916/441–5961. 98 rooms. Restaurant, lounge, pool, laundry service, free parking. AE, D, DC, MC, V.*

$$–$$$ **Holiday Inn Capitol Plaza.** Despite its somewhat dreary ambience, this hotel has the best location for visiting Old Sacramento and the Downtown Plaza. It's also within walking distance of the Capitol. ☎ *300 J St., 95814,* ☎ *916/446–0100 or 800/465–4329,* FAX *916/446–0100. 368 rooms. Restaurant, lounge, air-conditioning, pool, 2 saunas, convention center, free parking. AE, DC, MC, V.*

Sonora

DINING

$ **Alfredos.** Brightly decorated with Mexican accessories, this large restaurant serves the most authentic food around. The large menu usually includes seafood specialties and steaks, and you'll find traditional combination plates—tacos, enchiladas, burritos, and quesadillas—but they are not smothered in cheese and salsa. The rice is deliciously delicate, as is the garlic soup. ✕ *123 S. Washington St.,* ☎ *209/532–8332. Reservations accepted for parties of 6 or more. MC, V.*

$ **Coyote Creek Cafe & Grill.** The friendly, low-key atmosphere of this centrally located restaurant is matched by its fresh southwestern-style decor. The fare here is multinational—lunch might include pasta Castroville (with artichoke hearts marinara), Zuni black-bean plate, or Szechuan chicken. Dinner selections include Spanish tapas or grilled steak and ethnic specialties. The weekend brunch menu is outstanding. ✕ *177 S. Washington St.,* ☎ *209/532–9115. No reservations. D, MC, V.*

LODGING

$$$–$$$$ **Ryan House Bed and Breakfast Inn.** One of the oldest houses in Sonora, this 1850s farmhouse is steps from town. Guest rooms are furnished with antiques; everyone has access to the three parlors (one has a TV) with woodstoves, and the sunny kitchen. The garden suite in the attic has a very large sitting area set in the gables, a pink and burgundy bathroom with double soaking tub, and a brass-and-iron bed. Room rates include full breakfast. ☎ *153 S. Shepherd St., 95370,* ☎ *209/533–3445 or 800/831–4897. 4 rooms. Air-conditioning. AE, MC, V.*

$–$$ **Sonora Inn.** This landmark inn, located in the heart of town, is steeped in California history. There are two buildings—the old inn built in 1896, and a newer motel unit. The older structure is built atop several underground tunnels (now sealed). There are secret rooms, staircases that go nowhere, and sealed chambers. The motel unit has smallish, functional rooms. ☎ *160 S. Washington St., 95370,* ☎ *209/532–7468 or 800/580–4667,* FAX *209/532–4542. 64 rooms. Restaurant, lounge, pool. AE, D, MC, V.*

Sutter Creek

DINING

$$$ ★ **Pelargonium.** Kent and Charlene Wilson truly enjoy being chef and hostess of their beautiful restaurant. Charlene is meticulous about the decor, setting out designer china, crystal, and silver and filling the place with bright geraniums. Kent lovingly prepares generous portions with sophisticated sauces and interesting side dishes, which include herb-flavored polenta and imaginative vegetables. His chicken madras on a bed of curry, yogurt, almond, and coconut is not to be missed. The chef can accommodate special diets. The selection of regional wines is fairly comprehensive. ✕ *Hwy. 49 and Hanford St.,* ☎ *209/267–5008. Reservations advised. No credit cards. Closed Sun. and Mon., last 2 wks in Jan. and 1st 2 wks in Feb. No lunch.*

$-$$ **Ron and Nancy's Palace.** This popular, unpretentious restaurant offers Continental cuisine, with daily specials such as chicken marsala and veal piccata. The lunch menu is hearty, offering a good sandwich selection and some of the same entrées available for dinner. The cozy bar is conducive to socializing. ✕ *76 Main St.,* ☏ *209/267–1355. Reservations advised. AE, D, DC, MC, V.*

LODGING

$$$$ ★ **Foxes Bed & Breakfast.** The rooms in this white clapboard house, built in 1857, are handsome, with high ceilings, antique beds, and lofty armoires topped with floral arrangements. All rooms have queen-size beds; four have wood-burning fireplaces and/or cable TV. A menu allows guests to select a full breakfast (included in room rate) cooked to order and brought to each room or to the gazebo in the garden on a silver service. *Box 159, 77 Main St., 95685,* ☏ *209/267–5882,* FAX *209/267–0712. 7 rooms. No pets. No smoking. D, MC, V.*

$$$-$$$$ **Gold Quartz Inn.** This inn on the edge of town has spacious rooms decorated in 19th-century style, with soft pastels, floral wallpaper, ruffled curtains, and period furnishings. All rooms have king-size beds, many have additional beds and spacious porches, and two are equipped for people with disabilities. The lobby resembles a Victorian parlor. Breakfast is served in the dining room and afternoon tea in the butler's pantry; both are included in the room rates. *15 Bryson Dr., 95685,* ☏ *209/267–9155 or 800/752–8738,* FAX *209/267–9170. 24 rooms. Laundry, meeting rooms. No smoking indoors. AE, MC, V.*

$$-$$$ **Aparicio's Hotel.** This new hotel is a good choice for budget-minded travelers. Large rooms contain two queen beds; they're attractively decorated with antique reproductions. *271 Hanford St., Box 1839, 95685,* ☏ *209/267–9177. 52 rooms. Restaurant, lounge. AE, D, MC, V.*

SACRAMENTO AND GOLD COUNTRY ESSENTIALS

Arriving and Departing

By Bus

Greyhound (☏ 800/231–2222) serves Sacramento, Auburn, and Placerville. It's a two-hour trip from San Francisco's Transbay Terminal at 1st and Mission streets to the Sacramento station at 7th and L streets.

By Car

Sacramento lies at the junction of I–5 and I–80, just under 90 miles northeast of San Francisco. It's about an eight-hour drive north from Los Angeles. I–80 continues northeast through the Gold Country toward Reno, about three hours from Sacramento; Lake Tahoe is two hours east of Sacramento via U.S. 50 or I–80.

By Plane

Sacramento Metro Airport (☏ 916/648–0700), 12 miles northwest of downtown Sacramento on I–5, is served by **American** (☏ 800/433–7300), **Delta** (☏ 800/221–1212), **Northwest** (☏ 800/225–2525), **Southwest** (☏ 800/435–9792), and **United** (☏ 800/241–6522). It is an hour's drive from Placerville, and a little closer to Auburn.

San Francisco International Airport (*see* Chapter 5, San Francisco) and **Oakland International Airport** (1 Airport Dr., Oakland 94621, ☏ 510/577–4000) are about two hours from Sacramento.

By Train

Amtrak (☎ 800/872–7245) runs trains to Sacramento frequently from Oakland's new Jack London Square station (245 2nd St.). Trains making this three-hour trip stop in Emeryville, Richmond, Martinez, and Davis; some stop at Berkeley and Suisin-Fairfield as well. Shuttle buses connect the Emeryville station (5885 Landregan St.) and San Francisco's Ferry Building (30 Embarcadero, at the foot of Market St.).

Getting Around

By Bus

Sacramento Transit Authority (☎ 916/321–2877) buses and light-rail trains transport passengers in Sacramento. Buses run 5 AM–10 PM; trains 4:30 AM–12:30 AM.

By Car

This is the most convenient way to see the Gold Country, since most of the area's towns are too small to provide a base for public transportation. From Sacramento, three highways fan out toward the east, all intersecting with Highway 49: I–80 heads 30 miles northeast to Auburn; U.S. 50 goes east 40 miles to Placerville; and Highway 16 angles southeast 45 miles to Plymouth. Highway 49 is an excellent two-lane road that winds and climbs through the foothills and valleys, linking the principal Gold Country towns.

Guided Tours

Ballooning, Rafting

Outdoor Adventure River Specialists (O.A.R.S.) (Box 67, Angels Camp 95222, ☎ 209/736–4677 or 800/346–6277, FAX 209/736–2902) operates a wide range of white-water rafting trips on the Stanislaus, American, Merced, and Tuolumne rivers from late March through early October.

Coloma Country Inn (Box 502, Coloma 95613, ☎ 916/622–6919) operates rafting and ballooning packages on the American River; these are in conjunction with bed-and-breakfast accommodations.

Prospecting

Gold Prospecting Expeditions (18170 Main St., Box 1040, Jamestown 95327, ☎ 209/984–4653, FAX 209/984–0711) takes would-be miners on a range of gold-panning excursions, from one-hour to two-week trips.

River Cruises

Capital City Cruises (1401 Garden Hwy., Suite 125, Sacramento 95833, ☎ 916/921–1111) runs two-hour narrated cruises, as well as brunch, dinner-dance, and murder-mystery cruises, on the Sacramento River year-round on the *River City Queen* and the steamer *Elizabeth Louise.*

Channel Star Excursions (110 L St., Sacramento 95814, ☎ 916/522–2933 or 800/433–0263) operates the *Spirit of Sacramento,* a paddlewheel riverboat that embarks on a variety of excursions, including a one-hour narrated cruise, happy hour, dinner, and luncheon cruises, and a champagne brunch.

Shopping

Hop Around (Gray Line/Frontier Tours, 2600 North Ave., Sacramento 95838, ☎ 916/927–2877 or 800/356–9838; adults $12, children $6) operates a shopping and narrated sightseeing shuttle stopping at most downtown tourist attractions. Buses stop at major hotels.

Important Addresses and Numbers

Doctors

These Sacramento hospitals have 24-hour emergency rooms: **Mercy Hospital of Sacramento Promptcare** (4001 J St., ☎ 916/453–4424), **Sutter General Hospital** (2801 L St., ☎ 916/733–8900), and **Sutter Memorial Hospital** (52nd and F Sts., ☎ 916/733–1000).

Emergencies

Dial 911 for **police** and **ambulance** in an emergency.

Visitor Information

Amador County Chamber of Commerce (125 Peek St., Box 596, Jackson 95642, ☎ 209/223–0350).

Auburn Area Chamber of Commerce (601 Lincoln Way, Auburn 95603, ☎ 916/885–5616 or 800/427–6463).

Columbia State Historic Park (Box 151, Columbia 95310, ☎ 209/532–0150).

El Dorado County Chamber of Commerce (542 Main St., Placerville 95667, ☎ 916/621–5885 or 800/457–6279).

Golden Chain Council of the Mother Lode (Box 49, Newcastle 95658).

Nevada City Chamber of Commerce (132 Main St., Nevada City 95959, ☎ 916/265–2692 or 800/655–6569 in CA and NV).

Nevada County/Grass Valley Chamber of Commerce (248 Mill St., Grass Valley 95945, ☎ 916/273–4667 or 800/655–4667 in CA and NV).

Placer County Tourism Authority (13460 Lincoln Way, Auburn, take Forest Hill exit off I–80, ☎ 916/887–2111 or 800/427–6463).

Sacramento Convention and Visitors Bureau (1421 K St., Sacramento 95814, ☎ 916/264–7777).

Old Sacramento Visitor Information Center (1104 Front St., Old Sacramento, ☎ 916/442–7644).

Tuolumne County Visitors Bureau (Box 4020, 55 W. Stockton St., Sonora 95370, ☎ 209/533–4420 or 800/446–1333).

7 Lake Tahoe

Lake Tahoe is famous for its deep blue water and as the largest alpine lake on the continent. It stands up well to its reputation, despite crowded areas around the Nevada casinos. Lake Tahoe is just under a four-hour drive from San Francisco along I–80; the traffic to the lake on Friday afternoon and to San Francisco on Sunday is horrendous. If you plan to visit in winter, remember to carry chains in your car. Summertime is generally cooler here than in the foothills, though sometimes it does get hot. Luckily, there are lots of beaches where you can swim.

Updated by Deke Castleman

LAKE TAHOE, one of California's most beautiful natural attractions, lies 6,225 feet above sea level in the Sierra Nevada mountains, straddling the state line between California and Nevada. The border gives this popular resort region a split personality. About half of the visitors here arrive intent on low-key sightseeing, hiking, fishing, camping, and boating. The rest head directly for the Nevada side of the lake, where bargain dining and big-name entertainment draw customers into the glittering casinos. Tahoe is also a popular wedding and honeymoon destination, with chapels all around the lake where couples can get married with no waiting period or blood tests. On Valentine's Day, four times as many licenses are sold than on other days. Incidentally, the legal marrying age in California and Nevada is 18 years, but one must be 21 to gamble or drink.

Summer's cool temperatures offer respite from the heat in the surrounding deserts and valleys. Although swimming in Lake Tahoe is always brisk—68°F is about as warm as it gets—the lake's beaches are generally crowded in summer. Those who prefer solitude can escape to the many state parks, national forests, and protected tracts of wilderness that ring the 22-mile-long, 12-mile-wide lake. From mid-autumn to late spring, multitudes of skiers and winter-sports enthusiasts are attracted to Tahoe's 15 downhill skiing resorts and 11 cross-country centers—North America's largest concentration of skiing facilities. Ski resorts try to open by Thanksgiving, if only with machine-made snow, and operate through May or even later. Most accommodations, restaurants, and some parks are open year-round, although September and October, when crowds have thinned but the weather is still pleasant, may be the most satisfying time to visit Lake Tahoe.

The first white man to find this spectacular region was Captain John C. Fremont in 1844, guided by famous scout Kit Carson. Not long afterward, silver was discovered in Nevada's Comstock Lode at Virginia City, and as the bonanza hit, the Tahoe Basin's forests were leveled to provide lumber for mine-tunnel supports. By the turn of the century, wealthy Californians were building lakeside estates here, some of which survive. Improved roads brought the less affluent in the 1920s and 1930s, when modest, rustic bungalows began to fill the shoreline, where the woods had grown again. The first casinos opened in the 1940s. Ski resorts brought another development boom as the lake became a year-round destination.

Lake Tahoe's water is 99.7% pure, cleaner than drinking water in most U.S. cities. The water is so clear that you can see as deep as 75 feet into it. Over the last few decades, however, road construction and other building projects have washed soil and minerals into the lake, leading to a growth of algae that threatens its fabled clarity. After the environmental movement gained strength in the 1970s, a moratorium on new shoreline construction was declared and a master plan developed for growth.

During some summer weekends it seems that absolutely every tourist—100,000 at peak periods—is in a car on the one main road that circles the 72-mile shoreline, looking for historic sights, uncrowded beaches, parking places, restaurants, or motels. But the crowds and congestion don't exist at a vantage point overlooking Emerald Bay early in the morning, or on a trail in the national forests that ring the basin, or on a sunset cruise on the lake itself. At such moments, one can forget all the nearby glitz and commercial development and just drink in the beauty.

EXPLORING

The most common way to explore the Lake Tahoe area is to drive the 72-mile road that follows the shore, through wooded flatlands and past beaches, climbing to vistas on the rugged west side of the lake and descending to the busiest commercial developments and casinos. There are plenty of parks, picnic areas, and scenic lookouts to stop at along the way, and many hiking trails are accessible from the shoreline highway.

Although it's easy to do the entire circuit in good weather, we've divided the tour into two sections. If you're arriving on U.S. 50, you'll begin in South Lake Tahoe, on the southern shore; if you drive in on I–80 then Highway 89, you'll hit the northern shore of the lake first, at Tahoe City, then swing around the eastern shore, which lies in Nevada.

Numbers in the margin correspond to points of interest on the Lake Tahoe map.

U.S. 50 reaches the lake at **South Lake Tahoe,** the largest community on the lake. The road is lined with motels, lodges, and restaurants, but as you head west the lakefront route becomes Highway 89, and commercial development gives way to more wooded national-forest lands. You'll notice pleasant bike trails well off the road.

❶ At **Pope-Baldwin Recreation Area**, take in the Tallac Historic Site, where a museum and three magnificently restored estates allow visitors a glimpse of the lifestyles of the 1920s wealthy. Cultural events take place from June to September. The Valhalla Renaissance Festival, re-creating the arts, culture, and entertainments of the 15th and 16th centuries, is held at Camp Richardson in June (call the Tahoe Tallac Association at 916/542–4166 for information). Guided tours of the Pope House and a museum at the Baldwin Estate are available in summer. ☛ *Free to Tallac Historic site. Pope House tour $2 (days and times vary, reservations necessary,* ☎ *916/541–5227).* ⏲ *Year-round dawn–dusk (Tallac Historic Site). Recreation Area open late May–Oct., dawn–dusk. Museum open June–Labor Day, daily 10–4; Labor Day–Sept., daily 10–3.*

❷ The **Lake Tahoe Visitors Center** on Taylor Creek, operated by the U.S. Forest Service, offers far more than answers to questions. This stretch of lakefront is a microcosm of the area's natural history. You can visit the site of a Washoe Indian settlement; walk self-guided trails through meadow, marsh, and forest; and inspect the Stream Profile Chamber, an underground, underwater display with windows letting visitors look right into Taylor Creek (in the fall you may see spawning salmon digging their nests). For those who are driving a car around the lake, the center offers a free cassette player and a tape that tells about points of interest along the way. ☎ *In season 916/573–2674.* ⏲ *June–Sept. daily and Oct. weekends 8–5:30.*

★ ❸ The winding road next takes you to **Emerald Bay,** famed for its jewel-like shape and colors. The road is high above the lake at this point; from Emerald Bay Lookout you can survey the whole scene, which includes Fannette, Tahoe's only island. From the Emerald Bay **lookout**
★ a steep, mile-long trail leads down to **Vikingsholm,** a 38-room estate completed in 1929. The owner, Lora Knight, had this precise replica of a 1,200-year-old Viking castle built out of materials native to the area, without disturbing the existing trees. She furnished it with Scandinavian antiques and hired artisans to custom build period reproductions. The sod roof sprouts wildflowers each spring. There are picnic tables nearby and a sandy beach for strolling. Be warned: The

Lake Tahoe

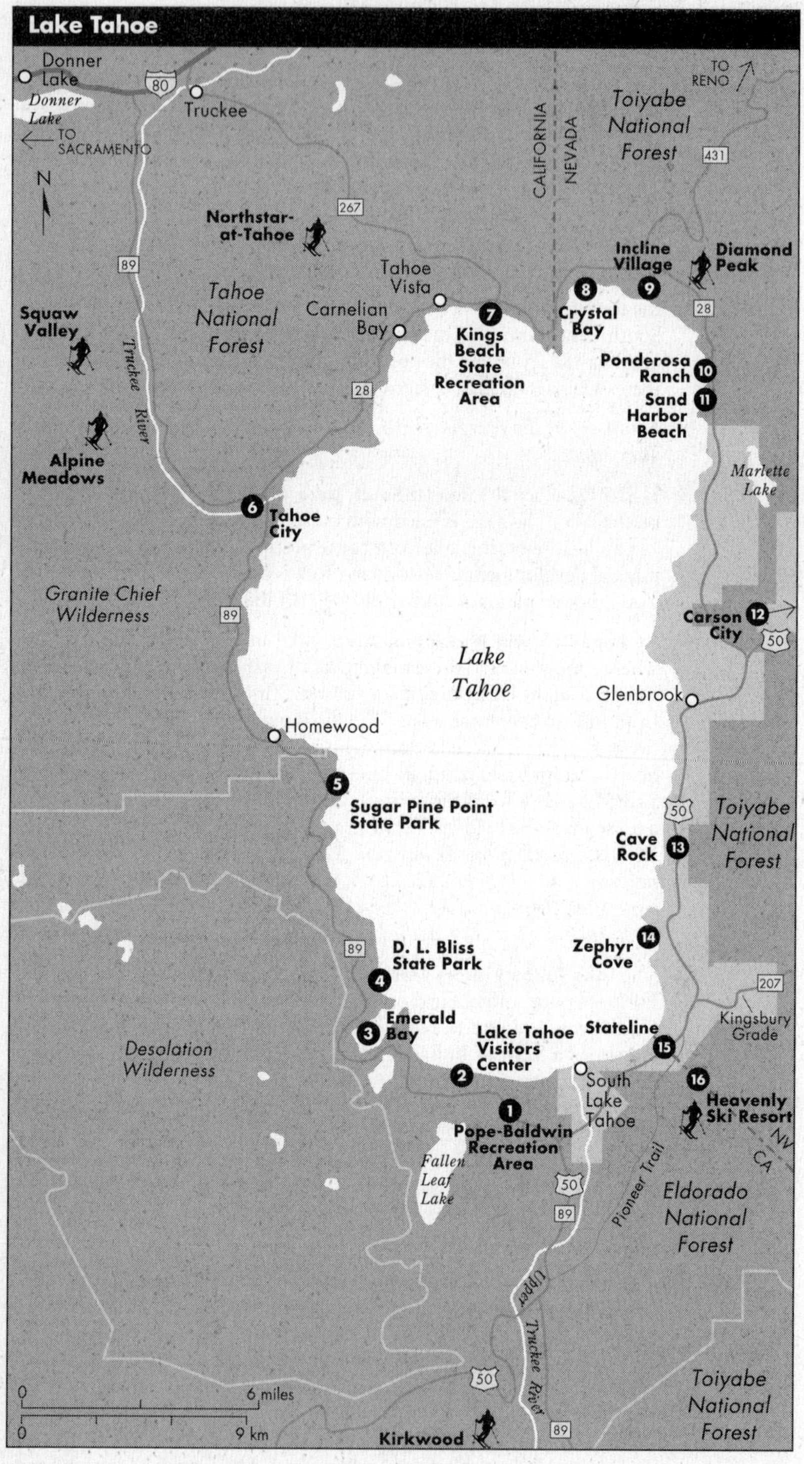
Donner Lake
Donner Lake
80
Truckee
TO SACRAMENTO
N
TO RENO
CALIFORNIA
NEVADA
Toiyabe National Forest
431
267
Northstar-at-Tahoe
89
Tahoe National Forest
Tahoe Vista
Carnelian Bay
Squaw Valley
Truckee River
28
Incline Village
Diamond Peak
28
8 Crystal Bay
9
7 Kings Beach State Recreation Area
Ponderosa Ranch 10
Sand Harbor Beach 11
Alpine Meadows
Marlette Lake
6 Tahoe City
Granite Chief Wilderness
89
Carson City 12
50
Lake Tahoe
Glenbrook
Homewood
5 Sugar Pine Point State Park
50
Toiyabe National Forest
Cave Rock 13
Zephyr Cove 14
89
D. L. Bliss State Park 4
207
Kingsbury Grade
3 Emerald Bay
Lake Tahoe Visitors Center
Stateline 15
Desolation Wilderness
2
South Lake Tahoe
16
Heavenly Ski Resort
1 Pope-Baldwin Recreation Area
NV
CA
Fallen Leaf Lake
Pioneer Trail
50
89
Eldorado National Forest
Upper Truckee River
50
0
6 miles
0
9 km
Kirkwood
89
Toiyabe National Forest

hike back up is steep. ☎ *916/525–7277.* ☛ *$2 adults, $1 children under 18.* ⏲ *Memorial Day–Labor Day, daily 10–4.*

4 Beyond Emerald Bay is **D. L. Bliss State Park,** which shares 6 miles of shoreline with the bay. At the north end of the park is **Rubicon Point,** which overlooks one of the lake's deepest spots. ☎ *916/525–7277.* ☛ *$5 per vehicle (day use).* ⏲ *Spring–fall.*

★ 5 The main attraction at **Sugar Pine Point State Park** is the **Ehrman Mansion,** a stately, stone-and-shingle 1903 summer home that displays the rustic aspirations of the era's wealthy residents. It is furnished in period style. ☎ *916/525–7232 year-round or 916/525–7982 in season.* ☛ *Free. State-park day-use fee: $5 per vehicle.* ⏲ *Memorial Day–Labor Day, daily 11–4.*

Tahoe City and the Nevada Shore

6 **Tahoe City** is a nice town to pass time in, with lots of stores and restaurants. The Truckee River, the lake's only outlet, flows through town. Before the severe drought of the late 1980s and early 1990s, you could look down and see the river's giant trout from **Fanny Bridge,** so called because you can usually see the backsides of rows of visitors leaning over the railing.

★ The **Gatekeeper's Log Cabin Museum** provides one of the best records of the area's past, displaying Washoe and Paiute artifacts as well as late-19th- to early 20th-century settlers' memorabilia. *130 W. Lake Blvd.,* ☎ *916/583–1762.* ☛ *Free.* ⏲ *May 15–Oct. 1, daily 11–5.*

The museum also oversees the nearby **Watson Cabin Living Museum,** a 1909 log cabin built by Robert M. Watson and his son and filled with turn-of-the-century furnishings. Costumed docents act out the daily life of a typical pioneer family. *560 N. Lake Blvd.,* ☎ *916/583–8717 or 916/583–1762.* ☛ *Free.* ⏲ *June 15–Labor Day, daily noon–4.*

At Tahoe City, Highway 89 turns north from the lake to Squaw Valley, Donner Lake, and Truckee (*see* Off the Beaten Track, *below*), while Highway 28 continues northeast around the lake. Traveling 8 miles in this direction on Highway 28 you will reach the 28-acre
7 **Kings Beach State Recreation Area**, one of the lakeshore parks open year-round.

TIME OUT The **Log Cabin Caffe** (8692 N. Lake Blvd., ☎ 916/546-7109) is a good choice for breakfast or lunch, serving health foods, sandwiches, ice cream, and freshly baked pastry.

You don't need a roadside marker to know when you've crossed from California into Nevada. The lake's water and the pine trees may be identical, but the flashing lights and elaborate marquees of casinos an-
8 nounce legal gambling with a bang. Right at the Nevada border, **Crystal Bay** has a cluster of four casinos; one, the **Cal-Neva Lodge** (*see* Lodging, *below*), is bisected by the state line. The next town is the re-
9 sort community of **Incline Village,** which has plenty of recreational diversions—hiking and biking trails, the area's greatest concentration of tennis courts, and a **Recreation Center** (980 Incline Way, ☎ 702/832–1300) with an eight-lane swimming pool, a cardiovascular-fitness area, a basketball court, a game room, and a snack bar. Highway 431 leads north out of Incline Village past the highest ski area in the region, Mt. Rose, and about 30 miles farther, to Reno.

★ 10 South of Incline Village on Highway 28 is the **Ponderosa Ranch,** a theme park inspired by the popular 1960s television series *Bonanza*. Attractions include the Cartwrights' ranch house, a western town, and a saloon. There's also a self-guided nature trail, free pony rides for children, and, if you're here from 8 to 9:30 in the morning, a breakfast hayride. ☎ *702/831–0691.* ☛ *$8.50 adults, $5.50 children 5–11 (children under 11 admitted free until mid-May), hayride $2.* ⏲ *Mid-Apr.–Oct., daily 9:30–5.*

★ 11 **Sand Harbor Beach** is one of the lake's finest and so popular it's sometimes filled to capacity by 11 AM on summer weekends. A pop-music festival is held here in July and a Shakespeare festival every August. *Festival information: Incline Village/Crystal Bay Visitors Bureau,* ☎ *702/832–1606 or 800/468–2463.*

Spooner Junction, where Highway 28 meets U.S. 50, offers several sightseeing options. If you turn east on U.S. 50, away from the lake, in 10 miles you reach U.S. 395, where you turn left and go 1 mile north to
12 **Carson City,** the capital of Nevada. It's one of the nation's smallest capital cities. Most of its historic buildings and other attractions are along U.S. 395, the main street through town. At the south end of town is the **Carson City Visitors Center** (1900 S. Carson St., ☎ 702/882–7474). About a half hour's drive northeast of Carson City (on Hwy. 342 off U.S. 50) is the fabled mining town of Virginia City, which has sites and activities of historical interest mixed in with touristy diversions.

If you continue south along the shore (now on U.S. 50 south), you'll
★ 13 pass through **Cave Rock,** 25 yards of solid stone. Tahoe Tessie, Lake Tahoe's version of the Loch Ness monster, is reputed to live in a cav-
14 ern below Cave Rock. Six miles farther south you'll come to **Zephyr Cove,** a tiny resort with a beach, marina, campground, picnic area, historic log lodge, and nearby riding stables.

A short distance past Zephyr Cove, Kingsbury Grade (Route 207) goes off to the east. This was originally a toll road used by wagon trains to get over the Sierras' crest. Now it leads to spectacular views of the Carson Valley. Turn left on Foothill Road (Route 206), which leads past **Walley's Hot Springs Resort** (2001 Foothill Rd., ☎ 702/782–8155), a small lodge with natural hot-spring pools (☛ $12; no children under 12). Beyond the resort you'll soon come to **Genoa** (population 250), the oldest settlement in Nevada. Along Main Street are some small museums and the state's oldest saloon.

Back on the lakeshore, you'll pass four major (and two minor) casi-
15 nos at **Stateline** before crossing back into California. Traveling southwest along U.S. 50, turn left at Ski Run Boulevard and drive up to the
16 **Heavenly Ski Resort.** Whether you're a skier or not, you'll want to ride
★ 2,000 feet up on the 50-passenger **Heavenly Tram,** which runs part way up the mountain, to 8,200 feet. There you'll find a memorable view of Lake Tahoe and the Nevada desert. When the weather's nice you can take one of three (successively more difficult) hikes around the mountaintop. ☎ *702/586–7000. Round-trip tram fare: $12 adults, $6 senior citizens and children under 12. Tram runs June–Sept., daily 10–10; Nov.–May, daily 9–4.*

TIME OUT At the top of the tram, **Monument Peak Cafe** (☎ 702/586-7000, ext. 6347), open daily during tram hours, offers basic American food and cafeteria service. It serves lunch, dinner, and Sunday brunch in summer and lunch in winter.

What to See and Do with Children

With its wealth of outdoor recreation, Lake Tahoe is an easy place to keep children and teenagers entertained. All the ski areas offer children's ski programs and most have child-care facilities. Although children are not allowed in the casinos' gambling areas, all these establishments have game arcades and some, like the Hyatt Regency in Incline Village, offer special youth-oriented activities all day. Among the lake's attractions, the **Ponderosa Ranch** (*see* Exploring, *above*) is usually a big hit with kids.

Commons Beach in the middle of Tahoe City has a playground for children. The **North Tahoe Beach Center** has a 26-foot hot tub, open year-round; in summer, the heat is turned down until 1 PM for youngsters. The beach has an enclosed swim area and four sand volleyball courts. This popular spot for families has a barbecue and picnic area, a fitness center, windsurfing and nonmotorized boat rentals, a snack bar, and a clubhouse with games. *7860 N. Lake Blvd., Kings Beach,* ☎ *916/546–2566. Daily fee: $7 adults, $3.50 children under 12.*

Magic Carpet Golf. This miniature golf course, video arcade, and electronic shooting gallery attracts all ages. *5167 Northlake Blvd., Carnelian Bay,* ☎ *916/546–4279; 2455 U.S. 50, S. Lake Tahoe,* ☎ *916/541–3787.* ☛ *$4 for 19 holes, $5.50 for 28 holes.* ⏲ *Easter–Nov., daily 10 AM–11 PM.*

In summer the **Lake Tahoe Visitors Center** (*see* Exploring, *above*) sets up discovery walks and nighttime campfires, with singing and marshmallow roasts.

Off the Beaten Track

Donner Memorial State Park (off I–80, 2 mi west of Truckee) commemorates the Donner Party, a group of 89 westward-bound pioneers who were trapped here in the winter of 1846–47 in snow 22 feet deep. Only 47 survived, some by cannibalism and others by eating animal hides. The Immigrant Museum offers a slide show hourly about the Donner Party's plight. Other displays relate the history of other settlers and of railroad development through the Sierras. ☎ *916/582–7892.* ☛ *$2 adults, $1 children 6–12.* ⏲ *Sept.–May, daily 10–4; June–Aug., daily 10–5; closed Thanksgiving and Dec. 25.*

Old West facades line the main street of nearby **Truckee,** a favorite stopover for people traveling from the Bay Area to the north shore of Lake Tahoe. Fine-art galleries and upscale boutiques are plentiful, but you will also find low-key diners, discount skiwear, and an old-fashioned five-and-dime store. For a map outlining a walking tour of historic Truckee, stop by the information booth in the Amtrak depot (Railroad St. at Commercial Rd.).

On the **Adventure Challenge Course,** set among 40- to 50-foot-high pines with riggings and cables, participants attempt feats of physical derring-do while safely tethered to mountaineering gear. Corporate groups, honeymoon couples, and families—all sorts of people—test their prowess with such stunts as jumping off a tall treetop holding a trapeze line that zips you to the ground and climbing an artificial wall. The course is a great confidence builder and a whole lot of fun. *Northstar Village Resort, off Hwy. 267, Truckee,* ☎ *916/562–1010 or 916/562–2285 direct; or contact Adventure Associates, 1030 Merced St., Berkeley, CA 94707,* ☎ *510/525–9391,* FAX *510/525–4673.* ☛ *$45 all ages.* ⏲ *To public July–Sept., daily noon–5; May–June and Oct. for groups only.*

SHOPPING

In South Lake Tahoe there's some good shopping south of town at the intersection of U.S. 50 and Highway 89 at the **Factory Outlet Stores.** In Tahoe City, try **Boatworks Mall** (780 N. Lake Blvd.), **Cobblestone Mall** (475 N. Lake Blvd.), and the **Roundhouse Mall** (700 N. Lake Blvd.).

SPORTS AND THE OUTDOORS

For most of the popular sports at Lake Tahoe, summer or winter, you won't have to bring much equipment with you, an important factor if you're traveling by air or have limited space. Bicycles and boats are readily available for rent at Lake Tahoe. Golf clubs can be rented at several area courses. All the major ski resorts have rental shops.

Golf

These courses in the Lake Tahoe area have food facilities, pro shops, cart rentals, and putting greens. **Edgewood Tahoe** (U.S. 50 and Lake Pkwy., behind Horizon Casino, Stateline, ☎ 702/588–3566) is an 18-hole, par-72 course with a driving range. Green fees include cart; the course is open 7–3. **Incline Championship** (955 Fairway Blvd., Incline Village, ☎ 702/832–1144) is another 18-hole, par-72 course with a driving range. Carts are mandatory. **Incline Executive** (690 Wilson Way, Incline Village, ☎ 702/832–1150) has 18 holes but is much easier: Par is 58. Carts are mandatory. **Lake Tahoe Golf Course** (U.S. 50 between Lake Tahoe Airport and Meyers, ☎ 916/577–0788) has 18 holes, par 70, and a driving range. **Northstar-at-Tahoe** (Hwy. 267 between Truckee and Kings Beach, ☎ 916/562–2490) has 18 holes, par 72, with a driving range. Carts are mandatory before 12:30. **Old Brockway Golf Course** (Hwys. 267 and 28, Kings Beach, ☎ 916/546–9909) is a nine-hole, par-35 course. **Resort at Squaw Creek Golf Course** (400 Squaw Creek Rd., Olympic Valley, ☎ 916/583–6300) is an 18-hole championship course designed by Robert Trent Jones, Jr. It's open 8–dusk. **Tahoe City Golf Course** (Hwy. 28, Tahoe City, ☎ 916/583–1516) is a nine-hole, par-33 course. Golfers use pull carts here. **Tahoe Paradise Golf Course** (U.S. 50 near Meyers, South Lake Tahoe, ☎ 916/577–2121) has 18 holes, par 66.

Hiking and Camping

Desolation Wilderness, a vast 63,473-acre preserve of granite peaks, glacial valleys, subalpine forests, the Rubicon River, and more than 50 lakes, offers hiking, fishing, and camping. Trails begin outside the wilderness preserve; Meeks Bay and Echo Lake are two starting points. Permits (free) are required for access and can be obtained from the U.S. Forest Service's **Lake Tahoe Visitors Center** (*see* Exploring, *above*), the **Desolation Wilderness** headquarters (870 Emerald Bay Rd., Suite 1, South Lake Tahoe 96150, ☎ 916/573–2600 or 916/573–2674), and **El Dorado National Forest** (☎ 916/644–6048). **D. L. Bliss State Park** (*see* Exploring, *above*) has 168 family campsites; the fee is $14 per campsite. There's a $5 day-use fee for entering the park; the park is closed in winter.

Scuba Diving

Scuba diving is a surprisingly popular activity at Lake Tahoe. Groups and clubs frequent Sand Harbor, the Rubicon River, and Emerald Bay, which are easily accessible. The water is clear enough to divulge shipwrecks, marine life, and incredible geologic forms. The **Diving Edge** (176 Shady La., Stateline, ☎ 702/588–5262) is a full-service PADI dive center offering rentals and instruction.

Skiing

The Tahoe Basin boasts the largest concentration of skiing in the country: 15 downhill ski resorts and 11 cross-country ski centers, with more cross-country skiing available on thousands of acres of public forests and parklands. The major resorts are listed below, but other, smaller places also offer excellent skiing. To save money, look for ski packages offered by lodges and resorts; some include interchangeable lift tickets that allow you to try different slopes. Midweek packages are usually lower in price, and most resorts offer family discounts. Free shuttle-bus service is available between most ski resorts and hotels and lodges.

DOWNHILL SKIING

Alpine Meadows Ski Area is a ski cruiser's paradise, with skiing from two peaks—Ward, a great open bowl, and Scott, for tree-lined runs. All main runs are groomed nightly. Alpine has some of Tahoe's most reliable skiing conditions and an excellent snowmaking system; it's usually the first in the area to open each November and the last to close, in May or even June. The base lodge contains rentals, a cafeteria, restaurant-lounge, bar, bakery, sports shop, ski schools for skiers of all skill levels and for skiers with disabilities, and a children's snow school; there's also an area for overnight RV parking. Beginner runs are close to the base lodge. Ski from every lift; there are no "transportation" lifts and snowboarding is prohibited. *6 mi northwest of Tahoe City off Hwy. 89, 13 mi south of I–80, Box 5279, Tahoe City, CA 96145, ☏ 916/583–4232; snow phone, ☏ 916/581–8374; information, ☏ 800/441–4423; FAX 916/583–0963. 2,000 acres, rated 25% easier, 40% more difficult, 35% most difficult. Longest run 2½ mi, base 6,835′, summit 8,637′. Lifts: 2 high-speed quads, 2 triples, 7 doubles, 1 surface.*

Diamond Peak has a fun, family atmosphere with many special programs and affordable rates. A learn-to-ski package, with rentals, lesson, and lift ticket, is $29; a parent-child ski package is $38, with each additional child's lift ticket $5. There is a half-pipe run just for snowboarding. Snowmaking covers 80% of the mountain, and runs are well groomed nightly. The ride up mile-long Crystal chair rewards you with the best views of the lake from any ski area. Diamond Peak is less crowded than some of the larger areas, and it offers free shuttles to lodging in nearby Incline Village. There's Nordic skiing here, too (*see* Cross-Country Skiing, *below*). *1210 Ski Way, Incline Village, NV 89450, off Hwy. 28 (Country Club Dr. to Ski Way), ☏ 702/832–1177 or 800/468–2463, FAX 702/832–1281. 655 acres, rated 18% beginner, 49% intermediate, 33% advanced. Longest run 2½ mi, base 6,700′, summit 8,540′. Lifts: 6 doubles, 1 quad.*

Heavenly Ski Resort gives skiers plenty of choices. Go up the Heavenly Tram on the California side (*see* Exploring, *above*) to ski the imposing face of Gunbarrel or the gentler runs at the top, or ride the Sky Express high-speed quad chair to the summit and choose wide cruising runs or steep tree skiing. Or drive over the Kingsbury Grade to the Boulder or Stagecoach lodges and stay on the Nevada-side runs, which are usually less crowded. Snowmaking covers both sides, top to bottom, for generally good conditions. The ski school, like everything else at Heavenly, is large and offers a program for everyone, beginner to expert. *Ski Run Blvd., Box 2180, Stateline, NV 89449, ☏ 916/541–1330 or 800/243–2836; snow information, ☏ 916/541–7544; FAX 916/541–2643. 4,800 acres, rated 20% beginner, 45% intermediate, 35% expert. Longest run 5½ mi, base 6,540′, summit 10,040′. Lifts: 24 total, including 3 high-speed quads.*

Kirkwood Ski Resort lies 36 miles south of Lake Tahoe in an Alpine-village setting, surrounded by incredible mountain scenery. Most of the runs off the top are rated expert only, but intermediate and beginning skiers have their own vast bowl, where they can ski through trees or wide-open spaces. This is a destination resort, with 120 condominiums, several shops, and restaurants in the base village, overnight RV parking, and a shuttle bus to Lake Tahoe. There's snowboarding on all runs, with lessons, rentals, and sales available. For Nordic skiing, *see* Cross-Country Skiing, *below. Hwy. 88, Box 1, Kirkwood, CA 95646,* ☎ *209/258–6000; lodging information, 209/258–7000; snow information, 209/258–3000;* FAX *209/258–8899. 2,000 acres, rated 15% beginner, 50% intermediate, 35% advanced. Longest run 2½ mi, base 7,800′, summit 9,800′. Lifts: 10 chairs, 1 surface.*

Northstar-at-Tahoe is the Sierras' most complete destination resort, with lots of activity in summer and winter. The center of action is the picturesque Village Mall, a concentration of restaurants, shops, recreation facilities, and lodging options from hotel rooms to condos and houses. Two northeast-facing, wind-protected bowls offer some of the best powder skiing around, including steep chutes and long cruising runs. Top to bottom snowmaking and intense grooming assure good conditions. For Nordic skiing, *see* Cross-Country Skiing, *below. Off Hwy. 267 between Truckee and North Shore, Box 129, Truckee, CA 96160, lodging reservations,* ☎ *916/562–1010 or 800/533–6787; snow information, 916/562–1330;* FAX *916/562–2215, 1,800 acres, rated 25% beginner, 50% intermediate, 25% advanced. Longest run 2.9 mi, base 6,400′, summit 8,600′. Lifts: 6-passenger express gondola, 3 doubles, 3 triples, 2 tows, 4 high-speed quads.*

Squaw Valley USA was the site of the 1960 Olympics. The immense resort has changed significantly since then, but the skiing is still first-class, with steep chutes and cornices on six Sierra peaks. Beginners delight in riding the tram to the top, where there is a huge plateau of gentle runs. At the top of the tram, you can find the High Camp Bath and Tennis Club in the lodge, with impressive views from its restaurants, bars, and outdoor ice-skating pavilion. Base facilities are clustered around the Village Mall, with shops, dining, condos, hotels, and lodges. The valley golf course doubles as a cross-country ski facility. On the other side of the golf course is the Resort at Squaw Creek, with its own run and quad chairlift that runs to Squaw's ski terrain. *Hwy. 89, 5 mi northwest of Tahoe City, Squaw Valley USA, CA 96146,* ☎ *916/583–6985; reservations, 800/545–4350; snow information, 916/583–6955;* FAX *916/581–7106. 4,000 acres, rated 25% beginner, 45% intermediate, 30% advanced. Longest run 3 mi, base 6,200′, summit 9,050′. Lifts: 6-passenger gondola, cable car, 3 quads, 8 triples, 15 doubles, 5 surface.*

CROSS-COUNTRY SKIING

With 11 areas to choose from on mountaintops and in valleys, this is a Nordic skier's paradise. For the ultimate in groomed conditions, there is America's largest cross-country ski resort, **Royal Gorge** (Box 1100, Soda Springs, CA 95728, ☎ 916/426–3871), which offers 197 miles of 18-foot-wide track for all abilities, 88 trails on 9,172 acres, two ski schools, and 10 warming huts, as well as four cafés, two hotels, and a hot tub and sauna. **Diamond Peak at Ski Incline** (☎ 702/832–1177) has 22 miles of groomed track with skating lanes. The trail system goes from 7,400 feet to 9,100 feet with endless wilderness to explore. The entrance is off Highway 431. **Kirkwood Ski Resort** (*see* Downhill Skiing, *above*) has 50 miles of groomed-track skiing, with skating lanes, instruction, and rentals. **Northstar-at-Tahoe** (*see* Downhill Skiing, *above*) gives cross-country skiers access to Alpine ski slopes for telemarking and also provides 40 miles of groomed, tracked trails with a wide skating lane. There's a ski shop, rentals, and instruction.

Skiers who want to tour the backcountry should check with the **U.S. Forest Service** (☎ 916/587–2158) prior to entering the wilderness for weather, conditions, avalanche warnings, and other information.

Sledding and Snow-Mobiling

There are five public **Sno-Park** areas in the vicinity, some for snowmobiling and cross-country skiing, as well as sledding. All are maintained by the Department of Parks and Recreation, and to use them you need to obtain a permit in advance. Call the department at 916/653–8569 or contact the Lake Tahoe Visitors Center (*see* Exploring, *above*).

Several companies in the area offer snowmobile tours. **Snowmobiling Unlimited** (Box 460, Carnelian Bay 96140, ☎ 916/583–5858), one of the area's oldest operators, offers guided tours and rentals, as well as a track to zoom around on, for $30 per half hour, $40 per hour for a single snowmobile and $60 for a double.

Swimming

There are 36 public beaches on Lake Tahoe. Swimming is permitted at many of them, but since Tahoe is a high mountain lake with fairly rugged winters, only the hardiest will be interested, except in midsummer. Even then the water warms to only 68°F. Lifeguards are on duty at some of the swimming beaches, and yellow buoys mark safe areas where motorboats are not permitted. Opening and closing dates for beaches vary with the climate and available park-service personnel. Parking fees range from $1 to $4.

GAMBLING

Nevada's major casinos are also full-service hotels and resorts, and they offer discounted lodging packages throughout the year. Five are clustered on a strip of U.S. 50 in Stateline—Caesars, Harrah's, Harvey's, Horizon, and Lakeside. Four others stand on the north shore: the Hyatt Regency, Cal-Neva, Tahoe Biltmore, and Crystal Bay Club. Open 24 hours a day, 365 days a year, these casinos offer more than 150 table games (craps, blackjack, roulette, baccarat, poker, keno, pai gow, bingo, and big six), race and sports books, and thousands of slot machines—1,750, for instance, at Harrah's. There is no charge to enter and there is no dress code.

Of the north-shore casinos, the Hyatt offers the most amenities. Frank Sinatra was once a part-owner of the Cal-Neva Lodge, one of Tahoe's original casinos. The other two are small, not luxurious properties.

Stateline is where the major Tahoe action takes place. The casinos share an atmosphere of garish neon and noise, but air-conditioning eliminates the smoky pall of the past, and today there are no-smoking areas. Each casino has its own distinctive decor in the lobby and common areas. Caesars is Greco-Roman, with lots of marble, real and simulated. Harrah's uses dark wood, red fabrics, and mirrors to the max. Harvey's has an elegant Continental decor that uses soft blues, crystal light fixtures, and period furnishings. The Horizon has a beaux arts look, very light (but only on the first level). Lakeside, the smallest, looks western-rustic, using dark wood and stone. Bill's, a "junior" casino owned by Harrah's (no lodging, but there's a McDonald's restaurant on the premises), appeals to younger and less-experienced players because it tends to have lower stakes.

The hotel-casinos attract visitors with shows, celebrity entertainers, and restaurants and lounges open around the clock. Gamblers are offered complimentary beverages. Valet parking, in enclosed garages, is technically free, but a $1–$2 tip is customary. High-stakes gamblers generally take advantage of the valet service; parking-lot robberies, though hardly epidemic, are not unheard of. In addition to the big casinos, in Nevada visitors will find slot machines in every conceivable location, from gas stations to supermarkets.

DINING AND LODGING

Dining

Restaurants at Lake Tahoe range from rustic rock-and-wood decor to elegant French, with stops along the way for Swiss chalet and spare modern. The food, too, is varied and may include delicate Continental or nouvelle-Californian sauces, mesquite- and olive-wood-grilled specialties, and wild game in season. On weekends and in high season, expect a long wait to be seated in the more popular restaurants. During slow seasons some places may close temporarily or limit their hours, so call ahead to verify.

Casinos use their restaurants to attract gaming customers, so their marquees might tout "$5.99 prime rib dinners" or "$2.99 full breakfasts." Some of these specials may not be top quality (meat is rarely "prime," and service is usually from a buffet), but the finer restaurants in casinos generally offer good food, service, and atmosphere at reasonable prices.

In Stateline, thanks to the cluster of hotel-casinos, there are no fewer than 22 restaurants concentrated in a block or two. Other choices on the south shore are limited to pizza, Mexican food, delis, and fast-food franchises, except for a handful of fine-dining establishments.

WHAT TO WEAR

Unless otherwise noted, dress is casual for all restaurants. Even the most elegant and expensive Tahoe eating places welcome customers in casual clothes—not surprising in this year-round vacation mecca—but don't expect to be served in a very expensive restaurant if you're barefoot and wearing beach clothes.

CATEGORY	COST*
$$$$	over $35
$$$	$25–$35
$$	$15–$25
$	under $15

**per person for a three-course meal, excluding drinks, service, and 7%–7¼% tax*

Lodging

Quiet inns on the water, motel rooms in the heart of the casino area, rooms at the casinos themselves, lodges close to ski runs—there's a wide range of lodging at Lake Tahoe. Just remember that during summer and ski season the lake is crowded; plan in advance. Spring and fall give you a little more leeway and lower—sometimes significantly lower—rates. Price categories listed below reflect high-season rates. Lake Tahoe has two telephone reservation services: **Tahoe North Visitors and Convention Bureau** (☎ 800/824–6348) and, for the south shore, the **Lake Tahoe Visitors Authority** (☎ 800/288–2463).

CATEGORY	COST*
$$$$	over $100
$$$	$75–$100
$$	$50–$75
$	under $50

**All prices are for a standard double room, excluding 9%–10% tax.*

Carnelian Bay

DINING

$$ **Gar Woods Grill and Pier.** This elegant but casual lakeside restaurant recalls the lake's past, with light-pine paneling and floor-to-ceiling picture windows overlooking the lake, a river-rock fireplace, and boating photographs. It specializes in grilled foods and pasta. It also serves Sunday brunch. ✕ *5000 N. Lake Blvd.,* ☎ *916/546–3366. Reservations accepted. AE, MC, V.*

Crystal Bay

LODGING

$$–$$$$ **Cal-Neva Lodge.** All the rooms in this hotel on Highway 28 at Crystal Bay have views of Lake Tahoe and the mountains. Most have recently been remodeled. There is an arcade with video games for children, cabaret entertainment, and, in addition to rooms in the main hotel, 12 cabins with living rooms and seven two-bedroom chalets. 🏨 *2 Stateline Rd., Box 368, 89402,* ☎ *702/832–4000 or 800/225–6382,* FAX *702/831–9007. 220 rooms. Restaurant, coffee shop, pool, hot tub, sauna, tennis courts, casino, 3 chapels. AE, D, DC, MC, V.*

Incline Village

DINING

$ **Azzara's.** This typical Italian trattoria with light, inviting decor serves a dozen pasta dishes and a variety of pizzas, as well as chicken, lamb, veal, and shrimp—but no beef. Dinners include soup or salad, vegetable, pasta, and garlic bread. This is a no-smoking restaurant. ✕ *930 Tahoe Blvd., Incline Center Mall,* ☎ *702/831–0346. MC, V.*

$ **Stanley's Restaurant and Lounge.** With its intimate bar and pleasant dining room, this casual local favorite is a good bet any time for straightforward American fare on the hearty side (barbecued pork ribs, beef Stroganoff). Lighter bites, such as seafood Cobb salad, are also available, along with ample breakfasts; try the eggs Benedict or a chili-cheese omelet. There's a deck for outdoor dining in summer and live music on Friday night. ✕ *941 Tahoe Blvd.,* ☎ *702/831–9944. No reservations. AE, MC, V.*

DINING AND LODGING

$$$–$$$$ **Hyatt Lake Tahoe Resort Hotel/Casino.** Some of the rooms in this luxurious, four-star hotel on the lake have fireplaces, but all the accommodations here are top-notch. A children's program and rental bicycles are available. The restaurants are Lone Eagle Grille (Continental, with steak, seafood, pasta, and rotisserie dishes), Ciao Mein Trattoria (Asian-Italian), and Sierra Cafe (open 24 hours). 🏨 *Lakeshore and Country Club Dr., Box 3239, 89450,* ☎ *702/831–1111 or 800/233–1234,* FAX *702/831–7508. 460 rooms. 2 restaurants, coffee shop, lounge, room service, pool, spa, 2 saunas, tennis courts, health club, casino, laundry service, valet parking. AE, D, DC, MC, V.*

Olympic Valley

DINING AND LODGING

$$$$ **Resort at Squaw Creek.** Adjacent to the base of Squaw Valley, this newer resort complex features a main lodge, an outdoor arcade of shops and boutiques, and a 405-room hotel. The decor suggests an opulent Sierra

lodge. Nearly half of the guest rooms are suites; some have a fireplace and full kitchen, and all feature original art, custom furnishings, and good views. Outdoors, just a few feet from the hotel entrance, you can get on a triple chairlift to Squaw Valley's slopes. The restaurants include Glissandi, for haute cuisine; the buffet-style Cascades; Montagne, the Italian room; and Sweet Potatoes, a pastry-and-coffee shop. There's also Bullwhackers Pub, a sports bar serving steak and seafood. ▣ *400 Squaw Creek Rd., 96146,* ☎ *916/583–6300,* FAX *916/581–6632. 405 rooms. 4 restaurants, bar, 3 pools, 4 hot tubs, sauna, 18-hole golf course, tennis center, exercise room, ice-skating. AE, D, DC, MC, V.*

South Lake Tahoe

DINING

$$–$$$ **Christiania Inn.** Located at the base of Heavenly Ski Resort's tram, this antiques-filled bed-and-breakfast is an old favorite for fine dining. The American-Continental menu emphasizes fresh seafood, prime beef, and veal. There's an extensive wine list. Midday buffets are served on holidays, and appetizers, soups, and salads are available in the lounge daily after 1:30, winter only. ✕ *3819 Saddle Rd.,* ☎ *916/544–7337. Reservations advised. MC, V.*

$$ **Nepheles.** In a quaint old house with stained-glass windows, this restaurant is on the road to the Heavenly Ski Resort. The creative California cuisine emphasizes fresh food freshly prepared. Entrées range from ahi with Asian peanut sauce and Indonesian ketchup to filet mignon with champagne-cognac cream sauce; in between are such standbys as baby back ribs and beef Stroganoff. Appetizers include Brie en brioche (Brie in pastry), escargots, and swordfish egg rolls. ✕ *1169 Ski Run Blvd.,* ☎ *916/544–8130. Reservations advised. AE, D, DC, MC, V. No lunch.*

$$ **Swiss Chalet.** The Swiss decor is carried out with great consistency. The Continental menu features Swiss specialties, charbroiled steaks, veal, fresh seafood, and homemade pastries. ✕ *2544 U.S. 50,* ☎ *916/544–3304. Reservations advised. AE, MC, V. Closed Nov. 25–Dec. 5. No lunch.*

$ **Red Hut Waffle Shop.** A vintage Tahoe diner, all chrome and red plastic, the Red Hut is a tiny place with a dozen counter stools and a few booths. It's a traditional breakfast spot for locals, who are attracted by the huge omelets and other good food. ✕ *2749 U.S. 50,* ☎ *916/541–9024. No reservations. No dinner. No credit cards.*

$ **Scusa!** This intimate Italian restaurant on the road to the Heavenly Ski Resort has smart, modern decor and delectable pasta. Besides the wide range of pasta dishes, there are hearty calzones, exotic pizzas, steak, chicken, and fresh fish entrées. The panfried calamari with red peppers and capers are a treat, and don't pass up the rosemary-flavored flat bread, baked fresh daily. A good wine list is presented. This is a no-smoking restaurant. ✕ *1142 Ski Run Blvd.,* ☎ *916/542–0100. Reservations advised. AE, MC, V. No lunch.*

DINING AND LODGING

$$$$ ★ **Embassy Suites.** In this opulent all-suite hotel, decorated in Sierra-lodge style, fountains and waterwheels splash in the soaring, nine-story atriums, where complimentary full breakfasts and evening cocktails are served daily. Glass elevators rise to guest suites, each with a living room, dining area, and separate bedroom. Restaurants include Pasquale's Pizza, Zachary's (casual Continental dining), and Julie's Deli. Turtles nightclub is on the ground floor. ▣ *4130 Lake Tahoe Blvd., 96150,* ☎ *916/544–5400 or 800/362–2779,* FAX *916/544–4900. 400 suites. 3 restaurants, indoor pool, spa, exercise room, nightclub, valet parking. AE, D, DC, MC, V.*

LODGING

$$$–$$$$ ★ **Inn by the Lake.** This luxury motel across the road from the beach is far from the flashy casinos but connected to them by free shuttle bus. The rooms and bathrooms are spacious and comfortable, furnished in contemporary style (blond oak and pale peach). All rooms have balconies; some have lake views, wet bars, and in-room kitchens. Room rates include Continental breakfast, and a senior-citizen discount is available. *3300 Lake Tahoe Blvd., 96150, 916/542–0330 or 800/877–1466, FAX 916/541–6596. 99 rooms. Pool, sauna, spa, bicycles, coin laundry. AE, D, DC, MC, V.*

$$$–$$$$ **Tahoe Seasons Resort.** This resort, among pine trees on the side of a mountain across from the Heavenly Ski Resort, has outfitted most rooms with a fireplace, and every room with a whirlpool and minikitchen. Rooms are done in teal and contemporary decor; all beds are queen-size. *3901 Saddle Rd., 96157, 916/541–6700, 916/541–6010, or 800/540–4874; FAX 916/541–0653. 183 suites. Restaurant, lounge, refrigerators, pool, hot tub, tennis courts, volleyball, indoor parking, valet garage, airport shuttle. AE, DC, MC, V.*

$$–$$$$ **Forest Inn Suites.** The location is excellent—5½ acres bordering a pine forest, a half block from Harrah's and Harvey's, and adjacent to a supermarket, cinema, and shops. Once considered old and staid, this property has changed its image to modern and dynamic with an extensive remodeling in the mid-1990s, which included redecorated rooms, and new landscaping and lobby. Ski rentals are available and a free shuttle to Heavenly Valley ski area is provided. *1101 Park Ave., Box 4300, 96150, 916/541–6655; in CA, 800/822–5950; FAX 916/544–3135. 124 units. Kitchens, 2 pools, 2 hot tubs, putting green, exercise room, health club, volleyball, boating, bicycles, coin laundry. AE, D, MC, V.*

$$–$$$$ **Lakeland Village Beach and Ski Resort.** A town house–condominium complex on 1,000 feet of private beach, Lakeland Village has a wide range of accommodations: studios, suites, and town houses, all with kitchens and fireplaces. *3535 Lake Tahoe Blvd., 96150, 916/544–1685 or 800/822–5969, FAX 916/544–0193. 208 units. Kitchens, 2 pools, wading pool, hot tub, 2 saunas, tennis courts, beach, boating, fishing, coin laundry. AE, MC, V.*

$–$$$$ **Travelodge.** There are three members of this national chain of well-run, clean budget lodges in South Lake Tahoe, all of them convenient to casinos, shopping, and recreation. All have some no-smoking rooms, and baby-sitting is available. Free local calls, HBO, and in-room coffee add to the budget appeal. *3489 U.S. 50 at Bijou Center, 96150, 916/544–5266 or 800/982–1466, FAX 916/544–6985, 59 rooms; 4011 U.S 50, Stateline 96150, 916/544–6000 or 800/982–3466, FAX 916/544–6869, 50 rooms; 4003 U.S. 50, South Lake Tahoe 96150, 916/541–5000 or 800/982–2466, FAX 916/544–6910, 66 rooms. Pool at each; Bijou Center has restaurant. AE, D, DC, MC, V.*

$$$ ★ **Best Western Station House Inn.** This pleasant inn has won design awards for its exterior and interior. The rooms are nicely appointed, with king- and queen-size beds and double-vanity bathrooms. The location is good, near a private beach yet close to the casinos. American breakfast is complimentary October–May, and a senior-citizen discount is available. *901 Park Ave., 96150, 916/542–1101 or 800/822–5953, FAX 916/542–1714. 102 rooms. Restaurant, lounge, pool, hot tub. AE, D, DC, MC, V.*

$$–$$$ **Best Western Lake Tahoe Inn.** Located near Harrah's Casino on U.S. 50, this large motel is nicely situated on 6 acres, with gardens and the Heavenly Ski Resort directly behind. Rooms are modern and decorated in soothing colors. *4110 Lake Tahoe Blvd., 96150, 916/541–*

2010 or 800/528–1234, FAX 916/542–1428. 400 rooms. Restaurant, lounge, 2 pools, hot tub, valet parking. AE, D, DC, MC, V.

$$ **Royal Valhalla Motor Lodge.** On the lake, at Lakeshore Boulevard and Stateline Avenue, this motel has simple, modern rooms, with queen-size beds and private balconies. There are elevators and some covered parking. It's popular with families because of its two- and three-bedroom suites with complete kitchens. Continental breakfast is complimentary, and a senior-citizen discount is available. *4104 Lakeshore Blvd., Box GG, 96157, ☎ 916/544–2233 or 800/999–4104, FAX 916/544–1436. 100 rooms. Pool, hot tub, coin laundry. AE, DC, MC, V.*

$–$$ ★ **Best Tahoe West Inn.** A long-established motel proud of its repeat business, Tahoe West is three blocks from the beach and downtown casinos. The exterior is rustic, rooms are neatly furnished, and beds are queen-size. Twelve rooms have kitchenette. Coffee and doughnuts are served in the lobby. Free shuttle to casinos and ski areas is provided. *4107 Pine Blvd., 96150, ☎ 916/544–6455 or 800/522–1021; in CA, 800/700–8246; FAX 916/544–0508. 60 rooms. Pool, hot tub, sauna, beach. AE, D, DC, MC, V.*

Stateline

DINING

$$–$$$ **Chart House.** It's worth the drive up the steep grade to see the view from here—try to arrive for sunset. The American menu of steak and seafood is complemented by an abundant salad bar. There is a children's menu. ✕ *329 Kingsbury Grade, ☎ 702/588–6276. Reservations accepted. AE, D, DC, MC, V. No lunch.*

$$–$$$ ★ **Llewellyn's Restaurant.** At the top of Harvey's, Llewellyn's deserves special mention. Elegantly decorated in blond wood and pastels, it offers one of the best views of Lake Tahoe from almost all tables. Dinner entrées—seafood, meat, and poultry—are served with unusual accompaniments, such as sturgeon in potato crust with saffron sauce, or veal with polenta, herbs, and pancetta. Lunches are reasonably priced, with gourmet selections as well as hamburgers. The adjacent bar (with the same view) is comfortable. ✕ *Harvey's Resort, U.S. 50, ☎ 702/588–2411 or 800/648–3361. Reservations accepted. AE, D, DC, MC, V.*

DINING AND LODGING

$$$$ **Harrah's Tahoe Hotel/Casino.** Harrah's is a luxurious 18-story hotel-casino on U.S. 50 in the casino area. All guest rooms have refrigerators (by request), private bars, and two full bathrooms, each with a television and telephone. All rooms have views of the lake and the mountains, but the least-obstructed views are from rooms on higher floors. There is an enclosed children's arcade on the lower level. Top-name entertainment is presented in the South Shore Room. Among its restaurants, the Summit (reservations advised, jacket and tie required) is a standout, offering romantic dining with spectacular views from the 16th floor. The menu changes nightly and includes creatively presented salads; lamb, venison, or seafood entrées with delicate sauces; and sensuous desserts. Other restaurants include the Forest (buffet), Cafe Andreotti (Italian bistro), North Beach Deli (New York–style), Asia (Pacific Rim), Friday's Station (steaks and seafood), and Sierra Restaurant (open 24 hours). There's also Bentley's Ice Cream Parlor. *U.S. 50, Box 8, 89449, ☎ 702/588–6611 or 800/648–3773, FAX 702/788–3274. 534 rooms. 7 restaurants, room service, indoor pool, hot tubs, barbershop, beauty salon, health club, casino, video games, laundry service, valet garage, kennel. AE, D, DC, MC, V.*

$$$$ **Harvey's Resort Hotel/Casino.** It started as a small cabin in 1944; owner Harvey Gross played an important role in convincing the state to keep U.S. 50 open year-round, making Tahoe accessible in winter. Harvey's is now the largest resort in Tahoe, and any description of the place runs to superlatives, from the 40-foot-tall crystal chandelier in the lobby to the 88,000-square-foot casino. Rooms feature custom furnishings, oversize marble baths, and minibars. The health club, spa, and pool are free to guests, a rarity for this area. Among its restaurants, Llewellyn's (*see* Dining, *above*) is outstanding. The Sage Room Steak House is also excellent, serving prime beef, veal, and seafood, as well as Continental dishes such as pheasant in puff pastry and frogs' legs. Other restaurants include the Seafood Grotto and more casual options. *U.S. 50, Box 128, 89449, ☎ 702/588–2411 or 800/648–3361, FAX 702/782–4889. 741 rooms. 8 restaurants, wading pool, health club, casino, chapel, valet parking. AE, D, DC, MC, V.*

$$$–$$$$ **Caesars Tahoe.** Most of the rooms and suites at this luxurious 16-story hotel-casino have oversize Roman tubs, king-size beds, two telephones, and a view of Lake Tahoe or the encircling mountains. The lavish casino encompasses 40,000 square feet. Top-name entertainers perform in the 1,600-seat Circus Maximus. Planet Restaurants include Empress Court (Chinese), Cafe Roma (24-hour coffee shop), Pisces (seafood), Primavera (Italian), Broiler Room, Planet Hollywood, and Yogurt Palace. *55 U.S. 50, Box 5800, 89449, ☎ 702/588–3515; reservations and show information, 800/648–3353; FAX 702/586–2068. 440 rooms. 7 restaurants, coffee shop, indoor pool, hot tub, saunas, tennis, health club, valet garage, parking lot. AE, D, DC, MC, V.*

$$–$$$$ **Horizon Casino Resort.** The guest rooms at this small Tahoe resort, formerly called the High Sierra, have recently been remodeled; many have beautiful lake views. The casino has a beaux arts decor, brightened by pale molded wood and mirrors. Entertainment is available at the Grande Lake Theatre, the Golden Cabaret, and the Aspen Lounge. Restaurants include Josh's (steaks, seafood, and pasta), the Four Seasons (open 24 hours), and Le Grande Buffet, with its nightly prime-rib special. *U.S. 50, Box C, 89449, ☎ 702/588–6211 or 800/322–7723, FAX 702/588–1344. 539 rooms. 3 restaurants, pool, wading pool, 3 hot tubs, exercise room, meeting rooms. AE, D, DC, MC, V.*

$$–$$$ **Lakeside Inn and Casino.** The smallest of the Stateline casinos, and not nearly as glitzy as the big four, Lakeside has a rustic look. Guest rooms are in lodges, away from the casino area. *U.S. 50 at Kingsbury Grade, Box 5640, 89449, ☎ 702/588–7777 or 800/624–7980, FAX 702/588–4092. 123 rooms. Restaurant. AE, D, MC, V.*

Tahoe City

DINING

$$$ ★ **Wolfdale's.** An intimate dinner house on the lake, Wolfdale's offers Japanese-California cuisine. The menu changes weekly and features a small number of imaginative entrées such as grilled Chinese pheasant with plum sauce and shiitake mushrooms, and baked Norwegian salmon with saffron-scallop sauce. ✕ *640 N. Lake Blvd., ☎ 916/583–5700. Reservations advised. MC, V. Closed Tues. No lunch.*

$$–$$$ **Christy Hill.** Panoramic lake views and fireside dining distinguish this restaurant, a favorite of locals. The California cuisine features fresh seafood and game, prepared by the owner-chef. ✕ *115 Grove St., Lakehouse Mall, ☎ 916/583–8551. Reservations advised. MC, V. Closed Sun. (spring and fall) and Mon. No lunch.*

$$ ★ **Jake's on the Lake.** Continental food is served in spacious, handsome rooms featuring oak and glass, on the water at the Boatworks Mall. There is an extensive seafood bar and a varied menu that includes meat

and poultry but emphasizes fresh fish. ✕ *780 N. Lake Blvd.,* ☏ *916/583–0188. Reservations accepted. AE, MC, V. No lunch in winter, except during holiday season.*

$–$$ **Grazie! Ristorante & Bar.** Northern Italian cuisine, emphasizing light sauces, is served here. There are a half dozen hearty pasta dishes and six pizza choices, but the stars are the antipasti and pasta salads. Chicken is cooked on a wood-burning rotisserie and rack of lamb on the grill, served with homemade sauces. ✕ *Roundhouse Mall, 700 N. Lake Blvd.,* ☏ *916/583–0233. Reservations advised. AE, D, DC, MC, V.*

DINING AND LODGING

$$$–$$$$ ★ **Sunnyside Restaurant and Lodge.** This quaint, sunny mountain lodge has a marina and an expansive lakefront deck with steps down to the beach. Rooms are decorated in a crisp, nautical style with prints of boats hanging on the pinstripe wall coverings, and sea chests as coffee tables. Each room has its own deck, with lake and mountain views. Continental breakfast is included in the rate, but this is not a full-service hotel. The lodge's very fine restaurant (which rates the star) continues the nautical theme. Seafood is the specialty of the Continental menu. The large lounge area has rock fireplaces, comfortable sofas, a seafood bar, and snacks. *1850 W. Lake Blvd.,* ☏ *916/583–7200 or 800/822–2754 in CA,* FAX *916/583–2551. 23 rooms. Restaurant (reservations accepted; no lunch in winter; $$–$$$), lounge, beach, marina facilities. AE, MC, V.*

LODGING

$$$$ ★ **Chinquapin Resort.** This deluxe development on 95 acres of forested lakeside land 3 miles northeast of Tahoe City includes roomy one- to four-bedroom town houses and condos with spectacular views of the lake and the mountains. Every one has a fireplace, a fully equipped kitchen, and laundry facilities. No two units are alike, since there are more than 20 floor plans, and decorating is done by the individual owners. *3600 N. Lake Blvd., 96145,* ☏ *916/583–6991 or 800/732–6721,* FAX *916/583–0937. 172 town houses and condos. Pool, saunas, 7 tennis courts, hiking, horseshoes. 1-wk minimum stay July–Aug., 2-night minimum stay in winter. No credit cards.*

$$ **Rodeway Inn.** This seven-story lake-view tower is within easy walking distance of the beaches, marina, shops, and restaurants of this quaint town. Rooms are clean and comfortable, if not luxurious, and offer some of the best lake views. *645 N. Lake Blvd., 96145,* ☏ *916/583–3711 or 800/228–2000,* FAX *916/583–6938. 51 rooms. Pool, hot tub, laundry. AE, D, DC, MC, V.*

Tahoe Vista

DINING

$$$ **Captain Jon's.** The dining room is small and cozy, with linen cloths and fresh flowers on the tables. On chilly evenings diners are warmed by a fireplace with a raised brick hearth. The lengthy dinner menu is country French, with two dozen daily specials; the emphasis is on fish and hearty salads. The restaurant's lounge, which serves light meals, is in a separate building on the water, with a pier where guests can tie up their boats. ✕ *7220 N. Lake Blvd.,* ☏ *916/546–4819. Reservations advised. AE, DC, MC, V. Closed Mon. No lunch in winter (usually Nov.–May).*

$$–$$$ **AJ's Ristorante.** Lakeside views and outdoor dining accompany authentic northern Italian cooking at this restaurant. Pizzas are delicate and varied, cooked quickly in an olive wood–fired brick oven. Other specialties are cooked on a mesquite rotisserie. There's an interesting appetizer menu; Sunday brunch is also served in the summer. The decor

is elegant rustic, with fine art, sculpture, and white-linen table coverings. ✕ *7320 N. Lake Tahoe Blvd.,* ☎ *916/546–3640. Reservations advised. AE, MC, V. No lunch in winter.*

Truckee

DINING AND LODGING

$$$–$$$$ **Northstar-at-Tahoe Resort.** This resort-village offers a peaceful, scenic getaway year-round. Accommodations range from hotel rooms to condos and private houses, all clustered around the shops and restaurants in the tiny village. Northstar is popular for meetings, seminars, and families because it offers all facilities, including loads of sports—downhill and cross-country skiing, mountain biking, horseback riding, tennis, and golf. Summer rates are lower than winter rates. *Off Hwy. 267 between Truckee and North Shore, Box 129, 96160,* ☎ *916/562–1010 or 800/533–6787,* FAX *916/562–2215. 230 units. 3 restaurants, deli, 18-hole golf course, 10 tennis courts, horseback riding, bicycles, skiing, snowmobiling, sleigh rides, recreation room, child-care center. AE, D, MC, V.*

NIGHTLIFE

Major nighttime entertainment is found at the larger casinos. The top venues are the **Circus Maximus** at Caesars Tahoe, the **Emerald Theater** at Harvey's, the **South Shore Room** at Harrah's, and Horizon's **Grand Lake Theatre.** Each theater is as large as a Broadway house. Typical headliners are Jay Leno, David Copperfield, Kenny Rogers, and Johnny Mathis. For Las Vegas–style production shows—fast-paced dancing, singing, and novelty acts—try Harrah's or the Horizon. The big showrooms also occasionally present performances of Broadway musicals by touring Broadway companies or by casts assembled for the casino.

Reservations are almost always required for superstar shows. Depending on the act, cocktail shows usually cost $12–$40, including Nevada's sales and entertainment taxes. Smaller casino cabarets sometimes have a cover charge or drink minimum. There are also lounges with no admission charge, featuring jazz and pop-music soloists and groups. Even these performers don't try to compete all night with gambling; the last set usually ends at 2:30 or 3 AM.

Lounges around the lake offer pop and country-music singers and musicians, and in winter the ski resorts do the same. Summer alternatives are outdoor music events, from chamber quartets to jazz bands and rock performers, at Sand Harbor and the Lake Tahoe Visitors Center amphitheater.

LAKE TAHOE ESSENTIALS

Arriving and Departing

By Bus

Greyhound Lines (☎ 800/231–2222) stops in Sacramento, Truckee, and Reno. The company offers reasonably priced three-day round-trip "casino fares" from San Francisco to Harrah's in Stateline, Nevada, in addition to regular coach tickets.

By Car

Lake Tahoe is 198 miles northeast of San Francisco, a drive of just under four hours when traffic and the weather cooperate. Avoid the heavy traffic leaving the San Francisco area for Tahoe on Friday afternoon and returning on Sunday afternoon.

The major route is I–80, which cuts through the Sierra Nevada about 14 miles north of the lake; from there state Highways 89 and 267 reach the north shore. U.S. 50 is the more direct highway to the south shore, taking about 2½ hours from Sacramento. From Reno, you can get to the north shore by heading west on Highway 431 off U.S. 395, 8 miles south of town (a total of 35 miles). For the south shore, continue south on U.S. 395 through Carson City, then head west on U.S. 50 (55 miles total).

By Plane

Reno–Tahoe International Airport (☎ 702/328–6400), 35 miles northeast of the closest point on the lake, is served by a number of national and regional airlines, including **American** (☎ 800/433–7300), **America West** (☎ 800/235–9292), **Continental** (☎ 800/525–0280), **Delta** (☎ 800/221–1212), **Northwest** (☎ 800/225–2525), **Sky West** (☎ 800/453–9417), **Southwest** (☎ 800/435–9792), **United** (☎ 800/241–6522), and **USAir** (☎ 800/428–4322). **Tahoe Casino Express** (☎ 702/785–2424 or 800/446–6128) has daily scheduled transportation from Reno to South Lake Tahoe, starting at 6:15 AM, then hourly from 8:15 to 3:15 PM, then 5:30, then every two hours until 12:30 AM.

Lake Tahoe Airport (☎ 916/542–6180) on U.S. 50, 3 miles south of the lake's shore, is served by **Transworld Express** (☎ 800/221–2000), which flies from Los Angeles and San Francisco.

By Train

Amtrak (☎ 800/872–7245) provides combined train/shuttle-bus service from San Francisco and Los Angeles to Lake Tahoe twice daily.

Getting Around

By Bus

South Tahoe Area Ground Express (STAGE, ☎ 916/573–2080) runs 24 hours along U.S. 50 and through the neighborhoods of South Lake Tahoe. On the lake's west and north shores, **Tahoe Area Regional Transit** (TART, ☎ 916/581–6365 or 800/736–6365) runs between Tahoma (from Meeks Bay in summer) and Incline Village daily 6:30–6:30. Free shuttle buses run among the casinos, major ski resorts, and motels of South Lake Tahoe.

By Car

The scenic 72-mile highway around the lake is marked Highway 89 on the southwest and west, Highway 28 on the north and northeast shores, and U.S. 50 on the southeast. It takes about three hours to drive, but allow plenty of extra time—heavy traffic on busy holiday weekends can prolong the trip, and there are frequent road repairs in summer.

During winter, sections of Highway 89 may be closed, making it impossible to complete the circular drive—call 800/427–7623 to check road conditions. I–80, U.S. 50, and U.S. 395 are all-weather highways, but there may be delays as snow is cleared during major storms. Carry tire chains from October to May (car-rental agencies provide them with rental cars).

By Taxi

Yellow Cab (☎ 916/542–1234) serves all of Tahoe Basin. **Sierra Taxi** (☎ 916/577–8888) serves the south shore. On the north shore, try **Tahoe Taxi** (☎ 916/583–8294).

Guided Tours

You can get to know Lake Tahoe by bus, boat, on foot, or in the air on the tours listed below. Discount coupons for most of these, plus other attractions listed in this chapter, are available at most lodgings—the savings add up, especially for families. Also check the *Lake of the Sky Journal,* in boxes on the street and elsewhere, for events listings and additional coupons.

Orientation

Gray Line (☎ 916/541–7223 or 800/822–6009) runs daily tours to South Lake Tahoe, Carson City, and Virginia City. Another tour provider is **Tahoe Limousine Service** (Box 9909, South Lake Tahoe 96158, ☎ 916/577–2727 or 800/334–1826).

Adventure

High Mountain Outback Adventures (2286 Utah Ave., South Lake Tahoe 96150, ☎ 916/541–5875) operates a trek skirting the Desolation Wilderness in four-wheel-drive all-terrain vehicles (ATVs), for $79 per half day and $139 per full day (you must be 18, have a driver's license, and be in good health). Those in very good physical shape can take a three-day, two-night Adventure Ride for $695. These rides are available starting in the late spring (depending on the weather) through October.

Air

CalVada Seaplanes Inc. (☎ 916/525–7143) provides rides over the lake for $45–$81 per person, depending on the length of the trip. Soaring rides on gliders over the lake and valley depart from the Douglas County Airport, Gardnerville. Try **High Country Soaring** (☎ 702/782–4944) or **Soar Minden** (☎ 702/782–7627).

Boat

The 500-passenger ***Tahoe Queen*** (☎ 916/541–3364 or 800/238–2463) is a glass-bottom stern-wheeler that makes 2½-hour lake cruises year-round from Ski Run Marina off U.S. 50 in South Lake Tahoe; sunset and dinner cruises are also offered. Fares are $14–$18 adults, $5–$9 children 1–11; in winter, the boat shuttles skiers to north-shore ski areas on weekdays for $18 round-trip.

The **MS *Dixie II*** (☎ 702/588–3508) sails year-round from Zephyr Cove Marina to Emerald Bay on lunch and dinner cruises. Fares are $14–$35 adults, $5–$10 children 4–11; food is additional.

The ***Woodwind*** (☎ 702/588–3000) is a glass-bottom trimaran that sails from Zephyr Cove Resort April–October. Fares are $14 adults, $7 children under 12; the evening champagne cruise is $20 for all passengers.

The ***Sierra Cloud*** (☎ 702/831–1111), a larger trimaran with a big trampoline lounging surface, cruises the North Shore area mornings and afternoons from the Hyatt Regency Hotel in Incline Village May–October. Fares are $25–$35 for adults, $10–$15 for children under 13.

Important Addresses and Numbers

Emergencies

Dial 911 for **police** or **ambulance** in an emergency, or call the **California Highway Patrol** (☎ 916/587–3510) or the **Nevada Highway Patrol** (☎ 702/687–5300).

Visitor Information

Lake Tahoe Visitors Authority (1156 Ski Run Blvd., South Lake Tahoe, CA 96150, ☎ 916/544–5050 or 800/288–2463) provides information and lodging reservations for the south shore.

Tahoe North Visitors and Convention Bureau (Box 5578, Tahoe City, CA 96145, ☎ 916/583–3494 or 800/824–6348, FAX 916/581–4081) provides information and lodging reservations for the California north shore.

Incline Village/Crystal Bay Visitors & Convention Bureau (969 Tahoe Blvd., Incline Village, NV 89451, ☎ 702/832–1606 or 800/468–2463) has information about the Nevada north shore.

Lake Tahoe Hotline (☎ 916/542–4636) gives out events information.

Ski Phone (☎ 415/864–6440) provides around-the-clock ski reports and weather information.

Road Conditions (☎ 916/445–7623 for California roads in and around Lake Tahoe, ☎ 702/793–1313 for roads on the Nevada side of the lake, and 415/557–3755 or 800/427–7623 for California roads approaching the Lake Tahoe area.

8 The Sierra National Parks

The highlight for many travelers to California is a visit to one of the Sierra Nevada's national parks. Yosemite is the state's most famous park and every bit as sublime as one expects. Its Yosemite-type or U-shape valleys were formed by the action of glaciers on the Sierra Nevada during recent ice ages. Other examples are found in Kings Canyon and Sequoia national parks (which are adjacent to each other and usually visited together). At all three parks there are fine groves of Big Trees (Sequoiadendron gigantea), some of the largest living things in the world.

Updated by Alan Frutkin

YOSEMITE, SEQUOIA, AND KINGS CANYON national parks are famous throughout the world for their unique sights and experiences. Yosemite, especially, should be on your "don't miss" list. Unfortunately, it's on everyone else's as well (the park hosts approximately 3.9 million visitors annually), so advance reservations are essential. During extremely busy periods—when snow closes high country roads in late spring or on crowded summer weekends—Yosemite Valley may be closed to all vehicles unless their drivers have overnight reservations, though this rarely happens. Because the parks are accessible year-round, it is possible to avoid these conditions. From mid-April to Memorial Day and from Labor Day to mid-October, the weather is usually hospitable and the parks less bustling.

We recommend allowing several days to explore the parks, but if your time is limited, a one-day guided tour will at least allow you a glimpse of the parks' wonders. We also recommend that you make your plans far enough in advance so you can stay in the parks themselves, not in one of the "gateway cities" in the foothills or Central Valley. You'll probably be adjusting to a higher altitude, dealing with traffic, and exercising a fair amount, so save your energy for exploring, not driving to and from the parks.

YOSEMITE NATIONAL PARK

Yosemite Valley is one of the most famous sights (or collection of sights) in California. The surrounding granite peaks and domes, such as El Capitan and Half Dome, rise more than 3,000 feet above the valley floor; two of the five waterfalls that cascade over the valley's rim are among the world's 10 highest; and the Merced River, placid here, runs through the valley. Such extravagant praise has been written of this valley (by John Muir and others) and so many beautiful photographs taken (by Ansel Adams and others) that you may wonder if the reality can possibly measure up. For almost everyone, it does; Yosemite is a reminder of what "breathtaking" and "marvelous" really mean.

Although Yosemite's 1,170 square miles of national park (about the size of Rhode Island) is 94½% undeveloped wilderness, accessible only to backpackers and horseback riders, many sites can be explored by the more than 1,000 miles of roads, hiking trails, and bicycle trails. The valley itself comprises only 7 square miles. Most visitor facilities are located in the Village. Yosemite is so large it functions as five parks: **Yosemite Valley** (open all year); **Hetch Hetchy and Wawona** (open all year, though Hetch Hetchy sometimes closes during severe weather); **Mariposa Grove** (open spring to fall) and the high country; **Tuolumne Meadows** (open for summer hiking); and **Badger Pass Ski Area** (winter only). Christmas is a very busy time, with lodging reservations best made up to a year in advance. The western boundary dips as low as 2,000 feet in the chaparral-covered foothills; the eastern boundary rises to 13,000 feet at points along the Sierra crest. Much of this country is accessible only to backpackers and horseback riders (and thus beyond the scope of this guide), but there are many sites to be explored by visitors who do not want to range too far from their cars.

The falls are at their most spectacular in May and June. By the end of the summer, however, some may have dried up, or very nearly so. They begin flowing again in late fall with the first storms, and during the winter, they may be dramatically hung with ice. Yosemite Valley is open year-round. Because the valley floor is only 4,000 feet high, snow there is never very deep, and it is possible to camp even in the winter (January highs are in the mid-40s, lows in the mid-20s). Tioga Pass Road is closed in winter (roughly late October–May), so you can't see Tuolumne Meadows then. The road to Glacier Point beyond the turnoff for Badger Pass is also not cleared in winter, but it is groomed for cross-country skiing.

A week's stay at the park costs $5 per car, $3 per person if you don't arrive in a car.

Exploring

Numbers in the margin correspond to points of interest on the Yosemite National Park map.

Yosemite Valley is the primary destination for many visitors, especially those who won't be making backpack or pack-animal trips. Because the valley is only 7 miles long and averages less than 1 mile wide, you can visit sites in whatever order you choose and return to your favorites at different times of the day.

Near the east end of Yosemite Valley, you'll find the park headquarters, restaurants, stores, a gas station, the Ahwahnee Hotel, Yosemite
❶ Lodge, a medical clinic, and a **Visitor Center,** where park rangers provide information and wilderness permits (necessary for overnight backpacking). There are exhibits on natural and human history as well as an adjacent Indian Cultural Museum, and a re-created Ahwahneechee village. ☏ *209/372–0264.* ⏲ *Daily 9–5, with extended hrs in summer.*

★ ❷ **Yosemite Falls** is the highest waterfall in North America and the fifth-highest in the world. The upper falls (1,430 feet), the middle cascades (675 feet), and the lower falls (320 feet) combine for a total of 2,425 feet and, when viewed from the valley, appear as a single waterfall. From the parking lot there is a ¼-mile trail to the base of the falls. The Yosemite Falls Trail is a strenuous 3½-mile climb rising 2,700 feet, taking you above the top of the falls. It starts from Sunnyside Campground.

If you arrive in Yosemite via the Wawona Road, your first view of the valley (in John Muir's words "a revelation in landscape affairs that en-
★ ❸ riches one's life forever") will include **Bridalveil Fall,** a filmy fall of 620 feet that is often diverted as much as 20 feet one way or the other by the breeze. Native Americans called it Pohono ("puffing wind"). There is a very short (¼-mile) trail from a parking lot on the Wawona Road to the base of the fall.

❹ Across the valley, **Ribbon Fall** (1,612 feet) is the valley's highest single fall, but it is also the first one to dry up in the summer.

Vernal and Nevada falls are on the Merced River at the east end of the
❺ valley. **Vernal Fall** (317 feet) is bordered by fern-covered black rocks,
❻ and rainbows play in the spray at the base. **Nevada Fall** (594 feet) is the first major fall as the river comes out of the high country. Both falls can be viewed from Glacier Point or visited on foot from Happy Isles nature area, east of Yosemite Village. The roads at this end of the valley are now closed to private cars, but a free shuttle bus runs frequently from the village. From late June through early September, the Happy Isles nature area is open daily 9–5 and features exhibits on ecology.

Yosemite National Park

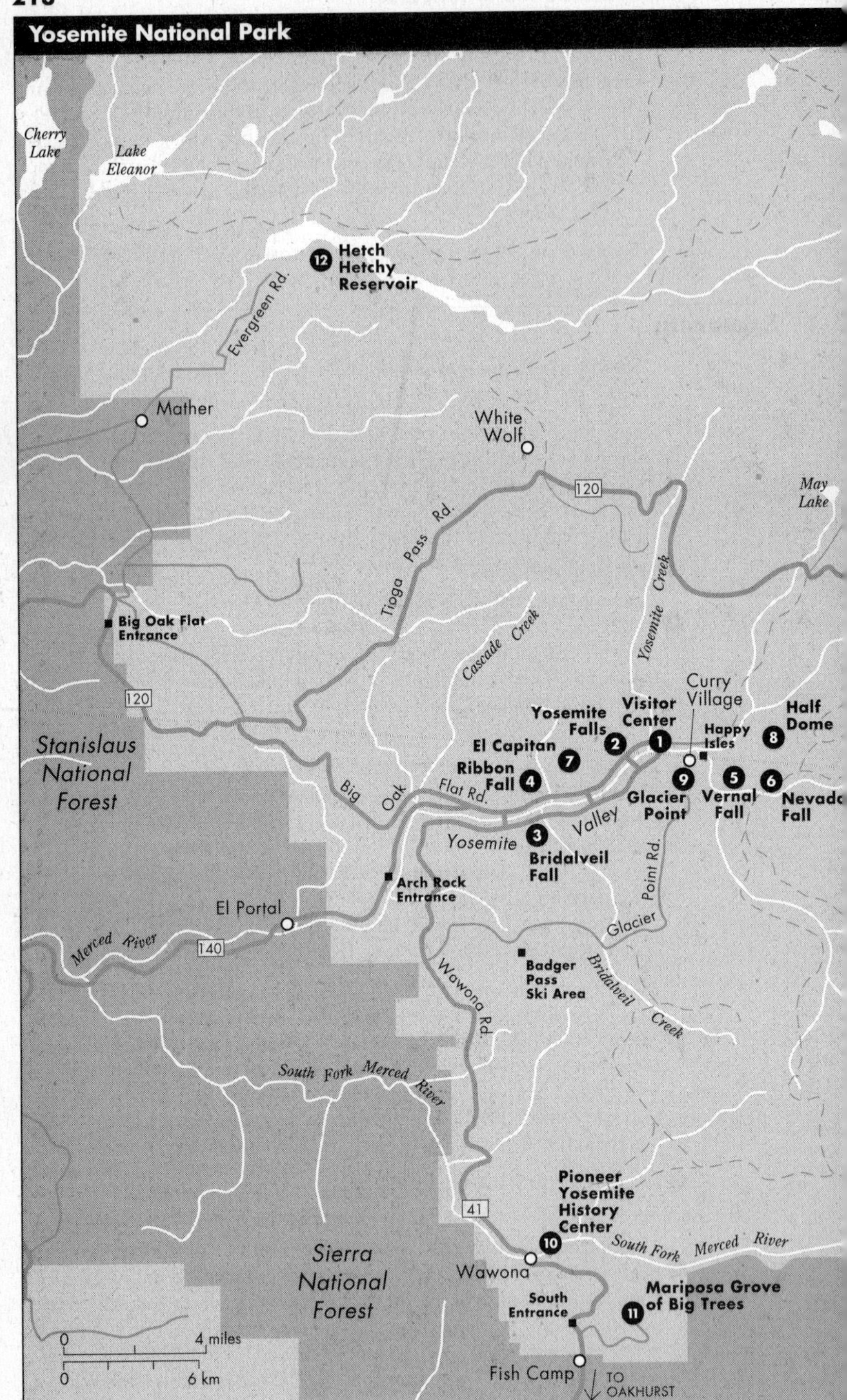
Cherry Lake
Lake Eleanor
12 Hetch Hetchy Reservoir
Evergreen Rd.
Mather
White Wolf
120
May Lake
Tioga Pass Rd.
Cascade Creek
Yosemite Creek
Big Oak Flat Entrance
120
Curry Village
Visitor Center
Yosemite Falls
Half Dome
Happy Isles
El Capitan
Stanislaus National Forest
Ribbon Fall
Big Oak Flat Rd.
Glacier Point
Vernal Fall
Nevada Fall
Yosemite Valley
Bridalveil Fall
Arch Rock Entrance
Glacier Point Rd.
El Portal
Merced River
140
Badger Pass Ski Area
Bridalveil Creek
Wawona Rd.
South Fork Merced River
Pioneer Yosemite History Center
41
South Fork Merced River
Sierra National Forest
Wawona
Mariposa Grove of Big Trees
South Entrance
0
4 miles
0
6 km
Fish Camp
TO OAKHURST

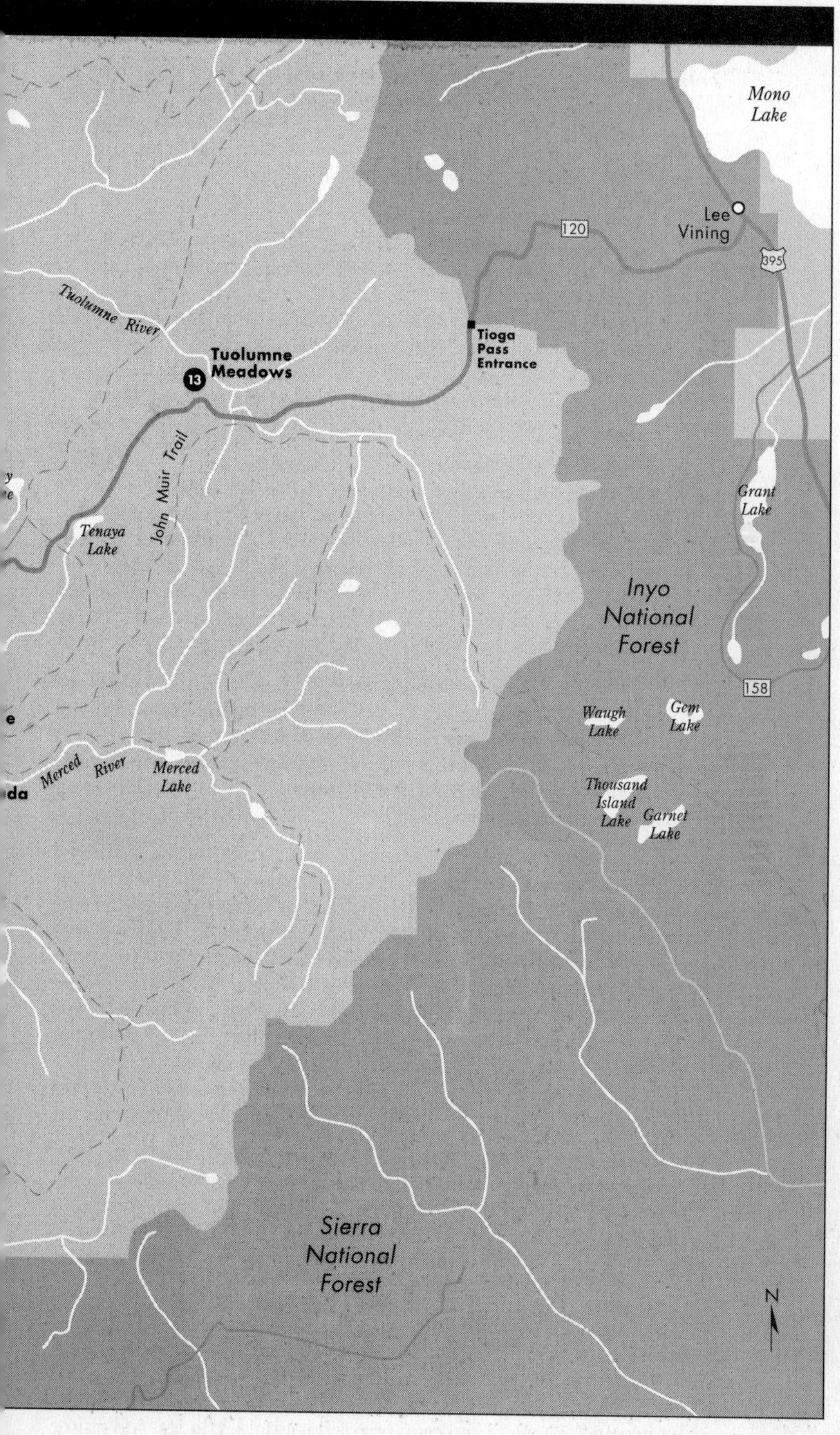
Mono Lake
Lee Vining
120
395
Tuolumne River
Tuolumne Meadows
13
Tioga Pass Entrance
John Muir Trail
Tenaya Lake
Grant Lake
Inyo National Forest
158
Waugh Lake
Gem Lake
Merced River
Merced Lake
Thousand Island Lake
Garnet Lake
Sierra National Forest
N

The hike on a paved trail from Happy Isles to the bridge at the base of Vernal Fall is only moderately strenuous and less than 1 mile long. It's another steep ¾-mile along the **Mist Trail,** open only in the warmer months, up to the top of the fall, and then an additional 2 miles to the top of Nevada Falls. Happy Isles Bridge is the beginning of the famous **John Muir Trail,** which leads south for more than 200 miles through the High Sierra to Mt. Whitney, in the southeastern section of Sequoia/Kings Canyon.

Most famous among Yosemite's peaks are El Capitan and Half Dome.
★ 7 **El Capitan** is the largest exposed granite monolith in the world, almost
twice the height of the Rock of Gibraltar. It rises 3,593 feet above the
valley, with an apparently vertical front thrust out from the valley's
★ 8 rim. **Half Dome** is the most distinctive rock in the region: The west side
of the dome is fractured vertically and cut away to form a 2,000-foot
cliff. Rising 4,733 feet from the valley floor, the top is at an altitude
of 8,842 feet above sea level.

★ 9 **Glacier Point** offers what may be the most spectacular view of the valley and the High Sierra that you can get without hiking. The Glacier Point Road leaves Highway 41 about 23 miles southwest of the valley; then it's a 16-mile drive, with fine views into higher country. From the parking area, walk a few hundred yards and you'll be able to see Nevada, Vernal, and Yosemite falls as well as Half Dome and other peaks. This road is closed beyond the turnoff for Badger Pass Ski Area in the winter.

10 At the **Pioneer Yosemite History Center** in Wawona (on Hwy. 41) are local historic buildings moved here from their original sites. A living history program in summer re-creates Yosemite's past, including stagecoach rides. The history program runs from late June to early September, Wednesday through Sunday 9 AM to 1 PM and 2 to 5 PM. However, the center is open year-round.

Farther down the Wawona Road (36 miles from the valley) is the
11 **Mariposa Grove of Big Trees.** This fine grove of *Sequoiadendron giganteum* can be visited on foot or on the one-hour tram rides in summer (☛ $7 adults, $6.25 for those 62 and older, $3.50 children 4–12; open May–Oct., daily 9–6). The Grizzly Giant is the oldest tree here; its age is estimated to be 2,700 years; its base diameter is 30.7 feet; its circumference is 96½ feet; and its height 210 feet. The Wawona Tunnel Tree—the granddaddy of Yosemite giants that was the centerpiece of many a vacation photo opportunity featuring family, car, and tree base—fell during the winter of 1968–69, but one other tunnel tree remains nearby. A museum, which doubles as a bookstore, presents information on the big trees (open in summer 9:30–4:30).

12 **Hetch Hetchy Reservoir** is about 40 miles from Yosemite Valley, via Big Oak Flat Road and Highway 120. The reservoir supplies water and power to San Francisco. Some say John Muir died of heartbreak when this beautiful valley was dammed and buried beneath 300 feet of water in 1913.

The Tioga Pass Road (Highway 120) crosses the Sierra Nevada and
meets U.S. 395 at Lee Vining. This scenic route (open only in summer)
13 will take you past **Tuolumne Meadows,** the largest subalpine meadow in the Sierra. There are campgrounds, a gas station, store (with very limited and expensive choice of provisions), stables, lodge, and visitor center (open late June–early Sept., daily 8–7:30). This is the trailhead for many backpack trips into the High Sierra, but there are also shorter

day hikes you can take. Remember, though, to give yourself time (a day or two, at least) to get acclimated to the altitude: 8,575 feet.

From Yosemite Valley, it's 55 miles to Tuolumne Meadows and 74 miles to Lee Vining. North of Lee Vining on Highway 395 is impressive Mono Lake, renowned for its striking "tufa towers" and nesting grounds for migratory birds. The tufa's visibility comes "courtesy" of the City of Los Angeles, which since the '40s (and not without great controversy) has been diverting water from streams that feed the lake, resulting in a lowering of its level. The **Mono Basin Visitors Center** (Hwy. 395, ☎ 619/647–3044 for brochures or information) in Lee Vining provides ranger- and naturalist-led tours of the tufa and other wildlife daily in the summer, weekends only (some on cross-country skis) in winter.

Off the Beaten Track

From early May to late October and during some holiday periods, actor Lee Stetson portrays noted naturalist John Muir, bringing to life Muir's wit, wisdom, and storytelling skill. Stetson's programs—"An Evening with a Tramp" and "The Spirit of John Muir"—are two of the park's best-loved shows. Locations and times are listed in the Yosemite Guide, the newspaper handed to you upon entering the park (and also found at the visitor center and at many local stores). Stetson, as John Muir, also leads free interpretive walks twice a week; the walks start at the visitor center.

Next door to the Narrow Gauge Inn in Fish Camp (*see* Lodging, *below*) is a major attraction: **Yosemite Mountain-Sugar Pine Railroad.** A 4-mile scenic historic steam-train excursion through the forest, this is especially interesting to children. A Saturday evening Moonlight Special excursion includes dinner and old-fashioned entertainment. There's also a small museum at Yosemite Mountain Railroad Station. *56001 Hwy. 41, Fish Camp 93623,* ☎ *209/683–7273. Trains run Mar.–Oct. and on limited basis in winter.*

Sports

Bicycling

Bicycles can be rented at **Yosemite Lodge** or **Curry Village** April–November. The cost is $4.50 per hour or $16 per day.

Fishing

All lakes and reservoirs within Yosemite are open to fishing year-round; appropriate state sportfishing licenses must be displayed. The park's annual stream- and river-fishing season begins the last Saturday in April and continues through November 15. On the Merced River in Yosemite Valley catch-and-release-only policy applies for native rainbow trout. Check with Yosemite Visitor Center or Pines Marina (*see* Water Sports, *below*) for information on specific locations.

Hiking

Hiking is the primary sport here. If you are hiking up any of the steep trails, remember to stay on the trail. Also consider the effect of the altitude on your endurance. If you plan to backpack overnight, you'll need a wilderness permit (free), available at visitor centers or ranger stations.

Rock Climbing

Yosemite Mountaineering (☎ 209/372–1244 Sept.–May or 209/372–1335 June–Aug.) conducts beginner through intermediate rock-climbing and backpacking classes. A one-day session includes a hands-on introduction to climbing. Classes are held April–September, weather permitting. In winter it offers cross-country ski instruction and snow camping trips.

Water Sports

Pines Marina (☎ 209/642–3565) at Bass Lake Reservoir rents ski boats, house and fishing boats, Jet Skis, and funabouts. It is open April 1 through October 31. Lodging facilities range from U.S. Forest Service campgrounds to luxury hotel-chalets.

Winter Sports

Badger Pass Ski Area, off the Glacier Point Road (☎ 209/372–1000), has nine runs serviced by one triple and three double chairlifts, and an excellent ski school. Gentle slopes make this an ideal beginners area. The cross-country center has a groomed and tracked 21-mile loop from Badger Pass to Glacier Point, where, with reservations, you can overnight in a hut and eat prepared meals. Snowshoeing is also available. There is an outdoor skating rink at **Curry Village.**

Dining

With precious few exceptions, the best meals available in our national parks are probably those cooked on portable grills at the various campgrounds. There is a snack bar in Yosemite Village, as well as coffee shops and a cafeteria at the Ahwahnee and Yosemite Lodge. Even so, if you are just there for a day, you will not want to waste precious time hunting about for food; instead, stop at a grocery store on the way in and fill up your hamper and ice chest with the makings of a picnic to enjoy under the umbrellas of giant fir trees.

What to Wear

Except where noted otherwise, dress is casual at Yosemite restaurants.

CATEGORY	COST*
$$$$	over $35
$$$	$25–$35
$$	$15–$25
$	under $15

**per person for a three-course meal, excluding drinks, service, and 7¾% tax*

In the Park

$$$ ★ **Ahwahnee Hotel.** With its 34-foot-tall trestle-beamed ceiling, full-length windows, and twinkling chandeliers, this is Yosemite's most impressive and romantic restaurant. Even if it's a splurge, you should dine here at least once during your stay in the valley. Classic American specialties focus on steak, trout, and prime rib, all competently prepared. Generations of Californians have made a ritual of spending Christmas and New Year's here, so make plans well in advance; reservation lotteries are conducted for both periods. ✕ *Yosemite Village,* ☎ *209/372–1489. Reservations advised. D, MC, V.*

$$ **Mountain Room Broiler.** The food becomes secondary when you see Yosemite Falls through the dining room's window-wall. Best bets are steaks, chops, roast duck, and a fresh herb-basted roast chicken. ✕ *Yosemite Lodge,* ☎ *209/372–1281. D, MC, V. No lunch.*

$$ **Wawona Hotel Dining Room.** You can watch deer graze on the meadow from the multipane windows of this romantic, candlelit restaurant dating back to the late 1800s. Vintage, hand-painted lamp shades and waitresses in ankle-length skirts set the scene for nostalgia. Classic American dishes focus on chicken, steak, and fish. ✕ *Wawona,* ☎ *209/375–6556. Reservations required for dinner. D, MC, V.*

$ **Four Seasons Restaurant.** The upscale rustic setting here features high-finish natural wood tables and lots of potted representatives of the local greenery and flora. The breakfast is hearty and all-American; dinner offerings cover the beef, chicken, and fish spectrum, plus vegetarian fare. ✕ *Yosemite Lodge,* ☎ *209/372–1269. D, MC, V. No lunch.*

Outside the Park

$$$$ ★ **Erna's Elderberry House.** As a special treat, stop at this countryside gem, where the owner, Vienna-born Erna Kubin, offers bountiful Continental-California cuisine, along with dishes from whatever country she's visited recently. Prix fixe, six-course dinners change nightly. ✕ *48688 Victoria La., Oakhurst,* ☎ *209/683–6800. Reservations advised. MC, V. Sun. brunch. Closed 1st 3 wks of Jan. No lunch Sat.–Tues.; no dinner Mon. and Tues. in winter, Tues. in summer.*

$$ **Ducey's on the Lake.** This lodge-style resort overlooking scenic Bass Lake attracts a lively crowd of boaters, locals, and tourists. The high-ceilinged, exposed-beam dining room serves prime rib, steaks, seafood, and pasta. Salmon Wellington prepared with mushrooms and spinach in phyllo dough is a popular dish. Sunday brunch is served from 10 to 2, twilight dinner specials ($9.95) from 4 to 6 daily. Burgers, sandwiches, and salads are the fare at the upstairs Bar & Grill. There is dancing and entertainment Friday and Saturday. Overnight guests can book lakefront suites at the Pines Resort. ✕ *54432 Rd. 432, Box 109, Bass Lake 93604,* ☎ *209/642–3131. Reservations advised for dining room, especially for brunch. AE, D, DC, MC, V.*

$ **Coffee Express.** If you're coming into Yosemite via Highway 120, this is a cozy, casual, and very inexpensive lunch spot with friendly service. Try the chicken salad with apples and alfalfa sprouts and at least a slice of the irresistible pies. The Iron Door Saloon, across the street, claims to be the oldest operating saloon in California. ✕ *Hwy. 120, Groveland,* ☎ *209/962–7393. No credit cards. No dinner.*

Lodging

Most accommodations inside Yosemite National Park can best be described as "no frills." Many have no electricity or plumbing. Other than the elegant Ahwahnee and Wawona hotels, lodging is geared toward those who prefer basic motels, rustic cabins, and campgrounds in natural, forest settings to full service and luxury. Except for the off-peak season, November to March, rates are pricey given the general quality of the lodging because of limited availability. Reservations for park lodging should be made well in advance, especially in summer. Surrounding towns such as Fish Camp, Oakhurst, and Bass Lake offer park visitors additional options. All are within an hour's drive of Yosemite Village. Price categories are based on the cost of a room for two people.

CATEGORY	COST*
$$$$	over $100
$$$	$75–$100
$$	$50–$75
$	under $50

**All prices are for a standard double room, excluding 9% tax.*

In the Park

All reservations are made through the **Yosemite Concession Services Corporation** (Central Reservations, 5410 E. Home Ave., Fresno 93727, ☎ 209/252–4848, FAX 209/456–0542).

$$$$ **Ahwahnee Hotel.** This grand, 1920s-style mountain lodge is constructed of rocks and sugar-pine logs, with exposed timbers and beau-

tiful scenery. The decorative style of the Grand Lounge and Solarium is a tribute to the local Miwoks and Paiutes, and the motifs continue in the room decor. *123 rooms. Restaurant, lounge, pool, tennis. D, MC, V.*

$$–$$$ **Wawona Hotel.** This 1879 National Historic Landmark is in the southern end of Yosemite National Park, near the Mariposa Grove of Big Trees. It's an old-fashioned Victorian estate of whitewashed buildings with wraparound verandas. Guests gather around the fire in the main hotel's parlor, where a pianist sings Cole Porter tunes on weekend evenings. Most rooms are small and half do not have private bath. There is a golf course adjacent to the hotel. *105 rooms. Restaurant, lounge, pool, tennis, horseback riding. D, MC, V.*

$$–$$$ **Yosemite Lodge.** The rooms in this lodge vary from fairly rustic motel-style units with two double beds and decorated in rust and green to very rustic cabins with no baths but within walking distance of Yosemite Falls. *495 rooms. Restaurant, lounge, pool. D, MC, V.*

$–$$ **Curry Village.** These are plain accommodations: cabins with bath and without and tent cabins with rough wood frames and canvas walls and roofs. It's a step up from camping (linens, blankets, and maid service are provided), but food and cooking are not allowed because of the animals. If you stay in a cabin without bath, showers and toilets are centrally located, as they would be in a campground. *180 cabins, 426 tent cabins, 8 hotel rooms. Cafeteria, pool, ice-skating. D, MC, V.*

$ **Housekeeping Camp.** These are also rustic tent cabins, set along the Merced River, but you can cook here on gas stoves rented from the front desk. The cabins are usually rented for several weeks at a time and are difficult to get; reserving at least 366 days in advance is advised. *282 tent cabins with no bath (maximum 4 per cabin). Toilet and shower in central shower house. D, MC, V.*

Outside the Park

$$$$ **Marriott's Tenaya Lodge.** One of the region's newest and largest hotels, this is for people who enjoy hiking in the wilderness but prefer coming home to full-service luxury. A southwestern motif prevails in the ample rooms, which are decorated in mauve, green, and rust. The hotel is about a one-hour drive from Yosemite Village. *1122 Hwy. 41, Box 159, Fish Camp 93623, ☎ 209/683–6555 or 800/635–5807, FAX 209/683–8684. 242 rooms. 2 restaurants, 2 lounges, room service, indoor-outdoor pools, health club, laundry and dry cleaning, meeting room. AE, D, DC, MC, V.*

$$–$$$ **Narrow Gauge Inn.** This is one of several B&Bs close to the park's Fish Camp entrance. It's comfortably furnished, with an old-fashioned decor and railroad memorabilia. Next door is the Yosemite Mountain-Sugar Pine Railroad (*see* Off the Beaten Track, *above*). The inn's restaurant is one of the best in Fish Camp. *48571 Hwy. 41, Fish Camp 93623, ☎ 209/683–7720, FAX 209/683–2139. 26 rooms. Restaurant, bar, pool, hot tub. D, MC, V. Closed Nov.–Mar.*

Camping

Reservations for camping are required year-round in Yosemite Valley and from spring through fall at three campgrounds outside the valley. They are strongly recommended at any time. Reservations for all campgrounds in Yosemite are made through **MISTIX** (Box 85705, San Diego, CA 92186-5705, ☎ 619/452–8787 or 800/365–2267 in the U.S. and Canada, TDD 800/284–7275). You can reserve campsites no sooner than eight weeks in advance, and you should indicate the campground and your first, second, and third choices of arrival dates. Campsites cost $14 per night in the valley, $12 outside the valley. If space is available, you can also make reservations in person at the Campground Reservations Office in Yosemite Valley, but we strongly recommend making them ahead of time. The campgrounds outside the valley that are not on the reservation system are first-come, first-served.

Words of warning: Park regulations mandate that visitors store food properly to prevent bears from getting it. Much property damage is caused when these animals go after food or trash, and the physical safety of campers is obviously at risk as well. Canisters for backpackers may be rented for $3 per day in most park stores. Also, keep an eye peeled for rattlesnakes below 7,000 feet. Though rarely fatal, bites require a doctor's attention. Marmots, small members of the squirrel family, have particular dining preferences. They enjoy getting under a vehicle and chewing on radiator hoses and car wiring! They aren't afraid of humans, considering their gear a source of food, including boots, backpacks, etc. Always check under the hood before driving away. Finally, don't drink the water directly from streams and lakes, as intestinal disorder may result.

SEQUOIA AND KINGS CANYON NATIONAL PARKS

The other two Sierra national parks are usually spoken of together. These adjacent parks share their administration and a main highway. Although you may want to concentrate on either Kings Canyon or Sequoia, most people visit both parks in one trip.

Like Yosemite, Sequoia and General Grant national parks were established in 1890. The General Grant National Park was added to over the years to include the Redwood Canyon area and the drainages of the south and middle forks of the Kings River, and eventually renamed Kings Canyon National Park. Both Sequoia and Kings Canyon now extend east to the Sierra crest. The most recent major addition was to Sequoia in 1978, to prevent the development of the Mineral King area as a ski resort.

The major attractions of both parks are the big trees (*Sequoiadendron giganteum*—the most extensive groves and the most impressive specimens are found here) and the stunning alpine scenery. These trees are the largest living things in the world. They are not as tall as the coast redwoods (*Sequoia sempervirens*), but they are much more massive and older. The exhibits at the visitor centers and the interpretive booklets that you can get there and take with you along the trails will explain the special relationship between these trees and fire (their thick, fibrous bark helps protect them from fire and insects) and how they live so long and grow so big.

The parks encompass land from only 1,200 feet above sea level to more than 14,000 feet. Mt. Whitney, on the eastern side of Sequoia, is the highest mountain (14,494 feet) in the contiguous United States. The greatest portion of both parks is accessible only on foot or with a pack animal. The Generals Highway (46 miles from Highway 180 in Kings Canyon National Park to the Ash Mountain Entrance in Sequoia National Park) links two major groves in the two parks and is open year-round (except during severe weather).

Summer is the most crowded season, but even then it is much less crowded than at Yosemite. Snow may remain on the ground in the sequoia groves into June but is usually gone by mid-month. The flowers in the Giant Forest meadows hit their peak in July. Fall is an especially good time to visit. The weather is usually warm and calm, and there are no crowds.

The entrance fee is $5 per car, $3 for pedestrians and cyclists, for a week's stay in both parks.

Exploring

Numbers in the margin correspond to points of interest on the Sequoia and Kings Canyon National Parks map.

If you take Highway 180 to the parks, you come into Kings Canyon National Park at the Big Stump Entrance. One mile later, head left (north) at the well-marked fork in the road, which keeps you on Highway 180
1 and takes you to **Grant Grove.** This is the grove (or what remained of a larger grove decimated by logging) that was designated as General Grant National Park in 1890 and is now the most highly developed area of Kings Canyon National Park. A walk along the 1-mile Big Stump Trail, starting near the park entrance, graphically demonstrates the effects of heavy logging on these groves.

At Grant Grove Village, you will find a visitor center, gas station, grocery store, campgrounds, coffee shop, and lodging. The visitor center has exhibits on *Sequoiadendron giganteum* and the area. Trail maps for this and the other major areas of the two parks may be purchased for $1 each here and at all the visitor centers. Horses are available for rent in this area.

A spur road leads west less than 1 mile to the General Grant Grove. An easy ⅓-mile paved trail leads through the grove and is fairly accessible to travelers with disabilities. The most famous tree here is the **General Grant.** In total mass it is not as large as the General Sherman Tree in Sequoia, but it is nearly as tall and slightly wider at its base. The **Gamlin Cabin** is one of several pioneer cabins that can be visited in the parks. A large sequoia was cut for display at the 1876 Philadelphia Centennial Exhibition; the **Centennial Stump** still remains.

2 **Hume Lake,** just outside the park, is a reservoir built early this century by loggers; today it is the site of many Christian camps, as well as a public campground. This is a pretty, small lake with views of high mountains in the distance. To reach it, follow Highway 180 north and east 8 miles from Grant Grove, then head south 3 miles on Hume Lake Road. The lake is also accessible by a side road off Generals Highway.

Beyond the turnoff for Hume Lake, Highway 180 (Kings Canyon Highway) is closed in winter (usually November–April). In summer you
★ 3 can take this road for a **spectacular drive to the Cedar Grove area**, a valley along the south fork of the Kings River. The drive takes one hour from Grant Grove to the end of the road, where you turn around for the ride back. Although it is steep in places, this is not a difficult road to drive. Built by convict labor in the 1930s, the road clings to some dramatic cliffs along the way, so you should watch out for falling rocks. The highway passes the scars where large groves of big trees were logged at the beginning of the century, and it runs along the south fork itself as well as through dry foothills covered with yuccas that bloom in the summer. There are amazing views down into the deepest gorge in the United States, at the confluence of the two forks, and up the canyons to the High Sierra.

Cedar Grove, named for the incense cedars that grow here, has campgrounds and lodging, a small ranger station, snack bar, convenience market, and gas station. Horses can be rented here; they are a good

Sequoia and Kings Canyon National Parks

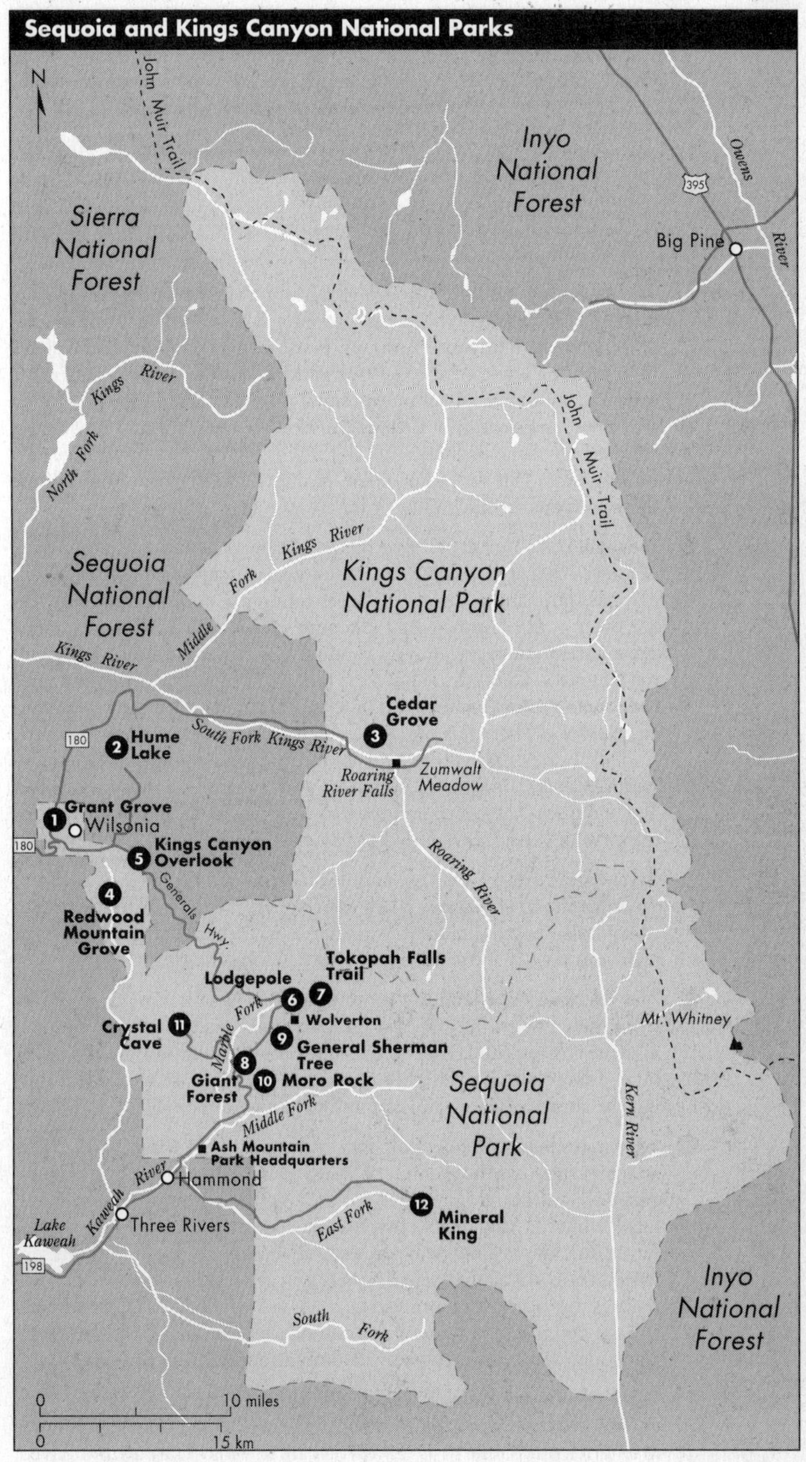
N
John Muir Trail
Inyo National Forest
Owens River
395
Sierra National Forest
Big Pine
Kings River
North Fork
John Muir Trail
Kings River
Middle Fork
Sequoia National Forest
Kings Canyon National Park
Kings River
Cedar Grove
Hume Lake
South Fork Kings River
180
Roaring River Falls
Zumwalt Meadow
Grant Grove
Wilsonia
180
Kings Canyon Overlook
Generals Hwy.
Roaring River
Redwood Mountain Grove
Tokopah Falls Trail
Lodgepole
Marble Fork
Wolverton
Crystal Cave
General Sherman Tree
Mt. Whitney
Giant Forest
Moro Rock
Sequoia National Park
Middle Fork
Ash Mountain Park Headquarters
Kern River
Kaweah River
Hammond
Lake Kaweah
Three Rivers
East Fork
Mineral King
198
Inyo National Forest
South Fork
0
10 miles
0
15 km

way to explore this country. There are also short trails (one around Zumwalt Meadow, one to the base of Roaring River Falls), and Cedar Grove is the trailhead for many backpackers. If you're staying at Grant Grove or Giant Forest, Cedar Grove is a lovely day trip.

The **Generals Highway** begins south of Grant Grove and runs through this smaller portion of Kings Canyon National Park, through a part of Sequoia National Forest, and then through Sequoia National Park to the Giant Forest and on to the southern entrance to these parks at Ash Mountain.

★ 4 The **Redwood Mountain Grove** is the largest grove of big trees in the world. There are several paved turnouts (about 4 miles from the beginning of the highway) from which you can look out over the grove (and into the smog of the Central Valley), but the grove is accessible only on foot or horseback. Less than 2 miles farther, on the north side
5 of the road, a large turnout, **Kings Canyon Overlook,** affords vistas across the canyon of the backcountry and mountain peaks. If you drive east on Highway 180 to Cedar Grove along the south fork, you will see these canyons at much closer range.

6 **Lodgepole,** in a U-shape canyon on the Marble Fork of the Kaweah River, is a developed area with a campground, gas station, store, public laundry, gift shop, and post office. An ice-cream parlor and public showers are open in the summer only. Lodgepole pines, rather than sequoias, grow here because the canyon conducts air down from the high country that is too cold for the big trees but is just right for lodgepoles. The
★ **Lodgepole Visitor Center** (☎ 209/565–3782; ⏲ Summer, daily 8–6; winter, daily 9–5) here has the best exhibits in Sequoia or Kings Canyon, a small theater that shows films about the parks, and the Walter Fry Nature Center (open in the summer), which features hands-on exhibits and activities that are geared toward children. You can buy tickets for the Crystal Cave (*see below*) at the visitor center.

A very short marked nature trail leads from behind the visitor center down to the river. Except when the river is flowing fast (be very cautious), this is a good place to rinse one's feet in cool water, because the trail runs past a "beach" of small rocks along the river.

7 The **Tokopah Falls Trail** is a more strenuous, 2-mile hike up the river from the campground (pick up a map at the visitor center), but it is also the closest you can get to the high country without taking a long hike. This is a lovely trail, but remember to bring insect repellent during the summer, when the mosquitoes can be ferocious.

8 Four miles beyond Lodgepole you will come to the **Giant Forest.** This area presently has the greatest concentration of accommodations (summer only), although plans call for moving these to the Wuksachi Village, which is under construction just north of Lodgepole. In the meantime, this is a magical place to stay because of the numerous and varied trails through a series of sequoia groves. During the summer, there is a grocery store, cafeteria, and two gift shops at Giant Forest Village and a wide range of accommodations at Giant Forest Lodge. The lodge also runs a full-service dining room during the summer.

Whether you are staying here or elsewhere in the parks, get the map of the local trails and start exploring. The well-constructed trails range in length from ⅓ mile to as far as you care to walk. They are not paved, crowded, or lined with barricades, so you quickly get the feeling of being on your own in the woods, surrounded by the most impressive trees you are ever likely to see.

Be sure to visit one of the meadows. They are lovely, especially in July when the flowers are in full bloom, and you can get some of the best views of the big trees. **Round Meadow,** just north of Giant Forest Village, is the most easily accessible, with its ⅓-mile, wheelchair-accessible "Trail For All People." **Crescent and Log meadows** are accessible by slightly longer trails. Tharp's Log, at Log Meadow, is a small and rustic pioneer cabin built in a fallen sequoia. There is also a log cabin at **Huckleberry Meadow** that children will enjoy exploring.

9 The most famous tree here is the **General Sherman Tree.** If you aren't up for hiking, you can still get to this tree. In summer there is usually a ranger nearby to answer questions, and there are benches so you can sit and contemplate one of the largest living things in the world. The tree is 274.9 feet tall and 102.6 feet around at its base, but what makes this the biggest tree is the fact that it is so wide for such a long way up: The first major branch is 130 feet up.

The Congress Trail starts here and travels past a series of large trees and younger sequoias. This is probably the most popular trail in the area, and it also has the most detailed booklet, so it is a good way to learn about the ecology of the groves. The booklet costs 50¢ and is available in summer from a vending machine near the General Sherman Tree.

A 2½-mile spur road takes off from the Generals Highway near the village and will lead you to other points of interest in the Giant Forest area as well as to the trails to Crescent and Log meadows. The road actually goes through the Tunnel Log (there is a bypass for RVs that are too tall—7 feet 9 inches and more—to fit). Auto Log is merely a fallen tree onto which you can drive your car for a photograph (if that seems like a reasonable idea to you).

★ 10 This is also the road to **Moro Rock,** a granite monolith 6,725 feet high, which rises from the edge of the Giant Forest. During the Depression, the Civilian Conservation Corps built a fabulous staircase to the top. There are 400 steps, and, although there is a railing along most of the route, the trail often climbs along narrow ledges over steep drops. The view from the top is striking. Southwest you look down the Kaweah River to Three Rivers, Lake Kaweah, and—on clear days—the Central Valley and the Coast Range. Northeast you look up into the High Sierra. Below, you look down thousands of feet to the middle fork of the Kaweah River.

★ 11 **Crystal Cave** is the best known of Sequoia's many caves. Its interior was formed from limestone that metamorphosed into marble and is decorated with stalactites and stalagmites. To visit the cave, you must first stop at the Lodgepole Visitor Center or the Foothills Visitor Center at Ash Mountain (on Generals Highway 1 mile inside Sequoia National Park) to buy a ticket—they're not sold at the cave. Then, drive to the end of a narrow, twisting, 7-mile road off the Generals Highway, 2.2 miles south of Giant Forest Village. From the parking area it is a 15-minute hike down a steep path to the cave's entrance. There are 45-minute guided tours daily on the half hour between 10 AM and 3 PM from mid-June through Labor Day and hourly Friday through Monday from mid-May to mid-June and after Labor Day through September. ☎ *209/565–3758 or 209/565–3134.* ☛ *$4 adults, $2 senior citizens and children 6–12.*

12 The **Mineral King** area is a relatively recent addition to the parks. In the 1960s the U.S. Forest Service planned to have Walt Disney Productions develop a winter-sports resort here, but the opposition of residents and conservation groups led to its incorporation into Sequoia

National Park in 1978. It is accessible in summer only by a narrow, twisty, and steep road (trailers and RVs not recommended) that takes off from Highway 198 several miles outside the park entrance. The road is only 25 miles long, but budget 90 minutes each way from Highway 198. This is a tough but exciting drive to a beautiful high valley. There are two campgrounds and a ranger station; facilities are very limited but some supplies are available. Many backpackers use this as a trailhead, and there are a number of fine trails for strenuous day hikes.

Sports

Hiking

As in Yosemite, hiking is the primary sport in these two parks. Talk to the rangers at the visitor centers about which trails they recommend when you are there. Keep in mind that you will have to become acclimated to the altitude (over 6,000 feet at Giant Forest) before you can exert yourself fully.

Horseback Riding

Horseback riding is available at Grant Grove, Cedar Grove, Wolverton (between Lodgepole and Giant Forest), and Mineral King. Ask at the visitor centers for specifics.

Swimming

If you get hot and need a swim, try Hume Lake (*see* Exploring, *above*). Don't try to swim in the fast-running Sierra rivers.

Winter Sports

In the winter there is cross-country skiing and snowshoeing. Networks of marked trails are found at Grant Grove and Giant Forest. Rentals, lessons, and tours are offered by Sequoia Ski Touring Center (☎ 209/565–3435) at Wolverton and Grant Grove.

Rangers lead snowshoe walks ($1 snowshoe rental or bring your own) through Grant Grove and Giant Forest on winter weekends. You can also use the shoes on the cross-country trails at these two areas. Snowshoes can be rented from Sequoia Ski Touring at Wolverton.

Year-Round Activities

Montecito Sequoia Resort provides year-round family-oriented recreation. Depending on the season, lodging rates include all meals or just breakfast and dinner. Winter activities include cross-country skiing and lessons. Summer activities, offered in a six-night Club Med–like package, include canoeing, sailing, waterskiing, horseback riding, a preschool program, volleyball, horseshoes, tennis, archery, nature hikes, and a heated pool. In spring and fall, most of the summer activities occur, but guests are able to book shorter stays. *Generals Hwy., 4 mi south of Hume Lake, ☎ 800/227–9900 for brochures and information, FAX 415/967–0540.*

Dining

Dining in Sequoia and Kings Canyon national parks is even less of a gourmet experience than dining in Yosemite, but acceptable food is available. Again, we suggest that you bring food (especially snacks, fresh fruit, and beverages) with you. It will give you more freedom in planning your day. Giant Forest Village has a market that is open during the summer only; year-round markets are at Lodgepole and Grant Grove. There are places to get a meal inside the parks, and the food is not expensive and will satisfy hunger pangs. All the restaurants within the parks are managed by **Sequoia Guest Services** (☎ 209/565–3381); dress is casual at all of them.

Food should never be left overnight in cars, because bears frequently break in to get it, causing significant property damage.

CATEGORY	COST*
$$	$15–$25
$	under $15

per person for a three-course meal, excluding drinks, service, and 7¼% tax

$–$$ Giant Forest Lodge Dining Room. This is the fanciest restaurant in the two parks, with tablecloths, soft lighting, picture windows overlooking the meadows, and a quiet atmosphere. The cuisine is basic American, featuring prime rib, shrimp, creamy pastas, halibut, and vegetarian pastas. Dinner is served daily, but breakfast is served on weekends only. ✕ *AE, MC, V. No lunch. Closed mid-Oct.–mid-May.*

$ Cedar Grove Restaurant. This self-serve restaurant serves trout, top sirloin, hamburgers, hot dogs, and sandwiches for lunch and dinner. Breakfast is eggs, bacon, and toast. You can take food from the restaurant to picnic tables along the river's edge. ✕ *No credit cards. Closed mid-Oct.–mid-May.*

$ Grant Grove Coffee Shop. This spacious family-style restaurant, with wood tables and chairs and a long counter, serves American standards for breakfast, lunch, and dinner: eggs, burgers, and steak. There are also chef's salads, fruit platters, and seasonal fish specials. ✕ *AE, MC, V.*

$ Village Cafeteria. A good selection of entrées, salads, desserts, and vegetables is served in a cafeteria-style setting. Breakfast, lunch, and dinner are served—the cafeteria is the place to feed a family on a budget without getting heartburn in the bargain. ✕ *No credit cards. Closed mid-Oct.–mid-May.*

Lodging

All the park's lodges and cabins are open during the summer months, but in winter only some of those in Grant Grove remain open. A variety of accommodations is offered, from rustic cabins without baths at Grant Grove to deluxe motels at Giant Forest. From November through April, excluding holiday periods, low-season rates are in effect, resulting in savings of 20%–30%. The town of Three Rivers on Highway 198 southwest of the park has a few more lodges and restaurants from which to choose.

Lodging facilities within the park are operated by **Sequoia Guest Services** (Box 789, Three Rivers 93271, ☎ 209/561–3314, FAX 209/561–3135; AE, MC, V). Reservations are recommended for visits at any time of the year because it's a long way out if there's no room at these inns.

CATEGORY	COST*
$$$	$75–$100
$$	$50–$75
$	under $50

**All prices are for a standard double room, excluding 10% tax.*

$$$ Cedar Grove Lodge. At the bottom of Kings Canyon, in one of the prettiest areas of the parks, is Cedar Grove, a good location for those who plan on staying a few days and doing a lot of day hiking. Although accommodations are close to the road and there is quite a bit of traffic through here, Cedar Grove manages to retain a quiet atmosphere. Those who don't want to camp will have to book way in advance—the motel-lodge has only 18 rooms. Each room is air-conditioned and carpeted and has a private shower and two queen-size beds. ☖ *Closed Oct.–late May.*

$-$$$ **Giant Forest Lodge.** There are seven different types of accommodations in this Sequoia National Park complex, including a deluxe motel, rustic cabins without bathrooms, and family cabins that sleep six. Facilities and decor vary: Some cabins have kerosene lamps and propane heat; motel rooms have carpeted floors and double- and queen-size beds. Prices range accordingly.

$$ **Grant Grove Village.** The nicest accommodations here are the carpeted cabins with private baths, electric wall heaters, and double beds. Other cabins are simpler, with woodstoves providing heat and kerosene lamps providing light. A central rest room and shower facility is nearby.

Camping

Campgrounds are the most economical ($5–$10 per night) accommodations in Sequoia and Kings Canyon, and probably the most fun. Located near each of the major tourist centers, the parks' campgrounds (☎ 209/565–3774 for general information) are equipped with tables, grills, drinking water, garbage cans, and either flush or pit toilets. The one campground that takes reservations, and only from Memorial Day through September, is Lodgepole in Sequoia (contact MISTIX, ☎ 800/365–2267). All others assign sites on a first-come, first-served basis, and on weekends in July and August they are often filled by Friday afternoon. Campgrounds permit a maximum of one vehicle and six persons per site.

Potwisha, Grant Grove, Lodgepole, Dorst, and Cedar Grove campgrounds are the only areas where trailers and RVs are permitted. Sanitary disposal stations are available year-round (snow permitting) in the Potwisha and Azalea campgrounds; from Memorial Day to October in Lodgepole and Dorst; and from May to mid-October in Sheep Creek and Cedar Grove. There are no hookups in the parks, and only a limited number of campsites can accommodate larger vehicles. The length limit for RVs is 40 feet, for trailers 35 feet.

Lodgepole, Potwisha, and Azalea campsites stay open all year, but Lodgepole is not plowed and camping is limited to recreational vehicles in plowed parking lots or snow tenting. Other campgrounds open some time from mid-April to Memorial Day or later in September or October. Some campgrounds in Sequoia National Forest (such as Landslide, a very small campground 3 miles from Hume Lake) are just about as convenient as those within the two national parks. Campers should be aware that the nights, and even the days, can be chilly into early June.

Bears can be a problem in every campground. You must use the metal food-storage boxes found at every site. Move all food, coolers, and items with a scent from your car to the storage box. Pets must be kept on a leash. Check bulletin boards and ask a ranger for further information. Failure to comply may result in a citation for you and the killing of the offending bear.

SIERRA NATIONAL PARKS ESSENTIALS

Arriving and Departing: Yosemite

By Bus

Yosemite VIA (☎ 209/384–2576 or 800/369–7275) runs four daily buses from Merced to Yosemite Valley, connecting with Greyhound (☎ 800/231–2222) and Amtrak (☎ 800/872–7245). The 2½-hour trip costs $30, which includes admission to the park.

By Car

Yosemite is a four- to five-hour drive from San Francisco and a six-hour drive from Los Angeles. From the west, Highways 41, 120, and 140 all intersect with Highway 99, which runs north–south through the Central Valley.

VIA HIGHWAY 41

As you come from the south, Highway 41 through Madera County is the most direct path to Yosemite from Fresno. Highway 41 (called Wawona Road inside the park) provides the most dramatic entrance, via the Wawona Tunnel, into Yosemite Valley. Sixty-four miles from Fresno (or 60 from Madera; connect with Highway 41 via Highway 145), Highway 41 leaves the San Joaquin Valley floor to climb through oak-studded hills before descending to the town of Oakhurst, the southern terminus of Highway 49, which links the Gold Country towns for 310 miles to the north. Highway 41 continues to the northeast past the Bass Lake turnoff into Fish Camp and on through the park's **South Entrance.** Two miles from this entrance is the **Mariposa Grove** of giant sequoias.

VIA HIGHWAY 140

Arch Rock Entrance is 75 miles northeast of Merced via Highway 140, the least mountainous road.

VIA HIGHWAY 120

Highway 120 is the northernmost route—the one that travels farthest and slowest through the foothills. You'll arrive at the park's **Big Oak Flat Entrance,** 88 miles east of Manteca. The more traveled routes are Highway 140 and Highway 41.

If you are coming from the east, you could cross the Sierra from Lee Vining on Highway 120 (Tioga Pass). This route takes you over the Sierra crest, past Tuolumne Meadows, and down the west slope of the range. It's scenic but the mountain driving may be stressful for some, and it's open only in the summer.

By Plane

You can fly into one of the large California airports (San Francisco or Los Angeles) and then either rent a car or take public transportation to Yosemite. **Fresno Air Terminal** (5175 Clinton Way, ☎ 209/498–4095) is the nearest major airport. It is served by **Delta** (☎ 800/221–1212), **American** (☎ 800/433–7300), **USAir** (☎ 800/428–4322), and several regional carriers. **United Express** (☎ 800/241–6522) serves Merced Airport (20 Macready Dr., administration ☎ 209/385–6873).

Getting Around Yosemite

Auto traffic in Yosemite National Park is sometimes restricted during peak periods. Check conditions before driving in.

Thanks to the free shuttle bus that runs around the eastern end of Yosemite Valley (7:30 AM–10 PM in the summer, 10–10 the rest of the year), it is possible to visit the park without your own car. From 9 to 5 in the summer, another free shuttle runs from Wawona to Big Trees. Large RVs and trailers are not allowed on this road. You should have tire chains when you drive in these mountains from November through April; the eastern entrance to the park at Tioga Pass is at nearly 10,000 feet.

Guided Tours

California Parlor Car Tours (Cathedral Hill Hotel, 1101 Van Ness Ave., San Francisco 94109, ☎ 415/474–7500 or 800/227–4250) offers several tours that include Yosemite (along with Monterey or Hearst Castle) and depart from either San Francisco or Los Angeles. All tours to Yosemite are round-trip. Lodging and some meals are included; you can choose to stay in either Yosemite Lodge or the Ahwahnee (there's a difference in price, of course). We recommend that you not consider any tour that leaves you less than one full day in the valley (and that is cutting it very short!).

Yosemite Concession Services (5410 E. Home, Fresno 93727, ☎ 209/372–1240) offers daily guided tours. Advance reservations are required for some. Tickets can also be purchased at Yosemite locations. A two-hour valley-floor tour covers the best sightseeing points. It costs $14.25 for adults, $13.25 for senior citizens, $7.25 children under 12. A six-hour trip to the Mariposa Grove of Big Trees costs $28 adults, $27.50 senior citizens, $13.75 children under 12. The Grand Tour (June–November) costs $38.50 adults, $35.25 senior citizens, $19 children under 12. Guided Saddle Trips start from three stables located in the park. Two-hour rides are $30, half-day rides $40, full-day rides $60. Reservations are recommended.

Arriving and Departing: Sequoia/Kings Canyon

By Bus

Greyhound (☎ 800/231–2222) serves Fresno and Visalia. **Amtrak** (☎ 800/872–7245) serves Fresno.

By Car

Under average conditions, it takes about six hours to reach Kings Canyon and Sequoia national parks from San Francisco and about five hours to do so from Los Angeles. Two major routes, Highways 180 and 198, intersect with Highway 99, which runs north–south through the Central Valley.

From the north, enter Kings Canyon National Park via Highway 180, 53 miles east of Fresno. From the south, enter Sequoia National Park via Highway 198, 36 miles from Visalia. If you are driving up from Los Angeles, take Highway 65 north from Bakersfield to Highway 198 east of Visalia.

By Plane

Fresno is the nearest major airport (*see* Arriving and Departing: Yosemite, *above*)

Getting Around Sequoia/Kings Canyon

By Car

Highways 180 and 198 are connected through the parks by the **Generals Highway,** a paved two-lane road that is open year-round but may be closed for weeks at a time during heavy snowstorms (carry chains in winter). Drivers of RVs and drivers who are not comfortable on mountain roads should probably avoid the southern stretch between the Potwisha Campground and Giant Forest Village. These very twisty 16 miles of narrow road rise almost 5,000 feet and are not advised for vehicles over 22 feet long. Few roads up the west slope of the Sierra rise so quickly through the foothills and offer such spectacular views of the high country. The rest of the Generals Highway is a well-graded, two-lane road and a pleasure to drive.

Highway 180 beyond Grant Grove to Cedar Grove and the road to Mineral King are open only in summer. Both roads, especially the latter, which is very steep and unpaved in sections, may present a challenge to inexperienced drivers. Large vehicles are discouraged. Campers and RVs are not advised on the Mineral King road. Trailers are not allowed in Mineral King campgrounds.

By Shuttle Bus

Sequoia Guest Services (☎ 209/565–3381) runs a shuttle bus between major points in the Giant Forest and Lodgepole. One-time fares are $1 per person, and $3 for a family of five or fewer; all-day passes are $3 per person, and $6 for a family of five or fewer.

Guided Tours

Sequoia Guest Services (☎ 209/565–3381) conducts an all-day van tour of **Kings Canyon** (mid-May–mid-Oct.; $22 adults, $20 senior citizens over 60, $11 children). A Giant Forest tour is being phased out, though it may still be offered in 1996. Sign up for tours at the Giant Forest Lodge.

Important Addresses and Numbers

Emergencies

Dial 911 for **police, medical,** and other emergencies.

Reservations

MISTIX (☎ 800/365–2267) handles reservations for all campgrounds in all three parks that are not offered on a first-come, first-served basis.

Sequoia Guest Services (Box 789, Three Rivers 93271, ☎ 209/561–3314) is the concessionaire for all lodgings in Sequoia and Kings Canyon national parks.

Yosemite Concession Services Corporation (Central Reservations, 5410 E. Home, Fresno, CA 93727, ☎ 209/252–4848) handles reservations for all lodgings in Yosemite National Park.

Road Conditions

Sequoia/Kings Canyon Road and Weather Information (☎ 209/565–3351).

Northern California Road Conditions (☎ 800/427–7623).

Yosemite Area Road and Weather Conditions (☎ 209/372–0200).

Visitor Information

National Park Service, Fort Mason (Bldg. 201, San Francisco, CA 94123, ☎ 415/556–0560) has information about Yosemite, Sequoia, and Kings Canyon national parks.

Sequoia and Kings Canyon National Parks (Three Rivers 93271, ☎ 209/565–3134; open daily 8–4:30).

Southern Yosemite Visitors Bureau (Box 1404, Oakhurst, CA 93644, ☎ 209/683–4636) provides brochures and information about areas in and around Madera County.

Yosemite National Park (National Park Service, Information Office, Box 577, Yosemite National Park, CA 95389, ☎ 209/372–0200 for a 24-hr connection to all recorded information, or ☎ 209/372–0264 weekdays 9–5).

9 Monterey Bay

The Monterey Peninsula has some of the state's most luxurious resorts and golf courses, interesting historic sites, and beautiful coastal scenery. Point Lobos is among the state's most treasured parks. Depending on which way you look, scenic 17-Mile Drive is rustic (cypress trees, craggy coastal views) or just plain elegant (the Crocker Marble Palace, the Pebble Beach Golf Links). There are many good restaurants in Monterey and Carmel and plenty of places to shop. The weather is usually mild, though visitors should prepare themselves for fog and cool temperatures.

THE INTEREST IS PERPETUALLY FRESH. On no other coast that I know shall you enjoy, in calm, sunny weather, such a spectacle of ocean's greatness, such beauty of changing color or such degrees of thunder in the sound." What Robert Louis Stevenson wrote of the Monterey Peninsula in 1879 is no less true today—it still provides a spectacle that is as exciting on the first visit as on the 23rd.

By Maria Lenhart and Vicki Elliott

Updated by Claudia Gioseffi

A semicircle about 90 miles (144 kilometers) across, Monterey Bay arcs into the coast at almost the exact halfway point between California's northern and southern borders. Santa Cruz sits at the top of the curve, and the Monterey Peninsula, including Monterey, Pacific Grove, and Carmel, occupies the lower end. In between, Highway 1 cruises along the coastline, passing windswept beaches piled high with sand dunes. Along the route are fields of artichoke plants, the towns of Watsonville and Castroville, and Fort Ord, which has begun its transition from army base to civilian mixed-use development.

The bay is blessed by nature. Here are deep green forests of Monterey cypress, oddly gnarled and wind-twisted trees that grow nowhere else. Here also is a vast undersea canyon, larger and deeper than the Grand Canyon, that supports a rich assortment of marine life, from fat, barking sea lions to tiny plantlike anemones.

Carefully preserved adobe houses and missions testify to the Monterey Peninsula's unique place in California history. With the arrival of Father Junípero Serra and Commander Don Gaspar de Portola from Spain in 1770, Monterey became both the military and ecclesiastical capital of Alta California. Portola established the first of California's four Spanish presidios, while Serra founded the second of 21 Franciscan missions, later moving it from Monterey to its current site in Carmel.

When Mexico revolted against Spain in 1822, Monterey remained the capital of California under Mexican rule. The town grew into a lively seaport, drawing Yankee sea traders who added their own cultural and political influence. Then, on July 7, 1846, Commodore John Sloat arrived in Monterey and raised the American flag over the Custom House, claiming California for the United States.

Monterey's political importance in the new territory was short-lived, however. Although the state constitution was framed in Colton Hall, the town was all but forgotten once gold was discovered at Sutter's Mill near Sacramento. After the Gold Rush, the state capital moved from Monterey and the town became a sleepy backwater.

At the turn of the century, however, the Monterey Peninsula began to draw tourists with the opening of the Del Monte Hotel, the most palatial resort the West Coast had ever seen. Writers and artists also discovered the peninsula, adding a rich legacy that remains to this day.

For visitors, the decline of Monterey as California's most important political and population center can be seen as a blessing. The layers of Spanish and Mexican history remain remarkably undisturbed, while the land and sea continue to inspire and delight.

EXPLORING

Despite its compact size, the Monterey Peninsula is packed with diversions—it would take more than a weekend just to get beyond the surface. Although most of the region's communities are situated only a few minutes' drive away from each other, each is remarkably different in flavor.

If you have an interest in California history and historic preservation, the place to start is in Monterey, where you need at least two full days to explore the adobe buildings along the Path of History, a state historic park encompassing much of the downtown area. Fans of Victorian architecture will want to explore the many fine examples in Pacific Grove. In Carmel you can shop till you drop, and when summer and weekend hordes overwhelm the town's boutiques, art galleries, houseware outlets, and gift shops, you can slip off to enjoy the incomparable loveliness of the Carmel coast.

A sweater or windbreaker is nearly always necessary along the coast, where a cool breeze is usually blowing and the fog is on the way in or out. Inland, temperatures in Salinas or Carmel Valley can be a good 15 or 20 degrees warmer than those in Carmel and Monterey.

Santa Cruz

Numbers in the margin correspond to points of interest on the Monterey Bay map.

❶ The beach town of **Santa Cruz** is sheltered by the surrounding mountains from the coastal fog to the north and south and from the smoggy skies of the San Francisco Bay area. The climate here is mild, and it is usually warmer and sunnier than elsewhere along the coast this far north. Something of a haven for those opting out of the rat race, and a bastion of '60s-style counterculture values, Santa Cruz has been at the forefront of such very Californian trends as health food, recycling, and environmentalism. It is less manicured than its upmarket neighbors to the south, but more urban than the agricultural towns between it and the Monterey Peninsula.

The town gets something of its youthful ambience from the nearby **University of California at Santa Cruz.** The school's harmonious redwood buildings are perched on the forested hills above the town, and the campus is tailor-made for the contemplative life, with a juxtaposition of sylvan settings and sweeping vistas over open meadows onto the bay. The humanities faculty offers a major in the "History of Consciousness," and this does seem to be the perfect spot for it.

The earthquake of 1989 laid low much of **Pacific Garden Mall,** in the historic downtown section. The epicenter of the quake was only a few miles away, in the Santa Cruz mountains, and the unreinforced masonry of the town's older buildings proved extremely vulnerable. Rebuilding has been a long process, especially along Pacific Avenue, in the heart of the downtown area, but the landscapers have been out replanting and widening the sidewalks for the café traffic, and the spirit of the place is alive and well again.

TIME OUT **Caffè Pergolesi** (418 Cedar St., ☎ 408/426–1775), a Victorian residence not far from the downtown area, has become a humming coffeehouse with a very European flair. You can read the newspaper and enjoy a pastry at one of the veranda tables, or have a light meal inside, surrounded by local artists' work.

Santa Cruz has been a seaside resort since the mid-19th century, and ★ its **Boardwalk**'s 1911 **Merry-Go-Round** and **Giant Dipper** monster roller-coaster are national historic landmarks. Elsewhere along the

Monterey Bay

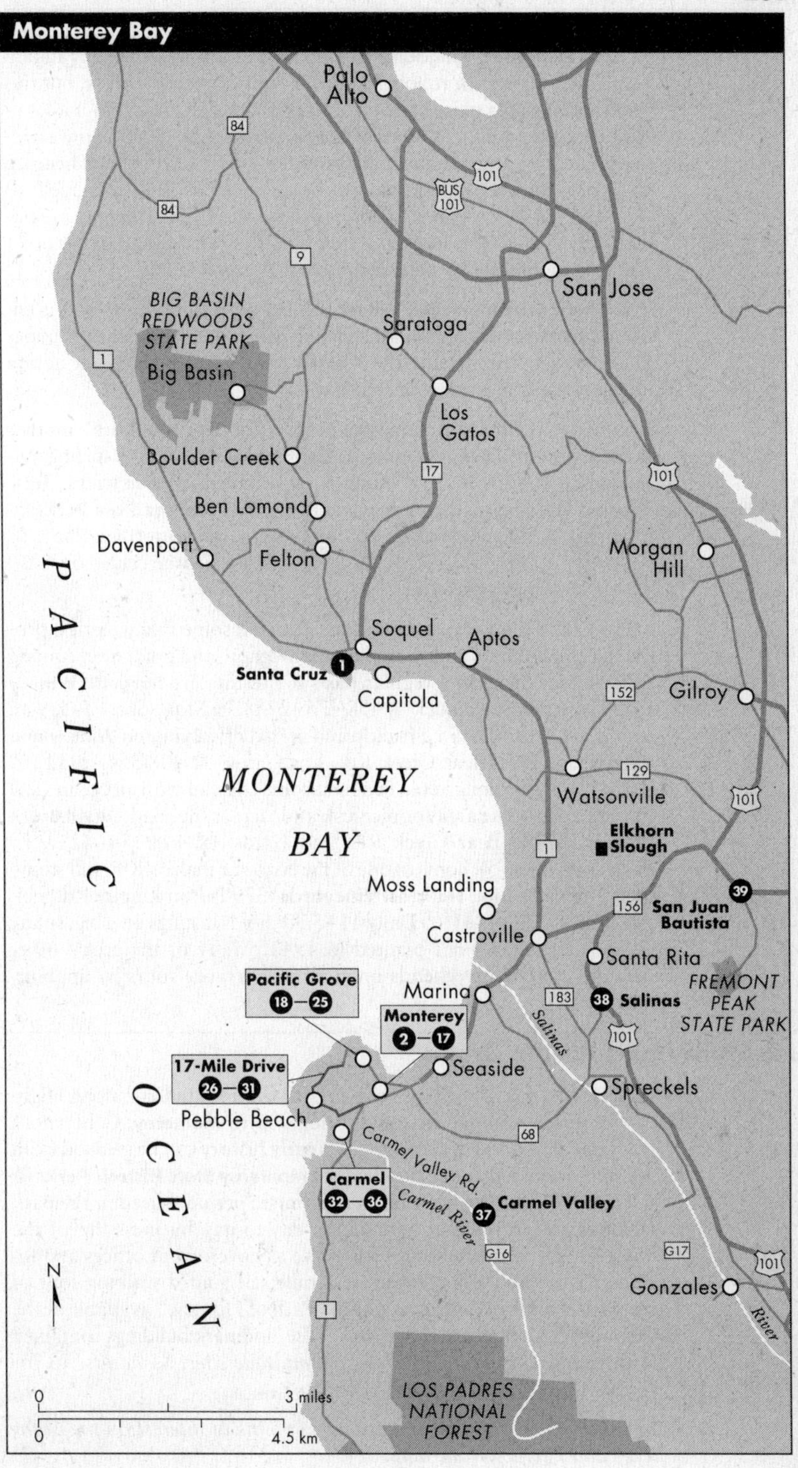

Boardwalk the **Casino Arcade** has its share of video-game technology, as does **Neptune's Kingdom,** which features a state-of-the-art miniature golf course with robotics and fiber-optics special effects, but this is still primarily a place of good old-fashioned fun. The colonnades of the turn-of-the-century **Cocoanut Grove** (☎ 408/423–2053), now a convention center and banquet hall, host a lavish Sunday brunch beneath the glass dome of its Sun Room. *Boardwalk,* ☎ *408/423–5590 or 408/426–7433. Day pass for unlimited rides, $17.95.* ⏲ *Daily Memorial Day–Labor Day, weekends and holidays rest of year; opens at 11 AM, closing times vary between dusk, 9 PM, and 11 PM.*

The **Santa Cruz Municipal Wharf** is lined with restaurants and is enlivened from below by the barking and baying of the sea lions that lounge in communal heaps under the wharf's pilings and shamelessly accept any seafood offerings tossed their way.

Down West Cliff Drive along the promontory are **Seal Rock,** another favored pinniped hangout, and the **Lighthouse,** which has a surfing museum (☎ 408/429–3429; ⏲ Noon–4, closed Tues.–Wed. in winter, Tues. in summer). The road continues on to **Natural Bridges State Park,** famous for its tide pools and a colony of monarch butterflies. *2531 W. Cliff Dr.,* ☎ *408/423–4609.* ⏲ *8 AM–sunset. Visitor center open 10 AM–4 PM. Parking fee: $6.*

Santa Cruz's temperate climate has attracted some fine wineries, producing chiefly chardonnay, cabernet sauvignon, and pinot noir. Among the wineries open on a regular basis for testing are **Bargetto Winery** (3535 N. Main St., Soquel, ☎ 408/475–2258; ⏲ Mon.–Sat. 10–5, Sun. 11–5), which also has a gift shop and art gallery; **Byington Winery and Vineyard** (21850 Bear Creek Rd., Los Gatos, ☎ 408/354–1111; ⏲ Daily 11–5), headquartered in a handsome château with an ocean view (there's a barbecue area for picnics); and, across the road, **David Bruce Winery** (21439 Bear Creek Rd., Los Gatos, ☎ 408/354–4214; ⏲ Wed.–Sun. noon–5), home to one of the last wine makers who still stomp their grapes by foot. **Hallcrest Vineyards** (379 Felton Empire Rd., Felton, ☎ 408/335–4441; ⏲ Daily 11–5:30) holds tastings on a big, sunny deck overlooking vines planted in 1941. Many of the area's other wineries are open weekends only; all will arrange tours by appointment.

Monterey and Pacific Grove

Follow the curve of the bay's coast south from Santa Cruz along High-
2 way 1, and a 45-mile drive will bring you to **Monterey,** California's first capital. A good deal of the city's early history can be gleaned from
★ the well-preserved adobe buildings of **Monterey State Historic Park** (☎ 408/649–7118). Far from being a hermetic period museum, the park facilities are an integral part of the day-to-day business life of the town—some of the buildings still serve as government offices and include a store and a restaurant. A 2-mile self-guided walking tour of the park is outlined in the brochure "Path of History," available at the Chamber of Commerce or at many of the landmark buildings contained in the park. *2-day tour package for multiple sites: $5 adults, $3 for youths 13–17, $2 children 6–12.*

Numbers in the margin correspond to points of interest on the Monterey and Pacific Grove map.

Monterey State Historic Park

3 A logical beginning to the walking tour is at the **Custom House** across from Fisherman's Wharf. Built by the Mexican government in 1827 and

Monterey and Pacific Grove

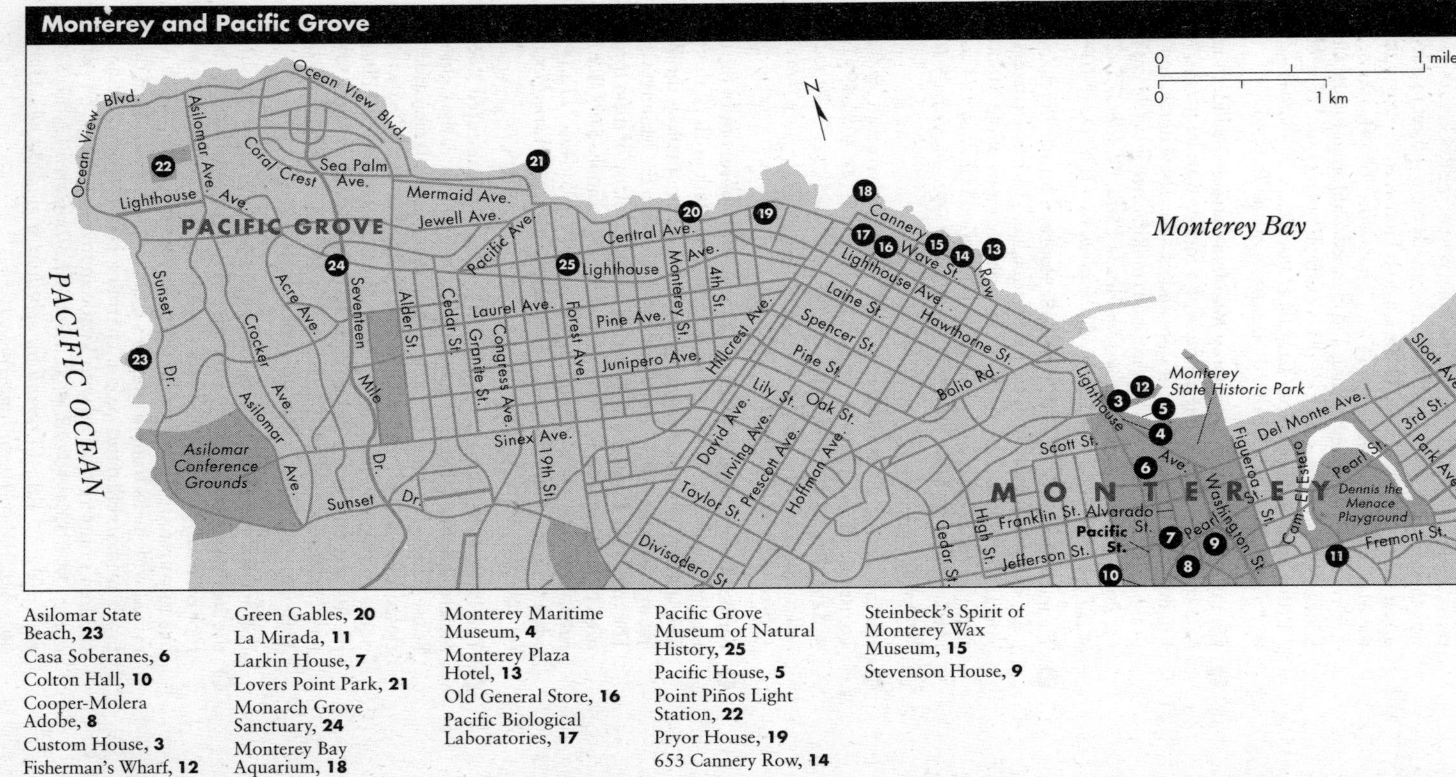

Asilomar State Beach, **23**
Casa Soberanes, **6**
Colton Hall, **10**
Cooper-Molera Adobe, **8**
Custom House, **3**
Fisherman's Wharf, **12**
Green Gables, **20**
La Mirada, **11**
Larkin House, **7**
Lovers Point Park, **21**
Monarch Grove Sanctuary, **24**
Monterey Bay Aquarium, **18**
Monterey Maritime Museum, **4**
Monterey Plaza Hotel, **13**
Old General Store, **16**
Pacific Biological Laboratories, **17**
Pacific Grove Museum of Natural History, **25**
Pacific House, **5**
Point Piños Light Station, **22**
Pryor House, **19**
653 Cannery Row, **14**
Steinbeck's Spirit of Monterey Wax Museum, **15**
Stevenson House, **9**

considered the oldest government building west of the Rockies, this adobe was the first stop for sea traders whose goods were subject to duty. An upper story was later added to the Custom House. At the beginning of the Mexican-American War in 1846, Commodore John Sloat raised the American flag over the building and claimed California for the United States. Now the lower floor displays examples of a typical cargo from a 19th-century trading ship. *1 Custom House Plaza,* ☎ *408/649–2909.* ☛ *Free.* ⏲ *Sept.–May, daily 10–4; June–Aug., daily 10–5.*

4 On the same plaza, the **Monterey Maritime Museum** includes the private collection of maritime artifacts of a former Carmel mayor, Allen Knight. Among the exhibits of ship models, scrimshaw items, and nautical prints, the highlight is the enormous multifaceted Fresnel Lens from the Point Sur Lighthouse. *5 Custom House Plaza,* ☎ *408/375–2553.* ☛ *$5 adults, $3 children 12–18, $2 children 6–11.* ⏲ *Daily 10–5.*

5 The next stop along the path is **Pacific House,** a former hotel and saloon, and now a museum of early California life. There are Native American artifacts, gold-rush relics, historic photographs of old Monterey, and a costume gallery displaying various period fashions. *10 Custom House Plaza,* ☎ *408/649–2907.* ☛ *Free.* ⏲ *Sept.–May, daily 10–4; June–Aug., daily 10–5.*

6 The low-ceilinged **Casa Soberanes,** a classic adobe structure, was once a Custom House guard's residence. *336 Pacific St.,* ☎ *408/649–7118.* ☛ *$2 adults, $1.50 children 13–17, $1 children 6–12.* ⏲ *Varied hrs; call for schedule of guided tours. Gardens open Sept.–May, daily 10–4; June–Aug., daily 10–5.*

7 Farther along the Path of History is the **Larkin House,** one of the most architecturally significant homes in California. Built in 1835, this two-story adobe with a veranda encircling the second floor reflects the blending of Mexican and New England influences into the Monterey style. The rooms are furnished with period antiques, many of them brought from New Hampshire to Monterey by the Larkin family. *510 Calle Principal, between Jefferson and Pacific Sts.,* ☎ *408/649–7118.* ☛ *$2 adults, $1.50 children 13–17, $1 children 6–12.* ⏲ *Varied hrs; call for schedule of guided tours.*

8 The largest site along the Path of History is the restored **Cooper-Molera Adobe,** a 2-acre complex that includes an early California house dating from the 1820s, a visitor center, and a large garden enclosed by a high adobe wall. The tile-roofed house is filled with antiques and memorabilia, mostly from the Victorian era, that illustrate the life of a prosperous pioneer family. *Polk and Munras Sts.,* ☎ *408/649–7118.* ☛ *$2 adults, $1.50 children 13–17, $1 children 6–12.* ⏲ *Varied hrs; call for schedule of guided tours.*

For literary and history buffs, one of the path's greatest treasures is
9 the **Stevenson House,** named in honor of Robert Louis Stevenson, author of *Treasure Island* and other classics, who boarded there briefly in a tiny upstairs room. In addition to Stevenson's room, which is furnished with items from his family's estate, there is a gallery of the author's memorabilia and several charming period rooms, including a children's nursery stocked with Victorian toys and games. *530 Houston St.,* ☎ *408/649–7118.* ☛ *$2 adults, $1.50 children 13–17, $1 children 6–12.* ⏲ *Varied hrs; call for schedule of guided tours. Gardens open Sept.–May, 10–6; June–Aug., 10–5.*

10 California's equivalent of Independence Hall is **Colton Hall,** where a convention of delegates met in 1849 to draft the first state constitu-

tion. Now the historic white building, which has served as a school, courthouse, and county seat, is a museum furnished as it was during the constitutional convention. The extensive grounds outside the hall also include a more notorious building, the Old Monterey Jail, where inmates languished behind thick granite walls. *500 block of Pacific St., between Madison and Jefferson Sts., ☎ 408/646–5640. ☛ Free. ⏲ Mar.–Oct., daily 10–noon and 1–5; Nov.–Feb., 10–noon and 1–4.*

Off the Path of History, just across the street from Colton Hall, is the **Monterey Peninsula Museum of Art.** It is especially strong on artists and photographers who have worked in the area, a distinguished lot that includes Ansel Adams and Edward Weston. Another focus is international folk art; the collection ranges from Kentucky hearth brooms to Tibetan prayer wheels. *559 Pacific St., ☎ 408/372–7591. ☛ $3 donation suggested. ⏲ Tues.–Sat. 10–5, Sun. 1–5.*

11 The newest addition to Monterey's art scene is **La Mirada,** a 19th-century adobe house filled with Asian and European antiques. A 10,000-square-foot gallery space, designed by architect Charles Moore, was added to house an extensive collection of Asian and Californian regional art. The permanent collection includes works by Armin Carl Hansen, as well as a large netsuke collection. The museum is also home to magnificent rose and rhododendron gardens. *720 Via Mirada, at Fremont St., ☎ 408/372–3689. ☛ $3 donation suggested. ⏲ Tues.–Sat. 10–4, Sun. 1–4.*

Fisherman's Wharf and Cannery Row

Inevitably, visitors are drawn to the waterfront in Monterey, if only because the mournful barking of sea lions that can be heard throughout the town makes its presence impossible to ignore. The whiskered
12 marine mammals are best enjoyed while walking along **Fisherman's Wharf,** an aging pier crowded with souvenir shops, fish markets, seafood restaurants, and popcorn stands.

Although tacky and touristy to the utmost, the wharf is a good place to visit, especially with children. For years, an organ grinder with a costumed monkey has entertained crowds at the entrance. Farther down, you can buy a bag of squid to feed the sea lions that beg from the waters below.

From the wharf, a footpath along the shore leads to **Cannery Row,** a street that has undergone several transformations since it was immortalized in John Steinbeck's 1945 novel of the same name. The street that Steinbeck described was crowded with sardine canneries processing, at their peak, nearly 200,000 tons of the smelly silver fish a year. During the mid-1940s, however, the sardines mysteriously disappeared from the bay, causing the canneries to close.

Over the years the old tin-roof canneries have been converted to restaurants, art galleries, and minimalls with shops selling T-shirts, fudge, and plastic otters. Recent tourist development along the row has been more tasteful, however, including several attractive inns and hotels. The
13 historic **Monterey Plaza Hotel** at 400 Cannery Row sits on the site of an estate built by Hugh Tevis for his bride, who died on their honeymoon. It's a good place to relax over a drink and watch for otters.

Although Steinbeck would have trouble recognizing Cannery Row today, there are still some historical and architectural features from its
14 colorful past. One building to take note of is **653 Cannery Row,** with its tiled Chinese dragon roof that dates from 1929. On a kitschy note,
15 characters from the novel *Cannery Row* are depicted in wax at **Stein-**

beck's Spirit of Monterey Wax Museum, which also features a 25-minute description of the history of the area over the past 400 years, with a recorded narration by Steinbeck himself. *700 Cannery Row,* ☏ *408/375–3770.* ☛ *$4.95 adults, $3.95 senior citizens and students, $2.95 children 6–12.* ⏲ *Daily 9–9.*

16 The building now called the **Old General Store** is the former Wing Chong Market that Steinbeck called Lee Chong's Heavenly Flower Grocery. Across the street, a weathered wooden building at 800 Cannery Row
17 was the **Pacific Biological Laboratories,** where Edward F. Ricketts, the inspiration for Doc in Steinbeck's novel, did much of his marine research.

★ 18 The most important attraction on Cannery Row is the spectacular **Monterey Bay Aquarium,** a $100 million window on the sea. A new wing, the first floor of which is scheduled to open in March 1996, will be devoted to open ocean and deep-sea habitats. Soupfin sharks, barracuda, pelagic stingrays, and other rarely displayed open ocean fish will find a home in Outer Bay, a million-gallon showcase. The addition will include the largest collection of jellyfish in the country. The aquarium is extremely popular—expect long lines and sizable crowds on weekends, especially during the summer. Braving the crowds is worth it, however, especially to see the three-story Kelp Forest exhibit, the only one of its kind in the world, and a re-creation of the sea creatures and vegetation found in Monterey Bay. Among other standout exhibits are a bat-ray petting pool, where the flat velvetlike creatures can be touched as they swim by; a 55,000-gallon sea-otter tank; and an enormous outdoor artificial tide pool that supports anemones, crabs, sea stars, and other colorful creatures. *886 Cannery Row,* ☏ *408/648–4888 or 800/756–3737 in CA for advanced tickets.* ☛ *$11.75 adults; $9.75 senior citizens, visitors with disabilities, and students; $5.75 children 3–12. (Note: Prices will rise when new wing opens in March 1996.)* ⏲ *Daily 10–6, 9:30–6 on holidays and summer.*

Pacific Grove

If not for the dramatic strip of coastline in its backyard, Pacific Grove could easily pass for a typical small town in the heartland. Beginning as a summer retreat for church groups more than a century ago, the town recalls its prim and proper Victorian heritage in the host of tiny board-and-batten cottages and stately mansions lining its streets.

Even before the church groups migrated here, however, Pacific Grove had been receiving thousands of annual guests in the form of bright orange-and-black monarch butterflies. Known as Butterfly Town USA, Pacific Grove is the winter home of monarchs that migrate south from Canada and the Pacific Northwest and take residence in the pine and eucalyptus groves between October and March. The site of a mass of butterflies hanging from the branches like a long fluttering veil is unforgettable.

A prime way to enjoy Pacific Grove is to walk or bicycle along its 3 miles of city-owned shoreline, a cliff-top area following Ocean View Boulevard that is landscaped with succulents and native plants and has plenty of park benches on which to sit and gaze at the sea. A variety of marine and bird life can be spotted here, including colonies of cormorants drawn to the massive rocks rising out of the surf.

On the other side of Ocean View Boulevard are a number of imposing turn-of-the-century mansions well worth your attention. One of
19 the finest is the **Pryor House** at number 429, a massive shingled struc-

ture with a leaded and beveled glass doorway built in 1909 for an early
20 mayor. At the corner of 5th Street and Ocean View is **Green Gables,**
a romantic Swiss Gothic-style mansion, now a bed-and-breakfast inn
(*see* Lodging, *below*), with steeply peaked gables and stained-glass win-
21 dows. At **Lovers Point Park,** located midway along the waterfront, there's
a pleasant grassy area with a gorgeous coastal view.

Farther out on the promontory stands the oldest continuously oper-
★ 22 ating lighthouse on the West Coast, the **Point Piños Light Station.** Visitors can learn about the lighting and foghorn operations and wander
through a small museum containing historical memorabilia from the
U.S. Coast Guard. *Asilomar Ave. between Ocean View Blvd. and
Lighthouse Ave., ☎ 408/648–3116. ☛ Free. ⏲ Weekends 1–4.*

★ 23 Another beautiful coastal area in Pacific Grove is **Asilomar State Beach,**
on Sunset Drive between Point Piños and the Del Monte Forest. The
100 acres of dunes, tide pools, and pocket-size beaches form one of
the region's richest areas for marine life. The deep tide pools support
210 species of algae and are alive with sea urchins, crabs, and other
creatures.

Although many of their original nesting grounds have vanished, the
24 **Monarch Grove Sanctuary,** adjacent to the Butterfly Grove Inn (1073
Lighthouse Ave.), is still a good spot for viewing butterflies.

If you are in Pacific Grove when the butterflies aren't, an approxima-
25 tion of this annual miracle is on exhibit at the **Pacific Grove Museum
of Natural History.** In addition to a finely crafted butterfly-tree exhibit,
the museum displays a collection of 400 mounted birds native to Monterey County and screens a film about the monarch butterfly. *165 Forest Ave., ☎ 408/648–3116. ☛ Free. ⏲ Tues.–Sun. 10–5.*

17-Mile Drive

Numbers in the margins correspond to points of interest on the Carmel and 17-Mile Drive map.

Although some sightseers balk at the $6.50-per-car fee, most agree that
★ 26 it is well worth the price to explore **17-Mile Drive,** an 8,400-acre microcosm of the Monterey coastal landscape. You can enter off Sunset
Drive in Pacific Grove, or, from the other end, off Highway 1 and North
San Antonio Avenue in Carmel.

Once inside, you see primordial nature preserved in quiet harmony with
palatial estates. Two landmarks of note near the beginning of the drive
27 28 are **Bird Rock** and **Seal Rock,** islands teeming with harbor seals, sea lions,
cormorants, and pelicans. All along 17-Mile Drive are rare Monterey
cypress, trees so gnarled and twisted that Robert Louis Stevenson once
described them as "ghosts fleeing before the wind." The most pho-
29 tographed of them all is the **Lone Cypress,** a weather-sculpted tree growing out of a precipitous, rocky outcropping above the waves. A parking
area makes it possible to stop for a view of the Lone Cypress, but walking out to it is no longer allowed.

Many of the stately homes along 17-Mile Drive reflect the classic
Monterey or Spanish Mission style typical of the region. A standout
30 is the **Crocker Marble Palace,** a waterfront estate designed after a
Byzantine castle. This baroque mansion is easily identifiable by its dozens
of marble arches. The estate's grounds feature a beach area with water
heated by underground pipes.

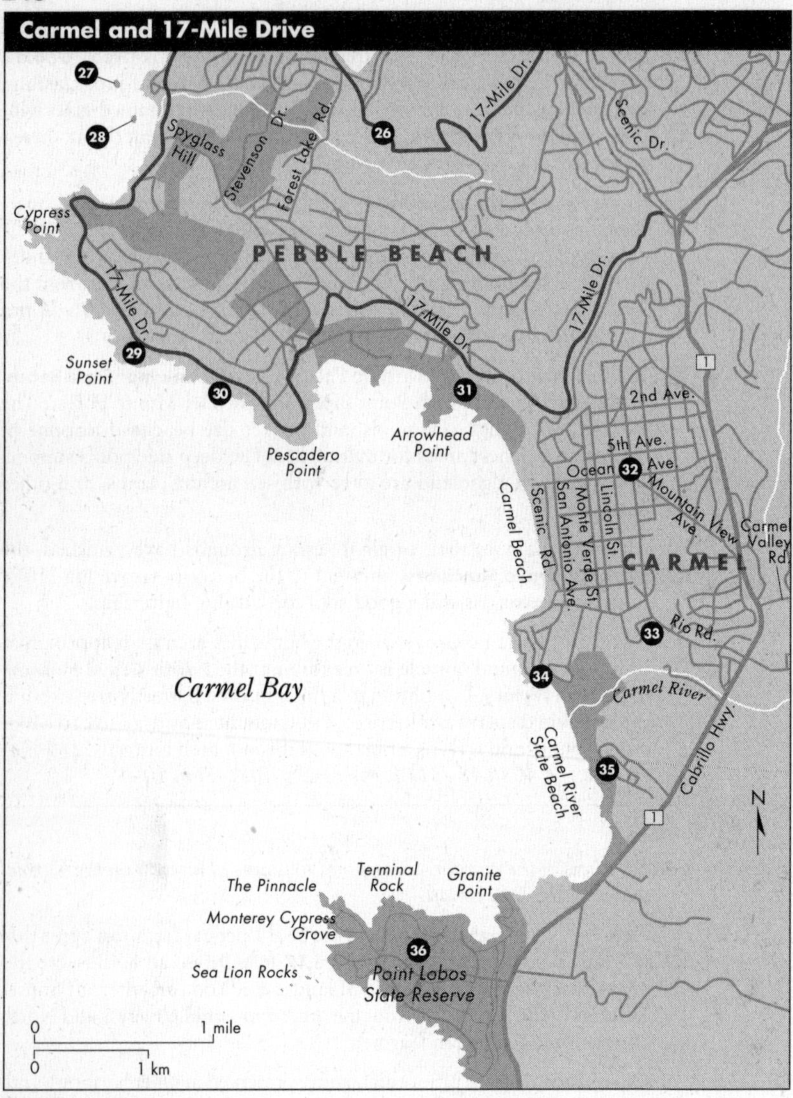

Bird Rock, **27**
Carmel Mission, **33**
Carmel Plaza, **32**
Carmel River State Park, **35**
Crocker Marble Palace, **30**
Lone Cypress, **29**
Pebble Beach Golf Links, **31**
Point Lobos State Reserve, **36**
Seal Rock, **28**
17-Mile Drive, **26**
Tor House, **34**

The man-made contributions to the scenery go beyond architecture:
Perhaps no more famous concentration of celebrated golf courses ex-
31 ists anywhere in the world. Most notable is the **Pebble Beach Golf Links,**
with its famous 18th hole, around which the ocean plays a major role.
Even if you're not a golfer, views of impeccable greens can be enjoyed
over a drink or lunch at the **Lodge at Pebble Beach** or the **Inn at Spanish Bay,** the two resorts located along the drive.

Carmel

Although the community has grown quickly over the years and its population quadruples with tourists on weekends and during the summer, Carmel retains its identity as a quaint village; buildings still have no street numbers and live music is banned in the local watering holes. You can wander the side streets at your own pace, poking into hidden courtyards and stopping at Hansel-and-Gretel-like cafés for tea and crumpets.

Downtown Carmel's chief lure is shopping. Its main street, **Ocean Avenue,** is a charming (except to architectural purists) mishmash of er-
32 satz English Tudor, Mediterranean, and other styles. **Carmel Plaza,** in
the east end of the village proper, is one of several newer malls. It has
more than 50 shops, restaurants, and small branches of major department
stores.

Before it became an art colony in the early 20th century and long before it became a shopping and browsing mecca, Carmel was an important religious center in the early days of Spanish California. That
heritage is preserved in one of the state's loveliest historic sites, the Mission San Carlos Borromeo del Rio Carmelo, more commonly known
★ 33 as the **Carmel Mission.** Founded in 1770 and serving as headquarters
for the mission system in California under Father Junípero Serra, the
Carmel Mission exists today with its stone church and tower dome beautifully restored. Adjoining the church is a tranquil garden planted with
California poppies and a series of museum rooms that depict an early
kitchen, Father Serra's spartan sleeping quarters, and the oldest college library in California. *Rio Rd. and Lasuen Dr.,* ☎ *408/624–3600.
$2 donation suggested.* ⏲ *Sept.–May, Mon.–Sat. 9:30–4:30, Sun.
10:30–4:30; June–Aug., Mon.–Sat. 9:30–7:30, Sun. 10:30–7:30.*

Scattered throughout the pines in Carmel are the houses and cottages
that were built for the steady stream of writers, artists, and photographers who discovered the area decades ago. Among the most impressive
34 dwellings is **Tor House,** a stone cottage built by the poet Robinson Jeffers in 1919 on a craggy knoll overlooking the sea. The low-ceilinged
rooms are filled with portraits, books, and unusual art objects, including
a white stone from the Great Pyramid in Egypt. The highlight of the
small estate is Hawk Tower, a detached edifice set with stones from
the Carmel coastline, as well as one taken from the Great Wall of China.
Within the tower is a Gothic-style room, which served as a retreat for
the poet's wife, Una, an accomplished musician. The docents who
lead tours are very well informed about the poet's work and life. Jeffers's home and life present a fascinating story, even if you are not a
fan of his poetry. *26304 Ocean View Ave.,* ☎ *408/624–1813 or
408/624–1840.* ☛ *$5 adults, $3.50 college students, $1.50 high-school
students. No children under 12.* ⏲ *Fri. and Sat. 10–3 for tours; reservations suggested.*

Carmel's greatest beauty is the rugged coastline with its pine and cy-
35 press forests and countless inlets. **Carmel River State Park** stretches for
106 acres along Carmel Bay. On sunny days the waters appear nearly

as turquoise as those of the Caribbean. The park has a sugar-white beach with high dunes and a nature preserve that provides excellent bird-watching for pelicans, kingfishers, hawks, and sandpipers. *Off Scenic Rd., south of Carmel Beach,* ☎ *408/626–4909.* ⏲ *Daily 9 AM–sunset.*

36 The park is overshadowed by **Point Lobos State Reserve,** a 456-acre headland just south of Carmel. There are few roads, and the best way to explore is to walk along one of the many hiking trails. The Cypress Grove Trail leads through a forest of rare Monterey cypress (one of only two natural groves remaining), clinging to the rocks above an emerald-green cove. Sea Lion Point Trail is a good place to observe sea lions. From the other trails you can spot otters, harbor seals, and (during certain times of year) migrating whales. Part of the reserve is an undersea marine park open to qualified scuba divers. If you have a dog, note that state law prohibits dogs within the reserve. Cars with dogs are turned away at the entrance. *Hwy. 1,* ☎ *408/624–4909, or 800/444–7275 to reserve for scuba diving.* ☛ *$6 per car, $5 if senior citizen is traveling.* ⏲ *May–Sept., daily 9–6:30; Oct.–Apr., daily 9–4:30.*

Numbers in the margin correspond to points of interest on the Monterey Bay map.

A world away from the cypress forests and tide pools of the coast are the pastoral ranch lands of Carmel Valley. The rolling meadows studded with oak trees are especially compelling in spring, when the grass is lush, green, and blooming with bright gold California poppies and blue lupines.

Carmel Valley Road, which turns inland at Highway 1 just south of Carmel, is the main thoroughfare through this secluded enclave of horse ranchers and other well-heeled residents who prefer the valley's perpetually dry, sunny climate to the fog and wind on the coast. You can spend a pleasant couple of hours rambling up the road and back. Stop
37 for a while in tiny **Carmel Valley** village, where there are several crafts shops and art galleries. If you want to stay longer, go to **Garland Ranch Regional Park** (☎ 408/659–4488), 10 miles east of Carmel. The park has hiking trails and picnic facilities.

A popular stop along this road, 5 miles off Highway 1, is the tasting room at the beautiful **Château Julien** winery, known for its chardonnay and merlot. Tours are at 10:30 AM and 2:30 PM but must be arranged by calling ahead. ☎ *408/624–2600.* ⏲ *Weekdays 8–5, weekends 11–5.*

An enjoyable loop drive can be added by turning off Carmel Valley Road about 7 miles out of town onto **Los Laureles Grade,** a 6-mile winding road that heads over the mountains to Highway 68, ending at a point about halfway between Monterey and Salinas. Located along Highway 68 is the award-winning **Ventana Vineyards.** Its tasting room is five minutes from downtown Monterey. ☎ *408/372–7415.* ⏲ *Daily 11–5.*

Salinas

38 While Monterey turns its face toward the sea, **Salinas,** a half hour inland and a world away in spirit, is deeply rooted as the population center of a rich agricultural valley. This unpretentious town may lack the sophistication and scenic splendors of the coast, but it is of interest to literary and architectural buffs.

Salinas's turn-of-the-century architecture has been the focus of ongoing renovation, much of which is centered on the original downtown area of South Main Street, with its handsome stone storefronts. The memory and literary legacy of Salinas native John Steinbeck are well honored here. The **Steinbeck Center Foundation** has information about local Steinbeck exhibits, tours of area landmarks mentioned in his novels, and a schedule of events for the annual Steinbeck festival. The foundation plans to build a conference center on South Main Street devoted to his life and writings. The ambitious complex will feature Steinbeck archives, film adaptations of his work, a gift shop, and a café with outdoor seating. *371 Main St., ☎ 408/753–6411. ⏲ Weekdays 9–4 and Sat. (May–Sept.) 10–2.*

The author's birthplace, a Victorian frame house, has been converted to a lunch-only restaurant, the **Steinbeck House,** run by the volunteer Valley Guild. The restaurant contains some Steinbeck memorabilia and presents a menu featuring locally grown produce. *132 Central Ave., ☎ 408/424–2735. Reservations requested. ⏲ Weekdays for 2 sittings at 11:45 AM and 1:15 PM.*

Steinbeck did much of his research for *East of Eden,* a novel partially ★ drawn from his Salinas boyhood, at what is now called the **Steinbeck Library.** The library features tapes of interviews with people who knew Steinbeck and a display of photos, first editions, letters, original manuscripts, and other items pertaining to the novelist. Entrance to the archives, which contain original manuscripts and first editions, is by appointment only. *350 Lincoln Ave., ☎ 408/758–7311. ☛ Free. ⏲ Mon.–Wed. 10–9, Thurs.–Sat. 10–6.*

Harvey-Baker House, a beautifully preserved redwood house built in 1868 for the city's first mayor, is one of the finest private residences built in Salinas during the 19th century. *238 E. Romie La., ☎ 408/757–8085. ☛ Free. ⏲ 1st Sun. of month 1–4 PM, and weekdays by appointment.*

Of even earlier vintage is the **Jose Eusebio Boronda Adobe,** the last unaltered adobe home from Mexican California open to the public in Monterey County. Located in the meadows above the Alisal Slough, the house contains furniture and artifacts from the period. *333 Boronda Rd., ☎ 408/757–8085. ☛ Free. ⏲ Weekdays 10–2, Sun. 1–4, Sat. by appointment.*

San Juan Bautista

A sleepy little hamlet tucked off U.S. 101 about 20 miles north of Sali-
39 nas, **San Juan Bautista** is a nearly unaltered example of a classic California mission village. Protected from development since 1933, when ★ much of it became **San Juan Bautista State Historic Park,** the village is about as close to early 19th-century California as you can get. On the first Saturday of each month, on Living History Day, costumed volunteers entertain visitors with such period events as quilting bees, tortilla making, and butter churning, and refreshments are served in the hotel's bar. *☎ 408/623–4881. ☛ $2 adults, $1 children 6–12. ⏲ Daily 10–4:30.*

The centerpiece for the village is a wide green plaza, ringed by historic buildings that include a restored blacksmith shop, a stable, a pioneer cabin, and a jailhouse. Running along one side of the square is **Mission San Juan Bautista,** a long, low colonnaded structure founded by Father Lasuen in 1797. A poignant spot adjoining it is **Mission Cemetery,** where more than 4,300 Native Americans who converted to Christianity are buried in unmarked graves. *408 S. 2nd St., 95045, ☎ 408/623–2127. ☛ $1 donation suggested. ⏲ Mar.–Oct., daily 9:30–5:30; Nov.–Feb., daily 9:30–4:30.*

After the mission era, San Juan Bautista became an important crossroads for stagecoach travel. The principal stop in town was the **Plaza Hotel,** a collection of adobe buildings with furnishings from the 1860s. Next door, the **Castro-Breen Adobe,** once owned by survivors from the Donner party and furnished with Spanish colonial antiques, presents a view of domestic life in the village.

More contemporary pursuits in San Juan Bautista include poking around in the numerous antiques shops and art galleries lining the side streets. On the first Sunday in August, the village holds a popular flea market.

What to See and Do with Children

Dennis the Menace Playground (Fremont St. and Camino El Estero, Monterey), in delightful Lake El Estero Park, is an imaginative playground whose name pays tribute to cartoonist and longtime local resident Hank Ketcham. The play equipment is on a grand scale and made for daredevils; there's a dizzyingly high rotating platform, a clanking suspension bridge, and a real Southern Pacific steam locomotive. Rowboats and paddleboats can be rented on U-shape Lake El Estero, home to a varied assortment of ducks, mud hens, and geese.

At **Edgewater Packing Co.** (640 Wave St., Monterey, ☎ 408/649–1899), a converted sardine cannery and processing plant, kids can sport on an antique carousel with hand-carved animals and mermaids, dating from 1905. A candy store and game arcade are among the other attractions.

Roller skates can be rented from the old-fashioned rink at **Del Monte Gardens** (2020 Del Monte Ave., Monterey, ☎ 408/375–3202).

Also in Monterey, children will enjoy the **Monterey Bay Aquarium,** the **Pacific Grove Museum of Natural History,** and the **Point Piños Light Station** (*see* Exploring, *above*). **Whale-watching expeditions** are also popular with children (*see* Spectator Sports, *below*).

Off the Beaten Track

A few miles north of Monterey, east of the tiny harbor town of Moss Landing, is one of only two federal research reserves in California, the **Elkhorn Slough** at the National Estuarine Research Reserve. Its 1,400 acres of tidal flats and salt marshes form a complex environment supporting more than 200 species of birds. A walk along the meandering waterways and wetlands can reveal hawks, white-tailed kites, owls, herons, and egrets, and sharks may be observed in the summer months. You can wander at leisure or, on weekends, take a guided walk (10 AM and 1 PM) to the heron rookery. To get to the reserve from Highway 1, head east on Dolan Road at Moss Landing, then north on Elkhorn Road. From San Juan Bautista head south on U.S. 101, and take the G-12/San Miguel Canyon Road exit. About 1 mile from U.S. 101, bear left at Castroville Boulevard, then head north on Elkhorn. *1700 Elkhorn Rd., Watsonville, ☎ 408/728–2822. ☛ $2.50 adults 16 and over, free with any California hunting or fishing license. ⏲ Wed.–Sun. 9–5.*

SHOPPING

Art Galleries

The gallery scene in Carmel is a varied one. **Masterpiece Gallery** (Dolores St. and 6th Ave., ☎ 408/624–2163) features early California Impressionists and Bay Area figurative art. Classic impressionism and traditional realism are the focus of the **Cottage Gallery** (Mission St.

and 6th Ave., ☎ 408/624–7888). The **LaRue Gallery** (Dolores St. between 5th and 6th Aves., ☎ 408/625–5636) has contemporary impressionism, western realism, and some folk art. The primary themes and styles at the **Bighorn Gallery** (26390 Carmel Rancho La., ☎ 408/625–2288) are western, wildlife, marine, aviation, African, and landscape. The **Highlands Sculpture Gallery** (Dolores St. between 5th and 6th Aves., ☎ 408/624–0535) is devoted to indoor and outdoor sculpture, primarily work done in stone, bronze, wood, and metal. **Photography West Gallery** (Ocean Ave. and Dolores St., ☎ 408/625–1587) exhibits 20th-century photography by artists such as Ansel Adams, who lived and worked in the region for many years.

The **Coast Gallery Pebble Beach** (The Lodge at Pebble Beach, 17-Mile Dr., Pebble Beach, ☎ 408/624–2002) presents the work of contemporary wildlife and marine artists.

Gift Ideas

In a region known for superb golf courses, you'll find the ultimate in golf equipment and accessories. **John Riley Golf** (601 Wave St., Monterey, ☎ 408/373–8855) purveys custom-made golf clubs. **Golf Arts and Imports** (Dolores St. and 6th Ave., Carmel, ☎ 408/625–4488) features antique golf prints and clubs, rare golf books, and other golfing memorabilia.

The **Mischievous Rabbit** (Lincoln Ave. between 7th and Ocean Aves., Carmel, ☎ 408/624–6854) sells toys, nursery bedding, books, music boxes, party supplies, china, and hand-painted and handmade clothing embellished with characters from some *Winnie the Pooh* tales.

SPORTS AND THE OUTDOORS

Participant Sports

Bicycling

Bicycle paths follow some of the choicest parts of the shoreline, including the Santa Cruz–area beaches, 17-Mile Drive, and the waterfront of Pacific Grove. Bikes can be rented from **Surf City Rentals** (46 Front St., Santa Cruz, ☎ 408/423–9050) and **Bay Bikes** (640 Wave St., Monterey, ☎ 408/646–9090). **Adventures by the Sea Inc.** (299 Cannery Row, Monterey, ☎ 408/372–1807) rents bikes, kayaks, roller skates, and Rollerblades. Mopeds, motorcycles, and bikes can be rented from **Monterey Moped Adventures** (1250 Del Monte Ave., Monterey, ☎ 408/373–2696); a driver's license is required.

Fishing

Rock cod is a relatively easy catch in Monterey Bay; salmon and albacore tuna are also possible. Several half- and full-day fishing trips leave from Fisherman's Wharf in Monterey, and rates often include equipment rental, bait, fish cleaning, and a one-day license. Try **Monterey Sport Fishing** (96 Fisherman's Wharf, ☎ 408/372–2203 or 800/200–2203), **Randy's Fishing Trips** (66 Fisherman's Wharf, ☎ 408/372–7440), and **Sam's Fishing Fleet** (84 Fisherman's Wharf, ☎ 408/372–0577). In Santa Cruz try **Stagnaro Fishing Trips** (center of the wharf, ☎ 408/427–2334).

Golf

With 19 golf courses, most of them commanding strips of choice real estate, it is not surprising that the Monterey Peninsula is sometimes called the golf capital of the world. Beginning with the opening of the Del Monte Golf Course in 1897, golf has been an integral part of the social and recreational scene. Greens fees for 18 holes run from $15 to $225, depending on the time and course.

Many hotels will help with golf reservations or offer golf packages; inquire when you make lodging reservations.

Several of the courses are within the exclusive confines of the 17-Mile Drive, where the Del Monte Forest and the surging Pacific help make the game challenging as well as scenic. The most famous of these courses is **Pebble Beach Golf Links** (17-Mile Dr., ☎ 408/625–8518), which takes center stage each winter during the AT&T Pro-Am (known for years as the "Crosby"), where show-business celebrities and pros team up for what is perhaps the world's most glamorous golf tournament. Golfers from around the world make this course one of the busiest in the region, despite greens fees of $225 plus $20 for a cart. Individual reservations for nonguests can only be made one day in advance on a space-available basis.

Another famous course in Pebble Beach is **Spyglass Hill** (Spyglass Hill Rd., ☎ 408/624–3811), where the holes are long and unforgiving. With the first five holes bordering on the Pacific, and the rest reaching deep into the Del Monte Forest, the views offer some consolation. Greens fees run $175 plus $20 for a cart; reservations are essential and may be made up to one month in advance.

Poppy Hills (17-Mile Dr., ☎ 408/625–2035), designed in 1986 by Robert Trent Jones, Jr., was named by *Golf Digest* as one of the world's top 20 courses. Greens fees for the general public are $105, cart $30 additional. Individuals may reserve up to one month in advance, groups up to a year.

The **Spanish Bay Golf Links** (☎ 408/624–3811) opened on the north end of the 17-Mile Drive in 1987. Spanish Bay, which hugs a choice stretch of shoreline, is designed in the rugged manner of a traditional Scottish course with sand dunes and coastal marshes interspersed among the greens. Fees are $135 per player plus $20 cart rental; individuals are advised to make reservations up to two months in advance.

Less-experienced golfers and those who want to sharpen their iron shots can try the shortest course in Pebble Beach, the nine-hole "pitch and putt" **Peter Hay** (17-Mile Dr., ☎ 408/624–3811). The course fee is $10 per person, no reservations necessary.

Just as challenging as the Pebble Beach courses is the **Old Del Monte Golf Course** (1300 Sylvan Rd., Monterey, ☎ 408/373–2436), the oldest course west of the Mississippi. The greens fees—$50 per player plus $15 cart rental, $18 twilight special after 2:30 in winter and 4:30 in summer—are the most reasonable in the region.

Another local favorite, with greens fees only a fraction of those in Pebble Beach, is **Pacific Grove Municipal Golf Course** (77 Asilomar Blvd., ☎ 408/648–3177). Designed by Jack Neville, who also designed the Pebble Beach Golf Links, and updated by H. Chandler Egan, the course features a back nine with spectacular ocean views and iceplant-covered sand dunes that make keeping on the fairway a must. The course is the only one on the peninsula to offer views of both Monterey Bay and the Pacific. Greens fees range from $24 to $28. Cart rental is $23. Tee times may be reserved up to seven days in advance.

Courses in Carmel Valley lack ocean views, but deer and quail wander across the greens. One of the choicest is **Rancho Cañada Golf Club** (Carmel Valley Rd., ☎ 408/624–0111) with 36 holes, some of them overlooking the Carmel River. Fees range from $15 to $70 plus $25 cart rental, depending on course and tee time selected. The club takes reservations up to 30 days in advance.

Up the road a few miles is the **Golf Club at Quail Lodge** (8000 Valley Greens Dr., ☎ 408/624–2770), whose course incorporates several lakes. Although private, the course is open to guests at the adjoining Quail Lodge and by reciprocation with other private clubs. The $90 greens fee ($115 for nonguests) includes cart rental.

Pete Dye designed the private **Carmel Valley Ranch Resort** course (1 Old Ranch Rd., ☎ 408/626–2510), whose front nine runs along the Carmel River and back nine reaches well up into the mountains for challenging slopes and spectacular views. Guests at the resort have access to the course; the $97 greens fee includes cart rental.

Seven miles inland from Monterey, off Highway 68, is **Laguna Seca Golf Club** (10520 York Rd., ☎ 408/373–3701), a course with an 18-hole layout updated by Robert Trent Jones, Jr., and open to the public. The greens fee for nonmembers is $55, cart rental $25.

Horseback Riding

A great way to enjoy the Del Monte Forest, which has 26 miles of bridle trails, is by reserving a horse from the **Pebble Beach Equestrian Center** (Portola Rd. and Alva La., ☎ 408/624–2756). You can ride in a group of six to eight, on a forest or beach trail, or schedule private rides.

Kayaking

Sea kayaking is increasingly popular in Monterey Bay, giving paddlers a chance to come face to face with otters, sea lions, and harbor seals. Kayak rentals, classes, and guided natural-history tours are offered by **Monterey Bay Kayaks** (693 Del Monte Ave., Monterey, ☎ 408/373–5357 or 800/649–5357 in CA).

Scuba Diving

Although the waters are cold, the marine life and kelp beds attract many scuba divers to Monterey Bay. Diving lessons, rental equipment, and guided dive tours are offered at **Aquarius Dive Shops** (2040 Del Monte Ave., Monterey, ☎ 408/375–1933; 32 Cannery Row, Suite 4, ☎ 408/375–6605). Call 408/657–1020 for local scuba-diving conditions.

Tennis

Public courts are available in Monterey and Pacific Grove; information is available through **Monterey Tennis Center** (☎ 408/372–0172) and **Pacific Grove Municipal Courts** (☎ 408/648–3129). Nonmembers are eligible to play on the courts for a small fee at the **Carmel Valley Inn Swim and Tennis Club** (Carmel Valley Rd. and Los Laureles Grade, Carmel Valley, ☎ 408/659–3131).

If tennis is a top vacation priority, you may want to stay at a resort where instruction and facilities are part of the scene. Best bets are the Lodge at Pebble Beach, the Inn at Spanish Bay, Hyatt Regency Monterey, Quail Lodge, and Carmel Valley Ranch Resort. *See* Lodging, *below,* for details.

Beaches

Surfers in Santa Cruz gather for the spectacular waves and sunsets at **Pleasure Point** (East Cliff Dr. and Pleasure Point Dr.) and **New Brighton State Beach** (1500 State Park Dr., Capitola), which also has campsites. **Manresa State Beach** (Manresa Dr., La Selva Beach, ☎ 408/761–1795), farther south, offers premium surfing conditions, and those who surf here tend to be very good—but although there is a lifeguard on duty during most of the summer season, the waters off this beach are notorious for treacherous currents and riptides; we recommend it only for sunbathing.

Around Monterey, the local waters are generally too cold and turbulent for much swimming. **Monterey Municipal Beach,** east of Wharf No. 2, has shallow waters that are warm and calm enough for wading. Another good beach for kids is **Lovers Point Park** on Ocean View Boulevard in Pacific Grove, a sheltered spot with a children's pool and picnic area. Glass-bottom boat rides, which permit viewing of the plant and sea life below, are available in summer.

Spectator Sports

Car Racing

Four major races take place each year on the 2.2-mile, 11-turn **Laguna Seca Raceway** (SCRAMP, Box 2078, Monterey 93942, ☎ 408/648–5100 or 800/327–7322; in CA, 800/367–9939). They range from Indianapolis 500–style IndyCAR races to a historic car race featuring more than 300 restored race cars from earlier eras.

Rodeo

One of the oldest and most famous rodeos in the West is the annual **California Rodeo** (Box 1648, Salinas 93902, ☎ 408/757–2951) in Salinas, which takes place during a week of festivities starting in mid-July.

Whale Watching

On their annual migration between the Bering Sea and Baja California, 45-foot gray whales can be spotted not far off the Monterey coast. Although they sometimes can be seen with binoculars from shore, a whale-watching cruise is the best way to view these magnificent mammals up close. The migration south takes place between December and March, while the migration north is from March to June. Late January is prime viewing time in Monterey Bay.

Even if no whales are in sight, bay cruises nearly always include some unforgettable marine-life encounter, anything from watching a cluster of sea lions hugging a life buoy to riding the waves alongside a group of 300 leaping porpoises. Whale-watching cruises, which usually last about two hours, are offered by **Monterey Sport Fishing** (96 Fisherman's Wharf, Monterey, ☎ 408/372–2203 or 800/200–2203), **Randy's Fishing Trips** (66 Fisherman's Wharf, Monterey, ☎ 408/372–7440), and **Sam's Fishing Fleet** (84 Fisherman's Wharf, ☎ 408/372–0577). In Santa Cruz, try **Stagnaro Fishing Trips** (center of the wharf, ☎ 408/427–2334).

DINING AND LODGING

Dining

There is little question that the Monterey area is the richest area for dining along the coast between Los Angeles and San Francisco. The surrounding waters abound with fish, there is wild game in the foothills, and the inland valleys are the vegetable basket of California; nearby Castroville prides itself on being the Artichoke Capital of the World. The region also takes pride in producing better and better wines.

WHAT TO WEAR

When it comes to dress, San Francisco's conservatism extends this far south. Except at beachside stands and the inexpensive eateries listed below, casual but attractive resort wear is the norm. The few places where more formal attire is required are noted below.

CATEGORY	COST*
$$$$	over $45
$$$	$30–$45
$$	$18–$30
$	under $18

per person for a three-course meal, excluding drinks, service, and 6½%–8¼% tax

Lodging

Monterey accommodations range from historic hotels to no-frills motels. Some of the newer upscale Monterey establishments are a bit impersonal and clearly designed for conventions, but others pamper the individual traveler in grand style. Here's a deal: Lodgings booked through Monterey's 800/555–9283 number include an informational brochure, two tickets to the Monterey Bay Aquarium, and discount coupons good at restaurants and shops.

Pacific Grove has quietly turned itself into the bed-and-breakfast capital of the region. Many of the town's landmark Victorian houses, some more than a century old, have been converted to charming inns with brass beds and breakfast buffets laden with such goodies as cranberry muffins and baked pears. Carmel and Carmel Valley also have fine bed-and-breakfasts; other lodgings vary from rustic beachside motels to luxury resorts. Even more luxurious are the resorts in exclusive Pebble Beach.

The rates below are for two people in the high season, April to October. Keep in mind that winter rates, especially at the larger hotels, drop by as much as 50%.

CATEGORY	COST*
$$$$	over $175
$$$	$120–$175
$$	$80–$120
$	under $80

**All prices are for a standard double room, excluding 10½% tax.*

Capitola

LODGING

$$$–$$$$ **Inn at Depot Hill.** This inventively designed hotel in a former rail depot has taken the *Orient Express* as its theme. Each double room or suite, complete with fireplace and feather beds, is inspired by a different European destination—Delft, the Netherlands; Portofino, Italy; Sissinghurst, England; the Côte d'Azur, France. One is decorated like a Pullman car for a railroad baron. Some accommodations have balconies with private Jacuzzis. Full breakfast is included, as well as wine and hors d'oeuvres. *250 Monterey Ave., Capitola-by-the-Sea 95010, ☎ 408/462–3376 or 800/572–2632, FAX 408/462–3697. 8 rooms. AE, MC, V.*

Carmel

DINING

$$$ **Anton and Michel.** Superb Continental cuisine is served at this elegant restaurant in Carmel's shopping district. The tender lamb dishes are fantastic and well complemented by the extensive wine list. The real treats, however, are the flaming desserts. Outdoor dining is available in the courtyard. ✕ *Ocean and 7th Aves., ☎ 408/624–2406. Reservations advised. AE, D, DC, MC, V.*

$$$ **Crème Carmel.** This bright and airy small restaurant has a California-French menu that changes according to season. Specialties include charbroiled Muscovy duck with celery root puree and green peppercorn, and beef tenderloin prepared with cabernet. ✕ *San Carlos St.,*

near 7th Ave., ☎ 408/624–0444. Reservations advised. AE, DC, MC, V. No lunch.

$$$ French Poodle. The service is attentive in this intimate dining room decorated in warm, raspberry tones and hung with landscapes by local California impressionists. Specialties on the traditional French menu include duck breast in port and an excellent abalone; for dessert, the "floating island" is delicious. ✕ *Junipero and 5th Aves., ☎ 408/624–8643. Reservations advised. AE, DC, MC, V. Closed Sun. and Wed. No lunch.*

$$ Flaherty's Seafood Grill & Oyster Bar. This is a bright blue-and-white-tiled fish house that serves bowls of steamed mussels, clams, cioppino, and crab chowder. Seafood pastas and daily fresh fish selections are also available. ✕ *6th Ave. and San Carlos St., ☎ 408/624–0311. Reservations taken for the grill. AE, MC, V.*

$$ Hog's Breath Inn. Actor and former Carmel mayor Clint Eastwood's eatery has a convivial publike atmosphere, complete with roaring fireplaces and rustic decor; you can eat either indoors or on an outdoor heated patio under an oak tree. The food is no-nonsense: meat and seafood entrées with sautéed vegetables. Many items—Dirty Harry Burger, Sudden Impact (Polish sausage) sandwich, et cetera—are named after Eastwood movies. Expect a wait at dinner. ✕ *San Carlos St. and 5th Ave., ☎ 408/625–1044. No reservations. AE, DC, MC, V.*

$$ La Bohème. This campy, offbeat restaurant offers a one-selection, fixed-price menu, which includes soup and salad. You may be bumping elbows with your neighbor in the cozy, faux-European-village courtyard, but the food is delicious, and the atmosphere is friendly. The cuisine is predominantly French with accents from throughout Europe. Vegetarian meals are available nightly. ✕ *Dolores St. and 7th Ave., ☎ 408/624–7500. Reservations not accepted. MC, V. No lunch.*

$$ Piatti. Here's one more link in this statewide chain of friendly, attractive trattorias that serve authentic, light Italian cuisine. ✕ *Junipero and 6th Sts., ☎ 408/625–1766. Reservations required for dinner, advised for lunch. AE, MC, V.*

$$ Pine Inn. An old favorite of locals, this Victorian-style restaurant offers traditional American fare. Outdoor dining is also available at tables set up around the gazebo. ✕ *Ocean Ave. and Monte Verde St., ☎ 408/624–3851. Reservations advised. AE, D, DC, MC, V.*

$$ Raffaello. A sparkling, elegant restaurant in one of the loveliest parts of Carmel, Raffaello offers excellent northern Italian cuisine. The menu includes superb pasta, Monterey Bay prawns with garlic butter, local sole poached in champagne, and the specialty of the house, veal Piemontese. ✕ *Mission St. between Ocean and 7th Aves., ☎ 408/624–1541. Reservations advised. AE, DC, MC, V. Closed Tues. and 1st wk in Jan. No lunch.*

$–$$ General Store. This Bavarian-influenced restaurant is decorated with artifacts that recall the building's origin as a blacksmith's shop, originating in the 1920s. California cuisine is served in the intimate dining room as well as on the adjacent brick patio and in a more casual saloon. Specialties include fresh seafood, steaks, and one of the best burgers in Carmel. ✕ *Junipero St. and 5th Ave., ☎ 408/624–2233. Reservations advised on weekend nights. AE, MC, V.*

$–$$ ★ Rio Grill. The best bets in this Santa Fe–style setting are the meat and seafood (such as fresh tuna or salmon) cooked over an oakwood grill. There's also a good California wine list. ✕ *101 Crossroads Blvd., Hwy. 1 and Rio Rd., ☎ 408/625–5436. Reservations advised. AE, MC, V.*

$ Friar Tuck's. This busy, wood-paneled coffee shop serves huge omelets at breakfast, and at lunch offers 16 varieties of hamburgers, including one topped with marinated artichoke hearts. ✕ *5th Ave. and Dolores St., ☎ 408/624–4274. No reservations. No credit cards. Closed for dinner except July–Aug.*

$ **Thunderbird Bookstore and Restaurant.** This well-stocked bookstore is also a good place to enjoy a light lunch or dinner, or you can order a cappuccino and a pastry and browse among the books. A hearty beef soup, sandwiches, popovers, and cheesecake are the best sellers. ✕ *3600 The Barnyard, Hwy. 1 at Carmel Valley Rd., ☎ 408/624–9414. AE, MC, V.*

DINING AND LODGING

$$$$ ★ **Highlands Inn.** The hotel's unparalleled location on high cliffs above the Pacific just south of Carmel gives it views that stand out even in a region famous for them. Accommodations are in plush spa suites and condominium-style units with wood-burning fireplaces and ocean-view decks; some have full kitchens. The specialties on the contemporary French menu at the inn's Pacific's Edge restaurant (☎ 408/624–0471; reservations advised) include fillet of beef with blue cheese potato gratin, roasted shallots, and a Portobello mushroom sauce; grilled Atlantic salmon wrapped in pancetta with local baby artichokes; and a succulent honey-roasted breast of duck. For dessert, crème brûlée and homemade sherbets are winners. *Hwy. 1, Box 1700, 93921, ☎ 408/624–3801 or 800/538–9525; in CA, 800/682–4811; FAX 408/626–1574. 142 rooms. 2 restaurants, lounges, pool, hot tub. AE, D, DC, MC, V.*

$$$$ **Quail Lodge.** One of the area's most highly regarded resorts is situated just outside of Carmel Valley on the grounds of a private country club. Guests have access to golf, tennis, and 853 acres of wildlife preserve, including 11 lakes, frequented by deer and migratory fowl. Spacious, modern rooms with European decor are clustered in several low-rise buildings. An elegant restaurant, the Covey at Quail Lodge (reservations advised, jacket required, no lunch), serves European cuisine in a romantic lakeside setting. Specialties include rack of lamb, mustard-crested salmon in beurre roupe with shrimp capellini, abalone, and mousseline of sole. *8205 Valley Greens Dr., Carmel 93923, ☎ 408/624–1581 or 800/538–9516, FAX 408/624–3726. 100 rooms. 2 restaurants, 2 lounges, piano bar, 2 pools, hot tub, golf, putting green, tennis. AE, DC, MC, V.*

LODGING

$$$$ **Carriage House Inn.** This attractive small inn with a rustic wood-shingled exterior has rooms with open-beam ceilings, fireplaces, down comforters, and sunken baths. Continental breakfast, wine, and hors d'oeuvres are included. *Junipero Ave. between 7th and 8th Aves., Box 1900, 93921, ☎ 408/625–2585 or 800/422–4732, FAX 408/624–2967. 13 rooms. AE, D, DC, MC, V.*

$$$–$$$$ **La Playa Hotel.** Now a pink, Mediterranean-style villa, the hotel was originally built in 1902 by Norwegian artist Christopher Jorgensen for his bride, a member of the famous Ghirardelli chocolate clan. The Terrace Grill and central garden, riotous with color, provide wonderful views of Carmel's magnificent coastline. All rooms are done in rose, beige, and blue tones, with hand-carved furniture. Some accommodations have ocean views. You can also opt for a cottage; all have full kitchens and a patio or terrace, and some have wood-burning fireplaces. *Camino Real at 8th Ave., Box 900, 93921, ☎ 408/624–6476 or 800/582–8900, FAX 408/624–7966. 80 rooms. Restaurant, pool, valet parking. AE, DC, MC, V.*

$$$–$$$$ **Tickle Pink Inn.** Just up the road from the Highlands Inn, this secluded inn has spectacular views. Accommodations are elegant but casual; 17

rooms are equipped with fireplace, most have private balcony or patios. The inn has a Jacuzzi available to all guests; some suites have private Jacuzzis. A separate cottage on the property sleeps four. Room rates include Continental breakfast and early evening wine and cheese. *155 Highland Dr., 93923, ☎ 408/624–1244 or 800/635–4774, FAX 408/626–9516. 34 rooms. AE, MC, V.*

$$–$$$$ **Lobos Lodge.** Pleasant white stucco units set amid cypresses, oaks, and pines on the edge of the business district feature fireplaces. Some rooms have private brick patios. Continental breakfast is included. *Monte Verde St. and Ocean Ave., Box L–1, 93921, ☎ 408/624–3874, FAX 408/624–0135. 30 rooms. AE, MC, V.*

$$–$$$$ **Mission Ranch.** Former mayor Clint Eastwood rescued this venerable inn, originally built in the 1850s and used as a dairy farm, and brought it back to life in 1992. Set in pastureland next to the ocean where sheep still graze, the main farmhouse has six rooms around a Victorian parlor; other accommodation options include cottages, hayloft, and bunkhouse. The details of rustic comfort include handmade quilts, princess-and-the-pea stuffed mattresses, and carved wooden beds. *26270 Dolores St., 93923, ☎ 408/624–6436 or 800/538–8221, FAX 408/626–4163. 31 rooms. Restaurant, piano bar, tennis courts, exercise room, pro shop. AE, D, DC, MC, V.*

$$–$$$$ ★ **Pine Inn.** This traditional favorite of generations of Carmel visitors features Victorian-style decor complete with grandfather clock, padded fabric panels, antique tapestries, and marble-topped furnishings. Located in the heart of the shopping district and only four blocks from the beach, the inn has its own brick courtyard of specialty shops. *Ocean Ave. and Lincoln St., Box 250, 93921, ☎ 408/624–3851 or 800/228–3851, FAX 408/624–3030. 49 rooms. Dining room. AE, D, DC, MC, V.*

$$$ ★ **Cobblestone Inn.** Recent renovations in this former motel have created an English-style inn with stone fireplaces in the guest rooms and in the sitting-room area. Quilts and country antiques, along with a complimentary gourmet breakfast buffet and afternoon tea (not to mention optional breakfast in bed), contribute to the homey feel. The inn is entirely no-smoking. *8th and Junipero Aves., Box 3185, 93921, ☎ 408/625–5222, FAX 408/625–0478. 24 rooms. AE, DC, MC, V.*

$$$ **Tally Ho Inn.** This is one of the few inns in Carmel's center that has good views out over the ocean. There are penthouse units with fireplaces and a pretty English garden courtyard. Continental breakfast and after-dinner brandy are included. *Monte Verde St. and 6th Ave., Box 3726, 93921, ☎ 408/624–2232 or 800/624–2290, FAX 408/624–2661. 14 rooms. AE, D, MC, V.*

$$–$$$ **Best Western Carmel Mission Inn.** This modern inn on the edge of Carmel Valley has a lushly landscaped pool and Jacuzzi area and is close to the Barnyard and Crossroads shopping centers. Rooms are large, some with spacious decks. *3665 Rio Rd., at Hwy. 1, 92923, ☎ 408/624–1841 or 800/348–9090, FAX 408/624–8684. 165 rooms. Restaurant, bar, pool, hot tub. AE, D, DC, MC, V.*

Carmel Valley

LODGING

$$$$ ★ **Carmel Valley Ranch Resort.** This all-suite resort, situated on 1,700 acres, well off the road on a hill overlooking the Carmel Valley, is a stunning piece of contemporary California architecture. Down-home touches include handmade quilts, wood-burning fireplaces, and watercolors by local artists. Rooms have cathedral ceilings, oversize decks, and fully stocked wet bars. *1 Old Ranch Rd., 93923, ☎ 408/625–9500 or*

800/422–7635, FAX 408/624–2858. 100 suites. Restaurant, pool, hot tub, saunas, golf, tennis courts. AE, DC, MC, V.

$$$$ **Stonepine Estate Resort.** The former estate of the Crocker banking family has been converted to an ultradeluxe (and ultraexpensive) inn nestled in 330 pastoral acres with riding trails and an equestrian center. The main house, richly paneled and furnished with antiques, offers eight individually decorated suites and a private dining room for guests only. Less formal but still luxurious rooms are also available in the ranch-style Paddock House. *150 E. Carmel Valley Rd., Box 1543, 93924, ☎ 408/659–2245, FAX 408/659–5160. 14 rooms. Dining room, pool, tennis, archery, exercise room, horseback riding, mountain bikes. AE, MC, V.*

$$–$$$$ **Robles Del Rio Lodge.** This pine-paneled charmer in a gorgeous setting of rolling meadows and oak forests dates from 1928. Rooms and cottages feature country-style decor with Laura Ashley prints, and the grounds include a large pool and sunbathing area, and hiking trails. Complimentary breakfast buffet is included. *200 Punta del Monte, 93924, ☎ 408/659–3705 or 800/833–0843, FAX 408/659–5157. 33 rooms. Restaurant, lounge, pool, hot tub, sauna, tennis. AE, MC, V.*

$$–$$$$ **Valley Lodge.** In this small, pleasant inn, there are rooms surrounding a garden patio and separate one- and two-bedroom cottages with fireplaces and full kitchens. Continental breakfast and morning paper are included. *Carmel Valley Rd. at Ford Rd., Box 93, 93924, ☎ 408/659–2261 or 800/641–4646, FAX 408/659–4558. 31 rooms. Pool, hot tub, sauna, exercise room. AE, MC, V.*

Monterey

DINING

$$$ ★ **Duck Club.** This elegant dining room in the Monterey Plaza Hotel (*see* Lodging, *below*) is built over the waterfront on Cannery Row. The California menu strongly emphasizes duck but also includes seafood, meat, and pasta. ✕ *400 Cannery Row, ☎ 408/646–1700. Reservations advised. AE, D, DC, MC, V.*

$$$ **Fresh Cream.** Nine out of ten local residents recommend this outstanding restaurant in Heritage Harbor, with its beautiful views over the bay. The cuisine is French, with light, imaginative California accents. Some favorites on the seasonal menu are the rack of lamb Dijonnaise and the roast boned duck in black-currant sauce. ✕ *99 Pacific St., Suite 100C, ☎ 408/375–9798. Reservations advised. AE, D, DC, MC, V. No lunch Sat.–Thurs.*

$$$ **Sardine Factory.** The interior of this old processing plant above Cannery Row has been turned into five attractive, separate dining areas, including a glass-enclosed garden room. The menu stresses fresh seafood, prepared in an elegant, Italian manner. There's a great wine list. ✕ *701 Wave St., ☎ 408/373–3775. Reservations advised. AE, D, DC, MC, V.*

$$–$$$ ★ **Whaling Station Inn.** A pleasing mixture of rough-hewn wood and sparkling white linen makes this restaurant a festive yet comfortable place in which to enjoy some of the best mesquite-grilled fish and meats in town. There are excellent artichoke appetizers and fresh salads. ✕ *763 Wave St., ☎ 408/373–3778. Reservations advised. AE, D, DC, MC, V. No lunch.*

$$ **Bradley's.** This restaurant—with possibly the best location on the harbor—offers regional American fare with various ethnic influences. The casual atmosphere recalls a 1920s European bistro. Menu highlights include avocado pancakes with salsa and fresh fish specials. Finish off your meal with one of the rich, delicious desserts. ✕ *32 Cannery*

Row at the Coast Guard Pier, ☏ *408/655–6799. Reservations advised. AE, D, DC, MC, V.*

$$ Cafe Fina. This understated restaurant on the wharf, with fine water views, specializes in Italian seafood dishes. Highlights include mesquite-grilled fish dishes and pasta Fina, a linguine in clam sauce with baby shrimp and tomatoes. The wine list is extensive. ✕ *47 Fisherman's Wharf,* ☏ *408/372–5200. Reservations advised. AE, D, DC, MC, V.*

$$ Domenico's. Under the same ownership as the Whaling Station Inn and nearby Abalonetti, this restaurant serves Italian seafood preparations, mesquite-grilled meats, and homemade pastas. The blue-and-white nautical decor keeps the place comfortably casual; white drapery lends an air of elegance lacking in most restaurants on the wharf. ✕ *50 Fisherman's Wharf,* ☏ *408/372–3655. Reservations advised. AE, D, DC, MC, V.*

$$ Ferrante's. Gorgeous rooftop views of both the town and the bay can be seen from this California-Italian restaurant at the top of the 10-story Monterey Marriott (*see* Lodging, *below*). The chicken cashew fettuccine with sun-dried tomatoes is especially good. Brunch is served Sunday. ✕ *350 Calle Principal,* ☏ *408/649–4234. Reservations advised. AE, D, DC, MC, V. No lunch.*

$$ ★ The Fishery. Popular with locals, this restaurant features a mixture of Asian and Continental influences, in both food and decor. Specialties include calamari, broiled swordfish with macadamia nut butter, and fresh Hawaiian tuna with teriyaki. ✕ *21 Soledad Dr.,* ☏ *408/373–6200. Reservations advised. MC, V. Closed Sun. and Mon. No lunch.*

$$ Old Monterey Cafe. Breakfast here, which is served until early afternoon, can include fresh-baked muffins and eggs Benedict. This is also a good place to relax with a cappuccino or coffee made from freshly ground beans. ✕ *489 Alvarado St.,* ☏ *408/646–1021. No reservations. DC, MC, V.*

$–$$ Abalonetti. From a squid-lover's point of view, this wharf-side restaurant is the best place in town, serving all kinds of squid dishes: deep-fried, sautéed with wine and garlic, or baked with eggplant. Abalone is another specialty, and the fresh fish is broiled or blackened and served with beurre blanc or pesto. Italian dishes such as seafood pasta and wood-fired pizza are also on the menu. ✕ *57 Fisherman's Wharf,* ☏ *408/373–1851. Reservations advised. AE, D, DC, MC, V.*

$–$$ Consuelo's. Housed in an 1886 Victorian Mansion, this doesn't look like a Mexican restaurant—only the food and music say "Mexico." Meals start with complimentary quesadillas, presented on a huge platter, then move into fare such as fajitas, tostadas, enchiladas, marinated chicken, and flautas. There's a children's menu as well. If the weather's nice you can sit outside under the shade of a huge Indian pine tree. ✕ *361 Lighthouse Ave.,* ☏ *408/372–8211. Reservations accepted. AE, MC, V.*

$–$$ Trattoria Paradiso. California and Mediterranean specialties and pizzas from a wood-burning oven are the luncheon fare at this Cannery Row establishment. Seafood is a good choice for dinner, which is served in a formal dining room that overlooks a lighted beachfront and lapping surf. ✕ *654 Cannery Row,* ☏ *408/375–4155. Reservations advised. AE, D, DC, MC, V.*

LODGING

$$$$ ★ Old Monterey Inn. Ann and Gene Swett provide quietly elegant accommodations in a historic Tudor-style home; Ann likes flea markets, as the Old Monterey's eclectic but tasteful decor illustrates. Most of the rooms or suites have fireplaces. Service here is outstanding, and the Swetts are happy to suggest touring ideas. Room rates include breakfast, served in front of the fireplace in the formal dining room at a table set for 14 with exquisite Oriental china; afternoon and evening refreshments are also complimentary and picnic baskets are available. *500 Martin St., 93940, ☎ 800/350–7344, FAX 408/375–6730. 8 rooms, 1 suite, 1 cottage suite. No credit cards. Closed Dec. 25.*

$$$$ ★ **Spindrift Inn.** This small hotel on Cannery Row boasts the street's only private beach and a rooftop garden overlooking Monterey Bay. Indoor pleasures include spacious rooms with sitting areas, Oriental rugs, fireplaces, canopied beds, down comforters, and other luxuries. Continental breakfast, brought to the room on a silver tray, and afternoon tea are also included. *652 Cannery Row, 93940, ☎ 408/646–8900 or 800/841–1879, FAX 408/646–5342. 41 rooms. AE, D, DC, MC, V.*

$$$–$$$$ **Best Western Victorian Inn.** Under the same ownership as the Spindrift Inn, this hotel two blocks above Cannery Row has a more casual feel but also offers such in-room comforts as fireplaces, private balconies or patios, and Continental breakfast. A few rooms have ocean views. Wine and cheese are served in the antiques-filled lobby during the afternoon. *487 Foam St., 93940, ☎ 408/373–8000 or 800/232–4141, FAX 408/373–4815. 68 rooms. Garage. AE, D, DC, MC, V.*

$$$–$$$$ **Doubletree Hotel.** Adjacent to the downtown conference center, this hotel is geared more toward convention groups and business travelers than toward vacationers seeking local ambience. Rooms, some with good views of Fisherman's Wharf and the bay, are attractively furnished. Resort amenities include a round swimming pool with adjoining Jacuzzi. *2 Portola Plaza, 93940, ☎ 408/649–4511 or 800/222–8733, FAX 408/649–4115. 374 rooms. Restaurant, pool, hot tub, parking (fee). AE, D, DC, MC, V.*

$$$–$$$$ **Hotel Pacific.** While other new hotels in downtown Monterey clash with the early California architecture and small-town ambience, the Hotel Pacific is an adobe-style addition that fits right in. All rooms are suites, handsomely appointed with four-poster feather beds, hardwood floors, Indian rugs, fireplaces, honor bars, and balconies or patios. Continental breakfast and afternoon tea are included. *300 Pacific St., 93940, ☎ 408/373–5700 or 800/554–5542 in CA, FAX 408/373–6921. 105 rooms. 2 hot tubs, garage. AE, D, DC, MC, V.*

$$$–$$$$ **Hyatt Regency Monterey.** Although rooms and atmosphere are less glamorous than at some other resorts in the region, the Hyatt does offer excellent facilities. *1 Old Golf Course Rd., 93940, ☎ 408/372–1234 or 800/233–1234; in CA, 800/824–2196; FAX 408/375–3960. 575 rooms. 2 restaurants, lounge, sports bar, 2 pools, 2 hot tubs, golf course, tennis court, exercise room. AE, D, DC, MC, V.*

$$$–$$$$ **Monterey Bay Inn.** This hotel, anchoring Cannery Row, is under the same ownership as the Spindrift Inn and demonstrates the same attention to detail. Spacious rooms, decorated in peach and green tones, offer private balconies, VCR, honor bar, terry-cloth robes, and binoculars for viewing marine life; most rooms have breathtaking bay views. In-room Continental breakfast is included. *242 Cannery Row, 93940, ☎ 408/373–6242 or 800/424–6242, FAX 408/373–7603. 47 rooms. 2 hot tubs, sauna, exercise room. AE, D, DC, MC, V.*

$$$–$$$$ ★ **Monterey Plaza Hotel.** This sophisticated full-service hotel commands a superb waterfront location on Cannery Row, where frolicking sea otters can be observed from the wide outdoor patio and from many of the room balconies. The architecture and decor blend early California and Mediterranean styles and retain a little of the old cannery design. *400 Cannery Row, 93940, ☎ 408/646–1700 or 800/631–1339; in CA, 800/334–3999; FAX 408/646–0285. 285 rooms. Restaurant, bar, exercise room, garage (fee). AE, D, DC, MC, V.*

$$–$$$$ **Best Western Monterey Beach Hotel.** Rooms here may be nondescript, but this hotel has a great waterfront location about 2 miles north of town, with panoramic views of the bay and the Monterey skyline. Grounds are pleasantly landscaped and feature a large pool with a sunbathing area. *2600 Sand Dunes Dr., 93940, 408/394–3321 or 800/242–8627, FAX 408/393–1912. 196 rooms. Restaurant, lounge, pool, hot tub. AE, D, DC, MC, V.*

$$–$$$$ **Cannery Row Inn.** This is a modern, small hotel on a street above Cannery Row with bay views from the private balconies of some rooms. Gas fireplaces and complimentary Continental breakfast are among the amenities. *200 Foam St., 93940, 408/649–8580 or 800/876–8580, FAX 408/649–2566. 32 rooms. Hot tub, garage. AE, D, MC, V.*

$$–$$$$ **Otter Inn.** This low-rise hotel with a rustic shingle exterior is one block above Cannery Row and has bay views from most of the rooms. Coffee and pastries are provided in rooms, which are spacious, with fireplaces and private hot tubs in some. *571 Wave St., 93940, 408/375–2299 or 800/385–2299, FAX 408/375–2352. 33 rooms. AE, MC, V.*

$$–$$$ **Monterey Hotel.** Originally opened in 1904, this quaint, small, downtown hotel reopened in 1987 after an extensive restoration that left its oak paneling and ornate fireplaces gleaming. Standard rooms are small but well appointed with reproduction antique furniture; master suites have fireplaces and sunken baths. Complimentary Continental breakfast and afternoon tea are included. *406 Alvarado St., 93940, 408/375–3184 or 800/727–0960, FAX 408/373–2894. 44 rooms. Parking (fee). AE, D, DC, MC, V.*

$$–$$$ **Monterey Marriott.** This large convention hotel sticks out like a 10-story sore thumb in the middle of Monterey's quaint downtown. Rooms are small, but many have good views of the town and bay. *350 Calle Principal, 93940, 408/649–4234 or 800/228–9290, FAX 408/372–2968. 341 rooms. 3 restaurants, lounge, pool, hot tub, health club, garage (fee). AE, D, DC, MC, V.*

$–$$ **Arbor Inn.** This stylish motel has a friendly, country-inn atmosphere. Continental breakfast is served in a pine-paneled lobby with a tile fireplace. There is an outdoor Jacuzzi, and rooms are light and airy, some with fireplaces and some with accessibility for visitors with disabilities. *1058 Munras Ave., 93940, 408/372–3381, FAX 408/372–4687. 55 rooms. Hot tub. AE, D, DC, MC, V.*

$–$$ ★ **Monterey Motor Lodge.** A pleasant location on the edge of Monterey's El Estero Park gives this motel an edge over its many competitors along Munras Avenue. Indoor plants and a large secluded courtyard with pool are other pluses. *55 Aguajito Rd., 93940, 408/372–8057 or 800/558–1900, FAX 408/655–2933. 45 rooms. Restaurant, pool. AE, D, DC, MC, V.*

Pacific Grove

DINING

$$$ **Melac's.** This intimate dining room has white tablecloths and lovely china and crystal. The menu of contemporary French cuisine changes almost weekly according to what's in season; some of the more characteristic dishes include sea bass wrapped in a potato crust and covered in red wine sauce, and roasted duck in balsamic vinegar. ✕ *663 Lighthouse Ave., 408/375–1743. Reservations advised. AE, D, DC, MC, V. Closed Sun.–Mon. No lunch Sat.*

$$$ ★ **Old Bath House.** A romantic, nostalgic atmosphere permeates this converted bathhouse overlooking the water at Lovers Point. The Continental menu here makes the most of local seafood and produce. When they're available, the salmon and Monterey Bay prawns are particularly worth ordering. The restaurant offers a less expensive menu for late-afternoon diners. ✕ *620 Ocean View Blvd.,* ☎ *408/375–5195. Reservations advised. AE, D, DC, MC, V. No lunch.*

$$ Fandango. With its stone walls and country furniture, this restaurant has the earthy feel of a southern European farmhouse. Complementing the ambience are the robust flavors of the cuisine, which ranges from southern France, Italy, Spain, and Greece to North Africa, from couscous and paella to cannelloni. ✕ *223 17th St.,* ☎ *408/372–3456. Reservations advised. AE, D, DC, MC, V.*

$$ The Tinnery. The simple, clean lines of this family-oriented restaurant are framed by picture-window views of Lovers Point. Breakfast items include pancakes, omelets, and fresh-squeezed orange juice. Burgers and other sandwiches are served at lunch. On the varied dinner menu are such dishes as broiled salmon with fresh Hollandaise sauce, mesquite-grilled meats, and English fish-and-chips. ✕ *631 Ocean View Blvd., at 17th St.,* ☎ *408/646–1040. No reservations. AE, D, DC, MC, V.*

$–$$ Gernot's. The ornate Victorian-era Hart Mansion that now houses this restaurant is a delightful setting in which to dine on seafood and game served with light sauces. Continental specialties include wild boar bourguignonne, roast venison, and veal medallions. ✕ *649 Lighthouse Ave.,* ☎ *408/646–1477. Reservations advised. AE, MC, V. Closed Mon. No lunch.*

$ Peppers. This cheerful white-walled café offers fresh seafood and traditional dishes from Mexico and Latin America. The red and green salsas are excellent. ✕ *170 Forest Ave.,* ☎ *408/373–6892. Reservations advised. AE, D, DC, MC, V. Closed Tues. No dinner except Sun.*

LODGING

$$$–$$$$ ★ Martine Inn. Most bed-and-breakfasts in Pacific Grove are Victorian houses; this one is a pink stucco Mediterranean-style villa overlooking the water. Its owners have assembled one of the most extensive antiques collections of any California B&B, including a mahogany suite exhibited at the 1893 Chicago World's Fair, movie costume designer Edith Head's bedroom suite, and an 1860 Chippendale Revival four-poster bed. There are many common areas; a glassed-in parlor affords a stunning ocean view. Full breakfast, wine, and hors d'oeuvres are included. *255 Oceanview Blvd., 93950,* ☎ *408/373–3388 or 800/852–5588,* FAX *408/373–3896. 20 rooms. AE, MC, V.*

$$–$$$$ ★ The Centrella. This handsome century-old Victorian mansion and garden cottages two blocks from Lovers Point Beach has an attractive garden, claw-foot bathtubs, and wicker and brass furnishings. Depending on the time of day, a sideboard in the large parlor is laden with breakfast treats, cookies and fruit, sherry and wine, or hors d'oeuvres. *612 Central Ave., 93950,* ☎ *408/372–3372 or 800/233–3372,* FAX *408/372–2036. 26 rooms, 2 share bath. AE, MC, V.*

$$–$$$ Gosby House Inn. Most of the rooms in this yellow Victorian bed-and-breakfast in the town center have private bath, some have fireplaces. The inn has an informal, country air; its innkeepers are knowledgeable and can offer tourism or restaurant suggestions. Full breakfast and afternoon hors d'oeuvres are served in a sunny parlor or by the fireplace in the living room. *643 Lighthouse Ave., 93950,* ☎ *408/375–1287 or 800/527–8828,* FAX *408/655–9621. 22 rooms, 2 with shared bath. AE, MC, V.*

$$–$$$ ★ Green Gables Inn. Stained-glass windows framing an ornate fireplace and other details compete with the spectacular bay views at this century-old house built by a sea captain to house his mistress. Guest rooms in a carriage house, perched on a hill out back, are larger, have ocean views, more modern amenities, and afford more privacy, though the rooms in the main house have more charm. The breakfast buffet is tempting, though breakfast in bed is also an option; afternoon hors d'oeuvres are served with wine, sherry, or tea. *104 5th St., 93950, 408/375–2095 or 800/722–1776, FAX 408/375–5437. 11 rooms, 4 share bath. AE, MC, V.*

$$ **Asilomar Conference Center.** A summer camp–like atmosphere pervades this assortment of 28 rustic but comfortable lodges in the middle of a 105-acre state park across from the beach. Breakfast is included. *800 Asilomar Blvd., Box 537, 93950, 408/372–8016, FAX 408/372–7227. 314 rooms. Cafeteria, pool. MC, V.*

Pebble Beach

DINING AND LODGING

$$$$ **Inn at Spanish Bay.** Under the same management as the Lodge at Pebble Beach (*see below*), this 270-room resort sprawls on a breathtaking stretch of shoreline along 17-Mile Drive. The resort has a slightly more casual feel, although the 600-square-foot rooms are no less luxurious. The inn has its own tennis courts and golf course, but guests also have privileges at all the Lodge facilities. For dinner, the excellent Bay Club restaurant (reservations advised), which serves haute Italian cuisine, overlooks the coastline and the golf links. *Box 1589, 2700 17-Mile Dr., 93953, 408/647–7500 or 800/654–9300, FAX 408/647–7443. 270 rooms. 3 restaurants, pool, tennis, health club. AE, DC, MC, V.*

$$$$ ★ **Lodge at Pebble Beach.** This renowned resort, built in 1919, features quietly luxurious rooms with fireplaces and wonderful views. The golf course, tennis club, and equestrian center are also highly regarded. Guests of the lodge have privileges at the Inn at Spanish Bay. Overlooking the 18th green, the very fine Club XIX restaurant (reservations advised) is an intimate, café-style spot serving classic French preparations of veal, lamb, and duck, as well as foie gras and caviar. *Box 1418, 17-Mile Dr., 93953, 408/624–3811 or 800/654–9300, FAX 408/625–8598. 161 rooms. 3 restaurants, coffee shop, lounge, pool, massage, sauna, golf, tennis, health club, horseback riding, beach, bicycles. AE, DC, MC, V.*

Santa Cruz

DINING

$$ ★ **Chez Renee.** This elegant retreat, owned by a husband-and-wife team, serves French-inspired cuisine. Specialties include sweetbreads with two sauces (Madeira and mustard); duck and home-preserved brandied cherries; deep-sea scallops garnished with smoked salmon and dill. Save room for the excellent dessert soufflés. ✕ *9051 Soquel Dr., Aptos, 408/688–5566. Reservations suggested. MC, V. No lunch Sat.*

$$ **El Palomar.** This spacious restaurant in the Palomar Hotel, with vaulted ceilings and wood beams, serves California Mexican cuisine with an emphasis on seafood. Homemade tamales, seviche, and chili verde are among the best dishes. ✕ *1336 Pacific Ave., 408/425–7575. No reservations. AE, D, MC, V.*

$$ **The Veranda.** The surroundings are attractive and the service cordial in this refurbished Victorian dining room in the Bayview Hotel. Homemade pâtés and terrines stand out among the appetizers, main-course offerings include baked salmon with a mustard-and-herb sauce and roast rack of lamb. The best-selling dessert is the white-chocolate macadamia nut cheesecake. Brunch is served Sunday ✕ *8041 Soquel Dr., 408/685–1881. Reservations accepted. AE, DC, MC, V. No lunch Sat.*

$–$$ **O Mei Sichuan Chinese Restaurant.** Not your run-of-the-mill chop-suey joint, this sophisticated, attractive place offers some unusual dishes: *gan pung* (boneless chicken crisp-fried and served with a spicy garlic sauce), *gan bian* (dried sautéed beef with hot pepper and ginger on crisp rice noodles), and rock cod prepared Taiwan style (filleted and breaded, with chili-vinegar sauce). ✕ *2316 Mission St. (Hwy. 1),* ☎ *408/425–8458. Reservations advised on weekends. AE, MC, V. No lunch weekends.*

$ **Scontriano's Dolphin Restaurant.** Occupying a scenic site at the end of the Municipal Wharf, this small, casual restaurant has a pleasant decor. Booths have bay views, ceiling fans whir, walls are the color of driftwood. The Dolphin serves up good breakfasts—hotcakes, French toast, omelets, cereals—plus seafood lunches and dinners. Typical fare is clam chowder, seafood sandwiches, salads, and fried squid or shrimp. ✕ *Santa Cruz Municipal Wharf (end of pier),* ☎ *408/426–5830. MC, V.*

LODGING

$$–$$$$ **Casablanca Motel.** Of the many motels along this hurly-burly waterfront, this is perhaps the most interesting. The main building was once the Cerf Mansion, built in 1918 in the Mediterranean style for a federal judge, and every room is individually decorated. There are brass beds, velvet drapes, and fireplaces. Most rooms have views of the ocean. The restaurant here serves innovative cuisine and has spectacular views. *101 Main at Beach, 95060,* ☎ *408/423–1570 or 800/644–1570,* FAX *408/423–0235. 34 rooms. Restaurant. AE, D, DC, MC, V.*

$$–$$$$ ★ **Darling House Bed and Breakfast by the Sea.** This superb 1910 mansion on the promontory overlooking the Pacific was built as a summer house for a rich Colorado family by William Weeks, architect of Santa Cruz's Cocoanut Grove. The decor, including antique furnishings and beveled glass, is authentic. Modern plumbing and electricity are among the few concessions made to the 1990s; in all other ways, the house retains an atmosphere of turn-of-the-century elegance. Continental breakfast is offered. No pets are allowed; smoking is outdoors only. *314 W. Cliff Dr., 95060,* ☎ *408/458–1958 or 800/458–1958. 8 rooms, 6 with shared bath. Hot tub. AE, D, MC, V.*

THE ARTS AND NIGHTLIFE

The Arts

The Monterey area's top venue for the performing arts is the **Sunset Community Cultural Center** (San Carlos, between 8th and 10th Aves., ☎ 408/624–3996) in Carmel, which presents concerts, lectures, and headline performers throughout the year. Facilities include the Sunset Theater and the Outdoor Forest Theater, the first open-air amphitheater built in California.

Festivals

Performing-arts festivals have a long tradition in the Monterey area, with the most famous drawing thousands of spectators. Ordering tickets as far in advance as possible is often essential. The **Carmel Bach Festival** (Box 575, Carmel 93921, ☎ 408/624–2046 or 800/513–2224) has presented the work of Johann Sebastian Bach and his contemporaries in concerts and recitals for more than 50 years. The highlight of the three-week event, which starts in mid-July, is a candlelit concert in the chapel of the Carmel Mission Basilica.

Nearly as venerable is the celebrated **Monterey Jazz Festival** (Box JAZZ, Monterey 93942, ☎ 408/373–3366), which attracts jazz and blues greats from around the world to the Monterey Fairgrounds on the third full weekend of September.

Another popular jazz event is **Dixieland Monterey** (177 Webster St., Suite A-206, Monterey 93940, ☎ 408/443–5260), held on the first full weekend of March, which features Dixieland bands performing in cabarets, restaurants, and hotel lounges on the Monterey waterfront, as well as a Saturday-morning jazz parade downtown and a program of Dixieland spirituals on Sunday.

For blues fans, there is the **Monterey Bay Blues Festival** (Box 1400, Seaside 93955, ☎ 408/394–2652), which is held in June at the Monterey Fairgrounds, featuring entertainment, arts and crafts, and a range of food booths.

The Custom House Plaza in downtown Monterey is the setting for free performances outdoors during the **Monterey Bay Theatrefest** (☎ 408/622–0700), which is held on weekend afternoons and evenings during most of the summer.

The **Cabrillo Music Festival** in Santa Cruz (104 Walnut Ave., Suite 206, Santa Cruz 95060, ☎ 408/426–6966, or box office 408/429–3444), one of the longest-running new music festivals, showcases contemporary sounds, particularly by American composers, for two weeks in early August.

Concerts

The highly regarded **Monterey County Symphony** (Box 3965, Carmel 93921, ☎ 408/624–8511) performs a series of concerts October through May in Salinas and Carmel. Programs range from classical to pop and include guest artists.

The **Chamber Music Society of the Monterey Peninsula** (Box 6283, Carmel 93921, ☎ 408/625–2212) presents a series of concerts featuring well-known chamber groups and holds an annual chamber-music contest for young musicians.

Theater

California's First Theater (Scott and Pacific Sts., Monterey, ☎ 408/375–4916) is home to the Troupers of the Gold Coast, who perform 19th-century melodramas in the country's oldest operating little theater, a historic landmark dating from 1846 on Monterey's Path of History.

Specializing in contemporary works, both comedy and drama, is the **Pacific Repertory Theater** (Box 222035, Carmel 93922, ☎ 408/622–0700). Also part of the acclaimed repertory company is the **Poetic Drama Institute,** which often presents solo dramatic performances and poetry readings.

American musicals and comedies, both old and new, are the focus of the **Wharf Theater** (Fisherman's Wharf, Monterey, ☎ 408/649–2332), where a local cast is sometimes joined by Broadway actors, directors, and choreographers.

Shakespeare Santa Cruz (Performing Arts Complex, University of California at Santa Cruz, 95064, ☎ 408/459–2121) puts on a six-week Shakespeare festival in July and August that also includes 20th-century works. Some performances are outdoors in the striking Redwood Glen.

Nightlife

Cabaret

Kalisa's (851 Cannery Row, Monterey, ☎ 408/372–3621). This long-established, freewheeling café in a Cannery Row landmark building offers a potpourri of entertainment that can include belly dancing, flamenco, jazz, folk dancing, and magic.

Bars and Nightclubs

Doc Ricketts' Lab (95 Prescott St., Monterey, ☎ 408/649–4241). Live bands perform nightly one block above Cannery Row. The varied program includes rock, blues, jazz, reggae, and folk.

McGarretts (Alvarado and Del Monte Sts., Monterey, ☎ 408/646–9244). This popular nightspot has dancing to Top 40 music Monday through Saturday, plus changing entertainment that includes country and western, burlesque, and male stripteasers.

Monterey Plaza Hotel (400 Cannery Row, Monterey, ☎ 408/646–1700). Automated piano music can be heard in a romantic setting overlooking the bay in the hotel's Duck Club.

Planet Gemini (625 Cannery Row, Monterey, ☎ 408/373–1449). Most nights, this club features comedy shows, followed by dancing to live rock music. There is country and western music and dancing Wednesday nights.

Safari Club (1425 Munras Ave., Monterey, ☎ 408/649–1020). Karaoke is featured Thursday through Saturday nights at this club in the Bay Park Hotel.

Sly McFlys (700 Cannery Row, Monterey, ☎ 408/649–8050). This popular local watering hole has a publike atmosphere.

Virgo's (2200 N. Fremont St., Monterey, ☎ 408/375–6116). This is Monterey's outpost for country-and-western music.

Piano Bars

Highlands Inn (Hwy. 1, Carmel, ☎ 408/624–3801). There is piano music nightly in the Lobos Lounge, dancing on weekends in the Fireside Lounge.

Lodge at Pebble Beach (17-Mile Dr., Pebble Beach, ☎ 408/624–3811). You'll find easy-listening entertainment in the Cypress Room and Terrace Lounge; there's a jazz band on Friday and Saturday evenings.

MONTEREY BAY ESSENTIALS

Arriving and Departing

By Bus

Greyhound Lines (☎ 800/231–2222) serves Monterey from San Francisco three times daily; the trip takes from three to five hours, depending on the number of stops.

By Car

The drive south from San Francisco to Monterey can be made comfortably in three hours or less. The most scenic way is to follow Highway 1 down the coast. Unless the drive is made on sunny weekends when locals are heading for the beach, the two-lane coast highway takes no longer than the freeway. (Note that portions of the road sometimes wash away during winter storms, in which case drivers are detoured inland.)

Of the freeways from San Francisco, a fast but enjoyable highway is Highway I–280 south to Highway 17, just south of San Jose. Highway 17 heads south and connects with Highway 1 in Santa Cruz. Another option is to follow U.S. 101 south through San Jose to Salinas, then take Highway 68 west to Monterey.

From Los Angeles, the drive to Monterey can be made in less than a day by heading north on U.S. 101 to Salinas and then heading west on Highway 68. The spectacular but slow alternative is to take U.S.

101 to San Luis Obispo and then follow the hairpin turns of Highway 1 up the coast. Allow at least three extra hours if you do.

By Plane

Monterey Peninsula Airport (☏ 408/648–7000) is 3 miles from downtown Monterey and is served by **American Eagle** (☏ 800/433–7300), **United Airlines** and **United Express** (☏ 800/241–6522), and **USAir** (☏ 800/428–4322).

By Train

Amtrak (☏ 800/872–7245) runs the *Coast Starlight* train between Los Angeles and Seattle, making a stop in Salinas (11 Station Pl.).

Getting Around

By Bus

Monterey-Salinas Transit (☏ 408/424–7695) provides frequent service between towns and many major sightseeing spots and shopping areas for $1.25 per ride, with an additional $1.25 for each zone you travel into, or $3.75 to $7.50 for a day pass, according to zone.

By Car

Highway 1 runs down the coast, past pumpkin and artichoke fields and the seaside communities of Half Moon Bay and Santa Cruz. Highway 17 crosses the redwood-filled Santa Cruz mountains between San Jose and Santa Cruz, where it intersects with Highway 1.

If your route takes you through San Jose, avoid the rush hour, which starts early and can be horrendous. Note also that parking is especially difficult in Carmel and in the vicinity of the Monterey Bay Aquarium on Cannery Row.

Guided Tours

Chardonnay II (Box 66966, Scotts Valley 95067, ☏ 408/423–1213), a "super yacht," accommodates 49 passengers for cruises on Monterey Bay, leaving from the yacht harbor in Santa Cruz. **California Parlor Car Tours** (☏ 415/474–7500 or 800/227–4250) and **Gray Line** (☏ 415/558–9400) operate motor-coach tours departing from San Francisco that feature the Monterey Peninsula in their northern California itineraries.

The **Rider's Guide** (Suite 255, 484 Lake Park Ave., Oakland 94610, ☏ 510/653–2553) produces a self-guided audiotape tour about the history, landmarks, and attractions of the Monterey peninsula and Big Sur, for $12.95, or $15.95 in vinyl binder, plus $2 postage.

Important Addresses and Numbers

Doctors

The **Monterey County Medical Society** (☏ 408/373–4197) will refer doctors on weekdays 9–5. For referrals at other times, call **Community Hospital of Monterey Peninsula** (23625 Holman Hwy., Monterey, ☏ 408/624–5311). The hospital has a 24-hour emergency room.

Emergencies

Dial 911 for **police** and **ambulance** in an emergency.

Pharmacies

Surf 'n' Sand in Carmel at 6th and Junipero streets (☏ 408/624–1543) has a pharmacy open weekdays 9–6:30, Saturday and holidays 9–2.

Visitor Information

The **Monterey Peninsula Chamber of Commerce** (Box 1770, 380 Alvarado St., Monterey 93942, ☎ 408/649–1770; ⌚ Weekdays 8:30—5).

Salinas Chamber of Commerce (119 E. Alisal St., Salinas 93902, ☎ 408/424–7611; ⌚ Weekdays 8:30–5).

The **Santa Cruz County Conference and Visitors Council** (701 Front St., Santa Cruz 95060, ☎ 408/425–1234 or 800/833–3494; ⌚ Mon.–Sat. 9–5, Sun. 10–4).

Santa Cruz Winegrowers (Box 3000, Santa Cruz 95063, ☎ 408/479–9463) has information on the region's 40 or so family-owned wineries.

10 The Central Coast

Highway 1 between Big Sur and Santa Barbara is a spectacular stretch of terrain, requiring concentration and nerve to drive. The road demands an unhurried pace, but even if it didn't you'd find yourself stopping often to take in the scenery. Don't expect much in the way of dining, lodging, or even history until you arrive at Hearst Castle. Santa Barbara flaunts its Spanish-Mexican heritage. The well-restored mission, a courthouse displaying some beautiful tile work and murals, and almost all of downtown, including some pleasant shopping areas, are done in Spanish-style architecture.

Updated by Colleen Dunn Bates

THE COASTLINE BETWEEN Carmel and Santa Barbara, a distance of just over 200 miles, is one of the most popular stretches of scenery in California—maybe one of the most popular anywhere. It is what many visitors to the state have come to see, and a drive that many Californians will take, whenever the opportunity presents itself. Except for a few smallish cities—Ventura and Santa Barbara in the south and San Luis Obispo in the north—the area is sparsely populated, with only a few small towns whose inhabitants relish their isolation among the redwoods at the sharp edge of land and sea. Between settlements, the landscape is dotted with grazing cattle and hillsides of wildflowers. Around Big Sur, the Santa Lucia mountains drop down to the Pacific with dizzying grandeur, but as you move south, the shoreline gradually flattens into the long sandy beaches of Santa Barbara and Ventura.

Big Sur has long attracted individualists—novelist Henry Miller comes to mind—drawn by the intractability of the terrain. But even the less precipitous junction of land and sea farther south has pulled in its share, most notably—and visibly—William Randolph Hearst, whose monumental home San Simeon is the most popular tourist attraction along the Central Coast.

Throughout the region are bed-and-breakfast inns and pleasant little towns, such as Cambria and Ojai, where resident artists create and sell their work. In the rolling hills of the Santa Ynez Valley are a growing number of wineries with steadily rising reputations. The Danish town of Solvang is a popular stopover for hearty Scandinavian fare and an architectural change of pace.

Santa Barbara is your introduction to the sand, surf, sun, and unhurried hospitality and easy living of southern California. Only 90 miles north of Los Angeles, Santa Barbara works hard to maintain its relaxed atmosphere and cozy scale. Wedged as it is between the Pacific and the Santa Ynez Mountains, it's never had much room for expansion. The city's setting, climate, and architecture combine to produce a Mediterranean feel that permeates not only its look but its pace.

Highway 1, which runs through most of this region, was the first in the country to be declared a scenic highway, in 1966. Barring fog or rain, the coast is almost always in view from the road. In some sections, the waves break on rocks 11,200 feet below; in other places, the highway is just 20 feet above the surf. The two-lane road is kept in good repair, but it twists, and traffic, especially in summer, can be very slow. Allow plenty of time for this drive, so that you can properly enjoy the breathtaking vistas.

EXPLORING

Most of the major sights and attractions of the region are right along the coastal route, or just a short detour away. The entire distance from Big Sur to Santa Barbara *could* be tackled in one long day of driving, but that would defeat the purpose of taking the slower, scenic coastal highway. A better option is to plan on taking several days, allowing time to explore Big Sur, Hearst Castle, the beaches, and Santa Barbara and to savor the changing scenery of the shoreline.

South Along Highway 1

Numbers in the margin correspond to points of interest on the Central Coast map.

❶ Just 13 miles south of Carmel is one of the quintessential views of California's coast, the elegant concrete arc of **Bixby Creek Bridge.** This view is a photographer's dream, and there is a small parking area on the north side from which to take a photo or to start a walk across the 550-foot span.

★ ❷ Five miles south is the **Point Sur Light Station,** standing watch from atop a sandstone cliff. The century-old beacon is open to the public on ranger-led tours (approximately 2½ hours; considerable walking is involved) on Saturday at 10 and 2, and Sunday mornings at 10. *Point Sur State Historical Park, ☏ 408/625–4419. ☛ $5 adults, $3 children 13–17, $2 children 5–12.*

The small developed area of the Big Sur valley begins a few miles south. Pfeiffer Big Sur State Park, gas, groceries, hotels, and restaurants are all clustered along the next 7 miles of the highway.

❸ One of the few places where you may actually set foot on the coastline you have been viewing from the road is at **Pfeiffer Beach.** The road to the beach turns off Highway 1 immediately past the Big Sur Ranger Station; follow it for 2 miles. The picturesque beach is at the foot of the cliffs, and a hole in one of the big sea-washed rocks lets you watch the waves break first on the sea side and then again on the beach side. The water is too cold and the surf too dangerous for swimming much of the year, however.

❹ On the ocean side of Highway 1, a towering 800 feet above the water, is **Nepenthe** (*see* Dining, *below*), a favorite hangout of tourists and locals. The restaurant's deck can be an excellent place to take a break from the rather stressful—though very beautiful—drive. Downstairs is a crafts and gift shop, displaying, among other items, the work of Kaffe Fassett, the famous knitting designer who grew up at Nepenthe.

❺ A few miles south is **Julia Pfeiffer Burns State Park** (☏ 408/667–2315), where a short and popular hike is a nice way to stretch your legs. The trail leads up a small, redwood-filled valley to a waterfall. You can go back the same (easier) way or continue on the trail and take a loop that leads you along the valley wall, with views out into the tops of the redwood trees you were just walking among. There are picnic and camping areas as well as access to the beach.

❻ For the next dozen miles' drive, it is just you, the road, and the coast—the gas station at Lucia is the first sign that you're returning to civilization. Among the many picnic areas and campgrounds between here and San Simeon is **Jade Cove,** one of the best-known areas on the coast in which to hunt for jade. Rock hunting is allowed on the beach, but you may not remove anything from the walls of the cliffs.

★ ❼ It's another 30 miles to **Hearst Castle,** known officially as the Hearst San Simeon State Historical Monument. Hearst Castle sits in solitary splendor atop La Cuesta Encantada (the Enchanted Hill); its buildings and gardens are spread over the 127 acres that were the heart of newspaper magnate William Randolph Hearst's 250,000-acre ranch.

Buses from the visitor center at the bottom of the hill take you to the neoclassical extravaganza above. Hearst devoted nearly 30 years and some $10 million to building this elaborate estate. He commissioned

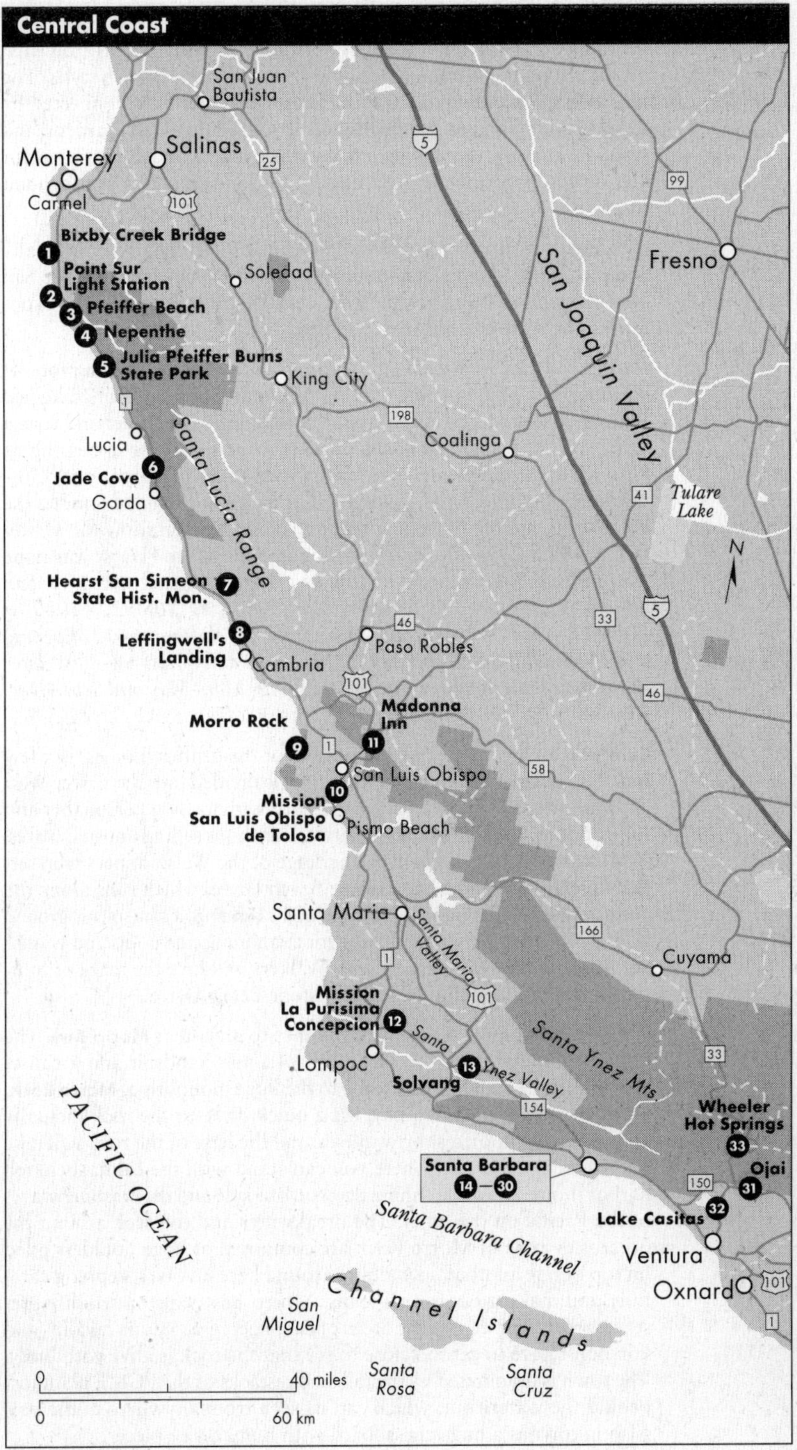

Central Coast
San Juan Bautista
Monterey
Salinas
Carmel
Bixby Creek Bridge
Point Sur Light Station
Pfeiffer Beach
Nepenthe
Julia Pfeiffer Burns State Park
Soledad
King City
Lucia
Jade Cove
Gorda
Santa Lucia Range
Coalinga
San Joaquin Valley
Fresno
Tulare Lake
N
Hearst San Simeon State Hist. Mon.
Leffingwell's Landing
Cambria
Paso Robles
Morro Rock
Madonna Inn
San Luis Obispo
Mission San Luis Obispo de Tolosa
Pismo Beach
Santa Maria
Santa Maria Valley
Cuyama
Mission La Purisima Concepcion
Lompoc
Santa Ynez Valley
Solvang
Santa Ynez Mts
Wheeler Hot Springs
Ojai
Santa Barbara
Lake Casitas
Ventura
Oxnard
PACIFIC OCEAN
Santa Barbara Channel
Channel Islands
San Miguel
Santa Rosa
Santa Cruz
0
40 miles
0
60 km

renowned architect Julia Morgan—who was also responsible for buildings at U.C. Berkeley—but was very much involved with the final product, a pastiche of Italian, Spanish, Moorish, and French styles. The art-filled main building and three guest "cottages" are connected by terraces and staircases and surrounded by reflecting pools, gardens, and statuary at every turn. In its heyday, this place was a playground for Hearst, Hollywood celebrities, and the rich and powerful from around the world.

Although construction began in 1919, the project was never officially completed. Work was halted in 1947 when Hearst had to leave San Simeon due to failing health. The Hearst family presented the property to the state of California in 1958.

Guides conduct four different daytime tours and one evening tour of various parts of the main house and grounds. Daytime tours take just under two hours. The evening tour, which begins at sunset and lasts a little over two hours, features docents in period dress appearing as Hearst's guests and staff. All tours include a half-mile walk and 150–400 stairs. An interesting free exhibit at the visitor center examines the life of this master of yellow journalism and inspiration for Orson Welles's film *Citizen Kane*—something about which Hearst was none too pleased. Reservations for the tours are a virtual necessity. *San Simeon State Park, 750 Hearst Castle Rd., ☎ 805/927–2020 or 800/444–4445. ☛ Day tour: $14 adults, $8 children 6–12. Evening tour: $25 adults, $13 children 6–12. Tours daily 8:20 AM–3 PM (later in summer) and most Fri. and Sat. evenings Mar.–May and Sept.–Dec. Reservations may be made up to 8 wks in advance. AE, D, MC, V.*

Cambria, an artists' colony full of turn-of-the-century homes, is a few minutes south of San Simeon. The town is divided into the newer West Village and the original East Village, each with its own personality and full of B&Bs, restaurants, art galleries, and shops selling unusual wares. You can still detect traces of the heritage of the Welsh miners who settled here in the 1890s. Moonstone Beach Drive, which runs along the
8 coast, is lined with motels, and **Leffingwell's Landing,** a state picnic ground at its northern end, is a good place for examining tide pools and watching otters as they frolic in the surf. Walkers will love the maze of footpaths along the beach side of Moonstone Beach Drive.

The coastal ribbon of Highway 1 comes to an end at **Morro Bay.** The bay is separated from the ocean by a 4½-mile sandspit and a cause-
★ 9 way, built in the 1930s, that leads to the huge monolith of **Morro Rock.** From the town of Morro Bay, it's a quick drive to the rock (actually an extinct volcano); a short walk around the base of the rock will take you to the breakwater, where you can stand with the calm, sheltered harbor (home of a large fishing fleet) on one side and the crashing waves of the Pacific on the other. The breakwater and the area around the ocean-side base of Morro Rock are composed of huge boulders piled on top of one another, so walking around here involves stepping carefully and making occasional leaps. Morro Bay is also a wildlife preserve, protecting the nesting areas of endangered peregrine falcons, and you don't have to get too close to see that the rock is alive with birds. The town is dominated by the tall smokestacks of the PG&E plant just behind the waterfront, which can be seen from anywhere in the bay. Also in town is a huge chessboard with human-size pieces.

South from Morro Bay, Highway 1 turns inland on its way to **San Luis Obispo,** the halfway point between San Francisco and Los Angeles and home to two decidedly different institutions: California Polytechnic State

University, known as Cal Poly, and the exuberantly goofy, garish Madonna Inn. The town has several restored Victorian-era homes, and the chamber of commerce offers a list of self-guided historic walks.
★ 10 Among the places to see is the **Mission San Luis Obispo de Tolosa** (782 Monterey St., ☎ 805/543–6850), one of the chain of missions established along the California coast by 18th-century Spanish missionary priests (*see also* La Purisima and Mission Santa Barbara, *below*). Nearby, several old warehouses along a stream have been renovated as shops. The **Ah Louis Store** (800 Palm St., ☎ 805/543–4332) was established in 1884 to serve the Chinese laborers building the Pacific Coast and Southern Pacific railroads and is still in business.

11 Even if you're not staying at the **Madonna Inn,** drop by the café and shops for a look at the gilt cherubs, pink bar stools, pink trash cans, pink lampposts, and all the other assorted outrageous kitsch that has put this place in a class by itself—a place way beyond any notions of good or bad taste. Begun in 1958 by Alex Madonna, a local highway contractor, and his wife, Phyllis, the inn has more than 100 rooms, each with its own played-to-the-hilt theme. The cave rooms, complete with waterfalls for showers, are among the most popular. *100 Madonna Rd. (take the Madonna Rd. exit from U.S. 101),* ☎ *805/543–3000.*

Highway 1 and U.S. 101 become one road for a short stretch just south of San Luis Obispo. A short detour off this road is **Avila Beach,** a usually quiet beach town that comes alive on weekends when Cal Poly students take over. A bit farther down the highway, 20 miles of wide sandy beaches begin at the town of **Pismo Beach,** where U.S. 101 and Highway 1 again go their separate ways. The action at this busy community centers on the shops and arcades near the pier, and there is camping near the beach.

Along the roads in and around **Lompoc** from May through August, you'll see vast fields of brightly colored flowers in bloom, and you will have little trouble in believing the town's boast of being the "Flower-Seed Capital of the World." Lompoc hosts a flower festival each June, and many of the petunias, poppies, marigolds, and other flowers grown here wind up on Rose Parade floats.

From Lompoc, take Highway 246 east to Mission Gate Road, which
★ 12 leads to the **Mission La Purisima Concepcion.** Founded in 1787, this is the most fully restored mission in the state, and its still-remote setting in this stark and serene landscape powerfully evokes the life of the early Spanish settlers in California. Once a month from March through September, costumed docents demonstrate crafts; every day, displays illustrate the secular as well as religious life of the mission. A corral near the parking area holds several farm animals, including sheep that are descendants of the original mission stock. *2295 Purisima Rd., Lompoc,* ☎ *805/733–3713 or 805/733–1303 to schedule a tour.* ☛ *$5 per vehicle, $4 if any passenger is over 62.* ⏲ *Daily 9–5; closed Thanksgiving, Dec. 25, Jan. 1.*

Southeast of Lompoc, inland along Highway 246 (or U.S. 101 to the
13 turnoff for 246 at Buellton), is the Danish town of **Solvang,** immortalized in William Castle's 1961 film *Homicidal.* You'll know when you've reached Solvang: The architecture suddenly turns to half-timbered buildings, windmills, and flags galore. Although it's aimed squarely at tourists, there is a genuine Danish heritage here—more than two-thirds of the town is of Danish descent. The 300 or so shops selling Danish goods and an array of knickknacks and specialty gift items are all within easy walking distance, many along Copenhagen Drive

and Alisal Road. Stop by the narrow and jammed coffee shop attached to the **Solvang Bakery,** at 460 Alisal Road, to try the Danish pastry. It is only one of a half-dozen aroma-filled bakeries in town.

From Buellton, U.S. 101 heads back to the coast, where it joins Highway 1 again and runs east to Santa Barbara, about 30 miles away.

Santa Barbara

14 The attractions in **Santa Barbara** begin with the ocean and end in the foothills of the Santa Ynez Mountains. In the few miles between the beaches and the hills, you pass the downtown and then reach the old mission and, a little higher up, the botanic gardens. A few miles farther up the coast, but still very much a part of Santa Barbara, is the exclusive residential district of Hope Ranch. To the east is the district called Montecito, where comics Charlie Chaplin, Fatty Arbuckle, and others built the Montecito Inn in 1928. Its first guests included movie stars Norma Shearer, W. R. Hearst mistress Marion Davies, Carole Lombard, and Wallace Beery. Montecito is also where the exclusive San Ysidro Ranch resort is located.

Because the town is on a jog in the coastline, the ocean is to the south, and directions can be confusing. "Up" the coast is west, "down" toward Los Angeles is actually east, and the mountains are north.

Everything in Santa Barbara is so close that the 8-mile drive to the airport seems like a long trip. A car is handy, but not essential, if you're planning on staying pretty much in town. The beaches and downtown are easily explored by bicycle or on foot, and the Santa Barbara Trolley takes visitors to most of the major hotels and sights, which can also be reached on the local buses.

The two visitor information centers (1 Santa Barbara St., at Cabrillo Blvd. and 504 State St., ☎ 805/965–3021) distribute a free guide to a scenic drive that circles the town with a detour into the downtown. It passes the harbor, beaches, Hope Ranch, and the old mission, offers fine views on the way to Montecito, then returns you to the beaches. You can pick up the drive, marked with blue SCENIC DRIVE signs, anywhere along the loop. A free guide to the downtown, the "Red Tile Walking Tour," is also available free from the visitor centers. It hits historical spots in a 12-block area.

The town of Goleta, the home of the University of California at Santa Barbara, is located a few miles up the coast via U.S. 101.

Numbers in the margin correspond to points of interest on the Santa Barbara map.

If you start at the Pacific and move inland, one of the first spots to visit
15 is **Stearns Wharf** on Cabrillo Boulevard at the foot of State Street. Although it's a nice walk from the Cabrillo Boulevard parking areas, you can drive out and park (for a fee) on the pier, then wander through the shops or stop for a meal at one of the wharf's restaurants or at the snack
16 bar. A major attraction on the wharf is **Sea Center** (*see* What to See and Do with Children, *below*), a branch of the Museum of Natural History that specializes in exhibits of marine life. Originally built in 1872 and reconstructed in 1981 after a fire, Stearns Wharf extends the length of three city blocks into the Pacific. The view from here back toward the city gives you a sense of the town's size and general layout.

17 The nearby **Santa Barbara Yacht Harbor** is sheltered by a man-made breakwater at the west end of Cabrillo Boulevard. You can take a ½-

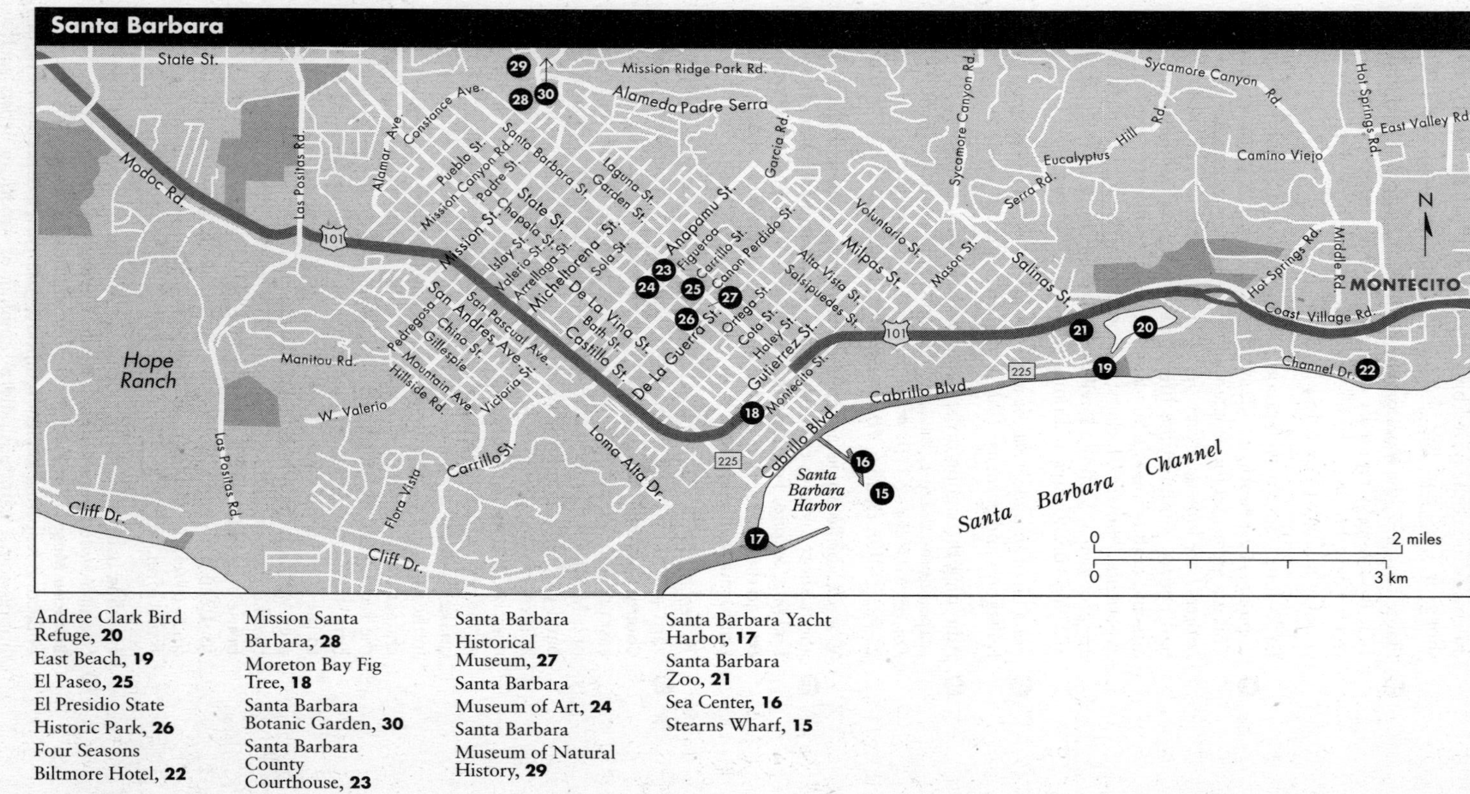

Andree Clark Bird Refuge, **20**
East Beach, **19**
El Paseo, **25**
El Presidio State Historic Park, **26**
Four Seasons Biltmore Hotel, **22**
Mission Santa Barbara, **28**
Moreton Bay Fig Tree, **18**
Santa Barbara Botanic Garden, **30**
Santa Barbara County Courthouse, **23**
Santa Barbara Historical Museum, **27**
Santa Barbara Museum of Art, **24**
Santa Barbara Museum of Natural History, **29**
Santa Barbara Yacht Harbor, **17**
Santa Barbara Zoo, **21**
Sea Center, **16**
Stearns Wharf, **15**

mile walk along the paved breakwater, check out the tackle and bait shops, or hire a boat from here.

18 Planted in 1877, the **Moreton Bay Fig Tree,** at Chapala Street and U.S. 101, is so huge it reputedly can provide shade for 10,000 people. In recent years, however, the tree has become a gathering place for an increasing number of homeless people.

Back along Cabrillo, well-groomed beaches stretch for miles. The most
19 popular is **East Beach,** a wide swath of sand at the east end of Cabrillo. This is a great spot for people-watching—an inordinate number of sunbathers here look as if they ought to be fashion models. Sand volleyball courts, summertime lifeguard and sports competitions, and arts-and-crafts shows on Sundays and holidays make for an often-lively experience. Showers, lockers, and beach rentals (also a weight room) are provided at Cabrillo **Pavilion Bathhouse** (1118 Cabrillo Blvd., ☎ 805/965–0509; days and times vary during the year).

20 For a bit of solitude, visit the nearby **Andree Clark Bird Refuge,** a peaceful lagoon and gardens. *1400 E. Cabrillo Blvd. ☛ Free.*

21 Adjoining the lagoon is the **Santa Barbara Zoo,** a small, lushly landscaped home to big-game cats, elephants, and exotic birds. *500 Niños Dr., ☎ 805/962–6310. ☛ $5 adults, $3 senior citizens and children 2–12. ⊙ Winter, daily 10–5; summer, daily 9–6.*

Where Cabrillo Boulevard ends at the lagoon, Channel Drive picks up
22 and, a short distance east, passes the **Four Seasons Biltmore Hotel** (*see* Lodging, *below*). For more than 60 years, Santa Barbara's high society and the visiting rich and famous have come here to indulge in quiet California-style elegance.

To reach the downtown area, retrace your route on Cabrillo Boule-
★ 23 vard and then head inland along State Street. The **Santa Barbara County Courthouse** in the center of downtown (from State Street head east one block on Ortega Street to Anacapa Street) has all the grandeur of a Moorish palace. As you wander the halls, admiring the brilliant hand-painted tiles and spiral staircase, you might just forget that you're in a courthouse until you spot a handcuffed group of offenders being marched by. This magnificent building was completed in 1929, as part of the rebuilding of Santa Barbara made necessary by a 1925 earthquake that destroyed much of downtown. At the time the city was also in the midst of a cultural awakening, and the trend was toward an architecture appropriate to the area's climate and history. The result is the harmonious Mediterranean-Spanish look of much of Santa Barbara's downtown area, especially its municipal buildings. An elevator to the courthouse tower takes visitors to a lovely, arched observation area with a panoramic view of the city and is a fine spot from which to take photos. In the supervisors' ceremonial chambers on the courthouse's second floor are murals painted by an artist who did backdrops for Cecil B. DeMille's silent films. *1100 block of Anacapa St., ☎ 805/962–6464. ⊙ Weekdays 8:30–4:45, weekends 9–5. Free 1-hr guided tours Mon.–Sat. 2 PM, Wed. and Fri. 10:30 AM and 2 PM.*

Heading back toward State Street on Anapamu Street, you'll pass the
24 Spanish-Style **Santa Barbara Public Library** on the way to the **Santa Barbara Museum of Art.** This fine small museum houses a permanent collection featuring ancient sculpture, Asian art, a collection of French Impressionist paintings, and a sampling of American artists such as Grandma Moses. *1130 State St., ☎ 805/963–4364. ☛ $4 adults, $3 senior citizens, $1.50 students with ID and children 6–16; free Thurs.*

and 1st Sun. of month. ⏲ *Tues.–Sat. 11–5 (until 9* PM *Thurs.), Sun. noon–5. Guided tours Tues.–Sat. 1* PM*, Sun. noon and 1* PM.

25 Walking south you'll pass **El Paseo,** a shopping arcade built around an
old adobe home. There are several such arcades in this area and also
26 many small art galleries. A few blocks east is **El Presidio State Historic Park.** Built in 1782, the presidio was one of four military strongholds established by the Spanish along the coast of California. The guardhouse, El Cuartel, is one of the two original adobe buildings that remain of the complex and is the oldest building owned by the state. *123 E. Cañon Perdido St.,* ☎ *805/966–9719.* ☛ *$1 donation suggested.* ⏲ *Daily 10:30–4:30.*

27 A block away is the **Santa Barbara Historical Museum,** with an array of items from the town's past. Adjacent is the **Gledhill Library,** a collection of books, photographs, maps, and manuscripts about the area. *136 E. De la Guerra St.,* ☎ *805/966–1601.* ☛ *$3 donation suggested to museum.* ⏲ *Museum: Tues.–Sat. 10–5, Sun. noon–5; library: Tues.–Fri. 10–4.*

A short distance from downtown (take State Street north and make a
★ 28 right on Los Olivos) at the base of the hills is **Mission Santa Barbara,** the gem of the chain of 21 missions established in California by Spanish missionaries in the late 1700s. One of the best preserved of the missions, it is still active as a Catholic church. *2201 Laguna St.,* ☎ *805/682–4713.* ☛ *$2 adults, children under 16 free.* ⏲ *Daily 9–5.*

29 Continuing north a block you pass the **Santa Barbara Museum of Nat-**
★ 30 **ural History** (2559 Puesta del Sol), and then the **Santa Barbara Botanic Garden,** 1½ miles north of the mission. The 65 acres of native plants are particularly beautiful in the spring. *1212 Mission Canyon Rd.,* ☎ *805/682–4726.* ☛ *$3 adults, $2 senior citizens, teens, and students with ID; $1 children 5–12.* ⏲ *Weekdays 9–4, weekends 9–5. Guided tours daily at 2* PM*; additional tour at 10:30* AM *on Thurs., Sat., and Sun.*

Ojai

Numbers in the margin correspond to points of interest on the Central Coast map.

A half-hour drive east of Santa Barbara over the narrow and winding
31 Highway 150 will put you in **Ojai,** a surprisingly rural town reminiscent of earlier days in California when agriculture was the uncontested king. You'll see acres of ripening orange and avocado groves that look like the picture-postcard images of southern California from decades ago. In recent years the area has seen an influx of show-biz types and other Angelenos who've opted for a life out of the fast lane. Moviemaker Frank Capra used the Ojai Valley as a backdrop for his 1936 classic, *Lost Horizon.* Be aware that the valley sizzles in the summer, when temperatures routinely reach 90°F.

The works of local artists can be seen in the Spanish-style shopping arcade along the main street. The **Art Center** (113 S. Montgomery, ☎ 805/646–0117) features art exhibits, theater, and dance. The **Ojai Valley Museum** (109 S. Montgomery, ☎ 805/646–2290; ☛ $1 over age 12; ⏲ Wed.–Mon. 1–4) documents the valley's history and displays Native American artifacts.

The compact town can be easily explored on foot, or hop on the new trolley (25¢), which takes riders on a 45-minute loop daily from 8:30

to 5:30. If you tell the driver you're a visitor, you'll get an informal guided tour. A stroll around town should include a stop at **Bart's Books** (302 W. Matilija, ☎ 805/646–3755), an outdoor store sheltered by native oaks and overflowing with used books. On Sunday, don't miss the **Farmers' Market** (on the plaza behind the arcade; ⏲ 10–2), where local organic and specialty farmers show their stuff. On Wednesday evenings in summer, the free all-American music played by the Ojai Band draws upward of 2,000 listeners to **Libbey Park** in the heart of town.

32 Nearby **Lake Casitas** on Highway 150 offers boating, fishing, and camping. It was the venue for the 1984 Summer Olympic rowing events.

One of the attractions in Ojai is a hot spring that makes use of natu-
33 ral mineral water from the nearby hills. The spa at **Wheeler Hot Springs** emerges like an oasis 7 miles north of town on Highway 33. Its tall palms and herb gardens are fed by an adjacent stream, and natural mineral waters fill the four redwood hot tubs and a large pool at the well-kept spa. Massage and skin-care services are also available. A restaurant on site offers dinner and live entertainment Thursday through Sunday, and Saturday and Sunday brunch. *16825 Maricopa Hwy.,* ☎ *805/646–8131 or 800/994–3353.* ⏲ *Mon.–Thurs. 9–9, Fri.–Sun. 9 AM–10 PM. Reservations advised at least a wk in advance for weekends, especially for spa.*

What to See and Do with Children

Sea Center on Stearns Wharf interests everyone from infants, who are lulled by the sight of fish in water, to teenagers and adults. Exhibits depict marine life from the Santa Barbara coastline to the Channel Islands: aquariums, life-size models of whales and dolphins, undersea dioramas, interactive computer-video displays, and remains of shipwrecks. The Touch Tank lets you handle marine invertebrates, fish, and marine plants collected from nearby waters. *211 Stearns Wharf,* ☎ *805/962–0885.* ☛ *$2 adults, $1.50 senior citizens, $1 children 3–17.* ⏲ *Mon., Wed., weekends, Sun. 10–5; Tues., Thurs., Fri. noon–5. Touch Tank open Thurs.–Tues. noon–4.*

At the **Santa Barbara Zoo,** youngsters particularly enjoy the scenic railroad and barnyard petting zoo. For children who quickly tire of the beach, there's an elaborate jungle gym play area at Santa Barbara's **East Beach,** next to the Cabrillo Bath House. Even more elaborate is the new **Kids' World** public playground (Santa Barbara St. near Micheltorena St.), a complex maze of fantasy climbing structures, turrets, and tunnels built by Santa Barbara's parents. Outside of Santa Barbara's **Museum of Natural History** is the skeleton of a blue whale, the world's largest creature. Kids are dwarfed by the bones and invited to touch them.

Off the Beaten Track

Channel Islands

Hearty travelers should consider a day visit or overnight camping trip to one of the five Channel Islands that often appear in a haze off the Santa Barbara horizon. The most often visited is Anacapa Island, 11 miles off the coast. The islands' remoteness and unpredictable seas protected them from development and now provide a nature enthusiast's paradise—both underwater and on land. In 1980 the islands became a national park; the water a mile around each is protected as a marine sanctuary.

On a good day, you'll be able to view seals, sea lions, and an array of bird life. From December through March, migrating whales can be seen close up. On land, tide pools alive with sea life are often accessible. Underwater, divers can view fish, giant squid, and coral. Off Anacapa Island, scuba divers can see the remains of a steamship that sank in 1853. Frenchy's Cove, on the west end of the island, has a swimming beach and fine snorkeling.

The waters of the channel are often rough and can make for a rugged trip out to the islands. You can charter a boat and head out on your own, but most visitors head to Ventura Harbor, a 40-minute drive south of Santa Barbara. From here a park-district concessionaire carries small groups to the islands for day hikes, barbecues, and primitive overnight camping.

Island Packers (1867 Spinnaker Dr., Ventura 93001, ☎ 805/642–1393) provides day trips to the islands and overnight camping to all five islands. Boats link up with national-park naturalists for hikes and nature programs. A limited number of visitors are allowed on each island, and unpredictable weather can limit island landings. Reservations are essential in the summer.

Wineries

Centered in the Solvang area, and spreading north toward San Luis Obispo, is a California wine-making region with much of the variety but none of the glitz or crowds of the Napa Valley in northern California. Most of the region's wineries are located in the rolling hills in the Santa Maria or Santa Ynez valleys. A leisurely tour of the entire area could take all day, but many wineries are just a short jog off U.S. 101. They tend to be fairly small, and only a few offer guided tours, but most have tasting rooms run by helpful staff, and wine makers will often act as your tour guide. Several of the wineries also have picnic areas on their properties.

Pamphlets with detailed maps and listings of each winery are readily available at lodgings and tourist centers all along the coast. A map for a self-guided driving tour is available free from the **Santa Barbara County Vintners' Association** (Box 1558, Santa Ynez 93460, ☎ 805/688–0881) and from **Paso Robles Wine Country** (1940 Spring St., Paso Robles 93446, ☎ 805/239–8463).

SHOPPING

State Street, the commercial hub of Santa Barbara, is a joy to shop: Thrift shops, elegant women's wear, bookstores, sporting goods, shopping centers, quirky storefronts—it's all here, and it's all accessible on foot. A smaller, swanker collection of boutiques lines Montecito's **Coast Village Road,** where the landed gentry pick up truffle oil, picture frames, and designer sweats.

Antiques

In Santa Barbara a dozen antiques and gift shops are clustered in restored Victorian buildings on Brinkerhoff Avenue, two blocks west of State Street at West Cota Street. For more serious antiques shopping, head east out of town a few miles to the beach town of **Summerland,** which is rife with antiques shops and markets. Wanda Livernois publishes a map and guide to area dealers available at 533 Brinkerhoff Avenue (or ☎ 805/962–4247 to have one mailed) and at other local shops.

Arcades

In all, 32 shops, art galleries, and studios share the courtyard and gardens of **El Paseo** (Cañon Perdido St., between State and Anacapa Sts., Santa Barbara), a shopping arcade rich in history. Lunch on the outdoor patio is a nice break from a downtown tour. Substantially larger and flashier, but still keeping in the Spanish-Moorish theme, is the newish, open-air **Paseo Nuevo** shopping center (700 and 800 blocks of State St.), home to such upscale chains as the Eddie Bauer Home Store, Nordstrom, and the California Pizza Kitchen—but more notable for such cherished local institutions as Stampa Barbara (rubber-stamp paradise) and children's clothier This Little Piggy.

Beach Wear

Pacific Leisure (808 State St., Santa Barbara, ☎ 805/962–8828) stocks the latest in California beachwear; it specializes in volleyball fashions, shorts, tops, and beach towels.

Books

The **Earthling Book Shop and Cafe** (1137 State St., ☎ 805/965–0926) is arguably Santa Barbara's cultural and intellectual center. Rambling yet homey, the Earthling holds book signings, poetry readings, a children's story time, and many other events. The book and magazine selection is terrific. **Chaucer's Bookstore** (3321 State St., ☎ 805/682–6787) is a well-stocked independent.

Clothing

Women can buy the quintessential casual southern California look at **Swept Away** (732 State St., Santa Barbara, ☎ 805/962–8291), a great place for sophisticated but beachy cotton clothing. Local clothier **Wendy Foster** (many locations, including Paseo Nuevo, ☎ 805/965–2634) also captures the fluid California style of women's wear. Men will find a more rugged equivalent at the **Territory Ahead** (515 State St., ☎ 805/962–5558), a high-quality, outdoorsy catalogue company whose only showroom is in Santa Barbara.

Kitchen

Los Angeles cooks and kitchen junkies have been known to drive two hours just to shop at **Jordano's** (614 Chapala St., ☎ 805/965–3031). Part professional restaurant supply, part gourmet store, part cooking school, this sprawling store stocks everything from seafood forks to espresso machines, flavored oils to herb pots.

SPORTS AND THE OUTDOORS

Participant Sports

Bicycling

Quadricycles, four-wheel carriages, and other types of bikes are available at **Surrey Cycle Rental** (1564 Copenhagen Dr.) and **Breezy's Carriages** (414 1st St.), both in Solvang at ☎ 805/688–0091.

Santa Barbara's waterfront boasts the level, two-lane Cabrillo Bike Lane. In just over 3 easy miles, you pass the zoo, a bird refuge, beaches, and the harbor. There are restaurants along the way, or you can stop for a picnic along the palm-lined path looking out on the Pacific. Rent bikes, quadricycles, and skates from **Beach Rentals** (8 W. Cabrillo Blvd., ☎ 805/966–6733; ⏲ daily 8–6 in winter, daily 8–dusk in summer). Bikes and quadricycles can be rented from the **Cycles 4 Rent** concession near the pool at Fess Parker's Red Lion Resort (633 E. Cabrillo, ☎ 805/564–4333, ext. 444).

Boating

Sailing Center of Santa Barbara (Santa Barbara Harbor, at the launching ramp, ☏ 805/962–2826 or 800/350–9090) offers sailing instruction, rents and charters sailboats, and organizes dinner cruises, sunset champagne cruises, and whale-watching expeditions.

Camping

There are many campsites along Highway 1, but they can fill up early anytime but winter. In **Big Sur,** campsites are at Pfeiffer Big Sur and Julia Pfeiffer Burns state parks. Near **Hearst Castle,** camping is available at several smaller state parks (San Simeon, Atascadero, Morro Bay, Montana de Oro, Avila Beach, and Pismo Beach). Most of the sites require reservations from MISTIX reservation service (☏ 800/444–7275 or 619/452–1950).

Fishing

There is access to freshwater- and surf-fishing spots all along the coast. For deep-sea trips, try **Virg's Sport Fishing** (☏ 805/772–1222) or **Bob's Sportfishing** (☏ 805/772–3340), both in Morro Bay.

At Santa Barbara, surface and deep-sea fishing are possible all year. Fully equipped boats leave the harbor area for full- and half-day trips, dinner cruises, island excursions, and whale watching from **SEA Landing** (Cabrillo Blvd. at Bath and breakwater, ☏ 805/963–3564).

Glider Rides

Scenic rides of 15–20 or 35–40 minutes are offered daily, 10–5, through **Windhaven Glider** (☏ 805/688–2517) at the **Santa Ynez Airport** near Solvang.

Golf

Play nine or 18 holes at the **Santa Barbara Golf Club** (Las Positas Rd. and McCaw Ave., ☏ 805/687–7087). **Sandpiper Golf Course,** 15 miles west (7925 Hollister Ave., Goleta, ☏ 805/968–1541), offers a challenging course that used to be a stop on the women's professional tour.

Hiking

There are miles of hiking trails in the **Ventana Wilderness,** with trailheads at state parks and picnic areas on Highway 1 from Big Sur to San Simeon. Another hiker's paradise is found in Ojai, home of the 9-mile **Ojai Valley Trail** as well as many miles of trails in the surrounding hills. The Ojai Chamber of Commerce recently published a regional trail map. Twelve miles east of Solvang is **Cachuma Lake,** a jewel of an artificial lake offering hiking as well as fishing and boating.

Horseback Riding

The **San Ysidro Ranch** hotel (900 San Ysidro La., Montecito, ☏ 805/969–5046) offers trail rides for parties of no more than six into the foothills by the hour. Reservations are required.

Tennis

Many Santa Barbara hotels have their own courts, but there are also excellent public courts. Day permits, for $3, are available at the courts. **Las Positas Municipal Courts** (1002 Las Positas Rd., Santa Barbara) has six lighted courts. Large complexes are also at the **Municipal Courts** (near Salinas St. and U.S. 101) and **Pershing Park** (Castillo St. and Cabrillo Blvd.).

Volleyball

The east end of Santa Barbara's **East Beach** has more than a dozen sandlots. There are some casual pickup games, but if you get into one, be prepared—these folks play serious volleyball.

Spectator Sports

Polo

The public is invited to watch the elegant game at the **Santa Barbara Polo Club,** 7 miles east in Carpinteria. *Take the Santa Claus La. exit from U.S. 101, turn left under the freeway and then left again onto Via Real. The polo grounds are ½ mi farther, surrounded by high hedges. ☎ 805/684–6683. ☛ $5 adults, children under 12 free. Games played Apr.–Oct., Sun.*

Beaches

Santa Barbara's beaches don't have the big surf of the beaches farther south, but they also don't have the crowds. A short walk from the parking lot can usually find you a solitary spot. Be aware that fog often hugs the coast until about noon in May and June.

East Beach, at the east end of Cabrillo Boulevard, is *the* beach in Santa Barbara. There are lifeguards, volleyball courts, a jogging and bike trail, and the Cabrillo Pavilion Bathhouse with a gym, showers, and changing rooms open to the public.

Arroyo Burro County Beach, a state beach just west of the harbor on Cliff Drive at Las Positas Road, has a small grassy area with picnic tables and sandy beaches below the cliffs. The usually gentle surf in this sheltered cove makes it ideal for families with young children. The Brown Pelican Restaurant on the beach serves a delicious breakfast.

Goleta Beach Park, north of Santa Barbara, in Goleta, is a favorite with the college students from the nearby University of California campus. The easy surf makes it perfect for beginning surfers and families with young children.

West of Santa Barbara on Highway 1 are **El Capitan, Refugio,** and **Gaviota state beaches,** each with campsites, picnic tables, and fire pits. East of the city is the state beach at **Carpinteria,** a sheltered, sunny, and often crowded beach.

DINING AND LODGING

Dining

Although you will find some chain restaurants in the bigger towns, the Central Coast from Big Sur to Solvang is far enough off the interstate to ensure that each restaurant and café has its own personality—from chic to down-home and funky. You'll find a few burger places, but they won't come with golden arches. In almost all cases, the restaurants will be right off Highway 1.

There aren't many restaurants along the coast from Big Sur until you reach Hearst Castle, where there is a large snack bar in the visitor center. From there south, the commercial fishing industry makes it possible for many of the restaurants to serve fresh fish every day. The stretch of Highway 1 in and around San Simeon is a popular tour-bus route, and restaurants catering to large groups offer solid, if routine, American fare: generous quantities of prime rib for dinner and bacon and eggs for breakfast. Cambria, true to its British-Welsh flavor, provides a taste of English cooking complete with peas and Yorkshire pudding, but the offerings range far beyond that. In Solvang, where the tone turns to Danish, count on traditional smorgasbord and sausages.

The variety of good food in Santa Barbara is astonishing for a town its size. Menu selections range from classic French to Cajun to fresh seafood. A leisurely brunch or lunch will take the best advantage of the beach and harbor views afforded by many restaurants and cafés. At the Biltmore's acclaimed and expensive Sunday brunch, however, all attention is on the spread of fresh fruits, seafood, and pastries. Served in the hotel's airy glass-roofed courtyard, it is perfect for special occasions.

If it is good, cheap food with an international flavor that you are after, follow the locals to Milpas Avenue on the east edge of Santa Barbara's downtown. You'll find everything from Thai to Greek to New Mexican and Hawaiian fare here. Freshly made tortillas are easily found in the markets on Milpas, particularly at La Super Rica, reputedly one of Julia Child's favorites for a quick, authentic Mexican snack.

WHAT TO WEAR

Dining attire on the Central Coast is generally casual, though slightly dressy casual wear is the custom at the expensive-to-very expensive restaurants listed below. Jacket or tie is not necessary unless noted.

CATEGORY	COST*
$$$$	over $45
$$$	$30–$45
$$	$18–$30
$	under $18

**per person for a three-course meal, excluding drinks, service, and 7¼%–7¾% sales tax*

Lodging

The choice of places to stay in Big Sur is limited, and there are few hotels or motels between Big Sur and San Simeon. From San Simeon to San Luis Obispo, however, there are many moderately priced hotels and motels—some nicer than others, but mostly just basic lodging. Only the loopy Madonna Inn in San Luis Obispo is worthy of a stay for its own sake. Make your reservations ahead of time, well ahead in the summer, because there very well may not be an alternative just down the road.

Bargain lodging is hard to come by in Santa Barbara, where high-end resorts are the staple. Long patronized by congestion-crazed Los Angeles residents, the resorts promise, and usually deliver, pampering and solitude in romantic settings. The beach area is most frequented and is certainly the most popular locale for lodging. Many places offer discounts in the winter season. Summer weekends, when 90% of the town's 46,000 motel and hotel rooms are filled, reservations made well in advance are strongly advised.

CATEGORY	COST*
$$$$	over $160
$$$	$100–$160
$$	$65–$100
$	under $65

**All prices are for a standard double room, excluding 9%–10% tax.*

Big Sur

DINING

$–$$ ★ Nepenthe. You'll not find a grander coastal view between Los Angeles and San Francisco than from here. The 800-foot-high cliff site, overlooking lush meadows to the ocean below, was once owned by Orson Welles and Rita Hayworth. The food is adequately average—from roast chicken with sage to sandwiches and hamburgers—so it is the location, in magnificent Big Sur, that rates the star. Nepenthe serves lunch and dinner; the outdoor Café Kevah serves breakfast and lunch. ✕ *Hwy. 1, south end of town,* ☏ *408/667–2345. Reservations for large parties only. AE, MC, V.*

DINING AND LODGING

$$$$ Ventana Inn. This getaway is essential California chic—restful and hip. Rooms are in buildings that are scattered in clusters on a hillside above the Pacific, done in natural woods with cool tile floors. Activities here are purposely limited to sunning at poolside—there is a clothing-optional deck—and walks in the hills nearby. The hotel's attractive stone and wood Ventana Restaurant serves California cuisine with Continental influences; the menu features oak-grilled salmon, grilled ahi tuna, and Black Angus sirloin steak. For a real event, come here for weekend brunch on the terrace, with spectacular views over golden hills down to the ocean. Room rates include Continental breakfast and complimentary afternoon wine and cheese buffet. *Hwy. 1, 93920,* ☏ *408/667–2331 or 800/628–6500,* FAX *408/667–2419. 59 rooms. Restaurant (reservations advised), 2 wading pools, hot tub, sauna, exercise room. AE, D, DC, MC, V. 2-night minimum stay on weekends and holidays.*

$$–$$$ Deetjen's Big Sur Inn. Built in bits and pieces in the '20s and '30s, this place has a certain rustic charm, at least for travelers not too attached to creature comforts. There are no locks on the doors (except from the inside), the heating is by wood-burning stove in half of the rooms, and your neighbor can often be heard through the walls. Still, it's a special place, set among redwood trees with each room individually decorated and given a name like Château Fiasco. The restaurant, which consists of four intimate dining rooms in the main house, serves stylish fare that includes Rock Cornish game hen, filet mignon, and lamb chops for dinner, wonderfully light and flavorful whole-wheat pancakes for breakfast (but no lunch). *Hwy. 1, south end of town, 93920,* ☏ *408/667–2377, restaurant* ☏ *408/667–2378. 19 rooms, 14 with bath. Restaurant (reservations required). No credit cards.*

LODGING

$$$$ ★ **Post Ranch Inn.** This luxurious retreat from the frenzy of urban life opened in 1992, the only commercial development to be approved in the Big Sur for 20 years and the ultimate in environmentally correct architecture. Visitors leave their cars at the gate and are bused up onto the cliff 1,200 feet above the ocean to the redwood guest houses, one butterfly-roofed, some on stilts, some built around trees, and all with dizzyingly splendid views of the Pacific. Each unit has its own spa tub, stereo system, private deck, and massage table, and because there are no televisions, there is every incentive to explore the glorious surrounding hiking country. Continental breakfast is included. *Hwy. 1, Box 219, 93920,* ☏ *408/667–2200 or 800/527–2200,* FAX *408/667–2824. 30 units. Restaurant, bar, 2 pools, spa, library. AE, D, DC, MC, V.*

$$$ Big Sur Lodge. This hostelry inside Pfeiffer Big Sur State Park is the best place in Big Sur for families. Motel-style cottages are set around a meadow surrounded by redwood and oak trees. Some have fireplaces, some kitchens. All rooms are without TV or phone. *Hwy. 1, Box 190, 93920,* ☏ *408/667–2171 or 800/424–4787,* FAX *408/667–3110. 61 rooms. Restaurant, pool, sauna. MC, V.*

Cambria

DINING

$–$$ ★ **Hamlet at Moonstone Gardens.** Set in the middle of a plant nursery, this restaurant has an enchanting patio garden that's perfect for lunch.

The upstairs dining room looks over the Pacific or the gardens. Service can be slow, but no one seems to mind. Fish of the day comes poached in white wine; other entrées range from hamburgers to rack of lamb. Downstairs is the International Wine Center, where you can taste wines from more than 50 wineries. ✕ *East side Hwy. 1,* ☏ *805/927–3535. Reservations accepted. MC, V. Closed Dec.*

$–$$ **Robin's.** "Multiethnic" only begins to describe the dining possibilities here: Tandoori prawns, quesadillas, fettuccine dishes with chow mein overtones, a Thai red curry, an array of salads (more for lunch than dinner), quite a few vegetarian entrées, hamburgers for the kids, and some truly fine desserts (house specialty: French apple pie with fresh whipped cream) are all on Robin's menu. ✕ *4095 Burton Dr.,* ☏ *805/927–5007. Reservations advised. AE, MC, V. Closed Sun. on nonholiday weekends.*

$ **Mustache Pete's.** This upbeat restaurant–sports bar serves Italian food—seafood, pasta, and poultry. ✕ *4090 Burton Dr.,* ☏ *805/927–8589. AE, D, DC, MC, V.*

LODGING

$$$ **Fog Catcher Inn.** Its beautifully landscaped gardens and 10 thatched-roof buildings lend the Fog Catcher the feel of an English country village. Most rooms (among them 10 minisuites) have ocean views. All have fireplaces and are done in floral chintz with light wood furniture. Breakfast is included. 🏨 *6400 Moonstone Dr., 93428,* ☏ *805/927–1400 or 800/425–4121. 60 rooms. Pool, hot tub. AE, D, DC, MC, V.*

$$$ **Squibb House.** The newest of several fine B&Bs in Cambria is housed in a Gothic Revival Italianate structure restored by its owner, Bruce Black, whose craftsmen built pine furniture in the 100-year-old carpentry shop next door. Black himself sought out old glass at flea markets, restored the gardens, and painted layers of soft colors in the bedrooms. Continental breakfast is included. 🏨 *4063 Burton Dr., Cambria 93428,* ☏ *805/927–9600. 5 rooms. Fireplaces. MC, V.*

$$–$$$ **Best Western Fireside Inn.** This modern motel has spacious rooms, with sofas and upholstered lounge chairs (plus refrigerators and coffeemakers). Some rooms have whirlpools or ocean views, and all have fireplaces. Continental breakfast is served in a room adjacent to the pool. The inn is just across from the beach, with fishing nearby. 🏨 *6700 Moonstone Beach Dr., 93428,* ☏ *805/927–8661 or 800/528–1234,* FAX *805/927–8584. 46 rooms. Pool, hot tub. AE, D, DC, MC, V.*

$$–$$$ ★ **Cambria Pines Lodge.** The lodge's buildings, from rustic cabins to fireplace suites, are set among 25 acres of pine trees above the town, with peacocks wandering the grounds. There is a big stone fireplace in the lounge, and all the furnishings—new and old—fit the decor of the 1920s, when the original lodge was established. The lodge's bar has live entertainment nightly. 🏨 *2905 Burton Dr., 93428,* ☏ *805/927–4200 or 800/445–6868,* FAX *805/927–4016. 125 rooms. Restaurant, bar, pool, hot tub, sauna, exercise room, volleyball. AE, D, MC, V.*

$–$$$ **Bluebird Motel.** Rooms at this garden motel, located near the East Village, range from simply furnished doubles to nicer creekside suites with fireplace and refrigerator. 🏨 *1880 Main St., 93428,* ☏ *805/927–4634 or 800/552–5434. 37 rooms. AE, D, DC, MC, V.*

$$ **San Simeon Pines Resort.** Set amid 9 acres of pines and cypresses, this motel-style resort has its own golf course and is directly across from Leffingwell Landing, a state picnic area on the rocky beach. The accommodations include cottages with their own landscaped backyards, and there are areas set aside for adults and families. Pets are not allowed (wildlife area). 🏨 *7200 Moonstone Beach Dr., Box 117, San*

Simeon 93452, ☎ 805/927–4648. 58 rooms. Pool, 9-hole golf course, croquet, playground. AE, MC, V.

Morro Bay

DINING

$–$$ **Dorn's.** This very pleasant seafood café overlooks the harbor. It looks like a Cape Cod cottage, with gray walls, mahogany wainscoting, awnings, and bay windows. Breakfast, lunch, and dinner are served; dinner features excellent fish and native abalone. ✕ *801 Market St., ☎ 805/772–4415. Weekend reservations advised. MC, V.*

$ ★ **Margie's Diner.** This clean and attractive, Mom-and-Pop diner-café serves generous portions of all-American favorites: ham or steak and eggs, three-egg omelets, chili, hot and cold sandwiches, chicken fried steak, deep-dish apple pie—you name it, and don't forget the milk shakes (or the 10 kinds of burger). Top-quality produce is used and service is excellent. ✕ *1698 N. Main St., ☎ 805/772–2510. No reservations. No credit cards.*

LODGING

$–$$ **Sea Air Inn.** Rooms in this modern, well-kept motel, a block from the waterfront, are clean and comfortable, decorated in blues and floral patterns. Some have ocean views, some have refrigerators, and all have coffeemakers. Location is the main drawing card. *845 Morro Ave., 93442, ☎ 805/772–4437. 25 rooms. AE, D, MC, V.*

Ojai

DINING

$$$ **L'Auberge.** Tasty country-French–Belgian food is paired with a terrific country setting. When the weather's fine, those in the know reserve an early table on the patio, so they can accompany their rack of lamb with a glorious sunset. ✕ *314 El Paseo Rd., ☎ 805/646–2288. Reservations advised. AE, MC, V. Closed Tues. No lunch weekdays.*

$$–$$$ **Wheeler Hot Springs Restaurant.** The menu, California Mediterranean in spirit, changes seasonally but always features herbs and vegetables grown in the spa's garden. It's 7 miles north of Ojai on Highway 33. The restaurant serves brunch on Saturday and Sunday, and offers packages including brunch and hot tub. ✕ *16825 Maricopa Hwy., ☎ 805/646–8131 or 800/994–3353. Reservations advised. AE, MC, V. Closed Mon.–Wed. No lunch.*

LODGING

$$$$ ★ **Oaks at Ojai.** This well-known, comfortable but not luxurious health spa boasts a solid fitness program that includes lodging, three nutritionally balanced, surprisingly good low-calorie meals, complete use of spa facilities, and 16 optional fitness classes. Various packages are offered. *122 E. Ojai Ave., 93023, ☎ 805/646–5573 or 800/753–6257, FAX 805/640–1504. 46 rooms. Dining room, pool, hot tubs, sauna, exercise room. D, MC, V. 2-day minimum stay.*

$$$$ **Ojai Valley Inn.** This outdoorsy, golf-oriented resort is set in landscaped grounds lush with flowers. The peaceful setting comes with hillside views in nearly all directions; nearby is the inn's 800-acre ranch, where guests can hike, mountain bike, ride horses, and bird-watch. Some of the nicer rooms are in the original adobe building and preserve such luxurious features as huge bathrooms and the original tiles. Families make use of popular Camp Ojai, held in summer and on holidays for kids 4–12, and the remarkable collection of miniature animals in the petting farm. The two restaurants tout "Ojai regional cuisine," featuring locally grown produce and locally made foods. *Country Club Rd., 93023, ☎ 805/646–5511 or 800/422–6524, FAX 805/646–*

7969. 207 units. 2 restaurants, bar, 2 pools, saunas, steam rooms, Senior PGA golf course, tennis courts, hiking, horseback riding, mountain bikes. AE, D, DC, MC, V.

$$–$$$ **Best Western Casa Ojai.** This spacious, modern hotel sits on Ojai's main street, across from Soule Park Golf Course. Rooms are simple and clean. Continental breakfast is included. *1302 E. Ojai Ave., 93023, ☎ 805/646–8175 or 800/255–8175, FAX 805/640–8247. 45 units. Pool, hot tub. AE, D, DC, MC, V.*

San Luis Obispo

DINING

$$ **Buona Tavola.** Locals favor this northern Italian restaurant, next door to the Fremont Movie Theater. Specialties include homemade agnolotti filled with scampi in a creamy saffron sauce and braised lamb shank with grilled polenta. Outdoor dining is also available on the flower-filled patio. ✕ *1037 Monterey St., ☎ 805/545–8000. Reservations required. D, MC, V.*

DINING AND LODGING

$$$–$$$$ ★ **Madonna Inn.** A designer's imagination run amok, this place is as much a tourist attraction as a place to stay. It is the ultimate in kitsch, from its rococo bathrooms to its pink-on-pink, froufrou dining areas. Each room is unique, to say the least: "Rock Bottom" is all stone, even the bathroom; the "Safari Room" is decked out in animal skins; "Old Mill" features a waterwheel that powers cuckoo-clock-like figurines. Even if you don't stay overnight, try a meal at the restaurant, where the food is perfectly adequate, with decor-matching desserts. *100 Madonna Rd., 93405, ☎ 805/543–3000 or 800/543–9666, FAX 805/543–1800. 109 rooms. Coffee shop, dining room (reservations advised). MC, V.*

LODGING

$$$–$$$$ ★ **Apple Farm.** The interior design is the strong point at this country-style hotel, where everything is meant to be soothing to the eye and no detail has been overlooked. Decorated to the hilt with floral bedspreads and wallpaper, and with watercolors by local artists, each room is individually appointed, some of them with canopy beds and cozy window seats. Complimentary coffee is served in the rooms. The adjoining restaurant serves such hearty country fare as chicken with dumplings and smoked ribs, and the breakfasts are copious. *2015 Monterey St., 93401, ☎ 805/544–2040 or 800/255–2040 in CA, FAX 805/546–9495. 101 rooms. Restaurant. AE, MC, V.*

$–$$ **Adobe Inn.** This clean, well-run inn, decorated in a spotless southwestern style, serves excellent full breakfasts, with fresh muffins and such daily specials as blueberry crepes or waffles topped with strawberries. *1473 Monterey St., 93401, ☎ 805/549–0321 or 800/676–1588. 15 rooms. AE, D, MC, V.*

San Simeon

DINING

$$ **Europa.** The menu here includes dishes from Germany, Hungary, and Italy—spätzle, egg dumplings and paprika, and homemade pasta. Crisp linen tablecloths brighten the small dining room. Steaks are featured as well as fresh fish specials. ✕ *9240 Castillo Dr. (Hwy. 1), ☎ 805/927–3087. Reservations accepted. MC, V. No lunch.*

$–$$ **San Simeon Restaurant.** This restaurant makes the most of its proximity to Hearst Castle, with a mind-boggling decor of imitation Greek columns, statues, and tapestries. There is a standard American menu; prime rib is the big draw. The dark dining room opens to views of the

Pacific across the highway. ✕ *East side Hwy. 1,* ☎ *805/927–4604. Reservations advised in summer. AE, DC, MC, V.*

LODGING

$–$$ **San Simeon Lodge.** This unpretentious motel is right across from the ocean. Many of its quite serviceable rooms have sea views. 🏨 *9520 Castillo Dr. (Hwy. 1), 93452,* ☎ *805/927–4601,* FAX *805/927–2374. 63 rooms. Restaurant, bar, lounge, pool. AE, DC, MC, V.*

$ **Motel 6.** This is a two-story motel with comfortable, if standard, rooms decorated in blue and rust, opening on an interior corridor. 🏨 *9070 Castillo Dr. (Hwy. 1), 93452,* ☎ *805/927–8691,* FAX *805/927–5341. 100 rooms. Pool. AE, D, DC, MC, V.*

Santa Barbara

DINING

$$$–$$$$ **The Stonehouse.** Set in a turn-of-the-century granite farmhouse, this atmospheric restaurant is part of the San Ysidro Ranch resort. The contemporary southern-American menu offers such treats as dry-aged New York steak with smoked tomato-horseradish sauce and clam hash, seared rare ahi wrapped in apple-smoked bacon, and an excellent four-course vegetarian menu. Even better than the generally wonderful food is the pastoral setting. Be sure to have lunch—salads, pastas, and sandwiches—on the tree-house-like outdoor patio. At night, the candlelit interior becomes seriously romantic. ✕ *900 San Ysidro La., Montecito,* ☎ *805/969–4100. Reservations required. AE, MC, V.*

$$$ ★ **Citronelle.** This offspring of Michel Richard's famed Citrus in Los Angeles has brought Santa Barbara folk some of the best California-French cuisine they've ever had this close to home. The accent is on Riviera-style dishes: light, delicate but loaded with intriguing good tastes. The desserts here are unmatched anywhere in southern California. There are splendid, sweeping views of the harbor from the dining room's picture windows—make sure to arrive before sunset. ✕ *901 E. Cabrillo Blvd.,* ☎ *805/963–0111. Reservations advised. AE, D, DC, MC, V.*

$$–$$$ **Palace Café.** A stylish and lively restaurant, the Palace has won acclaim for its Cajun and Creole dishes such as blackened redfish and jambalaya with dirty rice. Caribbean fare here includes delicious coconut shrimp. Just in case the dishes aren't spicy enough for you, each table has a bottle of hot sauce. The Palace offers dinner only; be prepared for a wait of up to 45 minutes on weekends. ✕ *8 E. Cota St.,* ☎ *805/966–3133. Reservations accepted weekdays, for 5:30 and 6 seatings on Fri. and 5:30 seating on Sat. AE, MC, V.*

$$ **Cold Spring Tavern.** Well worth the drive out of town, this century-old roadhouse is located on the former stagecoach route through the San Marcos Pass. It's part Harley-biker hangout, part romantic country hideaway, a mix that works surprisingly well. Game dishes—rabbit, venison, quail—are the specialty, along with such American standards as ribs, steak, and a great chili. It's a one-of-a-kind spot. ✕ *5995 Stagecoach Rd., San Marcos Pass,* ☎ *805/967-0066. Reservations advised for dinner. AE, MC, V.*

$$ **Pane & Vino.** This tiny trattoria, and its equally small sidewalk dining terrace, sits in a tree-shaded, flower-decked shopping center in Montecito, just east of Santa Barbara. The cold antipasto is very good, as are grilled meats and fish, pastas, and salads. ✕ *1482 E. Valley Rd., Montecito,* ☎ *805/969–9274. Reservations advised. MC, V. No lunch Sun.*

$–$$ **Brigitte's.** The quintessential California café, Brigitte's serves lively Mediterranean-influenced food and local wines at relatively low prices to a handsome crowd of locals and tourists. The individual pizzas are always worth trying, as are the pastas (penne with rock shrimp and golden chanterelles), grilled mahimahi or salmon, and roast lamb. Smart service. ✕ *1327 State St.,* ☏ *805/966–9676. Reservations accepted. MC, V. No lunch Sun.*

$–$$ **Castagnola Seafood Restaurant.** This unassuming spot just two blocks from the beach serves wonderfully good, fresh broiled fish. The homemade clam chowder is excellent. ✕ *205 Santa Barbara St.,* ☏ *805/962–8053. No reservations. AE, D, MC, V.*

$–$$ **Harbor Restaurant.** This sparkling spot on the pier is where locals like to take out-of-town guests for great views and average American food. The casual, nautical bar and grill upstairs serves sandwiches, large salads, and a huge variety of appetizers; the outdoor terrace is a glorious spot for a sandwich or a beer on a sunny day. Downstairs you'll find healthy portions of fresh seafood, prime rib, and steaks. Every seat has a harbor view. ✕ *210 Stearns Wharf,* ☏ *805/963–3311. AE, MC, V.*

$–$$ ★ **Montecito Café.** The ambience is upscale yet casual at this pleasant restaurant serving contemporary California-American cuisine—fresh fish, grilled chicken, steak, and pasta. It's one of the best values in Santa Barbara. The salads and lamb dishes are particularly inventive. ✕ *1295 Coast Village Rd.,* ☏ *805/969–3392. Reservations accepted for dinner. AE, MC, V.*

$ ★ **La Super-Rica.** This tiny, tacky food stand serves the best and hottest Mexican dishes between Los Angeles and San Francisco. Fans drive for miles to fill up on the soft tacos and incredible beans. ✕ *622 N. Milpas St., at Alphonse St.,* ☏ *805/963–4940. No credit cards.*

$ **Roy.** Voted best new restaurant by a local paper, this tiny downtown storefront is a real bargain. Owner-chef Leroy Gandy serves a $10 fixed-price dinner and Sunday brunch menu that includes a small salad, fresh soup, and a tempting roster of Cal-Mediterranean main courses: shrimp ravioli, marinated leg of lamb with eggplant ratatouille, grilled salmon with pineapple-orange-mango chutney and a mint-butter sauce. Expect a long wait on weekends. ✕ *7 W. Carrillo St.,* ☏ *805/966–5636. No reservations. AE, MC, V. Closed Mon. No lunch (open Sun. for brunch).*

LODGING

$$$$ ★ **Four Seasons Biltmore Hotel.** This hotel is Santa Barbara's grande dame. Its decor of muted pastels and bleached woods gives the cabanas behind the main building a light, airy touch without sacrificing the hotel's reputation for understated elegance. Surrounded by lush gardens and palm trees galore, the Biltmore is a bit more formal than other properties in town. *1260 Channel Dr., 93108,* ☏ *805/969–2261 or 800/332–3442,* FAX *805/969–4682. 234 rooms. 2 restaurants, bar, 2 pools, hot tub, putting green, tennis courts, croquet, health club, shuffleboard. AE, DC, MC, V.*

$$$$ ★ **San Ysidro Ranch.** At this luxury "ranch" you can feel at home in jeans and cowboy boots, but be prepared to dress for dinner. A hideout for the Hollywood set, this romantic place hosted John and Jackie Kennedy on their honeymoon. Guest cottages, some with down comforters and all with wood-burning stoves or fireplaces, are scattered among 14 acres of orange trees and flower beds. There are 500 acres more left in open space to roam at will on foot or horseback. The hotel, which welcomes children and pets, offers 24-hour room service. *900 San Ysidro La., Montecito 93108,* ☏ *805/969–5046 or 800/368–6788,* FAX *805/565–1995. 44 rooms. Restaurant, pool, beauty salon, massage, spa, tennis courts, boccie, exercise room, horseback riding, horseshoes. AE, MC, V. 2-day minimum stay on weekends, 3 days on holidays.*

$$$–$$$$ **Santa Barbara Inn.** Directly across the street from East Beach, this three-story, gussied-up motel has a crisp exterior and a sophisticated interior decor featuring light woods, teal accents, and subdued tones.

Unfortunately, the cheap motel construction compromises the attempt at elegance. The location—many of the rooms have ocean views—and the excellent restaurant, Citronelle, are the real draws, not the inn itself. *901 E. Cabrillo Blvd., 93103, 805/966–2285 or 800/231–0431, FAX 805/966–6584. 71 rooms. Restaurant, pool, hot tub. AE, D, DC, MC, V.*

$$$–$$$$ ★ **Simpson House Inn.** Traditional B&B fans will enjoy the beautifully appointed Victorian main house of this inn, set on a quiet acre in the heart of town. Those seeking total privacy and sybaritic comfort should choose one of the exceptional new cottages or century-old barn suites, each complete with wood-burning fireplace, luxurious bedding, state-of-the-art electronics, and whirlpool-equipped bath. Room rates include full breakfast. *121 E. Arrellaga St., 93101, 805/963–7067 or 800/676–1280, FAX 805/564–4811. 14 rooms. 2-night minimum stay on weekends. AE, D, MC, V.*

$$$–$$$$ **The Upham.** This handsomely restored Victorian hotel, situated on an acre of gardens in the midst of historic downtown, was established in 1871. Period furnishings and antiques adorn the rooms and cottages, some of which have fireplaces and private patios. Some rooms are quite small. Continental breakfast and afternoon wine and cheese are served in the lobby and on the garden veranda. *1404 De La Vina St., 93101, 805/962–0058 or 800/727–0876, FAX 805/963–2825. 49 rooms. AE, D, DC, MC, V.*

$$–$$$$ **Villa Rosa.** Inside this 60-year-old hotel, a red-tile-roofed Spanish-style house of stucco and wood, the rooms and intimate lobby are decorated in an informal southwestern style. The Villa Rosa is just one block from the beach. Rates include Continental breakfast, wine and cheese in the afternoon, and port and sherry in the evening. *15 Chapala St., 93101, 805/966–0851, FAX 805/962–7159. 18 rooms. Pool, hot tub. AE, MC, V.*

$$–$$$ **Ambassador by the Sea.** The wrought-iron trim and mosaic tiling on this Spanish-style building near the harbor and Stearns Wharf make it seem the quintessential California beach motel. The rooms have verandas, and sundecks overlook the ocean and the bike path. Two units have kitchenettes. *202 W. Cabrillo Blvd., 93101, 805/965–4577, FAX 805/965–9937. 32 rooms. Pool. AE, D, DC, MC, V.*

$$–$$$ **Miramar Resort Hotel.** Accommodations at this longtime favorite with families are in motel-type rooms and suites with private patios or balconies overlooking either the ocean or one of the pools, or in cottages with up to four bedrooms. Between May and October, there's a two-night minimum stay on weekends, a three-night minimum on holiday weekends. *1555 S. Jameson St. (3 mi south of Santa Barbara on U.S. 101), Box 429, Santa Barbara 93102, 805/969–2203 or 800/322–6983 in CA. 213 rooms. 2 restaurants, 2 pools, saunas, spa, tennis courts, exercise room, playground. AE, MC, V.*

$$–$$$ **Old Yacht Club Inn.** Built in 1912 as a private home in the California Craftsman style, this inn near the beach was one of Santa Barbara's first bed-and-breakfasts. The rooms have turn-of-the-century furnishings and Oriental rugs. Guests receive complimentary full breakfast and evening wine, along with the use of bikes and beach chairs. There is no smoking. *431 Corona del Mar Dr., 93103, 805/962–1277 or 800/676–1676; in CA, 800/549–1676; FAX 805/962–3989. 9 rooms. Dining room (open Sat. only for guests). AE, D, MC, V.*

$ **Motel 6.** The low price and location near the beach are the pluses for this no-frills place. Reserve well in advance all year. *443 Corona del Mar Dr., 93103, 805/564–1392. 52 units. Pool. AE, D, DC, MC, V.*

Solvang

DINING

$$ ★ **Danish Inn.** The smorgasbord here is popular, but there are also steaks and an extensive array of Continental-style items—rack of lamb, Rahm schnitzel, and Danish *morbrad* (medallions of pork sautéed with red wine, shallots, and mushrooms), for example. The atmosphere is more formal than in most other Solvang restaurants, but the fireplace and lace curtains keep it cozy. Breakfast is served on the weekends. ✕ *1547 Mission Dr., ☎ 805/688–4813. Reservations advised. AE, D, DC, MC, V.*

$–$$ **Restaurant Molle-Kroen.** A busy upstairs dining room serves smorgasbord and other Danish specialties. It has a cheerful, light setting, with fresh flowers on the tables and booths. The local folks come here when they want a good meal at a good price. ✕ *435 Alisal Rd., ☎ 805/688–4555. AE, D, DC, MC, V.*

$–$$ ★ **Royal Scandia Restaurant.** The three dining rooms here are decorated like a quaint old Danish cottage, with vaulted ceilings, rafters, and lots of brass and frosted glass. There is also dining on an enclosed patio. The menu caters to traditional American tastes but includes a Danish smorgasbord every evening. There is also a Sunday champagne brunch. ✕ *400 Alisal Rd., ☎ 805/688–8000. Reservations advised. AE, D, DC, MC, V.*

LODGING

$$–$$$$ **Chimney Sweep Inn.** All the rooms are pleasant, but it is the cottages in the backyard that are extra special (and expensive) here. Built in a half-timbered style, they were inspired by the C. S. Lewis children's books, *The Chronicles of Narnia*. The cottages have kitchens and fireplaces; some have private Jacuzzis. In the garden are a waterfall and fishpond. Room rates include Continental breakfast. 🏨 *1554 Copenhagen Dr., 93463, ☎ 805/688–2111 or 800/824–6444, FAX 805/688–8824. 28 rooms. Hot tub. AE, D, MC, V.*

$$–$$$ **Best Western Kronborg Inn.** Rooms at this comfortable motel three blocks from the center of town are spacious; most have balconies overlooking the pool and Jacuzzi. Two rooms have whirlpool baths. Continental breakfast is included. 🏨 *1440 Mission Dr., 93463, ☎ 805/688–2383, FAX 805/688–1821. 39 rooms. Pool, hot tub. AE, D, DC, MC, V.*

$$–$$$ **Solvang Royal Scandinavian Inn.** The look inside and out here reflects the town's Danish feel. Rooms—Scandinavian modern style, of course—have nice touches, like hand-painted furniture. The large, brick-walled, dark-timbered lobby has a fireplace and overstuffed chairs. 🏨 *400 Alisal Rd., 93464, ☎ 805/688–8000 or 800/624–5572, FAX 805/688–0761. 133 rooms. Restaurant, lounge, pool, hot tub. AE, D, DC, MC, V.*

THE ARTS AND NIGHTLIFE

The Arts

Santa Barbara prides itself on being a top-notch cultural center. It supports a professional symphony and chamber orchestra and an impressive art museum. The proximity to the University of California at Santa Barbara assures an endless stream of visiting artists and performers.

The enormous Moorish-style **Arlington Theater,** 1317 State Street, is home to the Santa Barbara Symphony. The Santa Barbara Civic Light Opera makes its home at the equally venerable, if slightly less grand, **Granada Theatre,** at 1216 State Street. The **Lobero,** a state landmark, at 33 East Cañon Perdido Street, shares its stage with community theater groups and touring professionals. Plays and readings are also staged at the **Center Stage Theatre,** on the second floor of Paseo Nuevo in the 700 block of State Street.

Music Festivals

Since 1971, the **San Luis Obispo Mozart Festival** (Box 311, San Luis Obispo 93406, ☎ 805/781–3008) has been held in late July and early August. The settings include the Mission San Luis Obispo de Tolosa and the Cal Poly Theater. Not all the music is Mozart; you'll hear Haydn and other composers. The Festival Fringe offers free concerts outdoors. This year marks the 50th anniversary of the **Ojai Music Festival** (☎ 805/646–2094), an internationally known event that attracts progressive and traditional musicians alike; last year's performers included France's Lyon Opera Company.

Theater

Boo and hiss the villains year-round at the **Great American Melodrama** (Hwy. 1, ☎ 805/489–2499) in the small town of Oceano, south of San Luis Obispo. The **Pacific Conservatory of the Performing Arts** (Box 1700, Santa Maria 93456, ☎ 805/922–8313 or 800/549–7272 in CA) presents a full spectrum of theatrical events, from classical to contemporary, with a few musicals thrown in, in different theaters in Solvang and Santa Maria. The Solvang Festival Theater has open-air performances.

Nightlife

Most of the major hotels offer nightly entertainment during the summer season and live weekend entertainment all year. To see what's scheduled at the hotels and many small clubs and restaurants, pick up a copy of the free weekly *Santa Barbara Independent* newspaper for an extensive rundown.

Bars

For a rowdy, collegiate outing, hit the venerable **Joe's Cafe** (536 State St., Santa Barbara, ☎ 805/966–4638), where steins of beer accompany hearty bar food. Those seeking quieter conversation, an early California feeling, and perhaps even romance should visit the **Plow & Angel** at the San Ysidro Ranch (900 San Ysidro La., Montecito, ☎ 805/969–5046); there's live jazz Thursday–Friday.

Dancing

Zelo (630 State St., Santa Barbara, ☎ 805/966–5792). This high-energy restaurant doubles as a progressive rock and punk dance club featuring offbeat videos and innovative lighting.

Music

Downtown Santa Barbara boasts several worthy music spots. Jazz lovers head for **21 Victoria Restaurant and Jazz Club** (21 W. Victoria St., ☎ 805/962–5222). Jazz is also featured on weeknights at **Soho** (1221 State St., ☎ 805/962–7776), a hip restaurant and hangout; on weekends, the mood livens with good blues and rock. Fans of easygoing California rock and people-watching should check out **State & A** (1201 State St., ☎ 805/966–1010), a very popular bar and grill.

CENTRAL COAST ESSENTIALS

Arriving and Departing

By Bus

Greyhound (☎ 800/231–2222) provides service from San Francisco and Los Angeles to San Luis Obispo and Santa Barbara.

Amtrak (☏ 800/872–7245) runs the *Coast Starlight* train from Los Angeles along the coast from Santa Barbara to San Luis Obispo. From there it heads inland for the rest of the route to the San Francisco Bay Area and Seattle. Local numbers are, in Santa Barbara, ☏ 805/963–1015; in San Luis Obispo, ☏ 805/541–0505.

By Car

The only way to see the most dramatic section of the Central Coast, the 70 miles between Big Sur and San Simeon, is by car. Heading south on Highway 1, you'll be on the ocean side of the road and will get the best views. Don't expect to make good time along here. The road is narrow and twisting with a single lane in each direction, making it difficult to pass slower traffic or the many lumbering RVs. In fog or rain, the drive can be downright nerve-racking. U.S. 101 from San Francisco to San Luis Obispo is the quicker, easier alternative, but it misses the coast entirely. U.S. 101 and Highway 1 join north of Santa Barbara. Both, eventually dividing, continue south through southern California.

By Plane

American and **American Eagle** (☏ 800/433–7300), **Skywest/Delta** (☏ 800/453–9417), **United** and **United Express** (☏ 800/241–6522), and **USAir Express** (☏ 800/428–4322) fly into **Santa Barbara Municipal Airport** (☏ 805/683–4011) 8 miles from downtown at 500 Fowler Road.

Santa Barbara Airbus (☏ 805/964–7759 or 800/733–6354) shuttles travelers between Santa Barbara and Los Angeles Airport. **Aero Airport Limousine** (☏ 805/965–2412) serves Los Angeles Airport (by reservation only). The **Santa Barbara Metropolitan Transit District** (☏ 805/683–3702) Bus 11 runs from the airport to the downtown transit center.

Getting Around

By Bus

From Monterey and Carmel, **Monterey–Salinas Transit** (☏ 408/899–2555) operates daily bus runs to Big Sur May–September. From San Luis Obispo, **Central Coast Transit** (☏ 805/541–2228) runs buses around the town and out to the coast on regular schedules. Local service is also provided by the **Santa Barbara Metropolitan Transit District** (☏ 805/683–3702).

By Car

Highway 1 and U.S. 101 run more or less parallel, with Highway 1 hugging the coast and 101 remaining a few miles inland. Along some stretches the two roads join and run together for a while. Plan on three to four hours' driving time for the 90 miles from Big Sur to Morro Bay on Highway 1—this is not a freeway, and you'll probably want to stop at some of the 300 scenic turnouts along this route. Once you start south from Carmel, there is no route off until Highway 46 heads inland from Cambria to connect with U.S. 101. At Morro Bay, Highway 1 moves inland for 13 miles and connects with U.S. 101 at San Luis Obispo. From here, south to Pismo Beach, the two highways run concurrently, and while you lose the dramatic coastal scenery, the driving is easier. The roads go their separate ways again near Gaviota, just north of Santa Barbara. You can drive between Santa Barbara and Los Angeles in just a couple of hours.

Guided Tours

California Parlour Car Tours (Cathedral Hill Hotel, 1101 Van Ness Ave., San Francisco 94109, ☏ 415/474–7500 or 800/227–4250) offers a number of tours that include the Central Coast. Lasting three to 10 days, these are one-way bus trips from San Francisco to Los Angeles (or vice versa) that travel along the coast, visiting Hearst Castle, Santa Barbara, and Monterey and may also include time in Yosemite or Lake Tahoe. (We recommend that you steer clear of any tour that takes you to Yosemite for less than one full day; readers have been disappointed in the past. Save Yosemite for a trip when you have enough time.)

Santa Barbara Trolley Co. (☏ 805/965–0353) has five daily, regularly scheduled runs from 10 AM to 4 PM in Santa Barbara. Motorized San Francisco–style cable cars deliver visitors to major hotels, shopping areas, and attractions. Stop or not, as you wish, and pick up another trolley when you're ready to move on. All depart from and return to Stearns Wharf. The fare for the whole day is $4 adults, $2 children and senior citizens.

Important Addresses and Numbers

Doctors

Emergency care is available at **St. Francis Hospital** (601 E. Micheltorena St., Santa Barbara, ☏ 805/962–7661).

Emergencies

Dial 911 for **police** and **ambulance** in an emergency.

Road Conditions

Dial 800/427–7623 for up-to-date information on road conditions throughout the Central Coast area.

Visitor Information

Big Sur Chamber of Commerce (Box 87, 93920, ☏ 408/667–2100).

California Dept. of Parks and Recreation (in Big Sur, ☏ 408/667–2315).

Cambria Chamber of Commerce (767 Main St., 93428, ☏ 805/927–3624).

Ojai Chamber of Commerce (Box 1134, 93024, ☏ 805/646–8126).

San Luis Obispo Chamber of Commerce (1039 Chorro St., 93401, ☏ 805/781–2777 or 800/756–5056).

San Simeon Chamber of Commerce (Box 1, 9255 Hearst Dr., 93452, ☏ 805/927–3500 or 800/342–5613).

Santa Barbara Conference and Visitors Bureau (510A State St., 93101, ☏ 805/966–9222 or 800/927–4688) will mail brochures and other information.

Santa Barbara Visitor Centers (1 Santa Barbara St., at Cabrillo Blvd., or 504 State St., ☏ 805/965–3021, ⏲ Mon.–Sat. 9–4, Sun. 10–4).

Solvang Conference and Visitors Bureau (Box 70, 1511A Mission Dr., 93464, ☏ 805/688–6144 or 800/468–6765).

11 Los Angeles

In certain lights Los Angeles displays its Spanish heritage, but much more evident is its cultural vibrancy as a 20th-century center on the Pacific Rim. Hollywood, the beaches, and Disneyland are all within an hour's drive. Also here are Beverly Hills, noted for its shops and mansions; important examples of 20th-century domestic architecture; and freeways. Everything about Los Angeles is grand—even overdone—which is part of the city's charm: It's all for show, but the show's usually a good one. Because things are so spread out here, visitors need to organize itineraries carefully.

YOU'RE PREPARING FOR YOUR TRIP to Los Angeles. You're psyching up with Beach Boys CDs and some Hollywood epics on the laser-disc player. You've pulled out your Hawaiian shirts and tennis shorts. You've studied the menu at Taco Bell. You're even doing a crash regimen at your local tanning salon and aerobics studio so you won't *look* so much like a tourist when you hit the coast.

Well, relax. *Everybody's* a tourist in LaLa Land. Even the stars are starstruck (as evidenced by the celebrities watching the other celebrities at Spago). Los Angeles is a city of ephemerals, of transience, and above all, of illusion. Nothing here is quite real, and that's the reality of it all. That air of anything-can-happen—as it often does—is what motivates thousands to move to and millions to vacation in this promised land each year. Visitors don't just come from the East or Midwest, mind you, but from the Far East, Down Under, Europe, and South America. It's this influx of cultures that's been the lifeblood of Los Angeles since its Hispanic beginning.

No matter how fast-forward Los Angeles seems to spin, the heart of the city—or at least its stomach—is still deep in the 1950s. Sure, the lighter, nouvelle-inspired California cuisine has made a big splash (no one here has ever been ridiculed as a "health-food nut" for preferring a healthier diet), but nothing is more quintessentially Californian than Johnny Rockets (a chrome-and-fluorescent burger paradise on Melrose) or Pink's (a beloved greasy spoon of a chili-dog dive on La Brea).

None of this was imagined when Spanish settlers founded their Pueblo de la Reina de Los Angeles in 1781. In fact, no one predicted a golden future for desert-dry southern California until well after San Francisco and northern California had gotten a head start with their own gold rush. The dusty outpost of Los Angeles eventually had oil and oranges, but the golden key to its success came on the silver screen: the movies. Although, if the early pioneers of Hollywood—religiously conservative fruit farmers—had gotten their way, their town's name would never have become synonymous with cinema and entertainment.

The same sunshine that draws today's visitors and new residents drew Cecil B. DeMille and Jesse Lasky in 1913 while searching for a place to make movies away from the East Coast. Lesser filmmakers had been shooting reels for the nickelodeons of the day in Hollywood, but DeMille and Lasky were the first to make a feature-length movie here. It took another 14 years to break through the sound barrier in cinema, but the silent-film era made Hollywood's name synonymous with fantasy, glamour, and, as the first citizens would snicker in disgust, with sin.

Outrageous partying, extravagant homes, eccentric clothing, and money, money, money have been symbols of life in Los Angeles ever since. Even the more conservative oil, aerospace, computer, banking, and import-export industries on the booming Pacific Rim have enjoyed the prosperity that leads inevitably to fun living. But even without piles of bucks, many people have found a kindred spirit in Los Angeles for their colorful lifestyles, be they spiritually, socially, or sexually unusual. At least in theory, tolerance reigns—which explains why you, too, may fit in.

The distance between places in Los Angeles explains why the ethnic enclaves have not merged, regardless of the melting-pot appearance of the city. Especially since the rioting in the spring of 1992, which—among other things—brought to the surface much long-simmering tension between various ethnic groups, it is impossible to gloss over the disparities of race, economics, and social mobility between neighborhoods. Nonetheless, at its best, and most notable for visitors, is the rich cultural and culinary diversity this mix of peoples creates.

Set off from the rest of the continent by mountains and desert, and from the rest of the world by an ocean, this incredible corner of creation has evolved its own identity that conjures envy, fascination, ridicule, and scorn—often all at once. Those from purportedly more sophisticated cities note what Los Angeles lacks. Others from more provincial towns raise an eyebrow at what it has. Yet 12.5 million people visit the city annually, and three-quarters of them come back for more. Indeed, you cannot do Los Angeles in a day or a week or even two. This second largest city in America holds too many choices between its canyons and its coast to be exhausted in one trip; it will exhaust you first.

EXPLORING

By Ellen Melinkoff

Updated and revised by Jane E. Lasky and William P. Brown

It's best to view Los Angeles as a collection of destinations, each to be explored separately, and not to jump willy-nilly from place to place. In this guide, we've divided up the major sightseeing areas of Los Angeles into eight major tours, starting Downtown and ending in the San Fernando Valley. After the eight tours, we highlight some of Los Angeles's other noteworthy attractions. For an orientation to the city's freeway system and a map, see Los Angeles Essentials at the end of this chapter.

Downtown Los Angeles

Numbers in the margin correspond to points of interest on the Downtown Los Angeles map.

All those jokes about Los Angeles being a city without a downtown are simply no longer true. This may have been true a few decades ago when Angelenos ruthlessly turned their backs on the city center and hightailed it to the suburbs. There had been a downtown, once, when Los Angeles was very young, and now the city core is enjoying a resurgence of attention from urban planners, real-estate developers, and downtown workers who have discovered the advantages of living close to the office.

Downtown Los Angeles can be explored on foot, or better yet, on DASH—Downtown Area Short Hop (*see below*). The natives might disagree, but these are the same natives who haven't been downtown since they took out a marriage license at city hall 30 years ago (unless they got hitched a second or third time as is often the case in LaLa Land); don't follow their lead. During the day, downtown is relatively safe (though be on your guard when you look around, just as you should be in any major city center).

Getting around to the major sites in downtown Los Angeles is actually quite simple, thanks to DASH. This minibus service travels in a loop past most of the attractions listed here, stopping every two blocks or so. Every ride costs 25¢, so if you hop on and off to see attractions, it will cost you every time. But the cost is worth it, since you can travel quickly and be assured of finding your way. DASH (☎ 213/626–4455) runs weekdays and Saturday 5 AM–10 PM. To follow the tour outlined below, get on Line A or B at ARCO Plaza (505 S. Flower St., between 5th and 6th Sts.).

Exploring Los Angeles *(Boxes Refer to Detail Maps)*

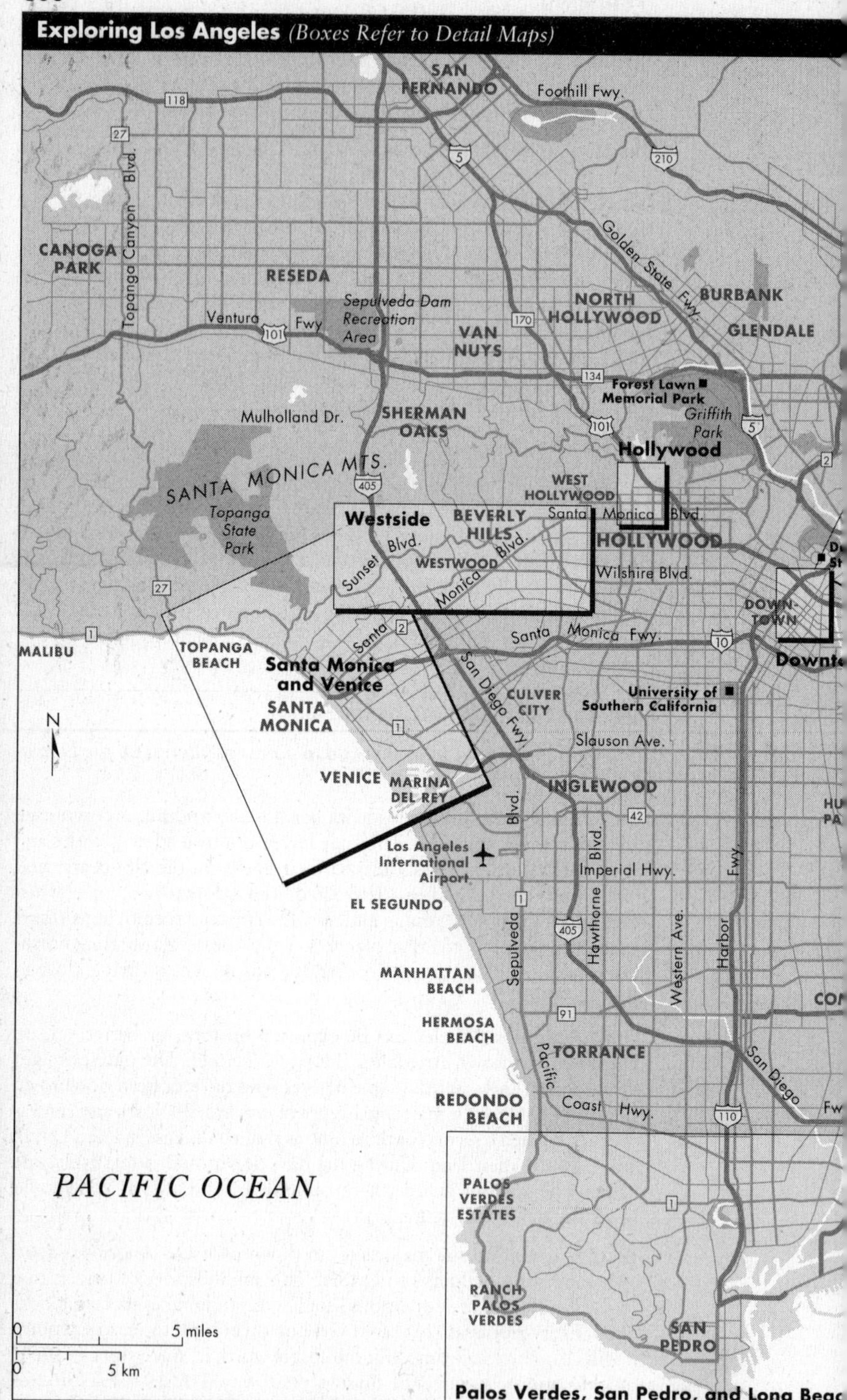

SAN FERNANDO
Foothill Fwy.
118
27
5
210
Topanga Canyon Blvd.
Golden State Fwy.
CANOGA PARK
RESEDA
Sepulveda Dam Recreation Area
NORTH HOLLYWOOD
BURBANK
GLENDALE
Ventura Fwy
101
170
VAN NUYS
134
Forest Lawn Memorial Park
Griffith Park
Mulholland Dr.
SHERMAN OAKS
Hollywood
SANTA MONICA MTS.
405
WEST HOLLYWOOD
Topanga State Park
Westside
BEVERLY HILLS
Santa Monica Blvd.
HOLLYWOOD
Sunset Blvd.
WESTWOOD
Wilshire Blvd.
DOWNTOWN
Downtown
Santa Monica Fwy.
10
MALIBU
TOPANGA BEACH
Santa Monica and Venice
SANTA MONICA
San Diego Fwy.
CULVER CITY
University of Southern California
Slauson Ave.
N
VENICE
MARINA DEL REY
INGLEWOOD
42
Los Angeles International Airport
Imperial Hwy.
EL SEGUNDO
Sepulveda Blvd.
Hawthorne Blvd.
Western Ave.
Harbor Fwy.
MANHATTAN BEACH
91
HERMOSA BEACH
TORRANCE
Pacific Coast Hwy.
San Diego Fwy.
REDONDO BEACH
110
PACIFIC OCEAN
PALOS VERDES ESTATES
RANCHO PALOS VERDES
SAN PEDRO
0
5 miles
0
5 km
Palos Verdes, San Pedro, and Long Beac

SAN GABRIEL MOUNTAINS
Angeles Crest Hwy.
Mt. Wilson
LA CAÑADA FLINTRIDGE
PASADENA
Highland Park, Pasadena, San Marino
Foothill Fwy.
Santa Anita Racetrack
SAN MARINO
Pasadena Fwy.
ARCADIA
ALHAMBRA
SAN GABRIEL
EL MONTE
San Bernardino Fwy.
Dodger Stadium
MONTEREY PARK
Downtown
Pomona Fwy.
Santa Ana Fwy.
Rosemead Blvd.
Fwy.
WHITTIER
HUNTINGTON PARK
DOWNEY
River
San Gabriel
Fwy.
COMPTON
Long Beach
Riverside Fwy.
Fwy.
LAKEWOOD
ANAHEIM
Pacific Coast Hwy.
GARDEN GROVE
San Diego Fwy.
LONG BEACH
Beach

Hidden directly under the twin ARCO towers, ARCO Plaza is a subterranean shopping mall that's jam-packed with office workers during the week, nearly deserted on weekends. The **Los Angeles Convention and Visitors Bureau** is nearby. It offers free information about attractions as well as advice on public transportation. *685 S. Figueroa St., between 7th St. and Wilshire Blvd.,* ☎ *213/689–8822.* ⌚ *Mon.–Sat. 8:30–5.*

❷ Just north of ARCO, the **Westin Bonaventure Hotel and Suites** (404 S. Figueroa St., ☎ 213/624–1000) is unique in the L.A. skyline: five shimmering cylinders in the sky, without a 90° angle in sight. Designed by John Portman in 1974, the building looks like science-fiction fantasy. Nonguests can use only one elevator, which rises through the roof of the lobby to soar through the air outside to the revolving restaurant and bar on the 35th floor. The food here is expensive; a better bet is to come for a drink (still overpriced) and nurse it for an hour as Los Angeles makes a full circle around you.

In the 19th century, the downtown area called Bunker Hill was the site of many stately mansions. Thanks to bulldozers, there's not much of a hill left, but the area is being redeveloped. Two major sites here showcase visual arts (painting, sculpture, and environmental work) and media and performing arts.

❸ The **Museum of Contemporary Art** houses a permanent collection of international scope, representing art from 1940 to the present. Included are works by Mark Rothko, Franz Kline, and Susan Rothenberg. The red sandstone building was designed by renowned Japanese architect Arata Isozaki and opened in 1986. Pyramidal skylights add a striking geometry to the seven-level, 98,000-square-foot building. Don't miss the gift shop or the lively Milanese-style café. *250 S. Grand Ave.,* ☎ *213/626–6222.* ☛ *$6 adults, $4 senior citizens and children, children under 12 free; free Thurs. 5–8.* ⌚ *Tues., Wed., Fri., and weekends 11–5, Thurs. 11–8.*

❹ Walk north to the **Music Center,** which has been the cultural center for Los Angeles since it opened in 1969. In spring, it's the site of the Academy Awards presentation: Limousines arrive at the Hope Street drive-through and celebrities are whisked through the crowds to the Dorothy Chandler Pavilion, the largest and grandest of the three theaters. It was named after the widow of the publisher of the *Los Angeles Times,* who was instrumental in fund-raising efforts to build the complex. The round building in the middle, the Mark Taper Forum, is a smaller theater. Most of its offerings are of an experimental nature, many of them on a pre-Broadway run. The Ahmanson, at the north end, is the venue for many musical comedies. The plaza has a fountain and sculpture by Jacques Lipchitz. *1st St. and Grand Ave.,* ☎ *213/972–7211. Free 45-min tours offered Tues.–Sat. 10–1:30. Schedule subject to change; call 213/972–7483 for reservations.*

❺ L.A.'s **Chinatown** runs a pale second to San Francisco's Chinatown but still offers visitors an authentic slice of life, beyond the tourist hokum. The neighborhood is bordered by Yale, Bernard, Alameda, and Ord streets. The main drag is North Broadway, where, every February, giant dragons snake down the center of the pavement during Chinese New Year celebrations. More than 15,000 Chinese and Southeast Asians actually live in the Chinatown area, but many thousands more regularly frequent the markets (filled with exotic foods unfamiliar to most Western eyes) and restaurants (dim-sum parlors are currently the most popular).

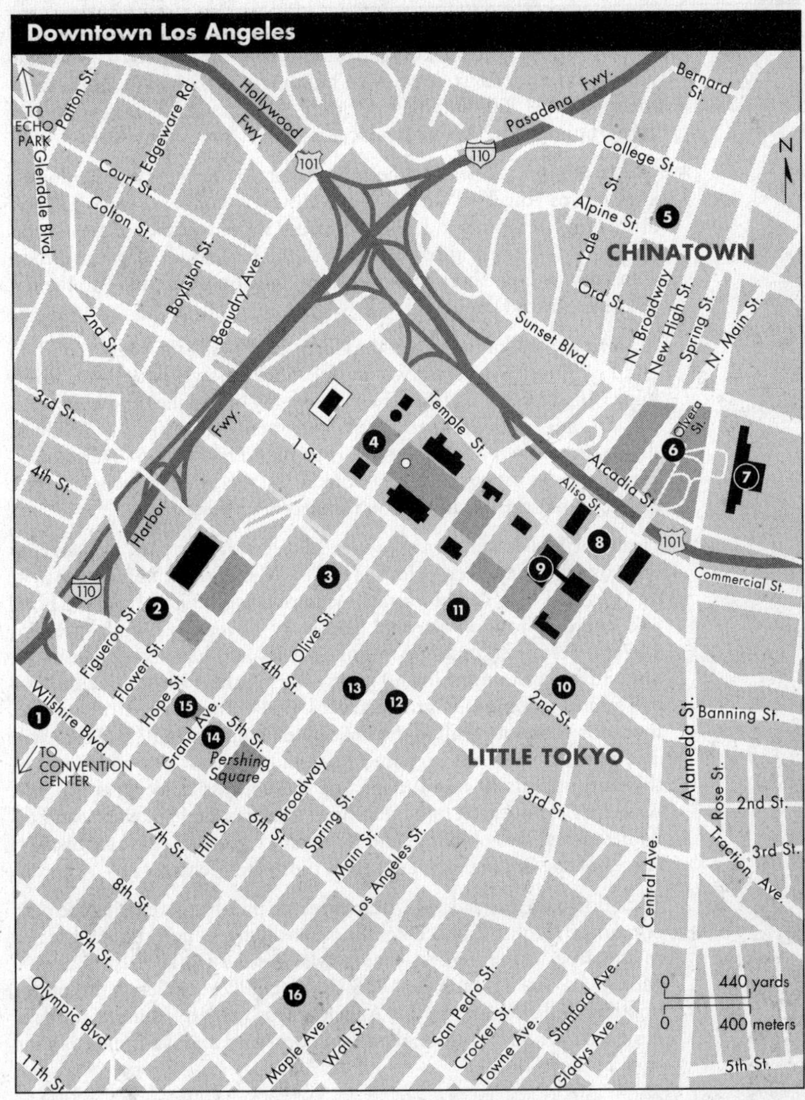

Biltmore Hotel, **14**
Bradbury Building, **12**
Central Library, **15**
Chinatown, **5**
El Pueblo de Los Angeles Historical Monument, **6**
Garment District, **16**
Grand Central Market, **13**
Little Tokyo, **10**
Los Angeles Children's Museum, **8**
Los Angeles City Hall, **9**
Los Angeles *Times* complex, **11**
Los Angeles Convention and Visitors Bureau, **1**
Museum of Contemporary Art, **3**
Music Center, **4**
Union Station, **7**
Westin Bonaventure Hotel and Suites, **2**

❻ **El Pueblo de Los Angeles Historical Monument** preserves the "birthplace" of Los Angeles (no one knows exactly where the original 1781 settlement was), the oldest downtown buildings, and some of the only remaining pre-1900 buildings in the city. The historical area covers 44 acres, bounded by Alameda, Arcadia, Spring, and Macy streets.

★ **Olvera Street** is the heart of the park and one of the most popular tourist sites in Los Angeles. With its tile walkways, piñatas, mariachis, and authentic Mexican food, Olvera Street should not be dismissed as merely some gringo approximation of the real thing. Mexican-American families come here in droves, especially on weekends—to them it feels like the old country.

Begin your walk of the area at the **Plaza,** on Olvera Street between Main and Los Angeles streets, a wonderful Mexican-style park shaded by a huge Moreton Bay fig tree. There are plenty of benches and walkways for strolling. On weekends there are often mariachis and folkloric dance groups here. You can have your photo taken in an oversize velvet sombrero, astride a stuffed donkey (a takeoff of the zebra-striped donkeys that are a tradition on the streets of Tijuana).

Head north up Olvera Street proper. Mid-block is the park's **visitor center,** housed in Sepulveda House (622 N. Main St., ☎ 213/628–1274; ⏲ Mon.–Sat. 10–3). The Eastlake Victorian was built in 1887 as a hotel and boardinghouse. **Pelanconi House** (17 Olvera St.), built in 1855, was the first brick building in Los Angeles and has been home to La Golondrina restaurant for 60 years. During the 1930s, famed Mexican muralist David Alfaro Siquieros was commissioned to paint a mural on the south wall of the **Italian Hall** building (650 N. Main St.). The patrons were not prepared for—and certainly not pleased by—this anti-imperialist mural depicting the oppressed workers of Latin America held in check by a menacing American eagle. It was promptly whitewashed into oblivion, and it remains under the paint to this day; copies of the original can be seen at the visitor center.

Walk down the east side of Olvera Street to mid-block, passing the only remaining sign of Zanja Ditch (mother ditch), which supplied water to the area in the earliest years. **Avila Adobe** (E–10 Olvera St.; ⏲ Mon.–Sat. 10–3), built in 1818, is generally considered the oldest building still standing in Los Angeles. This graceful, simple adobe is designed with the traditional interior courtyard and is furnished in the style of the 1840s.

On weekends, the restaurants are packed, and there is usually music in the plaza and along the street. Two Mexican holidays, Cinco de Mayo (May 5) and Independence Day (September 16), also draw huge crowds—and long lines for the restaurants. To see Olvera Street at its quietest and perhaps loveliest, visit on a late weekday afternoon. The long shadows heighten the romantic feeling of the street and there are only a few strollers and diners milling about.

South of the plaza is an area that has undergone renovation but remains, for the most part, only an ambitious idea. Although these magnificent old buildings remain closed, awaiting some commercial plan (à la Ghirardelli Square in San Francisco) that never seems to come to fruition, docent-led tours explore the area in depth. Tours depart Tuesday–Saturday 10–1, on the hour, from the **Old Firehouse** (south side of plaza, ☎ 213/628–1274), an 1884 building that contains early fire-fighting equipment and old photographs. Buildings seen on tours include the Merced Theater, Masonic Temple, Pico House, and the Garnier Block—all ornate examples of the late-19th-century style.

TIME OUT The dining choices on Olvera Street range from fast-food stands to comfortable, sit-down restaurants. The most authentic Mexican food is at **La Luz del Dia** (107 Paseo de la Plaza, ☎ 213/628–7495). Here they serve traditional favorites such as *chile rellenos* and pickled cactus, as well as handmade tortillas patted out in a practiced rhythm by the women behind the counter. **La Golondrina** (☎ 213/628–4349) and **El Paseo** (☎ 213/626–1361) restaurants, across from each other in mid-block, have delightful patios and extensive menus.

7 **Union Station** (800 N. Alameda St.), directly east of Olvera Street across Alameda, is one of those quintessential Californian buildings that seemed to define Los Angeles to moviegoers all over the country in the 1940s. Built in 1939, its Spanish Mission style is a subtle combination of Streamline Moderne and Moorish. The majestic scale of the waiting room alone is worth the walk over.

8 **Los Angeles Children's Museum** was the first of several strictly-for-kids museums now open in the city. All the exhibits here are hands-on, from Sticky City (where kids get to pillow fight with abandon in a huge pillow-filled room) to a TV studio (where they can put on their own news shows) to the Cave (where hologram dinosaurs lurk, seeming almost real). *310 N. Main St., ☎ 213/687–8800. ☛ $5, children under 2 free. ⏲ Weekends 10–5; also Tues.–Fri. 11:30–5 during summer vacation.*

9 **Los Angeles City Hall** is another often-photographed building, well known from its many appearances on *Dragnet, Superman,* and other television shows. Opened in 1928, the 27-story City Hall remained the only building to break the 13-story height limit (earthquakes, you know) until 1957. There is a 45-minute tour and ride to the top-floor observation deck. *200 N. Spring St., ☎ 213/485–4423. Tours by reservation only, weekdays at 10 and 11.*

10 **Little Tokyo** is the original ethnic neighborhood for Los Angeles's Japanese community. Most have deserted the downtown center for suburban areas such as Gardena and West Los Angeles, but Little Tokyo remains a cultural focal point. Nisei Week ("Nisei" is the name for second-generation Japanese) is celebrated here every August with traditional drums, dancing, a carnival, and a huge parade. Bounded by 1st, San Pedro, 3rd, and Los Angeles streets, Little Tokyo has dozens of sushi bars, tempura restaurants, trinket shops, and even a restaurant that serves nothing but eel. The **Japanese American Cultural and Community Center** (244 S. San Pedro St., ☎ 213/628–2725) presents such events as Kabuki theater straight from Japan.

11 The **Los Angeles *Times* complex** is made up of several supposedly architecturally harmonious buildings. Actually, the various styles from many eras look pretty much like a hodgepodge. *202 W. 1st St., ☎ 213/237–5000. 2 public tours weekdays after 2 and on Sat. morning (tour times vary): 35-min tour of old plant and 45-min tour of new plant; reservations required. Free parking at 213 S. Spring St.*

Broadway between 1st and 9th is one of Los Angeles's busiest shopping streets. The shops and sidewalk vendors cater primarily to the Hispanic population with bridal shops, immigration lawyers, and cheap stereo equipment. Be on your guard, as pickpockets and homeless people may approach you on the street, but this can be an exhilarating slice-of-life walk, past the florid old movie theaters like the **Orpheum** (842 S. Broadway) and the **Million Dollar** (310 S. Broadway) and the
12 perennially classy **Bradbury Building** (304 S. Broadway, ☎ 213/626–1893), a marvelous specimen of Victorian-era commercial architecture

at the southeast corner of 3rd Street and Broadway. Once the site of turn-of-the-century sweatshops, it now houses somewhat more genteel law offices. The interior courtyard, with its glass skylight and open balconies and elevator, really is picture perfect and, naturally, a popular movie locale. The building is only open Monday through Saturday 9–5; its owners prefer that you not wander too far past the lobby.

13 **Grand Central Market** (317 S. Broadway, ☎ 213/624–2378) is the most bustling market in the city and a testimony to the city's diversity. It's open Monday–Saturday 9–6, Sunday 10–5. This block-long marketplace of colorful and exotic produce, herbs, and meat draws a faithful clientele from the Latino community, senior citizens on a budget, and Westside matrons for whom money is no object. Even if you don't plan to buy anything, Grand Central Market is a delightful place in which to browse.

14 The **Biltmore Hotel** (506 S. Grand Ave.), built in 1923, rivals Union Station for sheer architectural majesty in the Spanish-Revival tradition. The public areas have been restored, with the magnificent hand-painted wood beams brought back to their former glory.

15 Around the corner on 5th Street, the city's **Central Library** reopened in 1993, after a six-year hiatus resulting from major fires. At twice its former size, it's now the third-largest public library facility in the nation. The original Goodhue building still stands, completely restored to its 1926 splendor, with shimmering Egyptian-style bas-reliefs around its roofline. Go inside, through wooden doors that resemble an old Spanish-era mission, to see Dean Cornwell's murals depicting the history of California. A 1½-acre outdoor garden within the library complex has a restaurant. *630 W. 5th St.,* ☎ *213/228–7000.* ☛ *Free.* ⏲ *Mon. and Thurs.–Sat. 10–5:30; Tues. and Wed. noon–8; Sun. 1–5.*

16 The **Garment District** (700–800 blocks of Los Angeles St.) is an enclave of jobbers and wholesalers that sell off the leftovers from Los Angeles's considerable garment industry production. The **Cooper Building** (860 S. Los Angeles St.) is the heart of the district and houses several of what local bargain hunters consider to be the best pickings.

Hollywood

Numbers in the margin correspond to points of interest on the Hollywood map.

"Hollywood" once meant movie stars and glamour. The big film studios were here; starlets lived in sorority-like buildings in the center of town; and movies premiered beneath the glare of klieg lights at the Chinese and the Pantages theaters.

Those days are long gone. Paramount is the only original major studio still physically located in Hollywood; and though some celebrities may live in the Hollywood Hills, there certainly aren't any in the "flats." In short, Hollywood is no longer "Hollywood." These days it is, even to its supporters, little more than a seedy town—though it's finally undergoing a large dose of urban renewal (some projects are, in fact, already completed). So why visit? Because the legends of the golden age of the movies are heavy in the air. Because this is where the glamour of Hollywood originated and where those who made it so worked and lived. Judy Garland lived here and so did Marilyn Monroe and Lana Turner. It is a tribute to Hollywood's powerful hold on the imagination that visitors can look past the junky shops and the lost souls who walk the streets to get a sense of the town's glittering past.

Besides, no visit to Los Angeles is truly complete without a walk down Hollywood Boulevard.

❶ Begin your tour simply by looking to the **HOLLYWOOD sign** in the Hollywood Hills that line the northern border of the town. Even on the smoggiest days, the sign is visible for miles. It is on Mt. Lee, north of Beachwood Canyon, which is approximately 1 mile east of Hollywood and Vine. The 50-foot-tall letters, originally spelling out "Hollywoodland," were erected in 1923 as a promotional scheme for a real-estate development. The "land" was taken down in 1949, and the remaining sign has become one of Los Angeles's best-known landmarks. Pranksters are constantly altering it, albeit temporarily, to say things like Hollyweed (in the 1970s, to commemorate the lenient marijuana laws), UCLA (during a football playoff game with local rival USC), and Perotwood (during the 1992 presidential election).

❷ **Hollywood and Vine** was once considered the heart of Hollywood. The mere mention of this intersection still inspires images of a street corner bustling with movie stars, starlets, and moguls passing by, on foot or in snazzy convertibles. But these days, Hollywood and Vine is far from the action, and pedestrian traffic is, well, pedestrian—no stars, no starlets, no moguls. The Brown Derby restaurant that once stood near the southeast corner is long gone, and the intersection these days is little more than a place for visitors to get their bearings.

❸ **Capitol Records Building** (1756 N. Vine St., 1 block north of Hollywood Blvd.) opened in 1956, is the very picture of '50s chic. When Capitol decided to build its new headquarters here, two of the record company's big talents of the day (singer Nat King Cole and songwriter Johnny Mercer) suggested that it be done in the shape of a stack of records. It was, and compared to much of what's gone up in L.A. since then, this building doesn't seem so odd. On its south wall, look at L.A. artist Richard Wyatt's mural *Hollywood Jazz, 1945–1972,* immortalizing such musical greats as Duke Ellington, Billie Holiday, Ella Fitzgerald, and Miles Davis. Murals play as important a role in Hollywood as billboards do along the Sunset Strip, so keep an eye out for others on several buildings in the immediate area. By the way, note the blinking light at the top of the Capital Records Building; those who don't know Morse Code will be interested to learn that the rooftop glow spells out Hollywood in this silent language.

❹ **The Palace** (1735 N. Vine St., ☏ 213/462–3000), just across the street from the Capitol Building, was opened in 1927 as the Hollywood Playhouse. It has hosted many shows over the years, from Ken Murray's *Blackouts* to Ralph Edwards's *This Is Your Life.* It is now the site of popular rock concerts and late-night weekend dancing.

❺ When the **Pantages Theater,** at 6233 Hollywood Boulevard, just east of Vine, opened in 1930, it was the very pinnacle of movie-theater opulence. From 1949 to 1959, it was the site of the Academy Awards and today hosts large-scale Broadway musicals.

❻ The **Hollywood Walk of Fame** is at every turn along the sidewalks as you make your way through downtown. The name of one or another movie star legend is embossed in brass, each at the center of a pink star embedded in a dark gray terrazzo circle. The first eight stars were unveiled in 1960 at the northwest corner of Highland Avenue and Hollywood Boulevard: Olive Borden, Ronald Colman, Louise Fazenda, Preston Foster, Burt Lancaster, Edward Sedgwick, Ernest Torrence, and Joanne Woodward (some of these names have stood the test of time better than others). In the 34 years since, more than 2,000 others have

Hollywood

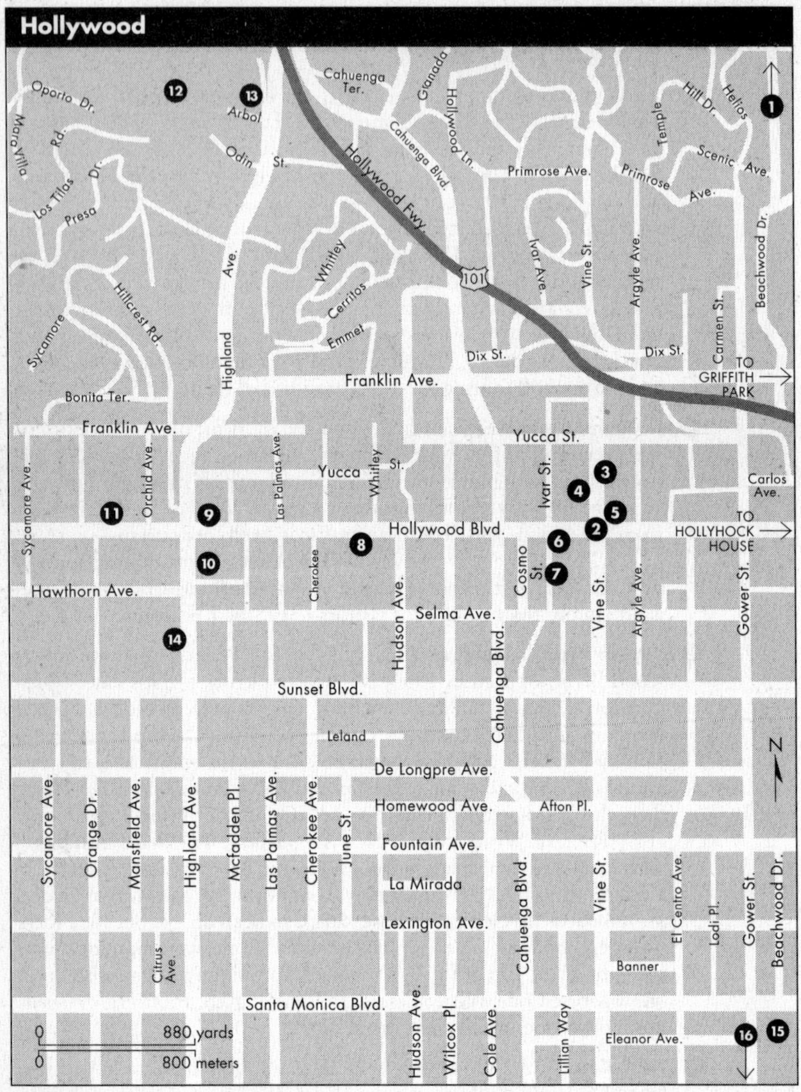

Capitol Records Building, **3**
Frederick's of Hollywood, **8**
Hollywood Bowl, **12**
Hollywood Farmer's Market, **7**
Hollywood High School, **14**
Hollywood Memorial Park Cemetery, **15**
Hollywood sign, **1**
Hollywood Studio Museum, **13**
Hollywood and Vine, **2**
Hollywood Walk of Fame, **6**
Hollywood Wax Museum, **9**
Mann's Chinese Theater, **11**
Max Factor Museum, **10**
The Palace, **4**
Pantages Theater, **5**
Paramount Studios, **16**

been added. But this kind of immortality doesn't come cheap—the personality in question (or more likely his or her movie studio or record company) must pay $5,000 for the honor. Walk a few blocks and you'll quickly find that not all the names are familiar. To aid in the identification, celebrities are classified by one of five logos: a motion picture camera, a radio microphone, a television set, a record, or theatrical masks. Here's a guide to a few of the more famous stars: Marlon Brando at 1765 Vine, Charlie Chaplin at 6751 Hollywood, W. C. Fields at 7004 Hollywood, Clark Gable at 1608 Vine, Marilyn Monroe at 6774 Hollywood, Rudolph Valentino at 6164 Hollywood, Michael Jackson at 6927 Hollywood, and John Wayne at 1541 Vine.

Every Sunday, a couple of blocks in this part of town are transformed into a festive street fair. Traffic is diverted so that no vehicle passes
★ 7 through the **Hollywood Farmer's Market,** situated on Ivar Street, between Hollywood Boulevard and Selma Avenue. Instead, some 20,000 people show up to sample ethnic foods and listen to lively musical entertainment as they peruse stalls packed with fruits, vegetables, crafts, and antiques. The Ivar Theater sponsors an outdoor coffee shop, where celebrities are often spotted.

After decades of sporting a gaudy lavender paint job, the exterior of
8 **Frederick's of Hollywood** (6608 Hollywood Blvd., ☎ 213/466–8506) has been restored to its original understated Art Deco look, gray with pink awnings. Fear not, however, that the place has suddenly gone tasteful: Inside is all the risqué and trashy lingerie that made this place famous. There is also a bra museum that features the undergarments of living and no-longer-living Hollywood legends.

TIME OUT At **Me & Me** (6687 Hollywood Blvd., ☎ 213/464-8448), you can munch on what just may be the city's best falafels.

9 **Hollywood Wax Museum** offers visitors sights that real life no longer can (Mary Pickford, Elvis Presley, and Clark Gable) and a few that even real life never did (Rambo and Conan). Recently added living legends on display include actors Kevin Costner and Patrick Swayze. *6767 Hollywood Blvd.,* ☎ *213/462–8860.* ☛ *$8.95 adults, $7.50 senior citizens, $6.95 children, under 6 free if with adult.* ⏲ *Sun.–Thurs. 10 AM–midnight, Fri.–Sat. 10 AM–2 AM.*

10 The **Max Factor Museum** lets civilians in on the beauty secrets of screen idols from flicks filmed as far back as the turn of the century. *1666 N. Highland Ave.,* ☎ *213/463–6668.* ☛ *Free.* ⏲ *Mon.–Sat. 10 AM–4 PM.*

★ 11 Angelenos no longer call **Mann's Chinese Theater** (6925 Hollywood Blvd., ☎ 213/464–8111) "Grauman's Chinese," and the new owners seem finally to have a firm hold on the place in the public's eye. The architecture is a fantasy of Chinese pagodas and temples as only Hollywood could turn out. Although you'll have to buy a movie ticket to appreciate the interior trappings, the courtyard is open for browsing, where you'll see the famous cement hand- and footprints. The tradition is said to have begun at the theater's opening in 1927, with the premiere of Cecil B. DeMille's *King of Kings,* when actress Norma Talmadge accidentally stepped into the wet cement. Now more than 160 celebrities have added their footprints or handprints, along with a few oddball prints like the one of Jimmy Durante's nose. Space has pretty much run out now, though there's always room to squeeze in another superstar, should Hollywood conjure one up.

12 Summer evening concerts at the **Hollywood Bowl** have been a tradition since 1922, although the band shell has been replaced several times.

The musical fare ranges from pop to jazz to classical; the L.A. Philharmonic has its summer season here. The 17,000-plus seating capacity ranges from boxes (where local society matrons put on incredibly fancy alfresco preconcert meals for their friends) to concrete bleachers in the rear. Some people actually prefer the back rows for their romantic appeal. *2301 N. Highland Ave., ☎ 213/850–2000. Grounds open daily sunrise–sunset. Call for schedule.*

13 The **Hollywood Studio Museum** sits in the Hollywood Bowl parking lot, east of Highland Boulevard. The building, recently moved to this site, was once called the Lasky–DeMille Barn; in it Cecil B. DeMille produced the first feature-length film, *The Squaw Man.* In 1927, the barn became Paramount Pictures, with the original company of Jesse Lasky, Cecil B. DeMille, and Samuel Goldwyn. The museum contains a re-creation of DeMille's office, original artifacts, and a screening room showing vintage film footage of Hollywood and its legends. A great gift shop sells such quality vintage memorabilia as autographs, photographs, and books. *2100 N. Highland Ave., ☎ 213/874–2276. ☛ $4 adults, $3 senior citizens and children, children under 6 free. Free parking. ⌚ Weekends 10–4.*

14 Such stars as Carol Burnett, Linda Evans, Rick Nelson, and Lana Turner attended **Hollywood High School** (1521 N. Highland Ave.).

15 Many of Hollywood's stars, from the silent-screen era on, are buried in **Hollywood Memorial Park Cemetery.** Walk from the entrance to the lake area and you'll find the crypt of Cecil B. DeMille and the graves of Nelson Eddy and Douglas Fairbanks, Sr. Inside the Cathedral Mausoleum is Rudolph Valentino's crypt (where fans and the press turn up every August 23, the anniversary of his death). Other stars interred in this section are Peter Lorre and Eleanor Powell. In the Abbey of Palms Mausoleum, Norma Talmadge and Clifton Webb are buried. *6000 Santa Monica Blvd., ☎ 213/469–1181. ⌚ Daily 8–5.*

16 Take Gower Street south to Melrose Avenue, turn right, and on the right-hand side you'll see the main gate of **Paramount Studios** (5555 Melrose Ave.). You can explore the studio lot on two-hour guided walking tours or by joining the audience for tapings of TV shows. *For tours or tapings, check in at 860 N. Gower St., ☎ 213/956–5575. ☛ $15. Tours held weekdays, on the hr, 9–2. No one under 10 admitted.*

Wilshire Boulevard

Wilshire Boulevard begins in the heart of downtown Los Angeles and runs west, through Beverly Hills and Santa Monica, ending at the cliffs above the Pacific Ocean. In 16 miles it moves through fairly poor neighborhoods populated by recent immigrants, solidly middle-class enclaves, and through a corridor of the highest priced high-rise condos in the city. Along the way, and all within a few blocks of each other, are many of Los Angeles's top architectural sites, museums, and shops.

This linear tour can be started at any point along Wilshire Boulevard, but to really savor the cross-section view of Los Angeles that this street provides, take the Bullocks-west-to-the-sea approach. If you have only limited time, it would be better to skip Koreatown and Larchmont and pare down the museum time than to do only one stretch. All these sites are on Wilshire or within a few blocks north or south.

"One" Wilshire, at the precise start of the boulevard in downtown Los Angeles, is just another anonymous office building. Begin, instead, a few miles westward, past the Harbor Freeway. As Wilshire Boulevard moves from its downtown genesis, it quickly passes through neighborhoods now populated by recent immigrants from Central America. Around the turn of the century, however, this area was home to many of the city's wealthy citizens, as the faded Victorian houses on the side streets attest.

As the population crept westward, the first suburban department-store branch, **Bullocks Wilshire** (3050 Wilshire Blvd.), was opened in 1929. The store closed in 1993, but this giant tribute to early Art Deco has been purchased by the Southwestern University School of Law, which is adapting the building to accommodate its law library and as office and classroom spaces. The exterior is often used as a background for films. Notice the behind-the-store parking lot—quite an innovation in 1929 and the first accommodation a large Los Angeles store made to the automobile age. On the ceiling of the porte cochere, a mural depicts the history of transportation.

Koreatown begins almost at Bullocks Wilshire's back door. Koreans are one of the latest and largest groups in this ethnically diverse city. Settling in the area south of Wilshire Boulevard, along Olympic Boulevard between Vermont and Western avenues, the Korean community has slowly grown into a cohesive neighborhood with active civic organizations and newspapers. The area is teeming with Asian restaurants (not just Korean but also Japanese and Chinese). Many of the signs in this area are in Korean only. For a glimpse of the typical offerings of Korean shops, browse the large **Koreatown Plaza** mall, on the corner of Western and San Marino avenues.

At the southeast corner of Wilshire and Western Avenue sits the **Wiltern Theater** (3780 Wilshire Blvd.), part of the magnificent Wiltern Center and one of the city's best examples of full-out Art Deco architecture. Inside, the theater is full of opulent detail at every turn. Originally a movie theater, the Wiltern is now a multiuse arts complex.

Continuing west on Wilshire, the residential real-estate values start to make a sharp climb. In the past, the official home of the mayor of Los Angeles was the **Getty House** (605 S. Irving Blvd., 1 block north of Wilshire), a white-brick, half-timber residence that was donated to the city by the Getty family. This area, known as Hancock Park, is one of the city's most genteel neighborhoods, remaining in vogue since its development in the 1920s. Many of L.A.'s old-money families live here in English Tudor homes with East Coast landscaping schemes that defy the local climate and history.

Drop back down to Wilshire Boulevard again and continue westward. **Miracle Mile,** the strip of Wilshire Boulevard between La Brea and Fairfax avenues, was so dubbed in the 1930s as a promotional gimmick to attract shoppers to the new stores. The area went into something of a decline in the '50s and '60s but is now enjoying a comeback, as Los Angeles's Art Deco architecture has come to be appreciated, preserved, and restored. Exemplary buildings like the **El Rey Theater** (5519 Wilshire Blvd., ☏ 213/936–6400) stand out as examples of period design (in spite of the fact that it now houses a nightclub). In **Callender's Restaurant** (corner of Wilshire and Curson), murals and old photographs effectively depict life on the Miracle Mile in its heyday.

Across Curson Avenue is **Hancock Park,** an actual park, not to be confused with Hancock Park, the residential neighborhood. This park is home to the city's world-famous fossil source, the **La Brea Tar Pits.** Despite the fact that *la brea* already means "tar" in Spanish and to say "La Brea Tar Pits" is redundant, the name remains firm in local minds.

About 35,000 years ago, deposits of oil rose to the earth's surface, collected in shallow pools, and coagulated into sticky asphalt. In the early 20th century, geologists discovered that the sticky goo contained the largest collection of Pleistocene fossils ever found at one location: more than 200 varieties of birds, mammals, plants, reptiles, and insects. More than 100 tons of fossil bones have been removed over 70 years of excavations. Statues of mammoths in the big pit near the corner of Wilshire and Curson depict how many of them were entombed: Edging down to a pond of water to drink, animals were caught in the tar and unable to extricate themselves. There are several pits scattered around Hancock Park; construction in the area has often had to accommodate these oozing pits, and in nearby streets and along sidewalks, little bits of tar occasionally ooze up, unstoppable.

The **George C. Page Museum of La Brea Discoveries,** a satellite of the Natural History Museum of Los Angeles County, is situated at the tar pits and set, bunkerlike, half underground. A bas-relief around four sides depicts life in the Pleistocene era, and the museum has more than 1 million Ice Age fossils. Exhibits include reconstructed, life-size skeletons of mammoths, wolves, sloths, eagles, and condors. In one permanent installation, a robotic saber-tooth cat attacks a woolly mammal. The glass-enclosed Paleontological Laboratory permits observation of the ongoing cleaning, identification, and cataloging of fossils excavated from the nearby asphalt deposits. A hologram magically puts flesh on "La Brea Woman," and an interactive tar mechanism shows visitors just how hard it would be to free oneself from the sticky mess. *5801 Wilshire Blvd.,* ☏ *213/936–2230.* ☛ *$6 adults, $3.50 senior citizens and students, $2 children 5–10; free 1st Tues. of month. Parking behind museum $4 with validation.* ⏲ *Tues.–Sun. 10–5.*

The **Los Angeles County Museum of Art,** just west of Hancock Park, is the largest museum complex in Los Angeles, comprising five buildings surrounding a grand central court. The Times Mirror Central Court provides both a visual and symbolic focus for the museum complex. The Ahmanson Building, built around a central atrium, houses the museum's collection of paintings, sculpture, costumes and textiles, and decorative arts from a wide range of cultures and periods. Highlights include a unique assemblage of glass from Roman times to the 19th century; the renowned Gilbert collection of mosaics and monumental silver; one of the nation's largest holdings of costumes and textiles; and an Indian and Southeast Asian art collection considered to be one of the most comprehensive in the world.

The Hammer Building features major special loan exhibitions as well as galleries for prints, drawings, and photographs. The Anderson Building features 20th-century painting and sculpture as well as special exhibitions. The museum's collection of Japanese sculpture, paintings, ceramics, and lacquerware, including the internationally renowned Shin'enkan collection of Japanese paintings and a collection of extraordinary netsuke, is on view in the Japanese Pavilion. The Contemporary Sculpture Garden comprises nine large-scale outdoor sculptures. The B. Gerald Cantor Sculpture Garden features bronzes by Auguste Rodin, Emile-Antoine Bourdelle, and George Kolbe. *5905 Wilshire Blvd.,* ☏ *213/857–6000; ticket information, 213/857–6010.* ☛ *$6 adults, $4 senior citizens and students, $1 children 6–17; free 2nd Wed. of month.* ⏲ *Tues.–Thurs. 10–5, Fri. 10–9, weekends 11–6.*

TIME OUT The County Museum's **Plaza Cafe** is a casual, cafeteria-style hangout with indoor-outdoor seating, serving such food as pizza frittatas, baked potatoes, and salad from an extensive salad bar.

The **Craft and Folk Art Museum,** across Wilshire Boulevard from Hancock Park, is worth checking out. The museum offers consistently fascinating exhibits of both contemporary crafts and folk crafts from around the world. Six to eight major exhibitions are planned each year. In the past, sunglasses, jewelry, masks, textiles, and architecture have been featured. *5800 Wilshire Blvd.,* ☎ *213/937–5544.* ☛ *$4 adults, $2.50 senior citizens and students, children under 12 free.* ⏲ *Tues.–Sun. 11–5, Fri. 11–8.*

Up the street is the **Carole & Barry Kaye Museum of Miniatures,** where a world of pint-size exhibits is showcased. You'll see landmarks such as the Hollywood Bowl and a complete set of First Ladies dolled up in their inaugural ball gowns. *5900 Wilshire Blvd.,* ☎ *213/937–6464.* ☛ *$7.50 adults, $6.50 senior citizens, $5 youths 13–21, $3 children 3–12.* ⏲ *Tues.–Sat. 10–5, Sun. 11–5.*

The **Petersen Automotive Museum** houses cars-of-the-stars exhibits, a gallery devoted to the motorcycle, rare French luxury cars, and race cars created in southern California. The gift shop's great, too. *6060 Wilshire Blvd.,* ☎ *213/930–2277.* ☛ *$7 adults, $5 senior citizens and students, $3 children 5–12.* ⏲ *Sat.–Thurs. 10–6, Fri. 10–9.*

West on Wilshire on the northeast corner of Fairfax Avenue is the former **May Co. department store,** another 1930s landmark, with a distinctive, gold-tiled curved corner. The L.A. County Museum of Art, which owns the building, plans to use it for a future expansion.

North on Fairfax a few blocks is the **Farmers' Market,** which has 30 American and international restaurants, some of which offer alfresco dining under umbrellas. Although this originally was a market, now in addition to food and produce you will find gifts, clothing, beauty shops, and even a shoe repair. Because it is next door to the CBS Television Studios, celebrities shop and dine here often. *6333 W. 3rd St.,* ☎ *213/933–9211.* ⏲ *Mon.–Sat. 9–6:30, Sun. 10–5; later hrs in summer.*

TIME OUT **Kokomo** (on 3rd St. side of market, ☎ 213/933–0773) is not only the best eatery inside the Farmers' Market, it's got some of the best new-wave diner food anywhere in L.A. Lively, entertaining service is almost always included in the reasonable prices.

The Westside

Numbers in the margin correspond to points of interest on the Westside map.

The Westside of Los Angeles—which to residents means from La Brea Avenue westward to the ocean—is where the rents are the most expensive, the real-estate prices sky-high, the restaurants (and the restaurateurs) the most famous, and the shops the most chic. It's the best of the good life, southern-California style, and to really savor (and understand) the Southland, spend a few leisurely days or half days exploring this area. Short on such traditional tourist attractions as amusement parks, historic sites, and museums, it more than makes up for those gaps with great shopping districts, exciting walking streets, outdoor cafés, and a lively nightlife.

The Westside can be best enjoyed in at least three outings, allowing plenty of time for browsing and dining. Attractions 1 through 4 are in the West Hollywood area; 5 through 9 in Beverly Hills; and 9 through 12 in Westwood. But the Westside is also small enough that you could pick four or five of these sites to visit in a single day, depending on your interests.

West Hollywood

Once an almost forgotten parcel of county land surrounded by the city of L.A. and Beverly Hills, West Hollywood became an official city in 1984. The West Hollywood attitude—trendy, stylish, and with plenty of disposable income—spills over beyond the official city borders.

★ 1 **Melrose Avenue** provides plenty of fodder for people-watching: post-punk fashion plates and folks in outlandish ensembles with spiked hairdos and earrings and tattoos on every conceivable body part. It's where panache meets paparazzi, and Beverly Hills chic meets Hollywood hip. The busiest stretch of Melrose is between Fairfax and La Brea avenues. Here you'll find one-of-a-kind boutiques and small, chic restaurants for more than a dozen blocks.

Park on a side street (and read the parking signs carefully: Parking regulations around here are vigorously enforced and a rich vein for the city's coffers) and begin walking. On the 7400 block are **Tempest** and **Notorious,** boutiques with the latest of California's trendsetting designers' clothes for women, along with **Mondial,** for men, and **Roppongi,** which supplies the sought-after Melrose look.

In the other direction—in more ways than one—**The Wasteland** (7428) is a great find for vintage clothing as well as resale items brought in by locals every day. **Melrose Place Antique Market** (7002 Melrose) is a collection of small items, vintage in nature, high in appeal. (*See* Shopping, *below,* for more store recommendations.)

That hulking monolith dominating the corner of La Cienega and Bev-
2 erly boulevards is the **Beverly Center** (8500 Beverly Blvd., ☎ 310/854–0070). Designed as an all-in-one stop for shopping, dining, and movies, it has been a boon to Westsiders—except for those who live so close as to suffer the consequences of the heavy traffic. Parking is on the second through fifth floors; shops on the sixth, seventh, and eighth floors; movies on the eighth floor; and restaurants on the eighth and at street level. (*See* Shopping, *below* for some of the center's stores.)

West Hollywood is the center of Los Angeles's thriving interior deco-
3 rating business. The **Pacific Design Center** (8687 Melrose Ave., ☎ 310/657–0800) is known to residents as the "Blue Whale." The blue-glass building, designed by Cesar Pelli in 1975, houses to-the-trade-only showrooms filled with the most tempting furnishings, wall coverings, and accessories. In 1988 the center added a second building by Pelli, this one clad in green glass. The building is open to the public (weekdays 9–5), who are allowed to browse in many of the more than 200 showrooms or opt for a free group tour at 10 AM. Note: Purchases can be made only through design professionals (a referral system is available). The **Murray Feldman Gallery,** featuring various art, design, and cultural exhibitions, sits on the adjacent 2-acre landscaped public plaza (open Tues.–Sat. noon–6).

"Robertson Boulevard," the area that surrounds the Blue Whale, has several more to-the-trade showrooms. These are not confined to the street Robertson Boulevard itself, being well represented also along Beverly Boulevard and Melrose Avenue. This area is exceptionally walk-

Westside

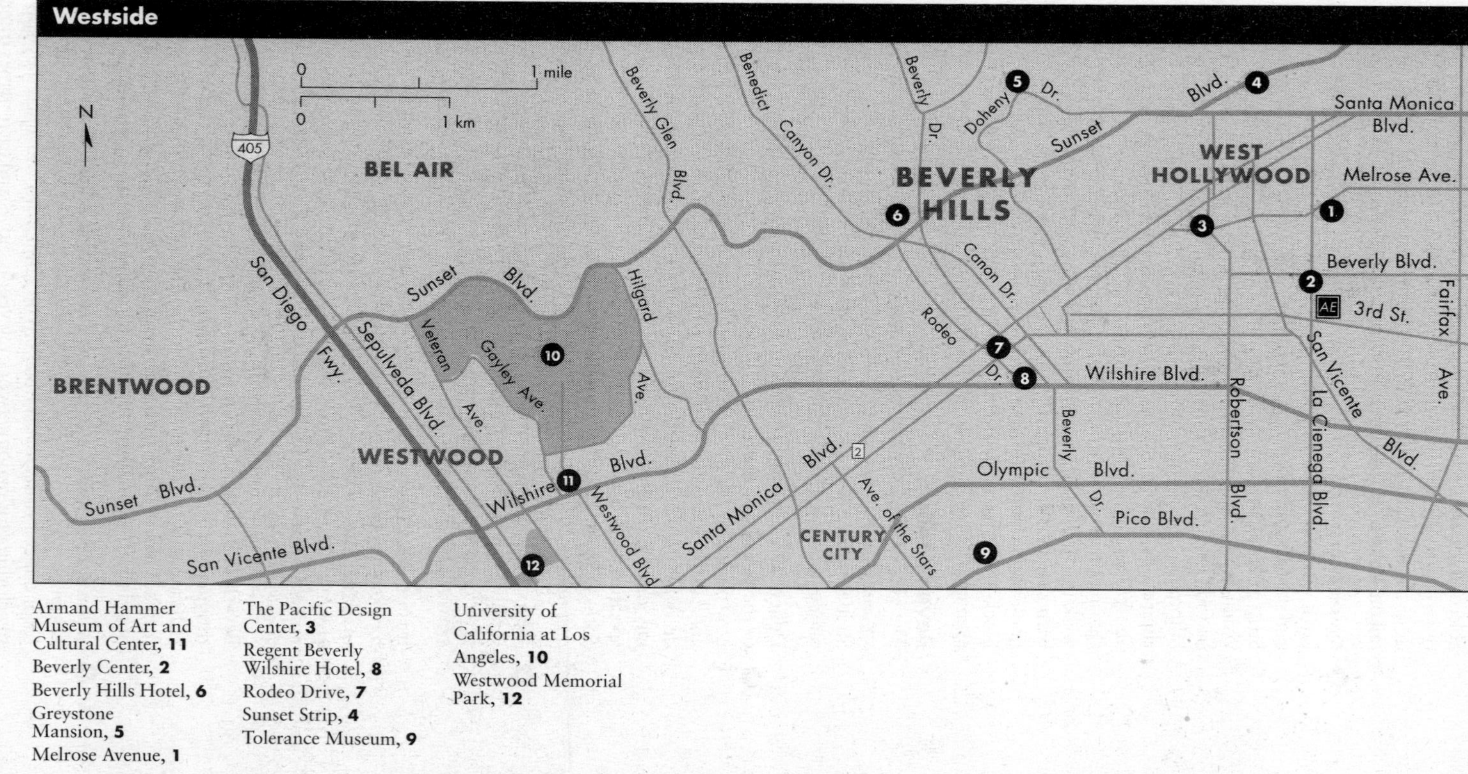

Armand Hammer Museum of Art and Cultural Center, **11**
Beverly Center, **2**
Beverly Hills Hotel, **6**
Greystone Mansion, **5**
Melrose Avenue, **1**
The Pacific Design Center, **3**
Regent Beverly Wilshire Hotel, **8**
Rodeo Drive, **7**
Sunset Strip, **4**
Tolerance Museum, **9**
University of California at Los Angeles, **10**
Westwood Memorial Park, **12**

able, and residents often walk their dogs here in the evening (even driving them here to then do their walking) so they can browse the well-lit windows. A few of the showrooms will accommodate an occasional retail buyer, so if you see something to die for, it's worth an inquiry inside.

4 **Sunset Strip** was famous in the '50s, as in the TV show *77 Sunset Strip*, but it was popular as far back as the 1930s, when nightclubs like Ciro's and the Mocambo were in their heyday and movie stars frequented the Strip as an after-work gathering spot. This winding, hilly stretch is a visual delight, enjoyed both by car (a convertible would be perfect) or on foot. Drive it once to enjoy the hustle-bustle, the vanity boards (huge billboards touting new movies, new records, new stars), and the dazzling shops. Then pick a section and explore a few blocks on foot. The Sunset Plaza area, a stretch of expensive shops and outdoor cafés (including the nouvelle Chinese favorite, **Chin Chin**), is especially nice for walking. At Horn Street, **Tower Records** (a behemoth of a CD store with two satellite shops across the street), **Book Soup** (L.A.'s literary bookstore), and Wolfgang Puck's famous restaurant **Spago** (a half block up the hill on Horn) make satisfying browsing, especially in the evening.

Beverly Hills

The glitz of Sunset Strip ends abruptly at Doheny Drive, where Sunset Boulevard enters the world-famous and glamorous Beverly Hills. Suddenly the sidewalk street life gives way to expansive, perfectly manicured lawns and palatial homes.

Doheny Drive is named for oilman Edward Doheny, the original owner
5 of the **Greystone Mansion,** built in 1927. This Tudor-style mansion, now owned by the city of Beverly Hills, sits on 18½ landscaped acres and has been used in such films as *The Witches of Eastwick* and *Indecent Proposal.* The gardens are open for self-guided tours and peeking (only) through the windows is permitted. Picnics are permitted in specified areas during hours of operation. *905 Loma Vista Dr.,* ☎ *310/550–4796.* ☛ *Free.* ⏲ *Daily 10–5 in fall and winter; 10–6 in spring and fall.*

6 West of Sunset Strip a mile or so is the **Beverly Hills Hotel** (9641 Sunset Blvd.), whose Spanish colonial revival architecture and soft pastel exterior have earned it the name "the Pink Palace." This landmark property reopened in 1995 after a multimillion-dollar renovation.

It is on this stretch of Sunset, especially during the day, that you'll see hawkers peddling maps to stars' homes. Are the maps reliable? Well, that's a matter of debate. Stars do move around, so it's difficult to keep any map up to date. But the fun is in looking at some of these magnificent homes, regardless of whether or not they're owned by a star at the moment.

Beverly Hills was incorporated as a city early in the century and has been thriving ever since. Within a few square blocks in the center of Beverly Hills are some of the most exotic, high-priced stores in southern California. Here you can find such items as a $200 pair of socks wrapped in gold leaf, and stores that take customers only by appointment.

★ 7 A fun way to spend an afternoon is to stroll famed **Rodeo Drive** between Santa Monica and Wilshire boulevards. Some of the Rodeo (pronounced ro-*day*-o) shops may be familiar to you since they supply clothing for major network television shows and their names often appear among the credits. Others, such as Gucci, have a worldwide reputation.

8 The **Regent Beverly Wilshire Hotel** (9500 Wilshire Blvd., ☎ 310/275–5200) anchors the south end of Rodeo Drive, at Wilshire. Opened in 1928, and vigorously expanded and renovated since, the hotel is often home to visiting royalty and celebrities. The lobby is quite small for a hotel of this size and offers little opportunity to meander; you might stop for a drink or meal in one of the hotel's restaurants.

A sobering but moving experience in the midst of all this glamour is
9 the **Museum of Tolerance,** adjacent to the Simon Weisenthal Center. Using state-of-the-art interactive technology, the museum challenges visitors to confront bigotry and racism. One of the most affecting sections of this museum covers the Holocaust—each visitor is issued a "passport" bearing the name of a child whose life was dramatically changed by the German Nazi rule and by World War II, and ultimately the museum goer learns the fate of that child. Anne Frank artifacts are part of the museum's permanent collection. Expect to spend at least three hours to see the whole museum. *9786 W. Pico Blvd., ☎ 310/553–8403. ☛ $8 adults, $6 senior citizens, $5 students, $3 children 3–12. ⏲ Sun. 10:30–5, Mon.–Thurs. 10–4, Fri. 10–1. Reservations advised.*

Westwood

Westward from Beverly Hills, Sunset continues to wind past palatial
10 estates and passes by the **University of California at Los Angeles.** Nestled in the Westwood section of the city and bound by Le Conte Avenue, Sunset Boulevard, and Hilgard Avenue, the parklike UCLA campus is an inviting place for visitors to stroll. The most spectacular buildings are the original ones, Royce Hall and the library, both in Romanesque style. In the heart of the north campus is the Franklin Murphy Sculpture Garden, with works by Henry Moore and Gaston Lachaise dotting the landscaping. For a gardening buff, UCLA is a treasure of unusual and well-labeled plants. The Mildred Mathias Botanic Garden is in the southeast section of campus and is accessible from Tiverton Avenue. Sports fans will enjoy the Morgan Center Hall of Fame (west of Campus bookstore), where memorabilia and trophies of the athletic departments are on display. Maps and information are available at drive-by kiosks at major entrances, even on weekends, and free 90-minute walking tours of the campus are given on weekdays. *Tours (☎ 310/206–8147) weekdays at 10:30 AM and 1:30 PM. Call for reservations. Meet at 10945 LeConte Ave., Room 1417, on south edge of campus, facing Westwood.*

Directly south of the campus is Westwood, once a quiet college town and now a busy place on weekend evenings—so busy that during the summer, many streets are closed to car traffic and visitors must park at the Federal Building (Wilshire Blvd. and Veteran Ave.) and shuttle over.

11 **Armand Hammer Museum of Art and Cultural Center** is small compared to other museums in Los Angeles, but the permanent collection here includes thousands of works by Honoré Daumier, and a rare portfolio of Leonardo da Vinci's technical drawings. The Hammer regularly features special blockbuster displays that cannot be seen elsewhere. *10899 Wilshire Blvd., ☎ 310/443–7000. ☛ $4.50 adults, $3 senior citizens, children under 18 free; free Thurs. 6–9. ⏲ Tues., Wed., Fri., Sat. 11–7, Thurs. 11–9, Sun. 11–5. Parking: $2.75.*

The Westwood stretch of Wilshire Boulevard is a corridor of cheek-by-jowl office buildings whose varying architectural styles can be jar-
12 ring. Tucked behind one of these behemoths is **Westwood Memorial Park** (1218 Glendon Ave.). In this very unlikely place for a cemetery

is one of the most famous graves in the city. Marilyn Monroe is buried in a simply marked wall crypt. Also buried here is Natalie Wood.

Santa Monica, Venice, Pacific Palisades, and Malibu

Numbers in the margin correspond to points of interest on the Santa Monica and Venice map.

The towns that hug the coastline of Santa Monica Bay reflect the wide diversity of Los Angeles, from the rich-as-can-be Malibu to the yuppie/seedy mix of Venice. The emphasis is on being out in the sunshine, always within sight of the Pacific. You would do well to visit the area in two excursions: Santa Monica to Venice in one day and Pacific Palisades to Malibu in another.

Santa Monica

Santa Monica is a tidy little city, about 2 miles square, where expatriate Brits tend to settle (there's an English music hall and several pubs here), attracted perhaps by the cool, foggy climate. The sense of order is reflected in the economic-geographic stratification: The most northern section has broad streets lined with superb, older homes. As you drive south, real estate prices drop $50,000 or so every block or two. The middle class lives in the middle and the working class, to the south, along the Venice border.

★ ❶ Begin exploring at **Santa Monica Pier,** located at the foot of Colorado Avenue and easily accessible for beachgoers as well as drive-around visitors. Cafés, gift shops, a psychic adviser, bumper-car rides, and arcades line the truncated pier, which was severely damaged in a storm a few years ago. The 46-horse carousel, built in 1922, has seen action in many movie and television shows, most notably the Paul Newman–Robert Redford film *The Sting.* ☎ *310/458–8900. Rides: 50¢ adults, 25¢ children.* ⏲ *Carousel: summer, Tues.–Sun. 10–9; winter, weekends 10–5.*

❷ **Palisades Park** is a ribbon of green that runs along the top of the cliffs from Colorado Avenue to just north of San Vicente Boulevard. The flat walkways are usually filled with casual strollers as well as joggers who like to work out with a spectacular view of the Pacific as company. It is especially enjoyable at sunset.

The **Santa Monica Visitor Information Center,** in the park at Santa Monica Boulevard, offers bus schedules, directions, and information on Santa Monica–area attractions. ☎ *310/393–7593.* ⏲ *Daily 10–4.*

Santa Monica has grown into a major center for the L.A. art commu-
❸ nity, and the **Santa Monica Museum of Art** is poised to boost that reputation. Designed by Frank Gehry, the well-known architect who's also a resident, the museum presents the works of performance and video artists and exhibits works of lesser-known painters and sculptors. *2437 Main St.,* ☎ *310/399–0433.* ☛ *Suggested $4 donation for adults, $2 artists, senior citizens, and students.* ⏲ *Wed. and Thurs. 11–6, Fri.–Sat. 11–10, Sun. 11–6.*

❹ The **California Heritage Museum,** housed in an 1894-vintage, late-Victorian home once owned by the founder of Santa Monica, was moved to its present site on trendy Main Street in the late 1970s. Three rooms have been fully restored: the dining room in the style of 1890 to 1910; the living room, 1910–20; and the kitchen, 1920–30. The second-floor galleries feature photography and historical exhibits as well as shows

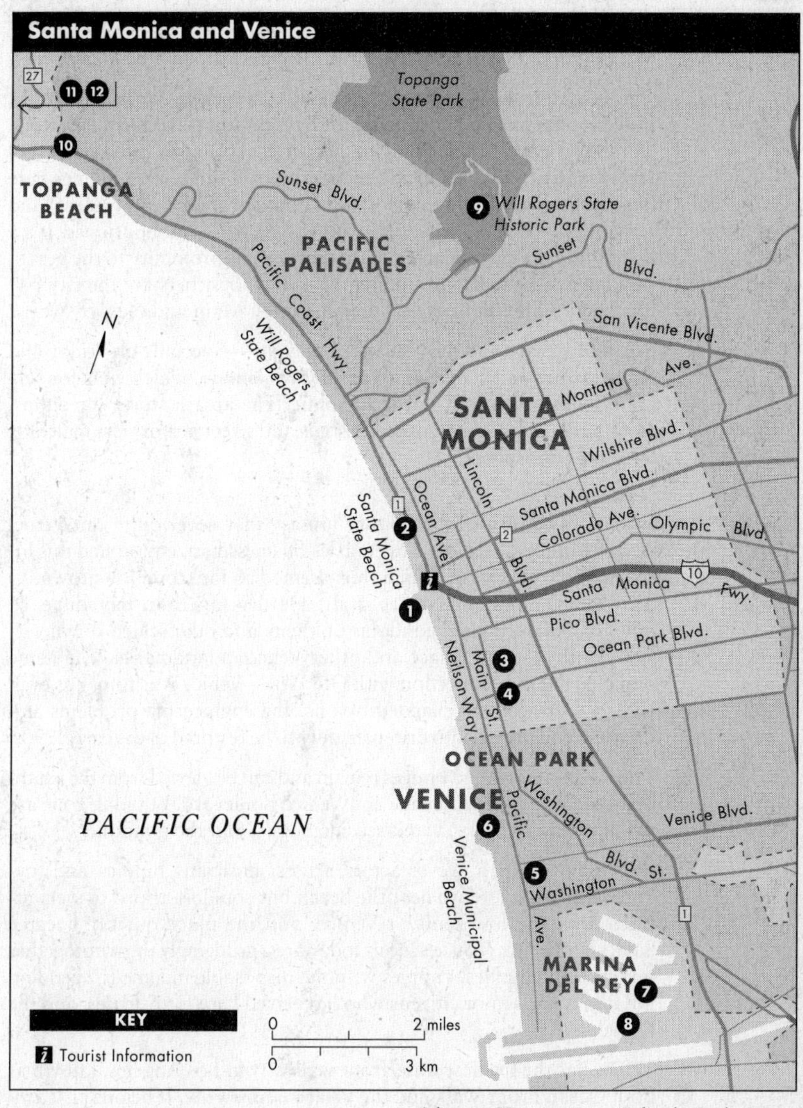

Adamson House, **11**
Burton Chase Park, **7**
California Heritage Museum, **4**
Canals, **5**
Fisherman's Village, **8**
J. Paul Getty Museum, **10**
Malibu Lagoon State Beach, **12**
Palisades Park, **2**
Santa Monica Museum of Art, **3**
Santa Monica Pier, **1**
Venice Boardwalk, **6**
Will Rogers State Historic Park, **9**

by contemporary California artists. *2612 Main St.*, ☎ *310/392–8537.* ☛ *$2 adults, children under 12 free.* ⏲ *Wed.–Sat. 11–4, Sun. noon–4.*

The museum faces a companion home, another Victorian delight moved to the site; it's now occupied by a catering company, **Monica's.** These two dowagers anchor the northwest corner of the funky **Main Street area** of Santa Monica. Several blocks of old brick buildings here have undergone a rejuvenation (and considerable rent increases) and now house galleries, bars, cafés, omelet parlors, and boutiques. It's a delightful area to walk around, though with its proximity to the beach, parking can be tight on summer weekends. Best bets are the city pay lots behind the Main Street shops, between Main and Neilsen Way.

Santa Moncians and tourists alike hang out—especially on Friday and Saturday nights—on the **Third Street Promenade,** which runs for several blocks north of Colorado Avenue. The area features hip shops, restaurants, night clubs; outdoor stalls and street performers make for a festive atmosphere.

Venice

Venice was a turn-of-the-century fantasy that never quite came true. Abbot Kinney, a wealthy Los Angeles businessman, envisioned this little piece of real estate, which then seemed so far from downtown, as a romantic replica of Venice, Italy. He developed an incredible 16 miles of canals, floated gondolas on them, and built scaled-down versions of the Doge's Palace and other Venetian landmarks. The name remains, but the connection with Old World Venice is as flimsy as ever. Kinney's project was plagued by ongoing engineering problems and disasters and drifted into disrepair, only to be restored in the early 1990s.

5 Three small **canals** and bridges remain and can be viewed from the southeast corner of Pacific Avenue and Venice Boulevard. But long gone are the amusement park, swank seaside hotels, and the gondoliers.

By the late 1960s, however, actors, artists, musicians, hippies, and anyone who wanted to live near the beach but couldn't afford to were attracted by the low rents in Venice, and the place quickly became SoHo-by-the-Sea. Venice's locals today are a grudgingly thrown-together mix of aging hippies, yuppies with the disposable income to spend on inflated rents, senior citizens who have lived here for decades, and the homeless.

Venice has the liveliest waterfront walkway in Los Angeles, known as
6 both Ocean Front Walk and the **Venice Boardwalk.** It begins at Washington Street and runs north. There is plenty of action year-round: Bicyclists zip along and bikini-clad roller and in-line skaters attract crowds as they put on impromptu demonstrations, vying for attention with the unusual breeds of dogs that locals love to prance along the walkway. A local bodybuilding club works out on the adjacent beach, and it's nearly impossible not to stop to ogle at the pecs as these strongmen lift weights.

At the south end of the boardwalk, along Washington Street, near the Venice Pier, in-line skates, roller skates, and bicycles (some with baby seats) are available for rent.

TIME OUT The boardwalk is lined with fast-food stands, and food can then be carried a few feet to the beach for a picnic. For a more relaxing meal, stand in line for a table at **Sidewalk Cafe** (1401 Ocean Front Walk, ☎ 310/399–5547). Wait for a patio table, where you can watch the free spirits on parade.

Marina del Rey

Just south of Venice is a quick shift of values. Forget about Venice—Italy or California—Marina del Rey is a modern and more successful, if less romantic, dream. It is the largest man-made boat harbor in the world, with a commercial area catering to the whims of boat owners and boat groupies. The stretch between Admiralty Way and Mindinao Way has some of the area's best restaurants—expensive but worth it. Most of the better hotel chains, such as the Ritz-Carlton, also have properties here.

For boatless visitors, the best place from which to view the marina is
7 **Burton Chase Park,** at the end of Mindinao Way. Situated at the tip of a jetty and surrounded on three sides by water and moored boats, this 6-acre patch of green offers a cool and breezy spot from which to watch boats move in and out of the channel, and it's great for picnicking.

8 **Fisherman's Village** is a collection of cute Cape Cod clapboards housing shops and restaurants (⏲ Daily 8 AM–9 PM). It's not much of a draw unless you stop in for a meal or a snack or take one of the 45-minute marina cruises offered by **Hornblower Dining Outs** that depart from the village dock. *13755 Fiji Way, ☎ 310/301–6000. Tickets: $7 adults, $4 senior citizens and children. Cruises leave June–Aug., weekdays noon–3 every hr; year-round, weekends 11–5.*

Pacific Palisades

From Santa Monica, head north on Pacific Coast Highway toward Malibu, a pleasant drive in daytime or evening. The narrow but expensive beachfront houses were home to movie stars in the 1930s.

9 Spend a few hours at **Will Rogers State Historic Park** in Pacific Palisades and you may understand what endeared America to this cowboy-humorist in the 1920s and 1930s. The two-story ranch house on Rogers's 187-acre estate is a folksy blend of Navajo rugs and Mission-style furniture. Rogers's only extravagance was raising the roof several feet (he waited till his wife was in Europe to do it) to accommodate his penchant for practicing his lasso technique indoors. The nearby museum features Rogers memorabilia. Short films show his roping technique and his homey words of wisdom. The tradition continues, with free games scheduled when the weather's good. The park's broad lawns are excellent for picnicking, and there's hiking on miles of eucalyptus-lined trails. Those who make it to the top will be rewarded with a panoramic view of the mountains and ocean. *1501 Will Rogers State Park Rd., Pacific Palisades, ☎ 310/454–8212. ☛ Free; parking: $5. Call for polo schedule.*

Malibu

★ 10 You'll want to plan in advance to visit the **J. Paul Getty Museum,** which contains one of the country's finest collections of Greek and Roman antiquities. The oil millionaire began collecting art in the 1930s, concentrating on three distinct areas: Greek and Roman antiquities, Baroque and Renaissance paintings, and 18th-century decorative arts. In 1946 he purchased a large Spanish-style home on 65 acres in a canyon just north of Santa Monica to house the collection. By the late 1960s, the museum could no longer accommodate the rapidly expanding collection and Getty decided to build this new building, which was completed in 1974. It's a re-creation of the Villa dei Papiri, a luxurious 1st-century Roman villa that stood on the slopes of Mt. Vesuvius overlooking the Bay of Naples, prior to the volcano's eruption in AD 79. The villa is thought to have once belonged to Lucius Calpurnius Piso, the father-in-law of Julius Caesar. The two-level, 38-gallery building and its extensive gardens (which include trees, flowers, shrubs, and herbs that might have grown 2,000 years ago at the villa) provide an appropriate and harmonious setting for Getty's classical antiquities. Note that in late 1997, everything except the classical antiquities will be moved to a new J. Paul Getty Center in Brentwood; now might be a good time to see the whole collection while it's still in one spot.

The main level houses sculpture, mosaics, and vases. Of particular interest are the 4th-century Attic stelae (funerary monuments) and Greek and Roman portraits. The decorative arts collection on the upper level features furniture, carpets, tapestries, clocks, chandeliers, and small decorative items made for the French, German, and Italian nobility, with a wealth of royal French treasures (Louis XIV to Napoléon). Richly colored brocaded walls set off the paintings and furniture to great advantage. All major schools of Western art from the late 13th century to the late 19th century are represented in the painting collection, which emphasizes Renaissance and Baroque art and includes works by Rembrandt, Rubens, de la Tour, Van Dyck, Gainsborough, and Boucher. Recent acquisitions include Old Master drawings, medieval and Renaissance illuminated manuscripts, works by Picasso, van Gogh's *Irises,* and a select collection of Impressionist paintings including some by Claude Monet. The only catch in visiting this museum is that parking is limited and reservations are necessary; they should be made one week in advance. The only other way in if you're not on a tour—handy if you've arrived too late to reserve a parking slot—is to take MTA Bus 434 from Santa Monica. The driver will give you an entrance pass. *17985 Pacific Coast Hwy., ☎ 310/458–2003. ☛ Free. ⌚ Tues.–Sun. 10–5.*

TIME OUT One of the best-located restaurants in Malibu is **Pierview** (22718 Pacific Coast Hwy., ☎ 310/456–6962), set right on the ocean just south of the pier. The menu ranges from sandwiches and pizzas to Mexican food, including shark fajitas.

11 **Adamson House** is the former home of the Rindge family, which owned much of the Malibu Rancho in the early part of the 20th century. Malibu was quite isolated then, with all visitors and supplies arriving by boat at the nearby Malibu Pier (and it can still be isolated these days when rock slides close the highway). The Moorish-Spanish home, built in 1928, has been opened to the public and may be the only chance most visitors get to be inside a grand Malibu home. The family owned the famous Malibu Tile Company, and their home is predictably encrusted with magnificent tile work in rich blues, greens, yellows, and oranges. Even an outside dog shower, near the servants' door, is a tiled delight. Docent-led tours help visitors to envision family life here as well as to learn about the history of Malibu and its real estate (you can't have one without the other). *23200 Pacific Coast Hwy., ☎ 310/456–8432. ☛ $2 adults, $1 children. ⌚ Wed.–Sat. 11–3. Parking (fee).*

12 Adjacent to Adamson House is **Malibu Lagoon State Beach Park** (23200 Pacific Coast Hwy.), a haven for native and migratory birds. Visitors must stay on the boardwalks so that the egrets, blue herons, avocets, and gulls can enjoy the marshy area. The signs that give opening and closing hours refer only to the parking lot; the lagoon itself is open 24 hours and is particularly enjoyable in the early morning and at sunset. Luckily, street-side parking is available then (but not at midday).

Palos Verdes, San Pedro, and Long Beach

Numbers in the margin correspond to points of interest on the Palos Verdes, San Pedro, and Long Beach map.

Palos Verdes

Palos Verdes Peninsula is a hilly haven for horse lovers and other gentrified folks, many of them executive transplants from east of the Mississippi. The real estate in these small peninsula towns, ranging from expensive to very expensive, is zoned for stables, and you'll often see riders along the streets (they have the right of way).

❶ **South Coast Botanic Garden** began life ignominiously—as a garbage dump–cum–landfill. It's hard to believe that as recently as 1960, truckloads of waste (3½ million tons) were being deposited here. With the intensive ministerings of the experts from the L.A. County Arboreta Department, the dump soon boasted lush gardens with plants from every continent except Antarctica, with all the plants eventually organized into color groups. Self-guided walking tours take visitors past flower and herb gardens, rare cacti, and a lake with ducks. Picnicking is limited to a lawn area outside the gates. *26300 S. Crenshaw Blvd., Rancho Palos Verdes, ☏ 310/544–6815. ☛ $5 adults, $1 senior citizens and children 5–12. ⏲ Daily 9–4:30.*

❷ **Wayfarers Chapel** (5755 Palos Verdes Dr. S, Rancho Palos Verdes, ☏ 310/377–1650) was designed by architect Lloyd Wright, son of Frank Lloyd Wright, in 1949. He planned this modern glass church to blend in with an encircling redwood forest. The redwoods are gone (they couldn't stand the rigors of urban encroachment), but another forest has taken their place, lush with ferns and azaleas, adding up to a breathtaking combination of ocean, vegetation, and an architectural wonder. This "natural church" is a popular wedding site, so avoid visiting on weekends.

San Pedro

San Pedro shares the peninsula with the Palos Verdes towns, but little else. Here, the cliffs give way to a hospitable harbor. The 1950s-vintage executive homes give way to tidy 1920s-era white clapboards, and horses give way to boats. San Pedro (locals steadfastly ignore the correct Spanish pronunciation—it's "San Peedro" to them) is an old seaport community with a strong Mediterranean and Eastern European flavor. There are enticing Greek and Yugoslavian markets and restaurants throughout the town.

❸ **Cabrillo Marine Aquarium** is a gem of a small museum dedicated to the marine life that flourishes off the southern California coast. It's set in a modern Frank Gehry–designed building right on the beach and is popular with school groups because its exhibits are especially instructive as well as fun. The 35 saltwater aquariums include a shark tank, and a see-through tidal tank gives visitors a chance to see the long view of a wave. On the back patio, docents supervise as visitors reach into a shallow tank to touch starfish and sea anemones. *3720 Stephen White Dr., ☏ 310/548–7562. ☛ Free; parking $6.50. ⏲ Tues.–Fri. noon–5, weekends 10–5.*

If you're lucky enough to visit at low tide, take time to explore the tide pool on nearby Cabrillo Beach (museum staff can direct you).

❹ **Ports O' Call Village** is a commercial rendition of a New England shipping village, an older version of Fisherman's Village in Marina del Rey, with shops, restaurants, and fast-food windows. Two companies run 1- to 1½-hour harbor cruises ($10 adults, $5 children) and whale-watching cruises, January–April ($15 adults, $5–$8 children). Cruises depart from the village dock; call 310/831–1073 for schedules.

Palos Verdes, San Pedro, and Long Beach

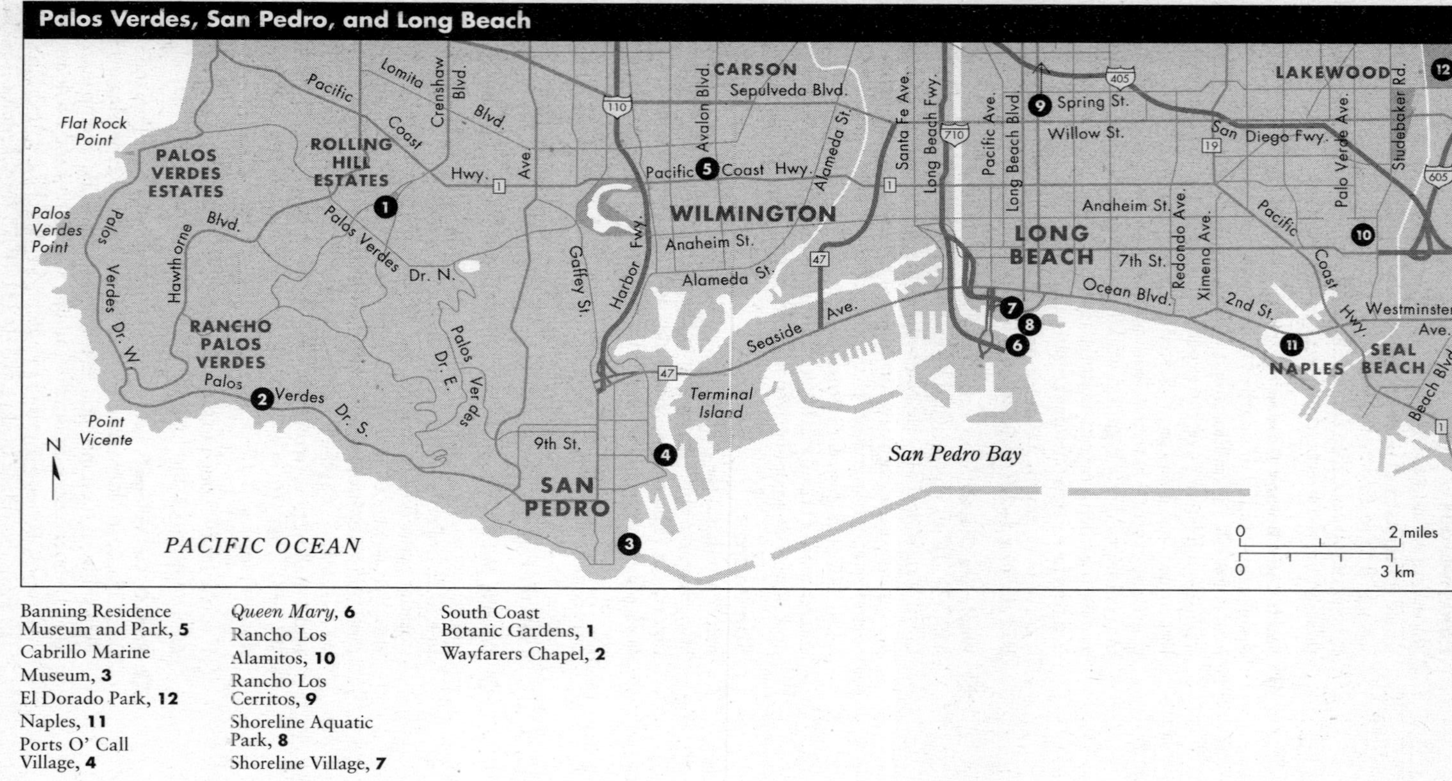

Banning Residence Museum and Park, **5**
Cabrillo Marine Museum, **3**
El Dorado Park, **12**
Naples, **11**
Ports O' Call Village, **4**
Queen Mary, **6**
Rancho Los Alamitos, **10**
Rancho Los Cerritos, **9**
Shoreline Aquatic Park, **8**
Shoreline Village, **7**
South Coast Botanic Gardens, **1**
Wayfarers Chapel, **2**

Wilmington

To preserve transportation and shipping interests for the city of Los Angeles, Wilmington was annexed in the late 19th century. A narrow strip of land, mostly less than ½ mile wide, it follows the Harbor Freeway from downtown south to the port. 5 **Banning Residence Museum and Park** is a pleasant, low-key stop here. General Phineas Banning, an early entrepreneur in Los Angeles, is credited with developing the harbor into a viable economic entity and naming the area Wilmington (he was from Delaware). Part of his estate has been preserved in a 20-acre park that offers excellent picnicking possibilities. A 100-year-old wisteria, near the arbor, blooms in the spring. The interior of the house can be seen on docent-led tours. *401 E. M St., Wilmington, ☎ 310/548–7777. ☛ To house: $2. House tours Tues.–Thurs. 12:30–2:30, Sat. and Sun. 12:30–3:30, on ½ hr.*

Long Beach

Long Beach began as a seaside resort in the 19th century and during the early part of the 20th century was a popular destination for midwesterners and Dust Bowlers in search of a better life. They built street after street of modest wood homes.

★ 6 The first glimpse of the ***Queen Mary***—the largest passenger ship ever built, now sitting snugly in Long Beach Harbor—is disarming. What seemed like sure folly when Long Beach officials bought her in 1964 put the city on the proverbial map. The 50,000-ton *Queen Mary* was launched in 1934, a floating treasure of Art Deco splendor. It took a crew of 1,100 to minister to the needs of its 1,900 passengers. Allow a generous half day to explore this most luxurious of luxury liners, admiring the extensive wood paneling, the gleaming nickel- and silver-plate handrails, and the hand-cut glass. Tours through the ship are available, and guests are invited to browse the 12 decks and witness close up the bridge, staterooms, officers' quarters, and engine rooms. There are several restaurants and shops on board. *Pier J, ☎ 310/435–3511. ☛ $10 adults, $8 senior citizens, $6 children under 12. Guided 1-hr tour ($3 extra adults and senior citizens, $1 children). ⏲ Daily 10–6.*

7 **Shoreline Village** is the most successful of the pseudo–New England harbors here. Its setting, between downtown Long Beach and the *Queen Mary,* is reason enough to stroll here, day or evening (when visitors can enjoy the lights of the ship twinkling in the distance). In addition to gift shops and restaurants there's a 1906 carousel with bobbing giraffes, camels, and horses. *Corner of Shoreline Dr. and Pine Ave., ☎ 310/435–2668. ☛ Carousel: $1 adults, children under 40" free with adult. ⏲ May–Sept., daily 10AM–11PM; Oct.–Apr., 10–10.*

TIME OUT Housed in a working lighthouse, the aptly named **Parker's Lighthouse** (435 Shoreline Village Dr. in Shoreline Village, ☎ 213/432–6500) does double duty: It's the best place to enjoy a view of the *Queen Mary* and surrounding harbor, and it offers the finest seafood in this part of town.

8 **Shoreline Aquatic Park** (205 Marina Dr.) is literally set in the middle of Long Beach Harbor and is a much-sought-after resting place for RVers. Kite flyers also love it because the winds are wonderful here. Casual passersby can enjoy a short walk, where the modern skyline, quaint Shoreline Village, the *Queen Mary,* and the ocean all vie for attention. The park's lagoon is off-limits for swimming, but aquacycles and kayaks can be rented during the summer months. Contact **Long Beach Water Sports** (730 E. 4th St., ☎ 310/432–0187) for information on sea kayaking lessons, rentals, and outings.

9 **Rancho Los Cerritos** is a charming Monterey-style adobe built by the Don Juan Temple family in 1844. Monterey-style homes can be easily recognized by two features: They are always two-storied and have a narrow balcony across the front. It's easy to imagine Zorro, that swashbuckling fictional hero of the rancho era, jumping from the balcony onto a waiting horse and making his escape. The 10 rooms have been furnished in the style of the period and are open for viewing. But don't expect an Old California–style Southwest fantasy, with primitive Mexican furniture and cactus in the garden. The Temple family shared the prevalent taste of the period, in which the American East Coast and Europe still set the style, emphasizing fancy, dark woods and Victorian bric-a-brac. The gardens here were designed in the 1930s by well-known landscape architect Ralph Cornell. *4600 Virginia Rd., ☏ 310/570–1755. ☛ Free. ⏲ Wed.–Sun. 1–5. Self-guided tours on weekdays. Free 50-min guided tours on weekends hourly 1–4.*

10 **Rancho Los Alamitos** is said to be the oldest one-story domestic building still standing in the county. It was built in 1806, when the Spanish flag still flew over California. There's a blacksmith shop in the barn. *6400 E. Bixby Hill Rd., ☏ 310/431–3541. ☛ Free. ⏲ Wed.–Sun. 1–5. Free 90-min tours leave every ½ hr until 4.*

11 The **Naples** section of Long Beach is known for its pleasant and well-maintained canals. Canals in *Naples,* you ask? Yes, this is a misnomer. But better misnamed and successful than aptly named and a bust. The developer who came up with the Naples canal idea learned from the mistakes and bad luck that did in Venice, just up the coast, and built the canals to take full advantage of the tidal flow that would keep them clean. Naples is actually three small islands in man-made Alamitos Bay. It is best experienced on foot—park near Bayshore Drive and 2nd Street and walk across the bridge, where you can begin meandering the quaint streets with very Italian names. This well-restored neighborhood boasts eclectic architecture: vintage Victorians, Craftsman bungalows, and Mission Revivals. You may spy a real gondola or two on the canals. You can hire them for a ride but not on the spur of the moment. **Gondola Getaway** offers one-hour rides, usually touted for romantic couples, although the gondolas can accommodate up to four people. *5437 E. Ocean Blvd., ☏ 310/433–9595. Rides: $55 per couple, $10 for each additional person. Reservations essential, at least 1 to 2 wks in advance. Cruises operate 4 PM–midnight.*

12 **El Dorado Park** (7550 E. Spring St.) hosted the 1984 Olympic Games archery competition and remains popular with local archery enthusiasts. Most visitors, however, come to this huge, 800-acre park for the broad, shady lawns, walking trails, and lakes. Several small lakes are picturesquely set among cottonwoods and pine trees. This is a wonderful picnicking spot. Fishing is permitted in all the lakes (stocked with catfish, carp, and trout), but the northernmost one is favored by local anglers. Pedal boats are available by the hour. The Nature Center is a bird and native plant sanctuary.

Highland Park, Pasadena, and San Marino

Numbers in the margin correspond to points of interest on the Highland Park, Pasadena, and San Marino map.

The suburbs north of downtown Los Angeles offer a rich architectural heritage as well as several fine museums. To take advantage of the afternoon-only hours of several sites, the Highland part of this tour is best scheduled in the afternoon. Pasadena could take a full day, more if you want to savor the museums' collections.

To reach this area, drive north on the Pasadena Freeway (110), which follows the curves of the arroyo (creek bed) that leads north from downtown. It was the main road north during the early days of Los Angeles when horses and buggies made their way through the chaparral-covered countryside to the small town of Pasadena. In 1942, the road became the Arroyo Seco Parkway, the first freeway in Los Angeles, later renamed the Pasadena Freeway. It remains a pleasant drive in non-rush-hour traffic, with the freeway lined with old sycamores and winding up the arroyo like a New York parkway.

Highland Park

Midway between downtown Los Angeles and Pasadena, Highland Park was a genteel suburb in the late 1800s, where the Anglo population tried to keep an eastern feeling alive in their architecture in spite of the decidedly southwestern landscape. The streets on both sides of the freeway are filled with faded beauties, classic old clapboards that have gone into decline in the past half century.

1 **Heritage Square** is the ambitious attempt by the Los Angeles Cultural Heritage Board to save from the wrecking ball some of the city's architectural gems of the 1865–1914 period. During the past 20 years four residences, a depot, a church, and a carriage barn have been moved to this small park from all over the city. The most breathtaking building here is **Hale House,** built in 1885. The almost-garish colors of both the interior and exterior are not the whim of some aging hippie painter but rather a faithful re-creation of the palette that was actually in fashion in the late 1800s. The **Palms Depot,** built in 1886, was moved to the site from the Westside of L.A. The night the building was moved, down city streets and up freeways, is documented in photomurals on the depot's walls. Docents dress in period costume. *3800 Homer St., off Ave. 43 exit, ☎ 818/449–0193. ☛ $5 adults, $4 senior citizens and children 13–17, $2 children 6–12. ⏲ Sat., Sun., and most holidays noon–4 PM. Tours every 45 min or so.*

2 **El Alisal** was the home of eccentric easterner turned westerner-with-a-vengeance Charles Lummis. This Harvard graduate was captivated by Native American culture (he founded the Southwest Museum; *see below*), often living the lifestyle of the natives, much to the shock of the staid Angelenos of the time. His home, built from 1898 to 1910, is constructed of boulders from the arroyo itself, a romantic notion until recent earthquakes made the safety of such homes questionable. The art-nouveau fireplace was designed by Gutzon Borglum, the sculptor of Mt. Rushmore. *200 E. Ave. 43 (entrance on Carlota Blvd.), ☎ 213/222–0546. ☛ Free. ⏲ Fri.–Sun. noon–4.*

3 You can spot the **Southwest Museum** from the freeway—it's the huge Mission Revival building standing halfway up Mt. Washington. Inside is an extensive collection of Native American art and artifacts, with special emphasis on the people of the Plains, Northwest Coast, Southwest U.S., and northern Mexico. The basket collection is outstanding. *234 Museum Dr., off Ave. 43 exit, ☎ 213/221–2163. ☛ $5 adults, $3 senior citizens and students, $2 children 7–18. ⏲ Tues.–Sun. 11–5.*

TIME OUT Just blocks down the street in either direction from the Southwest Museum you'll discover authentic Mexican food that is downright cheap. The first, **Señor Fish** (5111 Figueroa St., ☎ 213/257–2498), looks like a taco stand—but don't pass it up. Intriguing selections include octopus tostada, scallop burritos, and refreshing ceviche. A few minutes' walk in

El Alisal, **2**
Gamble House, **5**
Heritage Square, **1**
Huntington Library, Art Gallery, and Botanical Gardens, **12**
Kidspace, **10**
The Norton Simon Museum, **7**
Old Town Pasadena, **8**
The Pacific Asia Museum, **9**
Pasadena Historical Society, **6**
Ritz-Carlton, Huntington Hotel, **11**
The Rose Bowl, **4**
The Southwest Museum, **3**

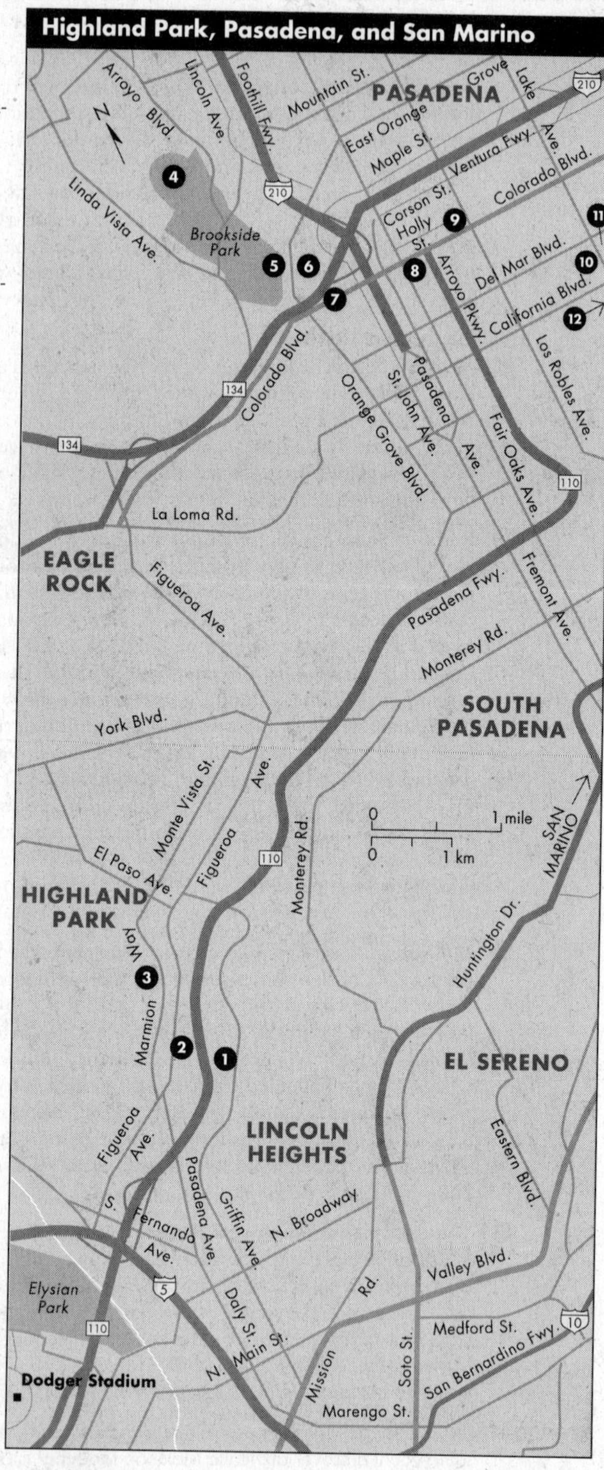

the other direction is **La Abeja** (3700 Figueroa St., ☎ 213/221-0474), a Mexican café that's been around for two-dozen years. The word inexpensive takes on new meaning at this hangout, known for its salsas and steak picado with chili.

Pasadena

Although now fully absorbed into the general Los Angeles sprawl, Pasadena was once a separate and distinctly defined—and refined—city. Its varied architecture, augmented by lush landscaping, is the most spectacular in southern California. Visitors with only a few hours to spend should consider at least driving past the Gamble House, through Old Town, and then on to the grand old neighborhood of the Huntington Library, spending most of their time there.

4 The **Rose Bowl** (991 Rosemont Ave.) is set at the bottom of a wide area of the arroyo in an older wealthy neighborhood that must endure the periodic onslaught of thousands of cars and party-minded football fans. The stadium is closed except for games and special events such as the monthly Rose Bowl Swap Meet. Held the second Sunday of the month, it is considered the granddaddy of West Coast swap meets.

5 **Gamble House,** built by Charles and Henry Greene in 1908, is the most spectacular example of Craftsman-style bungalow architecture. The term "bungalow" can be misleading, since the Gamble House is a huge two-story home. To wealthy easterners such as the Gambles, this type of vacation home seemed informal compared with their accustomed mansions. What makes visitors swoon here is the incredible amount of hand craftsmanship: the hand-shaped teak interiors, the Greene-designed furniture, the Louis Tiffany glass door. The dark exterior has broad eaves, with many sleeping porches on the second floor. It's on a private road, which is not well marked; take Orange Grove Boulevard to the 300 block to find Westmoreland Place. *4 Westmoreland Pl.,* ☎ *818/793–3334.* ☛ *$4 adults, $3 senior citizens, $2 students, children under 13 free.* ⏲ *Thurs.–Sun. noon–3. 1-hr tours every 15–20 min.*

6 The **Pasadena Historical Society** is housed in Fenyes Mansion. The 1905 building still holds the original furniture and paintings on the main and second floors; in the basement, the focus is on Pasadena's history. There are also 4 acres of well-landscaped gardens. *470 W. Walnut St.,* ☎ *818/577–1660.* ☛ *$4 adults, $3 senior citizens and students, children under 12 free.* ⏲ *Thurs.–Sun. 1–4. 1-hr docent-led tours.*

7 The **Norton Simon Museum** will be familiar to television viewers of the Rose Parade: The sleek, modern building makes a stunning background for the passing floats. Like the more famous Getty Museum, the Norton Simon is a tribute to the art acumen of an extremely wealthy businessman. In 1974, Simon reorganized the failing Pasadena Museum of Modern Art and assembled one of the world's finest collections, richest in its Rembrandts, Goyas, Degas, and Picassos—and dotted with Rodin sculptures throughout. Rembrandt's development can be traced in three oils—*The Bearded Man in the Wide Brimmed Hat, Self Portrait,* and *Titus.* The most dramatic Goyas are two oils—*St. Jerome* and the portrait of *Dona Francisca Vicenta Chollet y Caballero.* Down the walnut-and-steel staircase is the Degas gallery. Picasso's renowned *Woman with Book* highlights a comprehensive collection of his paintings, drawings, and sculptures. The museum's collections of Impressionist (van Gogh, Matisse, Cézanne, Monet, Renoir, et al.) and Cubist (Braque, Gris) work is extensive. Older works include Southeast Asian artwork from 100 BC and bronze, stone, and ivory

sculptures from India, Cambodia, Thailand, and Nepal. The museum also has a wealth of Early Renaissance, Baroque, and Rococo artwork: Church works by Raphael, Guariento, de Paolo, Filippino Lippi, and Lucas Cranach give way to robust Rubens maidens and Dutch landscapes, still lifes, and portraits by Frans Hals, Jacob van Ruisdael, and Jan Steen, and a magical Tiepolo ceiling highlights the Rococo period. *411 W. Colorado Blvd., ☎ 818/449–6840. ☛ $4 adults, $2 senior citizens and students, children under 12 free. ⏲ Thurs.–Sun. noon–6.*

8 A half mile east of the museum is **Old Town Pasadena,** which once fell into seedy decay, but in the 1990s, the area was revitalized as a blend of restored brick buildings with a yuppie overlay. Rejuvenated buildings include bistros, elegant restaurants, and boutiques. On Raymond Street, the Hotel Green, now the Castle Apartments, dominates the area. Once a posh resort hotel, the Green is now a faded Moorish fantasy of domes, turrets, and balconies reminiscent of the Alhambra but with, true to its name, a greenish tint. Holly Street, between Fair Oaks and Arroyo, is home to several shops offering an excellent selection of vintage '50s objects, jewelry, and clothes; it's an area that's best explored on foot. Old Town is bisected by Colorado Boulevard, which west of Old Town rises onto the **Colorado Street Bridge,** a raised section of roadway on graceful arches built in 1912 and restored in 1993. On New Year's Day throngs of people line Colorado Boulevard to watch the Rose Parade.

9 The **Pacific Asia Museum** is the gaudiest Chinese-style building in Los Angeles outside of Chinatown. Designed in the style of a northern Chinese imperial palace with a central courtyard, it is devoted entirely to the arts and crafts of Asia and the Pacific Islands. *46 N. Los Robles Dr., ☎ 818/449–2742. ☛ $3 adults, $1.50 senior citizens and students, children free; free the 3rd Sat. of the month. ⏲ Wed.–Sun. 10–5.*

10 **Kidspace** is a children's museum housed in the gymnasium of an elementary school. Here kids can talk to a robot, direct a television or radio station, dress up in the real (and very heavy) uniforms of a firefighter, an astronaut, a football player, and more. "Critter Caverns" beckons with its large tree house and secret tunnels for exploring insect life up close (don't worry, the bugs are fake). *390 S. El Molino Ave., ☎ 818/449–9143. ☛ $5 adults, $3.50 senior citizens, $2.50 children 1–2. ⏲ Sept.–May, Wed. 2–5, weekends 12:30–5; school vacations, weekdays 1–5 and weekends 12:30–5; June–Aug., Tues.–Fri. 1–5.*

11 The **Ritz-Carlton, Huntington Hotel** (1401 S. Oak Knoll Ave., ☎ 818/568–3900) is situated in Pasadena's most genteel neighborhood, Oak Knoll, close to San Marino. The hotel, built in 1906, underwent extensive renovations before reopening in 1991. The original design was scrupulously preserved, including the Japanese and Horseshoe Gardens. Murals along the gables of the historic Picture Bridge depict scenes of California.

San Marino

If you only have time for one stop in the Pasadena area, it should be
★ 12 the **Huntington Library, Art Gallery, and Botanical Gardens,** the area's most important site. Railroad tycoon Henry E. Huntington built his hilltop home in the early 1900s; since then it has established a reputation as one of the most extraordinary cultural complexes in the world. The library contains 6 million items, including a Gutenberg Bible, the earliest known edition of Chaucer's *Canterbury Tales,* George Washington's genealogy in his own handwriting, and first editions by Ben Franklin and Shakespeare. The art gallery, devoted to British art

from the 18th and 19th centuries, contains the original *Blue Boy* by Gainsborough; *Pinkie,* a companion piece by Lawrence; and the monumental *Sarah Siddons as the Tragic Muse* by Reynolds.

The Huntington's 130-acre garden, formerly the grounds of the estate, includes a 12-acre Desert Garden featuring the largest group of mature cacti and other succulents in the world, all arranged by continent. The Japanese Garden holds traditional Japanese plants, stone ornaments, a moon bridge, a Japanese house, a bonsai court, and a Zen rock garden. Besides these gardens, there are collections of azaleas and 1,500 varieties of camellias, the world's largest public collection. The 1,000-variety rose garden displays its collection historically so that the development leading to today's strains of roses can be observed. There are also herb, palm, and jungle gardens plus a Shakespeare garden, where plants mentioned in Shakespeare's works are grown.

The Huntington Pavilion, built in 1980, offers visitors unmatched views of the surrounding mountains and valleys and houses a bookstore, displays, and information kiosks as well. Both the east and west wings of the pavilion display paintings on public exhibition for the first time. The Ralph M. Parsons Botanical Center at the pavilion includes a botanical library, a herbarium, and a laboratory for research on plants.

Visitors to this vast property have several options, including a 12-minute slide show introducing the Huntington; a 1¼-hour guided tour of the gardens; a 45-minute audiotape about the art gallery (which can be rented for a nominal fee); a 15-minute introductory talk about the library; and inexpensive, self-guided tour leaflets. *1151 Oxford Rd.,* ☎ *818/405–2100.* ☛ *$7.50 adults, $6 senior citizens, $4 children 12–18 (suggested donation).* ⏲ *Tues.–Fri. 1–4:30, weekends 11–4:30.*

The San Fernando Valley

Although there are other valleys in the Los Angeles area, this is the one that people refer to simply as "the Valley." City people still see it as a mere collection of bedroom communities, not worth serious thought. But the Valley has come a long way since the early 20th century, when it was mainly orange groves and small ranches. Now home to more than 1 million people, this large portion of Los Angeles is an area of neat bungalows and ranch-style homes situated on tidy parcels of land, with shopping centers never too far away. Fine restaurants and several major movie and television studios are an integral part of this community.

We group the major attractions of the Valley into one Exploring section to give you a sense of the place, but because the Valley is such a vast area, focus on one or two attractions and make them the destination for a half- or full-day trip. Rush-hour traffic jams on the San Diego and Hollywood freeways can be brutal.

Universal City

If you drive into the area on the Hollywood Freeway, through the Cahuenga Pass, you'll come first to Universal City, a one-industry town, and that industry is Universal Studios. Its history goes back decades as a major film and television studio, but in the past few years Universal has also become a major tourist attraction. Today this hilly area boasts the Universal Studios Tour, the Universal Amphitheater, CityWalk (fun shopping and dining along a narrow thoroughfare that resembles a movie back lot), a major movie complex, and two major hotels.

★ **Universal Studios Hollywood and CityWalk** is the best place in Los Angeles for seeing behind the scenes of the movie industry. The five-to seven-hour Universal tour is an enlightening and amusing (if a bit sensational) day at the world's largest television and movie studio. The complex stretches across more than 420 acres, many of which are traversed during the course of the tour by trams featuring usually witty running commentary by enthusiastic guides. You can experience the parting of the Red Sea, an avalanche, and a flood; meet a 30-foot-tall version of King Kong; live through an encounter with a runaway train; be attacked by the ravenous killer shark of *Jaws* fame; and endure a confrontation by aliens armed with death rays—all without ever leaving the safety of the tram. And now, thanks to the magic of Hollywood, you can also experience the perils of the Big One—an all-too-real simulation of an 8.3 earthquake, complete with collapsing earth, deafening train wrecks, floods, and other life-threatening amusements such as *Backdraft*: 10,000 Degrees of Excitement. There is a New England village, an aged European town, and a replica of an archetypal New York street. Other favorites are *Back to the Future,* a \$60 million flight simulator disguised as a DeLorean car that shows off state-of-the-art special effects, and *Lucy: A Tribute to Lucille Ball,* a 2,200-square-foot heart-shape museum containing a re-creation of the set from the *I Love Lucy* television show, plus other artifacts from the hit 1950s program. Scheduled to open in 1996 is *Waterworld*: A Live Sea War Spectacle, a stunt show based on the Kevin Costner film. At the Entertainment Center, the longest and last stop of the day, you can stroll around to enjoy various shows: In one theater animals beguile you with their tricks; in another you can pose for a photo session with the Incredible Hulk; at Castle Dracula you'll confront a variety of terrifying monsters; and at the Star Trek Theater, you can have yourself filmed and inserted as an extra in a scene from a galactic adventure already released. Bedrock is represented in the "Flintstone's Live Musical Extravaganza," a stunning Stone Age revue. CityWalk opened in 1993, with a slew of quaint shops and restaurants, including Spago, a copy of the star-studded Sunset Strip restaurant. *100 Universal City Pl., ☎ 818/508–9600. ☛ \$33 adults, \$27 senior citizens 60 and over, \$25 children 3–11. ⏲ Box office: daily 9–7.*

Burbank

Warner Brothers Studios offers a two-hour tour, which involves a lot of walking, so you should dress comfortably and casually. This tour is somewhat technically oriented and centered more on the actual workings of filmmaking than the one at Universal. It also varies from day to day to take advantage of goings-on on the lot. Most tours see the back-lot sets, prop construction department, and sound complex. *4000 Warner Blvd., ☎ 818/954–1744. ☛ \$27. Tours on the hr, weekdays 9–4. No children under 10 permitted. Reservations essential, 1 wk in advance. AE, MC, V.*

NBC Television Studios are also in Burbank, as any regular viewer of *The Tonight Show* can't help knowing. For those who wish to be part of a live studio audience, free tickets are made available for tapings of the various NBC shows, and studio tours are offered daily. *3000 W. Alameda Ave., Burbank, ☎ 818/840–3537. ☛ \$6 adults, \$3.75 children. Tours daily 1–3.*

San Fernando

San Fernando, in the northeast corner of the valley of that bears its name, has only one important attraction: **Mission San Fernando Rey de España,** established in 1797 and named in honor of King Ferdinand

III of Spain. Fifty-six Native Americans joined the mission to make it a self-supporting community. By 1833, after Mexico extended its rule over California, a civil administrator was appointed for the mission and the priests were restricted to religious duties. The Native Americans began leaving, and what had been flourishing one year before became unproductive. Over time, the mission buildings were neglected; settlers stripped roof tiles, and the adobe walls were ravaged by the weather. Finally in 1923 a restoration program was initiated. The mission has been used in countless film and TV productions, among them *Gunsmoke, Dragnet,* and the 1991 Steve Martin comedy *L.A. Story.* The church's interior is decorated with Native American designs and artifacts of Spanish craftsmanship depicting the mission's 18th-century culture. *15151 San Fernando Mission Blvd.,* ☎ *818/361–0186.* ☛ *$4 adults, $3 senior citizens and children 7–15.* ⏲ *Daily 9–5.*

Calabasas

Calabasas, in the southwest corner of the Valley, was once a stagecoach stop on the way from Ventura to Los Angeles. The name means "pumpkins" in Spanish. The little town has retained some of the flavor of its early days. The **Leonis Adobe** is one of the most charming adobes in the county, due in part to its fairly rural setting and barnyard animals, especially the Spanish red hens. With a little concentration, visitors can imagine life in the early years. The house was originally built as a one-story adobe, but in 1844 Miguel Leonis decided to remodel rather than move and added a second story with a balcony. Voilà! A Monterey-style home. *23537 Calabasas Rd.,* ☎ *818/222–6511.* ☛ *Free.* ⏲ *Wed.–Sun. 1–4.*

TIME OUT The **Sagebrush Cantina** (23527 Calabasas Rd., ☎ 818/222-6062),just next door to the Leonis Adobe, is a casual, outdoorsy place and perfect for families. The specialty here, as the name suggests, is Mexican fare.

Other Places of Interest

Scattered across Los Angeles County are attractions that don't fit neatly into any organized drive or walk. Some, such as Dodger Stadium, are major sites. Others, such as the Gene Autry Museum, recall the West of days gone by.

Dodger Stadium has been home of the Los Angeles Dodgers since 1961, when Chavez Ravine was chosen as the site of the newly arrived-from-Brooklyn team's home base. The stadium seats 56,000 and parking is fairly easy. *1000 Elysian Park Ave.,* ☎ *213/224–1400, accessible from Pasadena Fwy. just north of downtown L.A.* ⏲ *Only during games.*

Exposition Park was the site of the 1932 Olympics and the impressive architecture still stands. Adjoining the University of Southern California (*see below*), Exposition Park is the location of two major museums: the **California Museum of Science and Industry** and the **Natural History Museum.** Also included in the 114-acre park is the **Los Angeles Swimming Stadium** (home of Los Angeles aquatic competitions), which is open to the public in summer, and **Memorial Coliseum,** the major stadium for the 1932 and 1984 Olympics, which was severely damaged in the 1994 earthquake. At press time (summer 1995) the swimming stadium was still closed for repairs. There are plenty of picnic areas on the grounds as well as a sunken rose garden. *Figueroa St. at Exposition Blvd., Los Angeles.*

Forest Lawn Memorial Park is more than just a cemetery: It covers 300 formally landscaped acres and features a major collection of marble statuary and art treasures, including a replica of Leonardo da Vinci's

The Last Supper done entirely in stained glass. In the Hall of the Crucifixion-Resurrection is one of the world's largest oil paintings incorporating a religious theme, *The Crucifixion* by artist Jan Styka. Forest Lawn was the model for the setting of Evelyn Waugh's novel *The Loved One.* Many celebrities are buried here, some more flamboyantly than others. Silent-screen cowboy star Tom Mix is said to be buried in his good-guy clothes: white coat, white pants, and a belt buckle with his name spelled out in diamonds. Markers for Walt Disney and Errol Flynn are near the Freedom Mausoleum. Inside the mausoleum are the wall crypts of Nat King Cole, Clara Bow, Gracie Allen, and Alan Ladd. Clark Gable, Carole Lombard, Theda Bara, and Jean Harlow are among the luminaries buried in the Great Mausoleum. *1712 S. Glendale Ave., Glendale,* ☎ *213/254–3131.* ⏲ *Daily 8–5.*

Forest Lawn Memorial Park–Hollywood Hills is the 340-acre sister park to Forest Lawn Glendale, situated just west of Griffith Park on the north slope of the Hollywood Hills. Dedicated to the theme of American liberty, it features bronze and marble statuary, including Thomas Ball's 60-foot Washington Memorial and a replica of the Liberty Bell. There are also reproductions of Boston's Old North Church and Longfellow's Church of the Hills. The film *The Many Voices of Freedom* is shown daily and Revolutionary War documents are on permanent display. Among the famous people buried here are Buster Keaton, Stan Laurel, Liberace, Charles Laughton, and Freddie Prinze. *6300 Forest Lawn Dr., Hollywood,* ☎ *213/254–7251.* ⏲ *Daily 8–5.*

Gene Autry Western Heritage Museum celebrates the American West, both the movie and real-life versions, with memorabilia, artifacts, and art in a structure that draws on Spanish Mission and early western architecture, located just north of the Los Angeles Zoo. The collection includes Teddy Roosevelt's Colt revolver, Buffalo Bill Cody's saddle, and Annie Oakley's gold-plated Smith and Wesson guns, alongside video screens showing clips from old westerns. *4700 W. Heritage Way, Los Angeles,* ☎ *213/667–2000.* ☛ *$7 adults, $5 senior citizens, $3 children 2–12.* ⏲ *Tues.–Sun. 10–5.*

★ **Griffith Park Observatory and Planetarium,** on the south side of Mt. Hollywood in the heart of Griffith Park, offers dazzling daily shows that duplicate the starry sky. A guide narrates the show and points out constellations. One of the largest telescopes in the world is open to the public for free viewing every clear night. Exhibits display models of the planets with photographs from satellites and spacecraft. The Laserium show is featured nightly, and other special astronomy shows are offered frequently. The outside decks and walkways offer a spectacular view of the city, very popular on warm evenings; you may recognize the location from *Rebel Without a Cause,* the James Dean movie classic. *Griffith Park,* ☎ *213/664–1191. Enter at Los Feliz Blvd. and Vermont Ave. entrance. Hall of Science and telescope are free. Planetarium shows: $4 adults, $3 senior citizens, $2 children. Laserium show: $6.50 adults, $5.50 children. Call for schedule.* ⏲ *Tues.–Fri. 2–10, weekends 12:30–10.*

Hollyhock House was the first of several houses Frank Lloyd Wright designed in the Los Angeles area. Built in 1921 and commissioned by heiress Aline Barnsdall, it exemplifies the pre-Columbian style Wright was fond of at that time. As a unifying theme, he used a stylized hollyhock flower, which appears in a broad band around the exterior of the house and even on the dining room chairs. Now owned by the city, as is Barnsdall Park, where it is located, Hollyhock House has been restored and furnished with original furniture designed by Wright and reproductions. His furniture may not be the comfiest in the world, but it sure looks perfect in his homes. *4800 Hollywood Blvd., Hollywood,*

☎ *213/662–7272.* ☛ *$2 adults, $1 senior citizens, children under 12 free. Tours conducted Tues.–Sun., at noon, 1, 2, and 3.*

Mulholland Drive, one of the most famous thoroughfares in Los Angeles, makes its very winding way from the Hollywood Hills across the spine of the Santa Monica Mountains west almost to the Pacific Ocean. Driving its length is slow, but the reward is sensational views of the city, the San Fernando Valley, and the expensive homes along the way. For a quick shot, take Benedict Canyon north from Sunset Boulevard, just west of the Beverly Hills Hotel, all the way to the top and turn right at the crest, which is Mulholland. There's a turnout within a few feet of the intersection, and at night, the view of the valley side is incredible.

University of Southern California (USC, or simply "SC" to locals) is the oldest major private university on the West Coast. The pleasant campus, which is home to nearly 30,000 students, is often used as a backdrop for television shows and movies. Two of the more notable of its 191 buildings are the Romanesque **Doheny Memorial Library** and **Widney Hall,** the oldest building on campus, a two-story clapboard dated 1880. The **Mudd Memorial Hall of Philosophy** contains a collection of rare books from the 13th through 15th centuries. *Bounded by Figueroa, Jefferson, Exposition, and Vermont, and adjacent to Exposition Park,* ☎ *213/740–2300. Free 1-hr campus tours weekdays 10–2, on the hr.*

Off the Beaten Track

El Mercado lies in East Los Angeles, the heart of the Mexican barrio. While Olvera Street draws both Mexican and gringo customers, this is the real thing: a huge, three-story marketplace that's a close cousin to places like Libertadad in Guadalajara. There are trinkets (piñatas and soft-clay pottery) to buy here, but the real draws are the authentic foods and mariachi music. The mid-level food shops offer hot tortillas, Mexican herbs, sauces, and cheeses. Upstairs is where the action is, especially on weekends, when several local mariachi bands stake out corners of the floor and entertain—all at the same time. The food on the top floor is only so-so, but the feeling of Old Mexico is palpable. *3425 E. 1st St., Los Angeles,* ☎ *213/268–3451.* ⏲ *Weekdays 10–8, later on weekends.*

The **Flower Market** (just east of downtown, in the 700 block of Wall Street) is a block-long series of stores and stalls that open up in the middle of the night to sell wholesale flowers and houseplants to the city's florists, who rush them to their shops to sell that day. Many of the stalls stay open until late morning to sell leftovers to the general public at the same bargain prices. And what glorious leftovers they are: Hawaiian ginger, Dutch tulips, Chilean freesia. The public is officially welcome after 9 AM, although many come earlier since the stock is quickly depleted. Even if you don't buy, it's a heady experience to be surrounded by so much fragile beauty.

Laurel and Hardy's Piano Stairway (923–927 Vendome St., in the Silver Lake section of Los Angeles, a few mi northeast of downtown) was the setting for the famous scene in 1932 film *The Music Box,* where Stan Laurel and Oliver Hardy try to get a piano up an outdoor stairway. The stairway remains today much as it was then.

Orcutt Ranch Horticultural Center (23600 Roscoe Blvd., Canoga Park, ☎ 818/883–6641; ☛ free), once owned by William Orcutt, a well-known geologist who was one of the excavators of the La Brea Tar Pits, is a surprisingly lush and varied garden in the west San Fernando Valley.

Orcutt is filled with interesting little areas to explore, such as the rose garden, herb garden, and streambank with shady trees and ferns (a wonderful picnic site). The first weekend after the 4th of July, the extensive orange and grapefruit groves are open for public picking. It's a chance to enjoy the Valley as it was in the years when groves like these covered the landscape for miles. You'll need an A-frame ladder or a special pole for dislodging the fruit up high. Bring along grocery sacks. ⏲ *Daily 8–5.*

Watts Towers is the folk-art legacy of an Italian immigrant tile-setter, Simon Rodia, and one of the great folk-art structures in the world. From 1920 until 1945, without helpers, this eccentric and driven man erected three cement towers, using pipes, bed frames, and anything else he could find, and embellished them with bits of colored glass, broken pottery, seashells, and assorted discards. The tallest tower is 107 feet. Plans are under way to stabilize and protect this unique monument, often compared to the 20th-century architectural wonders created by Barcelona's Antoni Gaudí. It's well worth a pilgrimage for art and architecture buffs (or anyone else, for that matter). *1765 E. 107th St., Los Angeles.*

SHOPPING

By Jane E. Lasky

When asked where they want to shop, visitors to Los Angeles inevitably answer, "Rodeo Drive." But this famous thoroughfare is only one of many enticing shopping streets in Los Angeles. There's also mall shopping, which in this metropolis is an experience unto itself—the mall is the modern-day Angeleno's equivalent of a main street, town square, back fence, malt shop, and county fair, all rolled into one. Distances between shopping spots can be vast, however, so don't choose too many different stops in one day—if you do, you'll spend more time driving than spending.

Most Los Angeles shops are open from 10 to 6, although many remain open until 9 or later, particularly at the shopping centers, on Melrose Avenue, and in Westwood Village during the summer. Melrose shops, on the whole, don't get moving until 11 AM but are often open Sunday, too. At most stores around town, credit cards are almost universally accepted and traveler's checks are also often allowed with proper identification. If you're looking for sales, check the *Los Angeles Times.*

Shopping Districts

Downtown

Although downtown Los Angeles has many enclaves to explore, we suggest that the bargain hunter head straight for the **Cooper Building** (860 S. Los Angeles St., ☎ 213/622–1139). Eight floors of small clothing and shoe shops (mostly for women) offer some of the most fantastic discounts in the city. Grab a free map in the lobby, and seek out as many of the 50 shops as you can handle. Nearby are myriad discount outlets selling everything from shoes to suits to linens.

Near the Hilton Hotel, **Seventh Street Marketplace** (735 S. Figueroa, ☎ 213/955–7150) is an indoor-outdoor multilevel shopping center with an extensive courtyard that boasts many busy cafés and lively music. The stores surrounding this courtyard include **G. B. Harb** (☎ 213/624–4785), a fine shop for fashion, and **Bullock's** (☎ 213/624–9494), a small version of the big department store, geared to the businessperson.

Melrose Avenue

West Hollywood, especially Melrose Avenue, is where young shoppers should try their luck, as should those who appreciate vintage styles in clothing and furnishings. The 1½ miles of Melrose from La Brea to a few blocks west of Crescent Heights is definitely one of Los Angeles's trendiest shopping areas, with loads of intriguing one-of-a-kind shops and bistros; both east and west of this delineation, Melrose has some other very worthwhile stores, too. *See* the Westside, *above,* for other stores along Melrose. A sampling of Melrose stores:

Betsey Johnson (7311 Melrose Ave., ☎ 213/931–4490) offers the designer's vivid, hip women's fashions. Watch for twice-yearly sales. **Comme des Fous** (7384 Melrose Ave., ☎ 213/653–5330) is an avant-garde (and pricey) clothing shop packed with innovative European designs. **Cottura** (7215 Melrose Ave., ☎ 213/933–1928) offers brightly colored Italian ceramics. **Emphasis** (7361 Melrose Ave., ☎ 213/653–7174) sells trendy women's clothing, as well as hats, belts, accessories, and a selection of unique lingerie. **Fantasies Come True** (8012 Melrose Ave., ☎ 213/655–2636) greets you with "When You Wish upon a Star" playing from a tape deck. The store, needless to say, is packed with Walt Disney memorabilia. **Fred Segal** (8118 Melrose Ave., ☎ 213/651–1935) has a collection of shops that provide stylish clothing for men and women. Among the designers and manufacturers they carry: Nancy Heller, New Man, Ralph Lauren, Calvin Klein. Children's clothing, accessories, and shoes—an impressive array—are also stocked at the Melrose store.

L.A. Eyeworks (7407 Melrose Ave., ☎ 213/653–8255) is a hip boutique; frame-wise, whatever's next in style around the globe will probably show up first in this leading-edge L.A. shop. **Modern Living** (8125 Melrose Ave., ☎ 213/655–3898) is a gallery of 20th-century design, representing renowned international furniture designers, including Philippe Starck, Ettore Sottsass, and Massino Iosaghini. **Off the Wall** (7325 Melrose Ave., ☎ 213/930–1185) specializes in "antiques and weird stuff": translation—20th-century nostalgia items such as rare Bakelite radios, vintage vending machines, and period furnishings. **Pole** (7378 Melrose Ave., ☎ 213/653–3784) offers very progressive women's clothing, with predominantly French labels like Morgan, Tehen, and Kookai. **Texas Soul** (7515 Melrose Ave., ☎ 213/658–5571) is a popular shop for western footwear made in the Lone Star State. **Time After Time** (7425 Melrose Ave., ☎ 213/653–8463), decorated to resemble a Victorian garden, has garments ranging from turn-of-the-century to the 1960s, especially antique wedding dresses. **Wacko** (7416 Melrose Ave., ☎ 213/651–3811) is a wild space crammed with all manner of blow-up toys, cards, and other semi-useless items that make good Los Angeles keepsakes. **The Wasteland** (7428 Melrose Ave., ☎ 213/653–3028) carries an extensive collection of retro clothing, both used and never-worn, all reasonably priced. It's a fun place to shop for '50s bowling shirts, '40s rayon dresses, funky ties, worn jeans, and leather jackets. **Wild Blue** (7220 Melrose Ave., ☎ 213/939–8434) is a fine shop-gallery specializing in functional and wearable art created by exceptional contemporary artists, many of whom hail from the L.A. area. **Wound and Wound** (7374 Melrose Ave., ☎ 213/653–6703) has an impressive collection of windup toys and music boxes.

Larchmont

One of L.A.'s most picturesque streets is Larchmont Boulevard, adjacent to the expensive residential neighborhood of Hancock Park. Stores that make Larchmont Village worth a detour include **Hollyhock** (214

N. Larchmont Blvd., ☎ 213/931–3400), for exceptional new and antique furnishings; **Lavender & Lace** (660 N. Larchmont Blvd., ☎ 213/856–4846), specializing in antique textiles, linens, and English pine furniture; **My Favorite Place** (202 N. Larchmont Blvd., ☎ 213/461–5713), for comfortable women's clothing—silks and ethnic pieces in particular; and **Robert Grounds** (119 N. Larchmont Blvd., ☎ 213/464–8304), for distinctive gifts and antiques.

Westwood

Westwood Village, near the UCLA campus, is a young and lively area for shopping. The atmosphere is invigorating, especially on summer evenings when there are movie lines around every corner, all kinds of people strolling the streets (an unusual phenomenon in L.A., where few folks walk anywhere), and cars cruising along to take in the scene. Among the shops worth scouting out in this part of the city:

Aah's (1083 Broxton, ☎ 310/824–1688) is good for stationery and fun gift items. **Copeland's Sporting Goods** (1001 Westwood Blvd., ☎ 310/208–6444) offers a cornucopia of sportswear, beachwear, shoes, and shorts, along with a variety of skiing, camping, and other outdoor equipment. **Morgan and Company** (1131 Glendon, ☎ 310/208–3377) is recommended for California jewelry. **Sisterhood Book Store** (1351 Westwood Blvd., ☎ 310/477–7300) stocks an incredible collection of women's books in all areas—history, health, and psychology among them. **Wilger Company** (10924 Weyburn, ☎ 310/208–4321) offers fine men's clothing with a conservative look, most of it carrying the store's own private label, though other lines like Polo are also stocked.

Beverly Center and Environs

The **Beverly Center** (☎ 310/854–0070), bound by Beverly Boulevard, La Cienega Boulevard, San Vicente Boulevard, and 3rd Street, covers more than 7 acres and contains some 200 stores. Call the Center for information about any of the shops. Examples are **By Design** for contemporary home furnishings; **Shauna Stein** and **Ice** for fashionable (and very pricey) women's clothes; **Alexio,** for fashionable men's garments; and two stores called **Traffic** for contemporary clothing for both genders. One of the more innovative and popular stores here is **MAC,** which offers a line of professional makeup at reasonable prices, sold by knowledgeable staff who help with quick-to-apply beauty hints.

The shopping center is anchored by **The Broadway** department store on one end and **Bullock's** on the other, and it has one of Los Angeles's finest multitheater complexes, with 14 individual movie theaters. Interesting restaurants include **California Pizza Kitchen** (though this may change in 1996) renowned for its unusual designer pies (like Tandoori Chicken Pizza and Thai Pizza) and healthy salads, and the **Hard Rock Cafe,** known for its bargain cuisine and fascinating decor, including a 1959 Caddy that dives into the roof of the building above the restaurant.

Directly across the street from the Beverly Center, on the east side of La Cienega between Beverly Boulevard and 3rd Street, is another mall, the **Beverly Connection** (100 N. La Cienega, ☎ 213/651–3611). Among the shops here: **Book Star** (☎ 213/289–1734) is a giant warehouse-like store selling every conceivable sort of reading material at low prices. **Old Navy** (☎ 213/658–5292) is a bottom-of-the-line clothing store hawking all sorts of sweats, shirts, and jeans. **Rexall Square Drug** (☎ 213/653–0880), a.k.a. "Drugstore of the Stars," is where people like Dustin Hoffman and Goldie Hawn have been seen lurking in the amply stocked aisles filled with over-the-counter drugs, cleaning supplies, jewelry, cosmetics, and lots of imaginative gifts. **Sports Chalet** (☎

213/657–3210) is one of the premier places in southern California to buy athletic equipment.

In the immediate neighborhood, **Charlie's** (8234 W. 3rd. St., ☎ 213/653–3657) sells a cornucopia of '40s, '50s, and '60s clothing, vintage evening gowns in impeccable condition and wild, wonderful hats designed by the namesake owner. **Cheap Frills** (8325 W. 3rd St., ☎ 213/653–9997) has an excellent selection of dance wear, from leotards to jazz shoes to cover-ups. **Freehand** (8413 W. 3rd St., ☎ 213/655–2607) carries contemporary American crafts, clothing, and jewelry, mostly by California artists. **Trashy Lingerie** (402 N. La Cienega, ☎ 310/652–4543) is just what the name suggests. This is a place for the daring; models try on the sexy garments to help customers decide what to buy.

Century City

Century City Shopping Center & Marketplace (☎ 310/277–3898), set among gleaming, tall office buildings on what used to be Twentieth Century Fox Film Studios' back lot, is an open-air mall. Besides Bullock's department store there are some excellent shops. **Wild Pair** (10250 Santa Monica Blvd., ☎ 310/203–8769) has trendy shoes and bags. The **Pottery Barn** (10250 Santa Monica Blvd., ☎ 310/552–0170) is a great source for contemporary furnishings and glassware. **Card Fever** (10250 Santa Monica Blvd., ☎ 310/553–7332) is a whimsical boutique with fun and funky messages to send. **Brentano's** (10250 Santa Monica Blvd., ☎ 310/785–0204) is one of the city's largest bookstores. **Gelson's** is a gourmet food market.

There are many restaurants on the premises, among them **Houston's,** which gets down with its American fare of grilled fish and steak, and **Stage Deli,** the kind of New York–style deli that previously was hard to find in L.A. Also at Century City is the **AMC Century** 14-screen movie complex.

West Los Angeles

The **Westside Pavilion** (☎ 310/474–6255) is a pastel-color postmodern mall on Pico and Overland boulevards, a couple minutes' drive from Century City. The three levels of shops and restaurants run the gamut from high-fashion boutiques for men and women to toy stores and housewares shops. Among them are the **Disney Store** (☎ 310/474–7022); **Robinsons-May** (☎ 310/475–4911) and **Nordstrom** (☎ 310/470–6155) department stores; **Mr. Gs for Toys** (☎ 310/475–9554), a good place for children's gifts; **Barami** (☎ 310/470–4742) for women's designer clothing; and **Victoria's Secret** (☎ 310/441-5007), a scented lingerie boutique. Worth visiting even if you're not here to shop is **Sisley Italian Kitchen** (☎ 310/446–3030), which serves California-Italian dishes, pizzas, and terrific salads.

Santa Monica

Third Street Promenade (☎ 310/393–8355) is a pedestrians-only street lined with boutiques, movie theaters, clubs, pubs, and restaurants. It's as busy at night as it is in the day, with wacky street performers to entertain as you mosey along.

Along **Montana Avenue,** a stretch of a dozen or so blocks from 7th to 17th streets, showcases boutique after boutique of quality goods, many of them exclusive to this street. Among the more interesting: **ABS Clothing** (1533 Montana Ave., ☎ 310/393–8770) sells contemporary sportswear designed in Los Angeles. **Brenda Cain** (1211 Montana Ave., ☎ 310/395–1559) features nostalgic clothes, antique jewelry, and an amazing array of Hawaiian shirts for men and women. **Brenda Himmel** (1126 Montana Ave., ☎ 310/395–2437) is known for its fine stationery, but antiques, frames, photo albums, and books also enhance this homey boutique. **Lisa Norman Lingerie** (1134 Montana Ave., ☎ 310/451–2026) sells high-quality lingerie from Europe and the United States—slips, camisoles, robes, silk stockings, and at-home clothes.

Weathervane II (1209 Montana, ☎ 310/393–5344) is one of the street's larger shops, with a friendly staff who make browsing among the classic and offbeat fashions more fun.

The stretch of **Main Street** leading from Santa Monica to Venice (Pico Blvd. to Rose Ave.) is another of those rare places in Los Angeles where you can indulge in a pleasant walk. While enjoying the ocean breeze, you'll pass some good restaurants and unusual shops and galleries. **Arts & Letters** (2665A Main St., ☎ 310/392–9076) is a stationery boutique carrying many picture frames and personalized gift items. **Bootz** (2736 Main St., ☎ 310/396–2466) stocks an incredible array of western footwear. **Malina** (2654C Main St., ☎ 310/392–2611) sells French fashions like Le Petit Bateau for children and Kenzo for women, as well as the store's own line.

Farther down the street, where Santa Monica turns into Venice, is an area known as **Abbott Kinney,** a quiet artists' colony amid what is otherwise the wilder part of town. Among its galleries, cafés, boutiques, and antiques shops, look for the **Psychic Eye Bookstore** (218 Main St., ☎ 310/396–0110), a spiritual haven selling wind chimes, incense, and crystal jewelry, as well as books on sorcery and other occult subjects.

San Fernando and San Gabriel Valleys

This is mall country; among the many from which to choose are **Sherman Oaks Galleria** (15301 Ventura Blvd., Sherman Oaks, ☎ 818/783–7100) and **The Promenade** (6100 Topanga Canyon Blvd., ☎ 818/884–7090) in Woodland Hills, **Glendale Galleria** (2148 Central Blvd., ☎ 818/240–9481) and **Encino Town Center** and **Plaza de Oro** (☎ 818/788–6100) in Encino. The **Cranberry House** (12318 Ventura Blvd., StudioCity, ☎ 818/506–8945) is a huge shopping arena covering half a city block, packed with 140 kiosks run by L.A.'s leading antiques dealers. Come here for vintage furniture, clothing, jewelry, and furnishings.

Beverly Hills

We've saved the most famous section of town for last. **Rodeo Drive** is often compared to such famous streets as 5th Avenue in New York and the Via Condotti in Rome. Along the couple of blocks between Wilshire and Santa Monica boulevards, you'll find an abundance of big-name retailers—but don't shop Beverly Hills without shopping the streets that surround illustrious Rodeo Drive. There are plenty of treasures to be purchased on those other thoroughfares as well.

Even Beverly Hills has a couple of shopping centers, although owners wouldn't dare call their collection of stores and cafés "malls." The **Rodeo Collection** (421 N. Rodeo Dr. ☎ 310/276–9600), between Brighton Way and Santa Monica Boulevard, is nothing less than the epitome of opulence and high fashion. Many famous upscale European designers opened their doors in this piazza-like area of marble and brass. Among them: **Fila** (☎ 310/276–1732), for the best in sports gear; **Mondi** (☎ 310/274–8380), for high-style German fashions; and **Gianni Versace** (☎ 310/276–6799), for trendsetting Italian designs.

A collection of glossy retail shops called **Two Rodeo Drive** (a.k.a. Via Rodeo, on the corner of Rodeo Dr. and Wilshire Blvd., ☎ 310/247-7040) is housed on a private cobblestone street that somewhat resembles a Hollywood back lot. Amid the Italianate piazza, outdoor cafés, and sculpted fountains of Two Rodeo are some two dozen boutiques, including **Christian Dior** (☎ 310/859-4700), for couture fashions known the world over; **Davidoff of Geneva** (☎ 310/278–8884), for the finest tobacco and accessories; **Gian Franco Ferre** (☎ 310/273–6311), for quality Italian designs; and **A. Sulka** (☎ 310/859–9940), a noted men's haberdasher.

The Beverly Hills branch of **Saks Fifth Avenue** (9600 Wilshire Blvd., ☎ 310/275–4211) isn't as impressive as the one you'll find next to St. Patrick's Cathedral in Manhattan. Still, the buyers have good taste. **Barneys New York** (9570 Wilshire, ☎ 310/276–4400) took up shop in Beverly Hills in 1994. The West Coast branch of this uptown and very hip Manhattan store is especially popular with Gen-Xers who come for the cutting-edge (and pricey) designer clothing (including threads by Comme des Garçons, Giorgio Armani, Donna Karan, and Azzedine Alaia), as well as a pristine collection of home furnishings in its Chelsea Passage department on the second floor. Don't forget your sunglasses when you visit; this cool, chic department store is so open and airy that it is not at all unusual to see shoppers donning shades as they scope the shelves and racks in this new neo-Spanish monument to the quintessential consumer.

Some of the many other shops, boutiques, and department stores in Beverly Hills:

FASHIONS AND HOME DECOR

Emporio Armani Boutique (9533 Brighton Way, ☎ 310/271–7790) hangs the lower-priced line of this famous Italian designer, as well as his accessories and perfumes. At the top of the premises is the upscale Italian restaurant **Armani Express** (☎ 310/271–9940). **Oilily** (9520 Brighton Way, ☎ 310/859–9145) features fun, colorful clothing and gift items (like stationery and umbrellas) for women, children, and even infants. All are exclusively designed in Holland for this store. **Polo/Ralph Lauren** (444 N. Rodeo Dr., ☎ 310/281–7200) serves up a complete presentation of Lauren's all-encompassing lifestyle philosophy. The men's area, reminiscent of a posh British men's club, offers rough wear and active wear. Some 200 antiques are used as a backdrop for the women's area. Upstairs resides the world's most extensive selection of Lauren's home-furnishing designs.

GIFTS

Hammacher-Schlemmer (309 N. Rodeo Dr., ☎ 310/859–7255) is a fabulous place to unearth those hard-to-find presents for adults who never grew up.

JEWELRY

Cartier (370 N. Rodeo Dr., ☎ 310/275–4272) offers all manner of luxury gifts and jewelry. **Tiffany and Company** (210 N. Rodeo Dr., ☎ 310/273–8880), the famous name in fine jewelry, silver, and more, packages each purchase in a signature blue Tiffany box. **Van Cleef and Arpels** (300 N. Rodeo Dr., ☎ 310/276–1161) sells expensive baubles and fine jewelry.

MEN'S FASHIONS

Alfred Dunhill of London (201 N. Rodeo Dr., ☎ 310/274–5351) is an elegant shop selling British-made suits, shirts, sweaters, and slacks. Pipes, tobacco, and cigars, however, are this store's claim to fame. **Battaglia** (306 N. Rodeo Dr., ☎ 310/276–7184) features accessories, shoes, and men's apparel—the richest Italian fashions in luxurious silks, woolens, cottons, and cashmeres. **Bernini** (362 N. Rodeo Dr., ☎ 310/278–6287) specializes in contemporary Italian designer fashions. Look for fine leather accessories from Giorgio Armani. **Bijan** (420 N. Rodeo Dr., ☎ 310/273–6544) is a store where it helps to make an appointment. Bijan claims that many Arabian sheikhs and other royalty shop here, along with some of the wealthiest men in the United States. Many designs are created especially by the owner. It's known for quality, service, and its exclusive clientele. **Cyril's** (370 N. Beverly Dr., ☎ 310/278–1330) features fine clothing in the latest European styles and carries labels like Cerruti and Haupt.

WOMEN'S FASHIONS

Alan Austin and Company (184 N. Canon Dr., ☎ 310/275–1162) has traditional clothing in a wide selection of fabrics. The store manufactures its own designs, so clothing can be made to order. **Ann Taylor** (357 N. Camden Dr., ☎ 310/858–7840) is the flagship shop of this chain of women's clothing stores, offering the epitome of the young executive look. **Celine** (460 N. Rodeo Dr., ☎ 310/273–1243) is for luggage, shoes, and accessories as well as traditionally tailored clothing made of fine fabrics. **Chanel** (400 N. Rodeo Dr., ☎ 310/278–5500), known for its fashions and cosmetics, now also features fine jewelry, including copies of the original Coco designs popular in the 1920s and '30s. **Fred Hayman** (273 N. Rodeo Dr., ☎ 310/271–3000) is an illustrious store where one does not merely shop for glitzy American and European clothing, accessories, and footwear; one also refreshes oneself at the stunning Oak Bar. **Theodore** (453 N. Rodeo Dr., ☎ 310/276–9691) offers trendy items in fabulous fabrics for men and women from Kenzo, Sonia Rykiel, Issey Miyake, and Donna Karan. Everything is done with a real eye for color.

Department Stores

All of the following have branches in and around Los Angeles:

The Broadway (the Beverly Center, 8500 Beverly Blvd., ☎ 310/854–7200) offers merchandise in the moderate price range, from cosmetics to housewares to linens to clothing for men and women.

Bullock's (the Beverly Center, 8500 Beverly Blvd., ☎ 310/854–6655), which is more upscale than The Broadway, carries an extensive collection of clothing for men and women, as well as housewares and cosmetics.

Nordstrom (Westside Pavilion, 10830 W. Pico Blvd., West Los Angeles, ☎ 310/470–6155) carries a wide selection of clothing and shoes for men and women. It's known for attentive customer service.

Robinsons-May (9900 Wilshire Blvd., ☎ 310/275–5464) is a high-end department store that has many women's selections, a few men's selections and a good housewares department.

Note: As we were going to press, it was announced that Federated Department Stores had bought the parent company of The Broadway and would begin converting the stores into Bullock's, Macy's, or Bloomingdale's stores in early 1996.

Specialty Shops

Antiques

La Cienega Boulevard, between Santa Monica Boulevard and Beverly Boulevard, is lined with antiques dealers selling everything from Chinese to French to Viennese collectibles. Nearby lies L.A.'s poshest antiquarian niche: the 8400 block of Melrose Place.

Books

Bodhi Tree (8585 Melrose Ave., West Hollywood, ☎ 310/659–1733) carries books on metaphysical subjects. **Book Soup** (8818 Sunset Blvd., West Hollywood, ☎ 310/659–3110) stocks a wide variety of volumes, with particularly strong photography, film, new fiction, and international magazines sections.

Leather

North Beach Leather (8500 Sunset Blvd., West Hollywood, ☎ 310/652–3224) has a great selection of clothing made of leather and suede, for both men and women.

Musical Recordings

Aron's Records (1150 N. Highland Ave., ☎ 213/469–4700) carries an extensive selection of old records, perhaps the largest on the West Coast, and has low prices on new albums. **Rockaway** (2395 Glendale Blvd., Silverlake, ☎ 213/664–3232) is one of L.A.'s best CD stores for hard-to-find and used discs.

SPORTS, FITNESS, BEACHES

Participant Sports and the Outdoors

There are almost as many sports in Los Angeles as there are people. The following list is a compilation of the more popular activities. For any additional information on facilities closer to where you're staying or on other sports not listed, two agencies can assist you: **City of Los Angeles Department of Recreation and Parks** (200 N. Main St., Suite 1380, City Hall East, Los Angeles 90012, ☎ 213/485–5515); **Los Angeles County Parks and Recreation Department** (433 S. Vermont Ave., Los Angeles 90020, ☎ 213/738–2961).

Bicycling

Perhaps the most famous bike path in the city, and definitely the most beautiful, can be found on the **Pacific Ocean beach,** from Temescal Canyon down to Redondo Beach. **San Vicente Boulevard** in Santa Monica has a nice, wide cycling lane next to the sidewalk that runs for about 5 miles. **Balboa Park** in the San Fernando Valley is another haven for two-wheelers, as is the marked path for cyclers that traverses **Griffith Park** (entrance is at intersection of Riverside Drive and Los Feliz Boulevard). **L.A. County Parks and Recreation Department** (*see above*) has a map of bike trails.

Billiards and Bowling

Hollywood Athletic Club (6525 W. Sunset Blvd., ☎ 213/962–6600) has full-size vintage snooker tables and a tournament room. Bowling hours vary at **Sports Center Bowl** in the Valley (12655 Ventura Blvd., Studio City, ☎ 818/769–7600) and **Hollywood Star Lanes** (5227 Santa Monica Blvd., East Hollywood, ☎ 213/665–4111).

Fishing

The best lakes for **freshwater fishing** in the area are Big Bear and Arrowhead in the San Bernardino National Forest, east of Los Angeles about two hours (*see* Excursion to Big Bear/Lake Arrowhead, *below*). Call for fishing information in the area (☎ 909/866–5796).

Shore fishing and surf casting are excellent on many of the beaches (*see* Beaches, *below*). The Malibu, Santa Monica, and Redondo Beach piers each offer nearby bait-and-tackle shops. If you want to break away from the piers, however, the **Malibu Pier Sport Fishing Company** (23000 Pacific Coast Hwy., ☎ 310/456–8030) offers boat excursions for $20 per half day. The **Redondo Sport Fishing Company** (233 N. Harbor Dr., ☎ 310/372–2111) has various excursions available. Half-day charters start at $19 per person and a full day goes for $65. You can rent a pole for $7 and you'll need a license, which will cost $6.55. Sea bass, halibut, bonita, yellowtail, and barracuda are the usual catch.

Skipper's Twenty Second Street Landing (141 W. 22nd St., San Pedro, ☎ 310/832–8304) offers an overnight charter. These boats, complete with bunk beds and full galley, leave at 10 PM and 10:30 PM and dock between 5 PM and 9 PM the next night. Per-person price is $60. Day charters are available as well, at $28–$40, with half-day excursions on weekends for $22.

The most popular and unquestionably the most unusual form of fishing in the L.A. area involves no hooks, bait, or poles. The great **grunion runs,** which take place March–August, are a spectacular natural phenomenon in which hundreds of thousands of small silver fish, called grunion, wash up on southern California beaches to spawn and lay their eggs in the sand. The **Cabrillo Marine Aquarium** in San Pedro (☎ 310/548–7562; *see* Palos Verdes, San Pedro, and Long Beach, *above*) has entertaining and educational programs about grunion throughout most of their spawning season. During certain months it is prohibited to touch the grunion, so please check with the Fish and Game Department (☎ 310/590–5132) before going to see them wash ashore.

Golf

The Department of Parks and Recreation lists seven public 18-hole courses in Los Angeles. **Rancho Park Golf Course** (10460 W. Pico Blvd., ☎ 310/838–7373) is a beautifully designed course. There's a two-level driving range, a nine-hole pitch 'n' putt (☎ 310/839–4374), a snack bar, and a pro shop where you can rent clubs.

Several good public courses are in the San Fernando Valley. The **Balboa and Encino Golf Courses** (16821 Burbank Blvd., Encino, ☎ 818/995–1170) are right next to each other. The **Woodley Lakes Golf Course** (6331 Woodley Ave., Van Nuys, ☎ 818/780–6886) is flat as a board and has hardly any trees. In summer, however, the temperature in the Valley can get high enough to fry an egg on your putter. Down the road in Pacoima is the **Hansen Dam Public Golf Course** (10400 Glen Oaks Blvd., ☎ 818/899–2200).

Perhaps the most concentrated area of golf courses in the city can be found in **Griffith Park. Harding Golf Course** and **Wilson Golf Course** (both at 4730 Crystal Springs Dr., ☎ 213/663–2555; 18 holes) are about 1½ miles inside the park entrance at Riverside Drive and Los Feliz Boulevard. The nine-hole **Roosevelt Course** (2650 N. Vermont Ave., ☎ 213/665–2011) can be reached through the park's Hillhurst Street entrance.

Also near Griffith Park is the nine-hole **Los Feliz Pitch 'n' Putt** (3207 Los Feliz Blvd., ☎ 213/663–7758). Other pitch 'n' putt courses include **Holmby Hills** (601 Club View Dr., West Los Angeles, ☎ 310/276–1604) and **Penmar** (1233 Rose Ave., Venice, ☎ 310/396–6228).

MINIATURE GOLF

Sherman Oaks Castle Park (4989 Sepulveda Blvd., Sherman Oaks, ☎ 818/756–9459) is the San Fernando Valley's Cadillac of minicourses. Another option: **Arroyo Seco Miniature Golf Course** (1055 Lohman La., South Pasadena, ☎ 213/255–1506).

Health Clubs

Bally's Nautilus Aerobics Plus and **Bally's Holiday Spa Health Club and Sports Connection** are the most popular local chains. The Holiday

Club between Hollywood and Sunset boulevards (1628 El Centro, ☎ 213/461–0227) is the flagship operation. This place has everything, including racquetball courts, indoor running tracks, pools, men's and women's weight and aerobics rooms, and a juice bar. To find the Bally's nearest you, call 800/695–8111. **Gold's Gym** has branches in Venice (358 Hampton Dr., ☎ 310/392–6004) and Hollywood (1016 N. Cole Ave., ☎ 213/462–7012); fees are $15 a day or $50 a week. At **Powerhouse Gym** (8053 Beverly Blvd., West Hollywood, ☎ 213/651–3636), fees are $10 a day and $40 a week.

DANCE AND WORKOUT STUDIOS

The trendy **Voight Fitness Center** (980 N. La Cienega Blvd., West Hollywood, ☎ 310/854–0741) provides the latest in hip hop, step, and funk moves. **Studio A's** (2306 Hyperion Ave., Silverlake, ☎ 213/661–8311) offers user-friendly aerobics, jazz, and ballet classes.

Hiking

Will Rogers Historic State Park, off Sunset Boulevard near Pacific Palisades, has a splendid nature trail that climbs from the polo fields to the mountaintop where you can get a spectacular view of the ocean. Other parks in the L.A. area that also have hiking trails include **Brookside Park, Elysian Park,** and **Griffith Park.** In the Malibu area, **Leo Carillo State Beach** and the top of **Corral Canyon** have incredible rock formations and caves to be explored on foot. For additional hiking information, contact the **Sierra Club** (3345 Wilshire Blvd., Suite 508, Los Angeles 90010, ☎ 213/387–4287).

Horseback Riding

Stables that rent horses are becoming an endangered species. Of the survivors, **Bar "S" Stables** (1850 Riverside Dr., Glendale, ☎ 818/242–8443) will rent you a horse for $13 an hour (plus a $10 deposit). Riders who come here can take advantage of more than 50 miles of beautiful bridle trails in the Griffith Park area. **Sunset River Trails** (Rush St., at end of Peck Rd., El Monte, ☎ 818/444–2128) offers riders the nearby banks of the San Gabriel River to explore at $15 an hour. **Los Angeles Equestrian Center** (480 Riverside Dr., Burbank, ☎ 818/840–8401) rents pleasure horses—English and Western—for riding along bridle paths throughout the Griffith Park hills. Horses cost $13 per hour. **Sunset Ranch** (3400 Beachwood Dr., Hollywood, ☎ 213/469–5450) offers a $35 adventure (not including the cost of dinner). At sunset riders take a trail over the hill into Burbank, where they tie up their horses and dine at a Mexican restaurant.

Ice-Skating

In the Valley, there's the **Pickwick Ice Center** (1001 Riverside Dr., Burbank, ☎ 818/846–0032). In Pasadena, try the **Ice Skating Center** (310 E. Green St., ☎ 818/578–0800) and, in Rolling Hills, try the **Culver City Ice Arena** (4545 Sepulveda Ave., ☎ 310/398–5718).

In-line and Roller Skating

The areas mentioned in Bicycling (*see above*) are also excellent for in-line and roller skating, though cyclists have the right of way. Venice Beach is the skating capital of the city—and maybe of the world. Two popular rinks are **Moonlight Rollerway** (5110 San Fernando Rd., Glendale, ☎ 818/241–3630) and **Skateland** (18140 Parthenia St., Northridge, ☎ 818/885–1491).

Jogging

Just about every local high school and college in the city has a track. Most are public and welcome runners. A popular scenic course for students and downtown workers can be found at **Exposition Park.** Circling the **Coliseum and Sports Arena** is a jogging-workout trail with pull-up bars and other simple equipment placed every several hundred yards. **San Vicente Boulevard** in Santa Monica has a wide grassy median that splits the street for several picturesque miles. The **Hollywood Reservoir,** just east of Cahuenga Boulevard in the Hollywood Hills, is encircled by a 3.2-mile asphalt path and has a view of the Hollywood sign. Within hilly **Griffith Park** are thousands of acres' worth of hilly paths and challenging terrain, while Crystal Springs Drive from the main entrance at Los Feliz to the zoo is a relatively flat 5 miles. Circle Drive, around the perimeter of **UCLA** in Westwood, provides a 2½-mile run through academia, L.A.-style.

Racquetball and Handball

Racquet Center (10933 Ventura Blvd., Studio City, ☎ 818/760–2303), in the San Fernando Valley, offers court time for $10–$14, depending on when you play. There's another Racquet Center in South Pasadena (920 Lohman La., ☎ 213/258–4178).

Tennis

Many public parks have courts that require an hourly fee. **Lincoln Park** (Lincoln and Wilshire Blvd., Santa Monica), **Griffith Park** (Riverside Dr. and Los Feliz Blvd.), and **Barrington Park** (Barrington just south of Sunset Blvd. in L.A.) all have well-maintained courts with lights. There are several nice courts on the campus of **USC** (off Vermont St. entrance), a few on the campus of **Paul Revere Junior High School** (Sunset Blvd. and Mandeville Canyon Rd., Brentwood), and a few more at **Palisades High School** (Temescal Canyon Rd., Pacific Palisades)—and that's only the tip of this iceberg. For a list of the public courts, contact the **L.A. Department of Recreation and Parks** (☎ 213/485–5515) or the **Southern California Tennis Association** (Los Angeles Tennis Center, UCLA Campus, 420 Circle Dr., Los Angeles 90024, ☎ 310/208–3838).

Water Sports

BOATING AND KAYAKING

Rent-A-Sail (13719 Fiji Way, Marina del Rey, ☎ 310/822–1868) will rent you everything from canoes to powerboats or 14- to 25-foot sailboats for anywhere from $16 to $36 per hour plus a $20 deposit. **Action Water Sports** (4144 Lincoln Blvd., Marina del Rey, ☎ 310/306–9539) rents kayaks for $35 per day during the summer.

SCUBA DIVING AND SNORKELING

Diving and snorkeling off Leo Carillo State Beach, Catalina, and the Channel Islands is considered some of the best on the Pacific coast. Dive shops, such as **New England Divers** (4148 Viking Way, Long Beach, ☎ 310/421–8939) and **Dive & Surf** (504 N. Broadway, Redondo Beach, ☎ 310/372–8423), will provide you with everything you need. Snorkeling equipment runs $9–$14 per day, while full scuba gear for certified divers runs $50–$62.50 per day, with prices cut for subsequent days.

SURFING

The signature water sport in L.A. is surfing. For the best surfing areas, *see* Beaches, *below.*

SWIMMING POOLS

Pacific Park Pool (☎ 818/247–1397), affiliated with the Glendale YMCA, in Glendale on the corner of Riverdale Drive and Pacific Avenue is a popular spot. The **Griffith Park** pool (☎ 213/665–4372) at the intersection of Los Feliz Boulevard and Riverside Drive is another favorite splash point, as is the **North Hollywood Park** public pool (☎ 818/763–7651) off the Hollywood Freeway at Magnolia Avenue, in the San Fernando Valley.

WATER PARKS AND WINDSURFING

Raging Waters (☎ 909/592–6453), off I–210 in San Dimas, is a sort of aquatic Disneyland. It's open daily mid-June–mid-September; weekends only, mid-April–mid-June and late September–October. There are a number of places from which to rent equipment for certified windsurfers. **Natural Progression** (22935 Pacific Coast Hwy., Malibu, ☎ 310/456–6302) leases windsurfing equipment for about $40 per day.

Spectator Sports

Some of the major sports venues in the area are **Anaheim Stadium** (2000 Gene Autry Way, Anaheim, ☎ 714/254–3100), **Great Western Forum** (3900 W. Manchester, Inglewood, ☎ 310/673–1773), **Los Angeles Memorial Coliseum** (3911 S. Figueroa, downtown, ☎ 213/748–6131), and **L.A. Sports Arena** (downtown, next to Coliseum, at 3939 S. Figueroa, ☎ 213/748–6131).

Baseball

The National League **Los Angeles Dodgers** play at Dodger Stadium (1000 Elysian Park Ave., exit off I–110, the Pasadena Fwy.; for ticket information, call 213/224–1400). The American League **California Angels** play at Anaheim Stadium (2000 Gene Autry Way, ☎ 714/634–2000).

Basketball

The **Los Angeles Lakers'** home court is the Forum; for ticket information, call 310/419–3182. L.A.'s "other" NBA team, the **Clippers,** make their home at the L.A. Sports Arena; for ticket information, call 213/748–8000. The **University of Southern California** (for tickets, ☎ 213/740–2311) plays at the L.A. Sports Arena, and the Bruins of the **University of California at Los Angeles** (for tickets, ☎ 310/825–2101) play at Pauley Pavilion on the UCLA campus.

Football

Los Angeles lost both its NFL teams in 1995, the Rams to St. Louis and the Raiders to Oakland. The city will likely get the league's next expansion team (or another city's franchise), perhaps as soon as 1997. The Los Angeles Memorial Coliseum is home turf for the **USC Trojans** (for tickets, ☎ 213/740–2311). The **UCLA Bruins** (for tickets, ☎ 310/825–2101) pack 'em in at the Rose Bowl in Pasadena.

Hockey

The **L.A. Kings** (for tickets, ☎ 310/673–6003) put their show on ice at the Forum and Disney's **Mighty Ducks** (for tickets, ☎ 714/704–2500) push the puck at The Pond in Anaheim, October–April.

Horse Racing

Santa Anita Race Track (Huntington Dr. and Colorado Pl., Arcadia, ☎ 818/574–7223; late Dec.–Apr., Oct.–mid-Nov.) is still the dominant site for thoroughbred racing. **Hollywood Park** (Century Boulevard and Prairie, ☎ 310/419–1500; Apr.–mid-July, mid-Nov.–Dec. 24) is another favorite racing venue. Since the completion of the Hollywood Park Casino in 1994, a sense of class and style has been restored to this nostalgic park. For harness racing, **Los Alamitos** (4961 Katella Ave., Anaheim, ☎ 714/995–1234) has both day and night racing.

Beaches

From downtown, the easiest way to hit the coast is by taking the Santa Monica Freeway (I–10) due west. Once you reach the end of the freeway, I–10 turns into the famous Highway 1, better known as the Pacific Coast Highway, or PCH, and continues up to Oregon. Other basic routes from the downtown area include Pico, Olympic, Santa Monica, Sunset, and Wilshire boulevards. The RTD bus line runs every 20 minutes to and from the beaches along each of these streets.

Los Angeles County beaches (and state beaches operated by the county) have lifeguards. Public parking (for a fee) is available at most. The following beaches are listed in north–south order. Some are excellent for swimming, some for surfing (check with lifeguards or call 310/578–0478 for current conditions), and others better for exploring.

Leo Carillo State Beach. This beach along a rough and mountainous stretch of coastline is the most fun at low tide, when a spectacular array of tide pools blossom for all to see. Rock formations on the beach have created some great secret coves for picnickers looking for solitude. There are hiking trails, sea caves, and tunnels, and whales, dolphins, and sea lions are often seen swimming in the offshore kelp beds. The waters here are rocky and best for experienced surfers and scuba divers; fishing is good. Picturesque campgrounds are set back from the beach. Camping fee is $16 per night. *35000 block of PCH, Malibu, ☎ 818/880–0350 or 800/444–7275. Facilities: parking, lifeguard, rest rooms, showers, fire pits.*

Zuma Beach County Park. This is Malibu's largest and sandiest beach, and a favorite spot of surfers. *30050 PCH, Malibu, ☎ 310/457–9891. Facilities: parking, lifeguard, rest rooms, showers, food, playground, volleyball.*

Westward Beach/Point Dume State Beach. Another favorite spot for surfing, this ½-mile-long sandy beach has tide pools and sandstone cliffs. *South end of Westward Beach Rd., Malibu, ☎ 310/457–9891. Facilities: parking, lifeguard, rest rooms, food.*

Paradise Cove. With its pier and equipment rentals, this sandy beach is a mecca for sportfishing boats. Though swimming is allowed, there are lifeguards during the summer only. *28128 PCH, Malibu, ☎ 310/457–9891. Facilities: parking, rest rooms, showers, food (concessions open summer only).*

Malibu Lagoon State Beach/Surfrider Beach. The steady 3- to 5-foot waves make this beach, just north of Malibu Pier, a great long-board surfing beach. The International Surfing Contest is held here in September. Water runoff from Malibu Canyon forms a natural lagoon, which is a sanctuary for many birds. There are also nature trails perfect for romantic sunset strolls. *23200 block of PCH, Malibu, ☎ 818/880–0350. Facilities: parking, lifeguard, rest rooms, picnicking, visitor center.*

Las Tunas State Beach. Las Tunas is small (1,300 feet long, covering a total of only 2 acres), narrow, and sandy, with some rocky areas, and set beneath a bluff. Surf fishing is the biggest attraction here. There is no lifeguard, and swimming is not encouraged because of steel groins set offshore to prevent erosion. *19400 block of PCH, Malibu, ☎ 310/457–9891. Facilities: parking, rest rooms.*

Topanga Canyon State Beach. This rocky beach stretches from the mouth of the Topanga Canyon down to Coastline Drive. Catamarans dance in these waves and skid onto the sands of this popular beach, where dolphins sometimes come close enough to shore to startle sunbathers. The area near the canyon is a great surfing spot. *18700 block of PCH, Malibu, ☎ 310/394–3266. Facilities: parking, lifeguard, rest rooms, food.*

Will Rogers State Beach. This wide, sandy beach is several miles long and has even surf. Parking in the lot here is limited, but there is plenty of beach, volleyball, and bodysurfing, attracting a predominantly gay crowd. *15800 PCH, Pacific Palisades, ☎ 310/394–3266. Facilities: parking, lifeguard, rest rooms.*

Santa Monica Beach. This is one of L.A.'s most popular beaches. In addition to a pier and a promenade, a man-made breakwater just offshore has caused the sand to collect and form the widest stretch of beach on the entire Pacific coast. And wider beaches mean more bodies. All in all, the 2-mile-long beach is well equipped with bike paths, facilities for people with disabilities, playgrounds, and volleyball. In summer, free rock and jazz concerts are held at the pier on Thursday nights. *West of PCH, Santa Monica, ☎ 310/394–3266. Facilities: parking, lifeguard, rest rooms, showers.*

Venice Municipal Beach. While the surf and sands of Venice are fine, the main attraction here is the boardwalk scene. Venice combines the beefcake of some of L.A.'s most serious bodybuilders with the productions of lively crafts merchants and street musicians. There are roller skaters, comedians, and rappers to entertain you, and cafés to feed you. You can rent bikes at Venice Pier Bike Shop (21 Washington St.) and skates at Skatey's (102 Washington St.). *1531 Ocean Front Walk, Venice, ☎ 310/394–3266. Facilities: parking, rest rooms, showers, food, picnicking.*

Playa del Rey. South of Marina del Rey lies one of the more underrated beaches in southern California. Its sprawling white sands stretch from the southern tip of Marina del Rey almost 2 miles down to Dockweiler Beach. One of the more attractive features of this beach is an area called Del Rey Lagoon, a grassy oasis in the heart of Playa del Rey. A lovely pond is inhabited by dozens of ducks, and barbecue pits and tables are available to picnickers. *6660 Esplanade, Playa del Rey, no ☎. Facilities: parking, lifeguard, rest rooms, food.*

Manhattan State Beach. Here are 44 acres of sandy beach for swimming, diving, surfing, and fishing. Polliwog Park is a charming, grassy landscape a few yards back from the beach that parents with young children may appreciate. Ducks waddle around a small pond, and picnickers enjoy some convenient facilities like showers and rest rooms. *West of Strand, Manhattan Beach, ☎ 310/372–2166. Facilities: volleyball, parking, lifeguard, rest rooms, showers, food.*

Redondo State Beach. The beach is wide, sandy, and usually packed in summer, and parking is limited. Excursion boats, boat launching ramps, and fishing are other attractions. There is a series of rock and jazz concerts held at the pier during the summer. *Foot of Torrance Blvd., Redondo Beach, ☎ 310/372–2166. Facilities: volleyball, parking, lifeguard, rest rooms, showers, food.*

DINING

By Bruce David Colen

Updated by Jane E. Lasky

Once Los Angeles was known only for its chopped Cobb salad, Green Goddess dressing, drive-in hamburger stands, and outdoor barbecues, but today it is home to many of the best French and northern Italian restaurants in the United States, and so many places featuring international cuisines that listing them would be like a roll call at the United Nations. Fierce competition among upscale restaurateurs has made L.A. one of the least-expensive big cities—here or abroad—in which to eat well.

Locals tend to dine early, between 7:30 and 9 PM, in part a holdover from when this was a "studio" town and the filmmaking day started at 6 AM (these days it's more to allow for early-morning jogging and gym time). Reservations are essential at the best restaurants, and at almost all restaurants on weekend evenings.

One caveat: The city recently enforced a no-smoking ordinance that applies to all restaurants. If you do want to smoke, there are ways around this—choose a restaurant with an outdoor area (smoking is allowed outdoors) or one that incorporates a full-scale bar (lounge areas are exempt from the no-smoking rule). Also, some of the incorporated cities like West Hollywood and Beverly Hills make their own rules, so call ahead to see if the place where you want to dine permits smoking.

What to Wear

Informality being a way of life in Los Angeles, casual dress is sufficient at most restaurants, though sometimes, as noted, casual chic is required or even jacket and tie. Remember, though, that Los Angeles is a style-conscious town; while you may not be turned away from most eateries if you come in looking like Al or Peg Bundy, you may feel out of place.

CATEGORY	COST*
$$$$	over $50
$$$	$30–$50
$$	$20–$30
$	under $20

**per person for a three-course meal, excluding drinks, service, and 8¼% tax*

American

BEVERLY HILLS

$$$ Grill on the Alley. This restaurant is known for great steaks, fresh seafood, chicken pot pies, and crab cakes. Repeat customers like the restaurant's creamy Cobb salad and homemade rice pudding. ✕ *9560 Dayton Way,* ☎ *310/276–0615. Reservations required. AE, DC, MC, V. Closed Sun. Valet parking in evening.*

$ Ed Debevic's. This is a good place to take the kids or to go yourself if you're feeling nostalgic. Old Coca-Cola signs, a blaring jukebox, gum-chewing waitresses in bobby socks, and meat loaf and mashed potatoes take you back to the diners of the '50s. ✕ *134 N. La Cienega,* ☎ *310/659–1952. Reservations for large parties only. AE, D, DC, MC, V. Valet parking.*

$ RJ's the Rib Joint. The large barrel of free peanuts at the door and the sawdust on the floor set a folksy atmosphere. An outstanding salad bar has dozens of fresh choices and return privileges, and there are gigantic portions of everything—from ribs, chili, and barbecued chicken to mile-high layer cakes. ✕ *252 N. Beverly Dr.,* ☎ *310/274–7427. Reservations advised. AE, D, DC, MC, V. Valet parking in evening.*

CENTURY CITY

$ **Dive!** When you walk in here, you'll feel as though you've just climbed down the hatch of a submarine. The sandwiches are nautical miles ahead of what you might find at a traditional deli, with such specialties as fajita sub cucina, a Chinese chicken salad sub, and a brick-oven-baked Tuscan steak sub. For dessert, try the Dive! s'mores, or lemon-bar concoction with white chocolate and raspberry sauce. ✕ *10250 Santa Monica Blvd.,* ☎ *310/788–3483. No reservations. AE, D, DC, MC, V.*

DOWNTOWN

$$$ **Pacific Dining Car.** This 70-year-old restaurant, one of L.A.'s oldest, is open around the clock. Best known for well-aged steaks, rack of lamb, and an extensive California wine list at fair prices, it's a favorite haunt of politicians and lawyers around City Hall and of sports fans after Dodger games. High tea is served every day from 3 to 5:30 PM. ✕ *1310 W. 6th St.,* ☎ *213/483–6000. Reservations advised. AE, DC, MC, V. Valet parking.*

$$–$$$ **Nicola.** Architect Michael Rotondi created the contemporary backdrop for this restaurant—celebrity chef Larry Nicola's latest venture—in the Sanwa Bank Building. The two-room restaurant provides a contrast in moods, one an intimate dining arena, the other more open and airy; both see a lot of business deals sealed over lunch and dinner. Although the seasonal menu is largely American, ethnic touches abound with entrées such as broiled Chilean sea bass with caramelized orange and ginger potatoes, roasted prime rib of pork with tomatillo sauce and corn succotash, and Mediterranean range chicken with tabbouleh and Lebanese fried potatoes. ✕ *601 S. Figueroa St.,* ☎ *213/485–0927. Reservations advised. AE, D, DC, MC, V. Closed Sun. No lunch Sat. Valet parking.*

SAN FERNANDO VALLEY

$ **Paty's.** Located near NBC, Warner Brothers, and the Disney Studio, Paty's is a good place for stargazing without having to mortgage your home to pay for the meal. Breakfast omelets are plump, and the biscuits are homemade and served with high-quality jam. Lunches and dinners include Swiss steak and a hearty beef stew that is served in a hollowed-out loaf of home-baked bread. All desserts are worth saving room for: New Orleans bread pudding with a hot brandy sauce is popular. ✕ *10001 Riverside Dr., Toluca Lake,* ☎ *818/760–9164. No reservations. No credit cards.*

WEST HOLLYWOOD

$$$–$$$$ ★ **Arnie Morton's of Chicago.** The West Coast addition to this ever-expanding national chain brought joy and cholesterol to the hearts of Los Angeles meat lovers, many of whom claim that Morton's serves the best steaks in town. In addition to a 24-ounce porterhouse, a New York strip, and a double-cut filet mignon, there are giant veal and lamb chops, thick cuts of prime rib, and imported lobsters at market prices. The baked potatoes are so huge they alone could be a meal. Although the prices are steep, the produce is prime, as are the service and private clublike atmosphere. ✕ *435 S. La Cienega Blvd.,* ☎ *310/246–1501. Reservations advised. Jacket required. AE, D, DC, MC, V. No lunch.*

$$$ **Morton's.** Steaks are the cornerstone of the menu of this restaurant, opened by Arnie Morton's (*see above*) son and daughter. Good broiled fish and chicken, as well as pasta, veal, and pizza, have since been added. Don't be intimidated by the celebrity-fawning waiters, all hoping for an acting job. ✕ *8764 Melrose Ave.,* ☎ *310/276–5205. Reservations required. Jacket required. AE, D, MC, V. Closed Sun. Valet parking.*

Downtown Los Angeles Dining and Lodging

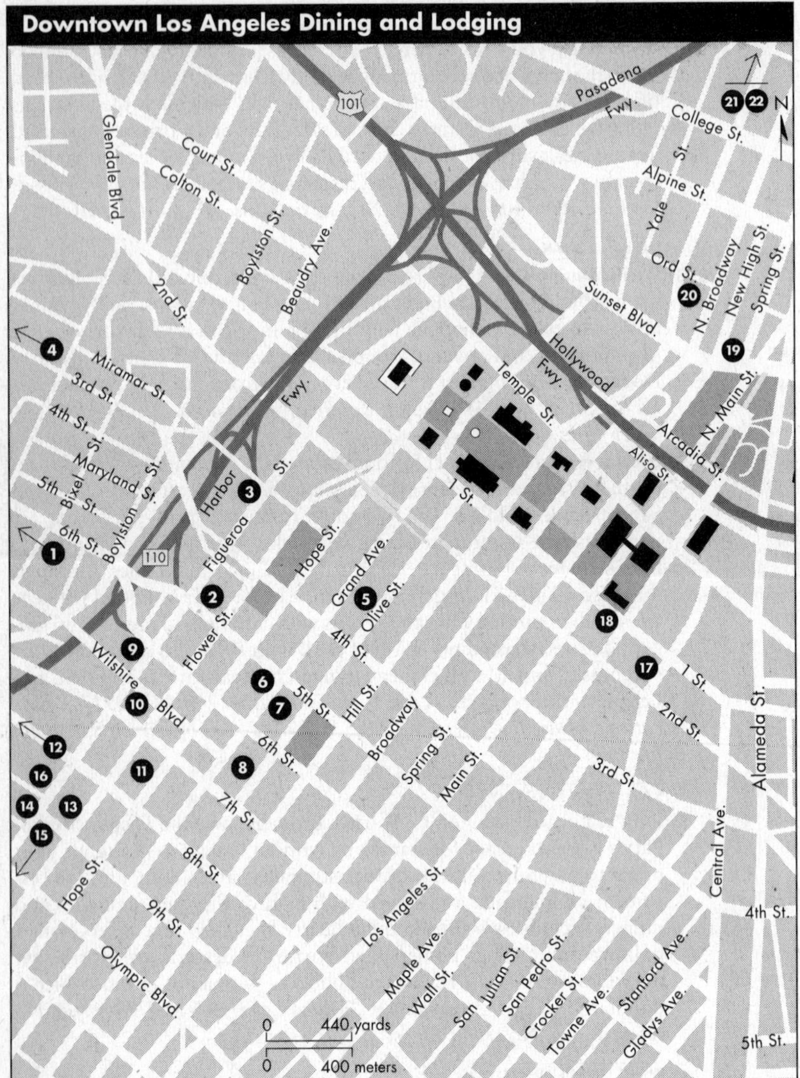

Dining
Clearwater Cafe, **22**
Mon Kee Seafood Restaurant, **19**
Nicola, **9**
Ocean Seafood Restaurant, **20**
Pacific Dining Car, **1**
Restaurant Horikawa, **17**
Rex Il Ristorante, **8**
Yujean Kang's Gourmet Chinese Cuisine, **21**

Lodging
Biltmore Hotel, **7**
EconoLodge, **4**
Figueroa Hotel, **14**
Holiday Inn L.A. Downtown, **12**
Hotel Inter-Continental Los Angeles, **5**
Hyatt Regency Los Angeles, **11**
The Inntowne, **16**
The Inn at 657, **15**
Los Angeles Hilton Hotel and Towers, **10**
New Otani Hotel and Garden, **18**
Orchid Hotel, **13**
Sheraton Grande Hotel, **3**
Westin Bonaventure Hotel and Suites, **2**
Wyndham Checkers Hotel, **6**

$$$ **The Palm.** A West Coast replay of the famous Manhattan steak house—down to the New York–style waiters rushing you through your Bronx cheesecake—this is where you'll find the biggest and best lobster, good steaks and chops, great french-fried onion rings, and paper-thin potato slices. The big deal for dinner, though, is the prime rib. However, if you have the corned-beef hash for lunch, you can skip dinner. A three-person-deep bar ups the noise level. ✕ *9001 Santa Monica Blvd.,* ☏ *310/550–8811. Reservations advised. AE, DC, MC, V. No lunch weekends. Valet parking.*

$$ **Hard Rock Cafe.** Big burgers, rich milk shakes, banana splits, BLTs, and other pre-nouvelle food delights, along with loud music and rock-and-roll memorabilia, have made this '50s-era barn of a café the favorite of local teenagers. ✕ *8600 Beverly Blvd.,* ☏ *310/276–7605. No reservations. AE, DC, MC, V. Valet parking in Beverly Center.*

$ **Roscoe's House of Chicken 'n' Waffles.** Come here for real down-home southern cooking: fried chicken, waffles, grits, and potatoes at bargain prices. ✕ *1514 N. Gower St.,* ☏ *213/466–9329. AE, D, DC, MC, V.*

WESTSIDE (COASTAL LOS ANGELES DINING MAP)

$$–$$$ ★ **West Beach Cafe.** Best bets at local restaurateur Bruce Marder's first big success (he also owns Rebecca's across the street) are Caesar salad, rack of lamb, ravioli with port and radicchio, fisherman's soup, and what many consider the best hamburger and fries in all of Los Angeles. There's also a fabulous selection of French wines and liqueurs. ✕ *60 N. Venice Blvd.,* ☏ *310/823–5396. Reservations advised. AE, D, DC, MC, V. Closed Mon. Valet parking.*

$$ **Gilliland's.** Gerri Gilliland was teaching cooking in her native Ireland, took a vacation in southern California, and never went back. Instead, she stayed and created this charming restaurant, which offers the best of both culinary worlds and showcases her fascination with Mediterranean dishes. The soda bread, Irish stew, and corned beef and cabbage are wonderful. A real treat are the Louisiana crab cakes served with fresh corn, herbs, onions, tomatillo sauce, and sour cream. All desserts are made on the premises; especially good is the lemon curd tart. The place is warm and friendly, just like its owner. ✕ *2424 Main St., Santa Monica,* ☏ *310/392–3901. Reservations advised. AE, MC, V.*

$–$$ **Broadway Deli.** This cross between a European brasserie and an upscale diner serves everything from a platter of assorted smoked fish or Caesar salad to shepherd's pie, carpaccio, steak, and broiled salmon with cream spinach. There are also excellent side dishes (such as corn muffins, mashed potatoes with mushroom gravy, and potato pancakes), desserts, and freshly baked breads. At the retail counter, fill a picnic basket's worth of delectable European and domestic delicacies. ✕ *1457 3rd St. Promenade, Santa Monica,* ☏ *310/451–0616. No reservations. AE, MC, V. Valet parking weekends and evenings.*

$ **Gladstone's 4 Fish.** This is undoubtedly the most popular restaurant along the southern California coast; it has spawned a sister restaurant in Universal Studios' CityWalk, also worth a visit. Perhaps the food is not the greatest, but familiar seashore fare is prepared adequately and in large portions, and the prices are certainly right. Best bets: crab chowder, steamed clams, three-egg omelets, hamburgers, barbecued ribs, and chili. ✕ *17300 Pacific Coast Hwy. (at Sunset Blvd.), Pacific Palisades,* ☏ *310/454–3474. Reservations advised. AE, D, DC, MC, V. Valet parking.*

Cajun

WESTSIDE (COASTAL LOS ANGELES DINING MAP)

$$–$$$ **Orleans.** The jambalaya and gumbo dishes are hot—in more ways than one—at this spacious eatery, where the cuisine was created with the help of New Orleans celebrity-chef Paul Prudhomme. The blackened

Beverly Hills & Hollywood Dining and Lodging

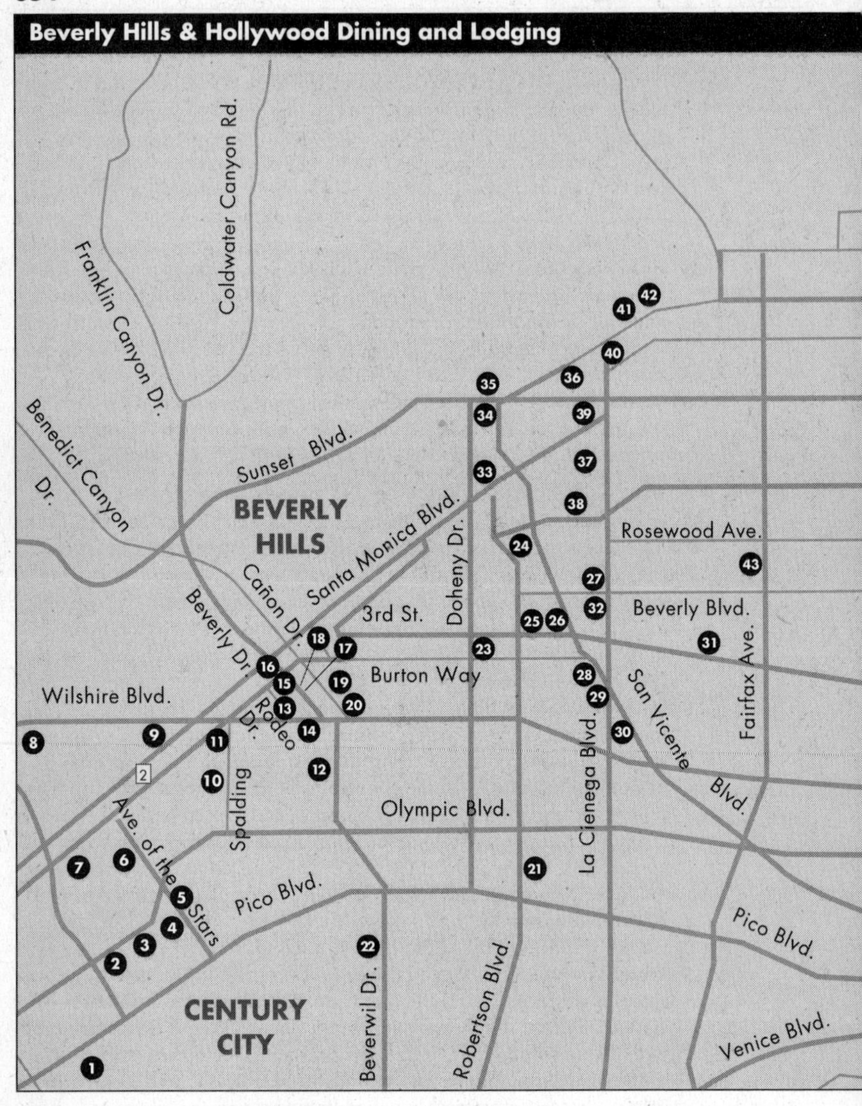

Dining

Antonio's Restaurant, **47**
Arnie Morton's of Chicago, **28**
The Bistro Garden, **20**
Ca'Brea, **46**
California Pizza Kitchen, **12**
Canter's, **43**
Cava, **26**
Cha Cha Cha, **56**
Chan Dara, **50**
Chopstix, **49**
Citrus, **51**
The Dining Room, **14**
Dive!, **7**
Ed Debevic's, **30**
El Cholo, **57**
The Grill on the Alley, **13**
Hard Rock Cafe, **32**
Harry's Bar & American Grill, **5**
Il Fornaio Cucina Italiana, **18**
Jimmy's, **10**
Le Dome, **36**
Locanda Veneta, **25**
L'Orangerie, **37**
The Mandarin, **15**
Morton's, **27**
Nate 'n' Al's, **17**
The Palm, **33**
Primi, **1**
Restaurant Katsu, **55**
RJ's the Rib Joint, **19**
Roscoe's House of Chicken and Waffles, **54**
Rustica, **16**
Sofi, **31**
Spago, **35**
Tarola Calda, **44**
Tommy Tang's, **48**
Trader Vic's, **11**

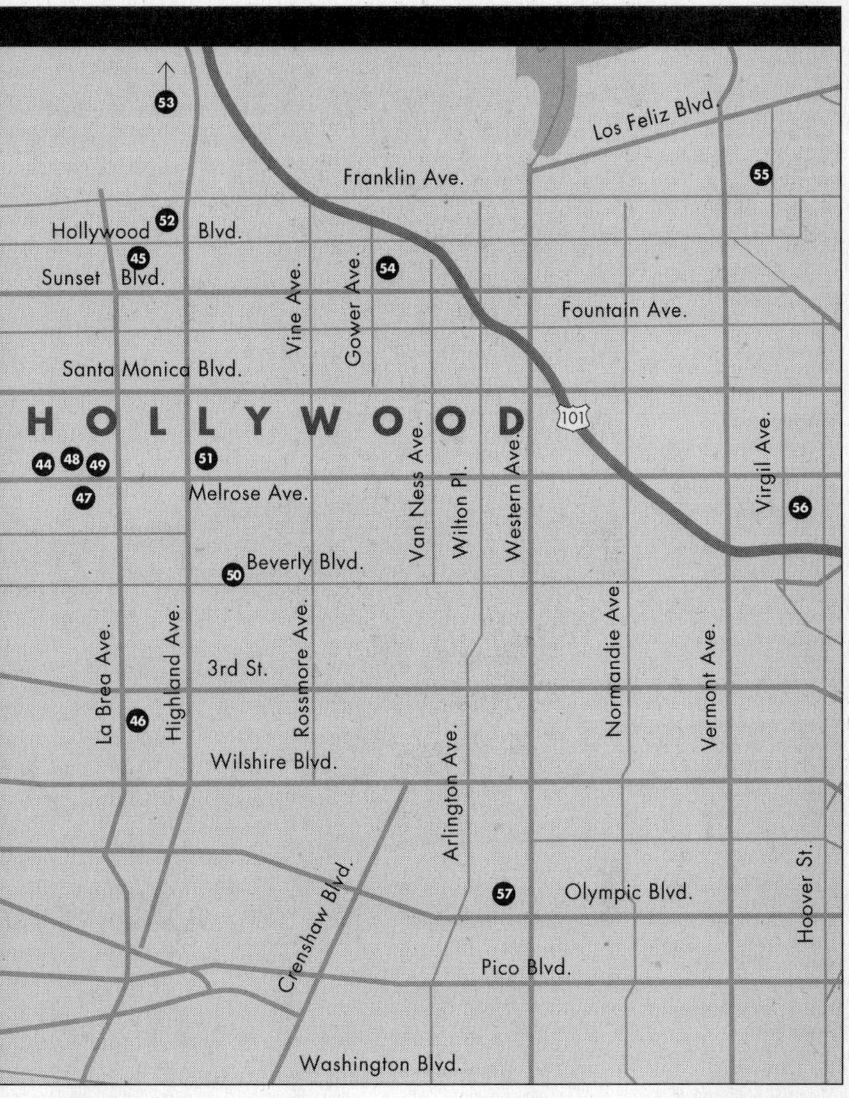

Lodging

The Argyle, **24**

Banana Bungalow Hotel and International Hostel, **53**

Beverly Hills Ritz Hotel, **8**

Beverly Hilton, **11**

Beverly Prescott Hotel, **22**

Carlyle Inn, **21**

Century City Courtyard by Marriott, **3**

Century City Inn, **2**

Century Plaza Hotel and Tower, **6**

Chateau Marmont Hotel, **42**

Four Seasons Los Angeles, **23**

Hollywood Holiday Inn, **52**

Hotel Nikko, **29**

Hotel Sofitel Ma Maison, **27**

Hyatt on Sunset, **41**

J.W. Marriott Hotel at Century City, **4**

Le Parc Hotel, **38**

Mondrian Hotel, **40**

Peninsula Beverly Hills, **8**

Radisson Hollywood Roosevelt, **45**

Regent Beverly Wilshire Hotel, **14**

Summerfield Suites Hotel, **39**

Wyndham Bel Age Hotel, **34**

Dining
Border Grill, **7**
Broadway Deli, **6**
Chinois on Main, **13**
Dynasty Room, **36**
Gilliland's, **14**
Gladstone's 4 Fish, **1**
Granita, **3**
Hotel Bel-Air, **38**
Orleans, **33**
Remi, **10**
Schatzi on Main, **15**
Tra di Noi, **2**
Valentino, **32**
Warszawa, **5**
West Beach Cafe, **17**

Lodging
Airport Marina Hotel, **23**
Barnabey's Hotel, **30**
Best Western Royal Palace Inn and Suites, **34**
Carmel Hotel, **4**
Century Wilshire, **35**
Crowne Plaza Redondo Beach and Marina Hotel, **29**
Doubletree Hotel LAX, **24**
Doubletree Marina del Rey L.A., **21**
Holiday Inn-LAX, **25**
Holiday Inn Santa Monica Beach, **12**
Hotel Bel-Air, **38**
Hyatt Hotel-LAX, **26**
Loews Santa Monica Beach Hotel, **8**
Marina del Rey Hotel, **20**
Marina del Rey Marriott Inn, **22**
Marina International Hotel, **18**
Marina Pacific Hotel & Suites, **16**
Miramar Sheraton, **9**
Palm Motel, **31**
Radisson Bel-Air, **37**
Red Lion Inn, **27**
The Ritz-Carlton, Marina del Rey, **19**
Sheraton Gateway Hotel at LAX, **28**
Shutters on the Beach, **11**
Westwood Marquis Hotel and Gardens, **36**

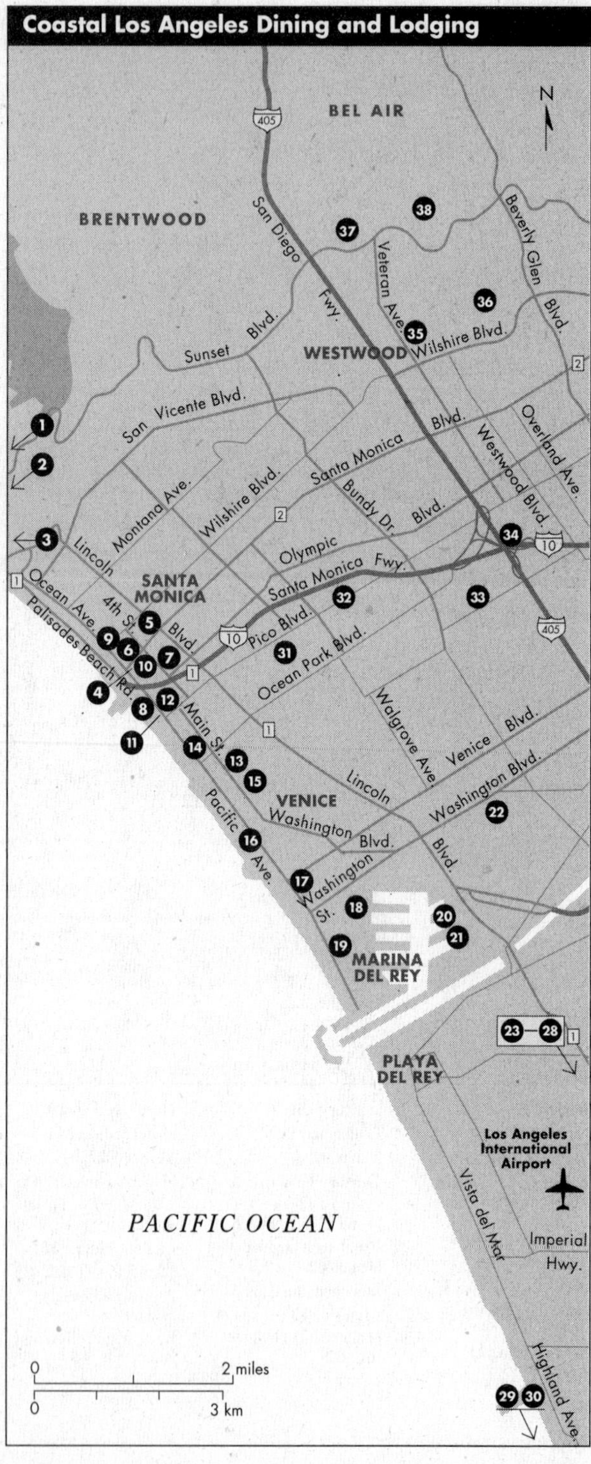

salmon is probably the best catch on the menu. Most menu items are available in low-sodium, low-fat versions; just ask. ✕ *11705 National Blvd., W. Los Angeles,* ☎ *310/479–4187. Reservations advised. AE, DC, MC, V. Valet parking.*

California

BEVERLY HILLS

$$$ **Bistro Garden.** The flower-banked outdoor dining terrace makes this the quintessential southern California "ladies who lunch" experience. It's chic and lively without being overly pretentious or too "Hollywood." There's excellent smoked salmon, fresh cracked crab, steak tartare, calves' liver with bacon, and a unique apple pancake. ✕ *176 N. Cañon Dr.,* ☎ *310/550–3900. Reservations required. Jacket and tie at dinner. AE, DC, MC, V. Closed Sun. Valet parking.*

$$$ ★ **Dining Room.** Located in the Regent Beverly Wilshire, this elegant, European-looking salon offers wonderful California cuisine (try the loin of Colorado lamb accompanied by eggplant and sweet pepper lasagna), plus splendid service, at prices that are relatively reasonable. A three-course fixed-price menu costs $38; a four-course sampler dinner is priced at $75. Adjoining the Dining Room is an equally attractive, sophisticated cocktail lounge, with romantic lighting and a pianist playing show tunes. ✕ *9500 Wilshire Blvd.,* ☎ *310/275–5200. Reservations advised. Jacket and tie. AE, D, DC, MC, V. Valet parking.*

$ **California Pizza Kitchen.** This member of the popular West Coast chain is the place to go for a good wood-fired pizza at a fair price, without the usual pizza-parlor surroundings. There's an immaculate, pleasingly modern dining room, plus counter service by the open kitchen, and a wide, rather esoteric choice of pizza toppings. Try the tandoori pie, which is made without cheese. The pastas are equally interesting and carefully prepared. The few sidewalk tables are in great demand. ✕ *207 S. Beverly Dr.,* ☎ *310/275–1101. No reservations. AE, D, DC, MC, V.*

WEST HOLLYWOOD

$$–$$$ ★ **Citrus.** One of L.A.'s most prominent chefs, Michel Richard, creates superb dishes by blending French and American cuisines. You can't miss with the delectable tuna burger, the impossibly thin angel-hair pasta, or the deep-fried potatoes, sautéed foie gras, rare duck, or carpaccio salad. For an unusual taste treat, try the chicken in mushroom skin. Get your doctor's permission before even looking at Richard's irresistible desserts. ✕ *6703 Melrose Ave.,* ☎ *213/857–0034. Reservations advised. Jacket required. AE, DC, MC, V. Closed Sun. Valet parking.*

$$–$$$ **Spago.** This is the restaurant that propelled owner-chef Wolfgang Puck into the international culinary spotlight. He deserves every accolade for raising California cuisine to a totally tantalizing gastronomic experience, using only the finest West Coast produce. The proof is in the tasting: roasted cumin lamb on lentil salad with fresh coriander and yogurt chutney, fresh oysters with green chili and black pepper mignonette, grilled free-range chickens, and grilled Alaskan baby salmon. The biggest seller is not on the menu, so ask: It's known as the Jewish pizza, with cream cheese and smoked salmon as toppings. As for Puck's incredible desserts, he's on Weight Watchers' Most Wanted List. This is the place to see *People* magazine live, but you'll have to put up with the noise in exchange. Be safe: Make reservations at least two weeks in advance. ✕ *1114 Horn Ave.,* ☎ *310/652–4025. Reservations required. Jacket required. D, DC, MC, V. No lunch. Valet parking.*

WESTSIDE (COASTAL LOS ANGELES DINING MAP)

$$$ **Hotel Bel-Air.** You couldn't ask for a lovelier setting, in a romantic country garden, and the menu matches—the California-Continental cooking is very good indeed, be it for breakfast, lunch, or dinner. Seasonal cartes use fresh fare in a fanciful way, like tuna and monkfish medallions with chive mashed potatoes; peppered swordfish medallions on a bed or artichokes, mushrooms, asparagus, and corn in a tarragon lobster sauce; and grilled whitefish with saffron couscous. A meal at the Bel-Air is a not-to-be-missed experience. ✕ *701 Stone Canyon Rd., Bel Air,* ☏ *310/472–1211. Reservations advised. Jacket and tie at dinner. AE, D, DC, MC, V. Valet parking.*

$$–$$$ ★ **Granita.** Wolfgang Puck's Granita has such stunning interior details as handmade tiles embedded with seashells, blown-glass lighting fixtures, and etched-glass panels with wavy edges. It's as close as you'll come to the beach without getting sand in your shoes. Even the blasé Malibu film colony is impressed. While Puck's menu here favors seafood items such as grilled John Dory with stir-fried vegetables and curry lime sauce, and grilled Atlantic salmon in lemongrass broth with seared carrots and wild mushrooms, the menu also features some of his standard favorites. Among the greats are spicy shrimp pizza with sun-dried tomatoes and herb pesto, roasted Chinese duck with dried fruit chutney, seared foie gras with caramelized walnuts and blood-orange port-wine glaze, and Caesar salad with oven-baked bruschetta. ✕ *23725 W. Malibu Rd., Malibu,* ☏ *310/456–0488. Reservations required far ahead, especially for weekends. D, DC, MC, V. No lunch Mon. and Tues.*

Caribbean

HOLLYWOOD

$–$$ **Cha Cha Cha.** Off the beaten path, this small shack of a Caribbean restaurant attracts a discerning, eclectic crowd—the place is hip, yet not pretentious or overly trendy. Sit indoors in a cozy room, or in the enclosed patio, very tropical in its decor, à la Carmen Miranda. There's Jamaican jerk chicken, swordfish brochette, fried plantain chips, and assorted flans. If you're in the mood for pizza, try Cha Cha Cha's Caribbean versions. A "Valley" branch (17499 Ventura Blvd., Encino, ☏ 818/789–3600) exists in much more stylish quarters. ✕ *656 N. Virgil Ave.,* ☏ *213/664–7723. Reservations advised. AE, D, DC, MC, V. Valet parking available (and advised).*

Chinese

BEVERLY HILLS

$–$$ ★ **The Mandarin.** Who said you only find great Chinese food in hole-in-the-wall places with oilcloth tabletops? Here is a good-looking restaurant with the best crystal and linens, serving an equally bright mixture of Szechuan and Chinese country-cooking dishes. Minced chicken in lettuce-leaf tacos, Peking duck (order ahead of time), a superb beggars chicken, scallion pancakes, and any of the noodle dishes are recommended. ✕ *430 N. Camden Dr.,* ☏ *310/859–0926. Reservations required. AE, DC, MC, V. No lunch weekends. Valet parking evening only.*

DOWNTOWN

$$ **Ocean Seafood Restaurant.** This is a great place to try garlic crab and catfish, and most customers—including the Chinese—consider its dim-sum menu the best in town. This noisy, vast Great Banquet Hall of a family-run place (since 1946, when it opened) becomes far more intimate when the staff drops by your table with dozens of tasty little Cantonese treats. The perfect spot for a Sunday breakfast or lunch. ✕ *750 N. Hill St.,* ☏ *213/687–3088. Reservations accepted. AE, D, MC, V.*

$–$$ ★ **Mon Kee Seafood Restaurant.** The fish here are morning-fresh, the garlic crab is addictive, and the steamed catfish is a masterpiece of gentle flavors. In fact, almost everything on the menu is excellent. Despite its wonderful cuisine, this is a crowded, messy place; be prepared to wait for a table. ✕ *679 N. Spring St.,* ☎ *213/628–6717. No reservations. AE, DC, MC, V. Parking (fee).*

PASADENA (DOWNTOWN LOS ANGELES DINING MAP)

$$–$$$ ★ **Yujean Kang's Gourmet Chinese Cuisine.** Mr. Kang, formerly of San Francisco, is one of the finest nouvelle-Chinese chefs in the nation. Forget any and all preconceived notions of what Chinese food should look and taste like. Start with the tender slices of veal on a bed of enoki and black mushrooms, topped with a tangle of quick-fried shoestring yams, or the sea bass with kumquats and a passion-fruit sauce, and finish with poached plums, or watermelon ice under a mantle of white chocolate. No MSG is used in any dish. ✕ *67 N. Raymond Ave.,* ☎ *818/585–0855. Reservations advised. AE, D, DC, MC, V.*

WEST HOLLYWOOD

$ **Chopstix.** Never underestimate the ability of Californians to adopt—and adapt—an ethnic-food vogue: in this case, dim sum, subtly doctored for non-Asian tastes. The result is MSG-free, nouvelle Asian fast food served in a mod setting, at high tables with stools, or at a diner-like counter. The dishes are interesting (spicy black bean beef, Thai tacos, Bangkok noodles), but don't expect a native Chinese to agree. There's another branch of Chopstix in Pasadena. ✕ *7229 Melrose Ave.,* ☎ *213/937–1111. No reservations. AE, D, MC, V.*

Continental

BEVERLY HILLS

$$–$$$ **Rustica.** Popular on sunny days (out back there's a retractable roof that allows you to dine alfresco when weather warrants), this contemporary bistro serves a mixture of California and Italian cuisine. It's one of Beverly Hills' most romantic spots, especially the cozy, dimly lit front room, and the service is ace. All entrées are under $25, which is very good for this part of town. Try the grilled swordfish; tricolor mushroom ravioli with sun-dried tomatoes, pesto, and Parmesan; and the blackened goat-cheese salad with roasted walnut vinaigrette. More than 200 wines make up the top-notch wine list. ✕ *435 N. Beverly Dr., Beverly Hills,* ☎ *310/247–9331. Reservations advised. AE, DC, MC, V. No lunch weekends. Valet parking.*

CENTURY CITY (BEVERLY HILLS AND HOLLYWOOD DINING MAP)

$$$–$$$$ **Jimmy's.** When Beverly Hills CEOs are not dining at home they often head here. Owner Jimmy Murphy provides the warmth in this expensive, decorator-elegant restaurant. The best dishes on the broad menu include peppered salmon, veal medallions with orange coffee-bean sauce, roast duckling, and chateaubriand. There's a fine steak or salmon tartare at lunch, and, if you're feeling flush, start your meal with beluga caviar. ✕ *201 Moreno Dr.,* ☎ *310/552–2394. Reservations required. Jacket and tie. AE, DC, MC, V. Valet parking.*

SAN FERNANDO VALLEY

$–$$ **Europa.** The menu here roams the world: great goulash, terrific teriyaki—even the occasional matzo-ball soup. The dining room is tiny, charming, and casual; reservations are a must, as this is a community favorite. ✕ *14929 Magnolia Blvd., Sherman Oaks,* ☎ *818/501–9175. Reservations advised. MC, V. No dinner Mon.; no lunch weekends.*

SANTA MONICA (COASTAL LOS ANGELES DINING MAP)

$$ **Schatzi on Main.** Owner Arnold Schwarzenegger has seen to it that the chef's dishes include his Austrian homeland favorites such as Wiener schnitzel, bratwurst, and smoked pork chops. The bulk of the dishes, however, range from Peking roast duck and pasta with shrimp to seared swordfish medallions and New York–style pizza. There's an indoor area and a patio. *3110 Main St., ☎ 310/399–4800. Reservations advised. AE, D, DC, MC, V. Valet parking.*

$$ **Warszawa.** At this Polish restaurant, the food is hearty and heartwarming. Regional Polish sausage with mashed potatoes and cabbage is a house favorite, as are the potato pancakes sprinkled with cinnamon and garnished with dried plums, sour cream, and apples. ✕ *1414 Lincoln Blvd., ☎ 310/393–8831. Reservations advised. AE, D, DC, MC, V. No lunch.*

WESTWOOD (COASTAL LOS ANGELES DINING MAP)

$$$ **Dynasty Room.** This peaceful, elegant dining room in the Westwood Marquis Hotel has a European flair and tables set far enough apart for privacy. The well-handled Continental fare includes grilled *opakapaka* (whitefish on a bed of couscous) with fennel and ahi (tuna) in Thai-curried seaweed. For dessert, the mixed-fruit tart is highly recommended. ✕ *930 Hilgard Ave., ☎ 310/208–8765. Reservations required. AE, D, DC, MC, V. No lunch. Valet parking.*

Deli

BEVERLY HILLS

$ **Nate 'n Al's.** A famous gathering place for Hollywood comedians, gag writers, and their agents, Nate 'n Al's serves first-rate matzo-ball soup, lox and scrambled eggs, cheese blintzes, potato pancakes, and the best deli sandwiches west of Manhattan. ✕ *414 N. Beverly Dr., ☎ 310/274–0101. No reservations. AE, MC, V. Free parking.*

SAN FERNANDO VALLEY

$ ★ **Art's Delicatessen.** One of the best Jewish-style delicatessens in the city, this Kosher mecca serves mammoth sandwiches named after celebrities and made from some of the best corned beef, pastrami, and other cold cuts around. Matzo-ball soup and sweet-and-sour cabbage soup are specialties, and there is good chopped chicken liver. ✕ *12224 Ventura Blvd., Studio City, ☎ 818/762–1221. No reservations. AE, D, DC, MC, V.*

WEST HOLLYWOOD

$ **Canter's.** Ex–New Yorkers claim that this granddaddy of delicatessens (it opened in 1928) is the closest in atmosphere, smell, and menu to a Big Apple corned-beef and pastrami hangout. The elderly waitresses even speak with New York accents. It's open 24 hours a day (attracting an eclectic late-night crowd) and has a yummy in-house bakery. ✕ *419 N. Fairfax Ave., ☎ 213/651–2030. Reservations accepted. MC, V. Valet parking.*

French

SAN FERNANDO VALLEY

$$–$$$ ★ **Pinot Bistro.** Joachim Spliechel, owner-chef of top-rated Patina, opened this perfectly designed synthesis of Parisian bistros. One can smell the fumes of perfectly seasoned escargots and the aroma of perfectly brewed espressos. Dishes are authentic: an array of fresh oysters, country pâtés, bouillabaisse, braised tongue and spinach, pot-au-feu, and steak with french fries. The pastry chef specializes in chocolate desserts. There's a long wine list. ✕ *12969 Ventura Blvd., ☎ 818/990–0500.*

Reservations advised. AE, DC, MC, V. No lunch weekends. Valet parking.

$$ **Barzac Brasserie.** Just north of Universal Studios, show-business types and other locals seeking French comfort food satiate themselves on chef Didier Poirier's Gallic menu. It's also an interesting place to eat, as the contemporary dining room surrounds an open kitchen, so you can watch your meal being prepared. Start with roasted potato shells with golden and black caviar, or sautéed baby escargots with shiitake mushrooms in a puffed pastry. Popular entrées are grilled baby coho salmon over couscous and curry sauce, and rack of lamb roasted with Dijon mustard and served with red Swiss chard. Don't skip dessert: The crème brûlée is superb. ✕ *4212 Lankershim Blvd., Universal City,* ☏ *818/760–7081. Reservations advised. AE, DC, MC, V. No lunch weekends. Valet parking.*

SANTA MONICA

$$–$$$ ★ **Chinois on Main.** The second of the Wolfgang Puck pack of restaurants, this one is designed in tongue-in-cheek kitsch by his wife, Barbara Lazaroff. Both the look of the place and Puck's merging of Asian and French cuisines are great fun. Specialties include grilled Mongolian lamb chops with cilantro vinaigrette and wok-fried vegetables, Shanghai lobster with spicy ginger curry sauce, and rare duck with a wondrous plum sauce. The best desserts are three differently flavored crèmes brûlées. This is one of L.A.'s most crowded spots—and one of the noisiest. ✕ *2709 Main St., Santa Monica,* ☏ *310/392–9025. Dinner reservations required. AE, D, DC, MC, V. No lunch Sat.–Tues. Valet parking.*

WEST HOLLYWOOD

$$$–$$$$ ★ **L'Orangerie.** For sheer elegance and classic good taste, it would be hard to find a lovelier restaurant in this country. And the cuisine, albeit nouvelle-light, is as French as the l'Orangerie at Versailles. Specialties include coddled eggs served in the shell and topped with caviar, duck with foie gras, John Dory with bay leaves, rack of lamb for two, and an unbeatable apple tart served with a jug of double cream. ✕ *903 N. La Cienega Blvd.,* ☏ *310/652–9770. Reservations required. Jacket and tie. AE, D, DC, MC, V. Closed Mon. No lunch. Valet parking.*

$$$ **Le Dome.** For some reason, local food critics have never given this brasserie as much attention as it deserves. Perhaps they are intimidated by the hordes of show- and music-biz celebrities that keep the place humming. By and large the food is honest, down-to-earth French: cockles in white wine and shallots; veal ragout; veal tortellini with prosciutto, sun-dried tomatoes, peas, and Parmesan sauce; and a genuine, stick-to-the-ribs cassoulet. ✕ *8720 Sunset Blvd.,* ☏ *310/ 659–6919. Reservations required. AE, DC, MC, V. Closed Sun. No lunch Sat. Valet parking.*

Greek

MID-WILSHIRE (BEVERLY HILLS AND HOLLYWOOD DINING MAP)

$ **Sofi.** Hidden down a narrow passageway is this friendly little taverna that makes you feel as if you've been transported straight to Mykonos. Enjoy your meal in the stone-walled dining room or under a vine-shaded patio. The food is authentic Greek cuisine: *dolmades* (stuffed grape leaves), lamb gyros, a sampling of traditional salads, phyllo pies, spanakopita, and souvlakia. ✕ *8030¾ W. 3rd St.,* ☏ *213/651–0346. Reservations advised. AE, D, DC, MC, V. No lunch Sun.*

Health Food

PASADENA (DOWNTOWN LOS ANGELES DINING MAP)

$-$$ **Clearwater Cafe.** Dishes here cater to low-fat, low-sodium palates, but that doesn't mean a loss in taste—the spicy catfish has a certain bite and the mixed vegetable grill with creamy polenta satisfies even the most discerning vegetarian. Sit in the courtyard patio of this two-level restaurant if the sun is shining. ✕ *168 W. Colorado Blvd.,* ☎ *818/356–0959. Reservations accepted. AE, D, MC, V. Valet parking.*

Italian

BEVERLY HILLS

$$-$$$ **Primi.** A younger, less expensive brother to Valentino (*see below*), Primi has a menu that features a wide variety of northern Italian treats, including pasta and salad selections. This is a cheerful, contemporary setting, with a pleasant outside terrace. ✕ *10543 W. Pico Blvd.,* ☎ *310/475–9235. Reservations advised. AE, DC, MC, V. Closed Sun. No lunch Sat. Valet parking.*

$-$$ ★ **Il Fornaio Cucina Italiana.** What was once a bakery-café has been transformed into one of the best-looking contemporary trattorias in California, and the food is more than worthy of the setting. From the huge brass-and-stainless-steel rotisserie come crispy roasted duck, herb-basted chickens, and juicy rabbit. Nearby, cooks paddle a tasty variety of pizzas and calzones in and out of the oakwood-burning oven. Also emerging from the latter is a *bomba,* a plate-size, dome-shape focaccia shell draped with strips of smoked prosciutto. The thick porterhouse steak alla Florentina at $17.95 is clearly the best beef buy around; another top choice is pasta stuffed with lobster, ricotta, and leeks, served with a lemon cream sauce. The wines come from vineyards Il Fornaio owns in Italy. Stop by for Sunday brunch; it's terrific. ✕ *301 N. Beverly Dr.,* ☎ *310/550–8330. Reservations accepted. AE, DC, MC, V. Valet parking.*

CENTURY CITY (BEVERLY HILLS AND HOLLYWOOD DINING MAP)

$$-$$$ **Harry's Bar & American Grill.** The decor and selection of dishes here are acknowledged copies of Harry's Bar in Florence. But for first-rate food—paper-thin carpaccio, grilled fish and steaks, and excellent pastas like ravioli filled with artichokes or tortellini with Maine lobster and shiitake sauce—the check will be far lower than it would be in Italy. ✕ *2020 Ave. of the Stars,* ☎ *310/277–2333. Reservations required. AE, DC, MC, V. No lunch weekends. Valet parking.*

DOWNTOWN

$$$$ ★ **Rex Il Ristorante.** Owner Mauro Vincenti remodeled two ground floors of a historic Art Deco building to resemble the main dining salon of the circa-1930 Italian luxury liner *Rex*. The cuisine, the lightest of *nuova cucina,* is equally special. Be prepared for small and costly portions of such delights as herb-breaded lamb chops with spinach or calamari with black squid-ink pasta. ✕ *617 S. Olive St.,* ☎ *213/627–2300. Reservations required. Jacket and tie. AE, DC, MC, V. Closed Sun. No lunch Sat.–Wed. Valet parking.*

SAN FERNANDO VALLEY

$$ **Posto.** Thanks to Piero Selvaggio, Valley residents no longer have to drive to the Westside for good modern Italian cuisine. His chef makes a tissue-thin pizza topped with flavorful ingredients, and the chicken, duck, and veal sausages are made each morning, as are the different herb breads, fried polenta, and wonderful risotto with porcini mushrooms. And, if you are not too stuffed after that, the desserts are delicious. ✕ *14928 Ventura Blvd., Sherman Oaks,* ☎ *818/784–4400. AE, MC, V. No lunch weekends.*

WEST HOLLYWOOD

$$ ★ **Ca'Brea.** Signoris de Mori and Tomassi were so successful with Locanda Veneta (*see below*) that they took a gamble and opened a much larger and lower-price place only 20 blocks away. Ca'Brea has turned into the Italian-restaurant smash hit of the penny-pinching '90s, and there isn't a pizza on the menu. You won't care, either, what with the osso buco, the linguine and baby clams, gnocchi with fresh herbs in a beef and veal sauce, grilled lamb chops covered in a black truffle and mustard sauce, roasted chicken and pork sausage with braised Napa Valley cabbage, and homemade mozzarella salads. Daily specials include soup, salad, pasta, and fish. ✕ *348 S. La Brea Ave.,* ☎ *213/938–2863. Reservations advised. AE, D, DC, MC, V. Closed Sun. No lunch Sat.*

$$ ★ **Locanda Veneta.** The food may be more finely wrought at one or two other spots, but the combination of a splendid Venetian chef, Antonio Tomassi, and a simpatico co-owner, Jean Louis de Mori, have re-created the atmospheric equivalent of a genuine Italian trattoria, at reasonable prices. Specialties include risotto with lobster, veal chop, potato dumplings with tomatoes and shrimp, linguine with clams, lobster ravioli with saffron sauce, and a delectable apple tart. ✕ *8638 W. 3rd St.,* ☎ *310/274–1893. Reservations required. AE, D, DC, MC, V. Closed Sun. No lunch Sat. Valet parking.*

$ **Tavola Calda.** This low-tech Italian nirvana draws the budget-watching crowd, who are attracted to the inexpensive entrées that are all under $10. Best bets on the limited menu are unusual gourmet pizzas and risotto that reminds you of being in Milan. ✕ *7371 Melrose Ave.,* ☎ *213/658–6340. No reservations. AE, DC, MC, V. Valet parking.*

WESTSIDE (COASTAL LOS ANGELES DINING MAP)

$$$–$$$$ ★ **Valentino.** Rated among the best Italian restaurants in the nation, Valentino is generally considered to have the best wine list outside Italy, although the 1994 earthquake wreaked havoc with the wine cellar. Owner Piero Selvaggio is the man who introduced Los Angeles to the best and lightest of modern-day Italian cuisine. There's superb prosciutto, fried calamari, lobster cannelloni, fresh broiled porcini mushrooms, and osso buco. ✕ *3115 Pico Blvd., Santa Monica,* ☎ *310/829–4313. Reservations required. AE, DC, MC, V. Closed Sun. No lunch Sat.–Thurs. Valet parking.*

$$ **Remi.** It's not easy to find authentic Venetian cuisine in southern California, but there's a top-rate source tucked away in Santa Monica's Third Street Promenade. Order the linguine with scallops, mussels, shrimp, and fresh chopped tomatoes; the grilled quail wrapped in bacon and served with radicchio and grilled polenta; the whole wheat crepes with ricotta and spinach, topped with a tomato, carrot, and celery sauce; or the roasted pork chop stuffed with smoked mozzarella and prosciutto. ✕ *1451 Third St. Promenade, Santa Monica,* ☎ *310/393–6545. Reservations required. AE, DC, MC, V. Parking in nearby multistory mall parking lots.*

$–$$ **Tra di Noi.** The name means "between us," and Malibu natives are trying to keep this charming, simple *ristorante* just that—a local secret. It's run by a mama (who does the cooking), son, and daughter-in-law. Regular customers, film celebrities and non–show-biz folk alike love the unpretentious atmosphere and bring their kids. There's nothing fancy or *nuovo* on the menu, just great lasagna, freshly made pasta, mushroom and veal dishes, and crisp fresh salads. ✕ *3835 Cross Creek Rd.,* ☎ *310/456–0169. Reservations advised. AE. No lunch Sun.*

Japanese

DOWNTOWN

$$–$$$ **Restaurant Horikawa.** A department store of Japanese cuisines includes sushi, teppan steak tables, tempura, sashimi, shabu-shabu, teriyaki, and a $75-per-person seven-course dinner. All are good or excellent, but the sushi bar is the best. The decor is traditional Japanese, with private dining rooms, where guests sit on tatami floor mats, for two to 24. ✕ *111 S. San Pedro St.,* ☎ *213/ 680–9355. Reservations advised. AE, MC, V. No lunch Sat. Valet parking.*

LOS FELIZ (BEVERLY HILLS AND HOLLYWOOD DINING MAP)

$$$ ★ **Restaurant Katsu.** A stark, simple, perfectly designed sushi bar with a small table area serves some of the most exquisite and delicious delicacies east of Japan. This is probably the most authentic Japanese restaurant in the city and definitely a treat for both the eye and the palate. ✕ *1972 N. Hillhurst Ave.,* ☎ *213/665–1891. Reservations advised. AE, DC, MC, V. No lunch weekends. Valet parking.*

Mexican

HOLLYWOOD

$ **El Cholo.** The progenitor of the upscale chain, this place has been packing them in since the '20s. It serves good-size margaritas, a zesty assortment of tacos, make-your-own tacos, and, from July through October, green-corn tamales. It's friendly and fun, with large portions for only a few pesos. ✕ *1121 S. Western Ave.,* ☎ *213/734–2773. Reservations advised. AE, DC, MC, V. Valet parking and parking meters.*

SANTA MONICA (COASTAL LOS ANGELES DINING MAP)

$–$$ **Border Grill.** This very trendy, very loud eating hall is owned by two talented female chefs with the most eclectic tastes in town. The menu ranges from Yucatán seafood tacos to vinegar-and-pepper-grilled turkey to spicy baby-back ribs. It's worth dropping by for the fun of it, if you don't mind the noise. ✕ *1445 4th St.,* ☎ *310/451–1655. Reservations advised. AE, D, DC, MC, V. No lunch.*

WEST HOLLYWOOD

$–$$ **Antonio's Restaurant.** Don't let the strolling mariachis keep you from hearing the daily specials: authentic (though mediocre) Mexico City dishes that still put this unpretentious favorite a couple of notches above the ubiquitous taco-enchilada cantinas. Be adventurous and try the *chayote* (squash) stuffed with ground beef; ricotta in a spicy tomato sauce; pork ribs in a sauce of pickled *chipotle* peppers; veal shank with garlic, cumin, and red pepper; or chicken stuffed with apples, bananas, and raisins. Have flan for dessert. ✕ *7472 Melrose Ave.,* ☎ *213/655–0480. Dinner reservations advised. AE, MC, V. Closed Mon. Valet parking evenings.*

Polynesian

BEVERLY HILLS

$$–$$$ **Trader Vic's.** Sure, it's corny, but this Trader Vic's, inside the Beverly Hilton, is the most restrained and elegant of the late Victor Bergeron's South Seas extravaganzas. The crab Rangoon, grilled cheese wafers, skewered shrimp, grilled pork ribs, and the steaks, chops, and peanut butter–coated lamb cooked in the huge clay ovens are just fine. As for the array of exotic rum drinks, watch your sips. ✕ *9876 Wilshire Blvd.,* ☎ *310/276–6345. Reservations required. Jacket and tie. AE, D, DC, MC, V. No lunch. Valet parking.*

Spanish

MID-WILSHIRE (BEVERLY HILLS AND HOLLYWOOD DINING MAP)

$$–$$$ **Cava.** The decor at this trendy tapas bar is artsy (larger-than-life roses are painted on the walls), the atmosphere a bit noisy but lots of fun, and the cuisine alluring. You can graze on tapas—tiny snacks such as baked artichoke topped with bread crumbs and tomato or a fluffy potato omelet served with crème fraîche—or feast on bigger entrées: The paella is a must, but you may also want to try *zarzuela* (lightly baked shrimp, scallops, clams, mussels, and fresh fish in a hearty tomato wine sauce) or *bistec flamenco* (aged New York steak with caramelized onions and a traditional Argentine steak sauce). ✕ *8384 W. 3rd St.,* ☏ *213/658–8898. Reservations advised. AE, D, DC, MC, V. Valet parking.*

Thai

HOLLYWOOD

$–$$ **Chan Dara.** Here you'll find excellent Thai food in a bright and shiny Swiss chalet! Try any of the noodle dishes, especially those with crab and shrimp. Also tops on the extensive menu are *satay* (appetizers on skewers) and barbecued chicken and catfish. ✕ *310 N. Larchmont Blvd.,* ☏ *213/467–1052. Reservations advised for parties of more than 4. AE, DC, MC, V. No lunch weekends.*

WEST HOLLYWOOD

$$ **Tommy Tang's.** At this grazing ground for yuppies and celebs, a lot of people-watching goes on. Although portions are on the small side, they are decidedly innovative. The kitchen features crisp duck marinated in ginger and plum sauce, blackened sea scallops, and a spinach salad tossed with grilled chicken. There is also a happening sushi bar overlooking the parade of eccentric people who frequent Melrose Avenue. ✕ *7313 Melrose Ave.,* ☏ *213/651–1810. Reservations advised. AE, DC, MC, V. Valet parking.*

LODGING

By Jane E. Lasky

Because Los Angeles is so spread out it's good to select a hotel room not only for its ambience, amenities, and price but also for a location that is convenient to where you plan to spend most of your time.

West Hollywood and Beverly Hills are at the heart of the city, equidistant from the beaches and downtown. These are also the primary shopping districts of Los Angeles, with Rodeo Drive the central axis of Beverly Hills, and Melrose Avenue the playground for trendier purchases. The more recently developed Century City, located between Westwood and Beverly Hills, has top-notch hotels, a terrific mall, movie and legitimate theaters, and quick access to Rodeo Drive shopping. It's also an important Los Angeles business center. Hollywood, unfortunately, has lost much of its legendary glamour, so don't book a room there expecting to be in the lap of luxury—parts of Hollywood are downright seedy.

Downtown is attractive if you are interested in Los Angeles's cultural offerings, since this is where the Music Center and the Museum of Contemporary Art are. It is also the heartland for Los Angeles's conventions.

For closest proximity to Pacific Ocean beaches, check out Santa Monica, Marina del Rey, or Malibu. The San Fernando Valley is a good place to stay if you're looking for a suburban setting and quarters close to the movie and television studios on that side of the hills.

It's best to plan ahead and reserve a room. Many hotels offer tickets to amusement parks or plays as well as special prices for weekend visits. A travel agent can help in making your arrangements.

Hotels listed below are organized according to their location, then by price category, following this scale:

CATEGORY	COST*
$$$$	over $160
$$$	$100–$160
$$	$65–$100
$	under $65

**All prices are for a standard double room, excluding 11%–14% tax.*

Downtown

$$$$ **Biltmore Hotel.** Since its 1923 opening, the Biltmore has hosted such notables as Mary Pickford, J. Paul Getty, Eleanor Roosevelt, Princess Margaret, and several U.S. presidents. The guest rooms in this historic landmark have been updated, with pastel color schemes and traditional French furniture and armoires. The lobby ceiling was painted by Italian artist Giovanni Smeraldi; imported Italian marble and plum-color velvet grace the Grand Avenue Sports Bar. There's also Bernard's, an acclaimed Continental restaurant. The swank health club has a Roman-bath motif. On the 9th and 11th floors, designated as the Executive floors, desks are specially equipped for business travelers. The 10th floor, the Club floor, comes complete with a concierge and a lounge that offers afternoon tea, Continental breakfast, board games, a fax machine, and big-screen TV. ☒ *506 S. Grand Ave., 90071,* ☎ *213/624–1011 or 800/245–8673,* FAX *213/612–1545. 683 rooms. 3 restaurants, lounge, no-smoking floors, room service, health club. AE, DC, MC, V.*

$$$$ **Hotel Inter-Continental Los Angeles.** Part of California Plaza (where the Museum of Contemporary Art is) and within walking distance of the Music Center, the sleek Inter-Continental boasts floor-to-ceiling views. Guest rooms are decorated in contemporary style, with glass-topped tables and desks, in color schemes of either ivory and peach or celadon and brown. The sculpture *Yellow Fin,* by Richard Serra, dominates the large lobby, and other artwork is on view throughout, on loan from the Museum of Contemporary Art. The Grand Cafe serves California cuisine in an arty atmosphere. ☒ *251 S. Olive St., 90012,* ☎ *213/617–3300 or 800/442–5251,* FAX *213/617–3399. 429 rooms. Restaurant, no-smoking floors, room service, outdoor pool, indoor pool, health club, business. AE, D, DC, MC, V.*

$$$$ **Hyatt Regency Los Angeles.** The Hyatt is in the heart of the downtown financial district, minutes away from the Convention Center, Dodger Stadium, and the Music Center. Each room, traditionally furnished with rich mahogany and cherry woods and marble baths, has a wall of windows with city views. Security is high at this downtown hotel, with well-lit hallways and no blind corners. The hotel is part of the Broadway Plaza, comprising 35 shops. Tennis is available nearby at an extra cost. ☒ *711 S. Hope St., 90017,* ☎ *213/683–1234 or 800/233–1234,* FAX *213/629–3230. 485 rooms, 41 suites. Restaurant, coffee shop, 2 lounges, no-smoking floors, health club, parking. AE, D, DC, MC, V.*

$$$$ **Los Angeles Hilton Hotel and Towers.** Located on Wilshire Boulevard, the Hilton is convenient to Dodger Stadium, museums, Chinatown, and the Music Center. The sparse-looking contemporary decor of the guest rooms is in beige, blue, and green. Among the hotel's restaurants, the standout is Cardini, a fine Italian eatery; the Gazebo, a standard hotel coffee shop, is the place to go if you're looking for a more casual set-

ting. Parking is expensive. *930 Wilshire Blvd., 90017, 213/629–4321 or 800/445–8667, FAX 213/612–3977. 900 rooms. 4 restaurants, coffee shop, lounge, exercise room, parking (fee). AE, D, DC, MC, V.*

$$$$ ★ Sheraton Grande Hotel. This 14-story hotel with its reflecting glass facade is near Dodger Stadium, the Music Center, and downtown's Bunker Hill District. Guest rooms are oversize, with wall-to-wall windows and awesome city views. The decor features dark wood furniture, sofas, and minibars; colors are mauve, peach, and gray; baths are marble. There's butler service with every room. If you can afford the rates, stay in the penthouse suite or in one of the executive-floor rooms, where you'll even have a chance to play Nintendo, as the hotel provides this electronic diversion. A limousine is available for Beverly Hills or downtown attractions. There are complimentary privileges at a local, state-of-the-art YMCA, and a lovely landscaped pool on the premises. *333 S. Figueroa St., 90071, 213/617–1133 or 800/524–7263, FAX 213/613–0291. 469 rooms. 3 restaurants, bar, room service, no-smoking floors, pool, 4 cinemas. AE, D, DC, MC, V.*

$$$$ Westin Bonaventure Hotel & Suites. This 35-story, five-tower, mirrored-glass high-rise is architect John Portman's striking contribution to downtown Los Angeles. Rooms—a number of which are on the small side—have a wall of glass, streamlined pale furnishings, and comfortable appointments. One tower is endowed with oversize suites, 94 in all. The outside elevators provide stunning city views; there are also 5 acres of ponds and waterfalls in the lobby. At the top of the hotel are the Bona Vista revolving lounge and Top of Five grill. A popular Sunday brunch is served in the five-story atrium lobby, where there is a thriving coffee bar. Parking is expensive. *404 S. Figueroa St., 90071, 213/624–1000 or 800/228–3000, FAX 213/612-4894. 1,368 rooms. 3 restaurants, lounge, no-smoking floors, pool, shops, parking (fee). AE, D, DC, MC, V.*

$$$$ Wyndham Checkers Hotel. Set in one of this neighborhood's few remaining historical buildings—it opened as the Mayflower Hotel in 1927—this hotel offers much the same sophistication and luxury as the Biltmore across the street, but on a smaller scale. Guest rooms are furnished with oversize beds, upholstered easy chairs, and writing tables and have marble baths. A library is available for small meetings or tea. *535 S. Grand Ave., 90071, 213/624–0000 or 800/996–3426, FAX 213/626-9906. 188 rooms. Restaurant, no-smoking floors, lap pool, spa, exercise room, valet parking (fee). AE, D, DC, MC, V.*

$$$–$$$$ ★ New Otani Hotel and Garden. For a quintessential Japanese hotel experience, visit this 21-story, ultramodern hotel, with its ½-acre rooftop Japanese-style garden. The decor is a serene blend of Westernized luxury and Eastern simplicity. Each room has a phone in the bathroom, a refrigerator, an alarm clock, and a color TV; most rooms have a *yukata* (robe). If you're so inclined, book a Japanese suite, where you'll sleep on a futon on the floor. *120 S. Los Angeles St., 90012, 213/629–1200, 800/421–8795; in CA, 800/273–2294; FAX 213/622-0989. 435 rooms. 3 restaurants, 3 lounges, room service, massage, sauna, parking (fee). AE, D, DC, MC, V.*

$$ Figueroa Hotel. This 12-story hotel, built in 1926, has managed to keep its charming Spanish style intact. Terra-cotta-color rooms carry out the Spanish look, with hand-painted furniture and, in many rooms, ceiling fans. The hotel boasts an Olympic-size swimming pool in a lush setting, complete with fountains and sculptures. *939 S. Figueroa St.,*

90015, ☎ *213/627–8971 or 800/421–9092,* FAX *213/689–0305. 285 rooms. 3 restaurants, coffee shop, lounge, pool, free parking. AE, DC, MC, V.*

$$ Holiday Inn L.A. Downtown. This six-floor hotel offers Holiday Inn's usual professional staff and services, and standard no-frills room decor. The hotel is convenient, close to the Museum of Contemporary Art, convention center, and Los Angeles Sports Arena. Guests can work out for free at the nearby Family Fitness Center at ARCO Plaza. *750 Garland Ave., 90017,* ☎ *213/628–5242 or 800/628–5240,* FAX *213/628–1201. 205 rooms. Restaurant, lounge, no-smoking floors, pool, free parking. AE, D, DC, MC, V.*

$$ The Inntowne. This three-story hotel with large beige-and-white rooms is 1½ blocks from the convention center and just down the street from the 24-hour Pantry restaurant, a favorite place for breakfast. The swimming pool is surrounded by palm trees and a small garden. *925 S. Figueroa St., 90015,* ☎ *213/628–2222 or 800/457–8520,* FAX *213/687–0566. 170 rooms. Lounge, coffee shop, pool, free parking. AE, D, DC, MC, V.*

$ EconoLodge. With its central location between downtown and Hollywood, near the Wilshire commercial district, this very plain, two-story hotel in four separate buildings is convenient for businesspeople. The guest rooms—modern, not overly large—are decorated in pastel colors with wood trimmings and have color TVs and VCRs. If you belong to AAA, ask for a discount. *3400 3rd St., 90020,* ☎ *213/385–0061 or 800/266–0061. 120 rooms. Coffee shop, pool, free parking. AE, D, DC, MC, V.*

$ ★ Inn at 657. This unassuming inn, run by retired attorney Patsy Carter, is reminiscent of a tiny European-style hotel. Suites are roomy and tastefully decorated and have stocked kitchens containing coffee, tea, and soft drinks, all included in the price. The rate also includes a hearty breakfast, local telephone calls, gratuities, taxes, and parking. The inn's location is convenient, close to the convention center and the University of Southern California campus. *657 W. 23rd St., 90027,* ☎ *213/741–2200 or 800/347–7512. 6 suites. No-smoking rooms, outdoor hot tub. No credit cards.*

$ Orchid Hotel. One of the smaller downtown hotels, this 1920s vintage property is very reasonably priced. There are no frills, but the standard rooms are clean, with modern decor in pastel tones. Note that there is no parking at the hotel, but public lots are close by. If you're staying at least a week, ask about lower weekly rates. *819 S. Flower St., 90017,* ☎ *213/624–5855,* FAX *213/624–8740. 63 rooms and 2 suites. Coin laundry. AE, D, DC, MC, V.*

Hollywood and West Hollywood

$$$$ The Argyle. Staying at this early Art Deco hotel is like checking into an exclusive private club—many a star called this address home, among them Marilyn Monroe, John Wayne, Clark Gable, and Errol Flynn. Ask for a city or mountain view. Both are great (although the rooms are a bit small by Los Angeles standards), but the city-side accommodations are more expensive. *8358 Sunset Blvd., West Hollywood 90069,* ☎ *213/654–7100 or 800/225–2637,* FAX *213/654–9287. 64 rooms. Restaurant, pool, sauna, health club, business services, meeting rooms. AE, DC, MC, V.*

$$$$ Mondrian Hotel. The exterior of this 12-story hotel is actually a giant surrealistic mural; inside there's fine artwork. Accommodations are spacious, with pale-wood furniture and curved sofas in the seating area. Ask for south-corner suites; they tend to be quieter than the rest. A chauffeured limousine is placed at each guest's disposal for a fee. The hotel is convenient to major recording, film, and TV studios and is popular with the rock-and-roll crowd. ☎ *8440 Sunset Blvd., West Hollywood 90069, ☎ 213/650–8999 or 800/525–8029, FAX 213/650–5215. 224 suites. Restaurant, room service, pool, health club, parking (fee). AE, D, DC, MC, V.*

$$$$ **Summerfield Suites Hotel.** This four-story luxury hotel features all suites, decorated in a modern style in shades of blue and pink. All have private balconies, fireplaces, and kitchens. Great for business travelers—it's near "Restaurant Row on La Cienega"—it's not as expensive as other hotels in this price category, and rates even include breakfast. ☎ *1000 Westmount Dr., West Hollywood 90069, ☎ 310/657–7400, 800/833–4353, FAX 310/854–6744. 109 suites. Bar, pool, health club, parking (fee). AE, D, DC, MC, V.*

$$$$ ★ **Wyndham Bel Age Hotel.** This elegant, European-style, all-suite hotel just off the Sunset Strip has a soothing, residential feel. The understated country-French decor is in dark woods and rose and mauve color schemes; the suites are spacious, with large living rooms. South-facing rooms have private terraces that look out over the Los Angeles skyline as far as the Pacific. Some touches are downright extravagant, such as multiline telephones with voice mail, original art, private terraces, and a daily newspaper. The hotel has a distinctive restaurant that serves fine Russian meals with a French flair. ☎ *1020 N. San Vicente Blvd., West Hollywood 90069, ☎ 310/854–1111 or 800/424–4443, FAX 310/854-0926. 200 suites. 3 restaurants, lounge, room service, pool, health club, concierge, parking (fee). AE, D, DC, MC, V.*

$$$ **Chateau Marmont Hotel.** Although planted on the Sunset Strip amid giant billboards and much sun-bleached Hollywood glitz, this castle of Old World charm and French Normandy design still promises its guests a secluded hideaway close to Hollywood's hot spots. A haunt for many reclusive show-biz personalities and discriminating world travelers since it opened in 1929, this is the ultimate in privacy. ☎ *8221 Sunset Blvd., Hollywood 90046, ☎ 213/656–1010 or 800/242–8328, FAX 213/655–5311. 63 rooms. Dining room, room service, pool, exercise room, concierge, free parking. AE, MC, V.*

$$$ **Hyatt on Sunset.** In the heart of the Sunset Strip, this Hyatt is a favorite of music-biz execs and rock stars who appreciate the two-line phones and voice mail available here. There are penthouse suites, and all rooms facing the boulevard have private patios. The rooms are decorated in peach colors and modern furniture; some have aquariums. ☎ *8401 Sunset Blvd., West Hollywood 90069, ☎ 213/656–1234 or 800/233–1234, FAX 213/650–7024. 262 rooms. Restaurant, lounge, no-smoking floors, pool, parking (fee). AE, D, DC, MC, V.*

$$$ **Radisson Hollywood Roosevelt.** The site of the first Academy Awards ceremony, this hotel across from Mann's Chinese Theatre has an Art Deco lobby and a pool decorated by David Hockney. Most rooms have pastel decor with pine furniture; for a treat, try one of the 40 Hollywood-theme suites such as the Gable/Lombard Suite or the Shirley Temple Suite. ☎ *7000 Hollywood Blvd., Hollywood 90028, ☎ 213/466–7000 or 800/950–7667, FAX 213/462–8056. 311 rooms. 3 restaurants, lounge, no-smoking floor, car rental, parking (fee). AE, D, DC, MC, V.*

$$ **Hollywood Holiday Inn.** You can't miss this hotel, one of the tallest buildings in Hollywood. The rooms are decorated in floral and pastels in standard-issue Holiday Inn fashion. There is a safekeeping box in each room. The hotel is only minutes from Hollywood attractions. ☎ *1755 N. Highland Ave., Hollywood 90028, ☎ 213/462–7181 or 800/465–4329, FAX 213/466–9072. 470 rooms. Restaurant, coffee shop, pool, coin laundry, parking (fee). AE, D, DC, MC, V.*

$ **Banana Bungalow Hotel and International Hostel.** Mostly hostel-style rooms are offered here, with three to six beds in each; you'll be sharing a room with people you don't know, unless you book one of the 12 double-occupancy rooms—be sure to specify what you want when booking. Checkout is early, by 10:30 AM. ☒ *2775 Cahuenga Blvd. W, Hollywood 90068,* ☎ *213/851–1129 or 800/446–7835,* FAX *213/851–1569. 56 rooms. Pool, exercise room, billiards, recreation room, theater, airport shuttle, free parking. MC, V.*

Beverly Hills

$$$$ **Beverly Hilton.** Most rooms here, decorated in warm tones, have balconies overlooking Beverly Hills or downtown. Of special interest to business travelers are a fax machine in the lobby and incredible deals on cellular phone rentals. There's also a complimentary town car that serves nearby shopping areas. ☒ *9876 Wilshire Blvd., 90210,* ☎ *310/274–7777 or 800/445–8667,* FAX *310/285–1313. 581 rooms. 3 restaurants, refrigerators, pool, wading pool, exercise room, parking (fee). AE, D, DC, MC, V.*

$$$$ ★ **Four Seasons Los Angeles.** Some say this property resembles a French château with the refinement of a European manor house. Rooms are eclectic, some done in pastels, others in a black-and-beige scheme. All suites have French doors and a balcony. There is an outstanding restaurant on the premises serving California cuisine, and there's great shopping only five minutes away on Rodeo Drive and Melrose Avenue. ☒ *300 S. Doheny Dr., Los Angeles 90048,* ☎ *310/273–2222 or 800/332–3442,* FAX *310/859–3824. 285 rooms. Restaurant, lounge, room service, pool, exercise room, free parking and parking (fee). AE, DC, MC, V.*

$$$$ **Hotel Nikko.** Distinctive Japanese accents distinguish this contemporary hotel located near Restaurant Row. Large guest rooms done in traditional pastels cater to business travelers: There are oversize desks and work areas with computer and fax hookup capabilities. Traditional Japanese soaking tubs dominate luxurious bathrooms, and a bedside remote-control conveniently operates in-room lighting, temperature, TVs, VCRs, and CD players. Pangaea, the hotel restaurant, serves Pacific Rim cuisine. ☒ *465 S. La Cienega Blvd., Los Angeles 90048,* ☎ *310/247–0400, 800/645–5687, or 800/645–5624;* FAX *310/247–0315. 300 rooms. Restaurant, lounge, room service, pool, fitness center, business services, parking. AE, D, DC, MC, V.*

$$$$ **Hotel Sofitel Ma Maison.** This hotel offers first-class service and the sort of intimacy you usually expect in small European-style hotels. The country-French guest rooms are done in terra-cotta and blues, with small prints. The hotel is across the street from two giant malls and a number of restaurants and movie theaters. The back of the property faces a large brick wall, so insist on a southern view. ☒ *8555 Beverly Blvd., Los Angeles 90048,* ☎ *310/278–5444 or 800/521–7772,* FAX *310/657–2816. 311 rooms. Restaurant, pool, sauna, fitness center, parking (fee). AE, DC, MC, V.*

$$$$ **Le Parc Hotel.** A boutique hotel housed in a modern low-rise building, the four-story Le Parc is in a lovely residential area. Suites are decorated in earth tones and shades of wine and rust with sunken living rooms, balconies, fireplaces, VCRs, and kitchenettes. The hotel is near the Farmers' Market, CBS Television City, and the Los Angeles County Museum of Art. ☒ *733 N. West Knoll, West Hollywood 90069,* ☎ *310/855–8888 or 800/578–4837,* FAX *310/659–5230. 154 suites. Restaurant, pool, tennis courts, health club, parking (fee). AE, DC, MC, V.*

$$$$ **Peninsula Beverly Hills.** A circular motor court surrounded by flowered hedges, poplar trees, and philodendrons greets guests in rare style.

The hotel's appearance is classic, done in French Renaissance architecture with contemporary overtones. Rooms are decorated like luxury homes, with antiques, rich fabrics, and marble floors. Minibars and refrigerators can be found behind armoire doors in all rooms, and all suites are equipped with compact disc players, fax machines, and individual security systems. ☎ *9882 Little Santa Monica Blvd., 90212,* ☎ *310/551–2888 or 800/462–7899,* FAX *310/788–2319. 195 rooms. 2 restaurants, bar, lap pool, health club, concierge, business services, parking. AE, D, DC, MC, V.*

$$$$ ★ **Regent Beverly Wilshire.** This landmark 12-story property has Italian Renaissance–style architecture with a French neoclassic influence; the guest rooms have appropriate period furnishings in subtle hues of soft beige and cream, wheat, peach, rose, and celery, and glorious marble bathrooms. The multilingual staff offers personal service (like private butlers) and many other extras, such as the fresh strawberries and cream and designer water that are delivered to your room upon arrival. The hotel's restaurants include the Dining Room, with its California-Continental menu, and the Lobby Lounge Cafe, which serves California cuisine. ☎ *9500 Wilshire Blvd., 90212,* ☎ *310/275–5200 or 800/421–4354; in CA, 800/427–4354;* FAX *310/274–2851. 300 rooms and 48 suites. 3 restaurants, no-smoking floors, pool, spa, concierge, business services, parking (fee). AE, D, DC, MC, V.*

$$$ ★ **Beverly Hills Ritz Hotel.** There's a very family-style European feel at this low-rise hotel; the friendly staff will get to know you by name, given half the chance. The cozy black-and-white lobby has overstuffed sofas and lots of plants. All the suites are off the pool. Furnishings are smart and contemporary; all feature kitchen–living room, one bedroom, and bath. ☎ *10300 Wilshire Blvd., 90024,* ☎ *310/275–5575 or 800/800–1234. 116 rooms. Restaurant, pool, exercise room, parking (fee). AE, D, DC, MC, V.*

$$$ **Beverly Prescott Hotel.** This small, 12-story luxury hotel is perched on a hill overlooking Beverly Hills, Century City, and the mighty Pacific. The open-air architecture is enhanced by soothing rooms decorated in warm salmon and caramel tones. Furnishings are stylish, and the rooms are spacious, with private balconies. Six suites are equipped with Jacuzzis. ☎ *1224 S. Beverwil Dr., 90035,* ☎ *310/277–2800 or 800/421–3212,* FAX *310/203–9537. 140 rooms. Restaurant, room service, pool, health club, business services, parking (fee). AE, D, DC, MC, V.*

$$$ **Carlyle Inn.** Service is the byword of this intimate, small hostelry in the city's design district. The four-story, contemporary property offers guests several extras: a buffet breakfast in the morning, a glass of wine in the late afternoon. Rooms are decorated in peach with light pine furniture and black accents. ☎ *1119 S. Robertson Blvd., 90035,* ☎ *310/275–4445 or 800/322–7595,* FAX *310/859–0496. 32 rooms. Restaurant, exercise room, parking (fee). AE, D, DC, MC, V.*

Century City

$$$$ ★ **Century Plaza Hotel and Tower.** Beside the 20-story hotel (on 10 acres of tropical plants and reflecting pools) is a 30-story tower, which is lavishly decorated with signature art and antiques. Rooms in both are furnished like a mansion, with a mix of classic and contemporary appointments. Each room has a refrigerator and balcony with an ocean or a city view. There are three excellent restaurants here. ☎ *2025 Ave. of the Stars, 90067,* ☎ *310/277–2000 or 800/228–3000,* FAX *310/551–3355. 1,072 rooms. 3 restaurants, 2 pools, health club, parking. AE, D, DC, MC, V.*

$$$$ ★ **J. W. Marriott Hotel at Century City.** The West Coast flagship for the multifaceted Marriott chain, this hotel has elegant, modern rooms

decorated in soft pastels and equipped with minibars, lavish marble baths, and facilities for travelers with disabilities. Ask for accommodations that overlook Twentieth Century Fox's back lot. The hotel offers complimentary limo service to Beverly Hills and provides excellent service. ☒ *2151 Ave. of the Stars, 90067,* ☎ *310/277–2777 or 800/228–9290,* FAX *310/785–9240. 367 rooms. Restaurant, indoor and outdoor pools, health club. AE, D, DC, MC, V.*

$$$ **Century City Courtyard by Marriott.** Located near the Century City business complex, this more-than-comfortable hotel mixes California architecture with traditional fabrics and furnishings in soft hues. The entrance is bold, though: A red welcome carpet and a red London phone booth are your first impressions. ☒ *10320 W. Olympic Blvd., Los Angeles 90067,* ☎ *310/556–2777 or 800/947–8521. 133 rooms. Restaurant, exercise room, free parking. AE, D, DC, MC, V.*

$$ **Century City Inn.** This hotel is small but designed for comfort. Rooms have a refrigerator, microwave oven, remote-control TV and VCR, as well as a 10-cup coffee unit with fresh gourmet-blend coffee and tea. Baths have whirlpool tubs and a phone. Complimentary Continental breakfast is served. ☒ *10330 W. Olympic Blvd., Los Angeles 90064,* ☎ *310/553–1000 or 800/553–1005,* FAX *310/277–1633. 48 rooms. Parking (fee). AE, D, DC, MC, V.*

Bel-Air, Westwood, and West Los Angeles

$$$$ ★ **Hotel Bel-Air.** This charming, secluded hotel—a celebrity mecca—is one of Los Angeles's best. Extensive exotic gardens and a creek complete with swans give it the ambience of a top-rated resort. The lovely rooms and suites are impeccably decorated in peach and earth tones. All are villa-bungalow style with Mediterranean decor offering the feel of fine homes. For their quietest accommodation, ask for a room near the former stable area. ☒ *701 Stone Canyon Rd., Bel-Air 90077,* ☎ *310/472–1211 or 800/648–4097,* FAX *310/476–5890. 92 rooms. Restaurant, lounge, pool, fitness center, parking (fee). AE, DC, MC, V.*

$$$$ **Westwood Marquis Hotel and Gardens.** This hotel near UCLA is a favorite of corporate and entertainment types. Each individualized suite in its 15 stories has a view of Bel Air, the Pacific Ocean, or Century City. South-facing suites overlooking the pool also offer expansive views of the city and sea. Breakfast and lunch are served in the Garden Terrace, which also has a popular Sunday brunch. The award-winning Dynasty Room restaurant features Continental cuisine. European teas are served in the afternoon in the Westwood Lounge. ☒ *930 Hilgard Ave., Los Angeles 90024,* ☎ *310/208–8765 or 800/421–2317,* FAX *310/824–0355. 257 suites. 2 restaurants, lounge, room service, no-smoking floor, 2 pools, health club, parking (fee). AE, D, DC, MC, V.*

$$$ **Radisson Bel-Air.** In its lovely garden setting, this two-story hotel feels very southern Californian, with patios and terraces overlooking the lush tropical greenery. Guest rooms are decorated in muted tones of cream and gray, with furniture in sleek, modern shapes and Art Deco–style fixtures. ☒ *11461 Sunset Blvd., Los Angeles 90049,* ☎ *310/476–6571 or 800/333–3333. 162 rooms. Restaurant, lounge, no-smoking rooms, pool, tennis courts, health club, concierge, business services, parking (fee). AE, D, DC, MC, V.*

$$–$$$ **Century Wilshire.** Most units in this three-story European-style hotel are suites with kitchenettes and tiled baths, all set in a homey English-style pastel decor. Within walking distance of UCLA and Westwood Village, this simple hotel has views of Wilshire and the courtyard. The clientele here is mostly European. ☒ *10776 Wilshire Blvd., West Los Angeles 90024,* ☎ *310/474–4506 or 800/421–7223 (outside CA),* FAX *310/474–2535. 99 rooms. Pool, free parking. AE, DC, MC, V.*

$ Best Western Royal Palace Inn and Suites. This small hotel located just off I–405 (San Diego Freeway) is decorated with modern touches, lots of wood, and mirrors. Guest rooms are done in rich greens and teals, with contrasting soft peach and rose tones. In-room morning coffee and tea are complimentary, as is parking to hotel guests. The Royal Palace is a good value for families: All the rooms are suites with a queen sleeper sofa in addition to the two queen-size beds in each unit; microwaves and refrigerators are also provided. ☐ *2528 S. Sepulveda Blvd., West Los Angeles 90064,* ☎ *310/477–9066 or 800/251–3888,* FAX *310/478–4133. 55 suites. Pool, exercise room, billiards, laundry service, free parking. AE, D, DC, MC, V.*

Santa Monica

$$$$ Loews Santa Monica Beach Hotel. This hotel is two blocks south of the landmark Santa Monica Pier. The property's centerpiece is a five-story glass atrium with views of the Pacific. Rooms are California casual with bleached rattan and wicker furniture and quilted bedspreads, in mauve, peach, coral, and sky-blue color schemes. Most have ocean views and private balconies, and all guests have direct access to the beach. ☐ *1700 Ocean Ave., 90401,* ☎ *310/458–6700 or 800/325–6397,* FAX *310/458–6761. 350 rooms, 35 suites. Restaurant, café, no-smoking floors, indoor-outdoor pool, fitness center, concierge, business services, parking (fee). AE, D, DC, MC, V.*

$$$$ Miramar Sheraton. This hotel, "where Wilshire meets the sea," is close to all area beaches, across the street from Pacific Palisades Park, and near deluxe shopping areas and many quaint eateries. Many rooms have balconies overlooking the ocean. ☐ *101 Wilshire Blvd., 90401,* ☎ *310/576–7777 or 800/325–3535. 302 rooms. 2 restaurants, lounge, pool, health club, parking (fee). AE, D, DC, MC, V.*

$$$$ Shutters on the Beach. Three separate buildings—just yards from the Pacific—are linked by trellises, balconies, and awnings, like resorts and cottages of the 1920s. Contemporary rooms are on the small side but tidily decorated. In the marble bathroom you'll find an oversize Jacuzzi tub with a glass window that opens to look across the room to the outdoors. ☐ *1 Pico Blvd., Santa Monica 90405,* ☎ *310/458–0030 or 800/334–9000,* FAX *310/458–4589. 198 rooms. 2 restaurants, no-smoking floors, in-room safes, pool, health club, concierge, parking (fee). AE, D, DC, MC, V.*

$$ Holiday Inn Santa Monica Beach. Close to many restaurants, major shopping centers, the beach, and Santa Monica Pier, this inn has standard Holiday Inn rooms and amenities. ☐ *120 Colorado Blvd., 90401,* ☎ *310/451–0676 or 800/947–9175,* FAX *310/393–7145. 132 rooms. Restaurant, lounge, pool, laundry service, parking. AE, D, DC, MC, V.*

$ Carmel Hotel. This charming four-story hotel built in the 1920s is one block from the beach and Santa Monica Place, as well as from movie theaters and many fine restaurants. The Art Deco–style lobby is appealing, and electric ceiling fans add to the simple room decor, done in wine, hunter green, and beige tones. ☐ *201 Broadway, 90401,* ☎ *310/451–2469 or 800/445–8695,* FAX *310/393–4180. 102 rooms, 8 suites. Restaurant, parking (fee). AE, D, DC, MC, V.*

$ Palm Motel. This quiet, unceremonious motel has old-fashioned rooms, in which the decorative highlight is the color TV. But the Palm does offer complimentary coffee, tea, and cookies at breakfast, and it's only a short drive away from several good restaurants and a mere mile from the beach. ☐ *2020 14th St., 90405,* ☎ *310/452–3822. 25 rooms. Coin laundry, free parking. MC, V.*

Marina del Rey

$$$$ ★ **Doubletree Marina del Rey L.A.** This luxurious, nine-story, high-rise property has a high-tech design softened by a pastel-toned decor accented in brass and marble. Ask for upper-floor rooms that face the marina. There are lovely touches in this Mediterranean-style hotel, such as a gazebo in the patio and rooms with water views. *4100 Admiralty Way, 90292, ☎ 310/301–3000, 800/222–8733, or 800/528–0444, FAX 310/ 301–6890. 375 rooms. Restaurant, lounges, pool, fitness center, business services airport shuttle, parking (fee). AE, D, DC, MC, V.*

$$$$ **Marina del Rey Hotel.** Completely surrounded by water, this deluxe waterfront hotel is on the marina's main channel, making cruises and charters easily accessible. Guest rooms (contemporary with a nautical touch) have balconies and patios, and many have harbor views. The hotel is within walking distance of shopping and only a bike ride away from Fisherman's Village. There are meeting rooms, a beautiful gazebo area for parties, and complimentary access to the nearby fitness club. *13534 Bali Way, 90292, ☎ 310/301–1000, 800/882–4000, or 800/862–7462 in CA; FAX 310/ 301–8167. 158 rooms. Restaurant, lounge, pool, putting green, airport shuttle, free parking. AE, DC, MC, V.*

$$$–$$$$ **Marina del Rey Marriott Inn.** Conveniently located in a lively area, this hotel is situated near great shopping at Fox Hills Mall (with 50 shops) and across the street from a movie theater. The contemporary rooms are decorated in cool greens and blues. Tropical trees and foliage enhance the pool area, as does the goldfish pond. *13480 Maxella Ave., 90292, ☎ 310/822–8555 or 800/228–9290, FAX 310/823–2996. 281 rooms. Restaurant, lounge, pool, health club, parking. AE, D, DC, MC, V.*

$$$–$$$$ **Marina International Hotel.** This hotel is across from a sandy beach within the marina. Each of the very private rooms offers a balcony or patio that faces the garden or the courtyard. Ask for one of the bungalows—they're huge. Boat charters are available for up to 200 people. *4200 Admiralty Way, 90292, ☎ 310/301–2000, 800/862–7462, or 800/529–2525; FAX 310/301–6687. 110 rooms, 25 bungalows. Restaurant, lounge, pool, health club, airport shuttle, free parking. AE, DC, MC, V.*

$$$–$$$$ **Ritz-Carlton, Marina del Rey.** This sumptuous property sits on some prime real estate at the northern end of a basin, offering a panoramic view of the Pacific. The well-appointed contemporary rooms have French doors, marble baths, honor bars, and plenty of amenities—from plush terry robes to maid service twice a day. *4375 Admiralty Way, 90292, ☎ 310/823–1700, FAX 310/823–7318. 306 rooms. 2 restaurants, pool, fitness center, tennis courts, business services, parking (fee). AE, D, DC, MC, V.*

$$ **Marina Pacific Hotel & Suites.** This hotel faces the Pacific and one of the world's most vibrant boardwalks; it's nestled among Venice's art galleries, shops, and elegant, offbeat restaurants. Comfortable accommodations include suites, conference facilities, full-service amenities, and a delightful sidewalk café. For active travelers, there are ocean swimming, roller skating along the strand, racquetball, and tennis nearby. *1697 Pacific Ave., Venice 90291, ☎ 310/399–7770 or 800/421–8151, FAX 310/452–5479. 57 rooms, 35 suites; 1-bedroom apartments available. Restaurant, laundry service, free parking. AE, D, DC, MC, V.*

South Bay Beach Cities

$$$–$$$$ **Crowne Plaza Redondo Beach and Marina Hotel.** Across the street from the Redondo Beach Pier, this swank five-story hotel overlooks the Pacific. The magnificent lobby has a 2,200-gallon saltwater aquarium as

the focal point, and there are plenty of amenities and special touches throughout the property, including indoor and outdoor dining, a nightclub, and the famous Gold's Gym. Rooms are decorated in a seaside theme with light woods and soft colors. *300 N. Harbor Dr., Redondo Beach 90277, 310/318–8888 or 800/368–9760, FAX 310/376–1930. 339 rooms. Restaurant, lounge, pool, sauna, tennis, exercise room, business services, parking (fee). AE, D, DC, MC, V.*

$$ ★ **Barnabey's Hotel.** Modeled after a 19th-century English inn, with four-poster beds, lace curtains, and antique decorations, Barnabey's also has an enclosed greenhouse pool. The London Pub resembles a cozy English hangout, with entertainment nightly; Barnabey's Restaurant serves Continental cuisine and has private, curtained booths. Complimentary English buffet breakfast is served. *3501 Sepulveda Blvd. (at Rosecrans), Manhattan Beach 90266, 310/545–8466 or 800/552–5285, FAX 310/545–8621. 126 rooms. 2 restaurants, lounge, no-smoking floor, pool, airport shuttle, free parking. AE, D, DC, MC, V.*

Airport

$$$–$$$$ **Sheraton Gateway Hotel at LAX.** This luxurious 14-story hotel suits business and leisure travelers alike. The contemporary rooms are decorated in muted shades and are not exceptional but adequate. Forty-eight of the rooms were designed especially for people with disabilities. *6101 W. Century Blvd., Los Angeles 90045, 310/642–1111 or 800/325–3535, FAX 310/645–1414. 807 rooms. 2 restaurants, lounges, pool, exercise room, concierge. AE, D, DC, MC, V.*

$$$ ★ **Doubletree Hotel LAX.** This three-wing hotel is a good place to stay if you want to be pampered but also need to be close to the airport. Rooms and suites are decorated in muted earth tones to complement the contemporary decor; many suites have private outdoor spas. The expansive, luxurious lobby is decorated in marble and brass. *5400 W. Century Blvd., Los Angeles 90045, 310/216–5858, FAX 310/670–1948. 729 rooms. 2 restaurants, lounge, pool, sauna, fitness center, business services, parking (fee). AE, D, DC, MC, V.*

$$$ **Hyatt Hotel–LAX.** Rich brown marble in the lobby entrance and dark wood columns delineate the neoclassical decor of this contemporary 12-story building close to LAX, Hollywood Park, the Forum, and Marina del Rey. The Hyatt keeps business travelers in mind, offering in-room fax machines, computer hookups, and voice mail, plus large meeting rooms with ample banquet space. The hotel's staff is multilingual. *6225 W. Century Blvd., Los Angeles 90045, 310/337–1234 or 800/233–1234, FAX 310/641–6924. 594 rooms. 2 restaurants, lounge, no-smoking floors, pool, health club, parking (fee). AE, D, DC, MC, V.*

$$ **Airport Marina Hotel.** Located in a quiet, residential area, perfect for jogging, tennis, and golf, is this contemporary hotel, with four separate wings and several buildings, the main one a 12-story high-rise. The rooms are warm, with plenty of wood; all have either pool, ocean, or airport views. A shuttle service goes to LAX, Marina del Rey, and Fox Hills Mall. *8601 Lincoln Blvd., Los Angeles 90045, 310/670–8111 or 800/800–6333, FAX 310/337–1883. 770 rooms. Restaurant, pool, airport shuttle. AE, D, DC, MC, V.*

$ **Holiday Inn–LAX.** This international-style hotel appeals to families as well as business types, with standard Holiday Inn rooms decorated in earth tones—beige, burgundy, orange, and green. Amenities include a California-cuisine restaurant and cocktail lounge, multilingual telephone operators, and tour information. ☏ *9901 La Cienega Blvd., Los Angeles 90045,* ☎ *310/649–5151 or 800/624–0025,* FAX *310/670–3619. 403 rooms. Restaurant, pool, exercise room, airport shuttle, parking (fee). AE, D, DC, MC, V.*

$ **Red Lion Inn.** Just 3 miles north of LAX and a few minutes from Marina del Rey, this deluxe hotel is convenient for business types. The oversize guest rooms on 12 floors have a '90s version of Art Deco–style decor. Extra special is the California Suite, with beautiful decorations and its own Jacuzzi. ☏ *6161 Centinela Ave., Culver City 90231,* ☎ *310/649–1776 or 800/547–8010,* FAX *310/649–4411. 368 rooms. 2 restaurants, lounge, no-smoking floors, pool, sauna, health club, free parking. AE, D, DC, MC, V.*

Pasadena

$$$–$$$$ **Ritz-Carlton Huntington Hotel.** The main building of this landmark hotel, a Mediterranean-style structure in warm-color stucco, fits perfectly with the lavish houses of the surrounding Oak Knoll neighborhood, Pasadena's best. Walk through the intimate lobby into the central courtyard, dotted with tiny ponds and lush plantings, to the wood-paneled grand lounge, where you can have afternoon tea while enjoying a sweeping view of Los Angeles in the distance. Guest rooms are traditionally furnished and handsome, although a bit small for the price; the large marble-fitted bathrooms also look old-fashioned. The landscaped grounds are lovely, with their Japanese and horseshoe gardens and the historic Picture Bridge, which has murals depicting scenes of California along its 20 gables. The food is excellent and the service attentive. ☏ *1401 S. Oak Knoll Ave., Pasadena 91106,* ☎ *818/568–3900 or 800/241–3333,* FAX *818/568–3700. 383 rooms. 2 restaurants, no-smoking floors, pool, tennis courts, health club, parking (fee). AE, D, DC, MC, V.*

San Fernando Valley

$$$$ **Universal City Hilton and Towers.** This 24-story glass tower blends contemporary luxury with the charm of an Old World European hotel. The pleasant rooms are decorated in warm tones of burgundy and hunter green, and the bathrooms have wall-to-wall marble. Breathtaking views of the San Fernando Valley and hills can be enjoyed through floor-to-ceiling windows. A popular place for TV location filming, the hotel is also close to the Universal Amphitheater, Universal Studios Tour, CityWalk, and the Hollywood Bowl. ☏ *555 Universal Terrace Pkwy., Universal City 91608,* ☎ *818/506–2500,* FAX *818/509–2058. 446 rooms. Restaurant, 2 lounges, no-smoking floors, pool, health club, parking (fee). AE, D, DC, MC, V.*

$$$ **Burbank Airport Hilton.** This contemporary Hilton is geared to business meetings—there's a state-of-the-art convention center on the premises. The mauve-and-pink lobby is large; rooms have standard-issue hotel decor with no particularly nice views. ☏ *2500 Hollywood Way, Burbank 91505,* ☎ *818/843–6000, 800/643–7400 in CA, 800/468–3576 outside CA;* FAX *818/842–9720. 500 rooms. Restaurant, in-room VCRs, pool, spa, parking (fee). AE, D, DC, MC, V.*

$$ **Sportsman's Lodge Hotel.** An English country–style building with a resort atmosphere, this hotel features beautiful grounds with waterfalls, a swan-filled lagoon, and a bright white gazebo. Guest rooms are large and are decorated in soft colors like mauve and blue. Studio suites with private patios are available, and there's an Olympic-size swimming pool. The hotel is close to the Universal Studios Tour and Universal Amphitheater. ☏ *12825 Ventura Blvd., North Hollywood 91604,* ☎ *818/*

769–4700 or 800/821–8511, FAX *213/877–3898. 193 rooms. 3 restaurants, pool, health club, free parking. AE, D, DC, MC, V.*

$ Safari Inn. Often used for location filming, this motel-like property near Warner Brothers Studios, encompassing two buildings, has a homey, neighborhood feel. The decor, in antique white and gold, has a modern flair, as for example in the rooms with sleek rattan-and-bamboo furniture. There's a fine Italian restaurant called Jane's Cucina on the premises. ⊡ *1911 W. Olive, Burbank 91506,* ☎ *818/845–8586 or 800/782–4373,* FAX *818/845–0054. 110 rooms. Restaurant, lounge, refrigerators, pool, free parking. AE, DC, MC, V.*

THE ARTS AND NIGHTLIFE

For the most complete listing of weekly events, get the current issue of *Los Angeles* magazine. The Calendar section of the *Los Angeles Times* also offers a wide survey of Los Angeles arts events, as do the more irreverent free publications, the *L.A. Weekly* and the *L.A. Reader.* For a telephone report on current music, theater, dance, film, and special events, plus a discount ticket source, call 213/688–2787.

Most tickets can be purchased by phone (with a credit card) from **Ticketmaster** (☎ 213/365–3500), **TeleCharge** (☎ 800/762–7666), **Good Time Tickets** (☎ 213/464–7383), **Tickets L.A.** (☎ 213/660–8587), or **Murray's Tickets** (☎ 213/234–0123).

The Arts

Theater

Los Angeles isn't quite the "Broadway of the West" as some have claimed—the scope of theater here really doesn't compare to that in New York. Still, there are plenty of offerings worth any visitor's time in this entertainment-oriented city.

The theater scene's growth has been astounding. In 1978 only about 370 professional productions were brought to stages in Los Angeles; now well over 1,000 are scheduled each year. Small theaters are blossoming all over town, and the larger houses, despite price hikes to $35 for a single ticket, are usually full.

Even small productions might boast big names from "the Business" (the Los Angeles entertainment empire). Many film and television actors love to work on the stage between projects or while on hiatus from a TV series as a way to refresh their talents or regenerate their creativity in this demanding medium. Doing theater is also an excellent way to be seen by those who matter in the glitzier end of show biz. Hence there is a need for both large houses—which usually mount productions that are road-company imports of Broadway hits or, on occasion, where Broadway-bound material gets a tryout—and a host of small, intimate theaters to showcase the talent that abounds in this city.

MAJOR THEATERS

The **Music Center** (135 N. Grand Ave., ☎ 213/972–7211). This big downtown complex includes three theaters: the newly renovated **Ahmanson Theatre,** with variable seating capacity, presenting both classics and new plays; the 3,200-seat **Dorothy Chandler Pavilion,** which offers a few plays in between performances of the L.A. Philharmonic, L.A. Master Chorale, and L.A. Opera; and the 760-seat **Mark Taper Forum,** under the direction of Gordon Davidson, which presents new works that often go on to Broadway, such as *Angels in America* and *Jelly's Last Jam.*

James A. Doolittle Theater (1615 N. Vine St., Hollywood, ☎ 213/972–0700, or call Ticketmaster, ☎ 213/365–3500). Located in the heart of Hollywood, this house offers an intimate feeling despite its 1,038-seat capacity. New plays, dramas, comedies, and musicals are presented here year-round.

John Anson Ford Theater (2580 Cahuenga Blvd., Hollywood, ☎ 213/744–3466). This 1,300-seat outdoor house in the Hollywood Hills is best known for its Shakespeare and free summer jazz, dance, and cabaret concerts.

Pantages (6233 Hollywood Blvd., Hollywood, ☎ 213/468–1770, or call Ticketmaster, ☎ 213/365–3500). Once the home of the Academy Awards telecast and Hollywood premieres, this house is massive (2,600 seats) and a splendid example of high-style Hollywood Art Deco, although the acoustics could use some updating. Large-scale musicals from Broadway are usually presented here.

Westwood Playhouse (10886 Le Conte Ave., Westwood, ☎ 310/208–6500 or 310/208–5454). An acoustically superior theater with great sight lines, the 498-seat playhouse showcases new plays in the summer, primarily musicals and comedies. Many of the productions here are on their way to or from Broadway. This is also where Jason Robards and Nick Nolte got their starts.

Wilshire Theater (8440 Wilshire Blvd., Beverly Hills, ☎ 213/468–1716 and 213/468–1799, or call Ticketmaster, ☎ 213/365–3500). The interior of this 1,900-seat house is Art Deco–style; musicals from Broadway are the usual fare.

SMALLER THEATERS

Cast Theater (804 N. El Centro, Hollywood, ☎ 213/462–0265). Musicals, revivals, and avant-garde improv pieces are done here.

The **Coast Playhouse** (8325 Santa Monica Blvd., West Hollywood, ☎ 213/650–8507). The specialty of this 99-seat house is excellent original musicals and new dramas.

Fountain Theater (5060 Fountain Ave., Hollywood, ☎ 213/663–1525). This theater, which seats 80, presents original American dramas and stages flamenco dance concerts. Marian Mercer and Rob Reiner got their starts here.

Japan America Theater (244 S. San Pedro St., downtown, ☎ 213/680–3700). This community-oriented 880-seat theater at the Japan Cultural Arts Center is home to local theater, dance troupes, and the L.A. Chamber Orchestra, plus numerous children's theater groups.

Santa Monica Playhouse (1211 4th St., Santa Monica, ☎ 310/394–9779). With 99 seats, this house is worth visiting for its cozy, library-like atmosphere; the good comedies, dramas, and children's programs presented here are further incentive.

Skylight Theater (1816½ N. Vermont Ave., Los Feliz, ☎ 213/666–2202). Many highly inventive productions have been hosted in this 99-seat theater.

Theatre/Theater (1713 Cahuenga Blvd., Hollywood, ☎ 213/871–0210). Angelenos crowd into this 70-seat house to view original works by local authors as well as international playwrights.

Concerts

Los Angeles is not only the focus of America's pop/rock music recording scene but now, after years of being denigrated as a cultural invalid, is also a center for classical music and opera.

MAJOR CONCERT HALLS

Dorothy Chandler Pavilion (135 N. Grand Ave., ☎ 213/972–7211). Part of the Los Angeles Music Center and—with the Hollywood

Bowl—the center of L.A.'s classical music scene, the 3,200-seat Pavilion is the home of the Los Angeles Philharmonic. The L.A. Opera presents classics from September through June.

The **Greek Theater** (2700 N. Vermont Ave., ☎ 213/665–1927). This open-air auditorium near Griffith Park offers some classical performances in its mainly pop/rock/jazz schedule from June through October. Its Doric columns evoke the amphitheaters of ancient Greece.

The **Hollywood Bowl** (2301 Highland Ave., ☎ 213/850–2000). A fixture of the local music scene since 1920, the Bowl is one of the world's largest outdoor amphitheaters, and located in a park surrounded by mountains, trees, and gardens. The Bowl's season runs early July–mid-September; the L.A. Philharmonic spends its summer season here. There are performances daily except Mondays (and some Sundays); the program ranges from jazz to pop to classical. Concert goers usually arrive early, bringing or buying picnic suppers. There are plenty of picnic tables, and box-seat subscribers can reserve a table right in their own box. Restaurant dining is available on the grounds (reservations recommended, ☎ 213/851–3588). The seats are wood, so you might bring or rent a cushion—and bring a sweater; it gets chilly here in the evening. A convenient way to enjoy the Hollywood Bowl experience without the hassle of parking is to take one of the Park-and-Ride buses, which leave from various locations around town; call the Bowl for information.

The **Shrine Auditorium** (665 W. Jefferson Blvd., ☎ 213/749–5123). Built in 1926 by the Al Malaikah Temple, the auditorium has decor that could be called Baghdad and Beyond. Touring companies from all over the world, along with assorted gospel and choral groups, appear in this one-of-a-kind, 6,200-seat theater.

The **Wilshire Ebell Theater** (4401 W. 8th St., ☎ 213/939–1128). The Los Angeles Opera Theater comes to this Spanish-style building, erected in 1924, as do a broad spectrum of other musical performers.

Wiltern Theater (Wilshire Blvd. and Western Ave., ☎ 213/380–5005 or 213/388–1400). Reopened in 1985 as a venue for the Los Angeles Opera Theater, the building was constructed in 1930 and is listed in the National Register of Historic Places. It is a magnificent example of Art Deco in its green terra-cotta glory.

Dance

You can find talented companies dancing around town at various performance spaces. Check the *L.A. Weekly* free newspaper under "dance" to see who is dancing where, or call the **Dance Resource Center** (☎ 213/622–0815) or the *Arts Line* (☎ 213/688–2787).

L.A. has one major resident company, the **Bella Lewistsky Dance Co.** (☎ 213/580–6338), which performs around town. Visiting companies such as Martha Graham, Paul Taylor, and Hubbard Street Dance Company perform in UCLA Dance Company's home space at **UCLA Center for the Arts** (405 N. Hilgard Ave., ☎ 310/825–2101).

Larger companies such as the Kirov, the Bolshoi, and the American Ballet Theater (ABT) perform at various times during the year at the **Shrine Auditorium** (665 W. Jefferson Blvd., ☎ 213/749–5123). Two prominent dance events occur annually: the Dance Fair in March and Dance Kaleidoscope in July. Both events take place at **Cal State L.A.'s Dance Department** (5151 State University Dr., ☎ 213/343–5124).

Movie Palaces

Mann's Chinese Theater (6925 Hollywood Blvd., Hollywood, ☎ 213/464–8111). This Chinese pagoda-style structure is perhaps the world's best-known movie theater. It still carries on one of the oldest of Hollywood traditions: its famous hand- and footprinting ceremony, which was supposed to have begun after actress Norma Talmadge accidentally stepped into wet cement at the theater's opening in 1927 (the film shown that night was Cecil B. DeMille's *King of Kings*). Today the Chinese houses three movie screens, and it still hosts many gala premieres.

Pacific Cinerama Dome (6360 Sunset Blvd., Hollywood, ☎ 213/466–3401). This futuristic, geodesic structure was the first theater designed specifically for Cinerama in the United States. The gigantic screen and multitrack sound system create an unparalleled cinematic experience.

Pacific's El Capitan (6838 Hollywood Blvd., Hollywood, ☎ 213/467–7674). Restored to its original Art Deco splendor, this classic movie palace reopened across the street from Mann's Chinese in 1991. First-run movies are on the bill.

The Silent Movie (611 N. Fairfax Ave., ☎ 213/653–2389). Though not a movie palace itself, this theater revives classics like Charlie Chaplin's *The Gold Rush* and the portfolio of Buster Keaton films. Screenings take place Wednesday, Friday, and Saturday evenings. The theater has a vintage organ.

Vista Theater (4473 Sunset Dr., Los Feliz, ☎ 213/660–6639). At the intersection of Hollywood and Sunset boulevards, this 70-year-old cinema was once Bard's Hollywood Theater, where both moving pictures and vaudeville played. A Spanish-style facade leads to an ornate Egyptian interior. D. W. Griffith's silent classic *Intolerance* was filmed on this site.

Television

Audiences Unlimited (100 Universal City Plaza, Bldg. 153, Universal City 91608, ☎ 818/506–0043) is a nifty organization that helps fill seats for television programs (and sometimes theater events, as well). There's no charge, but the tickets are on a first-come, first-served basis. Tickets can be picked up at Fox Television Center (5746 Sunset Blvd., Van Ness Ave. entrance, weekdays 8:30–6, weekends 11–6) or at the Glendale Galleria Information Desk between 10 and 9 daily. Note: You must be 16 or older to attend a television taping. For a schedule, send a self-addressed envelope a couple of weeks prior to your visit to the address above.

Nightlife

Despite the high energy level of the nightlife crowd, Los Angeles nightclubs aren't known for keeping their doors open until the wee hours. This is still an early-to-bed city, and it's safe to say that by 2 AM, most jazz, rock, and disco clubs have closed for the night. Perhaps it's the temperate climate and the daytime sports orientation of the city: Most Angelenos want to be on the tennis court or out jogging first thing in the morning, making a late-night social life out of the question.

The accent in this city is on trendy rock clubs, smooth country-and-western establishments, intimate jazz spots, and comedy clubs. Consult *Los Angeles* magazine for current listings. The Sunday *Los Angeles Times* Calendar section and the free *L.A. Weekly* and *L.A. Reader* also provide listings.

The Sunset Strip, which runs from West Hollywood to Beverly Hills, offers a wide assortment of nighttime diversions. Comedy stores, restaurants with piano bars, cocktail lounges, and hard-rock clubs proliferate. Westwood, home of UCLA, is a college town, and this section of Los Angeles comes alive at night with rock and new-wave clubs playing canned and live music. It's one of the few areas in the city with a true neighborhood spirit. In past years, downtown Los Angeles hasn't offered much in the way of nighttime entertainment (with the exception of the Music Center for concerts and theater), but that has gradually changed with the openings of more theaters and trendy clubs. Some of Los Angeles's best jazz clubs, discos, and comedy clubs are scattered throughout the San Fernando and San Gabriel valleys.

Dress codes vary depending on the place you visit. Jackets are expected at cabarets and hotels. Discos are generally casual, although some will turn away the denim-clad. The rule of thumb is to phone ahead and check the dress code, but on the whole, Los Angeles is oriented toward casual wear.

Jazz

Atlas Bar & Grill (3760 Wilshire Blvd., ☎ 213/380–8400). The eclectic entertainment at this snazzy supper club includes torch singers as well as a jazz band.

Baked Potato (3787 Cahuenga Blvd. W, North Hollywood, ☎ 818/980–1615). In this tiny club they pack you in like sardines to hear a powerhouse of jazz. The featured item on the menu is baked potatoes; they're jumbo and stuffed with everything from steak to vegetables.

House of Blues (8430 Sunset Blvd., Hollywood, ☎ 213/650–1451). The most happening nightclub on the Sunset Strip, this house has an impressive following, with three bars surrounding the large dance floor. Past performers include Etta James, Lou Rawls, Joe Cocker, and the Commodores.

Jax (339 N. Brand Blvd., Glendale, ☎ 818/500–1604). This intimate club serves a wide variety of food, from ribs to pasta; live music is an added draw.

Jazz Bakery (3221 Hutchison, Culver City, ☎ 310/271–9039). On weekends Jim Britt opens his photography studio, adjacent to the Helms Bakery Building, to serve coffee, desserts, and a nice selection of world-class jazz, enhanced by great acoustics and a smoke- free environment. The $15 cover (no credit cards) includes refreshments.

Marla's Jazz Supper Club (2323 W. Martin Luther King Jr. Blvd., Los Angeles, ☎ 213/294–8430). Owned by comedy star Marla Gibbs of *The Jeffersons* and *227*, the room pops with blues, jazz, and easy listening. James Ingram plays here from time to time. The appetizer menu boasts Cajun tidbits.

Folk, Pop, and Rock

Blue Saloon (4657 Lankershim Blvd., North Hollywood, ☎ 818/766–4644). For rock and roll, this is the place to go. (You'll also catch a smattering of country and blues at times.)

Club Lingerie (6507 Sunset Blvd., Hollywood, ☎ 213/466–8557). One local describes this place as "clean enough for the timid, yet seasoned quite nicely for the tenured scenester."

Ghengis Cohen Cantina (740 N. Fairfax Ave., West Hollywood, ☎ 213/653–0640). At this longtime music industry hangout, you can hear up-and-coming talent, usually in a refreshingly mellow format like MTV's "Unplugged" performances. A plus is the restaurant's Chinese cuisine.

Kingston 12 (814 Broadway, Santa Monica, ☎ 310/451–4423). This Santa Monica club is known for its rap music, although reggae is also on tap, as is a menu of fine Jamaican food.

McCabe's Guitar Shop (3101 Pico Blvd., Santa Monica, ☎ 310/828–4497; concert information, 310/828–4403). Folk, acoustic rock, bluegrass, and soul concerts are featured in this guitar store on weekend nights.

The Palace (1735 N. Vine St., Hollywood, ☎ 213/462–3000). The "in" spot for the upwardly mobile, this plush Art Deco palace boasts lively entertainment, a fabulous sound system, full bar, and dining upstairs. The patrons here dress to kill.

Pier 52 (52 Pier Ave., Hermosa Beach, ☎ 310/376–1629). From Wednesday through Saturday dance bands play pure rock and roll; Sunday is designated the day of blues.

The Roxy (9009 Sunset Blvd., West Hollywood, ☎ 310/276–2222). The premier Los Angeles rock club, classy and comfortable, offers performance art as well as theatrical productions.

The Strand (1700 S. Pacific Coast Hwy., Redondo Beach, ☎ 310/316–1700). This major concert venue covers a lot of ground, hosting hot new acts or such old favorites as Asleep at the Wheel, blues man Albert King, rock vet Robin Trower, and Billy Vera.

The Troubadour (9081 Santa Monica Blvd., West Hollywood, ☎ 310/276–6168). One of the hottest clubs of the 1970s is rolling again, this time with up-and-coming talent.

Viper Room (8852 Sunset Blvd., West Hollywood, ☎ 310/358–1880). This musicians' hangout, part-owned by actor Johnny Depp, devotes itself to music and dance in the pop, rock, blues, and jazz/fusion genres. Celebrities tend to be attracted to the place.

Whiskey A Go Go (8901 Sunset Blvd., West Hollywood, ☎ 310/652–4202). This, the most famous rock-and-roll club on the Sunset Strip, has hosted everyone from Otis Redding to AC/DC and now presents up-and-coming alternative, very hard rock, and punk bands.

Cabaret

L.A. Cabaret (17271 Ventura Blvd., Encino, ☎ 818/501–3737). This two-room club features a variety of comedy acts as well as karaoke. Famous entertainers often make surprise appearances.

Luna Park (665 Robertson Blvd., West Hollywood, ☎ 310/652–0611). This New York–style cabaret features an eclectic mix of music, with three stages and two bars. Locally (in)famous drag queens strut their stuff here.

Queen Mary (12449 Ventura Blvd., Sherman Oaks, ☎ 818/506–5619). Female impersonators vamp it up as Diana Ross, Barbra Streisand, and Bette Midler in this small club. Drinks are the only refreshment served, so eat first. Cross-dressers parade among the colorful clientele, which is never boring. It's open Wednesday–Sunday.

Dance Clubs

Bar One (9229 Sunset Blvd., Beverly Hills, ☎ 310/271–8355). A hot, hip place for dancing, this restaurant and bar also has a pool table and comfortable lounging areas.

Circus Disco and Arena (6655 Santa Monica Blvd., Hollywood, ☎ 213/462–1291 or 213/462–1742). A gay and mixed crowd flocks to these two huge side-by-side discos, which feature techno and rock music.

Coconut Teaszer (8117 Sunset Blvd., Los Angeles, ☎ 213/654–4773). Dancing to live music, a great barbecue menu, and killer drinks make for lively fun. Pool tables are always crowded.

Crush Bar Continental Club (1743 Cahuenga Ave., Hollywood, ☎ 213/463–7685). If 1960s music appeals to you, stop by this happening dance club, open Friday and Saturday evenings.

Florentine Gardens (5951 Hollywood Blvd., Hollywood, ☎ 213/464–0706). Here's one of Los Angeles's largest dance areas, with spectacular lighting to match. It's open Friday through Sunday.

Glam Slam (333 S. Boylston, Los Angeles, ☎ 213/482–6626). A New York–style club, this hot spot has a restricted entrance policy—there's a large celebrity clientele, and everybody's dressed to kill. There's a large dance floor, live bands, balcony bar, and restaurant. It's open Friday and Saturday until 4 AM. This club is in a terrible neighborhood, so be prepared to shell out for valet parking.

Moonlight Tango Cafe (13730 Ventura Blvd., Sherman Oaks, ☎ 818/788–2000). This high-energy club-restaurant, big on the swing era, really gets moving in the wee hours, when a conga line inevitably takes shape on the dance floor.

Country Music

In Cahoots (223 N. Glendale Ave., Glendale, ☎ 818/500–1665). At this raucous dance hall, à la Nashville, you can learn how to two-step if you don't already know how. All week long there's live music.

The Palomino (6907 Lankershim Blvd., North Hollywood, ☎ 818/764–4010). There's occasionally a wild crowd at this premier country showcase, where good old boys and urban cowboys meet and everybody has a good time.

Comedy and Magic

Comedy Act Theater (3339 W. 43rd St., near Crenshaw, ☎ 310/677–4101). This club features comedy by and for the black community, Thursday through Saturday nights. Past performers have been *Hollywood Shuffle*'s Robert Townsend and *Night Court*'s Marcia Warfield.

Comedy and Magic Club (1018 Hermosa Ave., Hermosa Beach, ☎ 310/372–1193). This beachfront club features many magicians and comedians seen on TV and in Las Vegas. The Unknown Comic, Elayne Boosler, Pat Paulsen, and Jay Leno have all played here.

Comedy Store (8433 Sunset Blvd., Hollywood, ☎ 213/656–6225). Los Angeles's premier comedy showcase has been going strong for more than a decade. Famous comedians, including Robin Williams and Steve Martin, occasionally make unannounced appearances.

Groundlings Theater (7307 Melrose Ave., Hollywood, ☎ 213/934–9700). The entertainment here consists of original skits, music, and improv, with each player contributing his/her own flavor to the usually hilarious performance.

Ice House Comedy Showroom (24 N. Mentor Ave., Pasadena, ☎ 818/577–1894). Three-act shows here feature comedians, celebrity impressionists, and magicians from Las Vegas, as well as from television shows.

Igby's Comedy Cabaret (11637 Pico Blvd., Los Angeles, ☎ 310/477–3553). You'll see familiar television faces, as well as up-and-coming comedians Wednesday through Sunday in this friendly club. Reservations are necessary.

The Improvisation (8162 Melrose Ave., West Hollywood, ☎ 213/651–2583). The Improv is a transplanted New York establishment showcasing comedians and some vocalists. This place was the proving ground for Liza Minnelli and Richard Pryor, among others. Reservations are recommended.

Bars

BEVERLY HILLS

La Scala (410 N. Canon, ☎ 310/275–0579). A quaint bar with an immense wine cellar, La Scala is honeycombed with celebrities nightly.

CENTURY CITY

Harper's Bar and Grill (2040 Ave. of the Stars, ☎ 310/553–1855). A central place to meet friends for cocktails before or after a show at the Shubert Theater, it offers warm decor and generous drinks.

DOWNTOWN

Dresden Room (1760 N. Vermont Ave., ☎ 213/665–4294). This unassuming '40s-style bar has been rediscovered by a happening '90s crowd.

El Coyote (7312 Beverly Blvd., ☎ 213/939–7766). For a pick-me-up margarita, stop by this kitschy restaurant-bar and get a glass of the best—and cheapest—in town.

Grand Avenue Sports Bar (506 S. Grand St., ☎ 213/612–1595). This sleek bar in the Biltmore Hotel serves until 2 AM. Bring a lot of money.

Musso & Frank's Grill (6667 Hollywood Blvd., ☎ 213/467–5123). Film-studio moguls and extras alike flock to this long-running hit, where the Rob Roys are just as smooth and the clientele just as eclectic as ever.

Rex (617 S. Olive St., ☎ 213/627–2300). This piano bar on the ground floor of the historic Oviatt Building radiates the Art Deco ambience of a 1930s cruise liner.

MARINA DEL REY/VENICE

The Warehouse (4499 Admiralty Way, ☎ 310/823–5451). Ex-cinematographer Burt Hixon collected tropical drink recipes on his South Seas forays and whips up one of the most sinfully rich piña coladas this side of Samoa.

MID-WILSHIRE

Tom Bergin's (840 S. Fairfax Ave., ☎ 213/936–7151). One of L.A.'s best Irish pubs, it's plastered with Day-Glo shamrocks perpetuating the names of the thousands of patrons who have passed through its door.

PASADENA

Beckham Place (77 W. Walnut, ☎ 818/796–3399). A rather fancy "Olde English" pub, it's known for its huge drinks, free roast beef sandwiches, and wingback chairs placed near a roaring fire.

SANTA MONICA AND THE BEACHES

Oar House (2941 Main St., ☎ 310/396–4725). Something old has been glued or nailed to every square inch of this place, from motorcycles to carriages. Drinks are downright cheap.

WEST HOLLYWOOD

Le Dome (8720 W. Sunset Blvd., ☎ 310/659–6919). The circular bar here draws the likes of Rod Stewart and Richard Gere. The best time to visit is after 11 PM, when it really starts to jump.

WESTWOOD/WESTSIDE

Hamburger Hamlet (11648 San Vicente Blvd., ☎ 310/826–3558). This is one of the Westside's hottest singles bars, so don't walk in here looking for solitude.

Q's (11835 Wilshire Blvd., West Los Angeles, ☎ 310/477–7550). This upscale pool hall and bar serves a yuppified clientele.

EXCURSIONS

Big Bear/Lake Arrowhead

Local legend has it that in 1845, Don Benito Wilson—General George Patton's grandfather—and his men charged up along the San Bernardino River in pursuit of a troublesome band of Native Americans. As Wilson entered a clearing, he discovered a meadow teeming with bears. The rest, of course, is history: Wilson later became mayor of Los Angeles, and the area he'd stumbled into was developed into a delightful mountain playground, centered on the man-made lakes of Arrowhead and Big Bear.

Visitors come in winter for downhill and cross-country skiing, and in summer to breathe cool mountain air, hike in the woods, sniff the daffodils, and play in the water. Along the edge of the San Bernardino Mountains, which connect Lake Arrowhead and Big Bear Lake, is a truly great scenic drive: the Rim of the World Scenic Byway. The alpine equivalent of the Pacific Coast Highway, it reaches elevations of 8,000 feet, offering views of sprawling San Bernardino and east toward Palm Springs.

Exploring

This tour begins near the western end of the byway, near its intersection with Highway 138. As you wind your way along the Rim of the World, there are several places to park, sip cool water from spring-fed fountains, and enjoy the view. At the village of Crestline, a brief detour off Highway 18 leads you to **Lake Gregory.** The newest of the high mountain lakes, Lake Gregory was formed by a dam constructed in 1938. Because the water temperature in summer is seldom extremely cold—as it can be in the other lakes at this altitude—this is the best swimming lake in the mountains, but it's open in summer only, and there's a minimum charge to swim. You can rent rowboats at Lake Gregory Village.

Continuing east on Highway 18, you will pass the **Baylis Park Picnic Ground,** where you can have a barbecue in a wooded setting. A little farther along, just past the town of Rim Forest, is the **Strawberry Peak** fire lookout tower. Visitors who brave the steep stairway to the tower are treated to a magnificent view and a lesson on fire spotting by the lookout staff.

Heading north on Highway 173 will lead you to **Lake Arrowhead Village** and the lake itself. Arrowhead Village draws mixed reviews: For some, it is a quaint alpine community with shops and eateries; for others, it has all the ambience of a rustic-theme shopping mall. The lake, on the other hand, is decidedly a gem, although it can become crowded with speedboats and water-skiers in summer. The ***Arrowhead Queen,*** operated daily by LeRoy Sports (☎ 909/336–6992, reservations needed in summer, price varies, the maximum is $9.50) provides 50-minute cruises around the lake, leaving from the waterfront marina. The **Lake Arrowhead Children's Museum** (lower level of the village, ☎ 909/336–3093; ☛ $3.50 adults and children, senior citizens $2.50) has plenty to entertain pint-size explorers: hands-on exhibits, a climbing maze, and a puppet stage. Call the Arrowhead Chamber of Commerce (☎ 909/337–3715) for information on events, camping, and lodging.

Those traveling with children may want to stop at nearby **Santa's Village,** which has a petting zoo, rides, riding stables, and a bakery filled with goodies. *Located on Hwy. 18, Box 638, Skyforest 92385, ☎ 909/337–2484. ☛ $10 adults and children (includes 12 rides). ⏲ Hrs vary depending on the season.*

Farther along the Rim drive, 5 miles east of Running Springs, is **Snow Valley** (☎ 909/867–5151), one of the major ski areas in the San Bernardinos, with a dozen lifts. Summer visitors will find hiking trails, horseback riding, and fishing here, too.

Beyond Snow Valley, the road climbs to **Lakeview Point,** where a spectacular view of the deep Bear Creek Canyon unfolds; Big Bear Lake is usually visible in the distance. A 15½-mile drive will take you completely around the lake, and **Big Bear Lake Village** is on the lake's south shore. The town is a pleasant combination of alpine and western-mountain style, with the occasional chaletlike building. The paddle wheeler ***Big Bear Queen*** (☎ 909/866–3218) departs daily, mid-March through October from Big Bear Marina for 90-minute scenic tours of the lake. Fishing-boat and equipment rentals are available from several lakeside marinas, including **Pine Knot Landing** (☎ 909/866–2628), adjacent to Big Bear Village. For information and lodging reservations, contact the Big Bear Resort Association (☎ 909/866–7000).

Snow Summit (☎ 909/866–5766) and **Bear Mountain Ski Resort** (☎ 909/585–2517) are both just to the southeast of the Village. Snow Summit, which has a 8,200-foot peak, is equipped with a high-speed quad chair, 12 chairlifts, and 20 miles of runs at all levels. Bear Mountain has 11 chairlifts and 35 trails, from beginner to expert. On busy winter weekends and holidays, your best bet is to reserve your tickets before you head for the mountain.

Dining

A three-course meal for one person, excluding drinks, service, and tax, costs between $15 and $25 at the following restaurants.

BIG BEAR

Blue Ox Bar and Grill. This rustic, casual restaurant, complete with peanut shells on the floor, serves oversize steaks, ribs, burgers, and chicken—all cooked simply but well. ✕ *441 W. Big Bear Blvd., Big Bear City,* ☎ *909/585–7886. AE, MC, V.*

ARROWHEAD VILLAGE

Woody's Boathouse. If you want to sit and relax, lakefront, choose this casual eatery for its juicy steaks, fresh seafood, and generous salad bar. ✕ *28200 Hwy. 189, Suite 13–100,* ☎ *909/337–2628. AE, MC, V.*

Lodging

Rates for Big Bear lodgings fluctuate widely, depending upon the season. When winter snow brings droves of Angelenos to the mountain for skiing, expect to pay sky-high prices for any kind of room. **Big Bear Lake Resort Association** (☎ 909/866–7000) can answer any questions you have and make arrangements for you.

CATEGORY	COST*
$$$$	over $100
$$$	$75–$100

**All prices are for a double room, excluding 8½% tax.*

BIG BEAR

$$$$ **Big Bear Inn.** This chateau-like inn's rooms are furnished with brass beds, antiques, and "bits and pieces from all over Europe," according to one of the friendly staff. ✉ *Box 1814, Big Bear Lake 92315,* ☎ *909/866–3471 or 800/232–7466 in CA. 80 rooms, 6 suites. Restaurant (breakfast daily; no lunch or dinner Mon.–Wed.), lounge, pool, hot tub, meeting rooms. AE, D, MC, V.*

$$$–$$$$ **Robinhood Inn and Lodge.** Near Snow Summit, this well-located property has reasonably priced rooms (with or without kitchen) and condos. Each room (some with fireplaces and/or Jacuzzis) is individually decorated with simple modern furniture and bright colors. All accommodations face a courtyard with an outdoor whirlpool spa. ✉ *Box 1881, Big Bear Lake 92315,* ☎ *909/866–4643. 21 rooms. Restaurant, spa. AE, MC, V.*

LAKE ARROWHEAD

$$$$ **Lake Arrowhead Resort.** The design and Old World graciousness of the lodge are reminiscent of the Alps. In addition to the lakeside luxury, guests receive membership privileges at the Village Bay Club and Spa (fee is $5). ✉ *Box 1699, 92352,* ☎ *909/336–1511 or 800/800–6791. 261 rooms. Restaurant, coffee shop, lounge, pool, tennis, health club, beach. AE, MC, V.*

$$$–$$$$ **Carriage House Bed and Breakfast.** Within walking distance of the lake and village, this New England–style country home offers lake views from all guest rooms. Breakfast and afternoon refreshments are included in the rates. ✉ *Box 982, 92352,* ☎ *909/336–1400. 3 rooms. MC, V.*

Big Bear/Lake Arrowhead Essentials

ARRIVING AND DEPARTING

By Car: Take I–10 east from Los Angeles to Highway 330, which connects with Highway 18—the Rim of the World Scenic Byway—at Running Springs. This is approximately the midpoint of the scenic drive, which hugs the mountainside from Big Bear Lake to Cajon Pass. The trip should take about 90 minutes to Lake Arrowhead, and two hours to Big Bear. Highway 38, the back way into Big Bear, is actually longer, but it can be faster when the traffic on the more direct route is heavy.

Catalina Island

When you approach Catalina Island through the typical early morning ocean fog, it's easy to wonder if perhaps there has been some mistake. What is a Mediterranean island doing 22 miles off the coast of California? Don't worry, you haven't left the Pacific—you've arrived at one of the Los Angeles area's most popular resorts.

Though lacking the sophistication of some European pleasure islands, Catalina does offer virtually unspoiled mountains, canyons, coves, and beaches. In fine weather, it draws thousands of southern California boaters, who tie up their vessels at moorings spotted in coves along the coast. The exceptionally clear water surrounding the island lures divers and snorkelers. Although there's not much sandy beach, sunbathing and water sports are also popular. The main town, Avalon, is a charming, old-fashioned beach community, where palm trees rim the main street and yachts bob in the crescent-shape bay.

Cruise ships sail into Avalon twice a week. The Catalina Island Company, which has a near-monopoly on sightseeing tours on the island beyond Avalon, has excellent service.

Discovered by Juan Rodriguez Cabrillo in 1542, the island has sheltered many dubious characters, from Russian fur trappers (seeking sea-otter skins), slave traders, pirates, and gold miners to bootleggers, filmmakers, and movie stars. In 1919, William Wrigley, Jr., the chewing-gum magnate, purchased controlling interest in the company developing the island. Wrigley had the island's most famous landmark, the Casino, built in 1929, and he made Catalina the site of spring training for his Chicago Cubs baseball team.

In 1975 the Santa Catalina Island Conservancy, a nonprofit foundation, acquired about 86% of the island to help preserve the natural resources here. Although Catalina can certainly be seen in a day, there are several inviting hotels that make it worth extending your stay for one or more nights. Between Memorial Day and Labor Day, be sure to make reservations *before* heading here. After Labor Day, rooms are much easier to find on shorter notice, rates drop dramatically, and a number of hotels offer packages that include transportation from the mainland and/or sightseeing tours.

Exploring

Everybody walks in Avalon, where private autos are restricted and there are no rental cars. But taxis, trams, and shuttles can take you to hotels, attractions, and restaurants. If you are determined to have a set of wheels, you can rent a bicycle (about $6 an hr) or a golf cart ($35 an hr, cash only) along Crescent Avenue as you walk in from the dock. To hike into the interior of the island you will need a permit, available free from Doug Bombard Enterprises (Island Plaza, Avalon, ☎ 310/510–7265).

The **Chamber of Commerce Visitors Bureau,** on Green Pier, is a good place to get your bearings, check into special events, and plan your itinerary. The **Catalina Island Company Visitors Center** (☎ 310/510–1520) is on the corner of Crescent and Catalina avenues, across from Green Pier.

On the northwest point of Crescent Bay is the **Casino,** Avalon's most prominent landmark. The circular structure, considered one of the finest examples of Art Deco architecture anywhere, has lots of Spanish-influenced details. Its floors and murals show off brilliant blue and green Catalina tiles. "Casino" is the Italian word for "gathering place" and has nothing to do with gambling here. Instead, you can visit the **Catalina Island Museum** (lower level of Casino, ☛ $1), which displays the history of the island; in the evening, you can see a first-run movie at the **Avalon Theater** (☎ 310/510–0179), which has a classic 1929 theater pipe organ; or on holiday weekends you can go to big-band dances similar to those that made the Casino famous in the 1930s and '40s.

If modern architecture interests you, be sure to stop by the **Wolfe House** (124 Chimes Tower Rd.). Built in Avalon in 1928 by noted architect Rudolph Schindler, its terraced frame is carefully set into a steep site, affording extraordinary views. The house is a private residence, rarely open for public tours, but you can get a good view of it from the path below it and from the street.

The **Wrigley Memorial and Botanical Garden** is 2 miles south of Avalon via Avalon Canyon Road. The garden displays only plants native to southern California, including several that grow only on Catalina Island: Catalina ironwood, wild tomato, and rare Catalina mahogany. The Wrigley family commissioned the garden as well as the monument, which has a grand staircase and a Spanish mausoleum that's decorated with colorful Catalina tile. Tram service between the memorial and Avalon is available daily between 8 AM and 5 PM. There is a nominal entry fee of $1.

El Rancho Escondido is a ranch in Catalina's interior, home to some of the country's finest Arabian horses. Horse shows are presented for passengers on the inland motor tour (*see* Guided Tours, *below*).

Snorkelers and divers can explore the crystal-clear waters of **Underwater Marine Park at Casino Point,** where moray eels, bat rays, spiny lobsters, halibut, and other sea animals cruise around kelp forests and along the sandy bottom.

Dining

Avalon restaurants cater to summer crowds; at other times of year, days and hours of operation can be sporadic.

CATEGORY	COST*
$$$	$25–$35
$$	$15–$25
$	under $15

**per person for a three-course meal, excluding drinks, service, and 8¼% tax*

$$–$$$ **Cafe Prego.** This waterfront restaurant specializes in pasta, seafood, and steak. ✕ *603 Crescent Ave., ☎ 310/510–1218. AE, D, DC, MC, V.*

$$–$$$ **Pirrone's.** Located on the second floor of the Vista del Mar hotel, Pirrone's has a bird's-eye view of the bay. The menu includes local seafood, prime rib, steaks, and pasta. ✕ *417 Crescent Ave.,* ☎ *310/510–0333. AE, D, DC, MC, V.*

$–$$ **Antonio's Pizzeria.** Here you'll find a spirited atmosphere, decent pizza, and appropriately messy Italian sandwiches. ✕ *230 Crescent Ave.,* ☎ *310/510–0008; 114 Sumner Ave.,* ☎ *310/510–0060. MC, V.*

$ **Sand Trap.** Basically an expanded taco stand on the way to the Wrigley Memorial, the Sand Trap specializes in omelets, burritos, *tortas* (layered tortilla casseroles), and quesadillas. ✕ *Falls Canyon,* ☎ *310/510–1349. No credit cards. No dinner.*

Lodging

CATEGORY	COST*
$$$$	over $100
$$$	$75–$100

**All prices are for a standard double room, excluding 9% tax.*

$$$$ **Hotel Metropole and Marketplace.** This romantic hotel has a French Quarter ambience: It overlooks a flower-decked courtyard of restaurants and shops. Some guest rooms have balconies, ocean views, fireplaces, and Jacuzzis. Continental breakfast is served in the lounge. ▣ *225 Crescent Ave., Avalon 90704,* ☎ *310/510–1884. 48 rooms. AE, MC, V.*

$$$$ **Inn on Mt. Ada.** Occupying the former Wrigley Mansion, the island's most exclusive hotel offers the comforts of a millionaire's mansion, beginning at $320 a night in summer. The six bedrooms are elegantly decorated, some with canopy beds, traditional furniture, and overstuffed chairs. The views across the water to the mainland are spectacular, and the service is discreet. All meals, beverages, snacks, and the use of a golf cart are complimentary. ▣ *Box 2560, Avalon 90704,* ☎ *310/510–2030. 6 rooms. MC, V.*

$$$–$$$$ **Hotel Vista del Mar.** This friendly, freshly decorated hotel offers surprisingly bright rooms, most of which open onto a skylighted atrium. There are fireplaces, Jacuzzis, wet bars, contemporary rattan decor, and abundant greenery. Two suites have ocean views. Rates include Continental breakfast. ▣ *417 Crescent Ave., Avalon 90704,* ☎ *310/510–1452. 15 rooms. AE, D, MC, V.*

$–$$ **Atwater Hotel.** Close to the beach, this budget hotel is operated by the Santa Catalina Island Company. Ask for a room with a water view. Appointments are very basic. ▣ *Box 737, 90704,* ☎ *800/851–0217. 108 rooms. AE, MC, V.*

Catalina Island Essentials

ARRIVING AND DEPARTING

By Boat: Catalina Express (☎ 310/519–1212 or 800/995–4386) makes the hour-long run from Long Beach or San Pedro to Avalon and Two Harbors; round-trip fare from Long Beach and San Pedro is $35 for adults, $32 for seniors, $26 for children 2–11, $2 for children under two. Service is also available from Newport Beach through **Catalina Passenger Service** (☎ 714/673–5245), which leaves from Balboa Pavilion at 9 AM, takes 75 minutes to reach the island, and costs $33 round-trip for adults, $30.50 for senior citizens, $16.50 for children 12 and under. The return boat leaves Catalina at 4:30 PM. You can make arrangements to boat in one direction and fly in the other, but you must make reservations separately. Reservations are advised.

By Plane: Island Express (☎ 310/436–2012) flies hourly from San Pedro and Long Beach. The trip takes about 15 minutes and costs $66 one-way, $121 round-trip.

Guided Tours

Santa Catalina Island Company (☎ 310/510–2000 or 800/428–2566) tours include coastal cruise to Seal Rocks (summer only), the *Flying Fish* boat trip (evenings, summer only) inland motor tour, the Skyline Drive, the Casino tour, the Avalon scenic tour, a traditional glass-bottom boat tour, and a submerged glass-bottom boat tour, where the vessel sinks 5 feet under. Reservations are highly recommended for the inland tours; the others are offered several times daily. Tours range in cost from $7.50 to $34.50 for adults; discounts are available for senior citizens over 55, children under 12, and for two or more tours booked in combination.

The **Catalina Conservancy** (☎ 310/510–1421) offers walks led by area docents.

LOS ANGELES ESSENTIALS

Arriving and Departing

By Bus

The Los Angeles **Greyhound Lines** terminal (☎ 800/231–2222) is at 208 East 6th Street, on the corner of Los Angeles Street.

By Car

Los Angeles is at the western terminus of I–10, a major east–west interstate highway that runs all the way east to Florida. I–15, angling down from Las Vegas, swings through the eastern communities around San Bernardino before heading on down to San Diego. I–5, which runs north–south through California, leads up to San Francisco and down to San Diego.

By Plane

The major gateways to Los Angeles are:

Los Angeles International Airport, commonly called LAX (☎ 310/646–5252). Departures are from the upper level and arrivals on the lower level. LAX is serviced by more than 85 major airlines. *See* Important Contacts A to Z *in* the Gold Guide for a list of all airlines serving LAX.

Burbank/Glendale/Pasadena Airport (☎ 818/840–8847) serves the San Fernando Valley with commuter and some longer flights. Alaska, American, America West, SkyWest, Southwest, and United airlines are represented.

Long Beach Airport (☎ 310/570–2600), at the southern tip of Los Angeles County, is served by America West and Sunjet International airlines.

John Wayne Airport, in Orange County (☎ 714/252–5006), is served by Alaska, American, American West, Continental, Delta, Northwest, Reno Air, Southwest, TWA, United, and USAir. Airport Coach (☎ 800/772–5299) provides ground transportation. (*See* Orange County Essentials *in* Chapter 12, for more details.)

Ontario International Airport (☎ 909/988–2700), located about 35 miles east of Los Angeles, serves the San Bernardino–Riverside area. (*See* Orange County Essentials *in* Chapter 12, for more details.)

Major carrier phone numbers: **Air Canada** (☎ 800/776–3000), **Alaska** (☎ 800/426–0333), **America West** (☎ 800/235–9292), **American** (☎ 800/433–7300), **British Airways** (☎ 800/247–9297), **Continental** (☎ 800/525–0280), **Delta** (☎ 800/221–1212), **Japan Air Lines** (☎ 800/525–

3663), **Midwest Express** (☎ 800/452–2022), **Northwest** (☎ 800/225–2525), **Reno Air** (☎ 800/736–6247), **Southwest** (☎ 800/435–9792), **Sunjet International** (☎ 800/478–6538), **TWA** (☎ 800/221–2000), **United** and **United Express** (☎ 800/241–6522), **SkyWest** (☎ 800/453–9417), and **USAir** and **USAir Express** (☎ 800/428–4322).

GROUND TRANSPORTATION FROM AIRPORT

A taxi ride to downtown from LAX can take 20 minutes—if there is no traffic. But in Los Angeles, that's a big if. Visitors should request the flat fee ($24 at press time) to downtown or choose from the several ground transportation companies that offer set rates.

SuperShuttle (☎ 310/782–6600) offers direct service between the airport and hotels. The trip to or from downtown hotels runs about $12 ($13 to Disneyland hotels); fares to private residences vary. The seven-passenger vans operate 24 hours a day. In the airport, phone 310/782–6600 or use the SuperShuttle courtesy phone in the luggage area; the van should arrive within 15 minutes. **Shuttle One** (9100 S. Sepulveda Blvd., No. 128, ☎ 310/670–6666) features door-to-door service and low rates ($10 per person from LAX to hotels in the Disneyland/Anaheim area). **Airport Coach** (☎ 714/938–8900 or 800/772–5299) provides service from LAX to the Pasadena ($12 one-way, $20 round-trip, $7/$12 children 3–11) and Anaheim ($14 one-way, $22 round-trip, $8/$14 children 3–11) areas.

The following limo companies charge a flat rate for airport service, ranging from $65 to $95: **Jackson Limousine** (☎ 213/734–9955), **A-1 West Coast Limousine** (☎ 213/756–5466), and **Dav-El Livery** (☎ 310/550–0070). Many of the cars have bars, stereos, televisions, and cellular phones.

Flyaway Service (☎ 818/994–5554) offers round-trip transportation between LAX and the central San Fernando Valley for $6. For the western San Fernando Valley and Ventura area, contact the **Great American Stage Lines** (☎ 800/287–8659). It charges $10–$20 one-way.

MTA (☎ 213/626–4455) also offers limited airport service to all areas of greater Los Angeles; bus lines depart from bus docks directly across the street from airport parking lot C. Prices vary from $1.25 to $3.10; some routes require transfers. The best line to take to downtown is the direct express line 439, which costs $1.50 and takes 45–50 minutes.

By Train

Los Angeles is a terminus for the **Amtrak** (☎ 800/872–7245). The *Coast Starlight,* which travels from the city to Seattle, with stops in Oakland–San Francisco and other northern California locations. The *Sunset Limited* goes to Los Angeles from New Orleans, the *Texas Eagle* from San Antonio, and the *Southwest Chief* and the *Desert Wind* from Chicago.

Union Station (800 N. Alameda St.) in Los Angeles is one of the grande dames of railroad stations.

Getting Around

By Bus and Subway

A bus ride on the **Metropolitan Transit Authority (MTA)** (☎ 213/626–4455) costs $1.10, with 25¢ for each transfer.

DASH (Downtown Area Short Hop) minibuses travel around the downtown area, stopping every two blocks or so. There are five different routes. You pay 25¢ every time you get on, no matter how far you go.

DASH (☎ 213/626–4455) runs weekdays 6:30 AM–6 PM, Saturday 10 AM–5 PM.

The **Metro Red Line** runs 4.4 miles through downtown, from Union Station to MacArthur Park, making five stops. The fare is $1.10.

The **Metro Blue Line** runs from downtown Los Angeles (corner of Flower and 7th Sts.) to Long Beach (corner of 1st St. and Long Beach Ave.), with 18 stops en route, most of them in Long Beach. The fare is $1.10 one-way.

By Car

In Los Angeles, it's not a question of whether wheels are a hindrance or a convenience: They're a necessity. More than 35 major companies (*see* Important Contacts A to Z *in* the Gold Guide) and dozens of local rental companies serve a steady demand for cars at Los Angeles International Airport and various city locations.

The freeway map below should help you to get around the maze. If you plan to drive extensively, consider buying a *Thomas Guide,* which contains detailed maps of the entire county. Despite what you've heard, traffic is not always a major problem, especially if you avoid rush hours (7–9 AM and 3–7 PM). Seat belts must be worn by all passengers at all times.

By Taxi

You probably won't be able to hail a cab on the street in Los Angeles. Instead, you should phone one of the many taxi companies. The metered rate is $1.60 per mile. Two of the more reputable companies are **Independent Cab Co.** (☎ 213/385–8294 or 310/569–8214) and **United Independent Taxi** (☎ 213/653–5050).

Guided Tours

Orientation

Los Angeles is so spread out and has such a wealth of sightseeing possibilities that an orientation bus tour may prove useful. The cost is between $25 and $40. All tours are fully narrated by a driver-guide. Reservations must be made in advance. Many hotels can book them for you.

L.A. Tours and Sightseeing (6333 W. 3rd St., at the Farmers' Market, ☎ 213/937–3361 or 800/286–8752) has a $38 tour covering various parts of the city, including downtown, Hollywood, and Beverly Hills. The company also operates tours to Disneyland, Universal Studios, Magic Mountain, beaches, and stars' homes.

Tourcoach Charter and Tours (6922 Hollywood Blvd., Hollywood 90028, ☎ 213/463–3333) picks up passengers from area hotels as well as around the corner from Mann's Chinese Theater (6925 Hollywood Blvd.). Sights such as Universal Studios, Sea World, Knott's Berry Farm, stars' homes, Disneyland, and other attractions are on this popular tour company's agenda. Price range is from $26 to $68.

A more personalized look at the city can be had by planning a tour with **Casablanca Tours** (Roosevelt Hotel, 7000 Hollywood Blvd., Cabana 4, Hollywood 90028, ☎ 213/461–0156), which offers a four-hour insider's look at Hollywood and Beverly Hills. Tours are in minibuses with a maximum of 14 people, and prices are equivalent to those for the large bus tours—about $33.

Los Angeles Freeways

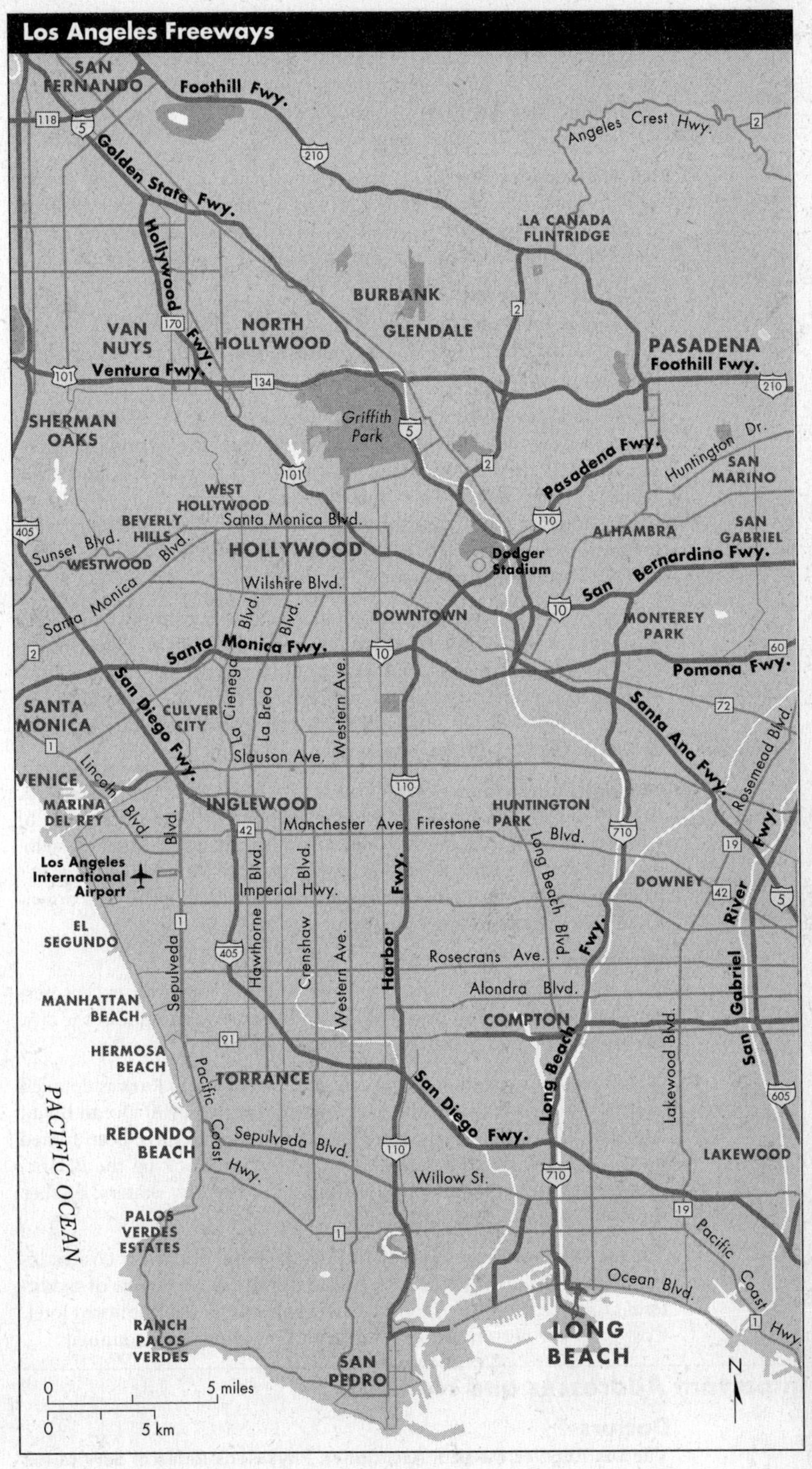
SAN FERNANDO
Foothill Fwy.
Angeles Crest Hwy.
Golden State Fwy.
Hollywood Fwy.
LA CAÑADA FLINTRIDGE
BURBANK
GLENDALE
VAN NUYS
NORTH HOLLYWOOD
PASADENA
Foothill Fwy.
Ventura Fwy.
SHERMAN OAKS
Griffith Park
Huntington Dr.
Pasadena Fwy.
SAN MARINO
WEST HOLLYWOOD
BEVERLY HILLS
Santa Monica Blvd.
SAN GABRIEL
Sunset Blvd.
WESTWOOD
HOLLYWOOD
ALHAMBRA
Dodger Stadium
San Bernardino Fwy.
Wilshire Blvd.
Santa Monica Blvd.
DOWNTOWN
MONTEREY PARK
Santa Monica Fwy.
Pomona Fwy.
SANTA MONICA
CULVER CITY
San Diego Fwy.
La Cienega Blvd.
La Brea
Western Ave.
Santa Ana Fwy.
Rosemead Blvd.
Slauson Ave.
VENICE
Lincoln Blvd.
MARINA DEL REY
INGLEWOOD
HUNTINGTON PARK
Manchester Ave.
Firestone Blvd.
Los Angeles International Airport
Hawthorne Blvd.
Crenshaw Blvd.
Imperial Hwy.
Long Beach Blvd.
DOWNEY
River Fwy.
EL SEGUNDO
Sepulveda Blvd.
Harbor Fwy.
Rosecrans Ave.
Long Beach Fwy.
MANHATTAN BEACH
Western Ave.
Alondra Blvd.
COMPTON
San Gabriel
HERMOSA BEACH
Lakewood Blvd.
PACIFIC OCEAN
Pacific Coast Hwy.
TORRANCE
San Diego Fwy.
REDONDO BEACH
Sepulveda Blvd.
LAKEWOOD
Willow St.
PALOS VERDES ESTATES
Pacific Coast Hwy.
Ocean Blvd.
RANCH PALOS VERDES
SAN PEDRO
LONG BEACH
N
0 5 miles
0 5 km
118
5
210
2
170
101
134
405
110
10
60
72
1
42
710
19
91
605

Personal Guides

Elegant Tours for the Discriminating (☎ 310/472–4090) is a personalized sightseeing and shopping service for the Beverly Hills area. Joan Mansfield offers her extensive knowledge of Rodeo Drive to one, two, or three people at a time. Lunch is included.

L.A. Nighthawks (Box 10224, Beverly Hills 90213, ☎ 310/392–1500) will arrange your nightlife for you. For a rather hefty price, you'll get a limousine, a guide (who ensures you're in a safe environment at all times), and immediate entry into L.A.'s hottest nightspots.

Special-Interest

Advantage Tours and Charters (Box 1192, Beverly Hills 90213, ☎ 310/823–0321 or 213/933–1475) specializes in touring area museums, both large and small.

Grave Line Tours (Box 931694, Hollywood 90093, ☎ 213/469–4149) is a clever, off-the-beaten-track tour that digs up the dirt on notorious suicides and visits the scenes of various murders, scandals, and other crimes via a luxuriously renovated hearse. Tours are daily at 9:30 AM for 2½ hours (a 12:30 PM tour will be scheduled if the morning one is full, and sometimes a 3:30 PM tour leaves as well); it's closed Monday, and the cost is $40 per person.

Visitors who want something dramatically different should check with Marlene Gordon of **The Next Stage** (Box 35269, Los Angeles 90035, ☎ 213/939–2688). This innovative tour company takes from four to 46 people, on buses or vans, in search of ethnic L.A., Victorian L.A., Underground L.A. (in which all the places visited are underground), as well as the very original Insomniac's Tour and Wacky L.A.

LA Today Custom Tours (14964 Camarosa Dr., Pacific Palisades 90272, ☎ 310/454–5730) also has a wide selection of offbeat tours, some of which tie in with seasonal and cultural events, such as theater, museum exhibits, and the Rose Bowl. Groups range from 8 to 800, and prices from $6 to $85. The least expensive is a two-hour walking tour of downtown Los Angeles architecture that costs $6.

Walking

Walking is something that Angelenos don't do much of, except perhaps in Westwood and Beverly Hills and in parks throughout the city. But there is no better way to see things close up.

A very pleasant self-guided walking tour of **Palisades Park** is detailed in a brochure available at the park's visitor center (1400 Ocean Blvd., Santa Monica). Many television shows and movies have been filmed on this narrow strip of parkland on a bluff overlooking the Pacific. The 26-acre retreat is always bustling with walkers, skaters, Frisbee throwers, readers, and sunbathers.

The **Los Angeles Conservancy** (☎ 213/623–2489) offers low-cost walking tours of the downtown area. Each Saturday at 10 AM one of six different tours leaves from the Olive Street entrance of the Biltmore Hotel. Cost is $5 per person. Make reservations, as group size is limited.

Important Addresses and Numbers

Doctors

The **Los Angeles Medical Association Physicians Referral Service** (☎ 213/483–6122) is open weekdays 8:45–4:45. Most larger hospitals in Los Angeles have 24-hour emergency rooms. Two are **Cedar-Sinai Medical Center** (8700 Beverly Blvd., ☎ 310/855–5000) and **Queen of**

Angels Hollywood Presbyterian Medical Center (1300 N. Vermont Ave., ☎ 213/413–3000).

Emergencies

Dial 911 for **police** and **ambulance** in an emergency.

24-Hour Pharmacies

The **Kaiser Bellflower Pharmacy** (9400 E. Rosecrans Ave., Bellflower, ☎ 310/461–4213) is open around the clock. The **Horton and Converse** pharmacies at 6625 Van Nuys Boulevard (Van Nuys, ☎ 818/782–6251) and at 11600 Wilshire Boulevard (W. Los Angeles, ☎ 310/478–0801) are open until 2 AM.

Visitor Information

The **Los Angeles Convention and Visitors Bureau** (633 W. 5th St., Suite 6000, 90071, ☎ 213/624–7300) will provide you with extensive free information about the region. "Destination Los Angeles," a packet of annually updated lists of entertainment and special events with lodging and dining suggestions, costs $2. Los Angeles also maintains a 24-hour toll-free multilingual line for information about community services (☎ 213/689–8822 or 800/339–6993).

In addition, there are visitor centers and chambers of commerce in many of the communities in the Los Angeles area, including:

Beverly Hills (239 S. Beverly Dr., 90212, ☎ 310/271–8174 or 800/345–2210).
Channel Islands (3810 W. Channel Islands Blvd., Suite 6, 93035, ☎ 800/994–4852).
Glendale (200 S. Louise St., Box 112, 91209, ☎ 818/240–7870).
Hollywood (7000 Hollywood Blvd., Suite 1, 90028, ☎ 213/469–8311).
Hollywood Visitors Center (6541 Hollywood Boulevard, ☎ 213/689–8822; ⏲ Mon.–Sat. 9–5).
Long Beach Area Convention and Visitors Council (1 World Trade Center, Suite 300, 90831, ☎ 310/436–3645).
Oxnard (715 S. A St., 93030, ☎ 800/269–6273).
Pasadena (171 S. Los Robles Ave., 91101, ☎ 818/795–9311).
Santa Monica Visitors Center (1400 Ocean Avenue, Palisades Park, ☎ 310/393–7593; ⏲ daily 10–4).
West Hollywood (8687 Melrose Ave. 90069, ☎ 310/289–2525).

12 Orange County

Orange County is one of California's top tourist destinations, and once you've arrived here it doesn't take long to see why. The county has made tourism its number-one industry, attracting nearly 40 million visitors annually. Two theme parks, Disneyland and Knott's Berry Farm, entice millions on their own. The California Angels baseball and Mighty Ducks of Anaheim hockey teams are also a draw. But Orange County is more than just Anaheim: It also boasts lively beaches, upscale shopping, some fine museums, and San Juan Capistrano, home of the famed annual swallow migration.

Updated by Jane E. Lasky and William P. Brown

ORANGE COUNTY IS SUCH A MAGNET for conventioneers and tourists it's easy to forget that people actually live here, too—many of them in high-priced Mediterranean-style suburbs strung along the 24-mile-long coastline. Orange County residents shop in the classy malls that lure visitors as well. Like visitors, locals can be found at the beach sunning themselves or waiting for the next big wave. Locals even dine and stay at the luxurious oceanfront resorts that perch on the edge of the Pacific.

Served by convenient airports and only an hour's drive from Los Angeles, Orange County is both a destination on its own and a very popular excursion from Los Angeles.

EXPLORING

Before visiting Orange County, select a primary attraction and then plan excursions to other sights. If Disneyland is the highlight, you'll probably want to organize your activities around the tourist attractions that fill the central county and take excursions to selected coastal spots. The reverse is true, of course, if you're planning to hang out on the beach. In that case, select a coastal headquarters and make forays to the Magic Kingdom.

If you're traveling with children, you could easily devote several days to the theme parks: a day or two for Disneyland, a day for Knott's Berry Farm, and perhaps a day driving to some of the area's lesser-known attractions.

Inland Orange County

Numbers in the margin correspond to points of interest on the Orange County map.

★ ❶ Perhaps more than any other place in the world, **Disneyland,** Walt Disney's first theme park, is a symbol of the eternal child in all of us. It's a place of delight and enchantment; an exceptionally clean and imaginatively developed wonder.

When Disney carved the park out of the orange groves in 1955, it consisted of four lands and fewer than 20 major attractions radiating from his idealized American Main Street. Much has changed in the intervening years, including the massive expansion of the park to include four more lands and some 40 more attractions. But Main Street retains its turn-of-the-century charm, and in ever-sharper contrast with the world just outside the gates of the park. Disney's vision of the Magic Kingdom was one of never-ending fantasy. Thus designers and engineers continue to devise new ways to tantalize and treat guests, among the more recent being the Indiana Jones Adventure, a chance to explore the ruins of an ancient excavation site to look for the lost Temple of the Forbidden Eye.

Disneyland is big and, during the busy summer season, crowded. Planning a strategy for your visit will help you get the most out of it. If you can, pick a rainy midweek day; surprisingly, most Disney attractions are indoors. Arrive early; the box office opens a half hour before the park's scheduled opening time. Go immediately to the most popular attractions: Space Mountain, Star Tours, Pirates of the Caribbean, Haunted Mansion, It's a Small World, and Splash Mountain. Mickey's Toontown tends to be most crowded in the mornings. Lines for rides will also be shorter during the evening Fantasmic! show, parades, and fireworks dis-

Anaheim Museum, **4**
Balboa Peninsula, **13**
Bolsa Chica Ecological Reserve, **10**
Bowers Museum of Cultural Art, **7**
Crystal Cathedral, **6**
Dana Point, **18**
Disneyland, **1**
Fiesta Marketplace, **8**
Huntington Beach, **11**
Irvine Museum, **9**
Knott's Berry Farm, **2**
Laguna Art Museum, **16**
Mission San Juan Capistrano, **20**
Movieland Wax Museum, **3**
Newport Harbor, **12**
Newport Harbor Art Museum, **14**
Orange County Marine Institute, **19**
Richard Nixon Birthplace and Library, **5**
Ritz-Carlton Laguna Niguel, **17**
San Juan Capistrano Library, **21**
Sherman Library and Gardens, **15**

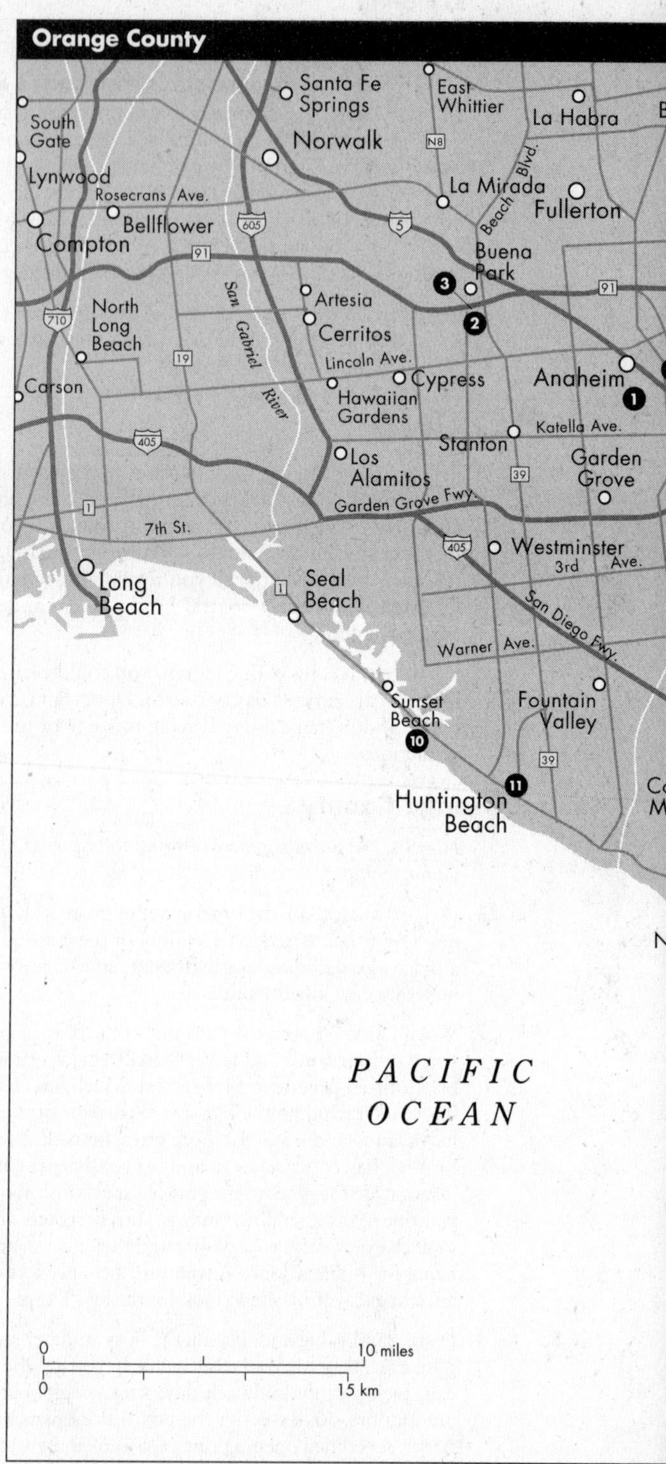

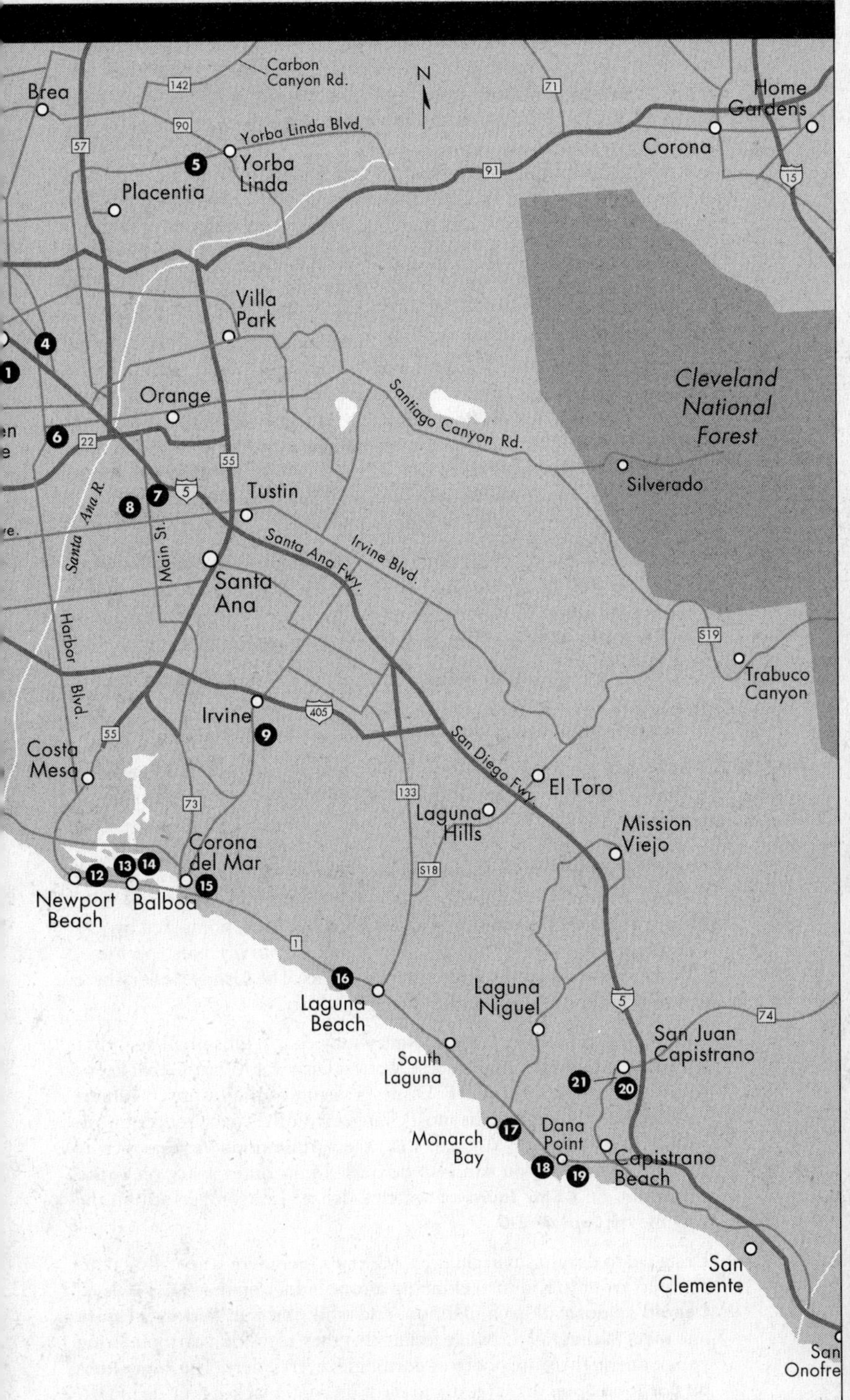

Brea
Carbon Canyon Rd.
N
Home Gardens
Corona
Yorba Linda Blvd.
Yorba Linda
Placentia
Villa Park
Orange
Cleveland National Forest
Santiago Canyon Rd.
Silverado
Tustin
Santa Ana R.
Main St.
Santa Ana
Santa Ana Fwy.
Irvine Blvd.
Harbor Blvd.
Trabuco Canyon
Irvine
Costa Mesa
San Diego Fwy.
El Toro
Laguna Hills
Mission Viejo
Corona del Mar
Newport Beach
Balboa
Laguna Beach
Laguna Niguel
South Laguna
San Juan Capistrano
Monarch Bay
Dana Point
Capistrano Beach
San Clemente
San Onofre

play (usually around 9:30), as well as near opening or closing times. Just the same, even on a slow day expect to wait in line for 15 minutes or so. As with the rides, strategize your eating as well. Restaurants are less crowded toward the beginning and end of meal periods. Also, fast-food spots abound, and you can now get healthy fare such as fruit, pasta, and frozen yogurt at various locations throughout the park. Whatever you wind up eating, food prices are higher than on the outside. When shopping, remember that there are lockers just off Main Street in which you can store purchases, and thereby avoid lugging bundles around all day or shopping just before the park's closing time when stores are crowded. If your feet get tired, you can move from one area of the park to another on the train or monorail, or even in a horse-drawn carriage.

Each of Disney's lands has its own theme rides. Stepping through the doors of Sleeping Beauty's castle into **Fantasyland** can be a dream come true for children. Mickey Mouse may even be there to greet them. Once inside, they can join **Peter Pan's Flight**; go down the rabbit hole with **Alice in Wonderland**; take an aerial spin with **Dumbo the Flying Elephant**; take **Mr. Toad's Wild Ride**; spin around in giant cups at the **Mad Tea Party**; swoosh through the **Matterhorn**; or visit **It's a Small World,** where figures of children from 100 countries worldwide sing of unity and peace.

In **Frontierland** you can take a cruise on the **steamboat *Mark Twain*** or the **sailing ship *Columbia*** and experience the sights and sounds of the spectacular **Rivers of America.** Kids of every age enjoy rafting to **Tom Sawyer's Island** for an hour or so of climbing and exploring.

Some visitors to **Adventureland** have taken the **Jungle Cruise** so many times that they know the patter offered up by the operators by heart. Other attractions here include shops with African and South Seas wares.

TIME OUT **Blue Bayou,** featuring Creole food, is a great place to eat. It is in the entrance to the Pirates of the Caribbean—you can hear the antics in the background.

The twisting streets of **New Orleans Square** offer interesting browsing and shopping, strolling Dixieland musicians, and the ever-popular **Pirates of the Caribbean** ride. The **Haunted Mansion,** populated by 999 holographic ghosts, is nearby. Theme shops purvey hats, perfume, Mardi Gras merchandise, and gourmet items. The **Disney Gallery** here has trendy (and expensive) original Disney art.

The animated bears in **Critter Country** may charm kids of all ages, but it's **Splash Mountain,** the steepest, wettest Disney adventure, that keeps them coming back for more. Disney's vision of the future in **Tomorrowland** has undergone the most changes over the years, reflecting advances in technology. You can still take a **Submarine Voyage** or ride the monorail, but you can also be hurled into outer space on **Space Mountain,** take **Star Tours,** or watch Michael Jackson perform in the 3-D movie ***Captain E-O*.**

Designed to delight small children, **Mickey's Toontown** is actually a pint-size playground. Kids can climb up a rope ladder on the **"Miss Daisy," Donald's Boat,** talk to a mailbox, and walk through **Mickey's House** and **meet Mickey,** all the while feeling that they're inside a cartoon. Bring your camera; there are photo opportunities everywhere. The **Roger Rabbit Car Toon Spin,** the largest and most unusual black-light ride in Disneyland history, is highly popular.

A stroll along **Main Street** evokes a small-town America, circa 1900, that never existed except in the popular imagination and fiction and films. Interconnected shops and restaurants line both sides of the street. The **Emporium,** the largest and most comprehensive of the shops, offers a full line of Disney products. But you'll also find magic tricks, crystal, hobby and sports memorabilia, clothing, and photo supplies here. *Disneyland: 1313 Harbor Blvd., Anaheim, ☎ 714/999–4565. ☛ $33 adults, $25 children 3–11. ⊙ June–mid-Sept., Sun.–Fri. 9 AM–midnight, Sat. 9 AM–1 AM; mid-Sept.–May, weekdays 10–6, Sat. 9–midnight, Sun. 9–10. Hrs and prices subject to change.*

★ 2 If Disneyland specializes in a high-tech brand of fantasy, **Knott's Berry Farm,** in nearby Buena Park, offers a dose of reality. The farm has been rooted in the community since 1934, when Cordelia Knott began serving chicken dinners on her wedding china to supplement the family's meager income. The dinners and the boysenberry pies proved more profitable than husband Walter's berry farm, so the family moved first into the restaurant business and then into the entertainment business. The park, with its Old West theme, is now a 150-acre complex with 100-plus rides and attractions, 60 eating places, and 60 shops.

Like Disneyland, the park has theme areas. **Ghost Town** offers a delightful human-scale visit to the Old West. Many of the buildings were relocated here from their original mining-town sites. You can stroll down the street, stop and chat with the blacksmith, pan for gold, crack open a geode, ride in an authentic 1880s passenger train, or take the **Gold Mine** ride and descend into a replica of a working gold mine. A real treasure here is the antique **Dentzel carousel** with a menagerie of animals. **Camp Snoopy** is a kid-size High Sierra wonderland where Snoopy and his Peanuts-gang friends hang out. Tall trees frame **Wild Water Wilderness,** where you can ride white water in an inner tube in **Big Foot Rapids** and commune with the native peoples of the Northwest coast in the spooky **Mystery Lodge.** Themes aside, thrill rides are placed throughout the park. Teenagers, especially, love the **Boomerang** roller coaster; **X-K-1,** a living version of a video game; **Kingdom of the Dinosaurs**; **Montezooma's Revenge,** a roller coaster that goes from 0 to 55 mph in less than five seconds; and the wild **Jaguar** roller coaster. Costumed interpreters offer insight into the natural and human history of the attractions.

Knott's also offers entertainment throughout the day with shows scheduled in Ghost Town, the Bird Cage Theater, and the Good Time Theater; occasionally stars appear here. *8039 Beach Blvd., Buena Park, ☎ 714/220–5200. ☛ $28.50 adults, $18.50 senior citizens and children 3–11. ⊙ June–early Sept., daily 9 AM–midnight; mid-Sept.–May, weekdays 10–6, Sat. 10–10, Sun. 10–7. Park closes during inclement weather. Hrs and prices subject to change.*

TIME OUT Don't forget what made Knott's famous: Mrs. Knott's fried chicken dinners and boysenberry pies at **Mrs. Knott's Chicken Dinner Restaurant.** It's just outside the park gates in Knott's California MarketPlace, a collection of 32 shops and restaurants.

Visitors will find more than 70 years of movie magic immortalized at
3 the **Movieland Wax Museum** in 400 wax sculptures of Hollywood's greatest stars, including Michael Jackson, Cindy Crawford, John Wayne, Marilyn Monroe, and George Burns. Figures are displayed in a maze of realistic sets from movies such as *Gone with the Wind, Star Trek, The Wizard of Oz,* and *Home Alone.* The Chamber of Horrors is designed to scare the daylights out of you. You can buy a combination ticket ($16.50 adults, $9.75 children) that also allows you entry to Ripley's Believe It or Not, the somewhat schlocky chain attraction across the street. *7711 Beach*

Blvd., 1 block north of Knott's, ☎ 714/522–1155. ☛ $12.95 adults, $6.95 children. ⏲ Sun.–Thurs. 9–7, Fri.–Sat. 9–8.

❹ The **Anaheim Museum,** housed in a 1908 Carnegie Library building, illustrates the history of Anaheim, including the original wine-producing colony. Changing exhibits include art collections, women's history, and hobbies. *241 S. Anaheim Blvd., ☎ 714/778–3301. Suggested ☛ $1.50, children free. ⏲ Wed.–Fri. 10–4, Sat. noon–4.*

★ ❺ About 7 miles north of Anaheim, off Highway 57 (Yorba Linda Blvd. exit), the **Richard Nixon Library and Birthplace** is the final resting place of the 37th president and his wife Pat. Displays illustrate the checkered career of Nixon, the only president forced to resign from office. Visitors can listen to Nixon's Checkers speech or to the so-called smoking-gun tape from the Watergate days, among other recorded material. Within the main building is a small but interesting gift shop that contains presidential souvenir items. *18001 Yorba Linda Blvd., Yorba Linda, ☎ 714/993–3393. ☛ $5.95 adults, $3.95 senior citizens, $2 children 8–11. ⏲ Mon.–Sat. 10–5, Sun. 11–5.*

❻ Garden Grove, a community just south of Anaheim and Buena Park, is the home of one of the most impressive churches in the country, the **Crystal Cathedral.** The domain of television evangelist Robert Schuller, this sparkling glass structure resembles a four-pointed star with more than 10,000 panes of glass covering a weblike steel truss to form translucent walls. *12141 Lewis St., Garden Grove, ☎ 714/971–4013. Donation requested. Guided tours Mon.–Sat. 9–3:30. Call for schedule. ☎ 714/544–5679 for reservations for Easter and Christmas productions.*

❼ The **Bowers Museum of Cultural Art,** once a quaint cultural-arts gallery, is now the largest museum in Orange County, having tripled in size after a $12 million expansion and restoration of its original 1936 Spanish-style buildings. The museum houses a first-rate, 85,000-piece collection of artwork by indigenous peoples from around the world. Permanent galleries illustrate sculpture, costumes, and artifacts from Oceania; sculpture from west and central Africa; Pacific Northwest wood carvings; dazzling beadwork of the Plains cultures; and California basketry. The museum's trendy Topaz Cafe offers an ethnically eclectic menu. *2002 N. Main St., Santa Ana, ☎ 714/567–3600. ☛ $4.50 adults, $3 senior citizens and students, $1.50 children, under 5 free. ⏲ Tues.–Wed. and Fri.–Sun. 10–4, Thurs. 10–9.*

❽ The **Fiesta Marketplace** along 4th Street in downtown Santa Ana offers a glimpse into contemporary Hispanic culture. The best time to visit is on the weekend, when the place takes on a lively fiesta atmosphere. You'll find bargain western wear, imports from Mexico and Guatemala, and authentic tacos and quesadillas. Just a block away is the **Old Orange County Courthouse,** which has been a backdrop for more than 30 movies and TV shows since 1915; it is now a county museum and historical center (400 W. Santa Ana Blvd.; ☛ Free; ⏲ Weekdays 9–5).

❾ To view the pristine California landscape as it was before development brought houses and freeways to hillsides, visit the **Irvine Museum.** Located on the 12th floor of a circular marble-and-glass office building, the museum displays a collection of California impressionist landscape paintings dated 1890 to 1930. The collection was assembled by Joan Irvine Smith, granddaughter of James Irvine, who once owned one-quarter of what is now Orange County. *18881 Von Karman Ave., Irvine, ☎ 714/476–2565. ☛ Free. ⏲ Tues.–Sat. 11–5.*

The Coast

Coastal Orange County, dotted with charming beach towns and punctuated with world-class resorts, offers the quintessential laid-back southern California experience. You can catch a monster wave with the bronzed local kids, get a glimpse of some rich and famous lifestyles, and take a walk through the shoreline's natural treasures. Sites and stops on this tour are strung out along some 42 miles of the Pacific Coast Highway, and we'll take this route north to south. Although there is bus service along the coast road, it's best to explore it by car.

★ 10 If you're interested in wildlife, a walk through **Bolsa Chica Ecological Reserve** (☎ 714/897–7003) will reward you with a chance to see an amazingly restored 300-acre salt marsh, which is home to 315 species of birds, plus other animals and plants. You can see many of them along the 1½-mile loop trail that meanders through the reserve. The walk is especially delightful in winter, when you're likely to see great blue heron, snowy and great egrets, common loons, and other migrating birds. The salt marsh, which is off the Pacific Coast Highway between Warner Avenue and Golden West Street, can be visited at any time, but a local support group, Amigos de Bolsa Chica, offers free guided tours from 9 to 10:30 AM on the first Saturday of the month, September through April.

11 **Huntington Beach,** with its 9 miles of white sand and sometimes towering waves, offers one of the hippest surf scenes in southern California. Each year it hosts the Pro Surfing Championships competition. This beach is a favorite of Orange County residents and has ample parking, food concessions, fire pits, and lifeguards. For years, the town itself was little more than a string of small, tacky buildings across the Pacific Coast Highway from the beach, containing surf shops, T-shirt emporiums, and hot-dog stands. In the early '90s, however, work began on a face-lift aimed at transforming the funky surf town into a shining resort area, with the newly reconstructed 1,800-foot-long **Huntington Pier** as its centerpiece. The **Pierside Pavilion,** across the Pacific Coast Highway from the pier, contains shops, a restaurant, a nightclub, and a theater complex. The **International Museum of Surfing** (411 Olive Ave., ☎ 714/960–3483; ☛ $2 adults, $1 students; ⏲ Wed.–Sun. noon–5) has an extensive collection of surfing memorabilia.

Newport Beach has a dual personality: It's best known as the quintessential (upscale) beach town, with its island-dotted yacht harbor and a history of such illustrious residents as John Wayne, author Joseph Wambaugh, and Watergate scandal figure Bob Haldeman. And then there's inland Newport Beach, just southwest of John Wayne Airport, a business and commercial hub with a major shopping center and a clutch of high-rise office buildings and hotels.

Even if you don't own a yacht and don't qualify as seaside high society, you can explore the charming avenues and alleys surrounding the
★ 12 famed **Newport Harbor,** which shelters nearly 10,000 small boats. To see it from the water, take a one-hour gondola cruise around the harbor (Gondola Company of Newport, 3404 Via Oporto, ☎ 714/675–1212). If you're here during the Christmas holidays, don't miss the Christmas boat parade—one of the best on the West Coast—with hundreds of brightly lighted and decorated yachts cruising through the channels. You can watch the parade from various restaurants overlooking the marina, but reserve a table early.

The waterside portion of Newport Beach consists of a U-shaped harbor
13 bor with the mainland along one leg and the **Balboa Peninsula** along

the other leg, separating the marina from the ocean. Set within the harbor are eight small islands, including Balboa and Lido, both well-known for their famous residents. The homes lining the shore may seem modest, but remember that this is some of the most expensive real estate in the world.

You can reach the peninsula from Pacific Coast Highway at Newport Boulevard, which will take you to Balboa Boulevard. Begin your exploration of the peninsula at the **Newport Pier,** which juts out into the ocean near 20th Street. Street parking is difficult here, so grab the first space you find and be prepared to walk. A stroll along Ocean Front reveals much of the character of this place. On weekday mornings head for the beach near the pier, where you're likely to encounter the dory fishermen hawking their predawn catches, as they've done for generations. On weekends the walk is alive with kids (of all ages) on skates, Rollerblades, skateboards, and bikes weaving among the strolling pedestrians and whizzing past fast-food joints, swimsuit shops, and seedy bars.

Continue your drive along Balboa Boulevard nearly to the end of the peninsula, where the charm is of quite a different character. On the bay side is the historic Victorian **Balboa Pavilion,** perched on the water's edge. Built in 1905 as a bath- and boathouse, it hosted big-band dances in the 1940s. Today it houses a restaurant and shops and is a departure point for harbor and whale-watching cruises. Adjacent to the pavilion is the three-car ferry, which connects the peninsula to Balboa Island. Several blocks surrounding the pavilion support restaurants, shops (all a little nicer than those at Newport Pier) and a small Fun Zone—a local hangout with a Ferris wheel, video games, rides, and arcades. On the ocean side of the peninsula the Balboa Pier juts into the surf, backed by a long, wide beach that seems to stretch forever.

14 The **Newport Harbor Art Museum** is internationally known for its impressive collection of abstract expressionist works and cutting-edge contemporary works by California artists. Historical art films are occasionally shown here, as well. Snacks are available in the Sculpture Garden Cafe. *850 San Clemente Dr., ☎ 714/759–1122. ☛ $4 adults, $2 students and senior citizens. ⏲ Tues.–Sat. 10–5, Sun. noon–5.*

Just south of Newport Beach, **Corona del Mar** is a small jewel of a town with an exceptional beach. You can walk clear out onto the bay on a rough-and-tumble rock jetty. Much of the beach around here is backed by short cliffs that resemble scaled-down versions of the northern California coastline. The town itself stretches only a few blocks along Pacific Coast Highway, but some of the fanciest stores in the county are here.

15 **Sherman Library and Gardens,** a lush botanical garden and library specializing in Southwest flora and fauna, offers diversion from sun and sand. You can wander among cactus gardens, rose gardens, a wheelchair-height touch-and-smell garden, and a tropical conservatory. *2647 E. Coast Hwy., Corona del Mar, ☎ 714/673–2261. ☛ $2; free Mon. ⏲ Gardens daily 10:30–4.*

The drive south to Laguna Beach passes some of southern California's most beautiful oceanfront; **Crystal Cove State Beach** stretches from Corona del Mar to Laguna, and its undersea park lures swimmers and divers. Each curve in the highway along here turns up a sparkling vista of crashing surf to one side and, to the other, gently rolling golden brown hills sweeping inland.

★ **Laguna Beach** has been called SoHo by the Sea, which is at least partly right. It is an artists' colony that, during the 1950s and '60s, attracted the beat, hip, and far-out, but it is also a colony of conservative wealth. The two camps coexist in relative harmony, with Art prevailing in the congested village, and Wealth entrenched in the canyons and on the hillsides surrounding the town. The November 1993 fire, which destroyed more than 300 homes in the hillsides surrounding Laguna Beach, miraculously left the village untouched.

Walk along Pacific Coast Highway in town or along side streets such as Forest or Ocean, and you'll pass gallery after gallery filled with art ranging from billowy seascapes to neon sculpture and kinetic structures. In addition, you'll find a wide selection of crafts, high fashion, beachwear, and jewelry shops.

16 The **Laguna Art Museum,** near Heisler Park, has historical and contemporary California art. Special exhibits change quarterly. *307 Cliff Dr., ☎ 714/494–6531. ☛ $5 adults, $4 students and senior citizens, children under 12 free. ⏲ Tues.–Sun. 11–5.*

TIME OUT The patio at **Las Brisas** (361 Cliff Dr., ☎ 714/497–5434), a restaurant next door to the museum, offers one of the loveliest views of the coastline available in Laguna Beach. Stop here for a snack, and drink in the scene.

In front of the Pottery Shack on Pacific Coast Highway is a bit of local nostalgia—a life-size **statue of Eiler Larsen,** the town greeter, who for years stood at the edge of town saying hello and goodbye to visitors. In recent years a man who calls himself Number One Archer has assumed the role of greeter, waving to tourists from a spot at the corner of Pacific Coast Highway and Forest Avenue.

Laguna's many arts festivals bring visitors here from all over the world. During July and August, the Sawdust Festival and Art-a-Fair, the Laguna Festival of the Arts, and the Pageant of the Masters take place. The **Pageant of the Masters** (☎ 714/494–1147) is Laguna's most impressive event, a blending of life and art. Live models and carefully orchestrated backgrounds are arranged in striking mimicry of famous paintings. Participants must hold a perfectly still pose for the length of their stay on stage. It is an impressive effort, requiring hours of training and rehearsal by the 400 or so residents who volunteer each year.

Going to Laguna without exploring its beaches would be a shame. To get away from the hubbub of Main Beach, go north to **Woods Cove,** off the Pacific Coast Highway at Diamond Street; it's especially quiet during the week. Big rock formations hide lurking crabs. As you climb the steps to leave, you'll see a stunning English-style mansion that was once the home of Bette Davis. At the end of almost every street in Laguna, there is a little cove with its own beach.

17 The **Ritz-Carlton Laguna Niguel** is the classiest hotel along the coast; it draws guests from around the world with its sweeping oceanside views, gleaming marble, and stunning antiques. Even if you're not a registered guest, you can enjoy the view and the elegant service by taking English tea, which is served each afternoon in the library. *1 Ritz-Carlton Dr., Dana Point, ☎ 714/240–2000.*

18 **Dana Point** is Orange County's newest aquatic playground, a small-boat marina tucked into a dramatic natural harbor surrounded by high bluffs. The harbor was first described more than 100 years ago by its namesake, Richard Henry Dana, in his book *Two Years Before the Mast.*

The marina has docks for small boats and marine-oriented shops and restaurants. Recent development includes a hillside park with bike and walking trails, hotels, small shopping centers, and a collection of eateries. A monument to Dana stands in a gazebo at the top of the bluffs in front of the Blue Lantern Inn. There's a pleasant sheltered beach and park at the west end of the marina. Boating is the big thing here. **Dana Wharf Sportfishing** (☎ 714/496–5794) has charters year-round and runs whale-watching excursions in winter, and the community sponsors an annual whale festival in late February.

A real treasure in Dana Point is the **Nautical Heritage Museum,** a collection of ship models, paintings, 18th- and 19th-century seafaring documents, and navigation instruments. *24532 Del Prado Ave., Dana Point,* ☎ *714/661–1001.* ☛ *Free.* ⏲ *Weekdays 10–4.*

19 The **Orange County Marine Institute** offers a number of programs and excursions designed to entertain and educate about the ocean. Three tanks containing touchable sea creatures are available on weekends. Anchored near the institute is *The Pilgrim,* a full-size replica of the square-rigged vessel on which Richard Henry Dana sailed. Tours of *The Pilgrim* are offered Sunday from 11 to 2:30. A gallery and gift shop are open daily. *24200 Dana Point Harbor Dr.,* ☎ *714/496–2274.* ⏲ *Daily 10–4:30.*

San Juan Capistrano is best known for its mission and, of course, for the swallows that migrate here each year from their winter haven in Argentina. The arrival of the birds on St. Joseph's Day, March 19, launches a week of festivities. After summering in the arches of the old stone church, the swallows head home on St. John's Day, October 23.

★ 20 Founded in 1776 by Father Junípero Serra, **Mission San Juan Capistrano** was the major Roman Catholic outpost between Los Angeles and San Diego. A main draw is a chance to see the original Great Stone Church, which is permanently supported by scaffolding. Many of the mission's adobe buildings have been restored to illustrate mission life, with exhibits of an olive millstone, tallow ovens, tanning vats, metal-working furnaces, and padres' living quarters. The bougainvillea-covered Serra Chapel is believed to be the oldest building still in use in California. The knowledgeable staff in the mission's visitor center can help you with a self-guided tour, or you can schedule your visit to coincide with the free walking tours offered every Sunday at 1. *Camino Capistrano and Ortega Hwy.,* ☎ *714/248–2048.* ☛ *$4 adults, $3 children under 13.* ⏲ *Daily 8:30–5.*

21 Near the mission is the postmodern **San Juan Capistrano Library,** built in 1983. Architect Michael Graves mixed classical design with the style of the mission to striking effect. Its courtyard has secluded places for reading, as well as a running water fountain. *31495 El Camino Real,* ☎ *714/493–3984.* ⏲ *Mon.–Tues. 11–9, Wed. 1–9, Thurs. noon–6, Sat. 10–5.*

The **Decorative Arts Study Center,** just up the street from the mission, presents exhibits and lectures on gardens and interior design, plus an annual antiques show and storytelling festival in October. *31431 Camino Capistrano,* ☎ *714/496–2132.* ⏲ *Tues.–Sat. 10–3.*

Galleria Capistrano, occupying the historic Egan House, is one of southern California's leading galleries devoted to the art of Native Americans. Exhibits include first-rate paintings, prints, jewelry, and sculpture from Southwest and Northwest artists. *31892 Camino Capistrano,* ☎ *714/661–1781.* ⏲ *Tues.–Sun. 11–6.*

TIME OUT The 1894 Spanish Revival **Capistrano Depot** (26701 Verdugo St., ☏ 714/496–8181) is not only the local Amtrak train station but also a restaurant. The eclectic menu runs from rack of lamb to southwestern fare to pasta. It's a perfect way to see San Juan if you are based in Los Angeles—a train ride, a meal, and then a little sightseeing.

SHOPPING

Shopping is Orange County's favorite indoor sport, and it's got the shopping malls to prove it. Some of the merchandise is available at venerable establishments like Tiffany, Chanel, and Brooks Brothers, but if these places are beyond your budget, you can always window-shop. The following is just a small selection of the shopping possibilities in the county.

South Coast Plaza (Bristol and Sunflower Sts., Costa Mesa), the most amazing of all the malls and the largest in Orange County, is actually two enclosed shopping centers, complete with greenery and tumbling waterfalls bisecting the wide aisles, plus a collection of boutiques and restaurants across the street. A free tram makes frequent runs among the three sections. The older section is anchored by **Nordstrom, Sears,** and **Bullock's;** the newer Crystal Court across the street has **The Broadway** department store as its centerpiece. It's the variety of stores, however, that makes this mall special. You'll find **Gucci, Burberry's, Armani, F.A.O. Schwarz, Saks Fifth Avenue,** and **Mark Cross** just up the aisle from **Sears.** Kids will want to browse through the **Disney** and **Sesame Street** stores. There's even an outpost of the **Metropolitan Museum of Art** just a few steps from **McDonald's** and **Eddie Bauer.** For literary buffs, there is a branch of the famous **Rizzoli's International Bookstore.** The mall is particularly festive during the holidays, when Santa's village fills the Carousel Court and a five-story Christmas tree soars to the top of the Crystal Court.

Fashion Island on Newport Center Drive in Newport Beach sits on a hilltop, where shoppers can enjoy the ocean breeze. It is an open-air, single-level mall of more than 200 stores. Major department stores here include **Neiman Marcus, Bullock's,** and **The Broadway** (note: at press time it was announced that this branch would likely close or be converted into another department store in 1996). The enclosed **Atrium Court** is a Mediterranean-style plaza with three floors of boutiques and stores such as Sharper Image, Benetton, and Caswell–Massey.

Main Place, just off I–5 in Santa Ana, has **Robinsons–May, Bullock's,** and **Nordstrom** as its anchors. Although many of the 190 shops are upscale, the mall resembles a warehouse. It's busy and noisy, and local teenagers tend to hang out here.

If you can look past the inflatable palm trees, unimaginative T-shirts, and other tourist novelties, there is some good browsing to be done in **Laguna Beach.** There are dozens of art galleries, antiques shops, one-of-a-kind crafts boutiques, and custom jewelry stores. Some of the best can be found along arty Forest Avenue and nearby thoroughfares, just a few steps off Pacific Coast Highway. **Tree Foxes Trot,** at 264 Forest Avenue, features a delightful selection of handcrafted items from around the world; **Georgeo's Art Glass and Jewelry,** at 269 Forest Avenue, contains a large selection of etched and blown-glass bowls, vases, glassware, and jewelry; **Rosovsky Gallery,** at 303 Broadway, showcases the work of three Russian artists; **Art Center Gallery,** at 1492 South Coast Highway, features works for locally renowned artists; and **Christie of Santa Fe,** at 202 Forest Avenue, specializes in southwestern art.

SPORTS AND BEACHES

Orange County has some of the best unplanned, casual spectator sports; besides seeing the surfers, you are bound to catch a vigorous volleyball or basketball game at any beach on any given weekend. For professional sports, *see* Spectator Sports *in* Chapter 11, Los Angeles.

Participant Sports and the Outdoors

Bicycling

Bicycles and roller and in-line skates are some of the most popular means of transportation along the beaches. A bike path spans the distance from Marina del Rey all the way to San Diego, with only some minor breaks. Most beaches have rental stands. In Laguna, try **Rainbow Bicycles** (☎ 714/494–5806) or, in Huntington Beach, **Team Bicycle Rentals** (☎ 714/969–5480).

Golf

Golf is one of the most popular sports in Orange County, and because of the climate, almost 365 days out of the year are perfect golf days. Here is a selection of golf courses:

Aliso Creek Golf Course (South Laguna, ☎ 714/499–1919); **Anaheim Hills Public Country Club** (☎ 714/748–8900); **Costa Mesa Public Golf and Country Club** (☎ 714/540–7500); **H.G. Dad Miller** (Anaheim, ☎ 714/774–8055); **Imperial Golf Course** (Brea, ☎ 714/529–3923); **Mile Square Golf Course** (Fountain Valley, ☎ 714/968–4556); **Newport Beach Golf Course** (☎ 714/852–8681); **San Juan Hills Country Club** (San Juan Capistrano, ☎ 714/837–0361).

Running

The **Santa Ana Riverbed Trail** hugs the Santa Ana River for 20.6 miles between the Pacific Coast Highway at Huntington State Beach and the Imperial Highway in Yorba Linda; there are entrances, as well as rest rooms and drinking fountains, at all crossings. The **Beach Trail** runs along the beach from Huntington Beach to Newport. Paths throughout **Newport Back Bay** wrap around a marshy area inhabited by lizards, squirrels, rabbits, and waterfowl.

Snorkeling

The fact that **Corona del Mar** is off-limits to boats—along with its two colorful reefs—makes it a great place for snorkeling. **Laguna Beach** is also a good spot for snorkeling and diving; the whole beach area of the city is a marine preserve.

Surfing

There are 50 surf breaks along the Orange County coastline, with wave action ranging from beginner to expert. If you are not an expert, you can get a sense of the action on a boogie board at one of the beginners' beaches. Surfing is permitted at most beaches year-round, except at **Huntington State Beach, Salt Creek Beach Park, Aliso County Beach, Capistrano Beach, Sunset Beach,** and **Newport Beach,** where it is permitted only in summer. "The Wedge" at **Newport Beach,** one of the most famous surfing spots in the world, is known for its steep, punishing shore break. Don't miss the spectacle of surfers, who appear tiny in the midst of the waves, flying through this treacherous place. San

Clemente surfers usually take a primo spot right across from the San Onofre Nuclear Reactor. Rental stands are found at all beaches.

Tennis

Most of the larger hotels have tennis courts. Here are some other choices; try the local Yellow Pages for additional listings.

ANAHEIM

Anaheim has 50 public tennis courts; phone Parks and Recreation for information (☎ 714/254–5191).

HUNTINGTON BEACH

Edison Community Center (21377 Magnolia St., ☎ 714/960–8870) has four courts available on a first-come, first-served basis in the daytime. The **Murdy Community Center** (7000 Norma Dr., ☎ 714/960–8895) has four courts, also first-come, first-served during the day. Both facilities accept reservations for play after 5 PM; both charge $2 an hour.

LAGUNA BEACH

Six metered courts can be found at **Laguna Beach High School,** on Park Avenue. Two courts are available at the **Irvine Bowl,** on Laguna Canyon Road, and six new courts are available at **Alta Laguna Park,** at the end of Alta Laguna Boulevard, off Park Avenue, on a first-come, first-served basis. For more information, call the City of Laguna Beach Recreation Department (☎ 714/497–0716).

NEWPORT BEACH

Call the recreation department (☎ 714/644–3151) for information about court use at **Corona del Mar High School** (2101 E. Bluff Dr.). There are eight public courts.

Newport Beach Marriott Hotel and Tennis Club (900 Newport Center Dr., ☎ 714/640–4000) has eight courts.

Water Sports

Rental stands for surfboards, Windsurfers, small powerboats, and sailboats can be found near most of the piers. **Hobie Sports** has three locations for surfboard and boogie-board rentals—two in Dana Point (☎ 714/496–2366) and one in Laguna (☎ 714/497–3304).

In the biggest boating town of all, Newport Beach, you can rent sailboats and small motorboats at **Balboa Boat Rentals** (☎ 714/673–7200; ⏲ Daily 11–5), in the harbor. Sailboats cost $25 an hour, and motorboats cost $29 an hour, half price for each subsequent hour. You must have a driver's license, and some knowledge of boating is helpful; rented boats are not allowed out of the bay.

Sportfishing is popular at **Davey's Locker** (☎ 714/673–1434; ⏲ Summer, daily 9–5:30) in the Balboa Pavilion. The cost is $35 per person, for a day's worth, half-day's cost is $22. Or, for $35 a half day you can rent a small motorboat to fish in the harbor for sea bass and other marine life.

In Dana Point, powerboats and sailboats can be rented at **Embarcadero Marina** (☎ 714/496–6177, ⏲ Weekdays 8–5, weekends 7–5:30, earlier June–Aug.), near the launching ramp at Dana Point Harbor. Boat sizes vary—sailboats range from $15 to $30 an hour, and motorboats are $20 an hour. Only cash is accepted.

Beaches

All the state, county, and city beaches in Orange County allow swimming. Make sure there is a staffed lifeguard stand nearby, and you should be pretty safe. Also keep on the lookout for posted signs about undertow: It can be mighty nasty around here. Most public beaches have fire rings, tidal pools, volleyball courts, showers, and rest rooms. Recently, beaches have begun closing at night. Moving from north to south along the coast, here are some of the best beaches:

Huntington Beach State Beach (☎ 714/536–1454) runs for 9 miles along the Pacific Coast Highway (Beach Blvd. from inland). There are changing rooms, concessions, fire pits, and vigilant lifeguards on the premises, and there is parking. **Bolsa Chica State Beach** (☎ 714/846–3460), just north of Huntington and across from the Bolsa Chica Ecological Reserve, has barbecue pits and is usually less crowded than its neighbor.

Lower Newport Bay provides an enclave sheltered from the ocean. This area, off Pacific Coast Highway on Jamboree Boulevard, is a 740-acre preserve for ducks and geese. Nearby **Newport Dunes Resort** (☎ 714/729–3863) offers RV spaces, picnic facilities, changing rooms, water-sports equipment rentals, and a place to launch boats.

Just south of Newport Beach, **Corona del Mar Beach** (☎ 714/644–3044) has a tidal pool and caves to explore. It also sports one of the best walks in the county—a beautiful rock pier that juts into the ocean. Facilities include fire pits, volleyball courts, food, rest rooms, and parking.

Crystal Cove State Park (☎ 714/494–3539, ☛ $6 per car), midway between Corona del Mar and Laguna, is a hidden treasure: 3½ miles of unspoiled beach with some of the best tidal pooling in southern California. Here you can see starfish, crabs, and lobster on the rocks, and rangers conduct nature walks on Saturday morning.

Located at the end of Broadway at Pacific Coast Highway, Laguna Beach's **Main Beach Park** has sand volleyball, two half-basketball courts, children's play equipment, picnic areas, rest rooms, showers, and road parking.

The county's best spot for scuba diving is in the **Marine Life Refuge** (☎ 714/494–6571), which runs from Seal Rock to Diver's Cove in Laguna. Farther south, in South Laguna, **Aliso County Park** (☎ 714/661–7013) is a recreation area with a pier for fishing, barbecue pits, parking, food, and rest rooms. Swim Beach, inside **Dana Point Harbor,** also has a fishing pier, barbecues, food, parking, and rest rooms, as well as a shower.

Doheny State Park (☎ 714/496–6171), at the south end of Dana Point, one of the best surfing spots in southern California, has an interpretive center devoted to the wildlife of the Doheny Marine Refuge, and there are food stands and shops nearby. Camping is permitted here, and there are picnic facilities and a pier for fishing. **San Clemente State Beach** (☎ 714/492–3156) is a favorite of surfers and other locals. It has ample camping facilities, RV hookups, and food stands.

DINING AND LODGING

Dining

In Orange County, restaurant choices used to be limited to fast food, fried chicken, and steak. You can still find fast food, but now there's also fancy French, inspired Italian, zesty Mexican, and savory seafood. Familiar chain restaurants pop up in minimalls on main streets throughout Orange County—north of Disneyland, for example, the corner of Orangethorpe and Harbor Boulevard supports more than two dozen such spots.

Central Orange County in particular boasts a number of ethnic restaurants, the result of an influx of people from all over the world. Some of these include **Sitar Indian Restaurant** (2632 W. La Palma Ave., Anaheim, ☎ 714/821–8333); **Phoenix Club** (1340 Sanderson Ave., Anaheim, ☎ 714/563–4164), a German restaurant; and **Sushi Seiha** (214 S. State College Blvd., Anaheim, ☎ 714/991–8980), a Japanese restaurant.

CATEGORY	COST*
$$$$	over $35
$$$	$25–$35
$$	$15–$25
$	under $15

**per person for a three-course meal, excluding drinks, service, and 7¾% tax*

Lodging

A general upgrading of the area surrounding Disneyland has increased the number of reliable inexpensive and moderately priced chain motels. There are four **Travelodge** (for reservations, ☎ 800/826–1616) properties here, two along West Street across the street from the park, one on Katella Avenue on the south side of the park, and one on Harbor Boulevard next to the parking lot entrance. Two **Days Inn** properties can be found on Harbor Boulevard, the eastern boundary of the park: Days Inn Suites (1111 S. Harbor Blvd., ☎ 714/533–8830, FAX 714/758–0573) and Days Inn Maingate (1604 S. Harbor Blvd., ☎ 714/635–3630, FAX 714/520–3290). A **Motel 6** (100 W. Freedman Way, ☎ 714/520–9696, FAX 714/533–7539) is about three blocks from the park.

Prices listed here are based on summer rates. Winter rates, especially near Disneyland, tend to be somewhat less. It pays to shop around for promotional and weekend rates.

CATEGORY	COST*
$$$$	over $100
$$$	$75–$100
$$	$50–$75
$	under $50

**All prices are for a standard double room; local hotel taxes vary.*

Anaheim

DINING

$$$$ ★ **JW's.** This is an elegant French surprise in the heart of convention-busy Anaheim. A quiet place where you can talk serious business or romance, the restaurant is a series of interconnected rooms. The decor is country French with fireplaces, books, subdued lighting, and original art on the walls. While French is the theme, the menu changes frequently to spotlight fresh seafood, game, and produce. The extensive wine list is fairly priced. ✕ *Marriott Hotel, 700 W. Convention Way, ☎ 714/750–8000. Reservations suggested. AE, D, DC, MC, V. Closed Sun. No lunch. Valet parking.*

$$$–$$$$ **Thee White House.** This mansion, built in 1909, which bears a striking resemblance to its namesake, is popular with conventioneers. There are several small dining rooms with crisp linens, candles, flowers, and some fireplaces. The northern Italian menu with French influence features a good selection from pasta to scaloppine, with a heavy emphasis on seafood. Vegetarian entrées are available. A four-course prix-fixe menu is available until 6:30 for $27.50 per person. ✕ *887 S. Anaheim Blvd., ☎ 714/772–1381. Reservations suggested. AE, DC, MC, V. No lunch weekends.*

Dining
Angelo's & Vinci's Cafe Ristorante, **1**
Antoine, **29**
Bangkok IV, **24**
The Beach House, **50**
The Cannery, **41**
The Catch, **19**
The Cellar, **2**
Chanteclair, **35**
The City Club, **20**
Crab Cooker, **40**
Delaney's Restaurant, **57**
The Dining Room, **56**
El Adobe, **62**
El Torito Grill, **38**
Emporio Armani Express, **25**
Etienne's, **64**
Five Feet, **53**
Hard Rock Cafe Newport Beach, **47**
JW's, **11**
Kachina, **52**
La Brasserie, **21**
La Vie en Rose, **4**
Le Biarritz, **42**
L'Hirondelle, **63**
Luciana's, **59**
Mandarin Gourmet, **37**
Marrakesh, **39**
Mulberry Street Ristorante, **3**
Pascal, **43**
Pavilion, **31**
Prego, **34**
Randall's, **23**
The Ritz, **44**
Tortilla Flats, **55**
Watercolors, **61**
Thee White House, **17**
Wolfgang Puck Cafe, **26**

Lodging
Anaheim Hilton and Towers, **10**
Anaheim Marriott, **11**
Atrium Marquis Hotel, **28**
Best Western Marina Inn, **60**
Blue Lantern Inn, **58**
Buena Park Hotel, **5**
Castle Inn and Suites, **14**
Country Side Inn and Suites, **36**
Dana Point Resort, **61**
Desert Palm Inn and Suites, **9**

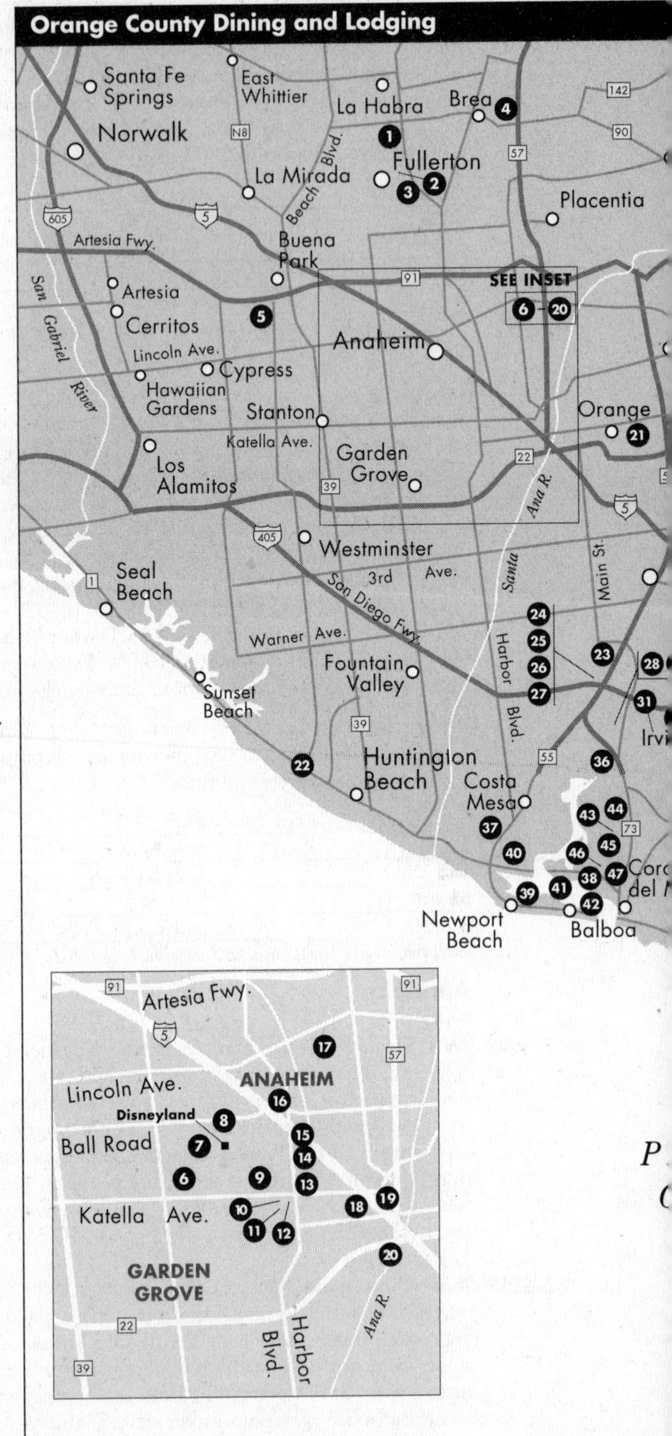

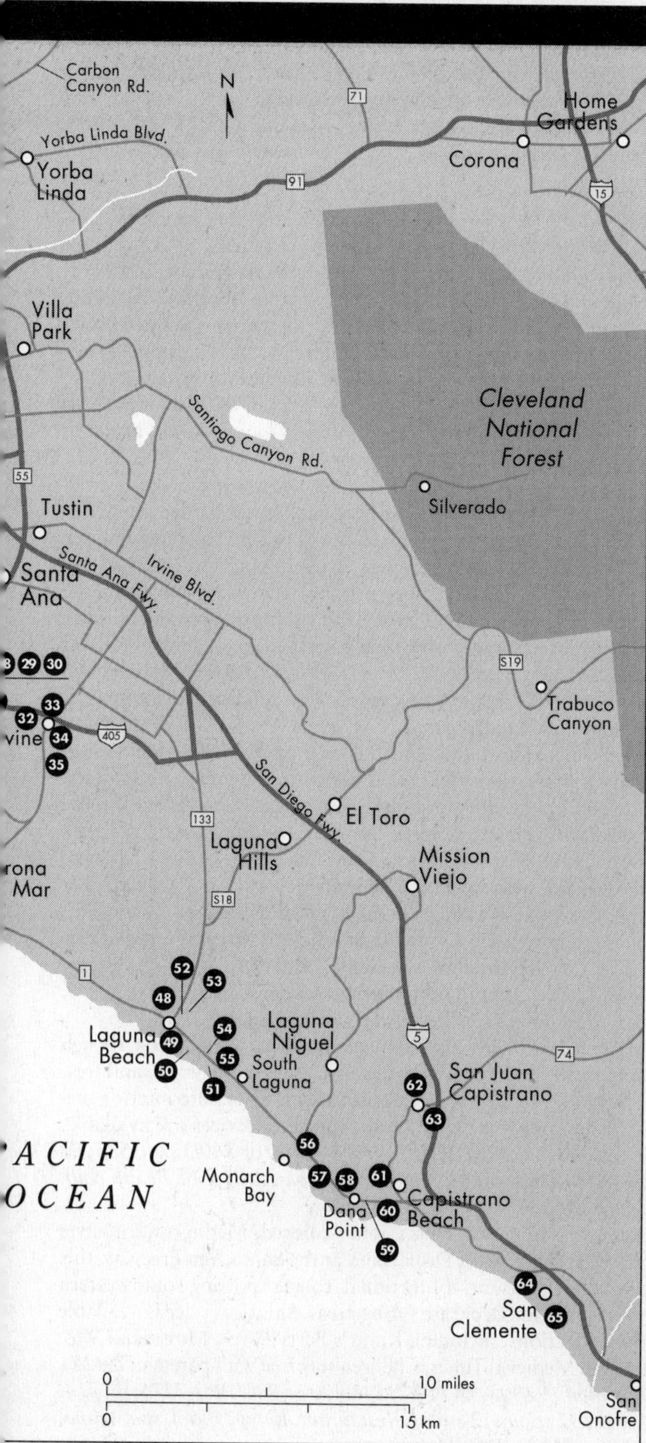

Disneyland Hotel, **7**
Doubletree Hotel
Orange County, **20**
Eiler's Inn, **54**
Four Seasons
Hotel, **45**
Hampton Inn, **18**
Holiday Inn
at the Park, **16**
Holiday Inn Maingate
Anaheim, **13**
Hotel Laguna, **49**
Hyatt Regency Irvine, **33**
Inn at Laguna Beach, **48**
Inn at the Park
Hotel, **12**
Irvine Marriott, **32**
Newport Beach
Marriott Hotel and
Tennis Club, **46**
Ramada Maingate/
Anaheim, **15**
Ritz-Carlton
Laguna Niguel, **56**
San Clemente Inn, **65**
Sheraton-Anaheim
Motor Hotel, **8**
Sheraton Newport
Beach, **30**
Stovall's Inn, **6**
Surf and Sand
Hotel, **51**
The Sutton Place
Hotel, **29**
Waterfront Hilton, **22**
Westin South Coast
Plaza, **27**

$$–$$$ **The Catch.** This very reliable restaurant across the street from Anaheim Stadium is popular with sports fans, who enjoy its sports-bar atmosphere and friendly service. Dining rooms have a comfortable denlike ambience. The menu features hearty portions of steak, seafood, and salads. ✕ *1929 S. State College Blvd., Anaheim, ☎ 714/634–1829. Reservations advised. AE, DC, MC, V. No lunch weekends.*

LODGING

$$$$ **Anaheim Hilton and Towers.** This hotel, the largest in southern California, is one of several choices convenient to the Anaheim Convention Center, which in fact is just a few steps from the front door. It is virtually a self-contained city—complete with its own post office. The lobby is dominated by a bright, airy atrium, and guest rooms are decorated in pinks and greens with light wood furniture. Because it caters to conventioneers, it can be busy and noisy, with long lines at restaurants. *777 Convention Way, 92802, ☎ 714/750–4321 or 800/222–9923, FAX 714/740–4252. 1,576 rooms. 4 restaurants, 3 lounges, outdoor pool, shops, fitness center ($10 charge), concierge. AE, D, DC, MC, V.*

$$$$ **Anaheim Marriott.** This contemporary hotel, which consists of two towers with 16 and 18 floors, is another headquarters for Convention Center attendees. The rooms are compact, but they have balconies and are well equipped for business travelers, with desks, two phones, and modem hookups. A concierge floor was added in 1994. Rooms on the north side have good views of Disneyland's summer fireworks shows. Discounted weekend and Disneyland packages are available. *700 W. Convention Way, 92802, ☎ 714/750–8000 or 800/228–9290, FAX 714/750–9100. 979 rooms, 54 suites. 3 restaurants, 2 lounges, 2 pools, fitness center, video games, concierge. AE, D, DC, MC, V.*

$$$$ ★ **Disneyland Hotel.** This hotel, which is connected to the Magic Kingdom by monorail, carries the Disney theme in the lobby, restaurants, entertainment, shops, and spacious guest rooms. Consisting of three towers surrounding lakes, streams, tumbling waterfalls, and lush landscaping, the hotel gleams with brass and marble. In Goofy's Kitchen, kids can breakfast with their favorite Disney characters. There are marina and park views, and rooms in the Bonita tower overlook the Fantasy Waters, a nighttime Disney-theme lighted fountain and music display. *1150 W. Cerritos Ave., 92802, ☎ 714/778–6600, FAX 714/778–5946. 1,136 rooms. 6 restaurants, 5 lounges, 3 pools, spa, beach, concierge floor, fitness center, business center. AE, DC, MC, V.*

$$$$ **Sheraton Anaheim Hotel.** This Tudor-style hotel has a bright look, though it keeps its castle theme in large tapestries, faux stone walls, and frescoes in the public areas. The large guest rooms open onto interior gardens. A Disneyland shuttle and multilanguage services are available. *1015 W. Ball Rd., 92802, ☎ 714/778–1700 or 800/325–3535, FAX 714/535–3889. 500 rooms. Dining room, bar, deli, pool, health club. AE, D, DC, MC, V.*

$$$ **Holiday Inn At The Park.** A big salmon-colored, Mediterranean-style building, set at the edge of Disneyland at the Santa Ana Freeway, this Holiday Inn has pleasant, if functional, rooms sporting southwestern decor, some including separate sitting areas. Shuttle service is available to nearby attractions, including Knott's Berry Farm, Movieland Wax Museum, and Medieval Times. Children stay free with parents. *1221 S. Harbor Blvd., 92805, ☎ 714/758–0900 or 800/545–7275, FAX 714/533–1804. 252 rooms, 2 suites. Restaurant, lounge, pool, spa, sauna, video games. AE, D, DC, MC, V.*

$$$ **Holiday Inn Maingate.** A trio of large glass chandeliers in the lobby sets the tone at this establishment one block south of Disneyland. The staff is known as one of the friendliest around. *1850 S. Harbor Blvd.,*

92802, ☎ 714/750–2801 or 800/624-6855, FAX 714/971–4754. 312 rooms, including 3 suites. Dining room, lounge, pool, video games. AE, D, DC, MC, V.

$$$ Inn at the Park Hotel. This hotel has the spacious rooms of an earlier era. All rooms have balconies, and those in the tower offer good views of Disneyland's summer fireworks shows. The hotel also has one of the most spacious and attractive pool areas around. The refreshingly bright lobby is inviting, with a tropical feel. *1855 S. Harbor Blvd., 92802, ☎ 714/750–1811 or 800/421–6662, FAX 714/971–3626. 500 rooms. Restaurant, coffee shop, lounge, pool, spa, exercise room, video games. AE, D, DC, MC, V.*

$$ Castle Inn and Suites. This colorful, cutesy motel across the street from Disneyland has been done up to resemble a castle. Children under 18 stay free. *1734 S. Harbor Blvd. 92802, ☎ 714/774–8111 or 800/521–5653, FAX 714/956–4736. 197 rooms. Refrigerators, pool, wading pool. AE, D, DC, MC, V.*

$$ Ramada Maingate/Anaheim. Clean and reliable, this chain hotel has pleasant guest rooms done in tones of mauve and room service from McDonald's. The property is across the street from Disneyland and offers free shuttle service to the park. *1460 S. Harbor Blvd., 92802, ☎ 714/772–6777 or 800/447–4048, FAX 714/999–1727. 465 rooms. Restaurant, pool. AE, D, DC, MC, V.*

$–$$ Desert Palm Inn and Suites. This budget hotel has many things going for it: It's midway between Disneyland and the Convention Center, it has large suites (some with balconies) that can accommodate as many as eight people, and every room has a microwave and a refrigerator. The brightly colored decor is attractive, though functional, and the staff is friendly. Book well in advance, especially when large conventions are in town. *631 W. Katella Ave., 92802, ☎ 714/535–1133, 800/635–5423, FAX 714/491–7409. 103 rooms and suites. Pool, sauna, exercise room, laundry service. D, MC, V.*

$–$$ Stovall's Inn. Very well kept, this motel stacks up well against area hotels in a similar price range. Nice touches include the topiary gardens, room decor in soft desert colors, and a friendly staff. Ask about discounts if you're staying several nights. *1110 W. Katella Ave., 92802, ☎ 714/778–1880, 800/854–8175, FAX 714/778–3805. 290 rooms. Restaurant, lounge, 2 pools. D, MC, V.*

$ Hampton Inn. Here you'll find basic lodging at a basic price. *300 E. Katella Way, 92802, ☎ 714/772–8713, FAX 714/778–1235. 136 rooms. Pool. AE, D, DC, MC, V.*

Brea

DINING

$$$$ ★ La Vie en Rose. A reproduction of a Norman farmhouse with a large turret, this restaurant across from the Brea Mall attracts visitors and locals for its artfully prepared French food. The fare includes seafood, lamb, veal, and melt-in-your-mouth pastries. With several cozy dining rooms, it has a warm atmosphere. ✕ *240 S. State College Blvd., 91621, ☎ 714/529–8333. Reservations suggested. AE, DC, MC, V. Closed Sun.*

Buena Park

LODGING

$$–$$$ Buena Park Hotel. At the center of a lobby of marble, brass, and glass, a spiral staircase winds up to the mezzanine. Rooms are done in green and peach tones. The hotel, which is adjacent to Knott's Berry Farm, offers complimentary shuttle service to Disneyland. *7675 Crescent Ave., 90620, ☎ 714/995–1111 or 800/854–8792, FAX 714/828–8590.*

350 rooms. Restaurant, coffee shop, lounge, pool, nightclub. AE, DC, MC, V.

Costa Mesa

DINING

$$–$$$ ★ **Bangkok IV.** This restaurant on the third floor of the Crystal Court shopping mall serves artistically prepared Thai cuisine. The decor is dramatic, with stylish flower arrangements and black-and-white appointments. Menu items designated as hot can be prepared with milder spices upon request. ✕ *3333 Bear St.,* ☎ *714/540–7661. Reservations required. AE, DC, MC, V.*

$$ **Mandarin Gourmet.** Dollar for bite, owner Michael Chang provides what the critics and locals consider the best Chinese cuisine in the area. His specialties include a crisp yet juicy Peking duck, cashew chicken, and, seemingly everyone's favorite, mu-shu pork. There is also a very good wine list. ✕ *1500 Adams Ave.,* ☎ *714/540–1937. Reservations accepted. AE, DC, MC, V.*

$ **Emporio Armani Express.** This classy storefront restaurant is adjacent to Armani fashions on the ground floor of South Coast Plaza. In typical Armani style, it's decorated with lots of light wood and accented with white linen, and fashion photos line the walls. The fare is Italian—salads, single-portion pizzas, pasta—and some portions seem a bit small. ✕ *3333 Bristol St.,* ☎ *714/754–0300. AE, DC, MC, V.*

$ **Wolfgang Puck Cafe.** The famous chef has tried here to create an institutional-style café (read school cafeteria), complete with high noise level. Just the same, it's always jammed. The menu lists Puck's famous pizzas, chicken salad, and pastas; the most popular item may be the half chicken with huge portions of garlic mashed potatoes. ✕ *South Coast Plaza, 3333 Bristol Ave.,* ☎ *714/546–9653. Reservations for parties of 5 or more only. MC, V.*

LODGING

$$$$ **Westin South Coast Plaza.** Rooms in this hotel sport soft colors, mostly cream and beige, and public areas are bright and pleasant. The hotel is a short walk from restaurants, theaters, and the South Coast Plaza shopping mall. Discounts are sometimes available on weekends. 🏨 *686 Anton Blvd., 92626,* ☎ *714/540–2500 or 800/228–3000,* FAX *714/662–6695. 390 rooms, including 17 suites. Restaurant, lounge, pool, 2 tennis courts, shuffleboard, volleyball, concierge floor. AE, D, DC, MC, V.*

$$–$$$ **Country Side Inn and Suites.** Rooms and lobbies are nicely decorated in Queen Anne–style furnishings with floral wall coverings. Breakfast is included in rates. Ask about discounts, which can reduce the price to well below this category. 🏨 *325 Bristol St., 91626,* ☎ *714/549–0300 or 800/322–9992,* FAX *714/662–0828. 300 rooms and suites. Restaurant, lounge, 2 pools, exercise room. DC, MC, V.*

Dana Point

DINING

$$$ **The Dining Room.** Long considered one of the best restaurants in Orange County, the Dining Room now boasts an innovative and very flexible prix-fixe menu featuring contemporary Mediterranean specialties: lobster risotto, grilled tuna chop, veal shank osso buco, almond soufflé. You can choose two to seven courses; the price depends on the number of courses. Like the hotel, this is an elegant room with subdued lighting, crystal chandeliers, original paintings on the walls, and antiques tucked into corners. ✕ *1 Ritz-Carlton Dr., Dana Point,* ☎ *714/240–2000. Reservations required. Jacket required. AE, D, DC, MC, V. No lunch Sun., Mon.*

$$–$$$ **Watercolors.** This light, cheerful dining room provides a cliff-top view of the harbor and an equally enjoyable Continental-California menu, along with low-calorie choices. Try the baked breast of pheasant, roast rabbit, grilled swordfish, and either the Caesar or poached spinach salad. ✕ *Dana Point Resort, ☎ 714/661–5000. Reservations advised. AE, D, DC, MC, V. Valet parking.*

$$ **Delaney's Restaurant.** Fresh seafood from nearby San Diego's fishing fleet is what this place is all about. Your choice is prepared as simply as possible. ✕ *25001 Dana Dr., ☎ 714/496–6195. Reservations advised. AE, D, DC, MC, V.*

$$ **Luciana's.** This intimate Italian restaurant is a real find, especially for couples seeking a romantic evening. Dining rooms are small, dressed with crisp white linens and warmed by fireplaces. The well-prepared food is served with care. ✕ *24312 Del Prado Ave., ☎ 714/661–6500. Reservations advised. AE, DC, MC, V. No lunch.*

LODGING

$$$$ **Blue Lantern Inn.** Perched atop the bluffs, this contemporary Cape Cod–style bed-and-breakfast has stunning harbor and ocean views. Rooms are individually decorated with period furnishings, fireplaces, stocked refrigerators, and jetted baths. Breakfast and afternoon refreshments are included in the price. 🏨 *34343 St. of the Blue Lantern, 92629, ☎ 714/661–1304, FAX 714/496–1483. 29 rooms. Concierge, exercise room, library. AE, MC, V.*

$$$$ ★ **Dana Point Resort.** This Cape Cod–style hillside resort is decorated in shades of sea-foam green and peach. The lobby is filled with large palm trees and original artwork, and most rooms have ocean views; all are done in rattan, with indoor plants. The ambience is casual yet elegant. In summer, the Capistrano Valley Symphony performs on the resort's attractively landscaped grounds. 🏨 *25135 Park Lantern, 92629, ☎ 714/661–5000 or 800/533–9748, FAX 714/661–5358. 350 rooms. Restaurant, 2 lounges, 3 pools, 3 spas, basketball, croquet, health club, volleyball, concierge floor. AE, D, DC, MC, V.*

$$$$ ★ **Ritz-Carlton Laguna Niguel.** This acclaimed hotel has earned world-class status for its gorgeous setting right on the edge of the Pacific, its sumptuous Mediterranean architecture and decor, and its reputation for flawless service. With colorful landscaping outside and an imposing marble-columned entry, it feels like an Italian country villa. Every possible amenity, and then some, is available to guests. Rooms feature traditional furnishings, sumptuous fabrics, marble bathrooms, and private balconies with ocean or garden views. Reduced-rate packages are sometimes available. Rental cars are available on the premises. 🏨 *1 Ritz-Carlton Dr., 92677, ☎ 714/240–2000 or 800/241–3333, FAX 714/240–0829. 393 rooms. 2 restaurants, lounge, 2 pools, beauty salon, golf privileges, 4 tennis courts, health club, concierge, nightclub. AE, D, DC, MC, V.*

$$ **Best Western Marina Inn.** Set right in the marina, this motel is convenient to docks, restaurants, and shops. Rooms vary in size from basic to family units with kitchens and fireplaces. Many rooms in this three-level motel have balconies and harbor views. 🏨 *24800 Dana Point Harbor Dr., 92629, ☎ 714/496–1203 or 800/255–6843, FAX 714/248–0360. 136 rooms. Pool, fitness facilities. AE, D, DC, MC, V.*

Fullerton

DINING

$$$$ **The Cellar.** Classic French cuisine that has been lightened for the California palate is served in an intimate subterranean dining room with beamed ceiling and stone walls, wine racks, and casks. The wine list is comprehensive. ✕ *305 N. Harbor Blvd.,* ☏ *714/525–5682. Reservations required. AE, DC, MC, V. Closed Sun., Mon. No lunch.*

$$ ★ **Mulberry Street Ristorante.** This friendly, noisy watering hole was designed to resemble a turn-of-the-century New York eatery. The kitchen serves up northern Italian fare, prodigious, highly seasoned portions of pasta, seafood, chicken, and veal. ✕ *114 W. Wilshire Ave.,* ☏ *714/525–1056. Reservations advised. AE, DC, MC, V. No lunch Sun.*

$ **Angelo's & Vinci's Cafe Ristorante.** Locally popular for huge portions of Sicilian-style pasta and pizza, this is a busy, noisy, riotously decorated place. ✕ *550 N. Harbor Blvd.,* ☏ *714/879–4022. Reservations accepted. AE, MC, V.* **$**

Huntington Beach

LODGING

$$$$ **Waterfront Hilton.** This oceanfront hotel rises 12 stories above the surf. The Mediterranean-style resort is decorated in soft mauves, beiges, and greens and offers a panoramic ocean view from many guest rooms. Ocean-view suites have balconies and wet bars. 🏨 *21100 Pacific Coast Hwy., 92648,* ☏ *714/960–7873 or 800/822–7873,* FAX *714/960–3791. 290 rooms. 2 restaurants, lounge, pool, 2 tennis courts, fitness center, bike and beach-equipment rentals, concierge floor. AE, DC, MC, V.*

Irvine

DINING

$$$ **Chanteclair.** This Franco-Italian country house is a lovely, tasteful retreat amid an island of modern high-rise office buildings. French Riviera–type cuisine is served, and the chateaubriand for two and rack of lamb are recommended. ✕ *18912 MacArthur Blvd.,* ☏ *714/752–8001. Reservations advised. Jacket required. AE, D, DC, MC, V. No lunch Sat.*

$$ **Pavilion.** Excellent Chinese food is offered in what resembles a formal eating hall in Taiwan. Specialties include steamed whole fish, ginger duck, and Hunan lamb. ✕ *14110 Culver Dr., 714/551–1688. Reservations advised. AE, DC, MC, V.*

$$ ★ **Prego.** A much larger version of the Beverly Hills Prego, this one is a local favorite of Orange County. Try the spit-roasted meats and chicken, pizzas cooked in an oak-burning oven, or charcoal-grilled fresh fish. California and Italian wines are reasonably priced. ✕ *18420 Von Karman Ave.,* ☏ *714/553–1333. Reservations advised. AE, DC, MC, V. No lunch weekends. Valet parking.*

LODGING

$$$$ **Hyatt Regency Irvine.** Offering all the amenities of a first-class resort, this hotel is elegantly decorated in contemporary colors, such as oatmeal, turquoise, jade, and salmon, and the marble lobby is flanked by glass-enclosed elevators. Soft cottons make guest furnishings comfortable and appealing. Special golf packages at nearby Tustin Ranch are available. The lower weekend rates are a great deal. 🏨 *17900 Jamboree Rd., 92714,* ☏ *714/975–1234,* FAX *714/852–1574. 526 rooms, 10 suites. 2 restaurants, 2 lounges, pool, 4 tennis courts, fitness facilities, bicycles, concierge. AE, D, DC, MC, V.*

$$$ **Atrium Marquis Hotel.** This hotel is across the street from John Wayne Airport and convenient to most area offices. The staff caters to business travelers, with rooms that have large work areas, coffeemakers, and two phones. All rooms have private balcony, some overlooking the pool and others looking out at the gardens. Special rates are available for weekend guests. 🏨 *18700 MacArthur Blvd., 92715,* ☏ *714/*

833–2770, FAX 714/757–1228. 209 rooms. 2 restaurants, 2 lounges, pool, fitness center. AE, D, DC, MC, V.

$$$ **Irvine Marriott.** This contemporary hotel towers over Koll Business Center, making it convenient for business travelers. Despite its size, the hotel has an intimate feel about it, due in part to the cozy lobby and the friendly staff. Asian-style rooms, all with small balconies, are slated for renovation in 1996. Weekend discounts and packages are usually available. *1800 Von Karman Ave., 92715, ☎ 714/553–0100, FAX 714/261–7059. 489 rooms, 24 suites. 2 restaurants, sports bar, indoor-outdoor pool, massage, spa, 4 tennis courts, health club, concierge floors, business services. AE, D, DC, MC, V.*

Laguna Beach

DINING

$$$–$$$$ ★ **Five Feet.** The first of a number of Chinese-European restaurants in Orange County, Five Feet continues to delight diners with its innovative culinary approaches. You'll find delicate pot stickers, wontons stuffed with goat cheese, and a salad featuring sashimi, plus steak and fresh fish. The decor showcases the work of local artists. ✕ *328 Gleneyre St., ☎ 714/497–4955. Reservations advised. AE, MC, V. No lunch Sat.–Thurs.*

$$ **Beach House.** A Laguna tradition, the Beach House has a water view from every table. Fresh fish, lobster, and steamed clams are the drawing cards. ✕ *619 Sleepy Hollow La., ☎ 714/494–9707. Reservations advised. AE, MC, V.*

$$ **Kachina.** The creation of Orange County star chef David Wilhelm, this tiny restaurant housed beneath an art gallery draws locals and visitors with contemporary southwestern-style cuisine and a boisterous atmosphere. Even hearty eaters can make a meal by selecting several items from the appetizer portion of the menu. Kachina is a good place for Sunday brunch. ✕ *222 Forest Ave., ☎ 714/497–5546. Reservations advised. AE, MC, V.*

$ **Tortilla Flats.** This hacienda-style restaurant specializes in first-rate chile rellenos, carne Tampiquena, soft-shell tacos, and beef or chicken fajitas. There's also a wide selection of Mexican tequilas and beers. Sunday brunch is served. ✕ *1740 S. Coast Hwy., ☎ 714/494– 6588. Dinner reservations advised. AE, MC, V.*

LODGING

$$$$ **Surf and Sand Hotel.** Laguna's largest hotel is situated right on the beach. The rooms are decorated in soft sand colors and bleached wood and have wooden shutters and private balconies. Weekend packages are available. *1555 S. Coast Hwy., 92651, ☎ 714/497–4477 or 800/524–8621, FAX 714/494–7653. 157 rooms, including 5 suites. 2 restaurants, 2 lounges, pool, beach, concierge. AE, DC, MC, V.*

$$$–$$$$ ★ **Inn at Laguna Beach.** This oceanfront Mediterranean-style inn, done in warm mauves and sea greens, has one of the best locations in town. It's close to Main Beach and Las Brisas restaurant and bar, one of Laguna's most popular watering holes, yet far enough away to be secluded. Set on a bluff overlooking the ocean, the inn has luxurious amenities and many rooms with views. *211 N. Coast Hwy., 92651, ☎ 714/497–9722 or 800/544–4479, FAX 714/497–9972. 70 rooms. Pool, free parking. AE, D, DC, MC, V.*

$$$ **Eiler's Inn.** A light-filled courtyard is the focal point of this European-style B&B. Rooms are on the small side, but each is unique and decorated with antiques. Breakfast is served outdoors, and in the afternoon there's wine and cheese, often to the accompaniment of live music. A

sun deck in back has an ocean view. 741 S. Coast Hwy., 92651, ☎ 714/494–3004, FAX 714/497–2215. 12 rooms. AE, MC, V.

$$$ **Hotel Laguna.** This downtown landmark, the oldest hotel in Laguna, has been redone, with four rooms now featuring canopy beds and reproduction Victorian furnishings. Lobby windows lookout onto manicured gardens, and a patio restaurant overlooks the ocean and the hotel's own private beach. *425 S. Coast Hwy., 92651,* ☎ *714/494–1151 or 800/524–2927,* FAX *714/497–2163. 65 rooms. 2 restaurants, lounge. AE, D, DC, MC, V.*

Newport Beach

DINING

$$$$ ★ **Antoine.** This lovely, candlelighted hotel dining room is made for romance and quiet conversation. It serves the best French cuisine of any hotel in southern California; the fare is nouvelle but is neither skimpy nor gimmicky. ✕ *Sutton Place Hotel, 4500 MacArthur Blvd.,* ☎ *714/476–2001. Reservations advised. Jacket and tie. AE, DC, MC, V. Closed Sun., Mon. No lunch.*

$$$$ ★ **Pascal.** Although it's in a shopping center, you'll think that you're in St. Tropez once you step inside this bright and cheerful bistro. And, after one taste of Pascal Olhat's light Provençale cuisine, the best in Orange County, you'll swear you're in the south of France. Try the sea bass with thyme, the rack of lamb, and the lemon tart. ✕ *1000 Bristol St.,* ☎ *714/752–0107. Reservations advised. AE, DC, MC, V. Closed Sun.*

$$$$ **The Ritz.** This is one of the most comfortable southern California restaurants—the bar area has red leather booths, etched-glass mirrors, and polished brass trim. Don't pass up the smorgasbord appetizer, the roast Bavarian duck, or the rack of lamb from the spit. This is one of those rare places that seem to please everyone. ✕ *880 Newport Center Dr.,* ☎ *714/720–1800. Reservations advised. AE, DC, MC, V. No lunch weekends.*

$$ **The Cannery.** The seafood entrées here are good, and the sandwiches at lunch are satisfying, but the wharfside views and lazy atmosphere are the real draw. If, however you're not into karaoke, you may want to consider booking elsewhere. ✕ *3010 Lafayette Ave.,* ☎ *714/675–5777. Reservations advised. AE, D, DC, MC, V.*

$$ **Le Biarritz.** Newport Beach natives have a deep affection for this restaurant, with its country-French decor, hanging greenery, and skylighted garden room. There's food to match the mood: a veal-and-pheasant pâté, seafood crepes, boned duckling and wild rice, sautéed pheasant with raspberries, and warm apple tart for dessert. ✕ *414 N. Old Newport Blvd.,* ☎ *714/645–6700. Reservations advised. AE, D, DC, MC, V. Closed Sun. No lunch Sat.*

$$ **Marrakesh.** In a casbah setting straight out of a Hope-and-Crosby road movie, diners become part of the scene—you eat with your fingers while sitting on the floor or lolling on a hassock. Chicken *b'stilla* (traditional chicken dish served over rice), rabbit couscous, and skewered pieces of marinated lamb are the best of the Moroccan dishes. It's fun. ✕ *1100 Pacific Coast Hwy.,* ☎ *714/645–8384. Reservations advised. AE, DC, MC, V. No lunch.*

$ **Crab Cooker.** If you don't mind waiting in line, this shanty of a place serves fresh fish grilled over mesquite at low-low prices. The clam chowder and coleslaw are quite good, too. ✕ *2200 Newport Blvd.,* ☎ *714/673–0100. No reservations. No credit cards.*

$ ★ **El Torito Grill.** Southwestern cooking incorporating south-of-the-border specialties is the attraction here. The just-baked tortillas with a green-pepper salsa, the turkey molé enchilada, and the miniature blue-corn duck tamales are good choices. The bar serves hand-shaken margaritas and 20 brands of tequila. ✕ *Fashion Island, 951 Newport Center Dr.,* ☎ *714/640–2875. Reservations advised. AE, D, DC, MC, V.*

$ **Hard Rock Cafe Newport Beach.** You can pick up your official Hard Rock Cafe T-shirt here while munching a hamburger or a sandwich. Like the other Hard Rocks, this one features an array of rock-star memorabilia and platinum records. ✕ *451 Newport Center Dr.,* ☎ *714/640–8844. No reservations. AE, DC, MC, V.*

LODGING

$$$$ ★ **Four Seasons Hotel.** This 20-story hotel lives up to its chain's reputation. Marble and antiques fill the airy lobby; all rooms—decorated with beiges, peaches, and southwestern touches—have spectacular views, private bars, and original art on the walls. Weekend golf packages are available in conjunction with the nearby Pelican Hill golf course, as well as fitness weekend packages. 🏨 *690 Newport Center Dr., 92660,* ☎ *714/759–0808 or 800/332–3442,* FAX *714/760–8073. 285 rooms. 2 restaurants, lounge, pool, massage, sauna, steam room, 2 tennis courts, health club, mountain bikes, concierge, business center. AE, D, DC, MC, V.*

$$$$ **Sutton Place Hotel.** The eye-catching ziggurat design is the trademark of this ultramodern hotel in Koll Center. The decor is southern Californian, with striking pastel accents. Luxuriously appointed rooms have minibars and built-in hair dryers. This is also the home of Antoine (*see above*), one of the best restaurants in Orange County. Special weekend theater and Pageant of the Masters packages are available. 🏨 *4500 MacArthur Blvd., 92660,* ☎ *714/476–2001 or 800/810-6888,* FAX *714/476–0153. 435 rooms. 2 restaurants, lounge, pool, 2 tennis courts, health club, concierge. AE, D, DC, MC, V.*

$$$ **Newport Beach Marriott Hotel and Tennis Club.** Overlooking Newport Harbor, this Mediterranean-style hotel attracts a large foreign clientele. Rooms, done in lavender, cream, and teal, are housed in two towers. They each have balconies or patios and overlook lush gardens or a stunning Pacific view. The hotel is across the street from Fashion Island shopping center. 🏨 *900 Newport Center Dr., 92660,* ☎ *714/640–4000 or 800/228–9290,* FAX *714/640–5055. 570 rooms. 2 restaurants, lounge, 2 pools, sauna, 8 tennis courts, golf, health club, business services, concierge. AE, D, DC, MC, V.*

$$$ **Sheraton Newport Beach.** Bamboo trees and palms decorate the lobby in this southern California beach-style hotel. Vibrant teals, mauves, and peaches make up the color scheme. Complimentary morning paper, buffet breakfast, and cocktail parties are offered Monday through Thursday. The hotel is convenient to John Wayne Airport. 🏨 *4545 MacArthur Blvd., 92660,* ☎ *714/833–0570,* FAX *714/833–3927. 335 rooms. 3 restaurants, lounge, pool, fitness center, 2 tennis courts. AE, D, DC, MC, V.*

Orange

DINING

$$ **La Brasserie.** It doesn't *look* like a typical brasserie, but the varied French cuisine befits the name over the door. One dining room in the multilevel house is done as an attractive, cozy library. The specialty here is veal chops. ✕ *202 S. Main St.,* ☎ *714/978–6161. Reservations advised. AE, MC, V. Closed Sun. No lunch Sat.*

$–$$ **City Club.** This restaurant, located in the Doubletree Hotel, specializes in steak and seafood. This dramatic two-story room has floor-to-ceiling windows, which reveal a garden and pond beyond. Service is welcoming. ✕ *100 The City Dr.,* ☎ *714/634–4500. AE, MC, V. Closed weekends.*

LODGING

$$$–$$$$ **Doubletree Hotel Orange County.** This contemporary, 20-story hotel has a dramatic lobby of marble and granite with waterfalls cascading down the walls. Guest rooms are large and come equipped with a small conference table. The hotel is near the shopping center called the City, UCI Medical Center, and Anaheim Stadium. Discount rates are available for summer weekends. ☎ *100 The City Dr., 92668, ☎ 714/634–4500 or 800/222–8733, FAX 714/978–3839. 435 rooms, 19 suites. 2 restaurants, lounge, pool, 2 tennis courts, health club, concierge floor. AE, D, DC, MC, V.*

San Clemente

DINING

$$$ **Etienne's.** This restaurant is housed in a white stucco historic landmark. Only the freshest fish is served; chateaubriand, frogs' legs, and other French favorites are on the menu, along with flaming desserts. ✕ *215 S. El Camino Real, ☎ 714/492–7263. Reservations advised. AE, D, DC, MC, V. Closed Sun. No lunch.*

LODGING

$$$ **San Clemente Inn.** This time-share condo resort is in the secluded southern part of San Clemente, adjacent to Calafia State Beach. Studio and one-bedroom units (accommodating as many as six) are equipped with minikitchens and Murphy beds. Limited space is available in summer. Ask about weekly discounts. *2600 Avenida del Presidente, 92672, ☎ 714/492–6103, FAX 714/498–3014. 96 units. Pool, sauna, tennis, exercise room, recreation room, playground. AE, DC, MC, V.*

San Juan Capistrano

DINING

$$ **El Adobe.** This early California–style eatery serves enormous portions of mildly seasoned Mexican food. Mariachi bands play Friday and Saturday nights and for Sunday brunch. ✕ *31891 Camino Capistrano, ☎ 714/830–8620. Weekend reservations advised. AE, D, MC, V.*

$$ ★ **L'Hirondelle.** There are only 12 tables at this charming Belgian inn. Duckling is the specialty, and it is prepared three different ways. ✕ *31631 Camino Capistrano, ☎ 714/661–0425. Reservations required. AE, MC, V. Closed Mon. No lunch.*

Santa Ana

DINING

$$$ **Randall's.** Located on the ground floor of an office building with lakeside views, this restaurant specializes in light Louisiana cuisine. Jazz and blues are presented nightly. ✕ *3 Hutton Centre Dr., Santa Ana, ☎ 714/556–7700. Reservations advised. AE, MC, V. No lunch Sun.*

THE ARTS AND NIGHTLIFE

The Arts

The **Orange County Performing Arts Center** (600 Town Center Dr., Costa Mesa, ☎ 714/556–2787) is the hub of the arts circle, hosting a variety of touring companies year-round. Groups that regularly schedule performances here include the New York City Opera, the American Ballet Theater, and the Los Angeles Philharmonic Orchestra, as well as touring companies of popular musicals such as *Les Misérables*. Information about current offerings can be found in the Calendar section of the *Los Angeles Times*.

Concerts

Irvine Meadows Amphitheater (8808 Irvine Center Dr., Irvine, ☎ 714/855–4515) is a 15,000-seat open-air venue offering a variety of musical events from May through October.

Pacific Amphitheater (Orange County Fairgrounds, Costa Mesa, ☎ 714/740–2000) offers musical entertainment from April through October.

Theater

South Coast Repertory Theater (655 Town Center Dr., Costa Mesa, ☎ 714/957–4033), near the Orange County Performing Arts Center, is an acclaimed regional theater complex with two stages that present both traditional and new works. A resident group of actors forms the nucleus of this facility's innovative productions.

La Mirada Theater for the Performing Arts (14900 La Mirada Blvd., La Mirada, ☎ 714/994–6310) presents a wide selection of Broadway shows, concerts, and film series.

Nightlife

Bars

Metropolis (4255 Campus Dr., Irvine, ☎ 714/725–0300) is the hottest nightclub ticket in Orange County, with iron-and-gilt decor, pool tables, a sushi bar, restaurant, entertainment, and dancing (you can even take a salsa class); the cover is $5. The **Cannery** (3010 Lafayette Ave., ☎ 714/675–5777) is a crowded Newport Beach bar that offers live entertainment. The **Studio Cafe** (100 Main St., Balboa Peninsula, ☎ 714/675–7760) presents jazz musicians every night. In Santa Ana, a young crowd gathers at **Roxbury** (2 Hutton Centre Dr., ☎ 714/662–0880) for entertainment and dancing Friday and Saturday evenings. The **Fullerton Hofbrau** (323 N. State College Blvd., ☎ 714/870–7400), a microbrewery, has live music nightly.

In Laguna Beach, the **Sandpiper** (1183 S. Pacific Coast Highway, ☎ 714/494–4694) is a tiny dancing joint that attracts an eclectic crowd. And Laguna's **White House** (340 S. Pacific Coast Hwy., ☎ 714/494–8088) has nightly entertainment that runs the gamut from rock to Motown, reggae to pop.

Comedy

Irvine Improv (4255 Campus Dr., Irvine, ☎ 714/854–5455) and **Brea Improv** (945 E. Birch St., Brea, ☎ 714/529–7878) present up-and-coming and well-known comedians nightly.

Country Music

Cowboy Boogie Co. (1721 S. Manchester, Anaheim, ☎ 714/956–1410) offers a popular country band's tune on Sunday night; music is piped in the rest of the week. The complex comprises three dance floors and four bars.

Dinner Theaters

Several nightspots in Orange County serve up entertainment with dinner.

Elizabeth Howard's Curtain Call Theater (690 El Camino Real, Tustin, ☎ 714/838–1540) presents a regular schedule of Broadway musicals.

Medieval Times Dinner and Tournament (7662 Beach Blvd., Buena Park, ☎ 714/521–4740 or 800/899–6600) takes guests back to the days of knights and ladies. Knights on horseback compete in medieval games, sword fighting, and jousting. Dinner, all of which is eaten with your hands, includes appetizers, whole roasted chicken or spareribs, soup, pastry, and beverages such as mead.

Tibbie's Music Hall (4647 MacArthur Blvd., Newport Beach, ☎ 714/252–0834) offers comedy shows along with prime rib, fish, or chicken Thursday through Sunday.

Wild Bill's Wild West Extravaganza (7600 Beach Blvd., Buena Park, ☎ 714/522–6414) is a two-hour action-packed Old West show featuring foot-stomping musical numbers, cowboys, Indians, can-can dancers, trick-rope artists, knife throwers, and audience participation in sing-alongs.

Nightclubs

Coach House (33157 Camino Capistrano, San Juan Capistrano, ☎ 714/496–8930) draws big local crowds for jazz and rock headliners.

ORANGE COUNTY ESSENTIALS

Arriving and Departing

By Bus

The **Los Angeles MTA** has limited service to Orange County. You can get the No. 460 to Anaheim from downtown; it goes to Knott's Berry Farm and Disneyland. **Greyhound** (☎ 714/999–1256 or 800/231–2222) has scheduled bus service to Orange County.

By Car

Two major freeways, I–405 (San Diego Freeway) and I–5 (Santa Ana Freeway), run north and south through Orange County. South of Laguna they merge into I–5. Avoid these during rush hours (6–9 AM and 3:30–6 PM), when they can slow to a crawl and back up for miles.

By Plane

Several airports are accessible to Orange County. **John Wayne Airport** (☎ 714/252–5252), in Santa Ana, is centrally located, and the county's main facility. It is serviced by **Alaska** (☎ 800/426–0333), **America West** (☎ 800/235–9292), **American** (☎ 800/433–7300), **Continental** (☎ 800/525–0280), **Delta** (☎ 800/221–1212), **Northwest** (☎ 800/225–2525), **Southwest** (☎ 800/435–9792), **TWA** (☎ 800/221–2000), **United** (☎ 800/241–6522), and several commuter airlines.

Ontario International Airport (☎ 909/988–2700), located about 35 miles east of Los Angeles, serves the San Bernardino–Riverside area. The airlines above that service John Wayne Airport fly to Ontario as well. **Reno Air** (☎ 800/736–6247), **United Express** (☎ 800/241–6522), and **USAir Express** (☎ 800/428–4322) are additional options.

BETWEEN THE AIRPORTS AND HOTELS

Airport Coach (☎ 800/772–5299), a shuttle service, carries passengers from John Wayne Airport and LAX to Anaheim, Buena Park, and Newport Beach. Fare from John Wayne to Anaheim is $10, from LAX to Anaheim $14.

Prime Time Airport Shuttle (☎ 800/262–7433) offers door-to-door service to LAX and John Wayne airports, hotels near John Wayne, and the San Pedro cruise terminal. The fare is $11 from Anaheim hotels to John Wayne and $12 from Anaheim hotels to LAX. Children under two ride free (but must have a car seat).

SuperShuttle (☎ 714/517–6600) provides 24-hour door-to-door service from all the airports to all points in Orange County. The fare to the Disneyland area is $10 a person from John Wayne, $34 from Ontario, $13 from LAX. Phone for other fares and reservations.

By Train

Amtrak (☏ 800/872–7245) makes several stops in Orange County: Fullerton, Anaheim, Santa Ana, San Juan Capistrano, and San Clemente. There are 11 departures daily, nine on weekends.

Getting Around

By Bus

The **Orange County Transportation Authority** (OCTA, ☏ 714/636–7433) will take you virtually anywhere in the county, but it will take time; OCTA buses go from Knott's Berry Farm and Disneyland to Huntington and Newport beaches. Bus 1 travels along the coast.

By Car

Highways 22, 55, and 91 go west to the ocean and east to the mountains: Take Highway 91 or Highway 22 to inland points (Buena Park, Anaheim) and take Highway 55 to Newport Beach. Caution: Orange County freeways are undergoing major construction; expect delays at odd times. Pacific Coast Highway (Highway 1; also known locally as PCH) allows easy access to beach communities and is the most scenic route. It follows the entire Orange County coast, from Huntington Beach to San Clemente.

SCENIC DRIVES

Winding along the seaside edge of Orange County on the **Pacific Coast Highway** is an eye-opening experience. Here, surely, are the contradictions of southern California revealed—the powerful, healing ocean vistas and the scars of commercial exploitation; the appealingly laid-back, simple beach life; and the tacky bric-a-brac of the tourist trail. Oil rigs line the road from Long Beach south to Huntington Beach and then suddenly give way to pristine stretches of water and dramatic hillsides. Stop in beach towns like Laguna Beach, Dana Point, and Corona del Mar along the route.

For a scenic mountain drive, try **Santiago Canyon Road,** which winds through the Cleveland National Forest in the Santa Ana Mountains. Tucked away in these mountains are Modjeska Canyon, Irvine Lake, and Silverado Canyon, of silver-mining lore.

Guided Tours

Boat

At the Cannery in **Newport Beach,** you can take a weekend brunch cruise around the harbor for $31. Cruises last two hours and depart at 10 AM and 1:30 PM. Call 714/675–5777 for information.

Catalina Passenger Service (☏ 714/673–5245) at the Balboa Pavilion offers a full selection of sightseeing tours and fishing excursions to Catalina and around Newport Harbor. The 45-minute narrated tour of Newport Harbor, at $6, is the least expensive. Whale-watching cruises (December–March) are especially enjoyable.

Hornblower Yachts (☏ 714/646–0155) offers Saturday dinner cruises with dancing for $56.95; Sunday brunch cruises are $34.05. Reservations are required.

General-Interest

Pacific Coast Sightseeing Tours (☏ 714/978–8855) provides guided tours from Orange County hotels to Disneyland, Knott's Berry Farm, Universal Studios Hollywood, and the San Diego Zoo.

Important Addresses and Numbers

Doctors

Orange County is so spread out and comprises so many communities that it is best to ask at your hotel for the closest emergency room. Here are a few: **Anaheim Memorial Hospital** (1111 W. La Palma, ☎ 714/774–1450), **Western Medical Center** (1025 S. Anaheim Blvd., Anaheim, ☎ 714/533–6220), **Hoag Memorial Hospital** (301 Newport Blvd., Newport Beach, ☎ 714/645–8600), **South Coast Medical Center** (31872 Pacific Coast Hwy., South Laguna, ☎ 714/499–1311).

Emergencies

Dial **911** for police and ambulance in an emergency.

Visitor Information

Anaheim/Orange County Convention and Visitors Bureau (Anaheim Convention Center, 800 W. Katella Ave., 92802, ☎ 714/999–8999) is the main source of tourist information. Its **Visitor Information Hot Line** (☎ 714/635–8900) offers recorded information on entertainment, special events, attractions, and amusement parks.

Other area chambers of commerce and visitors bureaus are generally open weekdays 9–5 and will help with information. These include:

Buena Park Visitors Bureau (6280 Manchester Blvd., 90261, ☎ 714/562–3560).

Dana Point Chamber of Commerce (24681 La Plaza, Suite 120, 92629, ☎ 714/496–1555).

Huntington Beach Conference and Visitors Bureau (2100 Main St., Suite 190, 92648, ☎ 800/729–6232).

Laguna Beach Hospitality (252 Broadway, 92651, ☎ 714/494–1018).

Newport Beach Conference and Visitors Bureau (366 San Miguel Dr., Suite 200, 92660, ☎ 800/942–6278).

San Juan Capistrano Chamber of Commerce and Visitors Center (26711 Verdugo Blvd., 92675, ☎ 714/493–4700).

13 San Diego

Spanish missionary Father Junípero Serra founded his first mission in Alta California (as opposed to Baja California, which is still part of Mexico) in San Diego in 1769. Some of the city's past is preserved in its Old Town section, but more than a century ago San Diego's focus moved closer to the water. A great place to take the kids, San Diego's daytime attractions include historical sites from Mexican and Victorian times, one of the best zoos in the country, and fine beaches. Dining and nightlife have improved in recent years, so the good times continue when the sun goes down.

EACH YEAR, SAN DIEGO ABSORBS thousands of visitors who are drawn by the climate: sunny, dry, and warm nearly year-round. They swim, surf, and sunbathe on long beaches facing the turquoise Pacific, where whales, seals, and dolphins swim offshore. They tour oases of tropical palms, sheltered bays fringed by golden pampas grass, and far-ranging parklands blossoming with brilliant bougainvillea, jasmine, ice plant, and birds of paradise. They run and bike and walk down wide streets and paths planned for recreation among the natives, who thrive on San Diego's varied health, fitness, and sports scenes.

San Diego County is the nation's sixth largest—larger than nearly a dozen U.S. states—with a population of more than 2.5 million. It sprawls east from the Pacific Ocean through dense urban neighborhoods to outlying suburban communities that seem to sprout on canyons and cliffs overnight. The city of San Diego is the state's second largest, after Los Angeles. It serves as a base for the U.S. Navy's 11th Naval District and a port for ships from many nations. A considerable number of its residents were stationed here in the service and decided to stay put. Others either passed through on vacation or saw the city in movies and TV shows and became enamored of the city and its reputation as a prosperous Sunbelt playground. From its founding San Diego has attracted a steady stream of prospectors, drawn to the nation's farthest southwest frontier.

Tourism is San Diego's third-largest industry, after manufacturing and the military. San Diego's politicians, business leaders, and developers have set the city's course toward a steadily increasing influx of visitors—which gives residents pleasant attractions as well as not-so-enjoyable distractions. With growth comes congestion, even in San Diego's vast expanse.

EXPLORING

By Maribeth Mellin

Updated by Edie Jarolim

Exploring San Diego is an endless adventure, limited only by time and transportation constraints, which, if you don't have a car, can be considerable. Many of the major attractions are at least 5 miles away from one another; if you are going to drive around San Diego, study your maps before you hit the road. The freeways are convenient and fast most of the time, but if you miss your turnoff or get caught in commuter traffic, you'll experience a none-too-pleasurable hallmark of southern California living—freeway madness.

If you stick with public transportation, plan on taking your time. San Diego's bus system covers almost all the county, but it does so slowly. Since many of the city's major attractions are clustered along the coast, you'll be best off staying there or in the Hotel Circle/Mission Valley hotel zone. Downtown and Fashion Valley Shopping Center in Mission Valley are the two major transfer points. Some buses have bicycle racks in the back, and a bike is a great mode of transportation here. The bike-path system, although never perfect, is extensive and well marked. Taxis are expensive, given the miles between various sights, and are best used for getting around once you're in a given area.

Downtown and the Embarcadero

Numbers in the margin correspond to points of interest on the Central San Diego map.

San Diego's politicians and business leaders have made a concerted effort to draw San Diegans to the downtown area, only 3 miles from the international airport but long ignored or avoided by the local populace. Thanks to a 15-year redevelopment effort, elegant hotels, upscale condominium complexes, and swank, trendy cafés now attract natives and visitors to a newly developed center city that has retained an outdoor character. Mirrored office and banking towers reflect the nearly constant blue skies and sunshine.

Downtown's natural attributes were easily evident to its original booster, Alonzo Horton, who arrived in San Diego in 1867. Horton looked at the bay and the acres of flatland surrounded by hills and canyons and knew he had found San Diego's center. Though Old Town, under the Spanish fort at the Presidio, had been settled for years, Horton understood that it was too far away from the water to take hold as the commercial center of San Diego. He bought 960 acres along the bay at 27½¢ per acre and literally gave away the land to those who would develop it or build houses. Within months, he had sold or given away 226 city blocks of land; settlers camped on their land in tents as their houses and businesses rose.

The transcontinental train arrived in 1885, and the land boom was on. Although the railroad's status as a cross-country route was short-lived, the population soared from 5,000 to 35,000 in less than a decade—a foreshadowing of San Diego's future. In 1887, the Santa Fe Depot was constructed at the foot of Broadway, two blocks from the water. Freighters chugged in and out of the harbor, and by the early 1900s, the navy had moved in.

As downtown grew into San Diego's transportation and commercial hub, residential neighborhoods blossomed along the beaches and inland valleys. The business district gradually moved farther away from the original heart of downtown, at 5th Avenue and Market Street, past Broadway, up toward the park. Downtown's waterfront fell into bad times during World War I, when sailors, gamblers, and prostitutes were drawn to one another and the waterfront bars.

But Alonzo Horton's modern-day followers, city leaders intent on prospering while preserving San Diego's natural beauty, have reclaimed the downtown area. Replacing old shipyards and canneries are hotel towers and waterfront parks; the Martin Luther King, Jr., Promenade project is slated to put 12 acres of greenery along Harbor Drive from Seaport Village to the convention center by the end of 1996. Nineteen ninety-two saw the completion of the part of the park near the $160 million, 760,000-square-foot San Diego Convention Center, which hosted its first events in early 1990. And a few blocks inland, the hugely successful Horton Plaza shopping center led the way for the hotels, restaurants, shopping centers, and housing developments that are now rising on every square inch of available space in downtown San Diego.

Your first view of downtown, regardless of your mode of transportation, will probably include the **Embarcadero,** a waterfront walkway on **Harbor Drive** lined with restaurants, sea vessels of every variety—cruise ships, ferries, tour boats, houseboats, and naval destroyers—and a fair share of seals and sea gulls. Many boats along the Embarcadero have been converted into floating gift shops, and others are awaiting restoration. If you plan to spend a good portion of your day in the area, either strolling or taking a harbor excursion, it's a good idea to park at the huge municipal lot ($3 per day) along the south side of the

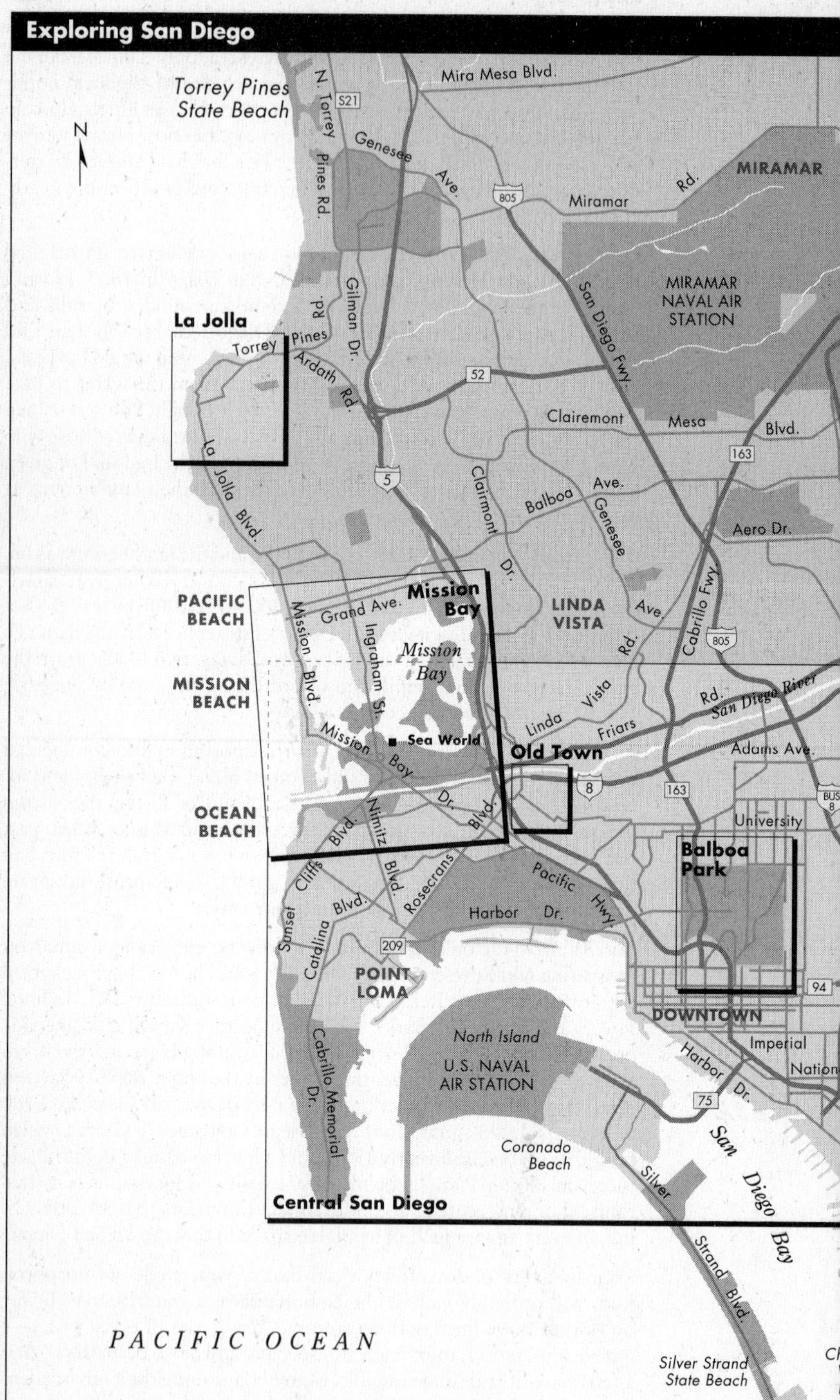
Torrey Pines State Beach
N. Torrey Pines Rd.
Mira Mesa Blvd.
S21
Genesee Ave.
805
Miramar Rd.
MIRAMAR
MIRAMAR NAVAL AIR STATION
San Diego Fwy.
Gilman Dr.
La Jolla
Torrey Pines Rd.
Ardath Rd.
52
Clairemont Mesa Blvd.
163
La Jolla Blvd.
5
Clairemont Dr.
Balboa Ave.
Genesee Ave.
Aero Dr.
Cabrillo Fwy.
PACIFIC BEACH
Grand Ave.
Mission Bay
Mission Blvd.
Ingraham St.
LINDA VISTA
805
MISSION BEACH
Linda Vista Rd.
Friars Rd.
San Diego River
Sea World
Mission Bay Dr.
Old Town
Adams Ave.
8
163
BUS 8
OCEAN BEACH
Nimitz Blvd.
University
Balboa Park
Sunset Cliffs Blvd.
Rosecrans
Pacific Hwy.
Harbor Dr.
Catalina Blvd.
209
POINT LOMA
94
DOWNTOWN
North Island
U.S. NAVAL AIR STATION
Imperial
Harbor Dr.
Cabrillo Memorial Dr.
75
Coronado Beach
San Diego Bay
Silver Strand Blvd.
Central San Diego
PACIFIC OCEAN
Silver Strand State Beach

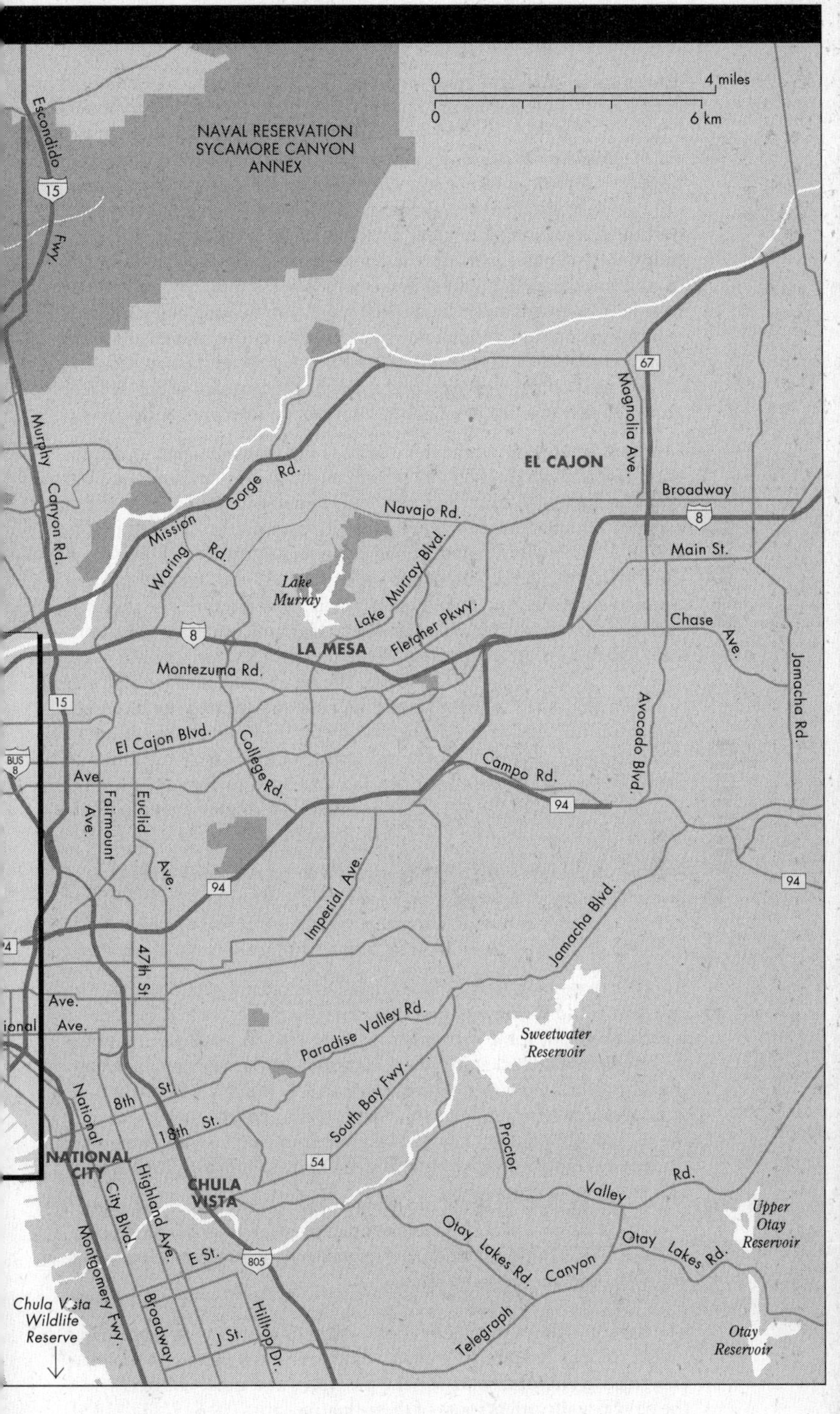
0
4 miles
0
6 km
NAVAL RESERVATION
SYCAMORE CANYON
ANNEX
Escondido
Fwy.
15
Murphy
Canyon Rd.
Mission
Gorge
Rd.
Waring
Rd.
Navajo Rd.
Lake Murray
Lake Murray Blvd.
Fletcher Pkwy.
EL CAJON
Magnolia Ave.
67
Broadway
8
Main St.
Chase
Ave.
Jamacha Rd.
LA MESA
Montezuma Rd.
El Cajon Blvd.
College Rd.
BUS 8
Ave.
Fairmount
Ave.
Euclid
Ave.
Campo Rd.
94
Avocado Blvd.
Imperial Ave.
Jamacha Blvd.
47th St.
Ave.
Ave.
Paradise Valley Rd.
Sweetwater Reservoir
South Bay Fwy.
54
8th St.
18th St.
National
NATIONAL CITY
CHULA VISTA
Proctor
Valley
Rd.
Upper Otay Reservoir
Otay Lakes Rd.
Canyon
Otay Lakes Rd.
City Blvd.
Highland Ave.
Montgomery Fwy.
E St.
805
Broadway
J St.
Hilltop Dr.
Telegraph
Chula Vista Wildlife Reserve
Otay Reservoir

B Street Pier building; much of the parking along Harbor Drive is limited to two-hour meters.

To get some historical perspective on your Embarcadero visit, begin your tour two blocks north of the parking lot at the foot of Ash Street, where the *Berkeley,* an 1898 riverboat, is moored. It's headquarters
1 for the **Maritime Museum,** a collection of three restored ships that may be toured for one entrance fee. The *Berkeley,* which served the Southern Pacific Railroad at San Francisco Bay until 1953, had its most important days during the great earthquake of 1906, when it carried thousands of passengers across San Francisco Bay to Oakland. Its carved wood paneling, stained-glass windows, and plate-glass mirrors have been restored, and its main deck serves as a floating museum, with exhibits on oceanography and naval history; permanent displays on the background of the America's Cup Race were recently installed. Anchored next to the Berkeley, the small Scottish steam yacht *Medea,* launched in 1904, may be boarded but has no interpretive displays.

The most interesting of the three ships is the ***Star of India,*** a beautiful windjammer built in 1863 and docked at the foot of Grape Street. The ship's high wooden masts and white sails flapping in the wind have been a harbor landmark since 1926. Built at Ramsey on the Isle of Man, the *Star of India* made 21 trips around the world in the late 1800s, when she traveled the East Indian trade route, shuttled immigrants from England to Australia, and served the Alaskan salmon trade. The ship languished after she was retired to San Diego Harbor, virtually ignored until 1959. Then a group of volunteers, organized by the Maritime Museum, stripped the wooden decks, polished the figurehead, and mended the sails. On July 4, 1976, the *Star of India* commemorated the bicentennial by setting sail in the harbor. The oldest iron sailing ship afloat in the world, she has made short excursions five times since then but for the most part stays moored at the pier and open to visitors. *1306 N. Harbor Dr., ☎ 619/234–9153. ☛ $6 adults, $4 senior citizens and students 13–17, $2 children 6–12, $12 families. Ships open daily 9–8.*

A cement pathway runs south from the *Star of India* along the water-
2 front to the pastel **B Street Pier,** used by ships from major cruise lines as both a port of call and a departure point. The cavernous pier building has a cruise-information center and a small, cool bar and gift shop.

Another two blocks south on Harbor Drive brings you to the foot of
3 Broadway and **Broadway Pier** (also known as the "excursion pier"), a gathering spot for day-trippers ready to set sail. A cluster of storefront windows sell tickets for the harbor tours and whale-watching trips that leave from the dock in January and February, when the gray whales migrate from the Pacific Northwest to southern Baja. One of the most traditional, and delightful, boat trips to take from the pier is the **Bay Ferry** to Coronado Island (*see* Coronado, *below,* for details).

TIME OUT Those waiting for their boats can grab a beer or ice cream at the diner-style **Bay Cafe** and sit on the upstairs patio or on benches along the busy pathway; it's a good vantage point for watching the sailboats, paddle wheelers, and yachts vie for space.

The navy's 11th Naval District has control of the next few waterfront blocks to the south, and a series of destroyers, submarines, and carriers cruise in and out, some staying for weeks at a time. On weekends, the navy usually offers tours of these floating cities (☎ 619/532–1431 for recorded information on hours and types of ships). A steady stream of joggers, bicyclists, and serious walkers on the Embarcadero pathway picks up speed at **Tuna Harbor,** the hub of San Diego's commercial tuna fishing, one of the city's earliest industries.

★ 4 **Seaport Village** (☎ 619/235–4013 for recorded events information or 619/235–4014) is the next attraction you'll reach if you continue south on Harbor Drive. Spread out across 14 acres are three connected shopping plazas, designed to reflect the architectural styles of early California, especially New England clapboard and Spanish Mission. A ¼-mile wooden boardwalk that runs along the bay, as well as 4 miles of simulated dirt-road and cobblestone paths, leads to a bustling array of specialty shops, snack bars, and restaurants—more than 75 in all. Seaport Village's shops are open daily 10–9 (10–10 in summer); a few eateries open early for breakfast, and many have extended nighttime hours, especially in summer.

The **Broadway Flying Horses Carousel,** created by I. D. Looff in Coney Island in 1890, was moved from its next home, Salisbury Beach in Massachusetts, and faithfully restored for the West Plaza of Seaport Village; tickets are $1. Strolling clowns, mimes, musicians, and magicians are also on hand throughout the village to entertain kids.

Seaport Village's center reaches out onto **Embarcadero Marine Park North,** an 8-acre grassy point into the harbor where kite-fliers, roller-skaters, and picnickers hang out in the sun. Seasonal celebrations with live music and fireworks are held here throughout the year.

Just beyond the mirrored towers of the San Diego Marriott Hotel and
5 Marina is the striking **San Diego Convention Center,** designed by Arthur Erickson; its nautical lines are complemented by the backdrop of blue sky and sea. The center often holds trade shows that are open to the public, and tours of the building are available.

Just south of the convention center, at the **Embarcadero Marina Park South,** the San Diego Symphony (☎ 619/699–4205) presents its annual Summer Pops concert series, complete with fireworks finales that light up the bay. These musical extravaganzas, increasingly popular in recent years, have gone upscale, offering cabaret seating as well as food and bar service.

One way to reach the heart of downtown is to walk up Market Street from Seaport Village. The **Olde Cracker Factory,** at Market and State streets, houses antiques and collectibles shops. Continue two blocks to Front Street and turn south one block to Island to reach the new facility of the **Children's Museum of San Diego.**

Another way to approach the central business district is to walk up Broadway from the Broadway Pier. Two blocks to the west of Harbor Drive, at Kettner Boulevard, you'll come to the Mission Revival–style
6 **Santa Fe Depot,** built in 1915 on the site of the original 1887 station. The terminal for north- and south-bound Amtrak passengers, the graceful, tile-domed depot hosts an unattended tourist information booth with bus schedules, maps, and brochures. The depot is overshadowed by **1 America Plaza** next door. At the base of this massive 34-story office tower, designed by architect Helmut Jahn, is a transit center that links the train, trolley, and city bus systems. (The Greyhound bus station is just a few blocks away at 120 West Broadway.) The building's signature crescent-shaped glass-and-steel canopy arching out over the trolley tracks calls attention to the new Sculpture Plaza that fronts the downtown branch of the **San Diego Museum of Contemporary Art.** The two-story building adjoining the transit center houses four small galleries, the main locus for exhibitions during the expansion of the orig-

B Street Pier, **2**
Broadway Pier, **3**
Cabrillo National Monument, **18**
Coronado Beach Historical Museum, **16**
Ferry Landing Marketplace, **12**
Gaslamp Quarter Association, **10**
Glorietta Bay Inn, **15**
Harbor Island, **22**
Horton Grand Hotel, **11**
Horton Plaza, **9**
Hotel del Coronado, **14**
Maritime Museum, **1**
Orange Avenue, **13**
San Diego Convention Center, **5**
Santa Fe Depot, **6**
Scott Street, **20**
Seaport Village, **4**
Shelter Island, **21**
Silver Strand Beach State Park, **17**
Spreckels Theater, **7**
Sunset Cliffs Park, **19**
U.S. Grant Hotel, **8**

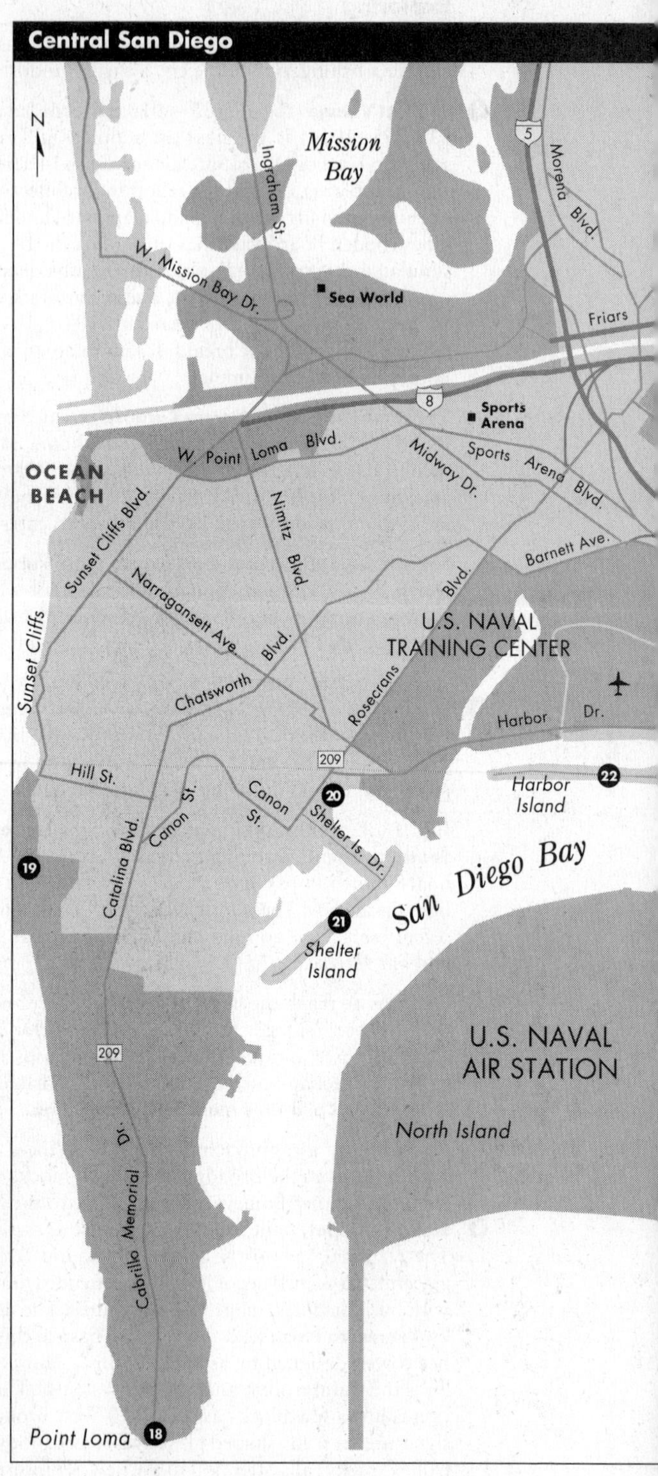

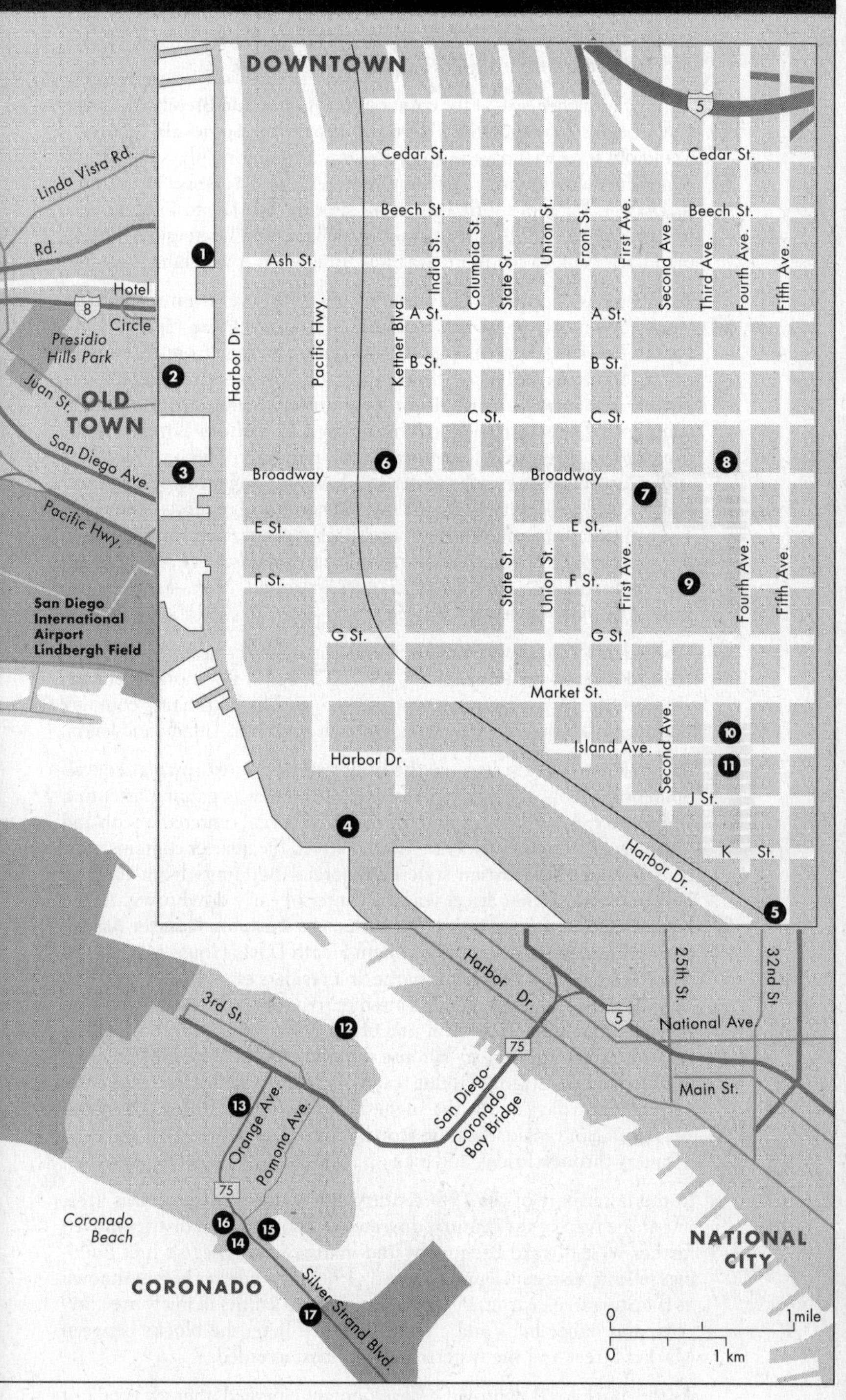

DOWNTOWN
Cedar St.
Beech St.
Ash St.
A St.
B St.
C St.
Broadway
E St.
F St.
G St.
Market St.
Island Ave.
J St.
K St.
Harbor Dr.
Pacific Hwy.
Kettner Blvd.
India St.
Columbia St.
State St.
Union St.
Front St.
First Ave.
Second Ave.
Third Ave.
Fourth Ave.
Fifth Ave.
Linda Vista Rd.
Rd.
Hotel
Circle
Presidio
Hills Park
Juan St.
OLD
TOWN
San Diego Ave.
Pacific Hwy.
San Diego
International
Airport
Lindbergh Field
3rd St.
Orange Ave.
Pomona Ave.
San Diego-
Coronado
Bay Bridge
Coronado
Beach
CORONADO
Silver Strand Blvd.
25th St.
32nd St
National Ave.
Main St.
NATIONAL
CITY
0
1mile
0
1 km

inal facility in La Jolla (scheduled for completion by early 1996). *1001 Kettner Blvd., ☎ 619/234–1001. ☛ $3 adults, $1 students and senior citizens, children under 13 free; free Fri. 5:30–8 PM. ⊙ Tues.–Thurs. and weekends 10:30 AM–5:30 PM, Fri. 10:30 AM–8 PM.*

Six blocks farther east, at the corner of 1st Avenue and Broadway, down-
7 town begins to come alive. Here you'll pass the **Spreckels Theater,** a grand old stage that presents pop concerts and touring plays these days.
8 Another block down and across the street, the **U.S. Grant Hotel,** built in 1910, is far more formal than most other San Diego lodgings; the massive marble lobby, gleaming chandeliers, and white-gloved doormen hark back to the more gracious time when it was built.

The theme of shopping in adventureland carries over from Seaport Vil-
★ 9 lage to downtown San Diego's centerpiece, **Horton Plaza** (☎ 619/238–1596). This shopping, dining, and entertainment mall fronts Broadway and G Street from 1st to 4th avenues and covers more than six city blocks. The **International Visitor Information Center,** operated in the complex by the San Diego Convention and Visitors Bureau, is the traveler's best resource for information on the city. The staff members and volunteers who run the center speak an amazing array of languages and are well acquainted with the myriad needs and requests of tourists. They dispense information on hotels, restaurants, and tourist attractions, including Tijuana. *11 Horton Plaza, street level at corner of 1st Ave. and F St., ☎ 619/236–1212. ⊙ Year-round, Mon.–Sat. 8:30–5; June–Aug., also open Sun. 11–5.*

Opened in 1992 across from Horton Plaza at 777 Front Street between G and F streets, the **Paladion** (☎ 619/232–1627) is a more recent addition to the thriving downtown retail scene. This ultrahaute complex features a collection of toney boutiques such as Cartier, Tiffany, and Gucci.

Before Horton Plaza became the bright star on downtown's redevelopment horizon, the nearby **Gaslamp Quarter** was gaining attention and respect. A 16-block National Historic District, centered on 5th and 4th avenues from Broadway to Market Street, the quarter contains most of San Diego's Victorian-style commercial buildings from the late 1800s, when Market Street was the center of early downtown. At the
10 farthest end of the redeveloped quarter, the **Gaslamp Quarter Association** is headquartered in the William Heath Davis House (410 Island Ave., ☎ 619/233–5227), one of the first residences in town. Davis was a San Franciscan whose ill-fated attempt to develop the waterfront area preceded the more successful one of Alonzo Horton. In 1850, Davis had this prefab saltbox-style house shipped around Cape Horn and assembled in San Diego. Walking tours of the historic district leave from here on Saturdays at 11; the suggested donation is $5 for those over 12. If you can't make the tour, stop by the house between 10 and 2:30 Monday through Friday and pick up a self-guiding brochure and map.

In the latter part of the 19th century, businesses thrived in this area, but at the turn of the century, downtown's commercial district moved farther west toward Broadway, and many of San Diego's first buildings fell into disrepair. During the early 1900s, the quarter became known as the Stingaree district. Prostitutes picked up sailors in lively area taverns, and dance halls and crime flourished here; the blocks between Market Street and the waterfront were best avoided.

As the move for downtown redevelopment emerged, there was talk of destroying the buildings in the quarter, literally bulldozing them and starting from scratch. In 1974, history buffs, developers, architects, and artists formed the Gaslamp Quarter Council. Bent on preserving the district, they gathered funds from the government and private benefactors and began the painstaking, expensive task of cleaning up the quarter, restoring the finest old buildings, and attracting businesses and the public back to the heart of New Town.

Across the street from the Gaslamp Quarter Association's headquar-
11 ters, at the corner of Island and 3rd avenues, is the **Horton Grand Hotel.** In the mid-1980s, this ornate, quintessentially Victorian hostelry was created by joining together two historic hotels, the Kahle Saddlery and the Grand Hotel, built in the boom days of the 1880s; Wyatt Earp stayed at the Kahle Saddlery (then called the Brooklyn Hotel) while he was in town speculating on real estate ventures and opening gambling halls. Doomed to demolition and purchased from the city for $1 each, the two hotels were dismantled and painstakingly reconstructed on a new site, about four blocks from their original locations. A small Chinese Museum serves as a tribute to the surrounding Chinatown district, a collection of modest homes that once housed Chinese laborers and their families.

Many of the quarter's landmark buildings are located on 4th and 5th avenues, between Island Avenue and Broadway. Among the nicest are the Backesto Building, the Louis Bank of Commerce, and the Mercantile Building, all on 5th Avenue, and the Keating Building on F Street. Johnny M's 801, at the corner of 4th Avenue and F Street, is a magnificently restored turn-of-the-century tavern with a 12-foot mahogany bar and a spectacular stained-glass domed ceiling.

As more and more artists—and art entrepreneurs—move to the area, the section of G Street between 6th and 9th avenues has become a haven for galleries; stop in at any one of them to pick up a map of the downtown arts district. For information about openings and other current events in the district, call the **Gaslamp Quarter Hot Line** (☎ 619/233–4691).

TIME OUT Fifth Avenue between F and G streets is lined with restaurants, a number of them with outdoor patios; **Trattoria La Strada** (702 5th Ave.) is a good place to sit out on a fine afternoon with a glass of wine and an antipasto. Many hip coffeehouses have also sprung up in the Gaslamp Quarter; you can nurse a double espresso at **Café LuLu** (419 F St.) for hours.

Coronado

Coronado Island, an incorporated city unto itself, is a charming, peaceful community. The Spaniards called the island Los Coronados, or "the Crowned Ones," in the late 1500s and the name stuck. Today's residents, many of whom live in grand Victorian homes handed down for generations, tend to consider their island to be a sort of royal encampment, safe from the hassles and hustle of San Diego proper.

North Island Naval Air Station was established in 1911 on the island's north end, across from Point Loma, and was the site of Charles Lindbergh's departure on his flight around the world. Today high-tech air- and seacraft arrive and depart continually from North Island, providing a real-life education in military armament. Coronado's long relationship with the navy has made it an enclave of sorts for retired military personnel.

Coronado is visible from downtown and Point Loma and accessible via the arching blue 2.2-mile-long San Diego–Coronado Bridge, a landmark just beyond downtown's skyline. There is a $1 toll for crossing the bridge into Coronado, but cars carrying two or more passengers may enter through the free car-pool lane. The bridge handles more than 20,000 cars each day, and rush hour tends to be slow, which is fine, since the view of the harbor, downtown, and the island is breathtaking, day and night. Until the bridge was completed in 1969, visitors and residents relied on the Coronado Ferry, which ran across the harbor from downtown. When the bridge was opened, the ferry closed down, much to the chagrin of those who were fond of traveling at a leisurely pace. In 1987, the ferry returned, and with it came the island's most ambitious development in decades. Coronado's residents and commuting workers have quickly adapted to this traditional mode of transportation, and the ferry has become quite popular with bicyclists, who shuttle their bikes across the harbor and ride the island's wide, flat boulevards for hours.

You can board the Bay Ferry (☎ 619/234–4111) at downtown San Diego's Embarcadero from the Broadway Pier, at Broadway and Harbor Drive. Boats depart every hour on the hour from San Diego and every hour on the half hour from Coronado from 9 AM to 9:30 PM Sunday through Thursday, until 10:30 PM Friday and Saturday; the fare is $2 each way (50¢ extra for bicycles). San Diego Harbor Excursion (☎ 619/235–TAXI) has recently instituted water taxi service from Seaport Village to Ferry Landing Marketplace, Le Meridien Resort, and the Hotel del Coronado; the fare is $5. Call for the exact schedules.

12 The Bay Ferry's point of disembarkation is the **Ferry Landing Marketplace** (1st St. and B Ave., ☎ 619/435–8895), which is actually a new development on an old site. Its buildings resemble the gingerbread domes of the Hotel del Coronado, long the island's main attraction. On a smaller scale, the Ferry Landing Marketplace is similar to Seaport Village, with little shops and restaurants and lots of benches facing the water. Nearby, the elegant Le Meridien Hotel accommodates many wedding receptions and gala banquets.

13 An electric trolley runs from the landing down **Orange Avenue,** the island's version of a downtown. It's easy to imagine you're on a street in Cape Cod when you stroll along this thoroughfare: The clapboard houses, small restaurants, and boutiques—many of them selling nautical paraphernalia—are in some ways more characteristic of New England than they are of California. But the East Coast illusion tends to dissipate as quickly as a winter fog here when you catch sight of one of the avenue's many citrus trees—or realize it's February and the sun is warming your face. The friendly volunteers at the Coronado Visitor Information center (1111 Orange Ave., ☎ 619/437–8788 or 800/622–8300) can answer your questions and provide you with an array of maps and brochures.

★ 14 At the end of Orange Avenue, the **Hotel del Coronado** is the island's most prominent landmark. Selected as a National Historic Site in 1977, the Del (as natives say) celebrated its 100th anniversary in 1988. Celebrities, royalty, and politicians marked the anniversary with a weekend-long party that highlighted the hotel's colorful history, integrally connected with that of the island itself.

The Del was the brainchild of wealthy financiers Elisha Spurr Babcock, Jr., and H. L. Story, who, in 1884, saw the potential of the island's virgin beaches and its view of San Diego's emerging harbor. The next year, they purchased a 4,100-acre parcel of land for $110,000 and threw a lavish Fourth of July bash for prospective investors in their hunting and fishing resort. By the end of the year, they had roused public interest—and had an ample return on their investment. The hotel was completed in 1888, and Thomas Edison himself threw the switch as the Del became the world's first electrically lighted hotel. It has been a dazzler ever since.

The Del's ornate Victorian gingerbread architecture is recognized all over the world because the hotel has served as a set for many movies, political meetings, and extravagant social happenings. It is said that the Duke of Windsor first met Wallis Simpson here. Eight presidents have been guests of the Del, and the film *Some Like It Hot,* starring Marilyn Monroe, was filmed at the hotel. Today, lower-level corridors are lined with historic photos from the Del's early days.

A red carpet leads up the front stairs to the main lobby, with its grand oak pillars and ceiling, and out to the central courtyard and gazebo. To the right is the Crown Room, a cavernous room with an arched ceiling made of notched sugar pine and constructed without nails. You can tell by looking at this space that the hotel's architect, James Reed, had previously designed railroad stations.

The Grand Ballroom overlooks the ocean and the hotel's long white beach. The patio surrounding the sky-blue swimming pool is a great place for just sitting back and imagining what the bathers looked like during the '20s, when the hotel rocked with good times. More rooms have been added in high-rise towers beside the original 400-room building, which is still the most charming place to stay. *1500 Orange Ave.,* ☎ *619/435–6611. 1-hr guided tours ($10) from lobby Thurs.–Sat. 10 and 11 AM. Headsets for self-guided tours ($5) can be rented at the Signature Lobby across from concierge desk.*

Coronado's other main attraction is its 86 historic homes—many of
15 them turn-of-the-century mansions—and sites. The **Glorietta Bay Inn,**
across the street from the Del, was the residence of John Spreckels, the original owner of North Island and the property on which the Hotel del Coronado now stands. On Tuesday, Thursday, and Saturday morning at 11, the inn is the departure point for a fun and informative 1½-hour walking tour of the area's historical homes. Sponsored by the Coronado Historical Association, the tour focuses on the Glorietta Bay Inn and the Hotel Del but also includes—from the outside only—some spectacular mansions along with the Meade House, where L. Frank Baum wrote *The Wizard of Oz* (some claim that Emerald City might be based on Coronado). The cost is $5; call 619/435–5892 or 619/435–5444 for information.

16 Just north of the Del is the **Coronado Beach Historical Museum** (1126
Loma Ave., ☎ 619/435–7242; ☛ free; ⏲ Wed.–Sat. 10–4, Sun. noon–4),
17 an interesting stop. Heading south from the Del is **Silver Strand Beach**
State Park, which runs along Silver Strand Boulevard to Imperial Beach. The view from the shore to Point Loma is lovely, and the long, clean beach is a perfect family gathering spot.

Point Loma, Shelter Island, and Harbor Island

Point Loma curves around the San Diego Bay west of downtown and the airport, protecting the center city from the Pacific's tides and waves. Although a number of military installations are based here and some main streets are cluttered with motels and fast-food shacks, Point Loma is an old and wealthy enclave of stately family homes for military officers, successful Portuguese fishermen, and political and professional leaders. Its bayside shores front huge estates, with sailboats and yachts packed tightly in private marinas.

★ 18 Take Catalina Drive all the way down to the tip of Point Loma to reach **Cabrillo National Monument,** named after the Portuguese explorer Juan Rodríguez Cabrillo. Cabrillo, who had earlier gone on voyages with Cortés, was the first European to come to San Diego, which he called San Miguel, in 1542. In 1913, government grounds were set aside to commemorate his discovery. Today his monument, a 144-acre preserve of rugged cliffs and shores and outstanding overlooks, is one of the most frequently visited of all National Park Service sites.

Begin your tour at the visitor center, where films and lectures about Cabrillo's voyage, the sea-level tidal pools, and the gray whales migrating offshore are presented frequently. The center has an excellent shop with an interesting selection of books about nature, San Diego, and the sea; maps of the region, posters of whales, flowers, shells, and the requisite postcards, slides, and film are also on sale. Rest rooms and water fountains are plentiful along the paths that climb to the monument's various viewpoints, but, except for a few vending machines at the visitor center, there are no food facilities. Exploring the grounds consumes time and calories; bring a picnic and rest on a bench overlooking the sailboats headed to sea.

Signs along the walkways that edge the cliffs explain the views, with posters depicting the various navy, fishing, and pleasure craft that sail into and fly over the bay. Directly south across the bay from the visitor center is the North Island Naval Air Station on the west end of Coronado Island. Directly left on the shores of Point Loma is the Naval Ocean Systems Center and Ballast Point; nuclear-powered submarines are now docked where Cabrillo's small ships anchored in 1542.

A statue of Cabrillo overlooks downtown from the next windy promontory, where visitors gather to admire the stunning panorama over the bay, from the snowcapped San Bernardino Mountains, some 200 miles northeast, to the hills surrounding Tijuana. The stone figure standing on the bluff looks rugged and dashing, but he is a creation of an artist's imagination—no portraits of Cabrillo are known to exist.

The oil lamp of the **Old Point Loma Lighthouse** was first lit in 1855. The light, sitting in a brass-and-iron housing above a painstakingly refurbished white wooden house, shone through a state-of-the-art lens from France and was visible from the sea for 25 miles. Unfortunately, it was too high above the cliffs to guide navigators trapped in southern California's thick offshore fog and low clouds. In 1891, a new lighthouse was built on the small shore under the slowly eroding 400-foot cliffs. The old lighthouse is open to visitors, and the coast guard still uses the newer lighthouse and a mighty foghorn to guide boaters through the narrow channel leading into the bay.

The western and southern cliffs of Cabrillo Monument are prime whale-watching territory in January and February, mostly in early morning. More accessible sea creatures can be seen in the tidal pools at the foot of the monument's western cliffs. Drive north from the visitor center to the first road on the left, which winds down to the coast guard station and the shore. *Cabrillo National Monument: 1800 Cabrillo Memorial Dr.,* ☎ *619/557–5450.* ☛ *$4 per car; $2 per person entering on foot or by bicycle; free for Golden Age Passport holders, people with disabilities, and children under 17.* ⏲ *Park: daily 9–5:15, Old Lighthouse 9–5, Bayside Trail 9–4, tidal-pool areas 9–*

4:30 in winter; in summer, the park is open until sunset and other areas have extended hrs.

Continue north on Catalina Boulevard to Hill Street and turn left to
19 reach **Sunset Cliffs Park,** at the western side of Point Loma near Ocean Beach. The cliffs are aptly named, since their main attraction is their vantage point as a fine sunset-watching spot. The dramatic coastline here seems to have been carved out of ancient rock. Certainly the waves make their impact, and each year more sections of the cliffs sport caution signs. Don't ignore these warnings: It's easy to lose your footing and slip in the crumbling sandstone, and the surf can get very rough. Small coves and beaches dot the coastline and are popular with surfers drawn to the pounding waves and locals from the neighborhood who name and claim their special spots. The homes along Sunset Cliffs Boulevard are lovely examples of southern California luxury, with pink stucco mansions beside shingle Cape Cod–style cottages.

Return to Catalina Boulevard and backtrack south for a few blocks to reach Canon Street, which leads toward the peninsula's eastern
20 (bay) side. Almost at the shore, you'll see **Scott Street,** which runs along Point Loma's waterfront from Shelter Island to the Marine Corps Recruiting Center on Harbor Drive. Lined with deep-sea fishing charters and whale-watching boats, this is a good spot from which to watch fishermen (and women) haul marlin, tuna, and puny mackerel off their boats.

TIME OUT The freshest and tastiest fish to be found along Point Loma's shores comes from **Point Loma Sea Foods,** off Scott Street at Emerson Street, behind the Vagabond Inn. There are a couple of places to sit outside, but most folks squeeze into tables in the small dining area behind the store.

21 Scott Street is bisected by Shelter Island Drive, which leads to **Shelter Island,** actually a peninsula that sits in the narrow channel between Point Loma's eastern shore and the west coast of Coronado. It is the center of San Diego's yacht-building industry, and boats in every stage of construction are visible in the yacht yards. A long sidewalk runs from the landscaped lawns of the **San Diego Yacht Club** (tucked down Anchorage Street off Shelter Island Drive), past boat brokerages to the hotels and marinas, which line the inner shore, facing Point Loma. On the bay side, fishermen launch their boats or simply stand on shore and cast. Families relax at picnic tables along the grass, where there are fire rings and permanent barbecue grills, while strollers wander to the huge Friendship Bell, given to San Diegans by the people of Yokohama in 1960.

Go back up Shelter Island Drive, turn right on Rosecrans Street, and
22 make another right on North Harbor Drive to reach **Harbor Island,** a peninsula adjacent to the airport that was created out of 3.5 million tons of rock and soil from the San Diego Bay. The bay shore has pathways, gardens, and picnic spots for sightseeing or working off the calories from the island restaurants' fine meals.

Balboa Park

Numbers in the margin correspond to points of interest on the Balboa Park map.

★ **Balboa Park** is set on 1,400 beautifully landscaped acres. Hosting the majority of San Diego's museums and a world-famous zoo, the park serves as the cultural center of the city, as well as a recreational paradise for animal lovers and folks who want to spend a day picnicking or strolling in a lush green space.

Many of the park's ornate Spanish-Moorish buildings were intended to be temporary structures housing exhibits for the Panama–California International Exposition of 1915. Fortunately, city leaders realized the buildings' value and incorporated them in their plans for Balboa Park's acreage, which had been set aside by the city founders in 1868. The Spanish theme first instituted in the early 1900s was carried through in new buildings designed for the California Pacific International Exposition of 1935–36.

The Laurel Street Bridge, also known as Cabrillo Bridge, is the park's official gateway; it leads over a vast canyon, filled with downtown commuter traffic on Highway 163, to El Prado, which, beyond the art museum, becomes the park's central pedestrian mall. At Christmas the bridge is lined with colored lights; bright pink blossoms on rows of peach trees herald the coming of spring. The 100-bell carillon in the California Tower tolls the hour. Figures of California's historic personages decorate the base of the 200-foot spire, and a magnificent blue-tiled dome shines in the sun. If you're driving in via the Laurel Street Bridge, the first parking area you'll come to is off the Prado to the left, going toward Pan American Plaza. Don't despair if there are no spaces here; you'll see more lots as you continue down along the same road.

1 A good place to begin a visit is at the **Balboa Park Visitors Center.** Maps and pamphlets—as well as the friendly volunteers who run the center—can help you decide what you'd like to see. The office sells the Passport to Balboa Park, which affords entry to nine museums for $18; it's worthwhile if you want to visit a number of them and aren't entitled to the other discounts that many give to children, senior citizens, and military personnel. On Tuesdays, the museums offer free entrance on a rotating basis; inquire here about the schedule.

Also available at the office is a schedule and route map for the free trams that operate around the park, giving you an alternative way to get back to your car or bus. From April through October (Daylight Saving Time), trams run 9:30–5:30, approximately every 8–12 minutes; the rest of the year, service is 11–5 and frequency is 12–24 minutes. Restoration of the center's usual home, the House of Hospitality, began in January 1995 and should take two years to complete. For the time being, the information facility is set up on the Plaza de Panama, adjacent to its old site. ☎ *619/239–0512.* ⏲ *Daily 9–4.*

2 Next door to the House of Hospitality, the **Casa de Balboa** houses four museums: the San Diego Hall of Champions Sports Museum, the Museum of Photographic Arts, the San Diego Historical Society–Museum of San Diego History, and the San Diego Model Railroad Museum.

Starting from the left as you enter, the **Museum of San Diego History** features rotating exhibits on local urban history after 1850, when California became part of the United States. The society's research library is in the building's basement. ☎ *619/232–6203.* ☛ *$4 adults; $3 senior citizens, military personnel, and students; $1.50 children 5–12.* ⏲ *Wed.–Sun. 10–4.*

Down the hall, the **San Diego Hall of Champions–Sports Museum** celebrates local heroes with a vast collection of memorabilia, uniforms, paintings, photographs, and computer and video displays. An amusing bloopers film is screened at the Sports Theater. ☎ *619/234–2544.* ☛ *$3 adults, 2 senior citizens, $1 children 6–17.* ⏲ *Daily 10–4:30.*

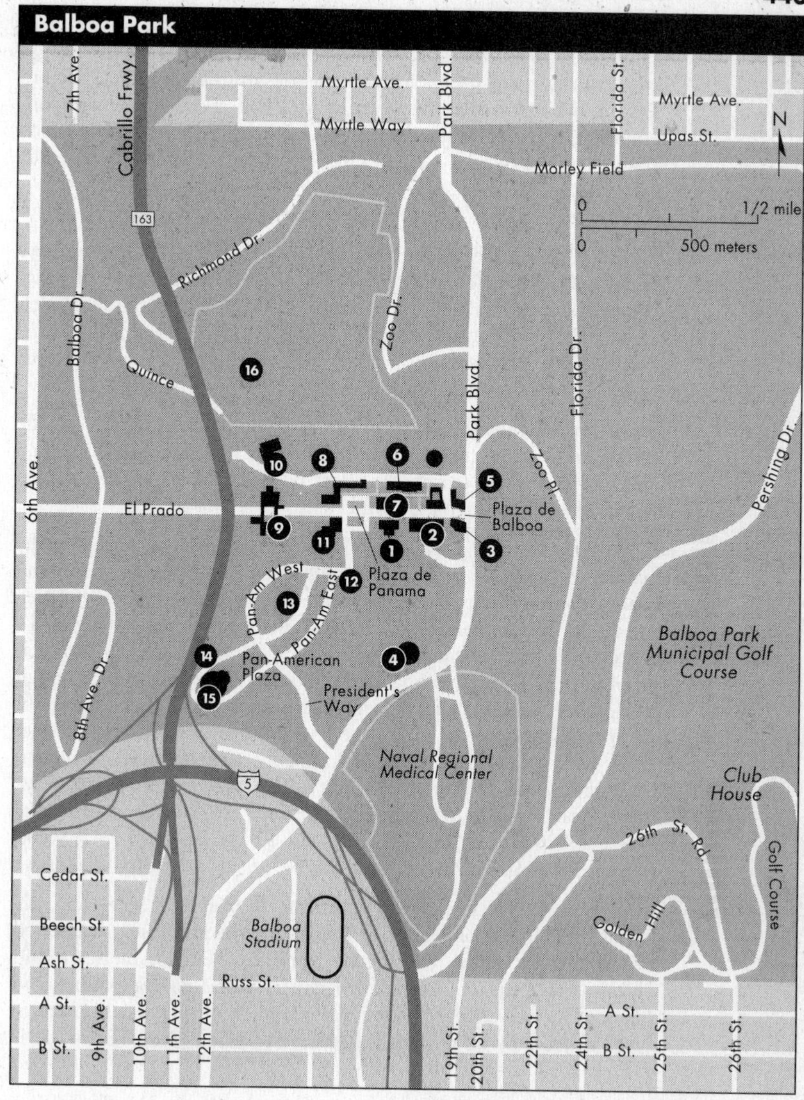

Balboa Park Visitors Center, **1**
Botanical Building, **6**
Casa Del Balboa, **2**
Centro Cultural de la Raza, **4**
House of Charm, **11**
House of Pacific Relations, **13**
The Museum of Man, **9**
Reuben H. Fleet Space Theater and Science Center, **3**
San Diego Aerospace Museum and International Aerospace Hall of Fame, **15**
San Diego Automotive Museum, **14**
San Diego Museum of Art, **8**
San Diego Natural History Museum, **5**
San Diego Zoo, **16**
Simon Edison Center for the Performing Arts, **10**
Spreckels Organ Pavilion, **12**
Timken Museum of Art, **7**

The **Museum of Photographic Arts** is one of the few in the country dedicated solely to photography. World-renowned photographers, such as Ansel Adams, Imogen Cunningham, Henri Cartier-Bresson, and Edward Weston, are represented in the museum's collection, along with contemporary artists. Volunteers lead tours through the exhibits, which change every six weeks. Gallery talks by artists are given on weekends at 1 PM. ☎ *619/239–5262.* ☛ *$3, children under 12 free.* ⏲ *Daily 10–5; closed national holidays and during installations.*

Below MOPA, in the basement of the Casa de Balboa, is the **San Diego Model Railroad Museum.** The room is filled with the sounds of chugging engines, screeching brakes, and shrill whistles when the six model-train exhibits are in operation. ☎ *619/696–0199.* ☛ *$3 adults; $2.50 senior citizens, students, and military personnel; children under 15 free.* ⏲ *Wed.–Fri. 11–4, weekends 11–5.*

If you continue walking down El Prado, you'll come to the Plaza de Balboa and a large central fountain. Just past the fountain, El Prado ends in a bridge that crosses over Park Boulevard to a perfectly tended rose garden and a seemingly wild cactus grove.

To the right of the Plaza de Balboa fountain, on the same side of the
★ 3 road as the Casa de Balboa, the **Reuben H. Fleet Space Theater and Science Center** features clever interactive exhibits that teach children and adults about scientific principles. The huge screen of the world's first IMAX Dome Theater premieres such exhilarating nature and science films as "Destiny in Space," which makes viewers feel as though they'd gone along on the 1993 expedition that fixed the ailing Hubble Space Telescope. At night, the Laserium presents laser shows set to rock music. ☎ *619/238–1233. Science Center* ☛ *$2.50 adults, $1.25 children 5–15 or included with price of theater ticket. Space Theater tickets: $6 adults, $4.50 senior citizens, $3.50 children 5–15; laser shows: $7.50 adults, $6 senior citizens, $5 children 5–15.* ⏲ *Mon., Tues. 9:30–6; Sun., Wed., Thurs. 9:30–9; Fri., Sat. 9:30 AM–10 PM.*

To the south, past the parking lots of the Reuben H. Fleet Space The-
4 ater, is the **Centro Cultural de la Raza,** an old water tower converted into a cultural center focusing on Mexican, Native American, and Chicano arts. Attractions include a gallery with rotating exhibits and a theater, as well as a permanent collection of mural art, a fine example of which may be seen on the tower's exterior. ☎ *619/235–6135.* ☛ *Free.* ⏲ *Wed.–Sun. noon–5.*

Across the Plaza de Balboa fountain from the Reuben H. Fleet Space
Theater and Science Center, a short flight of steps will take you up to
5 the **San Diego Natural History Museum,** which features displays on the plants and animals of southern California and Mexico. Children seem particularly impressed by the dinosaur bones and the live-insect zoo. The Hall of Mineralogy hosts an impressive collection of gems. ☎ *619/232–3821. Admission: $4 adults, $3 senior citizens and military personnel, $2 children 6–17.* ⏲ *Daily 9:30–4:30, until 6:30 Thurs.*

6 In the next section of El Prado is the graceful **Botanical Building.** Built for the 1915 exposition, the latticed, open-air nursery houses more than 500 types of tropical and subtropical plants. The orchid collection is stunning, and there are benches beside cool, miniature waterfalls for resting in the shade. The Lily Pond, filled with giant koi fish and blooming water lilies, is popular with photographers. ☎ *619/235–1116.* ☛ *Free.* ⏲ *Fri.–Wed. 10–4.*

7 On the other side of the Lily Pond is the only privately owned building in the park, operated by the Putnam Foundation. The small **Timken Museum of Art** houses a selection of minor works by major European and American artists, as well as a fine collection of Russian icons. ☎ *619/239–5548.* ☛ *Free.* ⌚ *Oct.–Aug., Tues.–Sat. 10–4:30, Sun. 1:30–4:30.*

8 Just behind the Timken on the Plaza de Panama, the **San Diego Museum of Art** is known primarily for its Spanish Baroque and Renaissance paintings, including works by El Greco, Goya, Rubens, and Van Ruisdale. The museum also has strong holdings of Southeast Asian art, Indian miniatures, and contemporary California art, and its Baldwin M. Baldwin wing displays more than 100 pieces by Toulouse-Lautrec. An interactive computer gallery lets you locate the highlights of the museum's holdings on screen and custom-design a tour based on your interests. An outdoor Sculpture Garden exhibits both traditional and modern pieces in a striking natural setting. ☎ *619/232–7931.* ☛ *$6 adults, $5 senior citizens, $2 students and children 6–17.* ⌚ *Tues.–Sun. 10–4:30.*

9 If you get back on El Prado and continue east, you'll come to the **Museum of Man,** located under the California Tower. Exhibits focus on southwestern, Mexican, and South American cultures; in 1993, the museum acquired a collection of ancient Egyptian artifacts. In the "Lifestyles and Ceremonies" section, high-tech gadgetry is employed in displays on biology, reproduction, and culture, offering a fascinating look at the costumes and rituals of San Diego's many ethnic communities. ☎ *619/239–2001.* ☛ *$4 adults, $2 children 13–18, $1 children 6–12.* ⌚ *Daily 10–4:30.*

10 The **Simon Edison Centre for the Performing Arts** (☎ 619/239–2255 or 619/23–GLOBE), including the Cassius Carter Centre Stage, the Lowell Davies Festival Theatre, and the Old Globe Theatre, sits beside the Museum of Man under the California Tower. Originally devoted to Shakespearean theater, the Globe now also holds first-rate productions by other playwrights, too. All three theaters are small and intimate, and evening performances on the outdoor stages are particularly enjoyable during the summer.

11 Across the Prado and back toward the Museum of Art, the **House of Charm** has been closed for a two-year renovation but by November 1995 should be the new home for the Mingei International Museum of Folk Art. The Mingei will share the space with rehearsal halls for the Old Globe Theater, and with the House of Charm's original tenant, the San Diego Art Institute, currently holding its shows in Mission Valley Shopping Center (1640 Camino del Rio N, Suite 1368, ☎ 619/220–4800 for information on hours).

At the Plaza de Panama parking lot, west of the Art Institute, another road heads south from El Prado. It's divided by a long island of flow-
12 ers as it curves around the **Spreckels Organ Pavilion** and the 4,445-pipe Spreckels Organ, believed to be the largest outdoor pipe organ in the world. You can hear this impressive instrument at one of the concerts offered at 2 PM on Sunday afternoons year-round. On summer evenings, local military bands, gospel groups, and barbershop quartets hold concerts, and at Christmas, the park's massive Christmas tree and life-size nativity display turn the pavilion into a seasonal wonderland. ☎ *619/226–0819.* ☛ *Free.* ⌚ *Fri.–Sun. 10–4.*

Northeast of the Organ Pavilion, the first phase of a new **Japanese Friendship Garden** includes an exhibit house, a traditional sand-and-stone garden, and a picnic area with a view of the canyon below. ☎ *619/232–2780.* ☛ *$2 adults; $1 senior citizens, military personnel, visitors with disabilities, students, and ages 7–18.* ⏲ *Fri.–Sun. and Tues. 10–4.*

13 To the right of the organ pavilion, on Pan American West road, the **House of Pacific Relations** (☎ 619/234–0739) is really a cluster of stucco cottages representing 31 foreign countries. The buildings are open on Sunday from 12:30–4:30 PM; from March through October, ethnic song and dance performances are held on the outdoor stage at 2 PM (check the schedule at the park information center).

14 Farther west, in the building used as the Palace of Transportation for the 1935–36 exposition, the **San Diego Automotive Museum** maintains a large collection of vintage cars and motorcycles and has an ongoing automobile restoration program. ☎ *619/231–2886.* ☛ *$5 adults, $4 senior citizens and active military, $2 children 6–17.* ⏲ *Daily 10–4:30.*

15 The southern road ends at the Pan American Plaza and the **San Diego Aerospace Museum and International Aerospace Hall of Fame.** Looking unlike any other structure in the park, the sleek, streamlined edifice was commissioned by the Ford Motor Company for the 1935–36 exposition; at night, with a line of blue neon outlining it, the round building looks like a landlocked UFO. Exhibits about aviation and aerospace pioneers line the rotunda, and a collection of real and replicated aircraft fills the center. ☎ *619/234–8291.* ☛ *$5 adults, $4.50 senior citizens, $1 children 6–17.* ⏲ *Daily 10–4:30.*

Next to the aerospace center, the **Starlight Bowl** (☎ 619/544–7800 or 619/544–STAR) presents live musicals during the summer on its outdoor stage; actors freeze in their places when planes roar overhead on their way to Lindbergh Field.

Fronting Park Boulevard is Balboa Park's most famous attraction, the
★ 16 100-acre **San Diego Zoo.** More than 3,200 animals of 777 species roam in expertly crafted habitats that spread down into, around, and above the natural canyons. Equal attention has been paid to the flora and the fauna, and the zoo is an enormous botanical garden with one of the world's largest collections of subtropical plants.

From the moment you walk through the entrance and face the swarm of bright pink flamingos and blue peacocks, you know you've entered a rare pocket of natural harmony. Exploring the zoo fully requires the stamina of a healthy hiker, but open-air trams that run throughout the day allow visitors to see 80% of the exhibits on their 3-mile tour. The animals are attuned to the buses and many like to show off; the bears are particularly fine performers, waving and bowing to their admirers. The Skyfari ride, which soars 170 feet above ground, gives a good overview of the zoo's layout and a marvelous panorama of the park, downtown San Diego, the bay, and the ocean, far past the Coronado Bridge.

Still, the zoo is at its best when you can wander the paths that climb through the huge enclosed Scripps Aviary, where brightly colored tropical birds swoop between branches just inches from your face. The Gorilla Tropics exhibit, beside the aviary, is one of the zoo's latest ventures into bioclimatic zone exhibits, where animals live in enclosed environments modeled on their native habitats. Throughout the zoo, walkways wind over bridges and past waterfalls ringed with tropical ferns; giant elephants in a sandy plateau roam so close you're tempted to pet them. The San Diego Zoo houses the only koalas outside Australia and three rare golden monkeys number among its impressive collection of endangered species; a small two-headed snake named Thelma and Louise holds court in the reptile house.

The Children's Zoo is worth a visit, no matter what your age. Goats and sheep beg to be petted and are particularly adept at snatching bag lunches, while bunnies and guinea pigs seem willing to be fondled endlessly. In the nursery windows, you can see baby lemurs and spider monkeys playing with Cabbage Patch kids, looking much like the human babies peering from strollers through the glass.

The Wedgeforth Bowl, a 3,000-seat amphitheater, holds various animal shows throughout the day, occasionally hosted by the zoo's ambassador of goodwill, Joan Embery, whose frequent appearances on Johnny Carson's *Tonight Show,* usually with some charming critter, made the San Diego Zoo a household name.

The zoo's simulated Asian rain forest, Tiger River, brings together 10 exhibits with more than 35 species of animals. As spectacular as the tigers, pythons, and water dragons are, they seem almost inconsequential among the $500,000 collection of exotic trees and plants. The mist-shrouded trails winding down a canyon into Tiger River pass by fragrant jasmine, ginger lilies, and orchids, giving the visitor the feeling of descending into a South American jungle. In Sun Bear Forest, playful cubs constantly claw apart the trees and shrubs that serve as a natural playground for climbing, jumping, and general rowdiness.

At the zoo's newest habitat, Hippo Canyon—a 2-acre African rain forest opened at the base of Tiger River in 1995—you can watch the huge but surprisingly graceful beasts frolicking underwater. However, these newcomers, along with the other zoo locals, are likely to be overshadowed for a while by two glamorous overseas visitors who arrived in the spring: Shi Shi and Bay Yun, a pair of giant pandas on 12-year loan from the People's Republic of China.

In many ways also a self-sustaining habitat for humans, the zoo rents strollers, wheelchairs, and cameras; it also has a first-aid office, a lost-and-found, two main gift shops, and an ATM. ☎ *619/234–3153.* ☛ *(including unlimited access to Skyfari ride and Children's Zoo): $13 adults, $6 children 3–11; bus tour: $3 adults, $2.50 children; senior citizens deluxe package (entrance and bus tour) $14.40; children under 12 free during Oct. Free entrance on Founder's Day, Oct. 3. D, MC, V.* ⏲ *Gates open fall–spring, daily 9–4 (visitors may remain until 5); summer, daily 9–9 (visitors may remain until 10).*

Old Town

Numbers in the margin correspond to points of interest on the Old Town San Diego map.

San Diego's Spanish and Mexican history and heritage are most evident in Old Town, just north of downtown at Juan Street, near the intersection of I–5 and I–8. Old Town didn't become a state historic park until 1968. Fortunately, private efforts kept the area's history alive until then, and a number of San Diego's oldest structures remain in good shape.

Although Old Town is often credited as being the first European settlement in southern California, the true beginnings took place overlooking Old Town from atop Presidio Park (*see below*). There, Father Junípero Serra established the first of California's missions, San Diego de Alcalá, in 1769. Some of San Diego's Native Americans, called the

San Diegueños by the Spaniards, were forced to abandon their semi-nomadic lifestyle and live at the mission. They were expected to follow Spanish customs and adopt Christianity as their religion, but they resisted these impositions fiercely; of all the California missions, San Diego de Alcalá was the least successful in carrying out conversions. For security reasons, the mission was built on a hill, but it didn't have an adequate water supply, and food became scarce as the number of Native Americans and Spanish soldiers occupying the site increased.

In 1774, the hilltop was declared a Royal Presidio, or fortress, and the mission was moved to its current location along the San Diego River, 6 miles east of the original site. Losing more of their traditional grounds and ranches as the mission grew along the riverbed, the Native Americans attacked and burned it in 1775, destroying religious objects and killing Franciscan padre Luis Jayme. Their later attack on the presidio was less successful, and their revolt was short-lived. By 1800, about 1,500 Native Americans were living on the mission's grounds, receiving religious instruction and adapting to Spanish ways.

The pioneers living within the presidio's walls were mostly Spanish soldiers, poor Mexicans, and mestizos of Spanish and Native American ancestry, many of whom were unaccustomed to farming San Diego's arid land. They existed marginally until 1821, when Mexico gained independence from Spain, claimed its lands in California, and flew the Mexican flag over the presidio. The Mexican government, centered some 2,000 miles away in Monterrey, stripped the missions of their landholdings, and an aristocracy of landholders began to emerge. At the same time, settlers were beginning to move down from the presidio to what is now called Old Town.

A rectangular plaza was laid out along today's San Diego Avenue to serve as the settlement's center. In 1846, during the war between Mexico and the United States, a detachment of marines raised the U.S. flag over the plaza on a pole said to have been a mainmast. The flag was torn down once or twice, but by early 1848, Mexico had surrendered California, and the U.S. flag remained. In 1850, San Diego became an incorporated city, with Old Town as its center.

Old Town's historic buildings are clustered around **Old Town Plaza,** bounded by Wallace Street on the west, Calhoun Street on the north, Mason Street on the east, and San Diego Avenue on the south; you can see the presidio from behind the cannon by the flagpole. These days, the plaza is a pleasant place for resting and regrouping as you plan your tour of Old Town and watch other visitors stroll by; art shows often fill the lawns around the plaza. San Diego Avenue is closed to traffic here, and the cars are diverted to Juan and Congress streets, both of which are lined with shops and restaurants. There are a number of free parking lots on the outskirts of Old Town, but they fill quickly. By the summer of 1996, the San Diego trolley should stop here; in the meantime, if you plan to visit on the weekend, come early to find a spot.

★ ❶ The **Old Town San Diego State Historic Park** office is in the **Robinson-Rose House,** on the west (Wallace Street) side of the plaza. This was the original commercial center of old San Diego, housing railroad offices, law offices, and the first newspaper press; one room has been restored and outfitted with period furnishings. Park rangers now show films and distribute information from the living room. An excellent free walking tour of the park leaves from here daily at 2 PM, weather permitting. From 10 to 1 every Wednesday and the first Saturday of the month, park staff and volunteers in period costume give cooking and crafts demonstrations at the Machado y Stewart adobe; adjacent to the Bandini House near Juan Street, you can watch a blacksmith hammering away at his anvil, starting at 10 every Wednesday and Saturday. *4002 Wallace St., ☎ 619/220–5422. ⊙ Daily 10–5; closed Thanksgiving, Dec. 25, Jan. 1.*

Many of Old Town's buildings were destroyed in a huge fire in 1872, but after the site became a state historic park in 1968, efforts were begun to reconstruct or restore the structures that remained. Eight of the original adobes are still intact. The tour map available at the Robinson-Rose House gives details on all of the historic houses on the plaza and in its vicinity; a few of the more interesting ones are noted below. Most of the houses are open to visitors daily 10–4 and most do not charge admission.

2 On Mason Street, at the corner of Calhoun Street, **La Casa de Bandini** is one of the loveliest haciendas in San Diego. Built in 1829 by a Peruvian, Juan Bandini, the house served as Old Town's social center during Mexican rule. Albert Seeley, a stagecoach entrepreneur, purchased the home in 1869, built a second story, and turned it into the Cosmopolitan Hotel, a comfortable way station for travelers on the day-long trip south from Los Angeles. These days, Casa Bandini's colorful gardens and main-floor dining rooms house a popular Mexican restaurant.

3 Next door on Calhoun Street, the **Seeley Stables** became San Diego's stagecoach stop in 1867 and were the transportation hub of Old Town until near the turn of the century, when the Southern Pacific Railroad became the favored mode of travel. The stables now house a collection of horse-drawn vehicles, western memorabilia, and Native American artifacts. There is a $2 entry fee for adults, $1 for children 6–17.

4 This fee also covers admittance to **La Casa de Estudillo,** built on Mason Street in 1827 by the commander of the San Diego Presidio, Jose Maria Estudillo. The largest and most elaborate of the original adobe homes, it was occupied by members of the Estudillo family until 1887. After being left to deteriorate for some time, it was purchased and restored in 1910 by sugar magnate and developer John D. Spreckels.

5 On Twigg Street and San Diego Avenue, the **San Diego Union Newspaper Historical Museum** is in the Casa de Altamirano, a New England–style wood-frame house prefabricated in Maine and shipped around Cape Horn in 1851. The building has been restored to replicate the newspaper's offices of 1868, when the first edition of the *San Diego Union* was printed.

Also worth exploring in the plaza area are the **Dental Museum, Mason Street School, Wells Fargo Museum,** and the **San Diego Courthouse.** Ask at the visitor center for locations.

6 Northwest of the plaza lies the unofficial center of Old Town, the **Bazaar del Mundo** (☎ 619/296–3161), a shopping and dining enclave built to represent a colonial Mexican square. The central courtyard is always in blossom, with magenta bougainvillea, scarlet hibiscus, and irises, poppies, and petunias in season. Ballet Folklorico and flamenco dancers perform on weekend afternoons, and the bazaar frequently holds arts-and-crafts exhibits and Mexican festivals in the courtyard. Colorful shops specializing in Latin American crafts and unusual gift items border the square. Although many of the shops here have high-quality wares, prices can be considerably higher than those at shops on the other side of Old Town plaza; it's a good idea to do some comparative shopping before you make any purchases.

Bazaar del Mundo, **6**
Heritage Park, **7**
La Casa de Bandini, **2**
Junípero Serra Museum, **9**
La Casa de Estudillo, **4**
Presidio Park, **8**
Robinson-Rose House, **1**
San Diego Union Newspaper Historical Museum, **5**
Seeley Stables, **3**

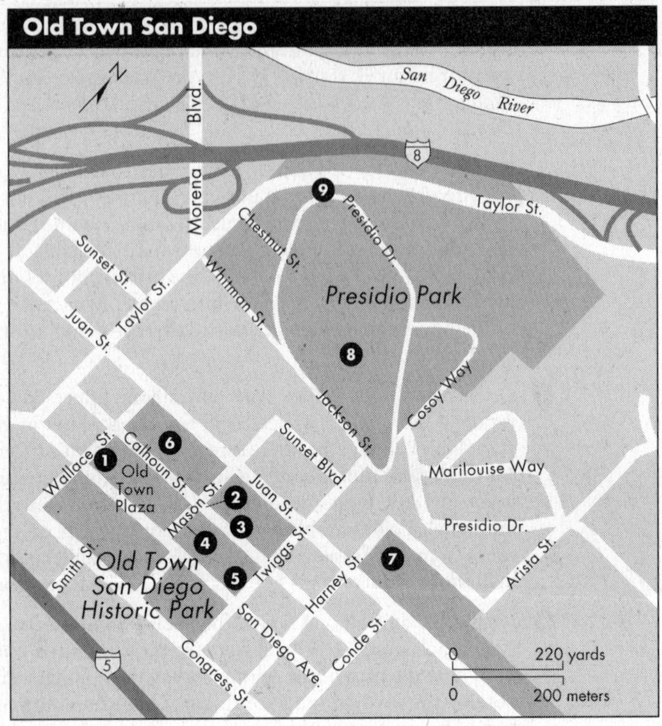

On San Diego Avenue beside the state park headquarters, **Dodson's Corner** is a modern retailer in a mid-19th-century setting; two of the shops in the complex, which sells everything from quilts and western clothing to pottery and jewelry, are reconstructions of homes that stood on the spot in 1848. Farther away from the plaza, art galleries and expensive gift shops are interspersed with curio shops, restaurants, and open-air stands selling inexpensive Mexican pottery, jewelry, and blankets.

7 **Heritage Park,** up the Juan Street hill near Harney Street, is the site of several grand Victorian homes and the town's first synagogue, all moved by the Save Our Heritage Organization (SOHO) from other parts of San Diego and restored. Some of the ornate houses may seem surprisingly colorful, but they are accurate representations of the bright tones of the era. The homes are now used for offices, shops, restaurants, and, in one case, a bed-and-breakfast inn. The climb up to the park is a bit steep, but the view of the harbor is great.

8 The rolling hillsides of the 40-acre **Presidio Park,** overlooking Old Town from the north end of Taylor Street, are popular with picnickers, and many couples have taken their wedding vows on the park's long stretches of lawn, some of the greenest in San Diego. You may encounter enthusiasts of a new sport, grass skiing, gliding over the grass and down the hills on wheels. Unless you love to climb, drive to the top of Presidio Park and then wander around on foot.

9 At the park's north end is the **Junípero Serra Museum,** which houses artifacts from San Diego's earliest days. *2727 Presidio Dr.,* ☎ *619/297–3258.* ☛ *$3 adults, children under 13 free.* ⏲ *Tues.–Sat. 10–4:30, Sun. noon–4:30.*

Mission Bay and Sea World

Numbers in the margin correspond to points of interest on the Mission Bay Area map.

San Diego's monument to sports and fitness, Mission Bay is a 4,600-acre aquatic park dedicated to action and leisure. Access to its 27 miles of bayfront beaches and 17 miles of ocean frontage is free. All you need for a perfect day is a bathing suit, shorts, and the right selection of playthings. Above the lawns facing I–5, the sky is flooded with the bright colors of huge, intricately made kites.

When explorer Juan Rodríguez Cabrillo first spotted the bay in 1542, he called it Baja Falso (False Bay) because the ocean-facing inlet led to acres of swampland inhospitable to boats and inhabitants. In the 1960s the city planners decided to dredge the swamp and build a bay with acres of beaches and lawns for play. Only 25% of the land was permitted to be commercially developed, and, as a result, only a handful of resort hotels break up the striking natural landscape.

❶ The **Visitor Information Center,** at the East Mission Bay Drive exit from I–5, is an excellent tourist resource for the bay and all San Diego. The center is a gathering spot for the runners, walkers, and exercisers who take part in group activities in the area. *2688 E. Mission Bay Dr., ☎ 619/276–8200. ⏲ Mon.–Sat. 9–5 (until 6 or 7 in summer), Sun. 9:30–4:30 (until 5:30 in summer).*

A 5-mile-long pathway runs through this section of the bay from the trailer park and miniature golf course, south past the high-rise Hilton Hotel to Sea World Drive. Playgrounds and picnic areas abound on the beach and low grassy hills of the park. Group gatherings, company picnics, and birthday parties are common along this stretch, where huge parking lots seem to expand to serve the swelling crowds on sunny days. On weekday evenings, a steady stream of joggers, bikers, and skaters releasing the stress from a day at the office line the path. In the daytime, swimmers, water-skiers, fishers, and boaters—some in single-person kayaks, others in crowded powerboats—vie for space in the water. The San Diego Crew Classic, which takes place in April, fills this section of the bay with teams from all over the country and college reunions, complete with flying school colors and keg beer. Swimmers should note signs warning about water pollution; certain areas of the bay are chronically polluted, and bathing is strongly discouraged.

❷ **Fiesta Island,** off East Mission Bay Drive and Sea World Drive, is a smaller, man-made playground popular with jet- and waterskiers. In July, the annual Over-the-Line Tournament, a competition involving a local variety of softball, attracts thousands of players and oglers, drawn by the teams' raunchy names and outrageous behavior.

Ingraham Street is another main drag through the bay, from the shores of Pacific Beach to Sea World Drive. The focal point of this part of the
❸ bay is **Vacation Isle.** You don't have to stay at the island's Princess Resort to visit its lushly landscaped grounds and bayfront restaurants. Ducks are as common as tourists here, and Vacation Isle's village is a great family playground. Powerboats take off from Ski Beach, across Ingraham Street, which is also the site of the Texaco Star Mart Cup hydroplane races, held in September. The noise from these boats is deafening, and the beach is packed from dawn till dark.

West Mission Bay Drive runs from the ocean beyond Mission Boulevard to Sea World Drive. The pathways along the Mission Beach side

Belmont Park, **4**
Fiesta Island, **2**
Sea World, **5**
Vacation Isle, **3**
Visitor Information Center, **1**

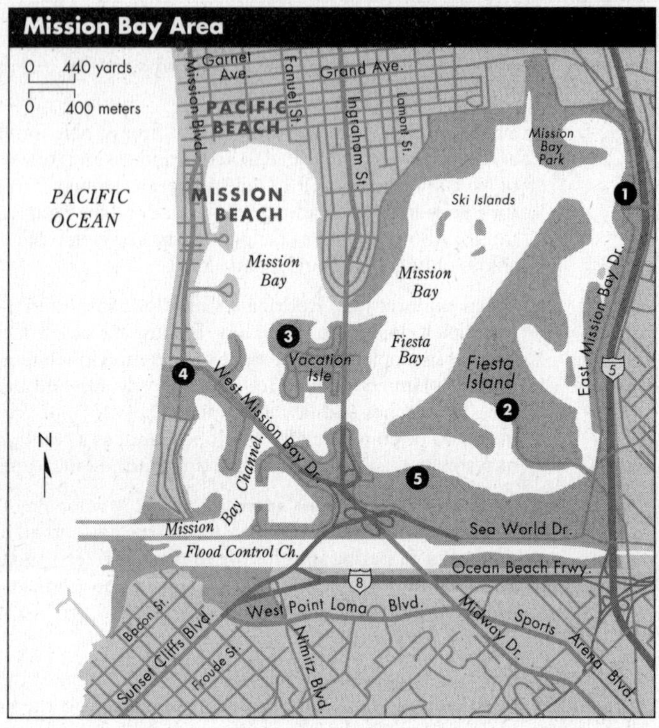

of the bay are lined with vacation homes, many of which can be rented
4 by the month. **Belmont Park,** once an abandoned amusement park at the corner of Mission Boulevard and West Mission Bay Drive, is now a shopping, dining, and recreation area between the bay and the Mission Beach boardwalk. Twinkling lights outline the refurbished old Belmont Park roller coaster on which screaming thrill-seekers ride. Nearby, younger riders enjoy the antique carousel, as well as the fresh cotton candy sold at the stand just next to it. The Plunge, an indoor freshwater swimming pool, has also been renovated and is open to the public, making Belmont Park a focal point for the ocean beach area.

Spread over 100 tropically landscaped bayfront acres, where a cool breeze
★ 5 always seems to rise from the water, **Sea World** is one of the world's largest marine-life amusement parks. A hospitality center to the right of the entrance reminds visitors that this popular attraction is owned by Anheuser-Busch: Adults can get two small free cups of beer in the building, which also houses a deli restaurant. Next door are stables for the huge Clydesdale horses that are hitched daily near the Penguin Encounter (*see below*).

The traditional favorite exhibit at Sea World is the Shamu show, with giant killer whales entertaining the crowds in a recently constructed stadium, but performing dolphins, sea lions, and otters at other shows also delight audiences with their antics. At another popular exhibit, the Penguin Encounter, a moving sidewalk passes through a glass-enclosed arctic environment, in which hundreds of emperor penguins slide over glaciers into icy waters (the penguins like it cold, so you may consider bringing a light sweater along for this one). Imaginative youngsters are especially fond of the Shark Encounter, which features a variety of species of the fierce-looking predators. The hands-on California Tide Pool exhibit gives visitors a chance to explore San Diego's indigenous marine life with a guide well versed in the habits of these creatures. At Forbidden Reef, you can feed bat rays and come nose to nose with creepy moray eels. Visitors to Rocky Point Preserve can interact with bottlenose dolphins and Alaskan sea otters that were treated after the 1989 *Exxon-Valdez* oil spill. Mission: Bermuda Triangle replicates the thrills of a submersible dive to the ocean bottom via a sophisticated motion-based film.

Not all the exhibits are water oriented. Children are entranced by Cap'n Kids' World, an enclosed playground with trampolines, swinging wood bridges, towers for climbing, and giant tubs filled with plastic balls. The Wings of the World show features a large assemblage of free-flying exotic birds. Those who want to head aloft themselves may consider the park's Sky Tower, a glass elevator that ascends 265 feet; the views of San Diego County from the ocean to the mountains are especially pleasing in early morning and late evening. A six-minute skytram ride that leaves from the same spot travels between Sea World and the Atlantis Hotel across Mission Bay. Tickets for the Sky Tower and the tram are $2 apiece or $3 for both.

Sea World is filled with souvenir shops and refreshment stands; it's difficult to come away from here without spending a lot of money on top of the hefty entrance and parking fees. Many hotels, especially those in the Mission Bay area, offer Sea World specials; some include price reductions, while others allow two days of entry for a single admission price—a good way to spread out what can otherwise be a very full day of activities. *Sea World Dr., at the west end of I–8, ☎ 619/226–3901 for recorded information or 619/226–3815. ☛ $28.95 adults, $20.95 children 3–11; parking $5. 90-min behind-the-scenes walking tours: $5 adults, $4 children 3–11, $3.50 senior citizens. D, MC, V. ⏲ Daily 10–dusk; extended hrs during summer. Call ahead to inquire about park hrs for the day you intend to visit.*

La Jolla

Numbers in the margin correspond to points of interest on the La Jolla map.

La Jollans have long considered their village to be the Monte Carlo of California, and with good cause. Its coastline curves into natural coves backed by verdant hillsides and covered with lavish homes worth millions. Though La Jolla is considered part of San Diego, it has its own postal zone and a coveted sense of class; old-monied residents mingle here with visiting film stars and royalty who frequent established hotels and private clubs. If development and construction have radically altered the once-serene and private character of the village, it has gained a cosmopolitan air that makes it a popular vacation resort for the international set.

The Native Americans called the site La Hoya, meaning "the cave," referring to the grottos dotting the shoreline. The Spaniards changed the name to La Jolla, meaning "the jewel," and its residents have cherished the name and its allusions ever since.

To reach La Jolla from I–5, take the Ardath Road exit if you're traveling north and drive slowly down Prospect Street so you can appreciate the breathtaking view. If you're heading south, get off at the La Jolla Village Drive exit, which will lead into Torrey Pines Road. For those who enjoy meandering, the best way to approach La Jolla from the south is to drive through Mission and Pacific beaches on Mission Boulevard, past the crowds of roller skaters, bicyclists, and sunbathers. The clutter and congestion ease up as the street becomes La Jolla Boulevard, where quiet neighborhoods with winding streets lead down to some of the best surfing beaches in San Diego. The boulevard here is lined with expensive restaurants and cafes, as well as a few take-out spots.

At the intersection of La Jolla Boulevard and Nautilus Street, turn to-
❶ ward the sea to reach **Windansea Beach,** made famous by Tom Wolfe's *The Pump House Gang,* which pokes fun at the So-Cal surfing culture. The surfing here is said to be as good as that in Hawaii. As you head north, streets curve past other neighborhood beaches where local surfers jealously guard their watery turf. Road signs along La Jolla Boulevard and Camino de la Costa direct drivers and bicyclists past some of La Jolla's loveliest homes—many designed by such famous architects as Frank Lloyd Wright and Irving Gill—toward the village.

As you approach the village, La Jolla Boulevard turns into Prospect Street, one of La Jolla's two main drags. The town's cultural center,
❷ the **Museum of Contemporary Art, San Diego** lies on the less trafficked southern end of Prospect. Housed in a remodeled Irving Gill home, the museum has a fine permanent collection of post-1950 art. Since early 1994, the facility has been undergoing expansion and renovation by (Robert) Venturi, Scott Brown and Associates. It is slated to reopen in early 1996. In the meantime, those interested in contemporary art must be content with visiting the much smaller downtown facility, opened in 1993 in the America Plaza complex (*see* Downtown and the Embarcadero, *above*). *700 Prospect St.,* ☎ *619/454–3541* ☛*: $4 adults, $1 senior citizens over 65 and students, free children under 14 and Fri. 5:30–8.* ⏲ *Tues.–Thurs. and weekends 10:30–5:30, Fri. 10:30–8.*

Continue north on Prospect and turn west onto Coast Boulevard to
❸ reach La Jolla's great natural coastal attraction, **Ellen Browning Scripps**
★ **Park** at the **La Jolla Cove.** Towering palms line the sidewalk along Coast Boulevard, where strollers in evening dress are as common as Frisbee-throwers. The **Children's Pool,** at the south end of the park, is aptly named for its curving beach and shallow waters protected by a seawall from strong currents and waves.

Just past the far northern point of the cove, in front of the La Jolla
❹ Cave and Shell Shop, a trail leads down to **La Jolla Caves**; it's some 133 steps down to the largest one, Sunny Jim Cave. *1325 Coast Blvd.,* ☎ *619/454–6080.* ☛ *To caves: $1.25 adults, 50¢ children 3–11.* ⏲ *Mon.–Sat. 10–5, Sun. 11–5, sometimes open later in summer.*

Like Prospect Street, Girard Avenue is lined with expensive shops and office buildings; it also hosts the village's only movie house, which tends to show nonmainstream films. The shopping and dining district has spread to Pearl and other side streets, where a steady parade of amblers and sightseers stroll about, chatting in many languages. Wall Street, a quiet tree-lined boulevard, was once the financial heart of La Jolla, but banks and investment houses can now be found throughout town. The La Jolla nightlife scene is an active one, with jazz clubs, piano bars, and watering holes for the elite younger set coming and going with the trends.

If you continue north of the cove on La Jolla Shores Drive, you'll come to the La Jolla Beach and Tennis Club, host of many tennis tourna-
❺ ments. **La Jolla Shores'** beaches are some of the finest in San Diego, with long stretches allotted to surfers or swimmers. Just beyond the beaches is the campus of the Scripps Institute of Oceanography, formerly the site of the marine institute's aquarium.

La Jolla

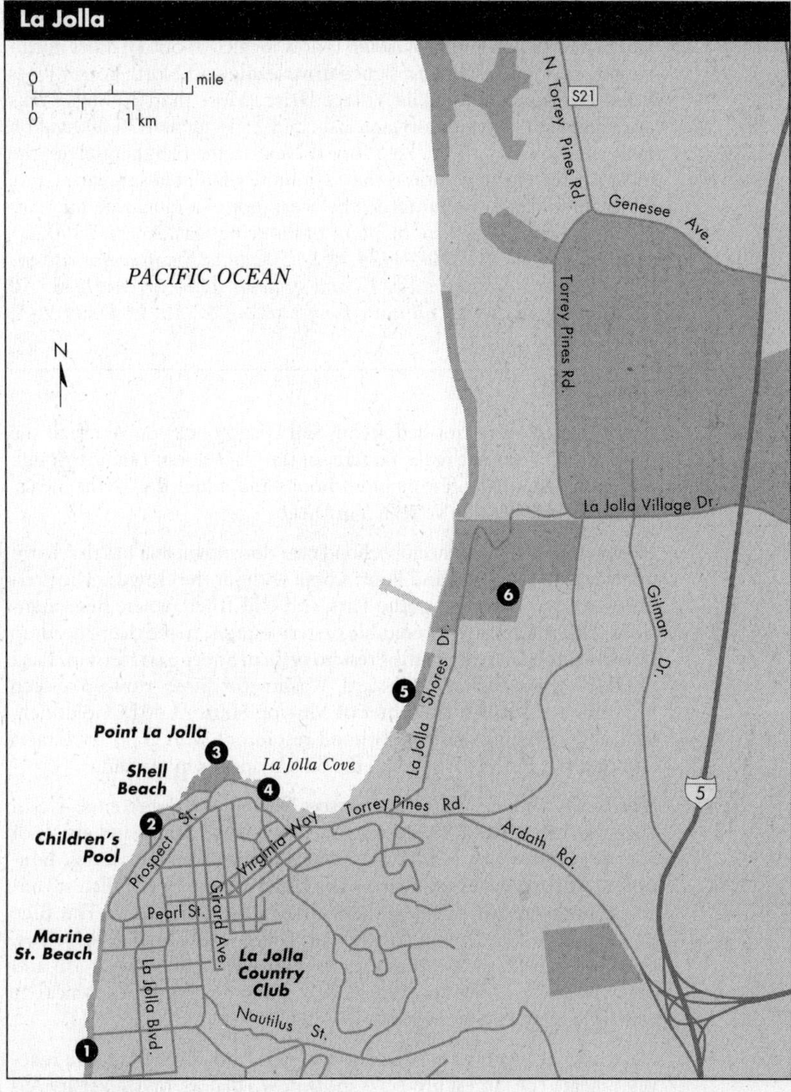

Ellen Browning Scripps Park, **3**
La Jolla Caves, **4**
La Jolla Shores, **5**
Museum of Contemporary Art, San Diego, **2**
Stephen Birch Aquarium-Museum, **6**
Windansea Beach, **1**

The largest oceanographic exhibit in the United States, Scripps's
6 **Stephen Birch Aquarium–Museum** is now located about 1½ miles northwest of its original site, on a signed drive leading off North Torrey Pines Road just south of La Jolla Village Drive. More than 30 huge tanks are filled with colorful saltwater fish, and a spectacular 70,000-gallon tank simulates a La Jolla kelp forest. Next to the fish themselves, the most interesting attraction is the 12-minute simulated submarine ride (children under 3 discouraged); the ocean noises and marine-life visuals are realistic almost to the point of inducing seasickness. *2300 Expedition Way,* ☎ *619/534–3474.* ☛ *$6.50 adults, $5.50 senior citizens 60 and older, $4.50 ages 13–17 and students with current ID, $3.50 children 3–12, active military free; parking $2.50.* ⏲ *Daily 9–5; closed Thanksgiving, Dec. 25.*

Off the Beaten Path

Don't think you've finished seeing San Diego once you've hit all the main attractions. The real character of the place doesn't shine through until you've visited a few neighborhoods and mingled with the locals. Then you can say you've seen San Diego.

Mission Hills is an older neighborhood near downtown that has the charm and wealth of La Jolla and Point Loma without the crowds. The prettiest streets are above Presidio Park and Old Town, where huge mansions with rolling lawns resemble eastern estates; to see them, head up Fort Stockton Drive from the Presidio or Juan Street past Heritage Park in Old Town to Sunset Boulevard. Washington Street runs up a steep hill from I–8 through the center of Mission Hills. At 4015 Goldfinch, visit the Gathering, a neighborhood restaurant with great breakfasts and outdoor tables for reading the Sunday paper in the sun.

Hillcrest, farther up Washington Street beginning at 1st Avenue, is San Diego's Castro Street, the center for the gay community and artists of all types. University, 4th, and 5th avenues are filled with cafés, boutiques, and excellent bookstores. The Guild Theater and Hillcrest Cinemas, both on 5th Avenue, show first-run foreign films. The Blue Door, next to the Guild, is one of San Diego's best small bookstores. Quel Fromage, a coffeehouse on University Avenue between 5th and 6th avenues, has long been the place to go to discuss philosophical or romantic matters over espresso.

Like most of San Diego, Hillcrest has been undergoing massive redevelopment. The largest project is the **Uptown District,** on University Avenue at 8th Avenue. This self-contained residential-commercial center was built to resemble an inner-city neighborhood, with shops and restaurants within easy walking distance of high-priced town houses.

Washington Street eventually becomes Adams Avenue, San Diego's Antiques Row, with shops displaying an odd array of antiques and collectibles. Adams Avenue leads into **Kensington** and **Talmadge,** two lovely old neighborhoods overlooking Mission Valley.

San Diego's large Vietnamese, Cambodian, and Korean communities congregate in **Linda Vista** and **North Park.** There are wonderful neighborhood restaurants here. The Mexican-American community is centered in **Barrio Logan,** under the Coronado Bridge. Chicano Park, just under the bridge supports, has huge murals depicting Mexican history, painted by artists from all over California.

SHOPPING

Shopping Districts

By Marael Johnson

Updated by Albert M. Columbo

San Diego's shopping areas are a mélange of self-contained megamalls, historic districts, quaint villages, funky neighborhoods, and chic suburbs.

Coronado

Across the bay, Coronado is accessible by car or ferry. **Orange Avenue,** in the center of town, has six blocks of ritzy boutiques and galleries. The elegant Hotel del Coronado, also on Orange Avenue, houses exclusive (and costly) specialty shops. **Old Ferry Landing,** where the San Diego ferry lands, is a waterfront center similar to Seaport Village.

Downtown

Horton Plaza, in the heart of center city, is a shopper's Disneyland—visually exciting, multilevel department stores; one-of-a-kind shops; fast-food counters; classy restaurants; a farmers' market; live theater; and cinemas. Surrounding Horton Plaza is the Gaslamp Quarter, a redevelopment area that features art galleries, antiques, and specialty shops housed in Victorian buildings and renovated warehouses.

The Paladion, just across 1st Avenue from Horton Plaza, is San Diego's answer to Rodeo Drive. This posh complex houses a collection of upscale boutiques—including Cartier, Tiffany, Gucci, Alfred Dunhill, Gianni Versace, and Salvatore Ferragamo.

Hotel Circle

The Hotel Circle area, northeast of downtown near I–8 and Freeway 163, has two major shopping centers. **Fashion Valley** and **Mission Valley Center** contain hundreds of shops, as well as restaurants, cinemas, and branches of almost every San Diego department store.

Kensington/Hillcrest

These are two of San Diego's older, established neighborhoods, situated several miles north and east of downtown. **Adams Avenue,** in Kensington, is Antiques Row. More than 20 dealers sell everything from postcards and kitchen utensils to cut glass and porcelain. The vicinity surrounding **University Avenue** at 5th Avenue (near the neon Hillcrest sign) is populated with designer clothes shops, specialty gift shops, bookstores, and music stores. **International Male** and **The Gap** are the anchor stores among boutiques like **California Man, Gamma Gamma, London Underground,** and **Tredair UK.** University Avenue is crossed one mile east by **Park Boulevard,** where you'll find **Babette Schwartz's** zany pop culture store and many "nostalgia" shops featuring clothing, accessories, furnishings, and bric-a-brac of the 1920s–60s. **Uptown District,** a shopping center on University Avenue, has the neighborhood's massive Ralph's grocery store, as well as several specialty shops.

La Jolla/Golden Triangle

La Jolla, about 15 miles northwest of downtown on the coast, is an ultra-chic, ultra-exclusive resort community. High-end and trendy boutiques line Girard Avenue and Prospect Street. Coast Walk, nestled along the cliffside of Prospect Street, offers several levels of sophisticated shops, galleries, and restaurants, as well as a spectacular ocean view. The Golden Triangle area, several miles east of coastal La Jolla, is served by **University Towne Centre,** between I–5 and Highway 805. This megamall features the usual range of department stores, specialty shops, sportswear chains, restaurants, and cinemas. Nearby **Costa Verde Centre,** on the corner of Genessee and La Jolla Village Drive, is an enormous strip mall of convenience stores and inexpensive eateries.

North County

This rapidly expanding area boasts an array of high-range shopping districts. One of the most attractive retail centers in the area, **Del Mar Plaza** (15th St. and Camino Del Mar) boasts a spectacular view of the Pacific and many excellent restaurants, boutiques, and specialty stores. Farther north in Encinitas is the **Lumberyard** (1st St. and Old Hwy. 1), an upscale strip mall where one can find everything from yogurt shops and stationery to sportswear and sushi. Inland from Del Mar in Escondido, one of the area's newest enclosed malls, **North County Fair** (Via Rancho Pkwy., east of Hwy. 15), is anchored by Nordstrom, Robinsons-May, and The Broadway.

Old Town

North of downtown, off I–5, this popular historic district is reminiscent of a colorful Mexican marketplace. Adobe architecture, flower-filled plazas, fountains, and courtyards highlight the shopping areas of **Bazaar del Mundo, La Esplanade,** and **Old Town Mercado,** where you will find international goods, toys, souvenirs, and arts and crafts.

Seaport Village

On the waterfront, a few minutes from downtown, **Seaport Village** offers quaint theme shops, restaurants, arts-and-crafts galleries, and commanding views of Coronado, the bridge, and passing ships.

Discount Outlet Shops

The Garment Center (1911 San Diego Ave., Old Town, ☎ 619/597–0788 or 619/453–6814). This is the place for manufacturers' end-of-season merchandise, discounted up to 60%.

Nordstrom Rack (Mission Valley Center, ☎ 619/296–0143). Top-of-the-line, end-of-season collections from Nordstrom department store, at about 50% off, are featured here.

San Diego Factory Outlet Center (Camino de la Plaza, San Ysidro, last exit off I–5 before the Mexican border, ☎ 619/690–2999). There are more than 25 discount factory outlets here, including Nike, Mikasa, Levi Strauss, and Eddie Bauer.

SPORTS, FITNESS, BEACHES

Participant Sports

Bicycling

On any given summer day, Old Highway 101, from La Jolla to Oceanside, looks like a freeway for cyclists. Never straying more than a quarter-mile from the beach, it is easily the most popular and scenic bike route around. Although the roads are narrow and winding, experienced cyclists like to follow Lomas Santa Fe Drive in Solana Beach east into beautiful Rancho Santa Fe, perhaps even continuing east on Del Dios Highway, past Lake Hodges, to Escondido. For more leisurely rides, Mission Bay, San Diego Harbor, and the Mission Beach boardwalk are all flat and scenic. For those who like to race on a track, San Diego even has a velodrome in Balboa Park. Call the Velodrome Office (☎ 619/296–3345) for more information. San Diego County also offers challenging mountain-bike trails. Local bookstores and camping stores sell trail guides.

Bikes can be rented at any number of places, including **Bicycle Barn** in Pacific Beach (746 Emerald St., ☎ 619/581–3665) and **Hamel's Action Sports Center** in Mission Beach (704 Ventura Pl, ☎ 619/488–5050). **Performance Bicycle Shop** (3619 Midway Dr., ☎ 619/223–5415) sells bicycles and bicycling accessories. A free map of all county bike paths is available from the local office of the **California Department of Transportation** (2829 Juan St., Old Town, ☎ 619/688–6699).

Diving

At La Jolla Cove, you'll find the **San Diego–La Jolla Underwater Park,** an ecological preserve. Farther north, off the south end of Black's Beach, the rim of **Scripps Canyon** lies in about 60 feet of water. The canyon plummets to more than 900 feet in some sections. Another popular diving spot is Sunset Cliffs in **Point Loma,** where a wide variety of sea life is relatively close to shore. Strong rip currents make it an area best enjoyed by experienced divers.

Diving equipment and boat trips can be arranged through **San Diego Divers Supply** (☎ 619/224–3439), **Ocean Enterprises** (☎ 619/565–6054), **Del Mar Ocean Sports** (☎ 619/792–1903) or at the several **Diving Locker** locations throughout the area. Spearfishing requires a license (available at most dive stores). For general diving information, contact the San Diego City Lifeguards' Office (☎ 619/221–8884).

Fishing

The Pacific Ocean is full of corbina, croaker, and halibut. No license is required to fish from a public pier, such as the Ocean Beach pier. A fishing license from the state Department of Fish and Game (☎ 619/525–4215), available at most bait-and-tackle stores, is required for fishing from the shoreline, although children under 15 won't need one. For general information on well-stocked freshwater lakes in the area, call 619/465–3474.

Several companies offer half-day, day, or multiday fishing expeditions in search of marlin, tuna, albacore, and other deep-water fish. **Fisherman's Landing** (☎ 619/221–8500), **H & M Landing** (☎ 619/222–1144), and **Seaforth Boat Rentals** (☎ 619/223–7584) are among the companies operating from San Diego. **Helgren's Sportfishing** (☎ 619/722–2133) offers trips from Oceanside Harbor.

Fitness

Many hotels have exercise rooms or full-scale health clubs. The dozen **Family Fitness Centers** in the area (including centers in Mission Valley, ☎ 619/281–5543; and Sports Arena/Point Loma area, ☎ 619/224–2902) allow nonmembers to use the facilities for a small fee.

Golf

Most public courses in the area offer an inexpensive current list of fees and charges for all San Diego courses. The **Southern California Golf Association** (☎ 818/980–3630 or 213/877–0901) publishes an annual directory with information on all member clubs. Another good resource for golfers is the **Southern California Public Links Information Service** (☎ 714/994–4747). A few choice courses are listed below:

PUBLIC COURSES

Coronado Golf Course (2000 Visalia Row, Coronado, ☎ 619/435–3121): 18 holes, driving range, equipment rentals, clubhouse. Views of San Diego Bay and the Coronado Bridge from the back nine holes on this good walking course make it very popular—and rather difficult to get on.

Mission Bay Golf Course (2702 N. Mission Bay Dr., San Diego, ☎ 619/490–3370): 18 holes, driving range, equipment rentals. A not-very-challenging executive (par 3 and 4) course, Mission Bay is lit for night play.

Rancho San Diego Golf Course (3121 Willow Glen Rd., El Cajon, ☎ 619/442–9891): 36 holes, driving range, equipment rentals. A good walking course, Rancho San Diego has nice putting greens and lots of cottonwood trees.

Redhawk Golf Course (45100 Redhawk Pkwy., Temecula, ☎ 909/695–1424 or 800/451–HAWK in CA): 18 holes, driving range, golf shop, snack bar. The extremely difficult design of this course will prove frustrating to those who are not experienced golfers, but experts should enjoy Redhawk.

Torrey Pines Municipal Golf Course (11480 N. Torrey Pines Rd., La Jolla, ☎ 619/452–3226): 36 holes, driving range, equipment rentals. Torrey Pines offers stunning views of the Pacific from every hole and is sufficiently challenging to host the Buick Invitational in February. It's not easy to get a good tee time, but every golfer visiting the area should try to play it at least once.

RESORTS

La Costa Resort and Spa (Costa del Mar Rd., Carlsbad, ☎ 619/438–9111 or 800/854–5000): 36 holes, driving range, clubhouse, equipment rental, pro shop. One of the premier golf resorts in southern California, La Costa hosts the annual PGA and Senior PGA Tournament of Champions in January. You'll find every golf amenity on the premises.

Singing Hills Country Club (3007 Dehesa Rd., El Cajon, ☎ 619/442–3425): 54 holes, driving range, equipment rentals. One of *Golf Digest*'s favorites, this lush, green course has lots of water hazards. Hackers will love the executive par-3 course; seasoned golfers can play the championship courses.

Horseback Riding

Holidays on Horseback (☎ 619/445–3997), in the East County town of Descanso, leads rides ranging from a few hours to a few days in the Cuyamaca Mountains. It rents special, easy-to-ride fox trotters to beginners. **Bright Valley Farm** (11990 Campo Rd., Spring Valley, ☎ 619/670–1861) is a wonderful place to ride. South of Imperial Beach, near the Mexican border, **Sandi's Rental Stables** (☎ 619/424–3124) leads rides through Border Field State Park.

In-Line Skating

The sidewalks at Mission Bay are perfect for rollerblading. You can rent Rollerblades at **Hamel's Action Sports Center** in Mission Beach (☎ 619/488–5050) and at the **Bicycle Barn** in Pacific Beach (☎ 619/581–3665).

Jogging

From downtown, the most popular run is along the Embarcadero, which stretches around the bay. There are nice, uncongested sidewalks through most of the area. Mission Bay, renowned for its wide sidewalks and basically flat landscape, may be the most popular jogging spot in San Diego. Trails head west around Fiesta Island from Mission Bay, providing distance as well as a scenic route. Del Mar has the finest running trails along the bluff; park your car near 15th Street and run south along the cliffs for a gorgeous view of the ocean. There are organized runs almost every weekend. For more information, call ***Competitor*** magazine (☎ 619/793–2711) or the **San Diego Track Club** (☎ 800/450–7382). **The Tinley Store** (1229 Camino Del Mar, ☎ 619/755–8015) has all the supplies and information you'll need for running in San Diego. Some tips: Don't run in bike lanes, and check the local newspaper's tide charts before heading to the beach.

Surfing

Beginners should paddle out at Mission, Pacific, Tourmaline, La Jolla Shores, Del Mar, or Oceanside Beach. Experienced surfers should hit Sunset Cliffs, the La Jolla reef breaks, Black's Beach, or Swami's (Sea Cliff Roadside Park) in Encinitas. Most public beaches have separate areas for surfers. Many local surf shops rent boards, including **Star Surfing Company** (☎ 619/273–7827) in Pacific Beach and **La Jolla Surf Systems** (☎ 619/456–2777) and **Hansen's** (☎ 619/753–6595) in Encinitas.

Swimming

The most spectacular pool in town is the **Mission Beach Plunge** (3115 Ocean Front Walk, ☎ 619/488–3110), in Belmont Park, where the public can swim weekdays 6–8 AM, noon–1, and 3:30–8, weekends 8–4. The fee is $2.25. The **Copley Family YMCA** (3901 Landis St., ☎ 619/283–2251) and the **Downtown YMCA** (500 W. Broadway Ave., ☎ 619/232–7451) are both centrally located.

Tennis

Public facilities in San Diego include **Morley Field** (☎ 619/295–9278), in Balboa Park, which has 25 courts, 19 of which are lighted. Nonmembers can make reservations after paying a nominal fee for the use of the courts; if you're lucky, a court may be available when you come in to pay the fee. The **La Jolla Recreation Center** (☎ 619/552–1658) offers 9 free public courts near downtown La Jolla, 5 of them lighted. There are 12 lighted courts at **Robb Field** (☎ 619/531–1563) in Ocean Beach, with a small day-use fee.

Hotel complexes with tennis facilities include the **Bahia Resort Hotel** (☎ 619/488–0551); **Hilton San Diego** (☎ 619/276–4010); the **Hotel del Coronado** (☎ 619/435–6611); the **Kona Kai Beach and Tennis Resort** (☎ 619/222–1191); the **LaCosta Resort and Spa** (☎ 619/438–9111); and the **Rancho Bernardo Inn and Country Club** (☎ 619/487–1611).

Water Sports

Mission Bay is one of the most popular waterskiing areas in southern California. Boats and equipment can be rented from **Seaforth Boat Rentals** (1641 Quivira Rd., near Mission Bay, ☎ 619/223–1681). Windsurfing rentals and instruction are available at the **Bahia Resort Hotel** (998 W. Mission Bay Dr., ☎ 619/488–0551) and other resorts in the Mission Bay area. **California Water Sports** (☎ 619/434–3089) has information about Jet Ski rentals and purchases.

Spectator Sports

For information on tickets to San Diego sports events, contact **Teleseat** (☎ 619/452–7328). **San Diego Jack Murphy Stadium** is at the intersection of I–8 and I–805.

Baseball

The National League **San Diego Padres** (☎ 619/283–4494) play from April into early October at San Diego Jack Murphy Stadium. Tickets range from $5 to $11 and are usually readily available.

Football

The NFL **San Diego Chargers** (☎ 619/280–2111) play at San Diego Jack Murphy Stadium August through December. The **San Diego State University Aztecs** compete in the Western Athletic Conference, with home games also at Jack Murphy.

Hockey

The **San Diego Gulls** (☎ 619/688–1800), competing in and dominating the International Hockey League, play October–April at the San Diego Sports Arena (☎ 619/224–4171), with ticket prices ranging from $6 to $15.50.

Horse Racing

Begun in the 1930s by Bing Crosby, Pat O'Brien, and their Hollywood cronies, the annual summer meeting of the **Del Mar Thoroughbred Club** (☎ 619/755–1141) on the Del Mar Fairgrounds attracts hordes of Beautiful People, along with the best horses and jockeys in the country. The meeting begins in July and continues through early September, every day except Tuesday. There's also a satellite wagering facility (*see* Excursion to the San Diego North Coast, *below*).

Beaches

San Diego's beaches are one of its greatest natural attractions. In some places, the shorefront is wide and sandy; in others, it's narrow and rocky or backed by impressive sandstone cliffs. You'll find beaches teeming with activities and deserted spots for romantic sunset walks. San Diego is a prime destination for surfers; the variety of breaks and their exposure to ocean swells make the surf off this portion of the Pacific Coast remarkably consistent and fun. For a surf and weather report, call 619/221–8884.

Overnight camping is not allowed on any San Diego city beaches, but there are campgrounds at some state beaches throughout the county; call 800/444–7275 for state beach camping reservations. Lifeguards are stationed at city beaches (from Sunset Cliffs to Black's Beach) in the summertime, but coverage in winter is provided by roving patrols only. Dogs are not permitted at most beaches in San Diego, and tickets for breaking the law can be very expensive. However, it is rarely a problem to bring your pet to isolated beaches during the winter.

Pay attention to all signs listing illegal activities; undercover police often patrol the beaches, carrying their ticket books in coolers. Glass is prohibited on all beaches, and fires are allowed only in fire rings or barbecues. Alcoholic beverages—including beer—are completely banned on some city beaches; others allow you to partake between 8 AM and 8 PM only. Check out the signs posted at the parking lots and lifeguard towers before you hit the shore with a six pack or some wine coolers. Imbibing in beach parking lots, on boardwalks, and in landscaped areas is always illegal; where drinking is permitted, stay on the sand. For more information on the beach-booze ban, call Pacific Beach Community Relations (☎ 619/581–9920) or Ocean Beach Community Relations (☎ 619/531–1540). For a general beach and weather report, phone 619/289–1212.

A selection of beaches, from south to north, is listed below. For information on Mission Bay, *see* Mission Bay and Sea World *in* Exploring, *above*.

South Bay

Border Field State Beach. The southernmost San Diego beach is different from the majority of California beaches. Located just north of the Mexican border, it is a marshy area with wide chaparrals and wildflowers, a favorite among horse riders and hikers. However, frequent sewage contamination from Tijuana makes the water dangerous for swimming. For this reason, the beach is often closed. There is ample parking, and there are rest rooms and fire rings. *Exit I–5 at Dairy Mart Rd. and head west along Monument Rd.*

South Beach. One of the few beaches where dogs are free to romp, this is a good spot for long, isolated walks. The often-contaminated water and rocky beach tend to discourage crowds. The downside: There are few facilities, such as rest rooms, and sewage contamination from Tijuana can create a health hazard at times. *Located at end of Seacoast Dr. Take I–5 to Coronado Ave. and head west on Imperial Beach Ave. Turn left onto Seacoast Dr.*

Imperial Beach. In July, this classic southern California beach is the site of one of the nation's largest annual sand-castle competitions. Surfers and swimmers flock here to enjoy the water, waves, and beach, which is an ideal playing field for the Frisbee games of the predominantly young crowd. There are lifeguards on duty during the summer, parking lots, food vendors nearby, and rest rooms. Note: Although the surf here can be excellent, this is another spot at which to be careful of sewage contamination. *Take Palm Ave. west from I–5 until it hits water.*

Coronado

Silver Strand State Beach. Farther north on the isthmus of Coronado (commonly mislabeled an island), Silver Strand was set aside as a state beach in 1932. The name is derived from the tiny silver seashells found in abundance near the water. The water is relatively calm, making this beach ideal for families. Four parking lots provide room for more than 1,500 cars. Parking is free from Labor Day through February; the rest of the year the cost is $4 per car. There is also an RV campground (cost: $14 per night) and a wide array of facilities but no hook-ups; spots are available on a first-come, first-served basis. ☎ *619/435–5184. Take the Palm Ave. exit from I–5 west to Hwy. 75; turn right and follow signs.*

Coronado Beach. With the famous Hotel del Coronado as a backdrop, this wide stretch of sandy beach is one of the largest and most picturesque in the county. It is surprisingly uncrowded on most days, since the locals go to the less touristy areas in the south or north. It's perfect for sunbathing or games of Frisbee and Smash Ball (played with paddles and a small ball). Parking can be a little difficult on the busiest days, but there are plenty of rest rooms and service facilities, as well as fire rings. The view (even for a brief moment) as you drive over the Coronado Bridge makes it a worthwhile excursion. *From bridge, turn left on Orange Ave. and follow signs.*

Point Loma

Sunset Cliffs. Beneath the jagged cliffs on the west side of the Point Loma peninsula is one of the more secluded beaches in the area, popular primarily with surfers and locals. The tide goes out each day to reveal tidal pools teeming with life at the south end of the peninsula, near Cabrillo Point. Farther north, the often-large waves attract surfers and the lonely coves attract sunbathers. Stairs are available at the foot of Bermuda and Santa Cruz avenues, but much of the access is limited to treacherous cliff trails. There are no facilities. Your visit here will be much more enjoyable at low tide; check the local newspaper for tide schedules. *Take I–8 west to Sunset Cliffs Blvd. and head south.*

San Diego

Ocean Beach. The north end of this beach, past the second jetty, is known as Dog Beach because it's the only one within the San Diego city limits that allows canines to romp around without a leash. The south end of Ocean Beach, near the pier, is a hangout for surfers and transients. Much of the area, though, is a haven for local volleyball players, sunbathers, and swimmers. You'll find food vendors and fire rings here; limited parking is available. *Take I–8 west to Sunset Cliffs Blvd. and head south. Turn right on Voltaire St., West Point Loma Blvd., or Newport Ave.*

Mission Beach. The boardwalk stretching along Mission Beach is popular with strollers, roller skaters, and bicyclists cruising at the posted 15-mph speed limit. Surfers, swimmers, and volleyball players congregate at the south end, which tends to get extremely crowded, especially on hot summer days. Toward the north end, near the Belmont Park roller coaster, the beach narrows and the water grows rougher—and the crowd gets even thicker. The refurbished Belmont Park is now a shopping and dining complex. Parking can be a challenge, but there are plenty of rest rooms and restaurants in the area. *Exit I–5 at Garnet Ave. and head west to Mission Blvd. Turn south and look for parking.*

Pacific Beach. The boardwalk turns into a sidewalk here, but there are still bike paths and picnic tables running along the beachfront. The beach is a favorite for families, teens, and surfers alike. Parking can be a problem, although there is a small lot at the foot of Ventura Place. *Exit I–5 at Garnet Ave. and head west to Mission Blvd. Turn north and look for parking.*

La Jolla

The beaches of La Jolla combine unusual beauty with good fishing, exciting scuba diving, and excellent surf. On the down side, they are very crowded and have limited parking facilities. Don't even think about bringing your pet—dogs are not even allowed on the sidewalks above some La Jolla beaches.

Tourmaline Surfing Park and **Windansea Beach.** These La Jolla beaches are two of the top surfing spots in the area. Tourmaline has the better parking area of the two and is more hospitable to tourists. The surf at Windansea is world-class, but the local crowd can be less than welcoming. *Take Mission Blvd. north (it turns into La Jolla Blvd.) and turn west on Tourmaline St. (for the surfing park) or Nautilus St. (for Windansea Beach).*

Marine Street Beach. This is an ideal stretch of sand for sunbathing and beach games. *Accessible from Marine St. off La Jolla Blvd.*

Children's Pool. For the tykes, a circular sea wall preserves this shallow lagoon. Small waves and no riptide provides a safe, if crowded, haven. *Follow La Jolla Blvd. north. When it forks, take the left, Coast Blvd.*

Shell Beach. Just north of the Children's Pool is a small cove, accessible by stairs, with a relatively secluded and beautiful beach. The exposed rocks just off the coast here have been designated a protected habitat for seals; you can watch them sun themselves and frolic in the water. *Continue along Coast Blvd. north from the Children's Pool.*

La Jolla Cove. Just north of Shell Beach is La Jolla Cove, one of the prettiest spots in the world. A beautiful, palm-tree-lined park sits on top of cliffs formed by the incessant pounding of the waves. At low tide the tidal pools and cliff caves provide an exciting destination for explorers. Divers explore the underwater delights of the San Diego–La Jolla Underwater Park, an ecological reserve. The cove is also a favorite of rough-water swimmers, for whom buoys mark distances. The beach below the cove is beautiful and great for kids over eight years old. *Follow Coast Blvd. north to signs, or take the La Jolla Village Dr. exit from I–5, head west to Torrey Pines Rd., turn left and drive down hill to Girard Ave. Turn right and follow signs.*

La Jolla Shores. This is one of the most popular and overcrowded beaches in the county. On holidays, such as Memorial Day, all access routes are usually closed. The lures are a wide sandy beach; fun surf for boogie-boarders, body-surfers, and regular surfers alike; and a concrete boardwalk paralleling the beach. There is also a wide variety of facilities, from posh restaurants to snack shops, within walking distance. Go early to get a parking spot. *From I–5 take La Jolla Village Dr. west and turn left onto La Jolla Shores Dr. Head west to Camino del Oro or Vallecitos St. Turn right and look for parking.*

Black's Beach. The late 1970s prohibition against public nudity doesn't stop nudists from frequenting this isolated beach. The cliffs should be avoided because of recent weakening by storms. Access along the shore should coincide with low tides. The powerful waves attract surfers, and secluded trails attract nudist nature lovers. There are no lifeguards on duty, and strong ebb tides are common: Only experienced swimmers should take the plunge. *Take Genessee Ave. west from I–5 and follow signs to glider port; easier access, via a paved path, is available on La Jolla Farms Rd., but parking there is limited to 2 hrs.*

Del Mar

Torrey Pines State Beach. This is one of the easiest and most comfortable beaches to visit in the area. The large parking lot (☛ $4) is rarely full. There is year-round lifeguard service, and fire rings are available for beach parties. Torrey Pines tends to get crowded during the summer, but more isolated spots under the cliffs are within a short walk in either direction. Exotic trails up into the hillside park offer lovely hikes. ☎ *619/755–2063. Take the Carmel Valley Rd. exit west from I–5.* ⏲ *Daily 9–sunset.*

Del Mar Beach. The numbered streets of Del Mar, from 15th to 29th, end at a wide, sandy beach, popular with volleyball players, surfers, and sunbathers. Although parking can be a problem on nice summer days, access is relatively easy, and the beach and water are both extremely comfortable. The portions of Del Mar south of 15th Street are lined with beautiful cliffs and are rarely crowded. *Take the Via de la Valle exit from I–5 west to Old Hwy. 101 (also known as Camino del Mar in Del Mar) and turn left.*

DINING

By Kathryn Shevelow

Updated by Albert M. Columbo

When it comes to cuisine, San Diego is not Los Angeles or San Francisco and perhaps will never be: There has not yet developed among San Diegans the kind of exacting culinary standards one finds in the demanding and vociferous residents of a truly great food city. In days gone by, "good food," with few exceptions, was the quasi-Continental fare served at the kind of indeterminate Chamber of Commerce restaurant humorist Calvin Trillin calls "La Maison de la Casa House."

Things have begun to change, though, with the excitement generated by the redevelopment of the downtown area. A substantial nightlife scene—something San Diego lacked before—has evolved, and with it has come a proliferation of clubs and good restaurants that is nothing short of astonishing. In addition to restaurants specializing in California cuisine and European (especially Italian) cooking, various immigrant groups have recently arrived in San Diego, bringing their culinary traditions with them. The city now boasts a rich selection of Latin American, Middle Eastern, and Asian cuisines. The many Vietnamese restaurants throughout the city are particularly noteworthy. Excellent Vietnamese restaurants, along with their equally good Chinese, Korean, and Japanese counterparts, can be found along Convoy Street and Linda Vista Road in Kearny Mesa; **Pho Hoa** (6921 Linda Vista Rd., ☎ 619/492–9108) and **Vietnam Seafood Restaurant** (6931 Linda Vista Rd., ☎ 619/292–8889) are just two of many.

What to Wear

San Diego is an informal city. The advised attire at most of the restaurants listed below is casual. Only one of the restaurants listed below requires men to wear ties.

CATEGORY	COST*
$$$$	over $50
$$$	$30–$50
$$	$20–$30
$	under $20

**per person for a three-course meal, excluding drinks, service, and 7¾% tax*

American

DOWNTOWN

$$$ ★ **Rainwater's.** This tony restaurant is as well known around town for the size of its portions as for the high quality of its cuisine. The menu includes a number of meat and fish dishes, but this is really the place to come if you crave a perfectly done, thick and tender steak. All the entrées are accompanied by such tasty side dishes as shoestring potatoes, onion rings, and creamed corn. The food is pricey, but the satisfaction level is high. ✕ *1202 Kettner Blvd. (2nd floor),* ☎ *619/233–5757. Reservations advised. AE, DC, MC, V. No lunch weekends.*

$$ **California Café.** On the top level of Horton Plaza, this stylish dining room with lots of windows and potted palms serves stylish California cuisine to match. The imaginative menu, which changes daily, may include smoked duck ravioli with basil and goat cheese, soba noodle salad with lemon wasabi dressing and wild mushrooms, or New Mexican chili fettuccine with shrimp and smoked corn. The crusty Italian bread is baked daily on the premises. ✕ *Upper Level, Horton Plaza,* ☎ *619/238–5440. Reservations advised. AE, D, DC, MC, V.*

$ **Croce's.** A tribute to the late singer-songwriter Jim Croce run by his widow, Ingrid, the popular Croce's used to be known more for its nightly jazz and pleasant, clublike ambience than for its cuisine. But with a new chef in the kitchen, Croce's now complements its high-quality music with high-quality food. The menu offers good salads and a range of appealing entrées; try the swordfish in grape leaves or the chicken cakes. Even those who are not jazz aficionados will find this restaurant a good bet for late-night dining, since Croce's kitchen doesn't close until midnight. ✕ *802 5th Ave.,* ☎ *619/233–4355. Reservations accepted. AE, D, DC, MC, V.*

$ **Dakota Grill & Spirits.** Housed in a historic building restored to a posh grandeur, Dakota's ambience is nothing short of elegant. Diners indulge themselves on a sensational American mixed-grill cuisine. House favorites are shrimp Tasso (shrimp sautéed with Cajun ham, sweet peas, and ancho-chile cream); basil-garlic linguine with steamed mussels; and Cowboy Steak (marinated skirt steak with smoked tomato salsa). Don't miss the homemade desserts like Key Lime pie or chocolate pecan torte covered in caramel sauce. ✕ *901 5th Ave. at E St.,* ☎ *619/234–5554. Reservations advised. AE, D, DC, MC, V. No lunch weekends.*

UPTOWN

$ **Hamburger Mary's.** Kin of the gay franchise, this outdoor restaurant is as popular for its casual atmosphere as for its burgers. Enjoy the Hawaiian-style Diamond Back Burger, the hearty Billy Burger, the savory Veggie Burger, or the delicious prime rib. Also enjoy the great domestic and imported beers like Warthog, Heineken, and Corona. ✕ *308 University Ave., Hillcrest,* ☎ *619/491–0400. No reservations. AE, MC, V.*

$ **Hob Nob Hill.** This comforting restaurant is still under the same ownership and management as it was when it started in 1944; with its dark wood booths and patterned carpets, Hob Nob Hill seems suspended in the 1950s. But you don't need to be a nostalgia buff to appreciate the bargain-priced American home cooking—dishes such as pot roast, fried chicken, and corned beef like your mother never really made. Reservations are particularly suggested on Sunday, when everyone comes for the copious breakfasts. ✕ *2271 1st Ave.,* ☎ *619/239–8176. Reservations accepted. AE, D, MC, V.*

LA JOLLA

$ **Choices.** Off the beaten path and rather low on atmosphere—it's in the Sports and Health Center at the north of the Scripps Clinic complex—this small cafeteria has indoor and outdoor tables with an ocean view, and very tasty, low-fat, low-cholesterol food. There's an excellent all-you-can-eat salad bar and a daily selection of healthy sandwiches and entrées. Choices is open for breakfast and lunch during the week but closes at 7 PM Monday–Thursday; it shuts down at 3 PM on Friday but reopens at 6 PM for dinner and folk music. ✕ *10820 N. Torrey Pines Rd.,* ☎ *619/554–3663. No reservations. AE, MC, V. Closed weekends.*

$ **Hard Rock Cafe.** This high-energy shrine to rock-and-roll and American food cranks its music up to ear-shattering decibels and hangs rock memorabilia on every available inch of wall space. This is not a place to come for intimate—or audible—conversation, but the burgers are fine. ✕ *909 Prospect St.,* ☎ *619/454–5101. No reservations. AE, DC, MC, V.*

$ **Pannikin Brockton Villa.** Connected with the local chain of trendy coffeehouses, this informal restaurant in a restored beach house overlooks La Jolla Cove and the ocean. Come here for good coffee, decent muffins and pastries, and stunning views. You'll have to fight the crowds on sunny weekends. The Pannikin opens for breakfast; call ahead for dinner hours (summer only). ✕ *1235 Coast Blvd.,* ☎ *619/454–7393. No reservations. AE, MC, V.*

Belgian

BEACHES

$$–$$$ **Belgian Lion.** The lace curtains at the windows of a rather forbidding white building, partially enclosed by a high wall, are the only hints of the cozy dining room within, where hearty Belgian dishes have been served to discerning diners for years. Among the signature dishes is the cassoulet, a wonderful rich stew of white beans, lamb, pork, sausage, and duck that makes you feel protected from the elements (even in San Diego, where there aren't many elements to be protected from). Lighter meals include sea scallops with braised Belgian endive or steamed

Dining
Anthony's Star of the Sea Room, **74**
Athens Market, **75**
Banana Bungalow, **31**
Bayou Bar and Grill, **76**
The Belgian Lion, **37**
Bella Luna, **80**
Berta's Latin American Restaurant, **50**
Cafe Japengo, **20**
Cafe Pacifica, **26**
California Café, **77**
California Cuisine, **60**
Calliope's Greek Cuisine, **78**
Canes California Bistro, **61**
Choices, **16**
Croce's, **96**
Dakota Grill & Spirits, **97**
Dobson's, **69**
El Indio Shop, **73**
Fio's, **70**
The Fish Market, **71**
George's at the Cove, **1**
Hamburger Mary's, **58**
Hard Rock Café, **9**
Hob Nob Hill, **79**
Karinya Thai, **29**
Old Town Mexican Café, **49**
Palenque, **24**
Panda Inn, **92**
Panevino, **50**
Pannikin Brockton Villa, **5**
Pizza Nova, **59**
Rainwater's, **93**
Ristorante Piatti, **14**
Sally D's, **62**
SamSon's, **15**
Star of India, **10**
Thai Chada, **94**
Thai Saffron, **95**
Top O' the Cove, **7**
Tosca's, **27**
Trattoria la Strada, **83**
Triangles, **22**

Lodging
Bahia Resort Hotel, **32**
Balboa Park Inn, **63**
Bay Club Hotel & Marina, **43**
The Bed & Breakfast Inn at La Jolla, **8**
Best Western Hacienda Hotel Old Town, **48**
Best Western Inn by the Sea, **12**
Best Western Posada Inn, **45**
Best Western Shelter Island Marina Inn, **41**
Catamaran Resort Hotel, **25**
Colonial Inn, **2**

San Diego Dining and Lodging

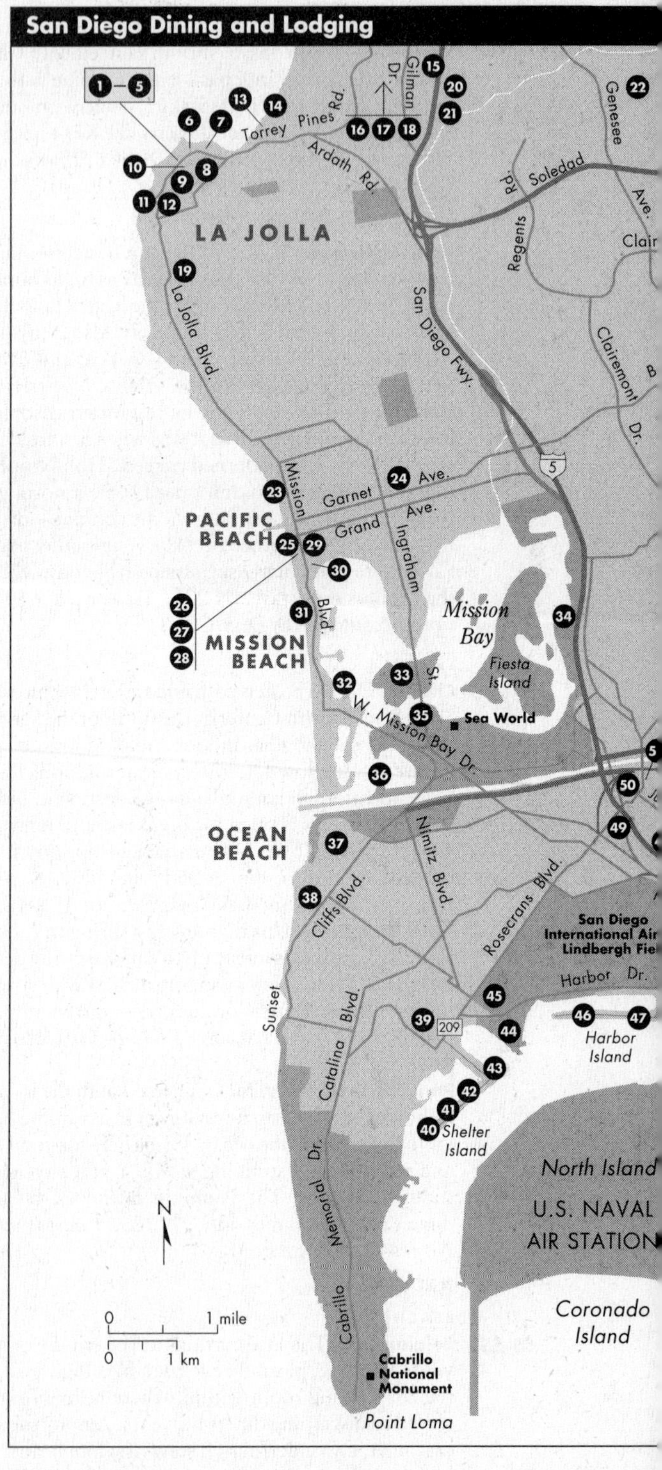

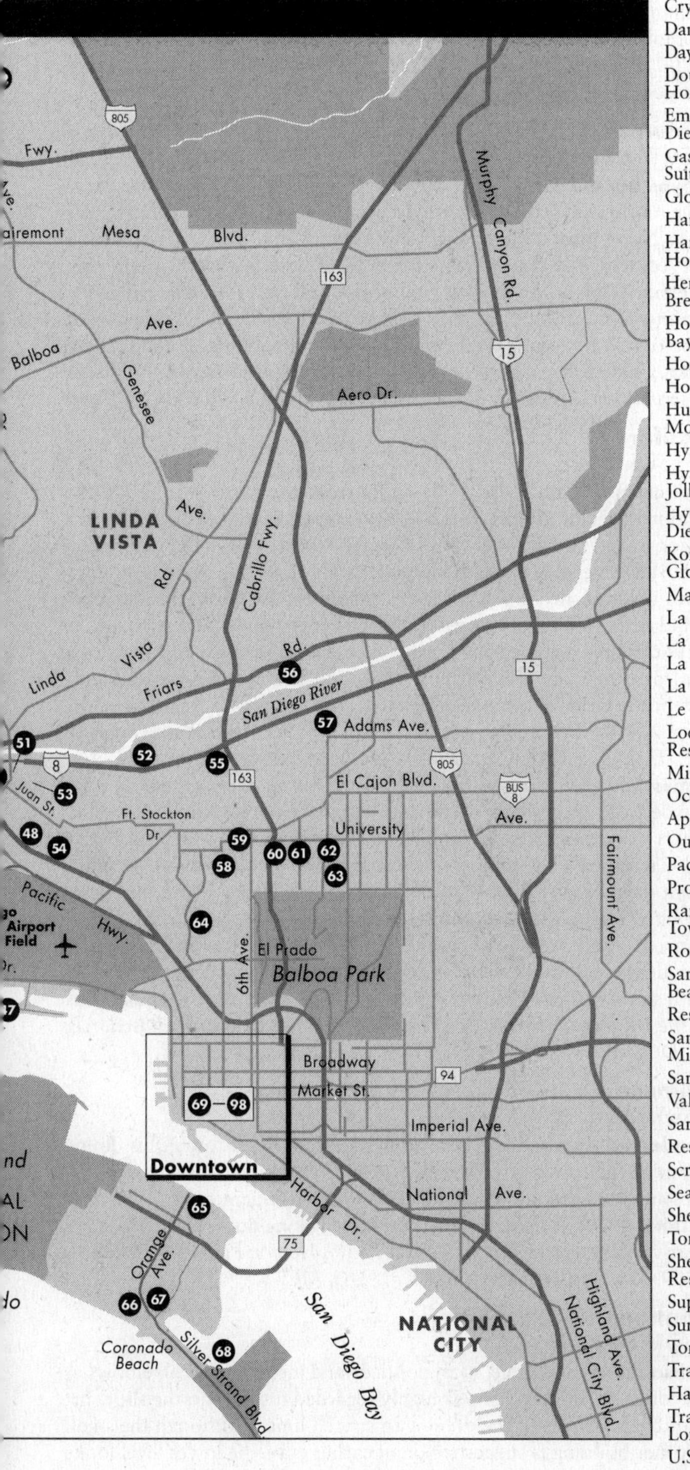

Crystal Pier Motel, **23**
Dana Inn & Marina, **35**
Days Inn Hotel Circle, **55**
Doubletree Hotel at Horton Plaza, **84**
Embassy Suites San Diego Bay, **85**
Gaslamp Plaza Suites, **90**
Glorietta Bay Inn, **67**
Hanalei Hotel, **52**
Harbor Hill Guest House, **64**
Heritage Park Bed & Breakfast Inn, **53**
Holiday Inn on the Bay, **86**
Horton Grand Hotel, **87**
Hotel del Coronado, **66**
Humphrey's Half Moon Inn, **42**
Hyatt Islandia, **36**
Hyatt Regency La Jolla, **21**
Hyatt Regency San Diego, **72**
Kona Kai Plaza Las Glorias Resort and Marina, **40**
La Jolla Cove Motel, **6**
La Jolla Palms Inn, **19**
La Pensione, **88**
La Valencia, **3**
Le Meridien, **65**
Loews Coronado Bay Resort, **68**
Mission Bay Motel, **30**
Ocean Manor Apartment Hotel, **38**
Outrigger Motel, **39**
Padre Trail Inn, **51**
Prospect Park Inn, **4**
Ramada Inn Old Town, **54**
Rodeway Inn, **89**
San Diego Hilton Beach and Tennis Resort, **34**
San Diego Marriott Mission Valley, **56**
San Diego Mission Valley Hilton, **57**
San Diego Princess Resort, **33**
Scripps Inn, **11**
Sea Lodge, **13**
Sheraton Grande Torrey Pines, **18**
Sheraton Harbor Island Resort, **47**
Super 8 Bayview, **98**
Surfer Motor Lodge, **28**
Torrey Pines Inn, **17**
Travelodge Hotel Harbor Island, **46**
Travelodge Point Loma, **44**
U.S. Grant Hotel, **91**
Westgate Hotel, **81**
Wyndham San Diego at Emerald Plaza, **82**

salmon with leeks. An impressive wine list was carefully designed to complement the food. ✕ *2265 Bacon St., Ocean Beach,* ☎ *619/223–2700. Reservations strongly advised. AE, D, DC, MC, V. No lunch. Closed Sun.–Wed.*

Cajun and Creole

DOWNTOWN

$–$$ ★ **Bayou Bar and Grill.** The ceiling fans revolving lazily over this attractive room, with dark-green wainscoting and light-pink walls, help create a New Orleans atmosphere for the spicy Cajun and Creole specialties served here. You may start with a bowl of superb seafood gumbo and then move on to the sausage, red beans, and rice, the duck esplanade, or any of the fresh Louisiana Gulf seafood dishes. A tempting selection of rich Louisiana desserts includes bread pudding, praline cheesecake, and Creole pecan pie. ✕ *329 Market St.,* ☎ *619/696–8747. Dinner reservations suggested. AE, D, DC, MC, V. No lunch Mon. or Tues.*

California

UPTOWN

$$ ★ **California Cuisine.** Across the street from the Uptown district, this minimalist chic dining room—gray carpet, stark white walls, and black-and-white photographs of urban landscapes—offers a suitably innovative menu. Daily selections may include grilled fresh venison served with wild mushrooms and mashed potatoes; the tasty warm chicken salad entrée is a regular feature. You can count on whatever you order to be carefully prepared and elegantly presented. Service is knowledgeable and attentive, the wine list is good, and the desserts are seriously tempting. Heat lamps make the back patio a romantic year-round option. ✕ *1027 University Ave.,* ☎ *619/543–0790. Reservations advised. AE, D, DC, MC, V. Closed Mon. No lunch weekends.*

$–$$ **Canes California Bistro.** A light-filled neighborhood bistro, whose walls are decked, appropriately enough, with canes of all kinds, Canes attracts a diverse group of diners, from senior citizens to families to Uptown trendies. They come for food that is similarly diverse—everything from meat loaf and mashed potatoes to hamburgers with sun-dried tomato *aioli* (garlic mayonnaise) to pastas with roasted garlic and gorgonzola—and consistently good. The weekend buffet brunch features excellent breakfast breads, French beef stew, and yellow corn pancakes with sour cream and golden caviar. ✕ *Vermont St. (at University Ave. in the Uptown District),* ☎ *619/299–3551. Reservations advised. AE, D, DC, MC, V.*

Chinese

DOWNTOWN

$–$$ ★ **Panda Inn.** Arguably the best Chinese restaurant in town, this dining room at the top of the Plaza serves subtly seasoned and attractively presented Mandarin and Szechuan dishes in an elegant setting. The fresh seafood dishes are noteworthy, as are the Peking duck, spicy Szechuan bean curd, and twice-cooked pork. ✕ *506 Horton Plaza,* ☎ *619/233–7800. Reservations advised. AE, D, DC, MC, V.*

Continental

DOWNTOWN

$$$ ★ **Dobson's.** At lunchtime, local politicos and media types rub elbows at the long, polished bar of this highly regarded restaurant; the show biz contingent arrives in the evening in stretch limos. Although the small two-tier building is suggestive of an earlier era—the lower level looks like a men's club and the upper level sports a wrought-iron balcony, elegant woodwork, and gilt cornices—there's nothing outdated about the cuisine. Among the range of carefully prepared entrées, which

change daily, you may find roasted quail with fig sauce or chicken risotto. The tasty house salad is laced with fennel and goat cheese, and Dobson's signature dish, a superb mussel bisque, comes topped with a crown of puff pastry. The wine list is excellent. ✕ *56 Broadway Circle,* ☎ *619/231–6771. Reservations advised. AE, DC, MC, V. Closed Sun. No lunch Sat.*

LA JOLLA

$$$ **Top O' the Cove.** Although the rather stolid menu of this La Jolla institution has been surpassed by glitzier newcomers, year after year San Diego diners give high marks for romance to this cozy, intimate spot with a beautiful ocean view. The filet mignon and roasted rack of lamb are reliable choices; calorie-counters may opt for the boneless chicken breast sautéed with shrimp and shellfish or sliced duck breast with Armagnac walnut sauce. The service is attentive but not overbearing, and the award-winning wine list is enormous. ✕ *1216 Prospect St.,* ☎ *619/454–7779. Reservations advised. AE, DC, MC, V.*

$$–$$$ **Triangles.** In an attractive, if slightly stiff, setting—clubby dark wood booths in a contemporary high-rise bank building—this bar and grill in the Golden Triangle area strives for variety. The menu, which changes daily, may include sautéed sweetbreads, potato knishes, ravioli stuffed with porcini mushrooms, or shrimp cassoulet. Along with rich dishes, you'll also find many lighter and vegetarian preparations—nice for the health-conscious diner or the overstuffed vacationer. A small patio, surrounded by lush landscaping, is pleasant at lunch. ✕ *4370 La Jolla Village Dr., in the Northern Trust Bldg.,* ☎ *619/453–6650. Reservations advised. AE, MC, V. Closed Sun. No lunch Sat.*

Deli

LA JOLLA

$ **SamSon's.** As close as you'll come to a real Jewish deli in San Diego, SamSon's has dill pickles set out on the tables; the menu and portions are enormous. If you're having trouble deciding, go for one of the daily soup-and-sandwich specials, especially the whitefish when it's available. And you can't go wrong with a lox plate for breakfast (SamSon's opens at 7 AM) or a corned beef sandwich for lunch. The two ample dining rooms are decorated in corny show-biz style, with movie stills covering the walls. ✕ *8861 Villa La Jolla Dr.,* ☎ *619/455–1462. Reservations accepted. AE, D, DC, MC, V.*

Greek

DOWNTOWN

$ **Athens Market.** As in many Greek restaurants, the appetizers here—such as *taramousalata* (fish roe dip) and stuffed grape leaves—can be superior to the somewhat heavy traditional beef and lamb entrées. Greek music, folk dancing, and belly dancers add to the festive atmosphere on weekend evenings. The adjacent Victorian-style coffeehouse, under the same ownership, keeps late hours for night owls in search of a caffeine fix. ✕ *109 W. F St.,* ☎ *619/234–1955. Reservations suggested. AE, D, DC, MC, V.*

UPTOWN

$–$$ **Calliope's Greek Cuisine.** Calliope moves beyond the standard Hellenic fare to offer tasty variations on traditional dishes. Included on the menu, along with a good moussaka and lamb souvlakia, are fettuccine Aegean, topped with shrimp, fresh fish, and mushrooms in a tomato wine sauce, and artichokes Athenian, served over linguine in a tomato-herb sauce. Fans of Greek wines will see not only the usual retsinas but also a selection of harder-to-find regional bottles. The white-walled dining room is light and airy. ✕ *3958 5th Ave.,* ☎ *619/291–5588. Reservations advised. AE, D, DC, MC, V.*

Indian

LA JOLLA

$$ **Star of India.** Star of India offers the best Indian food in town in a soothing setting of bamboo and quiet pastels. Particularly recommended are the chicken *tikka masala,* prepared tandoori style in a cream and tomato curry, and *saag gosht,* lamb in a spinach curry. Seafood dishes are generally the least successful. The excellent nan bread, baked in the tandoor oven, comes either plain or stuffed with a variety of fillings. An all-you-can-eat buffet lunch, available daily, is a good way to satisfy your curiosity about a variety of different dishes. ✕ *1000 Prospect St.,* ☎ *619/459–3355; 423 F St.,* ☎ *554–9891. Reservations advised, especially weekends. AE, D, DC, MC, V.*

Italian

DOWNTOWN

$$–$$$ **Bella Luna.** A recent, welcome addition to the "Italianization" of 5th Avenue, this small, stylish restaurant, whose owner hails from the island of Capri, more than holds its own against its longer-established neighbors. The menu features dishes from all over Italy: Try the stuffed mozzarella appetizer or the calamari in tomato sauce. Pastas are particularly recommended, especially the linguine *alle vongole verace* (with clams in their shells), the fettuccine with salmon, and the black squid-ink linguine served with a spicy seafood sauce; if you still have room for an entrée, consider the rack of lamb. ✕ *748 5th Ave.,* ☎ *619/239–3222. Reservations advised. AE, MC, V.*

$$–$$$ ★ **Trattoria la Strada.** La Strada specializes in Tuscan cuisine prepared so well that your taste buds will be convinced they've died and gone to Italy. Try the *antipasto di mare,* with tender shrimp and shellfish, or the salad La Strada, with wild mushrooms, walnuts, and delectable shaved Parmesan. The pastas, particularly the *pappardelle all'anitra* (wide noodles with a duck sauce), are excellent. The noise level can be high in the two high-ceilinged dining rooms. ✕ *702 5th Ave.,* ☎ *619/239–3400. Reservations advised. AE, D, DC, MC, V. No lunch weekends.*

$$ **Fio's.** Glitzy young singles mingle with staid business-suit types in this lively, popular place, one of the earliest of the trendy Italian restaurants now proliferating in the Gaslamp Quarter. Contemporary variations on traditional Italian cuisine are served in a high-ceilinged, brick-and-wood dining room overlooking the 5th Avenue street scene. The menu includes a range of imaginative pizzas baked in the wood-fired oven and classic Italian dishes. ✕ *801 5th Ave.,* ☎ *619/234–3467. Reservations advised. AE, D, DC, MC, V. No lunch weekends.*

$$ **Panevino.** This brick-walled Italian café is often crowded with diners who prefer its casual bistro atmosphere to the more trendy tone of neighboring restaurants. But the menu here is as au courant as any other in San Diego. Particularly recommended is the imaginative selection of pizzas and pastas: The spinach ravioli is always a good bet. You could easily make a meal of one of the excellent stuffed focaccias and a salad or a plate of grilled vegetables, although a range of tasty and sometimes ambitious entrées is also offered; if it's available, try the quail cooked in balsamic vinegar. Panevino is one of the few good downtown restaurants outside of Horton Plaza that are open for lunch on weekends. ✕ *722 5th Ave.,* ☎ *619/595–7959. Reservations advised. AE, D, DC, MC, V.*

UPTOWN

$ Pizza Nova. Voted "Best Pizza Restaurant" by *San Diego Magazine* and *San Diego Home and Garden,* Pizza Nova serves up 22 delicious varieties, including Roasted Garlic Chicken, Shrimp Pesto, and Mexican Lime. Just as appetizing are the 14 mouthwatering pasta entrées; Chicken Tequila Fettuccine is one of the most popular. ✕ *3955 5th Ave., Suite 101, The Village Hillcrest,* ☎ *619/296–6682. Reservations accepted. AE, D, DC, MC, V.*

$ Sally D's. A step above the old family tradition, this friendly establishment is a favorite among locals who return for great Italian food cooked up by Sally. Try Shrimp D's Pizza, baked mostoccolia and veal, or eggplant parmigiana. ✕ *1288 University Ave., Hillcrest Colonnade,* ☎ *619/291–1288. Reservations accepted. AE, D, MC, V.*

BEACHES

$ Tosca's. This popular Pacific Beach eatery is in some ways typical of pizza restaurants everywhere, with its fluorescent lighting and red-checkered vinyl tablecloths. But you are, after all, in California, which means you can opt for wheat or semolina crusts for your individually sized pizzas or calzones; choose toppings or fillings from an array of exotic ingredients, including artichokes, pesto, and feta cheese; and wash it all down with a microbrew from Sierra Nevada (on tap, yet). The young servers are cheerful and helpful. ✕ *3780 Ingraham St.,* ☎ *619/274–2408. AE, D, DC, MC, V.*

LA JOLLA

$$ Ristorante Piatti. On weekends, this trattoria-style restaurant is filled to overflowing with a lively mix of trendy singles and local families, who keep returning for the excellent country-style Italian food. A wood-burning oven turns out excellent breads and pizzas, and imaginative pastas include the *pappardelle fantasia* (wide saffron noodles with shrimp, fresh tomatoes, and arugula) and a wonderfully garlicky spaghetti *alle vongole* (served with clams in the shell). Among the *secondi* are good versions of roast chicken and Italian sausage with polenta. A fountain splashes softly on the tree-shaded patio, where heat lamps allow diners to sit out even on chilly evenings. ✕ *2182 Av. de la Playa,* ☎ *619/454–1589. Reservations strongly advised. AE, MC, V.*

Latin American

OLD TOWN

$–$$ Berta's Latin American Restaurant. A San Diego rarity—and particularly surprising in a section of town where the food often leans toward the safe and touristy—Berta's features a wide selection of Latin American regional dishes and a nice list of Latin American wines. While the wines are largely Chilean, the food, which manages to be wonderfully tasty and health-conscious at the same time, ranges all over the map. Try the Brazilian seafood *vatapa,* shrimp, scallops, and fish served in a sauce flavored with ginger, coconut, and chilis, or the Peruvian *pollo a la huancaina,* chicken with chilis and a feta cheese sauce. Service is friendly and helpful. The simple dining room is small, but there's also a patio. ✕ *3928 Twiggs St.,* ☎ *619/295–2343. Reservations advised weekends. AE, MC, V.*

$ Old Town Mexican Café. Singles congregate at the bar and families crowd into the wooden booths of this boisterous San Diego favorite, decked out with plants and colorful piñatas; an enclosed patio takes the overflow from both groups. You'll find all the Mexican standards here, as well as specialties, such as *carnitas,* chunks of roast pork served with fresh tortillas and condiments. The enchiladas with spicy ranchero or green chili sauce are nice variations on an old theme. You can watch the corn tortillas being handmade on the premises and pick up a dozen to take home with you. ✕ *2489 San Diego Ave.,* ☏ *619/297–4330. Reservations accepted for 10 or more. AE, D, MC, V.*

UPTOWN

$ **El Indio Shop.** El Indio has been serving some of the city's best Mexican fast food since 1940. The menu is extensive; try the large burritos, the *tacquitos* (fried rolled tacos) with guacamole, or the giant quesadillas. You can eat at one of the indoor tables or on the patio across the street; El Indio is also perfect for beach-bound takeout. ✕ *3695 India St.,* ☏ *619/299–0333; 115 W. Olive Dr., San Ysidro,* ☏ *619/690–1122. D, MC, V. San Ysidro shop closed Sun.*

BEACHES

$–$$ ★ **Palenque.** A welcome alternative to the standard Sonoran-style café, this family-run restaurant in Pacific Beach serves a wonderful selection of regional Mexican dishes. Recommendations include the chicken with mole, served in the regular chocolate-based or green chili version, and the mouthwatering *camarones en chipotle,* large shrimp cooked in a chili and tequila cream sauce (an old family recipe of the proprietor). Piñatas and paper birds dangle from the thatched ceiling, and seating is in comfortable round-backed leather chairs; a small deck in front is nice for warm-weather dining. Palenque is a bit hard to spot from the street and service is often slow, but the food is worth your vigilance and patience. ✕ *1653 Garnet Ave., Pacific Beach,* ☏ *619/272–7816. Reservations advised. AE, D, DC, MC, V.*

Pacific Rim

$$$ **Cafe Japengo.** In one of the most stylish dining rooms in town, framed by elegant marbled walls, accented with leafy bamboo trees, and dotted with unusual black-iron sculptures, Cafe Japengo serves excellent Pacific Rim cuisine. The inspiration for this eclectic and imaginative menu is largely Asian, with many North and South American touches. There's a selection of grilled, wood-roasted, and wok-fried entrées for dinner; try the 10-ingredient fried rice, the shrimp and scallops with dragon noodles, or the grilled swordfish with wild mushrooms. The curry fried calamari and the Japengo potstickers appetizers are guaranteed to stimulate your taste buds. You can also order fine sushi from your table or from a seat at the sushi bar. Unfortunately, the quality of the service doesn't match that of the food. ✕ *8960 University Center La.,* ☏ *619/450–3355. Reservations advised. AE, D, DC, MC, V. No lunch weekends.*

Seafood

DOWNTOWN

$$$ **Anthony's Star of the Sea Room.** The Anthony's chain of local seafood restaurants, one of the oldest in San Diego, has long been serving up adequately prepared seafood dishes to tourists and residents alike. The flagship of the Anthony's fleet, the Star of the Sea Room, is much more formal and expensive than the others. The menu offers an enormous selection of fresh fish from around the world, and if the recipes are less exciting than those at other seafood restaurants, the magnificent harbor views go far in the way of compensation. Many of the dishes are prepared at the table. ✕ *1360 N. Harbor Dr.,* ☏ *619/232–7408. Reservations strongly advised. Jacket and tie. AE, D, DC, MC, V. No lunch.*

$–$$$ **The Fish Market.** This bustling, informal restaurant offers diners a choice from a large variety of extremely fresh fish, mesquite grilled and served with lemon and tartar sauce. Also good are shellfish dishes, such as steamed clams or mussels. Enormous plate-glass windows look directly out onto the harbor, and if you're lucky enough to get a windowside table, you can practically taste the salt spray. This is one of the rare places where families with young children can feel comfortable without sacrificing their taste buds. A more formal and expensive upstairs restaurant, the Top of the Market, offers a good Sunday brunch. ✕ *750 N. Harbor Dr.,* ☎ *619/232–3474 for the Fish Market or 619/234–4867 for the Top of the Market; also in Del Mar, at 640 Via de la Valle,* ☎ *619/755–2277. Reservations accepted upstairs and for 8 or more downstairs, and at Del Mar. AE, D, DC, MC, V.*

OLD TOWN

$$–$$$ **Cafe Pacifica.** The menu here changes daily and features an impressive array of imaginative appetizers, salads, pastas, and entrées; it also does a crème brûlée worth blowing any diet for. The emphasis here is on seafood, however, and this restaurant serves some of the best in town. You can't go wrong with any of the fresh fish preparations grilled over mesquite and served with an herb-butter sauce, a Mexican-inspired salsa, or a fruit chutney. Other good bets include the tasty pan-fried catfish; yummy, greaseless fish tacos; and superb crab cakes. ✕ *2414 San Diego Ave.,* ☎ *619/291–6666. Reservations advised. AE, D, DC, MC, V.*

LA JOLLA

$$$ ★ **George's at the Cove.** At most restaurants you get either good food or good views; at George's, you don't have to choose. The elegant main dining room, with a wall-length window overlooking La Jolla Cove, is renowned for its daily fresh seafood specials; the menu also offers several good chicken and meat dishes. The delectable three-mushroom soup, accented with sherry and rosemary, or the salmon-and-shrimp sausage make fine starters. The charbroiled apple-smoked salmon entrée is highly recommended, as are any of the shellfish pastas. Desserts are uniformly excellent. For more informal dining, try the Cafe ($$) on the second floor. The outdoor Terrace ($$), on the top floor, affords a sweeping view of the coast; wonderful for breakfast, lunch, or brunch on a fine day, the Terrace (like the Cafe) does not take reservations, so you may have a wait. ✕ *1250 Prospect St.,* ☎ *619/454–4244. Reservations advised for main dining room. AE, D, DC, MC, V.*

Thai

UPTOWN

$–$$ ★ **Thai Chada.** Don't be put off by appearances. Although it's housed in a corner building that looks like a hamburger joint, this is one of the best Thai restaurants in town; the large windows and comfortable booths provide a low-key setting for consistently excellent food. Try any of the noodle dishes, especially the *pad thai,* rice noodles fried with fresh shrimp, egg, bean sprouts, scallions, and ground peanuts; the Tom Ka Kai chicken soup, with coconut milk, lemon grass, lime juice, and scallions; or the roast duck curry. A sister restaurant, Thai Chada 2, has recently opened in Pacific Beach. ✕ *142 University Ave.,* ☎ *619/297–9548; Thai Chada 2, 1749 Garnet Ave.,* ☎ *619/270–1888. Reservations advised. AE, D, DC, MC, V. Sat. lunch at Thai Chada 2 only; no lunch Sun. at both.*

$ **Thai Saffron.** In recent years, San Diego has seen an upsurge in the growth of take-out restaurants offering tasty, health-conscious food. Saffron is one of the earliest and best of the eateries that specialize in chicken spit-roasted over a wood fire, accompanied by an appealing selection of side dishes. The chicken is wonderfully moist and comes with a choice of sauces: Try the peanut or chili. Among the accompaniments, the Cambodian salad is particularly fresh and crunchy. There's limited outdoor seating, but this is an ideal place to pick up lunch or dinner to take to

Mission Bay or the beach. ✕ *3731B India St.,* ☏ *619/574–0177. No reservations. MC, V.*

BEACHES

$–$$ **Karinya Thai.** This popular restaurant in Pacific Beach serves excellent Thai cuisine in a relaxed but pretty setting; in one room, diners recline on colorful floor cushions at low tables. It's hard to go wrong with any of the dishes on the extensive menu. You could concoct a meal from appetizers alone: The stuffed chicken wings and spicy fish cakes are particularly recommended. Among the entrées, the scallops in three sauces, beef strips with broccoli, and pad thai noodles are all worth a try. ✕ *4475 Mission Blvd.,* ☏ *619/270–5050. Reservations advised. No lunch Sat.–Mon. MC, V.*

LODGING

By Sharon K. Gillenwater and Edie Jarolim

San Diego is very spread out, so the first thing to consider when selecting lodgings here is location. The various neighborhoods are rather diverse: You can choose to stay in the middle of a bustling metropolitan center or to kick back in a serene beach getaway. If you plan to do a lot of sightseeing, take into account a hotel's proximity to the attractions you most want to visit. Even the most expensive areas offer some reasonably priced—albeit modest—rooms.

Oakwood Apartments (Oakwood Mission Bay West, 3866 Ingraham St., 92109; Oakwood Mission Bay East, 3883 Ingraham St., 92109, ☏ 619/490–2100 booking for both) offers comfortable, furnished apartments in the Mission Bay area with maid service and linens; there's a minimum 30-day stay. At **San Diego Vacation Rentals** (1565 Hotel Circle S, Suite 390, 92108, ☏ 619/296–1000 or 800/222–8281), you can rent a coastal home or condo at competitive weekly and monthly rates; brochures of rentals are available on request.

Bed & Breakfast Guild of San Diego (☏ 619/523–1300) lists 11 high-quality member inns. **Bed & Breakfast Directory for San Diego** (Box 3292, 92136, ☏ 619/297–3130 or 800/619–ROOM) covers San Diego County.

CATEGORY	COST*
$$$$	over $165
$$$	$110–$165
$$	$70–$110
$	under $70

**All prices are for a standard double room in high (summer) season, excluding 10½% San Diego room tax.*

Coronado

Quiet, out-of-the-way Coronado feels as though it exists in an earlier, more gracious era. With boutiques and restaurants lining Orange Avenue, the main street, and its fine beaches, Coronado is great for a getaway, but if you plan to see many of San Diego's attractions, you'll probably spend a lot of time commuting across the bridge or riding the ferry.

$$$$ ★ **Le Meridien.** Flamingos greet you at the entrance of this 16-acre, lushly landscaped resort. The low-slung, Cape Cod–style buildings perfectly capture Coronado's understated old-money ambience. The large rooms and suites are done in a cheerful, California–country French fashion, with colorful Impressionist prints; all rooms have separate showers and tubs and come with plush robes and Limoge bath accessories. (Watch out for what looks like a gift basket on the vanity, though—it's an extension of the minibar.) The spa facilities are top-notch, as is the award-winning Marius Restaurant, which serves innovative French Provençale cuisine. ☒ *2000 2nd St., 92118,* ☎ *619/435-3000 or 800/543-4300,* FAX *619/435-3032. 300 rooms (including 7 suites and a 28-unit villa complex). 2 restaurants, 3 pools, massage, sauna, spa, steam room, 6 tennis courts, aerobics, exercise room, marina. AE, D, DC, MC, V.*

$$$$ **Loews Coronado Bay Resort.** You can park your boat at the 80-slip marina of this resort, set on a 15-acre private peninsula on the Silver Strand. Or you can rent one here. Rooms are somewhat formally but tastefully decorated, with pale yellows, pinks, and greens, and flowered bedspreads; all have furnished balconies with views of water—either bay, ocean, or marina. The Commodore Kids Club offers a nice variety of programs for children ages 4–12. ☒ *4000 Coronado Bay Rd., 92118,* ☎ *619/424-4000 or 800/235-6397,* FAX *619/424-4400. 438 rooms, 25 suites. 3 restaurants, deli, 3 pools, 2 spas, 5 tennis courts, fitness center, marina, windsurfing, boating, jet skiing, bicycles. AE, D, DC, MC, V.*

$$$–$$$$ **Hotel del Coronado.** Built in 1888, "the Del" is a historic and social landmark (*see* Exploring, *above,* for details). The rooms and suites in the original ornate Victorian building are charmingly quirky. Some have sleeping areas that seem smaller than the baths, while others are downright palatial; two are even said to come with a resident ghost. The public areas are grand, if perhaps a bit dark for modern tastes; a lower-level shopping arcade lined with historic photographs is fascinating, but tear yourself away to stroll around the hotel's lovely manicured grounds. More standardized accommodations are available in the newer high-rise. Service can be a bit chaotic; there's often a long line at the front desk. ☒ *1500 Orange Ave., 92118,* ☎ *619/435-6611 (hotel), 619/522-8000 or 800/468-3533 (reservations),* FAX *619/522-8262. 691 rooms. 3 restaurants, deli, pool, sauna, steam room, 8 tennis courts, croquet, bicycles, beach. AE, D, DC, MC, V.*

$$–$$$ **Glorietta Bay Inn.** The main building of this property—located across the street from the Del, adjacent to the Coronado harbor, and near many restaurants and shops—was built in 1908 for sugar baron John D. Spreckels, who once owned most of downtown San Diego. Rooms here and in the newer motel-style buildings are attractively furnished, with flowered bedspreads and green rugs; all have refrigerators. Tours of the island's historical buildings depart from the inn's lobby three mornings a week (cost: $5). ☒ *1630 Glorietta Blvd., 92118,* ☎ *619/435-3101 or 800/283-9383,* FAX *619/435-6182. 98 rooms. Pool, bicycles. AE, D, DC, MC, V.*

Downtown

There is much to see within walking distance of downtown accommodations—Seaport Village, the Embarcadero, the historic Gaslamp Quarter, a variety of theaters and night spots, and the spectacular Horton Plaza shopping center. The zoo and Balboa Park are also nearby. In addition, some good restaurants have opened in this part of town in the past few years. Visitors should be aware, however, that the area is still transitional; many streets are deserted at night, and street hustlers and homeless people mingle with tourists and office workers during the daytime.

$$$$ ★ **Hyatt Regency San Diego.** This high-rise adjacent to Seaport Village successfully combines Old World opulence with California airiness and space. Palm trees pose next to ornate tapestry couches in the high-ceiling, light-filled lobby, and the British Regency–style guest rooms have

views of the water. Although its proximity to the convention center attracts a large business trade (who can take advantage of an excellent Business Plan), this hotel also offers well-heeled leisure travelers a superb location and facilities. ☒ *One Market Place,* ☎ *619/232–1234 or 800/233–1234,* FAX *619/233–6464. 875 rooms (including 55 suites and Regency Club rooms). 2 restaurants, lobby lounge, piano bar, pool, 4 tennis courts, health club, boating. AE, D, DC, MC, V.*

$$$–$$$$ **Horton Grand Hotel.** A delightful Victorian confection in the heart of the historic Gaslamp Quarter, the Horton Grand comprises two 1880s hotels moved brick by brick from nearby locations. It features delightfully retro rooms, individually furnished with period antiques, ceiling fans, and gas-burning fireplaces. The choicest rooms are those overlooking a garden courtyard, which twinkles with miniature lights each night. There's high tea in the afternoon and jazz in the evening. The place is a charmer, but service can be a bit erratic. ☒ *311 Island Ave., 92101,* ☎ *619/544–1886 or 800/542–1886;* FAX *619/239–3823. 132 rooms. Restaurant, lounge. AE, D, DC, MC, V.*

$$$–$$$$ **Westgate Hotel.** A nondescript modern high-rise hides what must be the most opulent hotel in town: The lobby, modeled after the anteroom at Versailles, has hand-cut Baccarat chandeliers; rooms are individually furnished with antiques, Italian marble counters, and bath fixtures with 14-karat-gold overlays. Afternoon high tea is served in the lobby to the accompaniment of harp music. If this is a bit formal for some tastes, breathtaking views of the harbor and the city from the ninth floor up will bring you back to the modern world. Horton Plaza is nearby and the Tijuana trolley stops right outside the door. ☒ *1055 2nd Ave., 92101,* ☎ *619/238–1818, 800/221–3802, or 800/522–1564 in CA;* FAX *619/557–3737. 223 rooms. 3 restaurants, lounge, beauty salon, barbershop, exercise room. AE, D, DC, MC, V.*

$$$ **Doubletree Hotel at Horton Plaza.** Although it is fronted by a startling lighted blue obelisk, this high-rise is all understated marble, brass, and glass inside. The rooms are similarly elegant and low-key, with muted sea-green and coral color schemes. ☒ *910 Broadway Circle, 92101,* ☎ *619/239–2200 or 800/528–0444,* FAX *619/239–0509. 450 rooms, 14 suites. Restaurant, lobby lounge, sports bar, pool, sauna, spa, 2 tennis courts, health club. AE, D, DC, MC, V.*

$$$ **Embassy Suites San Diego Bay.** It's a short walk to the convention center, the Embarcadero, and Seaport Village from one of downtown's most popular hotels. The front door of each spacious suite opens out onto the hotel's 12-story atrium. The contemporary-style decor is pleasant, and the views from rooms facing the harbor are spectacular. Business travelers will find it easy to set up shop here, and families can make good use of the in-room refrigerators, microwaves, and separate sleeping areas. A cooked-to-order breakfast and afternoon cocktails are complimentary, as are airport transfers. ☒ *601 Pacific Hwy., 92101,* ☎ *619/239–2400 or 800/362–2779,* FAX *619/239–1520. 337 suites. Restaurant, sports bar, pool, sauna, exercise room. AE, D, DC, MC, V.*

$$$ **Holiday Inn on the Bay.** On the Embarcadero and overlooking San Diego Bay, this high-rise hotel is convenient for vacationers as well as business travelers. Rooms are unsurprising but very spacious and comfortable, and views from the balconies are hard to beat. ☒ *1355 N. Harbor Dr., 92101,* ☎ *619/232–3861 or 800/465–4329,* FAX *619/232–4914. 600 rooms, 17 suites. Restaurant, bar, pool, laundry, airport and Amtrak shuttle. AE, D, DC, MC, V.*

$$$ ★ **U.S. Grant Hotel.** Built in 1910 and reopened in 1985, this San Diego classic is just across the street from Horton Plaza. Crystal chandeliers and polished marble floors in the lobby and Queen Anne–style mahogany furnishings in the rooms hark back to a more gracious era when such

dignitaries as Charles Lindbergh and Franklin D. Roosevelt stayed here. The Grand Heritage group, which bought this hotel in 1994, has gone to great pains to be historically accurate in its refurbishing. ⌂ *326 Broadway, 92101,* ☎ *619/232–3121 or 800/237–5029;* FAX *619/232–3626. 280 rooms (including 60 suites). Restaurant, piano bar, exercise room. AE, D, DC, MC, V.*

$$$ Wyndham San Diego Hotel at Emerald Plaza. Business travelers especially like this striking pink hotel (formerly the Pan Pacific Hotel), but the Wyndham is also fine for vacationers who want to be near all downtown shopping and restaurants; many of the upper-floor accommodations offer panoramic views of the city. The green prismlike sculpture that hangs from the 100-foot central atrium is a bit overwhelming, and the rather bland, beige-dominated standard rooms are not overly large, but this hotel has a very good health club and such extras as a complimentary airport shuttle. ⌂ *400 W. Broadway, 92101,* ☎ *619/239–4500 or 800/996–3426,* FAX *619/239–3274 (guest) or 619/234–4527 (hotel). 436 rooms. 2 restaurants, bar, pool, spa, health club, business services. AE, D, DC, MC, V.*

$$–$$$ Balboa Park Inn. Directly across the street from Balboa Park, this B&B is housed in four Spanish colonial–style 1915 residences connected by courtyards. Prices are reasonable for the romantic one- and two-bedroom suites. Each has a different flavor, including contemporary versions of Italian, French, Spanish, or early Californian; some have fireplaces, wet bars, whirlpool tubs, patios, and kitchens. Continental breakfast and a newspaper are delivered to guests every morning. ⌂ *3402 Park Blvd., 92103,* ☎ *619/298–0823 or 800/938–8181,* FAX *619/294–8070. 26 suites with baths. Bar. AE, D, DC, MC, V.*

$$ Harbor Hill Guest House. This B&B, within walking distance of the harbor and Balboa Park, offers comfortable rooms in a three-story home, with a private entryway and full kitchen on each level. There's a pretty back garden and sun porch, and a carriage house connected to the main house provides a romantic getaway. Not fancy or antiques-filled, this is a cheerful, friendly place that's excellent for families as well as for couples or singles. Continental breakfast is included. ⌂ *2330 Albatross St., 92101,* ☎ *619/233–0638. 6 rooms with bath. MC, V.*

$–$$ ★ Gaslamp Plaza Suites. Built in 1913 as San Diego's first "skyscraper," this 11-story structure in the Gaslamp Quarter is only a block from Horton Plaza. It's listed on the National Register of Historic Places; elegant public areas boast lovely old marble, brass, and mosaic. Accommodations—either petite- or one-bedroom suites—are done in shades of burgundy and pink in attractive European style, with contemporary dark wood furniture. Guests can enjoy the view and a complimentary Continental breakfast on the rooftop terrace. Many of the rooms rent as time shares; book ahead if you're visiting in high season. ⌂ *520 E St., 92101,* ☎ *619/232–9500 or 800/874–8770,* FAX *619/238–9945. 60 suites. Restaurant, airport and Amtrak shuttle. AE, D, DC, MC, V.*

$–$$ Rodeway Inn. Situated on one of the better streets downtown, this property is clean, comfortable, and nicely decorated. Continental breakfast is included in the room rate. ⌂ *833 Ash St., 92101,* ☎ *619/239–2285, 800/228–2000, or 800/522–1528 in CA,* FAX *619/235–6951. 45 rooms. Sauna. AE, D, DC, MC, V.*

$ ★ La Pensione. This downtown budget hotels offers daily, weekly, and monthly rates, and it's pleasant enough for one to want an extended stay. Rooms are modern, clean, and well designed, with good working areas and kitchenettes. The hotel is convenient to the restaurants of the city's version of Little Italy, and the café downstairs is a lovely place to linger over a cappuccino or provolone and prosciutto sandwich. ⌂ *1700*

India St., 92101, ☎ 619/236–8000 or 800/232–4683, FAX 619/236–8088. 81 rooms. Kitchenettes, laundry. AE, MC, V.

$ **Super 8 Bayview.** There's nothing fancy about this motel, but the location is less noisy than those of other low-cost establishments. The accommodations are nondescript but clean, and there are rooms for nonsmokers, and some with refrigerators. Continental breakfast is included in the room rate. *1835 Columbia St., 92101, ☎ 619/544–0164 or 800/537–9902, FAX 619/237–9940. 101 rooms. Laundry, airport and Amtrak shuttle, free parking. AE, DC, MC, V.*

Harbor Island/Shelter Island/Point Loma

Two man-made peninsulas between downtown and the lovely community of Point Loma, Harbor Island and Shelter Island are both bordered by grassy parks, tree-lined paths, lavish hotels, and good restaurants. Harbor Island is closest to the downtown area and less than five minutes from the airport, while narrower Shelter Island is nearer to Point Loma. Both locations command breathtaking views of the bay and the downtown skyline. Not all the lodgings listed here are on the islands themselves, but all are in their vicinity.

$$$$ **Sheraton Harbor Island Resort.** This resort consists of two formerly separate Sheraton properties. The East Tower, upgraded and expanded in a 1994 renovation, has the better sports facilities. The smaller, more intimate West Tower, which reopened in March 1995, has larger rooms, with a separate area suitable for business entertaining. Rooms throughout are California-style spiffy, and views from the upper floors of both sections are superb, but because the West Tower is closest to the water, it affords fine outlooks from the lower floors, too. *1380 Harbor Island Dr., 92101, ☎ 619/291–2900 or 800/325–3535, FAX 619/692–2337. 1,048 rooms. 3 restaurants, 2 bars, deli, 3 pools, massage, sauna, spa, 4 tennis courts, health club, jogging, boating, airport shuttle. AE, D, DC, MC, V.*

$$$ **Bay Club Hotel & Marina.** Rooms in this appealing low-rise Shelter Island property are large, light, and attractively furnished with rattan tables and chairs and Polynesian tapestries; all have refrigerators and offer views of either the bay or the marina from outside terraces. A buffet breakfast and limo service to the airport or Amtrak are included in the room rate. *2131 Shelter Island Dr., 92106, ☎ 619/224–8888 or 800/672–0800, 800/833–6565 in CA, FAX 619/225–1604. 105 rooms. Restaurant, pool, spa, exercise room, bicycles, free parking. AE, D, DC, MC, V.*

$$$ **Travelodge Hotel Harbor Island.** This more upscale Travelodge offers visitors the views and amenities of more expensive hotels, plus such perks as in-room coffeemakers and complimentary parking, airport shuttle, and local phone calls. Those staying on the two executive floors also get free Continental breakfast as well as afternoon hors d'oeuvres and champagne. The attractive public areas and guest rooms are light and airy. The Waterfront Cafe & Club overlooks the marina; sometimes singer Florence Henderson pulls her boat into a slip and joins in the karaoke evenings here. *1960 Harbor Island Dr., 92101, ☎ 619/291–6700 or 800/578–7878, FAX 619/293–0694. 207 rooms. Restaurant, bar, pool, exercise room, jogging, car rental. AE, D, DC, MC, V.*

$$–$$$ **Humphrey's Half Moon Inn.** This sprawling South Seas–style resort has many grassy open areas with palm trees and tiki torches. The rooms are attractive, with rattan furnishings and nautical-style lamps; some have harbor or marina views. Locals throng to Humphrey's, the on-premises seafood restaurant, and to the jazz lounge; the hotel also hosts outdoor jazz concerts June–October. *2303 Shelter Island Dr., 92106,*

☎ *619/224–3411 or 800/542–7400 (weekdays 8–5), 800/345–9995 (reservations),* FAX *619/224–3478. 182 rooms. Restaurant, bar, pool, putting green, spa, croquet, Ping-Pong, boating, bicycles, airport and Amtrak shuttle. AE, D, DC, MC, V.*

$$–$$$ Kona Kai Plaza Las Glorias Resort and Marina. This 11-acre property was gutted in 1994 and rebuilt from the ground up. It hadn't yet opened when we visited, but the Kona Kai's prime location—with San Diego Bay on one side, a marina on the other—and its expansive new recreational facilities make it well worth checking out. Accommodations include two-level town houses along with standard rooms and suites. *1551 Shelter Island Dr., 92106,* ☎ *619/222–1191, 800/566–2524 or 800/342–2644,* FAX *619/222–9738. 207 units. Restaurant, 2 pools, sauna, spa, 2 tennis courts, jogging, volleyball, beach, airport and Amtrak shuttle, free parking. AE, D, DC, MC, V.*

$$ Best Western Posada Inn. One of the more upscale members of the Best Western chain, the Posada Inn is not on Harbor Island but is located on one of the neighboring thoroughfares adjacent to Point Loma. Many of the rooms, which are clean, comfortable, and nicely furnished, have wonderful views of the harbor. *5005 N. Harbor Dr., 92106,* ☎ *619/224–3254 or 800/528–1234,* FAX *619/224–2186. 112 rooms. Restaurant, bar, pool, spa, exercise room, airport shuttle. AE, D, DC, MC, V.*

$$ Best Western Shelter Island Marina Inn. This waterfront inn, with an airy, skylit lobby, is a good choice if you have a boat to dock; guest slips are available in the adjacent marina. Both harbor- and marina-view rooms are available. Standard accommodations are fairly small; if you're traveling with family or more than one friend, the two-bedroom suite with an eat-in kitchen is a good deal. *2051 Shelter Island Dr., 92106,* ☎ *619/222–0561 or 800/922–2336,* FAX *619/222–9760. 68 rooms, 29 suites. Restaurant, bar, pool, spa, free parking. AE, D, DC, MC, V.*

$ Outrigger Motel. A good bet for those traveling as a family, this motel, adjacent to the two resort peninsulas, is less expensive than its offshore counterparts and offers large rooms with eat-in kitchens. It's a short, scenic walk along the bay from here to Harbor Island. Rooms have gotten a bit shabby in recent years, but the price is still right. *1370 Scott St., 92106,* ☎ *619/223–7105. 37 rooms with kitchens. Pool, laundry. AE, D, DC, MC, V.*

$ Travelodge Point Loma. For far less money, you'll get the same view here as at the higher-priced hotels. Of course, there are fewer amenities and the neighborhood (near the navy base) isn't as serene, but the rooms, all with coffeemakers, are adequate and clean. *5102 N. Harbor Dr., 92106,* ☎ *619/223–8171 or 800/525–9055,* FAX *619/222–7330. 45 rooms. Pool. AE, D, DC, MC, V.*

Hotel Circle/Mission Valley/Old Town

Lining both sides of the stretch of I–8 that lies between Old Town and Mission Valley are a number of moderately priced accommodations that constitute the so-called Hotel Circle. A car is an absolute necessity here, since the only nearby road is the busiest freeway in San Diego. Although not particularly scenic or serene, this location is convenient to Balboa Park, the zoo, downtown, the beaches, the shops of Mission Valley, and Old Town. Mission Valley hotels, near movie theaters and restaurants as well as shops, are more upscale than those of Hotel Circle but generally less expensive than comparable properties at the beaches. Old Town itself has a few picturesque lodgings and is developing a crop of modestly priced chain hotels along nearby I–5;

when you're making reservations, request a room that doesn't face the freeway.

$$$ **Best Western Hacienda Hotel Old Town.** This pretty white hotel, with balconies and Spanish tile roofs, is in a quiet part of Old Town, away from the freeway and the main retail bustle. The accommodations are not really large enough to earn the "suite" label the hotel gives them, but they're decorated in tasteful southwestern style and equipped with microwaves, coffeemakers, minifridges, clock radios, and VCRs. *4041 Harney St., 92110, ☎ 619/298–4707 or 800/888–1991, FAX 619/298–4771. 150 suites. Restaurant, pool, free parking. AE, D, DC, MC, V.*

$$$ ★ **San Diego Marriott Mission Valley.** This high-rise sits in the middle of the San Diego River valley in a commercial zone with sleek office towers and sprawling shopping malls. It has facilities for business travelers but also caters to vacationers, with comfortable rooms, a friendly staff, a piano lounge, and free transportation to the malls. *8757 Rio San Diego Dr., 92108, ☎ 619/692–3800 or 800/228–9290, FAX 619/692–0769. 52 rooms. Restaurant, bar, pool, sauna, tennis court, exercise room, free parking. AE, D, DC, MC, V.*

$$–$$$ **Heritage Park Bed & Breakfast Inn.** One of the beautifully restored mansions in Old Town's Heritage Park, this romantic 1889 Queen Anne has eight quaint guest rooms and a suite decorated with period antiques. Breakfast and afternoon refreshments are included in the room rate. *2470 Heritage Park Row, 92110, ☎ 619/295–7088 or 800/995–2470. 6 rooms with bath, 2 rooms with shared bath, 1 2-bedroom suite. AE, MC, V.*

$$–$$$ **Ramada Inn Old Town.** The most established of the new hotels and motels springing up along I–5 at Old Town, the hacienda-style Ramada has Spanish colonial–style fountains, courtyards, and painted tiles, and Southwest-style decor in the rooms. Breakfast, cocktail reception, and transfers to the airport, bus, and Amtrak are all complimentary. *2435 Jefferson St., 92110, ☎ 619/260–8500 or 800/272–6232, FAX 619/297–2078. 152 rooms. Restaurant, pool, airport and Amtrak shuttle. AE, D, DC, MC, V.*

$$–$$$ **San Diego Mission Valley Hilton.** Directly fronting I–8, this property has soundproofed rooms decorated in contemporary southwestern style. When you're indoors, the attractive modern accommodations, along with the stylish public areas and lush greenery in the back, make you forget this business-oriented hotel's proximity to the freeway. Children stay free, and small pets are accepted ($25). *901 Camino del Rio S, 92108, ☎ 619/543–9000, 800/733–2332, or 800/445–8667, FAX 619/543–9358. 350 rooms. Restaurant, bar, sports bar, pool, spa, fitness center, airport shuttle, free parking. AE, D, DC, MC, V.*

$$ ★ **Hanalei Hotel.** As its name suggests, the theme of this friendly Hotel Circle property is Hawaiian: Palm trees, waterfalls, koi ponds, and tiki torches abound here. A two-story complex offers poolside rooms, and a high-rise building surrounds a lovely Hawaiian-style garden. The rooms were refurbished in 1993–94 with tropical prints in rich colors; some have tile floors, and others have wall-to-wall carpeting. Guests have access to an adjacent golf course, and free transport is provided to local malls and Old Town. *2270 Hotel Circle N, 92108, ☎ 619/297–1101 or 800/882–0858, FAX 619/297–6049. 412 rooms. 2 restaurants, bar, pool, spa, free parking. AE, D, DC, MC, V.*

$ **Days Inn Hotel Circle.** Rooms in this large complex are generally par for the chain-motel course but have the perk of minifridges; some units also have stoves. *543 Hotel Circle S, 92108, ☎ 619/297–8800 or 800/227–4743 (weekdays 8–4:30), 800/325–2525 (central reser-*

vations); FAX *619/298–6029. 280 rooms. Restaurant, pool, beauty salon, spa, laundry. AE, D, DC, MC, V.*

$ **Padre Trail Inn.** This standard, family-style motel is located slightly southwest of Mission Valley. Old Town, shopping, and dining are all within walking distance. *4200 Taylor St., 92110,* ☎ *619/297–3291 or 800/255–9988,* FAX *619/692–2080. 100 rooms. Restaurant, bar, pool. AE, D, DC, MC, V.*

La Jolla

Million-dollar homes line the beaches and hillsides of La Jolla, one of the world's most beautiful, prestigious communities. The village—the heart of La Jolla—is chock-a-block with expensive boutiques, galleries, and restaurants. Don't despair, however, if you're not old money or even nouveau riche; this popular vacation spot has sufficient lodging choices for every pocket, even those on a budget.

$$$$ ★ **Sheraton Grande Torrey Pines.** The view of the Pacific from this low-rise, high-class property atop the Torrey Pines cliffs is superb. The hotel blends into the clifftop, looking rather insignificant until you step inside the luxurious lobby and gaze out at the sea and the 18th hole of the lush green Torrey Pines public golf course. Amenities include complimentary butler service—just pick up the phone in the morning and a carafe of Starbucks coffee and a newspaper will be delivered to your room, gratis. The oversize accommodations, tastefully decorated in muted tones, are simple but elegant; all have balconies or terraces. Guests have privileges at the excellent health club/sports center next door ($7.50). *10950 N. Torrey Pines Rd., 92037,* ☎ *619/558–1500 or 800/325–3535,* FAX *619/450–4584. 400 rooms, including 17 suites. Restaurant, bar, in-room safes, pool, 3 tennis courts, exercise room, bicycles. AE, D, DC, MC, V.*

$$$–$$$$ ★ **La Valencia.** A La Jolla landmark, this pink Art Deco confection drew film stars down from Hollywood in the 1930s and '40s for its lovely setting and views of La Jolla Cove. The clientele is a bit older and more staid these days, but the hotel is still in prime condition. Many of the individually decorated rooms have a genteel European look, with antique pieces and plush, richly colored rugs. The restaurants are excellent, the Whaling Bar is a popular gathering spot, and the hotel is ideally located near the shops and restaurants of La Jolla village and what is arguably the prettiest beach in San Diego. Prices are quite reasonable if you're willing to look out on the village, but on a clear, sunny day, the ocean views may be worth every extra penny. *1132 Prospect St., 92037,* ☎ *619/454–0771 or 800/451–0772,* FAX *619/456–3921. 100 rooms. 3 restaurants, bar, pool, hot tub, exercise room, library. AE, D, DC, MC, V.*

$$$–$$$$ **Sea Lodge.** This low-lying compound, on the excellent La Jolla Shores beach, has a definite Spanish flavor to it, with its palm trees, fountains, red-tiled roofs, and Mexican tile work. The attractive rooms feature rattan furniture, nautical-design bedspreads, and terra-cotta lattice-board walls; all have hair dryers, coffeemakers, refrigerators, and irons as well as wooden balconies that overlook lush landscaping and the sea. Early reservations are a must; families will find plenty of room and distractions for both kids and parents. *8110 Camino del Oro, 92037,* ☎ *619/459–8271 or 800/237–5211,* FAX *619/456–9346. 128 rooms, 19 with kitchenettes. Restaurant, bar, pool, hot tub, sauna, 2 tennis courts, golf course, Ping-Pong, beach. AE, D, DC, MC, V.*

$$$ **Colonial Inn.** A tastefully restored Victorian-era building, this is the oldest hotel in La Jolla, offering turn-of-the-century elegance in its public spaces; in keeping with the period, rooms are a bit formal and

staid. Ocean views cost more than village views. On one of La Jolla's main thoroughfares but not in the thick of its busiest people traffic, the Colonial Inn is near boutiques, restaurants, and the cove. ☐ *910 Prospect St., 92037,* ☎ *619/454–2181, 800/832–5525, or 800/826–1278 in CA;* FAX *619/454–5679. 75 rooms. Restaurant, bar, pool. AE, DC, MC, V.*

$$$ Hyatt Regency La Jolla. Designed by Michael Graves, the Hyatt is the cornerstone of the Aventine complex in La Jolla's Golden Triangle, about 10 minutes from the beach and the village. The postmodern mix of design elements of the striking lobby is carried out into the spacious, comfortable rooms, where warm cherry wood furnishings contrast with austere gray closets (their stainless-steel handles make them look rather like large wall safes). The hotel's four trendy restaurants include the excellent Cafe Japengo (*see* Dining, *above*); you can work off some of the calories at one of the best health clubs in the city. Rates are lower on the weekends at this business-oriented hotel. ☐ *3777 La Jolla Village Dr., 92122,* ☎ *619/552–1234 or 800/233–1234,* FAX *619/552–6066. 400 rooms and suites. 4 restaurants, bar, pool, spa, 2 tennis courts, basketball, health club, jogging. AE, D, DC, MC, V.*

$$$ Scripps Inn. You'd be wise to make reservations well in advance for this small, quiet inn tucked away on Coast Boulevard; its popularity with repeat visitors ensures that it is booked year-round. Available kitchen facilities and lower weekly and monthly rates (not available in the summer season) make it particularly attractive to long-term guests. All the rooms are individually decorated; all offer ocean views and two have fireplaces. Continental breakfast is served in the lobby each morning. ☐ *555 Coast Blvd. S,* ☎ *619/454–3391,* FAX *619/459–6758. 13 rooms. Kitchenettes. AE, D, MC, V.*

$$–$$$ Bed & Breakfast Inn at La Jolla. Built in 1913 by Irving Gill, this B&B is located in a quiet section of La Jolla just down the street from the Museum of Contemporary Art. The individually decorated rooms cover a wide range of sizes and styles—some are done in Laura Ashley prints, others feature wicker or rattan furnishings—but all are pretty and well tended and come with fresh fruit, sherry, and terry robes. The lovely gardens in the back were planned by Kate Sessions, who was instrumental in landscaping Balboa Park. ☐ *7753 Draper Ave., 92037,* ☎ *619/456–2066. 16 rooms, 15 with private bath. Refrigerators, library. MC, V.*

$$–$$$ Best Western Inn by the Sea. In a quiet section of La Jolla Village, within five blocks of the beach, the five-story Inn by the Sea has all the modern amenities at reasonable rates for La Jolla. Rooms are done in cheerful pastel tones and have private balconies with views of either the sea or the village. Continental breakfast, newspaper, and local phone calls are on the house. ☐ *7830 Fay Ave., 92037,* ☎ *619/459–4461 or 800/462–9732,* FAX *619/456–2578. 132 rooms. Pool, exercise room, free parking. AE, D, DC, MC, V.*

$$–$$$ La Jolla Cove Motel. Offering studios and suites, some with spacious oceanfront balconies, this motel overlooks the famous La Jolla Cove beach. If it doesn't have the charm of some of the older properties of this exclusive area, this motel gives its guests the same first-class views at much lower rates. A complimentary Continental breakfast is included in the room rate. The free underground lot is also a bonus in a section of town where a parking spot is a prime commodity. ☐ *1155 S. Coast Blvd., 92037,* ☎ *619/459–2621 or 800/248–2683. 117 rooms. Kitchenettes, pool, spa, putting green, coin laundry. AE, D, MC, V.*

$$–$$$ ★ Prospect Park Inn. This European-style inn rents a wide variety of appealing rooms, many with sweeping ocean views from their balconies. Located in a prime spot in La Jolla village, it's near some of the best shops and restaurants in town and one block away from the beach. Continental breakfast is included in the very reasonable room rate, and parking is free. There is no smoking on the premises. ☐ *1110 Prospect St., 92037,* ☎ *619/454–0133 or 800/433–1609,* FAX *619/454–2056. 23 rooms. Bar, kitchenettes. AE, D, DC, MC, V.*

$$ **La Jolla Palms Inn.** In the southern section of La Jolla, near some excellent beaches, this modest motel is also near a wide variety of shops and restaurants. Many of the rooms are remarkably large, with huge closets; some have kitchenettes, and three suites offer separate eat-in kitchens. The rooms are nothing to write home about, but this is an excellent value for families who want to stay in this tony area and still have a few dollars left over for shopping. Complimentary Continental breakfast is provided. New owners are planning substantial renovations and room upgrades. ☐ *6705 La Jolla Blvd., 92037,* ☎ *619/454–7101 or 800/451–0358,* FAX *619/454–6957. 58 rooms. Pool, spa, billiards, laundry. AE, D, DC, MC, V.*

$$ ★ **Torrey Pines Inn.** Located on a bluff between La Jolla and Del Mar, this hotel commands a view of miles and miles of coastline. It's adjacent to the public Torrey Pines Golf Course, one of the best in the county, and very close to scenic Torrey Pines State Beach and nature reserve; the village of La Jolla is a 10-minute drive away. Most of the rooms have been renovated with dark wood furnishings and Asian fabrics. This off-the-beaten-path inn is a very good value, especially for golfers. ☐ *11480 N. Torrey Pines Rd., 92037,* ☎ *619/453–4420, 800/995–4507 (hotel central), or 800/777–1700 for central reservations,* FAX *619/453–0691. 74 rooms. Restaurant, 2 bars, coffee shop, pool. AE, D, DC, MC, V.*

Mission Bay and Beaches

Staying near the water is a priority for most people who visit San Diego. Mission and Pacific beaches have the highest concentration of small hotels and motels. Both these areas have a casual atmosphere and a busy coastal thoroughfare offering endless shopping, dining, and nightlife possibilities. Mission Bay Park, with its beaches, bike trails, boat-launching ramps, golf course, and grassy parks, is also a hotel haven. You can't go wrong with any of these locations, as long as the frenzy of hundreds at play doesn't bother you.

$$$–$$$$ ★ **Catamaran Resort Hotel.** If you check in at the right time, parrots will herald your arrival at this appealing hotel, set between Mission Bay and Pacific Beach; the two resident birds are often poised on a perch in the lushly landscaped lobby, replete with a koi fish pond. The grounds are similarly tropical, and tiki torches light the way for guests staying at one of the six two-story buildings or the 14-story high-rise (the view from the upper floors of the latter is spectacular). The popular Cannibal Bar hosts Top 40s and rock-and-roll groups, while a classical or jazz pianist tickles the ivories at the Moray Bar; Catamaran guests can also take advantage of the entertainment facilities at the sister Bahia Hotel. Children 18 or under stay free. ☐ *3999 Mission Blvd., 92109,* ☎ *619/488–1081, 800/288–0770, or 800/233–8172 in Canada,* FAX *619/490–3328 (reservations) 619/488–1619 (front desk). 312 rooms. Restaurant, bar, coffee shop, piano bar, pool, spa, exercise room, nightclub. AE, D, DC, MC, V.*

$$$–$$$$ **Crystal Pier Motel.** You can drive your car onto the Crystal Pier and park in front of one of this classic motel's blue-and-white cottages, equipped with kitchenettes and patios overlooking the sea. A landmark since the 1930s, this place is no longer the bargain it once was, nor does it have the amenities of the other properties in its price category; you're paying for character and a unique proximity to the ocean. But

it retains a loyal following nevertheless; call four to six weeks in advance for reservations. Weekly and monthly rates are available in winter. The more people you come with, the more reasonable this place is: The cottages sleep up to four but cost the same no matter what the occupancy. ⊞ *4500 Ocean Blvd.,* ☎ *619/483–6983 or 800/748–5894,* FAX *619/483–6811. 26 cottages. Kitchenettes. 3-night minimum stay June 15–Sept. 15, 2-night minimum rest of yr. D, MC, V.*

$$$–$$$$ **San Diego Princess Resort.** This 44-acre resort is so beautifully landscaped that it's been the setting for a number of movies, and it offers a wide range of recreational activities, as well as access to a marina. A major renovation in 1993–94 brightened up rooms with colorful new fabrics and plush carpeting; unfortunately, the walls between them remain motel thin. All rooms have private patios and coffeemakers, and a number have kitchens. Of the resort's various eateries, the Barefoot Bar and Grill is the most fun; guests and visitors come here to kick off their shoes and boogie in a sand-filled, strobe-lit setting. ⊞ *1404 W. Vacation Rd., 92109,* ☎ *619/274–4630 or 800/344–2626,* FAX *619/581–5929. 462 cottages. 3 restaurants, 2 bars, 5 pools, sauna, 6 tennis courts, 18-hole putting golf course, croquet, health club, jogging, volleyball, boating, bicycles. AE, D, DC, MC, V.*

$$$ **Bahia Resort Hotel.** This huge complex, on a 14-acre peninsula in Mission Bay Park, offers tastefully furnished studios and suites with kitchens; many have wood-beamed ceilings and attractive tropical decor. The hotel's *Bahia Belle* cruises Mission Bay at sunset, and guests can return for yucks at the on-premises Comedy Isle club. Rates are reasonable for a place so well located—within walking distance of the ocean—and offering so many amenities, including use of the facilities at the Catamaran Hotel. ⊞ *998 W. Mission Bay Dr., 92109,* ☎ *619/488–0551, 800/288–0770, or 800/233–8172 in Canada,* FAX *619/490–3328 (reservations) or 619/488–7055. 321 rooms. Restaurant, bar, piano bar, pool, spa, 2 tennis courts, bicycles, rollerblading, comedy club. AE, D, DC, MC, V.*

$$$ **Hyatt Islandia.** Located in Mission Bay Park, one of San Diego's most appealing seashore areas, the Islandia has rooms in several low-level, lanai-style units, as well as marina suites and rooms in a high-rise building. Many of the tastefully modern accommodations overlook the hotel's gardens and fish pond; others have dramatic views of the bay area. This hotel is famous for its lavish Sunday champagne brunch. In winter, whale-watching expeditions depart from the Islandia's marina. ⊞ *1441 Quivira Rd., 92109,* ☎ *619/224–1234 or 800/233–1234,* FAX *619/224–0348. 422 rooms. 2 restaurants, pool, spa, exercise room, marina, boating. AE, D, DC, MC, V.*

$$$ **San Diego Hilton Beach and Tennis Resort.** Spread out on the picturesque grounds of this deluxe resort, low-level bungalows are surrounded by trees, Japanese bridges, and ponds; a high-rise building offers accommodations with lovely views of Mission Bay Park. The Kids Club Program offers complimentary day care for children over age 5 (daily during the summer, on weekends the rest of the year), and the sports facilities on the property are excellent. Tickets (and discounts) for various area attractions can be picked up at the concierge desk and charged to your room. The property underwent a $25 million renovation in 1994–95, with rooms redone in a contemporary version of Spanish-colonial style. ⊞ *1775 E. Mission Bay Dr., 92109,* ☎ *619/276–4010 or 800/445–8667,* FAX *619/275–7991. 357 rooms. Restaurant, bar, coffee shop, pool, putting greens, 5 tennis courts, exercise room, boating, marina, bicycles, playground, car rental. AE, D, DC, MC, V.*

$$–$$$ **Dana Inn & Marina.** This hotel, which has an adjoining marina, is a bargain in the Mission Bay area. If accommodations are not as grand as those in the nearby hotels, they're more than adequate. There are many on-premises sports facilities, and the Dana Inn is within walking distance of Sea World, the beach, and a pleasant park. *1710 W. Mission Bay Dr., 92109, ☎ 619/222–6440, 800/DANA–INN, or 800/345–9995 (central reservations), FAX 619/222–5916. 196 rooms. Restaurant, pool, spa, 2 tennis courts, Ping-Pong, shuffleboard, boating. AE, D, DC, MC, V.*

$$ **Surfer Motor Lodge.** This high-rise is right on the beach and directly behind a shopping center with many restaurants and boutiques. Rooms are plain, but those on the upper floors have excellent views. *711 Pacific Beach Dr., 92109, ☎ 619/483–7070 or 800/787–3373, FAX 619/274–1670. 52 rooms. Restaurant, bar, pool, bicycles. AE, DC, MC, V.*

$–$$ ★ **Ocean Manor Apartment Hotel.** Some folks have been returning for 20 years to this well-priced Ocean Beach hotel, which rents units by the day (three-day minimum for those with kitchens), week, or month in winter; you'll need to reserve months in advance. Ocean Manor offers lovely views; the beach below has long since washed away, but other beaches are within walking distance and Point Loma is a 10-minute drive away. The comfortable studios and one- and two-bedroom suites are furnished plainly in the style of the 1950s—which is when the amiable owners took over the place. There is no maid service, but fresh towels are always provided. A limited number of garages are available for $1 a night. *1370 Sunset Cliffs Blvd., 92107, ☎ 619/222–7901 or 619/224–1379 (guest calls). 22 units. Pool, Ping-Pong, shuffleboard. MC, V.*

$ **Mission Bay Motel.** Located a half-block from the beach, this motel offers centrally located, modest units, some with kitchenettes. Great restaurants and nightlife are within walking distance, but you may find the area a bit noisy. *4221 Mission Blvd., 92109, ☎ 619/483–6440. 50 rooms. Pool. MC, V.*

Hostels

Banana Bungalow San Diego (707 Reed Ave., Mission Beach 92109, ☎ 619/273–3060 or 800/546–7835); **YWCA of San Diego** (1012 C St., San Diego 92101, ☎ 619/239–0355).

THE ARTS AND NIGHTLIFE

The Arts

By Marael Johnson

Updated by Albert M. Columbo

Top national touring companies perform regularly at the Civic Theatre, Golden Hall, Symphony Hall, and East County Performing Arts Center. Local universities and community colleges present a wide variety of performing-arts programs. The daily *San Diego Union* lists current attractions and movie schedules. The *Reader,* a free weekly that comes out each Thursday, devotes an entire section to cultural events, as well as current theater and film reviews. *San Diego* magazine publishes a monthly "What's Doing" column that lists events throughout the county and reviews of current films, plays, and concerts.

Half-price tickets to most theater, music, and dance events can be bought on the day of performance at the **TIMES ARTS TIX Ticket Center** (Horton Plaza, ☎ 619/238–3810). Only cash is accepted. Advance full-price tickets may also be purchased through ARTS TIX.

Visa and MasterCard holders may buy tickets for many scheduled performances through **Ticketmaster** (☎ 619/220–8497). Service charges vary according to the event, and most tickets are nonrefundable.

Theater

Blackfriars Theatre (121 Broadway, Suite 203, ☎ 619/232–4088), formerly the Bowery, is acclaimed by critics and theater goers for its premieres of high-quality works by both famous playwrights and soon-to-be-discovered artists.

Coronado Playhouse (1775 Strand Way, Coronado, ☎ 619/435–4856), a cabaret-type theater near the Hotel del Coronado, stages regular dramatic and musical performances. Dinner packages are offered on Friday and Saturday.

Diversionary Theatre (4545 Park Blvd., University Heights, ☎ 619/574–1060) is a gay and lesbian theater that stages comedies and dramas on gay themes for the whole community.

Gaslamp Quarter Theatre at the Hahn Cosmopolitan Theatre (444 4th Ave., ☎ 619/234–9583). The resident theater company stages comedies, dramas, mysteries, and musicals.

La Jolla Playhouse (Mandell Weiss Center for the Performing Arts, University of California at San Diego, ☎ 619/550–1010). From May to November, look for exciting and innovative presentations, under the artistic direction of Michael Greif. Many Broadway productions have previewed here before heading for the East Coast.

Lawrence Welk Resort Theatre (8860 Lawrence Welk Dr., Escondido, ☎ 619/749–3448 or 800/932–9355). About a 45-minute drive from downtown, this famed dinner theater puts on polished Broadway-style productions.

Old Globe Theatre (Simon Edison Centre for the Performing Arts, Balboa Park, ☎ 619/239–2255) is the oldest professional theater in California, performing classics, contemporary dramas, experimental works, and putting on the famous summer Shakespeare Festival at the Old Globe and its sister theaters, the Cassius Carter Centre Stage and the Lowell Davies Festival Theatre.

San Diego Comic Opera (Casa del Prado Theatre, Balboa Park, ☎ 619/231–5714) has four different productions of Gilbert and Sullivan and similar works from October through July.

San Diego Repertory Theater (79 Horton Plaza, ☎ 619/235–8025), San Diego's first resident acting company, performs contemporary works year-round on two different stages.

Sledgehammer Theatre (1620 6th Ave., ☎ 619/544–1484) is one of the cutting-edge theaters in San Diego; it stages avant-garde pieces in St. Cecilia's church.

Sushi Performance and Visual Art (633 9th Ave., ☎ 619/235–8466), a nationally acclaimed group, provides an opportunity for well-known performance artists to do their thing.

Concerts

Copley Symphony Hall (1245 7th Ave., ☎ 619/699–4200). The San Diego Symphony Orchestra performance season runs October–May, with a series of outdoor pop concerts held near Seaport Village during the summer.

Open-Air Theatre (San Diego State University, ☎ 619/594–6884). Top-name rock, reggae, and popular artists pack in the crowds for summer concerts under the stars.

Organ Pavilion (Balboa Park, ☎ 619/226–0819). Robert Plimpton performs free concerts on the giant 1914 pipe organ at 2 PM on most Sunday afternoons and on most Monday evenings in summer.

Sherwood Auditorium (700 Prospect St., La Jolla, ☎ 619/454–2594). Many classical and jazz events are held in the 550-seat auditorium in the San Diego Museum of Contemporary Art. August–May, La Jolla Chamber Music Society presents internationally acclaimed chamber ensembles, orchestras, and soloists. San Diego Chamber Orchestra, a 35-member ensemble, performs once a month, October–April.

Sports Arena (2500 Sports Arena Blvd., ☎ 619/224–4176). Big-name rock concerts play to more than 14,000 fans.

Spreckels Theatre (121 Broadway, ☎ 619/235–9500). This beautiful downtown theater, built more than 80 years ago and designated a landmark in 1972, hosts a wide range of musical events—everything from Mostly Mozart to small rock concerts. Ballets and theatrical productions are also held here.

Opera

Civic Theatre (202 C St., ☎ 619/236–6510). The San Diego Opera draws international artists and has developed an impeccable reputation. The season of five operas runs January–April in the 3,000-seat, state-of-the-art auditorium.

Dance

California Ballet (☎ 619/560–5676). Four high-quality contemporary and traditional works, from story ballets to Balanchine, are performed September–May. The *Nutcracker* is staged annually at the Civic Theatre; other ballets take place at Poway Center for the Performing Arts (15500 Espola Rd., Poway, ☎ 619/748–0505), the Lyceum, and Nautilus Bowl at Sea World.

Issacs McCaleb & Dancers (☎ 619/296–9523). Interpretative dance presentations, incorporating live music, are staged at major theaters and concert halls around San Diego County.

Nightlife

By Dan Janeck

Updated by Alberto Columbo

Music at local nightclubs ranges from danceable contemporary Top 40 to original rock and new wave. Discos and bars in the Gaslamp Quarter and at Pacific and Mission beaches are crowded weekends, but don't let that discourage you from visiting these quintessential San Diego hangouts. Live pop and fusion jazz have become especially popular in recent years. Country-western music is also plentiful. Should your tastes run to softer music, piano bars abound as well. Check the free weekly *Reader* for band information or *San Diego* magazine's "Restaurant & Nightlife Guide" for the full range of possibilities.

Bars and nightclubs usually stop serving at about 1:40 AM. You must be 21 to purchase and consume alcohol; most places will insist on current identification. Be aware that California also has some of the most stringent drunk-driving laws in the United States; roadblocks are not uncommon.

Bars and Nightclubs

Club Fifth Avenue. This is a popular destination for young professionals. There's a dress code (no jeans, T-shirts, or tennis shoes) Friday and Saturday nights. *835 5th Ave., downtown,* ☎ *619/238–7191.* ⏲ *Wed.–Sun. 8 PM–2 AM. AE, D, DC, MC, V.*

Club 66. Located under the restaurant Dakota's, this impressive club with stainless-steel decor and gas-station memorabilia is modeled after Route 66. *901 5th Ave., downtown,* ☎ *619/234–4166.* ⏲ *Wed.–Sat. 8 PM–2 AM. AE, D, DC, MC, V.*

E Street Alley. Off the street down a short alley, this club is a marvel for the senses. The Blue Room is a plush lounge of blue velvet covered walls, artwork, big velvet seats romantically paired in mood lighting and a handsome bar with live jazz on Thursdays and blues the rest of the week. Club E is a smartly designed spacious dance club with a DJ spinning Top 40 tunes. Chino's is an exquisite restaurant featuring an American cuisine with a Southeast Asian flare open 11:30 AM–2:30 PM and 5:30 PM–11 PM. *914 4th Ave. (on E St. between 4th and 5th), downtown,* ☎ *619/231–9200.* ⏲ *Tues.–Thurs. 10 PM–2 AM, Fri. and Sat. 8 PM–2 AM. AE, D, DC, MC, V.*

Megalopolis. This funky little club hosts an eclectic roster of blues, rock, and folk bands. *4321 Fairmount Ave., Kensington,* ☎ *619/584–7900.* ⏲ *Tues.–Sat. 8 PM–2 AM. No credit cards.*

Patrick's II. This downtown pub with definite Irish tendencies hosts live New Orleans–style jazz, blues, and rock. *428 F St., downtown,* ☎ *619/233–3077. Entertainment nightly 9 PM–2 AM. No credit cards.*

Jazz Clubs

Croce's. Superb acoustic-jazz musicians and an interesting menu are the draws here. Next door, Croce's Top Hat puts on live R&B nightly 9 PM–2 AM. *802 5th Ave., Gaslamp Quarter,* ☎ *619/233–4355.* ⏲ *Nightly 7:30 PM–2 AM. AE, D, DC, MC, V.*

Elario's. This club, on the top floor of the Summer House Inn, has an ocean view and an incomparable lineup of internationally acclaimed jazz musicians every month. *7955 La Jolla Shores Dr., La Jolla,* ☎ *619/459–0541. Nightly shows at 8:20, 9:45, and 11. AE, DC, MC, V.*

Humphrey's. This is the premier promoter of the city's best jazz, folk, and light-rock summer concert series held out on the grass. The rest of the year the music moves indoors for some first-rate jazz Sunday and Monday. *2241 Shelter Island Dr.,* ☎ *619/523–1010 for taped concert information. Entertainment 8 PM–midnight. AE, D, DC, MC, V.*

Rock Clubs

Belly Up Tavern. This eclectic live-concert venue hosts critically acclaimed artists who play reggae, rock, new wave, Motown, and other music. The Belly Up attracts people of all ages. Sunday nights are usually free and feature local R&B artists. *143 S. Cedros Ave., Solana Beach,* ☎ *619/481–9022.* ⏲ *Daily 11 AM–1:30 AM. Entertainment 9:30 PM–1:30 AM. MC, V.*

Bodie's. This Gaslamp Quarter bar hosts the best rock and blues bands in San Diego and some from out of town. *528 F St.,* ☎ *619/236–8988.* ⏲ *Daily 6 AM–2 AM. No credit cards.*

Casbah. This small club showcases rock, reggae, funk, and every other kind of band—except Top 40. *2501 Kettner Blvd., near the airport,* ☎ *619/232–4355. Live bands nightly at 9:30. No credit cards.*

Spirit. This original-music club emphasizes the top local alternative and experimental-rock groups. *1130 Buenos Ave., Bay Park, near Mission Bay,* ☎ *619/276–3993.* ⏲ *Nightly 8 PM–1 AM. No credit cards.*

Winston's Beach Club. Local bands, reggae groups, and, occasionally, '60s rock bands play this bowling alley turned rock club. The crowd here can get rowdy. *1921 Bacon St., Ocean Beach,* ☎ *619/222–6822. Live bands nightly 9 PM–2 AM. MC, V.*

Country-Western Clubs

Big Stone Lodge. This rustic dance hall showcases the two-steppin' tunes of the owners' band. Free dance lessons are given some nights. *12237 Old Pomerado Rd., Poway,* ☎ *619/748–1135. Entertainment Tues.–Thurs. 8 PM–12:30 AM, Fri. and Sat. 9 PM–1:30 AM, Sun. 5:30 PM–9:30 PM. DC, MC, V.*

In Cahootz. A great sound system, a large dance floor, occasional big-name performers, and free dance lessons every day except Wednesday are among this bar's many lures. *5373 Mission Center Rd., Mission Valley, ☎ 619/291–8635. ⏲ Weeknights 5 PM–2 AM, weekends 5:30 PM–2 AM. AE, D, MC, V.*

Leo's Little Bit O' Country. This is one of the largest country-western dance floors in the county. Leo's is another fun place to come for free dance lessons. *680 W. San Marcos Blvd., San Marcos, ☎ 619/744–4120. ⏲ Tues.–Sat. 5 PM–1 AM, Sun. 4 –midnight. Entertainment 8:30 PM–1 AM, Sun. 6:30 PM–midnight. Closed Mon. MC, V.*

Wrangler's Roost. This is a country-western haunt that appeals to both the longtime cowboy customer and the first-timer. Free dance lessons are offered Tuesday–Saturday nights. *6608 Mission Gorge Rd., ☎ 619/280–6263. ⏲ Daily 2 PM–2 AM. Entertainment Wed.–Sat. 9 PM–2 AM. MC, V.*

Zoo Country. Enjoy live music and free dance lessons Friday through Sunday or a DJ seven nights a week at this new hangout. *1340 Broadway, El Cajon, ☎ 619/442–9900. ⏲ Tues.–Sun. 5:30 PM–11 PM. AE, D, MC, V.*

Comedy Clubs

Comedy Isle. This club in the Bahia Resort Hotel books local and national talent. *998 W. Mission Bay Dr., Mission Bay, ☎ 619/488–6872. Shows Wed., Thurs., and Sun. 8:30 PM, Fri. and Sat. 8:30 and 10:30 PM. Reservations accepted. AE, DC, MC, V.*

The Comedy Store. National touring and local talent performs here. *916 Pearl St., La Jolla, ☎ 619/454–9176. Shows Tues.–Thurs. 8 PM, Fri. and Sat. 8 and 10:30 PM, Sun. 8:30 PM. AE, MC, V.*

Discos

Club Emerald City. Alternative dance music and an uninhibited clientele keep this beach-town spot hopping. *945 Garnet Ave., Pacific Beach, ☎ 619/483–9920. ⏲ Tues.–Sun. 8:30 PM–2 AM. No credit cards.*

Club Tremors. This impressive disco with nonstop dance music is a definite hot spot for those on the (21–35) singles scene. *860 Garnet Ave., Pacific Beach, ☎ 619/272–7278. ⏲ Tues.–Sun. 8:30 PM–2 AM. AE, D, MC, V.*

Johnny M's. Get down to '70s and '80s dance music at this huge disco. A blues room is open Wednesday, Friday, and Saturday from 10 PM to 1:30 AM, and the DJ plays from 8 PM until 1:30 AM. *801 4th St., Gaslamp Quarter, ☎ 619/233–1131. ⏲ Tues.–Sat. 8 PM–2 AM, restaurant open daily 11 AM–midnight. AE, D, MC, V.*

Olé Madrid. Slick back your hair and enjoy the loud, continuous beat at this Euro-style disco for the very chic. *755 5th Ave., Gaslamp Quarter, ☎ 619/557–0146. ⏲ Weekdays 11:30 AM–2 AM, weekends 5 PM–2 AM. AE, MC, V.*

Singles Bars

Dick's Last Resort. On weekends, fun-loving party people line up to get into this enormous barnlike restaurant and bar featuring live Dixieland music and an extensive beer list. *345 4th Ave., downtown, ☎ 619/231–9100. ⏲ Daily 11 AM–2 AM. AE, MC, V.*

El Torito. Notable happy hours and the central location attract yuppies and students to this Mission Valley Mexican restaurant. *445 Camino del Rio S, ☎ 619/296–6154. ⏲ Daily 11 AM–2 AM. AE, D, DC, MC, V.*

The U. S. Grant Hotel. This place is the classiest spot in town for meeting fellow travelers while relaxing with a scotch or martini at the mahogany bar. The best local Latin, jazz, and blues bands alternate appearances during the week. It's definitely for the over-30 business set. *326 Broadway, downtown,* ☎ *619/232–3121.* ⏲ *Daily 11:30 AM–1:30 AM. AE, D, DC, MC, V.*

Piano Bars/Mellow

Hotel del Coronado. The fairy-tale hostelry features beautiful piano music in its Crown Room and Palm Court, with dance-oriented standards in the Ocean Terrace Lounge. *1500 Orange Ave., Coronado,* ☎ *619/435–6611.* ⏲ *Daily 10:30 AM–1:30 AM. AE, D, DC, MC, V.*

Top O' the Cove. Show tunes and standards from the '40s to the '80s are the typical fare at this magnificent Continental restaurant in La Jolla. *1216 Prospect St.,* ☎ *619/454–7779. Entertainment Wed.–Sun. 8 PM–11 PM. AE, DC, MC, V.*

Westgate Hotel. One of the most elegant settings in San Diego offers piano music in the Plaza Bar. *1055 2nd Ave., downtown,* ☎ *619/238–1818.* ⏲ *Daily 11 AM–2 AM. Entertainment Mon.–Sat. 8:30 PM–closing. AE, D, DC, MC, V.*

Gay Bars and Discos

Bourbon Street. This classy piano bar with relaxing surroundings and a courtyard out back has live entertainment nightly. *4612 Park Blvd., University Heights,* ☎ *619/291–0173.* ⏲ *Weekdays noon–2 AM, Sat. 11 AM–2 AM, Sun. 9 AM–2 AM. D, MC, V.*

The Flame. A San Diego landmark, this friendly dance club caters to lesbians most of the week. On Tuesday, the DJ spins for the very popular Boys' Night, and on Friday there's a drag show. *3780 Park Blvd., Hillcrest,* ☎ *619/295–4163.* ⏲ *Daily 5 PM–2 AM. No credit cards.*

Flicks. Here you'll find a video bar with music and comedy—if you're not too busy looking at everyone else. *1017 University Ave., Hillcrest,* ☎ *619/297–2056.* ⏲ *Daily 2 PM–2 AM. No credit cards.*

West Coast Production Company. This three-story discotheque is really three clubs in one: two dance floors and a rooftop video bar overlooking the downtown skyline. *2028 Hancock St., Middletown,* ☎ *619/295–3724.* ⏲ *Wed., Fri., Sat. 9 PM–2 AM. MC, V.*

EXCURSIONS

The San Diego North Coast

By Kevin Brass

Updated by Albert M. Columbo

To say the north coast area of San Diego County is different from the city of San Diego is a vast understatement. From the northern tip of La Jolla to Oceanside, a half-dozen small communities each developed separately from urban San Diego—and from one another. The rich and famous were drawn early on to Del Mar, for example, because of its wide beaches and thoroughbred horse-racing facility. Just a couple of miles away, agriculture, not paparazzi, played a major role in the development of Solana Beach and Encinitas. Up the coast, Carlsbad still reveals elements of roots directly tied to the old Mexican rancheros and the entrepreneurial instinct of John Frazier, who told people the area's water could cure common ailments. In the late 19th century, not far from the current site of the posh La Costa Hotel and Spa, Frazier attempted to turn the area into a massive replica of a German mineral springs resort.

Today, the north coast is a booming population center. An explosion of development throughout the 1980s turned the area into a northern extension of San Diego. The freeways started to take on the typically cluttered characteristics of most southern California freeways.

Beyond the freeways, though, the communities have maintained their charm. Some of the finest restaurants, beaches, and attractions in San

Diego County can be found in the area, a true slice of southern California heritage. From the plush estates and rolling hills of Rancho Santa Fe and the beachfront restaurants of Cardiff to Mission San Luis Rey, a well-preserved remnant of California's first European settlers in Oceanside, the north coast is a distinctly different place.

Exploring

Numbers in the margin correspond to points of interest on the San Diego North Coast map.

Any journey around the north coast area naturally starts at the beach, and this one begins at **Torrey Pines State Beach,** just south of Del Mar. At the south end of the wide beach, perched on top of the cliffs, is the
1 **Torrey Pines State Reserve,** one of only two places (the other place is Santa Rosa Island off the coast of northern California) where the Torrey pine tree grows naturally. ☎ *619/755–2063.* ☛ *$4 per car.* ⏲ *Daily 9–sunset.*

2 To the east of the state beach is **Los Penasquitos Lagoon,** one of the many natural estuaries that flow inland between Del Mar and Oceanside. Following Old Highway 101, the road leads into the small village of **Del Mar,** best known for its chic shopping strip, celebrity visitors, and wide beaches. Years of spats between developers and res-
3 idents have resulted in the **Del Mar Plaza,** hidden by boulder walls and clever landscaping at the corner of Old Highway 101 and 15th Street. The upper level has a large deck and a view out to the ocean, and the restaurants and shops are excellent barometers of the latest in southern California style. A left turn at 15th Street leads to Seagrove Park, a small stretch of grass overlooking the ocean, where concerts are performed on summer evenings. A right turn on Coast Boulevard provides access to Del Mar's beautiful beaches, particularly popular with Frisbee and volleyball players.

Less than a half-mile north, Coast Boulevard merges with Old High-
4 way 101. Across the road are the **Del Mar Fairgrounds,** home to more than 100 different events a year, ranging from a cat show to an auto race. *Via de la Valle Rd. exit west from I–5,* ☎ *619/259–1355 for recorded events line.*

The fairgrounds also host the annual summer meeting of the **Del Mar Thoroughbred Club** (aka "Where the Turf Meets the Surf"). The track brings the top horses and jockeys to Del Mar, along with a cross section of the rich and famous, eager to bet on the ponies. Crooner Bing Crosby and his Hollywood buddies, Pat O'Brien, Gary Cooper, and Oliver Hardy, among others, organized the track in the '30s, primarily because Crosby thought it would be fun to have a track near his Rancho Santa Fe home. Del Mar soon developed into a regular stop for the stars of stage and screen.

During the off-season, horse players can still gamble at the fairgrounds, thanks to a satellite wagering facility. Races from other California tracks are televised, and people can bet as if the races were being run right there. Times vary, depending on which tracks in the state are operating. ☎ *619/755–1167. Racing season: July–Sept., Wed.–Mon. Post time 2* PM.

Next to the fairgrounds, on Jimmy Durante Boulevard, is a small exotic bird-training facility, **Freeflight,** which is open to the public. Visitors are allowed to handle the birds—a guaranteed child pleaser. *2132 Jimmy Durante Blvd.,* ☎ *619/481–3148.* ☛ *$1.* ⏲ *Daily 10–4.*

Following Via de la Valle Road east from I–5 will take you to the exclusive community of **Rancho Santa Fe.** Groves of huge, drooping eu-

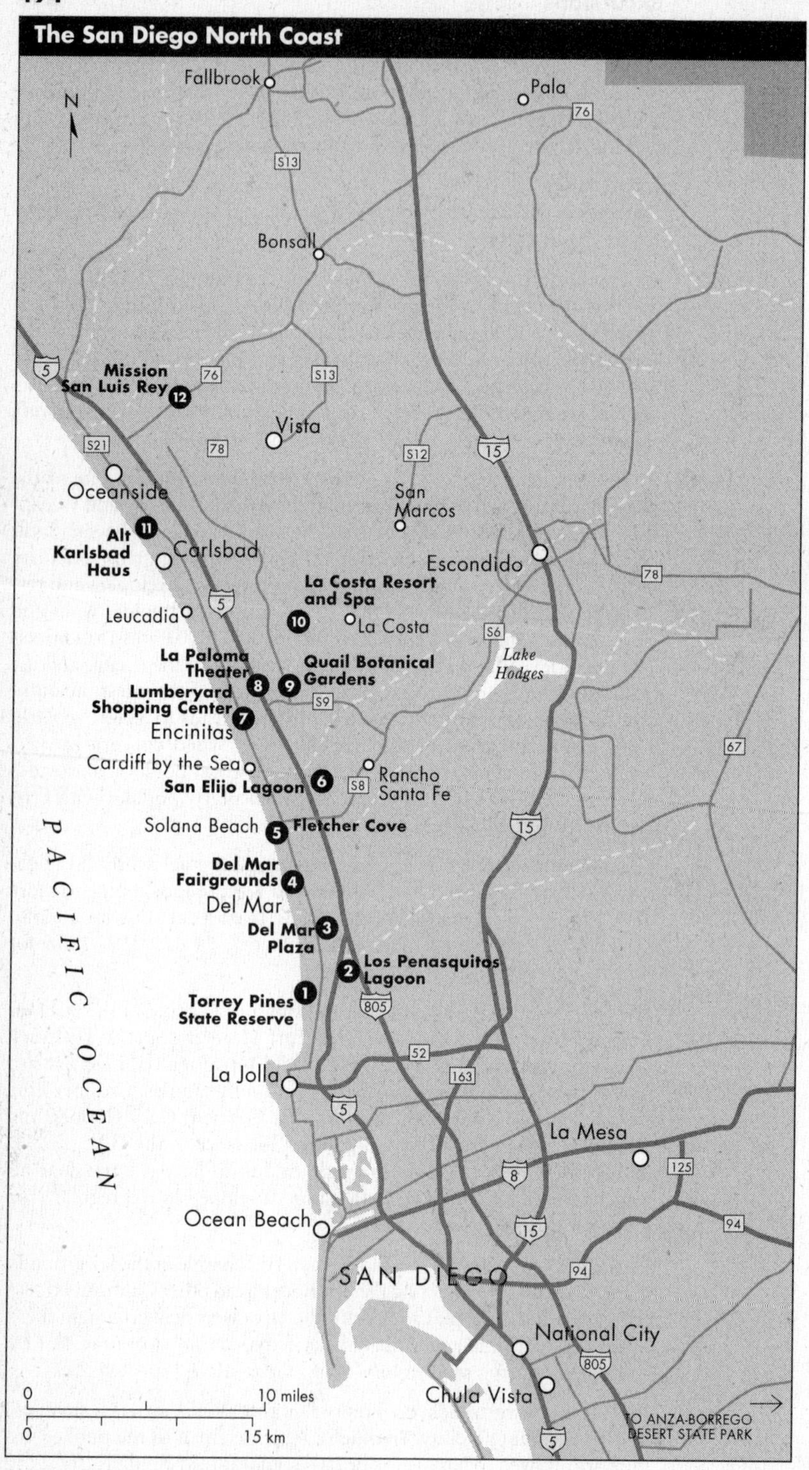
The San Diego North Coast
N
Fallbrook
Pala
76
S13
Bonsall
5
Mission San Luis Rey
12
76
S13
Vista
S21
78
S12
15
Oceanside
San Marcos
11
Alt Karlsbad Haus
Carlsbad
Escondido
78
La Costa Resort and Spa
5
Leucadia
10
La Costa
S6
La Paloma Theater
8
9
Quail Botanical Gardens
Lake Hodges
Lumberyard Shopping Center
7
S9
Encinitas
67
Cardiff by the Sea
Rancho Santa Fe
San Elijo Lagoon
6
S8
Solana Beach
5
Fletcher Cove
15
Del Mar Fairgrounds
4
Del Mar
Del Mar Plaza
3
2
Los Penasquitos Lagoon
1
Torrey Pines State Reserve
805
PACIFIC OCEAN
52
La Jolla
163
5
La Mesa
8
125
Ocean Beach
15
94
SAN DIEGO
94
National City
805
0
10 miles
Chula Vista
0
15 km
TO ANZA-BORREGO DESERT STATE PARK
5

calyptus trees, first imported to the area by a railroad company in search of trees to grow for railroad ties, cover the hills and valleys, hiding the posh estates. The little village of Rancho has some elegant and quaint—and overpriced—shops and restaurants. But it is no accident that there is little else to see or do in Rancho; the residents guard their privacy religiously.

Back along the coast, along Old Highway 101 north of Del Mar, is the
quiet little oceanside community of **Solana Beach.** A highlight of Solana
5 Beach is **Fletcher Cove,** located at the west end of Lomas Santa Fe Drive.
Early Solana settlers used dynamite to blast the cove out of the over-
hanging cliffs. Called Pill Box by the locals because of a bunkerlike
lifeguard station that overlooks it, the Fletcher Cove beach is easy to
reach and has a large parking lot.

6 To the north, separating Solana Beach from Cardiff, is the **San Elijo Lagoon,** home to many migrating birds. Trails wind around the entire area.

As you continue along Old Highway 101, past the cluster of hillside homes that make up Cardiff and beyond the campgrounds of the San Elijo State Beach, the palm trees of Sea Cliff Roadside Park (Swami's to the locals) and the golden domes of the Self-Realization Fellowship mark the entrance to downtown **Encinitas.** The Self-Realization Fellowship was built at the turn of the century and is a retreat and place of worship for the followers of a Native American religious sect. Its beautiful gardens are open to the public.

A recent landmark of Encinitas (which was incorporated as a city in
1986, including the communities of Cardiff, Leucadia, and Olivenhain)
7 is the **Lumberyard Shopping Center,** a collection of small stores and
restaurants that anchors the downtown shopping area.

8 An older landmark of Encinitas is the **La Paloma Theater** (471 lst St., near the corner of Encinitas Blvd., ☎ 619/436–7469), at the north end of town. Built in the 1920s as a stop for traveling vaudeville troupes, it has served as a concert hall, movie theater, and meeting place for the area ever since. Plays are still being rehearsed and performed here.

Encinitas is best known as the Flower Capital of the World, and although the flower industry is not as prevalent as it once was, the city
is still home to Paul Ecke Poinsettias, the largest producer of the popular Christmas blossom. A sampling of the area's dedication to horti-
9 culture can be found at the **Quail Botanical Gardens,** home to thousands
of different varieties of plants, especially drought-tolerant species.
Horticultural lectures are given here, and there are often plant sales.
*230 Quail Gardens Dr. (take Encinitas Blvd. east from I–5 and turn
left on Quail Gardens Dr.), ☎ 619/436–3036. Parking: $1. ⏲ Daily
8–5; closed 1st Mon. of month.*

Old Highway 101 continues north through **Leucadia** (named after a
famous Greek promontory), a small community best known for its small
art galleries and stores. At the north end of Leucadia, La Costa Avenue meets Old Highway 101. Following La Costa Avenue east, past
10 the Batiquitos Lagoon, you'll come to **La Costa Resort and Spa** (*see*
Lodging, *below*), once famous for its high-profile guests and reputed
mafia ties and now noted for its excellent golf and tennis facilities.

La Costa is technically part of the city of **Carlsbad,** which is centered farther north, west of the Tamarack Avenue and Elm Avenue exits of I–5. In Carlsbad, Old Highway 101 is called Carlsbad Boulevard. Large rancheros owned by wealthy Mexicans were the first settle-

ments inland; the coastal area was developed by an entrepreneur, John Frazier, who lured people to the area with talk of the healing powers of mineral water bubbling from a coastal well. The water was found to have the same properties as water from the German mineral wells of Karlsbad—hence the name of the new community. Remnants from
11 the era, including the original well, are found at the **Alt Karlsbad Haus,** a small museum–gift shop carrying northern European wares. *2802A Carlsbad Blvd., ☎ 619/729–6912. ⏲ Mon.–Sat. 10–5, Sun. noon–5.*

North of Carlsbad is **Oceanside,** home of Camp Pendleton, the country's largest marine base, as well as a beautiful natural harbor teeming with activity. **Oceanside Harbor** (☎ 619/966–4570) is the north-coast center for fishing, sailing, and all ocean-water sports. Salty fisherman types tend to congregate at Oceanside Pier.

Also in Oceanside is the **California Surf Museum,** which charts the history of surfing from balsa-wood boards up through the present Fiberglas state-of-the-art. *308 N. Pacific St., ☎ 619/721–6876. ☛ Free, donations appreciated. ⏲ Thurs.–Mon. noon–4, expanded hrs in summer.*

12 Oceanside is also home to **Mission San Luis Rey,** built by Franciscan friars in 1798 to help educate and convert local Native Americans. One of the best-preserved missions in the area, San Luis Rey was the 18th and largest of the California missions. Retreats are still held here, but a picnic area, gift shop, and museum are also on the grounds today. Self-guided tours are available. *4050 Mission Ave. (take Mission Ave. east from I–5), ☎ 619/757–3651. ☛ $3 adults, $1 children. ⏲ Mon.–Sat. 10–4:30, Sun. noon–4:30.*

Dining

Given the north coast's reputation as a suburban area, there is a surprisingly large selection of top-quality restaurants here. In fact, San Diegans often take the drive north to enjoy the variety of cuisines offered here.

WHAT TO WEAR

"Dressy casual" is the norm when dining at the more expensive north-coast establishments.

CATEGORY	COST*
$$$	over $30
$$	$20–$30
$	under $20

**per person for a three-course meal, excluding drinks, service, and 7¾% tax*

CARDIFF

$$ **The Chart House.** The beach and the sunset above the Pacific are the chief attractions of this surfside dining spot. Entrées include fresh fish, seafood, and beef dishes; there's also a good salad bar. ✕ *2588 Hwy. 101, ☎ 619/436–4044. Reservations advised. AE, D, DC, MC, V. No lunch; Sun. brunch.*

DEL MAR

$$$ **Tourlas.** Impressive California cuisine is served at the restaurant at Del Mar's posh L'Auberge resort. Such appetizers as corn meal–covered crab cakes might be followed by rack of lamb on couscous or halibut coated in pine nuts. The setting is lovely, and the service is attentive. ✕ *1540 Camino del Mar, ☎ 619/259–1515. Reservations advised. AE, D, DC, MC, V.*

$$ **Cilantro's.** Creative Mexican and southwestern-style dishes full of subtle spices are served here, including shark fajitas and spit-roasted chicken with a mild chili sauce. The inexpensive tapas menu, with such delicacies as crab tostadas and three-cheese quesadillas, is a little easier on the wallet. ✕ *3702 Via de la Valle,* ☎ *619/259–8777. Reservations advised. AE, MC, V.*

$$ **Epazote.** The sister restaurant to Cilantro's, located in the Del Mar Plaza, Epazote serves a similar menu of Cal-Mex cuisine with a southwestern touch. ✕ *1555 Camino del Mar, Suite. 322,* ☎ *619/259–9966. Reservations advised. AE, MC, V.*

$$ **Il Fornaio.** Located within the Del Mar Plaza, Il Fornaio features northern Italian cuisine, such as fresh seafood, homemade pastas, and crispy pizzas. The outdoor piazza affords a splendid ocean view. ✕ *1555 Camino del Mar, Suite 301,* ☎ *619/755–8876. Reservations advised. AE, DC, MC, V.*

$$ **Pacifica Del Mar.** Yet another fine Del Mar Plaza restaurant boasting a stunning view, Pacifica Del Mar emphasizes an imaginative California cuisine of fresh ingredients prepared with southwestern, Cajun, Italian, and Pacific Rim touches. Start with the scrumptious smoked corn, chicken, and black-bean chowder, and then go on to the grilled prawn salad, blackened catfish, or one of the free-range chicken dishes. Desserts are tasty, and the wine list is excellent. ✕ *1555 Camino del Mar, Suite 321,* ☎ *619/792–0476. Reservations advised. AE, D, DC, MC, V.*

$ **Johnny Rockets.** This '50s-style malt-and-burger joint, on the Del Mar Plaza's lower level, dishes up juicy burgers, thick malts, and fries. ✕ *1555 Camino del Mar, Suite 102,* ☎ *619/755–1954. MC, V.*

ENCINITAS

$ **Rico's Taco Shop.** Short on frills but long on great food, this Mexican fast-food café is a local favorite. Come here for excellent chicken taquitos, carne asada burritos, and the best fish burritos and tacos in town. The owners are friendly and health conscious, too: No lard is used in the recipes. Rico's is open daily for breakfast, lunch, and dinner. ✕ *165-L S. El Camino Real, in the Target Shopping Center,* ☎ *619/944–7689. No credit cards.*

$ **Vigilucci's.** This Italian trattoria has a cozy, bistrolike atmosphere, knowledgeable Italian waiters, and a stylish menu. The pastas are particularly good: Try the *spaghetti al funghetto,* with a fresh mushroom sauce, or the *tagliatelle alla bolognese,* with ground duck, chicken, and veal in a tomato sauce. The locally made bread is excellent, but the wine list needs upgrading. ✕ *505 1st St. (Hwy. 101),* ☎ *619/942–7332. Reservations advised. AE, D, DC, MC, V. No lunch weekends.*

RANCHO SANTA FE

$$$ ★ **Mille Fleurs.** Within a mile of Chino's, the county's most famous vegetable farm, where the chef shops daily, this is a most romantic hideaway, with tempting cuisine to enhance the mood. ✕ *6009 Paseo Delicias,* ☎ *619/756–3085. Reservations advised. AE, D, DC, MC, V. No lunch weekends.*

SOLANA BEACH

$ **California Pizza Kitchen.** Bright, noisy, and cheerful, this popular restaurant in the Boardwalk shopping center produces a selection of designer pizzas from its wood-fired oven. If Caribbean-shrimp, tuna-melt, or moo-shu-chicken pizzas are too exotic for you, try the duck sausage (particularly recommended), the mixed-grill vegetarian, or the five-cheese and tomato pizzas. ✕ *437 S. Hwy. 101,* ☎ *619/793–0999. No reservations. AE, D, DC, MC, V.*

$ **Chung King Loh.** One of the better Chinese restaurants along the coast, Chung King Loh offers an excellent variety of Mandarin and Szechuan dishes. ✕ *552 Stevens Ave.,* ☎ *619/481–0184. Reservations advised. AE, D, DC, MC, V. No lunch Sun.*

$ **Fidel's.** Both Fidel's restaurants serve a wide variety of well-prepared Mexican dishes in a low-key, pleasant atmosphere. The original restaurant in Solana Beach, a two-story building with an outdoor patio area, is particularly nice and draws a lively crowd. ✕ *607 Valley Ave.,* ☎ *619/755–5292; 3003 Carlsbad Blvd., Carlsbad,* ☎ *619/729–0903. Reservations accepted for 8 or more only. MC, V.*

Lodging

CATEGORY	COST*
$$$$	over $165
$$$	$110–$165
$$	$70–$110
$	under $70

**All prices are for a standard double room in high (summer) season, excluding 10% tax.*

CARLSBAD

$$$$ **La Costa Resort and Spa.** Don't expect glitz and glamour at this famous resort; it's surprisingly low-key, with low-slung buildings and vaguely Southwest contemporary–style rooms decorated in neutral tones. The sports facilities, especially golf and tennis, are excellent, and La Costa includes such other amenities as supervised children's activities and a movie theater. A variety of nutrition and stress-reduction classes are available. 🏨 *2100 Costa del Mar Rd., Carlsbad 92009,* ☎ *619/438–9111 or 800/854–5000,* FAX *619/438–9007. 480 rooms. 5 restaurants, pool, beauty salon, massage, spa, golf, 23 tennis courts, exercise room, theater. AE, D, DC, MC, V.*

$$$–$$$$ **Carlsbad Inn Beach Resort.** The palm trees seem a bit out of place on the manicured lawn of this sprawling European-style inn, with its gabled roofs and stone supports, but this is Carlsbad after all, where *alte* Germany meets southern California. The public areas and rooms are decorated in appealing Old World style; all the accommodations have VCRs, many offer kitchenettes, and some have fireplaces and private spas. 🏨 *3075 Carlsbad Blvd., 92008,* ☎ *619/434–7020 or 800/235–3939,* FAX *619/729–4853. 60 rooms. Pool, sauna, health club. AE, D, DC, MC, V.*

$$ **Best Western Beach View Lodge.** Reservations are essential at this reasonably priced hotel near the beach. A Mediterranean-style low-rise building hosts a variety of attractively decorated rooms with light-wood or whitewashed furnishings; all have refrigerators, and kitchens, private balconies, and fireplaces are also available. Families tend to settle in for a week or more. Complimentary Continental breakfast is included in the rates. 🏨 *3180 Carlsbad Blvd., 92008,* ☎ *619/729–1151, 800/535–5588 or 800/232–2488 in CA,* FAX *619/729–1151. 41 rooms. In-room safes, pool, sauna. AE, D, DC, MC, V.*

DEL MAR

$$$–$$$$ **L'Auberge Del Mar Resort and Spa.** Across the street from the Del Mar Plaza and one block from the ocean, L'Auberge is modeled on the Tudor-style Hotel Del Mar, playground for Hollywood's elite in the early 1900s. The inn is filled with dark-wood antiques, fireplaces, and lavish floral arrangements. Spacious rooms and suites are tastefully, if not memorably, decorated, with beige dominating the color scheme. The grounds are attractively landscaped, with stone paths leading to gazebos and pools; the spa specializes in European herbal wraps and treatments.

☎ *1540 Camino del Mar, Del Mar 92014,* ☎ *619/259–1515 or 800/553–1336,* FAX *619/755–4940. 123 rooms. Restaurant, bar, café, 2 pools, beauty salon, spa, 2 tennis courts, exercise room. AE, D, DC, MC, V.*

$$ **Stratford Inn.** The inn offers a pleasant atmosphere just outside the center of town and three blocks from the ocean. Rooms are large, with ample closet space and dressing areas; some have ocean views. Suites with kitchenettes are available. Continental breakfast is complimentary. ☎ *710 Camino del Mar, 92014,* ☎ *619/755–1501 or 800/446–7229,* FAX *619/755–4704. 98 rooms. 2 pools, refrigerators. AE, D, DC, MC, V.*

ENCINITAS

$$ **Moonlight Beach Hotel.** This folksy, laid-back motel is the closest to the beach at Encinitas. Rooms are basic but spacious and clean; all have kitchenettes. Weekly rates are available. ☎ *233 2nd St., 92024,* ☎ *619/753–0623 or 800/323–1259. 24 rooms. AE, MC, V.*

$$ **Radisson Inn Encinitas.** This attractively designed low-rise blends nicely into an Encinitas hillside just east of Old Highway 101. Rooms have plush, richly colored rugs and comfy upholstered chairs; some have kitchenettes and/or ocean views. Continental breakfast is complimentary. ☎ *85 Encinitas Blvd., 92024,* ☎ *619/942–7455 or 800/333–3333,* FAX *619/632–9481. 91 rooms. Restaurant, bar. AE, D, DC, MC, V.*

$ **Budget Motels of America.** Shag carpeting and kitschy murals decorate the rooms at this motel, but the place is clean, low-priced, and convenient to the beach and the freeway. No-smoking rooms are available, and Continental breakfast is included in the room rate. ☎ *133 Encinitas Blvd., 92024,* ☎ *619/944–0260 or 800/795–6044,* FAX *619/944–2803. 124 rooms. AE, MC, V.*

LEUCADIA

$ **Pacific Surf.** This motel is clean, comfortable, and near all the shops and restaurants of Encinitas. All rooms have kitchens, and there are discounts for extended stays. ☎ *1076 Rte. 101N, 92024,* ☎ *619/436–8763 or 800/795–1466. 30 rooms. Laundry. AE, D, DC, MC, V.*

OCEANSIDE

$ **Oceanside Travelodge.** It's near the beach and centrally located. ☎ *1401 N. Hill St., 92054,* ☎ *619/722–1244 or 800/255–3050,* FAX *619/722–3228. 28 rooms. Laundry. AE, D, DC, MC, V.*

RANCHO SANTA FE

$$$$ **Rancho Valencia.** The sister hotel to La Jolla's La Valencia, this resort is so luxurious that magazines have chosen it for fashion backdrops and have named it the most romantic hideaway in the United States. The suites are in red-tile-roofed casitas with fireplaces and private terraces. Tennis is the other draw here, with 18 courts and a resident pro; rates include unlimited use of the courts. ☎ *5921 Valencia Circle, 92067,* ☎ *619/756–1123 or 800/548–3664,* FAX *619/756–0165. 43 suites. Restaurant, pool, 18 tennis courts, pool, sauna, croquet. AE, DC, MC, V.*

North Coast Essentials

ARRIVING AND DEPARTING

By Bus: The **San Diego Transit District** covers the city of San Diego up to Del Mar, where the **North County Transit District** (☎ 619/722–6283) takes over, blanketing the area with efficient, on-time bus service.

Greyhound (☎ 619/722–1587 in Oceanside, or 800/231–2222) has regular routes connecting San Diego to points north, with stops in Del Mar, Solana Beach, Encinitas, Escondido, Vista, and Oceanside.

By Car: Interstate 5, the main freeway artery connecting San Diego to Los Angeles, follows the coastline. To the west, running parallel to it, is Old Highway 101, which never strays more than a quarter-mile from the ocean. Beginning north of La Jolla, where it is known as Torrey Pines Road, Old Highway 101 is a designated scenic route, providing access to the beauty of the coastline.

By Plane: Palomar Airport (☎ 619/431–4646), located in Carlsbad, 2 miles east of I–5 at 2198 Palomar Airport Road, is a general aviation airport run by the county of San Diego and open to the public. Commuter airlines sometimes have flights from Palomar to Orange County and Los Angeles.

By Taxi: Several companies are based in North County, including **Bernardo Cab Co.** (☎ 619/549–8445, or 619/592–9787 from Rancho Bernardo; ⏲ 7 AM–7 PM) and **Bill's Cab Co.** (☎ 619/755–6737).

By Train: Amtrak (☎ 619/481–0114 in Del Mar, 619/722–4622 in Oceanside, or 800/872–7245) operates trains daily between Los Angeles, Orange County, and San Diego, with stops in Solana Beach and Oceanside. The last train leaves San Diego at approximately 9 PM each night; the last arrival is at approximately midnight.

GUIDED TOURS

Civic Helicopters (2192 Palomar Airport Rd., ☎ 619/438–8424) offers whirlybird tours of the area. The tours run about $70 per person per half hour and go along the beaches to the Del Mar racetrack.

IMPORTANT ADDRESSES AND NUMBERS

Carlsbad Convention and Visitors Bureau (Box 1246, Carlsbad 92008, ☎ 619/434–6093).

Del Mar Chamber of Commerce (1401 Camino del Mar, Suite 101, Del Mar 92014, ☎ 619/793–5292).

Oceanside Chamber of Commerce (928 North Hill St., Oceanside 92051, ☎ 619/722–1534).

Anza-Borrego Desert State Park

Every spring, the stark desert landscape east of the Cuyamaca Mountains explodes with color. It's the blooming of the wildflowers in the Anza-Borrego Desert State Park, less than a two-hour drive from central San Diego. The beauty of this annual spectacle, as well as the natural quiet and blazing climate, lures tourists and natives to the area.

The area features a desert and not much more, but it is one of the favorite parks of those Californians who travel widely in their state. People seeking bright lights and glitter should look elsewhere. The excitement in this area stems from watching a coyote scamper across a barren ridge or a brightly colored bird resting on a nearby cactus or from a waitress delivering another cocktail to a poolside chaise longue. For hundreds of years, the only humans to linger in the area were Native Americans from the San Dieguito, Kamia, and Cahuilla tribes, but the extreme temperature eventually forced the tribes to leave, too. It wasn't until 1774, when Mexican explorer Captain Juan Bautista de Anza first blazed a trail through the area as a shortcut from Sonora to San Francisco, that modern civilization had its first glimpse of the oddly beautiful wasteland.

Today, more than 600,000 acres of desert are included in the Anza-Borrego Desert State Park, making it the largest state park in the contiguous 48 states. It is also one of the few parks in the country where people can camp anywhere. No campsite is necessary; just follow the trails and pitch a tent wherever you like.

Five hundred miles of road traverse the park, and visitors are required to stay on them so as not to disturb the ecological balance of the park. However, 28,000 acres have been set aside in the eastern part of the desert near Ocotillo Wells for off-road enthusiasts. General George S. Patton conducted field training in the Ocotillo area to prepare for the World War II invasion of North Africa, and the area hasn't been the same since.

The little town of Borrego Springs acts as an oasis in this natural playground. Not exactly like Palm Springs—it lacks the wild crowds and preponderance of insanely wealthy residents—Borrego is basically a small retirement community, with the average age of residents about 50. For visitors who are uninterested in communing with the desert without a shower and pool nearby, Borrego provides several pleasant hotels and restaurants.

We recommend visiting this desert between October and May to avoid the extreme summer temperatures. Winter temperatures are comfortable, but nights (and sometimes days) are cold, so bring a warm jacket.

Exploring

The **Anza-Borrego Desert State Park** is too vast even to consider exploring in its entirety. Most people stay in the hills surrounding Borrego Springs. An excellent underground **Visitor Information Center** (☎ 619/767–5311) and museum are reachable by taking the Palm Canyon Drive spur west from the traffic circle in the center of town. The rangers are helpful and always willing to suggest areas for camping or hiking. A short slide show about the desert is shown throughout the day. For a listing of the interpretive programs scheduled for the year, pick up a copy of the free park newspaper.

One of the most popular camping and hiking areas is **Palm Canyon,** just a few minutes west of the Visitor Information Center. A 1½-mile trail leads to a small oasis with a waterfall and palm trees. If you find palm trees lining city streets in San Diego and Los Angeles amusing, seeing this grove of native palms around a pool in a narrow desert valley may give you a new vision of the dignity of this tree. The Borrego Palm Canyon campground (on the desert floor, a mile or so below the palm oasis) is one of only two developed campgrounds with flush toilets and showers in the park. (The other is Tamarisk Grove Campground at the intersection of Route 78 and Yaqui Pass Road.)

Another point of interest is **Split Mountain** (take Split Mountain Road south from Route 78 at Ocotillo Wells), a narrow gorge with 600-foot perpendicular walls. You can drive the mile from the end of the paved road to the gorge in a passenger car if you are careful (don't get stuck in the sand). Don't attempt the drive in bad weather, when the gorge can quickly fill with a torrent of water; even if the sky is clear when you arrive, check ahead at the visitor center to find out if current road conditions allow for a safe trip.

On the way to Split Mountain (while you are still on the paved road), you'll pass a grove of the park's unusual **elephant trees** (10 feet tall, with swollen branches and small leaves). There is a self-guided nature trail; pick up a brochure at the parking lot.

You can get a good view of the Borrego Badlands from **Font's Point,** off Borrego–Salton Seaway (S22). The badlands are a maze of steep ravines that are almost devoid of vegetation and are best navigated by a four-wheel-drive vehicle.

In **Borrego Springs** itself, there is little to do besides lie or recreate in the sun. Borrego Roadrunner Club (☎ 619/767–5374) has an 18-hole golf course. Borrego Resorts International Tennis (☎ 619/767–9748) has courts that are open to the public, as does La Casa del Zorro (☎ 619/767–5323). One of the best and most appreciated deals in town is the Borrego Springs High School pool (☎ 619/767–5337), at the intersection of Saddle and Cahuilla roads and open to the public during the summer.

Most people prefer to explore the desert in a motorized vehicle. While it is illegal to drive off the established trails in the state park, the **Ocotillo Wells State Vehicular Recreation Area** (☎ 619/767–5391), reached by following Route 78 east from Borrego, is a popular haven for off-road enthusiasts and those who drive vehicles that are not street legal. The sand dunes and rock formations are challenging as well as fun. Camping is permitted throughout the area, but water is not available. The only facilities are in the small town (really no more than a corner) of Ocotillo Wells.

To the east of Anza-Borrego is the **Salton Sink,** a basin that (although not as low as Death Valley) consists of more dry land below sea level than anywhere else in this hemisphere. The Salton Sea is the most recent of a series of lakes here, divided from the Gulf of California by the delta of the Colorado River. The current lake was created in 1905–7, when the Colorado flooded north through canals meant to irrigate the Imperial Valley. The water is extremely salty, even saltier than the Pacific Ocean, and it is primarily a draw for fishermen seeking corbina, croaker, and tilapia. Some boaters and swimmers also use the lake. The state runs a pleasant park, with sites for day camping, recreational vehicles, and primitive camping. *Take Rte. 78E to Rte. 111N,* ☎ *619/393–3059.*

Bird-watchers will love the **Salton Sea National Wildlife Refuge.** A hiking trail and observation tower make it easy to spot the dozens of varieties of migratory birds stopping at Salton Sea. *At the south end of Salton Sea, off Rte. 111,* ☎ *619/348–5278.*

Dining

Quality, not quantity, is the operable truism of dining in the Borrego area. Restaurants are scarce and hard to find, and many close on holidays during the summer, but the best are high quality. Dress is casual at both the restaurants listed below.

$ **Chinese Panda Restaurant.** The only business in a Quonset hut in Borrego Springs, this friendly Chinese restaurant serves tasty versions of Mandarin and Szechuan dishes. ✕ *818 Palm Canyon Dr.,* ☎ *619/767–3182. Reservations accepted. MC, V. Closed Mon. and Aug.*

$ **Mi Tenampa Cafe.** It may seem odd to find good Mexican seafood in the desert, but no stranger, perhaps, than this low-key restaurant's location—just off Christmas Circle. ✕ *747 Palm Canyon Dr., no* ☎. *No reservations. No credit cards. Closed Mon., Tues.*

Lodging

If camping isn't your thing, there are two very nice resorts near Borrego Springs that offer fine amenities minus the overdevelopment of Palm Springs.

CATEGORY	COST*
$$$	over $165
$$	$110–$165
$	$70–$110

**All prices are for a standard double room in high (summer) season, excluding 9% tax.*

$–$$$ La Casa del Zorro. This is a small, low-key resort complex in the heart of the desert. You need walk only a few hundred yards to be alone under the sky, and you may well see roadrunners crossing the highway. There are 17 different types of accommodations, set in comfortable one- to three-bedroom ranch-style houses complete with living rooms and kitchens; some three-bedroom suites have private pools, while other suites come with baby grand pianos. The elegant Continental restaurant puts on a good Sunday brunch. *3845 Yaqui Pass Rd., 92004, ☎ 619/767–5323 or 800/824–1884, FAX 619/767–5963. 52 suites, 16 rooms, 19 casitas. Restaurant, 3 pools, 6 tennis courts, bicycles. AE, D, DC, MC, V.*

$–$$ Palm Canyon Resort. This is one of the largest properties in the area, with a hotel, an RV park, a restaurant, and recreational facilities. *221 Palm Canyon Dr., 92004, ☎ 619/767–5342 or 800/242–0044 in CA only, FAX 619/767–4073. 44 rooms. Restaurant, 2 pools, coin laundry. AE, D, DC, MC, V.*

Desert Essentials

ARRIVING AND DEPARTING

By Bus: The **Northeast Rural Bus System** (NERBS, ☎ 619/765–0145) connects Julian, Borrego Springs, Oak Grove, Ocotillo Wells, Agua Caliente, Ramona, and many of the other small communities with El Cajon, 15 miles east of downtown San Diego, and the East County line of the San Diego trolley, with stops at Grossmont shopping center and North County Fair. Service is by reservation, and buses do not run on Sundays or on some holidays.

By Car: Take I–8 east to Route 79 north. Turn east on Route 78.

IMPORTANT ADDRESSES AND NUMBERS

For general information about the Borrego and desert areas, contact the **Borrego Springs Chamber of Commerce** (622 Palm Canyon Dr., Box 66, Borrego Springs 92004, ☎ 619/767–5555). For details on the state park, phone or write the visitor center, **Anza-Borrego Desert State Park** (Box 299, Borrego Springs 92004, ☎ 619/767–5311). During the spring blooming season, a special **wildflower hot line** (☎ 619/767–4684) gives 24-hour recorded information on what is flowering at the time of your call and what is expected to bloom shortly. For campsite reservations, call **MISTIX** (☎ 800/444–7275).

SAN DIEGO ESSENTIALS

Arriving and Departing

By Bus

Greyhound (☎ 619/239–8082 or 800/231–2222) operates more than 20 buses a day between the downtown terminal at 120 West Broadway and Los Angeles, connecting with buses to all major U.S. cities. Many buses are express or nonstop; others make stops at coastal towns en route.

By Car

Interstate 5 stretches from Canada to the Mexican border and bisects San Diego. Interstate 8 provides access from Yuma, Arizona, and points east. Drivers coming from Nevada and the mountain regions beyond can reach San Diego on I–15.

By Plane

San Diego International Airport/Lindbergh Field (☎ 619/231–2100) is the main gateway to San Diego. The airport is a five-minute drive from downtown.

Carriers serving San Diego include **Aeromexico** (☎ 800/237–6639), **Alaska Airlines** (☎ 800/426–0333), **America West** (☎ 800/235–9292), **American** (☎ 800/433–7300), **Continental** (☎ 800/525–0280), **Delta** (☎ 800/221–1212), **Mark Air** (☎ 800/627–5247), **Midwest Express** (☎ 800/452–2022), **Northwest** (☎ 800/225–2525), **Reno Air** (☎ 800/736–6247), **SkyWest** (☎ 800/453–9417), **Southwest** (☎ 800/435–9792), **TWA** (☎ 800/221–2000), **United** (☎ 800/241–6522), and **USAir** (☎ 800/428–4322).

BETWEEN THE AIRPORT AND DOWNTOWN

San Diego Transit (☎ 619/233–3004) Route 2 buses leave every 10 to 15 minutes Monday through Friday and every 15 to 20 minutes Saturday and Sunday from about 5:30 AM to 1 AM. Buses depart from the front of East Terminal's USAir section and travel along Broadway, downtown. The fare is $1.50 per person, 75¢ for senior citizens.

Cloud 9 Shuttle (☎ 619/278–8877 or 800/974–8885 in San Diego) and **Public Shuttle** (☎ 619/990–8770) offer van shuttles that take you directly to your destination, often for less than a cab would cost.

Taxi fare is $6–$8 plus tip to most center-city hotels.

If you have rented a car at the airport, you can take Harbor Drive, at the perimeter of the airport, to downtown, only about 3 miles away.

By Train

Amtrak trains (☎ 800/872–7245) from Los Angeles arrive at Santa Fe Depot (1050 Kettner Blvd., corner of Broadway, near the heart of downtown, ☎ 619/239–9021). There are additional stations in Del Mar (☎ 619/481–0114) and Oceanside (☎ 619/722–4622), both in north San Diego County. Eight trains operate daily in either direction.

Getting Around

By Bus

The **San Diego Transit Information Line** (☎ 619/233–3004, TTY/TDD 619/234–5005; ⏲ Daily 5:30 AM–8:30 PM) can provide details on getting to and from any location.

The **Day Tripper Transit Pass** is good for unlimited trips on the same day on San Diego Transit buses and on the trolley and the ferry for $5; there's also a four-day pass for $15. Passes are available at the **Transit Store** (449 Broadway, ☎ 619/234–1060) as well as at the ferry landing and the downtown Amtrak station.

Regional bus companies that service areas outside the city include **ATC Van Co.** (☎ 619/427–5660), for Coronado, the Silver Strand, and Imperial Beach; **Chula Vista Transit** (☎ 619/233–3004), for Bonita and Chula Vista; **National City Transit** (tel. 619/474–7505), for National City; **North County Transit District** (☎ 619/722–6283), for the area bound by the ocean, east to Escondido, north to Camp Pendleton, and south to Del Mar; and **Northeast Rural Bus System** (☎ 619/765–0145) or

Southeast Rural Bus System (☎ 619/478–5875), for access to rural county towns.

By Car

A car is essential for San Diego's sprawling freeway system and comes in handy for touring Baja California, although it's not necessary in Tijuana. Avoid the freeways during rush hour when possible.

All the major car-rental companies are represented in San Diego. For a list, *see* Car Rentals *in* the Gold Guide. Rates in San Diego begin at $25 a day and $179 a week for an economy car with unlimited mileage.

Limousine companies offer airport shuttles and customized tours. Rates vary and are per hour, per mile, or both, with some minimums established. Companies that offer a range of services include **Advantage Limousine Service** (☎ 619/563–1651), **La Jolla Limousines** (☎ 619/459–5891), **Limousines by Linda** (☎ 619/234–9145), and **Olde English Livery** (☎ 619/232–6533).

By Ferry

The **San Diego-Coronado Ferry** (☎ 619/234–4111) leaves from the Broadway Pier daily, every hour on the hour, 9 AM–9:30 PM Sunday–Thursday, until 10:30 PM Friday and Saturday. The fare is $2 each way.

By Taxi

Taxi fares are regulated at the airport—all companies charge the same rate (generally $2 for the first mile, $1.40 for each additional mile). Fares vary among companies on other routes, however, including the ride back to the airport.

Cab companies that serve most areas of the city are **Coast Shuttle** (☎ 619/477–3333), **Co-op Silver Cabs** (☎ 619/280–5555), **Coronado Cab** (☎ 619/435–6211), **La Jolla Cab** (☎ 619/453–4222), **Orange Cab** (☎ 619/291–3333), and **Yellow Cab** (☎ 619/234–6161).

By Trolley

The **San Diego Trolley** (☎ 619/233–3004) travels from downtown to within 100 feet of the U.S.–Mexican border, stopping at 21 suburban stations en route. The basic fare is $1.75 one way. The trolley also travels from downtown to Encanto, Lemon Grove, La Mesa, and El Cajon in East County. Tickets must be purchased before boarding. Ticket-vending machines, located at each station, require exact change. Trolleys operate daily, approximately every 15 minutes, 5 AM–9 PM, then every 30 minutes until 1 AM. The Bayside line serves the Convention Center and Seaport Village; lines to Old Town, Mission Valley, and North County are under construction.

Guided Tours

Orientation

Gray Line Tours (☎ 619/491–0011 or 800/331–5077) and **San Diego Mini Tours** (☎ 619/477–8687) offer two daily sightseeing excursions for about $25.

Old Town Trolley (☎ 619/298–8687) travels to almost every attraction and shopping area on open-air trackless trolleys. Drivers double as tour guides. You can take the full two-hour, narrated city tour or get on and off as you please at any of the nine stops. An all-day pass costs $16 for adults, $7 for children 6–12. The trolley, which leaves every 30 minutes, operates daily 9–5 in summer, 9–4 in winter.

Free two-hour trolley tours of the downtown redevelopment area, including the Gaslamp Quarter, are hosted by **Centre City Development Corporation's Downtown Information Center** (☏ 619/235–2222). Groups of 35 passengers leave from 255 G Street, downtown, the first and third Saturday of each month at 10 AM. Reservations are necessary. The tour may be canceled if there aren't enough passengers.

San Diego Harbor Excursion (☏ 619/234–4111) and **Hornblower Invader Cruises** (☏ 619/234–8687) sail on narrated cruises of San Diego Harbor, departing from Broadway Pier. Both companies offer one-hour cruises ($10), departing several times daily, and a two-hour tour ($15) each day at 2 PM (additional tours in summer). No reservations are necessary, and both vessels have snack bars on board. **Classic Sailing Adventures** (☏ 619/224–0800) has morning and afternoon tours of the harbor and San Diego Bay and nighttime summer cruises for $45 per person.

Special-Interest

The **Gaslamp Quarter Association** (410 Island Ave., ☏ 619/233–5227) leads 1½-hour architectural tours of the restored downtown historic district on Saturday at 11 AM ($5 adults, $3 senior citizens and students). Self-guided tour brochures are available at the office, weekdays 10–4:30.

Six-passenger hot-air balloons lift off from San Diego's North Country. Most flights are at sunrise or sunset and are followed by a traditional champagne celebration. Companies that offer daily service, weather permitting, are **Air Affaire** (☏ 619/560–6373 or 800/331–1979), **Pacific Horizon** (☏ 619/756–1790 or 800/244–1790), and **Skysurfer** (☏ 619/481–6800 or 800/660–6809 in CA). Balloon flights average $145 per person for early morning or late afternoon.

Civic Helicopters (☏ 619/438–8424 or 800/438–4354) has helicopter tours starting at $69 per person per half hour.

On weekends, the State Park Department (☏ 619/220–5422) gives free walking tours of **Old Town.** Groups leave from 4002 Wallace Street at 2 PM daily, weather permitting.

Walkabout (☏ 619/231–7463) offers several different free walking tours throughout the city each week.

Gray whales migrate south to Mexico and back north from mid-December to mid-March. As many as 200 whales pass the San Diego coast each day, coming within yards of tour boats. During whale-watching season, ***The Apollo*** (☏ 619/221–8500), a luxury motor yacht, offers narrated tours twice a day. **Classic Sailing Adventures** (☏ 619/224–0800) tailors whale-watching expeditions for up to six people. **H&M Landing** (☏ 619/222–1144) and **Seaforth Sportfishing** (☏ 619/224–3383) have daily whale-watching trips in large party boats.

Burbury Wine Tour (2554 Lincoln Blvd., No. 525, Marina del Rey, CA 90291, ☏ 310/208–0980) offers picnic wine tours to wineries in Temecula Valley.

Important Addresses and Numbers

Doctors

Hospital emergency rooms, with physicians on duty, are open 24 hours. Major hospitals are **Mercy Hospital and Medical Center** (4077 5th Ave., ☏ 619/294–8111), **Scripps Memorial Hospital** (9888 Genesee Ave., La Jolla, ☏ 619/457–4123), **Veterans Administration Hos-**

pital (3350 La Jolla Village Dr., La Jolla, ☎ 619/552–8585), and **UCSD Medical Center** (200 W. Arbor Dr., Hillcrest, ☎ 619/543–6222).

Doctors on Call (☎ 619/275–2663) offers 24-hour medical service to guests at San Diego hotels.

The **San Diego County Dental Society** (☎ 619/275–0244) can provide referrals Monday through Friday to those with dental emergencies. Doctors on Call (*see above*) provides 24-hour dental emergency referrals.

Emergencies

Dial 911 for **police, ambulance,** and **fire** departments in an emergency.

Visitor Information

For information before your trip, contact the **San Diego Convention & Visitors Bureau** (401 B St., Suite 1400, San Diego 92101, ☎ 619/232–3101) for *The San Diego Official Visitors Guide.* The **Visitor Information Center** (2688 E. Mission Bay Dr., San Diego 92109, ☎ 619/276–8200) can make your lodging reservations and publishes a newspaper, *Pathfinder* (enclose a SASE when requesting a copy).

When you're in San Diego, stop in at the **International Visitor Information Center** (11 Horton Plaza, at 1st Ave. and F St., ☎ 619/236–1212; ⊙ Mon.–Sat., 8:30–5 year-round, also Sun. 11–5 June–Aug.) at the **Balboa Park Visitors Center** (1549 El Prado, in Balboa Park, ☎ 619/239–0512; ⊙ Daily 9–4), or at the **Mission Bay Visitor Information Center** (2688 E. Mission Bay Dr., off I–5 at the Mission Bay Dr. exit, ☎ 619/276–8200; ⊙ Mon.–Sat. 9–5, Sun. 9:30–4:30 in winter, ⊙ later in summer). Call the **San Diego City Beach and Weather Conditions Information Line** (☎ 619/221–8884).

You can get information about other communities within San Diego County from the visitors bureaus or chambers of commerce, including:

Carlsbad (Box 1246, 92018, ☎ 619/434–6093).
Coronado (1111 Orange Ave., Suite A, 92118, ☎ 619/437–8788 or 800/622–8300).
Del Mar (1104 Camino del Mar, 92014, ☎ 619/755–4844).
San Diego North County Convention & Visitors Bureau (720 N. Broadway, Escondido, 92025, ☎ 619/745–4741 or 800/848–3336).
La Jolla (1055 Wall St., Box 1101, 92038, ☎ 619/454–1444).
Oceanside (928 N. Hill St., 92054, ☎ 619/722–1534 or 800/350–7873).

14 Palm Springs Desert Resorts

Palm Springs and the new cities nearby are filling up with resorts with elaborate gardens, waterfalls, serpentine sidewalks, and golf courses. This is a different type of "desert experience" than you'll get in the outlying areas, but with all their creature comforts (not to mention great winter weather) the desert resorts are a good base for exploration. Joshua Tree National Park is an easy day trip from Palm Springs. The northern part is High Desert and the southern part Low Desert, so you can see the difference between these very different types of terrain.

Revised by Bobbi Zane

WHAT DO YOU GET when you start with dramatic scenery, add endless sunshine, mix in deluxe resorts, and spice things up with a liberal dash of celebrities? Palm Springs desert resorts, a magnet for socialites, sun worshipers, and stargazers.

The fashionable community, once limited to the village of Palm Springs, has expanded into other Coachella Valley towns in recent years. Now you'll find resorts stretching all the way from the foot of 10,831-foot Mt. San Jacinto in the northwest to once-sleepy Indio in the southeast. Streets are named for the celebrities who live here in unmarked gated estates—Frank Sinatra, Betty Ford, Bob Hope. Although the social, sports, shopping, and entertainment scenes now revolve around Palm Desert, you'll also find resorts and attractions in Indian Wells, Rancho Mirage, Desert Hot Springs, La Quinta, Cathedral City, and Indio.

During the "season" (January–April) resident celebrities and wealthy winter visitors present a nearly nightly round of parties and balls in conjunction with an endless round of world-class golf and tennis tournaments to support their favorite charities. They play during the day, too. There are more than 85 golf courses in a 20-mile radius, more than 600 tennis courts, 35 miles of bicycle trails, horseback paths, 10,000 or so swimming pools, and even cross-country skiing atop Mt. San Jacinto. Shopping is a serious pursuit here with clutches of chic boutiques to be found along main streets and fashionable department stores in enclosed malls. The McCallum Theater in Palm Desert presents top-name entertainment.

This is the place for stargazing. Hollywood stars, sports personalities, politicians, and other luminaries can be spotted at charity events and restaurants and on the golf course. Roseanne, Jay Leno, Leslie Nielsen, and even Dr. Ruth have done stints at the Westin Mission Hills Resort, and Goldie Hawn and Kurt Russell have been seen poolside at the Ingleside Inn (where Greta Garbo once hung out). Michael Jackson and Sylvester Stallone escape the crowds at La Quinta resort.

The desert became a Hollywood hideout in the 1920s, when La Quinta Hotel opened the Coachella Valley's first golf course. But it took a pair of tennis-playing celebrities to put Palm Springs on the map in the 1930s; actors Charlie Farrell and Ralph Bellamy bought 200 acres of land for $30 an acre and opened the Palm Springs Racquet Club, which soon listed Ginger Rogers, Humphrey Bogart, and Clark Gable among its members. Farrell served as the town's mayor in the '50s.

Developers have been careful not to overshadow the stunning beauty of the desert setting: City buildings are restricted to a height of 30 feet; flashing, moving, and neon signs are restricted, preserving an intimate village feeling; and 50% of the land consists of open spaces with palm trees and desert vegetation.

This beauty is particularly evident in the canyons surrounding Palm Springs. Lush Tahquitz Canyon, one of the five canyons that line the San Jacinto Mountains, was the setting for Shangri-La in an early movie version of *Lost Horizon*. The Agua Caliente Band of Cahuilla Indians settled this area about 1,000 years ago. They considered the mineral springs to be sacred, with great curative and restorative powers. The springs became a tourist attraction in 1871 when the tribe built a bathhouse on the site to serve passengers on a pioneer stage route. The Agua Caliente still own about 32,000 acres of Palm Springs desert,

6,700 of which lie within the city limits of Palm Springs. The Indians, while dedicated to preserving their historic homeland, will doubtless account for the next "boom" in the desert. Following the lead of nearby tribes, which operate profitable bingo parlors in Indio and Cabazon, the Agua Caliente have opened a small card room in the Spa Hotel in downtown Palm Springs.

One brief comment on the weather: Although daytime temperatures average a pleasantly warm 88°F, you are still in the desert. And that means during the middle of the day in the summer it is going to be very hot—sometimes uncomfortably so. You'll be told that "it is a dry heat." And it is. But it is still desert hot: Plan activities in the morning and late afternoon, and wear a hat and plenty of sunscreen if you're out for a midday stroll. Any time of the year be sure to drink plenty of water to prevent dehydration.

EXPLORING

Numbers in the margin correspond to points of interest on the Palm Springs map.

Physically, Palm Springs proper is easy to understand. Palm Canyon Drive runs north–south through the heart of downtown; the intersection with Tahquitz Canyon Way is pretty much the center of the main drag. Heading south, Palm Canyon Drive splits. South Palm Canyon Drive leads you to the Indian Canyons. East Palm Canyon Drive becomes Highway 111, taking you east through the resort areas of Cathedral City, Rancho Mirage, Palm Desert, La Quinta, and Indio. The Aerial Tramway is at the northern limits of Palm Springs. Joshua Tree National Park is about an hour's drive north.

Most Palm Springs desert resort attractions can be seen in anywhere from an hour or two to an entire day, depending upon your interests. Do you want to take the tram up Mt. San Jacinto, see the view, and come right back down, or spend the day hiking? Would you rather linger for a picnic lunch in one of the Indian Canyons, or double back for a snack and people-watching at a sidewalk café along El Paseo? Your best bet is to think of the list of sights and activities as if it were an à la carte menu and pick and choose according to your appetite. To help you organize your outings, we will start in the north and work our way south and southeast. A separate tour of Joshua Tree follows.

Palm Springs and Environs

★ ❶ Take the **Palm Springs Aerial Tramway** to get a stunning overview of the desert. The 2½-mile ascent brings you to an elevation of 8,516 feet in less than 20 minutes. On clear days, which are common, the view stretches some 75 miles from the peak of Mt. San Gorgonio to the north and the Salton Sea in the southeast. At the top you'll find several diversions. Mountain Station has an alpine buffet restaurant, cocktail lounge, apparel and gift shops, a theater screening a 22-minute film on the history of the tramway, and picnic facilities. ☎ *619/325–1391.* ☛ *$15.95 adults, $9.95 children 5–12.* ⏲ *Tram cars depart at least every 30 min from 10 AM weekdays and 8 AM weekends. Closed Aug. for maintenance.*

You can take the tram or hike into **Mt. San Jacinto State Park.** The park and the adjacent **Mt. San Jacinto State Wilderness** have 54 miles of hiking trails and camping and picnic areas; guided wilderness mule rides are available here during snow-free months. During winter the

Nordic Ski Center has cross-country ski equipment for rent. The tram is a popular attraction; lines can sometimes be long. ☎ *909/659–2607 for park information, 619/325–4227 for ski and weather conditions.* ☛ *Free, but permits (also free) are required for day or overnight wilderness hiking.*

Once one of the most fashionable shopping streets in southern California, **Palm Canyon Drive** is not quite as posh these days, but it's undergoing a renaissance into an entertainment and dining center. This is a lively and interesting place to take a stroll. You can take the Palm Springs Starwalk, stars imbedded in the sidewalk (à la the Hollywood Walk of Fame) honoring celebrities; pop into a coffeehouse for a cup of espresso; or cruise through the tiny but illuminating Showbiz Museum, adjacent to the historic Plaza Theater. Palm Canyon Drive is par-
★ ticularly lively on Thursday nights when the **Village Fest** street fair fills a three-block section of the drive. There are street musicians, food stalls, handcrafted gifts at low prices, antiques, sculpture, paintings, and a farmers' market. Things have also been picking up on weekends of late, with kids, tourists, senior citizens, and families hanging out on the street or taking in jazz or other live music.

Downtown Palm Springs is not without hidden historical treasures. The
2 **Village Green Heritage Center** illustrates pioneer life in Palm Springs in three museums. McCallum Adobe, dating back to 1885, displays the collections of the Palm Springs Historical Society and McCallum family memorabilia. Miss Cornelia White's House, dating back to 1894, exhibits this pioneer family's memorabilia, including an extensive collection of bibles, clothing, tools, books, paintings, even the first telephone in Palm Springs. Roddy's General Store Museum dates from a later pioneer era, the 1930s and 1940s, and displays signs, packages, and products of the period. *221 and 223 S. Palm Canyon Dr.,* ☎ *619/323–8297.* ☛ *Nominal admission.* ⏲ *House: Wed. and Sun. noon–3, Thurs.–Sat. 10–4; store: Thurs.–Sun. 10–4; summer hrs flexible.*

If further evidence is needed to prove that the desert is no barren
3 wasteland, there is the dramatic **Palm Springs Desert Museum.** This surprisingly large facility contains galleries devoted to western and Native American art. The display on the natural history of the desert alone is worth a visit. On the grounds are several striking sculpture gardens. Plays, operas, lectures, and other cultural events are presented at the museum's Annenberg Theater. *101 Museum Dr., just north of Tahquitz Way, on south side of Desert Fashion Plaza,* ☎ *619/325–7186.* ☛ *$5 adults, $2 children under 17; free 1st Fri. of month.* ⏲ *Late Sept.–May, Tues.–Thurs. and weekends 10–4, Fri. 1–8.*

A short drive or distinctly long walk farther south on Palm Canyon is
4 the **Moorten Botanical Garden.** More than 2,000 plant varieties cover the 4-acre site in settings that simulate the plants' original environments. Indian artifacts and rock, crystal, and wood forms are exhibited. *1701 S. Palm Canyon Dr.,* ☎ *619/327–6555.* ☛ *$2 adults, 75¢ children.* ⏲ *Mon.–Sat. 9–4:30, Sun. 10–4.*

5 The **Indian Canyons,** 5 miles south of downtown Palm Springs, are the ancestral home of the Agua Caliente Band of Indians. The Indians selected these canyons for their lush oases, abundant water, and wildlife. Even now visitors can see remnants of this life: rock art, house pits and foundations, irrigation ditches, bedrock mortars, pictographs, and stone houses and shelters built atop high cliff walls. Four canyons are open to visitors: Palm Canyon, noted for its lush stand of Washingtonia palms, the largest such stand in the world; Tahquitz, noted

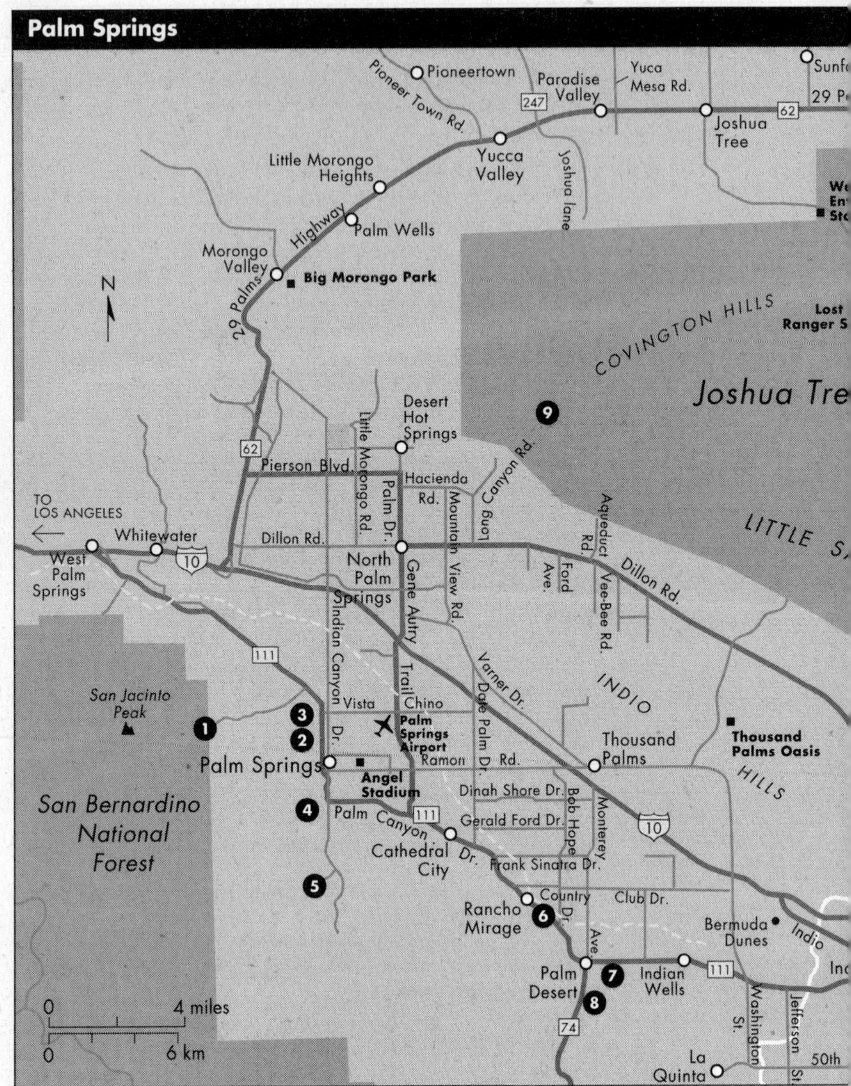
Palm Springs
Pioneertown
Pioneer Town Rd.
Paradise Valley
Yuca Mesa Rd.
Sunf
29 P
247
62
Joshua Tree
Yucca Valley
Joshua lane
Little Morongo Heights
Palm Wells
Highway
Morongo Valley
Big Morongo Park
29 Palms
N
COVINGTON HILLS
Lost Ranger S
Joshua Tre
Desert Hot Springs
9
Little Morongo Rd.
62
Pierson Blvd.
Hacienda Rd.
Palm Dr.
Mountain View Rd.
Long Canyon Rd.
Aqueduct Rd.
LITTLE S
TO LOS ANGELES
Whitewater
Dillon Rd.
West Palm Springs
10
North Palm Springs
Gene Autry Trail
Ford Ave.
Vee-Bee Rd.
Dillon Rd.
111
Indian Canyon Dr.
Varner Dr.
Date Palm Dr.
INDIO
San Jacinto Peak
1
3
2
Vista
Chino
Palm Springs Airport
Thousand Palms
Thousand Palms Oasis
Palm Springs
Ramon Rd.
Angel Stadium
HILLS
San Bernardino National Forest
4
Dinah Shore Dr.
Bob Hope Dr.
Monterey Ave.
Palm Canyon Dr.
111
Gerald Ford Dr.
10
Cathedral City
Frank Sinatra Dr.
5
Country Club Dr.
Rancho Mirage
6
Bermuda Dunes
Indio
Palm Desert
7
Indian Wells
111
8
0 4 miles
0 6 km
74
Washington St.
Jefferson St.
La Quinta
50th

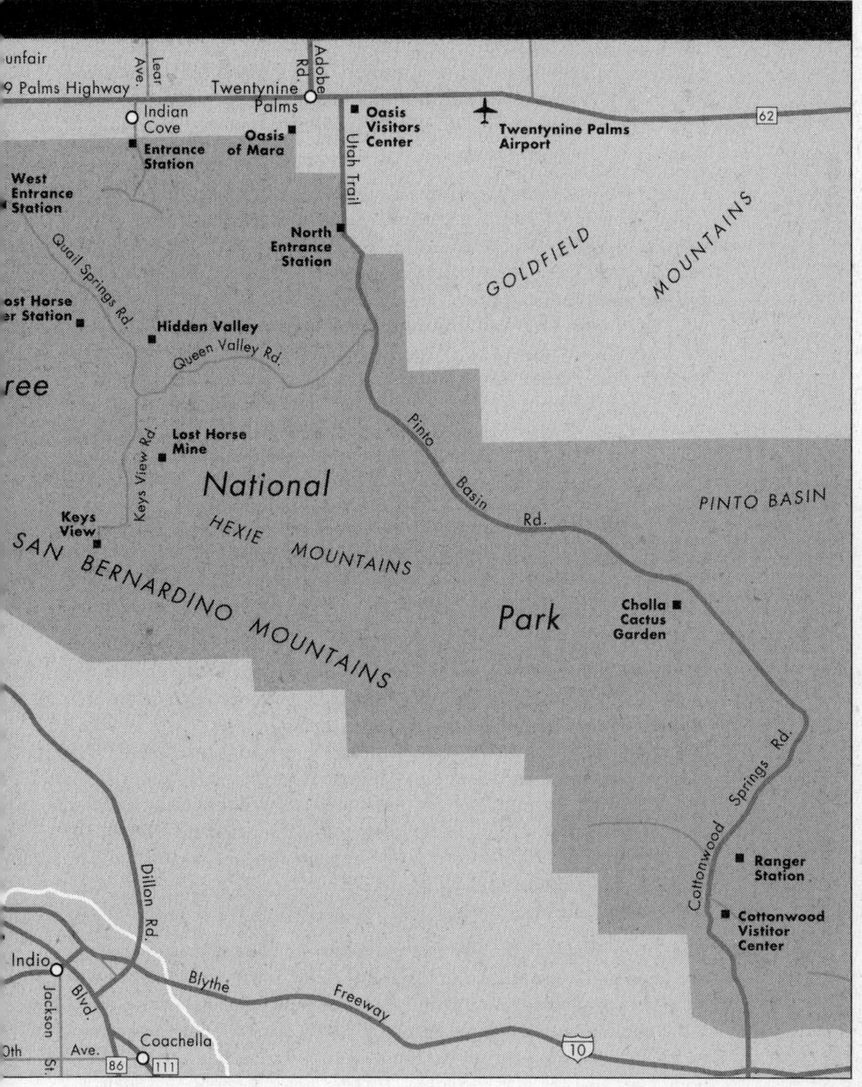
unfair
9 Palms Highway
Lear Ave.
Adobe Rd.
Twentynine Palms
Indian Cove
Entrance Station
Oasis of Mara
Oasis Visitors Center
Utah Trail
Twentynine Palms Airport
62
West Entrance Station
North Entrance Station
GOLDFIELD MOUNTAINS
Quail Springs Rd.
ost Horse
er Station
Hidden Valley
Queen Valley Rd.
ree
Pinto Basin Rd.
Keys View Rd.
Lost Horse Mine
National
PINTO BASIN
Keys View
HEXIE MOUNTAINS
SAN BERNARDINO MOUNTAINS
Park
Cholla Cactus Garden
Cottonwood Springs Rd.
Ranger Station
Dillon Rd.
Cottonwood Visitor Center
Indio
Jackson St.
Blvd.
Blythe Freeway
Coachella
0th Ave.
86
111
10

for waterfalls and pools; Murray, home of Peninsula bighorn sheep and a herd of wild ponies; and Andreas, where a stand of fan palms contrasts with sharp rock formations. A Trading Post in Palm Canyon has hiking maps, refreshments, Indian art, jewelry, and weavings. *End of S. Palm Canyon Dr., ☏ 619/325–5673. ☛ $3.50 adults, $1 children. ⏲ Sept.–June, daily 8–5.*

6 Elegant resorts, fine dining, world-class golf and tennis tournaments, and celebrity residents come together in **Rancho Mirage.** The city holds the famed Eisenhower Medical Center and Betty Ford Center, as well as the estates of such celebrities as Walter Annenberg, the late Ginger Rogers, and Frank Sinatra. Near the Eisenhower Medical Center is the new **Heartland California Museum of the Heart.** Walk through the huge heart-valve portal and experience interactive exhibits such as the 14-foot-tall "Plaque Attack" walk-in replica of a coronary artery, or grab a healthful bite at the Heart Rock Cafe. *39-600 Bob Hope Dr., ☏ 619/324–3278. ☛ Suggested donation: $2.50 adults, $2 senior citizens over 61, 50¢ children 6–17, students, or military with ID. ⏲ Weekdays 7–7 (also Sat. 8–noon Sept.–May).*

7 Some of the best desert people-watching, shopping, and dining can be found along trendy **El Paseo,** a 2-mile avenue just west of Highway 111 in Palm Desert. The flower-decked avenue is lined with apparel shops, specialty stores, art galleries, and restaurants.

★ 8 One of the most unique zoological gardens in the country, the **Living Desert Wildlife and Botanical Park** provides eyeball-to-eyeball views of coyotes, mountain lions, bighorn sheep, golden eagles, and owls. A number of easy to challenging trails go through desert gardens populated with plants of the Mojave, Colorado, and Sonoran deserts. One exhibit pinpoints the famed San Andreas earthquake fault across the valley. During the holidays, the park presents Wildlights, an evening light show. Shuttle service, interpretive tours, strollers, and wheelchairs are available. *47-900 Portola Ave., less than 2 mi south of Hwy. 111, ☏ 619/346–5694. ☛ $7 adults, $3.50 children 3–15. ⏲ Daily 9–5; closed mid-June–Aug.*

TIME OUT Pamper yourself with the Spa Experience, a sampling of the services available at the **Spa Hotel and Mineral Springs.** Sink into a tub filled with naturally hot mineral water from the original Agua Caliente spring, rest in the cool white relaxation room, swim in the outdoor mineral pool, or let the sauna warm your spirits. Massages, skin care, and beauty and body therapies are also available. *100 N. Indian Canyon Dr., Palm Springs, ☏ 619/325–1461. ☛ Spa Experience: $17.25 (includes gratuity), massages: $69–$92. ⏲ Sun.–Thurs. 9–6, Fri.–Sat. 9–7.*

Joshua Tree National Park

★ 9 **Joshua Tree National Park,** about a one-hour drive from Palm Springs, is immense, complex, and ruggedly beautiful. Its mountains of jagged rock, lush oases shaded by tall, elegant fan palms, and natural cactus gardens mark the meeting place of the Mojave and Colorado deserts. This is prime hiking, rock climbing, and exploring country, where you can expect to see such wildlife as coyotes and desert pack rats, and exotic plants such as the red-tipped ocotillo, sharp-barbed cholla cactus, smoke trees, and creamy white yucca. Extensive stands of Joshua trees give the park its name. The trees were named by early white settlers who felt their unusual forms resembled the biblical Joshua raising his arms toward heaven. ☏ *619/367–7511.* ☛ *$5 per car (good for 7 days' entry to park). Park open 24 hrs.*

If you have limited time to explore, visit the **Cottonwood Visitor Center,** reached by way of Cottonwood Springs Road, off I–10 east of Mecca. In spring this is one of the desert's best wildflower viewing areas, covered with carpets of white, yellow, purple, and red flowers stretching as far as the eye can see on the hillsides east of the freeway. A small museum illustrates the natural history of the park, and a man-made oasis, located a short walk from the parking lot, usually has water and contains a stand of palm trees. There are picnic tables, rest rooms, and water at the Cottonwood Visitor Center, but most of the rest of the park is dry. It is essential to carry your own water and food, as facilities are limited elsewhere. *Visitor Center open daily 8–4:30.*

You can see some of the best scenery in a long single day by taking a loop drive in the opposite direction. From highway I–10 north, take Highway 62 through the High Desert areas of Yucca Valley and Twentynine Palms. Enter the park through the Oasis Visitor Center and follow park roads to a number of points of interest. Exit through the Cottonwood complex and return to the desert cities via I–10.

The **Oasis Visitor Center** has an excellent selection of free and low-cost brochures, books, posters, and maps as well as several educational exhibits. Rangers are on hand to answer questions and offer advice. Paved trails (one is 12 mile, the other 14 mile) from the visitor center lead to the **Oasis of Mara.** Inhabited first by Indians and later by prospectors and homesteaders, the oasis now provides a home for birds, small mammals, and other wildlife. *74485 National Park Dr., Twentynine Palms 92277,* ☏ *619/367–7511.* ⏲ *Visitor center: daily 8–5.*

Within the park, you will find nine campgrounds with tables, fireplaces, and primitive rest rooms, and five organized picnic areas for day use. Major sights are the **Hidden Valley,** a legendary cattle rustlers' hideout reached by a trail winding through massive boulders; the **Cholla Cactus Garden,** an impressive stand of the legendary "jumping cactus"; the **Lost Horse Mine,** a remnant of the gold-mining days; and **Keys View,** an outstanding scenic point commanding a superb sweep of valley, mountain, and desert. Sunrise and sunset are magic times to be here, when the light throws rocks and trees into high relief before (or after) bathing the hills in brilliant shades of red, orange, and gold.

Off the Beaten Track

On the northern route to Joshua Tree, you may want to consider stopping at **Big Morongo Canyon Preserve,** which was once an Indian village and later a cattle ranch. Now a park, the preserve is a serene natural oasis with a year-round stream and waterfalls that support a wide variety of plants, birds, and animals. There is a shaded meadow for picnics and choice hiking trails. *From I–10 or Indian Canyon Dr., take Hwy. 62 east to East Dr.,* ☏ *619/363–7190.* ☛ *Free.* ⏲ *Wed.–Sun. 7:30–sunset.*

The **Eldorado Polo Club** (50-950 Madison St., Indio, ☏ 619/342–2223), known as the "Winter Polo Capital of the West," is home of world-class polo events. You can pack a picnic and watch practice matches free during the week; there's a $6 per person charge on weekends.

Hadley's Fruit Orchards (48980 Seminole Dr., just off I–10, Cabazon, ☏ 909/849–5255; ⏲ Daily 7 AM to 9 PM) contains a vast selection of dried California fruit, plus nuts, date shakes, and wines. Taste samples before you buy.

Several date gardens are open to the public for touring and tasting. **Oasis Date Gardens** (59-111 Hwy. 111, Thermal, ☎ 619/399–5665) conducts twice-a-day tours that show how dates are pollinated, grown, sorted, stored, and packed for shipping. Included are an educational video and a free shake with promotional coupon (widely available in the Palm Springs area) or purchase. The ranch has a store at 80-755 Highway 111 in Indio, which shows the video. Shakes are free with coupon or purchase. **Shields Date Gardens** (80-225 Hwy. 111, Indio, ☎ 619/347–0996) presents a continuous slide program on the history of the date and sells shakes.

The **Jude E. Poynter Golf Museum** at the Victor J. LoBue Institute of Golf College at College of the Desert (Fred Waring Dr. at San Pablo Ave., Palm Desert, ☎ 619/341–2491; ⏲ Daily 8–8) exhibits golf memorabilia, artwork, photos, and golf clubs.

SHOPPING

The Palm Springs area is full of toney boutiques and lively art galleries. The resort community also has several large air-conditioned indoor malls with major department stores and chic shops. Large and small strip malls lining most major streets contain chain stores such as Kmart, Target, and Walmart. El Paseo in nearby Palm Desert is the desert's fanciest shopping mecca, with its own collection of upscale and elegant galleries and shops. Most stores are open Monday–Saturday 10–5 or 6, and a fair number are open Sunday, typically noon–5.

Shopping Districts

Palm Canyon Drive is Palm Springs' main shopping destination, although many of the major stores have moved to Palm Desert. What began as a dusty two-way dirt road is now a one-way, three-lane thoroughfare with parking on both sides. Its shopping core extends from Alejo Road on the north to Ramon Road on the south. Anchoring the center of the drive is the **Desert Fashion Plaza,** now a more functional than fashionable mall, which features **Saks Fifth Avenue, Gucci,** and **Sabina Children's Fashions.**

El Paseo contains French and Italian fashion boutiques, shoe salons, jewelry designers, children's shops, nearly 30 galleries, and restaurants are clustered around fountains and courtyards along this 2-mile Mediterranean-style avenue. Specialty shops include **Polo/Ralph Lauren** (73-111 El Paseo, ☎ 619/340–1414), featuring Lauren's classic fashions and accessories for men and women, and **Cabale Cachet** (73-151 El Paseo, ☎ 619/346–5805), a collection of European haute couture.

The **Palm Desert Town Center** (Hwy. 111 at Monterey Ave., ☎ 619/346–2121) is an enclosed mall anchored by major department stores **Bullocks, J.C. Penney,** and **Robinson's-May.** There are 150 specialty shops ranging from **The Gap** and **Contempo Casuals** to upmarket **Cache** and **Miller Stockman,** as well as 10 movie theaters, five restaurants, fast food, and an **Ice Capades Chalet** skating rink.

The Atrium (69-930 Hwy. 111, Rancho Mirage) is a fantasyland for interior designers, containing an array of enterprises selling custom accessories, art objects, and furnishings.

Specialty Shops

DISCOUNT

Although Palm Springs is known for glamour and high prices, the city does offer bargains if you know where to look. **Desert Hills Factory Stores** (48650 Seminole Rd., Cabazon, ☎ 619/849–6641) is an outlet center with more than 150 name-brand fashion shops selling at a discount; **Spa Gear** here sells fashionable spa attire at a fraction of what you'd pay at hotel boutiques.

GOLF EQUIPMENT

Lady Golf (42-412 Bob Hope Dr., Rancho Mirage, ☎ 619/773–4949) features a large selection of apparel and accessories, custom golf-club fitting, and a practice and teaching facility.

Nevada Bob's Discount Golf & Tennis (4721 E. Palm Canyon Dr., Palm Springs, ☎ 619/324–0196) offers a large selection of golf and tennis equipment, clothing, and accessories.

SPORTS AND THE OUTDOORS

Participant Sports

The "Desert Guide" from *Palm Springs Life* magazine, available at most hotels and visitor information centers, contains a listing called "Courts and Courses." A complete listing of desert golf courses, including information about public availability and greens fees, is contained in the *Vacation Planner* published by Palm Springs Desert Resorts Convention and Visitors Bureau; it's available at most hotels. A listing of public golf courses also appears in the front of the GTE phone book.

Bicycling

There are more than 35 miles of bike trails, with six mapped-out city tours. Trail maps are available at the **Palm Springs Recreation Department** (401 S. Pavilion Way, ☎ 619/323–8272) and bike-rental shops. You can rent a bike at **Palm Springs Cyclery** (611 S. Palm Canyon Dr., Palm Springs, ☎ 619/325–9319) and at **Mac's Bicycle Rental** (70-053 Hwy. 111, Rancho Mirage, ☎ 619/321–9444), which will deliver mountain, three-speed, and tandem bikes to area hotels.

Golf

Palm Springs is known as the "Winter Golf Capital of the World," and a number of the courses are open to the public. Among these are the **Palm Springs Golf Course** (1885 Golf Club Dr., ☎ 619/328–1005) and **Tommy Jacobs' Bel-Aire Greens Country Club** (1001 S. El Cielo Rd., Palm Springs, ☎ 619/327–0332). **Mission Hills Resort Golf Club** (71-501 Dinah Shore Dr., Rancho Mirage, ☎ 619/328–3198), a challenging Pete Dye–designed course, is also home to major tournaments. Don't be surprised to spot well-known politicians and Hollywood stars on the greens.

Hiking

Nature trails abound in the **Indian Canyons, Mt. San Jacinto State Park and Wilderness,** and **Living Desert Wildlife and Botanical Park** (*see* Palm Springs and Environs *in* Exploring, *above*), in **Joshua Tree National Park** (*see* description of park *in* Exploring, *above*), and at **Big Morongo Canyon Preserve** (*see* Off the Beaten Track *in* Exploring, *above*). The Palm Springs Recreation Department (*see* Bicycling, *above*) has trail maps for $2.

Physical Fitness

In a resort town featuring the "most beautiful bodies money can buy," you'll find a wide selection of fitness facilities. Among the hotels that have health clubs, **Marriott's Desert Springs Resort and Spa** is the most luxurious. Exercise facilities include a 30-station gym, Lifecycles, fitness classes, personal training, and sauna and steam rooms. ☎ *619/341–1856.* ☛ *$24 daily membership includes workout clothing.* ⏲ *Daily 5:30 AM–7:30 PM.*

Tennis

Of the 600 or so tennis courts in the area, the following are open to the public: the **Palm Springs Tennis Center** (1300 Baristo Rd., ☎ 619/320–0020), with nine lighted courts; **Ruth Hardy Park** (Tamarisk and Caballeros, no ☎), with eight lighted courts and no court fee; and **Demuth Park** (4375 Mesquite Ave., no ☎), with four lighted courts.

Spectator Sports

Golf

More than 100 golf tournaments are presented in Palm Springs; the two most popular are the **Bob Hope Desert Classic** (January–February) and the **Dinah Shore LPGA Championship** (March or April). Call the Palm Springs Desert Resorts Convention and Visitors Bureau Events Hotline (☎ 619/770–1992) for exact dates and places.

Tennis

The **Evert Cup Women's Professional Tennis Tournament** and the ***Newsweek*** Champions Cup (both in February or March), held at Hyatt Grand Champions Resort in Indian Wells, attract top-ranked players on the international grand-slam circuit. For tickets, ☎ 619/341–2757.

DINING AND LODGING

Dining

Palm Springs area resorts have become weekend and winter homes to so many big-city types that it's not surprising to see the names of familiar restaurants—Morton's of Chicago, Ruth's Chris Steak House. While there are many expensive, trendy eateries in the desert, diligent diners can also get a good meal quite inexpensively at storefront restaurants, diners, and chains that cater to local clientele. Those who are careful about fat and cholesterol will find that most desert restaurant menus contain a selection of heart-healthy items. Most of the restaurants listed here are on or near Highway 111 between Palm Springs and La Quinta.

WHAT TO WEAR

Dining is generally casual at desert restaurants; a dress code may mean only that men must wear collared shirts.

CATEGORY	COST*
$$$$	over $50
$$$	$30–$50
$$	$20–$30
$	under $20

**per person for a three-course meal, excluding drinks, service, and 7¾% tax*

Lodging

One of the reasons the Palm Springs desert resorts attract so many celebrities, entertainment-industry honchos, and other notables is its stock of luxurious hotels. There is a full array of resorts, inns, clubs, spas, lodges, and condos, from small and private to big and bustling. Room rates cover an enormous range—from $40 to $1,600 a night—and also vary widely from summer to winter season. It is not unusual for a hotel to drop its rates from 50% to 60% during the summer (June through early September). For a growing number of off-season travelers, the chance to stay in a $180 room for $60 is an offer they just can't refuse. If you're seeking budget or moderate accommodations, you're more likely to find them in Palm Springs than in the newer resort areas. Also, discounts are sometimes given for extended stays.

Don't even think of visiting here during winter and spring holiday seasons without advance reservations. The **Palm Springs Chamber of Commerce** (☎ 619/325–1577) and **Palm Springs Visitor Information Center** (2781 N. Palm Canyon, ☎ 800/347–7746), which publishes a Visitor Guide, can help with lodging reservations. The *Vacation Planner,* available from the Convention and Visitors Bureau (☎ 800/967–3767), lists major hotels, motels, and resorts, including seasonal rates. To accommodate the increasing number of gay men and lesbians who vacation in the desert, the guide lists gay-friendly establishments, and a guide to restaurants and nightclubs is also available.

CATEGORY	COST*
$$$$	over $160
$$$	$100–$160
$$	$65–$100
$	under $65

**All prices are for a standard double room, excluding 9%–11% tax.*

RENTALS

Condos, apartments, and even individual houses may be rented by the day, week, month, or for longer periods. Some hotels, including Marriott's Desert Springs Resort and Spa (*see below*), have houses and villas for rent. Rates start at about $500 a week for a one-bedroom condo, $2,500 for two bedrooms, and $3,500 for a three-bedroom house for a month. Contact the **Rental Connection** (Box 8567, Palm Springs 92263, ☎ 619/320–7336 or 800/462–7256), or **Sunrise Co.** (76-300 Country Club Dr., Palm Desert 92260, ☎ 800/869–1130).

Cathedral City

DINING

$ **Red Bird Diner.** Hosts Art and Gayla Morris offer comfort food along with a hearty laugh for guests at their '50s-style diner, which even has counter service. This is a cute place with life-size murals of the decade's icons: James Dean, Ed Sullivan, and a bright red T-Bird. The specialty here is lamb, but Art also cooks country-fried steak, liver and onions, and chicken and dumplings. ✕ *Mission Plaza Center, 35-955 Date Palm Dr.,* ☎ *619/324–7707. AE, D, DC, MC, V.*

LODGING

$$$ **Doubletree Resort at Desert Princess.** This 345-acre luxury golf resort has attractively decorated rooms and condo units with balconies or terraces, and refrigerators; some rooms have views. *67-967 Vista Chino, 92234,* ☎ *619/322–7000 or 800/222–8733,* FAX *619/322–6853. 276 rooms, 13 suites and condos. 2 restaurants, lounge with entertainment, pool, hot tub, golf course, 10 tennis courts, health club, racquetball. AE, D, DC, MC, V.*

Indian Wells

LODGING

$$$$ **Hyatt Grand Champions Resort.** This stark white resort on 34 acres of natural desert is home to the *Newsweek* Champions Cup tennis tournament, which is played in the largest stadium in the West. Nicely appointed rooms are suite-style and are either split-level, one- or two-bedroom garden villas, or penthouses. All have balconies or terraces, living areas, and minibars. Some have fireplaces and private butler service. *44-600 Indian Wells La., 92210, ☎ 619/341–1000 or 800/233–1234, FAX 619/568–2236. 336 units. 3 restaurants, lounge, 4 pools, hot tubs, driving range, 2 golf courses, putting green, 12 tennis courts, health club, pro shop. AE, D, DC, MC, V.*

$$$$ **Stouffer Renaissance Esmeralda Resort.** The centerpiece of this luxurious Mediterranean-style resort is an eight-story atrium lobby with a fountain, surrounded by a dual grand staircase, which flows through a rivulet in the lobby floor to cascading pools and outside to lakes surrounding the property. Given its size, the hotel has a surprisingly intimate ambience. Spacious, well-appointed guest rooms are decorated in light wood with green and blue accents; they have sitting areas, balconies, refreshment centers, two TV sets, and travertine-marble vanities in bathrooms. One pool has a sandy beach. Golf and tennis instruction are available. *44-400 Indian Wells La., 92210-9971, ☎ 619/773–4444 or 800/552–4386, FAX 619/773–9250. 560 rooms, 44 suites. 2 restaurants, lounge with entertainment, 3 pools, 2 outdoor hot tubs, 2 golf courses, 7 tennis courts, health club. AE, D, DC, MC, V.*

La Quinta

DINING

$–$$ ★ **La Quinta Cliffhouse.** This popular "concept" restaurant perched halfway up a hillside offers sweeping mountain views at sunset, the early California ambience of a western movie set, and an eclectic international menu that includes grilled shrimp Provençal, Caesar salad with chicken, ahi Szechuan style, and tiramisù. Sunday brunch is popular here. ✕ *78-250 Hwy. 111, ☎ 619/360–5991. Reservations advised. AE, DC, MC, V.*

LODGING

$$$$ ★ **La Quinta Resort and Club.** Opened in 1926, this lush green oasis with red-roofed, blue-trimmed casitas is the oldest resort in the desert. Rooms are in historic adobe casitas separated by broad expanses of lawn and in newer, two-story units surrounding individual swimming pools and brilliant gardens. Furnishings are simple; there are fireplaces, robes, stocked refrigerators, and fruit-laden orange trees right outside the door. The atmosphere is discreet and sparely luxurious, and a premium is placed on privacy, which accounts for La Quinta's continuing lure for the brightest Hollywood stars. Frank Capra, for example, lived here for many years, and it's said that Greta Garbo roamed the grounds bumming cigarettes from guests. Contemporary stars such as Michael Jackson, Clint Eastwood, and Natalie Cole still seek tranquillity here. Now managed jointly with PGA West, La Quinta arranges access to some of the most celebrated golf courses in the area: Jack Nicklaus Resort Course, PGA West TPC Stadium Course (home of the Skins Game), and the Mountain Course. Golf packages include accommodations, breakfast daily, and rounds of golf. Pros John and Tracy Austin direct the Tennis Center, which provides clinics, private lessons, junior programs, and competitions. *49-499 Eisenhower Dr., 92253, ☎ 619/564–4111 or 800/854–1271, FAX 619/564–7656. 640 rooms (includes 22 suites). 5 restaurants, wine bar, lounge with entertainment,*

25 pools, 35 outdoor hot tubs, beauty salon, 4 golf courses, 30 tennis courts, health club, children's program. AE, D, DC, MC, V.

Palm Desert

DINING

$$–$$$ **Ristorante Mamma Gina.** Among the best Italian restaurants in the Palm Springs area, this attractive, simply furnished trattoria was opened by the son of the original Mamma Gina in Florence, Italy. There is an open kitchen where you can watch the chef from Tuscany prepare such specialties as deep-fried artichokes, fettuccine with porcini mushrooms, and prawns with artichokes and zucchini. The soups are robust. ✕ *73-705 El Paseo,* ☎ *619/568–9898. Reservations required. AE, DC, MC, V.*

$$ **Palomino Euro Bistro.** One of the hot spots in the desert, this restaurant specializes in grilled and roasted entrées: spit-roasted garlic chicken, oak-fired thin-crust pizza, and oven-roasted prawns. It's an interesting if noisy setting, with huge reproductions of famous French Impressionist paintings filling the walls. ✕ *73-101 Hwy. 111,* ☎ *619/773–9091. Reservations suggested. AE, D, DC, MC, V. No lunch Sat.*

$–$$ **Café des Beaux Arts.** This desert version of a sidewalk café has good garlicky French food and a trendy ambience, particularly at lunchtime, when the place is very busy. ✕ *73-640 El Paseo,* ☎ *619/346–0669. AE, MC, V. No dinner Tues.*

$ **Daily Grill.** The smell of cookies baking might make you more hungry than you thought you were. Good thing, because portions are huge at this bustling deli–coffee shop. A dinner plate–size chicken pot pie is but one fine example. Best buys are the blue-plate specials, which include soup or salad, along with turkey meat loaf, beef-dip sandwiches, turkey steak, and unlimited thirst-quenching lemonade. ✕ *73-061 El Paseo,* ☎ *619/779–9911. Lunch reservations advised. AE, DC, MC, V.*

$ ★ **La Donne Cucina Italiana.** This busy storefront restaurant-deli located in a shopping center is very popular with families. The menu features huge portions of wonderful homemade pasta, risotto, and chicken. ✕ *72-624 El Paseo,* ☎ *619/773–9441. Reservations essential. D, MC, V.*

LODGING

$$$$ **Marriott's Desert Springs Resort and Spa.** This sprawling hotel is the most spectacular-looking resort in the desert. It's a U-shape building with arms wrapped around the largest private lake in the desert, with 3 miles of shoreline. The centerpiece is an indoor, stair-stepped waterfall that flows right into the lake. From the base of the fall, guests and visitors can board boats for a worthwhile 10-minute tour of the grounds or a cruise to one of the hotel's restaurants. Nicely appointed rooms have lake or mountain views, balconies, oversize bathrooms, and minibars. There are long walks from lobby to rooms; if driving, request one close to the parking lot. Because the resort hosts business groups and conventions, guests will find it busier and dressier than most other desert hotels, with group activities often occupying pool and lawn areas. 🏨 *74-855 Country Club Dr., 92260,* ☎ *619/341–2211 or 800/228–9290,* FAX *619/341–1730. 891 rooms, 51 suites. 5 restaurants, barbecue grills, 2 lounges, 3 pools, hot tubs, spa, 2 golf courses, putting green, 21 tennis courts, badminton, croquet, health club, jogging, volleyball. AE, D, DC, MC, V.*

$$–$$$ **Tres Palmas Bed and Breakfast.** This contemporary B&B located just a few steps from El Paseo is also near the Living Desert. Spacious and bright, the inn's design is highlighted by enormous windows, high open-beamed ceilings, whitewashed wood, and textured peach tile floors. Southwestern decor in common areas and guest rooms (which are functional rather than luxurious) includes some fine old Navajo

rugs from the innkeepers' collection. Landscaped gardens include a gurgling fountain, succulents, and cactus. Breakfast is included. ☎ *73-135 Tumbleweed La., ☎ 619/773–9858. 5 rooms with private baths. Pool, outdoor hot tub. MC, V.*

Palm Springs

DINING

$$$ **Bono Restaurant and Racquet Club.** Owned by the Palm Springs area's Congressman Sonny Bono, this restaurant serves southern Italian dishes like those his mother used to make. It's a favorite feeding station for show-biz folk and the curious, and a fair place for pasta, chicken, veal, and scampi dishes. Outdoor dining is available. ✕ *1700 N. Indian Canyon Dr., ☎ 619/322–6200. Reservations advised. Valet parking. AE, D, DC, MC, V. No lunch.*

$$$ **Cafe St. James.** From the plant-filled balcony you can watch the passing parade below and dine on Mediterranean-Italian cuisine, Indian curries, or vegetarian dishes. ✕ *254 N. Palm Canyon Dr., ☎ 619/320–8041. Reservations advised. AE, DC, MC, V.*

$$ **Las Casuelas Original.** A longtime favorite among residents and visitors alike, this restaurant offers great (in size and taste) margaritas and average Mexican dishes: crab enchilada, carne asada, lobster Ensenada. It gets very, very crowded during the winter months. ✕ *368 N. Palm Canyon Dr., ☎ 619/325–3213. Reservations advised. AE, DC, MC, V.*

$ **Louise's Pantry.** A local landmark near the downtown Plaza Theater, this 1940s-style diner—bright yellow decor, with booths and a long counter—serves down-home cooking such as chicken and dumplings and short ribs of beef. You can get soup, salad, entrée, beverage, and dessert for under $15. There's usually a line to get in. Breakfast is served all day. ✕ *124 S. Palm Canyon Dr., ☎ 619/325–5124. No reservations. No credit cards.*

LODGING

$$$$ **Hyatt Regency Suites.** Located adjacent to the downtown Desert Fashion Plaza, this hotel's striking six-story asymmetrical atrium lobby holds a fountain and an enormous metal sculpture suspended from the ceiling. There are nicely decorated one- and two-bedroom suites with private balcony. Ask for the ones in the back of the hotel; they have pool and mountain views. Guests here have golf privileges at Rancho Mirage Country Club. ☎ *285 N. Palm Canyon Dr., 92262, ☎ 619/322–9000 or 800/233–1234, FAX 619/322–4027. 194 suites. 2 restaurants, lounge, pool, outdoor hot tub, beauty salon, health club. AE, D, DC, MC, V.*

$$$$ ★ **La Mancha Private Pool Villas and Court Club.** Only four blocks from downtown Palm Springs, this Spanish-Moroccan Hollywood-style retreat blocks out the rest of the world with plenty of panache. Opulently appointed villas, surrounded by lushly landscaped gardens, have kitchens, fireplaces, and private pools; four have private tennis courts. Convertibles for local transportation are available for rental. ☎ *444 N. Avenida Caballeros, 92262, ☎ 619/323–1773 or 800/647–7482, FAX 619/323–5928. 54 villas. Restaurant, pool, putting greens, 4 tennis courts, croquet, health club, paddle-tennis court, bicycles. AE, DC, MC, V.*

$$$$ **Palm Springs Hilton Resort and Racquet Club.** The cool, white marble elegance of this plant-filled resort hotel, just off Palm Canyon Drive, and its two superb restaurants make it a popular choice for visitors to the city. Rooms have private balconies and refrigerators. ☎ *400 E. Tahquitz Way, 92262, ☎ 619/320–6868 or 800/522–6900, FAX 619/323–2755. 189 rooms, 71 suites. 2 restaurants, pool, hot tub, 6 tennis courts, health club, pro shop. AE, D, DC, MC, V.*

$$$$ Wyndham Palm Springs Hotel. The main appeal of this hotel is its location adjacent to the Palm Springs Convention Center. The terra-cotta Spanish-colonial building surrounds the largest swimming pool in Palm Springs. Rooms are well equipped with hair dryers, "on-command TV," and huge walk-through bathrooms in the suites. Because the majority of the Wyndham's customers are on business, the atmosphere here is more serious than at other desert establishments. *888 Tahquitz Canyon Way, 92262, ☎ 619/322–6000 or 800/996–3426, FAX 619/322–5551. 410 rooms, including 158 suites. 2 restaurants, lounge, pool, wading pool, beauty salon, 2 outdoor hot tubs, spa, health club, bicycles, video arcade, business services. AE, D, DC, MC, V.*

$$$–$$$$ Abby West. This historic inn located in a quiet residential neighborhood at the north end of town is a knockout with black-and-white decor reflecting the art deco style of Hollywood in the 1930s. Large rooms have private entrances and patios, galley kitchens, and VCRs. There are several tree-shaded patios including a clothing-optional sunbathing area. Room rates include breakfast and lunch served buffet style. The inn, which caters to a gay clientele, is part of the Harlow Club Hotels group (*see below*). *772 Prescott Circle, 92262, ☎ 619/325–0229 or 800/223–4073, FAX 619/322–8534. 17 rooms. Pool, outdoor hot tub, exercise room. AE, D, DC, MC, V.*

$$$–$$$$ Harlow El Alameda. A historic resort now catering to a gay clientele, this is ideal for those seeking secluded accommodations in a lush garden setting. Smallish rooms are located in hacienda-style buildings surrounding a pool; many have fireplaces, private patios, and unusually large bathrooms. Crimson bougainvillea cascades from the rooftops; 10 varieties of date palms grow on the property, also fruit-laden orange, tangerine, and grapefruit trees. There's a secluded clothing-optional sunbathing area. Room rates include breakfast and lunch. *175 E. El Alameda, 92262, ☎ 619/323–3977 or 800/223–4073, FAX 619/320–1218. 15 rooms. Pool, outdoor hot tub, exercise room. AE, D, DC, MC, V.*

$$$–$$$$ Inn at the Racquet Club. Built by actors Charlie Farrell and Ralph Bellamy in the 1930s, this legendary resort (formerly the Palm Springs Racquet Club) brought the movie stars to the Springs. Once a private club, notable for Hollywood high jinks, partying, and the "discovery" of Marilyn Monroe, it was later opened to the public to mixed reviews. New owners have reduced the scale and renovated 24 of the original red-roofed cottages used by the stars; most have fireplaces and private patios. *2743 N. Indian Canyon Dr., 92262, ☎ 619/325–1281, FAX 619/325–3429. 86 units. Restaurant, lounge (weekends only), 3 pools, 3 hot tubs, sauna, 12 tennis courts, exercise room. AE, DC, MC, V.*

$$$–$$$$ Spa Hotel and Mineral Springs. With its brilliant pink facade, you can't miss the Spa as you drive through the Springs. This hotel has had its ups and downs since it was built in 1963 over the original Agua Caliente springs. Now owned by the Agua Caliente tribe, it underwent extensive renovation a few years back, its rooms decorated in soft desert pinks and blues and light-wood furniture. Not trendy or splashy, the Spa appeals to an older crowd that appreciates its soothing waters and downtown location. *100 N. Indian Canyon Dr., 92262, ☎ 619/778–1507 or 800/854–1279, FAX 619/325–3344. 230 rooms, 20 suites. Restaurant, 2 lounges, pool, outdoor hot tubs, beauty salon, spa, exercise room. AE, D, DC, MC, V.*

$$–$$$$ Casa Cody. This very clean, western-style bed-and-breakfast is just a few steps from the Palm Springs Desert Museum. Simply furnished spacious studios and one- and two-bedroom suites are individually decorated. Service is personal and gracious; room rates include Continental breakfast. *175 S. Cahuilla Rd., 92262, ☎ 619/320–9346 or*

800/231–2639, FAX 619/325–8610. 17 units. Kitchens, 2 pools. AE, D, DC, MC, V.

$$–$$$$ **Ingleside Inn.** Like many desert lodgings, this hacienda-style inn attracts its share of Hollywood personalities, who appreciate good service and relative seclusion. Rooms are individually decorated. Many have antiques, fireplaces, whirlpool tubs and steam showers, stocked refrigerators, and private patios. Those in the main building are dark and cool, even in summer. The adjacent Melvyn's Restaurant is locally popular. *200 W. Ramon Rd., 92264, ☎ 619/325–0046 or 800/772–6655, FAX 619/325–0710. 29 rooms. Pool, hot tub. AE, D, DC, MC, V.*

$$–$$$$ **Villa Royale.** Each room in this bed-and-breakfast is individually decorated with a European theme. Some have private Jacuzzis, fireplaces, and kitchens. The grounds feature lush gardens. *1620 Indian Trail, 92264, ☎ 619/327–2314 or 800/245–2314, FAX 619/322–3794. 34 rooms. Restaurant, lounge, 2 pools, hot tub. AE, MC, V.*

$$–$$$ **Korakia Pensione.** This historic Moorish-style home, built in the 1920s by Scottish artist Gordon Coutts, has long been a haven for the creative set. Winston Churchill came here to paint; more recently photographer Annie Leibovitz has enjoyed the home's scenic mountain view. Inside, rooms are furnished with antiques, handmade furniture, and Oriental rugs; some have fireplaces, and most have kitchens. Room rates include Continental breakfast. *257 S. Patencio Rd., ☎ 619/864–6411. 12 rooms. Pool. No credit cards.*

$$ **Bee Charmer Inn.** This southwestern-style inn with red-tile roof and terra-cotta tile floors caters exclusively to women. Spacious rooms surround a pool and tropical courtyard; comfortably but not lavishly decorated in soft pastel colors, they come with refrigerators and microwaves. Three rooms have wet bars, and one has a whirlpool bath. Owner Judy Nelson occasionally has barbecues and afternoon entertainment. Rates include Continental breakfast. *1600 E. Palm Canyon Dr., 92264, ☎ 619/778–5883. 14 rooms. Pool. AE, D, MC, V.*

$–$$ **Howard Johnson Lodge.** This typical motel-style property is popular with tour groups. Ask for special discounts. *701 E. Palm Canyon Dr., 92262, ☎ 619/320–2700 or 800/854–4345, FAX 619/322–5354. 206 rooms. Coffee shop, lounge, 2 pools. AE, D, DC, MC, V.*

$–$$ **Vagabond Inn.** Rooms are smallish at this centrally located motel but clean and comfortable. The Vagabond offers good value for budget prices. *1699 S. Palm Canyon Dr., 92264, ☎ 619/325–7211 or 800/522–1555, FAX 619/322–9269. 120 rooms. Coffee shop (no dinner), pool, outdoor hot tub, 2 saunas. AE, D, DC, MC, V.*

Rancho Mirage

DINING

$$$$ **Morton's of Chicago.** The desert version of this national steak-house chain lures in the meat-and-potatoes crowd with its selection of prime beef and seafood, contemporary hors d'oeuvres, and traditional desserts. Huge LeRoy Neiman serigraphs hang in the bustling dining room. The bar is quiet and clubby. ✕ *74-880 Country Club Dr., ☎ 619/340–6865, FAX 619/340–2645. Reservations suggested. AE, DC, MC, V. No lunch.*

$$$ **Wally's Desert Turtle.** If price is no object, and you like plush, gilded decor, then this is where to come. You'll be surrounded by the golden names of Palm Springs and Hollywood society and served old-fashioned French cooking: rack of lamb, imported Dover sole, braised sea bass, veal Oscar, chicken Normande, and dessert soufflés. ✕ *71-775 Hwy. 111, ☎ 619/568–9321. Reservations required. Jacket required. Valet parking. AE, D, DC, MC, V. No lunch Sat.–Thurs.*

$$ ★ **Bangkok V.** Dedicated spicy-food fans gather here at lunch or early evening to savor beautifully prepared and artistically presented Thai cuisine. When you order be sure to tell them how hot you want your food. It's a lovely place, whether you eat in the bright dining rooms or outside at an umbrella-shaded table. ✕ *72-930 Hwy. 111,* ☎ *619/770–9508. Reservations suggested. AE, DC, MC, V. No lunch weekends.*

$$ **Shame on the Moon.** This contemporary bistro recently moved to Rancho Mirage from Cathedral City. Dishes are American and Continental; specialties include pasta, fresh fish, and filet mignon. ✕ *69-950 Frank Sinatra Dr.,* ☎ *619/324–5515. Reservations advised. No lunch weekends. AE, MC, V.*

$$ **Zorba's Greek Islands.** This festive spot, tucked away in a shopping center, is a bit hard to locate but is worth seeking out for its tasty Greek food and entertainment. Kebabs, Greek salad, dolmas, and other Mediterranean dishes are served; celebrity photos, live music, dancing, and singing waiters contribute to a most convivial atmosphere. ✕ *42-434 Bob Hope Dr.,* ☎ *619/340–3066. Reservations advised. No lunch weekends. AE, DC, MC, V.*

LODGING

$$$$ ★ **Ritz-Carlton Rancho Mirage.** This hotel is tucked into a hillside in the Santa Rosa Mountains with sweeping views of the valley below. Sheep from the surrounding bighorn preserve frequently visit the hotel grounds. The surroundings are elegant, with gleaming marble and brass, original artwork, deep plush carpeting, and remarkable comfort. All rooms are spacious and meticulously appointed with antiques, fabric wall coverings, marble bathrooms, and often two phones and two TVs. Service is impeccable, anticipating your every need. 🏨 *68-900 Frank Sinatra Dr., 92270,* ☎ *619/321–8282 or 800/241–3333,* FAX *619/321–6928. 221 rooms, 19 suites. 3 restaurants, lounge with entertainment, pool, outdoor hot tub, spa, 10 tennis courts, 9-hole pitch-and-putt golf, health club, basketball, croquet, hiking, volleyball, children's programs, business services. AE, D, DC, MC, V.*

$$$$ **Westin Mission Hills Resort.** This sprawling Moroccan-style resort on 360 acres, adjacent to the annual Nabisco Dinah Shore LPGA Classic, is surrounded by fairways and putting greens. Rooms are in two-story buildings enveloping patios and fountains scattered throughout the property. Nicely furnished, the rooms have soft desert colors, terra-cotta tile floors, shuttered windows, and private patios or balconies; amenities include double sinks, in-room coffeemakers, and refrigerators. Paths and creeks meander through the complex, encircling a lagoon-style swimming pool with a 60-foot water slide. It's a place to spot the famous (and used-to-be-famous): Jay Leno, Walter Cronkite, Carol Burnett, Sargent Shriver, Beverly Sills, Chad Everett, Terry Bradshaw, and Magic Johnson have all graced these premises. 🏨 *71-333 Dinah Shore Dr., 92270,* ☎ *619/328–5955 or 800/228–3000,* FAX *619/321–2955. 512 rooms. 7 restaurants, lounge with entertainment, 3 pools, outdoor hot tubs, 2 18-hole golf courses, 7 tennis courts, health club, children's programs. AE, D, DC, MC, V.*

THE ARTS AND NIGHTLIFE

For complete listings of upcoming events, pick up a copy of *Palm Springs Life* magazine or *Palm Springs Life*'s "Desert Guide," a free monthly publication found in any hotel; gay nightlife is covered in *Bottom Line* (☎ 619/323–0552), available at gay establishments.

The Arts

The **McCallum Theatre** (73-000 Fred Waring Dr., Palm Desert, ☎ 619/340–2787), site of the **Palm Springs International Film Festival** in January, is the principal cultural venue in the desert, offering a number of arts series November through May. Programs include film, classical music, opera, ballet, popular music, and theater.

The **Annenberg Theater** (Palm Springs Desert Museum, 101 Museum Dr., north of Tahquitz Way, ☎ 619/325–7186 or 619/325–4490) is the other film-festival venue. The 450-seat theater hosts film series, Sunday-afternoon chamber concerts, lectures, Broadway shows, and opera.

Of the many arts festivals held in the desert, **La Quinta Arts Festival** (☎ 619/564–1244), normally the third weekend in March, displays the best work and has the classiest entertainment, food, and celebrities.

Theater

The **Fabulous Palm Springs Follies,** the hottest show in the desert, presents 10 sellout performances each week. A vaudeville-style revue, starring extravagantly costumed retired (but very much in shape) showgirls, singers, and dancers, is presented afternoons and evenings at the Plaza Theater (128 S. Palm Canyon Dr., ☎ 916/327–0225; ☛ $24.50–$39, call for schedule).

Starlight Theater (1426 N. Palm Canyon Dr., Palm Springs 92262, ☎ 619/778–6535), a new small theater, presents family-oriented musicals and dramas year-round.

Nightlife

Two good sources for finding current nightlife attractions are the *Desert Sun* (the local newspaper) and *Guide* magazine, a monthly publication distributed free at most downtown merchants' counters.

Live entertainment, ranging from soft dinner music to song-and-dance numbers, is frequently found in the city's hotels and restaurants. The piano bar at Melvyn's at the **Ingleside Inn** (200 W. Ramon Rd., Palm Springs) is popular.

Dancing

Between the flashing lights of its Top-40 disco and the retro-memorabilia in its new '50s–'60s room, **Cecil's on Sunrise** (1775 E. Palm Canyon Dr., ☎ 619/320–4202) is bound to keep you dancing. There's dancing to live country music at the **Cactus Corral** (67-501 E. Palm Canyon Dr., Cathedral City, ☎ 619/321–8558). **C. C. Construction Company** (68-449 Perez Rd., Cathedral City, ☎ 619/324–4241) is the largest gay nightclub in the desert, catering to a mixed crowd with dancing nightly. **Costas** (Marriott's Desert Springs, 74-855 Country Club Dr., Palm Desert, ☎ 619/341–1795) has live bands for dancing in a lakeside setting. **Zelda's** (169 N. Indian Canyon Dr., Palm Springs, ☎ 619/325–2375) is another active spot featuring talent and fashion shows, hot-body competitions, and limbo contests.

Jazz

Peabody's Jazz Studio and Coffee Bar (134 S. Palm Canyon Dr., Palm Springs, ☎ 619/333–1877) presents jazz in a warm atmosphere.

Lincoln View Coffee House (278-C N. Palm Canyon Dr., Palm Springs, ☎ 619/327–6365) has Sunday-afternoon jam sessions and live jazz Friday and Saturday nights.

PALM SPRINGS ESSENTIALS

Arriving and Departing

By Bus

Greyhound (☏ 800/231–2222) services Palm Springs from Los Angeles and San Diego. The Palm Spring depot (☏ 619/325–2053) is at 311 North Indian Canyon Drive.

By Car

Palm Springs is about a two-hour drive east of Los Angeles and a three-hour drive northeast of San Diego. Highway 111 brings you right onto Palm Canyon Drive, the main thoroughfare in Palm Springs and connecting route to other desert communities. From Los Angeles take the San Bernardino Freeway (I–10E) to Highway 111. From San Diego, I–15N connects with the Pomona Freeway (Highway 60) leading to the San Bernardino Freeway (I–10E) east. Exits are clearly marked: Highway 111 for Palm Springs, Monterey for Palm Desert, Washington for La Quinta. If you're coming from the Riverside area, you might want to try the scenic Palms-to-Pines Highway (Highway 74). This 130-mile route begins in Hemet and connects directly with Highway 111; the trek from snowcapped peaks to open desert valley is breathtaking.

By Plane

Major airlines serving **Palm Springs Regional Airport** include **Alaska** (☏ 800/426–0333), **American** and **American Eagle** (☏ 800/433–7300), **America West** (☏ 800/235–9292), **Continental** (☏ 800/525–0280), **Delta** (☏ 800/221–1212), **SkyWest/Delta Connection** (☏ 800/453–9417), **United** and **United Express** (☏ 800/241–6522), and **USAir Express** (☏ 800/428–4322). The airport is about 2 miles east of the city's main downtown intersection; most hotels provide service to and from the airport.

By Train

Amtrak (☏ 800/872–7245) passenger trains serve the Indio area, 20 miles east of Palm Springs. From Indio, Greyhound Lines bus service is available to Palm Springs.

Getting Around

By Bus

SunBus serves the entire Coachella Valley from Desert Hot Springs to Coachella with regular routes. Call 619/343–3451 for route and schedule information. Some hotels have free or low-cost passes for use on **SunBus.**

By Car

The desert resort communities occupy about a 20-mile stretch between I–10 in the east and Palm Canyon Drive in the west. Although some areas such as Palm Canyon Drive in Palm Springs and El Paseo are walkable, having a car is the best way to get around.

By Taxi

Desert Cab (☏ 619/325–2868) and **Valley Cabousine** (☏ 619/340–5845) serve the Palm Spring desert resorts area. **Dial-a-Cab** (☏ 619/327–8708), operating 7:30 AM–5:15 PM Monday–Saturday, offers door-to-door service and will take customers anywhere within Rancho Mirage or to nearby shopping centers for $1.75.

Guided Tours

Aerial

Fantasy Balloon Flights (☎ 619/398–6322) and **Sunrise Balloons** (☎ 800/548–9912) organize trips across the valley (trip lengths and prices vary); Sunrise also arranges customized helicopter tours.

Celebrity

Gray Line Tours (☎ 619/325–0974) conducts a 1½-hour tour of Palm Springs proper that covers its history, points of interest, and celebrity residences. The cost is $12 for adults, $10 for senior citizens 60 or over (50 or over with AARP card), and $9 for children three to 11 (under three free). Buses leave at 9 and 11 AM.

Palm Springs Celebrity Tours (☎ 619/325–2682) has two tours. An hour-long one covers Palm Springs history, points of interest, and its Native American heritage. Included are 30 to 40 celebrity homes. A 2½-hour tour takes in the above, plus Rancho Mirage and other areas in the Coachella Valley. Prices range from $11 to $16 for adults, $10 to $14 for senior citizens over 60, $6 to $8 for students under 16.

Desert

Covered Wagon Tours (☎ 619/347–2161) takes visitors on an old-time, two-hour exploration of the desert with a cookout at the end of the journey.

Desert Adventures (☎ 619/864–6530) takes to the wilds with Jeep tours of Indian canyons, off-road in the Santa Rosa Mountains and into a mystery canyon.

Golden Eagle Tours (☎ 800/428–1833) conducts visits to windmill turbine fields that cover the desert hillsides.

Important Addresses and Numbers

Emergencies

Dial 911 for **police** and **ambulance** in an emergency.

Desert Hospital (☎ 619/323–6511).

Dental emergency service is available from **Gregory Yates, D.D.S.** (☎ 619/327–8448), 24 hours each day.

Visitor Information

Palm Springs Desert Resorts Convention and Visitors Bureau (69-930 Hwy. 111, Suite 201, Rancho Mirage 92270, ☎ 619/770–9000 or 800/417–3529) mails brochures to prospective visitors and runs an **Activities Hotline** (☎ 619/770–1992).

Palm Springs Visitor Information Center (2781 N. Palm Canyon Dr., Palm Springs 92262, ☎ 800/347–7746) also provides tourist information.

15 The Mojave Desert and Death Valley

When most people assemble their "must-see" list of California attractions, the desert isn't often among the top contenders. What with its heat and vast, sparsely populated tracts of land, the desert is no Disneyland. But that's precisely why it deserves a closer look. The natural riches here are overwhelming: rolling waves of sand dunes, black cinder cones thrusting up hundreds of feet into the air from a blistered desert floor, riotous sheets of wildflowers, bizarrely shaped Joshua trees basking in an orange glow at sunset, and an abundant silence that is both dramatic and startling.

By Aaron Sugarman

Updated by Deke Castleman

THE MOJAVE DESERT begins just north of the San Bernardino mountains, along the northern edge of Los Angeles, and extends north 150 miles into the Eureka Valley and east 200 miles to the Colorado River. Death Valley lies north and east of the Mojave, jutting into Nevada near Beatty. The Mojave, with elevations ranging from 3,000 to 5,000 feet above sea level, is known as the High Desert; Death Valley, the Low Desert, with points at almost 300 feet below sea level, is the lowest spot in the United States.

Because of the vast size of California's deserts, an area about as big as Ohio, and the frequently extreme weather, careful planning is essential for an enjoyable desert adventure. Conveniences, facilities, trails, gas stations, and supermarkets do not lurk just around the corner from many desert sights. Be sure to fill your tank before entering Death Valley—fuel is cheaper on the interstates and you'll avoid running out. Also, check your vehicle's oil and its water and tire pressure. It is advisable on the steeper grades to shut off your air-conditioning to avoid engine overheating. Different regions of the desert can be easily handled in day trips, but more extensive exploring will require overnight stays. Reliable maps are a must, as signage is limited, and, in some places, nonexistent. Other important accessories include a compass, extra food and water (3 gallons per person per day is recommended, plus additional radiator water), sunglasses, extra clothes (for wind or cool nights), and a hat (if you're going to do any walking around in the sun). Bring along sufficient clothing to block the sun's rays. A pair of binoculars can come in handy, and don't forget your camera: You're likely to see things you've never seen before.

What is probably most surprising about the desert is its accessibility. A large portion of the desert can be seen from the comfort of an air-conditioned car. And don't despair if you are without air-conditioning—just avoid the middle of the day and the middle of the summer, good advice for all desert travel. Believe everything you've ever heard about desert heat; it can be brutal. A temperature of 134°F was once recorded at Furnace Creek in Death Valley, the hottest place on the planet. But during mornings and evenings, particularly in the spring and fall, the temperature ranges from cool and crisp to pleasantly warm and dry: perfect for hiking and driving.

EXPLORING

The Mojave Desert

Numbers in the margin correspond to points of interest on the Mojave Desert map.

Although the Mojave Desert is a sprawling space, many of its visitable attractions are conveniently situated on a north–south axis along U.S. 395 and Highway 178 and an east–west axis that runs between I–15 and I–40. We'll describe tours stretching roughly 120 miles along each axis, and a third tour that winds its way through Death Valley, which is between the two routes. If you plan to stop overnight en route to Death Valley, both Lone Pine and Ridgecrest on U.S. 395 offer tourist services and accommodations, as do Barstow and Baker on I–15.

The Western Mojave

On I–15, just before you reach U.S. 395 on the northbound tour, you
1 cross Cajon Pass, riding over the infamous **San Andreas Fault**—an apocalyptic way to start a desert trip.

2 About 70 miles farther on U.S. 395, you enter the **Rand Mining District,** consisting of the towns of Randsburg, Red Mountain, and Johannesburg. Randsburg is one of the few authentic gold-mining communities that haven't become ghost towns. The town first boomed with the discovery of gold in the Rand Mountains in 1895 and, along with the neighboring settlements, grew to support the successful Yellow Aster Mine. Rich tungsten ore was discovered during World War I, and silver was found in 1919. All told, the money brought in by these precious metals is estimated at more than $35 million. Randsburg still sports its authentic Old West heritage. The picturesque town has some original Gold Rush buildings, plus a few antiques shops, a general store, and the city jail.

3 Just to the northwest of the Rand Mining District is **Red Rock Canyon State Park.** The canyon is a feast for the eyes with its layers of pink, white, red, rust, and brown rocks. Entering the park from the south, you pass through a steep-walled gorge and enter a wide bowl tinted pink by what was once hot volcanic ash. The human history of this area goes back some 20,000 years to the canyon dwellers known only as the Old People. Mojave Indians roamed the land for several hundred years until Gold Rush fever hit the region in the mid- to late 1800s; remains of mining operations dot the countryside. The canyon was later invaded by filmmakers and has starred in westerns. The state park can be found on either side of Highway 14, about 10 miles south of where it meets U.S. 395. The ranger station is northwest on Abbott Drive from Highway 14.

4 Heading northwest, you will find **Short Canyon** about a half mile from the intersection of Highway 14 and U.S. 395. Sierra snows and natural springs feed the stream that flows down the rocky canyon, spills over a falls, and then sinks into the sand. In good years, there are large beds of wildflowers, and, even in very dry years, there are still some splashes of color. In the spring, a half-mile hike along the stream brings you to a 20-foot waterfall. Head west on the canyon road you'll find just south of Brady's Cafe on U.S. 395, but only after checking on current road conditions with the BLM (☎ 619/375–7125).

From Short Canyon, take U.S. 395 east to Highway 178 and continue east to **Ridgecrest,** a good hub for further exploration in this area. You'll find a range of stores dining possibilities here. The town's **Maturango Museum,** well worth a visit, contains interesting exhibits detailing the natural and cultural history of the northern Mojave. *100 E. Las Flores Ave., at China Lake Blvd., 93555, ☎ 619/375–6900, FAX 619/375–0479. ☛ $2 adults; $1 senior citizens over 55, military with ID, and children 6–18. ⏲ Wed.–Sun. 10–5.*

On weekends in the spring and fall, the Maturango Museum arranges
★ 5 the only tours to one of the desert's most amazing spectacles, the **Petroglyph Canyons.** (Call ahead; space is limited on these full-day excursions). The two canyons, commonly called Big and Little Petroglyph, are in the Coso mountain range on the million-acre **U.S. Naval Weapons Center at China Lake,** which allows only limited access. Each of the canyons holds a superlative concentration of rock art, the largest of its kind in the Northern Hemisphere. Scratched or pecked into the shiny desert varnish (oxidized minerals) that coats the canyon's dark basaltic rocks are thousands of images. Some are figures of animals and people, some seemingly abstract—it isn't clear to historians whether they're mythology of an ancient people or hunting records. All are exceptionally preserved and protected; the feeling of living history is incredible here.

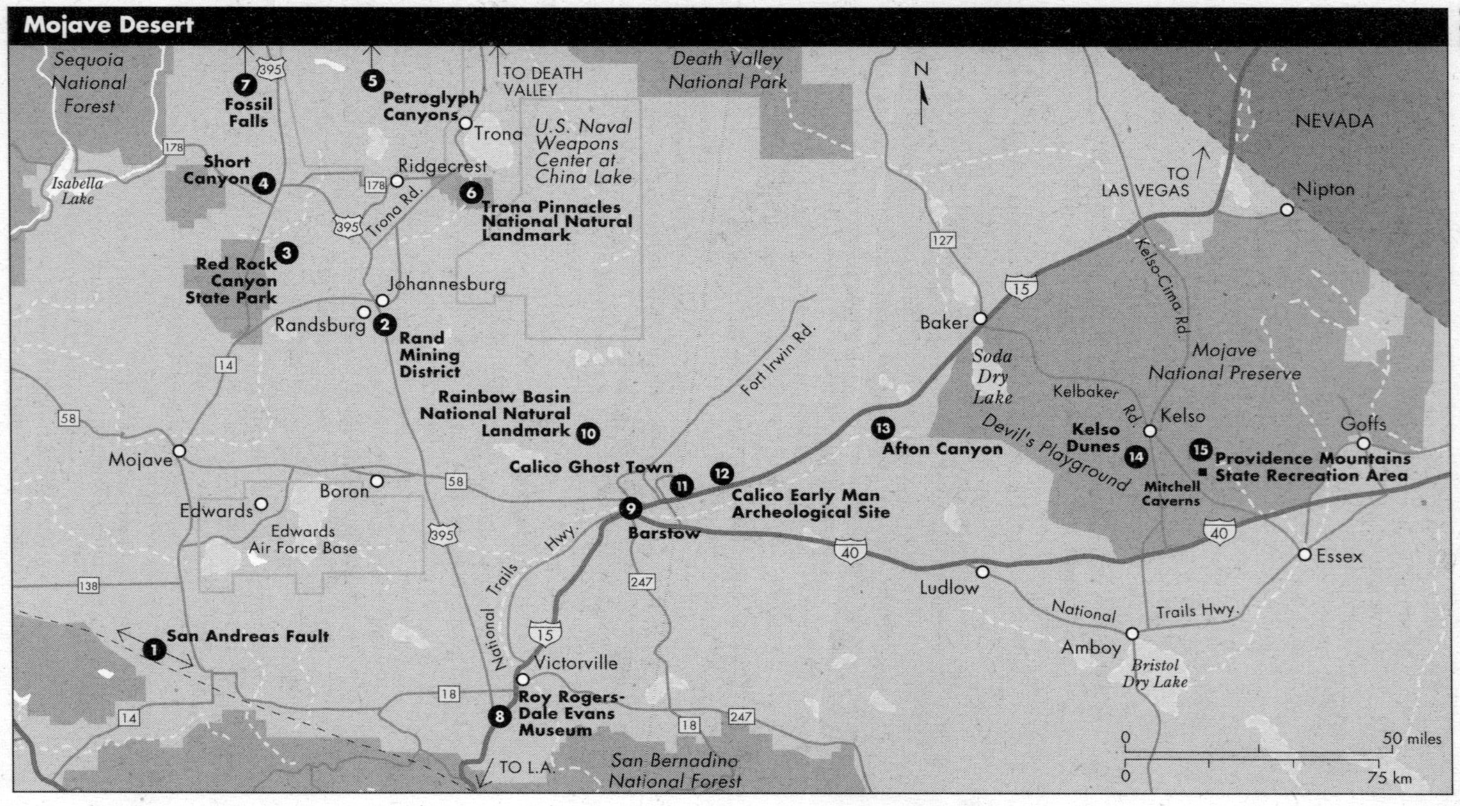
Mojave Desert
Sequoia National Forest
Isabella Lake
7 Fossil Falls
5 Petroglyph Canyons
TO DEATH VALLEY
Death Valley National Park
Trona
U.S. Naval Weapons Center at China Lake
4 Short Canyon
Ridgecrest
6 Trona Pinnacles National Natural Landmark
Trona Rd.
3 Red Rock Canyon State Park
Johannesburg
Randsburg
2 Rand Mining District
Rainbow Basin National Natural Landmark 10
Mojave
Boron
Edwards
Edwards Air Force Base
Calico Ghost Town
11
12 Calico Early Man Archeological Site
9 Barstow
National Trails Hwy.
Victorville
8 Roy Rogers-Dale Evans Museum
TO L.A.
1 San Andreas Fault
San Bernadino National Forest
Fort Irwin Rd.
Baker
Soda Dry Lake
13 Afton Canyon
Devil's Playground
Kelbaker Rd.
Kelso
Kelso Dunes 14
Mitchell Caverns
15 Providence Mountains State Recreation Area
Mojave National Preserve
Kelso-Cima Rd.
TO LAS VEGAS
Nipton
NEVADA
Goffs
Essex
Ludlow
Amboy
Bristol Dry Lake
National Trails Hwy.
N
395
178
14
58
138
18
247
15
40
127
0 50 miles
0 75 km

☛ *$20, children under 6 not admitted; $40 for less regular "extended trips" for photographers and others who want to see sunrise and sunset in the Little Petroglyph Canyon. Tours given Mar.–1st weekend in July and Sept.–1st weekend in Dec.*

Off the Beaten Track

The desert is not a particularly well-beaten track to begin with, but some spots are a bit farther out of the way, or more difficult to reach.

6 **Trona Pinnacles National Natural Landmark,** just 20 miles east of Ridgecrest and 10 miles south of the town of Trona (*see* Mojave Desert map), is not easy to reach—the best road to the area changes with the weather and can be impassable after a rain. But it's worth the effort, especially to sci-fi buffs, who will recognize the pinnacles as *Star Trek*'s Final Frontier. These fantasy formations of calcium carbonate, known as tufa, were formed underwater along cracks in the lake bed—first as hollow tubes, then mounds, and finally as the spires visible today. A ½-mile trail winds around this surreal landscape. Wear sturdy shoes—tufa cuts like coral! For information about the region, contact the **Ridgecrest Resource Area Office** (300 S. Richmond Rd., Ridgecrest 93555, ☏ 619/375–7125). *From the Trona—Red Mountain Rd., take Hwy. 178 east for 7.7 mi. Or, from its junction with U.S. 395, take Hwy. 178 for 29 mi to dirt intersection; turn southeast and go ½ mi to a fork. Continue south via right fork, cross railroad tracks, and continue about 5 mi to pinnacles.*

7 **Fossil Falls** is 20 miles up U.S. 395 from Highway 14, then ½ mile east on Cinder Cone Road. On the way, you'll pass Little Lake, a good place to see migrating waterfowl in the spring and fall, including several varieties of ducks and geese and probably pelicans as well. The area just north of the lake is often covered with wildflowers. As you pass the lake, Red Hill comes into view ahead of you. The hill is a small volcano that was active about 20,000 years ago. Approaching the falls you cross a large volcanic field; the falls themselves drop an impressive distance along the channel cut by the Owens River through the hardened lava flows.

The Eastern Mojave

We'll start the eastward tour in **Victorville,** less than 20 miles from Cajon Pass. The bit of water flowing along the eastern side of I–15, near **Mojave Narrows Regional Park,** is one of the few places where the Mojave River runs aboveground. For the most part, the 150-mile-long river flows from the San Bernardino mountains north and east underneath the desert floor. The park has boat rentals, an equestrian center, fishing, and camping. *Mojave Narrows Regional Park, 18000 Yates Rd.,* ☏ *619/245–2226.* ☛ *$4 per vehicle weekdays, $5 weekends; dry camping $10 a night, camping with utilities $15 a night.* ⏲ *Wed.–Mon. 7:30–sunset.*

8 Also within Victorville is the **Roy Rogers–Dale Evans Museum,** which exhibits the personal and professional memorabilia of the famous stars. Yes, Roy's faithful horse, Trigger, is here. *Take Roy Rogers Dr. exit off I–15 (mailing address: 15650 Seneca Rd.),* ☏ *619/243–4547.* ☛ *$4 adults, $3 senior citizens and children 13–16, $2 children 6–12.* ⏲ *Daily 9–5; closed Thanksgiving and Dec. 25.*

9 Continue north on I–15 to **Barstow,** established in 1886 when a subsidiary of the Atchison, Topeka, and Santa Fe Railroad began construction of a depot and hotel at this junction of its tracks and the 35th-parallel transcontinental lines. The **Desert Information Center** (831 Barstow

Rd., ☎ 619/256–8313) contains exhibits about desert ecology, wildflowers, wildlife, and other features of the desert environment. Travelers information is provided at 1610 AM on the radio dial.

10 **Rainbow Basin National Natural Landmark,** 8 miles north of Barstow, looks as if it could be on Mars, perhaps because so many sci-fi movies depicting the red planet have been filmed here. There is a tremendous sense of upheaval; huge slabs of red, orange, white, and green stone tilt at crazy angles like ships about to capsize. At points along the spectacularly scenic 6-mile drive it is easy to imagine you are alone in the world, hidden among the colorful badlands that give the basin its name. Hike the many washes and you are likely to see the fossilized remains of creatures that roamed the basin 12 million to 16 million years ago: mastodons, large and small camels, rhinos, dog-bears, birds, and insects. Leave any fossils you find where they are—they are protected by federal law. *Take Fort Irwin Rd. about 5 mi north to Fossil Bed Rd., a graded dirt road, and head west 3 mi. Call the Desert Information Center in Barstow (☎ 619/256–8313) for more information.*

After a 10-mile drive northeast from Barstow, you can slip into the more
11 recent past at **Calico Ghost Town.** Calico became a wild—and rich—mining town after a rich deposit of silver was found around 1881. In 1886, after more than $85 million worth of silver, gold, and other precious metals were harvested from the multicolored "calico" hills, the price of silver fell and the town slipped into decline. Frank "Borax" Smith helped revive the town in 1889 when he started mining the unglamorous but profitable mineral borax, but that boom busted by the turn of the century. The effort to restore the ghost town was started by Walter Knott of Knott's Berry Farm fame in 1960. Knott handed the land over to San Bernardino County in 1966, and it became a regional park. Today, the 1880s come back to life as you stroll the wooden sidewalks of Main Street, browse through several western shops, roam the tunnels of Maggie's Mine, and take a ride on the Calico–Odessa Railroad. Special festivals in March, May, October, and November add to Calico's Old West flavor. It's wise to make campground reservations (*see* Camping, *below*) several months in advance for these popular festivals. *Ghost Town Rd., 3 mi north of I–15,* ☎ *619/254–2122.* ☛ *$5 adults, $2 children 6–15.* ⏲ *Daily 9–5.*

★ 12 If you're at all curious about life 200,000 years ago, the **Calico Early Man Archaeological Site** is a must-see. Nearly 12,000 tools—scrapers, cutting tools, choppers, hand picks, stone saws, and the like—have been excavated from the site since 1964. Prior to finding the site, many archaeologists believed the first humans came to North America "only" 10,000 to 20,000 years ago. Dr. Louis Leakey, the noted archaeologist, was so impressed with the findings that he became the Calico Project director from 1963 to his death in 1972; his old camp is now a visitor center and museum. The Calico excavations provide a rare opportunity to see artifacts, buried in the walls and floors of the excavated pits, fashioned by the earliest known Americans. The only way in is by guided tour, and visitors are required to wear hard hats. *15 mi northeast of Barstow via I–15; take Minneola Rd. north for 3 mi,* ☎ *619/256–8313 (for information only). Guided tours of the dig are conducted Wed. at 1:30 and 3:30 and Thurs.–Sun. at 9:30, 11:30, 1:30, and 3:30.*

13 Because of its colorful, steep walls, **Afton Canyon** is often called the Grand Canyon of the Mojave. The canyon was carved out over many thousands of years by the rushing waters of the Mojave River, which makes another of its rare aboveground appearances here. And where

you find water in the desert, you'll find trees, grasses, and wildlife. The canyon has been popular for a long time; Indians and later white settlers following the Mojave Trail from the Colorado River to the Pacific coast often set up camp here, near the welcome presence of water. *About 38 mi from Barstow on I–15; take the Afton turnoff and follow a good dirt road about 3 mi southwest.*

Although there is a broad range of terrain that qualifies, nothing says "desert" quite like graceful, wind-blown sand dunes. And the white-
14 sand **Kelso Dunes,** about 40 miles southeast of Baker, are perfect, pristine desert dunes. They cover 70 square miles, often at heights of 500–600 feet, and can be reached in an easy half-mile walk from where you have to leave your car. When you reach the top of one of the dunes, kick a little bit of sand down the lee side and find out why they say the sand "sings." In Kelso there is a Mission Revival depot dating from 1925, one of the very few of its kind still standing. *I–15 to Baker, then take Kelbaker Rd. south 35 mi to town of Kelso; dunes are 7 mi ahead.*

15 East of the dunes are the **Providence Mountains State Recreation Area** and the **Mitchell Caverns Natural Preserve.** The recreation area's visitor center, at an elevation of 4,300 feet, offers spectacular views of mountain peaks, dunes, buttes, rocky crags, and desert valleys. The caves, known as El Pakiva and Tecopa, offer a rare opportunity to see all three types of cave formations—dripstone, flowstone, and erratics—in one place. The year-round 65°F temperature is also a nice break from the heat. If you're coming from the Kelso Dunes, there is a rough and at times unpaved (and unmarked) road that goes directly to Providence Mountains State Recreation Area, but the state parks department recommends heading south to I–40: From there: *Take I–40 east from Barstow 100 mi to Essex Rd., then head northwest for 16 mi to state recreation area,* ☎ *805/942–0662.* ☛ *$4 adults, $2 children. Guided tours of caves offered Sept.–June, weekdays at 1:30, weekends and holidays at 1:30 and 3; July and Aug., weekends only. Tours gather at visitor center.*

Death Valley

Numbers in the margin correspond to points of interest on the Death Valley map.

Distances are deceiving in **Death Valley National Park,** which comprises an area slightly smaller than Connecticut. It's a good idea to plan excursions carefully; the trip to Scotty's Castle, for example, can take a half day. Fees of $5 per vehicle, collected at entrance stations and at the visitor center, are valid for seven days.

The topography of Death Valley is a minilesson in geology. Two hundred million years ago, seas covered the area, depositing layers of sediment and fossils. Between 35 million and 5 million years ago, faults in the earth's crust and volcanic activity pushed and folded the ground, causing mountain ranges to rise and the valley floor to drop. The valley was then filled periodically by lakes, which eroded the surrounding rocks into fantastic formations and deposited the salts that now cover the floor of the basin. Today, the area has 14 square miles of sand dunes, 200 square miles of crusty salt flats, 11,000-foot mountains, hills, and canyons of many colors. There are more than 1,000 species of plants and trees—21 of which are unique to the valley, like the yellow Panamint daisy and the blue-flowered Death Valley sage.

In 1994 Death Valley National Monument was upgraded to Death Valley National Park as part of the California Desert Protection Act. The act added 1.3 million acres to the park's existing 2.1 million acres, making it the largest national park in the lower 48 states. It also transferred the 1.4-million-acre East Mojave National Scenic Area from the Bureau of Land Management to the park service and renamed it the Mojave National Preserve (*see* The Mojave Desert, *above*).

1 Starting from the northernmost point, **Scotty's Castle** is an odd apparition rising out of a canyon. This $2.5 million Moorish mansion, begun in 1924 and never completed, takes its name from Walter Scott, better known as Death Valley Scotty. An ex-cowboy, prospector, and performer in Buffalo Bill's Wild West Show, Scotty always told people the castle was his, financed by gold from a secret mine. That secret mine was, in fact, a Chicago millionaire named Albert Johnson, who was advised by doctors to spend time in a warm, dry climate. The house sports works of art, imported carpets, handmade European furniture, and a tremendous pipe organ. Guided tours feature costumed rangers portraying life at the castle in 1939. Tours are conducted frequently, but waits up to two hours can be expected during busy seasons. *From Hwy. 190 approximately 6 mi east of Stovepipe Wells, follow signs for castle and head north (the road is sometimes marked Rte. 5 on maps) for 38 mi.* ☎ *619/786–2392.* ☛ *$8 adults, $4 senior citizens and children 6–11.* ⏲ *Daily 8 AM–7 PM; tours 9–5.*

Back on Highway 190 heading south and east from the turnoff for
2 Scotty's Castle, you'll come to the remains of the famed **Harmony Borax Works,** from which the renowned 20-mule teams hauled borax to the railroad town of Mojave. Those teams were a sight to behold: 20 mules hitched up to a single massive wagon, carrying a load of 10 tons of borax to a town 165 miles away through burning desert. The teams plied the route between 1884 and 1907, when the railroad finally arrived in Zabriskie. You can visit the ruins of the Harmony Borax Works. The Borax Museum, 2 miles farther south, houses original mining machinery and historical displays in a building that used to serve as a boardinghouse for miners; the adjacent structure is the original mule-team barn. *Look for Harmony Borax Works Rd. on Hwy. 190, about 50 mi south of Scotty's Castle; take road west a short distance to ruins.*

3 Between the ruins and the museum you will see a sign for the **Visitor Center at Furnace Creek.** The center provides guided walks, exhibits, publications, and helpful rangers. The center is open 8 AM–7 PM. Call the national park service in Death Valley (☎ 619/786–2331) for more information on visitor-center services.

4 **Zabriskie Point,** about 4 miles south of the visitor center off Highway 190, is one of the park's most scenic spots. Not particularly high—only about 710 feet—it overlooks a striking badlands panorama with wrinkled, multicolored hills. You may recognize it—or at least its name—from the film *Zabriskie Point* by the Italian director Michelangelo Antonioni. Where Highway 178 splits off from Highway 190, fol-
5 low it south to the turnoff for Artists Drive; **Artists Palette** overlooks more badlands and the back sides of the hills viewed from Zabriskie Point. Thirteen miles south of Furnace Creek on Highway 178 is
★ 6 **Dante's View.** This viewpoint is more than 5,000 feet up in the Black Mountains. In the dry desert air, you can see most of the 110 miles the valley is stretched across. The oasis of Furnace Creek is a green spot to the north. The view up and down is equally astounding: The tiny blackish patch far below you is Badwater, the lowest point in the country at 280 feet below sea level; on the western horizon is Mt. Whitney, the highest spot in the continental United States at 14,494 feet. Those

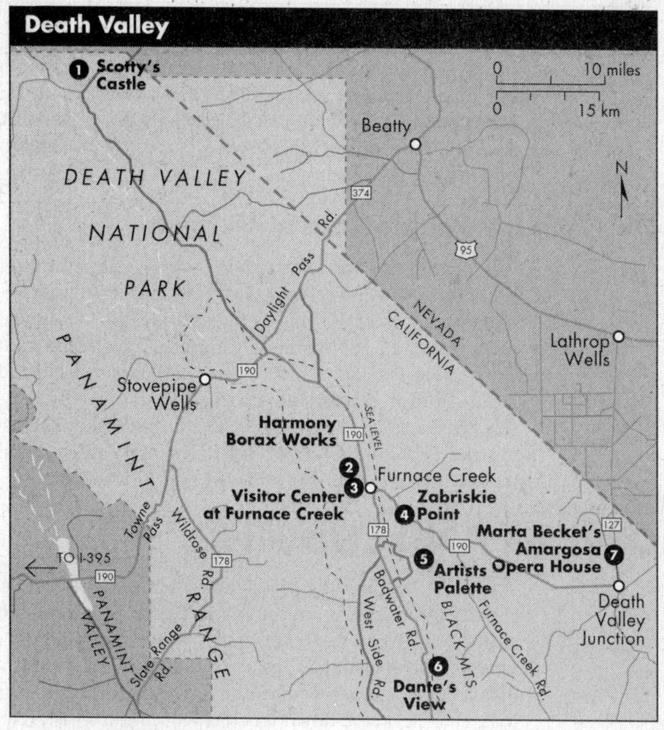

in great shape may want to try the 14-mile hike up to Telescope Peak. The view, not surprisingly, is breathtaking—as is the 3,000-foot elevation gain of the hike. The best time to visit any of these viewpoints is early morning or late afternoon when the colors and shapes of the surrounding desert are highlighted.

Just outside the park, at Death Valley Junction, is an unexpected plea-
7 sure to rival Scotty's Castle—**Marta Becket's Amargosa Opera House.** Marta Becket is an artist and dancer from New York who first saw the town of Amargosa while on tour in 1964. Three years later she came back, had a flat tire in the same place, and on impulse decided to buy a boarded-up theater amid a complex of run-down Spanish colonial buildings. Today, the population of the town is up to five people and about a dozen cats, but three nights a week, cars, motor homes, and buses roll in to catch the show she has been presenting for more than 20 years. To compensate for the sparse crowds her show attracted in the early days, Becket painted herself an audience, turning the walls and ceiling of the theater into a trompe l'oeil masterpiece. Now she often performs her blend of classical ballet, mime, and 19th-century melodrama to sell-out crowds. After the show, you can meet her in the adjacent art gallery, where she sells her paintings and autographs her posters and books. *Amargosa Opera House, Box 8, Death Valley Junction, CA 92328, ☎ 619/852–4441 or 800/952–4441. Call ahead for reservations. ☛ $8 adults, $5 children. Performances Nov., Feb., Mar., and Apr., Fri., Sat., and Mon. at 8:15 PM; Oct., Dec., Jan., and May, Sat. only.*

What to See and Do with Children

Many of the desert's attractions should delight children. The following are of particular interest: **Rand Mining District;** the **Roy Rogers–Dale Evans Museum** in Victorville, **Calico Ghost Town, Mitchell Caverns, Marta Becket's Amargosa Opera House.** For more information, *see* Exploring, *above.*

Off-Highway-Vehicle Recreation Areas

The Bureau of Land Management has developed special desert access areas for off-highway-vehicle (OHV) recreational activities. One popular route is the 130-mile Mohave Road, also known as Old Government Road, an 1860s wagon trail once traveled by mountain men Kit Carson and Jedediah Smith. The road runs parallel to and between I–40 and I–15 from Needles to just east of Barstow. The BLM's Needles office (☎ 619/326–3896) oversees this and other access areas, including the 660-mile East Mohave Heritage Trail (actually a series of trails), which begins and ends off I–40 in Needles.

DINING AND LODGING

Plan to eat as carefully as you plan the rest of your desert trip. Dining choices in this section of the desert are limited to the Fred Harvey–operated restaurants in Death Valley, which range from a cafeteria to an upscale nouveau-Italian restaurant, and to fast-food and chain establishments in Victorville and Barstow. Restaurants in other towns tend to be chancy at best, downright unappetizing at worst. Experienced desert travelers carry an ice chest well stocked with food and beverages.

CATEGORY	COST*
$$$$	over $100
$$$	$75–$100
$$	$50–$75
$	under $50

**All prices are for a standard double room, excluding tax.*

Barstow

$$ **Best Western Desert Villa.** This is a slightly above-average AAA-approved motel with some smallish suites in addition to standard-size rooms. Some units have private whirlpools. 🏨 *1984 E. Main St.,* ☎ *619/256–1781,* FAX *619/256–9265. 95 rooms. Restaurant (dinner only), pool, whirlpool, coin laundry. AE, D, DC, MC, V.*

Death Valley

$$$$ **Furnace Creek Inn.** This historic rambling stone structure tumbling down the side of a hill is something of a desert oasis; the creek meanders through its beautifully landscaped gardens. There are pleasantly cool dining rooms, a naturally warm spring-fed pool, tennis courts, golf, horseback riding, and a cocktail lounge with entertainment. The attractively decorated rooms have views. 🏨 *Box 1, Death Valley National Park 92328,* ☎ *619/786–2345,* FAX *619/786–2514. 67 rooms and suites. Jackets required evenings in dining room. AE, DC, MC, V. Closed mid-May–mid-Oct.*

$$$–$$$$ **Furnace Creek Ranch.** About a mile away from the Furnace Inn on the valley floor, this was originally crew headquarters for a borax company. A newer section consisting of four two-story buildings adjacent to the golf course has motel-type rooms. The ranch also features a swimming pool, tennis courts, guided carriage rides and hay rides, stables, a coffee shop, steak house, cocktail lounge, and a general store. 🏨 *Box*

1, Death Valley National Park 92328, ☎ *619/786–2345,* FAX *619/786–2514. 225 rooms. AE, DC, MC, V.*

$$ **Stovepipe Wells Village.** A landing strip for light aircraft is an unusual touch for a motel, as is a heated mineral pool, but the rest is pretty basic. The property includes a dining room (open only for breakfast 7–10 AM and dinner 7–10 PM), grocery store, pool, and cocktail lounge. *Hwy. 190,* ☎ *619/786–2387,* FAX *619/786–2389. 82 rooms. AE, D, MC, V.*

Ridgecrest

$$$ **Heritage Inn.** This hotel has pleasantly appointed rooms, all with king- or queen-size beds. The hotel is geared toward business travelers—there is a business center with fax, modem, laser printing, and other services—but the inn's staff is equally attentive to tourists' concerns. Room rates include complimentary breakfast. A sister property nearby is an all-suites hotel. *1050 N. Norma, 93555,* ☎ *619/446–6543 or 800/843–1586,* FAX *619/446–2884. 124 rooms. 2 restaurants, bar, pool, hot tub, coin laundry, business services, meeting rooms. AE, D, DC, MC, V.*

Victorville

$$–$$$ **Best Western Green Tree Inn.** This member of the chain sits right off I–15. Pluses here include a shaded lawn and many suite-size rooms that make the inn a good choice for families. The decor is no-nonsense but clean. *14173 Green Tree Blvd., 92392,* ☎ *619/3245–3461 or 800/528–1234. 168 rooms. Restaurant, coffee shop, bar, pool, hot tub, shuffleboard, meeting rooms. AE, D, DC, MC, V.*

Camping

The Mojave Desert and Death Valley have about two dozen campgrounds in a variety of desert settings. Listed below is a sampling of what is available. For further information the following booklets are useful: *High Desert Recreation Resource Guide,* from the Mojave Chamber of Commerce (15836 Sierra Hwy., Mojave, CA 93591); *San Bernardino County Regional Parks,* from the Regional Parks Department (825 E. 3rd St., San Bernardino, CA 92415); and *California Desert Camping,* from the Bureau of Land Management (California Desert District Office, 6221 Box Springs Blvd., Riverside, CA 92507).

Death Valley

Most campgrounds have no telephone number—simply show up when you arrive and hope there's a space open.

Furnace Creek (adjacent to the Furnace Creek Visitors Center). One hundred thirty-five RV and tent sites (some shaded), tables, fireplaces, flush and pit toilets, water, dump station. Pay showers, laundry, and swimming pool at Furnace Creek Ranch. *Reservations from MYSTIX,* ☎ *800/365–2267.* ☛ *$8.* ⏲ *Year-round.*

Mahogany Flat (east of Hwy. 178). Ten well-shaded tent spaces in a forest of juniper and piñon pine. Tables, pit toilets; no water. ☛ *Free.* ⏲ *Mar.–Nov.*

Mesquite Springs (Hwy. 190 near Scotty's Castle). Sixty tent or RV spaces, some shaded, with stoves or fireplaces, tables, flush toilets, water. ☛ *$5.*

Wildrose (west of Hwy. 178). Thirty-nine tent or RV sites, some shaded, in a canyon. Stoves or fireplaces, tables, pit toilets. No water in winter. ☛ *Free.* ⏲ *Year-round.*

Mojave Desert

Afton Canyon Campground (38 mi east of Barstow via I–15, 3 mi south on Afton Canyon Rd.). Twenty-two sites, 1,408 feet up in a wildlife area where the Mojave River surfaces. Surrounded by high desert scenic cliffs and a mesquite thicket. ☛ *$4.* ⏲ *Year-round.*

Calico Ghost Town Regional Park (8 mi east of Barstow on Ghost Town Rd., 3 mi north of I–15). Two-hundred-fifty sites (*see* description of Calico Ghost Town, *above*). Cabins and bunkhouse accommodations are also available. *For reservations,* ☎ *619/254–2122.* ☛ *$15 per night for tent camping, $19 for full RV hook-ups, 2-night minimum (includes Ghost Town admission).* ⏲ *Year-round.*

Mid-Hills Campground (123 mi east of Barstow via I–40). Hiking, horseback riding, in a wooded setting. Thirty campsites, pit toilets, water. ☛ *$4.* ⏲ *Year-round.*

Mojave Narrows (I–15). Eighty-seven camping units, hot showers. Secluded picnic areas and two lakes surrounded by cottonwoods and cattails. Fishing, rowboat rentals, bait shop, specially designed trail for visitors with disabilities.

Owl Canyon Campground (12 mi north of Barstow and 1 mi east of Rainbow Basin). Thirty-one camping units, cooking grills, pit toilets, water, hiking trails. ☛ *$4.* ⏲ *Year-round.*

MOJAVE DESERT AND DEATH VALLEY ESSENTIALS

Getting Around

By Car

The Mojave is shaped like a giant *L,* with one leg north and the other east. To travel north through the Mojave, take I–10 east out of Los Angeles to I–15 north. Just through Cajon Pass, pick up U.S. 395, which runs north through Victor Valley, Boron, the Rand Mining District, and China Lake. To travel east, continue on I–15 to Barstow. From Barstow there are two routes: I–40, which passes through the mountainous areas of San Bernardino County, whisks by the Providence mountains and enters Arizona at Needles; or the more northerly I–15, which passes south of Calico, near Devil's Playground and the Kelso Sand Dunes, and then veers northeast toward Las Vegas.

Some travelers may wish to avoid Cajon Pass, elevation 4,250 feet. To do this, take I–210 north of Los Angeles to Route 14 north. Head east 67 miles on Route 58 to the town of Barstow and pick up I–15 there. Continue east on I–15 to Highway 127, a very scenic route north through the Mojave to Death Valley.

Death Valley can be entered from the southeast or the west. Exit U.S. 395 at either Highway 190 or 178 to enter from the west. From the southeast: Take Highway 127 north from I–15 and then link up with either Highway 178, which travels west into the valley and then cuts north past Funeral Peak, Badwater, Dante's View, and Zabriskie Point before meeting up with Highway 190 at Furnace Creek, or continue on Highway 127 north for 28 miles and then take Highway 190 west straight into the middle of Death Valley.

Guided Tours

The following organizations regularly sponsor hikes, tours, and outings in the California deserts:

Audubon Society (Western Regional Office, 555 Audubon Pl., Sacramento, CA 95825, ☎ 916/481–5332).

California Native Plant Society (1722 J St., #17, Sacramento, CA 95814, ☎ 916/447–2677).

Furnace Creek Inn (☎ 619/786–2345, ext. 222). The transportation department of this inn conducts daily bus tours to Death Valley attractions, including Scotty's Castle, Dante's View, and the Amargosa Opera House from mid-October to Mother's Day.

The **Nature Conservancy** (201 Mission St., 4th Floor, San Francisco, CA 94105, ☎ 415/777–0487).

The **Sierra Club** (730 Polk St., San Francisco, CA 94109, ☎ 415/776–2211).

Important Addresses and Numbers

Emergencies

BLM Rangers (☎ 619/255–8700).

San Bernardino County Sheriff (☎ 619/256–1796).

Community Hospital (Barstow, ☎ 619/256–1761).

Visitor Information

Bureau of Land Management (BLM) (California Desert District Office, 6221 Box Springs Blvd., Riverside 92507, ☎ 909/697–5200 or 800/697–5200) provides information about BLM campgrounds and other recreational activities in the desert areas. Also consult:

Barstow Area Chamber of Commerce (222 E. Main St., Suite 216, Barstow 92311).

California Desert Information Center (831 Barstow Rd., Barstow 92311, ☎ 619/255–8760).

Death Valley Chamber of Commerce (Box 157, Shoshone 92384, ☎ 619/852–4524).

Interagency Visitor Center (Junction, Hwy. 136 and U.S. 395, Drawer R, Lone Pine 93545, ☎ 619/876–6222).

San Bernardino County Regional Parks Department (825 E. 3rd St., San Bernardino 92415, ☎ 909/387–2594).

16 Portraits of California

LIVING WITH THE CERTAINTY OF A SHAKY FUTURE

THERE'S NEVER been any question whether there will be another earthquake in San Francisco. The question is how soon. Even the kids here grow up understanding that it's just a matter of time, and from grade school on, earthquake safety drills become routine. *At the first rumble, duck under your desk or table or stand in a doorway,* they are instructed. *Get away from windows to avoid broken glass. When the shaking stops, walk—don't run—outdoors, as far away from buildings as possible.*

Sure as there are hurricanes along the Gulf of Mexico and blizzards in Maine, San Francisco's earthquakes are inevitable. Nobody here is surprised when the rolling and tumbling begins—it happens all the time. Just in the six months following the jarring 1989 earthquake, for instance, seismologists reported hundreds of aftershocks, ranging from the scarcely perceptible to those strong enough to bring down buildings weakened by October's jolt.

The Bay Area itself was created in upheaval such as this. Eons ago, a restless geology of shifting plates deep in the earth gave birth to the Sierra Mountains and the Pacific Coast Range. Every spring when the snows melted, the runoff rushed down from the mile-high Sierra peaks westward across what would eventually be known as California. Here, the runoff ran up against the coastal range, and a vast inland lake was formed.

The rampaging waters from the yearly thaw eventually crashed through the quake-shattered Coast Range to meet the Pacific Ocean, creating the gap now spanned by the Golden Gate Bridge. This breakthrough created San Francisco Bay, one of the world's great natural harbors, its fertile delta larger than that of the Mississippi River. What a fabulous setting for the city-to-be—surrounded on three sides by water, set off by dramatic mountainscapes to the north and south, and blessed by cool ocean breezes.

All this and gold, too. The twisting and rolling of so-called terra firma exposed rich veins of gold at and near ground level that otherwise would have remained hidden deep underground. The great upheaval pushed the Mother Lode to the surface and set the scene for the Gold Rush. But before the '49 miners came the Europeans. In the late 15th century, the Spanish writer Garci Ordóñez de Montalvo penned a fictional description of a place he called California, a faraway land ruled by Queen Califia, where gold and precious stones were so plentiful the streets were lined with them. Montalvo's vision of wealth without limit helped fuel the voyages of the great 15th- and 16th-century European explorers in the New World. They never did hit pay dirt here, but the name California stuck nevertheless.

Northern California was eventually settled, and in 1848, the population of San Francisco was 832. The discovery of gold in the California hills brought sudden and unprecedented wealth to this coastal trading outpost and its population exploded; by the turn of the century San Francisco was home to 343,000 people.

En route to its destiny as a premier city of the West, San Francisco was visited by innumerable quakes. Yet while the city's very foundations shook, residents found that each new rattler helped to strengthen San Francisco's self-image of adaptability. Robert Louis Stevenson wrote of the quakes' alarming frequency: "The fear of them grows yearly in a resident; he begins with indifference and ends in sheer panic." The big shaker of 1865 inspired humorist Mark Twain to look at the quakes in a different light by writing an earthquake "almanac" for the following year, which advised:

Oct. 23—Mild, balmy earthquakes.

Oct. 26—About this time expect more earthquakes; but do not look for them . . .

Oct. 27—Universal despondency, indicative of approaching disaster. Abstain from smiling or indulgence in humorous conversation . . .

Oct. 29—Beware!

Oct. 31—Go slow!

Nov. 1—Terrific earthquake. This is the great earthquake month. More stars fall and more worlds are slathered around carelessly and destroyed in November than in any month of the twelve.

Nov. 2—Spasmodic but exhilarating earthquakes, accompanied by occasional showers of rain and churches and things.

Nov. 3—Make your will.

Nov. 4—Sell out.

On the whole, those who settled in San Francisco were more inclined toward Twain's devil-may-care attitude—those who succumbed to Stevenson's panic didn't stick around for long. Certainly the multitude of vices that saturated the metropolis were sufficient to distract many men from their fears; throughout Chinatown and the infamous Barbary Coast opium dens, gin mills, and bordellos operated day and night.

Money flowed. Money tempted. Money corrupted. The city was built on graft, and city hall became synonymous with corruption under the influence of political crooks like Blind Chris Buckley and Boss Ruef. The very building itself was a scandal. Planned for completion in six months at a cost of half a million dollars, the city hall ultimately took 29 years to build at a graft-inflated cost of $8 million, an astronomical sum at the dawning of the 20th century. When the San Andreas Fault set loose the 1906 earthquake, the most devastating ever to hit an American city, city hall was one of the first buildings to come crashing down. Its ruins exposed the shoddiest of building materials, an ironic symbol of the city's crime-ridden past.

The 1906 earthquake and fire has come to define San Francisco both for itself and the outside world. In the immediate aftermath of the catastrophe, San Franciscans wondered whether they ought to believe the preachers and reformers who declared that this terrible devastation had been wrought upon their wicked city by the avenging hand of God. San Franciscans asked themselves whether, somehow, they had earned it.

BUT THE CITY was quick to prove its character. Fifty years earlier, six separate fires had destroyed most of San Francisco—yet each time it was rebuilt by a citizenry not ready to give up on either the gold or the city that gold had built. Now, in 1906, heroic firefighters dynamited one of the city's main thoroughfares to prevent the inferno from spreading all the way to the Pacific. The mood of San Franciscans was almost eerily calm, their neighborliness both heartwarming and jaunty. "Eat, drink, and be merry," proclaimed signs about town, "for tomorrow we may have to go to Oakland." No sooner had the flames died than rebuilding began—true to San Francisco tradition. Forty thousand construction workers poured into town to assist the proud, amazingly resilient residents.

The 1906 earthquake provided a chance to rethink the hodgepodge, get-rich-quick cityscape that had risen in the heat of Gold Rush frenzy. City fathers imported the revered urban planner Daniel Burnham, architect of the magnificent 1893 Chicago World's Fair, to reinvent San Francisco. "Make no little plans," Burnham intoned. "They have no power to stir men's souls."

The city's new Civic Center, built under Burnham's direction, was raised to celebrate the city's comeback and is regarded as one of America's most stately works of civic architecture. Its city hall stands as a monument to the city's will to prevail—from its colonnaded granite exterior to its exuberant interior, once described by Tom Wolfe as resembling "some Central American opera house. Marble arches, domes, acanthus leaves . . . quirks and galleries and gilt filigrees . . . a veritable angels' choir of gold." The inscription found over the mayor's office seems to sum it all up: "San Francisco, O glorious city of our hearts that has been tried and not found wanting, go thou with like spirit to make the future thine."

In 1915, San Francisco dazzled the world with its Panama–Pacific International Exposition, designed to prove not only that it was back but that it was back bigger and better and badder than ever before. An architectural wonderland, the Expo was built on 70 acres of marshy landfill, which later became the residential neighborhood called the Marina District. When the October 1989 earthquake struck, this neighborhood was badly damaged and became a focus as the entire nation tuned in to see how San Francisco and its people would fare this time around.

Like the gold that surfaced in the Mother Lode, the 1989 quake once again brought out the best in this region's people. Out at Candlestick Park, 62,000 fans were waiting for the start of the World Series between the San Francisco Giants and the Oakland A's when everything started shaking. They cut loose with big cheers after the temblor subsided. One San Francisco fan quickly hand-lettered a sign and held it aloft: "That was Nothing—Wait Til the Giants Bat." When it became apparent that there would be no ball played that night, the fans departed from the ballpark, just like in a grade-school earthquake safety drill, quietly and in good order.

This was what millions of TV viewers across the nation first saw of the local response to this major (7.1) earthquake, and, by and large, the combination of good humor and relative calm they observed was an accurate reflection of the prevailing mood around the city. San Franciscans were not about to panic. Minutes after the quake struck, a San Francisco couple spread a lace tablecloth over the hood of their BMW and, sitting in the driveway of their splintered home, toasted passersby with champagne. Simultaneously, across San Francisco Bay, courageous volunteers and rescue workers set to work digging through the pancaked rubble of an Oakland freeway in the search for survivors, heedless that they, too, could easily be crushed in an aftershock. Throughout the Bay Area, hundreds volunteered to fight the fires, clear away the mess, assist survivors, and donate food, money, and clothing.

San Francisco's city seal features the image of a phoenix rising from the flames of catastrophe, celebrating the city's fiery past and promising courage in the face of certain future calamity. The 1989 shake possessed only about one fortieth the force of the legendary 1906 quake, and all projections point to the inevitability of another Big One, someday, on at least the scale of '06. Often people from other, more stable parts of the world have trouble understanding how it is possible to live with such a certainty.

The *San Francisco Bay Guardian,* shortly after the 1989 quake, spoke for many Bay Area residents: "We live in earthquake country. Everybody knows that. It's a choice we've all made, a risk we're all more or less willing to accept as part of our lives. We're gambling against fate, and last week our luck ran out. It was inevitable—as the infamous bumper sticker says, 'Mother Nature bats last.' "

Former San Francisco mayor Dianne Feinstein explained it this way: "Californians seem undaunted. We [know] we'll never be a match for Mother Nature. But the principal thing that seems to arise from the ash and rubble of a quake is the strong resolve to rebuild and get on with life."

— *John Burks*

THERE MUST BE A THERE HERE SOMEWHERE

"Hollywood is a town that has to be seen to be disbelieved."

—Walter Winchell

WHILE HOSTING a British broadcaster-friend on his first trip to Los Angeles, I reluctantly took him to the corner of Hollywood and Vine. Driving toward the renowned street-corner, I explained (again) that this part of town isn't the "real" Hollywood. But he wasn't listening. He was on a pilgrimage and too filled with the anticipation of coming upon a sacred place to hear my warning. When we reached the intersection, his reaction was written all over his face: He was, as he later said, "gobsmacked."

As we pulled up to the light, a bedraggled hooker crossed Hollywood Boulevard. Otherwise, nothing was happening. Worse, this looked like someplace where nothing noteworthy or memorable ever had, would, or could happen. The area has been called squalid, but that gives it too much credit for being interesting. All there was to see were a few small and struggling businesses, the hulk of a long-defunct department store, and a couple of unremarkable office buildings.

To rescue the moment from disaster, I went into my standard routine: I pointed out that the northeast corner is where the Brown Derby restaurant once stood. I hoped this would conjure a strong enough image of movie stars dining in a giant hat to blot out the sun-bleached desolation before our eyes. I then recounted historian Richard Alleman's theory about how this unprepossessing street-corner got so famous. Alleman, who wrote *The Movie Lover's Guide to Hollywood,* believes that, because the radio networks, which maintained studios in the vicinity during the 1930s and 1940s, began their broadcasts with the words "brought to you from the corner of Hollywood and Vine . . ." the intersection became glamorous by association—at least to radio listeners who'd never seen it.

Any first-time visitor to Tinseltown is bound for some initial disappointment because, like a matinee idol, the place looks somehow smaller in person. Between the world-famous landmarks and the stars' names embedded in the sidewalks are long stretches of tawdriness that have resisted more than a decade of cleanup and restoration and look all the worse under the vivid glare of the southern California sun. Even the best of Hollywood looks a little wan and sheepish in broad daylight, as if caught in the act of intruding upon a reality in which it does not belong.

Pressed to show my British friend the "real" Hollywood, I took him on a tour of the more outstanding architecture along Hollywood Boulevard. He was duly captivated by the lunatic exuberance of Hollywood's art deco movie palaces, exemplified in the zigzaggy Moderne contours of the Pantages, and by the flamboyant absurdity of such thematically designed theaters as Mann's Chinese, the Egyptian, the baroque El Capitan, and other architectural treasures in and around Hollywood that have nothing directly to do with movies yet are spiritual cousins. Among these are the Tail O' the Pup hotdog stand; the Capitol Records building, looking—deliberately, mind you—like a 14-story stack of 45s; and an assortment of mock Mayan, Mission, Moorish, Moderne, and made-up-style structures housing video stores, fast-food franchises, and offices.

Yet despite the grand movie houses, the famous names underfoot, and the impressively zany architecture, my friend still felt he'd missed the enchantment, the excitement . . . the movies.

It's hard to fault the intrepid visitor for expecting a more dynamic, glitzier dream capital. Even seasoned locals, who understand that Hollywood is a state of mind more than a geographical location, can only just manage to intellectualize the concept, and still secretly hunger for evidence that all the magic and glamour come from an appropriately magical and glamorous place. But, except for the occasional gala premiere, you're not likely to see any movie stars in Hollywood. The workaday world of filmmaking and the off-duty hangouts of the movie crowd have largely moved elsewhere. There is only one movie studio—Paramount—still operating within Hollywood's city limits. Universal Studios and the Warner Brothers Studios are both in the San Fernando Valley, across the hills to the north, as are most network-television studios. And, although firmly rooted in the spirit of Hollywood, Disneyland is a world away in Anaheim.

Even a cursory glance at Hollywood's history raises serious doubts that the town was ever as glamorous as we insist it no longer is, and pinning down exactly when its star-studded golden era was is a slippery business. Most people point to the 1930s and 1940s, and the images evoked by those days are irresistible: tan, handsome leading men posed, grinning, with one foot on the running board of a snazzy convertible; heartbreakingly beautiful actresses clad in slinky silk gowns and mink, stepping from long black limousines into the pop of photographers' flash bulbs. Hollywood was an industry—an entire city—whose purpose was to entertain and that further dazzled us with its glittering style of life. The view from ground zero, naturally, was a bit different: long hours; the tedium of the filmmaking process; the rarity of achieving and maintaining a successful career, much less stardom; and, for those who did achieve it, the precarious tightrope walk balancing publicity and privacy. Both sides of the equation are well known and much documented. Indeed, for a place so enamored of its own appeal, Hollywood has never been shy about depicting itself in an unflattering light. Some of the most memorable films ever are rather grim portrayals of the movie business: *A Star Is Born, Sunset Boulevard,* and, most recently, *The Player.* That there is a very seamy side to the movie business is very old news and is as much a part of the legend as are fame and fortune. Scandal is a long-running subplot in Hollywood's epic history and has often proved as much a box-office draw as a liability.

THE TRICK to seeing Hollywood is knowing *how* to look at it, as well as where to look for it. The magic of movies is that reality, at least on film, can be made to look any way the filmmakers want it to look. The problem with visiting Hollywood is that your own field of vision isn't as selective as a movie camera's lens, and you're working without a script. It may be helpful to think of Hollywood the town as something of a relic, a symbol of past grandeur (both real and imagined), an open-air museum of artifacts and monuments, but hardly the whole story. Tennessee Williams said, "Ravaged radiance is even better than earnest maintenance," and, as regards Hollywood, I couldn't agree more. It helps a bit to visit in the evening, when the neon, theater marquees, and orchestrated lighting show off the extravagant buildings' shapes to advantage.

It may be that in order to fully experience Hollywood, you have to go outside it.

Only after we'd driven through the canyons, Beverly Hills, and Bel Air and were rounding the last corner of Sunset that leads to the Pacific Coast Highway and out to Malibu did my British visitor feel truly satisfied. "Yes, well," he said finally, "this is really much more like it, then," and seemed almost physically relieved to have found someplace that matched his expectations of luxurious living. And these are physically lovely places, fitting backdrops for a Hollywood lifestyle, and, in fact, where successful movie people live.

The variety of fun and fanciful buildings you'll see throughout Los Angeles reveals, I think, the essence of Hollywood. How else to explain the incongruous jumble of architectural styles sitting side by side in almost any neighborhood? A '50s futuristic house next door to a Queen Anne Victorian, a Craftsman bungalow abutting a French château, a redbrick Georgian across the street from a tile-roof Spanish revival—all on the same block—can be viewed as an extrapolation of a movie-studio back lot, on which a New York street is steps from a Parisian sidewalk café, and both are just a stone's throw from an antebellum plantation house.

If it's celebrity sightings you want, you'll have to take your chances. Many Angelenos live long, happy, and productive lives without ever personally sighting a movie star, but, for the visitor, not seeing one can be a bigger letdown than a rainy week at the beach. Here are a few things you can do to greatly improve the odds of seeing somebody famous: Book a table (weeks in advance) at Spago, Wolfgang Puck's star-studded hot spot off Sunset; dine at Musso & Franks, Hollywood's oldest restaurant and a favorite celebrity hangout for more than 60 years; wander Rodeo Drive on a sunny afternon, paying close attention to Fred Hayman of Beverly Hills and the Alaia Chez Gallery, known for their high-profile clientele; stroll Melrose Avenue between La Brea and Fairfax during the dinner hour; stop by Tower Records on Sunset, especially if some blockbuster CD has just been released.

Although it's almost become an amusement-park thrill ride, Universal Studio's tour does give a good in-person approximation of the excitement you get from the movies, and, in the bargain, offers a fun look behind the scenes of filmmaking. Universal Studios aside, the business of Hollywood is making movies and getting people into theaters, not drumming up tourism for the town where it all started. And, besides, there are limits to what even movie magicians can do, especially in broad daylight. Given that the original appeal of Hollywood to moviemakers was the perpetual sunshine that allowed them to shoot outdoors on virtually any day of the year (and thereby make more movies and, therefore, more money) and the ready access to dozens of different landscapes, it is no small irony that over the years the most compelling reason to shoot a movie in Hollywood has become the ready access to soundstages in which the world (this one and others) can be re-created and the weather made to perform on cue. Hollywood has never hesitated to substitute reality with a more convenient or photogenic stand-in. This is an industry whose stock-in-trade is sleight of hand. Along with romance, car chases, and happy endings.

Whatever Hollywood is or isn't, I like the place just the way it is: flawed, scarred, energetic, and full of mysteries and contradictions. Living nearby and seeing it often haven't harmed my love of movies or taken any of the enchantment from the experience of sitting in a darkened theater and giving myself over to the doings on screen. After all, that's where to find the real Hollywood.

—*Jane E. Lasky*

IDYLLING IN SAN DIEGO

I'VE NEVER BEEN TO SEA WORLD; performing fish give me the willies. And during the two years I lived within striking distance of Balboa Park, I had to take visiting friends to the San Diego Zoo so many times I began having nightmares about koalas. But if I came to dislike various theme-park aspects of the city, I nevertheless loved San Diego. At first sight.

A typical easterner, I went out to San Diego in the late 1970s expecting to find a smaller version of Los Angeles. The freeways were there, along with a fair share of traffic congestion, but so was an oceanscape of surprisingly pristine beauty. The first drive I took from the University of California, where I was doing graduate research, knocked me for a loop: I rounded a curve on La Jolla Shores Drive to confront a coastline that could match any on the French Riviera.

I was also taken by the distinctiveness of the many shoreline communities. For one thing, the beaches tend to get funkier as you head south from the old-money enclave of La Jolla: Pacific Beach, with its Crystal Pier, looks like an aging Victorian resort taken over by teenagers, while transients and surfers share the turf at Ocean Beach. To the north, Del Mar has a strip of shops that rival those of Rodeo Drive, while Carlsbad and Oceanside show the democratizing influence of nearby Camp Pendleton.

Unlike Los Angeles, San Diego is still strongly defined by its relationship to the ocean—to some degree by default. A building boom in the 1880s was largely based on the assumption that San Diego would become the western terminus of the Santa Fe Railroad line; it hoped in this way to compete with Los Angeles, which was already connected by rail to San Francisco and thus to the national railroad network. The link was completed in 1885 but it proved unsuccessful for a variety of reasons, including the placement of the line through Temecula Canyon, where 30 miles of track were washed out repeatedly in winter rainstorms. The Santa Fe soon moved its West Coast offices to San Bernardino and Los Angeles, and to this day there is no direct rail service from San Diego to the eastern part of the United States.

Instead, San Diego's future was sealed in 1908, when President Theodore Roosevelt's Great White Fleet stopped here on a world tour to demonstrate U.S. naval strength. The navy, impressed during that visit by the city's excellent harbor and temperate climate, decided to build a destroyer base on San Diego Bay in the 1920s; the newly developing aircraft industry soon followed (Charles Lindbergh's plane *Spirit of St. Louis* was built here). Over the years San Diego's economy became largely dependent on the military and its attendant enterprises, which provided jobs as well as a demand for local goods and services by those stationed here.

San Diego's character—conservative where Los Angeles's is cutting edge—was formed in large part by the presence of its military installations, which now occupy more than 165,000 acres of land in the area. And the city conducts most of its financial business in a single neighborhood, the district fronting San Diego Bay, in this way resembling New York more than its economic rival up the coast. San Diego has set some of its most prestigious scientific facilities on the water—Scripps Institute of Oceanography, naturally, but also Salk Institute. Jonas Salk didn't need the Pacific marine environment for his research, but his regular morning runs along Torrey Pines Beach no doubt cleared his head.

San Diego also has the ocean to thank for its near-perfect weather. A high-pressure system from the north Pacific is responsible for the city's sunshine and dry air; moderating breezes off the sea (caused by the water warming and cooling more slowly than the land) keep the summers relatively cool and the winters warm, and help clear the air of pollution. In the late spring and early summer the difference between the earth and water temperatures generates coastal fogs. This phenomenon was another of San Diego's delightful surprises: I never tired of watching the mist roll in at night, wonderfully romantic, as thick as any I'd ever seen in London and easier to enjoy in the balmy air.

If I loved San Diego from the start, I had a hard time believing in its existence. It was difficult to imagine that a functioning American city could be so attractive, that people lived and worked in such a place every day. Rampant nature conspires in a variety of ways to force you to let your guard down here. In northern East Coast cities, plants are generally orderly and prim: shrubs trimmed, roses demurely draped around railings, tulips in proper rows, the famed cherry blossoms of Washington, DC, profuse in neat columns. In San Diego, the flora, whimsical at best, sometimes border on obscenity. The ubiquitous palms come in comedic pairs: Short, squat trees that look like overgrown pineapples play Mutt to the Jeff of the tall, skinny variety. The aptly named bottlebrush bushes vie for attention with bright red flame trees, beaky orange birds of paradise, and rich purple bougainvillea spilling out over lush green lawns. Only in Hawaii had I previously encountered anthurium, a waxy red plant with a protruding white center that seems to be sticking its tongue out at you. "We're still on the mainland," I felt like telling them all on some days. "Behave yourselves."

Ironically, it was the Victorians who were largely responsible for this indecorous natural profusion. Difficult as it is to imagine now, it's the sparse brown vegetation of San Diego's undeveloped mesas that accurately reflects the climate of the region, technically a semiarid steppe. When Spanish explorer Juan Rodríguez Cabrillo sailed into San Diego Bay in 1542, looking for a shortcut to China, he and his crew encountered a barren, desolate landscape that did not inspire them to settle here, or even stop for very long.

IT WASN'T UNTIL the late 19th century, when the Mediterranean in general and Italy in particular were all the rage among wealthy residents, that the vegetation now considered characteristic of southern California was introduced to San Diego. In 1889, money raised by the Ladies Annex to the Chamber of Commerce was used to plant trees in Balboa Park, and between 1892 and 1903 a wide variety of exotic foliage was brought into the city: eucalyptus, cork oak, and rubber trees, to name a few. As homeowners in the area can attest, most of the landscaped local vegetation couldn't survive if it were not watered regularly.

No doubt both the natural setting and the relentlessly fine weather help contribute to the clash of cultures that exists here. The conservative traditionalism of the military presence in town is posed against the liberal hedonism of visiting sunseekers as well as a large local student population. Nude bathing is popular at Black's Beach in La Jolla, a spot that's reasonably private because it's fairly inaccessible: You have to hike down steep cliffs in order to get to the water. Rumor has it that every year a few navy men are killed when they lose their footing on the cliffs, so intent are they at peering through their binoculars.

Nods to certain So-Cal conventions notwithstanding, San Diego has never come close to approaching the much-touted libertinism of Los Angeles. It has the porno theaters and sleazy clubs you'd expect in a liberty port, but little entertainment of a more sophisticated nature. Celebrities who came down from Hollywood in the 1920s and '30s sought out suites at the La Valencia Hotel and other chic La Jolla locales for the privacy, not the nightlife; the gambling they did at Del Mar racetrack to the north was of the tony, genteel sort. Those who sought thrills—and booze during Prohibition—headed farther south to Mexico. Raymond Chandler, who spent most of his last 13 years in La Jolla and died there in 1959, wrote a friend that the town was "a nice place . . . for old people and their parents."

For all its conservatism, the one thing San Diego didn't conserve was its past—in some cases because there was little to save. When Father Junípero Serra arrived in 1769 to establish the first of the California missions, he did not find the complex dwellings that characterized so many of the Native American settlements he had encountered in Mexico. Nor did his fellow Spaniards improve much upon the site during their stay; the town that the

Mexicans took over in 1822 was rudimentary, consisting mostly of rough adobe huts. The mission church had been moved to a new site in 1774, and the original Spanish presidio, abandoned in the 1830s, was in ruins by the next decade; some grass-covered mounds and a giant cross built in 1913 on Presidio Hill, incorporating the tiles of the original structure, are all that's left of it.

Though a romanticized version of the city during the Mexican period (1822–49), today's Old Town district gives a rough idea of San Diego's layout at that time, when somewhat more impressive structures such as Casa Estudillo and the Bandini House were built. San Diego didn't really begin to flourish, however, until 1850, the year that California became a state. At this point the dominant architectural influence came from the East Coast; their enthusiasm for becoming American caused San Diegans to reject their Spanish and Mexican roots as inappropriately "foreign." Thus the first brick structure in the state, the Whaley House (1856), was built in typical New England nautical style. Most of the original Old Town was destroyed by fire in 1872, and a good deal of what was left fell victim to the construction of I–5.

DURING THE VICTORIAN ERA (1880–1905), the site of the city's development moved south; entrepreneur Alonzo Horton may have miscalculated the success of the rail link to the East Coast, but when he bought up a huge lot of land in 1867 for his "Addition," he knew the city's future lay on the harbor. It was in this area, now the city's financial district, that many of the neo-Gothic structures characteristic of the period were built. Perhaps it's perversely fitting that a number of the Victorian relics in downtown San Diego were removed in conjunction with the 15-block Horton Redevelopment Project, of which the huge Horton Plaza shopping complex is the center.

San Diego finally began to reject the East Coast architectural style at the turn of the century, and at the Panama–California Exposition of 1915 the city celebrated its Spanish roots—as well as a Moroccan and Italian past it never had—with a vengeance. The beautiful Spanish-style structures built for the occasion fit right into the Mediterranean landscape that had been cultivated in Balboa Park during the Victorian era; today these buildings house most of the city's museums. San Diego became even more thoroughly Hispanicized during the 1920s and '30s as Spanish colonial–style homes became popular in new suburbs such as Mission Hills and Kensington, as well as in the beach communities that were developing. Downtown buildings began looking like Italian palaces and Moorish towers.

In some ways, as residents and visitors alike have long feared, San Diego is coming to look more like Los Angeles. Faceless developments are cropping up all over once-deserted canyons and mesas, and the huge, castlelike Mormon temple rising along I–5 north of La Jolla wouldn't look out of place in Disneyland. But in the years since I lived there, San Diego has also become more like a city—that is, what easterners know to be the city in its divinely ordained form.

As recently as 10 years ago, virtually no one went downtown unless required to. It was a desolate place after dark, and people who worked there during the day never stayed around in the evening to play. Gentrification of sorts began in the mid-1970s, as the low rents attracted artists and real-estate speculators. At about the same time the city designated the formerly rough Stingaree neighborhood as the Gaslamp Quarter, but revitalization, in the form of street-level shops and art galleries, didn't really take until Horton Plaza was completed in 1985, and for many years the newly installed gaslights illuminated only the homeless.

The poor and disenfranchised are still here—indeed, many lost their homes to various redevelopment projects—but now the staff at the recently renovated historic U. S. Grant Hotel offers to accompany its guests across the street to Horton Plaza at night so they won't be bothered by vagrants. For the first time there's a concentration of good restaurants, and a serious art and theater scene is developing in the district, too. I like the infusion of life into downtown San Diego, and I even like Horton Plaza, which, with its odd angles and colorful banners, looks like it was designed by Alice in Wonderland's Red Queen. But maybe I miss that spot of unadulterated blight that once helped me to believe in San Diego's reality.

Would I move back to San Diego? In a minute. Like many temporary residents, I left the city vowing to return; unlike many, I've never managed to do more than visit. I used to think that if I had the chance I'd live in Hillcrest, a close-knit inland community with lots of ethnic restaurants and theaters that show foreign films, but I've come to realize that would only be transplanting my East Coast life into the sun. Now I think I'll wait until I'm rich and can afford to move to La Jolla; no doubt I'll be old enough by then to fit in, so I'll fully enjoy that suite in the La Valencia Hotel overlooking the cove.

— *Edie Jarolim*

MORE PORTRAITS

San Francisco

BOOKS➢ Many novels are set in San Francisco, but none come better than *The Maltese Falcon,* by Dashiell Hammett, the founder of the hard-boiled school of detective fiction. *The Barbary Coast: An Informal History of San the Francisco Underworld,* published in 1933 and still in print, is Herbert Asbury's searing look at life in what really was a wicked city before the turn of the century. Another standout is Vikram Seth's *Golden Gate,* a novel in verse about life in San Francisco and Marin County in the early '80s. Others are John Gregory Dunne's recent *The Red White and Blue,* and Alice Adams's *Rich Rewards.*

Two books that are filled with interesting background information on the city are Richard H. Dillon's *San Francisco: Adventurers and Visionaries* and *San Francisco: As It Is, As It Was,* by Paul C. Johnson and Richard Reinhardt.

Armistead Maupin's soap-opera-style *Tales of the City* stories are set in San Francisco; they were made into a successful 1993 PBS series.

VIDEOS➢ *San Francisco,* starring Clark Gable and Jeanette MacDonald, re-creates the 1906 earthquake with outstanding special effects. In *Escape from Alcatraz,* Clint Eastwood plays the prisoner who allegedly escaped from the famous jail on a rock in the San Francisco Bay. *The Times of Harvey Milk,* about San Francisco's first openly gay elected official, won the Academy Award for best documentary feature in 1984. Alfred Hitchcock immortalized Mission Dolores and the Golden Gate Bridge in *Vertigo,* the eerie story of a detective with a fear of heights, starring Jimmy Stewart and Kim Novak. A few other noteworthy films shot in San Francisco are *Dark Passage,* with Humphrey Bogart; the 1978 remake of *Invasion of the Body Snatchers*; and the 1993 comedy *Mrs. Doubtfire,* starring Robin Williams.

Los Angeles

BOOKS➢ Much has been written about the fascinating city of Los Angeles. *Los Angeles: The Enormous Village, 1781–1981,* by John D. Weaver, and *Los Angeles: Biography of a City,* by John and LaRee Caughey, will give you a fine background in how it came to be the city it is today. The unique social and cultural life of the whole southern California area is explored in *Southern California: An Island on the Land,* by Carey McWilliams.

One of the most outstanding features of Los Angeles is its architecture. *Los Angeles: The Architecture of Four Ecologies,* by Reyner Banham, relates the physical environment to the architecture. *Architecture in Los Angeles: A Compleat Guide,* by David Gebhard and Robert Winter, is exactly what the title promises and is very useful.

Many novels have been written with Los Angeles as the setting. One of the very best, Nathanael West's *Day of the Locust,* was first published in 1939, but still rings true. Budd Schulberg's *What Makes Sammy Run?,* Evelyn Waugh's *The Loved One,* and Joan Didion's *Play It As It Lays* are unforgettable. Other novels that give a sense of contemporary life in Los Angeles are *Sex and Rage,* by Eve Babitz, and *Less Than Zero,* by Bret Easton Ellis. Raymond Chandler and Ross Macdonald have written many suspense novels with a Los Angeles background.

VIDEOS AND TV➢ *Day of the Locust* and *Play It As It Lays* were made into two of the grimmer cinematic portraits of life in Los Angeles. Billy Wilder's *Sunset Boulevard* is a classic portrait of a faded star and her attempt to recapture past glory. Roman Polanski's *Chinatown,* arguably one of the best American films ever made, is a fictional account of the wheeling and dealing that helped make L.A. what it is today. Southern California's varied urban and rural landscapes are used to great effect (as is an all-star cast that includes Ethel Merman and Spencer Tracy) in Stanley Kramer's manic *It's a Mad, Mad, Mad, Mad World.*

Around the State

BOOKS➢ John Steinbeck immortalized the Monterey-Salinas area in numerous books, including *Cannery Row* and *East of Eden.* Joan Didion captured the heat—solar, political, and otherwise—of the Sacramento Delta area in *Run River.* Helen Hunt Jackson's romantic novel *Ramona* takes place in San Diego's Old Town. Richard Henry Dana, Jr.'s *Two Years Before the Mast,* based on the author's experiences as a merchant sailor, provides a masculine perspective on early San Diego history. Mark Twain's *Roughing It* and Bret Harte's *The Luck of Roaring Camp* evoke life during the Gold Rush. Tom Wolfe's *The Pump House Gang* tweaks the La Jolla surfing scene.

VIDEO➢ Steinbeck's *East of Eden* was a hit film starring James Dean and later a television movie; both are on video now. Buster Keaton's masterpiece *Steamboat Bill, Jr.* was shot in Sacramento. The cult favorite *Harold and Maude* takes place in the San Francisco Bay Area. The exteriors in Alfred Hitchcock's *Shadow of a Doubt* were shot in Santa Rosa, and his ultracreepy *The Birds* was shot in Bodega Bay, along the North Coast. *Shack Out on 101* is a loopy 1950s beware-the-Commies caper also set on the California coast.

Erich von Stroheim used a number of northern California locations for his films: *Greed* takes place in San Francisco but includes excursions to Oakland and other points in the East Bay. Carmel is one of the locations for his *Foolish Wives.* As we note in the Mojave Desert chapter, the various *Star Trek* movies and Michelangelo Antonioni's *Zabriskie Point* are among the features that have made use of the eastern desert region. Initial footage of Sam Peckinpah's western *Ride the High Country* was shot in the Sierra Nevada mountains before his studio yanked him back to southern California, where he blended the original shots with ones of the Santa Monica Mountains and the Hollywood Hills.

INDEX

D

G

H

M

N

O

P

Q

R

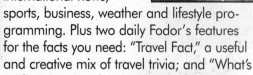

DESTINATIONS

Worldview covers more than 160 destinations worldwide. Choose the destination(s) that match your itinerary from the list below:

Europe
- Amsterdam
- Athens
- Barcelona
- Berlin
- Brussels
- Budapest
- Copenhagen
- Dublin
- Edinburgh
- Florence
- Frankfurt
- French Riviera
- Geneva
- Glasgow
- Lausanne
- Lisbon
- London
- Madrid
- Milan
- Moscow
- Munich
- Oslo
- Paris
- Prague
- Provence
- Rome
- Salzburg
- Seville
- St. Petersburg
- Stockholm
- Venice
- Vienna
- Zurich

United States (Mainland)
- Albuquerque
- Atlanta
- Atlantic City
- Baltimore
- Boston
- Branson, MO
- Charleston, SC
- Chicago
- Cincinnati
- Cleveland
- Dallas/Ft. Worth
- Denver
- Detroit
- Houston
- Indianapolis
- Kansas City
- Las Vegas
- Los Angeles
- Memphis
- Miami
- Milwaukee
- Minneapolis/St. Paul
- Nashville
- New Orleans
- New York City
- Orlando
- Palm Springs
- Philadelphia
- Phoenix
- Pittsburgh
- Portland
- Reno/Lake Tahoe
- St. Louis
- Salt Lake City
- San Antonio
- San Diego
- San Francisco
- Santa Fe
- Seattle
- Tampa
- Washington, DC

Alaska
- Alaskan Destinations

Hawaii
- Honolulu
- Island of Hawaii
- Kauai
- Maui

Canada
- Quebec City
- Montreal
- Ottawa
- Toronto
- Vancouver

Bahamas
- Abaco
- Eleuthera/ Harbour Island
- Exuma
- Freeport
- Nassau & Paradise Island

Bermuda
- Bermuda Countryside
- Hamilton

British Leeward Islands
- Anguilla
- Antigua & Barbuda
- St. Kitts & Nevis

British Virgin Islands
- Tortola & Virgin Gorda

British Windward Islands
- Barbados
- Dominica
- Grenada
- St. Lucia
- St. Vincent
- Trinidad & Tobago

Cayman Islands
- The Caymans

Dominican Republic
- Santo Domingo

Dutch Leeward Islands
- Aruba
- Bonaire
- Curacao

Dutch Windward Island
- St. Maarten/St. Martin

French West Indies
- Guadeloupe
- Martinique
- St. Barthelemy

Jamaica
- Kingston
- Montego Bay
- Negril
- Ocho Rios

Puerto Rico
- Ponce
- San Juan

Turks & Caicos
- Grand Turk/ Providenciales

U.S. Virgin Islands
- St. Croix
- St. John
- St. Thomas

Mexico
- Acapulco
- Cancun & Isla Mujeres
- Cozumel
- Guadalajara
- Ixtapa & Zihuatanejo
- Los Cabos
- Mazatlan
- Mexico City
- Monterrey
- Oaxaca
- Puerto Vallarta

South/Central America
- Buenos Aires
- Caracas
- Rio de Janeiro
- San Jose, Costa Rica
- Sao Paulo

Middle East
- Istanbul
- Jerusalem

Australia & New Zealand
- Auckland
- Melbourne
- South Island
- Sydney

China
- Beijing
- Guangzhou
- Shanghai

Japan
- Kyoto
- Nagoya
- Osaka
- Tokyo
- Yokohama

Pacific Rim/Other
- Bali
- Bangkok
- Hong Kong & Macau
- Manila
- Seoul
- Singapore
- Taipei

INTERESTS

For your personalized Travel Update, choose the eight (8) categories you're most interested in from the following list:

1.	Business Services	Fax & Overnight Mail, Computer Rentals, Protocol, Secretarial, Messenger, Translation Services
	Dining	
2.	All-Day Dining	Breakfast & Brunch, Cafes & Tea Rooms, Late-Night Dining
3.	Local Cuisine	Every Price Range—from Budget Restaurants to the Special Splurge
4.	European Cuisine	Continental, French, Italian
5.	Asian Cuisine	Chinese, Far Eastern, Japanese, Other
6.	Americas Cuisine	American, Mexican & Latin
7.	Nightlife	Bars, Dance Clubs, Casinos, Comedy Clubs, Ethnic, Pubs & Beer Halls
8.	Entertainment	Theater – Comedy, Drama, Musicals, Dance, Ticket Agencies
9.	Music	Classical, Opera, Traditional & Ethnic, Jazz & Blues, Pop, Rock
10.	Children's Activites	Events, Attractions
11.	Tours	Local Tours, Day Trips, Overnight Excursions
12.	Exhibitions, Festivals & Shows	Antiques & Flower, History & Cultural, Art Exhibitions, Fairs & Craft Shows, Music & Art Festivals
13.	Shopping	Districts & Malls, Markets, Regional Specialties
14.	Fitness	Bicycling, Health Clubs, Hiking, Jogging
15.	Recreational Sports	Boating/Sailing, Fishing, Golf, Skiing, Snorkeling/Scuba, Tennis/Racket
16.	Spectator Sports	Auto Racing, Baseball, Basketball, Golf, Football, Horse Racing, Ice Hockey, Soccer
17.	Event Highlights	The best of what's happening during the dates of your trip.
18.	Sightseeing	Sights, Buildings, Monuments
19.	Museums	Art, Cultural
20.	Transportation	Taxis, Car Rentals, Airports, Public Transportation
21.	General Info	Overview, Holidays, Currency, Tourist Info

Please note that content will vary by season, destination, and length of stay.

Name

Address

City **State** **Country** **ZIP**

Tel # ( ) - **Fax #** ( ) -

Title of this Fodor's guide:

Store and location where guide was purchased:

INDICATE YOUR DESTINATIONS/DATES: You can order up to three (3) destinations from the previous page. Fill in your arrival and departure dates for each destination. **Your Travel Update itinerary (all destinations selected) cannot exceed 30 days from beginning to end.**

		Month		Day		Month		Day
(Sample) **LONDON**	From:	**6**	/	**21**	To:	**6**	/	**30**
1	From:		/		To:		/	
2	From:		/		To:		/	
3	From:		/		To:		/	

CHOOSE YOUR INTERESTS: Select up to eight (8) categories from the list of interest categories shown on the previous page and circle the numbers below:

1 2 3 4 5 6 7 8 9 10 11 12 13 14 15 16 17 18 19 20 21

CHOOSE WHEN YOU WANT YOUR TRAVEL UPDATE DELIVERED (Check one):

❑ Please send my Travel Update immediately.

❑ Please hold my order until a few weeks before my trip to include the most up-to-date information.

Completed orders will be sent within 48 hours. Allow 7–10 days for U.S. mail delivery.

ADD UP YOUR ORDER HERE. SPECIAL OFFER FOR FODOR'S PURCHASERS ONLY!

	Suggested Retail Price	Your Price	This Order
First destination ordered	~~$ 9.95~~	$ 7.95	$ 7.95
Second destination (if applicable)	~~$ 6.95~~	$ 4.95	+
Third destination (if applicable)	~~$ 6.95~~	$ 4.95	+

DELIVERY CHARGE (Check one and enter amount below)

	Within U.S. & Canada	Outside U.S. & Canada
First Class Mail	❑ $2.50	❑ $5.00
FAX	❑ $5.00	❑ $10.00
Priority Delivery	❑ $15.00	❑ $27.00

ENTER DELIVERY CHARGE FROM ABOVE: +

TOTAL: $

METHOD OF PAYMENT IN U.S. FUNDS ONLY (Check one):

❑ AmEx ❑ MC ❑ Visa ❑ Discover ❑ Personal Check (U. S. & Canada only)

❑ Money Order/International Money Order

Make check or money order payable to: Fodor's Worldview Travel Update

Credit Card__/__/__/__/__/__/__/__/__/__/__/__/__/__/__/__/ **Expiration Date:**__/__

Authorized Signature

SEND THIS COMPLETED FORM WITH PAYMENT TO:
Fodor's Worldview Travel Update, 114 Sansome Street, Suite 700, San Francisco, CA 94104

OR CALL OR FAX US 24-HOURS A DAY

Telephone **1-800-799-9609** • Fax **1-800-799-9619** (From within the U.S. & Canada)
(Outside the U.S. & Canada: Telephone 415-616-9988 • Fax 415-616-9989)

(Please have this guide in front of you when you call so we can verify purchase.)
Code: FTG Offer valid until 12/31/97